THE APOCRYPHAL NEW TES

To Harvey
from Wantage Parish Church Choir
with affectionate thanks
for creating
" Into the Light "
15th November 2008

The Apocryphal New Testament

A Collection of Apocryphal Christian Literature in an English Translation

■

J. K. ELLIOTT

CLARENDON PRESS · OXFORD

OXFORD
UNIVERSITY PRESS

Great Clarendon Street, Oxford OX2 6DP
Oxford University Press is a department of the University of Oxford.
It furthers the University's objective of excellence in research, scholarship,
and education by publishing worldwide in

Oxford New York

Auckland Cape Town Dar es Salaam Hong Kong Karachi Kuala Lumpur
Madrid Melbourne Mexico City Nairobi New Delhi Shanghai Taipei Toronto

With offices in

Argentina Austria Brazil Chile Czech Republic France Greece
Guatemala Hungary Italy Japan Poland Portugal
Singapore South Korea Switzerland Thailand Turkey Ukraine Vietnam

Oxford is a registered trade mark of Oxford University Press
in the UK and in certain other countries

Published in the United States
by Oxford University Press Inc., New York

© The Oxford University Press 1993

The moral rights of the author have been asserted

Database right Oxford University Press (maker)

First published in paperback 2005
Reprinted 2006, 2007

All rights reserved. No part of this publication may be reproduced,
stored in a retrieval system, or transmitted, in any form or by any means,
without the prior permission in writing of Oxford University Press,
or as expressly permitted by law, or under terms agreed with the appropriate
reprographics rights organization. Enquiries concerning reproduction
outside the scope of the above should be sent to the Rights Department,
Oxford University Press, at the address above

You must not circulate this book in any other binding or cover
and you must impose this same condition on any acquirer

British Library Cataloguing in Publication Data

Data available

Library of Congress Cataloging in Publication Data

The Apocryphal New Testament: a collection of apocryphal Christian
literature in an English Translation / J K. Elliot.
Rev and newly translated ed. of: Apocryphal New Testament /
translated by Montague Rhodes James. 1924.
Includes bibliographical references and indexes.
I. Apocryphal books (New Testament). 2 Apocryphal books (New
Testament)- Criticism, interpretation, etc I. Elliot, J. K.
(James Keith). II. James, M. R. (Montague Rhodes), 1862-1936.
BS2832.A2   1994 1994 229'.92055208-dc20   92-38129
ISBN 978-0-19-826182-7
ISBN 978-0-19-826181-0 (Pbk.)

Printed in Great Britain
on acid-free paper by
Biddles Ltd., King's Lynn, Norfolk

Contents

Preface	ix
General Bibliography	xvi
Lists of Apocryphal Works	xxiii

I. APOCRYPHAL GOSPELS

Lost Gospels
1. Jewish-Christian Gospels: Introduction — 3
    - (*a*) The Gospel according to the Hebrews — 9
    - (*b*) The Gospel of the Nazaraeans — 10
    - (*c*) The Gospel of the Ebionites — 14
2. The Gospel of the Egyptians — 16
3. The Traditions of Matthias — 19
4. The Preaching of Peter (Kerygma Petrou) — 20
5. Other Lost Gospels — 24

Agrapha — 26

Fragments of Gospels on Papyrus — 31
1. Oxyrhynchus Papyrus 840 — 31
2. Oxyrhynchus Papyrus 1081 — 34
3. Oxyrhynchus Papyrus 1224 — 35
4. Papyrus Cairensis 10735 — 36
5. Papyrus Egerton 2 — 37
6. The Strasbourg Fragment — 41
7. Papyrus Berolinensis 11710 — 42
8. The Fayyum Fragment — 43
9. Papyrus Merton 51 — 45

BIRTH AND INFANCY GOSPELS

Introduction	46
The Protevangelium of James	48
The Infancy Gospel of Thomas	68
The Gospel of Pseudo-Matthew	84
The Arabic Infancy Gospel	100
Arundel 404 (Liber de Infantia Salvatoris)	108
The History of Joseph the Carpenter	111

Other Infancy Narratives — 118

GOSPELS OF THE MINISTRY AND PASSION

The Gospel of Thomas (including Coptic Thomas and P. Oxy. 1, 654, 655) — 123
The 'Secret' Gospel of Mark — 148
The Gospel of Peter — 150
The Gospel of Gamaliel — 159
Coptic Narratives of the Ministry and Passion — 161

THE PILATE CYCLE

The Gospel of Nicodemus — 164
   The Acts of Pilate — 169
   Christ's Descent into Hell — 185
Other Pilate Texts — 205
   The Letter of Pilate to Claudius — 205
   The Letter of Pilate to Tiberius — 206
   Paradosis Pilati — 208
   Anaphora Pilati — 211
   Vindicta Salvatoris — 213
   Mors Pilati — 216
   The Narrative of Joseph of Arimathaea — 217
   The Letters of Pilate and Herod — 222
   The Letter of Tiberius to Pilate — 224

II. APOCRYPHAL ACTS

Introduction — 229
The Acts of Andrew — 231
The Acts of John — 303
   Secondary Acts of John — 347
The Acts of Paul — 350
   Secondary Acts of Paul — 388
The Acts of Peter — 390
   Secondary Acts of Peter — 427
The Pseudo-Clementine Literature — 431
The Acts of Thomas — 439
Other Apocryphal Acts — 512

III. APOCRYPHAL EPISTLES

Introduction — 537
Shorter Epistles — 538

The Letters of Christ and Abgar	538
The Letter of Lentulus	542
The Epistle to the Laodiceans	543
The Correspondence of Paul and Seneca	547
The Epistle to the Alexandrians	553
The Epistle of the Apostles (Epistula Apostolorum)	555

IV. APOCRYPHAL APOCALYPSES

Introduction	591
The Apocalypse of Peter	593
Appendix: The Sibylline Oracles	613
The Apocalypse of Paul (Visio Pauli)	616
The Apocalypse of Thomas	645
The Questions of Bartholomew and the Book of the Resurrection of Jesus Christ by Bartholomew the Apostle	652
The Letter of James	673
Other Apocryphal Apocalypses	682
Appendix: The Assumption of the Virgin	689
Indexes	725
1. Apocryphal Writings with detailed lists of Contents	727
2. Subjects and Proper Names	733
3. Biblical and other Citations	740
4. Ancient Authorities	746

Preface

Montague Rhodes James, *The Apocryphal New Testament* was published by Oxford University Press in 1924. Since then it has been regularly reprinted. A modest revision was made in 1953, and the text of the Egerton Papyrus 2 and portions of the Acts of Paul were added as an appendix.

Much has happened in the study of New Testament apocrypha in recent years. Other new gospel-type fragments have come to light, and these need to be set alongside the fragments known from earlier this century. The vast find at Nag Hammadi in particular has added significantly to our knowledge of early Christian and Gnostic literature and has profoundly influenced our understanding of those early centuries when Christianity was expanding and when the bulk of our apocryphal texts had their genesis. New manuscripts of previously known texts have also been discovered in the libraries and monasteries of the world: their publication has sometimes revealed hitherto unknown portions of those texts; elsewhere the new texts have necessitated adjustments to published editions. Also in recent years, new projects have been initiated by scholars who are preparing critical editions. Some of these have started publication, most notably the *Corpus Christianorum: Series Apocryphorum* and the Society of Biblical Literature's *Christian Apocrypha* series.

Since 1924 other collections of apocryphal texts in translation such as those edited by Hennecke–Schneemelcher, de Santos Otero, Erbetta, Moraldi, and others have helped to spread knowledge of these texts. A growing number of scholars now pays attention to the significance of this body of early Christian literature.

As a result of this flurry of activity and the consequent renewed interest in the literature and theology of early Christianity, it was decided by Oxford University Press that the time had come to revise James's *Apocryphal New Testament*. As a one-volume collection in English, 'James' has been a valued introduction to these texts for generations of theologians, historians, and Biblical scholars, and it has also been a ready reference tool for clergy, art historians, and indeed for general readers too.

The Press allowed me *carte blanche* for this revision. When I began to examine the issues involved it became clear that nothing less than a thorough rewriting would suffice. Mere tinkering with the original, the adding of footnotes or further appendixes, seemed inadequate. This volume is therefore a complete reworking of the original. Nevertheless, it was my intention that it should be recognizable as a replacement of 'James'. The length and scope of the original and certain other features have been preserved. Unlike certain other modern collections the 'new James', like the old, includes some later, medieval, texts and does not limit itself exclusively to early writings. Despite reservations expressed in some quarters, one cannot really tie the production of apocryphal texts to a limited period up to, say, the fourth century. The creation of apocryphal literature and the revision of earlier texts did not cease with the formation and acceptance of the New Testament canon.

The purpose of this new edition is the same as its predecessor's: to allow readers access to the contents of this vast range of literature without overburdening the translations with excessive textual or critical notes.

One change I immediately decided upon was to replace the consciously archaizing English style that James affected with a translation, which I hope will be acceptable to modern readers. In the 1920s those who were likely to turn to a volume entitled *The Apocryphal New Testament* were probably familiar with the Bible, in the Authorized Version, and so it was appropriate for James to employ a style intended to remind the reader of it. Nowadays those who refer to apocryphal texts are not necessarily Bible readers and, even if they are, they are more likely to use a modern version. Thus the present translation is similarly in modern style.

Another major change in the present book is the inclusion of a formal introduction to each text. James's editorial insertions or introductory remarks were not always consistent or as complete as one might wish for. I have therefore tried to provide introductory notes that are more informative. The length of these introductions inevitably varies and is obviously dependent on the importance of the text being introduced and the amount of discussion it has generated in the specialist literature. Some secondary literature may have taken up matters such as the complexities of the manuscript evidence for a particular text, or its reconstruction and other critical questions. My intention in revealing such issues in the introductions is to alert readers to the debate, although I have tried to be a neutral observer where controversy is current. Wherever scholarly debate is raging or when old problems remain unsolved or unsettled it seemed best in a book designed in part as a reference book not to take sides. The bibliographies attached to each introduction should alert readers to the relevant secondary literature, and to the existence of differing views.

My decision to give fairly detailed (although by no means exhaustive) bibliographical references was prompted by the companion volume, *The Apocryphal Old Testament*, edited by H. F. D. Sparks (Oxford, 1984). There, a useful bibliography is appended to each introduction: in it are references to editions, translations, and general studies. I too have included references to critical editions of the texts in the original languages, and to ancient versions as well as to modern translations (principally into English, French, German, Italian, and Spanish). Articles or studies of a more general nature are added either in the bibliography to the separate text or at the beginning of the volume.

It will be noted in the bibliographies that I have occasionally included references to older printed editions and to earlier translations. This is not only to satisfy historical interests and show the extent to which a particular text might have been known to the scholarly world, but also because some of these earlier studies yield information not always repeated or available in later publications. The bibliographies are thus intended as a starting-point for those readers who wish to get behind a simple English rendering and read the text in its original language or to research the history of scholarly investigation on the text or, of course, to study the wider critical, literary, historical, or theological issues raised by the text.

There is a need to justify the retention of James's title for this book. In 1924 James himself devoted some space in his Preface to castigate the impression given by Hone's *Apocryphal New Testament* of 1820, which had been until then the main vehicle in English for popularizing some of the so-called apocryphal texts. Part of James's complaint was that Hone had given the impression that a book entitled *The Apocryphal New Testament* comprised a recognized collection of texts that had deliberately been excluded from the canon. Such an impression was encouraged by Hone's subtitle which stated that the apocryphal texts were 'not included in the New Testament by its compilers'. But even without such an addition the mere title *The Apocryphal New Testament* could imply that this is indeed a fixed body of literature. Unlike the Apocrypha to the Old Testament, which is in general universally identifiable, the texts included under a title such as *The New Testament Apocrypha* represent an amorphous and wide-ranging group. Unlike the New Testament, which is distinct and stable, and was written over only a short period of time, a collection of 'apocryphal' texts such as the present one does not constitute an agreed, settled, entity written within a defined time scale. In fact one noteworthy feature of this literature—possibly because it lacked the sanctity of texts afforded canonical status—is that the contents of its books were frequently revised, expanded, epitomized, and rewritten. Thus several texts re-emerge in a new guise that James liked to describe as a *réchauffé*.

One may even take exception to the words 'New Testament' in the title. Many of the texts translated here have no obvious link with the genres of literature to be found in the canonical New Testament. I have followed the convention of subdividing the texts into Gospels, Acts, Epistles, and Apocalypses, but many of them do not fit sensibly into these categories. The Epistle of the Apostles is no real letter as understood in terms of the New Testament epistles: rather it is a type of apocalyptic literature better designated as 'Dialogues of the Risen Jesus'. As such it could really stand alongside the Apocryphon of James among the apocalypses. Similarly, few of the apocryphal gospels are correctly classified as gospels in the normal understanding of this term. In style, theology, and content they are hardly comparable to the canonical Gospels. Some fragmentary apocryphal gospels may be mere homilies. Others are restricted to only certain periods in Jesus' career and are infancy gospels or passion gospels or are accounts of his descent to the underworld. Even the apocryphal acts and apocalypses, although at first sight having closer ties to their canonical counterparts, are in fact very different in character: the former seem to owe much to pagan romances, the latter to have been inspired by Jewish apocalyptic rather than the Book of Revelation. A justification for the use of the words 'New Testament' in the title may be that many, but probably not all, the apocrypha selected have been inspired by events, or gaps, in the New Testament narratives or, at the very least, have made use of the New Testament's *dramatis personae*. But, from the theological and literary points of view, the linking of these apocryphal works to the New Testament has suggested some common identity between the two sets of texts thus making their interrelationship closer and more significant than it sometimes ought to be.

Even the word 'apocrypha' in the title is not ideal! The majority of texts now normally to be found under such a title are not apocryphal in the sense of hidden or secret (although a few may have been intended as secret writings for an inner circle: the Apocalypse of Paul claims to have been hidden and only rediscovered later). The more normal meanings of apocryphal as spurious, fictitious, or false are also not ideal for the books included here, bizarre and fanciful though many of them are, but it is in this modern sense of the word that it is applied *faute de mieux* to the documents in this collection.

So if *The Apocryphal New Testament* is not the right title, why use it? Possibly one answer is that most readers turning to a book with this title are usually aware of the sort of literature they expect to find within its covers. Having become a conventional title it is now difficult to substitute for it another that would be more accurate yet still be recognized for what it is. Suggested alternatives such as 'Early Non-Canonical Christian Writings' or 'Christian Apocrypha' are occasionally to be heard as possibilities, but even these are not as clear, watertight, or inclusive as one might wish. I have tried to alleviate the problem of the title by adding a qualifier as a subtitle, 'A Collection of Apocryphal Christian Literature', and this may further inform the uninitiated browser about the range of contents.

Now to the selection of texts. First, it must be said that in compiling a collection of these apocryphal texts a major problem is that far more documents are available than could conceivably be included in a single volume planned to be roughly the same length and format as its predecessor. Nowadays the exclusion of the Apostolic Fathers is taken for granted. Similarly one can justify the exclusion of the bulk of Gnostic texts. Most of them—especially those from the Nag Hammadi library—are readily accessible in good modern editions and translations. (The Coptic Gospel of

Preface

Thomas has, however, been included because of its obvious importance for scholars of early Christianity. The Apocryphon (or Letter) of James from Nag Hammadi, which is a 'dialogue gospel' is also included here in a new translation from the Coptic. After deliberation I decided on balance not to include the Gospel of Philip; it is however readily available in publications of the Nag Hammadi material.) Following James's example I also exclude those books such as the Apostolic Constitutions that deal with church order and with liturgy. James excluded all the so-called Clementine literature, but I decided to include samples from the pseudo-Clementine *Recognitions* and *Homilies* as a supplement to the chapter on the Acts of Peter.

The vast number of apocryphal texts, especially martyrdoms, in Coptic, Ethiopic, and other oriental languages do not merit space in this volume and are generally referred to only when they relate to texts available to us in other languages. All Rabbinic and Islamic traditions about Jesus are omitted. Similarly, Christian or Christianized books bearing the name of Old Testament worthies are not included. Most of these are to be found in collections of Old Testament pseudepigrapha.

In general the criterion for the inclusion of texts in this book is that they should be either among the oldest or most important and influential or merely the most popular of those that have come down to us.

Montague Rhodes James was a pioneer—he discovered, identified, and published many apocryphal texts. His erudition and encyclopaedic knowledge of the world of early Christianity are clearly evident in his writings. The present volume owes a great deal to his inspiration and example. However, I could not have attempted to revise his *Apocryphal New Testament*, or have the audacity to replace it, without the encouragement and advice of many scholars whose help is gratefully acknowledged. They include François Bovon and members of the Association pour l'étude de la littérature apocryphe chrétienne, especially Jean-Daniel Kaestli, Eric Junod, Willy Rordorf, Gérard Poupon, and Yves Tissot, who gave of their time and expertise on matters relating to the apocryphal Acts during my stay in Switzerland in 1988. Others associated with this European enterprise to revive interest in apocryphal texts are Jean-Daniel Dubois, Albert Frey, Jean-Marc Prieur, Jan Gijsel, and Sever Voicu: I sought advice from them on various of the texts and I thank them for the help they rendered so readily.

Among American scholars at work in this field I wish to thank most warmly Ron Cameron for his translation of the Letter of James, and Dennis MacDonald for permission to base my translation of the Acts of Andrew on his work. Richard Pervo gave valuable comments on my draft of the Acts of John.

A. F. J. Klijn and Georg Strecker generously answered my queries concerning the Jewish-Christian Gospels and the Pseudo-Clementine literature respectively. Christopher Tuckett advised on aspects of the Coptic Gospel of Thomas; David Wright helped with the Gospel of Peter. My thanks are extended to them all.

Robin Wilson of St Andrews has been most supportive and has offered wise counsel throughout the years of planning and work on this volume. Richard Bauckham gave bibliographical help on the apocalyptic traditions. J. Martin Plumley readily answered queries on aspects of Coptic texts. These all deserve fulsome praise. I also wish to acknowledge with gratitude the help of H. F. D. Sparks and T. C. Skeat and the late A. J. B. Higgins, who gave me the benefit of their expertise at the early planning stages of this revision.

With thanks duly proffered, with all explanations made, with all the labours completed, there still remains the need to justify the publication of a volume of such literature. Why should anybody bother to read or study these texts? What is their significance and importance? In attempting to provide a justification I think I can most fittingly cite a few paragraphs written by M. R. James in the Preface to his 1924 edition:

Interesting as they are—and I will try to show later why they are interesting—they do not achieve either of the two principal purposes for which they were written, the instilling of true religion and the conveyance of true history.

As religious books they were meant to reinforce the existing stock of Christian beliefs: either by revealing new doctrines—usually differing from those which held the field; or by interpreting old ones—again, usually in a fresh sense; or by extolling some special virtue, as chastity or temperance; or by enforcing belief in certain doctrines or events, e.g. the Virgin birth, the resurrection of Christ, the second coming, the future state—by the production of evidence which, if true, should be irrefragable. For all these purposes the highest authority is claimed by the writings; they are the work, they tell us, of eyewitnesses of the events, or they report the utterances of the Lord himself. As books of history they aim at supplementing the scanty data (as they seemed) of the Gospels and Acts, and in this they resemble many of the Jewish Midrashim and apocrypha....

But, as I have said, they fail of their purpose. Among the prayers and discourses of the apostles in the spurious Acts some utterances may be found which are remarkable and even beautiful: not a few of the stories are notable and imaginative, and have been consecrated and made familiar to us by the genius of mediaeval artists. But the authors do not speak with the voices of Paul or of John, or with the quiet simplicity of the three first Gospels. It is not unfair to say that when they attempt the former tone, they are theatrical, and when they essay the latter, they are jejune. In short, the result of anything like an attentive study of the literature, in bulk and in detail, is an added respect for the sense of the Church Catholic, and for the wisdom of the scholars of Alexandria, Antioch, and Rome...

But, it may be said, if these writings are good neither as books of history, nor of religion, nor even as literature, why spend time and labour on giving them a vogue which on your own showing they do not deserve? Partly, of course, in order to enable others to form a judgement on them; but that is not the whole case. The truth is that they must not be regarded only from the point of view which they claim for themselves. In almost every other aspect they have a great and enduring interest.

If they are not good sources of history in one sense, they are in another. They record the imaginations, hopes, and fears of the men who wrote them; they show what was acceptable to the unlearned Christians of the first ages, what interested them, what they admired, what ideals of conduct they cherished for this life, what they thought they would find in the next. As folk-lore and romance, again, they are precious; and to the lover and student of mediaeval literature and art they reveal the source of no inconsiderable part of his material and the solution of many a puzzle. They have, indeed, exercised an influence (wholly disproportionate to their intrinsic merits) so great and so widespread, that no one who cares about the history of Christian thought and Christian art can possibly afford to neglect them.

The Translations

The source(s) for the translations are given in the introductory matter to each new text. I have tried to avoid extensive scholarly footnotes to the translations. Occasionally, significant variant readings or obscure passages are noted in the margin. The footnotes are generally reserved for references to Biblical citations in the text. Direct quotations from Biblical books are referred to: the footnote is preceded by 'cf.' if the citation is not exact. Allusions to a Biblical text are not noted: the nature of many of these apocryphal documents is such that their authors were so steeped in Biblical or liturgical language that many echoes of scriptural passages occur throughout the writings without being conscious quotations.

Translation is always a difficult art. My aim has been to produce as readable and coherent an English version as the original Greek and Latin allows. Lacunae in the originals are noted by dots '. . .' in the translation; significant additions to the original usually occur in round brackets. Occasionally, silent corrections to the originals have been accepted. Translations of texts in oriental languages have in the main been taken over with modest changes from James's edition. But for all the translations I have consulted other editions old and new in English, German, and Italian. The translation of Epistula Apostolorum has been taken directly from the English translation of Hennecke-Schneemelcher[5]: the permission granted by the publishers is herewith acknowledged. The translation of the Acts of Andrew and of the Acts of Andrew and Matthias is used with the permission of D. R. MacDonald.

This reprint (2005) incorporates a number of refinements, corrections, and extra bibliographical references.

General Bibliography

Generally, journals and series are abbreviated in conformity with Siegfried Schwertner, *International Glossary of Abbreviations for Theology and Related Subjects* (Berlin, 1974). The Corpus Christianorum series are abbreviated *CCA* for the Series Apocryphorum and *CCL* for the Latin series. The volumes of Oxyrhynchus Papyri when abbreviated appear as *OP*.

EDITIONS OF TEXTS AND EARLY VERSIONS

Greek and Latin

Fabricius = J. A. Fabricius, *Codex Apocryphus Novi Testamenti*, 4 vols. (Hamburg, ²1719).
Jones = J. Jones, *A New and Full Method of Settling the Canonical Authority of the New Testament*, 3 vols. (London, 1726–7; ²Oxford, 1798; ³1827).
Birch = A. Birch, *Auctarium Codicis Apocryphi Novi Testamenti Fabriciani*, i (Copenhagen, 1804).
Thilo = J. C. Thilo, *Codex Apocryphus Novi Testamenti*, i (Leipzig, 1832).
Giles = J. A. Giles, *Codex Apocryphus Novi Testamenti: The Uncanonical Gospels and Other Writings* (London, 1852).
Tischendorf, *Apoc. Apoc.* = C. Tischendorf, *Apocalypses Apocryphae* (Leipzig, 1866; repr. Hildesheim, 1966).
Tischendorf, *EA* = id., *Evangelia Apocrypha* (Leipzig, ²1876; repr. Hildesheim, 1966 and 1987). [Tischendorf's dissertation on apocryphal gospels acts as an introduction to his collection of texts (the first edition of which was published in 1852): *De evangeliorum apocryphorum origine et usu* (The Hague, 1851).]
James, *Apoc. Anec.* = M. R. James, *Apocrypha Anecdota*, 2 vols. (Cambridge, 1893 and 1897; repr. Nendeln, Liechenstein, 1967) (= *Texts and Studies* 2.3 and 5.1).
Lipsius–Bonnet = R. A. Lipsius and M. Bonnet, *Acta Apostolorum Apocrypha*, 3 vols. (Leipzig, 1891, 1898, 1903; repr. Hildesheim, 1959).
Preuschen = E. Preuschen, *Antilegomena* (Giessen, 1901; ²1905).
Klostermann, *Apocrypha* = E. Klostermann, *Apocrypha*, i (Bonn, 1903; ²1908, 1921; ³Berlin, 1929) (= *Kleine Texte* 3, ed. H. Lietzmann); *Apocrypha*, ii (Bonn, 1904; ²1910; ³Berlin, 1929) (= *Kleine Texte* 8, ed. H. Lietzmann); *Apocrypha*, iii (Bonn, ²1911) (= *Kleine Texte* 11, ed. H. Lietzmann).
Lührmann = D. Lührmann and E. Schlarb, *Fragmente apokryph gewordener Evangelien in griechischer und lateinischer Sprache* (Marburg, 2000) (= *Marburger Theologische Studien* 59).

Coptic

Guidi, *AAL.R/Giornale* = I. Guidi, 'Frammenti copti', *Atti della Reale Accademia dei Lincei. Rendiconti. Classe di scienze morali, stòriche e filologiche* (Rome, 1884–7); Italian translations in 'Gli atti apocrifi degli Apostoli nei testi copti, arabi ed etiopici', *Giornale della Società Asiatica Italiana* 2 (1888).

O. von Lemm, *Koptische apokryphe Apostelakten*, i (St Petersburg, 1890) (= *Mélanges Asiatiques* 10.1).

P. Lacau, *Fragments d'apocryphes coptes* (Cairo, 1904) (= *Mémoires publiés par les membres de l'institut français d'archéologie orientale du Caire* 9).

E. Revillout, *Les Apocryphes coptes*, i. *Les Évangiles des douze apôtres et de S. Barthélemy* (Paris, 1907 and 1913) (= *PO* 2.2 and 9).

F. Morard, 'Notes sur le recueil copte des actes apocryphes des apôtres', *RTP* 113 (1981), 403–13.

Syriac

Wright, *Contributions* = W. Wright, *Contributions to the Apocryphal Literature of the New Testament* (London, 1865).

Wright, *Apoc. Acts* = id., *Apocryphal Acts of the Apostles*, 2 vols. (London and Edinburgh, 1871; repr. Amsterdam, 1968).

Armenian

Leloir, *CCA* = L. Leloir, *Écrits apocryphes sur les apôtres: Traduction de l'édition arménienne de Venise*, i. *Pierre, Paul, André, Jacques, Jean* (Turnhout, 1986) (= *CCA* 3); ii. (Turnhout, 1992) (= *CCA* 4).

Ethiopic

Malan = S. C. Malan, *The Conflicts of the Holy Apostles* (London, 1871).

Wallis Budge, *Contendings* = E. A. Wallis Budge, *The Contendings of the Apostles*, 2 vols. (London, 1899 and 1901; ²1935; repr. London, 1976).

Arabic

Smith Lewis, *Acta Myth./Myth. Acts* = A. Smith Lewis, *Acta Mythologica Apostolorum*; Eng. trans. *The Mythological Acts of the Apostles* (London, 1904) (= *Horae Semiticae* 3 and 4).

Graf = G. Graf, *Geschichte der christlichen arabischen Literatur*, i (Vatican City, 1944) (= *Studi e Testi* 118).

Georgian

Kurcikidze = C. Kurcikidze, [Georgian versions of the Apocryphal Acts of the Apostles] (Tblisi, 1959).

Slavonic

de Santos Otero, *Altslav. Apok.* = A. de Santos Otero, *Die handschriftliche Überlieferung der altslavischen Apokryphen* 2 vols. (Berlin and New York, 1978, 1981) (= *Patristische Texte und Studien*, 20 and 23).

xviii   *General Bibliography*

SYNOPSES OF THE GREEK NEW TESTAMENT

References to the index pages of the following synopses are given when these editions include an apocryphal text among the parallels displayed.

Aland[13] = K. Aland, *Synopsis Quattuor Evangeliorum* (13th edn., Stuttgart, 1985).
Huck–Greeven[13] = A. Huck, *Synopse der drei ersten Evangelien; Synopsis of the First Three Gospels* 13th edn., rev. H. Greeven (Tübingen, 1981).
Boismard = M.-E. Boismard and A. Lamouille, *Synopsis Graeca Quattuor Evangeliorum* (Leuven and Paris, 1986).

PATRISTIC REFERENCES

The works below appear in the text in abbreviated form.

Augustine, *c. Adimantum* = *contra Adimantum*, ed. J. Zycha, *CSEL* 25.1 (Vienna, Prague, Leipzig, 1891).
—— *c. Faust.* = *contra Faustum Manicheum*, ed. J. Zycha, *CSEL* 25.1 (Vienna, Prague, Leipzig, 1891).
Clement of Alexandria, *Strom.* = *Stromateis*, ed. O. Stählin: vol. ii, *GCS* 52 (15) (Leipzig, 1906; [3]rev. L. Früchtel and U. Treu, Berlin, 1960; [4]rev. U. Treu, Berlin, 1985); vol. iii, *GCS* 17[2] (Leipzig, 1909; [2]rev. L. Früchtel and U. Treu, Berlin, 1970).
Epiphanius, *adv. Haer.* = *Panarion* or *adversus LXXX Haereses*, ed. K. Holl, *GCS* 25 (Leipzig, 1915); *GCS* 31 (Leipzig, 1922; [2]rev. J. Dummer, Berlin, 1980).
Eusebius, *HE* = *Historia Ecclesiastica*, ed. E. Schwartz, *GCS* 9.1 and 9.2 (Leipzig, 1903, 1908).
Hippolytus, *Haer.* = *Refutatio Omnium Haeresium* or *Philosophoumena*, ed. P. Wendland, *GCS* 26 (Leipzig, 1916).
Irenaeus, *adv. Haer.* = *adversus Haereses*, ed. A. Rousseau, *SC* (Paris, 1965–82).
Jerome, *de Vir. Ill.* = *de Viris Illustribus*, ed. E. C. Richardson, *TU* 14.1 (Leipzig, 1896).
—— *on Matt.* = *Commentary on Matthew*, ed. D. Hurst and M. Adriaen, *CCL* 77 (Turnhout, 1969).
John of Damascus, *Parall.* = *Sacred Parallels*, ed. K. Holl, *TU* 20.1 (Leipzig, 1899).
Origen, *on Matt.* = *Commentary on Matthew*, ed. E. Klostermann and E. Benz, *GCS* 40.1 (Leipzig, 1935).
—— *Hom. on Luke* = *Homilies on Luke*, ed. M. Rauer, *GCS* 49 (35) (Berlin, [2]1959).
—— *on John* = *Commentary on John*, ed. E. Preuschen, *GCS* 10 (Berlin, 1903).

MODERN TRANSLATIONS

English

Hone = W. Hone, *The Apocryphal New Testament* (London, 1820).
Walker = A. Walker, *Apocryphal Gospels, Acts and Revelations* (Edinburgh, 1870) (= A. Roberts and J. Donaldson (eds.), *Ante-Nicene Christian Library* 16).
Cowper = B. H. Cowper, *The Apocryphal Gospels and Other Documents relating to the History of Christ* (Edinburgh and London, [2]1867).

General Bibliography

A. Menzies (ed.), *Ante-Nicene Christian Library: Additional Volume* (Edinburgh, 1897) = Vol. ix following the American edition of the eight volumes of *ANCL* produced as the *Ante-Nicene Fathers* (Buffalo, 1880: rev. and suppl., Grand Rapids, 1967).

Pick = B. Pick, *The Apocryphal Acts of Paul, Peter, John, Andrew, and Thomas* (London, 1909).

Westcott = A. Westcott, *The Gospel of Nicodemus and Kindred Documents* (London, 1915).

James, *ANT* = M. R. James, *The Apocryphal New Testament* (Oxford, 1924; corrected edn., 1953).

H. J. Schonfield, *Readings from the Apocryphal Gospels* (London, 1940).

Grant and Freedman = R. M. Grant and D. N. Freedman, *The Secret Sayings of Jesus* (London, 1960).

Hennecke[3] = E. Hennecke, *New Testament Apocrypha*, ed. W. Schneemelcher, Eng. trans. ed. R. McL. Wilson, 2 vols. (London, 1963 and 1965).

Hennecke[5] = W. Schneemelcher (ed.), *New Testament Apocrypha*, Eng. trans. by R. McL. Wilson, 2 vols. (Cambridge and Louisville, 1991, 1992).

Cartlidge and Dungan = D. R. Cartlidge and D. L. Dungan, *Documents for the Study of the Gospels* (Philadelphia, 1980).

Cameron = R. Cameron, *The Other Gospels: Non-Canonical Gospel Texts* (Philadelphia, 1983).

Jacques Hervieux, *The New Testament Apocrypha* ET (New York, 1960).

French

Migne, *Dictionnaire* = J. P. Migne, *Dictionnaire des Apocryphes*, 2 vols. (Paris, 1856 and 1958; repr. Turnhout, 1989) (= *Troisième et dernière encyclopédie théologique* 23 and 24).

Michel = C. Michel, *Évangiles apocryphes*, i (Paris, 1911; ²1914) (= H. Hemmer and P. Lejay (eds.), *Textes et documents pour l'étude historique du Christianisme* 13).

Vouaux = L. Vouaux, *Les Actes de Paul et ses lettres apocryphes* (Paris, 1913) (= *Les apocryphes du Nouveau Testament*, ed. J. Bousquet and E. Amann).

Amiot = F. Amiot, *La Bible apocryphe: Évangiles apocryphes* (Paris, 1952) (= *Textes pour l'histoire sacrée*, ed. H. Daniel-Rops).

F. Quéré, *Évangiles apocryphes* (Paris, 1983).

Éac = F. Bovon and P. Geoltrain (eds.), *Écrits apocryphes chrétiens* I (Paris, 1997).

German

Clemens = R. Clemens, *Die geheimgehaltenen oder sogenannten apokryphen Evangelien*, 2 vols. (Stuttgart, 1850).

Michaelis = W. Michaelis, *Die apokryphen Schriften zum Neuen Testament* (Bremen, 1956; ³1962) (= *Sammlung Dieterich* 129).

Hennecke[1] = E. Hennecke, *Neutestamentliche Apokryphen in deutscher Übersetzung* (Tübingen and Leipzig, 1904; ²1924).

Handbuch = E. Hennecke, *Handbuch zu den Neutestamentlichen Apokryphen* (Tübingen, 1904).

Hennecke[3] = E. Hennecke, *Neutestamentliche Apokryphen in deutscher Übersetzung*, 3rd edn. by W. Schneemelcher, 2 vols. (Tübingen, 1959 and 1964).
Hennecke[5] = E. Hennecke, *Neutestamentliche Apokryphen in deutscher Übersetzung*, 5th edn. by W. Schneemelcher, 2 vols. (Tübingen, 1987 and 1989). [The sixth edition is a corrected reprinting of the fifth.]
W. Rebell, *Neutestamentliche Apokryphen und Apostolische Väter* (Munich, 1992).
Schneider = G. Schneider, *Evangelia Infantiae Apocrypha. Apocryphe Kindheitsevangelien* (Freiburg, 1995) (= *Fontes Christiani* 18).

Italian

Bonaccorsi = G. Bonaccorsi, *Vangeli Apocrifi*, i (Florence, 1948).
Cravieri = M. Cravieri, *I Vangeli apocrifi* (Turin, 1969).
Moraldi = L. Moraldi, *Apocrifi del Nuovo Testamento*, 2 vols. (Turin, 1971) (= *Classici delle religioni*, v. *Le altre confessioni cristiane*, ed. L. Firpo). 2nd. ed. 3 vols. 1994.
Erbetta = M. Erbetta, *Gli apocrifi del Nuovo Testamento*, 3 vols. (Casale Monferrato, i.1, 1975; i.2, 1981; ii, 1966, ²1978; iii, 1981).

Spanish

González-Blanco = E. González-Blanco, *Los Evangelios Apócrifos*, 3 vols. (Madrid, 1934).
de Santos Otero = A. de Santos Otero, *Los Evangelios Apócrifos* (Madrid, ²1963) (= *Biblioteca de Autores Cristianos*, Sección i. *Sagradas Escrituras* 148). [The 6th edn. of 1988 is used only for the Coptic Gospel of Thomas. Otherwise the 2nd edn. is cited; the pagination differs in the 6th edn.]

Dutch

A. F. J. Klijn, *Apokriefen van het Nieuwe Testament*, 2 vols. (Kampen, 1985).

Afrikaans

J. J. Müller, *Nuwe-Testamentiese Apokriewe* (Cape Town, Bloemfontein, Johannesberg, 1959, ²1976).

Polish

M. Starowieysky, *Apokryfy Nowego Testamentu*, 2 vols. (Lublin, 1980).

Norwegian

E. Thomassen and H. Moxnes, *Apokryfe Evangelier. (Verdens hellige Skrifter)* (Oslo, 2001).

Czech

Jan Dus and Petr Pokorný, *Neznámá Evangelia* (Prague, 2001); Jan Dus, *Příběhy Apoštolů* (Prague, 2003).

REFERENCE AND GENERAL

Variot = J. Variot, *Les Évangiles apocryphes: Histoire littéraire, forme primitive, transformations* (Paris, 1878).
Lipsius = R. A. Lipsius, *Die apokryphen Apostelgeschichten und Apostellegenden*, 3 vols. and supplement (Brunswick, 1883–90; repr. Amsterdam, 1976), esp. i. 1–117.
Zahn, *Kanon* = T. Zahn, *Geschichte des neutestamentlichen Kanons: Das Neue Testament vor Ongines*, 2 vols. (i, Leipzig, 1888–9; ii, Erlangen and Leipzig, 1890–2).
Harnack = A. von Harnack, *Geschichte der altchristlichen Literatur bis Eusebius.* i. *Die Überlieferung und der Bestand*; ii. *Die Chronologie*, (i) bis Irenäus, (ii) von Irenäus bis Eusebius (Leipzig, i, 1893; ii(i), 1897; ii (ii), 1904).

W. Bauer, *Das Leben Jesu im Zeitalter der neutestamentlichen Apokryphen* (Tübingen, 1909).
Findlay = A. F. Findlay, *Byways in Early Christian Literature* (Edinburgh, 1923).
Rosa Söder, *Die apokryphen Apostelgeschichten und die romanhafte Literatur der Antike* (Stuttgart, 1932; repr. Stuttgart, Berlin, Cologne, Mainz, 1969).
M. Blumenthal, *Formen und Motive in den apokryphen Apostelgeschichten* (Leipzig, 1933) (= *TU* 48.1).
Ehrhard = A. Ehrhard, *Überlieferung und Bestand der hagiographischen und homiletischen Literatur der griechischen Kirche von den Anfängen bis zum Ende des 16. Jahrhunderts*, 2 vols. (Leipzig, 1937-8) (= *TU* 50, 51). [Vol. iii published posthumously (Berlin, 1952 = *TU* 52).]
K. L. Schmidt, *Kanonische und apokryphe Evangelien und Apostelgeschichte* (Basle, 1944) (= *Abhandlungen zur Theologie des Alten und Neuen Testaments* 5).
J. Quasten, *Patrologie*, i (Utrecht and Brussels, 1950).
B. Altaner, *Patrology* (Edinburgh and London, 1958). [Eng. trans. of *Patrologie*, 5th German edn. (Freiburg, 1958).]
Hennecke[3], ii. 110-25 (W. Schneemelcher and K. Schäferdiek); Eng. trans. ii. 167-88.
Hennecke[5], ii. 71-93 (W. Schneemelcher and K. Schäferdiek); Eng. trans. ii. 75-100.
[Cf. E. Hennecke, in Hennecke[1], 346-51, and *Handbuch*, 351-8.]
A. Hamman, '"Sitz im Leben" des actes apocryphes du Nouveau Testament', in F. L. Cross (ed.). *Studia Patristica* 8.2 (Berlin, 1960), 62-9 (= *TU* 93).
Bauer = J. B. Bauer, *Die neutestamentlichen Apokryphen* (Düsseldorf, 1968) (= *Die Welt der Bibel* 21).
F. F. Bruce, *Jesus and Christian Origins outside the New Testament* (London, 1974; [2]1984).
Plümacher = A. Plümacher, 'Apokryphe Apostelakten', in G. Wissowa *et al.* (eds.), *Paulys Realencyclopädie der classischen Altertumswissenschaft*, Supplementband 15 (Munich, 1978), cols. 11-70.
S. L. Davies, *The Revolt of the Widows: The Social World of the Apocryphal Acts* (Carbondale, Edwardsville, London, Amsterdam, 1980).
F. Bovon (ed.), *Les Actes apocryphes des apôtres: Christianisme et monde païen* (Geneva, 1981) (= *Publications de la Faculté de Théologie de l'Université de Genève* 4).
D. R. MacDonald (ed.), *The Apocryphal Acts of the Apostles* (Decatur, Ga., 1986) (= *Semeia* 38).
R. I. Pervo, *Profit with Delight: The Literary Genre of the Acts of the Apostles* (Philadelphia, 1987). [He finds closer links between the canonical Acts and the apocryphal Acts than is often allowed for.]

For general introductions to apocryphal literature:

Vielhauer = P. Vielhauer, *Geschichte der urchristlichen Literatur: Einleitung in das Neue Testament, die Apokryphen und die apostolischen Väter* (Berlin and New York, 1975), 613-718.
R. McL. Wilson, 'Apokryphen II: Apokryphen des Neuen Testaments' *TRE* iii. 317-62.
Helmut Koester, 'Apocryphal and Canonical Gospels', *HTR* 73 (1980), 105-30.

Helmut Koester, *Introduction to the New Testament*, ii. *History and Literature of Early Christianity* (Berlin and New York, 1982). [Eng. trans. of part of *Einführung in das Neue Testament*.]

R. W. Funk, *New Gospel Parallels*, 2 vols. (Philadelphia, 1985) (= *Foundations and Facets* 5 and 6). [For cross-references to canonical and other apocryphal works.]

B. M. Metzger, *The Canon of the New Testament: Its Origin, Development, and Significance* (Oxford, 1987).

Charlesworth = J. H. Charlesworth and J. R. Mueller, *The New Testament Apocrypha and Pseudepigrapha: A Guide to Publications* (Metuchen and London, 1987) (= *American Theological Library Association Bibliography Series* 17).

J. H. Charlesworth, 'Research on the New Testament Apocrypha and Pseudepigrapha', *ANRW* 2.25.5, 3919–68.

S. Gero, 'Apocryphal Gospels: A Survey of Textual and Literary Problems', *ANRW* 2.25.5, 3979–84.

Bentley Layton, *The Gnostic Scriptures* (London, 1987).

J. M. Robinson (ed.), *The Nag Hammadi Library in English* (Leiden, 1977; ³1988).

R. McL. Wilson, 'New Testament Apocrypha', in E. J. Epp and G. W. Macrae (eds.), *The New Testament and its Modern Interpreters* (Philadelphia and Atlanta; 1989), 429–55 (= D. A. Knight (ed.), *The Bible and its Modern Interpreters* 3).

William D. Stroker, *Extracanonical Sayings of Jesus* (Atlanta: Scholars Press, 1989) (= *Society of Biblical Literature Resources for Biblical Study* 18).

Helmut Koester, *Ancient Christian Gospels: Their History and Development* (London and Philadelphia, 1990).

Hans-Josef Klauck, *Apokryphe Evangelien. Eine Einführung* (Stuttgart, 2002); *ET Apocryphal Gospels: An Introduction* (London and New York, 2003).

Fred Lapham. *An Introduction to the New Testament Apocrypha* (London/New York, 2003).

Lists of Apocryphal Works

Lists that were drawn up to indicate which writings were apocryphal are instructive in telling us which books were known at a certain period, and are helpful for discussing the history of the canon. The so-called Decretum Gelasianum is one such. The critical edition of E. von Dobschütz, *Das Decretum Gelasianum, De libris recipiendis et non recipiendis, im kritischen Text* (Leipzig, 1912) (= *TU* 38.4) gives an enumeration of the sixty-one apocryphal works listed in the Decree together with his attempted identification of the several writings. The Decree is likely to date from the sixth century but could contain even older parts.

Excluding from the sixty-one titles those that are titles of Old Testament apocryphal works, and patristic writings, the Shepherd of Hermas, and the Clementine Recognitions, the following remain (the numbers are as in von Dobschütz):

2. Actus nomine Andreae apostoli (extant).
3. Actus nomine Thomae apostoli (extant).
4. Actus nomine Petri apostoli (extant).
5. Actus nomine Philippi apostoli (extant).
6. Evangelium nomine Matthiae (Traditions of Matthias).
7. Evangelium nomine Barnabae.
8. Evangelium nomine Iacobi minoris (Protevangelium Iacobi, *q.v.*)
9. Evangelium nomine Petri apostoli (extant).
10. Evangelium nomine Thomae quibus Manichei utuntur (extant).
11. Evangelia nomine Bartholomaei (extant).
12. Evangelia nomine Andreae (? Acts of Andrew).
13. Evangelia quae falsavit Lucianus.
14. Evangelia quae falsavit Hesychius.
15. Liber de Infantia Salvatoris (Pseudo-Matthew *q.v.*)
16. Liber de nativitate Salvatoris et de Maria vel obstetrice (Pseudo-Matthew *q.v.*)
18. Libri omnes quos fecit Leucius (cf. Acts of John).
19. Liber qui appellatur Fundamentum.
20. Liber qui appellatur Thesaurus.
23. Liber qui appellatur Actus Theclae et Pauli (extant).
26. Revelatio quae appellatur Pauli (extant).
27. Revelatio quae appellatur Thomae (extant).
28. Revelatio quae appellatur Stephani (extant).

29. Liber qui appellatur Transitus sanctae Mariae (Pseudo-Melito, Assumption of the Virgin).
36. Liber qui appellatur Sortes Apostolorum.
37. Liber qui appellatur Lusa Apostolorum.
38. Liber qui appellatur Canones Apostolorum (extant).
56. Epistula Iesu ad Abgarum (extant).
57. Epistula Abgari ad Iesum (extant).

Where a title corresponds or is likely to correspond to an extant work this is indicated in brackets above. However, some of the identifications are debatable (e.g. 15) and a fuller discussion is to be found where appropriate in the section of the present book dealing with the text in question.

In addition to von Dobschütz's work, the following are studies of the Decretum, especially its origin and relationship to St Gelasius:

C. H. Turner, 'Latin Lists of the Canonical Books, i. The Roman Council under Damasus, AD 382' *JTS* 1 (1899–1900), 554–60.
J. Chapman, 'On the "Decretum Gelasianum de libris recipiendis et non recipiendis"', *Rev. Bén.* 25 (1913), 187–207 and 315–33.
E. Amann, reviews of Chapman and von Dobschütz, *Rev. Bib.* 10 (1913), 602–8.
E. Schwartz, 'Zum Decretum Gelasianum', *ZNW* 29 (1930), 161–8.

The List of the Sixty Books (given by James, *ANT*, 23[1]), dating from the seventh century, includes the following New Testament apocryphal works (the numbers are from James):

15. History of James (Protevangelium).
16. Apocalypse of Peter (extant).
17. Travels and Teachings of the Apostles (Apocryphal Acts).
19. Acts of Paul (extant).
20. Apocalypse of Paul (extant).
24. Gospel according to Barnabas.
25. Gospel according to Matthias (Traditions of Matthias).

The Epistle of Barnabas, the writings of Ignatius and Polycarp, and the Apostolic Constitutions are also listed.

The Stichometry of Nicephorus is likely to go back as far as the fourth century. It was added to the Chronology of Nicephorus in the ninth century. Among other writings it refers to the Apocalypse of John, the Apocalypse of Peter (extant), and the Gospel of the Hebrews (*q.v.*) as 'disputed' books. The apocryphal books of the New Testament include:

The Travels of Paul (Acts of Paul).
The Travels of Peter (Acts of Peter).

[1] See also T. Zahn, *Geschichte des neutestamentlichen Kanons*, ii (Erlangen and Leipzig, 1890–2), 289 f.

The Travels of John (Acts of John).
The Travels of Thomas (Acts of Thomas).
Gospel of Thomas (extant).

The text of the Stichometry may be seen in C. de Boor, *Nicephori archiepiscopi Constantinopolitani opuscula historica* (Leipzig, 1880), 132; cf. Zahn, op. cit. ii. 297–301, and E. Preuschen, *Analecta*, ii (Tübingen, ²1910), 62–4.

Jones lists apocryphal writings known to patristic authors from the second–fifth centuries. He gives an alphabetical list of apocryphal works not extant in his day on pp. 107–11 and discusses them in sequence in Part II (pp. 133–52).

Studies of the history of the canon of the New Testament often include details of the books deemed to be canonical and uncanonical by various patristic writers. Such information may be seen in B. M. Metzger, *The Canon of the New Testament* (Oxford, 1987).

See also:

F. W. Grosheide, *Some Early Lists of the Books of the New Testament* (Leiden, 1948) (= *Textus Minores* 1).

I

APOCRYPHAL GOSPELS

Lost Gospels

References are to be found in lists of disputed texts and in the writings of the church fathers to gospels which cannot now be identified with any extant works. The contents of parts of some of these can be ascertained, but our knowledge is second-hand. It is not surprising to discover that gospels that were deemed to be unorthodox eventually disappeared from view: what is surprising is that so many apocryphal works did survive, often despite official disapproval.

In the following pages some of the more significant lost gospels are described. Those known only by a mere title are listed at the end of this section (number 5).

1. Jewish-Christian Gospels:
    (a) The Gospel according to the Hebrews
    (b) The Gospel of the Nazaraeans
    (c) The Gospel of the Ebionites
2. The Gospel of the Egyptians
3. The Traditions of Matthias
4. The Preaching of Peter
5. Other Lost Gospels.

1. JEWISH-CHRISTIAN GOSPELS

Clement of Alexandria, Origen, Eusebius, Epiphanius, Jerome, and probably Didymus the Blind were acquainted with gospels of a Jewish-Christian character and quoted from them. The question is whether their quotations are from one, two, or more gospels, and whether these gospels originated within one or more of the Jewish-Christian sects mentioned in early Christian literature.

Early Christian writers usually connected Jewish-Christian gospel tradition with the supposed Aramaic or Hebrew version of the Gospel of Matthew. They all assumed that only one Jewish-Christian gospel existed, although possibly in various versions and languages, and attributed it to one or other of the well-known Jewish-Christian sects such as the Ebionites and the Nazaraeans (cf. Eusebius, *HE* 3. 27, 4 (Schwartz, *GCS* 9.1, p. 256) on the Gospel according to the Hebrews, and Epiphanius in his description of the Nazaraeans in *adv. Haer.* 29 and of the Ebionites in *adv. Haer.* 30 (Holl, *GCS* 25, pp. 372–5)). These ideas have been criticized during the last two centuries. It appears that some of the ancient presuppositions can be explained from historical facts, but the conclusions which have been drawn from those have to be corrected.

The existence of the original Aramaic or Hebrew version of the Gospel of Matthew is still a matter of dispute, but a relation between Matthew and a Jewish-Christian gospel used by Palestinian Christians called Nazaraeans is evident. The nature of this relationship is not quite clear, but both gospels must have had roots in the same environment and the use of similar sources cannot be denied. This Jewish-Christian gospel must have been present in the famous library of Caesarea, where it was probably read by Eusebius, who speaks in his *Theophania* of a gospel 'in Hebrew letters', and by Jerome, who adds that he also received the gospel from the Nazaraeans themselves (*de Vir. Ill.* 3 (Richardson, pp. 8–9)). This gospel enjoyed a great popularity because it was supposed to be a witness to the Aramaic version of Matthew. It was referred to until well into medieval times, but such references were usually based merely on Jerome's writings. From the time of Jerome a tendency has existed to ascribe (*a*) interesting historical traditions not known from the canonical Gospels and (*b*) supposed Semitisms in their text to the 'Jewish-Christian Gospel'.

Further evidence of the existence of a Jewish-Christian gospel is provided by marginal notes in some New Testament manuscripts dated around the tenth century that refer to *To Ioudaïkon*, 'The Jewish (Gospel)'. Their origin is unknown, but they may have been taken from a commentator on Matthew unknown to us.

This Aramaic gospel has to be distinguished from that quoted by Clement of Alexandria, Origen, and Didymus the Blind[1] under the name 'Gospel according to the Hebrews', since it is evident from their quotations that that gospel must have been written in Greek. The text does not show a relationship with the Gospel of Matthew. It seems to have been the gospel of Jewish-Christians in Egypt, but not those who belonged to a particular sect. From one of these references to this gospel (concerning Jesus' words about his mother, the Holy Spirit) we know that Jerome used it in his own works, but he erroneously supposed it to be from the gospel in Aramaic (cf. *on Micha* 7. 6 and *de Vir. Ill.* 2 infra).

This means we are not always certain whether Jerome is quoting from the Aramaic gospel or the Gospel according to the Hebrews. But it is usually assumed that those of his references to a Jewish-Christian gospel that have obviously been taken from a Greek original and are of a non-Matthaean character are from the Gospel according to the Hebrews, and it is on this basis that Jerome's citations have been divided between (*a*) and (*b*) below.

---

[1] *Comm. in Ps.* 33. See M. Gronewald (ed.), *Didymos der Blinde: Psalmenkommentare* (Tura-Papyrus), iii (Bonn, 1969), 198 f. (= *Papyrologische Texte und Abhandlungen* 8).

Epiphanius quoted from a Jewish-Christian gospel in his chapter about the Ebionites (*adv. Haer.* 30). The contents of the references show that this gospel has been composed with the help of the three synoptic Gospels of the New Testament. Its contents widely differ from that of the two gospels mentioned earlier. Epiphanius was convinced that this gospel is a heavily distorted version of the Aramaic Gospel of Matthew. It does not bear a particular name, but some modern scholars suppose that its title may have been 'The Gospel of the Twelve', an apocryphal gospel mentioned under this name by Origen (*Hom. 1 on Luke* (Rauer, pp. 3 ff.)).

(*a*) *The Gospel according to the Hebrews*
This Gospel was quoted by Clement, Origen, and probably by Didymus the Blind. Jerome also appears to be a witness for its contents. The Gospel must have been written at the beginning of the second century in Egypt in the Greek language. Its theology appears to be based upon Jewish Wisdom thinking.

The citations from the patristic sources are given below.

(*b*) *The Gospel of the Nazaraeans*
A number of references come from Jerome's works, particularly from his Commentary on Matthew. References to the 'Gospel according to the Hebrews' in the Latin translation—though not in the original Greek version—of Origen's Commentary on Matthew seem also to be to the present gospel. They show a definite Matthean character. References to *To Ioudaïkon* are present in the margin of the Greek text of some manuscripts of the Gospel of Matthew, and because one of them can also be found in Jerome we may assume that we are dealing with the Gospel of the Nazaraeans. The gospel would have been used by the Nazaraeans who lived in the neighbourhood of Beroea, and would have been written in (Palestinian) Aramaic in the first half of the second century.

Patristic citations and the annotations in New Testament Greek cursives 4, 273, 566, 899, 1424 are given below.

(*c*) *The Gospel of the Ebionites*
This is the name given by modern scholars to a gospel supposed to have been used by the Ebionites. All our knowledge of it is derived from Epiphanius, *adv. Haer.* 30. 3, 13 f., 16, 22. Attempts to locate citations from this gospel in other places have not been convincing.

Origen (*Hom. 1 on Luke*), Ambrose, and Jerome (*on Matt.* prol. and *Dialogi contra Pelagianos* 3. 2) refer to a 'Gospel of the Twelve' or a Gospel 'according to the Apostles', and it has been convincingly argued (by Zahn) that this is to be identified with the Gospel of the Ebionites, on the ground that in the fragments located in Epiphanius it is the apostles who are the narrators.

The fragments we have in Epiphanius show that its contents included accounts of the Baptism (with which the work is said to have begun), the Last Supper, and the Passion and Easter (for which details are lacking). Its original language was Greek, and there is a familiarity with the contents of the canonical Gospels (especially the synoptics). In character it is likely to have been of the synoptic type.

The ignoring of the birth of Jesus seems to have been deliberate in so far as the Ebionites' Christology denied the virgin birth. The account of the Baptist's food (eliminating locusts) points to the vegetarianism practised by Ebionites. These and other elements are said to confirm the origin of this Gospel as being not only separate from any other Jewish-Christian gospel but belonging to the Jewish Christianity of the Ebionites.

The work seems to have originated in the first half of the second century (Irenaeus knew of its existence by hearsay). Its provenance is likely to have been Transjordan, which is where the Ebionites were based, and where Epiphanius is known to have worked.

Extracts are given below.

THE GOSPEL ACCORDING TO THE HEBREWS AND THE GOSPEL OF THE NAZARAEANS

The extracts are set out in:

Preuschen, 3–8, 136–41.

Klostermann, *Apocrypha*, ii. (2)4–9. [Cf. Michaelis (General Bibl., under 'Modern Translations, German'), 112–28 and 131 f.]

de Santos Otero, 29–47 (with Spanish trans.).

Lührmann, 40–55.

Passages from *To Ioudaïkon* can be seen in:

A. Schmidtke, *Neue Fragmente und Untersuchungen zu den judenchristlichen Evangelien* (Leipzig, 1911) (= *TU* 37.1).

MODERN TRANSLATIONS

English

James, 1–8.
Hennecke[3], i. 139–53, 158–65, and see Introduction, 117–39.
Hennecke[5], i. 155–64, 172–8, and see Introduction, 135–53.

German

Hennecke[1], 11–21 (A. Meyer); cf. *Handbuch*, 21–38.
Hennecke[3], i. 90–100, 104–8 (P. Vielhauer), and see Introduction, 75–90.

Hennecke[5], i. 128–38, 142–7 (P. Vielhauer and G. Strecker), and see Introduction, 114–28.

French

Migne, Dictionnaire, ii, cols. 247–52 (cf. Variot (General Bibl., under Reference and General), 331–78).
Éac, 433–45, 455–62.

Italian

Bonaccorsi, i, pp. xii–xiv, 2–8.
Erbetta, i.1, 114–31.
Moraldi, i. 359–61, 367–9, 373–82.

GENERAL

E. B. Nicholson, *The Gospel according to the Hebrews: Its Fragments translated and annotated* (London, 1879).
R. Handmann, *Das Hebräerevangelium* (Leipzig, 1888) (= *TU* 5.3).
A. S. Barnes, 'The Gospel According to the Hebrews', *JTS* 6 (1905), 356–71.
V. Burch, 'The Gospel according to the Hebrews: Some New Matter chiefly from Coptic Sources', *JTS* (1920), 310–5. [Cf. *JTS* 22 (1921), 160–1 (M. R. James).]
M.-J. Lagrange, 'L'Évangile selon les Hébreux', *Rev. Bib.* 31 (1922), 161–81, 321–49.
R. Dunkerley, 'The Gospel According to the Hebrews', *ExpT* 39 (1927–8), 437–42, 490–5.
A. Schmidtke, 'Zum Hebräerevangelium', *ZNW* 35 (1936), 24–44.
H. Waitz 'Neue Untersuchungen über die sogennanten judenchristlichen Evangelien', *ZNW* 36 (1937), 60–81.
P. Parker, 'A Proto-Lukan Basis for the Gospel According to the Hebrews', *JBL* 59 (1940), 471–8.
A. A. T. Ehrhardt, 'Judaeo-Christians in Egypt, the Epistula Apostolorum and the Gospel to the Hebrews', in F. L. Cross (ed.), *Studia Evangelica* iii (Berlin, 1964), 360–82 (= *TU* 88).
A. F. J. Klijn, 'The Question of the Rich Young Man in a Jewish-Christian Gospel', *NovT* 8 (1966), 149–55.
S. P. Brock, 'A New Testimonium to the "Gospel According to the Hebrews" ', *NTS* 18 (1971), 220–2.
A. F. J. Klijn, 'Patristic Evidence for Jewish Christian and Aramaic Gospel Tradition', in E. Best and R. McL. Wilson (eds.), *Text and Interpretation* (Cambridge, 1979), 169–77.
—— 'Das Hebräer- und das Nazoräerevangelium', *ANRW* 2.25.5, 3997–4033.
Dieter Lührmann, *Die apokryph gewordenen Evangelien* (Leiden, 2004), 182–258 (= *Supplements* to *Novum Testamentum* 112).
M. Herbert and M. McNamara, *Irish Biblical Apocrypha* (Edinburgh, 1989), esp. pp. xv and xxi.

A. F. J, Klijn, *Jewish-Christian Gospel Tradition* (Leiden, 1992) (= *Supplements to Vigiliae Christianae* 17).
Klauck, 53–72: ET 36–54.

SYNOPSES

Aland[13], 584–6. [Aland provides cross-references to the Gospel of the Hebrews (including medieval texts not given above).]
Huck – Greeven[13], 285–6.
Boismard, 414–15.

THE GOSPEL OF THE EBIONITES

The extracts are set out in:

Preuschen, 9–12, 141–3.
Klostermann, *Apocrypha*, ii. [(2)] 9–12.
de Santos Otero, 47–53 (with Spanish trans.).
Lührmann, 32–9.
[Cf. Fabricius, i. 346–9.]

MODERN TRANSLATIONS

English

James, 8–10.
Hennecke[3], i. 153–8. Hennecke[5], i. 166–72.

French

Éac, 447–53.

German

Hennecke[1], 24–7 (A. Meyer); id., *Handbuch*, 42–7.
Hennecke[3], i. 100–4 (P. Vielhauer).
Hennecke[5], i. 138–42 (P. Vielhauer and G. Strecker).

Italian

Moraldi i. 358–9, 371–3; [2] i. 433–5, 445–7.
Cravieri, 261–4.

GENERAL

H. Waitz, 'Das Evangelium der zwölf Apostel (Ebioniten-evangelium)', *ZNW* 13 (1912), 338–48; 14 (1913), 38–64, 117–32.
M.-E. Boismard; 'Évangile des Ebionites et problème synoptique: Mc 1.2–6 et par.', *Rev. Bib.* 73 (1964), 321–52.
D. A. Bertrand, 'L'Évangile des Ebionites: une harmonie évangelique antérieure au Diatessaron', *NTS* 26 (1980), 548–63.
G. Howard, 'The Gospel of the Ebionites', *ANRW* 2.25.5, 4034–52.
F. Neirynck, 'The Apocryphal Gospels and the Gospel of Mark', in J.-M. Sevrin (ed.), *The New Testament in Early Christianity* (Leuven, 1989), 123–75, esp. 157–60 (= *BETL* 86).
Klauck, 72–6: ET 51–4.
Jörg Frey, 'Die Scholien aus dem jüdischen Evangelium und das sogenannte Nazoräerevangelium', *ZNW* 94 (2003), 122–37.

SYNOPSES

Aland[13], 584–6.
Huck–Greeven[13], 285–6.
Boismard, 414.

1 (a). THE GOSPEL ACCORDING TO THE HEBREWS

Patristic Citations

Clement of Alexandria, *Strom.* 2. 9. 45 (Stählin, *GCS* 52 (15), p. 137):

As it is also written in the Gospel of the Hebrews, 'He who wonders shall reign, and he who reigns shall rest.' 1

Cf. *Strom.* 5. 14. 96 (Stählin, *GCS* 52 (15), p. 389): With these words agrees the sentence: 'He who seeks will not rest till he finds, and when he finds he will wonder, and wondering he shall reign, and reigning he shall rest.'[1]

(Cf. also Coptic Thomas, logion 2, and P. Oxy. 654—below, pp. 135–6.)

Origen, *on John* 2. 12 (Preuschen, p. 67):

If any should lend credence to the Gospel according to the Hebrews, where the Saviour himself says, 'My mother, the Holy Spirit, took me just now by one of my hairs and carried me off to the great Mount Tabor', he will have difficulty in explaining how the Holy Spirit can be the mother of Christ. 2

Cf. id., *on Jer.* 15. 4 (ed. E. Klostermann, *GCS* 6 (Leipzig, 1901), p. 128): If anyone receives the word, 'My mother, the Holy Spirit, took me just now and carried me off to the great Mount Tabor', he could see his mother.

(See also Jerome, *on Micha* 7. 6f. (ed. M. Adriaen, *CCL* 76 (Turnhout, 1976), p. 513); id., *on Is.* 40. 9–11 (ed. M. Adriaen, *CCL* 73 (Turnhout, 1963), p. 459); id., *on Ezek.* 16. 3 (ed. F. Glorie, *CCL* 75 (Turnhout, 1964), p. 168).)

Jerome, *on Eph.* 5. 4 (Migne, *PL* 26, cols. 552 C–D):

As we read in the Hebrew Gospel where the Lord says to his disciples, 'Never be glad unless you are in charity with your brother.'[2] 3

Id., *de Vir. Ill.* 2 (Richardson, p. 8):

The Gospel also entitled 'according to the Hebrews' which I lately translated into Greek and Latin, and which Origen[3] often quotes, contains the following narrative after the Resurrection: 'Now the Lord, when he had given the cloth to the servant of the priest, went to James and appeared to him.' For 4

---

[1] Cf. Matt. 11: 28 f.
[2] Cf. Luke 15: 31 f.
[3] 'Adamantius', according to the text cited by Klijn, *ANRW* 2.25.5, 4011.

James had taken an oath that he would not eat bread from that hour on which he had drunk the cup of the Lord till he saw him risen from the dead. Again a little later the Lord said, 'Bring a table and bread', and forthwith it is added: 'He took bread and blessed and broke it and gave to James the Just and said to him, "My brother, eat your bread, for the Son of Man is risen from those who sleep."'

Cf. ibid. 16, which attributes the following passage from Ignatius, *ad Smyrn.* 3. 1–2, to the Gospel of the Hebrews: I know and believe that after his resurrection he lived in the flesh. For when the Lord came to Peter and to the Apostles, he said to them, 'Lay hold, handle me, and see that I am not an incorporeal spirit.' And immediately they touched him and believed, being convinced by his flesh and spirit.

Id., *on Ezek.* 18. 7 (ed. F. Glorie, *CCL* 75 (Turnhout, 1964), p. 237):

5   In the Gospel of the Hebrews which the Nazarenes are in the habit of reading it belongs to the greatest sins when 'one afflicts the spirit of his brother'.

Id., *on Isa.* 11. 2 (ed. M. Adriaen, *CCL* 73 (Turnhout, 1963), pp. 147–8):

6   But in the Gospel which is written in Hebrew and which the Nazarenes read, 'the whole fountain of the Holy Spirit shall descend upon him'. And the Lord is spirit, and where the Spirit of the Lord is, there is liberty. And in the Gospel referred to above I find this written: 'And it came to pass, as the Lord came up out of the water, the whole fountain of the Holy Spirit descended upon him and rested upon him and said to him, "My son, in all the prophets I expected that you might come and that I might rest upon you. You are my rest, you are my firstborn Son, who reigns in eternity."'[4]

Eusebius, *HE* 3. 39. 17 (Schwartz, *GCS* 9.1, p. 292):

7   He (Papias) gives a history of a woman who had been accused of many sins before the Lord, which is also contained in the Gospel of the Hebrews.

1(b). THE GOSPEL OF THE NAZARAEANS

Patristic Citations

(Pseudo-) Origen, *on Matt.* 15. 14 (Latin) (ed. E. Benz and E. Klostermann, x, *GCS* 40 (Leipzig, 1935), pp. 389–90):

1   It is written in a certain Gospel, which is styled 'according to the Hebrews', if any one pleases to receive it, not as an authority, but as an illustration of the subject before us: Another rich man said to him, 'Master, what good thing

---

[4] Cf. Mark 1: 9–11 and parallels.

shall I do to live?' He said to him, 'O man, fulfil the law and the prophets.' He replied, 'I have done that.' He said to him, 'Go, sell all that you possess and distribute it to the poor, and come, follow me.' But the rich man began to scratch his head and it did not please him. And the Lord said to him; 'How can you say, "I have fulfilled the law and the prophets", since it is written in the law: You shall love your neighbour as yourself, and lo! many of your brethren, sons of Abraham, are clothed in filth, dying of hunger, and your house is full of many goods, and nothing at all goes out of it to them.' And returning to Simon, his disciple, who was sitting by him, he said, 'Simon, son of Jonas, it is easier for a camel to enter the eye of a needle than for a rich man (to enter) into the kingdom of heaven.'[5]

Eusebius, *Theophania*, 4. 12 (Syriac) (ed. H. Gressmann, GCS 11.2 (Leipzig, 1904), pp. 182*–4*) (cf. *Theophania Syriaca*, ed. S. Lee (London, 1842):

The cause therefore of the divisions of souls that take place in houses Christ himself taught, as we have found in a place in the Gospel existing among the Jews in the Hebrew language, in which it is said: 'I will choose for myself the best which my Father in heaven has given me.'[6]

2

Id., *Theophania*, 4. 22 (Greek) (Klostermann, p. 9 (no. 15); Migne, *PG* 24, cols. 685–8):

Since the Gospel which has come down to us in the Hebrew language pronounces the threat not against the man who hid the money, but against him who spent it in riotous living ... (The master) had three servants; one spent the substance of the master with harlots and with flute girls; the second multiplied it; the third hid the talent; then one was received, another was blamed, and the other was cast into prison. I imagine that according to Matthew the threat which was spoken after the word addressed to the idle one does not concern him, but, by way of epanalepsis, the one mentioned before who had eaten and drunk with the drunkard.[7]

3

Jerome,[8] *Epistle 20 to Damasus* (ed. I. Hilberg, CSEL 54 (Vienna and Leipzig, 1910), p. 110):

Matthew who wrote a Gospel in Hebrew put it thus: 'Osanna Barrama', i.e. Hosanna in the highest.

4

Id., *de Vir. Ill.* 3 (Richardson, pp. 9 f.):

Now this Hebrew (viz. Matthew) is preserved to this day in the library at Caesarea, which Pamphilus the Martyr so diligently collated. I also obtained

5

---

[5] Matt. 19: 16–24.
[6] Cf. John 6: 37–9.
[7] Matt. 25: 14–30.
[8] Jerome's references to this gospel span writings normally dated between 383 and 415.

permission from the Nazarenes of Beroea in Syria, who use this volume, to make a copy of it. In this it is to be observed that, throughout, the evangelist, when quoting the witness of the Old Testament, either in his own person or in that of the Lord and Saviour, does not follow the authority of the Seventy translators, but the Hebrew Scriptures, from which he quotes these two sayings: 'Out of Egypt have I called my Son'[9] and 'hence he shall be called a Nazarene'.[10]

Id., *on Matt.* 2. 5 (Hurst and Adriaen, p. 13):

6 'Bethlehem of Judaea'. This is a mistake of the scribes, for I believe that the evangelist wrote it as we read it in the Hebrew 'of Judah' not Judaea.

Ibid. 6. 11 (Hurst and Adriaen, p. 37):

7 In the Gospel of the Hebrews for the 'supersubstantial bread' I found 'Maḥar' which signifies 'tomorrow's', so that the meaning would be: 'give us this day the bread for the morrow.'[11]

Cf. id., *on Ps.* 135 (ed. G. Morin, *CCL* 78 (Turnhout, 1958), p. 295): In the Hebrew Gospel according to Matthew it is thus: 'Our bread of the morrow give us this day'; that is 'the bread which you will give us in your kingdom give us this day'.

Ibid. 12. 13 (Hurst and Adriaen, p. 90):

8 In the Gospel that the Nazarenes and Ebionites use, which I recently translated from the Hebrew into Greek and which most people designate as the authentic text of Matthew, we read that the man with the withered hand[12] was a mason, who asked for help with these words: 'I was a mason, working for my bread with my hands. I pray to you, Jesus, restore me to health so that I do not eat my bread in disgrace.'

Ibid. 23. 35 (Hurst and Adriaen, p. 219):

9 In the Gospel which the Nazarenes use we find it written for 'Son of Barachias'[13] 'Son of Johoiada'.

Ibid. 27. 16 (Hurst and Adriaen, p. 265):

10 In the so-called Gospel of the Hebrews, Barabbas who was condemned for sedition and murder is interpreted by 'son of their teacher'.

Ibid. 27. 51 (Hurst and Adriaen, p. 275):

11 In the Gospel often mentioned we read that 'the very great lintel of the Temple broke and fell into pieces'.

---

[9] Matt. 2: 15.
[10] Matt. 2: 23.
[11] Matt. 6: 11; Luke 11: 3.
[12] Matt. 12: 9–14 and parallels.
[13] Matt. 23: 35.

Cf. *Epistle to Hedibia*, 120. 8 (ed. I. Hilberg, *CSEL* 55 (Vienna and Leipzig, 1912)), pp. 489-92: But in the Gospel that is written in Hebrew letters we read not that the veil of the temple was rent but that a lintel of the temple of wondrous size fell.

Id., *on Isa.*, pref. to book 18 (ed. M. Adriaen, *CCL* 73 (Turnhout, 1963), p. 741):

For when the apostles thought him to be a spirit or, in the words of the Gospel of the Hebrews which the Nazarenes read, 'a bodiless demon' he said to them...

Id., *Dialogi contra Pelagianos*. 3. 2 (ed. Migne, *PL* 23, cols. 597B-598A):

In the Gospel of the Hebrews which is written in the Syro-Chaldaic tongue but in Hebrew characters, which the Nazarenes make use of at this day, and which is also called the 'Gospel of the Apostles', or as many think, 'that of Matthew', and which is in the library of Caesarea, the following narrative is given: 'Behold, the mother of the Lord and his brothers said to him, "John the Baptist baptizes for the remission of sins; let us go and be baptized by him".' But he said, 'What have I committed, that I should be baptized of him, unless it be that in saying this I am in ignorance?"[14]. In the same volume (i.e. in the Gospel of the Hebrews) we read, 'If your brother has sinned in word against you and has made satisfaction, forgive him up to seven times a day.' Simon, his disciple, said to him, 'Seven times?"[15] The Lord answered saying, 'Verily I say to you: until seventy times seven! For even in the prophets the word of sin is found after they have been anointed with the Holy Spirit.'

Cf. variant in cursive 566 at Matt. 18: 22 below.

New Testament Greek cursive manuscripts (biblical reference, marginal note, and cursive number)

Matt. 4: 5. The Jewish copy has not 'to the holy city' but 'in Jerusalem'. 566
Matt. 5: 22. The word 'without cause' is not inserted in some copies, nor in the Jewish. 1424
Matt. 7: 5. The Jewish has here: 'If you are in my bosom and do not do the will of my Father which is in heaven, out of my bosom will I cast you away.' 1424 (2 Clement 4: 5 has: The Lord said, 'If you are with me gathered together in my bosom and do not do my commandments, I will cast you away and say to you, "Depart from me: I do not know where you come from, you workers of wickedness".')
Matt. 10: 16. The Jewish has '(wise) more than serpents' instead of 'as serpents'. 1424

---

[14] Matt. 3: 13-14.
[15] Matt. 18: 21-2.

Matt. 11: 12. (The kingdom of heaven suffers violence.) The Jewish has: 'is ravished (or plundered)'. 1424

Matt. 11: 25. (I thank you [lit. confess to you], O Father.) The Jewish: 'I give you thanks.' 1424

Matt. 12: 40. The Jewish does not have: 'three days and three nights (in the heart of the earth)'. 899

Matt. 15: 5. The Jewish: 'Corban, by which you shall be profited by us.' 1424

Matt. 16: 2, 3. Omitted by the Jewish (as by many extant manuscripts). 1424

Matt. 16: 17. The Jewish: '[Simon] son of John.' 566, 1424

Matt. 18: 22. The Jewish has, immediately after the seventy times seven: 'For in the prophets, after they were anointed with the Holy Spirit, there was found in them a word (matter) of sin.' 566, 899

Matt. 26: 74. The Jewish: 'and he denied and swore and cursed.' 4, 273, 566, 899, 1424

Matt. 27: 65. The Jewish: 'And he delivered to them armed men, that they might sit opposite the cave and keep watch on it day and night.' 1424

1 (c). THE GOSPEL OF THE EBIONITES

Patristic Citations

Epiphanius, *adv. Haer.* 30. 3 (Holl, *GCS* 25, pp. 335 f.):

1   And they only accept the Gospel of Matthew. This alone they use, as do also the followers of Cerinthus and Merinthus. They call it the Gospel of the Hebrews. To tell the truth, Matthew wrote only in Hebrew and in Hebrew letters the narrative and preaching of the Gospel in the New Testament. Others again have asserted that the Gospel of John is kept in a Hebrew translation in the treasuries of the Jews—namely at Tiberias—and that it is hidden there as some converts from Judaism have told us accurately. Even the book of the Acts of the Apostles translated from the Greek into the Hebrew is said to be kept there in the treasuries, so that the Jews, who told us this and read it, came in this way to belief in Christ.

Ibid. 30. 13:

2   In the Gospel of Matthew used by them—not in a perfect but in a mutilated and castrated form—called the Gospel of the Hebrews it is recorded: 'And there was a man named Jesus, and he was about thirty years old; he has chosen us and he came into Capernaum and entered into the house of Simon, surnamed Peter, and he opened his mouth and said, "As I walked by the sea of Tiberias, I chose John and James, the sons of Zebedee, and Simon and Andrew and Thaddaeus and Simon Zelotes, and Judas Iscariot; you also, Matthew, when you were sitting at the receipt of custom,

did I call and you followed me. According to my intention you shall be twelve apostles for a testimony to Israel".'[16]

And it came to pass when John baptized, that the Pharisees came to him and were baptized, and all Jerusalem also. He had a garment of camels' hair, and a leathern girdle about his loins. And his meat was wild honey, which tasted like manna, formed like cakes of oil.[17]

The beginning of their Gospel reads thus: 'It came to pass in the days of Herod, King of Judaea, that John came and baptized with the baptism of repentance in the river Jordan; he is said to be from the tribe of Aaron and a son of Zacharias the priest and of Elizabeth, and all went out to him.'[18]

And after many other words it goes on: 'After the people had been baptized, Jesus came also, and was baptized by John. And as he came out of the water, the heavens opened, and he saw the Holy Spirit descending in the form of a dove and entering into him. And a voice was heard from heaven, "You are my beloved Son, and in you am I well pleased." And again, "This day have I begotten you." And suddenly a great light shone in that place. And John, seeing him, said, "Who are you, Lord?" Then a voice was heard from heaven, "This is my beloved Son, in whom I am well pleased." Thereat John fell at his feet and said, "I pray you, Lord, baptize me." But he would not, saying, "Suffer it, for thus it is fitting that all should be accomplished".'[19]

Ibid. 30. 14:

They also deny that he is a man, basing their assertion on the word which he said when he was told: 'Behold your mother and your brethren stand outside.' 'Who is my mother and who are my brethren?' And he stretched forth his hand toward his disciples and said, 'My brethren and my mother and sisters are those who do the will of my Father.'[20]

Ibid. 30. 16:

They say that he is not begotten by God the Father but created like one of the archangels, being greater than they. He rules over the angels and the beings created by God and he came and declared, as the gospel used by them records: 'I have come to abolish the sacrifices: if you do not cease from sacrificing, the wrath [of God] will not cease from weighing upon you.'

Ibid. 30. 22:

Those who reject meat have inconsiderately fallen into error and said, 'I have no desire to eat the flesh of this Paschal Lamb with you.' They leave the

---

[16] Matt. 10: 1–4 and parallels.
[17] Mark 1: 5–6 and parallel.
[18] Mark 1: 4 and parallel.
[19] Matt. 3: 14 f.
[20] Mark 3: 31–5 and parallels.

true order of words and distort the word which is clear to all from the connection of the words and make the disciples say: 'Where do you want us to prepare for you to eat the Passover?' To which he replied, 'I have no desire to eat the flesh of this Paschal Lamb with you.'[21]

2. THE GOSPEL OF THE EGYPTIANS[22]

This apocryphal gospel is likely to have originated in Egypt in the middle of the second century. Clement of Alexandria and Origen knew it, which indicates its circulation within Egypt itself. In Origen's first *Homily on Luke* he refers to those who composed the Gospel of the Egyptians as an example of those who attempted to write gospels prior to Luke (Luke 1: 1). It was accepted at an early date as canonical in Egypt although by the time of Origen it was numbered among the books to be rejected.

The contents of this gospel are known from the following references in the works of church fathers, in particular from Clement of Alexandria:

Clement, *Strom.* 3. 6. 45; 3. 9. 63–6; 3. 13. 92 f.
Hippolytus, *Haer. (Philosophoumena)*, 5. 7
Epiphanius, *adv. Haer.* 62. 2. 4; *Excerpta ex Theodoto*, 67.

In so far as they can be reconstructed from the above passages, the contents suggest that this is a secondary gospel with a distinct doctrinal tendency, namely to promote Encratism, especially the rejection of marriage (e.g. in *Strom.* 3. 6. 45 Clement reports that when Salome asked how long death should have power she is told that it is 'as long as you women give birth to children'). The gospel was also used to prove the doctrines of the Naassenes and the Sabellians.

It resembles Gnostic works in assigning an important role to the female disciples, especially in this case to Salome. Other teaching (e.g. as reported by Clement, *Strom.* 3. 13. 92) encourages the elimination of the sexual differences between male and female, a doctrine to be found for instance in the Coptic Gospel of Thomas (logia 22 and 114).

Attempts to identify the Gospel of the Egyptians with other apocryphal writings (by Schneckenburger and others) are discussed in full by Schneemelcher in Hennecke[3] or [5], i, who shows that these are not convincing. Likewise it is improbable that works known to us from the Oxyrhynchus and other papyri fragments should be assigned to this gospel.

The extracts are set out in:

[21] Mark 14: 12–16 and parallels.
[22] This Greek gospel is not to be confused with a Gospel of the Egyptians found at Nag Hammadi.

The Gospel of the Egyptians

Preuschen, 2 f., 135 f.
Klostermann, *Apocrypha*, ii. [(2)]12–13.
de Santos Otero, 53–7 (with Spanish trans.).
Lührmann, 26–31.
[Cf. Fabricius, i. 346–9.]

SYNOPSES

Aland[13], 584–6. [The passages from Hippolytus are attributed to the Gospel of the Naassenes.]
Huck–Greeven[13], 285 f.
Boismard, 415.

MODERN TRANSLATIONS

English

James, 10–12.
Hennecke[3], i. 166–78.
Hennecke[5], i. 209–15.

French

Migne, *Dictionnaire*. ii. cols. 217–20
Éac, 473–7.

German

Hennecke[1], 21–3 (E. Hennecke); cf. *Handbuch* 38–42.
Hennecke[3], i, 109–17 (W. Schneemelcher).
Hennecke[5], i. 174–9 (W. Schneemelcher).

Italian

Bonaccorsi, i. xv, 14–15
Erbetta, i. 1, 147–52
Moraldi, i. 361–2, 383–5; [2] i. 437–8, 456–8.

GENERAL

M. Schneckenburger, *Über das Evangelium der Ägyptier* (Berne, 1834).
Klauck, 77–82: ET 55–9.

Patristic Citations

Epiphanius, *adv. Haer.* 62. 2 (Holl, *GCS* 31, p. 391):

    Their (the Sabellians') entire error has its cause and strength in some   1
apocrypha, especially in the so-called Gospel of the Egyptians to which some

have ascribed this name. For in it many such things are transmitted as esoteric doctrine of the Lord, as if he had taught his disciples that the Father, the Son, and the Holy Spirit are one and the same.

Hippolytus, *Haer.* 5. 7 (Wendland, p. 81):

2   [The Naassenes] say that the soul is something which is hard to find and hard to know. For it remains not in one fashion and in one form, nor also in one affection so that it could be called after one pattern or perceived in its nature. These manifold strange notions they find in the so-called Gospel of the Egyptians.

Clement of Alexandria, *Strom.* 3. 9. 63 (Stählin, GCS 52 (15), p. 225):

3   Those who are opposed to God's creation because of continence, which has a fair-sounding name, also quote the words addressed to Salome which I mentioned earlier. They are handed down, as I believe, in the Gospel of the Egyptians. For they say: the Saviour himself said, 'I have come to undo the works of the female', by the female meaning lust, and by the works birth and decay.

Ibid. 3. 9. 64 (Stählin, p. 225):

4   Salome asked correctly when the Logos spoke of the end, 'How long shall death prevail?'... Wherefore the Lord very aptly answered, 'As long as you women bear children'.

Cf. ibid. 3. 6. 45 (Stählin, p. 217) and id., *Excerpta ex Theodoto*, 67 (ed. O. Stählin, iii, GCS 17^2 (Leipzig, 1909; rev. L. Früchtel and U. Treu, Berlin, 1970), p. 129).

Ibid. 3. 9. 66 (Stählin, p. 226):

5   Why do they (heretics who reject marriage) not also quote the following words which were spoken to Salome, they, who sooner follow everything else than the true evangelical canon? For when she said, 'Then I have done well in not giving birth', imagining that it is not permitted to bear children, the Lord answered, 'Eat of every herb, but the bitter one eat not.'

Ibid. 3. 13. 92 (Stählin, p. 238):

6   When Salome asked when it shall be made known the Lord said, 'When you tread under foot the covering of shame and when out of two is made one, and the male with the female, neither male nor female.' And this word we have not in the four gospels transmitted to us but only in the Gospel of the Egyptians.

Cf. 2 Clem. 12. 2, 4, 5:[23] For the Lord himself, being asked by someone when his Kingdom would come, replied, 'When two shall be one, that which is without as that

---

[23] Ed. K. Bihlmeyer, *Die Apostolischen Väter*, i (Tübingen, ²1956), 76 (= *Sammlung ausgewählter kirchen- und dogmengeschichtliche Quellenschriften*, ii. 1).

which is within, and the male with the female, neither male nor female.' Now, two are one when we speak the truth one to another, and there is unfeignedly one soul in two bodies. And 'that which is without as that which is within' means this: He calls the soul 'that which is within', and the body 'that which is without'. As, then, your body is visible to sight, so also let your soul be manifest by good works. And 'the male with the female, neither male nor female', this he said, that brother seeing sister may have no thought concerning her as female, and that she have no thought concerning him as male. 'If you do these things', he says, 'the Kingdom of my Father shall come.'

3. THE TRADITIONS OF MATTHIAS

Origen (*Hom. 1. 1 on Luke*) says he knows of a Gospel according to Matthias. The name recurs in the writings of Ambrose, Jerome, and Eusebius. It is condemned in the Gelasian Decree, and occurs in the List of the Sixty Books. Clement of Alexandria refers in *Strom.* 2. 9. 45; 3. 4. 6; 7. 13. 82; 7. 17. 108 to a treatise known as the Traditions of Matthias and it is possible that this is the same work as Origen refers to.

The work seems to have been composed before the third century. Its Gnostic origin is assumed by Hennecke, which assigns it to that category of gospel, although H.-C. Puech (Hennecke[3], i. 224 f; Hennecke[5], i. 307; Eng. trans., [3]i. 308 f; [5]i. 382–6) is cautious about identifying its origin to Gnostic circles.

The extracts are set out in:

Preuschen, 12.
Klostermann, *Apocrypha*, ii [(2)]13 ff.
de Santos Otero, 58–60.
Lührmann, 140–1.
[Cf. Fabricius, i. 341.]

SYNOPSES

Aland[13], 584–6; Huck–Greeven[13], 285–6; Boismard, 415.

MODERN TRANSLATIONS

English

James, 12–13.
Hennecke[3], i. 308–13.
Hennecke[5], i. 382–6.

French

Éac, 467–71.

German

Hennecke[1], 167 (E. Hennecke); cf. *Handbuch*, 238f.

Hennecke³, i. 224–8 (H.-C. Puech).
Hennecke⁵, i. 306–9 (H.-C. Puech and B. Blatz).

Italian

Bonaccorsi, i. pp. xvi–xvii, 28–31.
Erbetta, i.1, 288–90.
Moraldi, i. 362–3, 385–6; ² i. 438, 458–9.

Patristic Citations

Clement of Alexandria, *Strom.* 2. 9. 45 (Stählin, *GCS* 52 (15), p. 137):

1   The beginning (of truth) is to wonder at things, as Plato says in the *Theaetetus*, and Matthias in the *Traditions*, advising us: 'Wonder at the things that are before you, making this the first step to further knowledge.'

Ibid. 3. 4. 26 (Stählin, *GCS* 52 (15), p. 208):

2   (The Gnostics) say that Matthias also taught thus: that we should fight with the flesh and abuse it, not yielding to it at all for licentious pleasure, but should make the soul grow by faith and knowledge.

Ibid. 7. 13. 82 (Stählin, *GCS* 17.2, p. 58):

3   They say that in the Traditions Matthias the apostle always states, 'If the neighbour of a chosen one sin, the chosen one has sinned: for had he behaved himself as the word enjoins, the neighbour also would have been ashamed of his way of life, so as not to sin.'

and perhaps also

Ibid. 4. 6. 35 (Stählin, *GCS* 52 (15), p. 263):

4   It is said that Zacchaeus (or, as some say, Matthias), the chief publican, when he had heard the Lord condescended to come to him said, 'Behold, the half of my goods I give in alms, Lord: and if I have defrauded any man of anything I restore it fourfold.' Whereupon the Saviour said, 'The son of man has come today and has found that which was lost.'

4. THE PREACHING OF PETER (KERYGMA PETROU)

This treatise, of which only a few fragments in patristic sources remain, was probably written in the first half of the second century. It was known to Clement of Alexandria. Its contents were intended to emphasize the superiority of Christian monotheism. The main references are *Stromateis* 1. 29. 182; 6. 5. 39–41, 43; 6. 6. 48; 6. 15. 128. Other possible allusions to this work are Origen, *Princ.* 1, prol. 8; Gregory of Nazianzus, *epp.* 16, 20; John of Damascus, *Parall.* A 12. James argues for an Egyptian provenance.

The genre is less likely to be a 'gospel' and should perhaps be classified as part of an apocryphal acts, although the Kerygma Petrou is unlikely to have formed part of the original Acts of Peter.

The extracts are set out in:

E. von Dobschütz, *Das Kerygma Petri kritisch untersucht* (Leipzig, 1893) (=*TU*, 11.1).
Preuschen, 52–4.
Klostermann, *Apocrypha*, i. [(3)]13–16.
[Cf. A. Hilgenfeld, 'Das *Kerygma Petrou (kai Paulou)*', *ZWT* 36 (1893), 518–41; and id., *Novum Testamentum extra Canonem Receptum*, iv (Leipzig, 1866; [2]1884), 52–67 (for introductory notes on the fragments).]

MODERN TRANSLATIONS

English

James, 16–19.
Hennecke[3], ii. 94–102.
Hennecke[5], ii. 34–41.

French

Migne, *Dictionnaire*, ii, cols. 691–2.
Éac, 5–22.

German

Hennecke[1], 168–72 (E. Hennecke); cf. *Handbuch*, 239–47.
Hennecke[3], ii. 58–63 (W. Schneemelcher).
Hennecke[5], ii. 34–41 (W. Schneemelcher).

Italian

Erbetta, ii. 237–9.

GENERAL

J. N. Reagan, *The Preaching of Peter: The Beginnings of Christian Apologetic* (Chicago, 1923).

Patristic Citations

Clement of Alexandria, *Strom.* 1. 29. 182 (Stählin, *GCS* 52 (15), pp. 111–12):

And in the Preaching of Peter you may find the Lord called 'Law and Word'.   1

Cf. *Strom.* 2. 15. 68 (Stählin, p. 149) and *Ecl. Proph.* 58 (Stählin, *GCS* 17², p. 137).

Ibid. 6. 5. 39–41 (Stählin, pp. 451–2):

2   But that the most notable of the Greeks do not know God by direct knowledge but indirectly, Peter says in his Preaching, 'Know then that there is one God who made the beginning of all things and has power over their end', and 'The invisible who sees all things, uncontainable, who contains all, who needs nothing, of whom all things stand in need and for whose sake they exist, incomprehensible, perpetual, incorruptible, uncreated, who made all things by the word of his power ... that is, the Son.' Then he goes on, 'This God you must worship, not after the manner of the Greeks ... showing that we and the notable Greeks worship the same God, though not according to perfect knowledge for they had not learned the tradition of the Son'. 'Do not', he says, 'worship'—he does not say 'the God whom the Greeks worship', but 'not in the manner of the Greeks': he would change the method of worship of God, not proclaim another God. What, then, is meant by 'not in the manner of the Greeks'? Peter himself will explain, for he continues, 'Carried away by ignorance and not knowing God as we do, according to the perfect knowledge, but shaping those things over which he gave them power for their use, wood and stones, brass and iron, gold and silver, forgetting their material and proper use, they set up things subservient to their existence and worship them; and what things God has given them for food, the fowls of the air and the creatures that swim in the sea and creep on the earth, wild beasts and four-footed cattle of the field, weasels too and mice, cats and dogs and apes; even their own foodstuffs do they sacrifice to animals that can be consumed and, offering dead things to the dead as if they were gods, they show ingratitude to God since by these practices they deny that he exists ...' He continues again in this fashion, 'Neither worship him as the Jews do for they, who suppose that they alone know God, do not know him, serving angels and archangels, the month and the moon: and if no moon be seen, they do not celebrate what is called the first sabbath, nor keep the new moon, nor the days of unleavened bread, nor the feast of tabernacles, nor the great day (of atonement).'

Then he adds the finale of what is required: 'So then learn in a holy and righteous manner that which we deliver to you, observe, worshipping God through Christ in a new way. For we have found in the Scriptures, how the Lord said, "Behold, I make with you a new covenant, not as the covenant with your fathers in mount Horeb." He has made a new one with us: for the ways of the Greeks and Jews are old, but we are Christians who worship him in a new way as a third generation.'

Cf. ibid. 6. 7. 57 (Stählin, p. 460): For there is indeed one God, who made the beginning of all things: meaning his first begotten Son; thus Peter writes,

The Preaching of Peter

understanding correctly the words: In the beginning God created the heaven and the earth.

Ibid. 6. 5. 43 (Stählin, p. 453) (= Agraphon 10, below):

Therefore Peter says that the Lord said to the apostles, 'If then any of Israel will repent and believe in God through my name, his sins shall be forgiven him: and after twelve years go out into the world, lest any say, "We did not hear".' 3

Ibid. 6. 6. 48 (Stählin, p. 456) (= Agraphon 9, below):

For example, in the Preaching of Peter the Lord says, 'I chose you twelve, judging you to be disciples worthy of me, whom the Lord willed, and thinking you faithful apostles I sent you into the world to preach the gospel to men throughout the world, that they should know that there is one God; to declare by faith in me [the Christ] what shall be, so that those who have heard and believed may be saved, and that those who have not believed may hear and bear witness, not having any defence so as to say, "We did not hear".' ... 4

And to all reasonable souls it has been said above: Whatever things any of you did in ignorance, not knowing God clearly, all his sins shall be forgiven him, if he comes to God and repents.

Ibid. 6. 15. 128 (Stählin, p. 496):

Peter in the Preaching, speaking of the apostles, says, 'But, having opened the books of the prophets which we had, we found, sometimes expressed by parables, sometimes by riddles, and sometimes directly and in so many words the name Jesus Christ, both his coming and his death and the cross and all the other torments which the Jews inflicted on him, and his resurrection and assumption into the heavens before Jerusalem was founded, all these things that had been written, what he must suffer and what shall be after him. When, therefore, we gained knowledge of these things, we believed in God through that which had been written of him.' 5

And a little after he adds that the prophecies came by divine providence, in these terms, 'For we know that God commanded them, and without the Scripture we say nothing.'

John of Damascus, *Parall.* A 12 (Migne, *PG* 95, col. 1158; cf. Holl, *TU* 20.2, p. 234, nos. 502 and 503):

(Of Peter): Wretched that I am, I remembered not that God sees the mind and observes the voice of the soul. Allying myself with sin, I said to myself, 'God is merciful, and will bear with me; and because I was not immediately smitten, I ceased not, but rather despised pardon, and exhausted the long-suffering of God.' 6

(From the Teaching of Peter): Rich is the man who has mercy on many, and, imitating God, gives what he has. For God has given all things to all his creation. Understand then, you rich, that you ought to minister, for you have received more than you yourselves need. Learn that others lack the things you have in superfluity. Be ashamed to keep things that belong to others. Imitate the fairness of God, and no man will be poor.

Origen, *on John* (Preuschen, pp. 435-6):

7   It is too much to set forth now the quotations of Heracleon taken from the book entitled The Preaching of Peter and dwell on them, inquiring about the book whether it is genuine or spurious or compounded of both elements: so we willingly postpone that, and only note that according to him (Heracleon) Peter taught that we must not worship as do the Greeks, receiving the things of matter, and serving stocks and stones: nor worship God as do the Jews, since they, who suppose that they alone know God, are ignorant of him, and serve angels and the month and the moon.

Id., *de Principiis* 1, prol. 8 (ed. P. Koetschau, *GCS* 22 (Leipzig, 1913), pp. 14-15):

8   But if any would produce to us from that book which is called The Doctrine of Peter, the passage where the Saviour is represented as saying to the disciples, 'I am not a bodiless demon', he must be answered in the first place that that book is not reckoned among the books of the church; and then it must be shown that the writing is neither by Peter nor by any one else who was inspired by the spirit of God.

Cf. Gospel according to the Hebrews, Jerome *de Vir. Ill.* 16 above, p. 10.

Gregory of Nazianzus, *epp.* 16 and 20 (*PG* 37, cols. 49-50 and 53-6):

9   'A soul in trouble is near to God', as Peter says somewhere—a marvellous utterance.[24]

5. OTHER LOST GOSPELS

De Santos Otero, 67-75, refers to other titles that are given in diverse patristic sources. These include:

(*a*) The Gospel of the Adversaries of the Law and the Prophets (Augustine, *Contra Adversarium Legis et Prophetarum*, 2. 3. 14).

(*b*) Memoria of the Apostles (Orosius, *Commonitorium de errore*..., 2). (Cf. James, 21; Hennecke[3] (English), i. 265-8, [5](English), i. 376-8; Hennecke[3], i. 188-90, [5]i. 301-3).

---

[24] Final words only in *ep.* 20; cf. also *ep.* 17 (*PG* 37, cols. 51-2).

(c) The Gospel of Judas Iscariot (Irenaeus, *adv. Haer.* 1. 31. 1; Epiphanius, *adv. Haer.* 38. 1; Theodoretus Cyrrhensis, *Haer. fabul. comp.* 1. 15).

(d) The Gospel of Eve (Epiphanius, *adv. Haer.* 26. 2–3). (Cf. Hennecke[3] (English), i. 241–3, [5](English), i. 358–60; Hennecke[3], i. 166–7, [5]i. 288–90; *Éac*, 479–82; Erbetta, i. 1, 537–8).

Jerome and Epiphanius refer to the Gospel of Apelles; Epiphanius to the Gospel of Cerinthus; Tertullian to the Gospel of Valentinus. Augustine knew of a Gospel of Andrew. The Gelasian Decree mentions other now lost works. These and others merely serve to remind us that many documents claiming to be or identified as gospels were in circulation and were known to or used by various sects, orthodox and heretical, Jewish and Gnostic.

(e) Gnostic gospels such as the Gospel of Philip, the Gospel of Truth, Sophia Jesu Christi, the two books of Jeu, the Dialogue of the Redeemer, and others are in existence and are discussed *inter alia* in Hennecke[3], i. by H.-C. Puech (cf. Hennecke[5], i. chapter rev. B. Blatz). On the Gospel of Philip see James, 12; de Santos Otero, 63; Hennecke[5], i. 148–73, (English), i. 179–208. The Gospel of Truth is translated in Hennecke[3] (English), ii. Appendix 2. The contents of these take us outside the scope of the present book, but reference to Hennecke[5] will provide up-to-date bibliographical details for further study. B. Layton (ed.), *The Gnostic Scriptures* (London, 1987), and J. M. Robinson (ed.), *The Nag Hammadi Library in English* (Leiden, 1977; 3rd edn., 1988) give many of these Gnostic texts in translation.

Agrapha

This inappropriate word is used conventionally to refer to sayings of Jesus not found in the canonical Gospels. Collections of agrapha have included words of Jesus that are found elsewhere in the New Testament canon (e.g. at Acts 20: 35) in individual manuscripts of the Greek New Testament (e.g. the longer text after Luke 6: 4 in Codex Bezae; the Freer logion in the longer ending of Mark), in the apocryphal texts, and in patristic works.

The relevance of including such material in a volume of apocryphal texts is debatable. Much of the material really belongs to the realm of New Testament textual criticism; other passages are best considered within a study of the individual patristic works. Yet convention seems to require at least a token recognition that such a category belongs in a collection of apocryphal material. This has been the case since Resch's pioneering work assembling such material. His second edition of 1906 included nearly 200 agrapha mainly from patristic sources. Ropes is credited with having provided an antidote to Resch's over-enthusiastic but often uncritical collection, by separating material likely to be authentic from that which is obviously secondary. Ropes eliminated many of Resch's agrapha and divided the remainder into valueless agrapha, possibly valuable agrapha, and valuable agrapha. The refining process was continued by Jeremias both in his *Unbekannte Jesusworte* and even more so in his section on the agrapha in Hennecke–Schneemelcher[3]. The process has been furthered by Jeremias' successor, Hofius, in Hennecke[5], where only seven agrapha are included. The criterion for the selection there seems to be their possible authenticity. Such a criterion is of interest in so far that it is theoretically possible that some *ipsissima verba* of Jesus continued to circulate independently as stray survivals from an unwritten tradition, and even after the circulation of the canonical Gospels, until they were eventually incorporated into later writings, but 'authenticity' and 'originality' are not normally the criteria applied to the selection of apocryphal texts. (Few would pass those tests!)

Agrapha illustrate the growth of tradition and the accretion of legend, as do the apocryphal texts themselves. Some may represent early tradition, which might be authentic; some result from false attribution (e.g. 1 Cor. 2: 9 appears as a saying of Jesus in Gospel of Thomas 17); some, embedded in apocryphal works, may have been composed *ad hoc* for the work concerned (and would have no claim to authenticity).

Included below is a sample of agrapha from the New Testament text and manuscripts and from patristic sources. Sayings found in papyrus fragments of apocryphal texts, in the apocryphal infancy narratives, the Gospel of Peter, the

Agrapha

Gospel of Nicodemus, and the like are to be found in their respective sections of this volume. Sayings in the Talmud and in Islamic sources are not included in this volume (but see the final section of the bibliography below).

COLLECTIONS OF AGRAPHA

A. Resch, *Agrapha: Ausserkanonische Evangelien-Fragmente* (Leipzig, 1889) (= *TU* 5.4).
——*Agrapha: Aussercanonische Schriftfragmente* (Leipzig, 1906; reprinted Darmstadt, 1967) (= *TU* 15 (= 30), 3–4).
J. H. Ropes, *Die Sprüche Jesus* (Leipzig, 1896) (= *TU* 14.2).
——'Agrapha' in J. Hastings (ed.), *A Dictionary of the Bible*, Extra Volume (Edinburgh 1904), 343–52.
E. Preuschen, *Antilegomena*, 26–31, 152–5.
B. Pick, *Paralipomena: Remains of Gospels and Sayings of Christ* (Chicago, 1908). [51 agrapha.]
J. Delobel, 'The Sayings of Jesus in the Textual Tradition: Variant Readings in the Greek Manuscripts of the Gospels', in J. Delobel (ed.), *Logia: Les Paroles de Jésus, The Sayings of Jesus* (Leuven, 1982), 431–57 (= *BETL* 59).
Klostermann, *Apocrypha*, iii.

SELECTIONS IN MODERN TRANSLATIONS OF NEW TESTAMENT APOCRYPHA

English

James, 33–7.
Hennecke[3], i. 85–90.
Hennecke[5], i. 88–91.

French

Amiot, 30–6.
Éac, 399–405, 487–95.

German

Hennecke[1], 7–11 (E. Hennecke); cf. *Handbuch*, 13–21 (E. Hennecke).
Hennecke[3] i, 52–5 (J. Jeremias).
Hennecke[5] i, 76–9 (O. Hofius).

Italian

Moraldi, i. 459–74; [2] i. 529–45.
Erbetta, i. 83–96.
Bonaccorsi, i. 48–57.

Spanish

de Santos Otero, 108–22.

GENERAL

W. Bauer, *Das Leben Jesu im Zeitalter der neutestamentlichen Apokryphen* (Tübingen, 1909), esp. 351–60 and 377–415 for a critical view of the agrapha.

R. Dunkerley, *The Unwritten Gospel: Ana and Agrapha of Jesus* (London, 1925).

H. Köster, 'Die ausserkanonische Herrenworte als Produkte der christlichen Gemeinde', *ZNW* (1957), 220–37.

J. Jeremias, *Unknown Sayings of Jesus* (Eng. trans. by R. H. Fuller) (London,²1964), 1–43 (German: *Unbekannte Jesusworte*, rev. O. Hofius (Gütersloh,³1963).

F. F. Bruce, *Knowing Christianity: Jesus and Christian Origins Outside the New Testament* (London. 1974), ch. 6, ' "Unwritten" Sayings and Apocryphal Gospels'.

M. Mees, *Ausserkanonische Parallelstellen zu den Herrenworte und ihre Bedeutung* (Bari, 1975).

O. Hofius, 'Unbekannte Jesusworte', in P. Stuhlmacher (ed.), *Das Evangelium und die Evangelien* (Tübingen, 1983), 355–82 (= *WUNT* 28).

W. D. Stroker, *Extracanonical Sayings of Jesus* (Atlanta, Georgia, 1989) (= SBL Resources for Biblical Study 18).

Klauck, 16–34: ET 6–21.

FOR AGRAPHA IN THE TALMUD AND IN ISLAMIC SOURCES

The Talmud

R. T. Herford, *Christianity in Talmud and Midrash* (London, 1903).

B. Pick, *Jesus in the Talmud: His Personality, his Disciples, and his Sayings* (Chicago, 1913).

J. Maier, *Jesus von Nazareth in der talmudischen Überlieferung* (Darmstadt, 1978).

Islam

D. S. Margoliouth, 'Christ in Islam: Sayings attributed to Christ by Mohammedan writers', *ExpT* 5 (1893–4), 59, 107, 177 f., 503 f., 561 (48 agrapha from Islamic sources are repeated in Ropes's article in Hastings' Dictionary').

M. Asin Y Palacios, *Logia et Agrapha Domini Jesu apud Moslemicos scnptores, asceticos praesertim, usitata* (Paris, 1919), 327–431 (= PO 13.3), and ibid. (Paris, 1926), 529–624 (= PO 19.4) (Arabic text and French trans.). Cf. id. Rev. Bib. 36 (1927), 76–83.

Agrapha found in the New Testament Text

1–4 Acts 20: 35; 1 Cor. 7: 10; 9: 14; 1 Thess. 4: 15 ff.

Agrapha found in New Testament Manuscripts

After Luke 6: 4 Uncial D adds:

5 The same day, seeing a certain man working on the sabbath, he said to him, 'Man, if indeed you know what you are doing, happy are you; but if not, you are accursed and a transgressor of the law.'

After Mark 16: 14 Uncial W adds:

6 And they excused themselves, saying, This age of lawlessness and unbelief is under Satan, who by his unclean spirits does not allow the true power of

God to be comprehended. Therefore now reveal your righteousness'. So they spoke to Christ; and Christ addressed them thus, 'The limit of the years of Satan's authority has been fulfilled, but other terrible things are drawing near, even to those sinners on whose behalf I was handed over to death, that they may turn to the truth and sin no more. In order that they may inherit the spiritual and incorruptible glory of righteousness in heaven (v. 15) go into all the world and preach the gospel to the whole creation'

This is known as the Freer Logion. Hennecke[5] includes it in the section 'Dialoge des Erlösers' (in Hennecke[3] this section, written by J. Jeremias, appeared under the heading 'Wechselgespräche Jesus mit seinen Jüngern nach seiner Auferstehung'). But it is perhaps best included, as in James (*ANT* 34), within the 'Agrapha'.

For studies of this text see:

H. A. Sanders, *American Journal of Archaeology*, II.12 (1908), 52–4.
H. B. Swete, *Zwei neue Evangelienfragmente* (Bonn, 1908, ²1924) (= *Kleine Texte* 31). [The other 'new fragment' is P. Oxy. 840 (below).]
C. R. Gregory, Das Freer Logion (Leipzig, 1908).
K. Haacker, 'Bemerkungen zum Freer-Logion', *ZNW* 63 (1972), 125–9.
W. L, Lane, *The Gospel according to Mark* (London, 1974), 606–11 (*New London Commentary on the New Testament*).
G. Schwarz, 'Zum Freer-Logion: Ein Nachtrag', *ZNW* 70 (1979), 119.
Jörg Frey, 'Zu Text und Sinn des Freer-Logion', *ZNW* 93 (2002), 13–34.

The text is included in the apparatus to most editions of the New Testament in Greek and in Greek synopses of the Gospels.

At Matt. 20: 28 D adds (with some Latin and Syriac support):

But seek to increase from smallness and from the greater to become less. And when you go in and are invited to dine, do not recline in the prominent place lest one more illustrious than you come in, and he who invited you to dinner say to you, 'Go even lower down; and you shall be put to shame.' But if you recline in the lesser place and a lesser man come in, he who invited you to dinner will say to you, 'Come up higher', and this will be profitable to you.

7

Cf. Luke 14: 8–10.

Agrapha found in Patristic Sources

Papias, cited in Irenaeus, *adv. Haer.* 5. 33. 3 (Rousseau, p. 415):

The Lord taught about those times and said, 'The days will come in which vines will bear 10,000 branches, each branch 10,000 twigs, each twig 10,000 clusters, each cluster 10,000 grapes, and each grape when pressed will yield twenty-five measures of wine. When any saint takes hold of one such cluster, another cluster will exclaim, 'I am a better cluster; take me; bless the Lord through me!' Similarly a grain of wheat will produce 10,000 ears, each ear will have 10,000 grains, and each grain will yield ten pounds of fine flour, bright and pure; and the other fruit, seeds, and herbs will be proportionately productive according to their nature, while all the animals which feed on these

8

products of the soil will live in peace and agreement one with another, yielding complete subjection to men.'

Cf. Encomium on John the Baptist cited in E. A. Wallis Budge, *Coptic Apocrypha in the Dialect of Upper Egypt* (London, 1913) 348, and James, *ANT*, 37.

Clement of Alexandria, *Strom.* 6. 6. 48 (Stählin, *GCS* 52 (15), p. 456):

9   See above, The Preaching of Peter, fr. 4.

Ibid. 6. 5. 43 (Stählin, *GCS* 52 (15), p. 453):

10 See above, The Preaching of Peter, fr. 3.

Origen, *on Jer. hom.* 3. 3 (Latin) (ed. W. A. Baehrens, *GCS* 33 (Leipzig, 1925), p. 312):

11 I have read somewhere that the Saviour said—and I question whether someone has assumed the person of the Saviour, or called the words to memory, or whether what is said is true—but at any rate the Saviour himself says, 'He who is near me is near the fire. He who is far from me is far from the kingdom.'

Cf. Didymus, *Comm. on Ps.* 88. 8 (Greek) (*PG* 39, col. 1488 (Greek)), and Coptic Gospel of Thomas 82.

Justin, *Dialogue with Trypho* 35. 3 (ed. E. J. Goodspeed, *Die ältesten Apologeten* (Göttingen, 1914), pp. 130–1):

12 For he said, 'Many shall come in my name clad outwardly with sheepskins, but within they are ravening wolves', and 'There shall be divisions (schisms) and heresies.'

Cf. Ps.-Clement, *Hom.* ii. 17, xvi. 21, and Coptic Gospel of Thomas 16.

Compare also:

Justin, *Dialogue with Trypho* 47 (Goodspeed (as above), p. 146), Clement of Alexandria, and many others:[1]

'Wherein I find you, there will I judge you.'

Origen, *on Prayer*, 2 (ed. P. Koetschau, *GCS* 3 (Leipzig, 1899), p. 299), quotes both parts of the following saying; Clement of Alexandria, *Strom.* 1. 24. 158 (Stählin, *GCS* 52 (15), p. 100), the first part only:

'Ask for the greater things, and the small shall be added to you; ask for the heavenly things, and the earthly shall be added to you.'

Clement of Alexandria, *Strom.* 1. 28. 177 (Stählin, *GCS* 52 (15), p. 109), and many others:

'Be competent money-changers.'

[1] J. H. Charlesworth, *The Old Testament Pseudepigrapha, i. Apocalyptic Literature and Testaments* (London, 1983), includes this (p. 495) as a fragment of the Apocryphon of Ezekiel.

Fragments of Gospels on Papyrus

In addition to quotations from lost gospels in the testimony of church fathers, in recent years papyrus fragments of non-canonical works have been discovered, most notably at Oxyrhynchus. In some cases (e.g. P. Oxy. 1, P. Oxy. 654, P. Oxy. 655) these are likely to be from the Gospel of Thomas (*q.v.*). In other cases (e.g. the Merton papyrus) it is not certain if we are dealing with a fragment of an apocryphal gospel. All those that are of a gospel type are included below in the following sequence:

1. P. Oxy. 840
2. P. Oxy. 1081
3. P. Oxy. 1224
4. P. Cairensis 10735
5. P. Egerton 2
6. The Strasbourg Fragment
7. P. Berolinensis 11710
8. The Fayyum Fragment
9. The Merton Fragment

For P. Rylands 463 see below, pp. 121–2.

1. OXYRHYNCHUS PAPYRUS 840

This text is found on one leaf of a miniature parchment book dating from the third century and discovered in 1905. The page is virtually complete, and contains part of a story that is of the synoptic type but does not appear in the canonical New Testament. It is not certain if the fragment belonged originally to a complete apocryphal gospel, or (as Preuschen, *ZNW* 9 (1908), was inclined to think) a tiny gospel book worn as a substitute for an amulet.

Interest in this fragment has centred on the details of the story, not least the title 'Saviour' used of Jesus: this is a title not found in the canonical Gospels. Although early reaction was unfavourable to the historical value of the story, especially as many of the details seemed not to ring true of Jewish practices, Jeremias, following Büchler, emphasized that the alleged inconsistencies are not as convincing as many early scholars believed.

James suggested that the story belonged originally to the Gospel of Peter (cf. also Arundel 404, below); Lagrange linked it to the Gospel according to the Hebrews. Neither suggestion has found wide acceptance.

The translation is of the Greek text as printed by de Santos Otero.

EDITIONS

B. P. Grenfell and A. S. Hunt, *Fragment of an Uncanonical Gospel from Oxyrhynchus* (Oxford, 1908); id. *OP* 5 (London, 1908).

H. B. Swete, *Zwei neue Evangelienfragmente* (Bonn, 1908; ²Berlin, 1924),[1] 3–9 (= *Kleine Texte* 31, ed. H. Lietzmann). [The other 'new fragment' is the Freer Logion (under Agrapha, above).]

Lührmann, 164–9.

SYNOPSES

Aland[13], 584.
Huck–Greeven[13], 285.
Boismard, 415.

MODERN TRANSLATIONS

English

James, 29–30.
Grant and Freedman, 49–51.
Hennecke[3], i. 92–4.
Hennecke[5], i. 94–5.

French

Éac, 407–10.

German

Hennecke[1], 18 and 31 (H. Waitz).
Hennecke[3], i. 57–8 (J. Jeremias).
Hennecke[5], i. 81–2 (J. Jeremias and W. Schneemelcher).

Italian

Bonaccorsi, i. 36–8.
Erbetta, i.1, 105–6.
Moraldi, i. 436–8.

Spanish

de Santos Otero, 80–2.

GENERAL

A. Büchler, 'The New "Fragment of an Uncanonical Gospel"', *JQR* 20 (Philadelphia, 1907–8), 330–46.

E. Preuschen, 'Das neue Evangelienfragment von Oxyrhynchos', *ZNW* 9 (1908), 1-11.

M. J. Lagrange, 'Nouveau fragment non canonique relatif à l'Évangile', *Rev. Bib.* 5 (1908), 538–53 (with French trans. of text).

T. Zahn, 'Neue Bruchstücke nichtkanonischer Evangelien', *NeuKirZ* 19 (1908), 371–86.

A. Harnack, 'Ein neues Evangelienbruchstück', *Preussische Jahrbücher*, 131 (Berlin, 1908), 201–10.

H. Riggenbach, 'Das Wort Jesu im Gespräch mit dem pharisäischen Hohenpriester nach dem Oxyrhynchus Fragment V n. 840', *ZNW* 25 (1926), 140–4.

E. Burrows, 'Oxyrhynchus Logion (1907 [sic]) V', *JTS* 28 (1926–7), 186.

R. Dunkerley, 'The Oxyrhynchus Gospel Fragments', *HTR* 23 (1930), 19–37, esp. 30–5.

J. Jeremias, 'Der Zusammenstoss Jesu mit dem pharisäischen Oberpriester auf den Tempelplatz. Zu Pap. Ox V 840', *Con NT* 11 (1947), 97–108; id., *The Unknown Sayings of Jesus* (London, ²1964), 9 f., 47–60, 104–5 (commentary).[1]

D. R. Schwartz. ' "Viewing the Holy Utensils", P. Ox. V, 840', *NTS* 32 (1986), 153–9. Klauck, 40–1: ET 26–7.

Michael J. Kruger, 'P. Oxy. 840: Amulet or Miniature Codex?' *JTS* 53 (2002), 81–94.

F. Bovon, 'Fragment Oxyrhynchos 840, Fragment of a Lost Gospel; Witness of an Early Christian Controversy over Purity', *JBL* 119 (2000), 705–28.

. . . before he does wrong he makes all kinds of ingenious excuses. 'But take care lest you also suffer the same things as they did, for those who do evil not only receive their chastisement from men but they await punishment and great torment.' Then he took them with him and brought them into the place of purification itself, and was walking in the temple. A Pharisee, a chief priest named Levi, met them and said to the Saviour, 'Who gave you permission to walk in this place of purification and look upon these holy vessels when you have not bathed and your disciples have not washed their feet? But you have walked in this temple in a state of defilement, whereas no one else comes in or dares to view these holy vessels without having bathed and changed his clothes.' Thereupon the Saviour stood with his disciples and answered him. 'Are you then clean, here in the temple as you are?' He said, 'I am clean, for I have bathed in the pool of David and have gone down by one staircase and come up by the other, and I have put on clean white clothes. Then I came and viewed the holy vessels.' 'Alas', said the Saviour, 'you blind men who cannot see!' You have washed in this running water, in which dogs and pigs have wallowed night and day, and you have washed and scrubbed your outer skin,

---

[1] O. Hofius, 'Unbekannte Jesusworte', in P. Stuhlmacher (ed.), *Das Evangelium und die Evangelien* (Tübingen, 1983), 372–3 (= *WUNT* 28) is more doubtful than Jeremias about the authenticity of the story as a piece of Jesus tradition.

which harlots and flute-girls also anoint and wash and scrub, beautifying themselves for the lusts of men while inwardly they are filled with scorpions and unrighteousness of every kind. But my disciples and I, whom you charge with not having bathed, have bathed ourselves in the living water which comes down from heaven. But woe to those who...'

2. OXYRHYNCHUS PAPYRUS 1081

This Greek text is included by de Santos Otero, but no translation is offered below. The fragment is clearly Gnostic. According to Puech (Hennecke[3], i. Eng. trans, p. 245) it is from the Sophia Jesu Christi (known in P. Berol. 8502[2] and from Nag Hammadi Codex III, 4). Klostermann included the text as the remains of an anonymous gospel or a Gnostic fragment. It dates from the third–fourth century and contains a conversation between Jesus and his disciples.

EDITIONS

B. P. Grenfell and A. S. Hunt, *OP* 8 (London, 1911), 16–19.
C. Wessely, *PO* 18 (Paris, 1924), 493–5.
Klostermann, ii. [(3)]25.
D. M. Parrott (ed.), *Nag Hammadi Codices III, 3–4, and V, 1, with papyrus Berolinensis 8502, 3 and Oxyrhynchus Papyrus 1081: Eugnostos and the Sophia of Jesus Christ* (Leiden, 1991) (= *NHS* 27).

MODERN TRANSLATIONS

English

Hennecke[3], i. 243–8.

German

Hennecke[3], i. 168–72 (H.-C. Puech).

Italian

Bonaccorsi, i. 40–1.
Moraldi, i. 438–9; [2] i. 508–10.

Spanish

de Santos Otero, 82–3.

---

[2] This manuscript also contains The Gospel of Mary and part of the Acts of Peter (*q.v.*)

GENERAL

H-C. Puech, 'Les nouveaux écrits gnostiques découverts en Haute-Egypte', in *Coptic Studies in Honour of W. E. Crum* (Boston, 1950), 91–154 (= *Bulletin of the Byzantine Institute* 2).

3. OXYRHYNCHUS PAPYRUS 1224

This dates from the fourth century. It is a part of a papyrus book; the page numbers (139, 174, 176) survive. It is in poor condition, and it is very uncertain if the fragments belong to a Gospel.

The translation is of the Greek text as printed by Klostermann.

EDITIONS

B. P. Grenfell and A. S. Hunt, *OP* 10 (London, 1914), 1–10.
C. Wessely, *PO* 18 (Paris, 1924), 266 ff.
Klostermann, *Apocrypha*, ii. (3)26.
Lührmann, 170–9.

SYNOPSES

Aland[13], 584; Huck–Greeven[13], 285; Boismard, 415.

MODERN TRANSLATIONS

English

Hennecke[3], i. 113–14.
Hennecke[5], i. 100.

French

Éac, 417–9.

German

Hennecke[3], i. 72–3 (W. Schneemelcher).
Hennecke[5], i. 85–6 (W. Schneemelcher).

Italian

Bonaccorsi, i. 40 (one fragment only).
Erbetta, i.i, 107.
Moraldi, i. 421, 447–8.

GENERAL

R. Dunkerley, *Beyond the Gospels* (Harmondsworth, 1957), 135–6. [Cf. id., 'The Oxyrhynchus Gospel Fragments', *HTR* 42 (1949), 19–37, esp. 35–7.]

J. Jeremias, *Unknown Sayings of Jesus* (London, ²1964), 96–7.
O. Hofius, 'Unbekannte Jesusworte', in P. Stuhlmacher (ed.), *Das Evangelium und die Evangelien* (Tübingen, 1983), 378 (= *WUNT* 28).

The two legible fragments are:

p. 175   And the scribes and [Pharisees
         and priests, when they saw him
         were angry [that with
         sinners in the midst he [reclined
         at table. But Jesus heard [it and said:
         The healthy do not need [the physician.[1]

p. 176   And pray for
         your enemies. For he who is not
         against you is with you.[2]
         He who today is far-off—tomorrow will be
         near to you . . .

4. PAPYRUS CAIRENSIS 10735

This page of a papyrus is dated sixth–seventh century. Grenfell and Hunt considered that it was part of a gospel. Deissmann entitled it 'The Supposed Fragment of a Gospel at Cairo' but argued that it is likely to have been a page of a homily or from a commentary.

The translation is of the Greek text as printed by de Santos Otero.

EDITIONS

B. P. Grenfell and A. S. Hunt, *Catalogue général des antiquités égyptiennes du Musée du Caire*, x (Oxford, 1903).
Klostermann, *Apocrypha*, ii. ⁽²⁾21.

SYNOPSES

Aland[13], 584–5.
Huck–Greeven[13], 285.
Boismard, 415.

MODERN TRANSLATIONS

English

Hennecke[3], i. 114–15.
Hennecke[5], i. 101–2.

---

[1] Cf. Mark 2: 16–17 and parallels.
[2] Cf. Matt. 5: 44; Mark 9: 40; Luke 9: 50.

German

Hennecke[3], i. 73–4 (W. Schneemelcher).
Hennecke[5], i. 86–7 (W. Schneemelcher).

Italian

Bonaccorsi, i. xviii, 32–3.
Erbetta i.1, 107–8.
Moraldi, i. 446–7; [2] i. 516–7.

Spanish

de Santos Otero, 86.

GENERAL

A. Deissmann, *Light from the Ancient East* (trans. L. R. M. Strachan, London, 1910), Appendix III, 441–5 (originally in *Archiv für Religionswissenschaft* 7 (1904), 387–92).

Recto:

    The angel of the Lord spoke, 'Joseph [
    take Mary, your wife, and
    flee to Egypt [

    .   .   .   .   .

    .   .   .   .   .

    every gift and if [
    his friends [
    of the King [[1]

Verso:[2]

    ... should interpret to you. The
    archistrategus] said to the virgin, 'Behold
    Elizabeth your] relative has also conceived
    and it is] the sixth month for her, who
    was barren.'] In the sixth, that is the month Thoth,
    his mother] conceived John.
    But] the archistrategus announced
    John beforehand] as the servant, who precedes
    the Lord's coming.[3]

5. PAPYRUS EGERTON 2

The fragments come from a papyrus codex (like P. Oxy. 1), not from a roll (like P. Oxy. 654, 655). The manuscript dates from *c*.150. The gospel it

---

[1] Cf. Matt. 2: 13.
[2] Based on Deissmann's reconstruction (Eng. trans., 441–5).
[3] Cf. Luke 1: 36.

contains may have been written at the turn of the century, thus making it and P⁵² (of the Gospel of John) the earliest Christian writing extant.

P. Egerton 2 contains two leaves and the remains of a third. The contents that show parallels with synoptic Gospel material are not verbally exact, but may represent reproduction of the synoptic stories from memory. The rewriting of stories taken from the canonical Gospels, or developed from the oral tradition behind the written Gospels, is a characteristic of much of the apocryphal material. The contents are not heretical. There is no need to connect this papyrus with other gospels known from antiquity (e.g. The Gospel according to the Hebrews, The Gospel of the Egyptians).

The translation is of the Greek text as printed by de Santos Otero.

EDITIONS

H. I. Bell and T. C. Skeat, *Fragments of an Unknown Gospel and other early Christian Papyri* (London, 1935) (*editio princeps*); and a more popular version: id., *The New Gospel Fragments* (London, 1935; repr. 1951, 1955).[1]

NB additional fragment published by M. Gronewald, 'Unbekanntes Evangelium oder Evangelienharmonie (Fragment aus dem "Evangelium Egerton")', in *Papyrologica Coloniensia*. vii. *Kölner Papyri* 6 (ed. M. Gronewald *et al.* Westdeutscher Verlag, 1987), 136–45 and plate V. Cf. D. Lührmann, *Die apokryph gewordenen Evangelien* (Leiden, 2004), 125–43 (= *Supplements* to *Novum Testamentum* 112); Lührmann, 142–53.

SYNOPSES

Aland¹³, 584; Huck–Greeven¹³, 285; Boismard, 415.

MODERN TRANSLATIONS

English

Hennecke³, i. 94–7. Hennecke⁵, i. 96–9.
James, Appendix i (5th imp. onwards), 569–70.

French

Éac, 411–6.

German

Hennecke³. i. 58–60 (J. Jeremias).
Hennecke⁵, i. 82–5 (J. Jeremias and W. Schneemelcher).

Italian

Bonaccorsi, i. 42–8. Erbetta, i.1, 102–6. Moraldi, i. 444–6 ² i. 514–6

---

[1] Reviews in *Rev. Bib.* 45 (1936). 272 (Benoit); *ZNW* (1935), 285–93 (Lietzmann).

Spanish

de Santos Otero, 95–100.

GENERAL

L. Cerfaux, 'Un nouvel évangile apocryphe', *ETL* 12 (1935), 579–81.

—— 'Parallèles canoniques et extracanoniques de l'Évangile Inconnu', *Le Muséon* 49 (1939), 55–78.

M.-J. Lagrange, 'Deux nouveaux texts relatifs à l'Évangile', *Rev. Bib.* 44 (1935), 321–43 (P. Egerton 2 = pp. 327–43).

H. Lietzmann, 'Neue Evangelienpapyri', *ZNW* 34 (1935), 285–93.

M. Gogue.l, 'Les nouveaux fragments évangeliques de Londres', RHR 113 (1936), 42–87 (with French translation of text).

C. H. Dodd, 'A New Gospel', *BJRL* 20 (1936), 56–92. (repr. in id., *New Testament Studies* (Manchester, 1953), 12–52).

J. Jeremias and K. F. W, Schmidt, 'Ein bisher unbekanntes Evangelienfragment', *Th. Blätt.* 15 (1936), cols. 34–45 (cf. I. Bell, ibid. cols. 72–4).

G. Mayeda, *Das Leben-Jesu-Fragment Papyrus Egerton 2 und seine Stellung in der urchristlichen Literaturgeschichte* (Berne, 1946).[2] [Gives the alternative reconstructions of lines 68–73 as proposed by Cerfaux, Dodd, and Lagrange.]

U. Gallizia, 'Il P. Egerton 2', *Aegyptus* 36 (1956), 29–72, 178–234.

F. Neirynck, 'Papyrus Egerton 2 and the Healing of the Leper'. *ETL* 61 (1985), 153–160.

D. F. Wright, 'Apocryphal Gospels (Pap. Egerton 2) and the Gospel of Peter', in D. Wenham (ed.), *The Jesus Tradition Outside the Gospels* (Sheffield, 1985), 207–32 (= *Gospel Perspectives* 5).

J. D. Crossan, *Four other Gospels: Shadows on the Contours of Canon* (Minneapolis, Chicago, New York, 1985).

D. F. Wright, 'Papyrus Egerton 2 (The Unknown Gospel)—Part of the Gospel of Peter?', *Second Century* 5 (1985–6), 129–50.

F. Neirynck, 'The Apocryphal Gospels and the Gospel of Mark', in J.-M. Sevrin (ed.), *The New Testament in Early Christianity* (Leuven, 1989), 123–75, esp. 161–7 (= BETL 86).

Klauck, 36–40: ET 23–6.

Fragment 1 verso, lines 1–20, with additional lines from P. Koln 255 (inv. 608) verso:

[And Jesus said] to the lawyers, '[Punish] every wrong-doer and transgressor, and not me . . . what he does as he does it.' Then, turning to the rulers of the people, he spoke this word, 'Search the scriptures, in which you think you have life; it is they which bear witness to me.[1] Do not think that I have come to accuse you to my Father; your accuser is Moses, on whom you have set your hope.'[2] When they said, 'We know well that God spoke to Moses; but as for you, we do not know [where you come from]'[3] Jesus said in reply, 'Now your unbelief is

---

[2] Reviews in *Rev. Bib.* 55 (1948), 472–4 (P Benoit); *Vig Chr.* 2 (1948), 120 (W. C. van Unnik); *HTR* 42 (1949), 53–63 (I. Bell); *HTR* 43 (1950), 103 (I. Bell).

[1] John 5: 39. [2] John 5: 45. [3] John 9: 29.

accused to the ones who were witnessed to by him. If you had believed [in Moses] you would have believed me, because he wrote to your fathers about me . . .'[4]

Fragment 1 recto, lines 22–41, with additional lines from P. Köln 255 (inv. 608) recto:

. . . collect stones and stone him. The rulers sought to lay their hands on him in order to arrest him and hand him over to the crowd; but they could not arrest him, because the hour of his betrayal had not yet come.[5] The Lord himself, passing out through their midst, escaped from them.[6]

And behold, a leper approached him and said, 'Teacher Jesus, while journeying with lepers and eating with them in the inn, I myself also became a leper. If, therefore, you are willing, I am cleansed.' The Lord said to him, 'I am willing: be cleansed.' And immediately the leprosy departed from him, and the Lord said, 'Go, show yourself to the priests and make an offering for your cleansing as Moses commanded, and sin no more . . .'[7]

Fragment 2 recto, lines 43–59:

. . . came to him to tempt him, saying, 'Teacher Jesus, we know that you have come from God,[8] for the things which you do bear witness beyond all the prophets. Tell us then: Is it lawful to render to kings what pertains to their rule? Shall we render it to them or not?'[9] But Jesus, knowing their mind, said to them in indignation, 'Why do you call me teacher with your mouth, when you do not do what I say? Well did Isaiah prophesy of you when he said: This people honours me with its lips, but their heart is far from me; in vain do they worship me, (teaching as doctrines merely human) commandments.'[10]

Fragment 2 verso, lines 60–75:

'. . . enclosed in its place, . . . placed below invisibly, . . . its weight immeasurable' . . . And when they were perplexed at his strange question, Jesus, as he walked, stood on the bank of Jordan and, stretching out his right hand, filled it [with seed] and sowed it on the river. Then . . . the water which had been sown [with seed] . . . in their presence and it produced much fruit . . . to their joy' . . .

Fragment 3 contains only a few isolated words.

---

[4] John 5: 46.
[5] John 7: 30.
[6] John 10: 39.
[7] Cf. Matt. 8: 2–4; Mark 1: 40–4; Luke 5: 12–14, 17: 14.
[8] John 3: 2.
[9] Cf. Matt. 22: 15–18; Mark 12: 13–15; Luke 20: 20–23; John 5: 14.
[10] Isa. 29: 13 (LXX); cf. Matt. 15: 7–8; Mark 7: 6–7.

6. THE STRASBOURG FRAGMENT

This is part of a fragmentary papyrus of the fourth–fifth century. Two leaves numbered 5 and 6 contain gospel-type material in Coptic, but the original language behind this text is uncertain; Greek is the most likely. Because the apostles speak in the first person plural, as they also do in the Gospel of the Twelve (possibly to be identified with the Gospel of the Ebionites (*q.v.*)), attempts have been made to connect the fragment with a Jewish-Christian gospel: these attempts have not been convincing. There is a resemblance between the contents of page 5 recto and the Acts of John 94–5.

EDITIONS

The fragments were first assembled and published by A. Jacoby, *Ein neues Evangelienfragment* (Strasbourg, 1900), but the critical interpretation is that by C. Schmidt in *Göttingische gelehrte Anzeigen* (1900), 481–506.

MODERN TRANSLATIONS

English

James, 30–1.
Hennecke[3], i. 227–30. Hennecke[5], i. 103–5.

French

Éac, 425–8.

German

Hennecke[1], 37–8 (E. Hennecke); cf. *Handbuch*, 88–94.
Hennecke[3], i. 155–8 (W. Schneemelcher).
Hennecke[5], i. 87–9 (W. Schneemeicher).

Italian

Erbetta, i.1, 109–10.
Moraldi, i. 448–51; 2 i. 518–9.

Spanish

de Santos Otero, 102–3.

GENERAL

Klauck, 41–2: ET 27–8.

Page 5 recto:

. . . that he may be known by his [hospitality] and be praised for his fruit, for . . . many of . . . Amen. Give me now your [strength], O Father, that [they] may endure the world with me. Amen. I have received the [diadem] of the kingdom . . . the diadem of him who is . . . lowliness, since they have not [recognized them]. I have become King [through you], Father. You will subject all things to me, [Amen]. Through whom shall [the last] enemy be destroyed? Through [Christ]. Through whom shall the sting of death be destroyed?[1] [Through the] only—begotten. Unto whom belongs the dominion? [To the son], Amen.

Page 5 verso:

Now when [Jesus] had completed the [prayer?] he turned to us and said, 'The hour has come when I shall be taken from you.[2] The spirit is willing but the flesh is weak.[3] Stay and watch with me.'[4] But we the apostles wept and said to him... [Son] of God... He answered and said to us, 'Do not fear the destruction [of the body] but [fear] rather... the power of [darkness?][5] Remember all I have said to you. If they have persecuted me, [they will] persecute you too.[6] Rejoice, because I have [overcome] the world and I have...'

Page 6 recto:

...may reveal to you all my glory and show you all your strength and the mystery of your apostleship... on the mountain...

Page 6 verso:

Our eyes penetrated all places. We beheld the glory of his Godhead and all the glory of his dominion. He clothed us with the power of our apostleship...

7. PAPYRUS BEROLINENSIS 11710

This fragment in two leaves dates from the sixth century and may be no more than an amulet text based on John 1: 49. It may, however, be a fragment of an apocryphal gospel. It is significant to note that Jesus in this text is titled Rabbi.

The translation is of the Greek text as printed by de Santos Otero.

EDITION

H. Lietzmann, 'Ein apokryphes Evangelien-fragment', *ZNW* 22 (1923), 153-4.

SYNOPSIS

Aland[13], 37.

---

[1] Cf. 1 Cor. 15: 25-6, 55.
[2] Matt. 9: 15; 26: 45 and parallels.
[3] Matt. 26: 41 and parallel.
[4] Matt. 26: 38 and parallels.
[5] Cf. Matt. 10: 28.
[6] John 15: 20.

MODERN TRANSLATIONS

French

Éac, 429–31.

Italian

Erbetta, i.1, 110. Moraldi, i. 448 ^{2} i. 518.
Cravieri, 286.

Spanish

de Santos Otero, 84.

... Nathanael] confessed and said 'Rabbi, Lord, you are the Son of God.' The Rabbi [answered him] and said, 'Nathanael, walk in the sun.' Nathanael replied and said to him, 'Rabbi, Lord, you are the lamb of God, who takes away the sins of the world.' The Rabbi answered him and said ...

8. THE FAYYUM FRAGMENT

The fragment was discovered in 1885 in Archduke Rainer's collection of papyri in Vienna. Its publication therefore preceded that of the Gospel of Peter or P. Oxy. 1 and aroused great interest. The manuscript is dated third century, and was found in the Fayyum district of Egypt.

As with some other fragments included in this section, it is not clear if this text comes from an unknown gospel, or if it is merely an adaptation of material known in the synoptic Gospels (in this case Matt. 26: 30–4 or Mark 14: 26–30).

The translation is of the Greek text as printed by de Santos Otero, following Harnack.

EDITIONS

G. Bickell, 'Ein Papyrusfragment eines nichtkanonischen Evangelium', *Zeitschrift für Katholische Theologie*, 9 (1885), 498–504; 10 (1886), 208–9.

—— *Mittheilungen aus der Sammlung der Papyrus Rainer*, i (Vienna, 1886), 53–61, ii and iii (1887), 41–2, v (1892), 78–82.

C. Wessely, 'Über das Zeitalter der Wiener Evangelienpapyrus', *Zeitschrift für katholische Theologie*, ii (1887), 507–15.

A. Harnack, 'Das Evangelienfragment von Fajjum', Appendix to A. Resch, *Agrapha* (Leipzig, 1889), 481–97 (= *TU* 5.4). [Includes short bibliography (pp. 483–4) of original notices.]

A. Resch, *Aussercanonische Paralleltexte zu den Evangelien*, ii (Leipzig, 1893–6), 28–34 (= *TU* 10).

Preuschen, 21–2.

Klostermann, *Apocrypha*, ii. $^{(2)}$20.

C. Bruston, *Fragments d'un ancien recueil de paroles de Jésus* (Paris, 1905), 27–9.

44 Fragments of Gospels on Papyrus

C. Wessely, 'Fragments de collections de prétendues sentences de Jésus', in *Les plus anciens monuments du Christianisme écrits sur papyrus: Textes grecs édités, traduits et annotés*', *PO* 4.2 (Paris, 1908), 173–7. [Also included is a bibliography of earlier notices (p. 173).]

SYNOPSES

Aland[13], 584; Huck–Greeven[13], 285; Boismard, 415.

MODERN TRANSLATIONS

English

James, 25.
Hennecke[3], i. 115–16.
Hennecke[5], i. 102.

French

Éac, 421–3.

German

Hennecke[1], 38 (E. Hennecke); cf. *Handbuch*, 88 f.
Hennecke[3], i. 74 (W. Schneemelcher).
Hennecke[5], i. 87 (W. Schneemelcher).

Italian

Bonaccorsi, i. 31–2.
Erbetta, i.1, 108.
Moraldi, i. 447; [2] i. 517.
Cravieri, 285.

Spanish

de Santos Otero, 85.

GENERAL

A. Hilgenfeld, 'Kein neuentdecktes Evangelium', *ZWT* 29 (1886), 50–6.
T. Zahn, *Geschichte des neutestamentlichen Kanons*, ii (Erlangen and Leipzig, 1890–2), 781 ff.
P. Savi, 'Le fragment évangélique de Fayoûm', *Rev. Bib.* 1 (1892), 321–44.

> [After supper as was the custom, he said,]
> 'All] in this night will be offended
> as] it is written: I will smite the [shepherd
> and the] sheep will be scattered.'[1]

[1] Matt. 26: 31 and Mark 14: 27.

When] Peter [said], 'Even if all, [not I',
Jesus said], 'Before the cock crows twice three times
today will you] deny me.'[2]

9. PAPYRUS MERTON 51

This dates from the third century and may be no more than a fragment of a homily or an exegesis of Luke 6: 7. On the other hand it may be a fragment of an uncanonical gospel. It has been included here on the advice of T. C. Skeat, who compares this fragment with his P. Egerton 2.

The translation is based on the text as printed in the *editio princeps*.

EDITION

B. R. Rees, H. I. Bell, and J. W. B. Barns, *A Descriptive Catalogue of the Greek Papyri in the Collection of Wilfred Merton F.S.A.*, ii (Dublin, 1959), 1–4.

Lührmann 155–7.

Recto:

... and all the] people and the taxgatherers
when they heard him] acknowledged the goodness of God[1]
confessed] their sins
but the Pharisees] were not baptized
by John] and rejected God's purpose[2]
and the command] of God
likewise God] rejected them ...

Verso:

... produce bad fruit [
] produce as from evil [
tree and when you send [from the good
treasure of the [heart
destroy ...[3]

[2] Mark 14: 30

[1] Luke 7: 29.
[2] John 7: 30.
[3] Luke 6: 45 or Matt 12: 35

Birth and Infancy Gospels

Introduction

Included in this section are translations of:
The Protevangelium of James
The Infancy Gospel of Thomas
and translations of extracts from:
The Gospel of Pseudo-Matthew
The Arabic Infancy Gospel
Arundel 404
The History of Joseph the Carpenter.

There then follows a section discussing other infancy narratives listed on p. 118, for which translations have not been given.

'Whenever biographical literature shows gaps, legend generally springs up, in the absence of reliable information, to supply the deficiency.' These words by Oscar Cullmann translated in Hennecke–Schneemelcher, *New Testament Apocrypha* (3rd edn., i. 364; 5th edn., i. 415), explain the origin of many of the infancy and birth stories to be found here.

Although some collections of apocryphal gospels subdivide the infancy narratives into birth stories and infancy stories (for example, de Santos Otero) it is convenient to group all these gospels under one head. They tell of events in the life of Jesus prior to his public ministry, and of his parentage.

As with much of the material to be found in the New Testament apocrypha as a whole, these infancy gospels fill gaps left by the nativity stories in the canonical Gospels. The other main gap in Jesus' life and ministry, in regard to which members of the early church were most curious but where the canonical Gospels did not satisfy their curiosity, was the three-day period between Jesus' death and his resurrection. As Bruce Metzger says,[1] 'When people are curious, they usually take steps to satisfy their curiosity, so we should not be surprised that members of the early Church drew up accounts

---

[1] B. M. Metzger, *The Canon of the New Testament: Its Origin, Development, and Significance* (Oxford, 1987), 166–7. See also id., 'Names for the Nameless in the New Testament: A Study in the Growth of Christian Tradition', in P. Granfield and J. A. Jungmann (eds.), *Kyriakon: Festschrift Johannes Quasten* (Münster, 1970), 79–99.

of what they supposed must have taken place.' The period covering Christ's death and afterlife will be considered below, under the heading 'Passion Gospels'.

Apart from the account of Jesus' birth, the canonical Gospels have only one story of Jesus' childhood, namely Luke's telling of Jesus in the Temple at the age of twelve, which doubtless inspired the many stories relating the generally miraculous events in Jesus' childhood that are to be found in the apocryphal infancy gospels. Elaborations of the actual nativity also have a place in the apocryphal traditions, and many of these are of a Gnostic character. Other accounts of Jesus' birth are there to glorify Mary and to emphasize her virginity. Episodes telling of Jesus' ancestry also occur, with accounts of Mary's parentage, her birth, and her early life, and with stories that treat of Joseph's first encounters with her and of his death. The sojourn of the Holy Family in Egypt is another theme in the apocryphal tradition that developed out of the canonical Gospels.

That many of the apocryphal infancy stories developed from, or were inspired by, the canonical Gospels permits us to refer to these works as 'gospels' although in many ways the genre of the apocryphal writings is not comparable to the literature of the New Testament Gospels.

The repetition of many of the pericopes within the apocryphal tradition is characteristic of the way in which this material was used and developed. Those interested in form- and redaction-criticism can readily pursue these literary concerns with much of the material, although the interrelationship of many of these texts is often speculative: definitive editions of many of the works are lacking, as will be clear from the introductory section to several of those included below. The repetition of stories and the repetitiveness of many of the types of stories is, however, a reason for my selecting and translating only samples from some derivative texts or in other cases for providing only introductory remarks and no text. The two seminal works, The Protevangelium of James and the Infancy Gospel of Thomas, are given in full, and extracts from four books that owe their inspiration to these two: Pseudo-Matthew, the Arabic Infancy Gospel, Arundel MS. 404, the History of Joseph the Carpenter. Other works are given briefer treatment.

Although theological and apologetic tendencies have shaped some of the material in the apocryphal infancy gospels, it is the narrative and biographical interest that predominates. The dominant theological concerns of the canonical birth stories (such as the fulfilment of prophecy, the Davidic descent of Jesus, the Bethlehem-Nazareth problem, the divine birth of Jesus, the relationship with the Baptist) are less significant in the apocryphal tradition. These texts were the popular literature of the pious for many centuries. Their influence in shaping belief, as well as their exposure of the beliefs that shaped their contents, are significant and important for all whose interests lie in the history of Christianity and Christian doctrine.

The Protevangelium of James

The Protevangelium of James (PJ) is one of the most important and influential of the apocryphal gospels. It represents the earliest written elaboration of the canonical infancy narratives that has survived: what has sometimes been described as a midrashic exegesis of Matthew's and Luke's birth narratives finds permanent expression in this document. Theories that stated that PJ was the source of the canonical Gospels' infancy narratives (Conrady) or that Matthew, Luke, and PJ were all dependent on a common written source (Resch) have not found general acceptance.

The influence of PJ was immense, and it may be said with some confidence that the developed doctrines of Mariology can be traced to this book. Together with the Infancy Gospel of Thomas PJ influenced other and later birth and childhood gospels such as Pseudo-Matthew and the Arabic, Armenian, and Latin infancy traditions.

It seems to have been a popular book, and over one hundred extant Greek manuscripts, some of them dating from the third century, contain all or part of PJ. Translations were made into Syriac, Ethiopic, Georgian, Sahidic, Old Church Slavonic, Armenian, and presumably into Latin (in so far as PJ was apparently known to the compiler of the Gelasian Decree). Thilo includes an early Arabic translation in his edition. In some cases (e.g. Ethiopic) the translation is very free, many liberties having been taken with the text. Others, such as the Syriac edited by A. Smith Lewis, are very literal. The absence of surviving early Latin translations[1] may be explained on two grounds. First, PJ was prohibited in the West because of its teaching about Joseph's first marriage. Secondly, the parallel development of Latin infancy gospels such as Pseudo-Matthew and *de Nativitate Mariae* (both of which were commended by introductory letters attributed to Jerome, who had denounced PJ), as well as the story of Joseph the Carpenter and the *Liber de Infantia*, all of which were based on PJ, obviated the need for its survival in Latin, as these other writings served to satisfy the same needs. In the Eastern church PJ continued to enjoy great popularity.

Printed editions have been known in the West since the mid-sixteenth century. The title by which the book is now known originated with Postel's Latin translation *Protevangelion sive de natalibus Jesu Christi et ipsius Matris virginis Mariae, sermo historicus divi Jacobi minoris* (Basle, 1552; ²Strasbourg,

---

[1] The Latin of Postel is a 16th-cent. translation of a contemporary Greek manuscript. But see the Bibliography (below) under 'Latin'.

The Protevangelium of James

1570), because he wished to imply that the contents of PJ were older than those in the canonical Gospels. The title in the Bodmer Papyrus V text is 'The Birth of Mary: Revelation of James'. The second half of the title is patently unsuitable, as PJ is in no sense apocalyptic. Even the first half is not entirely accurate because much more is related than Mary's birth. Variations of this title occur in other manuscripts. Origen refers to the book as that of James.

In PJ 25. 1 the author claims to be James the step-brother of Jesus by Joseph's first marriage, and the Gelasian Decree identifies him with James the Less of Mark 15: 40. In fact the author is unknown. He is not likely to have been a Jew: there is in PJ a great ignorance not only of Palestinian geography but also of Jewish customs (e.g. Joachim is forbidden to offer his gifts first because of childlessness; Mary is taken to be a ward of the Temple; Joseph plans to go from Bethlehem to Judea).

Most scholars now date PJ, or at least the bulk of the first draft of PJ, to the second half of the second century. It may well be that one of the motives behind the original composition was to counter the views of Celsus expressed *c*.170 (see further below). Attempts to prove that links between Justin (died 165) and PJ (e.g. *Apology* 1. 33 and PJ 11. 3 link Luke 1: 35 and Matt. 1: 21; cf. also *Dialogue with Trypho* 100. 5 and PJ 12. 2; *Apology* 1. 33, 36 and PJ 11. 2) are due to Justin's familiarity with PJ have not generally been accepted, and the counter-arguments of de Strycker, pp. 414–17, are significant. There is, however, no doubt that a *terminus ad quem* may be found in the patristic testimony of Origen (died 254) and Clement of Alexandria (died 215). The oldest explicit reference to the existence of PJ is in Origen, *on Matt.* 10. 17 (Klostermann and Benz, pp. 21–2): Origen is aware of the teaching about Joseph's first marriage (*on Matt.* 9. 2; 17. 1 (ibid. pp. 575 f.)) and of the birth in a cave (*c. Cels.* 1. 51 (ed. P. Koetschau, *GCS* 2 (Leipzig, 1899), p. 101)). Clement's testimony is to be found in *Strom.* 7. 16. 93 (Stählin, *GCS* 17², p. 661). The Bodmer Papyrus V has been dated to the third century and already shows secondary developments.

The Ascension of Isaiah 11 written early in the second century has a similar account of the birth to that found in PJ, but dependence of one on the other is difficult to prove. Ignatius, *ad Eph.* 19, implies virginity *in partu*, and the Odes of Solomon 19 also shows knowledge of this. All that this need suggest is a common provenance, possible Syrian.

As apocryphal texts were not sacred scripture they were subjected to a greater degree of alteration, addition, and abridgement than canonical writings. It may well be that some parts of PJ printed below are later than the second century.

The unity of PJ has often been questioned. PJ 22–4 in particular, the so-called Apocryphum Zachariae, seems not to have been known to Origen, who gives in his writings a reason for Zacharias' death that differs from the version in PJ. These chapters have been seen as a later addition based on the analogy of the Jesus–John stories of Luke, and the death of Zacharias as an elaboration of Matt. 23: 35. Peeters, in Michel, i. p. xvii, assigned the composition of these chapters to the sixth century. Other scholars in the last hundred years, such as Harnack, were prepared to argue that three separate documents (PJ 1–16, 17–20, and 22–4) were combined in the fourth century and chapters 21 and 25 then added. Recent discoveries have tended to undermine such arguments for disunity. The Pistelli fragment, of the fourth century, contains chapters 13–23 and thus cuts across the three sections. The Bodmer Papyrus V has certain abbreviations, especially in chapters 19 and 20, but the unity of 1–25 is not in question. É. de Strycker's major study of PJ argues for the homogeneity of the book on literary, linguistic, and paleographical grounds.

This does not, however, mean that the author did not make use of earlier written material in the composition of his work. The stories of Mary, of Jesus' birth, and of Zacharias' death may all have reached him from separate sources. Joseph's first-person narrative in 18. 2–7 probably came from an earlier written source, and invites comparison with the 'We' sections of the Acts of the Apostles. It is absent from P. Bodmer V. The story of the midwife could also have reached the author from another source. Certainly, Salome and the midwife are very suddenly introduced into the narrative. Other arguments for disunity (such as the apparent difference in attitude to Judaism between the piety of the Jews in the Temple caring for Mary their ward, and the lamenting Jews of 17. 2) can be explained on other grounds, not least the author's inconsistencies as a storyteller, about which more below.

Although the birth of Jesus is recounted, the main motive behind the composition is to glorify Mary by telling of her birth, childhood, and marriage. In accord with the demands of popular piety responsible for the growth of much apocryphal material, PJ sets out to satisfy curiosity about Jesus' antecedents by filling in the gaps left in the canonical material. Unlike much apocryphal literature, it is relatively restrained in its style. Its approach is sincere, although it is apologetic. One motive behind the composition seems to have been the defence of aspects of Christianity in the light of attacks on it by such as Celsus. Our author is concerned to tell us that Jesus' parents were not poor: Joseph is a building contractor; Mary spins, but not for payment. Another apologetic motive is to defend the conception of Jesus against charges of sexual irregularity: Mary's virginity is vindicated before Joseph (14. 2) and the priests (16).

A strong dogmatic motive lies behind the writing, too. The author wishes to stress that not only is Jesus' conception virginal but that his birth too preserved Mary's virginity. Virginity *in partu* is combined with a belief in Mary's perpetual virginity: the siblings of Jesus known from the canonical Gospels are explained in PJ as being Joseph's children of a previous marriage. Subsequent church opinion in the West found such teaching unacceptable: Jerome was instrumental in condemning this teaching in PJ as wrong, and he argued that Jesus' siblings were his cousins. Jerome's explanations met with papal approval and were responsible for the decline in the use of PJ in the West.

The biographical interest in this book centres on Mary, her miraculous birth (not her immaculate conception), her youth, and her marriage. The teaching in PJ includes the Davidic descent of Mary, itself of apologetic significance once the Davidic descent of Jesus through Joseph is rendered of no significance after Joseph is presented only as the supposed father of Jesus. Also of relevance for encouraging the enhancement of Mary is that she is seen in PJ as an instrument of divine salvation in her own right.

The catalepsy of all creation at Jesus' birth seems to be innovative although it may be compared to other nature miracles such as the earthquake and eclipse at the time of the crucifixion.

The historical value of the stories in PJ is insignificant. The names of Mary's parents, the names of Reuben, Zacharias, and Samuel are all fictitious. Zacharias is wrongly identified with Zacharias of Matt. 23: 35. Simeon was not a high-priest. The water of jealousy was not administered to men. The oracular plate on the forehead is not known outside PJ. Other peculiar details include the contradiction of the angelic annunciation (12. 2, cf. 11) and the warning given to the Magi not to go to Judea when they were already there (21. 4).[2] Such details do not necessarily indicate the author's use of variant sources; they may result from his own lack of interest in, or awareness of, such apparent inconsistencies.

The main inspiration and sources behind PJ have been the birth stories in Matthew and Luke and the Old Testament. Like Luke 1-2 the language of PJ is heavily influenced by the LXX. The name of Mary's mother, Anna, may have come from Luke's birth story, but the figures of Hannah, Samuel's mother, Susanna in the additions to Daniel, and Manoah's wife in Judges 13 have been models for Anna. The name Joachim may have been suggested by Susanna's husband in the additions to Daniel, but Manoah and Elkanah in 1 Samuel have also been models. 1 Samuel in particular seems to have served the author of PJ as a source. The popularity of the LXX version of 1 Samuel and of the story of Susanna in the second century AD seems evident.

Most surviving Greek manuscripts of PJ are later than the tenth century. The eighteen used by Tischendorf are all late; details are given in his Prolegomena. Since his time four earlier manuscripts have come to light:

1. B. P. Grenfell, *An Alexandrian Erotic Fragment and other Greek Papyri chiefly Ptolemaic* (Oxford, 1896), pp. 13-19 (contains PJ 16. 1-21. 4). Fifth-sixth century.

---

[2] Among other inconsistencies Mary is 12 in 8. 2-3, but 16 in 12. 3; Joseph has many sons according to 9. 2, 17. 1, 18. 3, but only one in 17. 2.

2. E. Pistelli, *Pubblicazioni della Società italiana per la ricerca dei papiri. Papiri greci e latini* (Florence, 1912), pp. 9–15 (contains PJ 13. 1–23. 3). Fourth century.
3. H. Schöne, 'Palimpsestblätter des Protevangeliums Jacobi in Cesena', in *Westfälische Studien* Festschrift A. Bömer, (Leipzig, 1928), pp. 263–76 (contains fragments of PJ 14; 15; 16. 2; 17. 1–2, 18; 18). Ninth century.
4. P. Bodmer V, published in 1958. Fourth century.

J. van Haelst, *Catalogue des papyrus littéraires juifs et chrétiens* (Paris, 1976) refers to other fragments. His 601 (P Grenf. 1. 8) contains PJ 7. 2–10. 1; his 602, which he plans to edit, contains 3. 3–4. 4. In addition *Oxyrhynchus Papyri*, vol. 50, publishes a sixth-century papyrus containing PJ 25. P. Ashmoleana inv. 9 contains a fragment of PJ 13. 3–14. 2 and 15. 2–4, to be published by J. Bingen in *Papyrologica Bruxellensia*.

The first edition of the printed Greek text, based on a now unknown manuscript, was by M. Neander (Neumann) in 1564. His text was used in the editions of Grynaeus, Fabricius, Jones, and Birch. Birch's may be seen as the first text-critical edition; in addition he made use of two Vatican manuscripts. Thilo's edition was based on Paris 1454 (= Tischendorf's C) with an apparatus that included seven other Paris manuscripts and Birch's two Vatican manuscripts. Suckow's text reproduced a Venice manuscript (= Tischendorf's A).

The composite new text created by Tischendorf from eighteen manuscripts, of which C is deemed to be the best, has been the most influential edition from which most modern versions have stemmed, although Hennecke gives prominence to the text of Bodmer V. É. de Strycker's attempt to establish the oldest form of PJ tries to combine the text of Tischendorf with that of Bodmer V.

My translation is based on Tischendorf.

EDITIONS

Greek

M. Neander, *Apocrypha... inserto etiam Protevangelio Iacobi graece, in Oriente nuper reperto, necdum edito hactenus* (Basle, 1564; ²1567), 340–92 (with Postel's Latin).
J. J. Grynaeus, *Monumenta SS. Patrum orthodoxographa* (Basle, 1568).
Fabricius, i. 66–125 (with Postel's Latin).
Jones, ii. 128–62 (with Eng. trans.).
Birch, i. 197–242.
Thilo, i. pp. xlv–lxxiii, 159–273 (with Postel's Latin).
C. A. Suckow, *Protevangelium Iacobi ex codice ms. Venetiano descripsit...* (Breslau, 1840).
Giles, i.
Tischendorf *EA*, 1–50.

M. Testuz, *Papyrus Bodmer* V (Cologny-Geneva, 1958) (with French translation and useful introduction).[3]

B. L. Daniels, 'The Greek Manuscript Tradition of the Protevangelium Jacobi' (unpublished Ph.D. thesis, Duke University. N. Carolina, 1956).[4]

Ronald F. Hock, *The Infancy Gospels of James and Thomas* (Santa Rosa, 1995) (= *The Scholars Bible* 2) (with English translation).

SYNOPSES

Aland[13] prints the Greek of PJ 11. 1-3, 12. 1-3, 12. 3-20. 4, 21. 1-4, 22. 1-24. 3, 24. 4 from Bodmer V and de Stacker's edition with the Lucan and Matthaean birth narrative See also extracts in Greek in Huck–Greeven[13] (8. 3, 10. 2, 11. 1-3, 12. 2-3, 14. 1-2, 17. 1-2, 21. 1-4, 22. 1-2, 23. 1-24. 2, 24. 3, 24. 4). and see Boismard, 415.

Coptic (Sahidic)

J. Leipoldt, 'Ein saïdisches Bruchstück des Jakobus-Protevangelium', *ZNW* 6 (1905), 106–7

F. Robinson, *Coptic Apocryphal Gospels* (Cambridge 1896) (= *TU* 4.2), 2–44 (Sahidic fragment of the life of the Virgin, with English translation).

Syriac

A. Smith Lewis, *Apocrypha Syriaca. The Protevangelium Jacobi and Transitus Mariae* (London and Cambridge, 1902) (= *Studia Sinaitica* 11) (with English translation).

Wright, *Contributions*, 1–5 (with English translation). [Syriac repr. in E. A. Wallis Budge, *The History of the Blessed Virgin Mary and the History of the Likeness of Christ* (London, 1899), i. 213–17 (= *Luzac's Semitic Text and Translation series* 4), but not translated in his vol. ii.]

E. Nestle, 'Ein syrisches Bruchstück aus dem Protevangelium Iacobi', *ZNW* 3 (1902), 86–7 (on Sachau's Berlin fragment).

Armenian

P. E. Tayecʻ i (or Daietsi), *Ankanon girkhʻ nor ktakaranacʻ(Tʻangaran Haykakan Hin ew Nor Dpruteancʻ*, ii (Venice, 1898).

(Latin translation by H, Quecke of Armenian fragments in Appendix to de Strycker, *La forme* . . . (below, 'General').)

F. C. Conybeare, 'Protevangelium Jacobi', *AJT* i (1897), 424–42 (English translation).[5]

---

[3] See O. Perler, 'Das Protevangelium des Jakobus nach dem Papyrus Bodmer V, *Freiburger Zeitschrift für Philosophie und Theologie*, 6 (1959); 25–35

[4] Daniels is the translator into English of PJ (based on the text of Bodmer V) in D. R. Cartlidge and D. L. Dungan (eds.) *Documents for the Study of the Gospels* (Cleveland, New York, London, 1980), 107–17.

[5] Strycker, (below, 'General': 1961), 44, suggests that the Armenian text translated by Conybeare is from part of a manuscript of the Armenian Gospel of the Infancy.

Georgian

G. Garitte, 'Le "Protévangile de Jacques" en géorgien', *Le Muséon*, 70 (1957), 233–65.

J. N. Birdsall, 'A Second Georgian Recension of the Protevangelium Jacobi', *Le Muséon*, 83 (1970), 49–72.

Ethiopic

M. Chaîne, 'Liber natiuitatis Mariae', in *Apocrypha de Beata Maria Virgine (Scriptores Aethiopici* series 1, 7; Rome, 1909; repr. Louvain, 1955), 3–19 (= *CSCO* 39, Aeth 22; Latin version in *CSCO* 40 = Aeth 23, 1–16).

Slavonic

For bibliography see de Santos Otero, *Altslav, Apok.* ii. 1–32.

N. Bonwetsch, in Harnack (below, 'General'), i. 902–17.

A. N. Pypin, [*False and Dismissed Books of Ancient Russia*] (St Petersburg, 1862), 78–80 (in Russian).

S. Novakovic ['The Apocryphal Proto-Gospel of James'], *Starine*, 10 (1878), 61–71 (in Russian).

I. I. Porfirjev, ['Apocryphal Sayings about New Testament People and Events in Manuscripts of the Solovetski Library'], *Sbornik otdelenija russkago jazyka i slovesnosti Imperstorskoj Akademii Nauk*, 52 (1890), 10–13, 136–48 (in Russian).

P. A. Lavrov, ['Apocryphal Texts'], *Nauk* 67 (1899), 52–69 (in Russian).

Cf. also A. Berendts, *Die handschriftliche Überlieferung der Zacharias- und Johannes-Apokryphen* (Leipzig, 1904), esp. 1–15, 17–79[6] (= *TU* 26.3).

N. Radovich, *Un frammento slavo del Protevangelio di Giacomo* (Naples, 1969).

Arabic

See Graf, i. 224 f.

According to Amann (below, 'Modern Translations, French'), 68, there are two manuscripts in the Bibliothèque Nationale containing the Protevangelium of James in Arabic written in Syriac script. These seem not to have been edited.

See also G. Garitte, '"Protevangelii Iacobi" Versio arabica antiquior', *Le Muséon*, 86 (1973), 377–96.

Latin

Possible extracts of PJ in a Latin version may be found in the chronicle known as the *Barbarus Scaligeri* (or *Excerpta Latina Barbarica*) of the fifth century. (Text in H. Gelzer, *Sextus Julius Africanus und die byzantinische Chronographie*, ii (Leipzig, 1885), 326–8).

J. A. de Aldama, 'Fragmentos de una versión latina del Protevangelio de Santiago y

---

[6] But see É. de Strycker's warnings (below, 'General': 1961), 46–7.

una nueva adaptación de sus primeros capítulos', *Biblica*, 43 (1962), 57–74. [Cf. id., *Studia Patristica*, 12 (1975), 79–82.]

E. de Strycker, 'Une ancienne version latine du Protévangile de Jacques avec des extraits de la Vulgate de Matthieu 1–2 et Luc 1–2', *Anal. Boll.* (1965), 365–402.

F. Vattioni, 'Frammento latino del Vangelo di Giacomo', *Augustinianum*, 17 (1977), 505–9.

See also bibliography to Arundel 404, below.

MODERN TRANSLATIONS

English

Hone, 24–37.
Cowper, 1–26.
Walker, 1–15.
James, 38–49.
J. B. Lightfoot, M. R. James, H. B. Swete, *et al.*, *Excluded Books of the New Testament* (London, 1927), 27–48.
Hennecke[3], i. 374–88.
Hennecke[5], i. 421–39.

French

G. Brunet, *Les Évangiles apocryphes traduits et annotés d'après l'édition de Thilo* (Paris, 1849; [2]1863).
Migne, *Dictionnaire*, i, cols. 1009–28.
E. Amann, *Le Protévangile de Jacques et ses remaniements latins* (Paris, 1910) (includes a detailed commentary) (= *Les apocryphes du Nouveau Testament*, ed. J. Bousquet and E. Amann).
Michel, i, pp. i–xviii, 1–51.
Amiot, 47–64.
H. Daniel-Rops, *Le Évangiles de la Vierge* (Paris, 1984), 132–48.
Éac, 73–104.

German

K. F. Borberg, *Bibliothek der neutestamentlichen Apokryphen gesammelt, übersetzt und erläutert* (Stuttgart, 1841), 11–56.
E. J. Lützelberger, *Das Protevangelium Iacobi, zwei Evangelien der Kindheit und die Akten des Pilatus* (Nuremberg, 1842).
Clemens, ii. 5–88.
Hennecke[1], 47–63 (A. Meyer); cf: *Handbuch*, 106–31.
Hennecke[3], i. 277–9 (O. Cullmann).
Hennecke[5], i. 334–49 (O. Cullmann).
Michaelis, 73–95.
J. Walterscheid, *Das Leben Jesu nach den neutestamentlichen Apokryphen* (Düsseldorf, 1953), 8–23.
Schneider, 96–145.

Italian

E. Pistelli, *Il Protevangelo di Jacopo* (Lanciano, 1919) (with parts of Pseudo-Matthew as an appendix).
Bonaccorsi, i. 58-109.
C. Rotunno and E. Bartoletti, *Il Protevangelo di Giacomo* (Venice, 1950) (= *Antichi Testi* 1).
Erbetta, i. 2, 7-43.
Moraldi, i. 57-87; [2] i. 77-139.
A. M. di Nola, *Il Protevangelo di Giacomo* (Parma, 1966).
Cravieri, 5-28.

Spanish

E. González-Blanco, i. 329-62.
de Santos Otero, 136-76.

GENERAL

Variot, 32-43, 141-96.
L. Conrady, 'Das Evangelium Jakob in neuer Beleuchtung', *ThStKr* 62 (1889), 728-84.
Harnack, i. 19-21, ii. 598-603.
A. Resch, *Das Kindheitsevangelium nach Lucas und Matthaeus unter Herbeiziehung der aussercanonischen Paralleltexte* (Leipzig, 1897).
A. Berendts, *Studien über Zacharias-Apokryphen und Zacharias-Legenden* (Leipzig, 1895) (cf. id., *Anal. Boll.* 16 (1907), 92-3).
L. Conrady, *Die Quelle der kanonischen Kindheits-geschichte Jesus: Ein wissenschaftlicher Versuch* (Göttingen, 1900).
P. Vannutelli, *Protevangelium Jacobi Synoptice* (Rome, 1939), 1-64 and (Rome, 1940), 65-96 (= *Synoptica* 4 and 5).
L. M. Peretto, 'La Vergine Maria nel pensiero di uno scrittore del secondo secolo (La Mariologia del Protevangelo di Giacomo)', *Marianum* 16 (1954), 228-65.
—— *La Mariologia del Protevangelo di Giacomo* (Rome, 1955).
É. de Strycker, *La forme la plus ancienne du Protévangile de Jacques* (Brussels, 1961) (= *Subsidia Hagiographica* 33).
—— 'Le Protévangile de Jacques: Problèmes critiques et exégétiques', in F. L. Cross (ed.), *Studia Evangelica*, iii (Berlin, 1964) 339-59 (= *TU* 88).
P. A. van Stempvoort, 'The Protevangelium Jacobi, the Sources of its Theme and Style and their Bearing on its Date', in Cross, op. cit., part II, 410-26.
H. R. Smid, *Protevangelium Jacobi: A Commentary* (Assen, 1965). [Gives a full bibliography.]
É. de Strycker, 'De griekse handschriften van het Protevangelie van Jacobus', in *Mededelingen van de Koninklijke Vlaamse Academie voor Wetenschappen, Letteren en Schone Kunsten van België. Kl der Letteren 30* (1968) (German version in D. Harlfinger, *Griechische Kodikologie und Textüberlieferung* (Darmstadt, 1980) 577-612).
F. Manns, *Essais sur le Judéo-Christianisme* (Jerusalem, 1977), esp. 106-114. [Tries to claim PJ as Jewish-Christian and to vindiate it as better acquainted with Jewish customs than usually allowed.]

A. Fuchs and C. Eckmair, *Die griechischen Apokryphen zum Neuen Testament*, ii. *Konkordanz zum Protevangelium des Jakobus* (Linz, 1978) (= *Studien zum Neuen Testament und seiner Umwelt* B3).

W. S. Vorster, 'The Protevangelium of James and Intertextuality', in T. Baarda *et al.* (eds.), *Text and Testimony: Essays in Honour of A. F. J. Klijn* (Kampen, 1988), 262–75.

E. Cothenet, 'Le Protévangile de Jacques: Origine, genre et signification d'un premier midrash chrétien sur la Nativité de Marie', *ANRW* 2.25.6, 4252–69.

Klauck, 89–90: ET 65–72.

1. 1. In the 'Histories of the Twelve Tribes of Israel' Joachim was a very rich man, and he brought all his gifts to the Lord twofold, saying. 'What I bring in excess shall be for the whole people, and what I bring as a sin-offering shall be for the Lord, as a propitiation for me.'

2. Now the great day of the Lord drew near, and the children of Israel were bringing their gifts. And Reuben stood up and said, 'It is not lawful for you to offer your gifts first, because you have begotten no offspring in Israel.'

3. Then Joachim became very sad, and went to the record-book of the twelve tribes of the people and said, 'I will look in the register to see whether I am the only one who has not begotten offspring in Israel', and he found that all the righteous had raised up offspring in Israel. And he remembered the patriarch Abraham to whom in his last days God gave a son, Isaac. 4. And Joachim was very sad, and did not show himself to his wife, but went into the wilderness; there he pitched his tent and fasted forty days and forty nights, saying to himself, 'I shall not go down either for food or for drink until the Lord my God visits me; my prayer shall be food and drink.'[1]

2. 1. Anna his wife sang two dirges and gave voice to a twofold lament:

> 'I will mourn my widowhood,
> and grieve for my childlessness.'

2. Now the great day of the Lord drew near, and Judith[2] her maid said, 'How long do you intend to humble your soul, because the great day of the Lord is near and it is not lawful for you to mourn. But take this headband, which the mistress of work gave me; it is not right for me to wear it because I am a servant and it bears a royal cipher.'[3]

3. But Anna said, 'Get away from me! I shall never do it. The Lord has greatly humbled me. Who knows whether a deceiver did not give it to you, and you have come to make me share in your sin!' Judith answered, 'Why should I curse you?[4] The Lord God has shut up your womb[5] to give you no fruit in Israel.'

4. And Anna was very sad, but she took off her mourning garments,

---

[1] Cf. John 4: 34.
[2] Variant: Euthine.
[3] Or 'you have a royal appearance'.
[4] Variant adds 'because you have not listened to me'.
[5] Cf. 1 Sam. 1: 6.

washed her head, put on her bridal garments, and about the ninth hour went into her garden to walk there. And she saw a laurel tree and sat down beneath it and implored the Lord saying, 'O God of our fathers, bless me and heed my prayer, just as you blessed the womb of Sarah and gave her a son, Isaac.'[6]

3. 1. And Anna sighed towards heaven and saw a nest of sparrows in the laurel tree and she sang a dirge to herself:

'Woe is me, who gave me life
What womb brought me forth?
For I was born a curse before them all and before the children of Israel,
And I was reproached, and they mocked me and thrust me out of the temple of the Lord.
2. Woe is me, to what am I likened?
I am not likened to the birds of the heaven;
for even the birds of the heaven are fruitful before you, O Lord.[7]
Woe is me, to what am I likened?
I am not likened to the beasts of the earth;
for even the beasts of the earth are fruitful before you, O Lord.
3. Woe is me, to what am I likened?
I am not likened to these waters;
for even these waters are fruitful before you, O Lord.
Woe is me, to what am I likened?
I am not likened to this earth;
for even this earth brings forth its fruit in its season[8] and praises you, O Lord.'

4. 1. And behold an angel of the Lord appeared to her and said, 'Anna, Anna, the Lord has heard your prayer. You shall conceive and bear,[9] and your offspring shall be spoken of in the whole world.' And Anna said, 'As the Lord my God lives, if I bear a child, whether male or female, I will bring it as a gift to the Lord my God, and it shall serve him all the days of its life.'[10]
2. And behold there came two angels, who said to her, 'Behold, Joachim your husband is coming with his flocks[11] for an angel of the Lord had come down to him and said to him, "Joachim, Joachim, the Lord God has heard your prayer. Go down from here; behold, your wife Anna shall conceive."'
3. And Joachim went down and called his herdsmen and said, 'Bring me here ten female lambs without blemish and without spot; they shall be for the Lord my God. And bring me twelve tender calves and they shall be for the priests and council of elders, and a hundred young he-goats for the whole people.'
4. And, behold, Joachim came with his flocks, and Anna stood at the gate and

---

[6] Cf. Gen. 21: 1-3.
[7] Some MSS add 'Woe is me, to what am I likened? | I am not likened to the dumb animals; for even the dumb animals are fruitful before you, O Lord'.
[8] Cf. Psalm 1: 3. [9] Luke 1: 13.   [10] Cf. 1 Sam. 2: 11; 1: 28.
[11] Variant adds 'and his shepherd and sheep and goats and oxen'.

saw Joachim coming and ran immediately and threw her arms around his neck saying, 'Now I know that the Lord God has greatly blessed me; for behold the widow is no longer a widow, and I, who was childless, shall conceive.'

And Joachim rested the first day in his house.

5. 1. The next day he offered his gifts, saying to himself, 'If the Lord God is gracious to me the frontlet of the priest will make it clear to me.'

And Joachim offered his gifts and observed the priest's frontlet when he went up to the altar of the Lord; and he saw no sin in himself. And Joachim said, 'Now I know that the Lord God is gracious to me and has forgiven all my sins.' And he came down from the temple of the Lord justified, and went to his house.

2. And her months were fulfilled; in the ninth[12] month Anna gave birth. And she said to the midwife, 'What have I brought forth?' And she said, 'A female.' And Anna said, 'My soul is magnified this day.' And she lay her down. And when the days were completed, Anna purified herself and gave suck to the child, and[13] called her Mary.

6. 1. Day by day the child grew strong; when she was six[14] months old her mother stood her on the ground to see if she could stand. And she walked seven steps and came to her bosom. And she took her up saying, 'As the Lord my God lives, you shall walk no more upon this earth until I bring you into the temple of the Lord.' And she made a sanctuary in her bedroom and did not permit anything common or unclean to pass through it. And she summoned the undefiled daughters of the Hebrews, and they served her.[15]

2. On the child's first birthday Joachim made a great feast, and invited the chief priests and the priests and the scribes and the elders and all the people of Israel. And Joachim brought the child to the priests, and they blessed her saying, 'O God of our fathers, bless this child and give her a name eternally renowned among all generations.' And all the people said, 'So be it, so be it, Amen.' And they brought her to the chief priests, and they blessed her saying, 'O God of the heavenly heights, look upon this child and bless her with a supreme blessing which cannot be superseded.' And her mother carried her into the sanctuary of her bedroom and gave her suck. And Anna sang this song to the Lord God:

'I will sing a praise to the Lord my God,
for he has visited me and removed from me the reproach of my enemies.
And the Lord gave me the fruit of his righteousness, unique yet
 manifold[16] before him.
Who will proclaim to the sons of Reuben that Anna gives suck?'[17]

---

[12] Variants: 'sixth', 'seventh', or 'eighth'.   [13] Variant adds 'on the eighth day'.
[14] Variant: 'nine'.   [15] Or 'cared for her amusement'.
[16] Cf. J. A. de Aldama, '*Poluplousios* dans l'Évangile de Jacques et l'*Adversus Haereses* d'Irénée', *RSR* 50 (1962), 86–9.
[17] Some MSS add 'Hearken, hearken, you twelve tribes of Israel: Anna gives suck'.

And she laid her down to rest in the bedroom of her sanctuary, and went out and served them. When the feast was ended they went down rejoicing and glorifying the God of Israel.[18]

7. 1. The months passed, and the child grew. When she was two years old Joachim said, 'Let us take her up to the temple of the Lord, so that we may fulfil the promise which we made, lest the Lord send some evil to us and our gift be unacceptable.' And Anna replied, 'Let us wait until the third year, that the child may then no more long for her father and mother.' And Joachim said, 'Let us wait.' 2. And when the child was three years old Joachim said, 'Call the undefiled daughters of the Hebrews, and let each one take a torch, and let these be burning, in order that the child may not turn back and her heart be tempted away from the temple of the Lord.' And they did so until they had gone up to the temple of the Lord. And the priest took her and kissed her and blessed her, saying, 'The Lord has magnified your name among all generations; because of you the Lord at the end of the days will reveal his redemption to the sons of Israel.' 3. And he placed her on the third step of the altar, and the Lord God put grace upon her and she danced with her feet, and the whole house of Israel loved her.

8. 1. And her parents returned marvelling, praising the Lord God because the child did not turn back. And Mary was in the temple of the Lord nurtured like a dove and received food from the hand of an angel. 2. When she was twelve[19] years old, there took place a council of the priests saying, 'Behold, Mary has become twelve[19] years old in the temple of the Lord. What then shall we do with her lest she defile the temple of the Lord?' And they said to the high priest, 'You stand at the altar of the Lord; enter the sanctuary and pray concerning her, and that which the Lord shall reveal to you we will indeed do.' 3. And the high priest took the vestment with the twelve bells and went into the Holy of Holies and prayed concerning her. And behold, an angel of the Lord appeared and said to him, 'Zacharias, Zacharias, go out and assemble the widowers of the people, and to whomsoever the Lord shall give a sign she shall be a wife.' And the heralds went forth through all the country round about Judaea; the trumpet of the Lord sounded, and all came running.

9. 1. And Joseph threw down his adze and went out to their meeting. And when they were gathered together, they took the rods and went to the high priest. He took the rods from them all, entered the temple, and prayed. When he had finished the prayer he took the rods, and went out and gave them to them; but there was no sign on them. Joseph received the last rod, and behold, a dove came out of the rod and flew on to Joseph's head. And the priest said to Joseph, 'You have been chosen by lot to receive the virgin of the

---

[18] Some MSS add 'And they gave her the name Mary because her name shall never fade'.
[19] Variants: 'fourteen' or 'ten'.

Lord as your ward.' 2. But Joseph answered him, 'I have sons and am old; she is but a girl. I object lest I should become a laughing-stock to the sons of Israel.' And the priest said to Joseph, 'Fear the Lord your God, and remember what God did to Dathan, Abiram, and Korah, how the earth was split in two and they were all swallowed up because of their rebellion. And now beware, Joseph, lest these things happen in your house too.' And Joseph was afraid and received her as his ward. And Joseph said to Mary', 'I have received you from the temple of the Lord, and now I leave you in my house and go away to build my buildings. I will return to you; the Lord will guard you.'

10. 1. Now there was a council of the priests saying, 'Let us make a veil for the temple of the Lord.' And the priest said, 'Call to me pure virgins of the tribe of David.' And the officers departed and searched and they found seven virgins. And the priest remembered the child Mary', that she was of the tribe of David and was pure before God. And the officers went and fetched her. 2. Then they brought them into the temple of the Lord and the priest said, 'Cast lots to see who shall weave the gold, the amiantus, the linen, the silk, the hyacinth-blue, the scarlet, and the pure purple'. The pure purple and scarlet fell by lot to Mary. And she took them and went home. At that time Zacharias became dumb,[20] and Samuel took his place until Zacharias was able to speak again. Mary took the scarlet and spun it.

11. 1. And she took the pitcher and went out to draw water, and behold, a voice said, 'Hail, highly favoured one,[21] the Lord is with you, you are blessed among women.' And she looked around to the right and to the left to see where this voice came from. And, trembling, she went to her house and put down the pitcher and took the purple and sat down on her seat and drew out the thread. 2. And behold, an angel of the Lord stood before her and said, 'Do not fear, Mary'; for you have found grace before the Lord of all things and shall conceive by his Word.' When she heard this she considered it and said, 'Shall I conceive by the Lord, the living God, and bear as every woman bears?' 3. And the angel of the Lord said, 'Not so, Mary; for the power of the Lord shall overshadow you; wherefore that holy one who is born of you shall be called the Son of the Most High. And you shall call his name Jesus; for he shall save his people from their sins.' And Mary said, 'Behold, (I am) the handmaid of the Lord before him: be it to me according to your word.'[22]

12. 1. And she made ready the purple and the scarlet and brought them to the priest. And the priest blessed her and said, 'Mary, the Lord God has magnified your name, and you shall be blessed among all generations of the earth'.[23] 2. And Mary rejoiced and went to Elizabeth her kinswoman and

---

[20] Cf. Luke 1: 20–2, 64.
[21] Luke 1: 28.
[22] Luke 1: 38.
[23] Luke 1: 42, 48.

knocked on the door. When Elizabeth heard it, she put down the scarlet and ran to the door and opened it, and when she saw Mary she blessed her and said, 'How is it that the mother of my Lord should come to me? For behold, that which is in me leaped and blessed you.'[24] But Mary forgot the mysteries which the archangel Gabriel had told her, and raised a sigh towards heaven and said, 'Who am I, Lord, that all generations of the earth count me blessed?' 3. And she remained three months with Elizabeth. Day by day her womb grew, and Mary was afraid and went into her house and hid herself from the children of Israel. And Mary was sixteen[25] years old when all these mysterious things happened.

13. 1. Now when she was in her sixth month, behold, Joseph came from his buildings and entered his house and found her with child. And he struck his face, threw himself down on the ground on sackcloth and wept bitterly saying, 'With what countenance shall I look towards the Lord my God? What prayer shall I offer for this maiden? For I received her as a virgin out of the temple of the Lord my God and have not protected her. Who has deceived me? Who has done this evil in my house and defiled the virgin? Has the story of Adam been repeated in me? For as Adam was absent in the hour of his prayer and the serpent came and found Eve alone and deceived her, so also has it happened to me.' 2. And Joseph arose from the sackcloth and called Mary and said to her, 'You who are cared for by God, why have you done this and forgotten the Lord your God? Why have you humiliated your soul, you who were brought up in the Holy of Holies and received food from the hand of an angel?' 3. But she wept bitterly, saying, 'I am pure, and know not a man.' And Joseph said to her, 'Whence is this in your womb?' And she said, 'As the Lord my God lives, I do not know whence it has come to me.'

14. 1. And Joseph feared greatly and parted from her, pondering what he should do with her. And Joseph said, 'If I conceal her sin, I shall be found to be in opposition to the law of the Lord. If I expose her to the children of Israel, I fear lest that which is in her may be from the angels and I should be found delivering innocent blood to the judgement of death. What then shall I do with her? I will put her away secretly.' And the night came upon him. 2. And behold, an angel of the Lord appeared to him in a dream, saying, 'Do not fear this child. For that which is in her is of the Holy Spirit. She shall bear a son, and you shall call his name Jesus; for he shall save his people from their sins.'[26] And Joseph arose from sleep and glorified the God of Israel who had bestowed his grace upon him, and he guarded her.

15. 1. And Annas the scribe came to him and said to him, 'Joseph, why have you not appeared in our assembly?' And Joseph said to him, 'Because I was weary from the journey and I rested the first day.' And Annas turned and

---

[24] Luke 1: 41–4.
[25] Variants: 'fourteen' or 'fifteen'.
[26] Cf. Matt. 1: 20f.

saw that Mary was pregnant. 2. And he went running to the priest and said to him, 'Joseph, for whom you are a witness, has grievously transgressed.' And the high priest said, 'In what way?' And he said, 'The virgin, whom he received from the temple of the Lord, he has defiled, and has secretly consummated his marriage with her, and has not disclosed it to the children of Israel.' And the priest said to him, 'Has Joseph done this?' And Annas said to him, 'Send officers, and you will find the virgin pregnant.' And the officers went and found as he had said, and brought her and Joseph to the court. And the priest said, 'Mary, why have you done this? Why have you humiliated your soul and forgotten the Lord your God, you who were brought up in the Holy of Holies and received food from the hand of an angel, and heard hymns, and danced before him? Why have you done this?' But she wept bitterly saying, 'As the Lord my God lives, I am pure before him and I know not a man.' And the priest said to Joseph, 'Why have you done this?' And Joseph said, 'As the Lord my God lives, I am pure concerning her.' And the priest said, 'Do not give false witness, but speak the truth. You have consummated your marriage in secret, and have not disclosed it to the children of Israel, and have not bowed your head under the mighty hand in order that your seed might be blessed.' And Joseph was silent.

16. 1. And the priest said, 'Give back the virgin whom you have received from the temple of the Lord.' And Joseph began to weep. And the priest said, 'I will give you both to drink the water of the conviction of the Lord, and it will make your sins manifest in your eyes.' 2. And the priest took it and gave it to Joseph to drink and sent him into the hill-country, and he returned whole. And he made Mary drink also, and sent her into the hill-country, and she returned whole. And all the people marvelled, because sin did not appear in them. And the priest said, 'If the Lord God has not revealed your sins, neither do I judge you.' And he released them. And Joseph took Mary and departed to his house, rejoicing and glorifying the God of Israel.

17. 1. Now there went out a decree from the king Augustus that all those in Bethlehem in Judaea should be enrolled.[27] And Joseph said, 'I shall enrol my sons, but what shall I do with this child? How shall I enrol her? As my wife? I am ashamed to do that. Or as my daughter? But all the children of Israel know that she is not my daughter. On this day of the Lord the Lord will do as he wills.' 2. And he saddled his she-ass and sat her on it; his son led, and Joseph followed. And they drew near to the third milestone. And Joseph turned round and saw her sad and said within himself, 'Perhaps the child within her is paining her.' Another time Joseph turned round and saw her laughing and said to her, 'Mary, why is it that I see your face at one moment laughing and at another sad?' And Mary said to Joseph, 'I see with my eyes two peoples, one weeping and lamenting and one rejoicing and exulting.'

---

[27] Luke 2: 1; Matt. 2: 1.

3. And having come half-way, Mary said to him, 'Joseph, take me down from the she-ass, for the child within me presses me to come forth.' And he took her down from the she-ass and said to her, 'Where shall I take you and hide your shame? For the place is desert.'

18. 1. And he found a cave there and brought her into it, and left her in the care of his sons and went out to seek for a Hebrew midwife in the region of Bethlehem. 2. Now I, Joseph, was walking, and yet I did not walk, and I looked up to the air and saw the air in amazement. And I looked up at the vault of heaven, and saw it standing still and the birds of the heaven motionless. And I looked down at the earth, and saw a dish placed there and workmen reclining, and their hands were in the dish. But those who chewed did not chew, and those who lifted up did not lift, and those who put something to their mouth put nothing to their mouth, but everybody looked upwards. And behold, sheep were being driven and they did not come forward but stood still; and the shepherd raised his hand to strike them with his staff but his hand remained upright. And I looked at the flow of the river, and saw the mouths of the kids over it and they did not drink. And then suddenly everything went on its course.

19. 1. And behold, a woman came down from the hill-country and said to me, 'Man, where are you going?' And I said, 'I seek a Hebrew midwife.' And she answered me, 'Are you from Israel?' And I said to her, 'Yes.' And she said, 'And who is she who brings forth in the cave?' And I said, 'My betrothed.' And she said to me, 'Is she not your wife?' And I said to her, 'She is Mary, who was brought up in the temple of the Lord, and I received her by lot as my wife, and she is not my wife, but she has conceived by the Holy Spirit.' And the midwife said to him, 'Is this true?' And Joseph said to her, 'Come and see.'[28] And she went with him. 2. And they stopped at the entrance to the cave, and behold, a bright cloud overshadowed the cave. And the midwife said, 'My soul is magnified today, for my eyes have seen wonderful things; for salvation is born to Israel.' And immediately the cloud disappeared from the cave and a great light appeared, so that our eyes could not bear it. A short time afterwards that light withdrew until the baby appeared, and it came and took the breast of its mother Mary. And the midwife cried, 'This day is great for me, because I have seen this new sight.' 3. And the midwife came out of the cave, and Salome met her. And she said to her, 'Salome, Salome, I have a new sight to tell you about; a virgin has brought forth, a thing which her condition does not allow.' And Salome said, 'As the Lord my God lives, unless I insert my finger and test her condition, I will not believe that a virgin has given birth.'

[28] P. Bodmer omits Joseph's monologue of ch. 18 and reads as follows at the beginning of ch. 19. And he found one who was just coming down from the hill-country, and he took her with him, and said to the midwife, 'Mary is betrothed to me; but she conceived of the Holy Spirit after she had been brought up in the Temple of the Lord.'

20. 1. And the midwife went in and said to Mary, 'Make yourself ready, for there is no small contention concerning you'.[29] And Salome inserted her finger[30] to test her condition. And she cried out, saying, 'Woe for my wickedness and my unbelief; for[31] I have tempted the living God; and behold, my hand falls away from me, consumed by fire!' 2. And she bowed her knees before the Lord saying, 'O God of my fathers, remember me; for I am the seed of Abraham, Isaac, and Jacob; do not make me pilloried for the children of Israel, but restore me to the poor. For you know, Lord, that in your name I perform my duties and from you I have received my hire'.[32] 3. And behold, an angel of the Lord appeared and said to her, 'Salome, Salome, the Lord God has heard your prayer. Bring your hand to the child and touch him and salvation and joy will be yours.' 4. And Salome came near and touched him, saying, 'I will worship him, for a great king has been born to Israel.' And Salome was healed as she had requested, and she went out of the cave.[33] And, behold, an angel of the Lord cried, 'Salome, Salome, do not report what marvels you have seen, until the child has come to Jerusalem.'

21. 1. And behold, Joseph was ready to go to Judaea. And there took place a great tumult in Bethlehem of Judaea. For there came wise men saying, 'Where is the new-born king of the Jews? For we have seen his star in the east and have come to worship him.' 2. When Herod heard this he was troubled and sent officers to the wise men, and sent for the high priests and questioned them, 'How is it written concerning the Messiah? Where is he born?' They said to him, 'In Bethlehem of Judaea; for thus it is written.' And he let them go. And he questioned the wise men and said to them, 'What sign did you see concerning the new-born king?' And the wise men said, 'We saw how an indescribably greater star shone among these stars and dimmed them, so that the stars no longer shone; and so we knew that a king was born for Israel. And we have come to worship him.' And Herod said, 'Go and seek, and when you have found him, tell me, that I also may come to worship him,' 3. And the wise men went out. And behold, the star which they had seen in the east, went before them[34] until they came to the cave. And it stood over the head of the cave.[35] And the wise men saw the young child with Mary his mother, and they took out of their pouch gifts: gold, and frankincense, and myrrh. 4. And having been warned by the angel that they should not go into Judaea, they went to their own country by another route.[36]

22. 1. But when Herod realized that he had been deceived by the wise

---

[29] Variant adds 'and when Mary heard this, she lay down in preparation'.
[30] P. Bodmer has only 'And Salome went in and made her ready'.
[31] P. Bodmer omits 'woe ... for'.
[32] P. Bodmer replaces all the preceding words in 20. 2 with 'And she prayed to the Lord'.
[33] Variant adds 'justified'; cf. Luke 18: 14.
[34] P. Bodmer manuscript abbreviates ch. 21 considerably.
[35] Or 'child'.
[36] For this chapter cf. Matt. 2: 1–12.

men he was angry and sent his murderers and commanded them to kill all the babies who were two years old and under.[37] 2. When Mary heard that the babies were to be killed, she was afraid and took the child and wrapped him in swaddling clothes and laid him in an ox-manger.[38]

3. But Elizabeth, when she heard that John was sought for, took him and went up into the hill-country. And she looked around to see where she could hide him, and there was no hiding-place. And Elizabeth groaned aloud and said, 'O mountain of God, receive a mother with a child.' For Elizabeth could not ascend. And immediately the mountain was rent asunder and received her. And a light was shining for them; for an angel of the Lord was with them and protected them.

23. 1. Herod was searching for John, and sent officers to Zacharias saying, 'Where have you hidden your son?' And he answered and said to them, 'I am a minister of God and serve in the temple of the Lord. I do not know where my son is.' 2. And the officers departed and told all this to Herod. Then Herod was angry and said, 'His son is to be king over Israel!' And he sent to him again saying, 'Tell the truth. Where is your son? You know that you are at my mercy.' And the officers departed and told him these things. 3. And Zacharias said, 'I am a witness of God. Pour out blood! But the Lord will receive my spirit, for you shed innocent blood at the threshold of the temple of the Lord.' And about daybreak Zacharias was slain. And the children of Israel did not know that he had been slain.

24. 1. But at the hour of the salutation the priests were departing, and the customary blessing of Zacharias did not take place. And the priests stood waiting for Zacharias, to greet him with prayer and to glorify the Most High. 2. But when he failed to come they were all afraid. But one of them took courage and went in and he saw beside the altar congealed blood; and a voice said, 'Zacharias has been slain, and his blood shall not be wiped away until his avenger comes.' And when he heard these words, he was afraid and went out and told the priests what he had seen. 3. And they took courage and entered and saw what had happened. And the ceiling panels of the temple wailed, and they split their clothes from the top to the bottom. And they did not find his body, but they found his blood turned into stone. And they were afraid, and went out and told all the people that Zacharias had been slain. And all the tribes of the people heard and they mourned him and lamented three days and three nights. 4. And after the three days the priests took counsel whom they should appoint in his stead and the lot fell upon Symeon. Now it was he to whom it had been revealed by the Holy Spirit that he should not see death until he had seen the Christ in the flesh.[39]

25. 1. Now I, James, wrote this history in Jerusalem when tumult arose on

---

[37] Cf. Matt. 2: 16.
[38] Cf. Luke 2: 7.   [39] Cf. Luke 2: 25–6.

the death of Herod, and withdrew into the desert until the tumult in Jerusalem ceased. And I praise the Lord God who gave me the wisdom to write this history. Grace shall be with all those who fear our Lord Jesus Christ, to whom be glory for ever and ever, Amen.

The Infancy Gospel of Thomas

Although various manuscripts contain collections of some infancy stories known now as the Gospel of Thomas, the superscriptions seem to avoid describing the work as a gospel. The usual designation is 'paidika' i.e. 'childhood events', and this form could be the oldest. This could represent a deliberate attempt to differentiate these stories from the full 'biographical' canonical Gospels. These childhood events fill in gaps left in the canonical Gospels, and they take their cue from the story of Jesus in the Temple at the age of twelve in Luke 2. The episodes in Thomas tell of Jesus at various ages prior to twelve.

The different forms in which infancy stories about Jesus have been preserved suggest that there was a continuing oral development of such episodes even after the first written accounts were circulating. Indeed the very existence of written accounts may have encouraged the development of other such accounts. The so-called Infancy Gospel of Thomas appears in various guises but must not be confused with the Nag Hammadi Gospel of Thomas in Coptic (*q.v.*). Following the example of M. R. James and Tischendorf, three versions are given here, translated from the texts by Tischendorf: Greek A, Greek B, and Latin.

Among the stories in the Thomas material, the episode of the dyer found in part in Paris manuscript 239 of Infancy Thomas finds a place also in the Armenian Infancy Gospel 21 and in the Arabic Infancy Gospel 37, and a variant of it even occurs in the Gnostic Gospel of Philip.[1] The free movement of such stories is also evidenced in the story of Jesus and the schoolmaster found three times in the Infancy Gospel of Thomas, Greek A and Latin, and also in the second-century anti-Gnostic work, the *Epistula Apostolorum* 4, as well as in Pseudo-Matthew 31 and 38, and the Arabic Infancy Gospel 49.

The theological teaching of these stories is minimal. The main thrust of the episodes is to stress in a crudely sensational way the miraculous powers of Jesus. Although they follow in the tradition found in the canonical Gospels, where Jesus is alleged to raise the dead, to pass through closed doors, to walk on water, and to still a storm at sea, the miracles in Thomas are often capricious and even destructive. Jesus is an *enfant terrible* who seldom acts in a Christian way! A reaction to this picture of Jesus as a ruthless infant prodigy may be seen in the differing picture of him in the History of Joseph the

---

[1] The story appears below under Arabic Infancy Gospel.

Carpenter (q.v.). Nevertheless, the vivid story-telling of the episodes creates a sequence of memorable incidents.

The earliest form of Infancy Thomas seems to be the Syriac, but the tradition seems to go back to a Greek model: the Greek alphabet figures in one story. Wright's Syriac text is based on a fifth-century manuscript that is close to Greek A (despite its being one thousand years older), and especially to the form of Greek A found in Paris 239. There are also links with the Vienna palimpsest in Latin. Peeters (*Évangiles apocryphes*, ii) tried to argue that all forms of Infancy Thomas, Greek and Latin, and the Armenian and Arabic expansions, go back ultimately to a Syriac original, but we should be wary of this and perhaps we ought to draw a sharp distinction between the direct traditions (Greek, Latin, Slavonic, Ethiopic, Wright's Syriac) and the infancy gospels in Armenian and Arabic. In favour of Peeters's view, however, is the argument that the later attribution of authorship to Thomas may indicate an East Syrian provenance, which is where most of the Thomas literature seems to have originated. More recently Gero has left the question of the language of the prototype open. Certainly there seems to have been a ninth-century Greek tradition from which Greek A, Greek B, Tischendorf's Latin, the Slavonic, and the Paris and the Athens Greek manuscripts developed, but whether that Greek is descended from an earlier Greek form of the text or from a Syriac original is not clear. Independent of that ninth-century Greek tradition there seems to have been a Syriac tradition, the text of which is close to that of Wright's manuscript.

Pseudo-Matthew part 2 seems to have been developed from the Greek tradition, and it is from Pseudo-Matthew that these stories gained the widest circulation in the West, especially in later Latin versions, and also in Provençal, Old French, and Anglo-Saxon.

It is obvious from Gero's sketch and the above summary that the precise interrelationship of the different Greek and versional infancy narratives needs careful scholarly investigation and ultimately demands a critical edition of the text(s). In the meantime, the infancy stories represent the encapsulating in writing at various points in history of a developing cycle of oral tradition. As with many of the canonical Gospel pericopae, many of the episodes in the Infancy Gospel are self-contained and only loosely connected with one another, thus facilitating changes. The changes in this tradition need not have been only in the direction of growth. It has been suggested that a shorter form of the infancy narratives, such as is found in Greek B, may in fact have been a deliberately shortened form of an originally longer document. In other words, the shorter versions may have been expurgated texts to render them suitable for the orthodox.

The Gnostic nature and origin of the infancy narratives is seen by some to exist not only in the stories themselves in which Jesus the *Wunderkind* is possessed of complete knowledge and wisdom and power *ab initio* and thus as a Gnostic revealer, but also in the reaction of early fathers to a Gospel of Thomas that seems to approximate to our Infancy Gospel. Their statements suggest a book of Gnostic origin that was adopted by the Naassenes and then popular with the Manichaeans. Cyril of Jerusalem (died 386), *Catecheses* 4. 36 and 6. 31 (*PG* 33. 500, 593), connects the Manichaeans with a Gospel of Thomas and notes that Thomas was one of the disciples of Manes. Hippolytus, *Haer.* 5. 7. 20 (Wendland, p. 83), refers to a Gospel of Thomas telling an episode (not actually in our Gospel of Thomas) of Jesus at the age of seven. The second Council of Nicaea in 787 condemned a Gospel of Thomas.

The book of Thomas referred to by the patristic writers may be Infancy Thomas in some form. If the Stichometry of Nicephorus refers to Infancy Thomas then it is known there in a much longer form, as a book of 1300 stichoi.

Attribution of authorship to Thomas possibly goes back to Origen, *Hom. 1 on Luke* (Rauer, *GCS* 49 (35), p. 5), who is aware of a Gospel of Thomas, but whether or not he is referring to our Infancy Gospel of Thomas is debatable. The infancy stories are attributed to Thomas in the titles of the Dresden, Sinai, and Bologna manuscripts. Authorship is attributed to James by the Athens manuscript. He is not named in the Paris fragment or in the Syriac, Georgian, or Ethiopic. The Vienna palimpsest lacks both the beginning and the end.

The titles of this work in the various forms include: 'The Account of Thomas the Israelite Philosopher concerning the childhood of the Lord', 'The Childhood of Jesus according to Thomas', 'The Book of the holy apostle Thomas concerning the life and childhood of the Lord', 'The Childhood of our Lord Jesus (Christ)'.

History of the Printed Text
Tischendorf's Greek A is the longest version and is based on two manuscripts both of the fifteenth century: one in Bologna (Univ. 2702), the other in Dresden (1187). Mingarelli's text had been based on the Bologna manuscript; Thilo added to this the Dresden manuscript and a fragment containing chapters 1–2 then in Vienna (and edited by Lambecius (see Tischendorf, *EA*, p. xliii)) but now lost. Athos Vatopedi 37 is unedited but is said to resemble Greek A. The fifteenth–sixteenth century Paris 239 containing chapters 1–7, edited originally by Cotelerius (and translated into English by M. R. James), is cited in Tischendorf's apparatus to the text of his Greek A. Delatte's publication of the Athens manuscript of the Greek came after Tischendorf's day. This manuscript shows links with the Latin, especially in Latin chapters 1–3. Both this fragment and the Latin try to provide a link with PJ: the Athens manuscript even attributes the authorship of both to James.

Tischendorf's Greek B was first edited by him from a fourteenth–fifteenth century manuscript he had discovered on Mount Sinai. It is shorter than his A text, with significant changes, such as the reversal in the order of the miracles in chapters 2 and 3, and the abridgement of chapter 7. The schoolmaster incident (and indeed other stories) bring it closer to Pseudo-Matthew than to the versions elsewhere in Thomas. At other places the wording of B is identical with that of A. A close textual and literary study of these two, and other versions, of Thomas needs to be undertaken along the lines of the study of the interrelationship of the canonical Gospels before its complicated history can be understood. S. Gero has pointed a way forward in his article in *NovT* 13.

Tischendorf's Latin is from a Vatican manuscript (Vat. Reg. 648). He was also aware of the fragmentary fifth-century Vienna palimpsest in Latin (Vindob. 563). Although Tischendorf's Latin resembles his Greek A, his version of Jesus the scholar is closer to Pseudo-Matthew 31–2.

Following the example of de Santos Otero, only the first three chapters of the Latin, which provide material not found in the Greek or Syriac, are reproduced below. These chapters concern the Holy Family in Egypt, and they provide a link with the end of the Protevangelium of James. The stories set in Egypt differ from those in Pseudo-Matthew the Arabic, and the Armenian. This link either encouraged the eventual merger of PJ with Thomas, as is the case in some of the apparently derivative apocryphal works such as Pseudo-Matthew and the Armenian infancy stories, or else is itself influenced by narratives already in existence that linked the birth and infancy narratives. Wright's Syriac manuscript contains PJ followed by Thomas, and both show links with Pseudo-Matthew. The blending of PJ and Thomas can also be seen in the later Latin of, say, Arundcl 404 or the Liber de Infantia Salvatoris (Paris 11867).

My translations are based on Tischendorf's editions.

EDITIONS

Greek

Fabricius, i. 159–67 (Greek with Latin trans.).
G. L. Mingarelli, *Nuova raccolta d'opuscoli scientifici e filologici*, xii (Venice, 1764), 73–155 (with Latin trans.).
Jones, ii. 273–9 (with Eng. trans.).
Thilo, i, pp. lxxiii–xci, 275–315 (and Latin version).
Giles, i (Greek text).
Tischendorf, *EA*, pp. 140–63 (Greek A, B).
A. Delatte, *Anecdota Atheniensia* i (*Bibliothèque de la faculté de philosophie et lettres de l'Université de Liège* 36; Paris and Liège, 1927), 264–71 (= Athens MS bibl. nat. gr. 355). [See M. R. James JTS 30 (1929), 51–4.]
Ronald F. Hock, *The Infancy Gospels of James and Thomas* (Santa Rosa, 1995) (= *The Scholars Bible* 2) (with English translation).

SYNOPSES

Aland[13] prints Greek A of Infancy Thomas 19. 1–5 together with the Latin version of the Arabic Infancy Gospel 50–3 alongside Luke 2: 41–52 (Jesus in the Temple at the age of twelve). Also shown in Huck-Greeven[13].

Latin

Tischendorf, *EA* 164–80.

G. Philippart, 'Fragments palimpsestes latins du Vindobonensis 563 (ve siècle ?): Évangile selon S. Matthieu, Évangile de Nicodème, Évangile de l'Enfance selon Thomas', *Anal. Boll.* 90 (1972), 391–411.

Syriac

Wright, *Contributions* 6–11 (Eng. trans.); repr. in E. A. Wallis. Budge, *The History of the Blessed Virgin*, i (London, 1899; repr. New York, 1976), 217–22 (= *Luzac's Semitic Text and Translation Society* 4 and 5).

Ethiopic

S. Grébaut, *PO* 12.4 (Paris, 1919), 565–6, 625–42; *PO* 14 (1921), 775–840; *PO* xvii (1923), 787–854 (with French trans.).

V. Arras and L. van Rompay, 'Les manuscrits éthiopiens des "Miracles de Jesus" ', *Anal. Boll.* 93 (1975), 133–46.

G. Gero, 'The Ta'āmra 'Īyasūs: A Study of Textual and Source-Critical Problems', in T. Beyene (ed.), *Proceedings of the Eighth International Conference of Ethiopian Studies 1984*, i (Addis Ababa and Frankfurt, 1988), 165–70.

A version of Infancy Thomas is found in the majority of Ethiopic manuscripts of the Miracles of Jesus based on Arabic, but these have close links to the Syriac and to the now lost Greek *Vorlage* of Infancy Thomas. Many Ethiopic manuscripts survive.

Georgian

L. Melikset-Bekov, in *Hristianskil Vostok* 6.3 (Tbilisi, 1922), 315–20 (Tiflis MS.); and cf. N. Marr, ibid. 343–7.

G. Garitte, 'Le fragment géorgien de l'évangile de Thomas', *RHE* 51 (1956), 513–20 (Latin trans.).

Slavonic

A. Popov, [*An Account of Manuscripts of the Books of the Church Seal of the Library of A. I. Chludov*] (Moscow, 1872), 320–5 (in Russian).

de Santos Otero, *Altslav. Apok.* i. 49–54.

S. Novaković, ['The Apocrypha of a Serbian-Cyrillic Collection of the Fourteenth Century'], *Starine*, 8 (1876), 48–55 (in Serbo-Croat).

P. A. Lavrov, ['Apocryphal Texts'], in *Sbornik otdelenija russkago jazyka i slovesnosti Imperistorskoj Akademii Nauk*, 67 (1899), 111–18 (Sofia MS. 69) (in Russian).

M. N. Sperasky, ['Slavic Apocryphal Gospels', in *The Work of the 8th Archaeological Conference in Moscow, 1890*], ii (Moscow, 1895), 73–92, 137–43 (in Russian).

A. de Santos Otero, *Das Kirchenslavische Evangelium des Thomas* (Berlin, 1967) (= *Patristische Texte und Studien* 6) (Slavonic text in German trans. with Greek retroversion and commentary).[2]

N. G. Bonwetsch, in A. von Harnack, *Geschichte der altchristlichen Litteratur bis Eusebius*, i (Leipzig, 1893), 910.

W. Lüdtke, 'Die slavischen Texte des Thomas-Evangeliums', *ByzNGrJ.* 6 (1927), 490–508.

P. Peeters, *Évangiles apocryphes*, ii. *L'Évangile de l'enfance* (Paris, 1914), Introduction, esp. section iii. (= *Textes et documents*, ed. H. Hemmer and P. Lejay 18).

L. Conrady, 'Das Thomasevangelium: Ein wissenschaftlicher kritischer Versuch', *ThStKr* 76 (1903), 377–459.

S. Gero, 'The Infancy Gospel of Thomas: A Study of the Textual and Literary Problems', *NovT* 13 (1971), 46–80.

CONCORDANCE

A. Fuchs and F. Weissengruber (with C. Eckmair), *Die griechischen Apokryphen zum Neuen Testament*, iii. *Konkordanz zum Thomasevangelium: Version A und B* (Linz, 1978) (= *Studien zum Neuen Testament und seiner Umwelt* B4).

MODERN TRANSLATIONS (OF GREEK A UNLESS OTHERWISE STATED)

English

Hone, 60–2 (Cotelerius' fragment).
Cowper, 128–69, 448–56 (Greek A, B, Latin, and Wright's Syriac).
Walker, 78–99 (Greek A, B, Latin).
James, 49–65 (Greek A, B, Latin).
Hennecke[3], i. 392–400 (Greek A, Syriac chs. 6–8).
Hennecke[5], i. 439–53.
D. L. Cartlidge, in Cartlidge and Dungan, 92–7.
C. Taylor, *The Oxyrhynchus Logia* (Oxford, 1899), Appendix I (Greek B).

French

Migne, *Dictionnaire*, i, cols. 1137–56 (Greek A, Latin).
Michel, i. pp. xxiii–xxxii, 161–89.
Éac, 191–204.

And see P. Peeters, *Évangiles apocryphes*, ii (Paris, 1914), 289–310, Appendice: 'Jésus à l'école de Zachée d'après les rédactions syriaque, latine et slavonne de pseudo-Thomas'.

German

K. F. Borberg, *Bibliothek der neutestamentlichen Apokryphen gesammelt übersetzt und erläutert* (Stuttgart, 1841), 57–84.

[2] See reviews by H. G. Lunt, *Slavonic and East European Journal* (1968), 488–90; J. Schutz, *ByzZ.* 62 (1969), 94–5; M. van Esbroeck, *Anal. Boll.* 87 (1969), 261–3.

Clemens, ii. 59–88.
Hennecke[1], 63–73 (A. Meyer); cf. *Handbuch* pp. 132–42.
Michaelis, 99–111.
J. Walterscheid, *Das Leben Jesu nach den neutestamentlichen Apokryphen* (Düsseldorf, 1953), 25–33.
Hennecke[3], i, 290–9 (O. Cullmann) (Greek A, Syriac chs. 6–8).
Hennecke[5], i. 349–61 (O. Cullmann) (Greek A, with Slavonic variants added by A. de Santos Otero, and Syriac chs. 6–8).
Schneider, 148–71.

Italian

Bonaccorsi, i, pp. xxiii–xxiv, 110–52 (Greek A).
Erbetta, i, 2, 78–101 (Greek A and B, Latin).
Moraldi, i. 247–79; [2] i. 269–97 (Greek A and B, Latin).
Cravieri, 29–61.

Spanish

González-Blanco, ii. 5–41.
de Santos Otero, 285–306 (Greek A, Latin chs, 1–3).

Irish

M. Herbert and M. McNamara, *Irish Biblical Apocrypha* (Edinburgh, 1989), 44–7 (sample of an Irish verse adaptation of Infancy Thomas).

GENERAL

R. A. Hofmann, *Das Leben Jesu nach den Apokrypha in Zusammenhang aus den Quellen erzählt und wissenschaftlich untersucht* (Leipzig, 1851), 144–65.
Variot, 44–50, 197–232.
W. Bauer, *Das Leben Jesu im Zeitalter der neutestamentlichen Apokryphen* (Tübingen, 1909), 87–100.
M. McNamara, 'Notes on the Irish Gospel of Thomas', *ITQ* 38 (1971), 42–66.
B. Bagatti, 'Nota sul Vangelo di Tommaso Israelite', *Euntes Docet* 29 (Rome, 1976), 482–9.
J. Noret, 'Pour une édition de l'évangile de l'Enfance selon Thomas', *Anal. Boll.* 90 (1972), 412.
S. Voicu, 'Notes sur l'histoire du texte de *l'Histoire de l'enfance de Jesus*', *Apocrypha: Le champ des Apocryphes*, ii (1991), 119–32.
Klauck, 99–105: ET 73–8.

THE INFANCY GOSPEL OF THOMAS

SUMMARY OF CONTENTS

Greek A

1 Introductory words.
2 Jesus forms birds out of mud and makes them come alive.

3 Jesus curses the son of Annas.
4–5 Jesus curses the boy who struck him on the shoulder; Joseph reprimands Jesus.
6–8 Jesus in school expounds the riddle of the alphabet.
9 Jesus raises Zeno who fell from the roof-top.
10 Jesus heals a man's foot.
11 Jesus carries water in his cloak.
12 Jesus reaps a miraculously great harvest.
13 Jesus stretches a plank of wood.
14–15 Jesus in school, and a variant of the story of the arcane meaning of the alphabet.
16 Jesus heals James, the son of Joseph, bitten by a viper.
17 Jesus raises a dead child.
18 Jesus raises a dead workman.
19 Jesus in the temple at the age of twelve.

Greek B

1 Introductory words.
2–3 follows A 2–3.
4–5 follows A 4–5.
6–7 follows A 6–8.
8 = A 9.
9 = A 10.
10 = A 11.
11 = A 13.

Latin

1 Flight to Egypt; Jesus revives a dead fish.
2 A teacher casts Jesus out of the city.
3 Jesus departs from Egypt.

A. Greek A

The account of Thomas the Israelite philosopher concerning the childhood of the Lord

1. I, Thomas the Israelite, announce and make known to you all, brothers from among the Gentiles, the mighty childhood deeds of our Lord Jesus Christ, which he did when he was born in our land. The beginning is as follows.

2. 1. When this boy Jesus was five years old he was playing at the crossing of a stream, and he gathered together into pools the running water, and instantly made it clean, and gave his command with a single word. 2. Having made soft clay he moulded from it twelve sparrows. And it was the sabbath

when he did these things. And there were also many other children playing with him. 3. When a certain Jew saw what Jesus was doing while playing on the sabbath, he at once went and told his father Joseph, 'See, your child is at the stream, and he took clay and moulded twelve birds and has profaned the sabbath.' 4. And when Joseph came to the place and looked, he cried out to him, saying, 'Why do you do on the sabbath things which it is not lawful to do?' But Jesus clapped his hands and cried out to the sparrows and said to them, 'Be gone!' And the sparrows took flight and went away chirping. 5. The Jews were amazed when they saw this, and went away and told their leaders what they had seen Jesus do.

3. 1. Now the son of Annas the scribe was standing there with Joseph; and he took a branch of a willow and with it dispersed the water which Jesus had collected. 2. When Jesus saw what he had done he was angry and said to him, 'You insolent, godless ignoramus, what harm did the pools and the water do to you? Behold, now you also shall wither like a tree and shall bear neither leaves nor root nor fruit.' 3. And immediately that child withered up completely; and Jesus departed and went into Joseph's house. But the parents of the boy who was withered carried him away, bemoaning his lost youth, and brought him to Joseph and reproached him. 'What kind of child do you have, who does such things?'

4. 1. After this he again went through the village, and a child ran and knocked against his shoulder. Jesus was angered and said to him, 'You shall not go further on your way', and immediately he fell down and died. But some, who saw what took place, said, 'From where was this child born, since his every word is an accomplished deed?' 2. And the parents of the dead child came to Joseph and blamed him and said, 'Since you have such a child, you cannot dwell with us in the village; teach him to bless and not to curse.[1] For he is killing our children.'

5. 1. And Joseph called the child to him privately and admonished him saying, 'Why do you do such things? These people suffer and hate us and persecute us.' But Jesus replied, 'I know that these words are not yours; nevertheless for your sake I will be silent. But these people shall bear their punishment.' And immediately those who had accused him became blind. 2. And those who saw it were greatly afraid and perplexed, and said concerning him, 'Every word he speaks, whether good or evil, was a deed and became a miracle.' And when they saw that Jesus had done this, Joseph arose and took him by the ear and pulled it violently. 3. And the child was angry and said to him, 'It is fitting for you to seek and not to find, and you have acted most unwisely. Do you not know that I am yours? Do not vex me.'

6. 1. Now a certain teacher, Zacchaeus by name, who was standing in a certain place, heard Jesus saying these things to his father, and marvelled greatly that, being a child, he voiced such things. 2. And after a few days he

---

[1] Cf. Rom. 12: 14.

came near to Joseph and said to him, 'You have a clever child, and he has understanding. Come, hand him over to me that he may learn letters, and I will teach him with the letters all knowledge, and how to address all the older people and to honour them as forefathers and fathers, and to love those of his own age.' 3. And he told him all the letters from Alpha to Omega distinctly, and with much questioning. But he looked at Zacchaeus the teacher and said to him. 'How do you, who do not know the Alpha according to its nature, teach others the Beta? Hypocrite, first if you know it, teach the Alpha, and then we shall believe you concerning the Beta.'[2] Then he began to question the teacher about the first letter, and he was unable to answer him. 4. And in the hearing of many the child said to Zacchaeus, 'Hear, teacher, the arrangement of the first letter, and pay heed to this, how it has lines and a middle stroke which goes through the pair of lines which you see, (how these lines) converge, rise, turn in the dance, three signs of the same kind, subject to and supporting one another, of equal proportions; here you have the lines of the Alpha'.[3]

7. 1. Now when Zacchaeus the teacher heard so many such allegorical descriptions of the first letter being expounded by the child, he was perplexed at such a reply and at his teaching and said to those who were present, 'Woe is me, I am in difficulties wretch that I am; I have brought shame to myself in drawing to myself this child. 2. Take him away, therefore, I beseech you, brother Joseph. I cannot endure the severity of his gaze, I cannot make out his speech at all. This child is not earth-born; he can even subdue fire. Perhaps he was begotten even before the creation of the world. What belly bore him, what womb nurtured him I do not know. Woe is me, my friend, he confuses me, I cannot attain to his understanding. I have deceived myself, thrice wretched man that I am. I desired to get a pupil, and have found I have a teacher. 3. My friends, I am filled with shame, that I, an old man, have been defeated by a child. I suffer despair and death because of this child, for I cannot in this hour look him in the face. And when all say that I have been conquered by a small child, what have I to say? And what can I tell concerning the lines of the first letter of which he spoke to me? I do not know, my friends, for I know neither beginning nor end of it. 4. Therefore I beg you, brother Joseph, take him away to your house. Whatever great thing he is, a god or an angel I do not know what I should say.

8. 1. And while the Jews were trying to console Zacchaeus, the child

---

[2] Irenaeus, *Adv. Haer.* 1. 20. 1 says that the Marcosian sect support their doctrines by a vast number of apocryphal writings. 'They adduce, too, this false invention, that when the Lord as a child was learning the alphabet, and his teacher said, as the custom is, "Say Alpha", he answered, "Alpha." But when the teacher bade him say Beta, the Lord answered, "First tell me what Alpha is, and then will I tell you what Beta is." And this they interpret as meaning that he alone knew the unknown mystery, which he manifested in the form of Alpha.'

[3] The text appears to be corrupt. Literally it seems to be: 'how it has lines and a middle stroke which you see, common to both, going apart, coming together, raised up on high, dancing (?), of three signs, like in kind (?) balanced, equal in measure.'

laughed aloud and said, 'Now let those who are yours bear fruit, and let the blind in heart see. I have come from above to curse them and to call them to the things above, as he who sent me ordained for your sakes.' 2. And when the child had ceased speaking, immediately all those who had fallen under his curse were saved. And no one after that dared to provoke him, lest he should curse him, and he should be maimed.

9. 1. Now after some days Jesus was playing in the upper story of a house, and one of the children who were playing with him fell down from the house and died. And when the other children saw it they fled, and Jesus remained alone. 2. And the parents of the one who was dead came and accused him.[4] But they threatened him. 3. Then Jesus leaped down from the roof and stood by the corpse of the child, and cried with a loud voice, 'Zeno'—for that is what he was called—'arise and tell me, did I throw you down?' And he arose at once and said, 'No, Lord, you did not throw me down, but raised me up.' And when they saw it they were amazed. And the parents of the child glorified God for the sign that had happened and worshipped Jesus.

10. 1. After a few days a certain man was cleaving wood in a corner,[5] and the axe fell and split the sole of his foot, and he was losing so much blood that he was about to die. 2. And there was a clamour, a crowd gathered, and the child Jesus also ran there, forced his way through the crowd, and took the injured foot, and it was healed immediately. And he said to the young man, 'Arise now, cleave the wood and remember me.' And when the crowd saw what happened, they worshipped the child, saying, 'Truly the spirit of God dwells in this child.'

11. 1. When he was six years old, his mother gave him a pitcher and sent him to draw water and bring it into the house. 2. But in the crowd he stumbled, and the pitcher was broken. But Jesus spread out the garment he was wearing, filled it with water and brought it to his mother. And when his mother saw the miracle, she kissed him, and kept to herself[6] the mysteries which she had seen him do.

12. 1. Again, in the time of sowing the child went out with his father to sow corn in their field. And as his father sowed, the child Jesus also sowed one grain of corn. 2. And when he had reaped it and threshed it, he brought in a hundred measures,[7] and he called all the poor of the village to the threshing-floor and gave them the corn, and Joseph took the residue. He was eight years old when he performed this sign.

13. 1. His father was a carpenter and made at that time ploughs and yokes. And he received an order from a rich man to make a bed for him. But when one beam was shorter than its corresponding one and they did not know what

---

[4] Syriac adds 'of having thrown him down. And Jesus replied, "I did not throw him down."'
[5] Variant: 'in the neighbourhood'.
[6] Luke 2: 19, 51.
[7] Luke 16: 7.

to do, the child Jesus said to his father Joseph, 'Lay down the two pieces of wood and make them even from the middle to one end.' 2. And Joseph did as the child told him. And Jesus stood at the other end and took hold of the shorter piece of wood, and stretching it made it equal to the other. And his father Joseph saw it and was amazed, and he embraced the child and kissed him, saying, 'Happy am I that God has given me this child.'

14. 1. And when Joseph saw the understanding of the child and his age, that he was growing to maturity, he resolved again that he should not remain ignorant of letters; and he took him and handed him over to another teacher. And the teacher said to Joseph, 'First I will teach him Greek, and then Hebrew.' For the teacher knew the child's knowledge and was afraid of him. Nevertheless he wrote the alphabet and practised it with him for many an hour; but he did not answer him. 2. And Jesus said to him, 'If you are indeed a teacher, and if you know the letters well, tell me the power of the Alpha, and I will tell you that of the Beta.' And the teacher was annoyed and struck him on the head. And the child was hurt and cursed him, and he immediately fainted and fell on his face to the ground. 3. And the child returned to Joseph's house. But Joseph was grieved and commanded his mother, 'Do not let him go outside the door, for all those who provoke him die.'

15. 1. And after some time yet another teacher, a good friend of Joseph, said to him, 'Bring the child to me to the school. Perhaps I by persuasion can teach him the letters.' And Joseph said to him, 'If you have the courage, brother, take him with you.' And he took him with fear and anxiety, but the child went gladly. 2. And he went boldly into the school and found a book lying on the lectern and picked it up, but did not read the letters in it; instead he opened his mouth and spoke by the Holy Spirit and taught the law to those that stood around. And a large crowd assembled and stood there listening to him, wondering at the beauty of his teaching and the fluency of his words, that, although an infant, he made such pronouncements. 3. But when Joseph heard it, he was afraid and ran to the school, wondering whether this teacher also was inexperienced. But the teacher said to Joseph, 'Know, brother, that I took the child as a disciple; but he is full of much grace and wisdom; and now I beg you, brother, take him to your house.' 4. And when the child heard these things, he at once smiled at him and said, 'Since you have spoken well and have testified rightly, for your sake shall he who was stricken be healed.' And immediately the other teacher was healed. And Joseph took the child and went away to his house.

16. 1. Joseph sent his son James to gather wood and take it into his house, and the child Jesus followed him. And while James was gathering the sticks, a viper bit the hand of James. 2. And as he lay stretched out and about to die, Jesus came near and breathed upon the bite, and immediately the pain ceased, and the creature burst, and at once James was healed.

17. 1. And after these things in the neighbourhood of Joseph a little

sick child[8] died, and his mother wept bitterly. And Jesus heard that great mourning and tumult arose, and he ran quickly, and finding the child dead, he touched his breast and said: 'I say to you child, do not die but live and be with your mother.' And immediately it looked up and laughed. And he said to the woman, 'Take him and give him milk and remember me.' 2. And when the people standing round saw it, they marvelled and said, 'Truly, this child was either a god or an angel of God, for every word of his is an accomplished deed.' And Jesus departed from there and played with other children.

18. 1. After some time a house was being built and a great disturbance arose, and Jesus arose and went there. And seeing a man lying dead he took his hand and said; 'I say to you, man, arise, do your work.' And immediately he arose and worshipped him. 2. And when the people saw it, they were amazed and said, 'This child is from heaven, for he has saved many souls from death, and is able to save them all his life long.'

19. 1. And when he was twelve years old his parents went according to the custom to Jerusalem to the feast of the passover with their companions and after the feast of the passover they returned to their house. And while they were returning, the child Jesus went back to Jerusalem. But his parents supposed that he was in the company. 2. And when they had gone a day's journey, they sought him among their kinsfolk, and when they did not find him, they were troubled, and returned again to the city seeking him. And after the third day they found him in the temple sitting among the teachers, listening[9] and asking them questions. And all paid attention to him and marvelled how he, a child, put to silence the elders and teachers of the people, elucidating the chapters of the law and the parables of the prophets. 3. And his mother Mary came near and said to him, 'Why have you done this to us, child? Behold, we have sought you sorrowing.' Jesus said to them, 'Why do you seek me? Do you not know that I must be about my father's affairs?'[10] 4. But the scribes and Pharisees said, 'Are you the mother of this child?' And she said, 'I am.' And they said to her, 'Blessed are you among women, because God has blessed the fruit of your womb.[11] For such glory and such excellence and wisdom we have never seen nor heard.' 5. And Jesus arose and followed his mother and was subject to his parents; but his mother stored up all that had taken place. And Jesus increased in wisdom and stature and grace.[12] To him be glory for ever and ever. Amen.

B. *Greek B*

Book of the holy Apostle Thomas concerning the conversation in childhood of the Lord

1. I, Thomas the Israelite, have thought it necessary to acquaint all the brethren who

---

[8] Mark 5: 38.
[9] Variant adds 'to the law'.
[10] Luke 2: 41–52.
[11] Luke 1: 42.
[12] Luke 2: 51 f.

The Infancy Gospel of Thomas

are Gentiles with the mighty childhood works which our Lord Jesus Christ did while he had his conversation bodily in the city of Nazareth, when he was five years old.

2. One day, when there was a shower, he went out of the house where his mother was and was playing on the ground where water was flowing down. And when he had made pools, the waters came down and the pools were filled with water. Then he said, 'I will that you waters become clear and good.' And straightway they became so. But a certain child of Annas the scribe passed by, carrying a stick of willow, and he broke up the pools with the stick and the waters gushed out. And Jesus turned and said to him, 'Wicked and lawless one, what harm did the pools do you that you emptied them? You shall not go on your way and you shall dry up like the stick which you are holding.' And as he was going, after a little while, he fell down and gave up the ghost. And when the young children who were playing with him saw it, they marvelled and went and told the father of the dead child. And he ran and found the child dead and went and complained to Joseph.

3. And Jesus made of that clay twelve sparrows; and it was Sabbath. And one young child ran and told Joseph saying, 'Behold your child is playing in the brook and has made sparrows of the clay, which is not lawful.' And having heard, he went and said to the child, 'Why do you do these things, profaning the Sabbath?' And Jesus did not answer, but looked at the sparrows and said, 'Go, fly away, and remember me while you live.' And at the word they took flight and went off into the air. And Joseph marvelled when he saw it.

4. And after some days, as Jesus was going through the middle of the city, a certain child threw a stone at him and hit him on the shoulder. And Jesus said to him, 'You shall not go on your way.' And straightway he too fell down and died. And those who happened to be there were astonished saying, 'Where does this young child come from that every word that he says has immediate effect?' They too went and complained to Joseph, saying, 'You will not be able to dwell with us in this city. But if you please, teach your child to bless and not to curse; for he slays our children and every word that he says has immediate effect.'

5. And when Joseph was seated upon his chair, the child stood before him. And taking hold of him by the ear, he pinched it hard. And Jesus looked intently at him and said, 'It is enough for you.'

6. And on the next day he took him by the hand and led him to a certain teacher named Zacchaeus and said to him, 'Take this child, teacher, and teach him letters.' And he said, 'Hand him over to me, brother, and I will teach him the Scripture and persuade him to bless everything and not to curse.' And when Jesus heard he laughed, and said to them, 'You say what things you know, but I understand more things than you; for before the ages I am. And I know when your fathers' fathers were born, and I understand how many are the years of your life.' And everyone who heard was astonished. And again Jesus said to them, 'Are you astonished because I said to you that I know how many are the years of your life? Truly I know when the world was created. Behold, you do not believe me now. When you see my cross then you will believe that I speak the truth.' And they were astonished when they heard these things.

7. And Zacchaeus wrote the alphabet in Hebrew and said to him, 'Alpha.' And the child said, 'Alpha.' And the teacher said again 'Alpha' and the child likewise. Then again the teacher said a third time, 'Alpha.' Then Jesus looking at the teacher said, 'You who do not know the Alpha, how will you teach another the Beta?' And the child,

beginning from the Alpha, said of his own accord the twenty-two letters. Then, again, he said, 'Hear, teacher, the arrangements of the first letter, and know how many strokes and rules it has, and marks that are common, diametral, and convergent.' And when Zacchaeus heard such attributes of the one letter, he was astonished, and could not answer him. And he turned to Joseph and said, 'Brother, truly this child is not earth-born; therefore take him away from me.'

8. And after these things, one day Jesus was playing with other children on a house-top. And one young child was pushed down by another headlong on to the ground and he died. And when the children playing with him saw it they fled; and Jesus was left alone standing upon the house-top from which the boy had been thrown down. And when the parents of the dead child learned it they ran weeping, and when they found the child lying dead on the ground and Jesus standing up above, supposed that the boy had been thrown down by him; they looked at him and reproached him. And Jesus, when he saw that, straightway leaped down from the house-top and stood at the head of the dead boy and said to him, 'Zeno, did I cast you down? Arise and speak'—for the boy was so called. And at the word the boy arose and he worshipped Jesus and said, 'Lord, you did not cast me down, but when I was dead you brought me to life.'

9. And after a few days, one of the neighbours while cleaving wood cut off the sole of his foot with his axe and from loss of blood was at the point of death. And many people ran up to him. Jesus also came with them there. And he touched the wounded foot of the young man, and immediately healed him; and he said to him, 'Arise, cleave your wood.' And he arose and worshipped him, giving thanks and cleaving the wood. Likewise, also, all who were there marvelled and gave thanks to him.

10. And when he was six years old, Mary, his mother, sent him to fetch water from the well. And as he went his pitcher broke. And going on to the well, he spread out his garment and drew water from the well and filled it, and took the water and brought it to his mother. And when she saw it she was astonished and embraced him and kissed him.

11. And when Jesus had reached his eighth year, Joseph was ordered by a certain rich man to construct a bed for him, for he was a carpenter. And he went out in the field to collect wood, and Jesus also went with him. And having cut two pieces of wood, he fashioned one and he laid it beside the other; and when he had measured it he found it too short. And when he saw it, he was grieved and sought to find another. And when Jesus saw it, he said to him, 'Lay these two together so as to make both equal at one end.' And Joseph, being in doubt what the child meant by this, did what was ordered. And he said to him again, 'Take hold firmly of the short piece of wood.' And Joseph wondered but took hold of it. Then Jesus taking hold of the other end pulled it and made that piece of wood equal to the other. And he said to Joseph, 'Grieve no more but do your work without impediment.' And he, when he saw, was exceedingly amazed and said within himself, 'Blessed am I that God gave me such a child.' And when they had gone away into the city, Joseph told Mary. And when she heard and saw the wonderful miracles of her Son, she rejoiced, glorifying him with the Father and the Holy Ghost, now and ever and unto the ages of the ages. Amen.

C. Latin

1. When a commotion had been raised, because a search had been made by Herod for our Lord Jesus Christ that he might slay him, then an angel said to Joseph, Take Mary

and her child, and flee into Egypt from the face of those who seek to slay him. Jesus was two years old when he entered Egypt.

And as he walked through a cornfield, he put out his hand, and took hold of the ears, and put them on the fire, and crushed them, and began to eat.

Now when they had come into Egypt, they found a lodging in the house of a certain widow, and they passed one year in the same place. And Jesus was three years old, and when he saw boys playing, he began to play with them. And he took a dry fish and put it in a basin, and ordered it to breathe, and it began to breathe. And he said again to the fish, 'Reject the salt which you have, and go into the water', and so it came to pass. But the neighbours, seeing what was done, told the widow in whose house Mary his mother was staying, and when she heard it, she cast them out of her house in great haste.

2. And as Jesus was walking with Mary his mother in the middle of the city, he looked up and saw a teacher teaching his pupils; and behold twelve sparrows which were quarrelling together fell from the wall into the lap of the teacher who was teaching the boys. But when Jesus saw it he laughed and stopped. When the teacher saw him laughing, in a great rage he said to his pupils, 'Go, fetch him to me.' Now when they had taken him, the master took hold of his ear, and said, 'What have you seen that has made you merry?' But he said, 'Behold master, my hand is full of corn. I showed it to them and scattered the corn, which, at their peril, they carry away; for it was this that they were fighting for—that they might divide the corn.' And Jesus did not depart from there until it was accomplished; and for this reason, the teacher cast him out of the city together with his mother.

3. And behold an angel of the Lord met Mary and said to her, 'Take the Child and return to the land of the Jews, for they are dead who sought his life.' And Mary arose with Jesus, and they went to the city of Nazareth, which is in the possession of her[1] father. Now when Joseph went out of Egypt after the death of Herod, he led him into the desert until there should be peace in Jerusalem from those who sought the child's life; and he thanked God that he gave him understanding, and that he found favour before the Lord God.

---

[1] Variant: 'his'.

The Gospel of Pseudo-Matthew

This work used to be known as the *Liber de Infantia* (sc. of both Mary and Jesus), or the *Historia de Nativitate Mariae et de Infantia Salvatoris*. It was very influential in the Middle Ages and was the main vehicle for popularizing the Protevangelium Jacobi (= PJ) and the Infancy Gospel of Thomas. Much medieval art is indecipherable without reference to books such as Pseudo-Matthew.[1]

Pseudo-Matthew 1–17 is based on PJ, and 26–34, 37–9, and 41 on Infancy Thomas.[2] For this reason, only extracts are translated here, namely the fictitious letters, 13–14, and the unique material (18–25, 35–6, 40, 42), preceded by a summary of the whole.

One of the reasons for the absence of extant manuscripts in Latin of the Protevangelium of James may be that the contents of PJ in Latin are to be found in Pseudo-Matthew, and in the Gospel of the Birth of Mary. The latter is derived from Pseudo-Matthew: the interrelationship of the two has been investigated by Amann (below, under 'Modern Translations, French'). (The citation of the contents of PJ as known to the Latin Fathers through the secondary works is set out by him too.) Conversely Pseudo-Matthew as such seems not to have been known in the East, or in the Eastern versions.

As far as detailed differences between Pseudo-Matthew and PJ are concerned, one may note the following: Anna's father, Achar, is mentioned only in Pseudo-Matthew; in Pseudo-Matthew Abiathar is high-priest when Mary is espoused to Joseph, in PJ it is Zacharias; Pseudo-Matthew embellishes PJ by including the circumcision and purification. Pseudo-Matthew does not include the catalepsy of nature, or John the Baptist, or Zacharias, absences which are possibly relevant in discussing the original form of PJ.

Links between the Gospel of the Birth of Mary and Pseudo-Matthew are strong. In both Mary at three years of age mounts the fifteen steps of the Temple (Pseudo-Matthew 4, Birth of Mary 6), but there are occasional differences. For instance in the Birth of Mary 8 Mary returns to her parents' home in Galilee after her espousal, whereas in Pseudo-Matthew (and PJ) the parents are not mentioned again after Mary is left by them in the care of the

---

[1] See, e.g. the plates in H. Daniel-Rops, *Les Évangiles de la Vierge* (Paris, 1948), and in de Santos Otero, Appendix. Cf. also Jacqueline Lafontaine-Dosogne, *Iconographie de l'enfance de la Vierge dans l'Empire byzantin et en occident*, 2 vols. (Brussels, 1964–5;[2] 1992) (= *Académie Royale de Belgique. Classe des Beaux Arts, Mémoires*, 2nd series, ii, fascicles 3, 3b). See also David R. Cartlidge and J. Keith Elliott, *Art and the Christian Apocrypha* (London, 2001)

[2] P. Peeters, *Évangiles apocryphes*, ii. *L'Évangile de l'enfance* (Paris, 1914), 1 f. (= H. Hammer and P. Lejay (eds.), *Textes et documents* 18), discusses the literary and historical relationship of the later infancy gospels to their sources.

Temple. The similarities and differences to be found, not only in these respects, but in all the forms in which the birth and infancy narratives are retailed, are characteristic of the way in which these narratives were subject to embellishment and alteration.

Even though much in Pseudo-Matthew has been derived from PJ and Infancy Thomas there are significant changes. Sometimes the sections of Pseudo-Matthew dependent on Infancy Thomas have a better text than is found in existing manuscripts of Infancy Thomas itself. At other times Pseudo-Matthew amplifies the material found in Infancy Thomas or alters it (sometimes to make Jesus less malevolent). Among the new details to be found in Pseudo-Matthew is that Joseph not only had children from his earlier marriage, but had grandchildren older than Mary (Pseudo-Matthew 8). Pseudo-Matthew 14 has an ox and an ass present at the birth of Jesus in fulfilment of Isaiah 1: 3.

The motive for writing Pseudo-Matthew seems to have been to further the veneration of Mary. To this end the writer attempted to combine two popular existing compilations with other miraculous material. Much of the matter in Pseudo-Matthew not derived from PJ and Thomas has affinities with the Arabic Infancy Narrative. Those who wish to study the textual tradition of Infancy Thomas (and indeed of PJ) need to take into account the use made of these sources in the secondary literature (i.e. Pseudo-Matthew, the Gospel of the Birth of Mary, the Arabic and Armenian infancy stories, and other Latin infancy gospels).

In the opinion of Gijsel the episodes of the *Infantia Salvatoris* (based on the Latin of Infancy Thomas) found in chs. 25–42 do not belong to Pseudo-Matthew: Tischendorf was mistaken to join these as a 'Pars Altera' to his edition of Pseudo-Matthew. These chapters are absent in most manuscripts and are not included in Thilo's edition of Pseudo-Matthew.

By way of introducing the book under good auspices the compiler has provided it with credentials in the form of pretended letters: (*a*) from two bishops, Cromatius and Heliodorus, to Jerome; (*b*) from Jerome to Cromatius and Heliodorus. In some manuscripts these letters are to be found prefacing the Gospel of the Birth of Mary,[3] but references in them to the infancy of Christ make it more likely that they belong to Pseudo-Matthew, seeing that the Gospel of the Birth of Mary stops short of Jesus' nativity. In so far as it was due to Jerome's disapproval of the teaching of Joseph's first marriage that PJ stood condemned in the West it is somewhat ironic that Pseudo-Matthew, which also preserves this teaching, was published with prefaces associated with Jerome's name. Their presence in some manuscripts of the Gospel of the Birth of Mary may be significant for the reason that in that gospel at

---

[3] The Latin Infancy Gospel, Arundel 404 (*q.v.*), also has the letters. In some manuscripts of the Gospel of the Birth of Mary there is a further letter ostensibly from Jerome to the bishops.

least the offending teaching about Joseph's first marriage is not mentioned. It was the reference to Matthew in letter (*a*) that encouraged Tischendorf to name this apocryphal work 'Pseudo-Matthew', following the title in one of his manuscripts (although it is to be noted that at least two other manuscripts have the name of James in the title).

The work seems to have been compiled in Latin, possibly in the eighth or ninth century, although the oldest manuscript extant is of the eleventh century. Hrsovit of Gandersheim made use of Pseudo-Matthew in the tenth-century *Historia Nativitatis laudabilisque conversationis intactae Dei Genitricis quam scriptam reperi sub nomine sancti Jacobi fratris Domini*: she therefore seems to have known the work by the title that attributes authorship to James.[4]

In the Gelasian Decree, no. 8 refers to *Evangelia nomine Jacobi minoris*, which Amann (p. 104) identifies with PJ, but de Strycker (*La Forme la plus ancienne...*, p. 43 n. 1) raises the possibility that this could be Pseudo-Matthew. If so, then Pseudo-Matthew must have been composed before the compilation of the Decree, and this would give it a date prior to the sixth century. No. 15 in the Decree is the *Liber de Infantia Salvatoris et de Maria vel obstetrice*. Amann (p. 104) takes this to be the source of Pseudo-Matthew. James agrees (p. 22) (although he suggests PJ as an alternative for no. 15), and gives Pseudo-Matthew for no. 16 (*Liber de Infantia Salvatoris*). Amann (p. 104) takes no. 16 to be the Arabic Infancy Gospel!

The first printed edition was Thilo's, based on a fourteenth-century manuscript (Paris 5559). This text ends with the Holy Family reaching Egypt. He published this under the title *Historia de Nativitate Mariae et Infantia Salvatoris*.[5] Thilo was also aware of another Paris manuscript (1652) that contained the same material as 5559 but concluded with miracles taken from Infancy Thomas, i.e. Pseudo-Matthew 25–42 (this second part is entitled *De Miraculis Infantiae Domini Jesu Christi*).

Tischendorf's text was based principally on Vatican 4578 of the fourteenth century[6] and on three other manuscripts, two of the fourteenth century (including Paris 5559) and one of the fifteenth (Paris 1652), which means he gives the full text and thus from ch. 25 is the first editor. Amann (p. 73) refers to other manuscripts of Pseudo-Matthew in Oxford, Cambridge, and Florence that have not been edited. There is apparently much textual variation between them all. Gijsel knows of over 180 Latin manuscripts which he has attempted to divide into different families.

My extracts are translated from Tischendorf.

---

[4] But see J. Gijsel, 'Zu welcher Textfamilie des Pseudo-Matthäus gehört die Quelle von Hrotsvits Maria?', *Classica et Mediaevalia* 32 (1979–80), 279–88.

[5] Cf. also O. Schade, *Liber de Infantia Mariae et Christi Salvatoris* (Halle, 1869), which seems to follow Paris 5559, although it is based on a Stuttgart manuscript (cited by Michel, i, p. xx). Tischendorf used Schade's Stuttgart manuscript for his second edition.

[6] This manuscript begins with the words 'Incipit Liber de Ortu Beatae Mariae et Infantia Salvatoris a beato Matthaeo evangelista hebraice scriptus et a beato Hieronymo presbytero in latinum translatus'.

EDITIONS

Latin

Jones, ii, 101–27.
Thilo, pp. cv–cxvii, 339–400.
Giles, i. 66–89.
Tischendorf, *EA*, pp. xxii–xxxi, 51–112.
J. Gijsel, *Libri de Nativitate Mariae* (Turnhout, 1997) (= CCSA 9).

MODERN TRANSLATIONS

English

Hone, 17–24 (first part).
Walker, 16–52.
Cowper, 27–83.
James, 70–9 (summary).
Hennecke³, i. 410–13 (chs. 14, 18–24).
Hennecke⁵, i. 462–6 (chs. 14, 18–24).

French

Migne, *Dictionnaire*, i, cols. 1059–88.
E. Amann, *Le Protévangile de Jacques et ses remaniements latins* (Paris, 1910), 272–339 (with Latin text, but translation only of the chapters corresponding to PJ, i.e. 1. 1–17. 2) (= *Les apocryphes du Nouveau Testament* ed. J. Bousquet and E. Amann).
Michel, i. 54–158.
Amiot, 65–79 (selection).
H. Daniel-Rops, *Les Évangiles de la Vierge* (Paris, 1948), 149–63 (chs. 3, 4, 8, 11, 14, 18–24). (Eng. trans. *The Book of Mary* (New York, 1960)).
Éac, 107–40.

German

E. Bock, *Die Kindheit Jesu: Zwei apokryphe Evangelien* (Munich, 1924) (= *Christus aller Erde* 14–15). [The other of the two gospels is the Arabic Infancy Gospel, below.]
Hennecke³, i. 306–9 (O. Cullmann) (chs. 14, 18–24).
Hennecke⁵, i. 367–369 (O. Cullmann) (chs. 14, 18–24).
Schneider, 214–55.

Italian

E. Pistelli, *Il Protevangelo di Jacopo* (Lanciano, 1919), Appendix.
Bonaccorsi, i. 152–231 (with Latin text).
Erbetta i. 2, 44–70.
Moraldi, i. 195–239; ² i. 343–85.
Cravieri, 63–111

Spanish

González-Blanco, i. 362–414.
de Santos Otero, 177–242 (with Latin text).

GENERAL

Variot, 51–9.

J. Gijsel, *Die unmittelbare Textüberlieferung des sogennanten Pseudo-Matthäus* (Brussels, 1981) (= *Verhandelingen van der Koninklijke Academie voor Wetenschappen Letteren en Schone Kunsten van Belgïe. Klasse der Letteren* 96).

G. Philippart, 'Le Pseudo-Matthieu au risque de la critique textuelle', *Scriptorium* 38 (1984), 121–31.

J. Gijsel, 'Nouveaux témoins du *Pseudo-Matthieu*' *Sacris Erudiri* 41 (2002), 17–37. Klauck, 105–9: ET 78–81.

Summary

1. In those days there was a man in Jerusalem, Joachim by name, of the tribe of Juda.

His whole care was his flocks. He offered double offerings. He divided his substance into three parts, one for the poor, one for the pious, the third for himself. God increased his wealth. This charity he had practised since he was fifteen years old. At twenty he married Anna, daughter of Ysachar of his own tribe; they lived twenty years childless.

2. Ruben rejects his offering. He goes to the mountains to his flocks for five months.

Anna has no news of him. She complains to God.

She sees a sparrow's nest, and laments her childlessness, and vows if she has a child to dedicate it in the temple. An angel comes and promises her a daughter. In fear and sorrow she throws herself on her bed for a whole day and night. She reproaches her maid (not named) for not coming to her. The maid answers her sharply and she weeps yet more.

3. A youth—an angel—comes to Joachim in the wilderness and promises him a daughter and predicts her glory. Joachim makes an offering: is urged by his servants to return. The angel comes again in a vision. They set off and journey thirty days.

The angel comes to Anna and bids her meet Joachim at the Golden Gate of the Temple, which she does.

4. Mary is born. At three years old she is taken to the temple and walks up fifteen steps.

5. Anna's thanksgiving.

6. Mary's beauty and chastity and wisdom and devoutness described at length. She is fed daily by angels.

7. Abiathar the priest offers many gifts that Mary may marry his son. She refuses, saying that she has vowed perpetual virginity.

8. When she was fourteen, a council was held and Israel was summoned to the temple on the third day. The high priest addressed them and said that since Solomon's time there had always been noble virgins brought up in the temple and married when they were of age. But Man had vowed virginity and it must be ascertained who should take charge of her. Those who had no wives were to bring rods. There was no sign, so Abiathar went in and prayed,

and an angel pointed out that one very small rod had not been returned to its owner. This was Joseph's. The dove appeared. Joseph resisted, but was overcome: he stipulated that some virgins should accompany Mary. Rebecca, Sephora, Susanna, Abigea, and Zahel were chosen. They cast lots for the colours of the veil. Mary had the purple: the others were jealous and called her in sport 'Regina virginum'. An angel rebuked them and said it was a true prophecy. They were abashed and asked Mary to pray for them.

9. Mary at the fountain addressed by an angel. On the next day as she wove he appeared again and completed the Annunciation.

10. Joseph returned from Capernaum and found Mary great with child. His lament. The virgins defended Mary, but Joseph lamented still.

11. The angel reassured him, and he asked pardon of Mary.

12. Rumour went forth, and Joseph and Mary were summoned by the priests. The water of jealousy administered by Abiathar. Joseph and Mary each went about the altar seven times and no sign appeared. All asked her pardon and took her home in triumph.

13–14. [Translated below.] Caesar's decree. They went to Bethlehem. On the third day Mary left the cave and went to a stable.

15. On the sixth day they went to Bethlehem, kept the sabbath, and circumcised the child on the eighth day. The Presentation: Symeon and Anna.

16. After the second year came the magi: told as in the Gospel.

17. Massacre of the Innocents; the warning to flee into Egypt.

18–25. [Translated below.]

26. When Jesus was in Galilee at the beginning of his fourth year he was playing by the Jordan, and made seven pools. A boy spoilt them, and was struck dead. The parents complained. Joseph asked Mary to admonish Jesus. She begged him not to do such things, and he, not willing to grieve her, 'smote the back side of the dead boy with his foot and bade him rise: which he did, and Jesus went on with his pools'.

27. He took clay from the pools and made twelve sparrows, on the sabbath. A Jew saw it and spoke to Joseph, who spoke to Jesus. Jesus clapped his hands and bade the sparrows fly away. All marvelled, and some went and told the chief priests and Pharisees.

28. The son of Annas the priest broke up the pools with a stick, and Jesus with a word withered him up.

29. Joseph was afraid and took Jesus home. On the way a boy ran against Jesus and got on his shoulder, meaning to hurt him. Jesus said, 'May you not return whole from the way you go.' He fell dead. Complaints of the parents, as in *Thomas*. Joseph to Jesus: 'Why do you do such things? Many are now complaining against you and hate us on your account, and we suffer injuries through you.' Jesus: 'No son is wise whom his father has not taught according to the knowledge of this age, and the curse of his father hurts no man except

those who do ill.' All reviled Jesus to Joseph and he was afraid. 'Then Jesus took the dead boy by the ear and held him up by it in the sight of all, and they saw Jesus speaking to him as a father to his son. And his spirit returned unto him and he lived again, and all marvelled.'

30. Master Zacchaeus spoke reproachfully to Joseph; 'You and Mary think more of your son than of the traditions of the elders.' Joseph: 'But who can teach him? if you can do so, we are very willing.' Jesus overhearing said, 'What you say is well for ordinary people: I have no earthly father. When I am lifted up from the earth I will make all mention of your descent to cease. I know when you were born and how long you have to live.' All cried out in wonder, 'We have never heard the like.' Jesus: 'Does this surprise you? I will tell you more. I have seen Abraham and spoken with him, and he has seen me.' None could answer. Jesus: 'I have been among you with the children, and you have not known me. I have spoken with you as with the wise and you have not understood my voice, for you are less than me, and of little faith.'

31. Zacchaeus said, 'Give him to me and I will take him to Levi who shall teach him letters.' Levi bade him answer to Aleph: he was silent. Levi smote him with a rod of storax on the head. Jesus: 'Why do you hit me? Know of a truth that he who is smitten teaches the smiter more than he is taught of him. For I can teach you the things that you yourself say. But all these who speak and hear are blind like sounding brass or a tinkling cymbal wherein is no perception of those things that are signified by their sound.' Further he said to Zacchaeus, 'Every letter from Aleph to Thau is discerned by the arrangement of it. First say what Thau is, and I will tell you what Aleph is.' And again he said, 'They who do not know Aleph, how can they tell Thau, hypocrites that they are? Say what Aleph is first and then will I believe you when you say Beth. He said to the master, 'Let the master of the law say what the first letter is, or why it has many triangles [eight adjectives follow].' Levi was stupefied and then began to lament, 'Ought he to live on the earth? Nay, rather is he worthy to be hung on a great cross. He can put out fire and escape all torments by guile. I think he was born before the flood, before the deluge. What womb bare him? What mother gave him birth? What breasts suckled him? I fly before him', etc., etc.

Jesus smiled and said with command to all the children of Israel that stood and heard him, 'Let the unfruitful bear fruit, and the blind see, and the lame walk straight, and the poor enjoy good things, and the dead revive, and every one return into a restored state, and abide in him who is the root of life and of everlasting sweetness.' All were healed who had fallen into evil infirmities. No one thereafter dared to say aught to him or hear aught of him.

32. At Nazareth the boy Zeno fell from the upper storey and was raised. Joseph, Mary, and Jesus went thence to Jericho.

33. Jesus' pitcher was broken by a child, and he brought water in his cloak.

34. He took a little corn out of his mother's barn and sowed it. When reaped it made three measures, which he gave away.

35-6. [Translated below.]

37. A bed of six cubits was ordered of Joseph, and he told his lad to cut a beam of the right length, but he made it too short. Joseph was troubled. Jesus pulled it out to the right length.

38. He went to school the second time. 'Say Alpha.' Jesus: 'Tell me first what Beta is, and I will tell you what Alpha is.' The master smote him and died.

Joseph said to Mary, 'Know that my soul is sorrowful even to death because of this boy. It may chance that any one may smite him in malice and he may die.' Mary said, 'O man of God, believe not that this can happen, but believe surely that he who sent him to be born among men will keep him from all malice and in his name preserve him from evil.'

39. For the third time they took him to school at the request of others, though they knew that it was not possible for a man to teach him. He entered the school, took the book from the master's hand, and taught—not what was written in it—like a torrent of water flowing from a living fountain. All marvelled, and the master adored him. Joseph ran there in fear. The master said, 'You have given me no scholar but a teacher! Who can ascertain his words?' Then was fulfilled the word: 'The river of God is full of water. You have prepared their food, for thus is the preparation thereof.'

40. [Translated below.]

41. They moved from Bethlehem to Capernaum [perhaps it should be vice versa]. Joseph sent his eldest son James into the garden to gather herbs for pottage. Story of the viper as in *Thomas*.

42. [Translated below.]

Translations
Here begins the book of the Birth of the Blessed Mary and the Infancy of the Saviour. Written in Hebrew by the blessed Evangelist Matthew, and translated into Latin by the Blessed Presbyter Jerome.

To their well-beloved brother Jerome the Presbyter, Bishops Cromatius and Heliodorus in the Lord, greeting.

The birth of the Virgin Mary, and the nativity and infancy of our Lord Jesus Christ, we find in apocryphal books. But considering that in them many things contrary to our faith are written we judged that they all ought to be rejected, lest perchance we should transfer the joy of Christ to Antichrist. While we were considering these things, there came holy men, Parmenius and Varinus, who said that your Holiness had found a Hebrew volume, written by the hand of the most blessed Evangelist Matthew, in which both the birth of the virgin mother herself and the infancy of our Saviour were written. Accordingly we entreat your charity through our Lord Jesus Christ himself, to render it from the Hebrew into Latin, not so much to ascertain those things which are the deeds of Christ, as to counteract the craft of heretics who, in order to teach bad doctrine, have mingled their own lies with the excellent nativity of Christ, that they might hide the bitterness of death under the sweetness of life. It will therefore be the purest piety on your part, either to listen to us as brethren entreating you, or to pay us as bishops, the debt of affection which you may deem due.

To my lords the holy and most blessed Bishops Cromatius and Heliodorus, Jerome, a humble servant of Christ, sends greetings in the Lord.

He who digs in ground where he knows that there is gold does not instantly snatch at whatever the ragged trench may pour forth; but, before the stroke of the spade he wields raises aloft the glittering mass, he meanwhile lingers over the sods to turn them over and lift them up, and still lives in hope because he has not added to his gains. An arduous task is enjoined upon me, since what your Blessedness has commanded me to translate, the holy Apostle and Evangelist Matthew himself did not write for the purpose of publishing. For if he had not done it somewhat secretly, he would have added it to his Gospel which he published. But he composed this book in Hebrew; and he published it so little that even today the book written in Hebrew by his own hand is in the possession of very religious men, to whom over long periods of time it has been handed down by their predecessors. And this book they never at any time gave to any one to translate, but have regularly reviled its text. And so it came to pass, that when it was published by a disciple of Manichaeus named Leucius, who also wrote the falsely styled Acts of the Apostles, this book afforded matter, not of edification, but of perdition; and the opinion of the Synod in regard to it was such that the ears of the church should not be open to it. Let the bites of those barking critics now cease; for we do not add this little book to the canonical writings, but we translate what was written by an apostle and evangelist, that we may disclose the falsehood of heresy. In this work, then, we obey the commands of pious bishops as well as oppose impious heretics. It is the love of Christ, therefore, to which we render service, believing that they who, thanks to our obedience, attain to a knowledge of the holy infancy of our Saviour, will assist us by their prayers.

13. And it came to pass some little time after, that an enrolment was made according to the edict of Caesar Augustus for all the world to be enrolled, each man in his native place. This enrolment was made by Cyrinus, the governor of Syria. It was necessary, therefore, that Joseph should enrol with Mary in Bethlehem, because they came from there, being of the tribe of Judah and of the house and family of David. When, therefore, Joseph and Mary

were going along the road which leads to Bethlehem, Mary said to Joseph, 'I see two peoples before me, the one weeping, and the other rejoicing.' And Joseph answered, 'Sit still on your beast, and do not speak superfluous words.' Then there appeared before them a beautiful boy, clothed in white raiment, who said to Joseph, 'Why did you say that the words which Mary spoke about the two peoples were superfluous? For she saw the people of the Jews weeping because they have departed from their God; and the people of the Gentiles rejoicing, because they have now approached and are near to the Lord, in accordance with what he promised to our fathers Abraham, Isaac, and Jacob: for the time is at hand when in the seed of Abraham a blessing should be bestowed on all nations.'

And when he had said this, the angel ordered the beast to stand, for the time when she should bring forth was at hand; and he commanded Mary to come down from the animal, and go into an underground cave, in which there never was light, but always darkness, because the light of day could not reach it. And when Mary had gone into it, it began to shine with as much brightness as if it were the sixth hour of the day. The light from God so shone in the cave that neither by day nor night was light wanting as long as Mary was there. And there she brought forth a son, and the angels surrounded him when he was being born. And as soon as he was born he stood upon his feet, and the angels adored him saying, 'Glory to God in the highest, and on earth peace to men of good will.'[1] Now, when the birth of the Lord was at hand, Joseph had gone away to seek midwives. And when he had found them, he returned to the cave and found with Mary the infant which she had brought forth. And Joseph said to Mary, 'I have brought two midwives, Zelomi and Salome; and they are standing outside by the entrance to the cave, not daring to come in because of the intense brightness.' And when Mary heard this she smiled; and Joseph said to her, 'Do not smile, but be prudent and allow them to visit you, in case you should require them for medication.' Then she ordered them to come to her. And when Zelomi had come in, she said to Mary, 'Allow me to touch you.' And when she had permitted her to make an examination the midwife cried out with a loud voice and said, 'Lord, Lord Almighty, mercy on us! It has never been heard or thought of that any one should have her breasts full of milk and that the birth of a son should show his mother to be a virgin. But there has been no spilling of blood in his birth, no pain in bringing him forth. A virgin has conceived, a virgin has brought forth, and a virgin she remains.' And hearing these words, the other midwife with the name Salome said, 'I will not believe what I have heard unless I also examine her'. And Salome entered and said to Mary, 'Allow me to handle you, and prove whether Zelomi has spoken the truth.' And Mary allowed her to handle her. And when she had withdrawn her hand from handling her it

---

[1] Luke 2: 14.

dried up, and through excess of pain she began to weep bitterly and to be in great distress, crying out and saying, 'O Lord God, you know that I have always feared you, and that without recompense I have cared for all the poor; I have taken nothing from the widow and the orphan, and the needy have I not sent empty away. And, behold, I am made wretched because of my unbelief, since without a cause I wished to test your virgin.'

And while she was speaking, there stood by her a young man in shining garments saying, 'Go to the child and worship him and touch him with your hand, and he will heal you, because he is the Saviour of the world and of all that hope in him.' And she went to the child with haste and worshipped him and touched the fringe of the clothes in which he was wrapped, and instantly her hand was cured. And going out she began to cry aloud and to tell the wonderful things which she had seen and which she had suffered and how she had been cured, so that many believed through her preaching.

And some shepherds also affirmed that they had seen angels singing a hymn at midnight, praising and blessing the God of heaven and saying, 'The Saviour of all, who is Christ the Lord has been born. Salvation shall be brought back to Israel through him.'

A great star, larger than any that had been seen since the beginning of the world, shone over the cave from the evening till the morning. And the prophets who were in Jerusalem said that this star pointed out the birth of Christ who should restore the promise not only to Israel but to all nations.

14. And on the third day after the birth of our Lord Jesus Christ, Mary went out of the cave and, entering a stable, placed the child in the manger, and an ox and an ass adored him. Then was fulfilled that which was said by Isaiah the prophet, 'The ox knows his owner, and the ass his master's crib.'[2] Therefore, the animals, the ox and the ass, with him in their midst, incessantly adored him. Then was fulfilled that which was said by Habakkuk the prophet, saying, 'Between two animals you are made manifest.'[3] Joseph remained in the same place with Mary for three days.

18. And having come to a certain cave, and wishing to rest in it, Mary dismounted from her beast, and sat down with the child Jesus in her lap. And on the journey there were with Joseph three boys, and with Mary a girl. And behold, suddenly there came out of the cave many dragons; and when the boys saw them they cried out in great terror. Then Jesus got down from his mother's lap and stood on his feet before the dragons; and they worshipped Jesus and then departed. Then was fulfilled that which was said by David the prophet, 'Praise the Lord from the earth, dragons, and all you ocean depths.'[4] And the child Jesus, walking before them, commanded them to hurt no-one.

---

[2] Isa. 1: 3.
[3] Hab. 3: 2 (LXX).
[4] Ps. 148: 7.

But Mary and Joseph were very much afraid lest the child should be hurt by the dragons. And Jesus said to them, 'Do not be afraid, and do not consider me to be a child, for I am and always have been perfect; and all the beasts of the forest must needs be docile before me.'

19. Likewise, lions and panthers adored him and accompanied them in the desert. Wherever Joseph and Mary went, they went before them showing them the way and bowing their heads; they showed their submission by wagging their tails, they worshipped him with great reverence. Now at first, when Mary saw the lions and the panthers and various kinds of wild beasts surrounding them, she was very much afraid. But the infant Jesus looked into her face with a joyful countenance and said, 'Be not afraid, mother, for they come not to do you harm, but they make haste to serve both you and me.' With these words he drove all fear from her heart. And the lions kept walking with them, and with the oxen and the asses and the beasts of burden, which carried what they needed, and did not hurt a single one of them, though they remained with them; they were tame among the sheep and the rams which they had brought with them from Judaea and which they had with them. They walked among wolves and feared nothing; and not one of them was hurt by another. Then was fulfilled that which was spoken by the prophet, 'Wolves shall feed with lambs; lion and ox shall eat straw together.'[5] There were two oxen and a waggon in which they carried their necessities, and the lions directed them in their path.

20. And it came to pass on the third day of their journey, while they were walking, that Mary was fatigued by the excessive heat of the sun in the desert; and, seeing a palm-tree she said to Joseph, 'I should like to rest a little in the shade of this tree.' Joseph therefore led her quickly to the palm and made her dismount from her beast. And as Mary was sitting there, she looked up to the foliage of the palm and saw it full of fruit and said to Joseph, 'I wish it were possible to get some of the fruit of this palm.' And Joseph said to her, 'I am surprised that you say so, for you see how high the palm-tree is, and that you think of eating its fruit. I am thinking more of the want of water because the skins are now empty, and we have nothing with which to refresh ourselves and our cattle.' Then the child Jesus, reposing with a joyful countenance in the lap of his mother, said to the palm, 'O tree, bend your branches and refresh my mother with your fruit.' And immediately at these words the palm bent its top down to the very feet of Mary; and they gathered from it fruit with which they all refreshed themselves. And after they had gathered all its fruit it remained bent down, waiting the order to rise from him who had commanded it to bend down. Then Jesus said to it, 'Raise yourself, O palm, and be strong and be the companion of my trees which are in the paradise of my Father; and open from your roots a vein of water which is hidden in the earth and let the waters flow,

---

[5] Isa. 65: 25.

so that we may quench our thirst.' And it rose up immediately, and at its root there began to gush out a spring of water exceedingly clear and cool and sparkling. And when they saw the spring of water, they rejoiced greatly and were all satisfied, including their cattle and their beasts and they gave thanks to God.

21. And on the day after, when they were setting out from there, and at the hour in which they began their journey, Jesus turned to the palm and said, 'This privilege I give you, O palm-tree, that one of your branches be carried away by my angels, and planted in the paradise of my Father. And this blessing I will confer upon you, that it shall be said to all who shall be victorious in any contest, "You have attained the palm of victory."' And while he was speaking, behold, an angel of the Lord appeared and stood upon the palm tree and, taking off one of its branches, flew to heaven with the branch in his hand. And when they saw this, they fell on their faces and were like dead men. And Jesus said to them, 'Why are your hearts possessed with fear? Do you not know that this palm, which I have caused to be transferred to paradise, shall be prepared for all the saints in the place of blessedness, as it has been prepared for us in this desert place?' And they were filled with joy; and being strengthened, they all arose.

22. After this, while they were going on their journey, Joseph said to Jesus, 'Lord, the heat is roasting us; if it please you, let us go by the sea-shore that we may be able to rest in the cities on the coast.' Jesus said to him, 'Fear not, Joseph; I will shorten the way for you, so that what you would have taken thirty days to traverse you shall accomplish in this one day.' And while they were speaking, behold, they looked ahead and began to see the mountains and cities of Egypt.

And rejoicing and exulting, they came into the regions of Hermopolis and entered into a certain city of Egypt, which is called Sotinen; and because they knew no one there from whom they could ask hospitality, they went into a temple, which was called the Capitol of Egypt. And in this temple there had been set up three hundred and sixty-five idols, to each of which on its own day divine honours and sacred rites were paid.

23. And it came to pass that, when Mary went into the temple with the child, all the idols prostrated themselves on the ground, so that all of them were lying on their faces shattered and broken to pieces; and thus they plainly showed that they were nothing. Then was fulfilled that which was said by the prophet Isaiah, 'Behold, the Lord will come upon a swift cloud and will enter Egypt, and all the handiwork of the Egyptians shall be moved before his face.'[6]

24. When this was told to Affrodosius, governor of that city, he went to the temple with his whole army. And when the priests of the temple saw

---

[6] Isa. 19: 1.

Affrodosius coming into the temple with all his army, they thought they would see him take vengeance on those who had caused the gods to fall down. But when he came into the temple and saw all the gods lying prostrate on their faces, he went up to Mary, who was carrying the Lord in her bosom, and worshipped him and said to his whole army and all his friends, 'Unless this were the God of our gods, our gods would not have fallen on their faces before him, nor would they be lying prostrate in his presence: therefore they silently confess that he is their Lord. Unless we do what we have seen our gods doing, we may run the risk of his anger and all come to destruction, just as it happened to Pharaoh king of the Egyptians who, not believing in powers so mighty, was drowned in the sea with all his army.' Then all the people of the city believed in the Lord God through Jesus Christ.

PARS ALTERA

25. After a short time the angel said to Joseph, 'Return to the land of Judah, for they are dead who sought the child's life.'

35. There is a road going out of Jericho and leading to the river Jordan, to the place where the children of Israel crossed; and there the ark of the covenant is said to have rested. And Jesus was eight years old, and he went out of Jericho and went towards the Jordan. And there was beside the road, near the bank of the Jordan, a cave where a lioness was nursing her whelps; and no one was safe to walk that way. Jesus, coming from Jericho, and knowing that in that cave the lioness had brought forth her young, went into it in the sight of all. And when the lions saw Jesus, they ran to meet him and worshipped him. And Jesus was sitting in the cavern and the lion's whelps ran round his feet, fawning and playing with him. And the older lions, with their heads bowed, stood at a distance and worshipped him and fawned upon him with their tails. Then the people who were standing afar off and who did not see Jesus, said, 'Unless he or his parents had committed grievous sins, he would not of his own accord have exposed himself to the lions.' And when the people were reflecting within themselves and were overcome with great sorrow, behold, suddenly in the sight of the people Jesus came out of the cave and the lions went before him, and the lion's whelps played with each other before his feet. And the parents of Jesus stood afar off with their heads bowed and they watched; likewise also the people stood at a distance on account of the lions, for they did not dare to come close to them. Then Jesus began to say to the people, 'How much better are the beasts than you, seeing that they recognize their Lord and glorify him; while you men, who have been made in the image and likeness of God, do not know him! Beasts know me and are tame; men see me and do not acknowledge me.'

36. After these things Jesus crossed the Jordan in the sight of them all with

the lions; and the water of the Jordan was divided on the right hand and on the left. Then he said to the lions so that all could hear, 'Go in peace and hurt no one; neither let man injure you, until you return to the place where you have come from.' And they, bidding him farewell, not only with their voices but with their gestures, went to their own place. But Jesus returned to his mother.

40. After these things Joseph departed with Mary and Jesus to go into Capernaum by the sea-shore, on account of the malice of his adversaries. And when Jesus was living in Capernaum, there was in the city a man named Joseph, exceedingly rich. But he had wasted away under his infirmity and died, and was lying dead in his couch. And when Jesus heard people in the city mourning and weeping and lamenting over the dead man, he said to Joseph, 'Why do you not grant the benefit of your favour to this man, seeing that he is called by your name?' And Joseph answered him, 'How have I any power or ability to grant him a benefit?' And Jesus said to him, 'Take the kerchief which is upon your head, go and put it on the face of the dead man and say to him, "Christ save you", and immediately the dead man will be healed and will rise from his couch.' And when Joseph heard this, he went away at the command of Jesus and ran and entered the house of the dead man, and put the kerchief, which he was wearing on his head, upon the face of him, who was lying in the couch and said, 'Jesus save you.' And forthwith the dead man rose from his bed and asked who Jesus was.

42. Joseph came to a feast with his sons, James, Joseph, and Judah, and Simeon, and his two daughters. Jesus met them, with Mary his mother, along with her sister Mary, the daughter of Cleophas, whom the Lord God had given to her father Cleophas and her mother Anna, because they had offered Mary the mother of Jesus to the Lord. And she was called by the same name, Mary, for the consolation of her parents.[7] And when they had assembled, Jesus sanctified and blessed them, and he was the first to begin to eat and drink; for none of them dared to eat or drink or to sit at table or to break bread until he had first sanctified them. And if he happened to be absent, they used to wait for him. And when he did not wish to come for refreshment,

---

[7] One of the manuscripts (Tischendorf's B) has: 'And when Joseph, worn out with old age, died and was buried with his parents, the blessed Mary lived with her nephews or with the children of her sisters; for Anna and Emerina were sisters. Of Emerina was born Elizabeth, the mother of John the Baptist. And as Anna, the mother of the blessed Mary, was very beautiful, when Joachim was dead she was married to Cleophas by whom she had a second daughter. She called her Mary, and gave her to Alphaeus to wife; and of her was born James the son of Alphaeus and Philip his brother. And her second husband having died, Anna was married to a third husband named Salome [sic] by whom she had a third daughter. She called her Mary likewise, and gave her to Zebedee to wife; and of her were born James the son of Zebedee, and John the Evangelist.

neither Joseph nor Mary, nor the sons of Joseph, his brothers, came. And, indeed, these brothers, keeping his life as a lamp before their eyes, observed him, and feared him. And when Jesus slept, whether by day or by night, the brightness of God shone upon him. To whom be all praise and glory for ever and ever. Amen, amen.

The Arabic Infancy Gospel

This is another collection of material that has made use of the Protevangelium of James (= PJ) and Infancy Thomas. Chapters 1–10 are based on PJ, and 36–55 show many similarities with Thomas (it is, however, difficult to use the Arabic Gospel to solve the literary and textual problems of Thomas). In between (i.e. chapters 11–35) the author has drawn on a large collection of fantasies, the origin of which is likely to be Egyptian. In this middle section the interest is focused on benevolent miracles wrought in particular by Mary during the sojourn in Egypt. The consistency of the book, as with other comparable collections, is not always faultless. In ch. 26 Joseph is told to go to Nazareth, yet in 27 onwards the story is resumed in Bethlehem. It may well be, therefore, that 26 is from a different source. Other similar inconsistencies can be detected, betraying the heterogeneous origin of many of the sources behind the composition.

Like the Armenian Infancy Gospel (see below), the Arabic is likely to go back to a Syrian archetype, which could be of the fifth–sixth century. Much of the material is embodied in the Syriac History of the Virgin[1], and a comparative study of the two is found in Peeters's introduction to his translation (p. vi). Although there may be no direct link between the two, such comparisons reinforce the argument for Syriac influence on the Arabic Infancy Gospel. Other links may be seen in the writings of the ninth-century Syriac father, Isho'dad of Merv, who seems to be aware of this Arabic Gospel in his commentary on Matthew. The title of this gospel, 'The Book of Joseph Caiaphas', may also be another significant indicator of its provenance in so far as Caiaphas was believed by Syrian Jacobites to have become a Christian (according to Cowper, p. lxxvii).

The Arabic text on which Sike's translation of 1697 was based has since been lost. Arabic manuscripts have, however, subsequently been discovered in Rome and Florence. The Laurentian manuscript now edited by Provera was described in Assemani's catalogue.[2] Sike's bilingual edition has been used, sometimes with emendations, in most subsequent Arabic editions and/or Latin translations.

---

[1] See the edition by E. A. Wallis Budge, *The History of the Blessed Virgin Mary and the History of the Likeness of Christ* (London, 1899; repr. New York, 1976) (= *Luzac's Semitic Text and Translation Series* 4 and 5).

[2] S. E. Assemani, *Bibliothecae Mediceae Laurentianae et Palatinae codicum manuscriptorum orientalium catalogus* (Florence, 1742), 72–3.

The Arabic Infancy Gospel

In his assessment of the worth of this book Cowper (p. lxxx) comments: 'Ignorance, folly and mendacity are here at least as conspicuous as piety'. Only a few sample chapters are translated here (13–15, 17, 25–4, 27, 57, 40), preceded by James's summary of the whole text. Most of them are typical of the racy and vivid style of the book as a whole. They smack of the 'Thousand and One Nights' rather than pious Christian literature. All of these chapters (but not 27) were included in Schonfield's selection from Walker's translation.[3] Chapter 23 tells of the meeting with the Good Thief, which is also to be found in the Acta Pilati (Greek B).

My extracts are translated from Tischendorf.

EDITIONS

Latin

H. Sike, *Evangelium Infantiae vel liber apocrphus de Infantia Salvatoris ex manuscripto edidit ac latina versione et notis illustravit* (Utrecht, 1697) (and in Arabic).
Fabricius, i. 168–212 (with introduction, 128–67).[4]
Jones, ii, 208–72 (with Eng. trans.).
C. C. L. Schmidius (= Schmid), *Corpus omnium veterum apocryphorum extra biblia*, i (Hadamar [Wiesbaden], 1804).[4]
Thilo, i, pp. xxvi-xliv, 63–158 (with Arabic text as revised by E. Rödiger).[4]
Tischendorf, *EA*, pp. xlviii-liii, 181–209 (text as revised by H. Fleischer).

Arabic

Giles, i. 12–32.
M. Provera, *Il Vangelo arabo dell' Infanzia* (Jerusalem, 1973).

SYNOPSES

Aland[13] prints a Latin version of the Arabic Infancy Gospel 50–3 and Greek A of Infancy Thomas 19. 1–5 with Luke 2: 41–52 (Jesus in the Temple at the age of twelve). Huck-Greeven[13] includes Fleischer's Latin version of 50 and 53.

MODERN TRANSLATIONS

English

Hone ('I Infancy'), 38–60.
Cowper, 170–216.
Walker, 100–24.

---

[3] H. J. Schonfield, *Readings From the Apocryphal Gospels* (London, 1940). In addition he gives 16, 18, 20–1, 22).
[4] All these editions are based on Sike's.

James, 80–2 (brief summaries, but the Miracle of the Dyer, Arabic ch. 37 (not 38, *pace* James, p. 66) and the Children in the Oven, Arabic ch. 40, are set out on pp. 66–8).
Hennecke[3], i. 400–1 and 408–9 (chs. 17, 23–4, 37, 40).
Hennecke[5], i. 452–3, 460–1. (chs. 17, 23–4, 37, 40).

French

Migne, *Dictionnaire*, i, cols. 973–1008.
P. Peeters, *Évangiles apocryphes*, ii *L'Évangiles de l'enfance* (Paris, 1914), i–xxix, 1–68. (= *Textes et documents*, ed. H. Hemmer and P. Lejay).
Amiot, 93–107 (extracts).
Éac, 207–38.

German

E. Bock, *Die Kindheit Jesu: Zwei apokryphe Evangelien* (Munich, 1924) (= *Christus Aller Erde* 14–15). [The other of the two gospels is Pseudo-Matthew, above.]
Hennecke[3], 299–300, 305–6 (O. Cullmann) (chs. 17, 23–4, 37, 40).
Hennecke[5], i. 360–1, 365–6 (O. Cullmann) (chs. 17 23–4, 37, 40).
Schneider, 174–95.

Italian

Bonaccorsi, i. 232–59.
Erbetta, i. 2, 102–23.
Moraldi, i. 281–311; [2] i. 299–305, 307–42.
A. M. Di Nola, *Evangelio Arabo dell' Infanzia* (Parma, 1963).
Cravieri, 113–48.

Spanish

González-Blanco, ii. 42–88.
de Santos Otero, 309–38 (with Latin).

GENERAL

Variot, 64–82.
P. Peeters, 'A propos de l'Évangile arabe de l'enfance: le manuscrit de J. Golius', *Anal. Boll.* 41 (1923), 132–4.
G. Graf, *Geschichte der christlichen arabischen Literatur*, i (*Studi e Testi* 118) (Vatican, 1944), 225–7.

Summary

1. States that it is found in the book of Joseph the high-priest in the time of Christ, who some say is Caiaphas, that Jesus in the cradle proclaimed his Godhead.

2. The decree of Augustus in the year 300 (or 304) of the era of Alexander. The Birth in a cave. An old Hebrew woman comes as midwife. 3. Her hands

The Arabic Infancy Gospel

are withered (?) because of her unbelief, and she is healed. [There is a gap in the text.] 4. The Shepherds. The midwife praises God. 5. The Circumcision. 6. The Presentation.

7. The Magi. 8. They bring back one of Jesus' swaddling cloths which is proof against fire and is preserved with veneration. 9. The Flight.

10–11. Arrival in Egypt. An idol announces the presence of a God, and falls. The demoniac son of a priest is healed. 12. Alarm of Joseph and Mary.

13. Robbers hear a noise of an approaching host and flee, leaving their captives. Joseph and Mary arrive, and the captives ask who is the king who is coming. Answer: 'He is coming on after us.'

14. A demoniac woman healed. 15. A dumb bride healed.

16. A woman oppressed by a demon-serpent relieved.

17. A leprous girl healed by water in which Jesus was washed.

18. A leprous child healed in like manner. 19. A husband and wife released from a spell. 20–21. The brother of two women, who had been changed into a mule, restored by having Jesus placed on his back. 22. The leprous girl of 17 married to the brother.

23. The robbers Titus and Dumachus (the good and bad thieves of the Crucifixion) capture them. Titus redeems them: Jesus prophesies his end.

24. At Matarieh in Egypt a spring bursts forth and balm originates from the sweat of Jesus. 25. They lived three years at Misr and saw Pharaoh. Many miracles were done which are not written in the Gospel of the Infancy or in the complete Gospel (probably the canonical Gospels are meant). 26. Return to Nazareth. 27. At Bethlehem a sick child healed. 28. A child diseased in the eyes healed. 29. Two women, mothers of children. One child dies, the other, Cleopas, is healed. The mother of the dead throws Cleopas first into an oven, then into a well: he is uninjured: she herself falls into the well and is killed. 30. One of two twin boys healed—the Bartholomew of the Gospels. 31. A leprous woman healed. 32. A leprous bride healed. 33, 34. A woman haunted by a dragon freed by one of Christ's swaddling cloths. 35. Judas, a child possessed by the devil, smites Jesus, and the devil leaves him in the form of a dog.

36. Jesus (seven years old) makes figures of all sorts of animals of clay, and makes them walk, fly, and feed. 37. The story of the Dyer Salem. 38. Jesus lengthens or shortens beams which Joseph had cut wrongly: for he was not clever at his trade. 39. A bed made for the king of Jerusalem pulled out to the right size. 40. The children in the oven (see above). 41. In the month of Adar the boys make Jesus their king, and passers by have to stop and salute him. 42. The parents of a child bitten by a snake come, and are stopped: Jesus goes with them to the snake's nest and makes it suck out the poison: it bursts: the child is healed: he was Simon Zelotes. 43. James bitten by the viper and healed. 44. Zeno falls from the house and is raised. 45. Jesus brings water in

his cloak. 46. The pools and sparrows of clay. The son of Hanan spoils the pools and is palsied. 47. The child who ran against Jesus falls dead. 48. Taught by Zacheus, who is confounded by his wisdom. 49. Taught by another master, who smites him and dies.

50. With the doctors at Jerusalem: questioned about the Law. 51. Questioned about astronomy. 52. And by a philosopher about philosophy: he answers all perfectly. 53. Is found by Mary and Joseph. Returns with them. 54. He lived in obscurity until his baptism. 55. Doxology.

Translations
13. Going out from there, they came to a place where there were robbers who had plundered many men of their baggage and clothes, and had bound them. Then the robbers heard a great noise, like the noise of a magnificent king going out of his city with his army, and his chariots and his drums; and at this the robbers were terrified, and left all that they had stolen. And their captives rose up, loosed each other's bonds, recovered their baggage, and went away. And when they saw Joseph and Mary coming up to the place, they said to them, 'Where is that king? When the robbers heard the magnificent sound of his approach they left us, and we have escaped safe?' Joseph answered them 'He will come behind us.'

14. Then they came into another city, where there was a demoniac woman whom the accursed and rebellious Satan had attacked when she had gone out by night for water. She could neither bear clothes, nor live in a house; and as often as they tied her up with chains and thongs, she broke them, and fled naked into desert places; and, standing in cross-roads and cemeteries, she threw stones at people, and brought great calamities upon her friends. And when the Lady Mary saw her, she pitied her; and immediately Satan left her, and fled away in the form of a young man, saying, 'Woe to me from you, Mary, and from your son.' So that woman was cured of her torment, and being restored to her senses, she blushed on account of her nakedness; and shunning the sight of men, went home to her friends. And after she put on her clothes, she gave an account of the matter to her father and her friends; and as they were the chief men of the city, they received the Lady Mary and Joseph with the greatest honour and hospitality.

15. On the day after, being supplied by them with provision for their journey, they went away, and on the evening of that day arrived at another town, in which a marriage was being celebrated; but, by the arts of accursed Satan and the work of enchanters, the bride had become dumb, and could not speak a word. And after the Lady Mary entered the town, carrying her son the Lord Christ, the dumb bride saw her, and stretched out her hands towards the Lord Christ, and drew him to her, and took him into her arms, and embraced him closely and kissed him, and leaned over him, rocking his body back and forwards. Immediately the knot of her tongue was loosened, and her

The Arabic Infancy Gospel

ears were opened; and she gave thanks and praise to God, because he had restored her to health. And that night the inhabitants of the town rejoiced, and thought that God and his angels had come down to them.

17. On the day after, a woman took scented water to wash the Lord Jesus; and after she had washed him, she took the water with which she had done it, and poured some of it upon a girl who was living there and whose body was white with leprosy, and washed her with it. And as soon as this was done, the girl was cleansed from her leprosy. And the townspeople said, 'There is no doubt that Joseph and Mary and this child are gods, not men.' And when they were ready to leave them, the girl who had suffered from the leprosy came up to them, and asked them to take her with them.

23. And departing from this place, they came to a desert; and hearing that it was infested by robbers, Joseph and the Lady Mary decided to cross this region by night. But on their way, behold, they saw two robbers lying in wait on the road, and with them a great number of robbers, who were their associates, sleeping. Now those two robbers into whose hands they had fallen were Titus and Dumachus. Titus therefore said to Dumachus, 'I beseech you to let these persons go free, so that our comrades do not see them.' And as Dumachus refused, Titus said to him again, 'Take forty drachmas from me, and have them as a pledge.' At the same time he held out to him the belt which he had had about his waist, that he should not open his mouth or speak. And the Lady Mary, seeing that the robber had done them a kindness, said to him, 'The Lord God will sustain you with his right hand, and will grant you remission of your sins.' And the Lord Jesus answered, and said to his mother, 'Thirty years hence, O my mother, the Jews will crucify me at Jerusalem, and these two robbers will be raised upon the cross along with me, Titus on my right hand and Dumachus on my left; and after that day Titus shall go before me into Paradise.' And she said, 'God keep this from you, my son.' And they went from there towards a city of idols, which, as they came near it, was transformed into sand-hills.

24. From there they went to that sycamore which is now called Matarea, and the Lord Jesus brought forth in Matarea a fountain in which the Lady Mary washed his shirt. And from the sweat of the Lord Jesus which he let drop there, balsam was produced in that region.

27. Thereafter, going into the city of Bethlehem, they saw there many and grievous diseases infesting the eyes of the children, who were dying in consequence. And a woman was there with a sick son, whom, being very near to death, she brought to the Lady Mary, who saw him as she was washing Jesus Christ. Then the woman said to her, 'O my Lady Mary, look upon this son of mine, who is suffering with a grievous disease.' And the Lady Mary

listened to her, and said, 'Take a little of that water in which I have washed my son, and sprinkle him with it.' She therefore took a little of the water, as the Lady Mary had told her, and sprinkled it over her son. And when this was done his illness abated; and after sleeping a little, he awoke safe and sound. His mother rejoiced at this, and took him again to the Lady Mary. And she said to her, 'Give thanks to God, because he has healed your son.'

37. One day, when Jesus was running about and playing with some children, he passed by the workshop of a dyer called Salem. They had in the workshop many cloths which he had to dye. The Lord Jesus went into the dyer's workshop, took all the pieces of cloth and put them into a tub full of indigo. When Salem came and saw that the cloths were spoiled, he began to cry aloud and asked the Lord Jesus, saying, 'What have you done to me, son of Mary? You have ruined my reputation in the eyes of all the people of the city; for everyone orders a colour to suit himself, but you have come and spoiled everything.' And the Lord Jesus replied, 'I will change for you the colour of any cloth which you wish to be changed', and he immediately began to take the cloths out of the tub, each of them dyed in the colour the dyer wished, until he had taken them all out. When the Jews saw this miracle and wonder, they praised God.

40.[1] On another day the Lord Jesus went out into the road, and seeing some boys who had met to play, he followed them; but the boys hid themselves from him. The Lord Jesus, therefore, having come to the door of a certain house, and seen some women standing there, asked them where the boys had gone; and when they answered that there was no one there, he said again, 'Who are these whom you see in the furnace?'[2] They replied that they were young goats of three years old. And the Lord Jesus cried out and said, 'Come out, O goats, to your Shepherd.' Then the boys, in the form of goats, came out, and began to skip round him; and the women, seeing this, were very much astonished, and were seized with trembling, and speedily supplicated the Lord Jesus, saying, 'O our Lord Jesus, son of Mary, you are truly that good Shepherd of Israel; have mercy on your handmaidens who stand before you, and who have never doubted: for you have come, O our Lord, to heal, and not to destroy.' And when the Lord Jesus answered that the sons of Israel were like the Ethiopians among the nations, the women said, 'You, O Lord, know all things, nor is anything hid from you; now, indeed, we

---

[1] James, 67-8, translates this story from the Syriac version found in E. A. Wallis Budge, *The History of the Blessed Virgin Mary and the History of the Likeness of Christ* (London, 1899; repr. New York, 1976), 76 (= *Luzac's Semitic Text and Translation Series 4 and 5*).

[2] Perhaps the correct reading is *fornice*, archway, and not *fornace*. The Syriac suggests 'cellar'.

beseech you, and ask you of your mercy to restore these boys, your servants, to their former condition.' The Lord Jesus therefore said, 'Come, boys, let us go and play.' And immediately, while these women were standing by, the kids were changed into boys.

Arundel 404 (Liber de Infantia Salvatoris)

This text (British Library Arundel 404) is one of two medieval Latin infancy gospels published originally by M. R. James, *Latin Infancy Gospels* (Cambridge, 1927). The other, in the chapter library of Hereford Cathedral, is also printed there in full, as the Hereford Manuscript. The Hereford manuscript attributes authorship to James, Arundel 404 to Matthew (cf. the similar confusion with Pseudo-Matthew). The Gospel in these two alternative forms is yet another derived ultimately from the earlier apocryphal infancy stories, the Protevangelium of James (= PJ), Pseudo-Matthew, and the Gospel of the Birth of Mary. It is another possible descendant of the long-lost Latin translation of PJ, but we cannot be certain how far the material in Arundel 404 common to PJ came from PJ directly or whether it reached Arundel 404 from Pseudo-Matthew.[1] But the version found here in Arundel 404 (a smoother version of the Hereford manuscript) gives a Latin rendering hitherto unknown. (The *Liber de Infantia* in Thilo and Tischendorf is a different work (now known as Pseudo-Matthew).)

James is of the opinion (*Latin Infancy Gospels*, p. xiii) that in the Gelasian Decree the *Liber de nativitate Salvatoris et de Maria vel obstetrice* may refer to the text known in the Arundel manuscript. (Here he differs from the view expressed in *ANT*, p. 22, that this title in the Decree could refer to Pseudo-Matthew or PJ.)

Arundel 404 is prefaced by the spurious correspondence between Jerome and the Bishops Cromatius and Heliodorus that is also to be found in manuscripts of Pseudo-Matthew and the Gospel of the Birth of Mary.[2] These letters were used to support and commend various infancy stories, and whatever their original context they seem especially to have been attached to unorthodox works such as Arundel 404.

James, *Latin Infancy Gospels*, tries to link this infancy gospel with the Gospel of Peter, claiming they both come from the same, docetic, source. Lagrange's review is sceptical of linking the two merely because of a common docetism. The chapters translated below (72–4), where most of the unique material is to be found, reflect second-century Greek docetic tendencies and may well be the *raison d'être* for the original composition, namely to give a Gnostic or docetic view of Jesus' birth.

---

[1] See Gijsel's article in Bibliography below.
[2] For translations of these letters, see above, under Pseudo-Matthew. James, *ANT* 71–2, gives a translation of another letter (from Jerome to the Bishops) sometimes prefacing manuscripts of the Gospel of the Birth of Mary. I have not included this text.

Arundel 404 contains the Zacharias story in full (equivalent to PJ 10, 22–4) suggesting that if PJ was indeed one of its sources then it was a longer text of PJ that was used. One other disputed section of PJ, namely the speech of Joseph (PJ 18. 2), is different in Arundel 404 where that speech is put into the mouth of the midwife. Elsewhere, if PJ was used, it has been adapted or replaced with material known to us in Pseudo-Matthew. In an interpretation of the two peoples of PJ 17 Arundel 404 ch. 61 identifies them as Jews and Gentiles as in Pseudo-Matthew 13 (not angels and demons as in the Armenian infancy narrative).

The translation of chs. 72–4 is from M. R. James's edition.

EDITION

Latin

M. R. James, *Latin Infancy Gospels* (Cambridge, 1927), (with Eng. of chs. 73–4 in Introduction, xx-xxi).[3]

Jean-Daniel Kaestli and Martin NcNamara, 'Latin Infancy Gospels: the J Compilation' in M. McNamara *et al.* (eds.), *Apocrypha Hiberniae I Evangelia Infantiae* (Turnhout, 2001), 621–880 (= *CCSA* 14).

MODERN TRANSLATIONS

English

Cartlidge and Dungan, 104–7 (extracts of chs. 68–9, 71–4).
Hennecke[3], i. 413–14 (chs. 73–4 only).
Hennecke[5], i. 466 (chs. 73–4 only).

German

Hennecke[3], i. 309–10 (O. Cullmann) (chs. 73–4 only).
Hennecke[5], i. 370 (O. Cullmann) (chs. 73–4 only).
Schneider, 198–211.

Italian

Bonaccorsi, i. xxv, 232–59 (with Latin text).
Erbetta, 1.2, 206–17 (selection).
Moraldi, i. 60, 105–93; 2 i. 167–267 (Arundel and Hereford).

Spanish

de Santos Otero, 260–75 (with Latin text).

---

[3] J. A. Robinson's review includes a translation of chs. 73–4 (*JTS* 29 (1928), 205–7). Another review: M. J. Lagrange, 'Un nouvel Évangile de l'Enfance édité par M. R. James', *Rev. Bib.* 37 (1928), 544–57.

Irish

M. McNamara, *The Apocrypha in the Irish Church* (Dublin, 1975), 42–6 (references to Irish versions close to Arundel).

GENERAL

J. Gijsel, 'Les "Évangiles latins de l'enfance" de M. R. James', *Anal. Boll.* 94 (1976), 289–302.

72. In that hour, a great silence descended with fear. For even the winds stopped, they made no breeze; there was no movement of the leaves on the trees, nor sound of water heard; the streams did not flow; there was no motion of the sea. All things born in the sea were silent; no human voice sounded and there was a great silence. For the pole itself ceased its rapid course from that hour. The measure of time almost stopped. Everyone was overwhelmed with great fear and kept silent; we were expecting the advent of the most high God, the end of the world.

73. As the time drew near, the power of God showed itself openly. The maiden stood looking into heaven; she became like a vine[1]. For now the end of the events of salvation was at hand. When the light had come forth, Mary worshipped him whom she saw she had given birth to. The child himself, like the sun, shone brightly, beautiful and most delightful to see, because he alone appeared as peace, bringing peace everywhere. In that hour when he was born the voice of many invisible beings proclaimed in unison, 'Amen.' And that light, which was born, was multiplied and it obscured the light of the sun itself by its shining rays. The cave was filled with the bright light and with a most sweet smell. The light was born just as the dew descends from heaven to the earth. For its perfume is fragrant beyond all the smell of ointments.

74. I,[2] however, stood stupefied and amazed. Fear seized me. I was gazing at the intense bright light which had been born. The light, however, gradually shrank, imitated the shape of an infant, then immediately became outwardly an infant like a child born normally. I became bold and leaned over and touched him. I lifted him in my hands with great awe, and I was terrified because he had no weight like other babies who are born. I looked at him; there was no blemish in him, but his whole body was shining, just as the dew of the most high God. He was light to carry, radiant to see. For å while I was amazed at him because he did not cry as new-born infants are accustomed to cry. While I held him, looking into his face, he smiled at me with a most joyful smile, and, opening his eyes, he looked at me intently, and suddenly a great light came forth from his eyes like a brilliant flash of lightning.

---

[1] J. A. Robinson, *JTS* 29 (1928), 207, conjectures *nivea* for *vinea*, arguing that the Latin translator mistook an original ὡς κιών (pillar) for ὡς χιών.

[2] The midwife is the narrator.

The History of Joseph the Carpenter

Like many apocryphal infancy gospels this book is likely to have been inspired by the Protevangelium of James. As a counterpart to the many legends that developed around the name of Mary, it tells of Joseph's death. The whole narrative is put into the mouth of Jesus (although there are lapses in chapters 30 and 32). An Egyptian provenance would readily account for much of the teaching on death, for which there are parallels in the Coptic accounts of the death of the Virgin. The work is known in Sahidic (from which a Bohairic version has been translated, according to Robinson, p. xvi), and in Arabic that has been based on the Coptic or possibly even on a Syriac version. According to Morenz, the original language is likely to have been Greek—from which the Coptic seems to have been translated.

The existence of the book in both main Coptic dialects is one of the arguments that have been put forward in favour of a fourth–fifth century date for its composition. Other arguments for this early date include the millenarian teaching of ch. 26: other eschatological teaching elsewhere is said by Tischendorf to support such a date. Others have opted for a later date on the ground that the book must belong to a period when saints' days were observed, since its purpose is clearly to glorify Joseph's feast day. As such it is another instance of a character in the canonical Gospels gaining greater significance in his or her own right in the apocryphal literature.

The extracts translated below are from the Bohairic version.

The Arabic text was edited and translated into Latin by Wallin; his Latin text was reproduced by Fabricius. The Arabic was revised by E. Rödiger for Thilo's edition, which also has a Latin translation. Tischendorf reproduced the Latin text as revised for him by H. Fleischer.

Joseph the Carpenter in Coptic is in the following manuscripts and editions:

Bohairic. The complete text in Borgia XXV is in Revillout, pp. 43–71, and described by Zoega (p. 33).[1] De Lagarde (pp. 1–37) published the text of Vat LXVI 11 (from which Borgia XXV was copied); Robinson's translation (pp. 130–47) relies on de Lagarde's text. A fragment in Bohairic (Crawford 39 = Rylands 440) is given by Robinson (pp. 221–9).

Sahidic. These are all fragments.

(a) Borgia 109 no. 116, formerly Zoega CXVI. One leaf containing chs. 4–8.

---

[1] G. Zoega, *Catalogus codicum copticorum manuscriptorum qui in Museo Borgiano Velitris adservantur* (Rome, 1810; repr. Hildesheim, 1973).

Described by Zoega (p. 223). Written and lithographed by Revillout (pp. 28-9), and printed with a translation by Robinson (pp. 146-9).
(b) Borgia 109, no. 121, formerly Zoega CXXI. Eight leaves containing chs. 14-24. Described by Zoega (p. 225), with selections from chapters 14-15, 21-23. These selections were translated into French by Dulaurier. Written and lithographed by Revillout (pp. 30-42). Printed by de Lagarde, from a transcript by Guidi[2] (pp. 9-29). Translated by Robinson (pp. 152-9). Given in the footnotes to Tischendorf's Latin text which translates the Arabic.
(c) BL Or 3581 B. One leaf containing chapters 13-15. Translated by Robinson (pp. 148-51).
(d) Paris fragments. Bibliothèque Nationale 127[17] fos. 13-16 (chs. 17. 17b-23. 2a) and 129[17] fo. 12 (chs. 7. 1b-9. 1). Published by Lefort, Sahidic with French translation.

EDITIONS

Arabic

G. Wallin,... *Historia Iosephi fabri lignarii. Liber apocryphus ex manuscripto Regiae Bibliothecae Parisiensis nunc primum arabice editus, nec non versione latina et notis illustratus* (Leipzig, 1722).
Fabricius, 309-36 (Latin from Arabic).
Thilo, pp. xv-xxvi, 1-61 (Latin and a revision of Wallin's Arabic by E. Röderer).
Giles, i (Arabic text).
Tischendorf, *EA*, pp. xxxii-xxxvi, 122-39 (Latin from Arabic).
P. de Lagarde, *Aegyptiaca* (Göttingen, 1883), 1-37 (following Wallin with corrections).
A. Battista and B. Bagatti, *Edizione critica del testo arabo della 'Historia Iosephi fabri lignarii' e ricerche sulla sua origine* (Jerusalem, 1978). (= *Studii Biblici Franciscani Collectio Minor* 20).

Coptic

E. Revillout, 'Apocryphes coptes du Nouveau Testament', i. *Études Égyptologiques* 7 (Paris, 1876), 28-71.
P. de Lagarde, *Aegyptiaca* (Göttingen, 1883).
F. Robinson, *Coptic Apocryphal Gospels* (Cambridge, 1896). (= *Texts and Studies* 4.2), 130-59, 220-35.
L. T. Lefort, 'A propos de l'histoire de Joseph le Charpentier', *Le Muséon* 66 (1953), 201-23.

---

[2] I. Guidi, 'Frammenti Copti', *Rendiconti della R. Accademia dei Lincei (Classe di scienze morali, storiche e filologiche)* ser. 4, vol. 3,2. (1887)

MODERN TRANSLATIONS

English

Cowper, 99–127.
Walker, 62–77.
James, 84–6 (summary of Arabic text).
Hennecke[5], i. 483–5 (includes summary)

French

E. Dulaurier, *Fragments des révélations apocryphes de S. Barthélemy...* (Paris, 1835), 23–9 (Borgia CXXI).
Migne, *Dictionnaire* i, cols. 1027–44.
P. Peeters, in Michel, *Évangiles apocryphes*, i. 191–243. (trans. of both the Bohairic and Arabic editions on facing pages, with the Sahidic fragment of ch. 23 from Borgia CXXI which gives a different version of this chapter (appendix, pp. 244–6).[3]
F. Amiot, 107–11.

German

L. Stern, *ZWT* 26 (1883), 267–94 (translation of Revillout's Sahidic and Bohairic with corrections).
G. Klameth, 'Über die Herkunft der Apokryphen "Geschichte Josephs des Zimmermanns"', *Angelos* 3 (Leipzig, 1928), 6–31 (translates chs. 19–24 of de Lagarde's Sahidic and Bohairic).
S. Morenz, *Die Geschichte von Joseph dem Zimmermann aus dem Bohairischen und Sahidischen übersetzt, erläutert und untersucht* (Berlin and Leipzig, 1951) (= *TU* 56) (translates Bohairic and Sahidic Borgia CXXI).[4]
Hennecke[5], i. 383–4 (W. A. Bienert) (includes summary).
Schneider, 272–83.

Italian

Erbetta, i. 2, 186–205 (summary of Bohairic).
Moraldi, i. 313–52; [2] i. 387–428 (trans. of Latin).
Cravieri, 227–56.

Spanish

González-Blanco, ii. 385–406 (from Coptic); 407 ff. (from Arabic).
de Santos Otero, 341–58 (trans. of Morenz's edition of the Bohairic).

---

[3] Review by M. R. James, *JTS* 13 (1912), 433–5.
[4] Reviews by P. Devos, *Anal. Boll.* 70 (1952), 382–5, and A. Böhlig, *ByzZ* 66 (1953), 142–5.

GENERAL

The major study and commentary are those of Morenz (see under 'German' above).
Variot, 83–92.
G. Giamberardini, 'San Giuseppe nella tradizione copta', *Studia Orientalia Christiana Collectanea* (Cairo, 1966), 5–291 (French translation (Montreal, 1969) (= *Cahiers de Joséphologie* 17/1)).
F. Manns, 'Le portrait de Joseph dans l'Histoire de Joseph le Charpentier', in id., *Essais sur le Judéo-Christianisme* (Jerusalem, 1977), 94–105.

Summary

Proem. 'This is the going forth from the body of our father Joseph the carpenter, the father of Christ according to flesh, whose life was one hundred and eleven years.' It was told by Christ to the apostles on Mount Olivet, was written down by them, and laid up in the library at Jerusalem. The day of the death was the 26th of the month Epep.

1. Christ on Mount Olivet addresses the apostles: on the certainty of death and the justice of God, etc.

2. There was a man whose name was Joseph, descended from a family of Bethlehem, a town of Judah, and the city of King David. This same man, being well instructed with wisdom and learning, was made a priest in the temple of the Lord. He was, also, skilful in his trade, which was that of a carpenter; and like all men, he married a wife. Moreover, he begot for himself sons and daughters in fact four sons, and two daughters. Now these are their names—Judas, Justus, James, and Simeon. The names of the two daughters were Assia and Lydia. At length the wife of righteous Joseph, a woman intent on the divine glory in all her works, died. But Joseph, that righteous man, my father after the flesh, and the spouse of my mother Mary, went away with his sons to his trade, practising the art of a carpenter.

3. Mary was being brought up in the Temple till she was twelve years old. The priests decided to give her to a husband.

4. The lot fell on Joseph. Mary brought up James and was called Mary of James. Two years passed.

5. 'I came and dwelt in her.' Joseph's perplexity.

6. Reassured by Gabriel.

7. Decree of Caesar. The Birth 'by the tomb of Rachel'.

8. Herod sought to slay me. The Flight: Salome was with us. A year in Egypt.

9. Return to Nazareth. Joseph worked at his trade.

10–11. [Translated below.]

12. Joseph's death drew near. He went to the temple and prayed at the altar.

13. His prayer to be saved from the terrors after death, 'the river of fire wherein all souls are purified before they see the glory of God'.

The History of Joseph the Carpenter

14. He returned to Nazareth and fell ill. The dates of his life: he was forty when he married, and was married forty-nine years: a year alone after his wife's death. Two years with Mary before the Nativity.

15-16. His strength gave way and he was troubled and uttered a lamentation over all the parts of his body, for their several transgressions.

17. [Translated below.]

18. I wept. My mother asked if Joseph must die, and I told her that it must be so.

19. I sat at his head, Mary at his feet. I felt his heart and found that the soul was in his throat.

20. Mary felt his feet and legs and found them cold as ice. The brethren and sisters were summoned. Lydia the eldest daughter ['who is the seller of purple', Sahidic: cf. Acts 16: 14] lamented: so did all.

21. I looked at the south of the door and saw Death, and Amente following with their satellites 'decani' armed with fire. Joseph saw them and feared. I rebuked them and they fled. Death hid himself behind the door. I prayed.

22. Prayer for protection for the soul of Joseph 'until it cross the seven aeons of darkness'. 'Let the river of fire be as water and the sea of demons cease vexing.' Address to the apostles on the terrors of death.

23. [Translated below.]

24. I sat down by the body and closed the eyes and mouth; and comforted Mary and the rest.

25. The people of Nazareth came and mourned till the ninth hour. Then I sent them all off, anointed and washed the body. 'I prayed to my Father with heavenly prayers which I wrote with my own fingers on the tables of heaven before I took flesh in the holy Virgin Mary.' Angels came and shrouded the body.

26. I blessed it from all corruption; pronounced blessings on all who celebrate his memory by good deeds or write the story of his death.

27. The chief men of the place came to prepare the body, and found it already shrouded. The burial. I wept.

28. The lament of Jesus.

29. The body was laid in the tomb beside Jacob his father.

30. We the apostles rejoiced to hear all this. We asked why Joseph should not have been exempted from death like Enoch and Elias.

31. Jesus speaks of the inevitableness of death, and tells how Enoch and Elias still have to die, and are in trouble until their death is over. Antichrist will shed the blood of two men like a cup of water, because of the reproaches they will heap upon him.

32. We asked: Who are the two whom he will slay? Answer: Enoch and Elias.

The book ends with a doxology of the apostles.

Translations

10. At length, by increasing years, the old man arrived at an advanced age. He did not, however, labour under any bodily weakness, nor had his sight failed, nor had any tooth perished from his mouth nor, for the whole time of his life, was he ever insane; but like a boy he always showed youthful vigour in his business and his limbs remained unimpaired, and free from all pain. His life, then, in total, amounted to one hundred and eleven years, his old age being prolonged to the utmost limit.

11. Now Justus and Simeon, the elder sons of Joseph, were married and had families of their own. Both the daughters were likewise married and lived in their own houses. So there remained in Joseph's house Judas and James the Less, and my virgin mother. I also lived with them, just as if I had been one of his sons. I passed all my life without fault. I called Mary my mother, and Joseph father, and I obeyed them in all that they said; nor did I ever resist them, but complied with their commands, just as other men whom earth produces are wont to do; nor did I at any time arouse their anger, or give any word or answer in opposition to them. On the contrary, I cherished them with great love, like the apple of my eye.

17. I now went in beside him and found his soul exceedingly troubled, for he was in great anguish. And I said to him, 'Hail! my father Joseph, you righteous man; how are you?' And he answered me, 'All hail! my well-beloved son. Indeed, the agony and fear of death have already surrounded me; but as soon as I heard your voice my soul was at rest. O Jesus of Nazareth! Jesus, my Saviour! Jesus, the deliverer of my soul! Jesus, my protector! Jesus! O sweetest name in my mouth, and in the mouth of all those that love it! O eye which sees, and ear which hears, hear me! I am your servant; this day I most humbly venerate you, and before your face I pour out my tears. You are my God; you are my Lord, as the angel has told me on many occasions, and especially on that day when my soul was tossed about with perverse thoughts about the pure and blessed Mary, who was carrying you in her womb, and whom I was thinking of secretly sending away. And while I was thus meditating, behold, there appeared to me in my sleep angels of the Lord, in a wonderful mystery, saying to me, "O Joseph, son of David, fear not to take Mary as your wife; and do not grieve, nor speak unbecoming words of her conception, because she is with child of the Holy Spirit, and shall bring forth a son, whose name shall be called Jesus, for he shall save his people from their sins." Do not for this cause wish me evil, O Lord! for I was ignorant of the mystery of your birth. I call to mind also, my Lord, that day when the boy died of the bite of the serpent. And his relations wished to deliver you to Herod, saying that you had killed him; but you raised him from the dead, and restored him to them. Then I went up to you, and took hold of your hand, saying, "My son, take care of yourself." But you said to me in reply, "Are you not my father after the flesh? I shall teach you who I am." Now therefore, O

The History of Joseph the Carpenter

Lord and my God, do not be angry with me, or condemn me on account of that hour. I am your servant, and the son of your handmaiden; but you are my Lord, my God and Saviour, most surely the Son of God'.

23. Therefore Michael and Gabriel came to the soul of my father Joseph, and took it, and wrapped it in a shining cloth. Thus he committed his spirit into the hands of my good Father, and he bestowed upon him peace. But as yet none of his children knew that he had fallen asleep. And the angels preserved his soul from the demons of darkness which were in the way, and praised God until they conducted it into the dwelling-place of the pious.

Other Infancy Narratives

No translations are given of any other infancy stories, as these are in general far removed from the earlier apocryphal material. Brief introductory comments are given below on:
1. The Armenian Infancy Gospel
2. Liber de Infantia Salvatoris
3. The Gospel of the Birth of Mary
4. Coptic Infancy Stories
5. Other Mary fragments

Later infancy material may be seen in the Ethiopic Miracles of Jesus:

S. Grébaut, *Les Miracles de Jésus: Texte éthiopien publié et traduit*, PO 12.4 (Paris, 1919)—cf. also M. Chaîne, *Liber Nativitatis Mariae*, in *CSCO* 1.7 (Paris, 1909), 13–16.

E. A. Wallis Budge, *Legends of our Lady Mary the Perpetual Virgin and her Mother Hanna translated from the Ethiopic manuscripts collected by King Theodore of Makdala and now in the British Museum* (London, 1922).

—— *One Hundred and Ten Miracles of our Lady Mary translated by Ethiopic Manuscripts* (Oxford, 1933).

1. THE ARMENIAN INFANCY GOSPEL

As with the Arabic Infancy Gospel, the Armenian is thought to have been derived from a Syriac archetype. It represents yet another expansion of the Protevangelium of James and Infancy Thomas. This is a very prolix rendering. Chapters not from PJ and Infancy Thomas show intermittent similarity with the Arabic Infancy Gospel. Its treatment of sources may be compared to the Armenian expansion of 4 Esdras. Peeters's edition of this gospel runs to over two hundred pages. He is disinclined to identify this infancy gospel with one brought to Armenia by Nestorian missionaries in 590. James similarly is not prepared to make this identification, preferring instead (p. 83) to connect the infancy gospel with the book of the infancy referred to by the twelfth-century Armenian writer Sargis Šnorholi in his commentary on the Catholic epistles.

Extracts in translation are given by Santos and by Amiot. The only full version (in French) is the one in Peeters. The first printed edition was Daietsi's (Tayecʻi's) based on two Armenian manuscripts in the Mechitarist library in Venice, of which the second manuscript is the longer. Other manuscripts are known in the Eds-midsin monastery and in Vienna (see Peeters, pp. xxxiv–xxxvi).

Other Infancy Narratives

EDITION

Armenian

P. I. Daietsi (Tayecʻi), *Ankanon Girkhʻ Nor Ktakaranacʻ*, i (Venice, 1898), 1–235.
For Armenian translations of manuscripts of the Protevangelium of James (PJ) rendered into Latin see H. Quecke in the Appendix to É. de Strycker, *La forme la plus ancienne du Protévangile de Jacques* (Brussels, 1961) (= *Subsidia Hagiographica* 33). de Strycker (p. 44), following Peeters (Introduction, p. xxix), claims that what is being translated by Conybeare in *AJT* I (1897) are six chapters from the Armenian Gospel of the Infancy rather than a manuscript of PJ in its own right (for Conybeare see PJ bibliography).

MODERN TRANSLATIONS

English

James, 83–4 (brief résumé of contents).

French

P. Peeters, *Évangiles apocryphes*, ii (Paris, 1914), xxix–l, 69–286 (= *Textes et Documents*, ed. H. Hemmer and P. Lejay).
Amiot, 81–93 (selection).

Italian

Erbetta, i.2, 124–85.
Moraldi, i. 89–94; [2] i. 141–6 (selection).
Cravieri, 149–213.

Spanish

González-Blanco, ii. 88–236.
de Santos Otero, 359–65 (selection).

2. LIBER DE INFANTIA SALVATORIS

Extracts from this are given in Latin with a Spanish translation by de Santos Otero, pp. 366–72, from the Bibliothèque Nationale, Paris, manuscript Latin 11867 of the thirteenth century. (The full text is given by Bonaccorsi, pp. 226–33.[1])

---

[1] See also O. Schade, *Narrationes de Vita et Conversatione Beatae Mariae Virginis et de Pueritia et Adolescentia Salvatoris* (Halle, 1870); R Reinsch, *Die Pseudo-Evangelien von Jesu und Maria's Kindheit in der romanischen und germanischen Literatur* (Halle, 1879); and the introduction in Erbetta, i,2, 217–20.

3. THE GOSPEL OF THE BIRTH OF MARY

This was Hone's title, following Fabricius and Thilo, but the use of the word 'gospel' is undesirable. Tischendorf's suggested title (*EA* 113, not p. xxii), *De Nativitate Mariae*, is to be preferred. The work is an amplification of the early chapters of Pseudo-Matthew, and thus represents a Latin version of material known in Greek in the Protevangelium of James. Some manuscripts preface it with letters to and from Jerome that are sometimes to be found introducing Pseudo-Matthew (above, pp. 91–2). It was included in Jacob de Voragine's *Golden Legend* of the thirteenth century, and as such influenced art and literature.

There are differences between the *De Nativitate Mariae* and other such narratives. For instance, Issachar (not Reuben) is the high-priest who rebukes Joachim. In ch. 9 the author explains that he is summarizing and paraphrasing other narratives. It is possible that the work goes back to the fifth–sixth centuries.

Genna Marias. The existence of such a text is known only from a reference in Epiphanius, *adv. Haer.* 26. 12. 1–4 (Holl, *GCS* 25, pp. 290–1). Its character is discussed in J. D. Dubois, 'Hypothèse sur l'origine de l'apocryphe Genna Marias', *Augustinianum* 23 (1983), 264–70. See also Hennecke[3], i. 255–6 (Eng. trans. i. 344–5); Hennecke[5], i. 316 (Eng. trans. i. 395–6); Erbetta, i.1, 297.

EDITIONS

Latin

Thilo, i, pp. xci–cv, 317–36.
Tischendorf, *EA*, pp. xxii–xxxi, 113–21.
Rita Beyers, *Libri de Nativitate Mariae* (Turnhout, 1997) (=CCSA 10).

MODERN TRANSLATIONS

English

Hone, 17–24.
Cowper, 84–98.
James, 79–80 (brief summary).

French

Migne, *Dictionnaire*, i., cols. 1045–56.
E. Amann, *Le Protévangile de Jacques et ses remaniements latins* (Paris, 1910), 340–64 (with Latin text) (= *Les apocryphes du Nouveau Testament*, ed. J. Bousquet and E. Amann).
Éac, 143–61.

German

G. Schneider, *Evangelia Infantiae Apocrypha. Apocryphe Kindheitsevangelien*, (Freiburg, 1995), 258–69 (= *Fontes Christiani* 18).

Italian

Erbetta, i.2, 71–7.
Moraldi, i. 95–104; [2] i. 147–66.
Cravieri, 215–25.

Spanish

González-Blanco, i. 414–23.
de Santos Otero, 243–58 (with Latin text).

4. COPTIC INFANCY STORIES

James (pp. 87–9) draws attention to some of the many Lives, Panegyrics, Discourses, etc. in Coptic, complete and fragmentary, which tell the story of the Virgin's birth. Some of these can be found in F. Robinson, *Coptic Apocryphal Gospels* (Cambridge, 1896), especially pp. 2–43 (= *Texts and Studies* 42), and E. A. Wallis Budge, *Miscellaneous Coptic Texts in the Dialect of Upper Egypt* (London, 1915).

These documents on the whole show great negligence in the use of ancient sources and great licence on the part of the writers. These characteristics seem commonplace in Christian literature from Egypt. Similar features can be seen in the other categories of apocryphal material in Coptic, such as in the Passion narratives and in the Acts and Apocalypses.

5. OTHER MARY FRAGMENTS

These concern Mary Magdalene, not the Virgin Mary, and it is therefore doubtful if they should belong here with the gospels of the infancy. This group of fragments in Greek and in Coptic comes from a Gospel of Mary (Magdalene), who figures quite prominently in some Gnostic literature:

(i) P. Oxy. 3525 (ed. P. J. Parsons, *OP* 50, pp. 12–14) is a fragment of a Gospel of Mary in Greek, dated third-century, which corresponds closely to a Coptic Gospel of Mary (P. Berol. 8502.1).[1]

(ii) Another portion of this Gospel of Mary is found in the Rylands fragment 463 (Greek). Hennecke gives extracts from this in combination with P. Berol. 8502.1 and de Santos Otero (pp. 100–1) prints the text with a Spanish translation.

---

[1] The Sahidic Coptic text is fifth-century (cf. W. Till, *Die gnostischen Schriften des Koptischen Payprus Berolinensis 8502* (Berlin, 1955), 66 ff. (= *TU* 60); and see rev edn. by H. M. Schenke (Berlin, 1972), 24–32, 62–79).

The *editio princeps* of the Rylands fragment is in C. H. Roberts (ed.), *Catalogue of the Greek and Latin Papyri in the John Rylands Library in Manchester*, iii. *Theological and Literary Texts* (Manchester, 1938), 18–23, with Greek text, English translation, and C. Schmidt's translation into German of the Coptic of the Berlin fragment. P. Ryl. 463 is third-century, and Roberts suggests that the original writing may be as old as the second century. This fragment also encourages those who look for Greek originals behind Coptic Gnostic texts.

A revised edition of P. Ryl. 463 may be seen in G. P. Carratelli in *La Parola del Passato* 2 (1946), 266 ff. (cf. G. Kapsamenos, in *Athena* 49 (1939), 177–86, and R. McL. Wilson 'The New Testament in the Gnostic Gospel of Mary', *NTS* 3 (1956–7), 233–43).

EDITIONS

R. McL. Wilson and G. W. MacRae, 'The Gospel of Mary', in D. M. Parrott, *Nag Hammadi Codices V 2–5 and VI with Papyrus Berolinens 8502, 1 and 4* (Leiden, 1979), 453–71 (= *NHS* 11) (with English trans.).

A. Pasquier, in *Bibliothèque copte de Nag Hammadi: Textes* 10 (Quebec, 1983) (with French trans.).

Lührmann, 62–5.

MODERN TRANSLATIONS

English

G. W. MacRae and R. McL. Wilson with D. M. Parrott, 'The Gospel of Mary (BG. 8502, 1)', in J. M. Robinson (ed.), *The Nag Hammadi Library in English* (Leiden, [3]1988), 523–7.

Hennecke[3], i. 340–5.

Hennecke[5], i. 301–5.

German

Hennecke[3], i. 250–5 (H.-C. Puech).

Hennecke[5], i. 313–16 (H.-C. Puech and B. Blatz).

Italian

Moraldi i. 453–8; [2] i. 523–7.

GENERAL

D. Lührmann, *Die apokryph gewordenen Evangelien* (Leiden, 2004), 105–24 (= *Supplements* to *Novum Testumentum* 112).

M. Tardieu and J. D. Dubois, *Introduction à la littérature gnostique*, i (Paris, 1986), 102–7 (general on Mary Magdalene).

Klauck, 207–18: ET 160–8.

Lührmann, 62–71.

Gospels of the Ministry and Passion

Included in this section are translations of:
  The Gospel of Thomas
  The 'Secret' Gospel of Mark
  The Gospel of Peter
and summaries of:
  The Gospel of Gamaliel
  Coptic Narratives of the Ministry and Passion

■

The Gospel of Thomas

In this section the arrangement is:

Introduction
  1. Coptic Thomas
  2. The Greek Fragments (P. Oxy. 1, 654, 655)
  3. Table: New Testament Parallels to the Gospel of Thomas
Translation (in which the passages occurring both in Coptic Thomas and in the Oxyrhynchus papyri are printed in parallel columns)

1. COPTIC THOMAS

Of all the apocryphal gospels this is the one that has probably received greatest attention in recent years.

This Coptic gospel was found among the codices in the so-called Gnostic library discovered at Nag Hammadi in 1945–6. The story of the finding and subsequent publication of this library is told by J. M. Robinson in the introduction to the English translation of these texts, *The Nag Hammadi Library* (Leiden, 1977, ³1988). This 'Gnostic' Gospel of Thomas received great publicity because of its sometimes close links with the canonical Gospels: modern synopses of the Gospels often include the parallels to

Thomas. A list of parallels precedes the translation below. The general public was alerted to the book by R. M. Grant and D. N. Freedman, *The Secret Sayings of Jesus* (London, 1960). In Britain, the *Sunday Times*, 15 and 22 November 1959, announced the discovery and published a translation of the sayings. A vast secondary literature has developed and a sample of the most significant is given in the bibliography below.

Ancient testimony about a 'Gospel of Thomas' includes Origen, *Hom 1 on Luke* (Rauer, p. 5) and Cyril of Jerusalem, *Catecheses* 4. 36 (*PG* 33. 500) and 6. 31 (*PG* 33. 593). The Gelasian Decree and the Stichometry of Nicephorus also refer to a Gospel of Thomas, but in none of these cases is it certain whether Coptic Thomas (or even the Infancy Gospel of Thomas (*q.v.*)) is intended. One indubitable testimonium to Coptic Thomas is Hippolytus, *Haer.* 5. 7. 20 (Wendland, p. 83). The date of Thomas is likely to be mid-second-century, although earlier dates have been proposed, and its provenance possibly Edessa: links with the Syriac Acts of Thomas are suggestive.

The Gospel is made up of 114 sayings (logia) mainly by Jesus. The existence of such a document has invited comparison with the contents of the hypothetical synoptic source Q, which is also a 'sayings source', and has helped to disprove the objection sometimes raised against Q that there is no evidence in early Christian literature of a document consisting only of sayings.

The possibility that at least some of the unique sayings of Jesus preserved in Coptic Thomas may ultimately go back to Jesus is generally conceded. The probability that where there are synoptic parallels the version in Thomas may preserve an earlier witness is less widely accepted; an influential group of scholars (e.g. Quispel, Koester, Crossan, Cameron, and others) would wish to argue that the Greek *Vorlage* of the Coptic version may well be independent of the synoptic Gospels.

The asceticism and Gnosticism of many of the sayings in Thomas are generally recognized as suggesting a Gnostic origin for the collection, but in so far as the sayings are likely to have come from the oral traditions of orthodox Christianity (if such a term is not an anachronism in the second century) it is not surprising that the character of the total is not entirely consistent. Although many of the sayings have a Gnosticizing tendency, the practical spirituality taught is not one that would have been untenable in catholic Christianity. A. J. B. Higgins (Bibliography below, under General) sets out the non-Gnostic sayings in Thomas.

Gilles Quispel has written extensively on Thomas: Charlesworth's bibliography lists thirty-five titles by him on this apocryphon (see also Scholer's bibliography). Some of his articles are concerned with links between Thomas and other sources, for example the Western Text, the Pseudo-Clementine literature, and the Diatessaron ('L'Évangile selon Thomas et les Clémentines', *VC* 12 (1958), 181–96; 'L'Évangile selon Thomas et le Diatessaron', *VC* 13 (1959), 87–113; 'L'Évangile selon Thomas et le "Texte Occidentale" du

Nouveau Testament', *VC* 14 (1960), 204–15). As van den Broek writes of Quispel in the introduction to the Quispel Festschrift,[1] p. viii, 'He defended from the beginning a two-fold thesis: (*a*) the Gospel of Thomas is essentially not a Gnostic but an encratite writing, and (*b*) it contains clear elements of an extra-canonical Jewish-Christian Gospel tradition.'

It is generally agreed that the original language of Coptic Thomas was Greek. The Oxyrhynchus Papyri 1, 654, and 655 preserve fragments of a Greek text that agrees closely with, but is not identical to, Coptic Thomas. For introductory notes on these papyri see below.

The translation of Coptic Thomas has been based on the edition by Bentley Layton in *Nag Hammadi Studies* 20.

The literature on Thomas is vast. The fullest bibliographic sources are D. M. Scholer, *Nag Hammadi Bibliography 1948–1969* (Leiden, 1971) (= *Nag Hammadi Studies* 1) and regular supplements in *Novum Testamentum*. Cf. also E. Haenchen, 'Literatur zum Thomasevangelium', *ThR* 27 (1961), 147–78, 306–38.

EDITIONS

P. Labib, *Coptic Gnostic Papyri in the Coptic Museum at Old Cairo*, i (Cairo, 1956) (plates 80, 10–99, 28). [Photographic edition.]

A. Guillaumont, H.-C. Puech, G. Quispel, W. Till, Yassah ʿAbd al Masih, *The Gospel According to Thomas* (London and Leiden, 1959) (with English trans.).[2] [*Editio princeps*.]

MODERN TRANSLATIONS

English

W. R. Schoedel, in R. M. Grant and D. N. Freedman, *The Secret Sayings of Jesus* (London, 1960), 112–86.

H. Koester and T. O. Lambdin, 'The Gospel of Thomas (II.2)', in J. M. Robinson (ed.), *The Nag Hammadi Library in English* (Leiden, 1977), 117–30.

B. M. Metzger, in Aland, *Synopsis*[13], 517–30.

D. R. Cartlidge, in D. R. Cartlidge and D. L. Dungan, 25–35.

Hennecke[3], i. 278–307, 511–22.

Hennecke[5], i. 110–34.

B. Layton, *The Gnostic Scriptures* (London, 1987), 376–99.

—— (ed.), *Nag Hammadi Codex II, 2–7, together with XIII, 2*, Brit. Lib. Or 4926(1) and P. Oxy 1, 654, 655*, i (Leiden, New York, Copenhagen, Cologne, 1989) (= *Nag Hammadi Studies* 20), 38–128 (Introduction by H. Koester, 38–49; Coptic text ed. B. Layton and English translation by T. O. Lambdin, 52–93). [For Appendix by H. W. Attridge on the Greek fragments, see below.]

---

[1] R. van den Broek and M. J. Vermaseren, *Studies in Gnosticism and Hellenistic Religions: Presented to Gilles Quispel on the Occasion of his Sixty-fifth Birthday* (Leiden, 1981) (= *Études préliminaires aux religions orientales dans l'Empire Romain* 91).

[2] French, German, and Castilian Spanish translations have also been published.

French

J. Doresse, *L'Évangile selon Thomas* (Paris, 1959).
R. Kasser, *L'Évangile selon Thomas* (Neuchâtel, 1961) (with Greek retroversion).
J.-É. Ménard, *L'Évangile selon Thomas* (Leiden, 1975) (= *Nag Hammadi Studies* 5).
Éac, 25-53.

German

J. Leipoldt, *Das Evangelium nach Thomas, Koptisch und Deutsch* (Berlin, 1967) (= *TU* 101).
E. Haenchen, in Aland, *Synopsis*[13], 517-30. [These pages also contain an Engl. trans. by B. M. Metzger and a Latin trans. by G. Garitte.]
Hennecke[3], i. 199-223 (H.-C. Puech).
Hennecke[5], i. 93-113 (B. Blatz). [Full German trans.]

Italian

Bonaccorsi, i. 30f.
Erbetta, i.1, 253-82.
Moraldi, i. 475-501; [2] i. 547-72.

Spanish

de Santos Otero ([6]1988), 678-705.

GENERAL

W. Michaelis, *Das Thomas-Evangelium* (Stuttgart, 1960) (= *Calwer Hefte* 34).
A. J. B. Higgins, 'The non-Gnostic Sayings in the Gospel of Thomas', *Nov T* 4 (1960), 292-306 (repr. in *The Tradition about Jesus: Three Studies* (Edinburgh, 1969), 30-47 (= *SJT Occasional Papers* 15)).
R. McL. Wilson, *Studies in the Gospel of Thomas* (London, 1960), cf. id., 'The Gospel of Thomas', in F. L. Cross (ed.), *Studia Evangelica* iii (Berlin, 1964) 447-59 (= *TU* 88).
—— 'Thomas and the Growth of the Gospels', *HTR* 53 (1960), 231-50.
W. R. Schoedel, 'Naassene Themes in the Coptic Gospel of Thomas', *VC* 14 (1960), 225-34.
B. Gärtner, *The Theology of the Gospel of Thomas* (London, 1961).
E. Haenchen, *Die Botschaft des Thomasevengeliums* (Berlin, 1961) (= *Theologische Bibliothek Töpelmann* 6) (with German trans.).
H. E. W. Turner and H. Montefiore, *Thomas and the Evangelists* (London, 1962) (= *Studies in Biblical Theology* 35).
G. C. Stead, 'Some Reflections on the Gospel of Thomas', in F. L. Cross (ed.), *Studia Evangelica* iii (Berlin, 1964) 390-402 (= *TU* 88).
M. Marcovich, 'Textual Criticism on the Gospel of Thomas', *JTS* 20 (1969), 53-74.
G. Quispel, *Gnostic Studies* (Istanbul, i, 1974; ii, 1975) (= *Uitgaven van het Nederlands historisch-archaeologisch instituut te Ishtanbul* 34).

E. Pagels, *The Gnostic Gospels* (New York, 1979).

G. Lüdemann, 'Zur Gleichnisinterpretation im Thomasevangelium', *ZNW* 71 (1980), 214–43.

G. Quispel, 'The Gospel of Thomas Revisited', in B. Barc (ed.), *Colloque international sur les textes de Nag Hammadi* (Leuven, 1981), 218–66.

B. Dehandschutter, 'L'Évangile de Thomas comme collection de paroles de Jésus', in J. Delobel (ed.), *Logia—The Sayings of Jesus* (Leuven, 1982), 507–15 (= *BETL* 59).

M. Lelyveld, *Les logia de la vie dans l'Evangile selon Thomas: A la recherche d'une tradition et d'une redaction* (Leiden, 1987) (= *Nag Hammadi Studies* 34).

F. T. Fallon and R. Cameron, 'The Gospel of Thomas: A *Forschungsbericht* and Analysis', *ANRW* 2.25.6, 4195–4251.

R. Valantasis, *The Gospel of Thomas* (London and New York, 1997).

Risto Uro, *Thomas: Seeking the Historical Context of the Gospel of Thomas* (London, 2003). Klauck, 142–62.

On the relationship of Thomas and the synoptic Gospels:

J. B. Bauer, 'The Synoptic Tradition in the Gospel of Thomas', in F. L. Cross (ed.), *Studia Evangelica* iii (Berlin, 1964), 314–17 (= *TU* 88).

W. Schrage, 'Evangelienzitate in den Oxyrhynchus-Logien und im koptischen Thomas-Evangelium', in *Apophoreta: Festschrift Ernst Haenchen* (Berlin, 1964), 251–68 (= *BZNW* 30).

—— *Das Verhältnis des Thomasevangeliums zur synoptischen Tradition und zu den koptischen Evangelienübersetzungen* (Berlin, 1964) (= *BZNW* 29).[3]

J. D. Crossan, *Four Other Gospels* (Minneapolis, Chicago, New York, 1985).

B. Chilton, 'The Gospel According to Thomas as a Source of Jesus' Teaching', in D. Wenham (ed.), *The Jesus Tradition outside the Gospels* (Sheffield, 1985), 155–75 (= *Gospel Perspectives* 5).

C. L. Blomberg, 'Tradition and Redaction in the Parables of the Gospel of Thomas', in Wenham, op. cit. 177–205.

J. M. Robinson, 'On Bridging the Gulf from Q to the Gospel of Thomas (and *vice versa*)', in C. W. Hedrick and R. Hodgson Jr. (eds.), *Nag Hammadi Gnosticism and Early Christianity* (Peabody, Massachusetts, 1986), 127–75.

C. M. Tuckett, 'Thomas and the Synoptics', *NovT* 30 (1988), 132–57.

F. Neirynck, 'The Apocryphal Gospels and the Gospel of Mark', in J.-M. Sevrin (ed.), *The New Testament in Early Christianity* (Leuven, 1989), 123–75, esp. 133–40 (= *BETL* 86).

On the relationship of Thomas with the Fourth Gospel:

R. E. Brown, 'The Gospel of Thomas and St. John's Gospel', *NTS* 9 (1963), 155–77.

SYNOPSES

For parallels between the Coptic Gospel of Thomas, Oxyrhynchus Papyri 1, 654, and 655, and the canonical Gospels see Aland[13], 585–6; Huck–Greeven[13], 286; Boismard, 415; J. S. Kloppenborg, *Q Parallels* (Sonoma, Calif., 1988); and the list preceding the translation below.

---

[3] Review by R. McL. Wilson, *VC* 20 (1966), 118–23.

2. THE GREEK FRAGMENTS (P. Oxy. 1, 654, 655)

It is convenient to group these three fragments together before introducing them separately. All three were discovered by Grenfell and Hunt at the same site: P. Oxy. 1, containing sayings of Jesus, was found in 1897 and published as the "ΛΟΓΙΑ ΙΗΣΟΥ". P. Oxy. 654 has similar characteristics and is also from a sayings document: this was found in 1903 and published as 'The New Sayings of Jesus'. P. Oxy. 655, found at the same time, was somewhat different in style: it contains a longer passage and was thought to be a fragment of a lost gospel. Evelyn White and Grenfell and Hunt, considered P. Oxy. 1 and 654 together as both coming from the same book. The heading to P. Oxy 654 attributes the collection to Thomas, and obviously a connection with a Gospel of Thomas known from ancient testimony was made. But it was only with the discovery of the Coptic Gospel of Thomas at Nag Hammadi in 1945-6 that parallels to the Oxyrhynchus fragments were noted. All three Oxyrhynchus fragments in fact, and not only 1 and 654, were found to resemble certain of the logia in 'Gnostic' Thomas, and as all three Greek fragments came from three different documents of varying dates this would seem to indicate the degree of popularity of the work. This Coptic text enabled scholars, who had long debated over the various reconstructions of the Oxyrhynchus fragments, to solve many of the problems. Hofius, Fitzmyer, Puech, and Kraft all took clues from the Coptic text to reconstruct the Greek fragments. Differences between the Greek and Coptic may be seen in H. Attridge, 'The Greek Fragments', in B. Layton (ed.), *Nag Hammadi Codex II 2-7* (Leiden, 1989), 99-101 (= *Nag Hammadi Studies* 20).

The discovery of the papyri generated a vast literature, some of which has been listed in Fitzmyer's article noted below in the bibliography. Many of the earlier articles were concerned with the originality of the sayings attributed to Jesus. Although this question of authenticity is still raised, both in connection with the Oxyrhynchus fragments and some of the sayings in Thomas, since the discovery of the Coptic text more attention has been given to that of the original language of these logia. The Oxyrhynchus sayings and the Coptic sayings are obviously related although one is not a direct translation of the other. The general consensus is that Coptic Thomas was originally in Greek although in a different recension from that found in the Oxyrhynchus fragments. Many of the arguments are set out by Garittte and by Guillaumont.

Another preoccupation of many of the earlier writers on the Oxyrhynchus texts was the source of the sayings, and links were presumed to exist with some of the 'missing' gospels such as the Gospel of the Egyptians (e.g. Harnack, Taylor, Preuschen) and the Gospel of the Hebrews (e.g. Grenfell and Hunt, Lagrange, Batiffol, Evelyn White, Bartlet). Here too, as with the problems of the links between the Greek texts, the discovery of Coptic Thomas has succeeded in eliminating previous speculation. Nevertheless, it is still acknowledged that the first saying in P. Oxy. 654 is attested by Clement of Alexandria (*Strom.* 5. 14. 96 ed. O. Stählin, *GCS* 52 (15) (⁴Berlin, 1985, rev. L. Früchtel and U. Treu) p. 389) and attributed to the Gospel of the Hebrews, but this merely indicates that a floating oral tradition of sayings attributed to Jesus sometimes came to ground in more than one place. Many of the Oxyrhynchus sayings are secondary constructions or variants of sayings already familiar in the synoptic Gospels.

My translations are based on the texts as printed by de Santos Otero and checked against H. W. Attridge, 'The Greek Fragments' in B. Layton (ed.), *Nag Hammadi Codex II, 2–7*, i. 112–18.

GENERAL ON THE OXYRHYNCHUS PAPYRI[1]

Preuschen, 22–6, 151 f.

C. Bruston, *Fragments d'un ancien recueil de paroles de Jésus* (Paris, 1905), esp. 1–27.

C. Taylor, *The Oxyrhynchus Sayings of Jesus found in 1903 with the Sayings called 'Logia' found in 1897* (Oxford, 1905).

V. Bartlet, 'The Oxyrhynchus "Sayings of Jesus"', *Contemporary Review* 87 (London, New York, 1905), 116–25. [Views developed in id., 'The Oxyrhynchus "Sayings of Jesus in a new Light"', *Expositor* VIII. 23 (London, 1922), 136–59.]

C. Taylor, 'The Oxyrhynchus and other Agrapha', *JTS* 7 (1906), 546–62, esp. 546–53.

E. Jacquier, 'Les Sentences du Seigneur extracanoniques (les Agrapha)', *Rev. Bib.* 15 (1918), 93–135, esp. 110–19.

R. Dunkerley, 'The Oxyrhynchus Gospel Fragments', *HTR* 42 (1949), 19–27.

R. M. Grant and D. N. Freedman, *The Secret Sayings of Jesus* (London, 1960), 44–51.

J. Jeremias, *Unknown Sayings of Jesus* (London, ²1964). [Treats the sayings in the wider context of the agrapha.]

An important study is:

J. A. Fitzmyer, 'The Oxyrhynchus *Logoi* of Jesus and the Coptic Gospel According to Thomas', *Theological Studies* 20 (1959), 505–60 (a major reconstruction of the Oxyrhynchus logoi based on the parallels in Coptic in 'Gnostic' Thomas, with a fairly complete bibliography in rough alphabetical order) repr. J. A. Fitzmyer, *Essays on the Semitic Background of the New Testament* (London, 1971), 355–433).

Prior to Fitzmyer's study, and antedating the discovery of Coptic Thomas, a major publication on the papyri is:

H. G. Evelyn White, *The Sayings of Jesus from Oxyrhynchus* (Cambridge, 1920). [Edits P. Oxy. 1 and 654 with his own reconstructions.][2]

Texts reproduced in:

C. Wessely, 'Fragments de collections de prétendues sentences de Jésus', in *Les plus anciens monuments du Christianisme écrits sur papyrus* (Paris, 1908), 151–72 (= *PO* 4).

---

[1] References to older literature may be found in B. Pick, *Paralipomena* (Chicago, 1908), 135–42.
[2] Review *JTS* 23 (1922), 293–300 (V. Bartlet).

Klostermann, *Apocrypha*, ii. (2)16–21 (with reconstructions of P. Oxy. 654 according to Grenfell and Hunt, Swete, Deissmann).

Lührmann, 106–31.

D. Lührmann, *Die apokryph gewordenen Evangelien* (Leiden, 2004), 144–181 (= *Supplements* to *Novum Testamentum* 112).

On the original language of the Oxyrhynchus fragments and of Thomas see:

G. Garitte, 'Les "Logoi" d'Oxyrhynque et l'apocryphe copte dit "Évangile de Thomas" ', *Le Muséon* 73 (1960), 151–72, 219–22; id., 'Les "Logoi" d'Oxyrhynque sont traduits du copte', ibid. 335–49.

A. Guillaumont, 'Les Logia d'Oxyrhynchos sont-ils traduits du copte?', *Le Muséon* 73 (1960), 325–33.

Reconstructions of the Oxyrhynchus Papyri in the light of the Gospel of Thomas may be seen in:

O. Hofius, 'Das koptische Thomasevangelium und die Oxyrhynchus-Papyri Nr. 1, 654 und 655', *Evangelische Theologie* 20 (1960), 21–42, 189–92.

Hennecke[3], i. 199–223 (H.-C. Puech) and 61–72 (W. Schneemelcher and J. Jeremias).

Hennecke[5], i. 98–100, 103–6 (B. Blatz).

Hennecke[3] (English), i. 278–307 and 97–113.

Hennecke[5] (English), i. 117–18 and 121–3.

The original identification of the Oxyrhynchus Papyri and Thomas is in H.-C. Puech, 'Un logion de Jésus sur bandelette funéraire', *Bulletin de la société E. Renan* 3 (Paris, 1954), 126–9. [This is acknowledged by G. Garitte, *Le Muséon* 70 (1957), 59–73.]

(a) P. Oxy. 1. 'Sayings of Jesus'

This papyrus leaf is dated c.200 and is part of a codex.

Editio princeps:

B. P. Grenfell and A. S. Hunt, ΛΟΓΙΑ ΙΗΣΟΥ: *Sayings of Our Lord from an Early Greek Papyrus* (London and New York, 1897);[1] cf. id., *OP* 1 (London, 1898), 1–3.

Early reactions may be seen in:

W. Lock and W. Sanday, *Two Lectures on the Sayings of Jesus recently discovered at Oxyrhynchus* (Oxford, 1897). [The Bibliography (p. 5) gives references to early reaction to the discovery of P. Oxy. 1.]

P. Batiffol, 'Les logia du papyrus de Behnesa', *Rev. Bib.* 6 (1897), 501–15.

C. Taylor, *The Oxyrhynchus Logia and the Apocryphal Gospels* (Oxford, 1899).

A. von Scholz, 'Zu den Logia Jesus', *ThQ* 82 (1900), 1–22.

Among attempted reconstructions of parts of P. Oxy. 1:

R. Reitzenstein, 'Ein Zitat aus den ΛΟΓΙΑ ΙΗΣΟΥ', *ZNW* 6 (1905), 203.

---

[1] Review by G. Heinrici, *ThLitZ* 22 (1897), cols. 449–55.

The Gospel of Thomas

MODERN TRANSLATIONS
(In addition to references given under 'GENERAL', above)

English

James, 26–8.

Italian

Bonaccorsi, i. 52–7.
Erbetta, i.1, 100–1.
Moraldi, i. 442–3; [2] i. 512–4.
Cravieri, 477–507.

Spanish

de Santos Otero, 87–91.

(*b*) P. Oxy. 654. 'New Sayings of Jesus'

This is a piece of a papyrus roll and is of the third century. The text appears on the back of a survey list of various pieces of land. There is an introductory title and five separate sayings. Before the connection with the Coptic Gospel of Thomas was known, those who published P. Oxy. 654 and P. Oxy. 1 together generally placed the sayings in 1 in a numerical sequence following those in 654 (hence the first saying in P. Oxy. 1 is often numbered Logion 6).

Editio princeps:

B. H. Grenfell and A. S. Hunt, *New Sayings of Jesus and Fragment of a Lost Gospel* (London, 1904); cf. id., *OP* 4 (London, 1904), 1–22.[1]

Early reactions may be seen in:

P. Batiffol, 'Nouveaux fragments évangéliques de Behnesa', *Rev. Bib.* NS. 1 (1904), 481–93 (incl. P. Oxy. 655).
H. B. Swete, 'The New Oxyrhynchus Sayings', *ExpT* 15 (1904), 488–95.
A. Deissmann, *Light from the Ancient East* (Eng. trans. by L. R. M. Strachan), Appendix II: 'On the text of the Second Logia Fragments from Oxyrhynchus'.

Among attempted reconstructions of P. Oxy. 654:

H. G. Evelyn White, 'The Fourth Oxyrhynchus Saying', *JTS* 14 (1912–13), 400–3.
—— 'The Second Oxyrhynchus Saying', *JTS* 16 (1915), 246–50.
—— 'The Introduction to the Oxyrhynchus Sayings', *JTS* 13 (1912), 74–6.
W. Schubart, 'Das zweite Logion Oxyrhynchus Pap IV 654', *ZNW* 20 (1921), 215–23.
M.-J. Lagrange, 'Une des paroles attribuées à Jésus', *Rev. Bib.* 30 (1921), 233–7.
—— 'La seconde parole d'Oxyrhynque', *Rev. Bib.* 31 (1922), 427–33.

---

[1] Reviews: *ZWT* 48 (1904–5), 343–53; cf. ibid. 47 (1904), 414–18, 567–73 (A. Hilgenfeld).

MODERN TRANSLATIONS
(In addition to references given under 'GENERAL', above)

English

James, 26.

Italian

Bonaccorsi, i, pp. xix–xx, 48–53.
Erbetta, i.1, 99–100.
Moraldi, i. 440–1; [2] i. 510–12.

Spanish

de Santos Otero, 91–5.

(c) P. Oxy. 655. 'Fragment of a Lost Gospel'

The eight pieces that make up this mutilated text all come from a papyrus scroll. Two pieces are now lost, and two have too little text to be identified. There have been various attempts at reconstructing the text, and links with Coptic Thomas 36–40 have been helpful guides. Usually P. Oxy. 655 is dated second–third century.

Editio princeps:

B. P. Grenfell and A. S. Hunt, *New Sayings of Jesus and Fragment of a Lost Gospel* (London, 1904); cf. id., *OP* 4 (London, 1904), 22–8.

Among attempted reconstructions of parts of P. Oxy. 655:

T. C. Skeat, 'The Lilies of the Field', *ZNW* 37 (1938), 211–14.
R. A. Kraft, 'Oxyrhynchus Papyrus 655 Reconsidered', *HTR* 54 (1961), 253–62.
T. F. Glasson, 'Carding and Spinning: Oxyrhynchus Papyrus No. 655', *JTS* 13 (1962), 31–2.
R. H. Gundry, 'Spinning the Lilies and Unravelling the Ravens. An Alternative Reading of Q12. 22b–31 and P. Oxy 655', *NTS* 48 (2002), 159–80.

MODERN TRANSLATIONS
(In addition to references given under 'GENERAL', above)

English

James, 28–9.

Italian

Bonaccorsi, i. 34–6.
Erbetta, i.1, 101–2.
Moraldi, i. 435–6; [2] i. 505–6.

Spanish

de Santos Otero, 76-8.

3. NEW TESTAMENT PARALLELS TO THE GOSPEL OF THOMAS[1]

GTh	Matthew	Mark	Luke	Other
1	—	—	—	John 8: 52
2	(7: 7-8)	—	(11: 9-10)	—
3	—	—	(17: 20-21)	—
4a	(11: 25)	—	(10: 21)	—
4b	19: 30; 20: 16	10: 31	13: 30	—
5	10: 26	4: 22	8: 17; 12: 2	—
6a	6: 1-8, 16-18	—	—	—
6b	10: 26	4: 22	8: 17; 12: 2	—
8	13: 47-50	—	—	—
9	13: 3-9	4: 3-9	8: 5-8	—
10	—	—	12: 49	—
11a	(24: 35)	(13: 31)	(21: 33)	—
12a	(18: 1)	(9: 34)	(9: 46)	—
13	16: 13-17	8: 27-30	9: 18-21	—
14a	6: 1-8, 16-18	—	—	—
14b	(10: 8)	—	10: 8-9	—
14c	15: 11, 17-18	7: 15, 18, 20	—	—
16a	10: 34a	—	12: 51a	—
16b	10: 34b	—	12: 51b	—
16c	—	—	12: 52	—
16d	10: 35	—	12: 53	—
17	—	—	—	1 Cor 2: 9
20	13: 31-32	4: 30-32	13: 18-19	—
21b	24: 43-44	—	12: 39-40	—
21c	—	—	12: 35	—
21d	—	4: 26-29	—	—
21e	13: 9	4: 9	8: 8	—
22a	19: 13-15 (18: 1-3)	10: 13-16 (9: 33-36)	18: 15-17 (9: 46-47)	—
24	6: 22-23	4: 21	11: 34-35	—
25	22: 39	12: 31	10: 27	—
26	7: 3-5	—	6: 41-42	—
30	18: 20	—	—	—
31	13: 57 (13: 58)	6: 4 (6: 5)	4: 24	John 4: 44

---

[1] See also Aland[13], Huck-Greeven[13], Boismard, and J. S. Kloppenborg, *Q Parallels* (Sonoma, Calif., 1988).

Gospels of the Ministry and Passion

GTh	Matthew	Mark	Luke	Other
32	5: 14	—	—	—
33a	10: 27	—	12: 3	—
33b	5: 15	4: 21	8: 16; 11: 33	—
34	15: 14	—	6: 39	—
35	12: 29	3: 27	11: 21–22	—
36	6: 25	—	12: 22	—
37	(16: 16)	—	—	—
38	(13: 16–17)	—	(10: 23–24; 17: 22)	John 7: 34–6
39a	23: 13	—	11: 52	—
39b	10: 16b	—	—	—
40	15: 13	—	—	—
41	13: 12; 25: 29	4: 25	8: 18; 19: 26	—
43	(7: 16a, 18; 12: 33)	—	(6: 43)	—
44	12: 31–32	3: 28–29	12: 10	—
45a	7: 16b	—	6: 44	—
45b	12: 35	—	6: 45a	—
45c	12: 34	—	6: 45b	—
46a	11: 11a	—	7: 28	—
46b	11: 11b; 18: 3	10: 15	7: 28b; 18: 17	—
47b	6: 24	—	16: 13	—
47c	—	—	5: 39	—
47d	9: 17	2: 22	5: 37	—
47e	9: 16	2: 21	5: 36	—
48	21: 21; 17: 20	11: 22–23	(17: 6)	—
54	5: 3	—	6: 20	—
55a	10: 37	—	14: 26	—
55b	10: 38; 16: 24	8: 34	14: 27; 9: 23	—
57	13: 24–30	—	—	—
59	—	—	—	John 7: 34; 8: 21; 13: 33
61a	(24: 40)	—	17: 34	—
61b	11: 27a	—	10: 22a	—
62a	13: 11	4: 11	8: 10	—
62b	6: 3	—	—	—
63	—	—	12: 16–21	—
64	22: 1–10	—	14: 15–24	—
65	21: 33–39	12: 1–8	20: 9–15	—
66	21: 42	12: 10	20: 17	—
67	16: 26	8: 36	9: 25	—
68	5: 11	—	6: 22	—
69a	5: 10–11	—	—	—
69b	5: 6	—	6: 21	—

GTh	Matthew	Mark	Luke	Other
71	26: 61	14: 58	—	John 2: 19
72	—	—	12: 13–14	—
73	9: 37–38	—	10: 2	—
76a	13: 44–46	—	—	—
76b	6: 20	—	12: 33	—
78	11: 7–8	—	7: 24–25	—
79a	—	—	11: 27–28	—
79b	(24: 19)	(13: 17)	23: 29 (21: 23)	—
82	—	(12: 34)	—	—
86	8: 20	—	9: 58	—
89	23: 25–26	—	11: 39–40	—
90	11: 28–30	—	—	—
91	16: 1–3	—	12: 56	—
92	7: 7	—	11: 9	—
93	7: 6	—	—	—
94	7: 8	—	11: 10	—
95	(5: 42)	—	6: 34–35	—
96	13: 33	—	13: 20–21	—
99	12: 47, 49	3: 32, 34	8: 20–21	—
100	22: 16–21	12: 14–17	20: 21–25	—
101a	10: 37	—	14: 26	—
102	23: 13	—	(11: 52)	—
103	24: 43	—	12: 37–39	—
104	9: 14–15	2: 18–20	5: 33–35	—
106	21: 21	11: 23	—	—
107	18: 12–13	—	15: 4–6	—
108	—	—	—	John 7: 37
109	13: 44	—	—	—
113	—	—	17: 20–21	—

THE GOSPEL OF THOMAS

Coptic
These are the secret words which the living Jesus spoke and Didymus Judas Thomas wrote down.
1. And he said, 'He who finds the interpretation of these sayings will not taste death.'
2. Jesus said, 'Let him who seeks

P. Oxy. 654
These are the [secret] words which... the living Jesus spoke and... and Thomas and spoke...
1. ... these words... shall not taste [death].   [Lines 1–4]
2. Let him who is seeking not

not cease in his seeking until he finds and, when he finds, he will be troubled. When he is troubled he will marvel and he will reign over the All.'

3. Jesus said, 'If those who lead you say to you, "Lo, the kingdom is in heaven", the birds of heaven will precede you. If they say to you, "It is in the sea", then the fish will precede you. Rather, the kingdom is within you and outside you. When you know yourselves, then you will be known, and you will know that you are sons of the living Father. But if you do not know yourselves, then you are in poverty and you yourselves are the poverty.'

4. Jesus said, 'The man advanced in days will not hesitate to ask an infant of seven days about the place of life, and he shall live. For many who are first will be last and they will become a single one.'

5. Jesus said, 'Recognize what is in front of your face and what is concealed from you will be revealed to you. For there is nothing hidden which will not be disclosed.'

6. His disciples asked him, 'Do you want us to fast? How shall we pray, and shall we give alms, and what diet shall we keep?' Jesus said, 'Do not lie and do not do what you hate, because all things are revealed in the sight of Heaven. For nothing is hidden that shall not be revealed, and nothing is covered that shall remain without being uncovered.'

7. Jesus said, 'Blessed is the lion which the man shall eat, so that the lion will become man; and cursed is the man whom the lion shall eat, and the lion will become man.'

cease...has found and when he has found...having been amazed, he will reign and...shall rest.
[Lines 5-9]

3. ...says Jesus...who lead us... the kingdom in heaven...the birds of the heaven...what is under the earth...the fish of the sea... you. And the kingdom...is inside you...knows will find this...you will know yourselves...you are of the Father of the...you know yourselves...and you are the poverty. [Lines 9-21]

4. [Jesus says] a man will not hesitate...to ask a [child]...about the place of...then many who are first will be...the last first and...
[Lines 21-7]

5. Jesus says...before your eye and...from you will be revealed... is hidden that will not be manifest and buried that will not be...
[Lines 27-31]

6. ...ask him...say, 'How shall we fast...pray and...and what shall we observe...Jesus says... do not do what you...truth... hidden...

7. ...blessed is... [Line 40]

Coptic

8. And he said, 'Man is like a wise fisherman who cast his net into the sea. He drew it out of the sea full of small fish. The wise fisherman found among them a large, good fish. He threw all the small fish back into the sea and chose the large fish without hesitation. He who has ears to hear, let him hear.'

9. Jesus said, 'Behold, the sower went out; he filled his hand, he sowed. Some seeds fell on the road. The birds came and gathered them up. Others fell on the rock and did not take root in the earth and did not produce ears up to heaven. Others fell among thorns. They choked the seed and the worm ate them. But others fell on good ground and it brought forth good fruit to heaven. These yielded sixty per measure and one hundred and twenty measures.'

10. Jesus said, 'I have cast fire on the world and, behold, I guard it until it blazes.'

11. Jesus said, 'This heaven will pass away and that which is above it will pass away, and the dead are not alive and the living will not die. In the days when you ate what is dead you made it alive; when you come into the light what will you do? On the day when you were one you became two. But when you have become two what will you do?'

12. The disciples said to Jesus, 'We know that you will go away from us; who will be our leader?' Jesus said, 'Wherever you are, go to James the just; heaven and earth came into being for him.'

13. Jesus said to his disciples, 'Compare me to someone and tell whom I am like.' Simon Peter said to him, 'You are like a righteous angel.' Matthew said to him, 'You are like a wise philosopher.' Thomas said to him, 'Master, my mouth is incapable of saying whom you are like.' Jesus said, 'I am not your master. Because you drank, you are drunk from the bubbling spring which I measured out.' And he took him and drew him aside and spoke three words to him. When Thomas returned to his companions they asked him, 'What did Jesus say to you?' Thomas said to them, 'If I tell you one of the words which he spoke to me, you will pick up stones and throw them at me. And fire will come from the stones and burn you up.'

14. Jesus said to them, 'If you fast, you will bring sin upon yourselves and, if you pray, you will condemn yourselves, and, if you give alms, you will do evil to your spirits. And when you enter any land and travel through the regions, if they receive you, eat whatever they set before you. Heal the sick among them. For that which enters your mouth will not defile you but that which comes out of your mouth is what will defile you.'

15. Jesus said, 'When you see him who was not born of woman, prostrate yourselves on your faces and worship him: that one is your father.'

16. Jesus said, 'Men might think that it is peace that I have come to impose on the world but they do not know that it is dissension I have come to cast on the earth: fire, sword, war. For there shall be five in a house: three shall be against two and two against three, the father against the son and the son against the father, and they shall stand as solitaries.'

17. Jesus said, 'I shall give you what no eye has seen and what no ear has heard and no hand has touched and what has not come into the heart of man.'

18. The disciples said to Jesus, 'Tell us in which way our end will occur.' Jesus said, 'Have you indeed discovered the beginning, that you search for the end? In the place where the beginning is, there the end will be. Blessed is he who will stand at the beginning: he will know the end and he will not taste death.'

19. Jesus said, 'Blessed is he who existed before he was created. If you become my disciples and you hear my words, these stones shall serve you. For you have five trees in paradise which do not move in summer or winter and their leaves do not fall. Whoever knows them shall not taste death.'

20. The disciples said to Jesus, 'Tell us, what is the Kingdom of Heaven like?' He said to them, 'It is like a grain of mustard seed, smaller than all seeds. But when it falls on cultivated ground the soil puts forth a large branch and provides a shelter for the birds of heaven.'

21. Mary said to Jesus, 'Whom are your disciples like?' He said, 'They are like little children dwelling in a field that is not theirs. When the owners of the field come, they will say, "Let us have our field." They strip naked before them and leave their field to them and give it back to them. Therefore I say, if the householder knows that the thief is coming he will keep awake before he comes and will not let him break into his house of his estate and carry away his goods. But you must keep watch against the world; arm yourselves with great power lest the robbers find a way to come upon you, because the difficulty you expect will materialize. Let there be a man of understanding among you. After the crop ripened he came quickly, his sickle in his hand and he reaped it. He who has ears to hear, let him hear.'

22. Jesus saw some infants being suckled. He said to his disciples, 'These children who are being suckled are like those who enter the kingdom.' They said to him, 'If we are children shall we enter the kingdom?' Jesus said to them, 'When you make the two one, and when you make the inner as the outer and the outer as the inner and the upper as the lower, and when you make the male and the female into a single one, so that the male is not male and the female not female, when you make eyes in place of an eye, and a hand in place of a hand, and a foot in place of a foot, an image in place of an image, then you shall enter the kingdom.'

23. Jesus said, 'I shall choose you, one from a thousand, and two from ten thousand, and they shall stand as a single one.'

24. His disciples said, 'Show us the place where you are, for we must seek it.' He said to them, 'He who has ears to hear let him hear. There is light within a man of light and it illuminates the whole world. When it does not shine, there is darkness.'[1]

---

[1] P. Oxy. 655, fragment d, contains part of this saying. Only the words 'light' and 'world' are clear.

25. Jesus said, 'Love your brother as your soul; guard him like the apple of your eye.'

Coptic

26. Jesus said, 'The splinter that is in your brother's eye you see but the plank in your own eye you do not see. When you have taken the plank out of your own eye, then you will see to remove the splinter from your brother's eye.'

27. [Jesus said], 'If you do not fast with respect to the world, you will not find the Kingdom; if you do not keep the Sabbath as Sabbath, you will not see the Father.'[2]

28. Jesus said, 'I stood in the midst of the world, and I appeared to them in the flesh. I found all of them drunk; I did not find any of them thirsting. And my soul was pained for the sons of men because they are blind in their heart, and they do not see that they came empty into the world; they seek to go empty out of the world. Now they are drunk. When they have shaken off their wine, then they will repent.'

29. Jesus said, 'If the flesh exists because of spirit, it is a miracle, but if spirit exists because of the body, it is a miracle of miracles. But I marvel at how this great wealth established itself in this poverty.'

30. Jesus said, 'Where there are three gods, they are gods; where there are two or one, I am with him.'

P. Oxy. 1

26. ... and you may clearly see to take out the splinter that is in the eye of your brother.
[Verso: Lines 1–4]

27. Jesus says, 'If you do not fast as regards the world, you will not find the Kingdom of God, and if you do not keep the Sabbath as a Sabbath you will not see the Father.'
[Lines 4–11]

28. Jesus says, 'I stood in the midst of the world and I was seen in the flesh by them and found all intoxicated and none among them did I find thirsting and my soul is afflicted for the sons of men because they are blind in their heart and do not see ...'.   [Lines 11–21]

29. ... the poverty.
[Recto: Line 22]

30. Jesus says, 'Wherever there are [three] they are without God and where there is one alone I say I am with him. Lift the stone and there

---

[2] See T Baarda, '"If you do not Sabbatize the Sabbath": The Sabbath as God or World in Gnostic Understanding (Ev. Thom. Log. 27),' in R. van der Broek, T. Baarda, and J. Mansfield (eds.), *Knowledge of God in the Graeco-Roman World* (Leiden, 1988), 178–201 (= *Études préliminaires aux religions orientales dans l'empire romain* 112).

31. Jesus said, 'No prophet is acceptable in his own village; a physician does not heal those who know him.'
32. Jesus said, 'A city built upon a high mountain and well-fortified cannot fall nor can it remain hidden.'
33. Jesus said, 'What you hear with your ear, preach in others' ears from your house-tops. For no one lights a lamp and puts it under a bushel nor does he put it in a hidden place, but he sets it on a lampstand so everyone who comes in and out may see its light.'
34. Jesus said, 'If a blind man leads a blind man both of them fall into a ditch.'[3]

you will find me: cleave the wood and I am there'. [Lines 23–30]
31. Jesus says, 'A prophet is not accepted in his own country neither does a physician heal those who know him.' [Lines 30–5]
32. Jesus says, 'A city which is built on the top of a high mountain and fortified cannot fall nor be hidden.' [Lines 36–41]
33. Jesus says, 'You hear in one of your ears...' [Lines 41–42]

Coptic
35. Jesus said, 'It is impossible for anyone to enter the house of the strong man and take it by force, unless he bind his hands; then he will be able to pillage his house.'

Coptic
36. Jesus said, 'Do not be anxious from morning to evening and from evening to morning about what you will wear.'

P. Oxy. 655
36. ...from early until...from evening...early neither...for you what you should eat nor about clothing...what you should wear. Much better are you than lilies which neither card nor spin. [And] having *one* clothing, ... you ... ? Who can add to your stature? He it is who will give you your cloak.

37. His disciples said, 'When will you be revealed to us and when shall we see you?' Jesus said, 'When you

37. His disciples say to him, 'When will you be revealed to us and when shall we see you?' He says,

---
[3] Cf. The Epistle of the Apostles 47 (below).

undress without being ashamed, and you take your clothes and put them under your feet like little children do and trample on them, then you will see the Son of the Living One and you will not fear.'

38. Jesus said, 'Many times have you desired to hear these words which I speak to you and you have no one else from whom to hear them. The days will come when you will seek me, and you will not find me.'

39. Jesus said, 'The Pharisees and the Scribes have received the keys of knowledge and they have hidden them. They did not enter and they did not allow those who wanted to enter to do so. But you be wise as serpents and as innocent as doves.'

'When you undress and are not ashamed...'
[Col. I, lines 1–23 (Fragment b)]

38. Fragment c contains col. II, lines 1–10. These are too fragmentary to include here, but seem to represent the equivalent of saying 38.

39. ... they have ... of the ... them they have hidden ... entered ... came in ... allowed ... be wise ... as ... guile ... doves ...
[Col. II, lines 14–23 (Fragment b)]

Coptic

40. Jesus said, 'A vine was planted without the Father, but because it did not become strong it will be uprooted and it will rot.'

41. Jesus said, 'He who has something in his hand, will receive more; and he who has nothing, even the little he has shall be taken away from him.'

42. Jesus said, 'Become passers-by.'

43. His disciples said to him, 'Who are you that you should say these things to us?' 'In what I say to you, you do not know who I am, but you have become like Jews. They love the tree but hate its fruit; they love the fruit but hate the tree.'

44. Jesus said, 'He who blasphemes against the Father will be forgiven, and he who blasphemes against the Son will be forgiven, but he who blasphemes against the Holy Spirit will not be forgiven, either on earth or in heaven.'

45. Jesus said, 'Grapes are not gathered from thorns nor figs from among thistles; they do not give fruit. A good man brings forth good from his treasure; a bad man brings forth evil from his evil treasure which is in his heart, and he speaks evil. For out of the abundance of his heart, he produces evil.'

46. Jesus said, 'From Adam to John the Baptist, among those born of women no one is greater than John the Baptist, so that his eyes...[4] But I said that

---

[4] Text uncertain.

whoever among you shall become as a child shall know the kingdom, and he will be superior to John.'

47. Jesus said, 'It is impossible for a man to mount two horses, or to draw two bows. A servant cannot serve two masters; he will honour the one and scorn the other. No one drinks vintage wine and immediately wants to drink new wine; and new wine is not put into old wine skins lest they burst, and vintage wine is not poured into new wine skins lest it spoil. No one sews an old patch on to a new garment, because there will be a tear.'

48. Jesus said, 'If two make peace with one another in the same house, they will say to the mountain, "Be moved!" and it will be moved.'

49. Jesus said, 'Blessed are the solitary and the chosen for you will find the kingdom. Because you have come from it you will go there again.'

50. Jesus said, 'If they say to you, "Where did you come from?", say to them, "We have come from the light, the place where the light came into existence alone of its own accord and revealed itself in their image." If they say to you, "Who are you?", say to them, "We are his sons and we are the chosen of the living Father." If they ask you, "What is the sign of your Father who is in you?", say to them, "It is a movement and a repose."'

51. His disciples said to him, 'On what day will the repose of the dead occur and when does the new world come?' He said to them, 'That repose you look for has come, but you have not recognized it.'

52. His disciples said to him, 'Twenty-four prophets spoke in Israel and all of them spoke in you.' He said to them, 'You have neglected the Living One in your presence and you have spoken only about the dead.'

53. His disciples said to him, 'Is circumcision profitable or not?' He said to them, 'If it were profitable, their father would beget them already circumcised from their mother. Rather true circumcision in the Spirit has become completely useful.'

54. Jesus said, 'Blessed are the poor for yours is the kingdom of heaven.'

55. Jesus said, 'He who does not hate his father and his mother cannot be my disciple and he who does not hate his brothers and his sisters and does not take up his cross as I have will not be worthy of me.'

56. Jesus said, 'He who has come to understand the world has found a corpse, and the world is not worthy of him who has found a corpse.'

57. Jesus said, 'The kingdom of the Father is like a man who had good seed. His enemy came by night; he sowed weeds among the good seed. The man did not let them pull up the weed. He said to them, "Do not do so, lest when you go to pull up the weed you pull up the wheat along with it." For on the day of the harvest the weeds will be conspicuous; they will be pulled up and burned.'

58. Jesus said, 'Blessed is the man who has laboured; he has found life.'

59. Jesus said, 'Look upon the Living One as long as you live, lest you die and seek to see him and you cannot see.'

60. They saw a Samaritan carrying a lamb as he was going to Judaea. He said to his disciples, 'Why does he carry the lamb?'[5] They said to him, 'That he may kill it and eat it.' He said to them, 'As long as it is alive he will not eat it but only if he has killed it and it has become a corpse.' They said, 'Otherwise he cannot do it.' He said to them, 'You yourselves must seek a place for repose, lest you become a corpse and be eaten.'

61. Jesus said, 'Two will be resting on a couch; one will die, the other will live.' Salome said, 'Who are you, man? You have mounted my bed and have eaten from my table.' Jesus said to her, 'I am he who derives his being from him who is undifferentiated. The things of my Father have been given to me.' (Salome said,) 'I am your disciple.' (Jesus said to her,) 'Therefore, I say, when he is united he will be filled with light, but if he is divided he will be filled with darkness.'

62. Jesus said, 'I tell my mysteries to those who are worthy of my mysteries. Let not your left hand know what your right hand does.'

63. Jesus said, 'There was a rich man who had considerable wealth. He said, "I will use my money to sow and reap and plant and fill my warehouses with fruit so that I will lack nothing." Such were his intentions. But in that night he died. He who has ears, let him hear.'

64. Jesus said, 'A man had the habit of receiving visitors and when he had prepared the banquet he sent his servant to invite the guests. He went to the first and said to him, "My master invites you." He replied, "Money is owed me by some merchants. They will come to me this evening; I must go and give them orders. I beg to be excused from the dinner." He went to another and said to him, "My master has invited you." He said to him, "I have just bought a house and am needed for a day. I have no time." He went to another and said to him, "My master invites you." He said to him, "My friend is about to be married and I have to prepare a wedding feast; I shall not be able to come. I beg to be excused from the dinner." He went to another and said to him, "My master invites you." He said to him, "I have bought a village and am on my way to collect the rent. I shall not be able to come. I beg to be excused from the dinner." The servant returned and said to his master, "Those whom you invited asked to be excused from the dinner." The master said to his servant, "Go out into the streets and bring in those whom you find so that they may dine." Buyers and merchants will not enter the places of my Father.'

65. He said, 'A good man had a vineyard. He leased it to some farmers so that they would cultivate it and he would receive the fruit from them. He sent his servant so that the tenants would give him the fruit of the vineyard. They seized his servant, beat him and almost killed him. The servant returned and told his master. His master said, "Perhaps they did not recognize him."[6] He sent another servant. The tenants beat him also. Then the master sent his

---

[5] Text uncertain.
[6] Corrected from 'he (the slave) did not recognize them'.

son. He said, "Perhaps they will respect my son." Those tenants knowing he was the heir of the vineyard seized him and killed him. He who has ears, let him hear.'

66. Jesus said, 'Show me the stone which the builders rejected. That is the cornerstone.'

67. Jesus said, 'He who knows the All but fails to know himself lacks everything.'[7]

68. Jesus said, 'Blessed are you when you are hated and persecuted, and where you have been persecuted they will find no place.'

69. Jesus said, 'Blessed are they who are persecuted in their heart; these are the ones who have truly known the Father. Blessed are those who are hungry for the belly of the needy will be filled.'

70. Jesus said, 'When you produce what is in you, what you have will save you. That which you do not have in you will kill you if you do not know it within you.'

71. Jesus said, 'I shall destroy this house and no one will be able to build it again.'

72. A man said to him, 'Tell my brothers to divide my father's possessions with me.' He said to him, 'O man, who made me a divider?' He turned to his disciples and said to them, 'I am not a divider, am I?'

73. Jesus said, 'The harvest is great but the labourers are few, so pray to the Lord to send labourers to the harvest.'

74. He said, 'Lord, there are many standing around the drinking trough, but no one in the well.'

75. Jesus said, 'Many are standing at the door but the solitary are the ones who will enter the bridal chamber.'

76. Jesus said, 'The kingdom of the Father is like a merchant who had goods and found a pearl. This merchant was wise. He sold the goods and bought the one pearl for himself. You also must seek the enduring treasure which does not perish, where no moth enters to eat, nor worm destroys.'

77. Jesus said, 'I am the light which is above everything, I am the All; the All came forth from me and the All has returned to me. Split the wood and I am there; lift up the stone and you will find me there.'

78. Jesus said, 'Why did you come out to the country? Was it to see a reed shaken by the wind or to see a man clothed in fine clothes like your kings and your great ones are? They are clothed with fine raiment and they do not know the truth.'

79. A woman in the crowd said to him, 'Blessed is the womb which bore you and the breasts which fed you.' He said to her, 'Blessed are those who have heard the word of the Father and have kept it in truth. For the days will come when you will say, "Blessed is the womb which has not conceived and the breasts that have not given suck."'

---

[7] Text corrupt.

80. Jesus said, 'He who has known the world has found the body, but he who has found the body, the world is not worthy of him.'

81. Jesus said, 'Let him who has become rich become king, and let him who has power renounce it.'

82. Jesus said, 'He who is near me is near fire but he who is far from me is far from the kingdom.'

83. Jesus said, 'The images are manifest to the man and the light in them is hidden in the image of the light of the Father. He will be revealed himself but his image is hidden by his light.'

84. Jesus said, 'When you see your likeness you rejoice. But when you see your images which came into being before you, which do not die nor are made manifest, how much will you bear?'

85. Jesus said, 'Adam came into existence from a great power and a great wealth and yet he was not worthy of you. For, if he had been worthy, he would not have tasted death.'

86. Jesus said, '[The foxes have] their earths and the birds have their nests but the Son of Man has nowhere to lay his head and rest.'

87. Jesus said, 'Wretched is the body which is dependent on a body and wretched is the soul which is dependent on them both.'

88. Jesus said, 'The angels and the prophets will come to you and they will give you that which belongs to you. You also give to them what is in your hands and say to yourselves, "On which day will they come and take what is theirs?"'

89. Jesus said, 'Why do you wash the outside of the cup? Do you not know that he who made the inside is also he who made the outside?'

90. Jesus said, 'Come to me, for my yoke is easy and my lordship is gentle and you will find your repose for yourselves.'

91. They said to him, 'Tell us who you are so that we may believe in you.' He said to them, 'You examine the face of the heavens and the earth, and yet you have not known that which is in front of your face nor do you know how to discern this present time.'

92. Jesus said, 'Seek and you will find, yet those things about which you asked me in former times I did not tell you then; now when I want to tell them you do not ask about them.'

93. (Jesus said,) 'Do not give what is holy to the dogs because they will throw it on the dung heap. Do not throw pearls to swine lest they make it . . .'[8]

94. Jesus [said,] 'He who searches, will find[9] . . . it will be opened to him.'

95. [Jesus said,] 'If you have money do not lend it out at interest, but give to those from whom you will not receive it back.'

96. Jesus [said,] 'The kingdom of the Father is like a woman who took a little leaven, (hid) it in dough and made it into large loaves. He who has ears let him hear.'

[8] Ending defective.
[9] Text defective.

97. Jesus said, 'The kingdom of the [Father] is like a woman who was carrying a jar which was full of meal. While she was walking on a long road the handle of the jar broke; the meal spilled out behind her on to the road. She did not notice it; she was unaware of the accident. When she came to her house she put the jar down and found it was empty.'

98. Jesus said, 'The kingdom of the Father is like a man who wanted to kill a powerful man. He drew the sword in his own house and he thrust it into the wall so that he would know if his hand would be strong enough. Then he killed the powerful one.'

99. The disciples said to him, 'Your brothers and your mother are standing outside.' He said to them, 'Those here who do the will of my Father are my brothers and mother; it is they who will enter the kingdom of my Father.'

100. They showed Jesus a gold coin and said to him, 'Caesar's men demand taxes from us.' He said to them, 'Give to Caesar what belongs to Caesar; give to God what belongs to God, and give to me what is mine.'

101. (Jesus said,) 'He who does not hate his [father] and his mother as I do will not be able to be my [disciple] and he who does [not] love [his father] and his mother as I do, will not be able to be my [disciple], for my mother . . . ,[10] but [my] true [mother] gave me life.'

102. Jesus said, 'Woe to them, the Pharisees, for they resemble a dog lying in the manger of oxen, for he neither eats nor lets the oxen eat.'

103. Jesus said, 'Blessed is the man who knows where the robbers will enter so that he may rise and gather his [strength] and arm himself before they invade.'

104. They said [to him], 'Come, let us pray today and let us fast.' Jesus said, 'Why? What sin have I committed or how have I been conquered? But after the bridegroom has left the bridechamber then let people fast and pray.'

105. Jesus said, 'He who knows father and mother will be called the son of a harlot.'

106. Jesus said, 'When you make the two one you shall become sons of man and when you say, "Mountain, be moved!", it will move.'

107. Jesus said, 'The kingdom is like a shepherd who had a hundred sheep. One of them, the largest, went astray. He left the ninety-nine and searched for that one until he found it. After he had laboured he said to the sheep, "I love you more than the ninety-nine."'

108. Jesus said, 'He who drinks from my mouth will be as I am, and I shall be that person, and the hidden things will be revealed to him.'

109. Jesus said, 'The kingdom is like a man who had a treasure [hidden] in his field without knowing of it. And [after] he died he left it to his [son] who also did not know: he inherited the field and sold it. The one who bought it [found] the treasure while he was ploughing. He began to lend money at interest to [whomever] he wished.'

[10] Text defective.

110. Jesus said, 'He who has found the world and becomes rich let him deny the world.'

111. Jesus said, 'The heavens and the earth will be rolled up in your presence and he who lives in the Living One will not see death.' Does not Jesus say, 'He who finds himself, of him the world is not worthy?'

112. Jesus said, 'Woe to the flesh which depends on the soul; woe to the soul which depends on the flesh.'

113. His disciples said to him, 'When will the kingdom come?' (He said,) 'It will not come when it is expected. They will not say, "Look here", or "Look there", rather the kingdom of the Father is spread out on the earth and men do not see it.'

114. Simon Peter said to them, 'Let Mary leave us, because women are not worthy of life.' Jesus said, 'Look, I shall lead her so that I will make her male in order that she also may become a living spirit, resembling you males. For every woman who makes herself male will enter the kingdom of heaven.'

The Gospel according to Thomas

The 'Secret' Gospel of Mark

The novelty value of this text and of the reporting of its find justifies the mention of it in this collection, but its antiquity and genuineness are questioned by many scholars. It was discovered by Morton Smith at Mar Saba monastery near Jerusalem in 1958 on the endpapers of a seventeenth-century book. The handwritten text dates from the eighteenth century and contains an otherwise unknown letter by Clement of Alexandria. Within the text are two citations that claim to come from a longer text of Mark than is found in manuscripts of the canonical Gospel. The main text in Marcan-style Greek tells of Jesus' raising a youth from the dead. The story has parallels with the Lazarus story of the Fourth Gospel.

TEXT AND DESCRIPTIONS

M. Smith, *Clement of Alexandria and a Secret Gospel of Mark* (Cambridge, Mass. 1973).
—— *The Secret Gospel: The Discovery and Interpretation of the Secret Gospel According to Mark* (New York, 1973).
Lührmann, 182–5.

MODERN TRANSLATIONS

English
Cameron, 67–71.
Hennecke[3], i. 106–9.

French
Éac, 57–69.

German
Hennecke[5], i. 89–92 (H. Merkel).

Italian
Erbetta, i.2, 342–3 (introduction).

GENERAL

R. E. Brown, 'The Relation of "The Secret Gospel of Mark" to the Fourth Gospel', *CBQ*, 36 (1974), 466–85.
F. F. Bruce, *The 'Secret Gospel' of Mark* (London, 1974) (= The Ethel M. Wood Lecture 1974); repr. F. F. Bruce, *The Canon of Scripture* (Glasgow, 1988), 298–315.
J. D. Crossan, Four Other Gospels (Minneapolis, 1985).

S, Levin, 'The Early History of Christianity in the Light of the "Secret Gospel" of Mark'. *ANRW* 2.25.6, 4270–92.
F Neirynck, The Apocryphal Gospels and the Gospel of Mark, in J.-M. Sevrin (ed.), *The New Testament in Early Christianity* (Leuven, 1989), 123–75, esp. 168–70, which include the text of 'Secret' Mark (= *BETL* 86).
M. W. Mever, 'The Youth in the *Secret Gospel of Mark*', in R. Cameron (ed.), *The Apocryphal Jesus and Christian Origins* (Atlanta, 1990), 129–53 (= *Semeia* 49). [Cf. response by J. D. Crossan ibid. 161–7.]
Klauck, 48–52: ET 32–5.

Citation I (follows Mark 10: 32–4):

And they came to Bethany, and there was a woman there whose brother had died. She came and prostrated herself before Jesus and said to him: 'Son of David pity me.' The disciples rebuked her, and Jesus in anger set out with her for the garden where the tomb was. Immediately a loud voice was heard from the tomb, and Jesus approached and rolled the stone away from the entrance to the tomb. And going in immediately where the young man was he stretched out his hand and raised him up, taking him by the hand. The young man looked on him and loved him, and began to beseech him that he might be with him. They came out of the tomb and went into the young man's house, for he was rich. After six days Jesus laid a charge upon him, and when evening came the young man came to him, with a linen robe thrown over his naked body; and he stayed with him that night, for Jesus was teaching him the mystery of the kingdom of God. When he departed thence, he returned to the other side of the Jordan.

Citation II (follows Mark 10: 46a):

And there was the sister of the young man whom Jesus loved and his mother and Salome; and Jesus did not receive them.

Note that the Greek text is set out in O. Stählin, *Clemens Alexandrinus* 2nd ed. by U. Treu IV *Register* part 1 (Berlin, ²1980) pp. xvii–xvm (= *GCS*).

The Gospel of Peter

Ancient testimony showing knowledge of the Gospel of Peter includes:

Origen, *on Matt.* 10. 17 (Klostermann, pp. 21, 26 ff.): a Gospel of Peter (and the Protevangelium of James) are mentioned *en passant*.

Eusebius, *HE* 6. 12 (Schwartz, *GCS* 9. 2, pp. 544–7): Serapion, bishop of Antioch *c.*190, found a church in Rhossus using an unorthodox book known as the Gospel of Peter.

Eusebius *HE* 3. 3. 2 (Schwartz, *GCS* 9. 1, pp. 188 ff.): the Gospel of Peter is named among writings not handed down among the catholic scriptures.

It was, however, only in 1886–7 that a document containing a Gospel of Peter (who is named in ch. 14 = §60) came to light during excavations in Akhmîm. This fragment was found together with fragments of Greek Enoch and the Apocalypse of Peter.[1] The manuscript is of the eighth century, but the composition of the Gospel of Peter is much earlier, as Eusebius' reference to Serapion indicates. Most scholars date its composition to the second half of the second century: Vaganay, Gardner-Smith, and Denker put it even earlier.[2] Another fragment of the same gospel has been found at Oxyrhynchus (P. Oxy. 2949) and is dated early in the third century. This shows considerable variation when compared with the Akhmîm fragment.

In many ways the Gospel of Peter can be compared with P. Egerton 2 (*q.v.*). Both betray early knowledge of the canonical Gospels but with differences that may be due to the influence of oral traditions.

One of the major questions raised in the numerous publications that followed quickly upon the first editions of the Gospel of Peter was its relationship to the canonical Gospels. Some features can easily be identified: for example, from Matthew has been taken the washing of hands, the sealing of the tomb, the bribing of the soldiers; from John the dating of the death, the crurifragium, and the appearance of the risen Jesus by the sea; from Luke the episode of the thief, and the involvement of Herod. But there are also significant differences and changes from incidents in the canonical Gospels. Although some commentators earlier this century over-estimated the dependence of Peter on the canonical tradition, few then or now would go to the other extreme and claim that this gospel represents an independent witness to

---

[1] See below for the Apocalypse of Peter.
[2] S. G. Hall, *Melito of Sardis: On Pascha* (Oxford, 1979), gives several references to the influence of the Gospel of Peter on Melito. The Gospel of Peter may also have influenced the Syriac Didascalia and Justin.

the Passion of Jesus. Crossan's views on the independence of Peter have been answered by R. E. Brown and F. Neirynck. Nowadays it is generally concluded that'this gospel is secondary to and dependent on the accounts of the passion in the canonical Gospels.

Another question that is often raised is the alleged Gnosticism or docetism in this writing. Certainly the cry from the cross, and Jesus' seeming inability to suffer pain and some other details have encouraged commentators to see Gnostic traits in the writing or to say that it was not Gnostic itself but prepared the way for fully Gnostic passion narratives.

The author's main aim seems to have been apologetic, especially in his attempts to blame the Jews and exonerate Pilate for Jesus' death. It is thoroughly anti-semitic in tone, for example attributing the crurifragium not to the fulfilment of Old Testament prophecies (as in the canonical Gospels) but to Jewish malevolence.

Gardner-Smith's verdict on this gospel (*JTS* 27 p. 260) was that '. . . "Peter" was hardly theologian enough to be a heretic: some passages may reflect heretical tendencies in his source, but "Peter" was probably unconscious of the fact'.

My translation is from the Greek as printed by Mara. The double numbering is maintained. The sixty verses originated in Harnack's edition, the fourteen chapters in J. A. Robinson's.

EDITIONS

U. Bouriant, 'Fragments du texte grec du livre d'Énoch et de quelques écrits attribués à Saint Pierre' (Paris, 1892), 137–42 (= *Mémoires publiés par les membres de la mission archéologique française au Caire*, 9.1. [*Editio princeps.*]

A. Lods, L'Évangile et l'Apocalypse de Pierre (Paris, 1893) (facsimile edition) (= *Mémoires publiés par les membres de la mission archéologique française au Caire* 9.3, 217–35).

—— *Evangelii secundum Petrum et Petri Apocalypseos quae supersunt ad fidem codicis in aegypto nuper inventi* (Paris, 1892), 2–28, 41–51. (French edition: id., *L'Évangile et l'Apocalypse de Pierre* . . . (Paris, 1893), 17–24, 44–84.)

Text reproduced in (among other places):

H. B. S. (= H. B. Swete), *The Apocryphal Gospel of Peter* (London, 1892; [2]1893).

O. von Gebhardt, *Das Evangelium und die Apokalypse des Petrus* (Leipzig, 1893) [facsimile edition].

H. von Schubert, *Das Petrusevangelium: Synoptische Tabelle nebst Übersetzung und kritischen Apparat* (Berlin, 1893) (Greek Synopsis); Eng. trans. J. Macpherson, *The Gospel of Saint Peter, Synoptical Tables, with Translation and Critical Apparatus* (Edinburgh, 1893). [Cf. H. von Schubert, *Die Composition des pseudo-petrinischen Evangelienfragments* (Berlin, 1893).]

Lührmann, 72–95.

Another synopsis in English showing the relationship of Peter with Matthew, Mark Luke and John by A. Rutherfurd is to be found in J. A. Robinson, 'The Gospel of Peter', in A. Menzies (ed.), *Ante-Nicene Christian Library* 9 (Edinburgh, 1897).

Klostermann, *Apocrypha*, i. ³3–8.
Preuschen, 15–20, 145–50.
J. Charlesworth, 'The Gospel of Peter and the Passion Narrative', *ANRW* 2.25.5, 3934–40, in id., 'New Testament Apocrypha and Pseudepigrapha', ibid. 3919–68 (Greek and English of verses 1–22).
D. Lührmann, *Die apokryph gewordenen Evangelien* (Leiden, 2004), 55–104 (= *Supplements* to *Novum Testamentum* 112).
Lührmann 72–95.
Thomas J. Kraus and Tobias Nicklas, *Die Petrusevangelium und die Petrusapokalypse* (Berlin and New York, 2004) (= *GCS* 11: *Neutestamentliche Apokryphen* 1).

Text of P. Oxy. 2949 in:

G. M. Browne *et al.*, *OP* 41 (1972), 15 f. (ed. R. A. Coles).
J. C. Treat, 'The Two Manuscript Witnesses to the Gospel of Peter', *SBL Seminar Papers* 1990) (Atlanta, 1990), 191–9 (with a reconstruction of P. Oxy. 2949).
Cf. P. Oxy. 4009 ed. D. Lührmann and P. Parsons, *OP* 60 (London, 1994) 1–5.

SYNOPSES

Aland[13], 585; Huck-Greeven[13], 285–6; Boismard, 415.

MODERN TRANSLATIONS

English

James, 90–4.
R. M. Grant and D. N. Freedman, *The Secret Sayings of Jesus* (London, 1960), 37–43.
Hennecke[3], i. 179–87.
Hennecke[5], i, 216–28.

French

C. Meunier, *L'Évangile selon Saint Pierre* (Boulogne, 1893) (with commentary).
Amiot, 137–44.
Éac, 241–54.

German

A. Harnack, *Bruchstücke des Evangeliums und der Apokalypse des Petrus* (Leipzig, ²1893) (= *TU* 9.2).
J. Walterscheid, *Das Leben Jesu nach den neutestamentlichen Apokryphen* (Düsseldorf, 1953), 39–45.
Michaelis, 45–61.
Hennecke[1], 27–33; ²59–63 (A. Stülcken); cf. *Handbuch*, 72–88.
Hennecke[3], i. 118–24 (C. Maurer).
Hennecke[5], i, 180–8 (C. Maurer and W. Schneemelcher).

Italian

Bonaccorsi, i. 16–27.
Erbetta, i.1, 137–45.
Moraldi, i. 503–17; ²i. 575–91
Cravieri, 289–98.

Spanish

González-Blanco, ii. 305–42.
de Santos Otero, 375–93.

GENERAL

J. A. Robinson and M. R. James, *The Gospel according to Peter and the Revelation of Peter* (London, ²1892), 13–33, 83–88 (Greek text).
H. B. Swete, ΕΥΑΓΓΕΛΙΟΝ ΚΑΤΑ ΠΕΤΡΟΝ: *The Akhmîm Fragment of the Apocryphal Gospel of St. Peter* (London, 1893) (trans. with notes and indices). [Trans. into English also included in J. B. Lightfoot, M. R. James, H. B. Swete, and others, *Excluded Books of the New Testament* (London, 1927), 111–17.]
J. R. Harris, *A Popular Account of the Newly-Discovered Gospel of Peter* (London, 1893).
T. Zahn, 'Das Evangelium des Petrus', *Neue Kirchliche Zeitschrift* 4 (Erlangen, 1893), 143–218, 181–218. [Reproduced in T. Zahn, *Das Evangelium des Petrus* (Leipzig, 1893).]
A. Sabatier, *L'Évangile de Pierre et les évangiles canoniques* (Paris, 1893). [Cf. H. von Soden, 'Das Petrusevangelium und die canonischen Evangelien', *ZTK* 3 (1893), 52–92.]
The Author of 'Supernatural Religion' (i.e. W. R. Cassels), *The Gospel according to Peter: A Study* (London, 1894), 1–11, 42–6, 107–33.
A. Resch, *Ausserkanonische Paralleltexte zu den Evangelien*, ii (Leipzig, 1894), 34–48 (= *TU* 10.2).
J. Macpherson, 'The Gospel of Peter', *ExpT* 5 (1894), 556–61.
J.-B. Semeria, 'L'Évangile de Pierre', *Rev. Bib.* 3 (1894), 522–60.
V. H. Stanton, 'The Gospel of Peter...', *JTS* 2 (1900), 1–25.
C. H. Turner, 'The Gospel of Peter', *JTS* 14 (1913), 161–87.
P. Gardner-Smith, 'The Gospel of Peter', *JTS* 27 (1926), 255–71.
—— 'The Date of the Gospel of Peter' ibid. 401–7.
L. Vaganay, *L'Évangile de Pierre* (Paris, ²1930) (= *Études bibliques*) (Text, French trans., commentary, and bibliography).
K. L. Schmidt, *Kanonische und apokryphe Evangelien und Apostelgeschichten* (Basle, 1944), ch. 3 (pp. 37–78): 'Die Reste des Petrusevangeliums im Rahmen der kanonischen und apokryphen Evangelien und Apostelgeschichten' (= *AThANT* 5).
E. Massaux, *Influence de l'Évangile de saint Matthieu sur la littérature chrétienne avant saint Irénée* (Louvain, 1950, ²1986) (= *BETL* 75) (pp. 358–88 deal with links between the Gospel of Peter and Matthew's Gospel).
M. G. Mara. *Évangile de Pierre* (Paris, 1973), (= *Sources chrétiennes* 201) (Text, French trans., detailed commentary, and bibliography).

J. Denker, *Die theologiegeschichtliche Stellung des Petrusevangeliums* (Berne and Frankfurt, 1975) (= *Europäische Hochschulschriften* series 23, vol. 36).

A. Fuchs, *Die griechischen Apokryphen zum Neuen Testament*, i. *Das Petrusevangelium* (Linz, 1978) (= *Studien zum Neuen Testament und seiner Umwelt* B2) (includes a concordance).

J. W. McCant, 'The Gospel of Peter: Docetism Reconsidered', *NTS* 30 (1984), 258–73.

D. F. Wright, 'Apocryphal Gospels (Pap. Egerton 2) and the Gospel of Peter', in D. Wenham (ed.), *Gospel Perspectives*, v. *The Jesus Tradition Outside the Gospels* (Sheffield, 1985), 207–32.

—— 'Apologetic and Apocalyptic: The Miraculous in the Gospel of Peter', in D. Wenham and C. Blomberg (eds.), *Gospel Perspectives*, vi. *The Miracles of Jesus* (Sheffield, 1986), 401–18.

J. D. Crossan, *Four Other Gospels* (Minneapolis, Chicago, New York, 1985), 125–81. [Answered by R. E. Brown, 'The *Gospel of Peter* and Canonical Gospel Authority', *NTS* 33 (1987), 321–43.]

D. Wright, 'Papyrus Egerton 2 (The Unknown Gospel)—Part of the Gospel of Peter?', *Second Century* 5 (1985–6), 129–50.

J. D. Crossan, *The Cross that Spoke* (San Francisco, 1988).

F. Neirynck, 'The Apocryphal Gospels and Mark', in J.-M. Sevnn (ed.). *The New Testament in Early Christianity* (Leuven, 1989), 123–75, esp. 140–57 and 171–5 (text) (= *BETL* 86).

A. J. Dewey, ' "Time to Murder and Create": Visions and Revisions in the *Gospel of Peter*', in R. Cameron (ed.). *The Apocryphal Jesus and Christian Origins* (Atlanta, 1990), 101–27 (= *Semeia* 49). [Cf. response by J. D. Crossan, ibid. 155–61.]

P. M. Head, 'On the Christology of the Gospel of Peter', *VC* 46 (1992), 209–24.

Klauck, 110–8: ET 82–8.

1. 1. . . . . But of the Jews none washed their hands,[1] neither Herod nor any of his judges. And as they would not wash Pilate stood up. 2. And then Herod the king commanded that the Lord should be taken off saying to them, 'What I have commanded you to do to him, do.'

2. 3. Now there stood there Joseph, the friend of Pilate and of the Lord, and knowing that they were about to crucify him he came to Pilate and asked for the body of the Lord for burial.[2] 4. And Pilate sent to Herod and asked for his body. 5. And Herod said, 'Brother Pilate, even if no one had asked for him we should bury him since the Sabbath is drawing on.[3] For it stands written in the law: "The sun should not set on one that has been put to death." '[4] And he delivered[5] him to the people before the first day of unleavened bread,[6] their feast.

3. 6. So they took the Lord and pushed him as they ran and said, 'Let us

---

[1] Cf. Man, 27: 24.
[2] Mark 15: 43 and parallels.
[3] Cf. Luke 23: 54.
[4] Cf. John 19: 31; Deut. 21: 22 ff.
[5] Cf. Mark 15: 15 and parallels.
[6] Cf. Mark 14: 12 and parallels.

drag the Son of God along now that we have got power over him.' 7. And they put upon him a purple robe and set him on the judgement seat and said, 'Judge righteously, O King of Israel!'[7] 8. And one of them brought a crown of thorns and put it on the Lord's head. 9. And others who stood by spat on his eyes, and others slapped him on the cheeks, others pricked him with a reed,[8] and some scourged him saying, 'With this honour let us honour the Son of God.'

4. 10. And they brought two malefactors and crucified the Lord between them.[9] But he held his peace[10] as (if) he felt no pain. 11. And when they had set up the cross they wrote: 'This is the King of Israel.'[9] 12. And having laid down his garments before him they divided them among themselves and cast lots for them.[9] 13. But one of the malefactors rebuked them saying, 'We are suffering for the deeds which we have committed, but this man, who has become the saviour of men, what wrong has he done you?'[11] 14. And they were angry with him and commanded that his legs should not be broken[12] so that he might die in torment.

5. 15. Now it was midday and darkness covered all Judaea. And they became anxious and distressed lest the sun had already set since he was still alive. It stands written for them: 'The sun should not set on one that has been murdered.'[13] 16. And one of them said, 'Give him to drink gall with vinegar.' And having mixed it they gave it to him to drink.[14] 17. And they fulfilled all things and accumulated their sins on their head.[15] 18. And many went about with lamps [and] as they supposed that it was night, they stumbled.[16] 19. And the Lord called out and cried, 'My power, O power, you have forsaken me!'[17] And having said this, he was taken up. 20. And at the same hour the veil of the temple in Jerusalem was torn in two.[18]

6. 21. And then the Jews drew the spikes[19] from the hands of the Lord and laid him on the earth. And the whole earth shook and there was great fear.[20] 22. Then the sun shone and it was found to be the ninth hour.[21] 23. And the Jews rejoiced and gave his body to Joseph that he might bury it since he had seen all the good deeds that he (Jesus) had done. 24. And he took the

---

[7] Cf. Justin, *Apol.* 1. 35; John 19: 13.
[8] Cf. Mark 14: 65; 15: 16–20.
[9] Cf. Mark 15: 24 ff. and parallels.
[10] Cf. Mark 14: 61 and parallel; 15: 5 and parallel.
[11] Cf. Luke 23: 39 ff.
[12] Cf. John 19: 31 ff.
[13] Mark 15: 33 and parallels; Amos 8: 9.
[14] Cf. Matt. 27: 34, 48 and parallel.
[15] Cf. John 19: 28, 30.
[16] Cf. John 11: 10. Von Gebhardt conjectured 'they went to bed'.
[17] Cf. Mark 15: 34 and parallel. Perhaps translate as a question 'Have you forsaken me?'
[18] Mark 15: 38 and parallel.
[19] John 20: 25, 27.
[20] Matt. 27: 51, 54.
[21] Cf. Mark 15: 33 and parallels.

Lord, washed him, wrapped him in linen,[22] and brought him into his own sepulchre, called Joseph's Garden.[23]

7. 25. Then the Jews and the elders and the priests, perceiving what great evil they had done to themselves, began to lament and to say, 'Woe on our sins, judgement has arrived and with it the end of Jerusalem.'[24] 26. But I mourned with my companions and, being wounded in heart, we hid ourselves for we were being sought after by them as if we were evil-doers and as persons who wanted to set fire to the temple. 27. Besides all these things we were fasting and sat mourning and weeping night and day until the Sabbath.[25]

8. 28. But the scribes and Pharisees and elders, being assembled and hearing that the people were murmuring and beating their breasts, said, 'If at his death these exceeding great signs happened, behold how righteous he was!'[26] 29. They were afraid and came to Pilate, entreating him and saying, (30) 'Give us soldiers that we may guard his sepulchre for three days, lest his disciples come and steal him away and the people suppose that he is risen from the dead, and do us harm.'[27] 31. And Pilate gave them Petronius the centurion with soldiers to guard the sepulchre. And with them there came elders and scribes to the sepulchre, and all who were there together rolled a large stone 32. and laid it against the door to the sepulchre to exclude the centurion and the soldiers, and they (33) put on it seven seals, pitched a tent there and kept watch.[28]

9. 34. Early in the morning, when the Sabbath dawned, there came a crowd from Jerusalem and the country round about to see the sealed sepulchre. 35. Now in the night in which the Lord's day dawned, when the soldiers were keeping guard, two by two in each watch, there was a loud voice in heaven, (36) and they saw the heavens open[29] and two men come down from there in a great brightness and draw near to the sepulchre. 37. That stone which had been laid against the entrance to the sepulchre started of itself to roll and move sidewards, and the sepulchre was opened and both young men entered.[30]

10. 38. When those soldiers saw this, they awakened the centurion and the elders, for they also were there to mount guard. 39. And while they were narrating what they had seen, they saw three men come out from the sepulchre, two of them supporting the other and a cross following them (40) and the heads of the two reaching to heaven, but that of him who was being led reached beyond the heavens. 41. And they heard a voice out of the

---

[22] Cf. Mark 15: 46 and parallels.
[23] John 19: 41.
[24] Cf. Luke 23: 48 v.l.
[25] Cf. Mark 2: 20 and parallels; 16: 10.
[26] Cf. Luke 23: 47 f.
[27] Cf. Matt. 27: 62–6.
[28] Cf. Mark 15: 46 and parallels; Matt. 27: 66.
[29] Cf. Matt. 3: 16 f. and parallels.
[30] Cf. Matt. 28: 1 f

heavens crying, 'Have you preached to those who sleep?',[31] 42. and from the cross there was heard the answer, 'Yes.'

11. 43. Therefore the men decided among themselves to go and report these things to Pilate. 44. And while they were still deliberating the heavens were again seen to open and a man descended and entered the tomb. 45. When those who were of the centurion's company saw this they hurried by night to Pilate, leaving the sepulchre which they were guarding, and reported everything that they had seen, being greatly agitated and saying, 'In truth he was (the) Son of God.'[32] 46. Pilate answered and said, 'I am clean from the blood of the Son of God; it was you who desired it.'[33] 47. Then they all came to him, beseeching him and urgently calling upon him to command the centurion and the soldiers to tell no one about the things they had seen. 48. 'For it is better for us', they said, 'to make ourselves guilty of the greatest sin before God than to fall into the hands of the people of the Jews and be stoned.'[34] 49. Pilate therefore commanded the centurion and the soldiers to say nothing.[35]

12. 50. At dawn on the Lord's day Mary Magdalene,[36] a woman disciple of the Lord—for fear of the Jews,[37] since they were inflamed with wrath—had not done at the sepulchre of the Lord what women are accustomed to do for their dead loved ones. 51. She took with her (women) friends and came to the sepulchre where he was laid. 52. And they were afraid lest the Jews should see them and said, 'Even though we could not weep and lament on that day when he was crucified, yet let us now do so at his sepulchre. 53. But who will roll away for us the stone that is across the entrance to the sepulchre, that we may go in and sit beside him and do what is due?'—(54) for the stone was great[38]—'and we fear lest any one see us. And if we cannot do so let us at least place by the entrance what we have brought as a memorial for him, and let us weep and lament until we go home.'

13. 55. But having arrived they found the sepulchre opened. And they came near, stooped down there, and saw a young man sitting in the middle of the sepulchre, comely, and clothed with a brightly shining robe. He said to them, (56) 'Why have you come? Whom do you seek? Not the man who was crucified? He is risen and gone. But if you do not believe, stoop this way and see the place where he lay for he is not there. For he is risen and is gone to the place from which he was sent.' 57. Then the women fled frightened.[39]

14. 58. Now it was the last day of unleavened bread and many went away

---

[31] Cf. 1 Pet. 3: 19.
[32] Mark 15: 39 and parallels.
[33] Cf. Matt. 27: 24.
[34] Cf. John 11: 50.
[35] With v. 47 cf. Matt. 28: 11–15.
[36] Cf. Matt. 28: 1 and parallels.
[37] Cf. John 20: 19.
[38] Cf. Mark 16: 3 f.
[39] Cf. Mark 16: 1–8.

and returned to their homes because the feast was at an end. 59. But we, the twelve disciples of the Lord, wept and mourned and each one, grieving for what had happened, returned to his own home. 60. But I, Simon Peter, and my brother Andrew took our nets and went to the sea.[40] And there was with us Levi, the son of Alphaeus, whom the Lord...

[40] Cf. John 21: 1 ff.

The Gospel of Gamaliel

No known document bears this title, and no such title is found in patristic literature. Modern scholarship is responsible for the identification. A certain confusion between a work attributed to Gamaliel and other works, including perhaps the Gospel of Bartholomew, was encouraged by the collection of Coptic fragments assembled by Revillout under the title 'Gospel of the Twelve Apostles', which Baumstark, James, and others subsequently divided into different texts; some may legitimately be read as fragments of the Gospel of Gamaliel, especially Revillout's fr. 15, actually attributed to Gamaliel, and perhaps 5, 10, 11, 13, 14 (others may be from the Gospel of Bartholomew (q.v.)). The book to which these fragments are said to have belonged was given the name 'Gospel' by Baumstark and by Ladeuze. It tells of the events of Good Friday and the days following. Some Arabic redactions have appeared and some Ethiopic fragments have come to light. The latter know this work as 'The Lament of Mary' although such a title is not appropriate to the whole of the contents as known in Ethiopic. Revillout's fragment 15 (= Lacau, no. 2) is found in the Ethiopic work. The original language is likely to have been Coptic and, according to van den Oudenrijn, could go back at least to the fifth century. The contents are orthodox and anti-Jewish in tone. The whitewashing of Pilate, revered as a saint in the Coptic church, is a dominant theme.

Only Revillout's fr. 15 is summarized here; others may be seen under 'Coptic Narratives of the Ministry and Passion' below.

P. Lacau, *Fragments d'apocryphes coptes* (Cairo, 1904) (= *Mémoires publiés par les membres de l'institut français d'archéologie orientale du Caire* 9).

E. Revillout, 'Les apocryphes coptes, i, Les Évangiles des douze apôtres et de Saint Barthélemy, in *PO* 2.2, ed. R. Graffin, (Paris, 1904; repr. 1946), 117–98.[1]

P. Ladeuze, 'Apocryphes évangeliques coptes. Pseudo-Gamaliel: Évangile de Barthélemy', *RHE* 7 (1906), 245–68.

A. Mingana, 'The Lament of the Virgin and the Martyrdom of Pilate', in *Woodbrooke Studies* 2, with introduction by J. R. Harris *BJRL* 12 (1928), 411–580 (Garshūni text with Eng. trans.).

F. Haase, 'Zur Rekonstruktion des Bartholomäusevangeliums', *ZNW* 16 (1915), 93–112. [Cf. M. A. van den Oudenrijn, *Gamaliel: Äthiopische Texte zur Pilatusliteratur* (Fribourg, 1959) (= *Spicilegium Friburgense: Texte zur Geschichte des kirchlichen Lebens* 4) (Ethiopic Lament of Mary with German trans. and commentary)].

---

[1] Reviewed by A. Baumstark, 'Les apocryphes coptes', *Rev. Bib.* NS 3 (1906), 245–65. esp. 253–9: 'Un Évangile de Gamaliel'.

M.-A. van den Oudenrijn, introduction to 'The Gospel of Gamaliel' in Hennecke[3], i. 376–8 (Eng. trans.[3], i. 508–10); Hennecke[5], i. 441–2 (Eng. trans.[5] i. 558–60).

MODERN TRANSLATIONS

English

James, 147–52 (brief summary).

Italian

Erbetta, i.2, 344–66 (from Ethiopic).
Moraldi, i. 655–82;[2] i. 777–801 (selection).

We find Pilate examining four soldiers as to their statement that the body of Jesus was stolen. One (the second: the testimony of the first is gone) says the eleven apostles took the body; the third says, Joseph and Nicodemus; the fourth, 'we were asleep.' They are imprisoned, and Pilate goes with the centurion and the priests to the tomb and finds the grave-clothes. He says, 'If the body had been stolen, these would have been taken too.' They say, 'These grave-clothes belong to some one else.' Pilate remembers the words of Jesus, 'Great wonders must happen in my tomb', and goes in, and weeps over the shroud. Then he turns to the centurion, who had but one eye, having lost the other in battle.

Here is a gap, in which no doubt the centurion's eye is healed by touching the grave-clothes, and he is converted. Also it is clear that Joseph and Nicodemus are sent for, and that the Jews point out to Pilate that in a well in the garden there is the body of a crucified man.

The other leaf begins with a dialogue between Pilate and the centurion. Then all go to the well. 'I, Gamaliel, followed them also among the band.' They see the body, and the Jews cry, 'Behold the sorcerer.'... Pilate asks Joseph and Nicodemus whether this is the body of Jesus. They answer, the grave-clothes are his, but the body is that of the thief who was crucified with him. The Jews are angry and wish to throw Joseph and Nicodemus into the well... Pilate remembers the words of Jesus, 'The dead shall rise again in my tomb', and says to the Jews, 'You believe that this is truly the Nazarene.' They say, 'Yes.' 'Then', says Pilate, 'it is but right to lay his body in his own tomb.'...

Here the leaf ends; but we can see that when the body is laid in Jesus' tomb it will revive and declare the truth.

Coptic Narratives of the Ministry and Passion

Forbes Robinson's *Coptic Apocryphal Gospels* and the fragments collected by Revillout and Lacau yield texts relating to the ministry and passion of Christ. Most are likely to have been homiletic. Some of Revillout's fragments may have belonged to the 'Gospel of Gamaliel' (*q.v.*) or to the Book of the Resurrection of Jesus Christ by Bartholomew the Apostle (*q.v.*), and these are referred to in those sections. Other summaries are given below based on the form set out by James, 147–52.

F. Robinson, *Coptic Apocryphal Gospels* (Cambridge, 1896), 162–85 (= *Texts and Studies* 4).
P. Lacau, *Fragments d'apocryphes coptes* (Cairo, 1904) (= *Mémoires publiés par les membres de l'institut français d'archéologie orientale du Caire* 9).
E. Revillout, 'Les apocryphes coptes, i. Les Évangiles des douze apôtres et de Saint Barthélemy', in *PO* 2.2, ed. R. Graffin (Paris 1904; repr. 1946), 117–98; and cf. id., 'Supplément à l'évangile des XII apôtres', in *PO* 9.2 (ed. R. Graffin and F. Nau) (Paris, 1913) pp. 133–9.

1. Robinson, p. 162. Birth and childhood of John Baptist. Birth of Christ. His star in the form of a wheel, its figure like a cross, letters on it: 'This is Jesus the Son of God'. The wise men see it and come to Herod.

2. Robinson, p. 163. The Feast at Cana. The wine has failed; the parents of the bridegroom complain to Mary, who is their sister, and ask her to approach Christ. She does so. He orders that the water-pots be filled. *We* (the servants) hastened and filled them.
This, then, belongs to a narrative written by an eyewitness.

3. Revillout, no. 1.
Herod accuses Philip to Tiberius.
Tiberius orders him to confiscate all Philip's goods.
Herod does so: Philip does not know the reason.

4. Revillout, no. 2. Robinson, p. 168.
This is one of the longest of the fragments. It begins with a passage addressed to the hearers, and quotes John the Evangelist on the feeding of the five thousand: the story is filled out with dialogue, and tells how Judas was the last to receive the bread and 'had no inheritance' in it. Thomas then says that he wishes to see the power of Christ displayed in the raising of the dead from their tombs, not only from the bier, as at Nain. Jesus replies in a long and rhetorical address of many clauses, beginning, 'Come with me, Didymus, to the tomb of Lazarus.' Then the raising of Lazarus is told, and the risen man

says that when the voice, 'Lazarus, come forth!', sounded in Amente (Hades), Adam knew it and bore witness to it.

We then hear of one Carius, a Roman officer appointed to look after the confiscated lands of Philip (see fragment 3). He came to see Jesus and reported his mighty works to Herod, saying that he ought to be made king. Herod threatened any one who consented thereto with death. Annas and Caiaphas went to Carius and accused Jesus—he is a magician, was born of fornication, breaks the sabbath, has abolished the synagogue of the Jews. Joseph and Nicodemus opposed them.

(Robinson's text ends here: Revillout's (p. 145) continues without break.)

Herod cast Joseph and Nicodemus into prison. Carius threatened the Jews with destruction if any ill befell them. Then Herod got a pound of gold from every one of the chiefs of the Jews and bribed Carius with it not to tell Tiberius. And Carius kept silence.

Joseph escaped to Arimathaea.

Carius sent the apostle John to Tiberius to tell him about Jesus, and the emperor honoured him, and wrote that Jesus should be made king: and as the Gospel says[1], 'Jesus departed to a mountain alone.'

After that he summoned the apostles; and now we have a lengthy blessing of Peter on the mountain, at the end of which Peter sees the seven heavens open, and the Trinity. All the armies of heaven and the very stones of the mountain cry out the trisagios to Peter.

5. Revillout, no. 4, Robinson, p. 176.

Jesus is comforting the apostles on the mountain. The messengers of Theophilus come to fetch him to make him king. 'My kingdom is not of this world.'

The 'authorities' of Tiberius prevailed the second time concerning Jesus, with Pilate also, to commend Jesus to make him king. Pilate advocated the plan strongly. Herod who was there abused him: 'You are a Galilaean foreign Egyptian Pontus!' There was enmity between Pilate and Herod, and Herod bribed the Roman authorities and slandered Jesus.

Jesus' address to the apostles, ending 'Let us go hence, for Herod seeks me to kill me.'

They came down from the mountain, and met the devil in the form of a fisherman with attendant demons carrying nets and hooks; and they cast their nets and hooks on the mount. The apostles questioned Jesus about this: John, Philip, and Andrew, in particular. John was sent to speak to the devil and ask him what he was catching. The devil said, 'It is not a wonder to catch fish in the waters: the wonder is in this desert, to catch fish there.' He cast his nets and caught all manner of fish (really men), some by their eyes, others by their lips, etc.

[1] John 6: 15.

(Here follows a fragment given only by Lacau, p. 108.) Jesus told John to tell the devil to cast his nets again. He did so, and a great smoke rose up, and the devil's power disappeared. John threw a stone at him and he fled, cursing. Bartholomew then asked to be permitted to see 'him whom you created to laugh at him' (Leviathan), and Jesus said that the sight was almost too terrible for human eyes; but the request was granted. A cloud—that of the Transfiguration—appeared in the heaven.

We next have a group of pieces relating to the Passion.

First we place two fragments relating to Judas and his wife.

6. Revillout no. 5.

A speaker tells how Judas used to take his ill-gotten gains home to his wife: sometimes he cheated her of them, and then she mocked him.

She counselled him to betray his master.

He listened to her as Adam did to Eve, and went and covenanted with the Jews. The prophecy was fulfilled.

He took the money to his wife.

7. Lacau, p. 34. Revillout, Appendix 1, p. 195.

Judas received the thirty pieces.

His wife was foster-mother to the child of Joseph of Arimathaea, who was seven months old. When the money was brought into the house, the child fell ill (or would not stop crying). Joseph was summoned: the child cried out, begging him to take it away 'from this evil beast, for yesterday at the ninth hour they received the price (of blood)'. Joseph took the child away.

Judas went to the priests. They arrested Jesus and took him to Pilate ... He was crowned with thorns and crucified, and said, 'Father forgive them.'

8. Revillout, no. 10. A dialogue between Christ and Pilate expanded from that in St. John.

9. Revillout, no. 11. A further piece of a similar dialogue, including long speeches of Jesus, and ending with *Ecce homo*.

The place and order of the two next is uncertain.

10. Revillout, no. 13. An address of Jesus (to Thomas) reminding him of the signs at the crucifixion, and exhorting him to touch him.

11. Revillout, no. 14. Mary (the Virgin) at the sepulchre. Jesus appears to her and addresses her, forbidding her to touch him. The scene is assimilated to that of the appearance to Mary Magdalene (as elsewhere in Coptic writings).

The Pilate Cycle

This section includes:
(a) Translations of the whole of:
 The Acts of Pilate (Tischendorf's Greek A)
 Christ's Descent into Hell (Tischendorf's Greek, Latin A and Latin B)
 Letter of Pilate to Claudius
 Letter of Pilate to Tiberius
 Paradosis Pilati
(b) Translation of selections of:
 Anaphora Pilati (Tischendorf's Greek B)
 Vindicta Salvatoris
 Mors Pilati
 The Narrative of Joseph of Arimathea
(c) Introductions to and summaries of:
 The Letter of Pilate to Herod
 The Letter of Herod to Pilate
 The Letter of Tiberius to Pilate

■

The Gospel of Nicodemus or Acts of Pilate

Both these titles are fairly late and are taken from the introductions to be found in some medieval Latin manuscripts. An Acts of Pilate was known in antiquity and mentioned in Justin, *Apology*, 35, 48 (ed. E. Goodspeed, *Die ältesten Apologeten* (Göttingen, 1914), pp. 50-1, 59-60). It is unlikely that Justin was referring to the present work: either he knew another treatise of this name or else merely assumed such a document must have existed. Eusebius, *HE* 9. 5. 1 (Schwartz, *GCS* 9.2, p. 810 (Greek), p. 811 (Latin of Rufinus, ed. T. Mommsen)) refers to a spurious Acts of Pilate officially published under Emperor Maximin in 311-12 for use against Christians. It is not impossible that the apocryphal Acts of Pilate originated as a Christian reaction to this publication. As so often with apocryphal texts, there is a dispute as to the likely date when the Gospel of Nicodemus was written, although the general consensus seems to be that both parts of the work, the Acts of Pilate proper and Christ's Descent into Hell (Descensus Christi ad Inferos), go back to the fifth–sixth century.

As with many apocryphal writings, the motive for the original composition was to satisfy the curiosity of those who found the canonical biblical writings inadequate. The role of Pilate in particular obviously intrigued early Christians, and the Pilate cycle in general—not just the Acts of Pilate but the associated literature—reflects the way in which the pious attempted to satisfy their curiosity. The same is true of the Descent: again the New Testament (here in particular 1 Peter 3: 19) whetted the appetite of Christians for further information about this aspect of their early history. The period of Christ's descent to Hades between Good Friday and Easter Day gave rise to many imaginative reconstructions. Fanciful and legendary though these stories and the Acts of Pilate are, they cannot be said to be unorthodox, and there is no evidence to connect their composition with heretical sects. In part of the tradition the names of the supposed authors of the Descent are said to be Leucius and Karinus, and Leucius Karinus (Charinus) is the name given by church writers to the author of the apocryphal Acts of John, Paul, Peter, Andrew and Thomas.

The genesis of the stories behind the Acts of Pilate may be much earlier than the fifth century: indeed Epiphanius, *adv. Haer.* 50.1 (Holl, *GCS* 31, p. 246), writing *c.*375, refers to details known to us now from the Acts. The stories were obviously growing over several centuries, and the texts published by Tischendorf represent at least three recensions of the Acts proper and three of the Descent, suggesting a continuing embellishment or abridgement of a common core of stories. Originally both parts were separate: there is no organic link or even natural connexion between them. It was originally only in some medieval Latin manuscripts that the text of one ran directly into the other. Although it is conventional to number the chapters of the Descent to follow the Acts, beginning at chapter 17, a new sequence beginning with 1 is provided below in parallel with the higher numbering. The Pilate legends became very popular in the Middle Ages and are the inspiration behind many of the legends concerning Joseph of Arimathea, the Holy Grail, and the Harrowing of Hell.

The original language of the Acts purports in the preface to be Hebrew, but it was in fact Greek. Tischendorf's edition of the Acts of Pilate and of the Descent prints an eclectic text which is increasingly criticized. For the Acts he gives two Greek texts and one Latin text. Greek A is based on eight manuscripts (not seven, as de Santos Otero claims),[1] and Greek B on three manuscripts. Greek B is a late reworking of A and is medieval in language:

---

[1] Nine according to Lake, who adds to Greek A the text of another MS. Nowadays over fifty Greek MSS (of A and B) are known.

none of the extant manuscripts is earlier than the fifteenth century. My translation of the Acts is based on Tischendorf's Greek A. (I have not provided a translation of Greek B.) Tischendorf's Latin of the Acts proper (not translated below) is based on twelve manuscripts. Coptic, Syriac, and Armenian and Georgian versions exist.

For the Descent I translate Tischendorf's Greek and his two Latin versions. His Latin A is preferable to Latin B and is older than the surviving Greek. Manuscripts of the Greek of the Descent are comparatively rare: Tischendorf based his edition on three Greek manuscripts, two of which he used also for the Acts. Most European versions of the Descent were based on the Latin text: many Latin manuscripts of the whole of the Gospel of Nicodemus have survived.[2] Tischendorf's Latin A was based on four manuscripts (all used in the Acts) and Latin B on three manuscripts (all used in the Acts). Latin B of the Descent is an abridged version of A although the introduction is longer in B than A. Latin A is closer to the Greek, but shows developments, especially in the conclusion. There are considerable differences between the text, and sequence of stories, in Latin A and Latin B.

EDITIONS

Greek and Latin

Fabricius, i. 238–98 (Latin text).
Jones, ii. 322–40 (Latin text and Eng. trans.).
Birch, i. 1–104.
Thilo, i. pp. cxviii–clx, 487–802.
Giles, chs. X and XI.
Tischendorf, *EA*, pp. liv–lxxvii, 210–432 (Acts: Greek A and B, Latin; Descent: Greek, Latin A and B; Turin Coptic cited in a Latin translation in footnotes to text of Part I Greek A).
K. Lake, 'Some Chapters of the Acta Pilati', in *Texts from Mount Athos* (Oxford, 1902), 152–63 (= *Studia Biblica et Ecclesiastica* 5) (Greek text of a Laura MS not used by Tischendorf).
G. Philippart, 'Fragments palimpsestes latins du Vindebonensis 563 (ve siècle?): Évangile selon S. Matthieu. Évangile de Nicodème, Évangile de l'enfance selon Thomas', *Anal. Boll.* 90 (1972), 391–411. cf. *id., ibid.* 107 (1989), 171–88.

Coptic

F. Rossi, 'Trascrizione di un codice copto del Museo egizio di Torino', *Memorie della Reale Accademia delle Scienze di Torino* ser. 2, 35 (1883), 163 ff.
E. Revillout, 'Les Apocryphes coptes, ii. Acta Pilati', in *PO* 9.2, ed. R. Graffin and F. Nau (Paris, 1913), 57–132.

[2] More than 350 MSS of the Latin *Evangelium Nicodemi* have recently been catalogued by Z. Izydorczyk.

P. Lacau, *Fragments d'apocryphes coptes* (with French trans.) (Cairo, 1904), 1–12[3] (= *Mémoires publiés par les membres de l'institut français d'archéologie orientale du Caire* 9).

J. W. B. Barns, 'Bodleian Fragments of a Sa'idic Version of the Acta Pilati', in *Coptic Studies in Honor of Walter Ewing Crum*, ed. M. Malinine (Boston, 1950), 245–50 (= *Bulletin of the Byzantine Institute* 2).

M. Vandoni and T. Orlandi, *Vangelo di Nicodemo* (Milan–Varese, 1966) (= *Testi e Documenti per lo Studio dell' Antiquità* 15) (new edition of the Turin papyrus).

Syriac

I. E. Rahmani, *Apocrypha hypomnemata Domini Nostri seu Acta Pilati: Antiqua Versio Syriaca* (Charfat, Lebanon, 1908) (= *Studia Syriaca* 2). [(German trans. by J. Sedláček in *Sitzungsberichte der Kgl. Böhm. Gesellschaft der Wissenschaften* 11 (Prague, 1908).]

Ethiopic

R. Beylot, 'Bref aperçu des principaux textes éthiopiens dérivés des Acta Pilati', *Langues orientales anciennes philologie et linguistique*, i. (Louvain, 1988), 181–95. [Cf. P. M. A. van den Oudenrijn, *Gamaliel: Äthiopische Texte und Pilatusliteratur* (Freiburg, 1959) (= *Spicilegium Friburgense* 4).]

Christian Palestinian Aramaic

S. P. Brock, 'A Fragment of the Acta Pilati in Christian Palestinian Aramaic', *JTS* 22 (1971), 157–9 (identifying texts published by F. Schultess in the *Abh. Kön. Ges. Wiss. zu Göttingen phil-hist-Kl.* NF 8.3 (Berlin, 1905), 134–6).

Armenian

Mechitarists' New Testament in Armenian (Venice, 1898), 313–45 (cf. F. C. Conybeare, *Acta Pilati* (Oxford, 1896) (= *Studia Biblica et Ecclesiastica* 4, 59–132)) (with retroversion of one MS into Greek and trans. of another into Latin).

Slavonic

M. N. Speransky, ['Slavic Apocryphal Gospels'], (Moscow, 1895), 92–133, 144–55 (= [*The Work of the Eighth Archeological Conference in Moscow*], 1890) (in Russian).

A. Vaillant, *Evangelium Nicodemi: Évangile de Nicodème: Texte slave et Latin* (Paris and Geneva, 1968) (= *Hautes Études Orientales* 2.1).

J. H. Charlesworth, *The New Testament Apocrypha and Pseudepigrapha: A Guide to Publications* (Metuchen and London, 1987) (includes several Russian and Serbo-Croat titles on the Gospel of Nicodemus in his section 57).

de Santos Otero, *Altslav. Apok.* ii. 61–98.

---

[3] Lacau also prints (ibid. 13–22) fragments of a possible apocryphal Gospel (Évangile(?) apocryphe') related to the Gospel of Nicodemus.

Georgian

Text edited by C. Kurcikidze (Tbilisi, 1985).

MODERN TRANSLATIONS

English

Hone, 63–91 (the Latin of Grynaeus' *Orthodoxographa*).
Cowper, pp. 227–388 (Greek A and B of Acts and Greek of Descent; Latin of Acts I and Latin A and B of Descent).
Walker, 125–222 (Greek A and Latin of Acts; Greek and Latin A and B of Descent).
A. Westcott, *The Gospel of Nicodemus and Kindred Documents* (London, 1915), 63–118 (Latin of both parts).
H. J. Schonfield, *Readings from the Apocryphal Gospels* (London, 1940) (selections).
James, 94–146 (Greek A with summary of Greek B of Acts, Greek and Latin A and B of Descent).
R. Cameron, *The Other Gospels* (Philadelphia, 1982), 163–83 (selections).
Hennecke[3], i. 444–81 (contents as for German edition).
Hennecke[5], i. 501–26 (contents as for German edition).

French

Migne, *Dictionnaire*, i, cols. 1087–1138.
Amiot, 145–56 (selection).
F. Quéré, *Évangiles apocryphes* (Paris, 1983), 125–59 (translates Greek A of Acts; Latin B of Descent).
Rémi Gounelle and Zbigniew Izydorczyk, *L'Évangile de Nicodème* (Turnhout, 1997) (= *Apocryphes* 9).

German

Hennecke[1], 74–6 (A. Stülcken); cf. *Handbuch*, 143–53.
Hennecke[3], i. 444–81 (F. Scheidweiler) (Greek A of Acts and Greek of Descent).
Hennecke[5], i. 395–418 (F. Scheidweiler) (as for Hennecke[3]).
Michaelis, 132–215.

Italian

Erbetta, i.2, 231–87 (Greek A with a summary of Greek B of Acts; Greek, Latin A and B of Descent).
Moraldi, i. 519–653; [2] i. 593–723 (Greek A, Turin Coptic, and Latin of Acts; Greek, Latin A and B of Descent).
Cravieri, 299–377.

Spanish

de Santos Otero, 396–471 (Greek A with variants in Greek B of Acts; Greek and Latin B of Descent).
González-Blanco, ii. 237–304.

Irish

R. Atkinson, *The Passions and the Homilies from Leabhar Breac* (Dublin, 1887), 113–24, 143–51, 359–71, 392–400 (= *Todd Lecture Series* 2) (text and trans. of Acts of Pilate found in the Leabhar Breac). [Cf. M. McNamara, *The Apocrypha in the Irish Church* (Dublin, 1975), 69–75.]

GENERAL

A. Lipsius, *Die Pilatenakten kritisch untersucht* (Kiel, 1871; ²1886).
L. Maury, 'Nouvelles recherches sur l'époque à laquelle a été composé l'ouvrage connu sous le nom d'Évangile de Nicodème', *Mémoires de la société des antiquaires de France* 20 (1850), 341–92.
Variot, 93–107, 233–328.
H. von Schubert, *Die Composition des pseudo-petrinischen Evangelienfragments* (Berlin, 1893), 175 f.
E. von Dobschütz, 'Der Process Jesu nach den Acta Pilati', *ZNW* 3 (1902), 89–114.
T. Mommsen, 'Die Pilatusacten', *ZNW* 3 (1902), 198–205.
A. M. Vitti, 'Descensus Christi ad Inferos iuxta Apocrypha', in *Verbum Domini* 7 (Rome, 1927), 138–44, 171–81.
P. Vannutelli, *Actorum Pilati textus synoptici* (Rome, 1938) (Greek texts in parallel with varants in Tischendorf's Greek A and Greek B MSS of the Acts of Pilate).
G. C. O'Ceallaigh, 'Dating the Commentaries of Nicodemus', *HTR* 56 (1963), 21–58.
I. Cazzaniga, 'Osservazioni critiche al testo del "prologo" del Vangeli di Nicodemo', *Instituto Lombardo: Accademia di Scienze e Lettere: Classe Lettere* 102 (Milan, 1968), 535–48.
D. D. R. Owen, *The Vision of Hell* (Edinburgh and London, 1970).
H. C. Kim (ed.), *The Gospel of Nicodemus: Gesta Salvatoris edited from the Codex Einsidlensis (Einsiedeln Stiftsbibliothek, MS 326)* (Toronto, 1973; ²1979) (= *Toronto Medieval Latin Texts* 2).
W. Speyer, 'Neue Pilatus-Apokryphen', *VC* 32 (1978), 53–9.
R. J. Hoffmann, 'Confluence in Early Christian and Gnostic Literature: The Descensus Christi ad Inferos (Acta Pilati, xvii–xxvii)', *JSNT* 10 (1981), 42–60.
M. Lowe, '*Ioudaioi* of the Apocrypha: A Fresh Approach to the Gospels of James, Pseudo-Thomas, Peter and Nicodemus', *Novum Testamentum* 23 (1981), 56–90, esp. 86–90.
G. W. H. Lampe, 'The Trial of Jesus in the *Acta Pilati*', in E. Bammel and C. F. D. Moule (eds.), *Jesus and the Politics of His Day* (Cambridge, 1984), 173–82.
Klauck, 118–31.

THE ACTS OF PILATE (GREEK A)

Prologue: I, Ananias, an officer of the praetorian guard, being learned in the law, came to know our Lord Jesus Christ from the sacred scriptures, which I approached with faith, and was accounted worthy of holy baptism. And having searched for the reports made at that period in the time of our Lord Jesus

Christ which the Jews committed to writing under Pontius Pilate, I found these acts in the Hebrew language and according to God's good pleasure I translated them into Greek for the information of all those who call upon the name of our Lord Jesus Christ, in the seventeenth year of the reign of our Emperor Flavius Theodosius and in the sixth year of the Nobility of Flavius Valentinianus, in the ninth indiction.

Therefore all you who read this and translate it into other books, remember me and pray for me that God may be gracious to me and forgive my sins which I have sinned against him. Peace be to those who read and hear it, and to their servants. Amen.

In the nineteenth year of the reign of the Roman Emperor Tiberius, when Herod was king of Galilee, in the nineteenth year of his rule, on the eighth day before the Kalends of April, that is, the 25th of March, in the consulate of Rufus and Rubellio, in the fourth year of the two hundred and second Olympiad, when Joseph Caiaphas was high priest of the Jews.

The things that Nicodemus recorded after the passion of the Lord upon the cross and delivered concern the conduct of the chief priests and the rest of the Jews. This same Nicodemus drew up his records in the Hebrew language.

1. 1. The chief priests and scribes assembled in council, Annas and Caiaphas, Semes, Dathaes and Gamaliel, Judas, Levi and Nephthalim, Alexander and Jairus, and the rest of the Jews, and came to Pilate accusing Jesus of many deeds. They said, 'We know that this man is the son of Joseph the carpenter and was born of Mary; but he says he is the Son of God and a king. Moreover he profanes the Sabbath and wishes to destroy the law of our fathers.' Pilate said, 'And what things does he do that he wishes to destroy it?' The Jews say, 'We have a law that we should not heal anyone on the Sabbath. But this man with his evil deeds has healed on the Sabbath the lame, the mutilated, the withered, the blind, the paralytic, the deaf, and the demoniacs.' Pilate asked them, 'With what evil acts?' They answered him, 'He is a sorcerer, and by Beelzebub the prince of the devils he casts out evil spirits, and all are subject to him.' Pilate said to them, 'It is not possible to cast out demons by an unclean spirit, but by the god Asclepius.'

2. The Jews said to Pilate, 'We beseech your excellency to place him before your judgment-seat and to try him.' And Pilate called them to him and said, 'Tell me! How can I, a governor, examine a king?' They answered, 'We do not say that he is a king; he says it of himself.' And Pilate summoned his messenger and said to him, 'Let Jesus be brought with gentleness.' So the messenger went out, and when he recognized him, worshipped him, and taking the scarf which was in his hand, he spread it upon the ground, and said to him, 'Lord, walk on this and go in, for the governor calls you.' But when the Jews saw what the messenger had done, they cried out against Pilate and said, 'Why did you not order him to come in by a herald, but by a messenger?

For as soon as he saw him the messenger worshipped him, and spread his scarf on the ground, and made him walk on it like a king.'

3. Then Pilate called for the messenger and said to him, 'Why have you done this, and spread your scarf on the ground and made Jesus walk on it?' The messenger answered him, 'Lord governor, when you sent me to Jerusalem to Alexander, I saw him sitting on an ass, and the children of the Hebrews held branches in their hands and cried out; and others spread their garments before him, saying, "Save now, you who are in the highest! Blessed is he that comes in the name of the Lord!"'

4. The Jews cried out to the messenger, 'The children of the Hebrews cried out in Hebrew; how do you know it in Greek?' The messenger replied, 'I asked one of the Jews, and said, "What is it that they cry out in Hebrew?" And he interpreted it to me.' Pilate said to them, 'And what did they cry out in Hebrew?' The Jews answered, 'Hosanna membrome baruchamma adonai.'[1] Pilate asked, 'And the Hosanna and the rest, how is it translated?' The Jews replied, 'Save now, you who are in the highest. Blessed is he that comes in the name of the Lord.' Pilate said to them, 'If you testify to these words spoken by the children, what sin has the messenger committed?' And they were silent. The governor said to the messenger, 'Go out and bring him in however you wish.' And the messenger went out and did as before and said to Jesus, 'Lord, enter, the governor calls you.'

5. Now when Jesus entered, and the ensigns were holding the standards, the images on the standards bowed down and worshipped Jesus. And when the Jews saw the behaviour of the standards, how they bowed down and worshipped Jesus, they cried out loudly against the ensigns. But Pilate said to them, 'Do you not marvel how the images bowed and worshipped Jesus?' The Jews said to Pilate, 'We saw how the ensigns lowered them and worshipped him.' And the governor summoned the ensigns and asked them, 'Why did you do this?' They answered, 'We are Greeks and servers of temples: how could we worship him? We held the images; but they bowed down of their own accord and worshipped him.'

6. Then Pilate said to the rulers of the synagogue and the elders of the people, 'Choose strong men to carry the standards, and let us see whether the images bow by themselves.' So the elders of the Jews took twelve strong men and made them carry the standards by sixes, and they stood before the judgement-seat of the governor. And Pilate said to the messenger, 'Take him out of the praetorium and bring him in again in whatever way you wish.' And Jesus left the praetorium with the messenger. And Pilate summoned those who had previously been carrying the images, and said to them, 'I have sworn by the salvation of Caesar that, if the standards do not bow down when Jesus enters, I will cut off your heads.' And the governor commanded Jesus to enter

---

[1] Corrupt transliteration of Psalm 118: 26.

in the second time. And the messenger did as before and begged Jesus to walk upon his scarf. He walked upon it and entered. And when he had entered, the standards bowed down again and worshipped Jesus.

2. 1. When Pilate saw this he was afraid, and tried to rise from the judgement-seat. And while he was still thinking of rising up, his wife sent to him saying, 'Have nothing to do with this righteous man. For I have suffered many things because of him by night'.[2] And Pilate summoned all the Jews, and stood up and said to them, 'You know that my wife is pious and prefers to practise Judaism with you.' They answered him, 'Yes, we know it.' Pilate said to them, 'See, my wife sent to me saying, "Have nothing to do with this righteous man. For I have suffered many things because of him by night."' The Jews answered Pilate, 'Did we not tell you that he is a sorcerer? Behold, he has sent a dream to your wife.' 2. And Pilate called Jesus to him and said to him, 'What do these men testify against you? Do you say nothing?' Jesus answered, 'If they had no power, they would say nothing; for each man has power over his own mouth, to speak good and evil. They shall see.'

3. Then the elders of the Jews answered and said to Jesus, 'What should we see? First, that you were born of fornication; secondly, that your birth meant the death of the children in Bethlehem; thirdly, that your father Joseph and your mother Mary fled into Egypt because they had no esteem among the people.' 4. Then some of the pious among Jews stood by, who said, 'We do not say that he came of fornication, for we know that Joseph was betrothed to Mary, and he was not born of fornication.' Pilate then said to the Jews who said that he came of fornication, 'Your statement is not true; for there had been a betrothal, as your compatriots say.' Annas and Caiaphas said to Pilate, 'We, the whole multitude, cry out that he was born of fornication, and we are not believed; these are proselytes and disciples of his.' And Pilate called to him Annas and Caiaphas and said to them, 'What are proselytes?' They answered, 'They are people who were born children of Greeks, and now have become Jews.' Then those who said that he was not born of fornication, namely Lazarus, Asterius, Antonius, Jacob, Amnes, Zeras, Samuel, Isaac, Phineës, Crispus, Agrippa, and Judas, said, 'We are not proselytes, but are children of Jews and speak the truth; for we were present at the betrothal of Joseph and Mary.'

5. And Pilate called to him these twelve men who denied that he was born of fornication, and said to them, 'I adjure you, by the salvation of Caesar, that your statement is true, that he was not born of fornication.' They said to Pilate, 'We have a law, not to swear, because it is a sin. But let *them* swear by the salvation of Caesar that it is not as we have said, and we will be worthy of death.' Pilate said to Annas and Caiaphas, 'Do you not answer these things?' And Annas and Caiaphas said to Pilate, 'These twelve men are believed who

---

[2] Matt. 27: 19.

say that he was not born of fornication. But we, the whole multitude, cry out that he was born of fornication, and is a sorcerer, and says he is the Son of God and a king, and we are not believed.' 6. And Pilate ordered the whole multitude to go out, except the twelve men who denied that he was born of fornication, and he commanded Jesus to be set apart. And he asked them, 'For what cause do they wish to kill him?' They answered Pilate, 'They are jealous because he heals on the Sabbath.' Pilate said, 'For a good work do they wish to kill him?' They answered him, 'Yes.'

3. 1. And Pilate was filled with anger and went out of the praetorium and said to them, 'I call the sun to witness that I find no fault in this man.' The Jews answered and said to the governor, 'If this man were not an evildoer, we would not have handed him over to you'.[3] And Pilate said, 'Take him yourselves and judge him by your own law.' The Jews said to Pilate, 'It is not lawful for us to put any man to death'.[4] Pilate said, 'Has God forbidden you to kill, but allowed me to do so?'

2. And Pilate entered the praetorium again and called Jesus and asked him privately, 'Are you the king of the Jews?' Jesus answered Pilate, 'Do you say this of your own accord, or did others say it to you about me?' Pilate answered Jesus, 'Am I a Jew? Your own nation and the chief priests have handed you over to me. What have you done?' Jesus answered, 'My kingship is not of this world; for if my kingship were of this world, my servants would fight, that I might not be handed over to the Jews. But now my kingship is not from here.' Pilate said to him, 'So you are a king?' Jesus answered him, 'You say that I am a king. For for this cause I was born and have come, that every one who is of the truth should hear my voice.' Pilate said to him, 'What is truth?'[5] Jesus answered him, 'Truth is from heaven.' Pilate said, 'Is there not truth upon earth?' Jesus said to Pilate, 'You see how those who speak the truth are judged by those who have authority on earth.'

4. 1. And Pilate left Jesus in the praetorium and went out to the Jews and said to them, 'I find no fault in him'.[6] The Jews said to him, 'He said: "I am able to destroy this temple and build it in three days"'.[7] Pilate said, 'What temple?' The Jews said: 'The one which Solomon built in forty-six years. This man says he will destroy it and build it in three days.' Pilate said to them, 'I am innocent of the blood of this righteous man; you see to it'. The Jews replied, 'His blood be on us and on our children'.[8] 2. And Pilate summoned the elders and the priests and the Levites and said to them secretly, 'Do not act in this way; for nothing of which you have accused him deserves death.

---

[3] John 18: 30.
[4] John 18: 31.
[5] John 18: 33–8.
[6] John 18: 38.
[7] Matt. 26: 61.
[8] Matt. 27: 24–5.

For your accusation concerns healing and profanation of the Sabbath.' The elders and the priests and the Levites answered, 'If a man blasphemes against Caesar, is he worthy of death or not?' Pilate said, 'He is worthy of death.' The Jews said to Pilate, 'If a man blasphemes against Caesar, he is worthy of death, but this man has blasphemed against God.'

3. Then the governor commanded the Jews to go out from the praetorium, and he called Jesus to him and said to him, 'What shall I do with you?' Jesus answered Pilate, 'As it was given to you.' Pilate said, 'How was it given?' Jesus said, 'Moses and the prophets foretold my death and resurrection.' The Jews had made enquiries and heard, and they said to Pilate, 'What more do you need to hear than this blasphemy?' Pilate said to the Jews, 'If this word is blasphemy, take him for his blasphemy and bring him into your synagogue and judge him according to your law.'[9] The Jews answered Pilate, 'Our law decrees that if a man sins against a man, he must receive forty strokes save one, but he who blasphemes against God must be stoned.'

4. Pilate said to them, 'Take him yourselves and punish him as you wish.' The Jews said to Pilate, 'We wish him to be crucified.' Pilate said, 'He does not deserve to be crucified.' 5. The governor looked at the multitudes of the Jews standing around, and when he saw many of the Jews weeping, he said, 'Not all the multitude wishes him to die.' But the elders of the Jews said. 'The whole multitude of us has come, for the purpose that he should die.' Pilate said to the Jews, 'Why should he die?' The Jews said: 'Because he called himself the Son of God and a king.'

5. 1. Now Nicodemus, a Jew, stood before the governor, and said, 'I beseech you, pious one, to allow me a few words.' Pilate said, 'Speak.' Nicodemus said, 'I said to the elders and the priests and the Levites and to all the multitude in the synagogue, "What do you intend to do with this man? This man does many signs and wonders, which no other has done nor will do. Release him and wish no evil against him. If the signs which he does are from God, they will stand; if they are from men, they will come to nothing.[10] For Moses also, when he was sent by God into Egypt, did many signs which God commanded him to do before Pharaoh, king of Egypt. And there were there physicians of Pharaoh, Jamnes and Jambres, and they also did not a few signs such as Moses did, and the Egyptians held Jamnes and Jambres as gods. And since the signs which they did were not from God, they themselves perished and those who believed them. And now let this man go, for he does not deserve death."'

2. The Jews said to Nicodemus, 'You became his disciple and speak on his behalf.' Nicodemus answered them, 'Has the governor also become his disciple, and speaks on his behalf? Did not Caesar appoint him to this high

---

[9] John 18: 31.
[10] Cf. Acts 5: 38–9.

office?' Then the Jews raged and gnashed their teeth against Nicodemus. Pilate said to them, 'Why do you gnash your teeth against him, when you hear the truth?' The Jews said to Nicodemus, 'Receive his truth and his portion.' Nicodemus said, 'Amen, may it be as you have said.'

6. 1. Then one of the Jews came forward and asked the governor that he might speak a word. The governor said, 'If you wish to say anything, say it.' And the Jew said, 'For thirty-eight years I lay on a bed in anguish and pain, and when Jesus came many demoniacs and those lying sick of various diseases were healed by him. And certain young men took pity on me and carried me with my bed and brought me to him. And when Jesus saw me he had compassion, and said to me, "Take up your bed and walk." And I took up my bed and walked.'[11] The Jews said to Pilate, 'Ask him what day it was on which he was healed.' The cured man said, 'On a Sabbath.' The Jews said, 'Did we not tell you, that he heals and casts out demons on the Sabbath?' 2. And another Jew hastened forward and said, 'I was born blind; I heard a man's voice, but did not see his face. And as Jesus passed by I cried with a loud voice, "Have mercy on me, Son of David." And he took pity on me and put his hands on my eyes and I saw immediately'.[12] And another Jew came forward and said, 'I was bowed, and he made me straight with a word.' And another said, 'I was a leper, and he healed me with a word.'

7. 1. And a woman called Bernice[13] crying out from a distance said, 'I had an issue of blood and I touched the hem of his garment, and the issue of blood, which had lasted twelve years, ceased'.[14] The Jews said, 'We have a law not to permit a woman to give testimony.'

8. 1. And others, a multitude of men and women, cried out, 'This man is a prophet, and the demons are subject to him.' Pilate said to those who claimed the demons were subject to him, 'Why are your teachers also not subject to him?' They said to Pilate, 'We do not know.' Others said, 'He raised Lazarus, who was dead, out of the tomb after four days.' Then the governor began to tremble and said to all the multitude of the Jews, 'Why do you wish to shed innocent blood?'

9. 1. And he called to him Nicodemus and the twelve men who said he was not born of fornication and said to them, 'What shall I do? There is dissension among the people.' They answered him, 'We do not know. They will see to it.' Again Pilate called all the multitude of the Jews and said, 'You know the custom that at the feast of unleavened bread one prisoner is released to you. I have in the prison one condemned for murder, called Barabbas, and this Jesus who stands before you, in whom I find no fault. Whom do you wish me to release to you?' But they cried out, 'Barabbas.' Pilate said, 'Then what

---

[11] Matt. 9: 1–8; Mark 2: 1–12; Luke 5: 17–26; John 5: 1–7.
[12] Mark 10: 46–7 and parallels.
[13] Latin: 'Veronica'.
[14] Mark 5: 25–9 and parallels.

shall I do with Jesus who is called Christ?' The Jews cried out, 'Let him be crucified'.[15] But some of the Jews answered, 'You are not Caesar's friend if you release this man,[16] for he called himself the Son of God and a king. You therefore wish him and not Caesar to be king.'

2. And Pilate was angry and said to the Jews, 'Your nation is always seditious and in rebellion against your benefactors.' The Jews asked, 'What benefactors?' Pilate answered, 'I have heard that your God brought you out of Egypt out of hard slavery, and led you safely through the sea as if it had been dry land, and in the wilderness nourished you and gave you manna and quails, and gave you water to drink from a rock, and gave you the law. And in spite of all these things you provoked the anger of your God: you wanted a molten calf and angered your God, and he wished to destroy you; and Moses made supplication for you, and you were not put to death. And now you accuse me of hating the emperor.' 3. And he rose up from the judgement-seat and was on his way out when the Jews cried out, 'We know as king Caesar alone and not Jesus. Wise men brought him gifts from the east, as for a king. And when Herod heard from the wise men that a king was born, he tried to slay him. But when his father Joseph knew that, he took him and his mother, and they fled into Egypt. And when Herod heard it, he destroyed the children of the Hebrews who were born in Bethlehem.'

4. When Pilate heard these words, he was afraid. And he silenced the multitudes, because they were crying out, and said to them, 'So this is he whom Herod sought?' The Jews replied, 'Yes, this is he.' And Pilate took water and washed his hands before the sun and said, 'I am innocent of this righteous blood. You will see to it.' Again the Jews cried out, 'His blood be on us and on our children'.[17] 5. Then Pilate commanded the curtain to be drawn before the judgement-seat on which he sat, and said to Jesus, 'Your nation has convicted you of being a king. Therefore I have decreed that you should first be scourged according to the law of the pious emperors, and then hanged on the cross in the garden where you were seized. And let Dysmas and Gestas, the two malefactors, be crucified with you.'

10. 1. Then Jesus went out from the praetorium, and the two malefactors with him. And when they came to the place, they stripped him and girded him with a linen cloth and put a crown of thorns on his head. Likewise they hanged up also the two malefactors. But Jesus said, 'Father, forgive them, for they know not what they do'.[18] And the soldiers parted his garments among them. And the people stood looking at him. And the chief priests and the rulers with them scoffed at him, saying, 'He saved others, let him save

---

[15] Cf. Matt. 27: 15–17.
[16] John 19: 12.
[17] Matt. 27: 24–5.
[18] Luke 23: 34.

himself. If he is the Son of God, let him come down from the cross.' And the soldiers also mocked him, coming and offering him vinegar with gall, and they said, 'If you are the king of the Jews, save yourself'.[19] And after the sentence Pilate commanded that the crime brought against him be written as a title in Greek, Latin, and Hebrew, that he was, as the Jews said, king of the Jews.[20].

2. One of the malefactors who were crucified said to him, 'If you are the Christ, save yourself and us.' But Dysmas answering rebuked him, 'Do you not fear God at all, since you are in the same condemnation? And we justly so. For we are receiving the due reward of our deeds. But this man has done nothing wrong.' And he said to Jesus, 'Lord, remember me in your kingdom.' And Jesus said to him, 'Truly, truly, I say to you, today you will be with me in paradise'.[21]

11. 1. And it was about the sixth hour, and there was darkness over the land until the ninth hour, for the sun was darkened. And the curtain of the temple was torn in two. And Jesus cried with a loud voice, 'Father, baddach ephkid rouel [sic]', which means: 'Into thy hands I commit my spirit.' And having said this he gave up the ghost. And when the centurion saw what had happened, he praised God, saying, 'This man was righteous.' And all the multitudes who had come to this sight, when they saw what had taken place, beat their breasts and returned home.[22]

2. But the centurion reported to the governor what had happened. And when the governor and his wife heard, they were deeply grieved, and they neither ate nor drank on that day. And Pilate sent for the Jews and said to them, 'Did you see what happened?' But they answered, 'There was an eclipse of the sun in the usual way.' 3. His acquaintances stood far off, and the women who had come with him from Galilee, and they saw these things. But a certain man named Joseph, a member of the council, from the town of Arimathaea, who also was waiting for the kingdom of God, went to Pilate and asked for the body of Jesus. And he took it down, and wrapped it in a clean linen cloth, and placed it in a rock-hewn tomb, in which no one had ever yet been laid.[23]

12. 1. When the Jews heard that Joseph had asked for the body, they looked for him and the twelve men who said that Jesus was not born of fornication, and for Nicodemus and for many others, who had come forward before Pilate and made known his good works. But they all hid themselves, and only Nicodemus was seen by them, because he was a ruler of the Jews. And Nicodemus said to them, 'How did you enter into the synagogue?' The Jews answered him, 'How did you enter into the synagogue? You are a

---

[19] Luke 23: 35–7.
[20] John 19: 19–20.
[21] Cf. Luke 23: 39–43.
[22] Cf. Luke 23: 44–8.
[23] Luke 23: 50–3.

sympathizer of his, and his portion shall be with you in the world to come.' Nicodemus said, 'Amen, amen.' Likewise Joseph came forth and said to them, 'Why are you angry with me, because I asked for the body of Jesus? See, I have placed it in my new tomb, having wrapped it in clean linen, and I rolled a stone in front of the door of the cave. And you have not done well with the righteous one, for you have not repented of having crucified him, but you even pierced him with a spear.'

Then the Jews seized Joseph and commanded him to be locked up until the first day of the week. They said to him, 'You know that the time prevents our doing anything against you, because the Sabbath dawns. But you also know that you will not even be counted worthy of burial, but we shall give your flesh to the birds of heaven.' Joseph said to them, 'This is the word of the boastful Goliath, who insulted the living God and the holy David. For God said through the prophet: "Vengeance is mine, I will repay, says the Lord."[24] And now he who is uncircumcised in the flesh, but circumcised in heart, took water and washed his hands before the sun, saying, "I am innocent of this righteous blood. You will see to it." And you answered Pilate, "His blood be on us and on our children".[25] And now I fear lest the wrath of God come upon you and your children, as you said.' When the Jews heard these words, they were embittered in their hearts, and laid hold on Joseph and seized him and shut him in a windowless house, and guards were stationed at the door. And they sealed the door of the place where Joseph was shut up.

2. And on the Sabbath the rulers of the synagogue and the priests and the Levites ordered that everybody should present himself in the synagogue on the first day of the week. And the whole multitude rose up early and took counsel in the synagogue by what death they should kill him. And when the council was in session they commanded him to be brought with great dishonour. And when they opened the door they did not find him. And all the people were astonished and filled with consternation because they found the seals undamaged, and Caiaphas had the key. And they dared no longer to lay hands on those who had spoken to Pilate on behalf of Jesus.

13. 1. And while they still sat in the synagogue wondering about Joseph, there came some of the guard whom the Jews had asked from Pilate to guard the tomb of Jesus, lest his disciples should come and steal him. And they told the rulers of the synagogue and the priests and the Levites what had happened, 'There was a great earthquake. And we saw an angel descend from heaven, and he rolled away the stone from the mouth of the cave, and sat upon it, and he shone like snow and like lightning. And we were in great fear, and lay like dead men.[26] And we heard the voice of the angel speaking to the women who waited at the tomb "Do not be afraid. I know that you seek Jesus

---

[24] Rom. 12: 19. Cf. Deut. 32: 35.
[25] Matt. 27: 25.
[26] Matt. 28: 2–4.

who was crucified. He is not here. He has risen, as he said. Come and see the place where the Lord lay. And go quickly and tell his disciples that he has risen from the dead and is in Galilee." '[27]

2. The Jews asked, 'Which women did he speak to?' The members of the guard answered, 'We do not know who they were.' The Jews said, 'At what hour was it?' The members of the guard answered, 'At midnight.' The Jews said, 'And why did you not arrest the women?' The members of the guard said, 'We were like dead men through fear, and gave up hope of seeing the light of day; how could we then have seized them?' The Jews said, 'As the Lord lives, we do not believe you.' The members of the guard said to the Jews, 'You saw so many signs in that man and you did not believe; and how can you believe us? You rightly swore, "As the Lord lives", for he *does* live.' Again the members of the guard said, 'We have heard that you shut up the man who asked for the body of Jesus, and sealed the door, and that when you opened it you did not find him. Therefore give us Joseph and we will give you Jesus.' The Jews said, 'Joseph has gone to his own city.' And the members of the guard said to the Jews, 'And Jesus has risen, as we heard from the angel, and is in Galilee.' 3. And when the Jews heard these words, they feared greatly and said, 'Take heed lest this report be heard and all turn to Jesus.' And the Jews took counsel, and offered a great sum of money and gave it to the soldiers of the guard, saying, 'Say that when you were sleeping his disciples came by night and stole him. And if this is heard by the governor, we will persuade him and keep you out of trouble.'[28]

14. 1. Now Phineës a priest and Adas a teacher and Angaeus a Levite came from Galilee to Jerusalem, and told the rulers of the synagogue and the priests and the Levites, 'We saw Jesus and his disciples sitting upon the mountain which is called Mamilch. And he said to his disciples, "Go into all the world and preach the gospel to the whole creation. He who believes and is baptized will be saved; but he who does not believe will be condemned. And these signs will accompany those who believe: in my name they will cast out demons; they will speak in new tongues; they will pick up serpents; and if they drink any deadly thing, it will not hurt them; they will lay their hands on the sick, and they will recover".[29] And while Jesus was still speaking to his disciples, we saw him taken up into heaven.'

2. Then the elders and the priests and the Levites said, 'Give glory to the God of Israel, and confess before him if you indeed heard and saw what you have described.' Those who related them said, 'As the Lord God of our fathers Abraham, Isaac, and Jacob lives, we heard these things and saw him taken up to heaven.' The elders and the priests and the Levites said to them, 'Did you come to tell us this, or did you come to offer prayer to God?' They answered, 'To offer prayer to God.' The elders and the chief priests and the

---

[27] Matt. 28: 5–7.
[28] Matt. 28: 12–14.
[29] Mark 16: 15–18.

Levites said to them, 'If you came to offer prayer to God, to what purpose is this idle tale which you have babbled before all the people?' Phineës the priest and Adas the teacher and Angaeus the Levite said to the rulers of the synagogue and priests and Levites, 'If the words which we spoke about what we saw are sin, behold, we stand before you. Do with us as it seems good in your eyes.' And they took the law and adjured them to tell these words to no one. And they gave them food and drink, and sent them out of the city, after having given them money and three companions, and they ordered them to depart to Galilee. And they went away in peace.

3. But when those men had departed to Galilee, the chief priests and the rulers of the synagogue and the elders assembled in the synagogue, and shut the gate, and raised a great lamentation, saying, 'Why has this sign happened in Israel?' But Annas and Caiaphas said, 'Why are you troubled? Why do you weep? Do you not know that his disciples gave money to the guards of the tomb and taught them to say that an angel descended from heaven and rolled away the stone from the door of the tomb?' But the priests and the elders replied, 'Let it be that his disciples stole his body. But how did the soul enter again into the body, so that Jesus now waits in Galilee?' But they, being scarcely able to give an answer, said, 'It is not lawful for us to believe the uncircumcised.'[30]

15. 1. And Nicodemus arose and stood before the council and said, 'What you say is right. You know, people of the Lord, that the men who came from Galilee fear God and are men of honour, that they hate covetousness, and are men of peace. And they have declared on oath, "We saw Jesus on the mountain Mamilch with his disciples." He taught them what you have heard from them, namely "We saw him taken up into heaven." And no one asked them in what manner he was taken up. Just as the book of the holy scriptures tells us that Elijah also was taken up into heaven, and Elisha cried with a loud voice, and Elijah cast his sheepskin cloak upon Elisha, and Elisha cast his cloak upon the Jordan, and crossed over and went to Jericho. And the sons of the prophets met him and said, "Elisha, where is your master Elijah?" And he said that he was taken up into heaven. But they said to Elisha, "Has perhaps a spirit caught him up and cast him on one of the mountains? But let us take our servants with us and search for him". And they persuaded Elisha, and he went with them. And they searched for him for three days and did not find him, and they knew that he had been taken up.[31] And now listen to me. Let us send to every mountain of Israel and see whether the Christ was perhaps taken up by a spirit and cast upon a mountain.' And this proposal pleased them all. And they sent to every mountain of Israel, and searched for Jesus and did not find him. But they found Joseph in Arimathaea and no one dared to seize him.

---

[30] Latin, Coptic and Armenian versions try to improve on this apparently illogical sentence.
[31] Cf. Kings 2: 1–18.

2. And they told the elders and the priests and the Levites, 'We went about to every mountain of Israel, and did not find Jesus. But Joseph we found in Arimathaea.' And when they heard about Joseph, they rejoiced and gave glory to the God of Israel. And the rulers of the synagogue and the priests and the Levites took counsel how they should meet with Joseph, and they took a roll of papyrus and wrote to Joseph these words, 'Peace be with you. We know that we have sinned against God and against you, and we have prayed to the God of Israel that you should deign to come to your fathers and your children, because we are all troubled. For when we opened the door we did not find you. We know that we devised an evil plan against you; but the Lord helped you, and the Lord himself has brought to nothing our plan against you, honoured father Joseph.'

3. And they chose from all Israel seven men who were friends of Joseph, whom Joseph himself was acquainted with, and the rulers of the synagogue and the priests and the Levites said to them, 'See! If he receives our letter and reads it, you know that he will come with you to us. But if he does not read it, you know that he is angry with us, greet him in peace and return to us.' And they blessed the men and dismissed them. And the men came to Joseph and greeted him with reverence, and said to him, 'Peace be with you!' He replied, 'Peace be with you and all Israel!' And they gave him the letter. Joseph took the roll, read the letter and kissed it, and blessed God and said, 'Blessed be God, who has delivered the Israelites from shedding innocent blood. And blessed be the Lord, who sent his angel and sheltered me under his wings.' And he set a table before them, and they ate and drank and lay down there. 4. And they rose up early in the morning and prayed. And Joseph saddled his she-ass and went with the men, and they came to the holy city Jerusalem. And all the people met Joseph and cried, 'Peace on your arrival.' And he said to all the people, 'Peace be with you!' And all kissed him, and prayed with Joseph, and were beside themselves with joy at seeing him. And Nicodemus received him into his house and made a great feast. He invited Annas and Caiaphas and the elders and the priests and the Levites to his house, and they rejoiced, eating and drinking with Joseph. And after singing a hymn each one went to his house; but Joseph remained in the house of Nicodemus.

5. And on the next day, which was the day of preparation, the rulers of the synagogue and the priests and the Levites rose up early and came to the house of Nicodemus. Nicodemus met them and said, 'Peace be with you!' They answered, 'Peace be with you and with Joseph and with all your house and with all the house of Joseph!' And he took them into his house. And the whole council sat down, and Joseph sat between Annas and Caiaphas. And no one dared to speak a word to him. And Joseph said, 'Why have you called me?' And they beckoned to Nicodemus to speak to Joseph. Nicodemus opened his mouth and said to Joseph, 'Father, you know that the honourable teachers and the priests and the Levites wish to learn something from you.' Joseph answered, 'Ask me.' And Annas and Caiaphas took the law and adjured

Joseph, saying, 'Give glory to the God of Israel and make confession to him. For Achan also, when adjured by the prophet Joshua, did not commit perjury, but told him everything and concealed nothing from him. So you too must not conceal from us a single word.' Joseph answered, 'I will not conceal anything from you.' And they said to him, 'We were very angry because you asked for the body of Jesus, and wrapped it in a clean linen cloth, and placed it in a tomb. And for this reason we secured you in a house with no window, and locked and sealed the door, and guards watched where you were shut up. And on the first day of the week we opened it, and did not find you, and we were very troubled, and all the people of God were amazed until yesterday. And now tell us what happened.'

6. And Joseph said, 'On the day of preparation about the tenth hour you shut me in, and I remained the whole Sabbath. And at midnight as I stood and prayed, the house where you shut me in was raised up by the four corners, and I saw as it were a flash of lightning in my eyes. Full of fear I fell to the ground. And someone took me by the hand and raised me up from the place where I had fallen, and moisture like water flowed from my head to my feet, and the myrrh came to my nostrils. And he wiped my face and kissed me and said to me, "Do not fear, Joseph. Open your eyes and see who it is who speaks with you." I looked up and saw Jesus. Trembling, I thought it was a phantom, and I recited the commandments. And he said them with me. Now as you well know, a phantom immediately flees if it meets anyone and hears the commandments. And when I saw that he said them with me, I said to him, "Rabbi Elijah!" He said, "I am not Elijah." And I said to him, "Who are you, Lord?" He replied, "I am Jesus, whose body you asked for from Pilate, whom you clothed in clean linen, on whose face you placed a cloth, and whom you placed in your new cave, and you rolled a great stone to the door of the cave." And I asked the one who spoke to me, "Show me the place where I laid you." And he took me and showed me the place where I laid him. And the linen cloth lay there, and the cloth that was upon his face. Then I recognized that it was Jesus. And he took me by the hand and placed me in the middle of my house, with the doors shut, and led me to my bed and said to me, "Peace be with you!" Then he kissed me and said to me, "Do not go out of your house for forty[32] days. For see, I go to my brethren in Galilee."'

16. 1. And when the rulers of the synagogue and the priests and the Levites heard these words from Joseph, they became like dead men and fell to the ground and fasted until the ninth hour. And Nicodemus and Joseph comforted Annas and Caiaphas and the priests and Levites, saying, 'Get up and stand on your feet, and taste bread and strengthen your souls. For tomorrow is the Sabbath of the Lord.' And they rose up and prayed to God, and ate and drank, and each went to his own house. 2. And on the Sabbath

---

[32] Variant: 'four'.

our teachers and the priests and the Levites sat and questioned one another, saying, 'What is this wrath which has befallen us? For we know his father and his mother.' Levi the teacher said, 'I know that his parents fear God and do not withhold their prayers and pay tithes three times a year. And when Jesus was born, his parents brought him to this place, and gave God sacrifices and burnt offerings. And the great teacher Simeon took him in his arms and said, "Lord, now let your servant depart in peace, according to your word; for my eyes have seen your salvation which you have prepared in the presence of all peoples, a light for revelation to the Gentiles, and for glory to your people Israel." And Simeon blessed them and said to Mary his mother, "I give you good tidings concerning this child." And Mary said, "Good, my lord?" And Simeon said to her, "Good. Behold, this child is set for the fall and rising of many in Israel, and for a sign that will be rejected, and a sword will pierce through your own soul also, and the thoughts out of many hearts will be revealed."'[33]

3. They said to Levi the teacher, 'How do you know this?' Levi answered them, 'Do you not know that I learned the law from him?' The council said to him, 'We wish to see your father.' And they sent for his father. And when they questioned him, he said to them, 'Why did you not believe my son? The blessed and righteous Simeon taught him the law.' The council said, 'Rabbi Levi, is the word true which you have spoken?' He answered, 'It is true.' Then the rulers of the synagogue and the priests and the Levites said among themselves, 'Come, let us send to Galilee to the three men who came and told us of his teaching and of his ascension, and let them tell us how they saw him taken up.' And this word pleased them all. And they sent the three men who had already gone to Galilee with them, and said to them, 'Say to Rabbi Adas and Rabbi Phineës and Rabbi Angaeus, "Peace be with you and all who are with you. Since an important inquiry is taking place in the council, we were sent to you to call you to this holy place Jerusalem."' 4. And the men went to Galilee and found them sitting and studying the law, and greeted them in peace. And the men who were in Galilee said to those who had come to them, 'Peace be to all Israel.' They answered, 'Peace be with you.' And again they said to them, 'Why have you come?' Those who had been sent replied, 'The council calls you to the holy city Jerusalem.' When the men heard that they were sought by the council, they prayed to God and sat down at table with the men and ate and drank, and then arose and came in peace to Jerusalem.

5. And on the next day the council sat in the synagogue and questioned them, saying, 'Did you indeed see Jesus sitting on the mountain Mamilch, teaching his eleven disciples? And did you see him taken up?' And the men answered them and said, 'We saw him taken up, as we have told you.'

---

[33] Luke 2: 28–35.

6. Annas said, 'Separate them from one another, and let us see if their words agree.' And they separated them from one another. And they called Adas first and asked him, 'How did you see Jesus taken up?' Adas answered, 'As he sat on the mountain Mamilch and taught his disciples, we saw that a cloud overshadowed him and his disciples. And the cloud carried him up to heaven, and his disciples lay on their faces on the ground.' Then they called Phineës the priest and asked him also, 'How did you see Jesus taken up?' And he said the same thing. And again they asked Angaeus, and he said the same thing. Then the members of the council said, 'At the mouth of two or three witnesses every word shall be established.'[34] Buthem the teacher said, 'It is written in the law, "Enoch walked with God, and was not, for God took him." '[35] Jairus the teacher said, 'Also we have heard of the death of the holy Moses, and we did not see him.[36] For it is written in the law of the Lord, "And Moses died as the mouth of the Lord determined, and no man knew of his sepulchre to this day." '[37] And Rabbi Levi said, 'Why did Rabbi Simeon say, when he saw Jesus, "Behold, this child is set for the fall and rising of many in Israel, and for a sign that is spoken against?" '[38] And Rabbi Isaac said, 'It is written in the law, "Behold, I send my messenger before your face. He will go before you to guard you in every good way. In him my name is named." '[39]

7. Then Annas and Caiaphas said, 'You have rightly said what is written in the law of Moses, that no one knows the death of Enoch and no one has named the death of Moses. But Jesus had to give account before Pilate; we saw how he received blows and spitting on his face, that the soldiers put a crown of thorns upon him, that he was scourged and condemned by Pilate and then was crucified at the place of a skull, and two criminals with him; he was given vinegar and gall to drink, and Longinus the soldier pierced his side with a spear. Our honourable father Joseph asked for his body; and, he says, he rose again. And the three teachers declare, 'We saw him taken up into heaven.[40] And Rabbi Levi spoke and testified to the words of Rabbi Simeon, "Behold, this child is set for the fall and rising of many in Israel, and for a sign that will be rejected." '[41] And all the teachers said to the whole people of the Lord, 'If this is from the Lord, and it is marvellous in your eyes, you shall surely know, O house of Jacob, that it is written, "Cursed is every one who hangs on a tree."[42] And another passage of scripture teaches, "The gods who did not make the heaven and the earth shall perish." '[43] And the priests

---

[34] Deut. 19: 15.
[35] Gen. 5: 24.
[36] Variant: 'We do not know how he died'.
[37] Deut. 34: 5–6.   [38] Luke 2: 34.
[39] Exod. 23: 20–1.
[40] One recension of the Latin adds here the Decensus (form 'A').
[41] Luke 2: 34.
[42] Deut. 21: 23.
[43] Jer. 10: 11.

and the Levites said to one another, 'If his memorial lasts to the year called Jubilee, he will reign for ever and create for himself a new people.' Then the rulers of the synagogue and the priests and the Levites admonished all Israel, 'Cursed is that man who shall worship the work of man's hand, and cursed is the man who shall worship created things alongside the creator.' And the people answered, 'Amen, amen.'

8. And all the people praised the Lord God and sang, 'Blessed be the Lord who has given rest to the people of Israel according to all that he spoke. Not one word of all the good which he promised to his servant Moses has failed. May the Lord our God be with us as he was with our fathers. May he not forsake us. May he not let us stop from turning our hearts to him, from walking in all his ways, and from keeping his commandments and laws which he gave to our fathers. And the Lord shall be king over all the earth on that day. And there shall be one God and his name shall be one, our Lord and king. He shall save us. There is none like you, O Lord. You are great, O Lord, and great is your name. Heal us, O Lord, in your power, and we shall be healed. Save us, Lord, and we shall be saved. For we are your portion and inheritance. The Lord will not forsake his people for his great name's sake, for the Lord has begun to make us his people.' Having sung hymns they all departed, every man to his house, glorifying God. For his is the glory for ever and ever. Amen.

CHRIST'S DESCENT INTO HELL

1(17). 1. Joseph said, 'Why then do you marvel that Jesus has been raised? This in itself is not marvellous, but what is marvellous is that he was not raised alone, but raised up many other dead who appeared to many in Jerusalem. And if you do not know the others, Simeon, who received Jesus, and his two sons, whom he raised up, you do at least know. For we buried them a little while ago. And now their sepulchres are to be seen opened and empty, but they themselves are alive and dwelling in Arimathaea.' They therefore sent men, and they found their tombs opened and empty. Joseph said, 'Let us go to Arimathaea and find them.' 2. Then arose the chief priests Annas and Caiaphas, and Joseph and Nicodemus and Gamaliel and others with them, and went to Arimathaea and found the men of whom Joseph spoke. So they offered prayer, and greeted one another. Then they went with them to Jerusalem, and they brought them into the synagogue, and secured the doors, and the chief priests placed the Old Testament of the Jews in the midst and said to them, 'We wish you to swear by the God of Israel and by Adonai and so speak the truth, how you arose and who raised you from the dead.' 3. When the men who had risen heard that, they signed their faces with the sign of the cross, and said to the chief priests, 'Give us paper and ink and pen.' So they brought these things. And they sat down and wrote as follows:

2(18). 1. O Lord Jesus Christ, the resurrection and the life of the world, give us grace that we may tell of your resurrection and of your miracles which you performed in Hades. We, then, were in Hades with all who have died since the beginning of the world. And at the hour of midnight there rose upon the darkness there something like the light of the sun, and it shone and lit us all, and we saw one another. And immediately our father Abraham, together with the patriarchs and the prophets, was filled with joy, and they said to one another, 'This light comes from a great illumination.' The prophet Isaiah, who was present there, said, 'This light comes from the Father and the Son and the Holy Spirit. This I prophesied when I was still living, "The land of Zabulon and the land of Nephthalim, the people that sit in darkness saw a great light."'[44]

2. Then there came into the midst another, an anchorite from the wilderness and the patriarchs asked him, 'Who are you?' He replied, 'I am John, the last of the prophets, who made straight the ways of the Son of God, and preached repentance to the people for the forgiveness of sins. And the Son of God came to me, and when I saw him afar off, I said to the people, "Behold, the Lamb of God, who takes away the sin of the world."[45] And with my hand I baptized him in the river Jordan, and I saw the Holy Spirit like a dove coming upon him, and heard also the voice of God the Father speaking thus, "This is my beloved Son, in whom I am well pleased."[46] And for this reason he sent me to you, to preach that the only begotten Son of God comes here, in order that whoever believes in him should be saved, and whoever does not believe in him should be condemned. Therefore I say to you all that when you see him, all of you worship him. For now only have you opportunity for repentance because you worshipped idols in the vain world above and sinned. At any other time this is impossible.'

3(19). 1. Now when John was thus teaching those who were in Hades, the first-created, the first father Adam, heard and said to his son Seth, 'My son, I wish you to tell to the forefathers of the race of men and to the prophets where I sent you when I was about to die.' And Seth said, 'Prophets and patriarchs, listen. My father Adam, the first-created, when he fell into mortal sickness, sent me close to the gate of paradise to pray to God that he might lead me by an angel to the tree of mercy, that I might take oil and anoint my father, so that he might arise from his sickness. This I did. And after my prayer an angel of the Lord came and asked me, "What do you desire, Seth? Because of the sickness of your father do you desire the oil that raises up the sick, or the tree from which flows such oil? This cannot be found now. Therefore go and tell your father that after the completion of 5,500 years from the creation of the world, the only-begotten Son of God shall then

---

[44] Isa. 9: 1–2.
[45] John 1: 29.
[46] Matt. 3: 16–17.

become man and shall descend upon the earth. And he shall anoint him with that oil. And he shall arise and wash him and his descendants with water and the Holy Spirit. And then he shall be healed of every disease. But this is impossible now."' When the patriarchs and prophets heard this, they rejoiced greatly.

4(20). 1. And while they were all so joyful, Satan the heir of darkness came and said to Hades, 'All devouring and insatiable one, listen to my words. There is one of the race of the Jews, Jesus by name, who calls himself the Son of God. But he is a man, and at our instigation the Jews crucified him. And now that he is dead, be prepared that we may secure him here. For I know that he is a man, and I heard him saying, "My soul is very sorrowful, even to death."[47] He caused me much trouble in the world above while he lived among mortals. For wherever he found my servants, he cast them out, and all those whom I had made to be crippled or blind or lame, leprous and the like, he healed with only a word, and many whom I had made ready for burial he also made alive again with only a word.' 2. Hades said, 'Is he so powerful that he does such things with only a word? And if he is of such power, are you able to withstand him? It seems to me that no one will be able to withstand such as he is. But if you say that you heard how he feared death, he said this to mock and laugh at you, wishing to seize you with a strong hand. And woe, woe to you for all eternity.' Satan answered, 'O all-devouring and insatiable Hades, did you fear so greatly when you heard about our common foe? I did not fear him, but worked upon the Jews, and they crucified him and gave him gall and vinegar to drink. Therefore prepare yourself to get him firmly into your power when he comes.'

3. Hades answered, 'O heir of darkness, son of perdition, devil, you have just told me that many whom you made ready for burial he made alive again with only a word. If then he freed others from the grave, how and with what power will he be held by us? A short time ago I devoured a certain dead man called Lazarus, and soon afterwards one of the living drew him up forcibly from my entrails with only a word. And I think it is the one of whom you speak. If, therefore, we receive him here, I fear lest we run the risk of losing the others also. For, behold, I see that all those whom I have devoured from the beginning of the world are disquieted. My belly is in pain. Lazarus who was snatched from me before seems to me no good sign. For not like a dead man, but like an eagle he flew away from me, so quickly did the earth cast him out. Therefore I adjure you by your gifts and mine, do not bring him here. For I believe that he comes here to raise all the dead. And I tell you this: By the darkness which surrounds us, if you bring him here, none of the dead will be left for me.'

5(21). 1. While Satan and Hades were speaking thus to one another, a loud

---

[47] Matt. 26: 38 and parallel.

voice like thunder sounded, 'Lift up your gates, O rulers, and be lifted up, O everlasting doors, and the King of Glory shall come in.'[48] When Hades heard this, he said to Satan, 'Go out, if you can, and withstand him.' So Satan went out. Then Hades said to his demons, 'Secure strongly and firmly the gates of brass and the bars of iron, and hold my bolts, and stand upright and keep watch on everything. For if he comes in, woe will seize us. 2. When the forefathers heard that, they all began to mock him, saying, 'O all-devouring and insatiable one, open, that the King of Glory may come in.' The prophet David said, 'Do you not know, blind one, that when I lived in the world, I prophesied that word: "Lift up your gates, O rulers"?'[49] Isaiah said, 'I foresaw this by the Holy Spirit and wrote, "The dead shall arise, and those who are in the tombs shall be raised up, and those who are under the earth shall rejoice.[50] O death, where is your sting? O Hades, where is your victory?"'[51] 3. Again the voice sounded, 'Lift up the gates.' When Hades heard the voice the second time, he answered as if he did not know it and said, 'Who is this King of Glory?' The angels of the Lord said, 'The Lord strong and mighty, the Lord mighty in battle.'[52] And immediately at this answer the gates of brass were broken in pieces and the bars of iron were crushed and all the dead who were bound were loosed from their chains, and we with them. And the King of Glory entered as a man, and all the dark places of Hades were illuminated.

6(22). 1. Hades at once cried out, 'We are defeated, woe to us. But who are you, who have such authority and power? And who are you, who without sin have come here, you who appear small and can do great things, who are humble and exalted, slave and master, soldier and king, and have authority over both the dead and the living? You were nailed to the cross, and laid in the sepulchre, and now you have become free and have destroyed all our power. Are you Jesus, of whom the chief ruler Satan said to us that through the cross and death you would inherit the whole world?' 2. Then the King of Glory seized the chief ruler Satan by the head and handed him over to the angels, saying, 'Bind with irons his hands and his feet and his neck and his mouth.' Then he gave him to Hades and said, 'Take him and hold him fast until my second coming.'

7(23). 1. And Hades took Satan and said to him, 'O Beelzebub, heir of fire and torment, enemy of the saints, through what necessity did you contrive that the King of Glory should be crucified, so that he should come here and strip us naked? Turn and see that not one dead man is left in me, but all that you gained through the tree of knowledge you have lost through the tree of the cross. All your joy is changed into sorrow. You wished to kill the King of

---

[48] Psalm 24: 7.
[49] Psalm 24: 7.
[50] Isa. 26: 19.
[51] 1 Cor. 15: 55.
[52] Psalm 24: 8.

Glory, but have killed yourself. For since I have received you to hold you fast, you shall learn by experience what evils I shall do to you. O arch-devil, the beginning of death, the root of sin, the end of all evil, what evil did you find in Jesus to procure his destruction? How did you dare to commit such great wickedness? How did you study to bring down such a man into this darkness, through whom you have been deprived of all who have died since the beginning?'

8(24). 1. While Hades was thus speaking with Satan, the King of Glory stretched out his right hand, and took hold of our forefather Adam and raised him up. Then he turned to the rest and said, 'Come with me, all you who have died through the tree which this man touched. For behold, I raise you all up again through the tree of the cross.' With that he sent them all out. And our forefather Adam was seen to be full of joy, and said, 'I give thanks to your majesty, O Lord, because you have brought me up from the lowest Hades.' Likewise all the prophets and the saints said, 'We give you thanks, O Christ, Saviour of the world, because you have brought up our life from destruction'. 2. When they had said this, the Saviour blessed Adam with the sign of the cross on his forehead. And he did this also to the patriarchs and prophets and martyrs and forefathers, and he took them and sprang up out of Hades. And as he went the holy fathers sang praises, following him and saying, 'Blessed be he who comes in the name of the Lord.[53] Alleluia. To him be the glory of all the saints.'

9(25). 1. Thus he went into paradise holding our forefather Adam by the hand, and he handed him and all the righteous to Michael the archangel. And as they were entering the gate of paradise, two old men met them. The holy fathers asked them, 'Who are you, who have not seen death nor gone down into Hades, but dwell in paradise with your bodies and souls?' One of them answered, 'I am Enoch, who pleased God and was removed here by him. And this is Elijah the Tishbite. We are to live until the end of the world. But then we are to be sent by God to withstand Antichrist and to be killed by him. And after three days we shall rise again and be caught up in clouds to meet the Lord.'

10(26). 1. While they were saying this there came another, a humble man, carrying a cross on his shoulder. The holy fathers asked him, 'Who are you, who have the appearance of a robber, and what is the cross you carry on your shoulder?' He answered, 'I was, as you say, a robber and a thief in the world, and therefore the Jews took me and delivered me to the death of the cross together with our Lord Jesus Christ. When he hung on the cross, I saw the wonders which happened and believed in him. And I appealed to him and said, "Lord, when you reign as king, do not forget me." And immediately he said to me, "Truly, truly, today, I say to you, you shall be with me in

---

[53] Psalm 118: 26.

paradise."[54] So I came into paradise carrying my cross, and found Michael the archangel, and said to him, "Our Lord Jesus Christ, who was crucified, has sent me here. Lead me, therefore, to the gate of Eden." And when the flaming sword saw the sign of the cross, it opened to me and I went in. Then the archangel said to me, "Wait a short while. For Adam also, the forefather of the race of men, comes with the righteous, that they also may enter in." And now that I have seen you, I have come to meet you.' When the saints heard this, they all cried with a loud voice, 'Great is our Lord, and great is his power.'

11(27). 1. All this we saw and heard, we two brothers who also were sent by Michael the archangel and were appointed to preach the resurrection of the Lord, but first to go to the Jordan and be baptized. We went there and were baptized with other dead who had risen. Then we went to Jerusalem and celebrated the passover of the resurrection. But now we depart, since we cannot remain here. And the love of God the Father and the grace of our Lord Jesus Christ and the fellowship of the Holy Spirit be with you all.[55]

When they had written this and had sealed the books, they gave half to the chief priests and half to Joseph and Nicodemus. And they immediately vanished. To the glory of our Lord Jesus Christ. Amen.

CHRIST'S DESCENT INTO HELL (LATIN A)

1(17). 1. And Joseph rose and said to Annas and Caiaphas, 'It is right and proper that you marvel at hearing that Jesus was seen to ascend into heaven alive from the dead. But what is more marvellous is that he did not rise from the dead alone, but has raised to life many other dead from their tombs, and they have been seen by many in Jerusalem. And hear me now, for we all know the blessed Simeon, the great priest, who in the temple took up the infant Jesus in his arms. Now this Simeon had two sons, full brothers, and we were all present at their falling asleep and at their burial. Go, therefore, and see their tombs for they are open, because they have risen again, and behold, they are in the city of Arimathaea, living together in prayer. And indeed they are heard crying out but speaking with no one, and they are silent as the dead. But come, let us go to them, and bring them back with all honour and gentleness. And if we put them on oath they will perhaps speak to us of the mystery of their resurrection.'

2. And they all rejoiced as they heard these things. And Annas and Caiaphas, Nicodemus and Joseph and Gamaliel, went and did not find them in their sepulchre; but, going to the city of Arimathaea, they found them there spending their time on bended knees in prayer. And they kissed them, and with all respect and fear of God led them to Jerusalem into the synagogue. And when the doors were shut they took up the law of the Lord and placed it in their hands, and adjured them by the God Adonai and the God of Israel who spoke to our fathers through the law and the prophets,

---

[54] Luke 23: 43.
[55] 2 Cor. 13: 14.

Christ's Descent into Hell 191

saying, 'Do you believe that it was Jesus who raised you from the dead? Tell us how you rose from the dead.'

3. Hearing this oath, Karinus and Leucius trembled in body, and being troubled in heart, groaned. And together, looking to heaven, they made the sign of the cross with their fingers upon their tongues and immediately spoke together and said, 'Give to each of us sheets of paper and let us write what we have seen and heard.' So they gave the paper to them. And they sat down and each wrote as follows:

2(18). 1. Lord Jesus Christ, the Resurrection and the Life, permit us to speak mysteries through your death on the cross for we have been adjured by you. For you have ordered your servants to tell to no man the secrets of your Divine majesty which you did in Hades. Now, when we were placed with all our fathers in the deep, in obscure darkness, suddenly there came a golden heat of the sun and a purple and royal light shining upon us. And immediately the father of all the human race with all the patriarchs and prophets rejoiced and said, 'That light is the author of everlasting light, who has promised to send to us the co-eternal light.' And Isaiah cried out and said, 'This is the light of the Father, the Son of God, as I foretold when I was living on the earth. The land of Zebulon and the land of Naphthalim beyond Jordan, Galilee of the Gentiles, the people who sat in darkness have seen a great light; and they who were in the region of the shadow of death, among them the light shone. And now it has come and shone on us who sit in death.'[1]

2. And when we all rejoiced in the light which shone upon us, our father Simeon came to us and said to us, rejoicing, 'Glorify the Lord Jesus Christ, the Son of God; for when born I took him up, an infant in my hands in the temple. And being compelled by the holy spirit I confessed to him, saying, "Now my eyes have seen your salvation which you have prepared in the sight of all peoples, a light for revelation of the Gentiles and the glory of your people Israel." '[2] And, hearing this, all the multitude of the saints rejoiced the more.

3. And after this there came up a man who looked like a dweller in the wilderness and he was asked by all, 'Who are you?' And he answered them and said, 'I am John, the voice and prophet of the Most High, who goes before the face of his coming to prepare his ways, to give knowledge of salvation to his people for the remission of their sins. And seeing him coming to me, compelled by the holy spirit, I said, "Behold the Lamb of God! Behold him who takes away the sins of the world!"[3] And I baptized him in the River Jordan and I saw the holy spirit descending upon him in the form of a dove, and I heard a voice from heaven saying, "This is my beloved son in whom I am well pleased." And now I have gone before his face and have come down to announce to you that the risen Son of God is about to visit us, coming from on high to us who are sitting in darkness and the shadow of death.'

3(19). 1. And when the first created man, Father Adam, had heard that Jesus was baptized in Jordan, he cried out to his son Seth, 'Tell your sons, the patriarchs and prophets, all that you heard from the archangel Michael, when I sent you to the gates of Paradise to pray to God that he would send to you his angel to give you oil from the tree of mercy to anoint my body when I was sick.' Then Seth, approaching the holy

---

[1] Isa. 9: 1-2.
[2] Luke 2: 30-2.
[3] John 1: 29.

patriarchs and prophets said, 'When I, Seth, was praying to the Lord at the gates of Paradise, behold, Michael, the angel of the Lord, appeared to me and said, "I am sent to you by the Lord for I am set over the human race. And to you, Seth, I say: Do not labour in praying and entreating with tears for the oil of the tree of mercy to anoint your father Adam for the pain of his body, for you will not be able to receive it except in the last days and times, nor until the five thousand and five hundred years[4] shall have been fulfilled. Then will come upon the earth the most beloved Son of God to raise the body of Adam and the bodies of the dead, and he, when he comes, shall be baptized in Jordan. And when he shall have come out from the water of Jordan, then with the oil of his mercy he will anoint all who believe in him, and that oil of mercy shall be for the generation of those who shall be born of water and the holy spirit to eternal life. Then descending into the earth the most beloved Son of God, Jesus Christ, shall bring our father Adam into paradise to the tree of mercy."' And hearing all these things from Seth, all the patriarchs and prophets rejoiced with great joy.

4(20). 1. And when all the saints were rejoicing, behold, Satan, the prince and leader of death, said to Hades, 'Prepare yourself to receive Jesus who boasts that he is the Son of God and is a man who fears death and says, "My soul is sorrowful even unto death."[5] And he has withstood me in very many things, doing me evil, and many whom I made blind, lame, deaf, leprous, and demoniacs, he has healed with a word; and those whom I brought to you dead, them has he taken from you.'

2. Hades, answering, said to prince Satan, 'Who is this man so powerful if he be a man who fears death? For all the powerful people of the earth whom you have brought into subjection by your might are held subject by my power. If, therefore, you are powerful, of what kind is that man Jesus, who, fearing death, resists your power? If he is so powerful in humanity, of a truth I say to you, he is all-powerful in divinity, and no one can resist his power. And when he says that he fears death he desires to capture you, and woe will be to you for everlasting ages.' And Satan, prince of Tartarus, answered and said, 'Why have you doubted and feared to receive that Jesus, your adversary and mine? For I have tempted him and stirred up my ancient people, the Jews, with zeal and wrath against him; I have sharpened a spear to pierce him, I have mingled gall and vinegar to give him drink, and I have prepared a tree to crucify him and thorns to prick him, and his death is close at hand that I may bring him to you, subject to you and me.'

3. Hades, answering, said, 'You have said to me that it is he himself who has drawn the dead from me. There are many who have been held here by me, who when they lived on the earth took from me the dead, not by their own powers but by prayers to God, and their almighty God drew them from me. Who is this Jesus, who by his own word has drawn the dead from me without prayers? Perhaps it is even he who by the word of his command restored Lazarus to life after he had been four days dead in stench and corruption, when I held him dead.' Then Satan, prince of death, answered and said, 'It is that same Jesus.' And hearing this, Hades said to him, 'I adjure you by your powers and mine that you do not bring him to me; for when I heard then the command of his word I trembled with fear and dread, and all my servants were confounded together with me. And we could not keep Lazarus; but shaking himself as

---

[4] Variant: 'five thousand, nine hundred, and fifty-two'.
[5] Matt. 26: 38.

an eagle with all alacrity and speed he sprang forth from us, and the very earth which held the dead body of Lazarus immediately gave him up alive. So now I know that the man who could do these things is God, powerful in dominion, mighty in humanity, and is the saviour of the human race. And if you bring him to me he will release all who are here shut up in the cruelty of prison and fettered with the unbreakable chains of their sins, and will bring them to the life of his divinity for ever.'

5(21). 1. And while prince Satan and Hades said these things, one to another, there came suddenly a voice as of thunder, and a cry of spirits, 'Lift up your gates, princes; and be lifted up you everlasting gates, and the King of Glory shall come in.'[6] And hearing this, Hades said to prince Satan, 'Go away from me and depart from my home. If you are a mighty fighter fight against the King of Glory. But what have you to do with him?' And Hades cast Satan forth from his realm. And Hades said to his wicked servants, 'Close the cruel gates of brass, and lay on them the bars of iron, and bravely resist, that we who hold captivity may not be taken captive.'[7]

2. And all the multitude of the saints, hearing these things, said to Hades, with the voice of reproof, 'Open your gates, that the King of Glory may come in.' And David cried out saying, 'When I was alive on the earth, did I not prophesy to you, "Let them confess to the Lord for his mercies and declare his wonders to the children of men; for he has shattered the gates of brass and broken the bars of iron; he has taken them up from the way of their iniquity"?'[8] And after this Isaiah likewise said, 'When I was alive on the earth, did I not prophesy to you, "The dead shall rise up, and they who are in the tombs shall rise again, and those who are on the earth shall rejoice, for the dew which is from the Lord is their healing"?[9] And again I said, "Where, O death, is your sting? Where, O Hades, is your victory?"'[10]

3. And when all the saints heard these words from Isaiah, they said to Hades, 'Open your gates. Now you are conquered and will be weak and powerless.' And again there came a great voice as of thunder saying, 'Lift up your gates, princes, and be lifted up, you gates of Hades, and the King of Glory shall come in.' And Hades, seeing that the voice had twice cried, said as if not knowing, 'Who is the King of Glory?' And David answered and said to Hades, 'I recognize the words of this cry, for I prophesied the same through his spirit. And now, as I said before, I say to you, "It is the Lord strong and mighty, the Lord mighty in battle, he is the King of Glory."'[11] And the Lord himself looked down from heaven on earth to hear the groans of the fettered and to release the sons of the slain. And now, O most vile and filthy Hades, open your gates, that the King of Glory may come in.' And while David spoke, the Lord of Majesty came upon Hades in the form of man, and lighted up the eternal darkness and broke the indissoluble chains, and the succour of invincible power visited us who were sitting in the deep darkness of trespasses and in the shadow of the death of sins.

6(22). 1. Then Hades and Death and their wicked servants, together with their cruel ministers, seeing this, were stricken with fear at the brightness so great a light revealed in their own dominions as they saw Christ suddenly in their abode and they

---

[6] Ps. 24: 7.
[7] Reading 'captevemur'.
[8] Ps. 107: 16–17.
[9] Isa. 26: 19.
[10] 1 Cor. 15: 55 (or Isa. 25: 8?).
[11] Ps. 24: 8.

cried out saying, 'We are conquered by you. Who are you who brings our master to confusion?[12] Who are you who, undestroyed by corruption, with proof of majesty undefiled, condemn with wrath our power? Who are you, so great and so small, so lowly and so high, soldier and commander, wondrous fighter in the form of a servant, and King of Glory, dead and alive, who, when slain, have carried the cross? You, who lay dead in the sepulchre, have descended to us alive; and in your death the whole creation trembled and all the stars were shaken, and now you have become free among the dead and disturb our legions. Who are you who release the prisoners who were held bound by original sin, and recall them to their former freedom? Who are you who shed divine and glorious and illuminating light on those who are blinded by the darkness of sins?' And in like manner all the legions of demons, terrified with similar fear because of their dreadful overthrow, cried out with one voice saying, 'Where do you come from, O Jesus, a man so strong and splendid in majesty, so glorious, without spot and clean from sin? For that earthly world which has always been subject to us until now and paid tribute to our profit has never sent to us such a dead man nor dispatched such gifts to the underworld. Who then are you, who have so fearlessly entered our bounds, and have not only no fear of our punishments but attempt in addition to deliver everyone from our chains? Perhaps you are that Jesus of whom our prince Satan said that by your death on the cross you would receive the dominion of the whole world.'

2. Then the King of Glory with his majesty trampled on Death and seizing Satan, its prince, delivered him to the power of Hades and drew Adam to his brightness.

7(23). 1. Then Hades, receiving prince Satan, said to him with great reviling, 'O prince of perdition and chief of destruction, Beelzebub, derision of angels, contempt of the righteous, why did you wish to do these things? Did you want to crucify the Lord of Glory in whose death you promised us such great spoils? Did you, as a fool, not know what you did? Behold now, this Jesus, with the splendour of his divinity, disperses all the darkness of death and has broken the firm foundations of our prisons, and has sent forth the prisoners and loosed those who were bound; and all who used to groan under our torments insult us, and by their prayers our dominion is stormed and our kingdom conquered, and the human race no longer fears us. And more than this, the dead, who were never proud over us and could not at any time be joyful as prisoners, now boldly threaten us. O prince Satan, father of all impious wretches and apostates, why did you wish to do this? They who from the beginning until now had despaired of salvation and life can no longer be heard howling, neither are their groans heard nor is the trace of tears found on the face of any of them. O prince Satan, possessor of the keys of the underworld, those riches of yours which you acquired by the tree of transgression and the loss of paradise you have now lost by the tree of the cross, and all your joy is perished. When you hanged that Christ Jesus, the King of Glory, you acted against yourself and against me. Henceforth you will know what eternal torments and endless punishments you are to suffer in my everlasting keeping. O prince Satan, author of death and source of all pride, you ought first to have considered the evil case of that Jesus. Why without reason did you dare unjustly to crucify him in whom you knew there to be no fault, and bring to our realm an innocent and righteous man, and release the guilty, wicked and unrighteous of the whole world?'

---

[12] Or variant: 'Who are you who directs your prayer to God for our confusion?'

2. And after Hades had spoken thus to prince Satan then the King of Glory said to Hades, 'Prince Satan shall be under your power for everlasting ages in the place of Adam and his sons, my righteous ones.'

8(24). 1. And the Lord, stretching forth his hand, said, 'Come to me, all you my saints who have my image and my likeness. You who by the tree and the devil and death had been condemned see now how by the tree the devil and death have been condemned.' And immediately all the saints were gathered together under the hand of the Lord. Then the Lord, holding the right hand of Adam, said to him, 'Peace be to you with all your sons, my righteous ones.' But Adam, falling at the knees of the Lord with tearful entreaty, prayed in a loud voice and said, 'I will exalt you, O Lord because you have taken me up and not made my foes to triumph me. O Lord God, I cried to you, and you, Lord, have healed me. You have brought my soul out of Hades and have saved me from those who go down into the pit. Sing to the Lord, all his saints, and give thanks to the remembrance of his holiness, for there is wrath in his indignation and life in his good pleasure.' In like manner all the saints of God knelt at the feet of the Lord and said with one voice, 'You have come, O redeemer of the world. What you foretold by the law and your prophets you have indeed fulfilled. You have redeemed the living by your cross, and by the death of the cross have descended to us that you might deliver us from the underworld and death by your majesty. O Lord, as you have set the name of your glory in heaven and have erected your cross on earth as the token of redemption, so, O Lord, set the sign of the victory of your cross in Hades that death may no more have dominion.'

2. And the Lord, stretching forth his hand, made the sign of the cross on Adam and on all his saints, and holding the right hand of Adam ascended from the underworld, and all the saints followed him. Then holy David cried aloud and said, 'Sing to the Lord a new song for he has done marvellous things. His right hand and his holy arm have brought salvation. The Lord has made known his salvation and revealed his righteousness in the sight of the nations.'[13] And all the multitude of the saints answered saying, 'This is glory for all his saints. Amen. Alleluia.'

3. And after this the prophet Habakkuk cried out saying, 'You went forth for the salvation of your people, to deliver your elect.'[14] And all the saints answered and said, 'Blessed is he who comes in the name of the Lord. The Lord is God and has shone his light upon us. Amen. Alleluia.' Likewise after this the prophet Micah cried out saying, 'Who is a God like you are, O Lord, taking away iniquities, and passing over sins? And now you restrain your anger for a testimony because you are desirous of mercy, and you turn away and have mercy on us, and forgive all our iniquities, and have made all our sins to sink in the multitude of death[15] as you did swear to our fathers in the days of old.'[16] And all the saints answered and said, 'This is our God for ever and world without end and he will rule us for ever. Amen. Alleluia.' Thus all the prophets, quoting sacred words from their praises, and all the saints crying, 'Amen. Alleluia!' followed the Lord.

9(25). 1. Then the Lord, holding the hand of Adam, delivered him to the archangel Michael, and all the saints followed the archangel Michael, and he brought them all

[13] Ps 98: 1–2.
[14] Hab. 3: 13.
[15] Perhaps 'depth of the sea', reading 'altitudine maris' for 'multitudine mortis'.
[16] Mic. 7: 18–20.

into the glorious grace of paradise. And there met them two men, ancients of days. And they were asked by the saints, 'Who are you who have not yet been dead in the underworld with us and have been placed in paradise in the body?' One of them answered and said, 'I am Enoch, who was translated here by the word of the Lord; and he who is with me is Elijah the Tishbite who was taken up in the chariot of fire. Up to this day we have not tasted death but have been waiting for the coming of Antichrist, to do battle with him with divine signs and wonders and, after having been slain by him in Jerusalem, to be again taken up alive in the clouds after three days and a half.'

10(26). 1. And while Enoch and Elijah were speaking with the saints, behold, another man, most wretched, came up, bearing on his shoulders the sign of the cross. And all the saints seeing him said to him, 'Who are you? Your appearance is that of a robber. And what is the sign that you bear on your shoulders?' And he answered them and said, 'You correctly say that I was a robber, doing all evil deeds on the earth. And the Jews crucified me with Jesus, and I saw the miracles which were done to creation by the cross of Jesus crucified, and I believed him to be the creator of all created things, and the King omnipotent, and I prayed to him, saying, "Remember me, O Lord, when you have come into your kingdom." And he, immediately receiving my prayer, said to me, "Amen, I say to you, this day you shall be with me in paradise."[17] And he gave me this sign of the cross saying, "Bearing this, walk into paradise, and if the angel who guards paradise will not permit you to enter show him the sign of the cross and you shall say to him, "Jesus Christ, the Son of God, who has now been crucified, has sent me." And when I had done this I said all this to the angel who guarded paradise. And when he heard this from me immediately he opened the gates and let me in and placed me on the right hand of paradise, saying, "Behold, wait a little and Adam, the father of all the human race, will enter with all his sons, the holy and just, after the triumph and glory of the ascension of Christ, the crucified Lord."' And hearing these words of the robber all the holy patriarchs and prophets said with one voice, 'Blessed be you, O Lord Almighty, the Father of eternal blessings and Father of mercies, who have given such grace to your sinners and have brought them into the joy of paradise and into your rich pastures; for this is spiritual life most sure. Amen, amen.'

11(27). 1. These are the divine and sacred mysteries which we saw and heard, I, Karinus, and Leucius. The other mysteries of God we are not permitted to tell further, as Michael the archangel adjured us and said, 'You shall go with your brethren to Jerusalem and continue crying in prayers and glorifying the resurrection of the Lord Jesus Christ, who raised you from the dead with himself. And you shall speak with no man, but shall sit dumb until the hour shall come when the Lord himself permits you to relate the mysteries of his divinty.' And the archangel Michael ordered us to go across Jordan into a rich and fertile spot where are many who rose with us in witness of the resurrection of the Lord Christ. But we who rose from the dead were only permitted three days to keep the passover of the Lord in Jerusalem with our living relatives in witness of the resurrection of Christ the Lord, and we have been baptized in the holy stream of Jordan, each one receiving a white robe. And after three days, having kept the Lord's passover, all who rose with us were carried up in the clouds and brought beyond Jordan, and have not been seen since by any man. But we were told to continue in prayer in the city of Arimathaea.

[17] Luke 23: 43.

2. These are the things which the Lord ordered us to relate to you. Give praise and thanks to him, and repent that he may have mercy on you. Peace be to you from the Lord Jesus Christ himself, the Saviour of us all. Amen.

3. And after they had finished writing on separate sheets of paper they rose. And Karinus gave what he had written into the hands of Annas and Caiaphas and Gamaliel; and in like manner Leucius gave what he had written into the hands of Nicodemus and Joseph. And they were suddenly transfigured and became exceeding white, and were seen no more. And their writings were found the same, neither more nor less by a letter.

4. And all the synagogue of the Jews, hearing all these wonderful words of Karinus and Leucius, said to one another, 'Of a truth all these things were done by the Lord and blessed be the Lord for ever and ever. Amen.' And they all went out with great anxiety, beating their breasts with fear and trembling, and departed, each to his own home.

5. And immediately Joseph and Nicodemus related to the governor all these things which were said by the Jews in their synagogue. And Pilate himself wrote all things that were done and said by the Jews concerning Jesus, and placed all the words among the public records of his praetorium.

12(28). 1. After this Pilate, having entered the temple of the Jews, gathered together all the chief priests and learned men and scribes and doctors of the law and entered with them into the sanctuary of the temple and ordered that all the gates should be shut, and said to them, 'We have heard that you have a great library in this temple. I therefore ask you that it be presented before us.' And when the collection of books, adorned with gold and precious stones, was brought by four servants, Pilate said to all, 'I adjure you by the God of your fathers, who commanded you to build this temple in the place of his sanctuary, that you do not hide the truth from me. You know all things that are written in this collection of books, so say now if you have found in the Scriptures that this Jesus whom you crucified is the Son of God, who should come for the salvation of the human race, and in how many years' time he ought to come. Show me if you crucified him in ignorance or with knowledge.'

2. Thus sworn, Annas and Caiaphas ordered all the others who were with them to go forth from the sanctuary, and they themselves shut all the gates of the temple and the sanctuary and said to Pilate, 'We have been adjured by you, O good judge, by the building of this temple, to give a clear and truthful explanation to you. After we crucified Jesus, not knowing that he was the Son of God but thinking that he did miracles by some charm, we held a great synagogue in this temple. And conferring with one another about the signs of the miracles which Jesus had done, we found many witnesses of our race who said that they had seen Jesus alive after the suffering of death, and that he had entered into the height of heaven. And we have seen two witnesses whom Jesus raised from the dead, who have declared to us many wonders which Jesus did among the dead, of which we have a written account in our hands. And it is our custom every year, before our synagogue, to open this sacred collection of books and seek out the testimony of God. And we have found in the first book of the Septuagint, where the archangel Michael spoke to the third son of Adam, the first man, about the five thousand and five hundred years after which Christ, the most dearly beloved Son of God, should come from heaven, and we have, moreover, considered that perhaps he was the God of Israel who said to Moses, "Make the ark of

the covenant of two cubits and a half in length, of one cubit and a half in width, and one cubit and a half in height."[18] In these five cubits and a half we have understood and recognized the structure of the ark of the Old Testament, that in five and a half thousands of years Jesus Christ should come in the ark of the body, and we have found that he is the God of Israel, the Son of God. Because after his suffering we, the chief priests, wondering at the signs which were done because of him, opened this collection of books seeking out all the generations up to the generation of Joseph, and reckoning that Mary, the mother of Christ, was of the seed of David; and we have found that from the time when God made heaven and earth and the first man until the flood are two thousand, two hundred, and twelve years; and from the flood until the building of the tower five hundred and thirty-one years; and from the building of the tower until Abraham, six hundred and six years; and from Abraham until the coming of the children of Israel four hundred and seventy years; from the Exodus of the children of Israel from Egypt to the building of the Temple five hundred and eleven years: and from the building of the Temple to the destruction of the same Temple four hundred and sixty-four years. Thus far have we found in the book of Ezra. We find, after search, that from the burning of the Temple to the coming of Christ and his birth are six hundred and thirty-six years. And these together are five thousand and five hundred years, as we find it written in the book that the archangel Michael foretold to Seth, the third son of Adam; so Christ, the Son of God, came in five and a half thousands of years. Until now we have told no one, that there may be no division in our synagogues; but now, O good judge, you have charged us on oath by this sacred collection of books of the testimonies of God and we declare it to you. And we have adjured you by your life and health to make these words known to no one in Jerusalem.'

13(29). 1. Pilate, hearing these words of Annas and Caiaphas, set them all in the acts of the Lord and Saviour in the public records of his praetorium and wrote a letter to Claudius, king of the city of Rome, saying:

Here follows the Letter of Pilate to Claudius. See below, pp. 205–6.

CHRIST'S DESCENT INTO HELL (LATIN B)

1(17). 1. Then Rabbi Adas, and Rabbi Fineës, and Rabbi Egias, the three men who had come from Galilee testifying that they had seen Jesus taken up into heaven, stood up in the midst of the multitude of the chiefs of the Jews and said before the priests and the Levites, who had been called together to the council of the Lord, 'When we came from Galilee we met at the Jordan a very great multitude of men, fathers, who had been some time dead. And present among them we saw Karinus and Leucius. And when they came up to us we kissed each other because they were dear friends of ours; and we asked them, "Tell us, friends and brothers, what is this soul and flesh? and who are those with whom you are going? and how is it that you, who have been some time dead, remain in the body?"'

2. And they said in answer, 'We rose with Christ from the underworld and he himself raised us up again from the dead. And from this you may know that the gates

---

[18] Exod. 25: 10.

of death and darkness have been destroyed, and the souls of the saints have been brought out from there, and have ascended into heaven along with Christ the Lord. And indeed we have been commanded by the Lord himself that for an appointed time we should walk over the banks of Jordan and the mountains; not, however, appearing to all nor speaking to all except to those to whom he has permitted us. And even now we could neither have spoken to you nor be seen by you unless we had been permitted by the Holy Spirit.'

3. And when they heard this all the multitude who were present in the council were struck with fear and trembling, and wondered whether these things had really happened which these Galileans testified. Then Caiaphas and Annas said to the council, 'What these have testified both before and after must shortly be made absolutely clear. If it is true that Karinus and Leucius remain alive in the body, and if we shall be able to behold them with our own eyes, then what they testify is altogether true; and if we find them they will inform us of everything; but if not, you may know that it is all lies.'

4. Then the council forthwith rose. And it seemed good to them to choose fit men, fearing God, who knew when they died and where they were buried: these would inquire diligently to see whether it was as they had heard. The men therefore proceeded to the same place, fifteen in number, who throughout had been present at their falling asleep, and had stood at their feet when they were buried, and had beheld their tombs. And they came and found their tombs open and very many others besides and found a sign neither of their bones nor of their dust. And they returned in all haste and reported what they had seen.

5. Then all their synagogue was in great grief and perplexity and they said to each other, 'What shall we do?' Annas and Caiaphas said, 'Let us turn to where we have heard that they are, and let us send to them men of rank asking and entreating them: perhaps they will deign to come to us. Then they sent to them Nicodemus and Joseph, and the three Galilean rabbis who had seen them to ask that they should deign to come to them. And they went and walked round all the region of Jordan and the mountains but returned without finding them.

6. And, behold, suddenly there appeared coming down from Mount Amalech a very great number, about twelve thousand men, who had risen with the Lord. And though they recognized very many there they were not able to say anything to them out of fear and the angelic vision; and they stood at a distance gazing at them and listening to them as they marched along singing praises and saying, 'The Lord has risen again from the dead as he had said; let us all exult and be glad since he reigns for ever.' Then those who had been sent were astonished and fell to the ground for fear and received the answer from them that they should see Karinus and Leucius in their own houses.

7. And they rose up and went to their houses and found them spending their time in prayer. And going in to them they fell on their faces to the ground, greeting them; and standing up, they said, 'O friends of God, all the multitude of the Jews have directed us to you, hearing that you have risen from the dead, asking and beseeching you to come to them that we all may know the great things of God which have happened around us in our times.' And they immediately, at a sign from God, stood up and came with them and entered their synagogue. Then the multitude of the Jews with the priests put the books of the law in their hands and adjured them by the God Heloi

and the God Adonai and by the law and the prophets, saying, 'Tell us how you have risen from the dead, and what are those wonderful things which have happened in our times, such as we have never heard to have happened at any other time; because already for fear all our bones have been benumbed and have dried up and the earth moves itself under our feet: for we have joined all our hearts to shed righteous and holy blood.'

8. Then Karinus and Leucius beckoned to them with their hands to give them a sheet of paper and ink. And this they did because the Holy Spirit did not allow them to speak to them. And they gave each of them paper and put them apart, the one from the other in separate cells. And they made with their fingers the sign of the cross of Christ and began to write on the separate sheets: and after they had finished they cried out as if out of one mouth from the separate cells, 'Amen.' And they rose, Karinus giving his paper to Annas, and Leucius to Caiaphas; and, greeting each other, they went out and returned to their sepulchres.

9. Then Annas and Caiaphas, opening the sheets of paper, began each to read it in secret. But all the people took it amiss and so all cried out, 'Read these writings to us openly; and after they have been read we shall keep them lest perchance this truth of God be turned through wilful blindness, by unclean and deceitful men, into falsehood.' At this Annas and Caiaphas, filled with trembling, delivered the sheet of paper to Rabbi Adas and Rabbi Fineës and Rabbi Egias, who had come from Galilee and announced that Jesus had been taken up into heaven. All the multitude of the Jews entrusted them to read this writing. And they read the paper containing these words:

2(18). 1. I Karinus. O Lord Jesus Christ, Son of the living God, permit me to speak of your wonders which you have done in the underworld. When we were kept in darkness and the shadow of death in the underworld suddenly there shone upon us a great light, and Hades and the gates of death trembled. And then was heard the voice of the Son of the Father most high as if the voice of a great thunder; and loudly proclaiming, he thus charged them, 'Lift up your gates, you princes; lift up the everlasting gates; the King of Glory, Christ the Lord, will come up to enter in.'[1]

2. Then Satan, the leader of death, came up, fleeing in terror, saying to his officers and the powers below, 'My officers and all the powers below, run together, shut your gates, put up the iron bars, and fight bravely, and resist, lest they lay hold of us and keep us captive in chains.' Then all his impious officers were troubled, and began to shut the gates of death with all diligence, and gradually to fasten the locks and the iron bars, and to hold all their equipment grasped in their hands, and to howl in a dreadful and most hideous voice.

3(19). 1. Then Satan said to Hades, 'Make yourself ready to receive him whom I shall bring down to you.' Thereupon Hades replied to Satan, 'That voice was nothing else than the cry of the Son of the Father most high because the earth and all the places of the world below so trembled under it: wherefore I think that myself and all my dungeons now lie exposed. But I adjure you, Satan, head of all evils, by your power and mine, do not bring him to me lest, when we wish to take him, we be taken captive by him. For if at his voice alone all my power had been thus destroyed what do you think he will do when he shall come in person?'

2. Satan, the leader of death, replied, 'What are you crying about? Do not be afraid,

---

[1] Ps. 24: 7.

my old most wicked friend, because I have stirred up the people of the Jews against him; I have told them to strike him with blows on the face and I have brought upon him betrayal by one of his disciples; and he is a man in great fear of death because out of fear he said, "My soul is sorrowful, even unto death",[2] and I have brought him to this, that he has just been lifted up and hanged on the cross.'

3. Then Hades said to him, 'If it is he who, by the mere word of his command made Lazarus fly away like an eagle from my bosom when he had already been dead four days, he is not a man in humanity but God in majesty. I entreat you not to bring him to me.' And Satan said to him, 'Make yourself ready nevertheless, be not afraid; because he is already hanging on the cross I can do nothing else.' Then Hades replied to Satan, 'If, then, you can do nothing else, behold, your destruction is at hand. I, indeed, shall remain cast down and dishonoured; you, however, will be tortured under my power.'

4(20). 1. And the saints of God heard the wrangling of Satan and Hades. They, however, were not as yet recognizing each other but, notwithstanding, did have knowledge. But our holy father Adam replied to Satan, 'O captain of death, why do you fear and tremble? Behold, the Lord is coming who will now destroy all your inventions; and you shall be taken by him and bound for ever.'

2. Then all the saints, hearing the voice of our father Adam and how boldly he replied to Satan, were strengthened in joy; and all ran together to father Adam and were crowded in one place. Then our father Adam, gazing on all that multitude, wondered greatly whether all in the world were descended from him. And embracing those who were standing everywhere around him and shedding most bitter tears, he addressed his son Seth, saying, 'Relate, my son Seth, to the holy patriarchs and prophets what the guardian of paradise said to you when I sent you to bring to me that oil of mercy to anoint my body when I was ill.'

3. Then he answered, 'When you sent me to the gates of paradise I prayed and entreated the Lord with tears and called upon the guardian of paradise to give it me. Then Michael the archangel came out and said to me, "Seth, why are you weeping? Know beforehand that your father Adam will not receive this oil of mercy now but after many generations of time. For the most beloved Son of God will come down from heaven into the world and will be baptized by John in the river Jordan; and then your father Adam shall receive of this oil of mercy and so will all who believe in him. And the kingdom of those who have believed in him will endure for ever."'

5(21). 1. Then all the saints, when they heard this, exulted in joy. And one of those standing there, Isaiah by name, cried out aloud and exclaimed, 'Father Adam and all standing round, hear my declaration. When I was on earth, by the teaching of the Holy Spirit I sang in prophecy of this light: "The people who sat in darkness have seen a great light; to them dwelling in the region of the shadow of death light has arisen."'[3] At these words father Adam and all of them turned and asked him, 'Who are you? What you say is true.' And he replied and said, 'My name is Isaiah.'

2. Then appeared another near him, as if a hermit. And they asked him, saying, 'Who are you, who wears such things on your body?' And he straightway answered, 'I am John the Baptist, voice and prophet of the Most High. I went before the face of the same Lord that I might make the desert and rough places into clear paths. With my

---

[2] Matt. 26: 38 and parallel.
[3] Isa. 9: 2.

finger I pointed out and made manifest the Lamb of the Lord, and Son of God, to the inhabitants of Jerusalem. I baptized him in the river Jordan. I heard the voice of the Father sounding from heaven over him and proclaiming, "This is my beloved Son, in whom I am well pleased."[4] I received from him the answer that he would descend to the underworld.' Then father Adam, hearing this, cried with a loud voice, exclaiming, 'Alleluia!' which means 'The Lord is certainly coming'.

6(22). 1. After that, another standing there, distinguished by a certain royal mark, David by name, cried out and said, 'When I was upon earth I made a revelation of the mercy of God and his visitation to the people prophesying future joys, saying, "Through all ages, let them make confession to the Lord of his tender mercy and his wonderful works to the sons of men because he has shattered the gates of brass and broken the bars of iron." '[5] Then the holy patriarchs and prophets began in turn to recognize each other and each to quote his prophecies. Then holy Jeremiah, examining his prophecies, said to the patriarchs and prophets, 'When I was upon earth I prophesied of the Son of God that he was seen upon earth and conversed with men.'

2. Then all the saints, exulting in the light of the Lord and in the sight of father Adam, and in answer to all the patriarchs and prophets, cried out saying, 'Alleluia! blessed is he who comes in the name of the Lord.' As a result of their crying out Satan trembled and sought a way of escape. And he could not, because Hades and his minions kept him bound in the underworld and guarded on all sides. And they said to him, 'Why do you tremble? By no means will we allow you to go forth. But receive this as you deserve from him whom you daily assailed, and know that, bound by him, you shall be in my custody.'

7(23). 1. And again there came the voice of the Son of the Father most high like great thunder, saying, 'Lift up your gates, you princes; and be lifted up, you everlasting gates, and the King of Glory will come in.' Then Satan and Hades cried out saying, 'Who is the King of Glory?' And the voice of the Lord answered them, 'The Lord strong and mighty, the Lord mighty in battle.'[6]

2. After this voice there came a man who had the appearance of a robber, carrying a cross on his shoulder, crying outside and saying, 'Open to me, that I may come in.' And Satan, opening to him a little, brought him inside into his abode and shut the door after him. And all the saints saw him clearly and said to him immediately. 'Your appearance is that of a robber. Tell us what it is you are carrying on your back.' And he answered and said humbly, 'Truly I was a robber, and the Jews hanged me up on a cross, along with my Lord Jesus Christ, the Son of the Father most high. I have come as his herald; he is coming immediately behind me.'

3. Then holy David, inflamed with anger against Satan, cried out aloud, 'Open your gates, most vile wretch, that the King of Glory may come in.' In like manner all the saints of God also rose up against Satan and tried to seize him and tear him in pieces. And again the cry was heard within, 'Lift up your gates, you princes; and be lifted up, you everlasting gates; and the King of Glory shall come in.' Hades and Satan at that clear voice again asked saying, 'Who is this King of Glory?'[7] And that wonderful voice replied, 'The Lord of hosts, he is the King of Glory.'

---

[4] Matt. 3: 17 and parallels.
[5] Ps. 107: 15–16.
[6] Ps. 24: 7–8.
[7] Ps. 24: 9–10.

8(24). 1. And behold, suddenly Hades trembled, and the gates of death and the bolts were shattered and the iron bars were broken and fell to the ground, everything was exposed. And Satan remained in the midst and stood confounded and downcast, bound with fetters on his feet. And behold, the Lord Jesus Christ, coming in the brightness of celestial light from on high, compassionate, great, and lowly, carrying a chain in his hand, bound Satan by the neck; and tying his hands behind him dashed him on his back into Tartarus and set his holy foot on his throat, saying, 'Through all the ages you have done many evils; you have never rested. Today I deliver you to everlasting fire.' And having quickly summoned Hades, he commanded him and said, 'Take this most wicked and impious one and have him in your keeping until that day when I shall command you.' And when he had received him he went down with him beneath the feet of the Lord into the depth of the abyss.

9(25). 1. Then the Lord Jesus, the Saviour of all, kind and gentle, greeted Adam and said to him, 'Peace be to you, Adam, with your children, through immeasurable ages of ages! Amen.' Then father Adam fell down at the feet of the Lord and then, rising, kissed his hands and shed many tears. And he testified to all, 'Behold the hands which fashioned me!' And he said to the Lord, 'You have come, O King of Glory, delivering men, and bringing them into your everlasting kingdom.' Then also our mother Eve in like manner fell at the feet of the Lord and, arising, kissed his hands and shed many tears. And she testified to all, 'Behold the hands which made me!'

2. Then all the saints, worshipping him, cried out saying, 'Blessed is he who comes in the name of the Lord! The Lord God has shone upon us through all ages. Amen. Alleluia for ever and ever! Praise, honour, power, glory, because you have come from on high to visit us.' Singing Alleluia and rejoicing together in his glory they ran together beneath the hands of the Lord. Then the Saviour, inquiring about all, smote Hades, immediately threw some down into Tartarus and led others with him to the world above.

10(26). 1. Then all the saints of God asked the Lord to leave as a sign of victory the sign of his holy cross in the underworld that its most impious officers might not retain as an offender any one whom the Lord had absolved. And so it was done. And the Lord set his cross in the midst of Hades and it is the sign of victory which will remain to eternity.

Then we all went forth with the Lord, leaving Satan and Hades in Tartarus. And to us and many others it was commanded that we should rise in the body to testify in the world of the resurrection of our Lord Jesus Christ and of those things which had been done in the underworld.

Dearest brethren, these are the things which we have seen and which, adjured by you, we testify. Our testimony is confirmed by him who died for us and rose. As it was written, so has it been done in all respects.

11(27). 1. And when the roll was completely read through, all who heard it fell on their faces, weeping bitterly and relentlessly beating their breasts, crying out and saying repeatedly, 'Woe to us! Why has this happened to us wretched men?' Pilate fled; Annas and Caiaphas fled; the priests and Levites fled; also the people of the Jews, weeping, said, 'Woe to us wretched! we have shed sacred blood upon the earth.'

For three days and three nights they did not taste bread and water at all, nor did any of them return to the synagogue. But on the third day the council was again assembled and the other paper (of Leucius) was read; and there was found in it neither more nor less, not even to a single letter, than that which the writing of Karinus contained. Then the synagogue was perplexed; and they all lamented forty days and forty nights, expecting destruction from God and the vengeance of God. But he, the Most High, grateful and merciful, did not immediately destroy them, generously giving them a means of repentance. But they were not found worthy to turn to the Lord.

These, beloved brethren, are the testimonies of Karinus and Leucius, concerning Christ the Son of God, and his holy deeds in the underworld. To him let us all give praise and glory through immeasurable ages of ages. Amen.

Other Pilate Texts

THE LETTER OF PILATE TO CLAUDIUS

The translation offered here is from the Latin version found attached to manuscripts of Latin A of the Descensus as given by Tischendorf (13(29). 1). The letter is also found in its original Greek form in the Acts of Peter and Paul 40–2 where the context has determined that the name of the emperor is Claudius—not Tiberius. The letter is also found in Greek in Pseudo-Marcellus, Passion of Peter and Paul 19. It could be the oldest of the Christian Pilate literature and might have originated at the end of the second century. Tertullian (*Apology* 5. 2 and 21. 24) (ed. H. Hoppe, *CSEL* 69 (Vienna and Leipzig, 1939) pp. 14, 58–9) and Eusebius *HE* 2. 2 (Schwartz, *GCS* 9.1, pp. 108, 110) knew of a dispatch from Pilate to Tiberius. An Armenian version exists and also a Syriac text found in the Mingana collection. The latter have few links with either the Greek or Latin forms.

EDITIONS

Latin

Tischendorf, *EA* 413–16.

Syriac

S. P. Brock, 'A Syriac Version of the Letters of Lentulus and Pilate', *Orientalia Christiana Periodica* 35 (1969), 45–62.

MODERN TRANSLATIONS

English

Cowper, 370–1.
Walker, 212, and see 264–5.
Westcott, 117–18.
James, 146.
Hennecke[3], i. 477–8.
Hennecke[5], 527.
Cartlidge and Dungan, 87.

German

Hennecke¹, 76 (A. Stülcken).
Hennecke³, i. pp. 353-4 (F. Scheidweiler).
Hennecke⁵, i. 419 (F. Scheidweiler).

Italian

Erbetta, iii, 131-2.
Moraldi, i. 641-2; ² i. 712-3.

Pontius Pilate to Claudius, his King, greeting.

There happened recently something which I myself brought to light. The Jews through envy have punished themselves and their posterity with a cruel punishment. For their fathers had a promise that God would send them from heaven his holy one, who would rightly be called their king and whom God had promised to send to earth by a virgin. Yet when he came to Judaea when I was governor, and they saw that he restored sight to the blind, cleansed lepers, healed paralytics, expelled evil spirits from men, and even raised the dead, and commanded the winds, and walked dry-shod upon the waves of the sea, and did many other miracles, and all the people of the Jews acknowledged him to be the Son of God, the chief priests were moved by envy against him and they seized him and delivered him to me, and telling one lie after another they said he was a sorcerer and acting contrary to their law. And I believed this was so and ordered him to be scourged, and handed him over to their will. And they crucified him and set guards over him after he was buried. But he rose again on the third day, while my soldiers kept watch. But the Jews were so carried away by their wickedness that they gave money to my soldiers saying, 'Say that his disciples stole his body.' But after receiving the money they were unable to keep silent about what had happened. For they testified that he had arisen and that they had seen it,[1] and that they had received money from the Jews. I have reported this lest anyone should lie about it and lest you should think that the lies of the Jews should be believed.

THE LETTER OF PILATE TO TIBERIUS

James suggests (p. 153) that some sort of report of Pilate to Tiberius was concocted very early. This letter represents one form of that report. The Anaphora (*q.v.*) is another. This letter, however, cannot be traced earlier than the Renaissance.

---

[1] Or 'For they testified that they had seen that he had risen'.

Tischendorf's text which is translated below is based on four manuscripts—all are in Latin, the original language of this letter.

EDITIONS

Fabricius, 300–1.
Thilo, 801–2.
Giles, ii. 14.
Tischendorf, *EA* lxxvii f., 433–4.

MODERN TRANSLATIONS

English

Cowper, 398–9.
Walker, 223.
Westcott, 119–20.
James, 153.

French

Migne, *Dictionnaire*, ii, cols. 757–60.

Italian

Erbetta, iii. 130.
Moraldi, i. 707; [2] i. 739.
Cravieri, 397.

Spanish

de Santos Otero, 472–3.

Pontius Pilate to the Emperor Tiberius Caesar greeting

On Jesus Christ, of whom I told you clearly in my last letter, a cruel punishment has been inflicted by the will of the people. I was unwilling and apprehensive about it. He was a man, by Hercules, so pious and upright no age has ever had nor will ever have. But the efforts of the people themselves, and the unanimity of all the scribes, chiefs, and elders to crucify this ambassador of truth, were remarkable, even though their prophets, like the Sibyls with us, warned against it. Supernatural signs appeared when he was hanging, and in the judgement of philosophers these threatened the destruction of the whole world. His disciples flourish, and in their work and temperate life they do not belie their master, but rather in his name they are most beneficent. Had I not greatly feared an uprising of the people, who were on the point of rebelling, that man would perhaps still be alive for us. Constrained more by fidelity to your dignity than led by my own will, I did not strive to the utmost of my power to prevent the loss and suffering of righteous blood, guiltless of every accusation. It was an injustice due to the malice of men, although, as the scriptures testify, it was to their own destruction.

Farewell.

The Fifth of the Kalends of April

PARADOSIS PILATI

The high regard for Pilate shown here betrays an Eastern provenance, for it was in the Coptic churches that Pilate was regarded as a saint.

The text is translated in full and is based on Tischendorf's Greek text, which he printed from five manuscripts, the earliest of which is twelfth-century.

It has been argued that the Acta Pilati developed from the traditions found in the Paradosis (and Anaphora).

EDITIONS

Birch, i. 176 ff.
Thilo, i. 803–16.
Giles, ii, ch. 14.
Tischendorf, *EA* lxxix f., 449–55.
M. D. Gibson, *Apocrypha Sinaitica* (London, 1896), 6–14 (= *Studia Sinaitica* 5) (Syriac and Arabic texts with Eng. trans.).

MODERN TRANSLATIONS

English

Cowper, 410–14.
Walker, 231–3.
Westcott, 126–30.
James, 154–5 (summary).
Hennecke[3], i. 482–4.
Hennecke[5], i. 530–3.

French

Migne, *Dictionnaire*, ii, cols. 751–4.

German

Hennecke³, i. 356–8 (F. Scheidweiler).
Hennecke⁵, i. 422–4 (F. Scheidweiler).

Italian

Erbetta, iii. 122–4.
Moraldi, i. 717–20; ² i. 748–50.
Cravieri, 386–8.

Spanish

González-Blanco, ii. 361–9.
de Santos Otero, 490–6.

GENERAL

Variot, 120–2.

1. When the report reached Rome and had been read to Caesar, with not a few standing by, all were amazed that it was because of the lawlessness of Pilate that the darkness and the earthquake had come upon the whole world; and Caesar, filled with anger, sent soldiers with orders to bring Pilate a prisoner.

2. And when he had been brought to the city of the Romans and Caesar heard that Pilate was there, he sat down in the temple of the gods in the presence of the whole senate and the whole army and all the multitude of his forces. And he commanded Pilate to stand forward[1] and said to him, 'How could you dare to do such a thing, you most impious one, when you had seen such great signs concerning that man? By daring to do an evil deed you have destroyed the whole world.'

3. Pilate answered, 'Almighty King, I am innocent of these things; it is the multitude of the Jews who are reckless and guilty.' Caesar asked, 'Who are they?' Pilate said, 'Herod, Archelaus, Philip, Annas and Caiaphas, and all the multitude of the Jews.' Caesar said. 'Why did you follow their advice?' Pilate said, 'This nation is rebellious and disorderly, and does not submit to your power.' Caesar said, 'As soon as they handed him over to you, you should have kept him secure and sent him to me, and not have obeyed them and crucified such a man who was righteous and did such wonderful signs as you have mentioned in your report. For it is clear from these signs that Jesus was the Christ, the king of the Jews.'

4. And when Caesar said this and named the name of Christ, all the

---

[1] Or 'in the entrance'.

multitude of the gods fell down, and became as dust where Caesar sat with the senate. And all the people who stood by Caesar trembled because of the utterance of the word and the fall of their gods, and gripped by fear, they all went away, each to his own house, marvelling at what had taken place. And Caesar commanded that Pilate should be guarded safely, in order that he might learn the truth about Jesus.

5. On the next day Caesar sat in the Capitol with all the senate and tried again to question Pilate. And Caesar said, 'Speak the truth, you most impious man, for through your godless behaviour against Jesus, even here the working of your evil deeds was shown in the overthrowing of the gods. Tell me now: Who is that crucified one, that his name destroyed all the gods?' Pilate answered, 'Truly, the charges made against him are true. For I myself was convinced by his deeds that he is greater than all the gods whom we worship.' Caesar said, 'Why then did you bring such audacious action against him if you were not ignorant of him, unless you wished to harm my kingdom?' Pilate answered, 'I did it because of the lawlessness and sedition of the lawless and godless Jews.'

6. Then Caesar, filled with anger, took counsel with all the senate and his forces, and ordered the following decree to be recorded against the Jews, 'To Licianus, chief governor of the East, greeting! I have been informed that recently those Jews who live in Jerusalem and the neighbouring Jewish towns have had the audacity to commit a lawless crime in forcing Pilate to crucify Jesus, who was acknowledged as God. Because of this crime of theirs the world was darkened and dragged down to destruction. Therefore by this decree proceed there with all speed with a strong body of troops and take them prisoner. Be obedient, and advance against them; by scattering them among all the nations enslave them and expel them from Judaea, making the nation so insignificant that it may no longer be seen anywhere, since they are full of evil.'

7. When this decree arrived in the East, Licianus obeyed it and destroyed the whole Jewish nation, and those who were left in Judaea he scattered as slaves among the nations, so that it was known to Caesar that these things had been done by Licianus against the Jews in the East, and he was pleased.

8. And again Caesar was determined to question Pilate, and commanded an officer called Albius to behead Pilate saying, 'As this man raised his hand against the righteous man called Christ, so shall he fall in the same way and find no salvation.'

9. And when Pilate came to the place of execution, he prayed silently, 'Lord, do not destroy me with the wicked Hebrews, for had it not been because of the nation of the lawless Jews, I would not have raised my hand against you, because they plotted a revolt against me. You know that I acted in ignorance. Therefore do not destroy me because of this sin, but pardon me, Lord, and your servant Procla, who stands with me in this hour of my death,

whom you taught to prophesy that you must be nailed to the cross. Do not condemn her also because of my sin, but pardon us and number us among your righteous ones.'

10. And behold, when Pilate had finished his prayer, there sounded a voice from heaven, 'All generations and families of the Gentiles shall call you blessed, because in your governorship everything was fulfilled which the prophets foretold about me. And you yourself shall appear as my witness at my second coming, when I shall judge the twelve tribes of Israel and those who have not confessed my name.' And the prefect cut off Pilate's head, and behold, an angel of the Lord received it. And when Procla his wife saw the angel coming and receiving his head, she was filled with joy, and immediately gave up the ghost and was buried with her husband.

ANAPHORA PILATI

There are two Greek texts behind Tischendorf's edition, which do not differ in essentials. The text edited by Abbott is combined with the Paradosis (*q.v.*)—normally the Anaphora and Paradosis are separate—and it differs from Tischendorf's text especially in its conclusion, which gives an account of the death of Annas and Caiaphas. The manner of Pilate's death in Abbott's text also differs from Tischendorf's, but approximates to the so-called Letter of Tiberius (*q.v.*), where the same episode is told of Annas. The Anaphora is close to the Letter of Pilate to Claudius (*q.v.*) and is probably an expansion of it.

Tischendorf printed his Greek A and his Greek B each on the basis of five manuscripts. The summary below is taken from James, and the translation of sections 7–8 from Tischendorf's Greek A.

EDITIONS

Fabricius, iii. 456–9.
Birch, i. 161–4.
Thilo, i. 803–16.
Giles, ii. 14.
Tischendorf, *EA*, pp. lxxviii f., 435–49.
M. D. Gibson, *Apocrypha Sinaitica* (London, 1896) (= *Studia Sinaitica* 5) (Syriac and Arabic texts with Eng. trans.).
G. F. Abbott, 'The Report and Death of Pilate', *JTS* 4 (1903), 83–6 (Greek text different from Tischendorf's).

MODERN TRANSLATIONS

English

Cowper, 400–9 (Tischendorf's A and B).

Walker, 224–30 (Tischendorf's A and B).
Westcott, 121–5 (Tischendorf's A).
James, 153–4 (summary).
Cartlidge and Dungan, 88–90.

French

Migne, *Dictionnaire*, ii, cols. 753–8.

Italian

Erbetta, iii. 119–21 (Greek B).
Moraldi, i. 710–13; (Greek A); 714–16 (Greek B); [2] i. 742–7.
Cravieri, 382–5.

Spanish

de Santos Otero, 477–84 (Tischendorf's A).

GENERAL

Variot, 117–20.

Summary

'I have received a communication, O most mighty, which oppresses me with fear and trembling.'

He goes on to say that in Jerusalem, a city of his province, the Jews delivered him a man named Jesus, charging him with much that they could not substantiate, and in particular with violating the sabbath. The miracles are then described with some rhetorical ornament, particularly in the case of Lazarus.

Jesus was delivered to him by Herod, Archelaus, Philip, Annas, Caiaphas, and all the people.

Translation

7. And at the time he was crucified there was darkness over all the world, the sun was darkened at midday, and the stars appeared but there appeared no lustre in them; and the moon, as if turned into blood, failed in her light. And the world was swallowed up by the nether regions, so that the very sanctuary of the temple, as they call it, was not seen by the Jews in their fall; and they saw below them a chasm in the earth, and rolling thunders that fell upon it. 8. And amid that terror dead men were seen risen, as the Jews themselves testified; and they said that it was Abraham, and Isaac, and Jacob, and the twelve patriarchs, and Moses and Job, who had died, as they say, three

thousand five hundred years ago. And there were very many whom I saw appearing in the body; and they were making a lamentation over the Jews, on account of the transgression that had come to pass because of them, and the destruction of the Jews and of their law.

Summary
On the first day of the week, at the third hour of night, there was a great light: the sun shone with unwonted brightness, men in shining garments appeared in the air and cried out to the souls in Hades to come up, and proclaimed the resurrection of Jesus.

The light continued all night. Many Jews disappeared in the chasms which the earthquake had caused, and all the synagogues except one fell down.

Under the stress of the consternation caused by all these portents Pilate writes to Caesar.

VINDICTA SALVATORIS
(or The Vengeance (or Avenging) of the Saviour)

Tischendorf's Latin text, based on two fourteenth-century manuscripts, is used for the summary and translation offered here. Like the Mors Pilati (*q.v.*) it is a medieval anti-Jewish Latin creation and is thus only given summary treatment. The legend of the death of Pilate here is a development that is thought to have originated in Aquitaine. An Anglo-Saxon version (of the eleventh century) exists.

EDITION

Tischendorf, *EA*, pp. lxxxii–v, 471–86.

MODERN TRANSLATIONS

English

Cowper, 432–47.
Walker, 245–55.
Westcott, 146–59.
James, 159–60 (summary).

French

Migne, *Dictionnaire*, i, cols. 1169–78.

Italian

Erbetta, i.2, 388–96.
Moraldi, i. 736–47; [2] i. 765–75.
Cravieri, 411–22.

Spanish

González-Blanco, ii. 343–60.
de Santos Otero, 512–32.

Anglo-Saxon

C. W. Goodwin, *The Anglo-Saxon Legends of St Andrew and St Veronica* (Cambridge, 1851).

GENERAL

Variot, 131–8.
E. Darley, *Les Acta Salvatoris: Un évangile de la passion et de la resurrection et une mission apostolique en Aquitaine* (Paris, 1913).
—— *Les actes du Sauveur, la lettre de Pilate, les missions de Volusien, de Nathan, la Vindicte: Leurs origines et leurs transformations* (Paris, 1919).

Summary

There was a king Titus under Tiberius, in Aquitaine, in a city of Libia called Burgidalla. He had a cancer in his right nostril and his face was eaten away up to his eye.

There was also a Jew named Nathan, son of Naum, whom the Jews had sent to Tiberius to bear a treaty to him. Tiberius, too, was ill of fever and ulcers and had nine kinds of leprosy. Nathan's ship was driven ashore at Titus' city. Nathan was sent for and told his story. Titus asked if he knew any one who could cure him. Nathan said, 'If you had been in Jerusalem lately there was a prophet called Emanuel' (the miracles are enumerated, and the Passion, descent into hell, and resurrection described). Titus said, 'Woe to you, Tiberius, in whose realm such things are done. I would have slain these Jews with my own hand for destroying my Lord.' At this word the wound fell from his face and he was healed, and so were all the sick who were there. Titus cried out, confessing his belief in Christ, and made Nathan baptize him.

Then he sent for Vespasian to come with all his forces, and he came with 5,000 men, and said, 'What do you want me for?' 'To destroy the enemies of Jesus.' So they sailed off to Jerusalem. Archelaus in terror gave his kingdom to his son, and stabbed himself. The son allied himself with other kings and fortified Jerusalem, which was besieged seven years, till the inhabitants had to eat earth. At last they took counsel to surrender, and gave the keys to Titus and Vespasian. Some were slain, some crucified head downwards, or pierced with lances, sold, cast lots upon, and divided into four parts, and the rest sold at thirty for a penny.

Then they made search for the likeness of Jesus and found Veronica, who had it. Pilate they delivered to four quaternions of soldiers. (Veronica was the woman healed of the issue of blood. She abode with Titus and Vespasian till the emperor's kinsman Velosian came.)

A message was sent by Titus to Tiberius to send Velosian. He told him to go to Jerusalem and bring some one to heal him, to whom he might promise half the kingdom.

Velosian arrived after a year and seven days, and first found Joseph and Nicodemus. Joseph told of the burial, of his imprisonment, and his deliverance by Jesus.

Then Veronica came and told of her healing. Velosian arraigned and imprisoned Pilate. He then examined Veronica, who denied that she had the likeness. He threatened her with torture; at last she confessed that she had it in (*or* on) a linen cloth and adored it every day. She produced it. Velosian adored it, took it, put it in a gold cloth and locked it in a box, and embarked for Rome. Veronica left all she had and insisted on coming with him. They sailed up the Tiber to Rome, after a year's journey.

Tiberius heard of their arrival and summoned Velosian, who told him all the story at length, including the destruction of the Jews...

Translation
31. And they seized Pilate, and gave him up to me, and I put him in prison, to be guarded by four quaternions of soldiers in Damascus. 32. Then they made a search with great diligence to seek the portrait of the Lord; and they found a woman named Veronica who had the portrait of the Lord. 33. Then the emperor Tiberius said to Velosian, 'How have you kept it?' And he answered, 'I have it in clean cloth of gold, rolled up in a shawl.' And the emperor Tiberius said, 'Bring it to me, and spread it before my face, that I may fall to the ground and bending my knees, may adore it on the ground.' Then Velosian spread out his shawl with the cloth of gold on which the portrait of the Lord had been imprinted; and the emperor Tiberius saw it. And he immediately adored the image of the Lord with a pure heart, and his flesh was cleansed and became as the flesh of a little child. And all the blind, the lepers, the lame, the dumb, the deaf, and those possessed by various diseases, who were there present, were healed, and cured, and cleansed. 34. And the emperor Tiberius bowed his head and bent his knees, and pondered the words, 'Blessed is the womb which bore you, and the breasts which you sucked',[1] and he groaned to the Lord, saying with tears, 'God of heaven and earth, do not permit me to sin, but confirm my soul and my body, and place

---
[1] Luke 11: 27.

me in your kingdom, because in your name do I always trust: free me from all evils, as you freed the three children from the furnace of blazing fire.'

35. Then the emperor Tiberius said to Velosian, 'Velosian, have you seen any of those men who saw Christ?' Velosian answered, 'I have.' He said, 'Did you ask how they baptize those who believed in Christ?' Velosian said, 'Here, my lord, we have one of the disciples of Christ himself.' Then he ordered Nathan to be summoned to come to him. Nathan therefore came and baptized him in the name of the Father, and of the Son, and of the Holy Ghost. Amen. Immediately the emperor Tiberius, made whole from all his diseases, ascended upon his throne, and said, 'Blessed are you, O Lord God Almighty, and worthy to be praised, who have freed me from the snare of death, and cleansed me from all my iniquities; because I have greatly sinned before you, O Lord my God, and I am not worthy to see your face.' And then the emperor Tiberius was instructed in all the articles of the faith, fully, and with strong faith.

MORS PILATI

Tischendorf's Latin text is that of a fourteeth-century manuscript. The Legend is a late creation. As it is a medieval composition it merits only brief treatment here, with merely the conclusion translated.

Like the Vindicta (*q.v.*) the story tells of Tiberius who is ill and who sends his emissary Volusian to seek out the healer Jesus. After learning of Jesus' death Volusian meets Veronica whose handkerchief has the wonder-working image of Jesus imprinted on it, and he takes her with him to Rome. Tiberius is thereby healed. Pilate is then punished and killed. In the Mors his dead body has several moves before finding its final resting place near Lake Lucerne. The bitter animosity shown to Pilate betrays not only a Western origin but also a late date.

EDITIONS

Tischendorf, *EA*, pp. lxxx f., 456–8.

G. F. Abbott, 'The Report and Death of Pilate', *JTS* 4 (1903), 83–6 (Greek text differing from Tischendorf's).

MODERN TRANSLATIONS

English

Cowper, 415–19.
Walker, 234–6.
Westcott, 131–5.
James, 157–8 (summary).

French

Migne, *Dictionnaire*, i, cols. 1177–80.

Italian

Erbetta i.2, 402–4.
Moraldi, i. 721–4; [2] i. 751–4
Cravieri, 389–92.

Spanish

González-Blanco, ii. 361–9.
de Santos Otero, 495–500.

GENERAL

Variot, 122–4.

When Caesar knew of the death of Pilate, he said, 'He has justly died a most disgraceful death, seeing that his own hand has not spared him.' He was therefore bound to a great block of stone, and sunk in the river Tiber. However, malignant and filthy spirits, rejoicing in his malignant and filthy body, kept moving in the waters, and in a terrible manner caused lightning and tempests, thunder and hail, so that everyone was in constant fear. Therefore the Romans pulled him out of the river Tiber and carried him off in derision to Vienne, and sunk him in the river Rhône. Vienne means the Way of Gehenna, because it became a place of cursing. But evil spirits were at work and did the same things there too, so the people, unwilling to endure a plague of demons, removed that vessel of malediction and sent him to be buried in the territory of Losania. The inhabitants there were also troubled by the same visitations, so they removed him and sunk him in a lake, surrounded by mountains, where to this day, according to the tales of some, sundry diabolical machinations occur.

THE NARRATIVE OF JOSEPH OF ARIMATHAEA

This is another medieval legend given only brief treatment here.[1] The earliest of Tischendorf's manuscripts is twelfth-century. The language is Greek.

James (p. 165) states: '. . . several phrases betray the influence of the same workshop that produced the Letters of Herod to Pilate. The ignorance of Jewish customs which it betrays is colossal."

---

[1] Chapter 3 is translated in full. The rest is given in summary form only.

EDITIONS

Birch, i. 183 ff.
Tischendorf, *EA*, pp. lxxxi f., 459–70.

MODERN TRANSLATIONS

English

Cowper, 420–31.
Walker, 237–44.
Westcott, 136–45.
James, 161–5 (summary).

French

Migne, *Dictionnaire*, ii, cols. 433–8.

Italian

Erbetta i.2, 397–401.
Moraldi, i. 683–92; i. 803–12.
Cravieri, 401–9.

Spanish

de Santos Otero, 501–12.

GENERAL

Variot, 125–31.

Summary

1. I, Joseph of Arimathaea, who begged the body of the Lord Jesus from Pilate, was imprisoned by the Jews on that account. These are the people who provoked their lawgiver Moses, and failing to recognize their God crucified his Son.

Seven days before the passion of Christ, two condemned robbers were sent from Jericho to Pilate, whose crimes were these.

The first, Gestas, used to strip and murder wayfarers, hang up women by the feet and cut off their breasts, drink the blood of babes: he knew not God nor obeyed any law, but was violent from the beginning.

The other, Demas, was a Galilean who kept an inn: he despoiled the rich but did good to the poor, even burying them, like Tobit. He had committed robberies on the Jews, for he stole the law itself at Jerusalem, and stripped the daughter of Caiaphas, who was a priestess of the sanctuary, and he took away even the mystic deposit of Solomon which had been deposited in the (holy) place.

Jesus also was taken at evening on the third day before the passover. But Caiaphas and the multitude of the Jews had no passover but were in great grief because of the robbery of the sanctuary by the thief. And they sent for Judas Iscariot who was brother's son to Caiaphas, and had been persuaded by the Jews to become a disciple of Jesus, not to follow his teachings, but to betray him. They paid him a didrachm of gold daily; and as one of Jesus' disciples, called John, says, he had been two years with Jesus.

On the third day before Jesus was taken, Judas said to the Jews, 'Let us assemble a council and say that it was not the robber who took away the law, but Jesus.' Nicodemus, who had the keys of the sanctuary, said, 'No': for he was a truthful man. But Sarra, Caiaphas' daughter, cried out that Jesus said in public, 'I can destroy the temple (etc.)'. All the Jews said, 'We believe you.' For they held her as a prophetess. So Jesus was taken.

2. On the next day, being Wednesday, at the ninth hour, they brought him into Caiaphas' hall, and Annas and Caiaphas asked him, 'Why did you take away the law?' He was silent. 'Why would you destroy the temple of Solomon?' He was silent.

In the evening the multitude sought the daughter of Caiaphas, to burn her with fire, because the law was stolen and they could not keep the passover. But she said, 'Wait a little, my children, and let us destroy Jesus, and the law will be found and the feast kept.' Then Annas and Caiaphas privily gave gold to Judas and said, 'Say as you said before, that it was Jesus who stole the law.' Judas agreed, but said, 'The people must not know that you have told me this: and you must let Jesus go, and I will persuade them.' So they fraudulently let Jesus go.

At dawn of the Thursday Judas went into the sanctuary and said to all the people, 'What will ye give me if I deliver to you the destroyer of the law and robber of the prophets?' They said, 'Thirty silver pieces of gold.' But they did not know that it was Jesus of whom he spoke, for many thought him to be the Son of God. And Judas received the thirty pieces.

At the fourth and fifth hours he went out and found Jesus walking in the street. Towards evening he obtained a guard of soldiers. As they went, Judas said, 'Whomsoever I shall kiss, take him: he it is that stole the law and the prophets.' He came to Jesus and kissed him, saying, 'Hail, Rabbi.' They took Jesus to Caiaphas and examined him. 'Why did you do this?' But he answered nothing. Nicodemus and I left the seat of the pestilent, and would not consent to perish in the council of sinners.

Translation

3. Having done many dreadful things against Jesus that night, they gave him to Pilate, the Procurator, at dawn on the day of preparation, so that he could

crucify him. They all came together for this purpose. After a trial, Pilate, the Procurator, ordered him to be nailed to the cross, alongside two robbers. They were nailed up along with Jesus, Gestas on the left, and Demas on the right.

And the man on the left began to cry out and said to Jesus, 'See how many evil deeds I did on earth. If I had known you were a king I would have destroyed you too. Why do you call yourself Son of God yet cannot help yourself when you are in need? How can you help someone else with your prayer? If you are the Christ, come down from the cross, so that I may believe in you. Now I see you are perishing along with me, not like a man but like a wild beast.' And he said many other things against Jesus, blaspheming and gnashing his teeth against him. The robber was taken alive in the snare of the devil.

But the robber on his right hand, whose name was Demas, saw the godlike grace of Jesus and said, 'Jesus Christ, I know you are the Son of God. I see you, Christ, adored by countless myriads of angels. Pardon me my sins. In my trial do not let the stars come against me, or the moon, when you will judge all the world, because it was at night-time when I did my wicked deeds. Do not urge the sun, darkened now on your account, to tell the evils of my heart, for I can give you no gift for the remission of my sins. Already death is coming upon me because of my sins; but yours is the propitiation. Deliver me, O Lord of all, from your fearful judgement. Do not give the enemy power to swallow me up or to become the inheritor of my soul, as he has the soul of him hanging on the left. I see how the devil joyfully takes his soul and his flesh disappears. Do not even order me to depart to the portion of the Jews; for I see Moses and the patriarchs lamenting, and the devil rejoices over them. O Lord, before my spirit departs, order my sins to be washed away, and remember me, the sinner, in your kingdom, when upon the great throne of the Most High you shall judge the twelve tribes of Israel.[1] For you have prepared great punishment for the world on your own account.'

And when the robber had said these things, Jesus said to him, 'Truly I say to you, Demas, that today you will be with me in paradise.[2] And the sons of the kingdom, the children of Abraham, and Isaac, Jacob and Moses, shall be cast into outer darkness. There shall be weeping and gnashing of teeth.[3] And you alone shall dwell in paradise until my second coming, when I am to judge those who do not confess my name.' And he said to the robber, 'Go and speak to the cherubim and the powers who wield the flaming sword, who have guarded paradise from the time that Adam, the first creation, was in paradise and sinned and did not keep my commandments and I cast him out from

---

[1] Matt. 19: 28.
[2] Luke 23: 43.
[3] Matt. 8: 11–12.

there. Say that none of the first shall see paradise until I come the second time to judge the living and the dead, it having been written that Jesus Christ, the Son of God, came down from the heights of heavens, and came forth from the bosom of the invisible Father without having been separated from him, and came down into the world to be made flesh and to be nailed to a cross, in order that I might save Adam, whom I fashioned. Say to my archangelic powers, the gatekeepers of paradise, to the officers of my Father: I require and order that he who has been crucified along with me should enter and receive remission of sins through me, and that, having put on an incorruptible body, he should go into paradise, and dwell where nobody has been able to dwell.'

After he had said this, Jesus gave up the ghost on the day of preparation at the ninth hour. And there was darkness over the whole earth, and there was a great earthquake. The sanctuary collapsed and the pinnacle of the temple fell.

Summary
4. And I, Joseph, begged the body and laid it in my new tomb. The body of Demas was not found: that of Gestas was in appearance like that of a dragon. The Jews imprisoned me on the evening of the sabbath.

When it was evening on the first day of the week, at the fifth hour of the night, Jesus came to me with the thief on the right hand. There was great light; the house was raised up by the four corners and I went forth: and I perceived Jesus first, and then the thief bringing a letter to him, and as we journeyed to Galilee there was a very great light, and a sweet fragrance came from the thief.

Jesus sat down in a certain place and read as follows: The cherubim and the six-winged that are commanded by your Godhead to keep the garden of paradise make known to you this by the hand of the robber that by your dispensation was crucified with you. When we saw the mark of the nails on the robber that was crucified with you and the light of the letters of your Godhead, the fire was quenched, being unable to bear the light of the mark, and we were in great fear and crouched down. For we heard that the maker of heaven and earth and all creation had come to dwell in the lower parts of the earth for the sake of Adam the first-created. For we beheld the spotless cross, with the robber flashing with light and shining with seven times the light of the sun, and trembling came on us, when we heard the crashing of them beneath the earth, and with a great voice the ministers of Hades said with us, 'Holy, Holy, Holy, is he that was in the highest in the beginning', and the powers sent up a cry, *saying*, 'Lord, you have been manifested in heaven and upon earth, giving joy unto the worlds and saving your own creation from death.'

5. And as I went with Jesus and the robber to Galilee, the form of Jesus was changed and he became wholly light, and angels ministered to him and he

conversed with them. I stayed with him three days, and none of the disciples were there.

In the midst of the days of unleavened bread his disciple John came, and the robber disappeared. John asked who it was, but Jesus did not answer. John said, 'Lord, I know that you have loved me from the beginning: why do you not reveal this man to me?' Jesus said, 'Do you seek to know hidden things? Are you wholly without understanding? Do you not perceive the fragrance of paradise filling the place? Do you not know who it was? The thief who was on the cross has become heir of paradise: verily, verily, I say to you, that it is his alone until the great day come.' John said, 'Make me worthy to see him.'

Then suddenly the thief appeared, and John fell to the earth: for he was now like a king in great might, clad with the cross. And a voice of a multitude was heard, 'You have come into the place of paradise prepared for you: we are appointed to serve you by him that sent you until the great day.' After that both the thief and I, Joseph, vanished, and I was found in my own house, and I saw Jesus no more.

All this I saw and have written, that all might believe in Jesus and no longer serve Moses' law, but believe in the signs and wonders of Christ, and believing obtain eternal life and be found in the kingdom of heaven.

For His is glory, might, praise, and majesty, world without end. Amen.

THE LETTERS OF PILATE AND HEROD

The text is known in Greek and in Syriac. The latter is a manuscript of the sixth–seventh century and differs slightly from the Greek text, which is of the fifteenth century. Greek is the original language of the letters.

Both Thilo (pp. cxxiii, cxxiv) and Tischendorf (*EA*, p. lxxx) knew of the Greek manuscript subsequently published by James (= Paris, Bibliothèque Nationale 929), but they themselves did not publish it. The letters belong to the cycle represented by the Anaphora and Paradosis of Pilate. The Paris manuscript in fact combines the letters with these works.

Summaries of the letters are offered here.

EDITIONS

Greek

James, *Apoc. Anec.* ii. pp. xlv–xlviii, 66–70 (with Eng. trans.).

Syriac

W. Wright, *Contributions*, 12–17 (Engl. trans. of Syriac also found in James, *Texts and Studies* 5.1 (above), 71–5).

I. E. Rahmani, *Hypomnemata Domini Nostri seu Acta Pilati* (Charfat, Lebanon 1908), 32–3 (= *Studia Syriaca* 2).

MODERN TRANSLATIONS

English

Cowper, 390–7.
James, 155–6 (summaries).

French

Variot, 112–16.

Italian

Erbetta, iii. 127–9.
Moraldi, i. 703–6; ² i. 735–8.
Cravieri, 393–4, 395–6.

Spanish

de Santos Otero, 484–9.

The Letter of Pilate to Herod

It was no good thing which I did at your persuasion when I crucified Jesus. I ascertained from the centurion and the soldiers that he rose again, and I sent to Galilee and learned that he was preaching there to above five hundred believers.

My wife Procla took Longinus, the believing centurion, and ten (*or* twelve) soldiers (who had kept the sepulchre), and went forth and found him 'sitting in a tilled field' teaching a multitude. He saw them, addressed them, and spoke of his victory over death and hell. Procla and the rest returned and told me. I was in great distress, and put on a mourning garment and went with her and fifty soldiers to Galilee. We found Jesus: and as we approached him there was a sound in heaven and thunder, and the earth trembled and gave forth a sweet odour. We fell on our faces and the Lord came and raised us up, and I saw on him the scars of the passion, and he laid his hands on my shoulders, saying, 'All generations and families shall call you blessed, because in your days the Son of Man died and rose again.'

The Letter of Herod to Pilate

It is in no small sorrow—according to the divine Scriptures—(i.e. as I might have anticipated from the teaching of Scripture) that I write to you.

My dear daughter Herodias was playing upon the water (i.e. the ice) and fell in up to her neck. And her mother caught at her head to save her, and it was cut off, and the water swept her body away. My wife is sitting with the head on her knees, weeping, and all the house is full of sorrow.

I am in great distress of mind at the death of Jesus, and reflecting on my sins in killing John Baptist and massacring the Innocents. 'Since, then, you are able to see the man Jesus again, strive for me and intercede for me: for to you Gentiles the kingdom is given, according to the prophets and Christ.'

Lesbonax my son is in the last stages of a decline. I am afflicted with dropsy, and worms are coming out of my mouth. My wife's left eye is blinded through weeping. Righteous are the judgements of God, because we mocked at the eye of the righteous. Vengeance will come on the Jews and the priests, and the Gentiles will inherit the kingdom, and the children of light be cast out.

And, Pilate, since we are of one age, bury my family honourably: it is better for us to be buried by you than by the priests, who are doomed to speedy destruction. Farewell. I have sent you my wife's earrings and my own signet ring. I am already beginning to receive judgement in this world, but I fear the judgement hereafter much more. This is temporary, that is everlasting.

THE LETTER OF TIBERIUS TO PILATE

Although this is a Greek text, it has a typically Western view of Pilate regarding him as a criminal. The Eastern churches, and the Coptic in particular, regarded him as a saint and martyr. It is late in date (possibly from the eleventh century), and has affinities with the Acta Pilati (Greek B).

Although Tischendorf knew the text of the letter in two separate manuscripts (Vindobon.-Nessel 246 and Paris 1771) according to his introduction to *EA* (pp. lxxix f.), he chose not to include it.

EDITIONS

Birch, i. 172 f. (text of Vindobon.-Ness. 246).
James, *Apoc. Anec.* ii. pp. lix–xl, 78–81.

MODERN TRANSLATIONS

English

James, 156–7.

Italian

Erbetta, iii. 125–6.
Moraldi, i. 707–9; ² i. 739–41.
Cravieri, 398–400.

Spanish

de Santos Otero, 473–7.

This was delivered to Pilate by means of the messenger Raab, who was sent with 2,000 soldiers to bring him to Rome.

Since you have given a violent and iniquitous sentence of death against Jesus of Nazareth, showing no pity, and having received gifts to condemn him, and with your tongue have expressed sympathy, but in your heart have delivered him up, you shall be brought home a prisoner to answer for yourself.

I have been exceedingly distressed at the reports that have reached me: a woman, a disciple of Jesus, has been here, called Mary Magdalene, out of whom he is said to have cast seven devils, and has told of all his wonderful cures. How could you permit him to be crucified? If you did not receive him as a God, you might at least have honoured him as a physician. Your own deceitful writing to me has condemned you.

As you unjustly sentenced him, I shall justly sentence you, and your accomplices as well.

Pilate, Archelaus, Philip, Annas, and Caiaphas were arrested.

Rachaab and the soldiers slew all the Jewish males, defiled the women, and brought the leaders to Rome. On the way Caiaphas died in Crete: the earth would not receive his body, and he was covered with a cairn of stones.

It was the old law that if a condemned criminal saw the face of the emperor he was spared: so Tiberius would not see Pilate, but shut him up in a cave.

Annas was sewed into a fresh bull's-hide, which, contracting as it dried, squeezed him to death. The other chiefs of the Jews were beheaded; Archelaus and Philip were crucified.

One day the emperor went out to hunt, and chased a hind to the door of Pilate's prison. Pilate looked out, trying to see the emperor's face, but at that moment the emperor shot an arrow at the hind, which went in at the window and killed Pilate.

II

APOCRYPHAL ACTS

Introduction

The first sections of Part II deal with the five major apocryphal Acts:
  The Acts of Andrew
  The Acts of John
  The Acts of Paul
  The Acts of Peter
  The Acts of Thomas
together with associated Acts linked with each of them. Minor Acts not connected with these texts are then discussed in a final section.

The five are the most influential and among the oldest of the apocryphal Acts, although they were not composed as a collection. It was originally held that all five were written by the same author. The name Leucius, the companion of John the Apostle, was given originally to the author of the Acts of John and then to the author of all five major acts. From the time of Photius he was named as Leucius Charinus. The names Leucius and Charinus (Karimus) appear in the Latin versions of the Descensus, and it may perhaps be assumed that there is some connection between these and the names given by Photius.

Recent scholarship is of the opinion that no two Acts were produced by the same author and the name of Leucius is not now usually applied to the authorship of any of them. They are anonymous works, but their literary interrelationship is clear. Language, style, sometimes theology, and occasionally even contents often show close connexions. The Acts of John shows links with the Acts of Andrew. (The Acts of John by Prochorus, a separate work, also seems to show a knowledge of the Acts of Andrew.) The relative sequence of the ancient Acts is difficult to determine, but the order of composition could be:
  1. (or 2) The Acts of Paul
  2. (or 1) The Acts of Peter
  3. The Acts of John
  4. The Acts of Andrew
  5. The Acts of Thomas

(Earlier scholars tended to place the Acts of John as the first written.) The Manichaeans gathered these five into a corpus which they substituted for the canonical Acts.

These Acts were composed in the second and third centuries and were intended to supplement stories and details about the apostles. To this extent therefore they belong to the apocryphal traditions based on the New Testament. They are part of the literature of popular piety tinged from time to time with Gnostic ideas and teaching, but which as pieces of literature belong to early orthodox Christianity as practised in various places in the second century.

The Acts of Andrew

The arrangement of this section is:
 Introduction
  The Acts of Andrew
  The Acts of Andrew and Matthias; the Acts of Peter and Andrew; the Acts of Andrew and Paul
 Texts
  A. The Acts of Andrew
  B. Papyrus Texts (P. Utrecht 1; Bodleian Fragment)
  C. Gregory of Tours' Epitome (summary)
  D. The Acts of Andrew and Matthias
  E. The Acts of Peter and Andrew (summary)
  F. The Acts of Andrew and Paul (summary)

INTRODUCTION

The oldest testimony for the existence of the apocryphal Acts of Andrew is in Eusebius *HE* 3. 25. 6 (Schwartz, *GCS* 9.2, pp. 252–3), which denounces the work (and others, including the Acts of John) as heretical. The Manichaean Psalter of about the same period relates certain events that are now thought to be from the Acts of Andrew (see Allberry, pp. 142 f., 192). Epiphanius, *adv. Haer.* 2. 47. 1; 2. 61. 1; 2. 63. 2 (Holl, *GCS* 31, pp 216, 381, 399), knew that some heretical groups including Encratites possessed the Acts of Andrew.

The use of the Acts of Andrew in the West is attested first by Philaster of Brescia towards the end of the fourth century in *Diversarum Hereseon Liber* 61 (ed. F. Marx, *CSEL* 38 (Vienna, Prague, Leipzig, 1898), pp. 48 f.). A few years later Innocent I in some manuscripts at least attributed the authorship of the Acts of Andrew to the philosophers Xenocharides and Leonides (see H. Wurm, *Apollinaris* 12 (1939), 57–78, esp. 77–8) and condemned its use. The Gelasian Decree includes the Acts in its list of apocryphal texts. Augustine, *c. Faust.* 14. 1; 22. 79; 30. 4 (Zycha, pp. 402, 681, 751), states that the Manichaeans in North Africa and the Priscillianists in Spain had a corpus of apocryphal Acts including the Acts of Andrew. See also references in Augustine, *Contra adv. legis* 1. 19. 38 (ed. K.-D. Daur, *CCL* 49 (Turnhout, 1985), p. 68) and *Contra felicem Manicheum* 2. 6 (ed. J. Zycha, *CSEL* 25.2 (Prague, Vienna, Leipzig, 1892), p. 833).

Our best authority for a general knowledge of the Acts of Andrew is

232   *The Acts of Andrew*

Gregory of Tours' epitome, *Liber de Miraculis Beati Andreae Apostoli* sometimes known as the *Virtutes Andreae*. This has been edited by M. Bonnet in *Monumenta Germaniae Historica*, I. *Scriptores rerum Merovingicarum. Gregorii Turonensis Opera* (ed. W. Arndt and B. Kruesch), vol. i, part 2 (Hanover, 1885), pp. 821–46. Gregory probably based his epitome on an earlier *de Virtutibus S. Andreae*. A modified version of M. R. James's abstract of Gregory's work appears below.

The references in the *Vita Andreae* by Epiphanius the Monk are also significant (*PG* 120, cols. 215–60) for a ninth-century view of the developments of the Andrew traditions, although there is no precise citation from the Acts of Andrew. Generally, there is a paucity of references in patristic testimony. One noteworthy exception is the following extract found in Evodius of Uzala, *De fide contra Manichaeos* 38 (ed. J. Zycha, *CSEL* 25.2 (Vienna, Prague, Leipzig, 1892), pp. 968–9), with its allusions which may refer to the original Acts of Andrew:

Observe, in the Acts of Leucius which he wrote under the name of the apostles, what manner of things you accept about Maximilla the wife of Egetes: who, refusing to pay her due to her husband (though the apostle had said 'Let the husband pay the due to the wife and likewise the wife to the husband' 1 Cor. 7. 3), imposed her maid Euclia upon her husband, decking her out, as is there written, with wicked enticements and paintings, and substituted her as deputy for herself at night, so that he in ignorance used her as his wife.

There also is it written, that when this same Maximilla and Iphidamia were gone together to hear the apostle Andrew, a beautiful child, who, Leucius would have us understand, was either God or at least an angel, escorted them to the apostle Andrew and went to the praetorium of Egetes, and entering their chamber feigned a woman's voice, as of Maximilla, complaining of the sufferings of womankind, and of Iphidamia replying. When Egetes heard this dialogue, he went away.

If original, these incidents could have occurred after chapter 35 of Gregory's outline (cf. Acts of Andrew 17). Evodius' work dates from the early fifth century.

Outside this ancient testimony, what survives in manuscript form are the following portions of the Acts of Andrew (as is usual with such literature the Martyrdom circulated separately from the Acts as a whole in many manuscripts):

(A) *The Acts of Andrew*
    (i) Sinai Gr. 526 (10th century) and Jerusalem S. Saba 103 (12th cent.) include a long extract covering Vatican Greek 808 and the complete Martyrdom. These form the basis of the translation below.
    (ii) Vatican Greek 808 (10th–11th cent.) published by Bonnet. This includes incidents prior to the martyrdom and may be part of the

original Acts. Some of the material is absent from the Sinai and Jerusalem manuscripts.
(iii) P. Utrecht 1 (4th cent.). In the view of its original editor, G. Quispel—a view generally shared by later commentators—this one 'Act of Andrew' is a Sahidic Coptic version taken from the original Acts of Andrew. It seems to have been not unusual for an isolated act of an apostle to be abstracted from the longer apocryphal acts. The story in the papyrus is found in a different, shorter, form in Gregory of Tours' epitome (18), but is ignored in Epiphanius the Monk's *Vita Andreae* and in the Laudatio (see below).
(iv) Bodleian Fragment, published by Barns. As with the Utrecht fragment, this too may have been another Sahidic Coptic extract from the original Acts of Andrew. An appearance of the risen Jesus is not uncharacteristic of the apocryphal Acts: Barns considers that this episode may have occurred near the beginning of the original Acts of Andrew. Its verbosity and its encratite tendency are consistent with the character of the rest of the Acts of Andrew, but Prieur is cautious about accepting it as an original part of the Acts.

(B) *The Martyrdom*

The Martyrdom exists in several adaptations:
(i) *Byzantine texts* (all published by Bonnet):
 (a) *Martyrium Andreae Prius* (based on two manuscripts, one of the 9th–10th cent., the other of the 12th cent.). This account is close to the Laudatio.
 (b) *Martyrium Andreae Alterum* (found in two recensions, one supported by two manuscripts, the other by one).
 (c) *Narratio*. An encomium that generally reproduces the *Martyrium Alterum* with additions that may come from the original Acts. (Based on four manuscripts of the 10th–11th cent.)
 (d) *Laudatio*. Another encomium attributed to Nicetas the Paphlagonian (ninth century). This is based on three manuscripts of the 11th–12th cent.
(ii) *Latin texts* (all published by Bonnet):
 (a) *The Epistle of the Presbyters and Deacons of Achaea*. Bonnet prints this text (found in several manuscripts) together with two Greek versions, also found in several manuscripts. He has argued that the Latin, edited in the sixth century, is the original language. The first Greek version is a literal translation of the Latin. The second of the two Greek versions he prints (beginning Ἅπερ τοῖς ὀφθαλμοῖς...) is a freer translation, which also incorporates some additional material

likely to have come from the original Acts. Flamion calls that second Greek the 'Épître grecque'. One manuscript of the Latin text goes back to the 8th cent.; most of the other Latin and the Greek manuscripts are 10th–12th cent.

(b) *Conversante et Docente*. These are the opening words of an account of a 6th-cent. martyrdom edited from four manuscripts dating from the 10th–12th cent.

(iii) *Armenian*: The important Armenian account of the martyrdom corresponds to the final part of the ancient Acts of Andrew, although it does not agree exactly with existing Greek editions. It also includes some episodes unknown in the Greek tradition, in particular speeches attributed to Andrew.

Some, but not all the above, represent a text close to that of the original Acts of Andrew. Precision is difficult, but the editions by Prieur (and MacDonald) are based primarily on A (i), A (ii), B (i) (b), with some support from B (ii) (a) (second Greek form), B (i) (a), B (i) (c), B (i) (d) and B (ii) (b). It is difficult to estimate the original length of the Acts of Andrew: the work is not included in the Stichometry of Nicephorus. It is, however, thought to have been the longest and most prolix of the five major apocryphal Acts. Because of its extreme asceticism and encratism the original Acts were expurgated and catholicized over the centuries. The famous epitome by Gregory of Tours (which in its prologue confesses that he has deliberately excised its 'excessive verbosity') selected only the miracles. This may give us some idea of the original scale. In addition, Gregory has often altered and censored some details, as may be seen where his epitome can be compared to parallel accounts elsewhere. The following list shows links between Gregory and accounts in other sources (a full list is to be seen in Prieur's article in *ANRW* (see bibliography below, under General), 4408–13, and see his *CCA* 5, 59–65):

Gregory

6 (exorcism at Nicaea). Cf. Narratio 4; Laudatio 18.

11 (wedding at Philippi). Cf. Epistle of Pseudo-Titus[1]: When, finally, Andrew also [John has been cited shortly before] had come to a wedding, he too, to manifest the glory of God, disjoined certain who were intended to marry each other, men and women, and instructed them to continue holy in the single state.

12 (incendiarism at Philippi). Cf. Manichaean Psalm Book (Allberry, p. 142: 'Andrew the Apostle: they set fire to the house beneath him').

---

[1] A Latin apocryphon that exists in an 8th-century MS. See Lipsius, ii.2, 401–6, and the text in D. de Bruyne, 'Nouveaux fragments des Actes de Pierre, de Paul, de Jean, d'André et de l'Apocalypse d'Élie', *Rev. Bén.* 25 (1908), 149–60.

18 (Virinus). Cf. Pap. Utrecht 1 (Varianus), and perhaps P. Oxy. 851, ed. B. P. Grenfell and A. S. Hunt, *OP* 6 (London, 1908), pp. 18-19.

22-3 (conversion of proconsul). Cf. Laudatio 34-6 and Martyrium Prius 3-7 (see Prieur, *CCA*, pp. 708-23). (MacDonald adds after Gregory ch. 23 Martyrium Prius 7 = Laudatio 36.)

30 (healing of Maximilla). Cf. Laudatio 38 and Epiphanius the Monk, *Vita*, col. 245 A-B.

31 (sick beggar). Cf. Laudatio 39 and *Vita*, col. 245 C.

32 (blind family). Cf. Laudatio 40 and *Vita*, col. 245 C.

33 (sick sailor). Cf. Laudatio 41 and *Vita*, col. 245 D. (See Prieur, *CCA*, pp. 728-33).

34 (exorcism of slave and conversion of Stratocles). Cf. Acts of Andrew 2-12, Laudatio 43, *Vita*, col. 248 B-C.

35 (the Maximilla incident and Aegeates' anger). Cf. Evodius (above, p. 232), and Acts of Andrew 17.

36 (imprisonment). Cf. Laudatio 44.

Gregory's work did not include the martyrdom of Andrew although he alludes to a passion in his ch. 37. The later Apostolic History of Pseudo-Abdias made use of Gregory's summary but added to it a martyrdom account similar to that found in *Conversante et Docente*.

An attempt to work back from the existing accounts of the martyrdom to a form close to that found in the original Acts was described by Flamion. The mosaic he suggested was accepted by James, who used this reconstructed text, and by Hennecke-Schneemelcher[3]. Other modern scholars, including Moraldi, have been sceptical of such a reconstruction and in their editions have preferred to include only translations of the actual manuscripts containing a version of the passion. The recent publication of the Jerusalem and Sinai manuscripts (together with support from an unpublished Ann Arbor manuscript of the Passion) has rendered this mosaic obsolete.

Authorship and Provenance

On the basis of similarities between the Acts of Andrew, the Acts of Peter, and the Acts of John, M. R. James (*Apoc. Anec.* ii, p. xxxi) was prepared to conclude that the works are by one and the same author 'who may be called, for the sake of convenience, Leucius', but such an identity of authorship or attribution to Leucius are not now generally accepted.

The provenance of the original work is not known. Syria or Egypt are possibilities.

Date

The strongly encratite character of the Acts has suggested an early date for its composition. Most commentators have decided on a date in the second or third century. Some of the arguments are dependent on the supposed interrelationship of these Acts and other apocryphal Acts (see Prieur, *CCA* 5, 385–403). An early third-century date for the Acts of Andrew is probable.

Character
The Gnostic character of the original Acts has been regularly referred to in modern studies ever since such an interpretation was popularized by Lipsius, but Flamion's study of the material led him to emphasize the orthodox and non-Gnostic character of the material. The publication of the Utrecht papyrus revived the theory of Gnostic influence, but Quispel has conceded that neither in that fragment nor in the other remains of the Acts of Andrew is there to be found a fully-fledged Gnosticism. As an early document it is not surprising that Gnostic and contemporary Hellenistic ideas were present in the original Acts without the work itself coming from Gnostic groups or from an author outside the catholic church.

Historical Value
The historical value of these Acts is minimal, but the tradition that the Byzantine church was founded on apostolic preaching became very significant from the seventh century onwards. Dvornik's study emphasizes that the original Andrew legends were based in Scythia (in the south of present-day Russia) rather than in Achaea. However, Epiphanius of Cyprus's list of disciples states bluntly that the Apostle Andrew instituted Stachys as first bishop of Byzantium; this list is likely to be from the eighth century. Traditions of Andrew's apostolic activity seem to have been known from at least the fourth century onwards by fathers of the church, and by the time of Gregory of Tours the Byzantine tradition concerning Andrew was well established.

The tradition that Andrew's apostolic activity was in Scythia may be found in Origen (see Eusebius, *HE* 3. 1 (Schwartz, *GCS* 9.2, p. 188)), but the original author of the Acts of Andrew (if the Acts of Andrew and Matthias are excluded from the original Acts) gave his account of a journey only from Pontus to Greece, where a belief in his martyrdom in Patras could be explained.

The stories set in Greece survived in the versions by Gregory of Tours and Pseudo-Abdias. The legends set in Scythia may be represented in the Acts of Andrew and Matthias and in the Acts of Peter and Andrew (see below).

Translation
The Acts of Andrew below is based on the translation by MacDonald from the text reconstructed by Prieur and by MacDonald on the evidence primarily of the Jerusalem and Sinai manuscripts.

EDITIONS

Greek and Latin

J. M. Prieur, *Acta Andreae*, 2 vols. (Turnhout, 1989) (= *CCSA* 5 and 6).
D. R. MacDonald, *The Acts of Andrew and the Acts of Andrew and Matthias in the City of the Cannibals* (Atlanta, 1990) (= *SBL Texts and Translations* 33; *Christian Apocrypha* 1).

Greek

T. Detorakis, Ἀνέκδοτο μαρτύριο τοῦ ἀποστόλου Ἀνδρέα, in *Acts of the Second International Congress of Peloponnesian Studies 1980*, i (Athens, 1981–2), 325–52 (= *Peloponnesiaca* Supplement 8).
Vat. 808: 'Ex Actis Andreae', Lipsius–Bonnet, ii. 1, 38–45.
Martyrium Prius: Lipsius–Bonnet, ii. 1, 46–57.
Martyrium Alterum: Lipsius–Bonnet, ii. 1, 58–64.
Narratio: M. Bonnet, 'Martyrium Sancti Apostoli Andreae', *Anal. Boll.*[2] 13 (1894), 353–72. [Eng. trans. (beginning at Narratio 4) in Peterson (below General), 49–58.]
Laudatio: M. Bonnet, 'Acta Andreae Apostoli cum laudatione contexta', *Anal. Boll.*[2] 13 (1894), 309–52
Passio (Epistle of the Presbyters and Deacons in Achaea): Lipsius–Bonnet, ii. 1, 1–37 (includes one Latin and two Greek texts) [Cf. C. C. Woog, *Presbyterorum et diaconorum Achaiae de Martyrio Sancti Andreae apostoli epistoli encyclica* (Leipzig, 1749) (Greek text), and Cf. Fabricius, ii. 747–59.]

Latin

Conversante et Docente: M. Bonnet. 'Passio Sancti Andreae Apostoli,' *Anal. Boll.*[2] 13 (1894), 373–8.
Gregory of Tours: see introduction above.
Pseudo-Abdias, *Apostolic History*, iii (ed. Fabricius, ii. 456–515) (joins a modified version of Gregory's epitome with Conversante et Docente). [General discussion in Lipsius, i. 117–78.]

Coptic

Utrecht 1: G. Quispel, 'An Unknown Fragment of the Acts of Andrew (Pap. Copt. Utrecht N.1)', *VC* 10 (1956), 129–48 and plate (repr. in G. Quispel, *Gnostic Studies*, ii (Istanbul, 1975), 271–87 (= *Uitgaven van het Nederlands historisch—archaeologisch Instituut te Ishtanbul 34*). [Reconstruction by Roelof van den Broek in Prieur, *CCA* 6, 653–71.]
Bodleian Fragment: J. Barns, 'A Coptic Apocryphal Fragment in the Bodleian Library', *JTS* 11 (1960), 70–6.

---

[2] The texts in *Anal. Boll.* were reprinted separately in M. Bonnet, *Supplementum Codicis Apocryphi*, ii (Paris, 1895).

Armenian

A French translation (with introductory notes) of the Armenian (based on MS 653 of Venice) as edited by C. Tsherakian, *Ankanon Girkh Arakhelakankh* (= Non-Canonical Apostolic Writings) (Venice, 1904), 146–67, has been made by Leloir, *CCA* 3, 228–57; cf. id, 'La version arménienne des actes apocryphes d'André et le Diatessaron', *NTS* 22 (1976), 115–39.

MODERN TRANSLATIONS

English

Walker, 335–48 (Greek of the Epistle of the Presbyters and Deacons of Achaea).
Pick, 220–21 (the fragments of Evodius, Vat. 808, and a mosaic based on parts of the Épître grecque and the Martyrium Prius).
James, 337–63.
Hennecke[3], ii. 390–425 (Flamion's mosaic of the martyrdom, the tract by Evodius, P. Utrecht 1, Vat. 808, and the Bodleian fragment).
Hennecke[5], ii. 101–51 (P. Utrecht 1, Vat. 808, Jerusalem–Sinai MSS, summary of Gregory of Tours' epitome).

French

Migne, *Dictionnaire*, ii, cols. 93–101 (Latin of the Epistle of the Presbyters and Deacons of Achaea).
Amiot, 252–61 (Latin of the Epistle of the Presbyters and Deacons of Achaea).
Éac, 877–972 (Greek Acts, Utrecht 1, Gregory of Tours' Epitome).
J.-M. Prieur, *Actes de l'apôtre André* (Turnhout, 1995) (= *Apocryphes. Collection de poche de l'AELAC* 7).

German

Hennecke[1], 459–73 (E. Schimmelpfeng) (Vat. 808, Evodius' citations, parts of Épître grecque, and Martyrium Prius 14); cf. *Handbuch*, 544–62.
Hennecke[3], ii. 270–97 (M. Hornschuh) (Bodleian Fragment, P. Utrecht 1, Vat. 808, the tract by Evodius, Flamion's mosaic of the martyrdom).
Hennecke[5], ii. 93–137 (J.-M. Prieur, W. Schneemelcher, G. Ahn) (P. Utrecht 1, Vat. 808, Jerusalem–Sinai MSS, summary of Gregory of Tours' epitome).
Michaelis, 379–401 (selection).

Italian

Erbetta, ii. 395–449 (Vat. 808, P. Utrecht 1, citations by Evodius and Pseudo-Titus, Gregory's 'Virtutes Andreae' in the collection of Pseudo-Abdias iii, the Latin of the Epistle of the Presbyters and Deacons of Achaea, Martyrium Prius, Martyrium Alterum A, and a summary of Epiphanius the Monk's testimony).
Moraldi, ii. 1351–1429, 1467–98; [2] ii. 429–507, 543–74. (Vat. 808, P. Utrecht 1, Bodleian Fragment, Gregory's 'Virtutes Andreae', Pseudo-Abdias iii, Épître grecque, Martyrium Prius).

Irish

See M. McNamara, *The Apocrypha in the Irish Church* (Dublin, 1975), 91-2.

GENERAL

Lipsius, i. 543-622.
M. Bonnet, 'La Passion de l'apôtre André en quelle langue a-t-elle été écrite?', ByzZ 3 (1894), 458-69.
James, *Apoc. Anec.* ii, pp. xxix-xxxi.
J. Flamion, *Les Actes apocryphes de l'apôtre André. Les Actes d'André et de Matthias, de Pierre et d'André et les textes apparentés* (Louvain, Paris, Brussels, 1911) (= *Recueil de travaux . . . d'histoire et de philologie* 33).[3]
M. Blumenthal, 'Zur Gesamtkomposition der Andreasakten', in *Formen und Motive in der apokryphen Apostelgeschichten* (Leipzig, 1933), 38-57 (= *TU* 48.1).
C. R. C. Allberry, *A Manichaean Psalm-Book* (Stuttgart, 1938) (= *Manichaean Manuscripts in the Chester Beatty Collection* 2).
F. Dvornik, *The Idea of Apostolicity in Byzantium and the Legend of the Apostle Andrew* (Cambridge, Mass., 1958) (= *Dumbarton Oaks Studies* 4).
P. M. Peterson, *Andrew, Brother of Simon Peter, His History and His Legends* (Leiden, 1958; repr. 1963) (= Supplements to *Novum Testamentum* 1) (includes details of works discussing the Andrew traditions in both the East and West from the New Testament up to the twelfth century).
Plümacher, cols. 30-4.
J.-M. Prieur, 'La figure de l'apôtre dans les actes apocryphes d'André', in F. Bovon (ed.), *Les Actes apocryphes des apôtres: Christianisme et monde païen* (Geneva, 1981), 121-39 (= *Publications de la Faculté de Théologie de l'Université de Genève* 4).
—— 'Les Actes apocryphes de l'apôtre André: Présentation des diverses traditions apocryphes et état de la question', *ANRW* 2.25.6, 4384-4414.
D. R. MacDonald, *Christianizing Homer* (New York and Oxford, 1994).
J. N. Bremmer (ed.), *The Apocryphal Acts of Andrew* (Leuven, 2000) (= *Studies on the Apocryphal Acts of the Apostles* 5).

[3] Review by M. R. James, *JTS* 13 (1912), 435-7.

The Acts of Andrew and Matthias; the Acts of Peter and Andrew; the Acts of Andrew and Paul

The Acts of Andrew and Matthias among the Cannibals was at one time thought to have belonged to the original Acts of Andrew. This apocryphon survives in Greek, Latin, Syriac, Coptic, Georgian, Ethiopic, Armenian, and Arabic. Gregory of Tours' epitome of the Acts of Andrew gives a short abstract of it in chs. 1 and 2, possibly because he found this apocryphon prefixed to his copy of the Acts of Andrew.

Flamion, in his study of all the Andrew traditions, argued on several grounds that it was unlikely that the Acts of Andrew and Matthias belonged to the Acts of Andrew, and that is the view accepted by Prieur, although MacDonald has recently attempted to revive the hypothesis that with the possible exclusion of chs. 11–15 it was part of the original Acts of Andrew. If MacDonald is corrrect, then this Acts must be of third-century rather than fifth-century composition. For MacDonald the Acts of Andrew including the Acts of Andrew and Matthias influenced the opening sequence in The Acts of Thomas, and this influence is also seen in the Martyrium Prius (of Andrew). He also claims that the Acts of Andrew and Matthias influenced the Acts of Philip, the Acts of John by Prochorus, and the Acts of Xanthippe and Polyxena.

The Old English poem attributed to Cynewulf is based on this work and it has been edited by, among others, K. R. Brooke, *Andreas and the Fates of the Apostles* (Oxford, 1961), who is of the opinion that the ultimate source is a Greek text but mediated through Latin (although not the Latin of Blatt's publications). Two Old English prose versions also exist, and these are independent of Andreas and of the Latin and Greek.

MacDonald's translation based on his eclectic text is reproduced below (with minor adaptations).

The Acts of Peter and Andrew is a sequel to the Acts of Andrew and Matthias and seems to be one of the attempts made to complete the Acts of Andrew and Matthias—presumably, on MacDonald's argument, after it had been detached from the rest of the Acts of Andrew. It exists in Greek and Slavonic and, in a different form, in Ethiopic. A summary, based on James, is given below.

Also included below is a summary of another apocryphon belonging to the Andrew cycle, the eighth–ninth century Acts of Andrew and Paul which has survived in Coptic.

ACTS OF ANDREW AND MATTHIAS

EDITIONS

(See MacDonald, under Bibliography to the Acts of Andrew.)

Greek

J. C. Thilo, *Acta SS. Apostolorum Andreae Graece*... (Halle, 1846).
Lipsius–Bonnet, ii.1, 65–116.
Tischendorf, *Apoc. Apoc.* 139–41.
J. B. Bauer, 'Ein Papyrusfragment der Acta Andreae et Matthiae', *JÖBG* 16 (1976), 35–8.

Latin

F. Blatt, *Die lateinischen Bearbeitungen der Acta Andreae et Matthiae apud Anthropophagos* (Giessen, 1930) (= *Beihefte zur Zeitschrift für die neutestamentliche Wissenschaft* 12). [Cf. B. Löfstedt, 'Zu den lateinischen Bearbeitungen der Acta Andreae et Matthiae apud Anthropopagos', *Habis* 6 (1975), 167–76.]

Syriac

'The History of Mār Matthew and Mār Andrew', in Wright, *Apoc. Acts*, i. 102–26; ii (Eng. trans.), 93–115.

Armenian

A French translation of the Armenian appears in Leloir, *CCA* 3, 191–227, and cf. pp. 258–65.

Coptic

[Cf. O. von Lemm, 'Koptische apokryphe Apostelacten', *Mélanges Asiatiques* 10 (St Petersburg, 1892), 148–66.]
E. Lucchesi and J.-M. Prieur, 'Fragments coptes des Actes d'André et Matthias et d'André et Barthélemy', *Anal. Boll.* 96 (1978), 339–50.

Arabic

Smith Lewis, *Acta Myth.* 109–118; *Myth. Acts*, pp. 126–9.

Ethiopic

Wallis Budge, *Contendings* i. 225–46, 307–35; ii (Eng. trans.), 267–88, 370–403.

Slavonic

de Santos Otero, *Altslav. Apok.* i. 69–83. [For further references see Hennecke[5], ii. 403 or MacDonald, 64.]

MODERN TRANSLATIONS

English

Walker, 348–68.
James, 453–8 (summary).
Hennecke[5], ii. 443–51 (description only).
Peterson (bibliography to Acts of Andrew), 56–66 (translation of most of text).

German

Hennecke[5], ii. 399–406 (description only).

Italian

Erbetta, ii. 493–505.
Moraldi, ii. 1613–15; [2] ii. 689–91 (summary).

GENERAL

Lipsius, i. 547–54; ii.2, 258–69.
D. R. MacDonald and J.-M. Prieur, 'The Acts of Andrew and Matthias and the Acts of Andrew', in D. R. MacDonald (ed.), *The Apocryphal Acts of Apostles* (Decatur, Ga., 1986), 9–33 (= *Semeia* 38).

ACTS OF PETER AND ANDREW

EDITIONS

Greek

Tischendorf, *Apoc. Apoc.* xlviii–l, 167–7 (= Bodleian MS).
Lipsius–Bonnet, ii.1, 117–27 (Bodleian and Vatican MSS with help from Slavonic and Ethiopic).

Coptic

Guidi, *AAL. R* 4, 3.1 (1887), 62–3; Italian trans., *Giornale*, 21–2.

Arabic

Smith Lewis, *Acta Myth.* 101–9; *Myth. Acts*, 120–5.

Slavonic

de Santos Otero, *Altslav. Apok.* i. 67–8.
N. Bonwetsch, 'Ein Beitrag zu den Akten des Petrus und Andreas', *KKG* 5 (1882), 506 9.

Ethiopic

Malan, 221–9.
Wallis Budge, *Contendings*, i. 296–306; ii (Eng. trans.), 296–306.

MODERN TRANSLATIONS

English

Walker, 368–73.
James, 458–60 (summary).

Italian

Erbetta, ii. 529–34.
Moraldi, ii. 1618–19; [2] ii. 693–4 (summary).

GENERAL

Lipsius, i. 554–7.

ACTS OF ANDREW AND PAUL

EDITIONS

X. Jacques, 'Les deux fragments conservés des "Actes d'André et de Paul"', *Orientalia* 38 (1969), 187–213 (Coptic and French trans.). [The two texts are in Cod. Borg. Copt. 109, fasc. 132.]
Tischendorf, *Apoc. Apoc.*, pp. xlvi–xlix (long footnote containing a résumé of a trans. of the Coptic).
Guidi, *AAL. R* 4, 3.2 (1887), 80–1; Italian trans., *Giornale*, 45–6.

MODERN TRANSLATIONS

English

James, 472–4 (summary).

French

X. Jacques, trans. (see above) repeated in *RSR* 58 (1970), 289–96.

Italian

Erbetta, ii. 537–8 (follows James).
Moraldi, ii. 1616–17; ² ii. 692 (summary).

GENERAL

Lipsius, i. 616–17.

OTHER ANDREW LEGENDS

Arabic

Smith Lewis, *Acta Myth.* 11–23; *Myth. Acts*, 11–29 ('The Preaching of Andrew', 'The Acts of Andrew and Bartholomew', 'The Martyrdom of Saint Andrew', 'The Preaching of Saint Matthias'). These developed from Coptic at a time when that language ceased to be generally understood in Egypt.

Ethiopic

Malan, 76–117, 147–63, 221–9 (Acts concerning Andrew but not directly connected with the Acts of Andrew, viz. 'The Conflict of Saint Andrew', 'The Conflict of Saints Andrew and Bartholomew', 'The Conflict of Saints Andrew and Philemon').
Wallis Budge, *Contendings*, i. 140–55, 156–83, 184–8; ii (Eng. trans.), 163–82, 183–214, 215–21 ('The Preaching of Saint Andrew', 'The Martyrdom of Saint Andrew in Scythia', 'The Acts of Saints Andrew and Bartholomew'). These texts probably reached Ethiopic from Coptic through Arabic.

Coptic

Guidi, *AAL. R* 4, 3.2 (1887), 19–20, 177–90, 368–72; Italian trans., *Giornale*, 22–6, 46–55.
E. Lucchesi and J-M. Prieur, 'Fragments coptes des Actes d'André et Matthias et d'André et Barthélemy', *Anal. Boll.* 96 (1978), 339–50, esp. 347–50; 98 (1980), 75–82.

A. THE ACTS OF ANDREW

SUMMARY OF CONTENTS

1–5 Andrew heals the slave of Stratocles, Aegeates' brother.
6–12 Stratocles himself is converted.
13–16 Maximilla refuses sexual relations with her husband, Aegeates.
17–21 She substitutes her servant Euclia to sleep with him instead.
22–4 Aegeates executes Euclia when he discovers the truth.

25–50 Maximilla refuses Aegeates' sexual advances. Andrew is imprisoned, but his followers listen to his preaching in prison.
51–4 Aegeates crucifies Andrew.
55–8 Andrew preaches for four days.
59–63 The crowd persuade Aegeates to release Andrew, but the apostle prefers to die.
64 Maximilla and Stratocles bury Andrew, then devote themselves to a life of piety. Aegeates commits suicide.

A. THE ACTS OF ANDREW

1. Stratocles, Aegeates' brother, who had petitioned Caesar not to serve in the army but to pursue philosophy, arrived in Patras from Italy at that very moment. Excitement overtook the entire praetorium of Aristocles, because Stratocles had not come to visit Aegeates for a long time. Maximilla too left the bedroom delighted to greet him, and when she had welcomed Stratocles, she went inside with him. At daybreak, she was alone while Stratocles fulfilled his duty to his friends, behaving gently towards everyone and greeting them all graciously and with decorum.

2. As he was thus engaged, one of the servants under the supervision of Aristocles, whom Stratocles loved dearly, was stricken by a demon and lay in filth, out of his mind. When Stratocles saw him he said, 'If only I had never come here but perished at sea this would not have happened to me? Friends I cannot live without him.' As he said this turning to those with him, he hit himself about the eyes and became disturbed and unfit to be seen.

When Maximilla heard about this, she emerged upset from her bedroom and said to Stratocles, 'Do not worry about your servant, brother. Soon he will be healed, for there is a most God-fearing man staying in this city who can not only dispel demons, but if a menacing and serious sickness overcomes someone, he cures it. We have therefore come to trust in him, but we say this as those who have put him to the test.' Iphidama likewise said such things to Stratocles to restrain him from performing some rash act, in his extreme anguish.

3. While both women were consoling Stratocles, Andrew, having agreed with Maximilla that he would go to the boy, arrived at the praetorium. On entering the gate he said, 'Some force is fighting inside; hurry brothers!' Without asking questions he burst inside to the place where Stratocles' servant was foaming at the mouth, entirely contorted.

Those who came dashing because of Stratocles' cries had no idea who Andrew was when they saw him smiling and pushing aside those who were present, making a path in order to get to the servant lying on the ground. Those who had already met Andrew and had seen him at work gave ground, fearing him as a god. Stratocles' servants, on the other hand, viewed him as a common man and tried to beat him. When the rest saw them maltreating him they rebuked them for not knowing what they were doing. When they settled down, they waited to see the outcome.

4. Just then someone told Maximilla and Iphidama that the blessed one had arrived. They were elated, ran from their rooms, and hurried to Stratocles: 'Come and you will see how your servant is healed.'

Stratocles also got up and walked with them, and when he saw the enormous crowd standing around his servant he said quietly, 'Alcman,' (this was the boy's name) 'you have become a spectacle by coming to Achaea!'

Andrew stared at Maximilla, and while looking at her he said the following: 'My child, what is most disconcerting to those who are turning to a faith in God away from a great tempest and wandering is to see these ailments cured which many considered beyond help. Look, even now I see what I am saying coming to pass. Magicians are standing here helpless to do anything. They have given up healing the servant. So have those charlatans whom we all see trading in public. Why have they been unable to expel this fearsome demon from the poor servant? Because they are kindred to it. It is useful to say this before the present crowd.'

5. Without delay he got up and said, 'O God who do not give heed to magicians, O God who do not offer yourself to the quacks, O God who withdraw from things foreign to yourself, O God who always offer your possessions to your own, even now, in the presence of all these people, grant my request quickly with respect to Stratocles' servant by banishing the demon whom those who are its kindred could not.'

Immediately the demon relented and said in a masculine voice, 'I flee, servant of God! I flee not only from this servant but also from this entire city.'

'I not only command you to flee from this city', Andrew told him, 'but I bar you from setting foot in any of those regions where there is so much as a trace of my brethren.'

When the demon had left, Alcman got up from the ground. Andrew extended his hand to him, and the lad walked with him, self-composed, steady on his feet, speaking normally, affectionately looking at Andrew and his master, and inquiring about the cause for the crowd inside. Andrew told him, 'There is no need for you to learn about anything alien to you. It is enough for us to see in you what we have seen.'

6. While they were thus occupied, Maximilla took Andrew and Stratocles by the hand and entered her bedroom along with all of the brethren who were there. Once seated, they fixed their eyes on the blessed Andrew so that he might speak. For the sake of Stratocles, Maximilla had been eager for the apostle to talk so that he might believe in the Lord. His brother Aegeates was altogether blasphemous and despicable with respect to what is superior.

7. 'O Stratocles,' Andrew began, 'I know well that you are moved by what has happened, but I am also certain that I must bring out into the open the person now latent within you. Your total bewilderment and pondering of the

source and cause of what has happened are the greatest proofs that the soul within you is troubled, and the perplexity, hesitation, and astonishment in you please me. Bring to birth the child you are carrying and do not give yourself over to labour pains alone. I am no novice at midwifery or divination. I desire what you are bearing. I love what you are suppressing. I will suckle what is within you. I know the one who is silent. I know the one who has hope. Already your new self speaks to me. Already I encounter those things he has suffered for so long. He is ashamed of his former religion; he mourns his former public conduct; he considers all his former worship vacuous; he has no idea what true religion is; he tacitly reproaches the useless gods of his past; having become a vagabond, he suffers in order to become educated. Whatever his former philosophy, he now knows that it was hollow. He sees that it is destitute and worthless. Now he learns that it promises nothing essential. Now he admits that it pledges nothing useful. Is that not so? Does the person inside you not say these things, Stratocles?'

8. After a loud groan, Stratocles answered as follows: 'Most prophetic man, truly a messenger of the living God, I too will not separate from you until I recognize myself by having despised all those things about which you rebuked me for idly squandering my time in them.'

Stratocles was with the apostle night and day and never left him, sometimes examining, learning from, and interrupting him, and other times remaining silent and enjoying himself, having truly become enamoured of saving attentiveness. Declaring that he would take leave of all his possessions, he decided to live alone, with no one else but the apostle. He ceased examining the blessed one when anyone else was present, but while the rest of the believers were doing something else, he questioned him in private. When the others fell asleep, he would lie awake and by his enthusiastic interruptions would not let Andrew sleep.

9. Andrew would not keep quiet but exposed Stratocles' inquiries to the brethren by telling him, 'Stratocles, double your harvest by asking me questions in private and by hearing the same in the presence of the brethren, for in this way what you desire and seek will all the more surely be stored up in you. It is not right for you to conceal your labour pains even from your peers. Take the example of a woman in labour: When the labour pains overcome her and the foetus is forced by some power to come forth—not to stay within but to be squeezed outside—the foetus becomes obvious and noticeable to the attending women who take part in such mysteries (it was the foetus itself that cried out when the mother cried out earlier). Then, after the birth, these initiates at last provide for the new-born whatever care they know, so that, in so far as it is up to them, the foetus might be born alive. Likewise, Stratocles my child, we too must not be passive but bring your offspring into the open, so that they may be registered and be brought to the gift of saving words by many kindred, whose associate I found you to be.'

10. Maximilla and Iphidama rejoiced that Stratocles was conducting himself in a pious manner, was at last firmly accepting all the words that were akin to him, and possessed a steady soul and a firm and unalterable faith in the Lord. Alcman, after his cure, no longer resisted the faith. Because they were rejoicing and being confirmed in Christ night and day, Stratocles, full of gratitude, Maximilla, Iphidama, Alcman, along with many of the other brethren, were deemed worthy of the Lord's seal.

11. 'My children,' Andrew told them, 'if you keep this seal's impression separate from other seals that imprint different designs, God will commend you and receive you to his domain. Because such a radiant image appears in your souls which are essentially set loose from your bodies, the punishing powers, evil authorities, fearsome rulers, fiery angels, hideous demons, and foul forces, who cannot endure being forsaken by you, since they have nothing to do with the symbol of the seal which is kindred to light, run aground and sink during their flight to their kindred: darkness, fire, gloom, and whatever other impending punishment one might imagine. But if you pollute the brilliance of the grace given you, those awful powers will taunt you and tease you by dancing here and there. Like an impostor or a tyrant, each will demand its own. Then it will do you no good to call on the God of your seal which you defiled by apostasizing from him. (12.) So, my children, let us guard the deposit entrusted to us. Let us return the deposit spotless to the one who entrusted it to us. When we arrive there, let us say to him, "Look, we brought you your gift unabused. Which of your possessions will you give us?" He will answer us at once, "I will give you myself. All that I am I give to my own. If you desire unflickering light, I am it. If you desire a life not subject to evolution, I am it. If you desire rest from futile labour, you have me as your rest. If you desire a friend who supplies goods not of this world, I am your friend. If you desire a father for those who are rejected on earth, I am your father. If you desire a legitimate brother to set you apart from false brothers, I am your brother. If you desire and seek anything more valuable to you, you have me with all that is mine, and all that is mine will be in you." Beloved, our Lord gives us this reply.'

After Andrew said these things, some of the brethren cried, others rejoiced, but because he had become a neophyte Stratocles in particular was so elevated in his mind that he forsook all his possessions and devoted himself to the word alone.

13. There was great joy among the brethren as they gathered together night and day at the praetorium with Maximilla. On the Lord's day, when the brethren were assembled in Aegeates' bedroom listening to Andrew, the proconsul arrived home. When her husband's arrival was announced to Maximilla she was troubled, anticipating the outcome, that he would find so many people inside.

When Andrew saw her perplexity, he said to the Lord, 'Do not permit

Aegeates to enter this bedroom, Lord Jesus, until your servants can leave here without fear, for they have come together for your sake, and Maximilla constantly pleads with us to meet and take our rest here. Inasmuch as you have judged her worthy to deserve your kingdom, may she be especially emboldened, and Stratocles too. Save us all by repelling that savage lion armed to attack us.'

As the proconsul Aegeates came in, he had stomach pains, asked for a chamber pot, and spent a long time sitting, attending to himself. He did not notice all the brethren leave in front of him. For Andrew laid his hand on each one and said, 'Jesus will screen your appearance from Aegeates, in order to secure your invisibility before him.' Last of all, Andrew sealed himself and left.

14. When this grace of the Lord was completed, Stratocles, because he had been away from his brother for a long time, went out and embraced Aegeates, with a smile on his face but with no joy in his soul. The rest of his servants and freedmen greeted him in the same manner.

But Aegeates, out of passion for Maximilla, rushed into the bedroom assuming she was still asleep. She was at prayer. When she saw him, she looked away toward the ground.

'First give me your right hand', he told her. 'I will kiss the woman I will call no longer "wife" but "queen", so that I may find relief in your chastity and love for me.'

For when the wretch found her at prayer, he supposed she was praying for him and was delighted to hear his own name mentioned while she prayed. This is what Maximilla actually said: 'Rescue me at last from Aegeates' filthy intercourse and keep me pure and chaste, giving service only to you, my God.' When he approached her mouth intending to kiss it, she pushed him back and said, 'Aegeates, after prayer a woman's mouth should never touch a man's.'

Taken back by the sternness of her face, the proconsul left her. Because he had just completed a long journey, he took off his travelling clothes, relaxed, and lay down to sleep.

15. Maximilla then told Iphidama, 'Sister, go to the blessed one so that he may come here to pray and lay his hand on me while Aegeates is sleeping.'

Without hesitation she ran to Andrew, and after she reported the request of faithful Maximilla, Andrew went and entered another bedroom where Maximilla was. Stratocles also entered with the apostle, having come with the blessed one from his guest house. After Stratocles had greeted his brother, he asked about the accommodation where the Lord's apostle was staying. Guided by a brother named Antiphanes, Stratocles entered with the blessed one.

16. Andrew laid his hand on Maximilla and prayed as follows, 'I pray to you, my God, Lord Jesus Christ, who knows the future, and I entrust to you my child, the worthy Maximilla. May your word and power be mighty in her, and may the spirit that is in her struggle even against Aegeates, that insolent

and hostile snake. O Lord, may her soul remain forever pure, sanctified by your name. In particular, protect her, O Master, from this disgusting pollution. With respect to our savage and unbearable enemy, cause her to sleep apart from her visible husband and wed her to her inner husband, whom you above all recognize, and for whose sake the entire mystery of your plan of salvation has been accomplished. If she has such a firm faith in you, may she obtain her own proper kinship through separation from those who masquerade as friends but are really enemies.' When he had prayed thus and entrusted Maximilla to the Lord, he left with Stratocles once again.

17. Maximilla then planned the following. She summoned a comely, exceedingly wanton servant-girl named Euclia and told her something that delighted her and met her desires. 'You will have me as a benefactor of all your needs, providing you scheme with me and carry out what I advise.' Because she wanted to live chastely from that time on, Maximilla told Euclia what she wanted and got her word agreeing to it, and so for some time she employed the following subterfuge. Just as a woman customarily adorns herself to look like her rival, Maximilla groomed Euclia in just such finery and put her forward to sleep with Aegeates in her stead. Having used her as his lover, he let her get up and go to her own bedroom, just as Maximilla used to. By so doing, Maximilla escaped detection for some time, and thereby got relief, rejoiced in the Lord, and never left Andrew.[1]

18. When eight months had elapsed, Euclia demanded that her lady procure her freedom. That same day, Maximilla granted her whatever she asked. A few days later she made more demands, this time a large sum of money, and Maximilla gave it to her without hesitation. When Euclia demanded some of her jewellery, Maximilla did not object. In a word, even though Euclia regularly took clothing, fine linen, and headbands from Maximilla, she was not content but flaunted the affair before the other servants, boasting and vaunting herself.

The slaves, though indignant at Euclia's bragging, at first curbed themselves from injuring her. But she would laugh at them when showing them the gifts her mistress had given her. Euclia's fellow servants recognized them but were at a loss about what to do. Wishing to provide even greater proof of what she was saying, Euclia stationed two of them at the head of her master's bed when he was drunk, in order to convince them that she was indeed sleeping with him as though she were Maximilla. When she woke him from a deep sleep, she and the fellow servants observing the situation heard: 'Maximilla, my queen, why do you come so late?' Euclia said nothing, and the attending servants left the bedroom without a sound.

19. But Maximilla, supposing that Euclia was true to her word and reliable because of the gifts given her, spent her nights resting with Andrew along with

---

[1] See Evodius of Uzala's paraphrase in the introduction above.

Stratocles and all the other brethren. Andrew saw a vision, and as Maximilla listened, he told the brethren, 'Today at the home of Aegeates some new contrivance is brewing, brimming with trouble and wrath.' Maximilla begged him to disclose what this might be, but he said, 'Do not be eager to learn from me what you are to recognize soon enough.'

20. She altered her customary attire and entered the praetorium gate in plain sight. The household servants who had known about the affair—how it was that every day she and Stratocles went to Andrew, and at what hour she returned to her own bedroom—took her to be a visitor. She entered the proconsul's praetorium at that hour trying to escape detection. When they had forcibly exposed her they noticed she was their mistress. Some of them wanted to divulge the ruse and to tell Aegeates, while the others, motivated by hypocrisy toward their mistress, feigned fondness for her and silenced the others, assaulted them as though they were insane, and drove them out. While the slaves were fighting each other Maximilla burst into her bedroom and prayed that the Lord would fend her from every evil.

21. One hour later, those who had fought on Maximilla's behalf against their fellow servants set upon her, fawning, expecting to receive some reward, as though they were servants of Aegeates. The blessed lady considered them deserving of their request and summoned Iphidama: 'Give them their due.' She ordered that those who had hypocritically simulated affection for her be given one thousand denarii and commanded them to disclose the matter to no one.

Even though they solemnly swore themselves to silence about what they had seen, at the instigation of their father the devil they went to their master immediately, money in hand, and told him the whole story, including how their own fellow servant submitted to the plan Maximilla devised because she no longer wanted to sleep with Aegeates, repulsed by sexual intercourse with him as a heinous and despicable act.

22. The proconsul learned everything in detail, how Euclia had shared his bed as though she were his spouse, and how she confessed to having done so to her fellow slaves. Through interrogation he also discovered her motivation, for under torture she confessed to all the payments she received from her lady for keeping quiet.

The proconsul, furious at her for boasting to her fellow servants and for saying these things in order to defame her mistress—he wanted the matter to be kept secret since he was still fond of his spouse—cut out Euclia's tongue, mutilated her, and ordered her thrown outside. She stayed there without food for several days before she became food for the dogs. The rest of the servants who had told their story to him—there were three of them—he crucified.

23. Stricken by grief, Aegeates stayed in seclusion that day and ate nothing at all, baffled by the great change in Maximilla's attitude toward him. After crying for some time and reproaching his gods, he went to his spouse, fell at

her feet weeping, and said, 'I cling to your feet, I who have been your husband now for twelve years, who always revered you as a goddess and still do because of your chastity and your refined character, even though it might have been tarnished, since even you are human. So if you are keeping some secret from me about another man—something I never would have suspected—I will make allowances and I myself will cover it up, just as you often put up with my follies. Or if there is something else even more serious than this that separates you from me, confess it and I will quickly remedy the situation, for I know it is entirely useless to contradict you.'

While he persistently cajoled and begged, she told him, 'I am in love, Aegeates. I am in love, and the object of my love is not of this world and therefore is imperceptible to you. Night and day it kindles and enflames me with love for it. You cannot see it for it is difficult to see, and you cannot separate me from it, for that is impossible. Let me have intercourse with it and take my rest with it alone.'

24. The proconsul left her as if he were a maniac, not knowing what to do. He did not dare commit any impropriety against the blessed woman, for her pedigree far outstripped his. He said to Stratocles who was walking with him, 'Brother and my only legitimate surviving relative, I do not know if my wife is in a state of ecstacy or lunacy.'

And as he dejectedly began to tell Stratocles something else, one of his attending servants whispered in his ear, 'Master, if you would learn of this affair in detail, ask Stratocles; he will satisfy your curiosity, for he knows all about your wife. But if you wish to know of the entire matter now, I will apprise you.'

25. He drew Aegeates aside and told him privately, 'There is a certain stranger sojourning here who has become renowned not only in this city but throughout Achaea. He performs great miracles and cures which exceed human strength, as I in part can corroborate in that I was present and saw him revive corpses. And so that you may know the whole story, he proclaims a reverence for the divine and truly shows it to be shining forth into public view. My mistress, following Iphidama's lead, became acquainted with this stranger. She has so given way to desire for him that she loves no one more than him, including you I would say. Not only has she become intimately involved with the man, she has enchained your brother Stratocles with the same passion for him that has enchained her. They confess but one God, the one that that man disclosed to them, denying the existence of every other on earth. But listen to what your brother did that was the most insane thing of all. Even though he is of noble stock, the most honoured man in Achaea, addressed as brother of the proconsul Aegeates, he carries his own little oil flask to the gymnasium. Even though he owns many slaves, he appears in public doing his own chores—buying his own vegetables, bread, and other necessities, and carrying them on foot through the centre of the city—without shame in the sight of everybody.'

26. While the youth was telling this to his master, who was taking a walk and staring at the ground all the time, he spotted Andrew from a distance and shouted out loud: 'Look, master! There is the man responsible for the present disruption of your household.' The entire crowd turned to see the cause of his shout. Without another word, the youth—who was as fearsome as Aegeates, as though he were his brother and not really his slave—ran from the proconsul, seized Andrew, and forcibly brought him to Aegeates, wrapping around his neck the towel that the blessed one used to wear over his shoulder.

When the proconsul saw him, he recognized him and said, 'You are the one who once cured my wife and who refused a considerable sum of money that I wanted to donate. Teach me too about your renown and what sort of power you have, such that you are praised, so I hear, by those who are rich and poor, including infants, even though you appear in this manner like a simple old man.'

The entire crowd there dearly loved the apostle, and when they learned that the proconsul was speaking with him but not knowing why, they ran to the place where he was talking with Andrew. Without hesitation, Aegeates ordered him to be locked up, saying, 'Corrupter! You will see my rewards to you for your benefactions to Maximilla.'

27. A short time later, Aegeates left and went to Maximilla and discovered her eating bread and olives with Iphidama, this being the normal time for it, and said to her, 'Maximilla, now that I have captured your teacher and locked him up, I bring you news about him: he will not escape from me but will suffer a horrible death.'

'My teacher is not someone who can be detained,' the blessed lady answered, 'for he is not apprehensible or perceptible. Inasmuch as you have never overpowered anyone like this, Aegeates, stop this boasting.' He went out smiling, leaving her to eat.

'Sister,' Maximilla said to Iphidama, 'here we are eating while our benefactor, second to the Lord himself, is imprisoned. Go to the garrison in the name of the Lord, Iphidama, and find out where the prison is. I believe that at nightfall we will be able to see the Lord's apostle and that no one will see me leaving except Jesus and you, my guide.'

28. Iphidama changed usual clothing and dutifully rushed off. Once she discovered where the prison was, she went there and saw a large crowd standing at the prison gate. She inquired why the crowd had formed, and someone told her, 'Because of the most pious Andrew, locked up by Aegeates.'

When the faithful Iphidama had stood there for an hour, she saw the prison gate opened, and encouraged by this, she said, 'Jesus, I ask you to go in with me to your servant.' No one detected her as she entered and found the apostle speaking with his fellow inmates, whom he had already strengthened by encouraging them to believe in the Lord.

29. When he turned and saw Iphidama, his soul was elated, and he said to

the Lord, 'Glory be to you, Jesus Christ, ruler of true words and promises, who instils courage in my fellow servants. All who make use of you conquer their enemies, for you alone exist. Behold your Iphidama, driven by desire for us, has come here. I know that she and her mistress are under surveillance. Shield her with your covering both now as she leaves and this evening when she returns with her mistress, so that they will be invisible to their enemies. For as long as I have been here, they have made every effort to be bound together with me. Guard them yourself, Lord, for they are affectionate and God-loving.'

When he had prayed for Iphidama, Andrew dismissed her and said, 'The prison gate will be opened before you get there, and when you and Maximilla return here this evening, it will have been opened, and you will rejoice in the Lord and leave again, so that by these events too you both might be confirmed in our Lord.'

30. Iphidama left at once and found everything to be just as Andrew had predicted. When she came to Maximilla, she informed her about the blessed one's noble soul and resolve; namely, that even though imprisoned he was not quiet, but in fact urged on his fellow inmates and extolled the Lord's power. She also recounted to her whatever else he said to her inside the prison that pertained to them both.

When Maximilla heard everything Iphidama told her about the apostle, she exulted in spirit and said, 'Glory be to you, O Lord, for I am about to see your apostle again without fear. Even if an entire legion kept me locked up under key, it would not be strong enough to prevent me from seeing your apostle. It would be blinded by the radiant appearance of the Lord and by the boldness of his servant before God.' Having said this, she waited for lamps to be lit so that she could leave.

31. The proconsul said to some of those who were with him, 'I know Maximilla's audacity, because she never obeys me. Therefore, leave the praetorium doors unguarded but have four men go off to the prison and tell the jailer, "At this moment secure the door for which you are responsible! See that you do not open it for any of the dignitaries, even if you are won over by intimidation or bribery—not even if I should come myself—or you will lose your head!"' He commanded four others posted around her bedroom to detect if she should come out. The first four sped to the prison, while the others paced up and down in front of the blessed woman's bedroom as ordered. The cursed Aegeates went to supper.

32. Maximilla prayed with Iphidama to the Lord for a long time, telling the Lord again, 'Lord, at last it is time for me to go to your servant.' She left the bedroom with Iphidama, saying, 'Lord, be with us and do not forsake those who are here.'

When she arrived at the prison gate she found a beautiful young boy standing before opened doors who told them, 'Both of you go in to your

Lord's apostle. He has been expecting you for some time.' Running ahead of them, he went to Andrew and told him, 'Look, Andrew, these women have come to you rejoicing in your Lord. May they be strengthened in him by your speech.' . . .

33(1)[2] '(. . .) is everything about you lax? Have you still not convinced yourselves that you do not yet bear his goodness? Let us stand in awe and rejoice with each other over our abundant partnership with him. Let us say to each other: "Blessed is our race, for someone has loved it. Blessed is our existence, for someone has shown it mercy. We are not cast to the ground, for we have been recognized by such a height. We do not belong to time, so as to be dissolved by time. We are not the product of motion, which disappears of its own accord, nor of earthly birth so as to die in the same condition. Rather, we are those who aspire to greatness. We belong to the one who indeed shows mercy. We belong to the better, therefore we flee the worse. We belong to the good, through whom we drive away the disgraceful; to the just, through whom we reject the unjust; to the merciful, through whom we abandon the unmerciful; to the saviour, through whom we have recognized the destroyer; to the light, through whom we have cast off the darkness; to the one, through whom we have turned from the many; to the heavenly, through whom we have learned about the earthly; to the enduring, through whom we see the transitory." What better cause do we have for desiring to give thanks, to speak boldly, to sing a hymn, or to boast before the God who had mercy on us than that we have been recognized by him.'

34(2). And after he had spoken with the women for some time he at last sent them away saying, 'Go in peace. For you well know, O maidservants of Christ, that because of his love I will never entirely abandon you, and that because of his mediation, you will never again abandon me.' Each one left for home.

For several days, while Aegeates had no thought of pressing charges against the apostle, there was great joy among them. Every day they were strengthened in the hope of the Lord; they convened fearlessly at the prison and were incessantly with Maximilla and Iphidama and the others, because they were protected by the guardianship and grace of the Lord.

35(3). One day, while Aegeates sat as judge, he remembered the case of Andrew. Like a maniac, he left the case at hand, rose from the bench, and dashed to the praetorium seething with anger at Maximilla but flattering her all the same. Maximilla got home from the prison before he arrived.

36(4). When he went in to her, he said, 'Maximilla, because your parents thought me worthy to be your husband, they pledged you to me in marriage without regard to wealth, heredity, or reputation, considering only the kindness of my soul. Just now I deliberately left the court and came here not to

---

[2] This alternative numbering is that conventionally given to Vat. 808, which begins here.

enumerate the many matters I had wanted to reproach you with—such as the benefits I enjoyed from your parents, or the honours and favours you received from me during our lives together, such as your designation as my queen—but simply to learn from you this one thing. If you would be the woman you once were, living together with me as we are accustomed to—sleeping with me, having sexual relations with me, bearing my children—I would treat you well in every way. What is more, I will release the stranger whom I have in prison. But if you should not choose this course, I will do you no harm—I am unable to–but I will torment you indirectly through the one you love more than me. Answer me tomorrow, Maximilla, after you have considered which of the two options you want, for I am fully prepared to carry out this threat.' Having said this, he left.

37(5). At the usual time, Maximilla again went with Iphidama to Andrew. Putting his hands on her eyes and then bringing them to her mouth, she kissed them and began to seek his advice about every aspect of Aegeates' ultimatum.

'O Maximilla my child,' Andrew replied, 'I know that you have been moved to resist any proposition of sexual intercourse and wish to be dissociated from a foul and filthy way of life. For a long time this conviction has dominated my thinking, but still you want me to give my opinion. I bear you witness, Maximilla: do not commit this act. Do not submit to Aegeates' threat. Do not be moved by his speech. Do not fear his disgusting schemes. Do not be conquered by his artful flatteries. Do not consent to yield yourself to his impure spells. Endure each of his tortures by looking to us for a while, and you will see him entirely numb and wasting away from you and from all of your kindred. Inasmuch as I do not keep silent in making the matter visible and actual through you, the most important thing I should say to you now comes to me: I rightly see in you Eve repenting and in me Adam converting. For what she suffered through ignorance, you—whose soul I seek—must now redress through conversion. The very thing suffered by the mind which was brought down with her and was estranged from itself, I make right with you, through your recognition that you are being raised up. You healed her deficiency by not experiencing the same passions, and I have perfected Adam's imperfection by fleeing to God for refuge. Where Eve disobeyed, you obeyed; what Adam agreed to, I flee from; the things that tripped them up, we have recognized. For it is ordained that each person should correct his or her own fall.

38(6). 'Having said these things as I have said them, I would also say this: You have done well, O nature being saved, for you are neither overbearing nor in hiding. You have done well, O soul crying out what you suffered and returning to yourself. You have done well, O man who learn what is not yours and speed on to what is yours. You have done well, O hearer of what is being said, for I know that you are greater than what is thought or said; I recognize that you are more powerful than those who presume to dominate you; more distinguished than those who cast you down to shame, than those who lead you away to captivity. O man, if you understand all these things in yourself—that you are immaterial, holy, light, akin to the unbegotten, intellectual, heavenly, translucent, pure, superior to the flesh, superior to the world, superior to the powers, superior to the authorities over whom you really are—if you perceive yourself in your condition, then take knowledge in what you excel, if you see your face in your own being, having broken every shackle—I mean not only those shackles acquired by birth but also those beyond the realm of birth, whose magnificent names we have presented to you—then desire to see him who was revealed to you without having been created, whom you alone soon will recognize, if you take courage.

39(7). 'I have said these things in your presence, Maximilla, because the force of what has been said applies also to you. Just as Adam died in Eve through his complicity with her, so also I now live in you through your observing the commandment of the Lord and through your transporting yourself to a state worthy of your being. Scorn Aegeates' threats, Maximilla, for you know that we have a God who has compassion on us. Do not let his threats move you but remain chaste. Let him not only avenge himself on me with the tortures of captivity, let him also throw me to the beasts, burn me with fire, and throw me off a cliff. What does it matter? Let him destroy this body as he wishes, for it is only one body and it is akin to him.

40(8). 'Once again my speech is for you, Maximilla. I say to you, do not yield yourself to Aegeates. Stand up against his ambushes, especially, Maximilla, since I saw the Lord saying to me, "Andrew, Aegeates' father, the devil, will use him to release you from this prison." So from now on keep yourself chaste and pure, holy, unsullied, unalloyed, unadulterated, separated from anything foreign to us, unbroken, undamaged, unweeping, unwounded, unvexed by storms, undivided, unfalling, unsympathetic to the works of Cain. For if you do not give yourself up to their opposites, Maximilla, I will rest, even if I am forcibly unloosed from this life for your sake—that is, for my sake. If I am driven from here, perhaps I can help others of my kindred because of you, but if you become won over by the seductions of Aegeates and the flatteries of the serpent, his father, so that you return to your former sexual acts, know this: I will be punished there because of you, until you yourself realize that I despised living this life because of an unworthy soul.

(41[9].) Therefore, I beg you, wise man [sic], that your clearsighted mind stand firm. I beg you, mind unseen, that you may be protected. I entreat you, love Jesus. Do not be overcome by the inferior. You whom I entreat as a man, assist me in my becoming perfect. Help me too, so that you may recognize your true nature. Suffer with my suffering, so that you may recognize what I suffer and escape suffering. See what I see, and what you see will blind you. See what you should, and you will not see what you should not. Hear what I say and throw off whatever you heard (from Aegeates). I have said these things to you and to any who hear, if perchance you might hear.'

42(10). 'But to you, Stratocles,' he said, looking at him, 'why are you afflicted with many tears and why do you groan out loud? Why do you despair? Why your great grief and great sorrow? You recognize what has been said, so why do I beg you, child, that you live accordingly? Do you know to whom I have said these things? Has each gripped your mind? Has it reached your intellect? Do I still have the one who listened to me? Do I find myself in you? Is there someone in you speaking whom I see as my own? Does he love the one who has spoken in me and does he desire to have fellowship with him? Does he wish to be united with him? Does he strive to become loved by him? Does he long to be yoked with him? Does he find any rest in him? Does he have anywhere to lay his head?[3] Surely there is nothing in you to resist him—nothing to be turbulent against him, nothing to counteract him, nothing to hate him, nothing to flee from him, nothing to be savage to him, nothing to shun him, nothing that has turned away from him, nothing to rush from him, nothing to be oppressed, nothing to fight him, nothing to associate with others, nothing to be flattered by others, nothing to conspire with others, no other things to disturb him, nothing in you alien to me, no opponent, no corrupter, no enemy, no magician, no charlatan, no pervert, no deceiver, no traitor, no misanthrope, no hater of rational discourse, no one similar to tyrants, no boaster, no arrogant man, no maniac, no kinsman of the snake, no weapon of the devil, no advocate for fire, no friend of darkness. Stratocles, surely there is no one in you to oppose my saying these things, is there? Who is it? Answer! I do not speak in vain, do I? I have not spoken in vain, have I? "No!", says the man in you who weeps once again, Stratocles.'

43(11). Then Stratocles approached Andrew weeping and wailing. Andrew took Stratocles' hand and said, 'I have the one I sought. I have found the one I desired. I hold the one I loved. I rest because of the one I have waited for. The very fact that you are still groaning louder and are weeping uncontrollably symbolizes for me that I have already achieved rest, because I have not spoken in vain to you the words which are akin to me.'

44(12). 'Most blessed Andrew,' Stratocles replied, 'do not think that there is anything that vexes me but you, for the words which came from you are like fiery javelins impaling me. Each of them strikes me and truly blazes and burns with love for you. The sensitive part of my soul, which is disposed toward what I have heard, is tormented in that it presages with anguish (what will take place). For you yourself may leave, and I know well that it is good that you do so. But after this, where and in whom will I seek and find your concern and love? I received the seeds of the words of salvation while you were my sower; for them to sprout and reproduce requires no one else but you, blessed

---

[3] Cf. Matt 8: 20 and Luke 9: 58.

Andrew. What do I have to say to you but this, servant of God? I need the great compassion and help that comes from you in order to be worthy of these seeds I already have from you, which I might not otherwise see undamaged and sprouting into the open without your willing it and praying for them and for my entire self.'

45(13). 'Child,' answered Andrew, 'these things are what I myself also found in you. I glorify my Lord that my estimation of you was not groundless, but knew what it said. So that you all may know, tomorrow Aegeates will hand me over to be impaled on a stake. Maximilla, the Lord's servant, will trouble the enemy in him to whom he belongs, and will not consent with him to do anything alien to her. By turning against me he will presume to console himself.'

46(14). Maximilla was not present when the apostle said this, for when she heard the words that applied to her and in some way was changed by them, she became what the words themselves had signified. She rushed out deliberately and resolutely and went to the praetorium. Because she had bidden farewell to her whole life as well as to wickedness, the mother of the flesh, and to things pertaining to the flesh, when Aegeates made the same severe demand which he had told her to ponder—namely, whether she would be willing to sleep with him—she rebuffed him. He turned attention at last to the destruction of Andrew and considered what kind of death he might impose on him. Of all the options crucifixion most preoccupied him. Then he went off with his friends and ate like an animal.

47[4](15). Maximilla, led by the Lord disguised as Andrew, went to the prison again with Iphidama. A great crowd of the brethren was inside when she found him speaking the following: 'Brethren, the Lord sent me as an apostle to these regions of which my Lord considered me worthy, not to teach anyone, but to remind everyone akin to these words that all people pass their time among ephemeral evils, revelling in their destructive fantasies, which I have continually encouraged you to shun. I have urged you to pursue things that are permanent, and to flee from all that is transient. Look, not one of you stands firm, but everything—including human conventions—is in flux. This happens because of the uneducated soul's wandering into nature and retaining the pledges of its mistake. Therefore, I consider blessed those who have obeyed the words preached and who through them observe, as in a mirror, the mysteries concerning their proper nature, for the sake of which all things were constructed. (48[16].) Therefore, I command you, beloved children, to build firmly on the foundation laid for you, which is unshakeable and impregnable to the stratagems of the wicked. Be rooted on this foundation. Stand firm, remembering everything that happened while I was living among all of you. You saw acts performed through me which you yourselves cannot disbelieve;

---

[4] The Armenian passion narrative begins here.

such signs performed that perhaps even mute nature would have cried out in acclaim. I have handed over to you words which I pray you received in the way the words themselves would want. Dear friends, stand firm in everything you have seen, heard, and participated in, and God, in whom you have believed, because he had mercy, will present you to himself as acceptable, eternally at rest. (49[17].) Do not let what is going to happen to me trouble you as though it were some strange marvel, namely that God's servant, by whom God himself provided many things through acts and words, will be violently driven from this passing life by a wicked man. This violence will not come upon me only, but also on all who have loved, believed, and confessed (Jesus). The devil, entirely void of shame, will arm his own children against them, so that they may join forces with him. But he will not obtain what he wants. I will tell you why he undertakes these things. From the beginning of all things, in other words, from that time when the one without beginning descended to that realm under him to drive away (...). The enemy, a stranger to peace, (oppresses) the one not belonging to him, but is merely one of the weaker, inconspicuous, and thus far unable to be recognized. And because this person does not understand, he has to wage war with him. In so far as the enemy also aspires to dominate him forever, he opposes him in a manner that makes their hostility resemble a friendship. In order to place him under his control, he often flaunted his own pleasure-loving and deceitful traits, supposing that through these he would subjugate him. By faking a friendship befitting his victim, he did not display himself openly as an enemy. (50[18].) This activity took place for so long that the victim forgot to recognize it. ⟨But⟩ the devil recognized it; that is, because of his gifts he (was not seen to be an enemy). But when the mystery of grace was set aflame, and the plan for rest was revealed, and the light of the word was set forth, and the race being saved was proved to have been previously at war with pleasures, and when the enemy saw himself scorned and his gifts, through which he thought to intimidate, ridiculed because of the goodness of the merciful one, he began to entangle us in hate, hostility, and insurrection. He has made it his business not to leave us alone until we give way to the things that he values. For when this was the case, our opponent had nothing to worry about, and he pretended to depict his status as friendly to us. He had no fear that we would revolt inasmuch as we had been deceived by him. But let us not stand aside from Christ by the deceit of the enemy, because the providence of God has been revealed to us and has enlightened us. He has weakened the enemy's power and arrogance. For the hidden aspect of the devil's nature and what seemed to be unnoticed, this Christ exposed and forced to confess what it was. Therefore, brethren, since we understand what will happen, let us awaken and separate ourselves from him. Let us not be vexed or agitated by the storm, and let us not bear in our souls traces of the devil which are not ours. But since we have been entirely buoyed up by the whole word, let us all eagerly anticipate the goal and let us take flight from him, so that at last he may be exposed for what he is by nature, as we fly off to those things which are ours.'[5]

51[6](1). Throughout the night Andrew spoke these things to the brethren and prayed, and all rejoiced together and were confirmed in the Lord. Early in the morning, Aegeates summoned Andrew from prison and said to him, 'The time to complete my judgement against you has arrived, you stranger, alien to this present life, enemy of my home, and corrupter of my entire house. Why did you decide to burst into places alien to you and corrupt a wife who used to please me in every way and never slept with another man? She has convinced me that she now rejoices in you and your God. So enjoy my gifts!'

He commanded that Andrew be scourged with seven whips. Then he sent him off to be crucified and commanded the executioners not to impale him with nails but to stretch him out tied up with ropes, ⟨and⟩ to leave his knees uncut, supposing that by so doing he would punish Andrew even more cruelly.

This matter became known to everyone, for it was rumoured throughout Patras that the stranger, the righteous one, the man who possessed God, was being crucified by the impious Aegeates, even though he had done nothing improper. All alike were outraged.

52(2). As the executioners led him to the place intending to carry out their orders, Stratocles, who had learned what was happening, arrived running and saw the executioners violently dragging off the blessed one like a criminal. Stratocles did not spare any of them but gave each a beating, ripped their clothing from top to bottom, tore Andrew away, and told them, 'Thank the blessed one for educating me and teaching me to check my violent temper. Otherwise, I would have demonstrated for you what Stratocles and Aegeates the rogue are capable of. For we (believers) have learned to endure our afflictions.' He grabbed the apostle's hand and went away with him to the seaside location where he was to be crucified.

53(3). The soldiers left and presented themselves to Aegeates explaining what had happened. 'Change your clothes', the proconsul answered, 'and go back there to perform your duties. When you rid yourselves of the convict's friends, then obey your orders. Avoid as best you can letting Stratocles see you, and do not argue if he should require from you anything at all. For I know the nobility of his soul, such that if provoked he probably would not even spare me.' They did exactly as Aegeates told them.

Stratocles walked with the apostle to the designated spot, but he was perturbed, furious with Aegeates, now and then railing against him under his breath.

'Stratocles my child,' Andrew responded, 'from now on I want you to keep your mind unwavering, and do not wait for advice from someone else, but take such advice from yourself—that you not be inwardly oriented toward seeming

---

[5] End of Vat. 808.
[6] The alternative numbering indicates the chapters of the martyrdom proper.

hardships nor attached to mere appearances—for it is fitting for a servant of Jesus to be worthy of Jesus. I will tell you and the brethren walking with me something else about people alien to us. As long as the demonic nature lacks its bloody food and cannot suck up its nutrition because animals are not slain, it weakens and recedes to nothingness, becoming entirely dead. But if it has what it longs for, it strengthens, expands, and rises up, growing by means of those foods it enjoys. This situation, child, obtains to those outside who die when we do not attach ourselves to what they are attached to. But even that self within ourselves which is contrary (to our true nature), when it dares to do something and cannot find anyone to consent with it, is beaten and totally crushed to the earth, dead, because it did not complete what it undertook. Let us keep this image always before our eyes, children, so that we not grow drowsy and the opponent intrude and slaughter us.[7] This is the end of my speech, for I think that while we were speaking we arrived at the appointed place. The cross planted there is a sign to me that this is the place.'

54(4). He left everyone, approached the cross, and spoke to it in a loud voice: 'Greetings, O cross! Greetings indeed! I know well that, though you have been weary for a long time, planted and awaiting me, now at last you can rest. I come to you, whom I have known. I recognize your mystery, why you were planted. So then, cross that is pure, radiant, full of life and light, receive me, I who have been weary for so long.'

The blessed one said these things standing on the ground looking intently at the cross. When he came to it, he commanded the brethren to summon the executioners, who were standing far away, to carry out their orders. When they came, they tied up only his feet and armpits, without nailing up his hands or feet nor severing his knees because of what the proconsul had commanded them, for Aegeates intended to torment him by being hung and being eaten by dogs if he were still alive at night.

55(5). The brethren stood around, so many they were nearly innumerable. When they saw that the executioners had withdrawn and had carried out against the blessed one none of the usual procedures suffered by those who are hung, they expected to hear something more from him, for even while hanging he moved his head and smiled.

'Why do you smile, Andrew, servant of God?', asked Stratocles. 'Should your laughter not make us mourn and weep because we are being deprived of you?'

'Shall I not laugh, Stratocles my child,' Andrew answered, 'at Aegeates' futile trap by which he intends to avenge himself on us? He has not yet been persuaded that we are alien to him and his designs. He is not able to hear, since if he were able, he would have heard that the person who belongs to Jesus and who has been recognized by him in the end cannot be punished.'

---

[7] The Armenian adds a long allegory about an eagle.

56(6). When Andrew had said these things, he addressed a general speech to everyone, for even the pagans had hurried to the site, infuriated at Aegeates' unjust decision. 'Men who are present with me, women, children, old, slaves, free, and any others who would hear: if you suppose this act of dying is the end of ephemeral life, leave this place at once. If you understand the conjunction of the soul with a body to be the soul itself, so that after the separation (of the two) nothing at all exists, you possess the intelligence of animals and one would have to list you among ferocious beasts. And if you love immediate pleasures and pursue them above all, in order to enjoy their fruits exclusively, you are like thieves. And if you suppose that you are merely that which can be seen and nothing more, you are slaves of folly and ignorance. And if you perceive that only this nocturnal light exists and nothing in addition to it, you are kindred to this night. And if you think that your earthly food is capable of creating bodily mass and the blood's constitutive power, you yourselves are earthly. And if you suppose that you are happy even though you have an inequitable body, you actually are miserable. And if your external prosperity makes you happy, you truly are most wretched. And if the pleasure and intercourse of marriage please you, and if the corruption which is from them, full of pain, makes you sad, and if you are in need of sustenance for your many children, and if the irritating poverty they cause is known to you, it will upset you. And if the rest of your possessions draw you to themselves as though you belonged to them, may their impermanence reproach you. (57[6].) What benefit is there for you who gain for yourselves external goods but do not gain your very selves? What pride issues from external ancestry if the soul in you is held captive, sold to desires? And why do we desire pleasure and childbearing, for later we have to separate? No one knows what he does. Who will take care of his wife when he is preoccupied merely by the passions of desire? Or why all the rest of the concern for externals, while you yourselves neglect what you actually are? I exhort you all rather to rid yourselves of this life which is painful, vain, senseless, boastful, empty, perishable, transitory, the friend of pleasures, the slave of time, the servant of drunkenness, the neighbour of debauchery, the possession of greed, the kindred of wrath, the umpire of treachery, the ally of murders, the prince of hatred, the patron of desire, the master of adulteries, the mediator of jealousies, the instigator of murders. I entreat you who have come here together for my sake, abandon this entire life and hasten to overtake my soul which speeds toward things beyond time, beyond law, beyond speech, beyond body, beyond bitter and lawless pleasures full of every pain. Observe now, even you, with the eyes of your souls, those things about which I speak. Follow my deep-seated love. Learn of my sufferings about which I am now speaking with you. Take my mind as a deposit. Participate in another fellowship for yourselves. Submit yourselves to my lashes, and cleanse your ears to hear what I say. Flee from everything merely temporal. Even now speed away with me. (58[6].) Even now I know that you are not inattentive to my words. Truly I see you mild as I want it, and to be far away from external forms, for the internal is our unity. I greet you with the grace of God and with love which is due him and even more with your consent to each other, to keep us away from those who do harm, and to apply to him, and to the good, and to the innocence which is to him and to the accord which is in them. For this reason men quietly take courage in the knowledge of our God. On the one hand, I am leaving to prepare routes there for those who align themselves with me and are equipped with a pure faith and with love for him; I am stifling the fire, banishing the shadows, extinguishing the furnace, killing the worm, eradicating the threat, gagging the demons, muzzling and destroying the ruling powers, dominating the authorities, throwing down the devil, casting out Satan, and punishing wickedness. On the other hand, with respect to those who have come here not out of love for God but out of hypocrisy and because of unfruitful pleasures, who have submitted themselves to superstition, disbelief, and every other ignorance, and who suppose nothing else exists after one's release from here, all these monsters fly out, become agitated, rush forth, take wing, ravage, fight, conquer, rule, wreak vengeance, enflame, rage, afflict, punish, and attack. They blaze, enact violence, and do not withdraw or relent, but rejoice, exult, smile, mock, and take their rest and delight in all who are similar to them, possessing those who succumbed to them by not believing in my God. Choose then which of the two paths you prefer, for the choice is yours to decide.'

59(6). When the crowds heard Andrew's speech, they were won over by him, so to say, and did not leave the spot. The blessed one proceeded to speak to them even longer than he had before, to such an extent that those who heard him took it as a sign. He spoke to them for three days and nights, and no one, no matter how weary, separated from him.

On the fourth day, when they observed his nobility, the adamance of his thought, the sheer abundance of his words, the value of his exhortation, the stability of his soul, the prudence of his spirit, the firmness of his mind, and the precision of his reasoning, they were furious with Aegeates and together ran off to the tribunal. As he sat there they cried out, 'What is this judgement of yours, O proconsul? You have judged wickedly! You have made an unjust decision! Your courts are a sacrilege! What crime did the man commit? What evil has he done? The city is in uproar! You are wronging us all! You are grieving us all! Do not betray the city of the emperor! Grant the Achaeans the just man! Grant us this God-fearing man! Do not kill this man possessed of God! Do not destroy this pious man! Even though he has been hanging for four days, he is still alive. Although he has eaten nothing, he has nourished us with his words. Bring the man down and we will all become philosophers! Untie the prudent one, and all Patras will be law-abiding! Release the wise man, and all Achaea will receive mercy!'

60(7). When Aegeates at first disregarded the crowd and gestured for them to leave the tribunal, they were enraged and were gaining courage to oppose him in some way; they numbered about two thousand. When the proconsul saw that they were in some way incensed he was terrified that he might suffer a revolution. He rose from the tribunal and went off with them, promising to release the blessed Andrew.

Some ran ahead to disclose to the apostle this very fact as well as the reason for Aegeates' coming to the place. The crowd was jubilant because the blessed Andrew was about to be untied, and when the proconsul arrived, all the brethren were rejoicing, among them Maximilla.

61(8). When Andrew heard this, he said, 'O the great lethargy of those I have taught! O the sudden fog engulfing us even after many mysteries! O, how much we have spoken up to the present, and we have not convinced our own! O, how much has happened so that we might flee the earthly! O, what strong statements have been spoken against carnal things, and yet they want more of the same! O, how many times I have prayed that I might lift them from these filthy habits, but instead they were encouraged to nothingness! Why this excessive fondness for the flesh? Why this great complicity with it? Do you again encourage me to be put back among things in flux? If you understood that I have been loosened from ropes but tied up to myself, you yourselves would have been eager to be loosened from the many and to be tied to the one. What should I say? I know well that what I am saying will happen, for you yourselves will I tie up with me, and after liberating myself, I will release myself from all things and become united with the one who came into being for all and who exists beyond all. (62[8].) But now that Aegeates is coming to me, I will keep quiet and embrace my children. Whatever I must resolve by speaking to him, these I will speak. Aegeates, why have you come to us again? Why should you who are foreign to us come to us? What do you want to attempt now? What do you want to contrive? Whom do you wish to summon? Say something! Have you come to untie us because you changed your mind? Even if you really did change your mind, Aegeates, I would never accede to you. Were you to promise all your possessions, I would stand aloof from them. Were you to say you yourself were mine, I would not trust you. Would you untie the one who is tied up, proconsul? Would you untie the one who has fled? Would you untie the one who was liberated? Would you untie the one recognized by his kindred, the one who received mercy, the one loved by him, the one alien to you, the stranger who appeared so only to you? I possess the one with whom I will always be. I possess the one with whom I will be a compatriot for countless ages. It is to him that I go. It is to him that I speed on, to the one who made me recognize even you by saying to me: "Mark Aegeates and his gifts. Do not let that rogue frighten you, and let him not suppose that he can seize you, for you are mine. He is your enemy. He is a corrupter, a cheat, a destroyer, a slanderer, merciless, a maniac, a plotter, a murderer, an insolent egotist, a flatterer, a magician, terrible, petulant, insensitive, and decorated on all sides by his material veneer." Inasmuch as I recognized you through your turning to me, I am released from you. Proconsul, I know well that you bewail and mourn because of what I am saying to you as I flee to the one beyond you. You will weep, beat your breast, gnash your teeth, grieve, despair, lament, anguish, and behave like your relative the sea, which you now see furiously troubled by waves because I am leaving all of you. The grace which came because of me is delightful, holy, just, true, charming, and articulate, along with all the things by which you seemed to have been adorned through me.'

When the proconsul heard these things he stood there speechless and as if stunned. Andrew looked at him again and said, 'Aegeates, enemy of us all, now you stand there watching. You stand there quiet and calm, unable to do anything you dare. My kindred and I speed on to things our own, leaving you to be what you are and what you fail to understand about yourself.'

63(9). And when Aegeates again attempted to approach the wood to untie Andrew, the entire city was in an uproar at him. The apostle Andrew shouted: 'O Master, do not permit Andrew, the one tied to your wood, to be untied again. O Jesus, do not give me to the shameless devil, I who am attached to your mystery. O Father, do not let your opponent untie me, I who am hanging upon your grace. May he who is little no longer humiliate the one who has known your greatness. But you yourself, O Christ, you whom I desired, whom I loved, whom I know, whom I possess, whom I cherish, whose I am, receive me, so that by my departure to you there may be a reunion of my many kindred, those who rest in your majesty.' When he had said these things and further glorified the Lord, he handed over his spirit, so that we wept and everyone grieved his departure.

64(10). After the departure of the blessed apostle, Maximilla, accompanied by Stratocles, completely disregarding those standing around her, came forward, untied the corpse of the blessed one, and having provided it with the necessary attention, buried it at nightfall.

She separated from Aegeates because of his savage soul and lawless public life. Thereafter, though he simulated good behaviour, she had nothing whatever to do with him. Choosing instead a life holy and quiet, provided for by the love of Christ, she spent her time happily with the brethren. Even though Aegeates often importuned her and offered her the opportunity to control his affairs, he was not able to persuade her. One night, undetected by anyone in his household, he threw himself from a great height and died.

Stratocles, Aegeates' brother according to the flesh, did not want so much as to touch the property Aegeates left—the wretch died childless. He said, 'May your possessions go with you, Aegeates! May Jesus be my friend and I his! Casting from me the entire lot of external and internal evils and entrusting to that one everything I own, I thrust aside everything averse to him.'

B. Papyrus Texts

65(11). Here let me make an end of the blessed tales, acts, and mysteries difficult—or should I say impossible—to express. Let this stroke of the pen end it. I will pray first for myself, that I heard what was actually said, both the obvious and also the obscure, comprehensible only to the intellect. Then I will pray for all who are convinced by what was said, that they may have fellowship with each other, as God opens the ears of the listeners, in order to make comprehensible all his gifts in Christ Jesus our Lord, to whom, together with the Father, be glory, honour, and power with the all-holy and good and life-giving Spirit, now and always, forever and ever, amen.

B. PAPYRUS TEXTS

(i) P. Utrecht 1[1]

p. 9   the apostle. But when Andrew
the apostle of Christ heard
that they had arrested those from the city on his account,
he arose and went out into the middle
of the street and said to the brethren
that there was no reason for dissimulating anything.
And while the apostle was speaking these
words, a young man was there,
one of the four soldiers, in
whose body was hidden a demon. When
that young man had come into
the presence of the apostle, the demon.
cried out, saying, 'O Varianus,
what have I done to you that you should send me
to this god-fearing man?'
When the young man had said this,
the demon cast him down, and made
him foam [at the mouth]. His fellow-soldiers,
however, seized him and persisted
in [holding him up]. But Andrew
pitied the young man and said
to his fellow-soldiers: 'Are you
ashamed, because you see your nature
exposing you? Why
do you take away the prize money so that
he does not appeal to his king, to receive
help so as to be able to fight

---

[1] Pages 1–8 are no longer extant.

against the demon who is hidden in his
limbs? Not only is he appealing
for this, but he is speaking in
the language of the palace, so that his
king will soon hear him. For I
hear him say: [O
Varianus, what [have I done to you
that you should [send me to this god-
fearing [man . . . An-
drew [

p. 10 against me. For this act which I have done,
I have not done it by myself, but
I have been compelled to do it. I will tell you, then,
the whole meaning of this matter. This
young man who is tormented in his body,
has a sister, a virgin,
who is a great ascetic
and athlete. Truly, I say,
she is near to God because of
her purity and her prayers and
her love. Now, to relate it
briefly, there was
somebody near her house, who was a great
magician. It happened
one day thus: one evening
the virgin went up on
her roof to pray, the young
magician saw her praying,
Semmath entered into him to
fight against this great athlete.
The young magician said within
himself: 'I have spent twenty years
under the instruction of my master until I was taught
this skill, behold! now
this is the beginning of my career; if I do not
prevail upon this virgin, I shall not
be able to do any work.'
And the young magician conjured up some
great powers upon the virgin
and sent them after her. And when
the demons went to tempt
her or to persuade her,
they acted like her brother and knocked

at the door. She arose and went down
to open the door, thinking that
it was her brother. But first she prayed
much, so that the demons became like
[flames of fire? *or* as the ... and fell]?
] and fled away
] little.

p. 13 The virgin wept
with Eirusia. Eirusia, however,
said to the virgin: 'Why
do you weep? Do you not know that those
who come here ... to weep [
for this is the place ... now
these powers come after you,
in order to tempt you (? *or*: in order to take you?) ... you weep,
while the sorrow [
Now however, if you weep over your brother
because a God (?) ... with
him,
to-morrow I shall send him to the
apostle Andrew, that he may
heal him. Not only so that I shall
heal him, but I shall make him enter into the (military) service
of the palace.'
When the demon had said this, the apostle said
to him: 'How did you acquire knowledge
concerning the hidden mysteries of
the height? A soldier, when
cast out of the palace, is not at all
allowed to learn the
mysteries of the palace; and how
will he learn the hidden mysteries
of the height?' The demon
said to him, 'I descended
into this night ... this
young man, while a power out of
the height entered into [
] virgin
in him out ... goes, while she
will go away ... this
her friend ... said
] sorrow (?)
befalls me [

the great power came out
of the height in this night [

p. 14 (The apostle is speaking)
'why then should you not tremble, since you speak (of)
the mysteries of the height.
I tremble completely in all my limbs
and I glorify the Receiver
who will come for the souls
of the saints. O athletes
of virtue, not in vain
have you fought. Behold! the judge of the contest
prepares for you the crown
imperishable. O fighters,
not in vain have you acquired
weapons and
shields, and not in vain have you
endured wars:
the king has prepared for you the
palace. O virgins,
not in vain have you guarded the
purity and not in vain have you
persevered in prayers,
your lamps burning at
midnight, until this
voice reached you: 'Arise,
go out to meet the
bridegroom.'[2] When the apostle
had said this, he turned
to the demon and said [to him],
'Now indeed it is time for you to come
out from this young man,
so that he may enter on (military) service at the
heavenly palace.' The demon said
to the apostle,
'Truly, O man of God,
I have never destroyed a limb of his
because of the holy hands
of his sister. Now, however,
I shall go out from this
young man, for I have done no harm
at all to his limbs.'

[2] Cf. Matt. 25: 6.

And when the demon had said this
he went out of [the young man].
When he had [gone out from]
the young [man]
[he put off his uniform]
p. 15   of soldiery and [cast it]
before the feet of the apostle,
saying, 'O man
of God, I have spent
twenty coins to
acquire this
ephemeral garment; but now
I desire to spend all that I have
to acquire the uniform
of your God.' His
fellow-soldiers said to him,
'Poor youth, if you
deny the garment of the king,
you will be punished.' Said
the young man to them, 'Indeed
I am a miserable fellow because of my
earlier sins; would that
my punishment were only because of this
that I denied the garment of the
king and not that I am punished
because I have despised the garment
of the immortal King of the Ages.
O ignorant ones, do you not see
what kind of man this is?
For he has no sword in his hand nor
any weapon of war and (yet)
these great miracles are performed
by him.'
                              The Act of Andrew

(ii) Bodleian Fragment

I^r   ... man ... to behold me in the member which is ...
Then said Jesus to
Andrew, 'Come near to
me, Andrew; your name
is the fire; blessed are you
among men.'

Andrew answered
and said unto the Saviour
'Allow me to speak.'
Then said he to him,
'Speak, Andrew, you
firmly established pillar.'
Andrew answered and said,
'As God lives
Who is your Father,
I^v I came out from
the house of my father and
my mother; and as
my soul lives, I have not
again gone
into it, and
I have not beheld the faces of my father
and my mother, neither have
I beheld the faces of my children
and my wife, but
I bore my cross
every day, following you
from morning till night
and I have not laid it down.'
Jesus answered and
said, 'I know this Andrew? ...'
II^v ... a lesser than one of
us who bear your name.
Two coats I have not desired
for myself; even this
coat which is upon me ...'

C. GREGORY OF TOURS' EPITOME

The famous triumphs of the apostles are, I believe, not unknown to any of the faithful, for some of them are taught us in the pages of the gospel, others are related in the Acts of the Apostles, and about some of them books exist in which the actions of each apostle are recorded; yet of the more part we have nothing but their Passions in writing.

Now I have come upon a book on the miracles (virtues, great deeds) of St Andrew the apostle, which, because of its excessive verbosity, was called by some apocryphal. And of this I thought good to extract and set out the 'virtues' only, omitting all that bred weariness, and so include the wonderful miracles within the compass of one small volume, which might both please the reader and ward off the spite of the adverse critic: for it is not the multitude of words but the soundness of reason and the purity of mind that produce unblemished faith.

1. After the Ascension the apostles dispersed to preach in various countries. Andrew began in the province of Achaea, but Matthew went to the city of Mermidona.[1]

2. Andrew left Mermidona and came back to his own allotted district. Walking with his disciples he met a blind man who said, 'Andrew, apostle of Christ, I know you can restore my sight', but I do not wish for that: only bid those with you to give me enough money to clothe and feed myself decently.' Andrew said, 'This is the devil's voice, who will not allow the man to recover his sight.' He touched his eyes and healed him. Then, as he had but a vile rough garment, Andrew said, 'Take the filthy garment off him and clothe him afresh.' All were ready to strip themselves, and Andrew said, 'Let him have what will suffice him.' He returned home thankful.

3. Demetrius of Amasea had an Egyptian boy of whom he was very fond, who died of a fever. Demetrius hearing of Andrew's miracles, came, fell at his feet, and besought help. Andrew pitied him, came to the house, held a very long discourse, turned to the bier, raised the boy, and restored him to his master. All believed and were baptized.

4. A Christian lad named Sostratus came to Andrew privately and told him, 'My mother cherishes a guilty passion for me: I have repulsed her, and she has gone to the proconsul to throw the guilt on me. I would rather die than expose her.' The officers came to fetch the boy, and Andrew prayed and went with him. The mother accused him. The proconsul bade him defend himself. He was silent, and so continued, until the proconsul retired to take counsel. The mother began to weep. Andrew said, 'Unhappy woman, you do not fear to cast your own guilt on your son.' She said to the proconsul, 'Ever since my son entertained his wicked wish he has been in constant company with this man.' The proconsul was enraged, ordered the lad to be sewn into the leather bag for parricides and drowned in the river, and Andrew to be imprisoned till his punishment should be devised. Andrew prayed, there was an earthquake, the proconsul fell from his seat, every one was prostrated, and the mother withered up and died. The proconsul fell at Andrew's feet praying for mercy. The earthquake and thunder ceased, and he healed those who had been hurt. The proconsul and his house were baptized.

5. The son of Gratinus of Sinope bathed in the women's bath and was seized by a demon. Gratinus wrote to Andrew for help: he himself had a fever and his wife dropsy. Andrew went there in a vehicle. The boy tormented by the evil spirit fell at his feet. He bade it depart and so it did, with outcries. He then went to Gratinus' bed and told him he well deserved to suffer because of

---

[1] The rest of 1 gives a short abstract of the Acts of Andrew and Matthew.

his loose life, and bade him rise and sin no more. He was healed. The wife was rebuked for her infidelity. 'If she is to return to her former sin, let her not now be healed: if she can keep from it, let her be healed.' The water came out of her body and she was cured. The apostle broke bread and gave it her. She thanked God, believed with all her house, and relapsed no more into sin. Gratinus afterwards sent Andrew great gifts by his servants, and then, with his wife, asked him in person to accept them, but he refused saying, 'It is rather for you to give them to the needy.'

6. After this he went to Nicaea where were seven devils living among the tombs by the wayside, who at noon stoned passers-by and had killed many. And all the city came out to meet Andrew with olive branches, crying, 'Our salvation is in you, O man of God.' When they had told him all, he said, 'If you believe in Christ you shall be freed.' They cried, 'We will.' He thanked God and commanded the demons to appear; they came in the form of dogs. Said he, 'These are your enemies: if you profess your belief that I can drive them out in Jesus' name, I will do so.' They cried out, 'We believe that Jesus Christ whom you preach is the Son of God.' Then he bade the demons go into dry and barren places and hurt no man till the last day. They roared and vanished. The apostle baptized the people and made Callistus bishop.

7. At the gate of Nicomedia he met a dead man borne on a bier, and his old father supported by slaves, hardly able to walk, and his old mother with hair torn, bewailing. 'How has it happened?', he asked. 'He was alone in his chamber and seven dogs rushed on him and killed him.' Andrew sighed and said, 'This is an ambush of the demons I banished from Nicaea. What will you do, father, if I restore your son?' 'I have nothing more precious than him, I will give him.' He prayed, 'Let the spirit of this lad return.' The faithful responded, 'Amen'. Andrew bade the lad rise, and he rose, and all cried, 'Great is the God of Andrew.' The parents offered great gifts which he refused, but took the lad to Macedonia, instructing him.

8. Embarking in a ship he sailed into the Hellespont, on the way to Byzantium. There was a great storm. Andrew prayed and there was calm. They reached Byzantium.

9. Thence proceeding through Thrace they met a troop of armed men who made as if to fall on them. Andrew made the sign of the cross against them, and prayed that they might be made powerless. A bright angel touched their swords and they all fell down, and Andrew and his company passed by while they worshipped him. And the angel departed in a great light.

10. At Perinthus he found a ship going to Macedonia, and an angel told him to go on board. As he preached the captain and the rest heard and were converted, and Andrew glorified God for making himself known on the sea.

11. At Philippi were two brothers, one of whom had two sons, the other two daughters. They were rich and noble, and said, 'There is no family as good as ours in the place: let us marry our sons to our daughters.' It was

agreed and the earnest paid by the father of the sons. On the wedding-day a word from God came to them, 'Wait till my servant Andrew comes: he will tell you what you should do.' All preparations had been made, and guests bidden, but they waited. On the third day Andrew came: they went out to meet him with wreaths and told him how they had been charged to wait for him, and how things stood. His face was shining so that they marvelled at him. He said, 'Do not, my children, be deceived: rather repent, for you have sinned in thinking to join together those who are near of kin. We do not forbid or shun marriage.[2] It is a divine institution: but we condemn incestuous unions.' The parents were troubled and prayed for pardon. The young people saw Andrew's face like that of an angel, and said, 'We are sure that your teaching is true.' The apostle blessed them and departed.

12. At Thessalonica was a rich noble youth, Exuos, who came without his parents' knowledge and asked to be shown the way of truth. He was taught, and believed, and followed Andrew, taking no care of his worldly estate. The parents heard that he was at Philippi and tried to bribe him with gifts to leave Andrew. He said, 'Would that you had not these riches, then you would know the true God, and escape his wrath.' Andrew, too, came down from the third storey and preached to them, but in vain: he retired and shut the doors of the house. They gathered a band and came to burn the house, saying, 'Death to the son who has forsaken his parents', and brought torches, reeds, and faggots, and set the house on fire. It blazed up. Exuos took a bottle of water and prayed, 'Lord Jesus Christ, in whose hand is the nature of all the elements, who moisten the dry and dry the moist, cool the hot and kindle the quenched, put out this fire that your servants may not grow evil, but be more enkindled unto faith.' He sprinkled the flames and they died. 'He is become a sorcerer', said the parents, and got ladders, to climb up and kill them, but God blinded them. They remained obstinate, but one Lysimachus, a citizen, said, 'Why persevere? God is fighting for these. Desist, lest heavenly fire consume you.' They were touched, and said, 'This is the true God.' It was now night, but a light shone out, and they received sight. They went up and fell before Andrew and asked pardon, and their repentance made Lysimachus say, 'Truly Christ whom Andrew preaches is the Son of God.' All were converted except the youth's parents, who cursed him and went home again, leaving all their money to public uses. Fifty days after they suddenly died, and the citizens, who loved the youth, returned the property to him. He did not leave Andrew, but spent his income on the poor.

13. The youth asked Andrew to go with him to Thessalonica. All assembled in the theatre, glad to see their favourite. The youth preached to them, Andrew remaining silent, and all wondered at his wisdom. The people

---

[2] This cannot be the author's original sentiment: it is contradicted by all that we know of the Acts.

cried out, 'Save the son of Carpianus who is ill, and we will believe.' Carpianus went to his house and said to the boy, 'You shall be cured to-day, Adimantus.' He said, 'Then my dream is come true: I saw this man in a vision healing me.' He rose up, dressed, and ran to the theatre, outstripping his father, and fell at Andrew's feet. The people seeing him walk after twenty-three years, cried, 'There is none like the God of Andrew.'

14. A citizen had a son possessed by an unclean spirit and asked for his cure. The demon, foreseeing that he would be cast out, took the son aside into a chamber and made him hang himself. The father said, 'Bring him to the theatre: I believe this stranger is able to raise him.' He said the same to Andrew. Andrew said to the people, 'What will it profit you if you see this accomplished and do not believe?' They said, 'Fear not, we will believe.' The lad was raised and they said, 'It is enough, we do believe.' And they escorted Andrew to the house with torches and lamps, for it was night, and he taught them for three days.

15. Medias of Philippi came and prayed for his sick son. Andrew wiped his cheeks and stroked his head, saying, 'Be comforted, only believe', and went with him to Philippi. As they entered the city an old man met them and entreated for his sons whom, for an unspeakable crime, Medias had imprisoned, and they were putrefied with sores. Andrew said, 'How can you ask help for your son when you keep these men bound? Loose their chains first, for your unkindness obstructs my prayers.' Medias, penitent, said, 'I will loose these two and seven others of whom you have not been told.' They were brought, tended for three days, cured, and freed. Then the apostle healed the son, Philomedes, who had been ill twenty-two years. The people cried, 'Heal our sick as well.' Andrew told Philomedes to visit them in their houses and bid them rise in the name of Jesus Christ, by which he had himself been healed. This was done, and all believed and offered gifts, which Andrew did not accept.

16. A citizen, Nicolaus, offered a gilt chariot and four white mules and four white horses as his most precious possession for the cure of his daughter. Andrew smiled. 'I accept your gifts, but not these visible ones: if you offer this for your daughter, what will you for your soul? That is what I desire of you, that the inner man may recognize the true God, reject earthly things and desire eternal . . .' He persuaded all to forsake their idols, and healed the girl. His fame went through all Macedonia.

17. Next day as he taught, a youth cried out, 'What have you to do with us? Have you come to turn us out of our own place?' Andrew summoned him: 'What is your work?' 'I have dwelt in this boy from his youth and thought never to leave him: but three days since I heard his father say, "I shall go to Andrew"; and now I fear the torments you bring us and I shall depart.' The spirit left the boy. And many came and asked, 'In whose name do you cure our sick?'

Philosophers also came and disputed with him, and no one could resist his teaching.

18. At this time, one who opposed him went to the proconsul Virinus and said, 'A man is arisen in Thessalonica who says the temples should be destroyed and ceremonies done away, and all the ancient law abolished, and one God worshipped, whose servant he says he is.' The proconsul sent soldiers and knights to fetch Andrew. They found his dwelling; when they entered, his face so shone that they fell down in fear. Andrew told those present the proconsul's purpose. The people armed themselves against the soldiers, but Andrew stopped them. The proconsul arrived; not finding Andrew in the appointed place, he raged like a lion and sent twenty more men. They, on arrival, were confounded and said nothing. The proconsul sent a large troop to bring him by force. Andrew said, 'Have you come for me?' 'Yes, if you are the sorcerer who says the gods ought not to be worshipped.' 'I am no sorcerer, but the apostle of Jesus Christ whom I preach.' At this, one of the soldiers drew his sword and cried, 'What have I to do with you, Virinus, that you send me to one who can not only cast me out of this vessel, but burn me by his power? Would that you would come yourself! You would do him no harm.' And the devil went out of the soldier and he fell dead. On this the proconsul came and stood before Andrew but could not see him. 'I am he whom you seek.' His eyes were opened, and he said in anger: 'What is this madness, that you despise us and our officers? You are certainly a sorcerer. Now will I throw you to the beasts for contempt of our gods and us, and we shall see if the crucified whom you preach will help you.' Andrew: 'You must believe, proconsul, in the true God and his Son whom he has sent, specially now that one of your men is dead.' And after long prayer he touched the soldier: 'Rise up: my God Jesus Christ raises you.' He arose and stood whole. The people cried, 'Glory be to our God.' The proconsul, 'Believe not, O people, believe not the sorcerer.' They said, 'This is no sorcery but sound and true teaching.' The proconsul: 'I shall throw this man to the beasts and write about you to Caesar, that you may perish for contemning his laws.' They would have stoned him, and said, 'Write to Caesar that the Macedonians have received the word of God, and forsaking their idols, worship the true God.'

Then the proconsul in wrath retired to the praetorium, and in the morning brought beasts to the stadium and had the apostle dragged thither by the hair and beaten with clubs. First they sent in a fierce boar who went about him thrice and did not touch him. The people praised God. A bull led by thirty soldiers and incited by two hunters, did not touch Andrew but tore the hunters to pieces, roared, and fell dead. 'Christ is the true God,' said the people. An angel was seen to descend and strengthen the apostle. The proconsul in rage sent in a fierce leopard, which left everyone alone but seized and strangled the proconsul's son; but Virinus was so angry that he said nothing of it nor cared. Andrew said to the people, 'Recognize now that this is the true God, whose power subdues the beasts, though Virinus knows him not. But that you may believe the more, I will raise the dead son, and confound the foolish father.' After long prayer he raised him. The people would have slain Virinus, but Andrew restrained them, and Virinus went to the praetorium, confounded.

19. After this a youth who followed the apostle sent for his mother to meet Andrew. She came, and after being instructed, begged him to come to their house, which was devastated by a great serpent. As Andrew approached, it hissed loudly and with raised head came to meet him; it was fifty cubits long: everyone fell down in fear. Andrew said, 'Hide your head, foul one, which you raised in the beginning for the hurt of mankind, and obey the servants of God, and die.' The serpent roared, and coiled about a great oak near by and vomited poison and blood and died.

Andrew went to the woman's farm, where a child killed by the serpent lay dead. He said to the parents, 'Our God who would have you saved has sent me here that you may believe on him. Go and see the slayer slain.' They said, 'We care not so much for the child's death, if we be avenged.' They went, and Andrew said to the proconsul's wife [her conversion has been omitted by Gregory], 'Go and raise the boy.' She went, nothing doubting, and said, 'In the name of my God Jesus Christ, rise up whole.' The parents returned and found their child alive, and fell at Andrew's feet.

20. On the next night he saw a vision which he related. 'Hearken, beloved, to my vision. I beheld, and lo, a great mountain raised up on high, which had on it nothing earthly, but only shone with such light, that it seemed to enlighten all the world. And lo, there stood by me my beloved brethren the apostles Peter and John; and John reached his hand to Peter and raised him to the top of the mount, and turned to me and asked me to go up after Peter, saying, "Andrew, you are to drink Peter's cup." And he stretched out his hands and said, "Draw near to me and stretch out your hands so as to join them unto mine, and put your head by my head." When I did so I found myself shorter than John. After that he said to me: "Would you know the image of that which you see, and who it is that speaks to you?", and I said, "I desire to know it." And he said to me, "I am the word of the cross whereon you shall hang shortly, for his name's sake whom you preach." And many other things he said to me, of which I must now say nothing, but they shall be declared when I come unto the sacrifice. But now let all assemble that have received the word of God, and let me commend them to the Lord Jesus Christ, that he may vouchsafe to keep them unblemished in his teaching. For I am now being loosed from the body, and go to that promise which he has vouchsafed to promise me, who is the Lord of heaven and earth, the Son of God Almighty, very God with the Holy Ghost, continuing for everlasting ages?'[3]

[3] John in the latter part of this vision has been substituted by Gregory for Jesus. The echoes of the Acts of John and of Peter are very evident here.

C. Gregory of Tours' Epitome

All the brethren wept and smote their faces. When all were gathered, Andrew said, 'Know, beloved, that I am about to leave you, but I trust in Jesus whose word I preach, that he will keep you from evil, that this harvest which I have sown among you may not be plucked up by the enemy, that is, the knowledge and teaching of my Lord Jesus Christ. But pray always and stand firm in the faith, that the Lord may root out all tares of offence and vouchsafe to gather you into his heavenly garner as pure wheat.' So for five days he taught and confirmed them: then he spread his hands and prayed, 'Keep, I beseech you, O Lord, this flock which has now known your salvation, that the wicked one may not prevail against it, but that what by your command and my means it has received, it may be able to preserve inviolate for ever.' And all responded, 'Amen.' He took bread, broke it with thanksgiving, gave it to all, saying, 'Receive the grace which Christ our Lord God gives you by me his servant.' He kissed everyone and commended them to the Lord, and departed to Thessalonica, and after teaching there two days, he left them.

21. Many faithful from Macedonia accompanied him in two ships. And all were desirous of being on Andrew's ship, to hear him. He said, 'I know your wish, but this ship is too small. Let the servants and baggage go in the larger ship, and you with me in this.' He gave them Anthimus to comfort them, and bade them go into another ship which he ordered to keep always near ... that they might see him and hear the word of God. And as he slept a little, one fell overboard. Anthimus roused him, saying, 'Help us, good master; one of your servants perishes.' He rebuked the wind, there was a calm, and the man was borne by the waves to the ship. Anthimus helped him on board and all marvelled. On the twelfth day they reached Patras in Achaea, disembarked, and went to an inn.

22. Many asked him to lodge with them, but he said he could only go where God bade him. That night he had no revelation, and the next night, being distressed at this, he heard a voice saying, 'Andrew, I am always with you and forsake you not,' and was glad.

Lesbius the proconsul was told in a vision to take him in, and sent a messenger for him. He came, and entering the proconsul's chamber found him lying as dead with closed eyes; he struck him on the side and said, 'Rise and tell us what has happened to you.' Lesbius said, 'I abominated the way which you teach, and sent soldiers in ships to the proconsul of Macedonia to send you bound to me, but they were wrecked and could not reach their destination. As I continued in my purpose of destroying your Way, two Ethiopes appeared and scourged me, saying, "We can no longer prevail here, for the man is coming whom you mean to persecute. So to-night, while we still have the power, we will avenge ourselves on you." And they beat me sorely and left me. But now do you pray that I may be pardoned and healed.' Andrew preached the word and all believed, and the proconsul was healed and confirmed in the faith.

23. Now Trophima, once the proconsul's mistress, and now married to

another, left her husband and joined Andrew. Her husband came to Lesbius' wife and said she was renewing her liaison wth the proconsul. The wife, enraged, said, 'This is why my husband has left me these six months.' She called her procurator and had Trophima sentenced as a prostitute and sent to the brothel. Lesbius knew nothing, and was deceived by his wife, when he asked about her. Trophima in the brothel prayed continually, and had the Gospel on her bosom, and no one could approach her. One day as someone attacked her the Gospel fell to the ground. She cried to God for help and an angel came, and the youth fell dead. After that, she raised him, and all the city ran to the sight.

Lesbius' wife went to the bath with the steward, and as they bathed an ugly demon came and killed them both. Andrew heard and said, 'It is the judgement of God for their usage of Trophima.' The lady's nurse, decrepit from age, was carried to the spot, and supplicated for her. Andrew said to Lesbius, 'Will you have her raised?' 'No, after all the ill she has done.' 'We ought not to be unmerciful.' Lesbius went to the praetorium; Andrew raised his wife, who remained shamefaced: he bade her go home and pray. 'First', she said, 'reconcile me to Trophima whom I have injured.' 'She bears you no malice.' He called her and they were reconciled. Callisto was the wife.

Lesbius, growing in faith, came one day to Andrew and confessed all his sins. Andrew said, 'I thank God, my son, that you fear the judgement to come. Be strong in the Lord in whom you believe.' And he took his hand and walked with him on the shore.

24. They sat down, with others, on the sand, and he taught. A corpse was thrown up by the sea near them. 'We must learn', said Andrew, 'what the enemy has done to him.' So he raised him, gave him a garment, and bade him tell his story. He said, 'I am the son of Sostratus, of Macedonia, lately come from Italy. On returning home I heard of a new teaching, and set forth to find out about it. On the way here we were wrecked and all drowned.' And after some thought, he realized that Andrew was the man he sought, and fell at his feet and said, 'I know that you are the servant of the true God. I beseech you for my companions, that they also may be raised and know him.' Then Andrew instructed him, and thereafter prayed God to show the bodies of the other drowned men: thirty-nine were washed ashore, and all there prayed for them to be raised. Philopator, the youth, said, 'My father sent me here with a great sum. Now he is blaspheming God and his teaching. Let it not be so.' Andrew ordered the bodies to be collected, and said, 'Whom will you have raised first?' He said, 'Varus my foster-brother.' So he was first raised and then the other thirty-eight. Andrew prayed over each, and then told the brethren each to take the hand of one and say, 'Jesus Christ the son of the living God raises you.'

Lesbius gave much money to Philopator to replace what he had lost, and he stayed with Andrew.

25. A woman, Calliopa, married to a murderer, conceived an illegitimate child and suffered in travail. She told her sister to call on Diana for help; when she did so the devil appeared to her at night and said, 'Why do you trouble me with vain prayers? Go to Andrew in Achaea.' She came, and he accompanied her to Corinth, Lesbius with him. Andrew said to Calliopa, 'You deserve to suffer for your evil life: but believe in Christ, and you will be relieved, but the child will be born dead.' And so it was.

26. Andrew did many signs in Corinth. Sostratus the father of Philopator, warned in a vision to visit Andrew, came first to Achaea and then to Corinth. He met Andrew walking with Lesbius, recognized him by his vision, and fell at his feet. Philopator said, 'This is my father, who seeks to know what he must do.' Andrew: 'I know that he is come to learn the truth; we thank God who reveals himself to believers.' Leontius the servant of Sostratus, said to him, 'Sir, do you see how this man's face shines?' 'I see, my beloved,' said Sostratus, 'let us never leave him, but live with him and hear the words of eternal life.' Next day they offered Andrew many gifts, but he said, 'It is not for me to take anything from you but your own selves. Had I desired money, Lesbius is richer.'

27. After some days he bade them prepare him a bath; and going there saw an old man with a devil, trembling exceedingly. As he wondered at him, another, a youth, came out of the bath and fell at his feet, saying, 'What have we to do with you, Andrew? Have you come here to turn us out of our abodes?' Andrew said to the people, 'Fear not', and drove out both the devils. Then, as he bathed, he told them, 'The enemy of mankind lies in wait everywhere, in baths and in rivers; therefore we ought always to invoke the Lord's name, that he may have no power over us.'

They brought their sick to him to be healed, and so they did from other cities.

28. An old man, Nicolaus, came with clothes rent and said, 'I am seventy-four years old and have always been a libertine. Three days ago I heard of your miracles and teaching. I thought I would turn over a new leaf, and then again that I would not. In this doubt, I took a Gospel and prayed God to make me forget my old devices. A few days after, I forgot the Gospel I had about me, and went to the brothel. The woman said, "Depart, old man, depart: you are an angel of God, do not touch me or approach me, for I see in you a great mystery." Then I remembered the Gospel, and am come to you for help and pardon.' Andrew discoursed for a long time against incontinence, and prayed from the sixth to the ninth hour. He rose and washed his face and said, 'I will not eat till I know if God will have mercy on this man.' A second day he fasted, but had no revelation until the fifth day, when he wept vehemently and said, 'Lord, we obtain mercy for the dead, and now this man that desires to know your greatness, why should he not return and you heal him?' A voice from heaven said, 'You have prevailed for the old man; but just as you are

worn with fasting, let him also fast, that he may be saved.' And he called him and preached abstinence. On the sixth day he asked the brethren all to pray for Nicolaus, and they did. Andrew then took food and permitted the rest to eat. Nicolaus went home, gave away all his goods, and lived for six months on dry bread and water. Then he died. Andrew was not there, but in the place where he was he heard a voice, 'Andrew, Nicolaus for whom you interceded, is become mine.' And he told the brethren that Nicolaus was dead, and prayed that he might rest in peace.

29. And while he was staying in that place Antiphanes of Megara came and said, 'If there be in you any kindness, according to the command of the Saviour whom you preach, show it now.' Asked what his story was, he told it. 'Returning from a journey, I heard the porter of my house crying out. They told me that he and his wife and son were tormented of a devil. I went upstairs and found other servants gnashing their teeth, running at me, and laughing madly. I went further up and found they had beaten my wife: she lay with her hair over her face unable to recognize me. Cure her, and I care nothing for the others.' Andrew said, 'There is no respect of persons with God. Let us go there.' They went from Lacedaemon to Megara, and when they entered the house, all the devils cried out, 'What are you doing here, Andrew? Go where you are permitted: this house is ours.' He healed the wife and all the possessed persons, and Antiphanes and his wife became firm adherents.

30. He returned to Patras where Aegeates was now proconsul, and one Iphidama, who had been converted by a disciple, Sosias, came and embraced his feet and said, 'My lady Maximilla, who is in a fever, has sent for you. The proconsul is standing by her bed with his sword drawn, meaning to kill himself when she expires.' He went to her, and said to Aegeates, 'Do yourself no harm, but put up your sword into its place. There will be a time when you will draw it on me.' Aegeates did not understand, but made way. Andrew took Maximilla's hand, she broke into a sweat, and was well: he bade them give her food. The proconsul sent him 100 pieces of silver, but he would not look at them.

31. Going thence he saw a sick man lying in the dirt begging, and healed him.

32. Elsewhere he saw a blind man with wife and son, and said: 'This is indeed the devil's work: he has blinded them in the soul and body.' He opened their eyes and they believed.

33. One who saw this said, 'I beg you come to the harbour; there is a man, the son of a sailor, sick fifty years, cast out of the house, lying on the shore, incurable, full of ulcers and worms.' They went to him. The sick man said, 'Perhaps you are the disciple of that God who alone can save.' Andrew said, 'I am he who in the name of my God can restore you to health', and added, 'In the name of Jesus Christ, rise and follow me.' He left his filthy rags and

followed, the pus and worms flowing from him. They went into the sea, and the apostle washed him in the name of the Trinity, and he was whole and ran naked through the city proclaiming the true God.

34. At this time the proconsul's brother Stratocles arrived from Italy. One of his slaves, Alcman, whom he loved, was taken by a devil and lay foaming in the court. Stratocles hearing of it said, 'Would the sea had swallowed me before I saw this.' Maximilla and Iphidama said, 'Be comforted: there is a man of God here, let us send for him.' When he came he took the boy's hand and raised him whole. Stratocles believed and became a follower of Andrew.

35. Maximilla went daily to the praetorium and sent for Andrew to teach there. Aegeates was away in Macedonia, angry because Maximilla had left him since her conversion. As they were all assembled one day, he returned, to their great terror. Andrew prayed that he might not be allowed to enter the place till all had dispersed. And Aegeates was at once seized with indisposition, and in the interval the apostle signed them all and sent them away, himself last. But Maximilla on the first opportunity came to Andrew and received the word of God and went home.

36. After this Andrew was taken and imprisoned by Aegeates, and all came to the prison to be taught. After a few days he was scourged and crucified; he hung for three days, preaching, and expired, as is fully set forth in his Passion. Maximilla embalmed and buried his body.

37. From the tomb comes manna like flour, and oil: the amount shows the barrenness or fertility of the coming season—as I have told in my first book of Miracles. I have not set out his Passion at length, because I find it well done by some one else.[4]

38. This much have I presumed to write, unworthy, unlettered, &c. The author's prayer for himself ends the book. May Andrew, on whose death-day he was born, intercede to save him.

D. THE ACTS OF ANDREW AND MATTHIAS

1. At that time, all the apostles were gathered together at one place and divided the regions among themselves by casting lots, so that each would leave for his allotted share. The lot fell on Matthias to go to the city called Myrmidonia.[1]

The people of that city ate no bread and drank no water, but ate human flesh and drank their blood. They would seize all who came to their city, gouge out their eyes, and make them drink a drug prepared by sorcery and magic. When forced by them to drink the drug, the victims' hearts became

---

[4] The Passion to which Gregory alludes is probably Conversante et Docente.

[1] Where 'Myrmidonia' occurs in the text, following Latin witnesses, note that the bulk of Greek support reads 'city (or region) of the cannibals'. Generally, I follow MacDonald throughout in preferring Myrmidonia with the Latin.

muddled and their minds deranged. Out of their minds and taken to prison, they would eat hay like cattle or sheep.

2. So when Matthias entered the gate of the city Myrmidonia, the people of that city seized him and gouged out his eyes. They made him drink the drug of their magical deceit, led him off to the prison, and gave him grass to eat.

He ate nothing, for his heart was not muddled and his mind not deranged when he took their drug, but he prayed to God weeping, 'Lord Jesus Christ, for whom we have forsaken everything to follow you, knowing that you help all who hope in you, pay attention and see what they have done to your servant Matthias, how they have nearly reduced me to the condition of beasts, for you know all. Therefore, if you have determined in my case that the lawless people of this city should devour me, I will not flee your plan. Restore to me, Lord, the light of my eyes, so that I can see what the lawless men of this city are undertaking against me. Do not abandon me, my Lord Jesus Christ, and do not hand me over to this bitter death.'

3. As Matthias was praying, a light shone in the prison, and a voice came out of the light saying, 'Beloved Matthias, receive your sight.' Immediately he received his sight. Again the voice came out saying, 'Brace yourself, our Matthias, and do not be terrified, for I will never abandon you. I will rescue you from every danger, not only you but also all your brothers and sisters who are with you, for I am with you every hour and always. But remain here twenty-seven days for the benefit of many souls, and then I will send Andrew to you who will lead you out of this prison, not only you but also all who are with you.' When the Saviour had said these things, he again said to Matthias, 'Peace be with you, our Matthias', and he returned to heaven.

Seeing this, Matthias said to the Lord, 'May your grace continue with me, my Lord Jesus!' Then Matthias sat in the prison and sang.

When the executioners came into the prison to carry people away to eat, Matthias would shut his eyes so they would not notice he could see. The executioners came to him, read the ticket on his hand, and said to each other, 'In three days we will take this one too from the prison and slaughter him.' (They would indicate for everyone they caught the date of their capture, and they tied a ticket to their right hands so that they would know the completion of thirty days.)

4. When twenty-seven days elapsed since Matthias had been captured, the Lord Jesus appeared in a city of Achaea where Andrew was teaching and said to him, 'Arise, go with your disciples to the city called Myrmidonia, and bring Matthias out of that place, for in three days the citizenry will bring him out and slaughter him for their food.'

'My Lord,' answered Andrew, 'I cannot travel there before the three day limit, so send your angel quickly to get him out of there. For you know, Lord, that I too am flesh and cannot go there quickly. I do not even know the route.'

D. The Acts of Andrew and Matthias

'Obey the one who made you,' he told Andrew, 'the one who can speak but a word and that city and all its inhabitants would be brought here. For if I were to command the horns of the winds, they would drive it here. But rise up early, go down to the sea with your disciples, and you will find a boat on the shore that you and your disciples should board.' Having said this, the Saviour again said, 'Peace to you, Andrew, and to those with you', and he went into the heavens.

5. Rising early in the morning, Andrew and his disciples went to the sea, and when he descended to the shore he saw a small boat and seated in the boat three men. The Lord by his own power had prepared the boat. He himself was in the boat like a human captain, and he had brought on board two angels whom he transformed to look like humans, and they were sitting in the boat with him.

When Andrew saw the boat and the three men in it, he was overjoyed. He went to them and said, 'Brothers, where are you going with this little boat?'

'We are going to the city of Myrmidonia', answered the Lord.

Andrew looked at Jesus but did not recognize him, because Jesus was hiding his divinity and appeared to Andrew as a human captain. 'I too am going to the city of the Myrmidons,' Andrew answered, "so take us to this city, brothers.'

'Everybody flees from that city', Jesus told him. 'How is it that you are going there?'

'We have a small task to perform there, and we must finish it,' Andrew answered. 'But if you can, do us the favour of taking us to the city of Myrmidonia where you too are now going.'

'If it is so very necessary for you,' Jesus answered, 'board this boat and travel with us.'

6. 'Young man,' said Andrew, 'I want to make something clear to you before we board your boat.'

'Say what you want', Jesus said.

'Listen brother: we have no fare to offer you,' Andrew said, 'and we have no bread to eat.'

'How then can you board if you have no fare for us and no bread to eat?', Jesus asked.

'Listen brother,' said Andrew to Jesus, 'do not think that we withhold our fare from you as an act of arrogance. We are disciples of our Lord Jesus Christ, the good God. He chose us twelve and gave us this command: "When you go to preach take on the road no money, no bread, no bag, no sandals, no staff, and no change of tunic."[2] So if you will do us the favour, brother, tell us straightaway. If not let us know and we will leave to find ourselves another boat.'

---

[2] Cf. Mark 6: 8–9; Matt. 10: 7–10; Luke 9: 3, 10: 4.

'If this is the command you received, and if you are carrying it out,' Jesus told Andrew, 'board my boat joyfully. In truth, I would rather bring aboard my boat you disciples of the one called Jesus than those who offer me gold and silver, for I am fully worthy that the apostle of the Lord should board my boat.'

'Brother,' responded Andrew, 'allow me. May the Lord grant you glory and honour.' Andrew and his disciples boarded the boat.

7. After boarding he sat down by the sail of the boat, and Jesus said to one of the angels, 'Get up and go below to the hold of the boat, bring up three loaves, and place them before all the brothers, so that the men may eat in case they are hungry from having come to us after a long trip.' He got up, went below to the hold of the boat, and brought up three loaves, just as the Lord had commanded him, and set out the bread for them.

Then Jesus said to Andrew, 'Brother, stand up with those in your party and take bread for nourishment, so that you may be strong enough to endure the turbulence of the sea.'

'My children,' Andrew told his disciples, 'we have experienced great generosity from this person, so stand up and take bread for nourishment, so that you might be strong enough to endure the turbulence of the sea.'

His disciples could not respond to him with as much as a word; they were already seasick. Then Jesus insisted that Andrew and his disciples take bread for nourishment.

'Brother,' said Andrew, unaware he was Jesus, 'may the Lord grant you heavenly bread from his kingdom. Just leave them alone, brother, for you see that the servants are queasy from the sea.'

'Perhaps the brothers have no experience of the sea,' Jesus told Andrew. 'Ask them if they want to return to land and wait for you until you finish your task and return to them again.'

Then Andrew asked his disciples, 'My children, do you want to return to land and wait for me there until I finish the task for which I was sent?'

'If we separate from you,' they answered Andrew, 'we may become strangers to the good things that you provided us. We shall be with you now wherever you go.'

8. Jesus said to Andrew, 'If you are indeed a disciple of the one called Jesus, tell your disciples the miracles your teacher did so that their souls may rejoice and that they may forget the terror of the sea, for we are about to push the boat off shore.' Jesus at once said to one of the angels, 'Cast off the boat', and he cast the boat off from land. Jesus went and sat at the rudder and piloted the craft.

Then Andrew encouraged and strengthened his disciples saying, 'My children, you who have handed over your souls to the Lord, do not be afraid, for the Lord will never abandon us. At that time when we were with our Lord, we boarded the boat with him, and he lay silently on board in order to test us;

he was not really sleeping. A great wind arose, and the sea swelled so much that the waves broke over the sail of the boat. Because we were terrified, the Lord stood up and rebuked the winds, and calm returned to the sea.[3] All things fear him, because they are his creations. So now, my children, do not be afraid, for the Lord Jesus will never abandon us.'

As the holy Andrew said this, he prayed in his heart that his disciples would be drawn off to sleep and no longer be terrified by the tempest. As Andrew prayed, his disciples fell asleep.

9. Andrew turned to the Lord, still not knowing it was the Lord, and said to him, 'There is something I would like to say to you.'

'Say what you wish', the Lord told him.

'Sir, show me your sailing technique, because from the moment I boarded until now I have constantly observed your piloting and I am astounded. I have never seen anyone sail the sea as now I see you doing. I sailed the seas sixteen times; this is my seventeenth, and I have never seen such skill. The ship actually responds as though it were on land. So, young man, show me your technique, for I eagerly desire to learn it.'

'We too have often sailed the sea and been in danger,' Jesus told Andrew, 'but because you are a disciple of the one called Jesus, the sea knew that you were righteous and so it was still and did not lift its waves against the boat.'

Then Andrew cried out in a loud voice, 'I bless you, my Lord Jesus Christ, that I have met a man who glorifies your name.'

10. 'Tell me, disciple of the one called Jesus,' Jesus asked Andrew, 'why did the faithless Jews not believe in him and say that he was not God but a human? How could a human do the miracles of God and his great wonders? Make it clear to me, disciple of the one called Jesus, for we heard that he revealed his divinity to his disciples.'

'Brother,' Andrew answered, 'he did indeed reveal to us that he was God, so do not suppose he is a human, for he himself created human beings'.

'Why then did the Jews not believe?', Jesus asked. 'Perhaps he performed no signs before them.'

'Have you not heard about the miracles he performed before them?', answered Andrew. 'He made the blind see, the lame walk, the deaf hear, he cleansed lepers and changed water into wine.[4] He took five loaves and two fish, made a crowd recline on grass, and after blessing the food gave it to them to eat. Those who ate were five thousand men and they were filled. They took up their excess, twelve baskets of leftovers.[5] And even after all these miracles they did not believe in him.'

'Perhaps he did these signs before the people and not before the high priests,' Jesus told Andrew, 'and for this reason they did not believe in him.'

[3] Cf. Matt. 8: 23–7; Mark 4: 35–41; Luke 8: 22–5.
[4] Cf. Matt. 11: 5; Luke 7: 22; John 2: 1–12.
[5] Cf. Matt. 14: 13–21; Mark 6: 32–44; Luke 9: 10–17.

11. 'Yes, brother,' answered Andrew, 'he did them also before the high priests, not only publicly but also privately, and they did not believe in him.'

'What kind of miracles did he do privately?', Jesus asked. 'Disclose them to me.'

'O you with an inquisitive spirit,' Andrew said, 'why do you test me?'

Jesus said, 'By saying these things to you, disciple of the one called Jesus, I am not testing you, but my soul rejoices and exults—and not only mine, but every soul that hears of his wonders.'

'O child,' Andrew said, 'the Lord will fill your soul with all joy and every good thing, since you asked me now to tell you the signs which our Lord did privately. (12.) When we twelve disciples went with our Lord into the temple of the Gentiles in order for him to make us recognize the devil's ignorance, because the high priests saw us following Jesus they told us, "O you wretches, how can you walk with the one who says, 'I am the son of God'? God does not have a son, does he? Which of you has ever seen God consorting with a woman? Is he not the son of Joseph the carpenter? Is his mother not Mary, and are not his brothers James and Simon?"[6]

'When we heard these words, our hearts turned weak. But Jesus, knowing that our hearts were giving way, took us to a desolate place, performed great signs before us, and demonstrated all of his divinity for us. And we said to the high priests, "You come too and see, for he has persuaded us."

13. 'When the high priests went with us and entered into the temple of the gentiles, Jesus showed us the form of heaven, so that we should know whether it was real or not. Thirty men of the people and four high priests entered with us. Looking to the right and left of the sanctuary, Jesus saw two sculpted marble sphinxes in the likeness of cherubim, which the priests of the idols worship and adore, one on the right and one on the left. Jesus turned to us and said, "Behold the replica of heaven, for these are similar to the cherubim and seraphim in heaven." Then Jesus looked at the sphinx on the right side of the temple and said to it, "I tell you, O model of that which is in heaven, which the hands of artists sculpted, be loosened from your place, come down, answer, disgrace the high priests, and prove to them that I am God and not a human."

14. 'And immediately, that very hour, the sphinx leaped up from its place, acquired a human voice, and said, "O foolish sons of Israel, the blindness of their own hearts is not enough for them, but they want to make others blind like themselves by saying God is a human. He it is who from the beginning formed the human and gave his breath to everything, who moves everything immovable. He it is who called Abraham, who loved his son Isaac, who returned his beloved Jacob to his land, appeared to him in the desert, and made for him many good things. He it is who led them out and gave them

---

[6] Cf. Matt. 13: 55.

D. The Acts of Andrew and Matthias

water from the gushing rock. He is the judge of the living and the dead. He it is who prepares marvellous things for those who obey him, and prepares punishment for those who do not believe in him. Do not suppose that I am merely a marble idol, for I tell you that the temples are more beautiful than your synagogue. Although we are stones, the priests gave us alone the name god, and the priests themselves who conduct worship in the temple purify themselves for fear of the demons. If they have sexual relations with women, they purify themselves seven days for fear they cannot enter into the temple because of us, and because of the name they gave us: 'god'. But when you fornicate, you take the law of God, go into God's synagogue, sit, read, and do not reverence the glorious words of God. Therefore, I tell you that the temples will abolish your synagogues, so that they even become churches of the unique son of God." Having said this, the sphinx was silent.

15. '"The sphinx's speech is trustworthy," we told the high priests, "because even the stones tell you the truth and put you to shame".

'The high priests of the Jews answered, "Observe and learn that this stone speaks through magic. You must not suppose that he is a god. Had you tested what the sphinx said to you, you would have known this, for you heard the stone claim that this is the one who spoke with Abraham. Where did he find Abraham or see him? Since Abraham died not a few years before this person was born, how did he know Abraham?"

'Again Jesus turned to the sphinx and said to it, "Why do these people not believe that I spoke with Abraham? Go and enter the land of the Canaanites, go to the double cave in the field of Mambre where lies the body of Abraham, and outside the tomb call, 'Abraham, Abraham, you whose body is in the cave, but whose soul is in paradise, thus says the one who moulded human beings at the beginning, the one who made you his own friend: "Arise with your son Isaac and Jacob, and go into the temples of the Jebusites in order that we might refute the high priests, that they may know that I knew you and you me."'"

'When it heard these words, immediately the sphinx walked before us all, went into the land of the Canaanites, to the field of Mambre, and called outside the tomb, just as Jesus had commanded it. At once the twelve patriarchs came out of the tomb alive and said to it, "To which of us were you sent?"

'"I was sent to the three patriarchs for evidence," the sphinx answered. "But as for you, go and rest until the time of resurrection."

'Hearing this, they went into the tomb and slept. The three patriarchs went with the sphinx, came to Jesus, and refuted the high priests. Then Jesus said to the patriarchs, "Go to your places." They left at once.

'Jesus turned to the sphinx and said, "Go up to your place", and immediately it arose and stood at its place. Even though the high priests saw these things, they did not believe in him. He showed us many other mysteries, which, should I narrate to you, brother, you would not be able to endure them.'

'I can endure them,' Jesus told him, 'for when the prudent hear useful words, their hearts rejoice. But when speaking with the perverted, you never—not until death—persuade their souls.'

16. When Jesus knew that the boat was nearing land, he laid his head on one of his angels, was still, and stopped speaking with Andrew. Seeing this, Andrew too laid his head on one of his disciples and fell asleep.

Jesus knew that Andrew was asleep and said to his angels, 'Spread out your hands, lift up Andrew and his disciples, and go and place them outside the gate of the city of the cannibals. Once you have set them on the ground, return to me.'

The angels did as Jesus commanded them: they lifted Andrew and his sleeping disciples, raised them aloft, and brought them outside the gate of the city of the cannibals. After putting them down, the angels returned to Jesus, and then Jesus and his angels ascended into heaven.

17. Early in the morning Andrew woke, looked up, and found himself sitting on the ground. When he looked, he saw the gate of the city of Myrmidonia. Looking about, he saw his disciples sleeping on the ground, and he woke them by saying, 'Get up, my children, and know the great event that has happened to us. Learn that the Lord was with us in the boat and we did not know him, for he transformed himself into a captain in the boat. He humbled himself and appeared to us as a mortal in order to test us.' When he had come to himself, Andrew said, 'Lord, I recognized your excellent speech, but I did not recognize you because you did not reveal yourself to me.'

'Father Andrew,' his disciples said, 'do not suppose that we were conscious when you spoke with him in the boat, for we were dragged off by a deep sleep. Eagles descended, carried away our souls, brought us to the heavenly paradise, and we saw great marvels. We saw our Lord Jesus sitting on a throne of glory and all the angels surrounding him. We saw Abraham, Isaac, Jacob, all the saints, and David singing a psalm with his harp. We saw you twelve apostles standing there before our Lord Jesus Christ, and outside you twelve angels circling you. One angel stood behind each of you, and they were like you in appearance. We heard the Lord say to the angels, "Listen to the apostles with regard to everything they ask of you." This is what we saw before you woke us, father Andrew, and they brought our souls into our bodies.'

18. When Andrew heard this he was exuberant that his disciples had been considered worthy to see these marvels. Andrew looked up into heaven and said, 'Appear to me, Lord Jesus Christ, for I know you are not far from your servants. Forgive me, for I beheld you on the boat as a human and spoke with you as with a human. Therefore, O Lord, reveal yourself now to me in this place.'

D. The Acts of Andrew and Matthias

After Andrew had said these things, Jesus came to him appearing like a most beautiful small child and said, 'Greetings, our Andrew.'

When Andrew saw him he fell to the earth, worshipped him, and said, 'Forgive me, Lord Jesus Christ, for on the sea I saw you as a human and spoke with you. My Lord Jesus, what sin had I committed that caused you not to reveal yourself to me on the sea?'

'You did not sin,' Jesus said to Andrew. 'I did these things to you because you said, "I cannot travel to the city of Myrmidonia in three days." I showed you that I can do anything and appear to each person in any form I wish. Now stand up, go to Matthias in the city, and bring him and all those strangers who are with him out of the prison. For behold, I show you, Andrew, before you enter their city what you must suffer. They will show you many terrible insults, contrive tortures, scatter your flesh on the public avenues and streets of their city. Your blood will flow on the ground like water. They will not be able to kill you, but they will contrive many afflictions. Stand firm, our Andrew, and do not respond in kind to their unbelief. Remember those many tortures my soul endured when they beat me, spat in my face, and said, "He casts out demons through Beelzebul."[7] Am I not able with the blink of my eyes to crush the heaven and the earth against those who sin against me? But I endured and forgave in order to provide a model for you all. So now, our Andrew, if they inflict on you these insults and tortures, endure them, for there are those in this city who are about to believe.' After the Saviour said these things, he ascended into the heavens.

19. Andrew rose up and went to the city with his disciples without anyone seeing him. They went to the prison, and Andrew saw seven guards standing at the door of the prison guarding it. He prayed silently, and the seven guards fell and died. When he came to the prison door, Andrew marked it with the sign of the cross and it opened automatically. On entering the prison with his disciples he saw Matthias sitting, singing psalms by himself. When he saw Andrew, Matthias rose, and they greeted each other with a holy kiss. 'O brother Matthias,' Andrew said, 'how is it that one finds you here? In three days they will take you out for slaughter, and you will become food for the people of this city. Where are the great mysteries you were taught? Where are the marvels with which we were entrusted, any of which would shake heaven and earth if you were to narrate them?'

'O brother Andrew,' Matthias answered, 'did you not hear the Lord say, "Behold, I send you as sheep in the midst of wolves?"[8] For as soon as they brought me into prison I prayed to the Lord, and he revealed himself to me saying, "Stand firm here for twenty-seven days, and then I will send you Andrew who will deliver you and everyone with you from the prison." Now look, I see you just as the Lord said I would. So now what should we do?'

[7] Cf. Matt. 9: 34; 12: 24, 27; Mark 3: 22; Luke 11: 15, 19.
[8] Cf. Matt. 10: 16; Luke 10: 3.

20. Then Andrew looked into the middle of the prison and saw the prisoners naked and eating grass like dumb beasts. Andrew beat his breast and said to himself, 'O Andrew, look and see what they have done to people like you, how they nearly reduced them to the state of irrational beasts.'

Then Andrew began rebuking Satan saying to him, 'Woe to you, Devil, enemy of God and his angels. These wretches and strangers did you no harm, so why have you brought this punishment upon them? O rogue, how long will you war with the human race? From the beginning you caused Adam to be expelled from paradise. God caused him to sow a diet of grain on the earth, but you turned his bread on the table into stones. Later, you entered into the minds of the angels, made them to be defiled with women, and made their unruly sons giants, so that they devoured the people of the earth,[9] until the Lord raged against them and brought a flood on them in order to obliterate every structure the Lord had made on the earth. But he did not obliterate his righteous one, Noah. Now you come to this city as well in order to make its residents eat humans and drink their blood so that they too may end up accursed and destroyed. For you assume that God will obliterate what he has moulded. Enemy! Have you not heard that God said, "I will never again bring a flood on the earth?"[10] If any punishment is prepared, it is for retaliation against you.'

21. Andrew and Matthias then rose up and prayed, and after the prayer Andrew put his hands on the faces of the blind men in the prison, and immediately they received their sight. He also put his hand on their hearts, and their minds regained human consciousness. Then Andrew said to them, 'Stand up, go to the lower parts of the city, and you will find along the road a large fig tree. Sit under the fig tree and eat its fruit until I come to you. Should I delay coming there, you will find enough food for yourselves, for the fruit of the fig tree will not fail. No matter how much you eat, it will bear more fruit and feed you, just as the Lord commanded.'

'Come with us, our lord,' the men said to Andrew, 'lest the lawless men of this city see us again, lock us up, and inflict tortures on us more dreadful and numerous than what they have inflicted on us so far.'

'Go!', Andrew answered them. 'For I tell you truly that when you go not even a dog will bark at you with his tongue.'

The men went off just as the blessed Andrew had told them. All the men whom Andrew released from prison numbered two hundred and forty-eight, and the women forty-nine. He made Matthias go with his disciples out of the city toward the east. Andrew commanded a cloud, and the cloud lifted Matthias and Andrew's disciples and placed them on the mountain where Peter was teaching, and they stayed with him.

---

[9] Cf. Gen. 6: 1–4.
[10] Cf. Gen. 9: 11.

D. The Acts of Andrew and Matthias

22. After Andrew left the prison, he walked about the city, and by a certain street he saw a pillar with a copper statue standing on it. He sat behind that pillar in order to see what would happen. When the executioners arrived at the prison to remove people for their food according to their daily custom, they found the doors of the prison opened and the seven guards lying dead on the ground. At once they went and told the rulers, 'We found the prison opened, and when we went inside we found no one, except for the guards lying dead on the ground.'

When the rulers of the city heard these things, they said to each other, 'What has happened? Have some people perhaps gone into the city prison, killed the guards, and released the prisoners?' Then they commanded the executioners, 'Go to the prison and bring the seven men so that we may eat them. Tomorrow let us go and gather together all the elderly of the city so that they can cast lots among themselves until the lots select seven. Let us slaughter seven each day, and they will be our food until we select some young men and appoint them to boats as sailors. They can invade the neighbouring territories and bring captives here for our food.'

The executioners went and brought out the seven dead men. An earthen oven had been erected in the middle of the city, and next to it lay a large trough where they used to slay people and their blood would flow into the trough, whence they would draw up the blood and drink it. They brought the men and placed them in the trough. When the executioners lifted their hands over them, Andrew heard a voice saying, 'Andrew, look what is happening in this city.'

Andrew looked and prayed to the Lord, 'My Lord Jesus Christ, you who commanded me to enter this city, do not let the residents of the city do any harm, but let the swords fall from their lawless hands, and may their hands be like stone.'

Immediately the swords fell from the executioners' hands, and their hands became stone. When the rulers saw what had happened, they cried, 'Woe to us, for there are magicians here who even went into the prison and led the people out! For look, they have put these men under a magic spell. What should we do? Go now, and gather up the elderly of the city; we are hungry.'

23. They went and gathered up all the old people of the city, and found two hundred and seventeen. They brought them to the rulers, made them cast lots, and the lot fell on seven old people. One of those selected said to the attendants, 'I beg you! I have a small son. Take him, slaughter him in my place, and let me go.'

The attendants answered him, 'We cannot take your son unless we first take the matter up with our superiors.'

The attendants went and informed the rulers, and the rulers answered the attendants: 'If he gives you his son in his place, let him go.'

When the attendants came to the old man, they told him, and the old man said to them, 'In addition to my son I also have a daughter. Take and slaughter them, only let me go.' He delivered up his children to the attendants for them to slaughter, and they dismissed him unharmed.

As they went to the trough, the children wept together, and begged the attendants, 'We beg you: do not kill us when we are so small, but let us reach full stature and then slaughter us.' But the attendants did not listen to the children or have compassion on them, but brought them weeping and begging to the trough.

As they brought them for slaughter, Andrew saw what was happening and cried. He looked into heaven weeping and said, 'Lord Jesus Christ, just as you listened to me in the case of the dead guards and did not let them be devoured, so now too, listen to me, so that the executioners may not bring death on these children. Loosen the swords from the hands of the executioners.'

Immediately the swords were loosened and fell from the hands of the executioners like wax in fire. At that, when the executioners saw what had happened, they were terrified. When Andrew saw what had happened, he glorified the Lord, because he had responded to him in every instance.

24. When the rulers saw what had happened, they wept terribly saying, 'Woe to us, for now we perish. What shall we do?'

Then the devil came looking like an old man and began to speak in the midst of them all, 'Woe to you, for now you are dying for lack of food. What good will sheep or cattle do you? They will never satisfy you. If you want my opinion, get up and search for a certain stranger here residing in the city named Andrew and kill him. If you do not, he will not allow you to carry out this practice ever again, for it is he who released the people from prison. Indeed, the man is in this city, and you do not recognize him. So now, arise, seek him out, so that at last you can gather your food.'

Andrew saw how the devil was speaking to the crowds, but the devil did not see the blessed Andrew. Then Andrew told the devil, 'O most cruel Belial, opponent of every creature, my Lord Jesus Christ will lower you into the abyss.'

When the devil heard these things he said, 'I hear your voice, and I recognize it, but I do not know where you are standing.'

'Why were you nicknamed Amael?', Andrew asked the devil. 'Was it not because you are blind, unable to see all the saints?'

Hearing this, the devil said to the citizens, 'Look around now for the one who is speaking with me, for he is the one.'

The citizens ran about, shut the city gates, and searched for the blessed one but did not see him. Then the Lord revealed himself to Andrew and said to him, 'Andrew, arise and reveal yourself to them, so that they may learn the power of the devil who sways them.'

25. Then Andrew arose before them all and said, 'Look, I am Andrew whom you seek.'

D. The Acts of Andrew and Matthias

The crowds ran to him, seized him, and said, 'What you have done to us we shall do to you.' They deliberated among themselves saying, 'How shall we kill him?' They said to each other, 'If we behead him, his death will not be agonizing for him.' Still others said, 'If we burn him with fire and give his body to feed our superiors, this death is not painful for him.'

Then one of them whom the devil had entered and possessed said to the crowd, 'As he has done to us, let us do to him. Let us invent the most heinous tortures for him. Let us go, tie a rope around his neck, and drag him through all the avenues and streets of the city each day until he dies. When he is dead, let us divide his body for all of the citizens and distribute for their food.'

Hearing this, the crowds did as he had said to them. They tied a rope around his neck and dragged him through all the avenues and streets of the city. As the blessed Andrew was dragged, his flesh stuck to the ground, and his blood flowed on the ground like water. When evening came, they threw him into the prison and tied his hands behind him. He was utterly exhausted.

26. Early the next morning, they brought him out again, tied a rope around his neck, and dragged him about. Again his flesh stuck to the ground and his blood flowed. The blessed Andrew wept and prayed, 'My Lord Jesus Christ, come and see what they have done to me your servant. But I endure because of your command which you commanded me when you said, "Do not respond in kind to their unbelief." Now Lord, observe how many tortures they bring upon me, for you, Lord, know human flesh. I know, Lord, that you are not far from your servants and I do not dispute the command which you gave me. Otherwise, I would have made them and their city plunge into the abyss. But I shall never forsake your command which you commanded me, even to the point of death, because you, Lord, are my help. Only do not let the enemy mock me.'

As the blessed Andrew said these things, the devil was walking behind him saying to the crowds, 'Hit his mouth to shut him up!'

At nightfall they took Andrew, threw him again into the prison, tied his hands behind him, and left him again until the next day.

Taking with him seven demons whom the blessed Andrew had cast out of the vicinity, the devil entered the prison, stood before the blessed Andrew, and jeered at him cruelly. The seven demons and the devil taunted the blessed Andrew, 'Now you have fallen into our hands. Where are your power, your awesomeness, your glory, and your grandeur, you who raise yourself up against us, dishonour us, narrate our deeds to the people in every place and region, you who make our temples deserted houses with the result that no sacrifices for our delight are offered up in them? For this reason we will retaliate. We will kill you as Herod killed your teacher called Jesus.'

27. The devil said to his seven wicked demons, 'My children, kill him who dishonours us, so that at last all the regions will be ours.' Then the seven demons came and stood before Andrew wanting to kill him. But when they saw the seal on his forehead which the Lord had given him, they were afraid

and were not able to approach him but fled. The devil said to them, 'My children, why do you flee from him and not kill him?'

The demons answered the devil, 'We cannot kill him, for we saw the seal on his forehead and were afraid of him, for we knew him before he came into this torment of his humiliation. You go and kill him if you can, for we do not obey you, lest God heal him and deliver us up to bitter tortures.'

'We cannot kill him,' said one of the demons, 'but come, let us mock him in this torment.'

The demons and the devil came to the blessed Andrew, stood before him, and mocked him saying, 'Look Andrew, you too have come to dishonourable shame and tortures. Who can rescue you?'

After the blessed Andrew heard these things he wept greatly, and a voice came to him saying, 'Andrew, why do you weep?' (The voice was the devil's, for the devil altered his voice.)

'I weep', answered Andrew, 'because my Lord commanded me, "Be patient with them." Had he not, I would have shown you my power.'

The devil answered Andrew, 'If you have some such power, use it.'

'Even if you kill me here', answered Andrew, 'I will never do your will but the will of Jesus Christ who sent me. For this reason then you do these things to me, so that I may neglect the command of my Lord, for if the Lord visits this city for my sake, I will punish you as you deserve.' When the seven demons heard these things, they fled with the devil.

28. The next morning they again fetched Andrew, tied a rope around his neck, and dragged him. Again his flesh stuck to the earth, and his blood flowed on the ground like water. As he was dragged, the blessed Andrew wept, saying, 'Lord Jesus Christ, these tortures are enough; I am exhausted. Look at what the enemy and his demons have done to me. Remember, O Lord, that you spent three hours on the cross and you weakened, for you said, "My Father, why have you forsaken me?"[11] Look, Lord, for three days I am dragged around in the avenues and streets of this city. Lord, especially because you know that human flesh is weak, command my spirit to leave me, my Lord, so that at last I may attain rest. Lord, where are your words which you spoke to us to strengthen us, telling us, "If you walk with me, you will not lose one hair from your head?"[12] Therefore, Lord, look and see that my flesh and the hairs of my head stick to the ground, for I have been dragged around in heinous tortures for three days, and you, my Lord, have not revealed yourself to me to fortify my heart. I am utterly exhausted.' The blessed Andrew said these things as he was dragged about.

Then a voice came to him in Hebrew, 'Our Andrew, heaven and earth will pass away, but my words will never pass away.[13] Therefore, look and see behind you at what has happened to your fallen flesh and hair.'

---

[11] Cf. Matt. 27: 46; Mark 15: 34.
[12] Cf. Luke 21: 18; Acts 27: 34.
[13] Cf. Matt. 24: 35; Mark 13: 21; Luke 21: 33.

D. The Acts of Andrew and Matthias

Andrew turned and saw large fruit-bearing trees sprouting, and he responded, 'I know, Lord, that you have not forsaken me.'

When evening came, they threw him into the prison. Already he was exceedingly weak. The men of the city said to each other, 'He will probably die during the night, for he is weak and his flesh exhausted.'

29. The Lord appeared in the prison, and extending his hand he said to Andrew, 'Give me your hand and stand up whole.'

When Andrew saw the Lord Jesus, he gave him his hand and stood up whole. He fell, worshipped him, and said, 'I thank you, my Lord Jesus Christ.'

When Andrew looked into the middle of the prison, he saw a standing pillar and on the pillar rested an alabaster statue. He stretched out his hands, and said to the pillar and the statue on it, 'Fear the sign of the cross, at which heaven and earth tremble, and let the statue sitting on the pillar spew from its mouth water as abundant as a flood, so that the residents of this city may be punished. Do not fear, O stone, and say "I am just a stone and unworthy to praise the Lord," for in fact you too have been honoured. The Lord moulded us from the earth, but you are pure. Therefore, God gave to his people the tablets of the law made from you. He did not write on gold or silver tablets but on tablets of stone. So now, O statue, carry out this plan.'

As soon as the blessed Andrew had said these things, the stone statue spewed from its mouth a great quantity of water as from a trench, and the water rose on the earth. It was exceedingly brackish and consumed human flesh.

30. When morning came, the men of the city saw what had happened and began to flee, saying to themselves, 'Woe to us, for now we die!' The water killed their cattle and their children, and they began to flee the city.

Then Andrew said to the Lord, 'Lord Jesus Christ, I already have undertaken and performed this sign in this city. Do not forsake me, but send your archangel Michael in a fiery cloud and wall up this city so that if any should want to flee it they will not be able to pass through the fire.'

Immediately a cloud of fire descended and encircled the entire city like a wall. When Andrew learned that the plan had been achieved, he blessed the Lord. The water rose to the necks of the men and was devouring them viciously.

'Woe to us,' they all cried and shouted, 'for all these things came upon us because of the stranger in prison whom we delivered over to tortures. What will we do? Let us go to the prison and free him, lest we die in this deluge of water. Let us all cry out, "We believe in you, O God of this stranger! Take this water from us."' All went out crying in a loud voice, 'O God of this stranger, remove this water from us.'

Andrew knew that their souls were submissive to him. Then the blessed Andrew said to the alabaster statue, 'Now at last stop spewing water from your mouth, for the time of rest has come. For behold, I am leaving to preach the word of the Lord. I say to you, stone pillar, that if the inhabitants of this city believe, I will build a church and place you in it, because you did this service for me.'

The statue ceased flowing and no longer emitted water. Andrew left the prison, and the water ran from the feet of the blessed Andrew. When the citizenry went to the doors of the prison, they cried out, 'Have mercy on us, God of this stranger. Do not treat us as we treated this man.'

31. The old man who had delivered up his children for slaughter in his place came and entreated at the feet of the blessed Andrew, 'Have mercy on me.'

'I am amazed', said the holy Andrew to the old man, 'that you can say, "Have mercy on me", when you did not have mercy on your own children but delivered them up in your place. Therefore I tell you, at that hour when the water recedes, you will go into the abyss, you and the fourteen executioners who killed people daily, and all of you will stay in Hades until I turn once again and raise you. So now, go into the abyss so that I may show these executioners the place of your murder and the place of peace, and this old man the place of love and the surrender of his children. Now everyone follow me.'

As the men of the city followed him, the water divided before the feet of the blessed Andrew until he came to the place of the trough where they used to slaughter people. Looking up into heaven, the blessed Andrew prayed before the entire crowd, and the earth opened and devoured the water along with the old man, and he and the executioners were carried down into the abyss.

When the men saw what happened, they were terrified and began to say, 'Woe to us, for this person is from God, and now he kills us for the torments which we inflicted on him. For look, what he said to the executioners and the old man has happened to them. Now he will command the fire and it will burn us.'

After hearing this, Andrew said to them, 'My little children, do not be afraid; for I will not let even them stay in Hades. They went there so that you should believe in our Lord Jesus Christ.'

32. Then the blessed Andrew commanded all those who had died in the water to be brought to him, but they were unable to bring them because a great multitude had died, of men, women, children, and beasts. Then Andrew prayed, and all revived.

Later, he drew up plans for a church and had the church built on the spot where the pillar in the prison had stood. After baptizing them, he handed on to them the commands of our Lord Jesus Christ telling them, 'Stand by these, so that you may know the mysteries of our Lord Jesus Christ, for his power is great. I will not hand them on to you now; instead, I am going to my disciples.'

'We beg you,' they all implored, 'stay with us a few days, so that we might drink our fill from your fountain, because we are neophytes.'

Even though they begged him, he was not persuaded but said to them, 'I will go first to my disciples.' And the children with the men followed behind weeping and begging, and threw ashes on their heads. He was still not persuaded by them but said, 'I will go to my disciples, and later I will return to you.' He went on his way.

33. The Lord Jesus, having become like a beautiful small child, descended and greeted Andrew saying, 'Andrew, why do you depart leaving them fruitless, and why do you have no compassion on the children following after you and on the men who implore, "Stay with us a few days"? Their cry and weeping rose to heaven. So now, turn back, go into the city, and stay there seven days until I strengthen their souls in the faith. Then you may leave this city and you will go into the city of the barbarians, you and your disciples. After you enter that city and preach my gospel there, you may leave them and again come into this city and bring up all the men in the abyss.'

Then Andrew turned and entered the city of Myrmidonia saying, 'I bless you, my Lord Jesus Christ who wants to save every soul, that you did not permit me to leave this city in my rage.' When he entered the city they saw him and were jubilant.

He spent seven days there teaching and confirming them in the Lord Jesus Christ. At the completion of seven days, the time came for the blessed Andrew to leave. All the people of Myrmidonia were gathered to him, young and old, and sent him off saying, 'One is the God of Andrew: the Lord Jesus Christ, to whom be glory and power forever. Amen.'

E. THE ACTS OF PETER AND ANDREW

1. When Andrew left the city of the cannibals, a cloud of light took him up and carried him to the mountain where Peter and Matthias and Alexander and Rufus were sitting. And Peter said, 'Have you prospered?' 'Yes,' he said, 'but they did me great harm.' 'Come then,' said Peter, 'and rest a while from your labours.' 2. And Jesus appeared in the form of a little child and greeted them, and told them to go to the city of the barbarians, and promised to be with them, and left them.

3. So the four set out. And when they were near the city Andrew asked Peter, 'Do many troubles await us here?' 'I do not know, but here is an old man sowing. Let us ask him for bread; if he gives it us, we shall know that we are not to be troubled, but if he says, "I have none", troubles await us.' They greeted him and asked accordingly. He said, 'If you will look after my plough and oxen I will fetch you bread...' 'Are they your oxen?' 'No, I have hired them.' And he went off. 4. Peter took off his cloak and garment, and said, 'It is no time for us to be idle, especially as the old man is working for us', and he took the plough and began to sow. Andrew protested and took it from him and sowed, and blessed the seed as he sowed. And Rufus and Alexander and

Matthias, going on the right, said, 'Let the sweet dew and the fair wind come and rest on this field.' And the seed sprang up and the corn ripened. 5. When the farmer returned with the bread and saw the ripe corn he worshipped them as gods. But they told him who they were, and Peter gave him the Commandments... He said, 'I will leave all and follow you.' 'Not so, but go to the city, return your oxen to the owner, and tell your wife and children and prepare us a lodging.' 6. He took a sheaf, hung it on his staff, and went off. The people asked where he got the corn, for it was the time of sowing, but he hastened home. 7. The chief men of the city heard of it and sent for him and made him tell his story. 8. And the devil entered them and they said, 'Alas! these are of the twelve Galileans who go about separating men from their wives. What are we to do?' 9. One of them said, 'I can keep them out of the city.' 'How?' 'They hate all women, and specially unchaste ones: let us put a naked wanton in the gate, and they will see her and flee.' So they did. 10. The apostles perceived the snare by the spirit, and Andrew said, 'Bid me, and I will chastise her.' Peter said, 'Do as you will.' Andrew prayed, and Michael was sent to hold her up by the hair till they had passed. 11. And she cried out, cursing the men of the city and praying for pardon. 12. And many believed at her word and worshipped the apostles, and they did many cures, and all praised God.

13. There was a rich man named Onesiphorus who said, 'If I believe, shall I be able to do wonders?' Andrew said, 'Yes, if you forsake your wife and all your possessions.' He was angry and put his garment about Andrew's neck and began to beat him, saying, 'You are a wizard, why should I do so?' 14. Peter saw it and told him to leave off. He said, 'I see you are wiser than he. What do you say?' Peter said, 'I tell you this: it is easier for a camel to go through a needle's eye than for a rich man to enter the kingdom of God.'[1] Onesiphorus was yet more angry, and took his garment off Andrew's neck and cast it on Peter's and pulled him along, saying, 'You are worse than the other. If you show me this sign, I and the whole city will believe, but if not you shall be punished.' 15. Peter was troubled and stood and prayed, 'Lord, help us at this hour, for you have entrapped us by your words.' 16. The Saviour appeared in the form of a boy of twelve years, wearing a linen garment smooth within and without, and said, 'Fear not: let the needle and the camel be brought.' There was a huckster in the town who had been converted by Philip; and he heard of it, and looked for a needle with a large eye, but Peter said, 'Nothing is impossible with God; rather bring a needle with a small eye.' 17. When it was brought, Peter saw a camel coming and stuck the needle in the ground and cried, 'In the name of Jesus Christ crucified under Pontius Pilate I command thee, camel, to go through the eye of the needle.' The eye opened like a gate and the camel passed through; and a second time, at

---

[1] Matt. 19: 24; Mark 10: 25; Luke 18: 25.

Peter's bidding. 18. Onesiphorus said, 'You are a great sorcerer: but I shall not believe unless I may send for a needle and a camel.' And he said secretly to a servant, 'Bring a camel and a needle, and find a defiled woman and some swine's flesh and bring them too.' And Peter heard it in the spirit and said. 'O slow to believe, bring your camel and woman and needle and flesh.' 19. When they were brought, Peter stuck the needle in the ground, with the flesh; the woman was on the camel. He commanded it as before, and the camel went through, and back again. 20. Onesiphorus cried out, convinced, and said, 'Listen. I have lands and vineyards, and 27 pounds of gold and 50 of silver, and many slaves: I will give my goods to the poor and free my slaves if I may do a wonder like you.' Peter said, 'If you believe, you shall.' 21. Yet he was afraid he might not be able, because he was not baptized; but a voice came, 'Let him do what he will.' So Onesiphorus stood before the needle and camel and commanded it to go through, and it went as far as the neck and stopped. And he asked why. 'Because you are not yet baptized.' He was content, and the apostles went to his house, and 1,000 souls were baptized that night. 22. Next day the woman who was hung in the air said, 'Alas that I am not worthy to believe like the rest! I will give all my goods to the poor and my house for a monastery of virgins. Peter heard it and went out to her, and at his word she was let down unhurt, and gave him for the poor 4 pounds of gold and many clothes and her house for a monastery of virgins. 23. And the apostles consecrated a church and ordained clergy and committed the people to God.

F. THE ACTS OF ANDREW AND PAUL

... We find the captain of a ship which has brought Andrew and Paul to some city. Andrew has gone towards the city; Paul has plunged into the sea to visit the underworld, and leaves a message for Andrew to bring him up again. The shipman's mother—dim of sight—comes to meet her son, and he, having Paul's cloak to bring to Andrew, accidentally touches her eyes with it, and she sees clearly. Andrew takes the cloak and goes to the city with the multitude; a man meets him and begs him to visit and cure his only son, twelve years old, who is dying. But the Jews oppose his entrance; he tells the father to return home: his boy will die, but he must not bury him till the morrow. The father goes home and finds him dead.

Andrew returns to the ship and makes the shipman point out the place where Paul dived into the sea. He takes a cup of fresh water, prays, and pours it into the sea, bidding the salt water retreat and the dry land appear. The abyss cleaves, and Paul leaps up, bearing a fragment of wood in his hand.

He has visited Amente and seen Judas and heard his story. Judas had repented and given back the money, and seen Jesus and pleaded for forgiveness. Jesus sent him to the desert to repent, bidding him fear no one but God. The prince of destruction came to him and threatened to swallow him up, and Judas was afraid and worshipped him. Then in despair he thought to go and ask Jesus again for pardon; but he had been taken away to the praetorium. So he resolved to hang himself and meet Jesus in Amente. Jesus came and took all the souls but his. The powers of Amente came and wept before Satan, who said, 'After all, we are stronger than Jesus; he has had to leave a soul with us.' Jesus ordered Michael to take away Judas' soul also, that Satan's boast might be proved vain, and told Judas how he had destroyed his own hopes by worshipping Satan and killing himself. Judas was sent back till the day of judgement. Paul tells also how he saw the streets of Amente desolate, and brought away a fragment of the broken gates in his hand. There were still some souls in punishment—the murderers, sorcerers, and those who cast little children into the water.

The apostles land, and with Apollonius the shipman go up to the city. The Jews refuse to let them in. They see 'a bird which is called True'[1] digging in a wall. Andrew says, 'You bird, go into the city to where the dead boy is, and tell them that we are at the gate and cannot enter; let them open to us.' The bird gives the message and the people threaten to stone the Jews. At this point the governor comes out; the matter is explained to him by the people and by the Jews, who add, 'If they are the disciples of the living God, why does he not open the gate for them?' The governor is impressed by this and calls on the apostles to open for themselves. They consult, and Paul, suddenly inspired, strikes the gates with the fragment of wood from Amente, and they are swallowed up in the earth.[2]

... The apostles say that the only thing is to order the dead man to be loosed. The Jews seek to flee, but they are held by the soldiers till the grave clothes are loosed. The apostles pray; the dead man rises and falls at the apostles' feet, saying, 'Forgive me for my folly', and tells everything that had happened. Andrew says to the Jews, 'Who is now the deceiver of the people? We or you?' It appears from this that the dead man in question has been an accomplice of the Jews in their trick, and is not the dead child whom the apostles were to raise, and doubtless did raise when they first entered the city. This is confirmed by the next words of the Jews: they fall at the apostles' feet and say, '... (we) killed him in folly, thinking that he would not rise.' They ask for baptism. And the act concludes with a general conversion—apparently of 27,000 Jews.

---

[1] This is really a scarabaeus, δίκαιρον in Greek, which word has been mistaken for δίκαιον.
[2] Here two leaves are lost.

The Acts of John

In the East the earliest unambiguous patristic attestation to the Acts of John is in Eusebius (*HE* 3. 25. 6 (Schwartz *GCS* 9.2, pp. 252 f.)) who condemns the Acts of John (and of Andrew) as heretical. Epiphanius (*adv. Haer.* 2. 47. 1 (Holl, *GCS* 31, p. 216)) notes that the Acts of John (and of Andrew and of Thomas) were used by encratite groups. The Manichaean Psalm Book used it as part of a Manichaean corpus of Acts[1] about AD 340 (according to C. R. C. Allberry). Western attestation includes Augustine (*Ep.* 237 (253) to Ceretius, ed. A. Goldbacher, *CSEL* 57 (Vienna and Leipzig, 1911), pp. 526–32) who cites in Latin some ten lines of the Hymn of Christ, which Ceretius claims to have found circulating as an independent text among the Priscillianists. The Acts were also mentioned by Innocent I (*Ep.* 6. 7, *PL* 20, col. 502) and by Turribius of Astorga (*Ep. ad Idacium et Ceponium* 5, *PL* 54, cols. 693–5). The Acts in Latin were also obviously known to the editor of the *Virtutes Johannis* in the collection of Pseudo-Abdias. The Acts were therefore known by the fourth century as a sectarian work and used by, among others, Priscillianists.

The Stichometry of Nicephorus calculates the Acts of John to have contained 2500 *stichoi*, making it comparable in length to the Gospel of Matthew. If Nicephorus' total represents the length of the original Acts (rather than a shortened version known in his day) then what we possess is likely to be only two-thirds of the original. These contents need to be re-established from several different manuscripts (with the help of later descriptions or allusions) as none of them contains the total remaining contents of the original Acts.

As may be seen in the bibliography below, Thilo, Tischendorf, Zahn, and James were responsible for publishing an increasing number of sections of the original Acts, but it was not until Bonnet's edition of 1898 that all the material then known was conveniently available. Only in recent years, thanks to the labours of Junod and Kaestli, has Bonnet's edition been significantly improved. Bonnet pieced together the various episodes in Greek that occur in different manuscripts, many of them containing the Acts of John of Prochorus, and published the Acts of John in 115 chapters. He was aware that there were gaps in the original story after his chs. 17, 55, 86, and 105. Another gap has been identified after ch. 36, although there is no break here in the manuscript tradition: this has been seen as relevant to the question of where chs. 87–105 belong. The Acts of John as published by Bonnet may thus be seen as consisting of separate sections:

---

[1] This also contained the Acts of Peter, Andrew, Thomas and Paul.

(a) 1–17, now considered not to belong to the original Acts of John.
(b) 18–36 and 37–55.
(c) 56–7 (asterisked by Bonnet as not original).
(d) 58–86.
(e) 87–105.
(f) 106–115.

A certain reordering of these sections is now normal, especially the insertion of chs. 87–105 after 36. The story of the partridge in 56–7 may not be part of the original Acts,[2] and Junod and Kaestli replace it with an episode found in two manuscripts of the Acts of John according to Prochorus concerning the healing of Antipatros' sons as their chs. 56–7. Both stories are included below.

The main sections are thus:

(i) Chs. 18–55, 58–86, contained in a few Greek manuscripts of Prochorus, notably Patmos 188.

(ii) Chs. 87–105, found in only one manuscript, published originally by M. R. James in *Apoc. Anec.* ii (with the Greek text and an English translation). Bonnet placed them immediately before the Metastasis (106–115). A better placing for them is after 36, and this is the position adopted here, following Hennecke–Schneemelcher and Junod and Kaestli.

(iii) The Metastasis (106–115), found in several Greek manuscripts and in Syriac, Armenian, Coptic (Sahidic), Ethiopic, Arabic, and Georgian. The Slavonic version, on which much work awaits to be done, also renders the Metastasis, but according to Hennecke[5], ii. 151 (Eng. trans., ii. 163), the Slavonic Metastasis is taken from the Acts of John of Prochorus.

Three recensions of the Metastasis have been identified by Junod and Kaestli, who print them separately in *CCA* 1 and 2. Their chart on p. 62 shows that the Ethiopic is descended from the Coptic through one of the two Arabic versions published by A. Smith Lewis. The other Arabic version comes from the Greek. The Georgian represents another version from the Greek. The Armenian represents a different tradition, as does the Syriac.

In addition, certain other episodes known from other sources are sometimes considered for inclusion in the lacunae as part of the original Acts of John or for additional support in editing the text of chs. 18–115:

(a) A sequence of stories found only in Latin (in Pseudo-Abdias, *Virtutes Iohannis* V–VIII (sometimes numbered 14–21) and in Pseudo-Melito, *Passio Iohannis*, is translated by James, pp. 257–64. The text of Pseudo-Abdias is

---

[2] It is a story known to John Cassian, *Conlationes* 24. 21 (ed. M. Petschenig, *CSEL* 13 (Vienna, 1886), pp. 697–8). This text is reproduced in a modified form in Jacob of Voragine's Golden Legend, and may be found in Slavonic (de Santos Otero, *Altslav. Apok.* i. 98, with reference to *BHG* ii. 906 and see under 'de ansere').

found in Nausea, or more conveniently in Fabricius, ii. 557–80,[3] Pseudo-Melito in *PG* 5, cols. 1242 B–1249 B. One of these stories is that of the poison cup to be found in a different form in the Acts of John in Rome (i.e. Lipsius–Bonnet, chs. 1–14, esp. 10). The relevant chapters are translated below ('Allied Texts (*a*)').

(*b*) P. Oxy. 850, a fourth-century fragment, refers in its text to the character named Andronicus. As he is introduced in Acts of John 31, the events recorded in the fragment could have occurred between that point and the Metastasis. They take place in Ephesus; as the Acts refer to two periods in Ephesus (chs. 31–55 and 62–115), the fragment is likely to have been located in one of the gaps following 36, 86 or 105. It is translated below ('Allied Texts (*b*)').

(*c*) In the citations from the Acts of John found in the fifth-century Epistle of Pseudo-Titus one quotation is close to ch. 113, ll. 10–11. The other two are from episodes now lost. James included these as having possibly originated in the Acts of John, and they appear below ('Allied Texts (*c*)').

(*d*) Junod and Kaestli, *CCA*, pp. 122–36, consider the possibility that the episode of the hay turned to gold and two other stories found in the Irish fifteenth-century Liber Flavus Fergusiorum[4] (which they include in an English version in *CCA*, pp. 113–16) are from the original Acts. The Liber Flavus has links with P. Oxy. 850 and with Evodius of Uzala (see *de fide contra Manichaeos* 40, ed. J. Zycha, *CSEL* 25.2 (Vienna, Prague, Leipzig, 1892), pp. 970–1).

The story of the hay concerns John's dealings with criticism of his success in receiving alms. He plucks some hay, which is turned to one hundred rods of gold. These he throws into the river, claiming that he prefers poverty for himself and that any alms he receives he distributes to the needy. This story is not translated below.

(*e*) The proceedings of the Second Council of Nicaea (AD 787) are contained in several Greek and Latin manuscripts, and also in the Latin version by Anastasius.[5] Citations in them from the Acts of John 27–8, 93–5, and 97–8 are valuable for establishing the Greek text at these points (see Junod and Kaestli *CCA*, pp. 344–68).

The condemnation of the Acts of John by the Second Council of Nicaea meant that the ancient Acts could only survive in clandestine copies after 787. Parts survived in the rewritings of the story of John found in Pseudo-Prochorus, and (in Latin) in Pseudo-Abdias and Pseudo-Melito. It is perhaps

---

[3] Also in Junod and Kaestli, *CCA*, pp. 814–27, and see their discussion on pp. 782–90.

[4] See M. Herbert and M. McNamara, *Irish Biblical Apocrypha* (Edinburgh, 1989), 91–4, esp. 93. The text is to be found in Hennecke[5] (German), ii. 191–3; (Eng. trans.), ii. 210–12.

[5] J. C. Thilo, *Colliguntur et commentariis illustrantur fragmenta actuum S. Johannis a Leucio Charino Conscriptum*, i. in *Universitatis Literariae Fridericianae Halis consociatae programma paschale* (Halle, 1847), 14 f.

an oversimplification to suggest that these later works represent Catholic expurgated editions of the original Acts, because much in the original Acts was not heretical and thus not in need of censorship anyway. The rewritings more accurately represent retellings of popular stories that were already well-known in the wider church. It may even be suggested that some rewriting was motivated by a desire to eliminate prolix passages.

Author
The name Leucius (Charinus) is often associated with the composition of the original Acts of John. From the fourth century onwards his name was added as the author of a large number of pious romances. Possibly he was the author of some early lives of apostles but whether he was the author of the Acts of John (and the Acts of Peter) or any of the other early Acts is not certain.

Date
This is normally given as late second-century, but some scholars (e.g. Zahn) who argued that the work was known to Clement of Alexandria[6] gave an earlier date. Modern scholars tend to agree that there is no firm evidence that the Acts of John was known before Eusebius.

Provenance
This is not clear, although a case could be made for an Egyptian origin.

Sources
The literary style is in general very simple, with ample borrowings from folklore and pagan literature. The canonical Acts of the Apostles seems not to have been a significant influence. The dislocated nature of the surviving scenes, the inclusion of some stories told in the first person, and the presence in various parts of the tradition of floating stories that might have belonged to an early Acts of John make it difficult to evaluate the character and intention of the original composition.

Orthodoxy
In the nineteenth century these Acts were considered to be Gnostic, but recent scholars (since Schmidt and Harnack) have been inclined to identify only docetic or modalist influences. In the most recent study by Junod and Kaestli the 'unorthodox' nature of the text has been identified as being restricted to only a few chapters, namely 94–102 and 109, where a Valentinian Gnostic influence has resulted in a differing Christology from that seen in chs. 87–93. They conclude that these chapters were added to the original

---

[6] 'Fragments', ed. O. Stählin, GCS 17 (Leipzig, 1909);[2] rev. L. Früchtel and U. Treu (Berlin, 1970) 210, with reference perhaps to Acts of John 93.

Acts of John and were not composed by the same author. Also included in the section 87–105 is the Hymn of Christ (set to music by Gustav Holst), which many scholars have argued is also likely to have come from a separate source.

Translation

The translation below is based on Bonnet 18–115, with attention to the edition of the Acts by Junod and Kaestli, *CCA*, especially with regard to their new chapters 56–7 and to certain textual variants within sections 58–81 and elsewhere. Gaps in the texts are indicated by dots (. . .) in the translation. Translations of P. Oxy. 850 and from Pseudo-Abdias and Pseudo-Titus are also included.

EDITIONS

Greek

Lipsius–Bonnet ii.1, 151–216.
James, *Apoc. Anec.* ii. 1–25, 144–53 (edition of Acts of John 87–105 MS C: Greek with Engl. trans.). [Cf. James's note in *JTS* 7 (1906), 566–8.]
P. Oxy. 850, ed. B. P. Grenfell and A. S. Hunt, *OP* 6 (London, 1908), 12–19.
E. Junod and J.-D. Kaestli, *Acta Iohannis* (Turnhout, 1983), 2 vols. (= *Corpus Christianorum; Series Apocryphorum* 1 and 2) (with full discussion of text, and with commentary. The story of the Sons of Antipatros occurs as Acts of John, chs. 56–7; see id., 'Un fragment inédit des Actes de Jean; la guérison des fils d'Antipatros à Smyrne', *Museum Helveticum* 31 (1974), 102).[7] [Abbreviated as Junod and Kaestli, *CCA*.]

VERSIONAL EVIDENCE FOR THE METASTASIS

Syriac

Wright, *Apoc. Acts*, i. 66–72; ii (Eng. trans.), 61–8. [Cf. Lipsius, i. 431–41.]

Coptic

E. A. Wallis Budge, 'The Repose of Saint John the Evangelist and Apostle' [British Museum MS Oriental 6782], in *Coptic Apocrypha in the Dialect of Upper Egypt* (London, 1913), 51–8; Eng. trans., 233–40.
Guidi, *AAL.R* 4, 3.2 (1887), 72–6, 251–70; Italian trans., *Giornale*, 38 ff., 56–66. [Cf. also *AAL.R* 5, 2.7 (1893), 513–30.]
W. E. Crum, *Catalogue of Coptic Manuscripts in the British Library* (London, 1905), 130.
Junod and Kaestli, *CCA* 376–97.

---

[7] Review by W. Schneemelcher, *Rivista di Storia e Letteratura Religiosa* 22 (1980), 358–71.

Armenian

J. Katergian, *Ecclesiae Ephesinae de obitu Ioannis Apostoli Narratio ex versione armeniaca saeculi V* (Vienna, 1877), 32–51 (with Latin trans.).

Malan, 244–8 (Eng. trans. of an apocryphal text in an edition of the Armenian Bible).

Georgian

M. van Esbroeck, 'Les formes géorgiennes des Acta Iohannis', *Anal. Boll.* 93 (1975), 11–19 (Latin trans. of Kekelidze's text and Latin version of a different Georgian text). [Cf. M. Tarchnišvili, *Geschichte der kirchlichen georgischen Literatur* (Rome, 1955), 342 f. (= *Studi e Testi* 185).

Arabic

Smith Lewis, *Acta Myth.* 46–51 (based on a Coptic original; an Arabic text from Syriac, but close to the Greek, is given on 144–6);[8] *Myth. Acts*, 54–9, 168–71. [Cf. Graf, i. 258–64.]

Slavonic

de Santos Otero, *Altslav. Apok.* i. 97–123; ii. 244–6.

The Slavonic Metastasis seems to be from the Acts of John of Pseudo-Prochorus (see Hennecke[5], ii. 151, 390; Eng. trans. ii. 163, 434–5).

Ethiopic

Malan, 137–45.
Wallis Budge, *Contendings*, i. 214–22; ii (Eng. trans.), 253–63.

MODERN TRANSLATIONS

English

Pick, 123–99 (includes 1–17).
James, 228–70.
Hennecke[3], ii. 188–259. Hennecke[5], ii. 152–209.

French

Amiot, 157–84 (extracts).
A.-J. Festugière, *Les Actes apocryphes de Jean et de Thomas* (Geneva, 1983), part I. *Actes de Jean* (= *Cahiers d'Orientalisme* 6).
Junod and Kaestli, *CCA* 160–315.
Éac, 975–1037.

---

[8] This continues an Arabic text of *The History of John, Son of Zebedee*, an independent story of John based on a Syriac original. (*Horae Semiticae* 2, 134–44; Eng. trans. ibid 4, 157–67.)

German

Hennecke[1], 423–59 (G. Schimmelpfeng); cf. id. Handbuch, 492–543.
Hennecke[3], ii. 125–76 (K. Schäferdiek).
Hennecke[5], ii. 138–93 (K. Schäferdiek).
Michaelis, 222–68.

Italian

Moraldi, ii. 1131–1212;[2] ii. 211–302 (Lipsius-Bonnet, chs. 18–105, acts from Ps.-Abdias and Ps.-Melito (some summarized), chs. 106–115, various conclusions, Borgia Coptic fragment, P. Oxy. 850, Ps.-Titus, 2nd. ed. includes Acts of John by Procurus).
Erbetta, ii. 29–67 (34–9 = Lipsius–Bonnet, chs. 1–17; 40–67 = chs. 18–115).

HYMN OF CHRIST (= Acts of John 94–7)

D. I. Pallas, "ὁ ὕμνος τῶν πράξεων τοῦ Ἰωάννου κεφ. 94–7", in *Mélanges offerts à Octave et Melpo Merlier* (Athens, 1956), ii. 221–64 (= *Collection de l'Institut français d'Athènes* 93).
J. S. MacArthur, 'The Words of the "Hymn of Jesus"', *ExpT* 36 (1924–5), 186–8.
W. C. van Unnik, 'A Note on the Dance of Jesus in the "Acts of John"', *VC* 18 (1964), 1–5.
J. J. Thierry, *Christ in Early Christian Greek Poetry* (Leiden, 1972), 32–7.
M. Brioso, 'Sobre el "Tanzhymnus" de *Acta Ioannis* 94–6', *Emerita* 40 (1972), 31–45.
A. J. Dewey, 'The Hymn in *The Acts of John*: Dance as Hermeneutic', in D. R. MacDonald (ed.), *The Apocryphal Acts of the Apostles* (Decatur, Ga., 1986), 67–80 (= *Semeia* 38) (with response by J.-D. Kaestli, 81–8).

GENERAL

P. Corssen, *Monarchianische Prologe zu den vier Evangelien: Ein Beitrag zur Geschichte des Kanons* (Leipzig, 1896), esp. 73–102 (= *TU* 15.1).
T. Zahn, 'Die Wanderungen des Apostels Johannes', *NKZ* 10 (Erlangen, 1899), 191–218.
Harnack, i. 124–7; ii. 1, 541–9.
Lipsius, i. 2, 348–542.
R. H. Connolly, 'The Original Language of the Syriac Acts of John', *JTS* 8 (1907), 249–61.
Findlay, 208–37.
W. von Loewenich, *Das Johannes-Verständnis im zweiten Jahrhundert* (Giessen, 1932) (= *BZNW* 13).
C. R. C. Allberry, *A Manichaean Psalm-Book* (Stuttgart, 1938) (= *Manichaean Manuscripts in the Chester Beatty Collection* 2).
S. G. Hall, 'Melito's Paschal Homily and the *Acts of John*', *JTS* 17 (1960), 95–8.
F. Corsaro, *Le Praxeis di Giovanni* (Catania, 1968) (= *Centro Studi sull'antico cristianismo: Miscellanea di studi di letteratura cristiana antica* 18).
J. D. Breckenridge, 'Apocrypha of Early Christian Portraiture', *ByzZ* 67 (1974), 101–9.

Vielhauer, 706–10.

E. Junod and J.-D. Kaestli, 'Les traits caractéristiques de la théologie des *Actes de Jean*', *Revue de Théologie et de Philosophie* 26 (1976), 125–45.

Plümacher, cols. 14–19.

E. Junod and J.-D. Kaestli, *L'Histoire des Actes apocryphes des apôtres du IIIe au IXe siècle: Le cas des Actes de Jean* (Geneva, Lausanne, Neuchâtel, 1982) (= *Cahiers de la Revue de Théologie et de Philosophie* 7).

K. Schäferdiek, 'Herkunft und Interesse der alten Johannesakten', *ZNW* 74 (1983), 247–67.

E. Junod and J.-D. Kaestli, 'Le Dossier des Actes de Jean: État de la question et perspectives nouvelles', *ANRW* 2.25.6, 4293–4362.

J.-D. Kaestli, 'Le mystère de la croix de lumière et le johannisme, Actes de Jean ch. 94–102', *Foi et Vie 86: Cahier Biblique* 26 (Paris, 1987), 35–46.

G. Sirker-Wicklaus, *Untersuchungen zu den Johannes-Akten* (Bonn, 1988).

J. N. Bremmer (ed.), *The Apocryphal Acts of John* (Kampen, 1995) (= *Studies on the Apocryphal Acts of the Apostles* 1).

P. Lalleman, *The Acts of John* (Leuven, 1998) (= *Studies on the Apocryphal Acts of the Apostles* 4).

THE ACTS OF JOHN

SUMMARY OF CONTENTS

18   From Miletus to Ephesus.

19–36   First Stay in Ephesus:
Lycomedes and Cleopatra raised from the dead by John (19–25). The portrait of John is painted by a friend of Lycomedes (26–9). John's sermon in the theatre prior to a healing of the sick women (absent from the text) (30–6).

Gap. Possibly includes the healing of the women and the story of Andronicus' conversion. The raising of Andronicus and his wife Drusiana is likely to have been included, leading to the sermon given as chs. 87–105 in Bonnet's numeration.

87–105   Discourse on the polymorphous nature of Christ. Hymn of Christ. The revelation of the mystery of the cross.

Stories taken from Pseudo-Abdias (the broken gems; rods and stones turned to gold and jewels; Dives and Lazarus retold and explained; Raising of Stacteus; Aristodemus and the poisoned cup) and P. Oxy. 850 (Zeuxis; John and the soldier) perhaps belong here. They appear in the following translation as an appendix (Allied Texts (*a*) and (*b*)).

37–55   End of First Stay in Ephesus:
Destruction of the Temple of Artemis and conversion of her followers (37–45). Raising of the priest of Artemis (46–7). Story of the parricide (48–54). Call to Smyrna.

Gap (= 56–7). Included are the stories of the healing of the sons of Antipatros, and the partridge. Probably stories concerning the characters referred to in ch. 59 would have occurred in this gap.

The Acts of John

58–61 Return to Ephesus (58–9). The obedient bedbugs (60–1).
62–86, 106–15 Second Stay in Ephesus:
The history of Drusiana and Callimachus (62–86). Final reunion of John and the brethren. John's last act of worship. Prayers and eucharist. John's death (106–15).

18. ...John hastened to Ephesus, prompted by a vision. For this reason Demonicus and his relative Aristodemus and the very rich Cleobius and the wife of Marcellus persuaded him with some difficulty to remain a day at Miletus and they rested with him. When they had left early in the morning and had covered about four miles, a voice from heaven was heard, 'John, you are to procure for your Lord at Ephesus the glory which you know, you and all your brethren with you, and some of those there who shall believe through you.' And John rejoiced, realizing what it might be that was to happen to him at Ephesus, and said, 'Lord, behold I go in accordance with your will. Your will be done.'

19. When we came near the city Lycomedes, the commander-in-chief of the Ephesians, a wealthy man, met us, fell down before John and asked him for help, with these words, 'Your name is John; the God whom you preach has sent you to help my wife, who has been paralysed for seven days and lies past recovery. But glorify your God and treat her out of compassion for us. Whilst I was reflecting what to do, a man came to me and said, "Desist, Lycomedes, from the evil thought which militates against you. Do not submit. For out of compassion for my servant Cleopatra I have sent you a man from Miletus, named John, who will comfort her and restore her to you cured." Delay not, therefore, servant of the God who announced you to me, but hasten to the ailing woman.' And John went at once from the gate with the brethren who were with him, and followed Lycomedes into his house. And Cleobius said to his servants, 'Go to my relative Callippus and make yourselves comfortable in his house—for I am coming there with his son— that we may find everything prepared!'

20. When Lycomedes and John had come into the house in which the woman was lying, he grasped his feet again, and said, 'See, Lord, the lost beauty, see the youth, see the much talked of bloom of my unhappy wife, the admiration of all Ephesus! Woe to me, unhappy man! I was envied, humbled, the enemy's eye was fixed on me. I never wronged anyone, although I could harm many. I envisaged this situation and I was always anxious to experience no sorrow or anything like it! Of what use is my care now, Cleopatra? What good was it to me, that I was called godly to this day? I suffer more than a heathen, seeing you, Cleopatra, suffering so. The sun in his circuit shall not see me, if you are no more with me. Cleopatra, I will die before you. I will not spare my life though I am still youthful. I will justify myself before the goddess of right, whom I served in righteousness, though I might indict her for her unrighteous sentence. I will avenge myself on her by coming as a shade. I will

say to her, 'You have forced me to leave the light of life, because you tore away Cleopatra. You are the cause of my death, by having prepared for me this fate. You have forced me to blaspheme Providence by destroying my joy.'

21. And Lycomedes spoke more to Cleopatra, went to her couch, and cried bitterly. But John drew him away and said, 'Abandon these tears and unbecoming words! It is not proper for you, who saw the vision, to be disbelieving. Know that your partner for life will be restored to you. Therefore join us, who have come for her sake, and pray to the God whom you saw, when he showed me to you in a vision! What is the matter, Lycomedes? Wake up and open also your soul! Cast from you heavy sleep! Call on the Lord, beseech him for your wife, and he will support her.' But he fell to the ground and wept dejectedly. And John said with tears, 'Woe to the treachery of the vision, woe to the new temptation prepared for me, woe to the new craft of him who devises cunnings against me! Did the voice from heaven, which came to me by the way, intend this for me, predicting to me what should here take place? Will it deliver me up to such a great multitude of citizens, for the sake of Lycomedes? The man lies here lifeless, and I know that I shall not leave this house alive. Why do you delay, Lord? Why have you deprived us of your gracious promise? I beseech you, Lord, let not him rejoice who delights in the sorrow of others. Let him not dance who always laughs at us! But let your holy name and your compassion come quickly! Waken the bodies of the two, who are against me!'

22. While John was crying, the city of Ephesus ran to the house of Lycomedes, supposing him dead. And when John saw the great multitude, he prayed to the Lord, 'Now the time of refreshing[1] and confidence has come with you, O Christ; now is the time for us weary ones to have help from you, physician, who heal freely. Keep my entrance here free from derision! I beseech you, Jesus, help such a great multitude to come to the Lord of the universe. Behold the affliction, behold those who lie here! Even those who came here, make holy instruments for your service, after they have seen your gift. For you have said yourself, O Christ, "Ask and it shall be given you."[2] We therefore beseech you, O King, not for gold, not for silver, not for riches, not for possession, nor for any transient, earthly goods, but for two souls through whom you will convert those present to your way, to your knowledge, to your confidence and to your infallible promise. For many of them shall be saved, after they have known your power through the resurrection of the departed. Give us, therefore, hope in you! I will go to Cleopatra and say, "Arise, in the name of Jesus Christ."'

23. And he went, touched her face, and said, 'Cleopatra, he whom every ruler fears, and every creature, power, abyss, and darkness and unsmiling death and the heights of heaven and the caverns of the lower world and the

---

[1] Cf. Acts 3: 19. [2] Matt. 7: 7 and parallel.

The Acts of John

resurrection of the dead and the sight of the blind and the whole power of the ruler of the world, and the pride of its prince, says, "Rise and become not a pretext for many who will not believe, and an affliction for souls who hope and could be saved."' And Cleopatra cried out at once, 'I will rise, master, save your handmaiden!' When she had risen after the seven days, the whole city of Ephesus was stirred by the miraculous sight. And Cleopatra asked for her husband Lycomedes. John answered, 'Cleopatra, if you have a steadfast and firm soul, you shall immediately see your husband beside you, provided you do not become excited and confounded by what took place, but believe in my God, who through me will give him to you alive. Follow me into another room, and you shall see him dead but he will rise up by the power of my God.'

24. And Cleopatra followed John into her room, and saw Lycomedes dead because of her. Her voice failed, she gnashed her teeth, bit her tongue, closed her eyes, and began to weep. And she looked silently at the apostle. And John felt sorry for Cleopatra and, seeing that she became neither distraught nor excited, he called upon the perfect mercy free from arrogance, saying, 'Lord Jesus Christ, you see this self-control; you see that she imposes restraint on herself; you see how Cleopatra's soul cries in silence. For she hides within herself insufferable grief. And I know that she will die yet because of Lycomedes.' And in a low voice she said to John, 'This I have in my mind, master, and nothing else.' And the apostle went to the couch, on which Lycomedes lay, seized the hand of Cleopatra, and said, 'Cleopatra, because of the people who stand by and because of your relatives who have come, call to your husband, "Arise, and glorify God's name, because he gives the dead to the dead!"' And she went and spoke to her husband as she was told, and immediately she raised him. Having risen, he fell down and kissed the feet of John. And he lifted him up and said, 'Man, kiss not my feet, but God's, by whose power both of you have risen!'

25. And Lycomedes said to John, 'I beseech and adjure you by the God in whose name you have revived us, stay with us, both you and your companions.' Likewise Cleopatra grasped his feet and said the same. And John answered, 'To-morrow I will be with you.' And they said again to him, 'We have no hope in your God, but would be revived in vain, if you did not stay with us.' And Cleobius, Aristodemus, and Demonicus, grieved to the very heart, said to John, 'Let us abide with them, that they remain unsullied before the Lord!' So he remained there with the brethren.

26. And a great multitude gathered together because of John. And while he was preaching to those present, Lycomedes, who had a talented painter as friend, ran to him and said, 'You see that I have come to you. Come quickly to my house, and paint the man whom I shall point out, without his perceiving it.' And the painter gave the necessary instruments and colours to some one, and said to Lycomedes, 'Point him out to me, and have no worry for the rest!'

And Lycomedes pointed out John to the painter, and brought him into a room close by, from which the apostle of Christ could be seen. And Lycomedes remained with the blessed man, united in faith and in the knowledge of our God; but rejoiced still more that he was to have him in a portrait.

27. On the first day the painter made the outline and left; on the following day he completed the picture and gave it to Lycomedes, who rejoiced. He took it, put it in his bedchamber, and put garlands on it. And John, who saw it much later said to him, 'My beloved child, what are you doing when upon leaving the bath you go alone into your bedchamber? Am I not to pray with you and the other brethren? Or are you hiding something from us?' Saying this and jesting, he entered the room with him. And he saw the crowned picture of an old man, and candlesticks and an altar before it. And he said to him, 'Lycomedes, what does this picture mean to you? Is it a picture of one of your gods? I see that you are still living like a heathen!' Lycomedes replied, 'He alone is my God who has revived me and my wife from the dead. But if one is permitted next to God to call those gods who are our benefactors, then it is you, father, who are painted in the picture, whom I crown, love, and worship as having become my good guide.'

28. And John who had never yet seen his own face, said to him, 'You mock me, child. Do I look like this? By your Lord, how will you convince me that the picture is like me?' And Lycomedes brought a mirror. And when John saw himself in the mirror, he said 'As the Lord Jesus Christ lives, the picture resembles me, child, but is not like me, only like the image of my body. For if that painter, who copied my face in the picture, will paint me, he would now lack the colours given to you as well as tables and opportunity (?) and access (?) and carriage and form and age and youth and everything visible.[3]

29. 'But, Lycomedes, you must be a good painter to me. You have colours, which Jesus gives you through me, who paints us all for himself, who knows the shape and form and gesture and disposition and image of our souls. And the colours which I bid you use are: belief in God, knowledge, fear of God, love, fellowship, meekness, goodness, brotherly love, chastity, integrity, firmness, fearlessness, cheerfulness, honesty. And the whole range of colours, which represents your soul in the picture, and already supports your prostrated members which rose, appeased, delivered from plagues, heals your wounds, arranges your entangled hair, washes your face, trains your eyes, purifies your heart, empties your stomach, and mutilates your abdomen. In short, if all such colours are combined and mixed in your soul, they will make it bold, intrepid, and firm, and bring it to our Lord Jesus Christ. But what you have done now is childish and imperfect: you have painted the dead picture of what is dead.'

30. And he ordered brother Verus, who ministered to him, to bring all the

---

[3] Text obscure.

old women in the whole of Ephesus, whilst he himself and Cleopatra and Lycomedes made the necessary preparations to care for them. And Verus came and told John, 'Of the more than sixty old women who live here, I found only four in a healthy state; of the rest some are paralysed and some otherwise sick.' When John heard it, he remained silent for some time, rubbed his face, and said, 'Oh, the indolence of those who dwell in Ephesus! Oh, the despair and weakness in the faith in God! Oh, devil who mocked all this time at the believers in Ephesus! Jesus, who gives me grace and the gift to trust in him, speaks quietly to me now, "Have the sick women brought, come with them to the theatre, and heal them through me! For of those who will come to this spectacle are some which I will convert by such cures, that they may be of some use."'

31. When all the people had met at Lycomedes' house on account of John, he dismissed them, saying, 'All of you who wish to know the power of God, come to the theatre tomorrow!' On the following day, while it was still dark, the people ran to the theatre. The proconsul also went there and sat among the people. A captain, Andronicus, at that time one of the most prominent Ephesians, said, 'John has promised impossible and incredible things. But if he can really do what I hear he boasts about let him come to the theatre naked, without holding anything in his hands; let him not pronounce that magic name which I heard him name!'

32. Upon hearing this and moved by these words, John had the old women brought to the theatre. When they were brought there on couches, some asleep, and after the whole city had gathered, a great silence ensued and John opened his mouth and spoke thus:

33. 'Men of Ephesus, first know why I visit your city... or what is my confidence towards you, which is so strong that it even became known to this assembly, to all of you. I have not been sent with a human message, nor a hopeless journey. I am no merchant who buys or exchanges goods; but Jesus Christ, of whom I preach, will, in his mercy and goodness, convert you all through me and deliver you from your error, who are domineered by unbelief and are sold into ignominious lusts. By his power I will also confound your captain in his unbelief by raising up those who are before us, whose external condition and diseases are visible to you all. And this I cannot do if they perish; so they shall be healed.

34. 'There is, however, one thing first which I would implant into your ear: I have come to you to care for your souls, so that you do not think that this time will last to all eternity, which is rather a time of bondage, and that you do not lay up for yourselves treasures upon earth, where everything withers away. Do not think, if you have children, to rest on them, and do not seek to rob and defraud on their account! Do not mourn, you who are poor, if you cannot serve your desires! For even those who are rich call you happy when they are sick. And you who are rich, rejoice not because you have treasures! For their

possession causes you unlimited sorrow, if you lose them. And again, when you have them, you must be afraid that some one might kill you because of them.

35. 'And you who are proud of bodily beauty, and give haughty looks, you will see the end of the promise only when you come to the grave. You who delight in adultery, know that law and nature revenge themselves on you, and above all the conscience! And you, adulteress, who trespassed against the law, you do not know where you will end up. If you kept your treasures without helping the poor, having left this body and being in the flames of the fire, you will find no one who will have mercy on you when you are begging for mercy. You who are hot-tempered and raging, know that you live like brutes. You drunkard and brawler, realize that you lose your senses by serving a vile, filthy passion!

36. 'You who have pleasure in gold and ivory and precious stones, do you see the things you love when the night has set in? You who indulge in soft raiment and depart this life, will these help you in the place you go to? Let the murderer know that the merited punishment is double in the time after he goes from here! In like manner the poisoner, sorcerer, robber, defrauder, sodomite, thief, and all who belong to that band, accompanied by your works you shall go into the fire that never shall be quenched, to utter darkness, to the pit of torture, and to external damnation. Therefore, men of Ephesus, repent; understand also that kings, rulers, tyrants, boasters, warmongers depart naked from this world, to suffer pain in everlasting torments!'
Having thus spoken, John healed all their diseases by the power of God...[4]

87.[5] ... Then those who were present inquired about the cause, and were especially perplexed because Drusiana had said, 'The Lord appeared to me in the tomb in the form of John and of a youth.' And as they were perplexed and in some ways were not yet confirmed in the faith, John said with patience:

88. 'Men and brethren, you have suffered nothing that is strange or incredible in your perception of the Lord, inasmuch as we also, whom he chose for himself as apostles, were tried in many ways. I, indeed, am able neither to set forth to you nor to write the things which I saw and heard. Now I must adapt them to your hearing; and in accordance with everyone's capabilities I will communicate to you those things whereof you are able to become hearers, that you may see the glory that surrounds him who was and is both now and for ever.

'For when he had chosen Peter and Andrew, who were brothers, he came to me and to my brother James, saying, "I have need of you, come unto me." And my brother said, "John, this child on the shore who called to us, what

---

[4] This summary sentence, often numbered as the beginning of ch. 37, must be an abridgement of a much longer narration. The manuscript does not indicate a break, but much text has been lost: this is likely to have included the conversion of Drusiana and Andronicus.

[5] Chs. 37–86 follow 87–105.

does he want?" And I said, "What child?" He replied, "The one who is beckoning to us." And I answered, "Because of our long watch that we kept at sea you are not seeing straight, brother James: but do you not see the man who stands there, fair and comely and of a cheerful countenance?" But he said to me, "Him I do not see, brother; but let us go and we shall see what it means." And so when we had landed the ship, we saw him helping us to beach the ship.

89. 'And when we left the place, wishing to follow him again, he again appeared to me, bald-headed but with a thick and flowing beard; but to James he appeared as a youth whose beard was just starting. We were perplexed, both of us, as to the meaning of what we had seen. But when we followed him, we both became gradually more perplexed as we thought on the matter. Yet to me there appeared a still more wonderful sight; for I tried to see him as he was, and I never at any time saw his eyes closing but only open. And sometimes he appeared to me as a small man and unattractive, and then again as one reaching to heaven. Also there was in him another marvel; when I sat at table he would take me upon his breast and I held him; and sometimes his breast felt to me to be smooth and tender, and sometimes hard, like stone, so that I was perplexed in myself and said, "What does this mean?" And when I was thinking of these things....[6]

90. 'At another time he took me and James and Peter to the mountain, where he used to pray, and we beheld such a light on him that it is not possible for a man who uses mortal speech to describe what it was like. Again in a similar way he led us three up to the mountain saying, "Come with me." And we went again and saw him at a distance praying. Now I, because he loved me, went to him quietly as though he should not see, and stood looking upon his back. And I saw that he was not dressed in garments, but was seen by us as naked and not at all like a man; his feet were whiter than snow, so that the ground there was lit up by his feet, and his head reached to heaven; so that I was afraid and cried out, and he turned and appeared as a man of small stature, and took hold of my beard and pulled it and said to me, "John, be not unbelieving, but believing, and not inquisitive." And I said to him, "What have I done, Lord?" And I tell you brethren, I suffered such pain for thirty days at the place where he took hold of my beard, that I said unto him, "Lord, if your playful tug has given me so much pain, what if you had given me a beating?" And he said to me, "Let it be your concern from henceforth not to tempt him who is not to be tempted."

91. 'But Peter and James were angry because I spoke with the Lord and beckoned me to come to them and leave the Lord alone. And I went, and they both said to me, "Who was speaking to the Lord when he was on top of the mountain, for we heard both of them speaking?" And I, when I considered his

---

[6] Gap in text.

great grace and his unity which has many faces, and his wisdom which without ceasing looked upon us, said, "This you shall learn if you ask him."

92. 'Again when all of us disciples were once sleeping in a house at Gennesaret, after wrapping myself up I watched what he did, and first I heard him say, "John, go to sleep." And thereupon I feigned to be asleep; and I saw another like him whom I also heard saying to my Lord, "Jesus, those whom you have chosen still do not believe in you." And my Lord said to him, "You are right, for they are men."

93. 'Another glory I will tell you, brethren. Sometimes when I meant to touch him, I met a material and solid body; and at other times again when I felt him, the substance was immaterial and bodiless and as if it were not existing at all. Now, if at any time he were invited by one of the Pharisees and went where he was invited, we went with him. And there was set before each one of us a loaf of bread by our host, and he also received a loaf. And he would bless his own and divide it amongst us; and from that little piece each of us was filled, and our own loaves were saved intact, so that those who had invited him were amazed. And often when I was walking with him I wished to see whether the print of his foot appeared upon the earth—for I saw him raising himself from the earth—but I never saw it. Now, these things, dear brethren, I speak to you to encourage you in your faith towards him, for we must at the present keep silent about his mighty and wonderful works, inasmuch as they are mysteries and doubtless cannot be uttered or heard.

94. 'Now, before he was arrested by the lawless Jews, who received their law from a lawless serpent, he gathered us all together and said, "Before I am delivered up to them, let us sing a hymn to the Father, and go forth to what lies before us." So he commanded us to make a circle, holding one another's hands, and he himself stood in the middle. He said, "Respond Amen to me." He then began to sing a hymn, and to say:

"Glory be to you, Father!"
And we circling him said, "Amen".
"Glory be to you, Word! Glory be to you, Grace!" "Amen."
"Glory be to you, Spirit! Glory be to you, Holy One! Glory be to the glory!" "Amen."
"We praise you, O Father. We give thanks to you, light, in whom darkness does not abide." "Amen."

95. "Now we give thanks, I say:
I will be saved, and I will save." "Amen."
"I will be loosed, and I will loose." "Amen."
"I will be pierced, and I will pierce." "Amen."
"I will be born, and I will bear." "Amen."
"I will eat, and I will be eaten." "Amen."

"I will hear, and I will be heard." "Amen."
"I will be understood, being wholly understanding." "Amen."
"I will be washed, and I will wash." "Amen."

Grace is dancing.

"I will pipe, dance all of you!" "Amen."
"I will mourn, lament all of you!" "Amen."
"An Ogdoad[7] is singing with us." "Amen."
"The Twelfth number is dancing above." "Amen."
"The whole universe takes part in the dancing." "Amen."
"He who does not dance, does not know what is being done." "Amen."
"I will flee and I will stay." "Amen."
"I will adorn, and I will be adorned." "Amen."
"I will be united, and I will unite." "Amen."
"I have no house, and I have houses." "Amen."
"I have no place, and I have places." "Amen."
"I have no temple, and I have temples." "Amen."
"I am a lamp to you who see me." "Amen."
"I am a mirror to you who perceive." "Amen."
"I am a door to you who knock on me." "Amen."
"I am a way to you, wayfarer." "Amen."

96. '"Now if you respond to my dancing, see yourself in me who speak; and when you have seen what I do, keep silence about my mysteries! You who dance, perceive what I do; for yours is this passion of mankind which I am to suffer! For you could not at all have comprehended what you suffer if I had not been sent to you as the Word by the Father. When you saw what I suffer, you have seen me as one suffering; and seeing that, you have not stood firm but were wholly moved. Moved to become wise, you have me for a support. Rest upon me! Who am I? You shall know when I go away. What I am now seen to be, that I am not. You shall see when you come. If you knew how to suffer, you would have had the power not to suffer. Learn suffering, and you shall have the power not to suffer. That which you do not know, I will teach you. I am your God, not that of the betrayer. I will that there be prepared holy souls for me. Know the word of wisdom! Say again with me:

Glory be to you, Father; glory be to you, Word;
Glory be to you, Holy Ghost!

Now concerning me, if you would know what I was: with a word I once deceived all things, and was not put to shame at all. I have leaped; but

---

[7] i.e. the eightfold power.

understand the whole, and having understood it say, "Glory be to you, Father!" "Amen."[8]

97. 'After this dance, my beloved, the Lord went out; and we were as men gone astray or dazed with sleep, and we fled all ways. Even I, when I saw him suffer, did not abide at his passion but fled to the Mount of Olives, weeping over what had taken place. And when he was hung upon the cross on Friday, at the sixth hour of the day, there came darkness over all the earth. And my Lord stood in the middle of the cave and lit it up, and said, "John, to the multitude down below in Jerusalem I am being crucified, and pierced with lances and reeds, and gall and vinegar is given me to drink. But to you I am speaking, and pay attention to what I say. I put it into your mind to come up to this mountain, so that you might hear matters needful for a disciple to learn from his teacher, and for a man to learn from his God."

98. 'And having said this, he showed me a cross of light set up, and around the cross a great multitude which had no one form; and in the cross was one form and one likeness. And the Lord himself I beheld above the cross, not having a shape, but only a voice, and a voice not such as was familiar to us, but a sweet and kind voice and one truly divine, and it said to me, "It is necessary that one man should hear these things from me, O John, for I have need of someone who will hear. This cross of light is sometimes called the Word by me for your sakes, sometimes Mind, sometimes Jesus, sometimes Christ, sometimes Door, sometimes Way, sometimes Bread, sometimes Seed, sometimes Resurrection, sometimes Son, sometimes Father, sometimes Spirit, sometimes Life, sometimes Truth, sometimes Faith, sometimes Grace. Thus it is called for man's sake. But in truth, as known in itself and as spoken to us, it is the marking off of all things and the uplifting and foundation of those things that are fixed but had been unstable, and the harmony of the wisdom and indeed the wisdom of the harmony. But there are on the right and on the left, powers, principalities, dominions and demons, operations, threatenings, wrath, devils, Satan and the inferior root, from which the nature of the transient things proceeded.

99. '"This, then, is the cross which has united all things by the Word, and marked off things transient and inferior, and then compacted all into one. But this is not the cross of wood which you will see when you go down here, neither am I he who is upon the cross, whom now you do not see, but only hear a voice. I was reckoned to be what I am not, not being what I was to

---

[8] Fragments of this hymn (chs. 95–6) cited in Augustine, *ep.* 237, are (Goldbacher's page and line):

I will save, and I will be saved. (530. 17)   I will loose, and I will be loosed. (529. 3 and 29)   I will be born. (531. 4)   I will sing, dance all of you. (531. 7 and 9)   I will lament, beat you all yourselves. (531. 12)   I will adorn, and I will be adorned. (531. 13 f.)   I am a lamp to you who see me. (531. 18)   I am a door to you who knock on me. (531. 20 f)   You who see what I do, keep silence about my works. (531. 26)   By the Word I mocked at all things, and I was not mocked at all. (532. 17 f.)

many others; but they will call me something else, which is vile and not worthy of me. Therefore, just as the place of rest is neither seen nor spoken of, much less shall I, the Lord of this place, be seen or spoken of.

100. '"Now the multitude about the cross which is the lower nature is not of one form; and those whom you see in the cross, do not have one form. That is because every member of him who came down has not yet been gathered together. But when the nature of man shall be taken up, and the race which comes to me in obedience to my voice, then he who now hears me shall be united with it and shall no longer be what it now is, but shall be above them, as I am now. For as long as you do not call yourself mine, I am not that which I was. But if you hear and hearken to me, then you shall be as I am, and shall be what I was, when I have you with myself. For from this you are.[9] Therefore, ignore the many, and despise those who are outside the mystery! Know that I am wholly with the Father, and the Father with me.

101. '"Therefore I have suffered none of the things which they will say of me: that suffering which I showed to you and to the rest in dance, I wish it to be called a mystery. For what you are, you see that I showed you; but what I am, that I alone know, and no one else. Let me, therefore, keep that which is my own, and that which is yours you must see through me. As for seeing me as I am in reality, I have told you this is impossible unless you are able to see me as my kinsman. You hear that I suffered, yet I suffered not; that I suffered not, yet I did suffer; that I was pierced, yet was I not wounded; hanged, and I was not hanged; that blood flowed from me, yet it did not flow; and, in a word, those things that they say of me I did not endure, and the things that they do not say those I suffered. Now what they are I will reveal to you for I know you will understand. Perceive in me the slaying of the Logos, the piercing of the Logos, the blood of the Logos, the wounding of the Logos, the hanging of the Logos, the passion of the Logos, the nailing of the Logos, the death of the Logos. And thus I speak, discarding manhood. Therefore, in the first place think of the Logos, then you shall perceive the Lord, and thirdly the man, and what he has suffered".

102. 'When he had spoken to me these things and others which I know not how to say as he would have me, he was taken up, without any of the multitude having seen him. And when I went down, I laughed them all to scorn, inasmuch as he had told me the things which they said about him; and I held firmly this one thing in my mind, that the Lord contrived all things symbolically and as a dispensation toward men, for their conversion and salvation.

103. 'Therefore, brethren, having seen the grace of the Lord and his affection toward us, let us worship him as those to whom he has shown mercy, not with our fingers, nor with our mouths, nor with the tongue, nor with any

---

[9] Text obscure.

part of our body whatsoever, but with the disposition of our soul: let us worship him, who became man apart from this body. And let us watch because he keeps watch even now over prisons for our sakes, and in tombs, in bonds and dungeons, in shame and reproaches, by sea and land, at scourgings, condemnations, conspiracies, plots, punishments, and, in a word, he is with all of us, and suffers with us when we suffer, brethren. When he is called by any one of us he does not allow himself to shut his ears to us, but being everywhere he hearkens to all of us, and just now has hearkened to both me and Drusiana—as he is the God of those who are imprisoned—bringing help to us by his own compassion.

104. 'You therefore must also be persuaded, beloved, that it is no man that I preach to you to worship, but God unchangeable, God invincible, God higher than all authority, and all power, and older and mightier than all the angels and creatures that are spoken of, and all ages. If then you abide in him, and are built up in him, you shall possess your soul indestructible.'

105. And when he had delivered these things to the brethren, John departed with Andronicus to walk; and Drusiana also followed afar off together with all, that they might behold the acts that were done and at all times hear his word in the Lord...[10]

37. And the brethren from Miletus said to John, 'We have remained a long time at Ephesus. If you agree, let us go to Smyrna. For we already hear that the wonderful works of God have been heard of there.' And Andronicus said, 'If it pleases the master, then let us go!' John said, 'First let us go to the temple of Artemis! For if we are seen there we shall be able to find ministers of the Lord.'

38. After two days the birthday of the idol's temple was celebrated. While everybody was dressed in white garments, John wore black and went to the temple. They laid hold of him and tried to kill him. But John said, 'Men, you are mad to lay hold of me, the servant of the only God.' And climbing on to the platform he spoke to them:

39. 'Men of Ephesus, you are in danger of behaving like the sea. Every discharging river and every precipitating spring, downpours and incessant waves and torrents rushing from the rock, are permeated by the bitter salt which is in the sea. Thus to this day you are unchangeably hostile to true piety, and you perish in your old idolatry. How many miraculous deeds did you see me perform, how many cures! And still you are hardened in the heart and cannot see clearly. What now, men of Ephesus? I have ventured now to come up to this idol's temple, to convince you that you are wholly without God and dead to human reasoning. Behold, here I stand. You all assert that Artemis is powerful. Pray to her, that I alone die! Or if you cannot accomplish this, I alone will call upon my God to kill you all because of your unbelief.'

---

[10] MS C adds 'now, always and for eternity, Amen'. Several episodes are missing at this point.

40. Since they already knew him and had seen the dead raised, they cried aloud, 'Do not treat us so and kill us, we beseech you, John; we know indeed that you can do it.' And John answered them, 'If you do not wish to die, let me convince you of your idolatry. And why? So that you may desist from your old error. Be now converted by my God or I will die at the hands of your goddess. For I will pray in your presence to my God, and ask him to have mercy upon you.'

41. After these words he prayed, 'God, who are God above all so-called gods, who to this day have been despised at Ephesus, you induced me to come to this place, which I never had in view. You have abrogated every form of worship through conversion to you. In your name every idol, every demon, and every unclean spirit is banished. May the deity of this place, which has deceived so many, now also give way to your name, and thus show your mercy on this place! For they walk in error.'

42. And with these words of John the altar of Artemis suddenly split into many parts, and the oblations put up in the temple suddenly fell to the ground, and its glory[11] broke, and so did more than seven of the idols. And half of the temple fell down, so that when the roof came down, the priest also was killed at one stroke. And the people of the Ephesians cried, 'There is only one God, that of John, only one God who has compassion for us; for you alone are God; now we have become converted, since we saw your miraculous deeds. Have mercy upon us, God, according to your will, and deliver us from our great error.' And some of them lay on their faces and cried; others bent their knees and prayed; others rent their garments and lamented; still others tried to escape.

43. And John stretched out his hands and prayed with uplifted soul to the Lord, 'Glory be to you, my Jesus, the only God of truth, who procure your servants in manifold ways!' And after these words he said to the people, 'Rise up from the ground, men of Ephesus, pray to my God, and know how his invisible power was made manifest and his miraculous deeds took place before your eyes! Artemis herself should have helped. Her servant should have received help from her and not have died. Where is the power of the deity? Where are the sacrifices? Where the birthday? Where the festivals? Where the garlands? Where the great enchantment and the poison allied to it?'

44. And the people rose up from the ground and made haste to destroy the remainder of the temple, crying, 'We know that the God of John is the only one, and henceforth we worship him, since we have obtained mercy from him.' And as John came down, many of the people touched him, saying, 'Help us, John, help us who die in vain! You see our intention; you see how the multitude following you cleaves to hope in your God. We have seen the way in

---

[11] Text obscure. Junod and Kaestli, p. 222, conjecture 'arch' from Greek 'toxon' instead of 'doxon' ('glory').

which we have gone astray when we were lost. We have seen that our gods were erected in vain. We have seen their great and disgraceful derision. But give us, we beseech you, help without hindrance, when we have come to your house! Receive us, who are desperate!'

45. John answered them, 'Men, believe that it was for your sakes that I remained at Ephesus, although I was anxious to go to Smyrna and the other cities, so that the people there may become converted to him as servants of Christ. But when I was about to leave and my mind was not yet completely at ease about you, I remained praying to my God and asked him that I should leave Ephesus only after I had strengthened you. Since I see that this is done, and is increasing, I shall not leave until I have weaned you like children from the milk of the nurse, and have set you upon a firm rock.'

46. So John remained with them, and received them in the house of Andronicus. And one of those gathered there placed the body of the priest of Artemis before the gate, for he was a relative, and quickly came in with the others without saying anything to anyone. After John's homily to the brethren, prayer and eucharist, and the laying on of hands on each person assembled, he said, moved by the Spirit, 'There is present someone, brought here through faith in God, who has laid the priest of Artemis before the gate and come in, because in the desire of his soul he placed the care for his soul first, reasoning thus within himself, "It is better to care for the living than for the body of my relative. For I know that by turning to the Lord and saving my own soul John will not refuse to raise the dead."' And John rose from his place and went to the place where the relative of the priest who had had these thoughts was standing, and taking him by the hand he said, 'Were these not your thoughts, as you came to me, child?' And he answered tremblingly, 'Yes, lord!', and fell down at his feet. And John said, 'Our Lord is Jesus Christ, who will prove his power on the body of your relative by raising him.'

47. And lifting up the young man, he took him by the hand, and said, 'It is not a great task for a man who is lord over great mysteries to bother himself with small things. Or is it important to drive away bodily diseases?' And still holding the young man by the hand he said, 'I say to you, son, go, and raise the dead man yourself without saying anything else but this: "The servant of God, John, says to you, Arise!"' And the young man went to his relative and said in the presence of many people these words only, and then returned to John bringing him in alive. When he saw him who had been raised, he said, 'You have been raised and are indeed not really living, and are not partaker and heir of the true life. Will you belong to him by whose name and power you have been raised? Believe now and you shall live in all eternity.' He immediately believed in the Lord Jesus and followed John.

48. On the following day, having seen in a vision that he was to walk three miles outside the gates, John did not hesitate, but rose early in the morning, and went with the brethren. And a young farmer, having been admonished by

his father not to take to himself the wife of his fellow labourer, as the other threatened to kill him, was offended at his father's warning, and suddenly killed him.[12] When John had perceived what had taken place, he said to the Lord, 'Lord, was it because of this that you told me to come here to-day?'

49. When the young man saw the hasty death, he was afraid of being seized, took the sickle from his girdle, and ran to the house. When John met him, he said, 'Stand still, you villainous demon! Where are you running with that bloodthirsty sickle?' The young man, confused, let the weapon drop to the ground, and said to him, 'I have knowingly committed a monstrous, inhuman deed; therefore, I resolve to do something more violent and more cruel to myself, to die once for all. For whilst my father always exhorted me to lead a chaste and honourable life, I could not tolerate his censure, and struck and killed him. And when I saw what had taken place, I intended to go to the woman on whose account I had become a parricide and try to kill her and her husband and finally myself. For I could not bear her husband seeing me being executed.'

50. And John said to him, 'I will not go away and leave you in danger nor shall I give a chance to him who would laugh and mock you. Come with me and show me where your father is! And if I raise him up for you, how will I keep you away from the woman who has become dangerous to you?' The young man replied, 'By giving me back my father alive, and by seeing and hearing him, I will keep away from her.'

51. And thus speaking, they came to the place where the body of the old man lay. Other travellers stood by. John said to the young man, 'Unhappy one, not even the age of your father was spared by you.' And he wept, tore his hair, and confessed he felt sorry. But the servant of the Lord, John, prayed, 'You who have this day shown me the way here, who knew that this deed was to take place, before whom no deed in human life can be hidden, who granted to me every healing and cure according to your will, grant to me also that the old man may live, since you see how the murderer became his own judge! And spare him, O Lord, although he did not spare his father, from whom he received such good advice!'

52. After these words he went to the old man and said, 'My Lord shall not be powerless to extend to you his good compassion and his mercy free from presumption. Arise, therefore, and give God glory for the present work.' And the old man said, 'I rise, Lord.' And he arose and, having seated himself, he said, 'I was delivered from a life of the most fearful pain. I had to suffer many fearful abuses and unkindness from my son; and now, man of the living God, you have called me back: to what purpose?' John replied: 'If you rise up to the same life, you would be better to remain dead. But rise up to a better!' And he took him, brought him to the city, and preached to him of the mercy of God, so that before he came into the gate the old man believed.

---

[12] Variant: 'kicked him and left him speechless'.

53. And when the young man saw the unexpected resurrection of his father and his own salvation, he took the sickle and cut off his genitals. And running into the house where he kept his adulteress, he flung them at her saying, 'On your account I became a parricide and should also become a murderer both of you two and myself. Here is the cause of all. God has had mercy upon me, because I have seen his power.'

54. He returned to John, and in the presence of the brethren told what he had done. But John said to him, 'The one who induced you, young man, to kill your father and to become the lover of another man's wife, has also made you cut off your genitals as if it were a righteous work. But you should not have destroyed your private parts for the temper which proved itself evil through the members. For your organs are not hurtful to man, but the hidden sources, by which every shameful inclination is stirred and becomes manifest. Repent, therefore, my son, this fault, and recognize Satan's cunnings, and you shall have God, who helps you in all that your soul needs.' And the young man led a quiet life in repentance for his former sins, that he might obtain forgiveness through God's goodness, and he did not leave John.

55. While he was performing these deeds at Ephesus, the people in Smyrna sent messengers to him saying, 'We hear that God whom you preach is an unenvious God, and has bidden you not to show partiality and remain in one place. Being the preacher of such a God, come to Smyrna and the other cities, that we may know your God and, knowing him, put our hope in him ...

(A gap follows. A travel narrative seems to have disappeared at this point. Many editors place here, as chs. 56-7, the story of John and the partridge, found in MS Q. Junod and Kaestli print as their chs. 56-7 a story set in Smyrna found in MSS L and S. Both are now translated below.)

A. John and the Partridge

56. One day John was seated and a partridge flew through the air and was playing in the sand before him. John looked at this with amazement. And a priest, one of the hearers, came to John and saw the partridge playing before him. He was offended and said to himself, 'Such a great man rejoices over a partridge playing in the sand!' But John perceived his thoughts and said to him, 'It would be better if you, too, my son, would look at a partridge playing in the sand, and not contaminate yourself with disgraceful and impure acts. He who expects the repentance and conversion of all has brought you here for this purpose. For I have no need of a partridge playing in the sand. The partridge is your soul.'

57. When the old man heard this and perceived that he was not unknown, but that Christ's apostle had said everything which was in his heart, he fell to the ground and said, 'Now I know that God dwells in you, blessed John. And blessed is he who has not tempted God in you! He who tempts you, tempts

him who cannot be tempted.' And he asked him to pray for him. And he instructed him, gave him commandments, dismissed him and praised God who is over all.

B. *John in Smyrna: The Sons of Antipatros*

56. Then leaving Ephesus we came to Smyrna. All the town gathered together when it learned of John's presence. And a man called Antipatros, a prominent resident of Smyrna, came to John and said, 'Servant of God, I have heard tell that you have performed many good and great wonders in Ephesus. Behold, I offer you a hundred thousand gold pieces. I have twin sons who since birth have been possessed of a demon and who have suffered terribly: they are thirty-four years old. In one moment both may fall faint, sometimes in the baths, sometimes while walking, often while eating, and sometimes even at a public gathering in town. You will see for yourself that they are well-built men, but they are overcome by this malady that possesses them every day. I pray you, assist me in my old age. I am quite prepared to take a deadly decision. As children they suffered slightly, but since becoming adults their demons have grown up too. Take pity on me and on them.' John said to him, 'My healer works without payment, and heals freely; in exchange for illness he accepts the souls cured. What are you prepared to give, Antipatros, in exchange for your sons? Give your soul to God and you will find your sons in good health by the power of Christ.' But Antipatros said, 'Until now you have neglected no one, do not neglect my sons. With the agreement of my kinsfolk I was prepared to end the derision and poison them, but you who have come as a faithful doctor invested by God, for their sake, enlighten them and help them.'

57. John, who had been called to help, said to the Lord, 'You who always console the downtrodden and who called me to aid, you who have never waited to be called to console because you are present before we seek your assistance, make the evil spirits be discharged from the sons of Antipatros.' And immediately they left them. John ordered the sons to come to him. When the father saw them in good health, he fell to the ground prostrate before John. John, having instructed them about Father, Son and Holy Ghost, baptized them. John besought Antipatros to give his money to those in need, and he dismissed them and they praised and blessed God.

FROM LAODICEA TO EPHESUS THE SECOND TIME[13]

58. Some time passed without any of the brethren being distressed by John. But now they were distressed when he said, 'Brethren, it is time for me to go

---
[13] Heading as in MSS M and O.

to Ephesus; for such is my agreement with those who live there, so that they may not become slack through being for a long time without their pastor. But you must direct your mind to God, who does not desert us. And when the brethren heard this, they became sad that they should be separated from him. And John said, 'Though I go from you, Christ is always with you. If you love him purely, you shall continually enjoy the blessing of his communion. For where he is loved, he loves those first who love him.'

59. Having spoken thus, and having instructed them, he left a large amount of money to the brethren for distribution, and went to Ephesus, leaving all the brethren sorrowing and weeping. Those who were with him from Ephesus were Andronicus and Drusiana, Lycomedes and Cleobius, and their attendants. They were followed by Aristobula, who had heard that her husband Tertullus had died on the way, Aristippus with Xenophon, and the chaste prostitute, and many others whom he always directed to the Lord and who would never leave him.

60. On the first day we came to a lonely inn, and when we were trying to find a bed for John we experienced a strange event. There was one bedstead without covers over which we spread our cloaks which we had brought and requested him to lie down and to rest, whilst we slept on the floor. He had hardly lain down, when he was molested by bugs. But as they became more and more troublesome, and as it was midnight already, we all heard him say to them, 'I say to you, you bugs, be considerate; leave your home for this night and go to rest in a place which is far away from the servants of God!' And while we laughed and talked, John fell asleep. And we conversed quietly, and thanks to him we remained undisturbed.

61. When it was day, I rose first, and with me Verus and Andronicus. And in the door of the room which we had taken was a mass of bugs. And having called all the brethren, we went outside to have a full view of them. John was still asleep. When he woke up we showed him what we had seen. And sitting up in bed and seeing them, he said, 'Since you have been wise to heed my warning, go back to your place!' When he had spoken and had risen from the bed, the bugs hastened from the door to the bed, ran up the legs into the joints and disappeared. And John said again, 'This creature heard the voice of a man and kept quiet and was obedient. We, however, hear God's voice, and yet irresponsibly transgress his commandments. And how long will this go on?'

62. After this we came to Ephesus. And when the brethren who lived there had learned that John had returned after this long time, they met in the house of Andronicus, where he also was staying, grasped his feet, put his hands to their faces, and kissed them because they had touched his clothes.[14]

63. And while great love and endless joy prevailed among the brethren,

---

[14] Variant deletes 'because ... clothes'.

one, a servant of Satan, coveted Drusiana, although he saw and knew that she was the wife of Andronicus. Very many people remonstrated with him, 'It is impossible for you to obtain this woman, especially since she has separated even from her husband out of piety. Or do you alone not know that Andronicus, who was not the godly man he now is, had locked her up in a tomb, saying, "Either I'll have you as a wife, as I had you before, or you must die!" And she preferred to die rather than to commit the repugnant act. Now, if out of piety she withheld her consent to sexual intercourse with her husband and master, but persuaded him to become like-minded, should she consent to you, who wish to commit adultery with her? Desist from your passion, which gives you no rest! Desist from your scheme, which you cannot accomplish!'

64. Though his intimate friends remonstrated with him, they could not persuade him. He was even so impudent as to send word to her. When Drusiana heard of his disgraceful passion and shameless demands, she became very despondent, and after two days she was feverish. She said, 'Oh, if I only had not come back to my native city where I have become a stumbling-block to a man who believes not in the worship of God! For if he were filled with God's word, he would not fall into such a passion. Therefore, O Lord, since I have become accessory to a blow which struck an ignorant soul, deliver me from this prison and take me soon to you!' And without being understood by anyone Drusiana departed this life in the presence of John, not rejoicing but sorrowing over the physical trouble of that man.

65. And Andronicus was sad and carried a hidden sorrow in his heart, and wept bitterly, so that John could only silence him by saying to him, 'Drusiana has departed this unjust life for a better hope.' To this answered Andronicus, 'Of this I am certain, John, and I have no doubt in the belief in my God. My hopes are grounded on the fact, that she departed this life pure.'

66. After she was interred, John took Andronicus aside, and having learned of the cause he sorrowed more than Andronicus. And he kept silence, considering the threats of the enemy, and sat still a little. When the brethren were assembled to hear which words he would say concerning the departed, he began to speak:

67. 'When the helmsman who crosses the ocean has landed with the ship and passengers in a quiet haven free from storms, he feels secure. The husbandman who sowed the seed-grains in the ground and cared for them with great pains is only then to enjoy a rest from his labours when he has harvested abundant corn in his barns. Whoever promises to take part in a race should rejoice only when he has obtained the prize. He whose name is entered on the list of prize-fighting should triumph only after he receives the crowns. And thus it is with all races and skills, when they do not fail at the end, but are carried out, as they were intended.

68. 'So I think it is with the faith which every one of us practises, and which can be decided as having been the true one only when it remains the

same to the end of life. For there are many obstacles which cause unrest to human reasoning: cares, children, parents, glory, poverty, flattery, youth, beauty, boasting, desire for riches, anger, pride, frivolity, envy, passion, carelessness, violence, lust, slaves, money, pretence, and all the other similar obstacles which exist in life; it is the same for the helmsman who takes his course for a quiet journey and is opposed by the adverse winds and a great tempest and a mighty wave, when the heaven is serene; it is the same for the husbandman who is opposed by untimely weather and blight and creeping worms appearing from the ground; for the athletes, the near miss, and for the craftsman the obstacles to their skills.

69. 'The believer must above all things consider the end and carefully examine how it will come, whether energetic[15] and sober and without impediment, or in confusion and flattering worldly things and bound by passions. Thus one can praise the beauty of the body only when it is completely naked; and the greatness of the general when he has happily finished the whole campaign as he promised; and the excellence of the physician when he has succeeded in every cure; and so one praises a soul filled with faith and worthy of God if it has happily accomplished that which it promised, not one which made a good beginning, and gradually descended into the errors of life and became weak, nor the numb soul which made an effort to attain higher things and was afterwards reduced to perishable, nor that which loved the temporal more than the eternal, nor that which exchanged the perishable for the lasting, nor that which honoured what was not to be honoured and loved works of dishonour, nor that which accepted pledges from Satan and received the serpent into its house, nor one which was reviled for God's sake and afterwards was ashamed, nor one which consented with the mouth but did not show it by the deed; but we praise one which refused to be inflamed by filthy lust, to succumb to levity, to be ensnared by thirst after money, or to be betrayed by the strength of the body and anger.'

70. While John continued to preach to the brethren that they despise earthly goods for the sake of the eternal ones, the lover of Drusiana, inflamed by the influence of the polymorphous Satan to the most ardent passions, bribed the greedy steward of Andronicus with money. And he opened the tomb of Drusiana and left him to accomplish on the body that which was once denied to him. Since he had not procured her during her lifetime, he continually thought of her body after she was dead, and exclaimed, 'Although when living you refused to unite with me in love, after your death I will dishonour your corpse.' Being in such a frame of mind he obtained the opportunity to execute his impious plan through the accursed steward, and both went to the tomb. Having opened the door, they began to take the graveclothes from the corpse, and said, 'What have you gained, unhappy

---

[15] Text unclear.

Drusiana? Could you not have done this while you were alive? It need not have grieved you if you had done it willingly.'

71. Whilst they spoke and only the shift remained, there appeared something wonderful, which people that do such things deserve to experience.[16] A serpent appeared from somewhere, bit the steward, and killed him. And the serpent did not bite the young man, but encircled his feet, hissing fearfully, and when he fell down, the serpent sat on him.

72. On the following day John and Andronicus and the brethren went at the break of day to the tomb in which Drusiana had been for three days, so that we might break bread there. And when we were about to start, the keys were not to be found. And John said to Andronicus, 'It is right that they are lost, for Drusiana is not in the tomb. Nevertheless, let us go, that you do not appear neglectful, and the doors will open of themselves, since the Lord has already given us many other things.'

73. When we came to the place, the doors opened at the master's[17] behest, and at the tomb of Drusiana we saw a beautiful youth smiling. When John saw him, he exclaimed and said, 'Do you come before us here also, noble one? And why?' And he heard a voice saying to him, 'For the sake of Drusiana, whom you are to raise up. I found her almost defiled on account of the dead man lying near the tomb.' And when the noble one had thus spoken to John he ascended to heaven before the eyes of all. And John turned to the other side of the tomb and saw a young man, the very prominent Ephesian Callimachus—for this is what he was called—and on him a huge snake sleeping, also the steward of Andronicus, named Fortunatus, dead. On seeing both, he stood helpless and said to the brethren, 'What does all this mean? Or why did the Lord not reveal to me what took place here, for he was always concerned for me?'

74. When Andronicus saw these bodies, he jumped up and went to the tomb of Drusiana. And when he saw her in her shift, he said to John, 'I understand what took place, blessed servant of God. This Callimachus loved my sister. And as he could not get her, although he tried it often, he no doubt bribed this accursed steward of mine with a great sum of money with the intention—as one can now see—to accomplish his purpose through him. For this Callimachus said to many, "If she will not yield to me alive, rape shall be committed on her death." This, O master, the noble one saw and did not allow her earthly remains to be violated. That is why those who engineered this are dead. And the voice which came to you "Raise Drusiana!" foretold this. For she departed this life through sorrow. And I believe him who said that this is one of the men who was led astray. For you were asked to raise him. As for the other I know that he does not deserve salvation. But one thing I ask of you. Raise Callimachus first, and he shall confess what took place.'

---

[16] Following MS M in Bonnet.   [17] Some MSS read 'John's'.

75. And John looked at the corpse and said to the poisonous snake, 'Depart from him who is to serve Jesus Christ!' Then he rose and prayed, 'God, whose name is rightly praised by us; God, who overcomes each harmful work; God, whose will is done, who always hears us, make your grace now efficacious on this youth! And if through him some dispensation is to take place, make it known to us, when he is raised!' And the young man immediately arose and kept silence for a whole hour.

76. When the man had regained his senses, John asked what his intrusion into the tomb meant. And having learned from him what Andronicus had already told him, how he passionately loved Drusiana, John asked further whether he had accomplished his wicked design to commit rape on the holy earthly remains. And he replied, 'How could I have accomplished this when this fearful beast killed Fortunatus with one bite before my eyes? And this deservedly so, for he encouraged me to such madness, after I had already desisted from the ill-timed and dreadful frenzy—but he frightened me and put me in the state in which you saw me, before I arose. But I will tell you another greater miracle, which nearly slew me and almost killed me. When my soul was seized with mad passion and the incurable disease was troubling me, when I had already robbed her of the grave-clothes with which she was dressed, and went from the grave to put them down as you see, I turned back to perpetrate the abominable deed. And I saw a beautiful youth covering her with this cloak. Rays of light fell from his face upon hers, and he turned to me also and said, "Callimachus, die, that you may live." Who it was, I knew not, servant of God. Since you have come here, I know that it was an angel of God. And this I truly know, that the true God is preached by you; and I am sure of it. But I pray you, see to it that I may be delivered from this fate and dreadful crime, and bring me to your God as a man who had gone astray in scandalous, abominable, deceit. On my knees I ask for your help. I will become one of those who hope in Christ so that the voice may also prove true, which spoke here to me, "Die to live!" And it is already fulfilled. For that unbeliever, godless, lawless man, is dead; I am raised by you as a believer, faithful and godly, that I may know the truth, which I ask of you to reveal to me.'

77. And John, rejoicing, contemplated the whole spectacle of the salvation of men and said, 'O Lord Jesus Christ, I do not know what your power is. I am amazed at your great mercy and endless forbearance. Oh, what greatness descended to servitude! O unspeakable freedom, which was enslaved by us! O inconceivable glory, which has come upon us! You have kept the grave from shame, and redeemed that man who contaminated himself with blood, and taught him to be chaste who meant to violate dead bodies. Father, full of mercy and compassion toward him who disregarded you, we praise, glorify, and honour you and thank you for your great goodness and long-suffering,

holy Jesus, for you alone are God and none else; you, against whose power all devices can do nothing now and in all eternity! Amen!'[18]

78. After these words, John took Callimachus, kissed him, and said, 'Glory be to our God, who had mercy upon you, child, and deemed me worthy to praise his power, and delivered you by a wise method from that madness and intoxication and called you to rest and renewal of life.'

79. When Andronicus saw that Callimachus had been raised from the dead, he and the brethren besought John to raise Drusiana also, and said, 'John, let her be raised and happily complete life's short space, which she gave up out of sorrow for Callimachus, because she thought she was a temptation to him! And when it pleases the Lord, he will take her to himself.' And without delay John went to the grave, seized her hand and said, 'You who alone are God, I call upon you, the immense, the unspeakable, the incomprehensible, to whom all worldly power is subject, before whom every authority bows, before whom every pride falls down and is silent, before whose voice the demons are confounded, at whose contemplation the whole creation surrenders in quiet meditation. Your name will be hallowed by us. Raise Drusiana that Callimachus be still further strengthened in you who alone can do what is wholly impossible with man, and have given salvation and resurrection, and let Drusiana come out comforted because, in consequence of the conversion of the youth, she no more has the least impediment to long for you!'[19]

80. Having spoken thus John said, 'Drusiana, arise!' And she arose and came from the tomb. And when she saw that she wore nothing but her shirt, she was perplexed how to explain what had happened. Having learned everything from Andronicus, while John was upon his face and Callimachus with tears praised God, she also rejoiced and praised God.

81. Having dressed herself and looked around, she saw Fortunatus. And she said to John, 'Father, he too shall rise, though he tried so much to become my betrayer.' When Callimachus heard her speaking thus, he said, 'No, I beg you, Drusiana. For the voice which I heard did not mention him, but only concerned you, and when I saw I believed. If he were good, God out of mercy would have certainly raised him through the blessed John. He knew that the man should have a bad death.' And John answered him, 'My son, we have not learnt to recompense evil with evil. For God has not recompensed the evil which we have done to him, but has given us repentance. And although we did not know his name, he did not forget us, but had mercy upon us. And when we reviled him, he forsook us not, but was merciful. And when we were disbelieving, he remembered not the evil. And when we persecuted his

---

[18] A different version of this prayer is given in *CCA* i. 278–81.
[19] Text obscure.

brethren, he did not requite us, but made us repent, turn away from sin, and called us to himself, as he called you also, child Callimachus, and, without remembering your former sins, made you his servant through his long-suffering mercy. If you do not wish me to raise Fortunatus, let Drusiana do it.'

82. Without wavering, but in the joy of her spirit and soul, she went to the body of Fortunatus and said, 'God of the ages, Jesus Christ, God of truth, you allowed me to see signs and wonders and granted me to partake of your name. You breathed into me your spirit with your polymorphous face, and showed much compassion. With your rich goodness, you protected me when my former husband, Andronicus, did violence to me, and gave me your servant Andronicus as a brother. Until now you have kept me, your maiden, pure. You raised me when I was dead through your servant John. To me, risen and freed from offence, you showed me him who was offended at me. You gave me perfect rest in you, and delivered me from the secret madness. I love you with all my heart. I beseech you, Christ, not to dismiss Drusiana's petition, who asks of you the resurrection of Fortunatus, though he tried so much to become my betrayer.'

83. And she took the hand of the dead man and said, 'Rise, Fortunatus, in the name of our Lord Jesus Christ!' And Fortunatus rose up. And seeing John in the tomb and Andronicus and Drusiana risen from the dead and Callimachus now a believer, he said, 'O how far the power of these awful people has spread! I wish I were not raised, but remained dead, so as not to see them.' And with these words he ran from the tomb.

84. And when John perceived the unchangeable soul of Fortunatus, he said, 'O nature, unchanged for the better! O source of the soul, remaining in the filth! O essence of corruption, full of darkness! O death, dancing among those belonging to you! O fruitless tree, full of fire![20] O wood, producing coal as fruit! O forest, with trees full of unhealthy shoots,[21] neighbour of unbelief! You showed us who you are, and you will always be convicted with your children. And the power of praising higher things is unknown to you, for you do not have it. Therefore as your issue is, so is your root and nature. Vanish away from those who hope in the Lord—from their thoughts, from their mind, from their souls, from their bodies, from their action, from their life, from their conversation, from their activity, from their deeds, from their counsel, from their resurrection to God, from their fragrance which you will share, from their fastings, from their prayers, from their holy baptism, from their eucharist, from the nourishment of their flesh, from their drink, from their dress, from their agape, from their acts of mourning, from their continence, and from their righteousness. From all these, most unholy and

---

[20] Variant adds 'O trunk, having a demon for reason'.
[21] Or 'O matter that dwells with the madness of matter'.

abominable Satan, shall Jesus Christ, our God and judge of those who are like you and your nature, remove you.'

85. After these words John prayed, fetched a loaf of bread to the tomb to break it, and said, 'We praise your name, who have converted us from error and unmerciful lusts. We praise you who have brought before our eyes that which we saw. We bear witness to your goodness manifested to us in various ways. We hallow your gracious name, Lord, and thank you who have convicted those who are convicted by you. We thank you, Lord Jesus Christ, that we believe in your unchangeable mercy.[22] We thank you that you are in need of a saved human nature. We thank you that you gave this sure faith, that you alone are God, now and for ever. We, your servants, thank you, O holy One, we who are assembled with good reason and risen from the dead.'

86. Having thus prayed and praised God, he made all the brethren partake of the eucharist of the Lord and then left the tomb. And when he had come into the house of Andronicus, he said to the brethren, 'Dear brethren, a spirit within me has prophesied that, in consequence of the bite of the serpent, Fortunatus would die of blood-poisoning.[23] Let someone make haste and inquire whether it is so!' And one of the young men ran and found him dead already, the poison[23] having spread and reached his heart. And he returned to John, reporting that he had been dead three hours already. And John said, 'You have your child, devil!'

Thus John rejoiced with the brethren in the Lord.[24]

106.[25] On the following day, which was the Lord's day, he began to say to them in the presence of the brethren, 'Brethren, fellow-servants, coheirs, and copartners in the kingdom of the Lord, you know the Lord, how many powers he has given you through me, how many miracles, what cures, signs, gifts, teachings, rulings, times for relaxation, services, knowledge, glories, graces, gifts, acts of faith, communion, which you have seen with your eyes, were given you by him, though they cannot be seen with these eyes and cannot be heard with these ears. Be strong, therefore, in him, remembering him in all your doings, knowing the mystery of the dispensation that has come to men, and why the Lord has so acted. He, then, through me, exhorts you, since he wishes you to remain without grief, without insult, without treachery, without punishment. For he also knows insult comes from you, he knows also dishonour, treachery, and punishment, if you disobey his commandments.

107. 'So let not our good God be grieved, the compassionate, the merciful, the holy, the undefiled, the immaterial, the only, the one, the immutable, the sincere, the guileless, the patient, he who is higher and more exalted than every name that we speak or think of, our God Jesus Christ! Let him rejoice

---

[22] Conjecture (Bonnet).
[23] Literally 'blackness'.
[24] *CCA* i. 292–3 links this sentence with the beginning of ch. 106.
[25] Chs. 87–105 follow ch. 36.

along with us, because we behave well; let him be glad because we live in purity. Let him be refreshed because our behaviour is sober. Let him be unconcerned because we are temperate, let him be pleased because we live in fellowship, let him smile because we are chaste, and let him be delighted because we love him! These things, brethren, I communicate to you, pressing on to the work prepared for me, already perfected for me by the Lord. For what else have I to say to you? You have the sureties of our God. You have the pledges of his goodness, you have his sure presence. And if you, then, sin no more, he will forgive you what you have done in ignorance. But if, after you have known him and he has had compassion upon you, you return to such deeds, even your former offences will be laid to your charge, and you shall have no part or mercy in his presence.'

108. And when he had said this to them, he prayed, 'Jesus, who have woven this crown by your twining, who have inserted these many flowers into the everlasting flower of your countenance, who have sown these words into my soul, who are the only protector and physician of your servants, who heal freely; you who are benign and not haughty, alone merciful and kind, alone a Saviour and righteous; you who always see what concerns all, and are in all, and everywhere present, comprising all and replenishing all, Christ Jesus, God, Lord, who with your gifts and your compassion protect those who hope in you; who know intimately all the cunnings and threats by which our adversary contrives against us everywhere. O Lord, only help your servants with your watchful care. So be it, Lord.'

109. And having asked for bread, he gave thanks, saying, 'What praise or what sort of offering or what thanksgiving shall we invoke as we break the bread, but you only, Lord Jesus? We glorify the name spoken by the Father. We glorify the name spoken through the Son. We glorify you as the entrance door; we glorify your resurrection manifested to us through you. We glorify your way; we glorify your seed, your word, your grace, your faith, your salt, your unspeakable pearl, your treasure, your plough, net, greatness, diadem, him called Son of man for our sakes, who has given us truth, rest, knowledge, power, commandment, trust, hope, love, freedom, and place of refuge in you. For you alone, O Lord, are the root of immortality and the fountain of incorruption, and seat of the ages; you have been called all these names for our sakes, so that now we, calling upon you through them, may recognize your greatness, which we cannot see at the present, but which is only visible to the pure, solely in the image of the man portrayed in you!'

110. And having broken the bread, he gave it to us, praying for each of the brethren, that he might be worthy of the grace of the Lord and his most holy eucharist. He also partook of it and said, 'To me also let there be a portion with you, and peace be with you, my beloved.'

111. And he said to Verus, 'Take two brethren with you with baskets and shovels and follow me!' And Verus did immediately what John, the servant of

God, had bidden him.[26] And the blessed John went from the house and walked outside the gates, having told the multitude to leave him. And having come to the tomb of one of our brethren, he told the young men, 'Dig, my sons!' And they dug, and he said to them, 'Let the trench be deeper.' And as they dug, he preached to them the word of God, and exhorted those who had come out of the house with him, building them up and preparing them for the majesty of God, and praying for each one of us. And when the young men had finished the trench as he had wished, while we were kept in ignorance, he took off the clothes he had on, and laid them, as if they were bedding, at the bottom of the trench; and standing in only his vest, stretched forth his hands, and prayed:

112. 'O God, who have chosen us for the apostleship among the Gentiles, who have sent us into this world; who have declared yourself through the Law and the prophets; who have never rested, but from the foundation of the world always save those who can be saved; who have made yourself known through all nature, even among the animals; who have made the lonely and wild soul quiet and peaceable; who have given yourself to it when thirsting after your words; who quickly showed yourself to it when about to die, and appeared as a law when it sank into lawlessness; who manifested yourself to it when overcome by Satan; who have overcome its adversary when it took refuge in you; who have given it your hand and raised it from the works of Hades; who did not allow it to walk in the body; who have shown it its own enemy; who have given it a pure knowledge of you, God Jesus, Father of the supernatural, ruler of those in heaven, law of things ethereal, the course of things in the air, guardian of those on earth and terror of those under the earth, and grace of your own people; receive also the soul of your John, which is certainly deemed worthy of you!'

113. 'You who have preserved me also till the present hour pure to yourself, and free from intercourse with a woman; who, when I inclined in my youth to marry, appeared to me and said, "I am in need of you, John"; who prepared for me beforehand my bodily weakness; who, on the third occasion when I wished to marry, prevented me immediately, and said to me at the third hour on the sea, "John, if you were not mine, I would let you marry"; who for two years blinded me, letting me mourn and be dependent on you; who in the third year opened up the spiritual eyes, and gave me back my visible eyes; who, when I regained my sight, disclosed to me the repugnance of gazing upon a woman; who delivered me from temporary show, and guided me to eternal life; who separated me from the foul madness of the flesh; who snatched me from bitter death, and presented me only to you; who silenced the secret disease of the soul, and cut off its open deed; who afflicted and banished him who rebelled in me; who established a spotless friendship to

---

[26] *CCA* i. 304–5 adds these two sentences to the end of ch. 110.

you; who prepared a safe way to you; who gave me undoubting faith in you; who have traced out for me pure thoughts toward you; who have given the due reward to every deed; who have set it in my soul to have no other possession than you alone—for what can be more precious than you? Now, since I have accomplished your stewardship with which I was entrusted, make me worthy, O Lord, of your repose, and give me my end in you, which is the unspeakable and ineffable salvation.'

114. 'And as I go to you, let the fire withdraw; let darkness be overcome; let chaos be powerless; let the furnace grow weak; let hell be extinguished, let the angels get behind me; let the demons be afraid; let the princes be shattered; let the power fall. Let the devil be brought to silence; let Satan be laughed to scorn; let his madness be tamed; let his wrath be broken; let his vengeance be disgraced; let his attack suffer sorrow. Let his children be trodden under foot, and let all his root be destroyed. And grant me to accomplish my journey to you, without suffering insults and abuses; and let me receive what you have promised to those who live in purity and love you only!'

115. And having sealed himself in every part, he stood and said, 'Be with me, Lord Jesus Christ'; he lay down in the grave in which he had spread out his garments. He then said to us, 'Peace be with you, brethren!', and peacefully yielded up the ghost.

ALLIED TEXTS

(a) *Virtutes Iohannis V–VIII*[27]

V. Now on the next day Craton, a philosopher, proclaimed in the market-place that he would give an example of the contempt of riches; and the spectacle was in this manner. He persuaded two young men, the richest of the city, who were brothers, to spend their whole inheritance and each of them buy a jewel, and these they broke in pieces publicly in the sight of the people. And while they were doing this, it happened by chance that the apostle passed by. And calling Craton, the philosopher, to him, he said, 'That is a foolish despising of the world which is raised by the mouths of men, but long ago condemned by the judgement of God. For as that is a vain medicine whereby the disease is not extirpated, so is it a vain teaching by which the faults of souls and of conduct are not cured. But indeed my master taught a youth who desired to attain to eternal life, in these words, saying that if he would be perfect, he should sell all his goods and give to the poor, and so doing he would gain treasure in heaven and find the life that has no ending.'[28] And

---

[27] Following Junod and Kaestli's numbering of the *Virtutes*. The chapters are usually given as 14–18, 20–1.

[28] Mark 10: 17–22 and parallels.

Craton said to him, 'Here the fruit of covetousness is set forth in the midst of men, and has been broken to pieces. But if God is indeed your master and wills that the sum of the price of these jewels should be given to the poor, cause the gems to be restored whole, that what I have done for the praise of men you may do for the glory of him whom you call your master.' Then the blessed John gathered together the fragments of the gems and, holding them in his hands, lifted up his eyes to heaven and said, 'Lord Jesus Christ, to whom nothing is impossible; who, when the world was broken by the tree of concupiscence, restored it again in your faithfulness by the tree of the cross; who gave to one born blind the eyes which nature had denied him; who recalled Lazarus, dead and buried, after the fourth day to the light, and have subjected all diseases and all sicknesses to the word of your power—so also now do with these precious stones which these men, not knowing the fruits of almsgiving, have broken in pieces for the praise of men: recover them, Lord, now by the hands of your angels, that by their value the work of mercy may be fulfilled, and make these men believe in you the unbegotten Father through your only-begotten Son Jesus Christ our Lord, with the Holy Ghost the illuminator and sanctifier of the whole Church, world without end.' And when the faithful who were with the apostle answered and said 'Amen', the fragments of the gems were forthwith so joined that no sign at all that they had been broken remained visible. And Craton, the philosopher, with his disciples, seeing this, fell at the feet of the apostle and believed immediately and was baptized, with them all, and began himself publicly to preach the faith of our Lord Jesus Christ.

Those two brothers, therefore, of whom we spoke, sold the gems which they had bought by the sale of their inheritance and gave the price to the poor; and thereafter a very great multitude of believers began to be joined to the apostle.

VI. And when all this was done, it happened that, after the same example, two honourable men of the city of the Ephesians[29] sold all their goods and distributed them to the needy, and followed the apostle as he went through the cities preaching the word of God. But it came to pass, when they entered the city of Pergamum, that they saw their servants walking abroad arrayed in silken raiment and shining with the glory of this world. It happened that they were pierced with the arrow of the devil and became sad, seeing themselves poor and clad with a single cloak while their own servants were powerful and prosperous. But the apostle of Christ, perceiving these wiles of the devil, said, 'I see that you have changed your minds and your countenances on this account, that, obeying the teaching of my Lord Jesus Christ, you have given all you had to the poor. Now, if you desire to recover that which you formerly possessed of gold, silver, and precious stones, bring me some straight rods,

---

[29] Or rather, as Pseudo-Melito has it, the same two brothers.

each of you a bundle.' And when they had done so, he called upon the name of the Lord Jesus Christ, and they were turned into gold. And the apostle said to them, 'Bring me small stones from the sea-shore.' And when they had done this also, he called upon the majesty of the Lord, and all the pebbles were turned into gems. Then the blessed John turned to those men and said to them, 'Go about to the goldsmiths and jewellers for seven days, and when you have proved that these are true gold and true jewels, tell me.' And they went, both of them, and after seven days returned to the apostle, saying, 'Lord, we have gone about the shops of all the goldsmiths, and they have all said that they never saw such pure gold. Likewise the jewellers have said the same, that they never saw such excellent and precious gems.'

Then the holy John said to them, 'Go, and redeem for yourselves the lands which you have sold, for you have lost the estates of heaven. Buy yourselves silken raiment, that for a time you may shine like the rose which shows its fragrance and redness and suddenly fades away. For you sighed at beholding your servants and groaned that you were poor. Flourish, therefore, that you may fade; be rich for the time, that you may be beggars for ever. Is not the Lord's hand able to make riches overflowing and unsurpassably glorious? But he has appointed a conflict for souls, that they who for his name's sake have refused temporal wealth may believe that they shall have eternal riches. Indeed, our master told us about a certain rich man[30] who feasted every day and shone with gold and purple, at whose door lay a beggar, Lazarus, who desired to receive even the crumbs that fell from his table, and no man gave anything to him. And it came to pass that on one day they both died, and that beggar was taken into the rest which is in Abraham's bosom, but the rich man was cast into flaming fire, out of which he lifted up his eyes and saw Lazarus, and prayed to him to dip his finger in water and cool his mouth, for he was tormented in the flames. And Abraham answered him and said, "Remember, son, that you received good things in your life, but this Lazarus, evil things. Wherefore rightly is he now comforted, while you are tormented, and besides all this, a great gulf is fixed between you and us, so that neither can they come thence hither, nor hither thence." But he answered, "I have five brothers: I pray that someone may go to warn them, that they do not come into this flame." And Abraham said to him, "They have Moses and the prophets, let them hear them." To that he answered, "Lord, unless one rise up again, they will not believe." Abraham said to him, "If they do not believe Moses and the prophets, neither will they believe, even if someone rise again." And these words our Lord and master confirmed by examples of mighty works: for when they said to him, "Who has come hither from there that we may believe him?", he answered, "Bring hither the dead whom you have." And when they had brought to him a young man who was dead, he was awakened by him as if he had been asleep, and confirmed all his words.

[30] Luke 16: 19–31.

'But wherefore should I speak of my Lord, when at this present there are those whom in his name and in your presence and sight I have raised from the dead; in whose name you have seen palsied men healed, lepers cleansed, blind men enlightened, and many delivered from evil spirits? But the riches of these mighty works they cannot have if they have desired to have earthly wealth. Finally, when you yourselves went to the sick and called upon the name of Jesus Christ, they were healed; you drove out devils and restored light to the blind. Behold, this grace is taken from you, and you have become wretched, you who were mighty and great. And whereas there was such fear of you by the devils that at your bidding they left the men whom they possessed, now you will be in fear of the devils. For he who loves money is the servant of Mammon, and Mammon is the name of a devil who is set over carnal gains, and is the master of those who love the world. But even the lovers of the world do not possess riches, but are possessed of them. For it is out of reason that for one belly there should be laid up so much food as would suffice a thousand, and for one body so many garments as would furnish clothing for a thousand men. In vain, therefore, is that stored up which does not come into use, and for whom it is kept no man knows, as the Holy Ghost says by the prophet, "In vain is every man troubled who heaps up riches and knows not for whom he gathers them."[31] Naked did our birth from women bring us into this light, destitute of food and drink; naked will the earth receive us which brought us forth. We possess in common the riches of the heaven; the brightness of the sun is equal for the rich and the poor, and likewise the light of the moon and the stars, the softness of the air and the drops of rain, and the gate of the church and the fount of sanctification, and the forgiveness of sins, and the sharing in the altar, and the eating of the body and drinking of the blood of Christ, and the anointing of the chrism, and the grace of the giver, and the visitation of the Lord, and pardon of sin—in all these the dispensing of the Creator is equal, without respect of persons. The rich man does not use these gifts after one manner and the poor after another.

'But wretched and unhappy is the man who would have something more than he requires; for of this come heats of fevers, rigours of cold, divers pains in all the members of the body, and he can be neither fed with food nor sated with drink; so that covetousness may learn that money will not profit it, which being laid up brings to the keepers thereof anxiety by day and night, and does not permit them even for an hour to be quiet and secure. For while they guard their houses against thieves, till their estate, ply the plough, pay taxes, build storehouses, strive for gain, try to baffle the attacks of the strong, and to strip the weak, exercise their wrath on whom they can, and hardly bear it from others, shrink not from playing at tables and from public shows, fear not to defile or to be defiled, suddenly they depart from this world naked, bearing only their own sins with them, for which they shall suffer eternal punishment.'

[31] Ps. 39 (38): 6.

VII. While the apostle was speaking, behold there was brought to him by his widowed mother a young man who thirty days before had married a wife. And all the people who were waiting upon the burial came with the widowed mother and cast themselves at the apostle's feet with groans, weeping, and mourning, and besought him that in the name of his God he would raise up this young man as he had done with Drusiana. And there was such great weeping that the apostle himself could hardly refrain from crying and tears. He therefore cast himself down in prayer and wept a long time; and rising from prayer he spread out his hands to heaven, and for a long period prayed within himself. And when he had so done three times, he commanded the body which was swathed to be loosed, and said, 'Young Stacteus,[32] who for love of your flesh have quickly lost your soul, youth which knew not your creator, nor perceived the Saviour of men, and were ignorant of your true friend, and therefore fell into the snare of the worst enemy: behold, I have poured out tears and prayers to my Lord for your ignorance, that you may rise from the dead, the bands of death being loosed, and declare to these two, to Atticus and Eugenius, what great glory they have lost, and what great punishment they have incurred.' Then Stacteus arose and worshipped the apostle, and began to reproach his disciples, saying, 'I beheld your angels weeping, and the angels of Satan rejoicing at your overthrow. For now in a little time you have lost the kingdom that was prepared for you, and the dwelling-places built of shining stones, full of joy, of feasting and delights, full of everlasting life and eternal light; and have obtained yourselves places of darkness, full of dragons, of roaring flames, of torments, and punishments unsurpassable, of pains and anguish, fear and horrible trembling. You have lost the places full of unfading flowers, shining, full of the sounds of instruments of music, and have on the contrary obtained places wherein roaring and howling and mourning does not stop day or night. Nothing else remains for you except to ask the apostle of the Lord that just as he raised me to life, he would raise you also from death to salvation and bring back your souls which now are blotted out of the book of life.'

Then both he who had been raised and all the people, together with Atticus and Eugenius, cast themselves at the apostle's feet and besought him to intercede for them with the Lord. The holy apostle gave them this answer: that for thirty days they should offer penitence to God, and in that space pray especially that the rods of gold might return to their nature and likewise the stones return to the baseness of which they were made. And it came to pass that after thirty days were accomplished, and neither the rods were turned into wood nor the gems into pebbles, Atticus and Eugenius came and said to the apostle, 'You have always taught mercy, and preached forgiveness, and urged that one man should spare another. And if God wills that a man should

---

[32] *v.l.* 'Syrice'.

forgive a man, how much more shall he, as he is God, both forgive and spare men. We are confounded for our sin; and whereas we have cried with our eyes which lusted after the world, we do now repent with eyes that weep. We pray you, Lord, we pray you, apostle of God, show in deed that mercy which you have always promised in words.' Then the holy John said to them as they wept and repented, and interceded for them, 'Our Lord God used these words when he spake concerning sinners: "I do not desire the death of a sinner, but I wish rather that he be converted and live."[33] For when the Lord Jesus Christ taught us about the penitent, he said, "Verily I say unto you, there is great joy in heaven over one sinner who repents and turns himself from his sins; and there is more joy over him than over ninety-nine who have not sinned."[34] Wherefore I would have you know that the Lord accepts the repentance of these men.' And he turned to Atticus and Eugenius and said, 'Go, carry back the rods to the wood from which you took them, for now they are returned to their own nature, and the stones to the sea-shore, for they have become common stones as they were before.' And when this was accomplished, they received again the grace which they had lost, so that again they cast out devils as before and healed the sick and enlightened the blind, and daily the Lord did many mighty works by their means...[35]

VIII. Now when Aristodemus, who was chief priest of all those idols, saw this he was filled with a wicked spirit, and stirred up sedition among the people, so that one group of people prepared themselves to fight against the other. And John turned to him and said, 'Tell me, Aristodemus, what can I do to take away the anger from your soul?' And Aristodemus said, 'If you want me to believe in your God, I will give you poison to drink, and if you drink it, and do not die, it will appear that your God is true.' The apostle answered, 'If you give me poison to drink, when I call on the name of my Lord it will not be able to harm me.' Aristodemus said again, 'First I wish you to see others drink it and die straightway, so that your heart may recoil from that cup.' And the blessed John said, 'I have told you already that I am prepared to drink it, that you may believe in the Lord Jesus Christ when you see me whole after drinking the cup of poison.' Aristodemus therefore went to the proconsul and asked of him two men who were to undergo the sentence of death. And when he had set them in the midst of the market-place before all the people, in the sight of the apostle he made them drink the poison; and as soon as they had drunk it, they gave up the ghost. Then Aristodemus turned to John and said, 'Hearken to me and depart from your teaching with which you call away the people from the worship of the gods; or take and drink this, that you may show that your God is almighty if, after you have drunk, you can remain

---

[33] Ezekiel 33: 11.
[34] Luke 15: 7.
[35] A paragraph omitted here tells of the destruction of the temple in Ephesus and the conversion of 12,000 people.

whole.' Then the blessed John, with those who had drunk the poison lying dead, like a fearless and brave man took the cup and, making the sign of the cross, said, 'My God, and the Father of our Lord Jesus Christ, by whose word the heavens were established,[36] unto whom all things are subject, whom all creation serves, whom all power obeys, fears, and trembles, when we call on you for succour; upon hearing whose name the serpent is still, the dragon flees, the viper is quiet, the frog is still and strengthless, the scorpion is quenched, the serpent vanquished, and the spider does no harm; in a word, all venomous things, and the fiercest reptiles and troublesome beasts are covered with darkness, and all roots hurtful to the health of men dry up. I say, quench the venom of this poison, put out its deadly workings, void it of the strength which it has in it, and grant in your sight to all these whom you have created eyes that they may see and ears that they may hear and a heart that they may understand your greatness.' And when he had said this, he armed his mouth and all his body with the sign of the cross and drank all that was in the cup. And after he had drunk, he said, 'I ask that those for whose sake I have drunk be turned to you, O Lord, and by your enlightening receive the salvation which is in you.' And when for the space of three hours the people saw that John was of a cheerful countenance, and that there was no sign at all of paleness or fear in him, they began to cry out with a loud voice, 'He whom John worships is the one true God.'

But even so Aristodemus did not believe, though the people reproached him. But he turned to John and said, 'This one thing I lack: if you in the name of your God raise up these who have died by this poison, my mind will be cleansed of all doubt.' When he said that, the people rose against Aristodemus, saying, 'We will burn you and your house if you go on to trouble the apostle further with your words.' John, therefore, seeing that there was a fierce sedition asked for silence, and said in the hearing of all, 'The first of the virtues of God which we ought to imitate is patience, by which we are able to bear with the foolishness of unbelievers. Wherefore if Aristodemus is still held by unbelief, let us loose the knots of his unbelief. He shall be compelled, even though late, to acknowledge his creator; for I will not cease from this work until a remedy shall bring help to his wounds, and like physicians who have in their hands a sick man needing medicine, so also, if Aristodemus be not yet cured by that which has already been done, he shall be cured by that which I will now do.' And he called Aristodemus to him, and gave him his coat, and he himself stood clad only in his mantle. And Aristodemus said to him, 'Why have you given me your coat?' John said to him, 'That you may even so be put to shame and depart from your unbelief.' And Aristodemus said, 'And how shall your coat make me depart from unbelief?' The apostle answered, 'Go and cast it upon the bodies of the dead, and say: "The apostle of our Lord

---

[36] Ps. 33 (32): 6.

Jesus Christ has sent me that in his name you may rise again, that all may know that life and death are servants of my Lord Jesus Christ."' When Aristodemus had done this, and had seen them rise, he worshipped John, and ran quickly to the proconsul and began to say with a loud voice, 'Hear me, hear me, proconsul; I think you remember that I have often stirred up your wrath against John and devised many things against him daily, and so I fear that I may feel his wrath; for he is a god hidden in the form of a man, and has drunk poison, and not only continues whole, but those who died by the poison he has recalled to life by my means, by the touch of his coat, and they have no mark of death upon them.' When the proconsul heard this he said, 'And what will you have me do?' Aristodemus answered, 'Let us go and fall at his feet and ask pardon, and whatever he commands us let us do.' Then they came together and cast themselves down and besought forgiveness. And he received them and offered prayer and thanksgiving to God, and he ordained them a fast of a week and when it was fulfilled he baptized them. And when they were baptized, with all their house and their servants and their kindred, they broke all their idols and built a church in the name of Saint John, wherein he himself was taken up, in the following way:[37]

(b) *Oxyrhynchus Papyrus 850*

Verso:[38]
... for him [
] groanings and [
] but John [
to Zeuxis having arisen and taken [
] who compelled me [
] thinking to strangle himself, who the desperate
] converts to yourself; you who to no man are known
] makes known; who weeps for the oppressed
] who raises up the dead [
] of the helpless: Jesus the comforter [
] we praise you and worship and give
thanks for all your gifts and for your present dispensation
] and service. And to Zeuxis only at the eucharist
] he gave to those who wished to receive [
] looking on him they did not dare, but the proconsul [
] the midst of the congregation to John
] said 'Servant of the unnameable [

---

[37] There then follows in Ps.-Abdias a version of the Metastasis.
[38] James places the incident told on the recto before the incident told on the verso.

346   *The Acts of John*

] has brought letters from Caesar
] and with...
Recto:
... departure [
] Andronicus and his]wife[39]
When a few days had passed John
went[with many brethren to [
] pass over a bridge under which a river ran [
] John went to the brethren [
a man came to him in soldier's clothing
and stood in his presence and said, 'John if [
my hands you shall shortly come.' And John [
said, 'The Lord shall quench your threatening and your wrath and
transgression.' And behold, the man vanished. When John
came to those he was visiting and found
them gathered together, he said, 'Rise up, my brethren
and let us bow our knees to the Lord who the great
enemy's unseen activity has brought to nothing
] bowed their knees together with them
] God...[40]

(c) *Epistle of Pseudo-Titus*[41]

As rendered by James (p. 266) one part reads:

Or is that outside the law which we are taught, how the very devils [when they] confessed to Dyrus (*read* Verus) the deacon as to the coming of John: consider what they said, 'Many will come to us in the last times to turn us out of our vessels (i.e. the bodies possessed by them), saying that they are pure and clean from women and are not held by desire of them: whom (MS while) if we desired, we (could) possess them also.'

Another reads (in brief):

Receive therefore in your heart the admonition of the blessed John, who, when he was bidden to a marriage, came only to promote the cause of chastity, and consider what he said: 'Little children, while yet your flesh is

---

[39] This is written as a title of the following episode.
[40] In the interest of presenting a reasonably logical sequence of English words from this fragmentary text no attempt has been made to indicate the *exact* lengths of the original lines. The brackets are meant to indicate the major gaps in the text.
[41] Ed. D. de Bruyne, 'Nouveaux fragments des Actes de Pierre, de Paul, de Jean, d'André et de l'Apocalypse d'Élie', *Rev. Bén.* 25 (1908), 149–60, sp. 155–7. The full text of Pseudo-Titus was edited by de Bruyne in *Rev. Bén.* 37 (1925), 47–72.

pure and you have your body untouched and not destroyed, and are not defiled by Satan, the great enemy and shameless (foe) of chastity: know therefore more fully the mystery of the nuptial union: it is the experiment of the serpent, the ignorance of teaching, injury of the seed, the gift of death, . . .[42] the impediment which separates from the Lord, the beginning of disobedience, the end of life, and death. Hearing this, little children, join yourselves together in an inseparable marriage, holy and true, waiting for the one true incomparable bridegroom from heaven, even Christ, the ever-lasting bridegroom.'

SECONDARY ACTS OF JOHN[1]

(i) *The Acts of John in Rome.* This account dating from the sixth century is given in two forms, both included by Lipsius–Bonnet as chs. 1–14 (ii.1, pp. 151–60).[2]

(ii) *The Acts of John attributed to Prochorus* of the fifth or sixth century is concerned mainly with miracles performed by John in Patmos. Some 150 manuscripts survive, and many are valuable in that they preserve extracts of the original Acts of John.

(iii) 'Pseudo-Abdias', *Virtutes Apostolorum: Virtutes Iohannis* (sixth century).[3]

(iv) *Passio Iohannis* of Pseudo-Melito (Mellitus) of the sixth century. This is close to, but shorter than, Pseudo-Abdias, *Virtutes*. The two works were independent of one another but are both likely to have developed from the same, now lost, Latin source, which was translated from the Greek.

(v) *Liber Flavus Fergusiorum.* This fifteenth-century Irish text contains stories about the life of John. Most of them are taken from Pseudo-Melito, but some of the others may have developed from the original Acts of John. There are links with P. Oxy. 850.[4]

(vi) *The Syriac Acts of John*, son of Zebedee, is independent of the preceding versions.[5] It is of the fifth–sixth century.

---

[42] Text corrupt.

[1] On the possibility that some episodes in these works may belong in the original Acts of John see above, pp. 304–6.

[2] Bonnet's chs. 15–17 (also a late composition) containing local stories based on Miletus and found in one manuscript of Prochorus were printed only as a footnote in his edition. Junod and Kaestli, *CCA*, pp. 862–80 and 881–6 also edit the Acts of John in Rome.

[3] Reproduces Acts of John 62–86 (used by Festugière for his trans.) and 106–15 in a version close to the Greek text.

[4] For details see Junod and Kaestli *CCA*, pp. 109–12.

[5] Wright, *Apoc. Acts* i. 4–65; ii (Eng. trans.), 3–60. See James, *ANT* 469–70, and Erbetta, ii. 130–1, for summaries in English and Italian respectively. The scene for this text is set in Ephesus. Included in these Acts is the story that John wrote his Gospel in one hour. An Arabic version exists (see bibliography above).

PROCHORUS, ACTS OF JOHN[6]

EDITIONS

Greek

T. Zahn, *Acta Joannis* (Erlangen, 1880; repr. Hildesheim, 1975).

Coptic

See under 'Metastasis' above.

Arabic

Smith Lewis, *Acta Myth.* 31–46; *Myth. Acts*, 37–53.

Ethiopic

Malan, 117–37.
Wallis Budge, *Contendings*, i. 189–213; ii (Eng. trans.), 222–52.

Armenian

L. Leloir, 'Actes de Jean par Prochore' (French trans. of Armenian), *CCA* 3, 289–407.

MODERN TRANSLATIONS

French

Migne, *Dictionnaire*, ii, cols. 759–86.

Italian

Erbetta, ii. 68–110.
Moraldi, ii. 1212–23; [2] ii. 292–302 (summary).

PSEUDO-ABDIAS, *VIRTUTES IOHANNIS*
(in Fabricius, ii. 531–90)

Junod and Kaestli *CCA*, 750–834, esp. 799–834. [Cf. Lipsius, i. 408–31.]

MODERN TRANSLATIONS

English

James, 257–64 (extracts).

---

[6] See Hennecke[5], ii. 385–91; Eng. trans., ii. 429–35.

French

Migne, *Dictionnaire*, ii, cols. 327-56.

Italian

Erbetta, ii. 111-29.
Moraldi, ii. 1507-33; [2] ii. 583-609.

PSEUDO-MELITO, *PASSIO IOHANNIS*

EDITIONS

(See Junod and Kaestli, *CCA* ii. 764-71.)
Fabricius, iii. 604-23.
G. Heine, *Bibliotheca Anecdotorum*, i (Leipzig, 1848), 109-17, and in *PG* 5, cols. 1239-50.
M. Herbert and M. McNamara, *Irish Biblical Apocrypha* (Edinburgh, 1989), 89-91, 96-8 (and 'Note' on 180f).

MODERN TRANSLATIONS

French

Migne, *Dictionnaire*, ii, cols. 597-610 (translates an interpolated Latin version of chs. 8-11 descended from Ps.-Melito).

Italian

See Erbetta, i.2, 635-40.

The Acts of Paul

Attestation

Tertullian, *de Baptismo* 17 (ed. A. Reifferscheid and G. Wissowa, *CSEL* 20 (Prague, Vienna, Leipzig, 1890), p. 215, or ed. J. W. P. Borleffs, *CCL* 1.2 (Turnhout, 1954), pp. 291–2), written at the end of the second century, knows of Thecla, and it may well be that he was aware of the existence of the Acts of Paul and Thecla which circulated separately, and indeed of the Acts of Paul as a whole. His testimony, however, is ambiguous. Borleff's edition speaks of the 'Acts of Paul', the *CSEL* edition of the 'writings attributed falsely to Paul'.[1] Certainly the details given by Tertullian do not fit the Acts of Paul and Thecla precisely. *de Bapt.* tells that the author was a presbyter in Asia who resigned from office for falsely claiming that, on the precedent of Thecla's action, women had a right to preach and to baptize.

Unlike Tertullian (if he is indeed referring to the Acts of Paul), some other fathers do not disapprove of these Acts. Hippolytus, *Commentary on Daniel* 3. 29, written about 204, refers to Paul and the lion without hesitation as orthodox (ed. G. N. Bonwetsch, *GCS* 1.1 (Leipzig, 1897), pp. 176–7).

The first explicit reference to the Acts of Paul by name is in Origen, *de Principiis* 1. 2. 3 (ed. P. Koetschau, *GCS* 22 (Leipzig, 1913), p. 30) and in his commentary on John 20, 12 (Preuschen, p. 342). Eusebius, *HE* 3. 3. 5, claims that the Acts of Paul does not belong to the undisputed books, but in *HE* 3. 25. 4 he distinguishes it from the lesser spurious works (Schwartz, *GCS* 9.1, pp. 190, 252). Jerome is more definite in rejecting the orthodoxy of the Acts of Paul. In his *de Vir Ill.* 7 (Richardson, pp. 11 ff.). the 'περίοδοι Pauli et Theclae' is one of the 'apocryphal writings'.

After it was known that the Manichaeans had made use of the Acts of Paul subsequent church opinion branded the work as apocryphal.[2] Thus it is rejected (twice) in the Gelasian Decree, in the Stichometry of Nicephorus, and in the Catalogue of the Sixty Canonical Books. But it is included in the canonical list inserted into Codex Claromontanus of the Pauline epistles (D).

Clement of Alexandria, *Strom.* 6. 5 (Stählin, *GCS* 52 (15), pp. 451–3) possibly shows knowledge of a work known as 'The Preaching of Paul'.

---

[1] See A. Souter, 'The "Acta Pauli" etc. in Tertullian', *JTS* 25 (1924), 292 and J. W. P. Borleffs, 'La valeur du Codex Trecensis pour la critique de texte dans le traité *de baptismo*', *VC* 2 (1948), 185–200.

[2] See E. Junod and J.-D. Kaestli, *L'Histoire des Actes apocryphes des apôtres du IIIe au IXe siècle: le cas des Actes de Jean* (Geneva, Lausanne, Neuchâtel, 1982) (= *Cahiers de la Revue de Théologie et de Philosophie* 7).

Similarly Pseudo-Cyprian in the third century, de *Rebaptismate* 17, (ed. G. Hartel, *CSEL* 3, Part 3 (Vienna, 1871), p. 90) refers to 'The Preaching of Paul', but there is no trace of a book with such a title, and it may well be that it is the Acts of Paul that are being referred to. W. Schneemelcher, in Hennecke[3], ii. 56; [5]ii. 33 (Eng. trans. [3]ii. 92 ff.; [5]ii. 31–2), is doubtful about connecting the Pseudo-Cyprian reference to the Acts of Paul (cf. E. von Dobschütz, *Das Kerygma Petri* (Leipzig, 1893), pp. 127–31 (= *TU* 11.1)). James, in *Apoc. Anec.* (ii. 54–7) and then in *ANT* drew attention to later writings that may be referring to portions of the Acts of Paul. These include John of Salisbury's *Policraticus* 4. 3 of the twelfth century, which includes the abstract of a sermon delivered by Paul in Athens that is not the Areopagus speech of Acts 18. The Latin text is given by James in *Apoc. Anec.* ii. 56, with an English rendering in *ANT*, p. 299, repeated here:

I make use of these examples[3] the more readily because I find that the apostle Paul when preaching to the Athenians made use of them also. That excellent preacher strove so to impress on their minds Jesus Christ and him crucified, that he might show by the example of heathens how the release of many came about through the shame of the cross. And this, he argued, could not happen save by the blood of the just, and of those who bore rule over the people. Further, no one could be found capable of freeing all, both Jews and Gentiles, save he unto whom the heathen are given for an inheritance, and the utmost parts of the earth assigned for his possession. And such a one he said could be no other than the Son of God Almighty, since no one but God has subjected to himself all nations and lands. As, then, he proclaimed the shame of the cross in such a way as gradually to purge away the foolishness of the heathen, little by little he raised the word of faith and the language of his preaching, up to the Word of God, the wisdom of God, and the very throne of the divine majesty: and, lest the power of the gospel should seem mean in the weakness of the flesh by dint of the slanders of Jews and the folly of heathens, he set forth the works of the crucified, which were confirmed by the witness of common report; since it was plain to all that none but God could do such things. But as report often falsifies, in both directions, report was assisted by the fact that *Christ's* disciples did even greater works, seeing that by the shadow of a disciple (Peter) the sick were healed of every kind of disease. What more? The ingenuities of an Aristotle, the subtleties of a Chrysippus, the traps of all the philosophers were defeated by the rising of one who had been dead.

Another text cited in its original Latin in *Apoc. Anec.* (ii. 54) and translated in *ANT* (p. 298) is from Commodianus, *Carmen de Duobus Populis* (cf. ed. J. Martin, *CC* 128 (Turnhout, 1960), p. 96):

And whatever he wills he can do: making dumb things to speak; he made Balaam's ass speak to him when he beat it; and a dog to say to Simon: 'You are called for by Peter!' For Paul when he preached, he caused mules[4] to speak of him: he made a lion speak

---

[3] i.e. the preceding stories in which he tells of the self-sacrifice of Codrus and Lycurgus (taken from the historian Justin).
[4] Reading 'muli' for 'multi' ('muti' is also a possible conjecture).

to the people with God-given voice. Lastly, a thing which our nature does not permit—he made an infant five months old speak in public.

The passage may refer to the Acts of Paul or to Nicephorus' account of the Ephesian lion (see later).

Echoes of these Acts are to be found in two manuscripts of the Greek New Testament, namely cursive 181p (of the eleventh century) and cursive 460 (of the thirteenth century). They make an addition at 2 Tim. 4: 19 seemingly from the Acts of Paul and Thecla. 181 alone makes a further addition (at 2 Tim. 3: 11) also from this source (see J. K. Elliott, *The Greek Text of the Epistles to Timothy and Titus* (Salt Lake City, 1968), ad. loc. (= *Studies and Documents* 36)).

The Stichometry of Nicephorus calculates 3600 lines to the Acts of Paul (cf. 2800 for the canonical Acts). Much is unaccounted for by the extant remains. The following fragments exist:

Greek. Eleven papyrus leaves in a third–fourth century Hamburg manuscript (P. Hamb.); and P. Michigan 1317, P. Michigan 3788, and P. Berlin 13893 of the fourth century (these belong together and for the most part overlap with a portion of the Hamburg manuscript p. 8, as shown in the footnotes to my translation). P. Michigan 3788 contains some lines absent from the Hamburg fragment. These extra lines appear below in the translation and are indicated in the footnote accordingly. The lines agree with a folio (pp. 79–80) of the Heidelberg Coptic manuscript (see below), which C. Schmidt, the original editor, identified as coming from an apocryphal gospel and thus printed separately in *Acta Pauli*, pp. 55*–6*. A German translation appears in *Acta Pauli*, pp. 237–8, and there are English translations by B. Pick, *Paralipomena: Remains of Gospels and Sayings of Christ* (Chicago, 1908), pp. 54–6, and by James, *ANT*, pp. 31–2. Four further texts, two from Oxyrhynchus (P. Oxy. 6 and 1602, the latter overlapping with part of P. Hamb. p. 8), one papyrus from Antinoopolis, and the small Fackelmann fragment now in the Münster Bibelmuseum, also survive. Other, later, manuscripts were used by Lipsius–Bonnet (as indicated below for the separate sections).

Coptic. The fifth–sixth century Heidelberg manuscript (P. Heid.) contains extensive remains of the whole of the Acts of Paul. They were pieced together by C. Schmidt from 2000 fragments. A fourth-century fragment in the Rylands library described by Crum has not yet been published: this seems to have belonged to the beginning of Acts. Kasser's unpublished Bodmer manuscript contains the Ephesus episode (see below).

For some time The Acts of Paul and Thecla, the Correspondence between Paul and the Corinthians (including the so-called 3 Corinthians), and the Martyrdom of Paul have been well-known, although it was not usually recognized that these three were originally to be found together in a larger work, the Acts of Paul.

(1) *The Acts of Paul and Thecla*
These acts tell the popular story of Thecla, a Greek girl who is converted by Paul's preaching. She breaks off her engagement and follows Paul as his assistant. She escapes persecutions and death in a miraculous way and finally retires to Seleucia. The cult of St Thecla became widespread in both East and West. The contents of this novel influenced Christian art and literature not least for its description of Paul. It is unlikely to be historical, despite mention of Queen Tryphaena of Pisidian Antioch, who is historically attested.

Lipsius–Bonnet based their edition on eleven Greek manuscripts, but over forty are now known to be extant. There are manuscripts of separate Latin translations that, according to von Gebhardt, represent an independent tradition. Syriac, Armenian, Slavonic, and perhaps Arabic[5] versions also survive.

Since the publication of Lipsius–Bonnet's edition, parts of the text of the Acts of Paul and Thecla are to be found in P. Heid. (pp. 6–28), the Antinoopolis fragment, P. Oxy. 6, and the Fackelmann papyrus.

The popularity of the Acts of Paul and Thecla and of the Acts of Paul as a whole is shown in various later writings, not least in hagiographical literature, which encouraged the spread of the legend of St Thecla. The separate circulation and the subsequent survival of the Acts of Paul and Thecla were also due to the veneration of Thecla, who was commemorated on 23 September (in the West) and on 24 September (in the East). The cult of Thecla seems to have reached a peak of popularity in the fifth century. Pseudo-Chrysostom's *Panegyric to Thecla* seems to have been composed about this time (text in *PG* 50, cols. 745–8, and in M. Aubineau (ed.), 'Le Panégyrique de Thecle, attribué à Jean Chrysostome *BHG* 1720: la fin retrouvée d'un texte mutilé', *Anal. Boll.* 93 (1975), 349–62.[6]

(2) *3 Corinthians*
The Correspondence of Paul with the Corinthians contains the Corinthians' letter to Paul and Paul's reply to them. These letters were included in the Syriac collection of the Pauline epistles: at one time the Syriac (and the Armenian) churches regarded them as authentic Pauline letters.

Five Latin manuscripts (one dating from the third century) betray varying texts. The correspondence is also known from the Armenian Bible and from Ephraem's commentary. Recently a Greek text of the third century (being the language of the original) was discovered and is now known as Bodmer X, but is not to be treated as infallible: the later Latin often seems to have the better reading. P. Heid. (pp. 45–50, 41, 42, 44) also contains this section.

---

[5] According to Lipsius–Bonnet, i, p. cii.
[6] See D. R. MacDonald and A. D. Scrimgeour, 'Pseudo-Chrysostom's Panegyric to Thecla: The Heroine of the *Acts of Paul* in Homily and Art', in D. R. MacDonald (ed.), *The Apocryphal Acts of the Apostles* (Decatur, Ga., 1986), 151–9 (= *Semeia* 38).

The Corinthian correspondence is likely to date from the second century and probably had a separate authorship and existence prior to its incorporation into the Acts of Paul. Its separate existence continued even after its incorporation into this larger work, as is evidenced by the Bodmer papyrus and by its inclusion as a separate entity in the Armenian Bible.

(3) *The Martyrdom of Paul*
This work deals with Paul's preaching and missionary work in Rome, the persecution by Nero, and the death of the apostle. The description of the death influenced Christian art. After his death Paul appears to the emperor and prophesies the judgement that will befall him. The work emphasizes the conflict between the soldiers of Christ the King and the cult of the emperor.

Lipsius–Bonnet's edition is based on two Greek manuscripts (which also contain the Acts of Peter), on a fragmentary Latin translation, and on Coptic, Slavonic, and Ethiopic versions. Vouaux added the Syriac edited by Nau. The Martyrdom also occurs in the Hamburg and Heidelberg manuscripts (P. Hamb. pp. 9–11; P. Heid. pp. 53–8).

As can be seen from the description above, P. Heid. contains elements of all these three sections, showing that originally all three belonged together in the Acts of Paul, and its finding thus confirmed the suspicions of those who had previously considered that the Acts of Paul and Thecla (and 3 Corinthians) had from an early date belonged with the Martyrdom of Paul to a larger work.

This manuscript also contains other parts of the original Acts including the following:

(a) A journey from Damascus to Jerusalem (probably corroborated in the Rylands fragment) (pp. 61, 62, and perhaps 60, 59)
(b) Paul in Antioch (pp. 1–6)
(c) Paul in Myra (pp. 28–35)
(d) Paul in Sidon (pp. 35–9)
(e) Paul in Tyre (p. 40)
(f) Paul in Corinth (also found in P. Hamb.) (pp. 44, 43, 51, 52)
(g) Paul's speech in Puteoli (cf. the Michigan manuscripts) (pp. 79–80)

P. Hamb., of *c*.300 in Greek, contains the following:

(a) Paul in Ephesus (also in the unpublished Bodmer manuscript) (pp. 1–5)
(b) Paul in Corinth (also found in P. Heid.) (pp. 6–7)[7]
(c) Paul *en route* from Corinth to Italy (portions of this section also found

---

[7] Thus P. Hamb. or its *Vorlage* deliberately omits the Corinthian correspondence and records nothing of Paul in Philippi despite the words 'from Philippi to Corinth' on p. 6 (top)—i.e. the back of p. 5.

in the Berlin, Oxyrhynchus 1602, and Michigan fragments, and in P. Heid. pp. 79–80) (pp. 7–8)

The sequence of Paul's travels can be reconstructed with a reasonable degree of confidence on the basis of the Heidelberg and Hamburg fragments. After journeys from Damascus to Jerusalem and then on to Antioch, Paul travels to Iconium where the famous Acts of Paul and Thecla is located. P. Heid. goes on to relate the acts of Paul in Myra, stating in its superscription that he set out for Myra from Antioch, and then leads into an episode in Sidon. Both these acts are incomplete, as is the next episode in Tyre, which is known from P. Heid. p. 40, though hardly anything of this scene survives. Schmidt printed the fragments numbered pp. 64, 63, 70, 69, 68, 67, 66, 65, 61, 62, 60, 59 at this point, and James followed this, but so little is decipherable on these pages that there is no certainty that they did in fact belong here; they are ignored in the present volume.

There is in any case a gap in the story at this juncture, and it is disputed at which point P. Heid. should be resumed. James decided that what came next was the episode of Longinus and Firmilla's daughter, Frontina, followed by the correspondence between Paul and the Corinthians, and then by an episode in Ephesus. Hennecke–Schneemelcher argued that the Ephesus episode should follow the act in Tyre. In the present work also it was decided that the unpublished Coptic text of the papyrus announced by Kasser and the first five pages of P. Hamb., which tell of events in Ephesus (following a visit to Smyrna), belong here after the episode in Tyre. James, who was unaware of either of these texts, printed his episode of the lion in Ephesus on the evidence of (*a*) Nicephorus, *Ecclesiastical History* 2. 25 (*PG* 145, col. 822)— which is possibly fourteenth-century although based on a tenth-century ancestor—with some support from the Acts of Titus by Pseudo-Zenas, which is dependent on the Acts of Paul, and (*b*) Hippolytus, *Commentary on Daniel* 3. 29 of the third century (ed. G. N. Bonwetsch, *GCS* 1.1 (Leipzig, 1897), p. 176). Both of these sources show the popularity of the lion story. (It is also to be found in Ethiopic literature in the Letter of Pelagia—see bibliography below under 'Ethiopic'.) The reference in Hippolytus vouches for the early date of the story; Nicephorus shows its source to be the Acts of Paul. James' judgement in *ANT* (pp. 291–2) that an episode in Ephesus belonged to the original Acts of Paul has thus been vindicated by later manuscript discoveries.

Hennecke–Schneemelcher's text then gives the correspondence with the Corinthians which is to be found in P. Heid. pp. 45–50 and in Armenian, Latin, Greek, and Syriac. This edition again deviates from James's sequence by *following* this correspondence with the Frontina episode. The correspondence places the episode in Philippi (3 Cor. 2: 1 states that the letter was brought to Paul, in prison, in Philippi). There is a gap in P. Heid. between the Corinthian correspondence and the conclusion of the Philippi episode, and thus it is uncertain where Schmidt's pp. 41-2, 44 (telling of the Frontina episode) belong. Hennecke-Schneemelcher's sequence is adopted here.

In the middle of Schmidt's p. 44 a new episode begins, which indicates a move from Philippi to Corinth; P. Hamb. is clear that the following episode takes place in Corinth. (P. Hamb. jumps from the episode in Ephesus straight to the incident in Corinth.) The next journey takes Paul from Corinth to Italy; the text is found in the Hamburg, Berlin, Oxyrhynchus 1602, and Michigan manuscripts. The two Michigan texts also overlap with P. Hamb. p. 8 and with P. Heid. pp. 79-80 (identified by Schmidt as coming from an apocryphal gospel (see above, p. 352) and accepted as such by James who provided a translation (*ANT* pp. 31-2) under the running title 'Fragments of Gospels'). P. Mich 3788 (= 1317) now anchors that leaf to a portion of the Acts of Paul. It also helps to fill the gap that is apparent between P. Hamb. p. 8 and p. 9 (p. 9 begins the Martyrdom). The final episode (in Rome) is also found in various versions and often circulated as a separate text.

I summarize here the contents of my translation and their manuscript attestation:

1. *From Damascus to Jerusalem*
   P. Ryl.; P. Heid. pp. 60-59, 61-2.[8]
2. *Antioch*
   P. Heid. pp. 1-6.
3. *Iconium (The Acts of Paul and Thecla)*
   Lipsius-Bonnet; P. Heid. pp. 6-28; P. Oxy. 6; P. Antinoopolis; P. Fackelmann.
4. *Myra*
   P. Heid. pp. 28-35 (one page missing after p. 30 (not indicated by Schmidt); one page missing after p. 34).
5. *Sidon*
   P. Heid. pp. 35-9 (two pages at least missing after p. 36; two pages at least missing after p. 38).
6. *Tyre*
   P. Heid p. 40 (James adds fragments pp. 64, 63, 70, 69, 68, 67, 66, 65 and (following Schmidt's original positioning[8]) pp. 61, 62, 60, 59).
7. *Ephesus*
   P. Hamb. pp. 1-5 (and a summary of the unpublished Coptic fragment).
8. *Philippi* (and text of 3 Corinthians)
   P. Heid. pp. 45-50, 41, 42 44a; P. Bod. X.
9. *Corinth*
   P. Heid. pp. 44b-3, 51-2; P. Hamb. pp. 6-7.

---

[8] Schmidt changed his mind after the original publication. See his ΠΡΑΞΕΙΣ ΠΑΥΛΟΥ, p. 118.

10. *Corinth to Italy*
    P. Hamb. pp. 7-8; P. Berlin 13893; P. Oxy. 1602; P. Michigan 1317, 3788; P. Heid. pp. 79-80 (and possibly fragments pp. 71-4).
11. *Martyrdom*
    Lipsius-Bonnet; P. Hamb. pp. 9-11; P. Heid. pp. 53-8.
(Unplaced fragments = P. Heid. pp. 75-8).

The work uses the conventions of contemporary preaching. Although not a theological treatise it is concerned to promote a simple faith (in contrast to Gnostic systems) and to encourage sexual continence. The main motive for its composition seems to have been to set already existing legends about Paul (some possibly oral) in sequence, as an act of devotion to his memory.

In contrast with the canonical Acts, Paul here undertakes one continuous missionary journey; the Christian communities were already in existence, and he is not founding new churches. It may well be that the author of the Acts of Paul was not familiar with the details of the canonical Acts. However, the popularity of Paul was doubtless enhanced by the canonical letters, including the Pastoral Epistles, that were written by him (or in his name) and by the circulation of the canonical Acts. The popularity bred the legends that were then included in the Acts of Paul.

The majority of scholars date the book at the end of the second century (a date confirmed if Tertullian was referring to the Acts of Paul). The provenance is likely to have been Asia Minor.

ACTS OF PAUL

EDITIONS[9]

Greek

Jones, ii. 431-69 (Paul and Thecla).
Fabricius, ii. 791-6 (Paul and Thecla).
Lipsius-Bonnet, i. 235-72 (Paul and Thecla).
B. P. Grenfell and A. S. Hunt, *OP* 1 (London, 1892), no. 6, pp. 9-10; *OP* 13 (London, 1919), no. 1602, pp. 23-5.
C. Schmidt, 'Ein Berliner Fragment der alten Πράξεις Παύλου,' *SPAW* (19 Feb. 1931), 37-40 (= P. Berlin 13893).
C. Schmidt with W. Schubart, Πράξεις Παύλου: *Acta Pauli nach dem Papyrus der Hamburger Staats- und Universitätsbibliothek* (Glückstadt and Hamburg, 1936) (= *Veröffentlichungen aus der Hamburger Staats- und Universitätsbibliothek*, ed. G. Wahl, ii) (with German translation).[10] [This publication was anticipated in C. Schmidt, 'Neue Funde zu den alten Πράξεις Παύλου', *SPAW* 7 (28 Feb. 1929), 176-83.]

---

[9] For 3 Corinthians see below, pp. 360 ff.
[10] Reviews: A. Baumstark, *Or. Chr.* 34 (1937), 122-6; H. I. Bell, *JTS* 38 (1937), 189-91.

H. A. Sanders, 'A Fragment of the *Acta Pauli* in the Michigan Collection', *HTR* 31 (1938), 70–90 (= P. Mich. 1317).

—— 'Three Theological Fragments', *HTR* 36 (1943), 165–7 (original publication of P. Mich. 3788).

G. D. Kilpatrick and C. H. Roberts, 'The *Acta Pauli*: A New Fragment', *JTS* 47 (1946), 196–9 (= P. Mich. 3788). [Identification and calculation by Kilpatrick, pp. 198 f., supersedes C. H. Roberts, 'A Fragment of an Uncanonical Gospel', *JTS* 47 (1946), 56–7; cf. also W. D. McHardy, 'A Papyrus Fragment of the *Acta Pauli*', *ExpT* 58 (1947), 279.]

C. H. Roberts, 'The Acts of Paul and Thecla', in *The Antinoopolis Papyri*, i (London and Metuchen, 1950), 26–8.

M. Gronewald, 'Einige Fackelmann-Papyri', *ZPE* 28 (1978), 274–5 and Table XIX d, e (the Fackelmann fragment).

W. Rordorf, 'Les Actes de Paul sur papyrus: problèmes liés aux P. Mich. 1317 et 3788', in *Proceedings of the XVIII International Congress of Papyrology 1986* (Athens, 1988), 453–6.

Greek and Latin

Lipsius–Bonnet, i. 104–17 (Passio).

Latin

O. von Gebhardt, *Passio S. Theclae virginis: Die lateinischen Übersetzungen der Acta Pauli et Theclae* (Leipzig, 1902) (= *TU* 22 (7). 2).

D. A. Wilmart, 'Extraits d'*Acta Pauli*', *Rev. Bén.* 27 (1910), 402–12.

D. de Bruyne, 'Nouveaux fragments des Actes de Pierre, de Paul, de Jean, d'André et de l'Apocalypse d'Élie', *Rev. Bén.* 25 (1908), 149–60, esp. 153.

Coptic

O. von Lemm, 'Koptische apokryphe Apostelacten', *Mélanges Asiatiques* 10 (St Petersburg, 1892), 354–81.

Guidi, *AAL. R* 4, 3.2 (1887), 65–7; Italian trans., *Giornale*, 36–7.

C. Schmidt, *Acta Pauli aus der Heidelberger Koptischen Papyrushandschrift Nr 1* (Leipzig, ²1905; repr. Hildesheim, 1965); *Tafelband*, with German translation (Leipzig, 1904; repr. Hildesheim, 1965).[11]

—— 'Ein neues Fragment der Heidelberger Acta Pauli', *SPAW* (4 Feb. 1909), 216–20 (extra portion of the Acts of Paul and Thecla).

W. Crum, 'New Coptic Manuscripts in the John Rylands Library', *BJRL* 5 (1920), 497–503, esp. 501 (description of the Rylands fragment, as yet unpublished).

R. Kasser, 'Acta Pauli 1959', *Revue d'histoire et de philosophie religieuses* 40 (1960), 45–57 (description of Bodmer Papyrus X and the (as yet unpublished) Coptic MS of the Ephesus episode).

---

[11] Reviewed by P. Corssen, *Göttingen Gelehrte Anzeigen* (1904), 702 ff., who denied the origin of the newly discovered fragments within the ancient Acts of Paul.

Syriac

Wright, i. 128–69; Eng. trans. ii. 116–45 (Paul and Thecla).
F. Nau, 'La version syriaque inédite des martyres de S. Pierre, S. Paul et S. Luc', *Revue de l'orient chrétien* 3 (1898), 39–57, 151–6, esp. 51–7.
A. Smith Lewis, *Select Narratives of Holy Women* (London, 1900) (= *Studia Sinaitica* 9), 190–205 (collation of the text of the Thecla story in the Sinai palimpsest against Wright's text).

Ethiopic

Malan, 11–15.
Wallis Budge, *Contendings*, i. 41–8, 437–598; ii (Eng. trans.), 43–8, 527–685 (generally a different tradition of the Acts, but the Martyrdom corresponds to the Greek).[12]
E. J. Goodspeed, 'The Book of Thekla', *American Journal of Semitic Languages and Literatures* 17 (1901), 65–95 (with Eng. trans.).
—— *The Book of Thekla* (Chicago 1901) (= *University of Chicago Historical and Linguistic Studies in Literature related to the New Testament*, i. *Ethiopic Texts*) (with Eng. trans.).

Epistle of Pelagia

For evidence of the Ephesus episode see E. J. Goodspeed *American Journal of Semitic Languages and Literatures* 20 (1904), 95–105, and G Krüger, 'Noch einmal der getaufte Löwe', *ZNW* 5 (1904), 261–3 (cf. id., ibid. 163–6). (Goodspeed's English translation is repeated by C. Schmidt, *Acta Pauli* (Leipzig,²1905), pp. xxi–xxv).

Arabic

Smith Lewis, *Acta Myth.* 184 ff.; *Myth. Acts*, 217–22.

Armenian

F. Conybeare, *The Apology and Acts of Apollonius and other Monuments of Early Christianity* (London, 1894; ²1896), 49–88 (Eng. trans. of Acts of Paul and Thecla from the Armenian).
Leloir, *CCA* 3, 77–86, 'Le Martyre de Paul' (includes a French trans. of the Martyrdom from an important Venice MS).

Slavonic

de Santos Otero, *Altslav. Apok.* i. 43–51 (Paul and Thecla).

---

[12] See review by M. R. James, *JTS* 3 (1902), 286–91 with special reference to the Acts of Paul.

MODERN TRANSLATIONS

English

Hone, 99–111 (Paul and Thecla).
Pick, 1–49.
James, 270–97, and (from 1953) Appendix II by J. W. B. Barns (pp. 570–8).
Hennecke[3], ii. 322–90.
Hennecke[5], ii. pp. 213–70.
Walker, 279–92 (Paul and Thecla).

French

Migne, *Dictionnaire*, ii, cols. 961–88 (Paul and Thecla).
Vouaux (Greek and Latin texts also given; and a good bibliography of the literature from 1887 to 1913) pp. 135–9.[13]
Amiot, 226–51.
Éac, 1117–77.

German

Michaelis, 268–317 (and cf. 442 ff.).
Hennecke[1], 357–83 (E. Rolffs); cf. *Handbuch*, 358–95.
Hennecke[3], ii. 221–70 (W. Schneemelcher and R. Kasser).
Hennecke[5], ii. 193–243 (W. Schneemelcher and R. Kasser).
[The third and fifth editions reconstruct the Acts and Martyrdom from all available sources in Greek and Coptic, including Kasser's unpublished fragment.]

Italian

Moraldi, ii. 1061–1130; [2] ii. 141–210 (translates Paul and Thecla with diverse endings; P. Heid.; P. Hamb.; P. Bod. X; Martyrdom). See also under 3 Corinthians below.
Erbetta, ii. 243–88 (follows Hennecke–Schneemelcher's contents, excluding Kasser's Coptic fragment, but including various accounts of Paul and the lion in Ephesus).

3 CORINTHIANS

EDITIONS

Greek

M. Testuz, *Papyrus Bodmer X–XII* (Cologny-Geneva, 1959) (X = *Correspondance apocryphe des Corinthiens et de l'apôtre Paul*, with French translation). [The text is the same codex as the text known as P. Bod. V, 'The Nativity of Mary', i.e. The Protevangelium Jacobi.]

---

[13] Reviewed by M. R. James, *JTS* 14 (1913), pp. 604–6.

Coptic

C. Schmidt, *Acta Pauli* (above, p. 358), esp. 125–45.

Armenian

P. Vetter, 'Der apokryphe dritte Korintherbrief', *TQ* 73 (1890), 610–39 (German translation of Armenian).

—— 'Eine rabbinische Quelle des apokryphen dritte Korintherbriefes', *TQ* 77 (1895), 622–33.

—— *Der apokryphe dritte Korintherbrief* (Vienna, 1894) (= *Tübinger Universitätsprogramm*) (cf. *Tübinger Universitätschriften* (1893–4), 41–52) (edition of Armenian based on 11 MSS.).

W. F. Rinck, *Das Sendschreiben der Korinther an den Apostel Paulus und das dritte Sendschreiben Pauli an die Korinther* (Heidelberg, 1823) (German translation of Armenian).

S. P. Cowe, 'Text Critical Investigation of the Armenian Version of *Third Corinthians*' in V. Calzolari Bouvier, J.-D. Kaestli and B. Outtier (eds.), *Apocryphes Arméniens* (Lausanne, 1999), 91–102 (= *Publications de L'Institut romand des sciences bibliques* 1).

Latin

A. Carrière and S. Berger, 'La correspondance apocryphe de Saint Paul et des Corinthiens', *Revue de Théologie et de Philosophie* 24 (1891), 333–51 (Latin text and also French trans. of Armenian).

A. M. Ceriani, *La Correspondance apocryphe de Saint Paul et des Corinthiens* (Paris, 1891) (Latin text and French trans. of Armenian).

E. Bratke, 'Ein zweiter lateinischer Text des apokryphen Briefwechsels zwischen den Apostel Paulus und den Korinthern', *TLZ* 17 (1892), cols. 585–88.

D. de Bruyne, 'Un nouveau manuscrit de la troisième lettre de Saint Paul aux Corinthiens', *Rev. Bén.* 25 (1908), 431–4 (Latin text).

—— 'Un quatrième manuscrit latin de la correspondance apocryphe de S. Paul avec les Corinthiens', *Rev. Bén.* 45 (1933), 189–95 (Latin text).

A. Harnack, *Apocrypha*, iv. *Die apokryphen Briefe des Paulus an die Laodicener und Korinther* (Bonn, [2]1912; Berlin, [3]1931), 6–23 (= *Kleine Texte* 12 ed. H. Lietzmann) (Latin text with Greek retroversion).

H. Boese, 'Über eine bisher unbekannte Handschrift des Briefwechsels zwischen Paulus und den Korinthern', *ZNW* 44 (1952), 66–76.

MODERN TRANSLATIONS

(See also under Acts of Paul above)

English

K. Lake, *The Earlier Epistles of St. Paul* (London, 1911), 236–40.

French

Migne, *Dictionnaire*, i, cols. 1289–94.
Amiot, 243–7.

Vouaux, 246–75 (a Latin reconstruction based on two Latin MSS and the Armenian, with a French trans.).

Italian

Moraldi, ii. 1723–30, 1740–8; ² ii. 98–106.

STUDIES OF 3 CORINTHIANS

K. Pink, 'Die pseudo-paulinischen Briefe I', *Biblica* 6 (1925), 68–91, esp. 70–91: 'I. Die Apokryphe Briefwechsel des hl. Paulus mit den Korinthern (3 Korbr.)'.

A. F. J. Klijn, 'The Apocryphal Correspondence between Paul and the Corinthians', *VC* 17 (1963), 2–23.

GENERAL STUDIES OF THE ACTS OF PAUL

The Acts of Paul has spawned a great deal of secondary literature. The bibliographies in Vouaux and in Charlesworth will furnish many more titles than can be included here. The following is only a selection of the more interesting, the seminal, and the most significant contributions.

C. Schlau, *Die Acten des Paulus und der Thecla und die altere Thecla-Legende* (Leipzig, 1877).

Lipsius, ii.1, 424–67.

Zahn, *Kanon*, i. 783–90; ii. 865–910.

A. Rey, *Étude sur les Acta Pauli et Theclae et la légende de Thecla* (Paris, 1890).

W. M. Ramsay, *The Church in the Roman Empire before AD 170* (London, New York, Toronto, ⁵1897), ch. 16.

A. Harnack, *Drei wenig beachtete Cyprianische Schriften und die 'Acta Pauli'* (Leipzig, 1899) (= *TU* 4.3b).

A. Baumstark, *Die Petrus- und Paulusacten in der litterarischen Ueberlieferung der syrischen Kirche* (Leipzig, 1902).

C. Clemen, 'Miszellen zu den Paulusakten', *ZNW* 5 (1904), 228–47.

P. Corssen, 'Die Urgestalt des Paulusakten', *ZNW* 4 (1903), 22–47; id., 'Der Schluss der Paulusakten', *ZNW* 6 (1905), 317–38.

C. Holzhey, *Die Thekla-Akten: Ihre Verbreitung und Beurtheilung in der Kirche* (Munich, 1905) (= *Veröffentlichungen aus dem kirchen-historischen Seminar* 2.7).

Findlay, 238–72.

C. Schmidt, 'Acta Pauli', *Forschungen und Fortschritte* 28 (1936), 352–4.

A. Kurfess, 'Zu dem Hamburger Papyrus der Πράξεις Παύλου', *ZNW* 38 (1939), 164–70.

E. Peterson, 'Die Acta Xanthippae et Polyxenae und die Paulusakten', *Anal. Boll.* 65 (1947), 57–60.

—— 'Einige Bemerkungen zum Hamburger Papyrus-fragment der Acta Pauli', *Vig. Chr.* 3 (1949), 142–62 (rev. in id., *Frühkirche, Judentum und Gnosis* (Rome, Freiburg, Vienna, 1959), 182–208.

P. Devos, 'Actes de Thomas et Actes de Paul', *Anal. Boll.* 69 (1951), 119–30 (against Peterson's argument that the Acts of Paul is dependent on the Acts of Thomas).

W. Schneemelcher, 'Die Acta Pauli: Neue Funde und neue Aufgaben', *ThLZ* 89 (1964), cols. 241–54 (repr. in W. Bienert and K. Schäferdiek (eds.), *Gesammelte Aufsätze zum Neuen Testament und zur Patristik* (Thessalonica, 1974), 182–203 (= *Analekta Vlatadon* 22).

—— 'Der getaufte Löwe in den Acta Pauli', in A. Striber and A. Hermann (eds.), *Mullus* (Festschrift Theodor Klauser) (Münster, 1964), 316–26. (= *Jahrbuch für Antike und Christentum, Ergänzungsband* 1) (repr. *Analekta Vlatadon* 22, 223–39).

—— 'Die Apostelgeschichte des Lukas und die Acta Pauli', in W. Eltester (ed.), *Apophoreta* (Festschrift Ernst Haenchen) (Berlin, 1974), 236–50 (= *Beiheft ZNW* 30) (repr. *Analekta Vlatadon* 22, 204–22).

Bauer, 71–5.

J. Rohde, 'Pastoralbriefe und Acta Pauli', in F. L. Cross (ed.), *Studia Evangelica* 5 (Berlin, 1968), part 2, 303–10 (= *TU* 103).

Vielhauer, 699–705.

Plümacher, cols. 24–30.

E. M. Howe, 'Interpretations of Paul in the Acts of Paul and Thecla', in D. A. Hagner and M. J. Harris (eds.), *Pauline Studies* (Festschrift for F. F. Bruce) (Exeter and Grand Rapids, 1980), 33–49.

W. Rordorf, 'Die Neronische Christenverfolgung im Spiegel der apokryphen Paulusakten', *NTS* 28 (1982), 364–75.

—— 'Tradition and Composition in the *Acts of Thecla*: The State of the Question', in D. R. MacDonald (ed.), *The Apocryphal Acts of the Apostles* (Decatur, Ga., 1986), 43–52 (= *Semeia* 38; French trans. in *TZ* 41 (1985), 272–83).

D. R. MacDonald, *The Legend and the Apostle: The Battle for Paul in Story and Canon* (Philadelphia, 1983).

Aldo Moda, 'Per una Biographia Paolina: La Lettura di Clemente, il Canone Muratoriana, la Letteratura Apocrifa', in *Testimonium Christi: Scritti in Onore di Jacques Dupont* (Brescia, 1985), 289–315.

S. L. Davies, 'Women, Tertullian, and the Acts of Paul', in MacDonald (above, under Rordorf), 139–43, with response by T. W. Mackay, 145–9 (= *Semeia* 38).

D. R. MacDonald and A. D. Scrimgeour, 'Pseudo-Chrysostom's Panegyric to Thecla: The Heroine of the *Acts of Paul* in Homily and Art', ibid. 151–9.

W. Rordorf, 'In welchem Verhältnis stehen die apokryphen Paulusakten zur kanonischen Apostelgeschichte und zu den Pastoralbriefen?', in T. Baarda, A. Hilhorst, G. P. Luttikhuizen, and A. S. van der Woude (eds.), *Text and Testimony* (Kampen, 1988), 225–41.

—— 'Nochmals Paulusakten und Pastoralbriefen', in G. F. Hawthorne and O. Betz (eds.), *Tradition and Interpretation in the New Testament* (Festschrift for E. E. Ellis) (Grand Rapids and Tübingen, 1987), 319–27.

—— 'Was wissen wir über Plan und Absicht der Paulusakten?' in D. Papandreou, W. A. Bienert, and K. Schäferdiek (eds.), *Oecumenica et Patristica* (Festschrift for W. Schneemelcher) (Geneva, 1989), 71–82.

J. N. Bremmer (ed.), *The Apocryphal Acts of Paul and Thecla* (Kampen, 1996) (=*Studies on the Apocryphal Acts of the Apostles* 2).

1. From Damascus to Jerusalem

The fragments tell that after his conversion outside Damascus Paul receives the command to go to Damascus and then Jerusalem. He enters Damascus 'with great joy' and finds the community fasting.

On his journey to Jericho the baptism of the lion occurs (according to Paul's later account in Ephesus).

2. Antioch

The fragments suggest that Paul has been summoned to raise the son of Panchares.[1] His wife rebukes Panchares for not mourning their dead son. Paul arrives and raises the boy. This irritates the townspeople. The following section is legible:

'... and I also believe, my brethren, that there is no other God save Jesus Christ, the son of the Blessed, to whom is glory for ever. Amen.' But when they saw that he would not turn to them they pursued Paul, laid hold of him and brought him back into the city, ill-using (?) him, and they cast stones at him and thrust him out of their city and out of their country. But Panchares would not requite evil with evil.

3. THE ACTS OF PAUL AND THECLA

1. As Paul was going to Iconium after his flight from Antioch, his fellow-travellers were Demas and Hermogenes, the copper-smith, who were full of hypocrisy and flattered Paul as if they loved him. Paul, looking only to the goodness of Christ, did them no harm but loved them exceedingly so that he made sweet to them all the words of the Lord and the interpretation of the gospel concerning the birth and resurrection of the Beloved; and he gave them an account, word for word, of the great deeds of Christ as they were revealed to him.

2. And a certain man, by name Onesiphorus, hearing that Paul was to come to Iconium, went out to meet him with his children Simmias and Zeno and his wife Lectra, in order that he might entertain him. Titus had informed him what Paul looked like, for he had not seen him in the flesh, but only in the spirit.

3. And he went along the royal road to Lystra and kept looking at the passers-by according to the description of Titus. And he saw Paul coming, a man small in size, bald-headed, bandy-legged, of noble mien, with eyebrows meeting, rather hook-nosed, full of grace. Sometimes he seemed like a man, and sometimes he had the face of an angel.

---

[1] James argued (*ANT* 271 f.) that the name in the manuscript (Anchares) was due to the Coptic translator mistaking the initial letter for the Coptic definite article and thus omitting it.

4. And Paul, seeing Onesiphorus, smiled; and Onesiphorus said, 'Hail, O servant of the blessed God.' And he said, 'Grace be with you and your house.' And Demas and Hermogenes were jealous and showed greater hypocrisy, so that Demas said, 'Are we not of the blessed God that you have not thus saluted us?' And Onesiphorus said, 'I do not see in you the fruit of righteousness, but if such you be, come also into my house and refresh yourselves.'

5. And after Paul had gone into the house of Onesiphorus there was great joy and bowing of knees and breaking of bread and the word of God about abstinence and the resurrection. Paul said, 'Blessed are the pure in heart, for they shall see God;[2] blessed are those who have kept the flesh chaste, for they shall become a temple of God; blessed are the continent, for God shall speak with them; blessed are those who have kept aloof from this world, for they shall be pleasing to God; blessed are those who have wives as not having them, for they shall experience God;[3] blessed are those who have fear of God, for they shall become angels of God.

6. 'Blessed are those who respect the word of God, for they shall be comforted;[4] blessed are those who have received the wisdom of Jesus Christ, for they shall be called the sons of the Most High;[5] blessed are those who have kept the baptism, for they shall be refreshed by the Father and the Son; blessed are those who have come to a knowledge of Jesus Christ, for they shall be in the light; blessed are those who through love of God no longer conform to the world, for they shall judge angels, and shall be blessed at the right hand of the Father; blessed are the merciful, for they shall obtain mercy[6] and shall not see the bitter day of judgement; blessed are the bodies of the virgins, for they shall be well pleasing to God and shall not lose the reward of their chastity. For the word of the Father shall become to them a work of salvation in the day of the Son, and they shall have rest for ever and ever.'

7. And while Paul was speaking in the midst of the church in the house of Onesiphorus a certain virgin named Thecla, the daughter of Theoclia, betrothed to a man named Thamyris, was sitting at the window close by and listened day and night to the discourse of virginity, as proclaimed by Paul. And she did not look away from the window, but was led on by faith, rejoicing exceedingly. And when she saw many women and virgins going in to Paul she also had an eager desire to be deemed worthy to stand in Paul's presence and hear the word of Christ. For she had not yet seen Paul in person, but only heard his word.

8. As she did not move from the window her mother sent to Thamyris. And he came gladly as if already receiving her in marriage. And Thamyris said to Theoclia, 'Where, then, is my Thecla ⟨that I may see her⟩?'[7] And

---

[2] Matt. 5: 8.   [3] 1 Cor. 7: 29; Rom 8: 17.
[4] Matt. 5: 4.   [5] Matt. 5: 9.   [6] Matt. 5: 7.
[7] Words bracketed are absent in Greek MSS.

Theoclia answered, 'I have a strange story to tell you, Thamyris. For three days and three nights Thecla does not rise from the window either to eat or to drink; but looking earnestly as if upon some pleasant sight she is devoted to a foreigner teaching deceitful and artful discourses, so that I wonder how a virgin of her great modesty exposes herself to such extreme discomfort.

9. 'Thamyris, this man will overturn the city of the Iconians and your Thecla too; for all the women and the young men go in to him to be taught by him. He says one must fear only one God and live in chastity. Moreover, my daughter, clinging to the window like a spider, lays hold of what is said by him with a strange eagerness and fearful emotion. For the virgin looks eagerly at what is said by him and has been captivated. But go near and speak to her, for she is betrothed to you.'

10. And Thamyris greeted her with a kiss, but at the same time being afraid of her overpowering emotion said, 'Thecla, my betrothed, why do you sit thus? And what sort of feeling holds you distracted? Come back to your Thamyris and be ashamed.' Moreover, her mother said the same, 'Why do you sit thus looking down, my child, and answering nothing, like a sick woman?' And those who were in the house wept bitterly, Thamyris for the loss of a wife, Theoclia for that of a child, and the maidservants for that of a mistress. And there was a great outpouring of lamentation in the house. And while these things were going on Thecla did not turn away but kept attending to the word of Paul.

11. And Thamyris, jumping up, went into the street, and watched all who went in to Paul and came out. And he saw two men bitterly quarrelling with each other and he said to them, 'Men, who are you and tell me who is this man among you, leading astray the souls of young men and deceiving virgins so that they should not marry but remain as they are? I promise you money enough if you tell me about him, for I am the chief man of this city.'

12. And Demas and Hermogenes said to him, 'Who he is we do not know. But he deprives the husbands of wives and maidens of husbands, saying, "There is for you no resurrection unless you remain chaste and do not pollute the flesh."'

13. And Thamyris said to them, 'Come into my house and refresh yourselves.' And they went to a sumptuous supper and much wine and great wealth and a splendid table. And Thamyris made them drink, for he loved Thecla and wished to take her as wife. And during the supper Thamyris said, 'Men, tell me what is his teaching that I also may know it, for I am greatly distressed about Thecla, because she so loves the stranger and I am prevented from marrying.'

14. And Demas and Hermogenes said, 'Bring him before the Governor Castellius because he persuades the multitude to embrace the new teaching of the Christians, and he will destroy him and you shall have Thecla as your wife. And we shall teach you about the resurrection which he says is to come,

that it has already taken place in the children whom we have[8] and that we rise again, after having come to the knowledge of the true God.

15. And when Thamyris heard these things he rose up early in the morning and, filled with jealousy and anger, went into the house of Onesiphorus with rulers and officers and a great crowd with batons and said to Paul, 'You have deceived the city of the Iconians and especially my betrothed bride so that she will not have me! Let us go to the governor Castellius!' And the whole crowd cried, 'Away with the sorcerer for he has misled all our wives!', and the multitude was also incited.

16. And Thamyris standing before the tribunal said with a great shout, 'O proconsul, this man—we do not know where he comes from—makes virgins averse to marriage. Let him say before you why he teaches thus.' But Demas and Hermogenes said to Thamyris, 'Say that he is a Christian and he will die at once.' But the governor kept his resolve and called Paul, saying, 'Who are you and what do you teach? For they bring no small accusation against you.'

17. And Paul, lifting up his voice, said, 'If I today must tell any of my teachings then listen, O proconsul. The living God, the God of vengeance, the jealous God, the God who has need of nothing, who seeks the salvation of men, has sent me that I may rescue them from corruption and uncleanness and from all pleasure, and from death, that they may sin no more. On this account God sent his Son whose gospel I preach and teach, that in him men have hope, who alone has had compassion upon a world led astray, that men may be no longer under judgement but may have faith and fear of God and knowledge of honesty and love of truth. If then I teach the things revealed to me by God what harm do I do, O proconsul?' When the governor heard this he ordered Paul to be bound and sent to prison until he had time to hear him more attentively.

18. And Thecla, by night, took off her bracelets and gave them to the gatekeeper; and when the door was opened to her she went into the prison. To the jailer she gave a silver mirror and was thus enabled to go in to Paul and, sitting at his feet, she heard the great deeds of God. And Paul was afraid of nothing, but trusted in God. And her faith also increased and she kissed his bonds.

19. And when Thecla was sought for by her family and Thamyris they were hunting through the streets as if she had been lost. One of the gatekeeper's fellow slaves informed them that she had gone out by night. And they examined the gatekeeper who said to them, 'She has gone to the foreigner in the prison.' And they went and found her, so to say, chained to him by affection. And having gone out from there they incited the people and informed the governor what had happened.

20. And he ordered Paul to be brought before the tribunal, but Thecla was

---

[8] 2 Tim. 2: 18.

riveted to the place where Paul had sat whilst in prison. And the governor ordered her also to be brought to the tribunal, and she came with an exceedingly great joy. And when Paul had been led forth the crowd vehemently cried out, 'He is a sorcerer. Away with him!' But the governor gladly heard Paul speak about the holy works of Christ. And having taken counsel, he summoned Thecla and said, 'Why do you not marry Thamyris, according to the law of the Iconians?' But she stood looking earnestly at Paul. And when she gave no answer Theoclia, her mother, cried out saying, 'Burn the wicked one; burn her who will not marry in the midst of the theatre, that all the women who have been taught by this man may be afraid.'

21. And the governor was greatly moved, and after scourging Paul he cast him out of the city. But Thecla he condemned to be burned. And immediately the governor arose and went away to the theatre. And the whole multitude went out to witness the spectacle. But as a lamb in the wilderness looks around for the shepherd, so Thecla kept searching for Paul. And having looked into the crowd she saw the Lord sitting in the likeness of Paul and said, 'As if I were unable to endure, Paul has come to look after me.' And she gazed upon him with great earnestness, but he went up into heaven.

22. And the boys and girls brought wood and straw in order that Thecla might be burned. And when she came in naked the governor wept and admired the power that was in her. And the executioners arranged the wood and told her to go up on the pile. And having made the sign of the cross she went up on the pile. And they lighted the fire. And though a great fire was blazing it did not touch her. For God, having compassion upon her, made an underground rumbling, and a cloud full of water and hail overshadowed the theatre from above, and all its contents were poured out so that many were in danger of death. And the fire was put out and Thecla saved.

23. And Paul was fasting with Onesiphorus and his wife and his children in a new tomb on the way which led from Iconium to Daphne. And after many days had been spent in fasting the children said to Paul, 'We are hungry.' And they had nothing with which to buy bread, for Onesiphorus had left the things of this world and followed Paul with all his house. And Paul, having taken off his cloak, said, 'Go, my child, sell this and buy some loaves and bring them.' And when the child was buying them he saw Thecla their neighbour and was astonished and said, 'Thecla, where are you going?' And she said, 'I have been saved from the fire and am following Paul.' And the child said, 'Come, I shall take you to him; for he has been mourning for you and praying and fasting six days already.'

24. And when she had come to the tomb Paul was kneeling and praying, 'Father of Christ, let not the fire touch Thecla but stand by her, for she is yours'; she, standing behind him, cried out, 'O Father who made the heaven and the earth, the Father of your beloved Son Jesus Christ, I praise you that you have saved me from the fire that I may see Paul again.' And Paul, rising

up, saw her and said, 'O God, who knows the heart, Father of our Lord Jesus Christ, I praise you because you have speedily heard my prayer.'

25. And there was great love in the tomb as Paul and Onesiphorus and the others all rejoiced. And they had five loaves and vegetables and water, and they rejoiced in the holy works of Christ. And Thecla said to Paul, 'I will cut my hair off and I shall follow you wherever you go.' But he said, 'Times are evil and you are beautiful. I am afraid lest another temptation come upon you worse than the first and that you do not withstand it but become mad after men.' And Thecla said, 'Only give me the seal in Christ, and no temptation shall touch me.' And Paul said, 'Thecla, be patient; you shall receive the water.'

26. And Paul sent away Onesiphorus and all his family to Iconium and went into Antioch, taking Thecla with him. And as soon as they had arrived a certain Syrian, Alexander by name, an influential citizen of Antioch, seeing Thecla, became enamoured of her and tried to bribe Paul with gifts and presents. But Paul said, 'I know not the woman of whom you speak, nor is she mine.' But he, being of great power, embraced her in the street. But she would not endure it and looked about for Paul. And she cried out bitterly, saying, 'Do not force the stranger; do not force the servant of God. I am one of the chief persons of the Iconians and because I would not marry Thamyris I have been cast out of the city.' And taking hold of Alexander, she tore his cloak and pulled off his crown and made him a laughing-stock.

27. And he, although loving her, nevertheless felt ashamed of what had happened and led her before the governor; and as she confessed that she had done these things he condemned her to the wild beasts. The women of the city cried out before the tribunal, 'Evil judgement! impious judgement!' And Thecla asked the governor that she might remain pure until she was to fight with the wild beasts. And a rich woman named Queen Tryphaena, whose daughter was dead, took her under her protection and had her for a consolation.

28. And when the beasts were exhibited they bound her to a fierce lioness, and Queen Tryphaena followed her. And the lioness, with Thecla sitting upon her, licked her feet; and all the multitude was astonished. And the charge on her inscription was 'Sacrilegious.' And the women and children cried out again and again, 'O God, outrageous things take place in this city.' And after the exhibition Tryphaena received her again. For her dead daughter Falconilla had said to her in a dream, 'Mother, receive this stranger, the forsaken Thecla, in my place, that she may pray for me and I may come to the place of the just.'

29. And when, after the exhibition, Tryphaena had received her she was grieved because Thecla had to fight on the following day with the wild beasts, but on the other hand she loved her dearly like her daughter Falconilla and said, 'Thecla, my second child, come, pray for my child that she may live in

eternity, for this I saw in my sleep.' And without hesitation she lifted up her voice and said, 'My God, Son of the Most High, who are in heaven, grant her wish that her daughter Falconilla may live in eternity.' And when Thecla had spoken Tryphaena grieved very much, considering that such beauty was to be thrown to the wild beasts.

30. And when it was dawn Alexander came to her, for it was he who arranged the exhibition of wild beasts, and said, 'The governor has taken his seat and the crowd is clamouring for us; get ready, I will take her to fight with the wild beasts.' And Tryphaena put him to flight with a loud cry, saying, 'A second mourning for my Falconilla has come upon my house, and there is no one to help, neither child for she is dead, nor kinsman for I am a widow. God of Thecla, my child, help Thecla.'

31. And the governor sent soldiers to bring Thecla. Tryphaena did not leave her but took her by the hand and led her away saying, 'My daughter Falconilla I took away to the tomb, but you, Thecla, I take to fight the wild beasts.' And Thecla wept bitterly and sighed to the Lord, 'O Lord God, in whom I trust, to whom I have fled for refuge, who did deliver me from the fire, reward Tryphaena who has had compassion on your servant and because she kept me pure.'

32. And there arose a tumult: the wild beasts roared, the people and the women sitting together were crying, some saying, 'Away with the sacrilegious person!', others saying, 'O that the city would be destroyed on account of this iniquity! Kill us all, proconsul; miserable spectacle, evil judgement!'

33. And Thecla, having been taken from the hands of Tryphaena, was stripped and received a girdle and was thrown into the arena. And lions and bears were let loose upon her. And a fierce lioness ran up and lay down at her feet. And the multitude of the women cried aloud. And a bear ran upon her, but the lioness went to meet it and tore the bear to pieces. And again a lion that had been trained to fight against men, which belonged to Alexander, ran upon her. And the lioness, encountering the lion, was killed along with it. And the women cried the more since the lioness, her protector, was dead.

34. Then they sent in many beasts as she was standing and stretching forth her hands and praying. And when she had finished her prayer she turned around and saw a large pit full of water and said, 'Now it is time to wash myself.' And she threw herself in saying, 'In the name of Jesus Christ I baptize myself on my last day.' When the women and the multitude saw it they wept and said, 'Do not throw yourself into the water!'; even the governor shed tears because the seals were to devour such beauty. She then threw herself into the water in the name of Jesus Christ, but the seals, having seen a flash of lightning, floated dead on the surface. And there was round her a cloud of fire so that the beasts could neither touch her nor could she be seen naked.

35. But the women lamented when other and fiercer animals were let loose; some threw petals, others nard, others cassia, others amomum, so that

The Acts of Paul

there was an abundance of perfumes. And all the wild beasts were hypnotized and did not touch her. And Alexander said to the governor, 'I have some terrible bulls to which we will bind her.' And the governor consented grudgingly, 'Do what you will.' And they bound her by the feet between the bulls and put red-hot irons under their genitals so that they, being rendered more furious, might kill her. They rushed forward but the burning flame around her consumed the ropes, and she was as if she had not been bound.

36. And Tryphaena fainted standing beside the arena, so that the servants said, 'Queen Tryphaena is dead.' And the governor put a stop to the games and the whole city was in dismay. And Alexander fell down at the feet of the governor and cried, 'Have mercy upon me and upon the city and set the woman free, lest the city also be destroyed. For if Caesar hear of these things he will possibly destroy the city along with us because his kinswoman, Queen Tryphaena, has died at the theatre gate.'

37. And the governor summoned Thecla out of the midst of the beasts and said to her, 'Who are you? And what is there about you that not one of the wild beasts touched you?' She answered, 'I am a servant of the living God and, as to what there is about me, I have believed in the Son of God in whom he is well pleased; that is why not one of the beasts touched me. For he alone is the goal of salvation and the basis of immortal life. For he is a refuge to the tempest-tossed, a solace to the afflicted, a shelter to the despairing; in brief, whoever does not believe in him shall not live but be dead forever.'

38. When the governor heard these things he ordered garments to be brought and to be put on her. And she said, 'He who clothed me when I was naked among the beasts will in the day of judgement clothe me with salvation.' And taking the garments she put them on.

And the governor immediately issued an edict saying, 'I release to you the pious Thecla, the servant of God.' And the women shouted aloud and with one voice praised God, 'One is the God, who saved Thecla', so that the whole city was shaken by their voices.

39. And Tryphaena, having received the good news, went with the multitude to meet Thecla. After embracing her she said, 'Now I believe that the dead are raised! Now I believe that my child lives. Come inside and all that is mine I shall assign to you.' And Thecla went in with her and rested eight days, instructing her in the word of God, so that many of the maidservants believed. And there was great joy in the house.

40. And Thecla longed for Paul and sought him, looking in every direction. And she was told that he was in Myra. And wearing a mantle that she had altered so as to make a man's cloak, she came with a band of young men and maidens to Myra, where she found Paul speaking the word of God and went to him. And he was astonished at seeing her and her companions, thinking that some new temptation was coming upon her. And perceiving this, she said

to him, 'I have received baptism, O Paul; for he who worked with you for the gospel has worked with me also for baptism.'

41. And Paul, taking her, led her to the house of Hermias and heard everything from her, so that he greatly wondered and those who heard were strengthened and prayed for Tryphaena. And Thecla rose up and said to Paul, 'I am going to Iconium.' Paul answered, 'Go, and teach the word of God.' And Tryphaena sent her much clothing and gold so that she could leave many things to Paul for the service of the poor.

42. And coming to Iconium she went into the house of Onesiphorus and fell upon the place where Paul had sat and taught the word of God, and she cried and said, 'My God and God of this house where the light shone upon me, Jesus Christ, Son of God, my help in prison, my help before the governors, my help in the fire, my help among the wild beasts, you alone are God and to you be glory for ever. Amen.'

43. And she found Thamyris dead but her mother alive. And calling her mother she said, 'Theoclia, my mother, can you believe that the Lord lives in heaven? For if you desire wealth the Lord will give it to you through me; or if you desire your child, behold, I am standing beside you.'

And having thus testified, she went to Seleucia and enlightened many by the word of God; then she rested in a glorious sleep.

(a) In some manuscripts after 'Seleucia' is to be found the following section (translated from Lipsius–Bonnet, i. 270–1):

'and dwelt in a cave seventy-two years, living upon herbs and water. And she enlightened many by the word of God.

44. And certain men of the city, being Greeks by religion and physicians by profession, sent to her pompous young men to corrupt her. For they said, 'She is a virgin and serves Artemis, and from this she has virtue in healing.' And by the providence of God she entered into the rock alive and went under ground. And she departed to Rome to see Paul and found that he had fallen asleep. And after staying there a short time, she rested in a glorious sleep and she is buried about two or three stadia from the tomb of her master Paul.

45. She was cast into the fire when seventeen years old and among the wild beasts when eighteen. And she was an ascetic in the cave, as has been said, seventy-two years so that all the years of her life were ninety. And after accomplishing many cures she rests in the place of the saints, having fallen asleep on the twenty-fourth of the month of September in Christ Jesus our Lord to whom be glory and strength for ever and ever. Amen.

[This section appears in Italian translation in Moraldi, ii. 1098–9, and Erbetta, ii. 268–9.]

(b) In manuscript G (as edited by Grabe) this final paragraph is expanded as follows (translated from Lipsius–Bonnet, i. 271–2):

And a cloud of light guided her. And having come into Seleucia she went outside the city one stade. And she was afraid of them for they worshipped idols. And it guided her to the mountain called Calaman or Rhodeon, and having found there a cave she went into it. And she was there many years and underwent many and grievous trials by the devil and bore them nobly, being assisted by Christ. And some of the well-born women, having learned about the virgin Thecla, went to her and learned the miracles of God. And many of them bade farewell to the world and lived an ascetic life with her. And a good report was spread everywhere concerning her; and cures were done by her. All the city, therefore, and the country around, having learnt this, brought their sick to the mountain, and before they came near the door they were speedily released from whatever disease they were afflicted with; and the unclean spirits went out shrieking, and all received their own people in health, glorifying God who had given such grace to the virgin Thecla. The physicians of the city of Seleucia were thought nothing of, having lost their trade, and no one any longer had regard to them. Being filled with envy and hatred, they plotted against the servant of Christ to decide what they should do to her. The devil then suggested to them a wicked device. One day, having assembled, they took counsel and consulted with each other, saying, 'This holy virgin has influence upon the great goddess Artemis and if she ask anything of her she hears her, being a virgin herself, and all the gods love her. Come, then, let us take unprincipled men and make them drunk with wine, and let us give them a great deal of money and say to them, "If you can corrupt and defile her we shall give you even more money."' The physicians said to themselves that if they should be able to defile her neither the gods nor Artemis would listen to her in the case of the sick. They therefore acted accordingly, and the wicked men went up to the mountain and rushed upon the cave like lions and knocked at the door. And the holy martyr Thecla opened it, emboldened by the God in whom she trusted, for she knew of their plot beforehand. And she said to them, 'What do you want, my children?' And they said, 'Is there someone here called Thecla?' And she said, 'What do you want with her?' They said to her, 'We want to sleep with her.' The blessed Thecla said to them, 'I am a poor old woman, a servant of my Lord Jesus Christ; and even though you want to do something unseemly to me you cannot.' They said to her, 'We must do to you what we want.' And having said this, they laid fast hold of her and wished to insult her. But she said to them with mildness, 'Wait, my children, that you may see the glory of the Lord.' And when they took hold of her she looked up into heaven and said, 'God, terrible and incomparable and glorious to your adversaries, who delivered me out of the fire, who did not give me up to Thamyris, who did not give me up to Alexander, who delivered me from the wild beasts, who saved me in the abyss, who has everywhere worked with me and glorified your name in me, now also deliver me from these lawless men and let them not insult my virginity which for your name's sake I have preserved till now because I love you and desire you and adore you, the Father, and the Son, and the Holy Ghost for ever. Amen.' And there came a voice out of the heaven saying, 'Fear not, Thecla, my true servant, for I am with you. Look and see where an opening has been made before you, for there shall be for you an everlasting house and there you shall obtain shelter.' And looking around, the blessed Thecla saw the rock opened far enough to allow a person to enter, and in obedience to what had been said to her she courageously fled from the lawless men and entered into the rock; and the rock was immediately shut together so that not even a joint could be seen. And they, beholding the extraordinary wonder, became distracted, and they were not able to stop the servant of God but only caught hold of her dress and were able to tear off a certain part. All this happened by the permission of God for the faith of those seeing the venerable place and for a blessing in the generations afterwards to those who believe in our Lord Jesus Christ out of a pure heart.

Thus, then, suffered the first martyr of God and apostle and virgin, Thecla, who came from Iconium when eighteen years of age. With her journeying and travels and the retirement in the mountain she lived seventy-two years more. And when the Lord took her she was ninety years old. And thus is her consummation. And her holy commemoration is celebrated on the twenty-fourth of the month of September, to the glory of the Father and the Son and the Holy Ghost, now and ever and to ages of ages. Amen.

[This ending is given in English translation by Hone, 110-11, and Pick, *Paralipomena: Remains of Gospels and Sayings of Christ* (Chicago, 1908), 32-4, and in Italian translation in Moraldi, ii. 1099-1101; Erbetta, ii. 267-8.]

4. Myra

(When he departed from) Antioch and taught in Myra

When Paul was teaching the word of God in Myra there was a man there named Hermocrates who had the dropsy. He stood in the sight of all and said to Paul, 'Nothing is impossible with God but especially with him whom you preach, for when he came he healed many, he whose servant you are. Lo, I and my wife and my children cast ourselves at your feet that I also may believe just as you believed in the living God.' Paul said to him, 'I will give you ... without reward, but through the name of Jesus Christ you shall become whole in the presence of all these.'

... and his belly opened and a great deal of water flowed out of him and he fell as if dead, so that some said, 'It is better for him to die, that he may not be in pain.' But when Paul had quietened the crowd he took his hand, raised him up, and asked him saying, 'Hermocrates, ... what you will.' But he said, 'I wish to eat.' And he took a loaf and gave it him to eat. He became whole in that hour, and received the grace of the seal in the Lord, he and his wife.

But Hermippus his son was angry with Paul and sought for an opportunity to rise up with those of his own age and destroy him. For he wished that his father should not be healed but die, so that he might quickly be master of his property. But Dion, his younger son, heard Paul gladly. All who were with his brother took counsel to fight Paul, so that Hermippus ... and tried to kill him ... Dion fell down and died, but Hermippus washed Dion with his tears. But Hermocrates mourned, for he loved Dion more than his other son. As he sat at Paul's feet he forgot that Dion was dead.

But when Dion was dead his mother Nympha rent her clothing and went to Paul and set herself before her husband Hermocrates and Paul. But when Paul saw her he was startled and said, 'Why are you doing this, Nympha?' But she said to him, 'Dion is dead.' And the whole crowd wept as they looked upon her. And Paul looked upon the mourning crowd; he sent young men and said to them, 'Go and bring him here to me.' So they went, but Hermippus took hold of the body in the street and cried out...[10]

But an angel of the Lord had said to him in the night, 'Paul, there is before you today a great conflict against your body, but God, the Father of his Son Jesus Christ, will (protect) you.' When Paul had arisen he went to his brethren and remained... saying, 'What does this vision mean?' But while Paul thought about this he saw Hermippus coming with a drawn sword in his hand, and with him many other young men with their cudgels. Paul said to them, 'I am not a robber, nor am I a murderer. The God of all things, the Father of Christ, will turn your hands backwards and your sword into its sheath and will transform your strength into weakness. For I am a servant of God, and I am alone, a stranger, small and of no significance among the heathen. But you, O God, look down upon their counsel and let me not be brought to nought by them.' As Hermippus... his sword... against Paul... he lost his sight, so that he cried aloud, saying, '... comrades, forget not... Hermippus. For I have sinned, Paul, I have pursued after... blood. Learn, you foolish and you of understanding, this world is nothing, gold is nothing, all possessions are nothing. I who glutted myself with all that is good am now a beggar and entreat you all. Hearken, all my companions and every one who dwells in Myra. I have mocked a man who saved my father, I have... raised up my brother... But entreat him, for behold he saved my father and raised up my brother. It is possible for him to deliver me too.' But Paul stood there weeping, alike before God because he had heard him quickly and also before men because the proud man was brought low. He turned and went up...

And they saw Hermippus their son in the form of... and how he touched the feet of each one, and also the feet of his parents, praying to them like one of the strangers that he might be healed. And his parents were troubled and lamented to every one who went in, so that some said, 'Why do they weep? For Dion is risen.' But Hermocrates... and brought the price to the... and took it and divided it...

But they and Paul prayed to God. And when Hermippus recovered his sight he turned to his mother Nympha, saying to her, 'Paul came and laid his hand upon me while I wept. And in that hour I saw all things clearly.' And she took his hand and brought him in to the widows and Paul.[11]

...And when Paul had confirmed the brethren who were in Myra he departed for Sidon.

5. *Sidon*

When he had departed from Myra and (wished to go to Sidon)

---

[10] One leaf is missing. [11] A leaf is probably missing here.

But when Paul departed from Myra and wished to go up to Sidon there was great sorrow among the brethren who were in Pisidia and Pamphylia since they yearned after his word and his holy presence, so that some from Perga followed Paul, namely Thrasymachus and Cleon with their wives Aline (?) and Chrysa, the wife of Cleon.

...[12] after the manner of strange men. Why do you presume to do things that are not seemly? Have you not heard of that which happened which God brought upon Sodom and Gomorrah, because they robbed...'

But they did not listen to him but took the men and put them into the temple of Apollo to keep them secure until the morning in order that they might assemble the city... Abundant and costly was the food they gave them, but Paul, who was fasting for the third day, testified all night long, sad at heart, and smiting his brow said, 'O God, look down upon their threats and do not allow us to fall and let not our adversary strike us down, but deliver us by bringing down quickly your righteousness upon us...'

They went away and proclaimed in the city, 'Apollo the god of the Sidonians has fallen and half of his temple.' And all the inhabitants of the city ran to the temple and saw Paul and those who were with him weeping at this tribulation, because they were to become a spectacle for everyone. But the crowd cried out, 'Bring them to the theatre!' The magistrates came to fetch them and they groaned bitterly in their soul...[13]

But he commanded them to go to Tyre... in safety (?), and they put Paul ⟨aboard a ship?⟩ and went with him.

6. *Tyre*

When he had departed from Sidon and wished to go to Tyre

But when Paul had entered into Tyre there came a crowd of Jews... in to him...

But immediately the demons fled. But when the crowd saw these things in the power of God they praised him who... to Paul. Now there was one named... rimos who had a ⟨son⟩ who had been born dumb...[14]

7. *Ephesus*

But Paul said to him, '... for you have no power over me except over my body, but my soul you can not kill. But hear in what manner you must be saved. And taking all my words to heart... and the earth and stars and

---

[12] The section immediately preceding these words is preserved only in fragments and at least two leaves are missing.

[13] At least two leaves are missing.

[14] James adds here the fragments found in Schmidt, nos. 64, 63, 70, 69, 68, 67, 66, 65, 61, 62, 60, 59.

dominions and ... and all the good things in the world for the sake of ... moulded ... of men ... led astray and enslaved ... by gold ... silver and precious stones ... and acts of adultery and drunkenness ..., which lead to deception through the afore-mentioned ... went and were slain. Now then since the Lord wishes us to live in God because of the error in the world and not to die in sins, he saves through the ... who preach, that you may repent and believe ... and one Christ Jesus and no other exists. For your gods are of ... and stone and wood and can neither take food nor see nor hear, nor even stand. Form a good resolve and be saved, lest God be wroth and burn you with unquenchable fire and the memory of you perish.' And when the governor heard this ... in the theatre with the people he said, 'You men of Ephesus, that this man has spoken well I know, but also that it is not yet time for you to learn these things. Decide now what you wish!' Some said he should be burned ..., but the goldsmiths said, 'To the beasts with the man!' And since a great tumult broke out Hieronymus condemned him to the beasts, after having him scourged. Now the brethren, since it was Pentecost, did not mourn or bow their knees, but rejoiced and prayed standing. But after six days Hieronymus made a display of animals: all who saw it were astonished at the size of the beasts. While Paul was bound ... he began to (? pray) ... he heard the noise of the waggons ... that carried the beasts ...

And when the lion came to the side door of the stadium where Paul was imprisoned it roared loudly, so that everybody cried out, 'The lion!' For it roared fiercely and angrily, so that even Paul broke off his prayer in terror. There was a certain Diophantes, a freedman of Hieronymus, whose wife was a disciple of Paul, and she sat beside him night and day, so that Diophantes became jealous and hastened on the conflict. And Artemilla, the wife of Hieronymus, wished to hear Paul pray and said to Eubula, the wife of Diophantes, '... to hear the beast-fighter's prayer.' And she went and told Paul, and Paul full of joy said, 'Bring her.' She put on darker clothes and came to him with Eubula. But when Paul saw her he groaned and said, 'Woman, ruler of this world, mistress of much gold, citizen of great luxury, splendid in your raiment, sit down on the floor and forget your riches and your beauty and your finery. For these will profit you nothing if you pray not to God, who regards as dross all that here is marvellous but graciously bestows what beyond is wonderful. Gold perishes, riches are consumed, clothes become worn out. Beauty grows old, and great cities are changed, and the world will be destroyed in fire because of the lawlessness of men. God alone abides, and the sonship that is given through him in whom men must be saved. And now, Artemilla, hope in God and he will deliver you; hope in Christ and he will give you forgiveness of sins and will bestow upon you a crown of freedom, that you may no longer serve idols and the savour of sacrifice but the living God and Father of Christ whose is the glory for ever and ever. Amen.' And when Artemilla heard this she with Eubula besought

Paul that he would forthwith baptize her in God. And the fight with the beasts was arranged for the next day.

And Hieronymus heard from Diophantes that the women sat night and day with Paul, and he was not a little angry with Artemilla and the freedwoman Eubula. And when he had dined Hieronymus withdrew early that he might quickly carry through the animal fight. But the women said to Paul, 'Do you wish us to bring a lock-smith that you may baptize us in the sea as a free man?' And Paul said, 'I do not wish it, for I have faith in God who delivered the whole world from its bonds.' And Paul cried out to God on the Sabbath as the Lord's day drew near, the day on which Paul was to fight with the beasts, and he said, 'My God, Jesus Christ, who redeemed me from so many evils, grant me that before the eyes of Artemilla and Eubula, who are yours, the fetters may be broken from my hands.' And as Paul thus testified there came in a youth very comely in grace and loosed Paul's bonds, the youth smiling as he did so. And straightway he departed. But because of the vision which was granted to Paul and the great miracle of his fetters his grief over the fight with the beasts departed and, rejoicing, he leaped as if in paradise. And taking Artemilla he went out from the narrow and dark place where the prisoners were kept.

...[15] 'O you who give light and shine, come to my help, so that the heathen may not say that Paul the prisoner fled after killing Artemilla.' And again the youth smiled, and the matron came to herself and went into the house as dawn was already breaking. But as Paul (?) went in the guards were asleep, and he broke bread and brought water, gave her to drink of the word, and sent her to her husband Hieronymus. But he himself prayed.

At dawn there was a cry from the citizens, 'Let us go to the spectacle! Come, let us see the man who possesses God fighting with the beasts!' Hieronymus himself joined them, partly because of his suspicion against his wife, partly because Paul had not fled; he commanded Diophantes and the other slaves to bring Paul into the stadium. He was dragged in, saying nothing but bowed down and groaning because he was led in triumph by the city. And when he was brought out he was immediately flung into the stadium. Everybody was angry at Paul's dignified bearing. But Artemilla and Eubula fell into a sickness and were in extreme danger because of Paul's likely destruction. Hieronymus was therefore not a little grieved over his wife, and also because the rumour was already abroad in the city and he did not have his wife with him. So when he had taken his place the ... ordered a very fierce lion which had but recently been captured to be set loose against him ...

...[16] 'Away with the sorcerer! Away with the poisoner!' But the lion looked

---

[15] The following section is fragmentary. In it is the account of Artemilla's baptism in the sea in the presence of the young man. As Artemilla faints this prayer occurs.

[16] In the gap would be found the lion's prayer and its conversation with Paul. There then follows this acclamation of the crowd.

at Paul, and Paul at the lion. Then Paul recognized that this was the lion which had come and been baptized. And borne along by faith Paul said, 'Lion, was it you whom I baptized?' And the lion in answer said to Paul, 'Yes.' Paul spoke to it again and said, 'And how were you captured?' The lion said with its own voice, 'Just as you were, Paul.' After Hieronymus had sent many beasts so that Paul might be slain, and archers that the lion too might be killed, a violent and exceedingly heavy hail-storm fell from heaven, although the sky was clear: many died and all the rest took to flight. But it did not touch Paul or the lion although the other beasts perished under the weight of the hail, which was so heavy that Hieronymus' ear was hit and torn off, and the people cried out as they fled, 'Save us, O God, save us, O God of the man who fought with the beasts!' And Paul took leave of the lion, which spoke no more, and went out of the stadium and down to the harbour and embarked on the ship which was sailing for Macedonia, for there were many who were sailing as if the city were about to perish. So he embarked too like one of the fugitives, but the lion went away into the mountains as was natural for it.

Now Artemilla and Eubula mourned not a little, fasting and in ... as to what had befallen Paul. But when it was night there came (a young man) visibly into the bedroom, where ... Hieronymus had a running sore in his ear. ...[17] 'Through the will of Christ Jesus heal the ear!' And it became whole, as the youth had commanded him, 'Treat yourself with honey.'

The unpublished Coptic fragment announced by Kasser[18] concerns Paul in Ephesus and overlaps the passages translated above. In this fragment Paul leaves Smyrna to go to Ephesus, where he lodges with Prisca and Aquila. At night an angel warns Paul of impending doom. Paul then gives a sermon in which he refers to his having baptized a lion in Judaea. The sermon results in Paul's converting many Ephesians but also in his arrest. He is brought to the proconsul, Hieronymus, and gives an account of himself. (This section overlaps with P. Hamb, p. 1).[19] This Coptic fragment is then too lacunose to be of value.

8. *Philippi*[20]

... The Corinthians were in great distress about Paul because he was going to die before his time. For men, Simon and Cleobius, had come to Corinth who said, 'There is no resurrection of the flesh but only of the spirit, and the body of man is not created by God, and God did not create the world and does not know the world, nor has Jesus Christ been crucified but only in appearance, and he was not born of Mary nor of the seed of David.' In a word, they taught

---

[17] In the gap it seems as if the women are comforted by the youth. Hieronymus then prays to Paul's God for help.
[18] See bibliography under 'Coptic'.
[19] The passages are set out in parallel columns in Moraldi's Italian translation, ii. 1114–15; ² ii 194–5.
[20] The beginning of this section is lost.

many things in Corinth, deceiving many others and deceiving themselves. When therefore the Corinthians heard that Paul was at Philippi they sent a letter to Paul in Macedonia by the hand of Threptus and Eutychus, the deacons. The letter was as follows:

[A. LETTER OF THE CORINTHIANS TO THE APOSTLE PAUL]

I

1. Stephanus and his fellow-presbyters Daphnus and Eubulus and Theophilus and Zeno to Paul, the brother in the Lord—greeting! 2. Two individuals have come to Corinth, named Simon and Cleobius, who overthrow the faith of some through pernicious words. 3. These you shall examine yourself. 4. For we never heard such things either from you or from the other apostles. 5. But we keep what we have received from you and from the others. 6. Since the Lord has shown us mercy, while you are still in the flesh we should hear this from you once more. 7. Come to us or write to us. 8. For we believe, as it has been revealed to Theonoe, that the Lord has delivered you from the hands of the godless. 9. What they say and teach is as follows: 10. They assert that one must not appeal to the prophets (11) and that God is not almighty, (12) there is no resurrection of the body, (13) man has not been made by God, (14) Christ has neither come in the flesh, nor was he born of Mary, (15) and the world is not the work of God but of angels. 16. Wherefore we beseech you, brother, be diligent to come to us that the Corinthian church may remain without stumbling and the foolishness of these men be confounded. Farewell in the Lord!

II[21]

1. The deacons, Threptus and Eutychus, took the letter to Philippi (2) and Paul received it, being himself in prison because of Stratonike, the wife of Apollophanes; and he became very sad, (3) and exclaimed saying, 'It would have been better had I died and were with the Lord than to abide in the flesh and to hear such words so that sorrow comes upon sorrow, (4) and to be in prison in the face of such great distress and behold such mischief where the wiles of Satan are busy!' 5. And in great affliction Paul wrote the answer to the letter.

[B. PAUL'S EPISTLE TO THE CORINTHIANS][22]

III

1. Paul, the prisoner of Jesus Christ, to the brethren at Corinth—greeting! 2. Being in many afflictions, I marvel not that the teachings of the evil one had

---

[21] Not in P. Bod.
[22] P. Bod. adds 'concerning the Flesh'.

such rapid success. 3. For my Lord Jesus Christ will quickly come, since he is rejected by those who falsify his teaching. 4. For I delivered to you first of all what I received from the apostles before me who were always with Jesus Christ, (5) that our Lord Jesus Christ was born of Mary of the seed of David, the Father having sent the spirit from heaven into her (6) that he might come into this world and save all flesh by his own flesh and that he might raise us in the flesh from the dead as he has presented himself to us as our example. 7. And since man is created by his Father, (8) for this reason was he sought by him when he was lost, to become alive by adoption. 9. For the almighty God, maker of heaven and earth, sent the prophets first to the Jews to deliver them from their sins, (10) for he wished to save the house of Israel; therefore he took from the spirit of Christ and poured it out upon the prophets who proclaimed the true worship of God for a long period of time. 11. For the wicked prince who wished to be God himself laid his hands on them and killed them and bound all flesh of man to his pleasure. 12. But the almighty God, being just, and not wishing to repudiate his creation had mercy (13) and sent his Spirit into Mary the Galilean,[23] (15) that the evil one might be conquered by the same flesh by which he held sway, and be convinced that he is not God. 16. For by his own body Jesus Christ saved all flesh, (17) presenting in his own body a temple of righteousness (18) through which we are saved. 19. They who follow them are not children of righteousness but of wrath, who despise the wisdom of God and in their disbelief assert that heaven and earth and all that is in them are not a work of God. 20. They have the accursed belief of the serpent. 21. Turn away from them and keep aloof from their teaching.[24] 24. And those who say that there is no resurrection of the flesh shall have no resurrection, (25) for they do not believe him who had thus risen. 26. For they do not know, O Corinthians, about the sowing of wheat or some other grain that it is cast naked into the ground and having perished rises up again by the will of God in a body and clothed. 27. And he not only raises the body which is sown, but blesses it manifold. 28. And if one will not take the parable of the seeds (29) let him look at Jonah, the son of Amathios who, being unwilling to preach to the Ninevites, was swallowed up by the whale. 30. And after three days and three nights God heard the prayer of Jonah out of deepest hell, and nothing was corrupted, not even a hair nor an eyelid. 31. How much more will he raise you up, who have believed in Christ Jesus, as he himself was raised up. 32. When a corpse was thrown on the bones of the prophet Elisha by one of the children of Israel the corpse rose from death; how much more shall you rise up on that day with a whole

---

[23] Verse 14 is found in Latin MSS: 'Who believed with all her heart and conceived by the Holy Spirit that Jesus could come into the world'.

[24] Verses 22-3 are not found in all authorities. These verses read (in the Milan and Paris MSS and in Armenian): '22. For you are not children of disobedience but of the beloved church. 23. Therefore is the time of the resurrection preached to all.'

body, after you have been thrown upon the body and bones and Spirit of the Lord.[25] 34. If, however, you receive anything else let no man trouble me, (35) for I have these bonds on me that I may win Christ, and I bear his marks that I may attain to the resurrection of the dead. 36. And whoever accepts this rule which we have received by the blessed prophets and the holy gospel, shall receive a reward,[26] (37) but for whomsoever deviates from this rule fire shall be for him and for those who preceded him therein (38) since they are Godless men, a generation of vipers. 39. Resist them in the power of the Lord. 40. Peace be with you.

Between 3 Corinthians and the conclusion of the episode in Philippi there is a gap. In it is likely to have occurred the story of Longinus' and Firmilla's daughter Frontina. The fragment begins in the middle of a speech probably by Longinus:

... nothing good has befallen my house.' And he advised that ... who were to throw down Frontina his daughter should also throw down Paul alive with her. Now Paul knew of the matter, but he laboured and fasted in great cheerfulness for two days with the prisoners. They commanded that on the third day ... bring out Frontina. But the ... followed her. And Firmilla and Longinus and the soldiers lamented. But the prisoners carried the bier. And when Paul saw the great mourning ... Paul alive with the daughter. But when Paul had taken the daughter in his arms he groaned to the Lord Jesus Christ because of Firmilla's sorrow; he threw himself on his knees in the mud ... and prayed for Frontina and her in one prayer. In that hour Frontina rose up. And all the crowd was afraid and fled. Paul took the daughter's hand and led her through the city to the house of Longinus. But the whole crowd cried with one voice, 'One is God, who has made heaven and earth, who has given life to the daughter ... of Paul' ...[27]

9. Corinth

From Philippi to Corinth

When Paul came from Philippi to Corinth, to the house of Epiphanius, there was joy; all our people rejoiced but at the same time wept as Paul related what he had suffered in Philippi in the workhouse and everywhere and what had befallen him so that his tears became ... and prayer was offered without

---

[25] Verse 33 is found in some MSS: 'Also Elijah the prophet: he raised up the widow's son from death: how much more shall the Lord Jesus raise you up from death at the sound of the trumpet, in the twinkling of an eye? For he has shown us an example in his own body.'

[26] Some manuscripts add: 'and when he is raised from the dead shall obtain eternal life'.

[27] Shortly after this Schmidt conjectured (incorrectly) the reading 'to Philippi'. It is *from* Philippi', as P. Hamb. p. 6 makes clear. Before the next episode the following words may be restored from P. Heid. p. 44: 'When he had departed from Philippi and wished to go (to Corinth)'.

ceasing by all for Paul, and he counted himself blessed that so single-heartedly every day they guided his affairs in prayer to the Lord. Unrivalled therefore was the greatness of the joy, and Paul's soul was uplifted because of the goodwill of the brethren so that for forty days he preached the word of perseverance, namely in what place anything had befallen him and what great deeds had been granted to him. So in every account he praised almighty God and Christ Jesus who in every place had been well pleased with Paul. But when the days were ended and the time drew near for Paul to depart for Rome grief came upon the brethren as to when they should see him again. And Paul, full of the Holy Spirit, said, 'Brethren, be zealous about... and love. For behold, I go away to a furnace of fire... and I am not strong except the Lord grant me power. For indeed David accompanied Saul... for Christ Jesus was with him... The grace of the Lord will go with me that I may fulfil the... dispensation with steadfastness.' But they were distressed and fasted. Then Cleobius was filled with the Spirit and said, 'Brethren, now must Paul fulfil his assignment and go up to the... of death... in great instruction and knowledge and sowing of the word and must suffer envy and depart out of this world.' But when the brethren and Paul heard this they lifted up their voice and said, 'O God,... Father of Christ, help Paul your servant, that he may yet abide with us because of our weakness.' But since Paul was cut to the heart and no longer fasted with them, when an offering was celebrated by Paul...

But the Spirit came upon Myrta so that she said, 'Brethren, why are you alarmed at the sight of this sign? Paul the servant of the Lord will save many in Rome and will nourish innumerable people with the word and he will become manifest above all the faithful, and greatly will the glory... come upon him so that there will be great grace in Rome.' And immediately, when the Spirit that was in Myrta was at peace, each one partook of the bread and feasted according to custom... amid the singing of psalms of David and of hymns. And Paul too was glad. On the following day, after they had spent the whole night according to the will of God, Paul said, 'Brethren, I shall set out on Friday and sail for Rome that I may not delay what is commanded and laid upon me, for to this I was appointed.' They were greatly distressed when they heard this, and all the brethren contributed according to their ability so that Paul might not be troubled, except that he was going away from the brethren.

10. *From Corinth to Italy*

As he embarked on the ship while they all prayed Artemon the captain of the ship was there. He had been baptized by Peter and... Paul that so much was entrusted to him... the Lord was embarking. But when the ship had set sail Artemon came together with Paul to glorify the Lord Jesus Christ in the grace of God since he had fore-ordained his plan for Paul. When they were on the open sea and it was quiet Paul fell asleep, fatigued by the fastings and the night watches with the brethren. And the Lord came to him, walking upon the sea, and he touched Paul and said, 'Stand up and see!' And he awoke and said, 'You are my Lord Jesus Christ, the king..., but why are you so gloomy and downcast, Lord? And if you... Lord, for I am not a little distressed that you are so.' And the Lord said, 'Paul, I am about to be crucified afresh.' And Paul said, 'God forbid, Lord, that I should see this!' But the Lord said to Paul, 'Paul, get up, go to Rome and admonish the brethren, that they abide in the calling to the Father.' And... walking on the sea, he went before them... showed (the way). But when the voyage was ended... Paul went... with great sadness, and he saw a man standing on the harbour who was waiting for Artemon the captain and when Artemon saw him he greeted him... and he[28] said to him, 'Claudius, see here Paul the beloved of the Lord, who is with me.'... Claudius embraced[29] Paul and greeted him. And without delay he and Artemon carried the baggage from the ship to his house. And he rejoiced greatly and informed the brethren about him, so that at once Claudius' house was filled with joy and thanksgiving. For they saw how Paul laid aside his mood of sadness and taught the word of truth and said, 'Brethren and soldiers of Christ, listen! How often did God deliver Israel out of the hand of the lawless! And as long as they kept the things of God he did not forsake them. For he saved them out of the hand of Pharaoh the lawless and of Og, a more ungodly king, and of Adar and the foreign people. And as long as they kept the things of God he gave them of the fruit of the loins, after he had promised them the land of the Canaanites, and he made the foreign people subject to them. And after all the things that he had provided for them in the desert and in the waterless country he sent them in addition prophets to proclaim our Lord Jesus Christ; and these in succession received a share and portion of the Spirit of Christ, and having suffered greatly were slain by the people. Having thus forsaken the living God according to their own desires they forfeited the eternal inheritance. And now, brethren, a great temptation lies before us. If we endure we shall have access to the Lord and shall receive as the refuge and shield of his good pleasure[30] Jesus Christ, who gave himself for us, if at least you receive the word as it is. For in these last times God for our sakes has sent down a spirit of power into the flesh,[31] that is, into Mary the Galilean, according to the prophetic word, which was conceived and borne by her as the fruit of her womb until she was delivered and gave birth to Jesus the Christ, our king, of Bethlehem in Judaea, brought up in Nazareth,[32] who went to Jerusalem and taught all Judaea, 'The kingdom of heaven is at hand! Forsake the darkness, receive the light, you who live in the darkness of death!

---

[28] P. Mich. 1317 begins here.
[29] P. Berlin 13893 begins here.
[30] P. Mich. 3788 begins.
[31] P. Mich. 1317 breaks off.
[32] P. Mich. 1317 resumes.

The Acts of Paul

A light has arisen for you!' And he did great and wonderful works, choosing from the tribes twelve men whom he had with him in understanding and faith, as he raised the dead, healed diseases, cleansed lepers, healed the blind,[33] made cripples whole, raised up paralytics, cleansed those possessed by demons...

P. Mich 1317 ends, but in the Berlin papyrus there follow the fragments of 23 further lines. Possibly the text of P. Heid. pp. 79/80 and P. Mich. 3788 was attached here (see James p. 31):

... wondered greatly and deliberated in their hearts. He said to them, 'Why are you amazed that I raise up the dead or that I make the lame walk or that I cleanse the lepers or that I raise up the sick or that I have healed the paralytic and those possessed by demons or that I have divided a little bread and satisfied many or that I have walked upon the sea or that I have commanded the winds? If you believe this and are convinced then are you great. For truly I say to you, "If you say to this mountain; "Be removed and be cast into the sea", and are not doubtful in your heart it will happen for you.'... when one of them was convinced whose name was Simon and who said, 'Lord, truly great are the works which you do. For we have never heard nor have we ever seen a man who has raised the dead, except you.' The Lord said to him, 'You will pray for the works which I myself will do... But the other works I will do at once. For these I do for the sake of a temporary deliverance in the time during which they are in these places, that they may believe in him who sent me.' Simon said to him, 'Lord, command me to speak.' He said to him, 'Speak, Peter!' For from that day he called them by name. He said, 'What then is the work that is greater than these except the raising of the dead and the feeding of such a crowd?' The Lord said to him, 'There is something that is greater than this, and blessed are they who have believed with all their heart.' But Philip lifted up his voice in wrath, saying, 'What manner of thing is this that you will teach us?' But he said to him, 'You...'

11. The Martyrdom of the Holy Apostle Paul[34]

1. Luke, who had come from Gaul, and Titus, who had come from Dalmatia, expected Paul at Rome. When Paul saw them he rejoiced and rented a barn outside Rome where he and the brethren taught the word of truth. He became famous and many souls were added to the Lord, so that it was noised about in Rome and a great many from the house of the emperor came to him and there was much joy.

A certain Patroclus, a cupbearer of the emperor, who had come too late to

---

[33] Here P. Hamb. p. 8 ends; the following words are from P. Berlin 13893.
[34] A small gap separates this section from the preceding.

the barn and could not get near to Paul on account of the throng of the people sat on a high window, and listened as he taught the word of God. But Satan, being wicked, became jealous of the love of the brethren and Patroclus fell down from the window and died; speedily it was reported to Nero. Paul, however, having learned it by the Spirit said, 'Brethren, the evil one has obtained a way to tempt you; go forth and you will find a boy who has fallen down and is dying. Lift him up and bring him here.' This they did. When the people saw him they were frightened. Paul said to them, 'Now, brethren, show your faith. Come, let us mourn to our Lord Jesus Christ, that the boy may live and we remain unharmed.' When all began to lament, the boy took breath and, having put him on an animal, they sent him away alive with all those who were of the emperor's house.

2. And Nero, having heard of Patroclus' death, became very sad, and as he came out from his bath he ordered another to be appointed for the wine. But his servants said, 'Emperor, Patroclus is alive and stands at the sideboard.' When the emperor heard that Patroclus was alive he was frightened and would not come in. But when he came in and saw Patroclus he cried out, 'Patroclus, are you alive?' He answered, 'I am alive, Caesar.' But he said, 'Who is he who made you alive?' And the boy, uplifted by the confidence of faith, said, 'Christ Jesus, the king of the ages.' The emperor asked in dismay, 'Is he to be king of the ages and destroy all kingdoms?' Patroclus said to him, 'Yes, he destroys all kingdoms under heaven, and he alone shall remain in all eternity, and there will be no kingdom which escapes him.' And he struck his face and cried out, 'Patroclus, are you also fighting for that king?' He answered, 'Yes, my lord and Caesar, for he has raised me from the dead.'

And Barsabas Justus the flat-footed and Urion the Cappadocian and Festus of Galatia, the chief men of Nero, said, 'And we, too, fight for him, the king of the ages.' After having tortured those men whom he used to love he imprisoned them and ordered that the soldiers of the great king be sought, and he issued an edict that all Christians and soldiers of Christ that were found should be executed.

3. And among the many Paul also was brought in fetters. Those who were imprisoned with him looked at him, so that the emperor observed that he was the leader of the soldiers. And he said to him, 'Man of the great king, now my prisoner, what induced you to come secretly into the Roman empire and to enlist soldiers in my territory?' But Paul, filled with the Holy Spirit, said in the presence of all, 'Caesar, we enlist soldiers not only in your territory but in all lands of the earth. For thus we are commanded to exclude none who wishes to fight for my king. If it seems good to you serve him, for neither riches nor the splendours of this life will save you; but if you become his subject and beseech him you shall be saved. For in one day he will destroy the world.'

Having heard this Nero commanded all the prisoners to be burned with fire, but Paul to be beheaded according to the law of the Romans. But Paul was not silent and communicated the word to Longus the prefect and Cestus the centurion. And Nero, being instigated by the evil one, raged in Rome and had many Christians executed without trial, so that the Romans stood before the palace and cried, 'It is enough, Caesar; these men are ours. You destroy the strength of the Romans.' Being thus convinced, he desisted and commanded that no Christian was to be touched till his case had been investigated.

4. After the issuing of the edict Paul was brought before him, and he insisted that he should be executed. And Paul said, 'Caesar, I live not merely for a short time for my king; and if you have me executed I shall do the following: I will rise again and appear to you, for I shall not be dead but alive to my king, Christ Jesus, who shall come to judge the earth.'

And Longus and Cestus said to Paul, 'Whence have you this king that you believe in him without changing your mind even at point of death?' And Paul answered and said, 'You men, who are now ignorant and in error, change your mind and be saved from the fire which comes over the whole earth. For we fight not, as you suppose, for a king who is from the earth but for one who is from heaven: he is the living God who comes as judge because of the lawless deeds which take place in this world. And blessed is he who will believe in him and live in eternity when he shall come with fire to purge the earth.' And they besought him and said, 'We entreat you, help us, and we will release you.' But he answered, 'I am not a deserter from Christ but a faithful soldier of the living God. If I knew that I should die I would still have done it, Longus and Cestus, but since I live to God and love myself I go to the Lord that I may come again with him in the glory of his Father.' And they said to him, 'How can we live after you have been beheaded?'

5. And while they were speaking Nero sent a certain Parthenius and Pheretas to see whether Paul had already been beheaded. And they found him still alive. He summoned them beside him and said, 'Believe in the living God who will raise me, as well as all those who believe in him, from the dead.' But they said, 'We will now go to Nero but when you have died and have been raised up we will believe in your God.'

But when Longus and Cestus continued to ask about salvation he said to them, 'In the early dawn come quickly to my grave and you will find two men at prayer, Titus and Luke; they will give you the seal in the Lord.'

And turning toward the east, Paul lifted up his hands to heaven and prayed at length; and after having conversed in Hebrew with the fathers during prayer[35] he bent his neck, without speaking any more. When the executioner cut off his head milk splashed on the tunic of the soldier. And the soldier and all who stood near by were astonished at this sight and glorified God who had thus honoured Paul. And they went away and reported everything to Caesar.

---

[35] P. Hamb. includes here the words 'Father (into your hands) I commit my spirit... receive it'.

6. When he heard of it he was amazed and did not know what to say. While many philosophers and the centurion were assembled with the emperor Paul came about the ninth hour, and in the presence of all he said, 'Caesar, behold, here is Paul, the soldier of God; I am not dead but live in my God. But upon you, unhappy one, many evils and great punishment will come because you have unjustly shed the blood of the righteous not many days ago.' And having spoken this Paul departed from him. When Nero had heard he commanded that the prisoners be released, Patroclus as well as Barsabas with his friends.

7. And, as Paul had told them, Longus and Cestus, the centurion, came in fear very early to the grave of Paul. And when they drew near they found two men in prayer and Paul with them, and they became frightened when they saw the unexpected miracle, but Titus and Luke, being afraid at the sight of Longus and Cestus, turned to run away.

But they followed and said to them, 'We follow you not in order to kill you, blessed men of God, as you imagine, but in order to live, that you may do to us as Paul promised us. We have just seen him in prayer beside you.' Upon hearing this Titus and Luke gave them joyfully the seal in the Lord, glorifying God and the Father of our Lord Jesus Christ to whom be glory for ever and ever. Amen.

SECONDARY ACTS OF PAUL[1]

(a) *Martyrium beati Pauli Apostoli*

Attributed to Pseudo-Linus (cf. a similar martyrdom of Peter by Pseudo-Linus; see under Acts of Peter), this is a Latin reworking of the conclusion to the Acts of Paul. Many manuscripts have survived.

EDITIONS

Lipsius–Bonnet, i. 23–44, and see esp. Prolegomena, pp. xiv–xxiii.
Fabricius, ii. 775 f.

MODERN TRANSLATIONS

French

Migne, *Dictionnaire*, ii, cols. 665–74.

Italian

Erbetta, ii. 289–96.

[1] Not translated.

(b) The Acts of Titus by Pseudo-Zenas

Brought to light by James, *Apoc. Anec.* i. 54–7, who dated it not earlier than the fifth century. His edition has been superseded by the publication of the text by F. Halkin, 'La légende crétoise de saint Tite' *Anal. Boll.* 79 (1961), 241–56.

This text is perhaps of value in helping to restore the text of the act of Paul in Antioch. When referring to the events known from the Coptic manuscript as the Myra and Sidon episodes the Acts of Titus places them after Paul's conversion in Damascus and puts the Panchores incident in Antioch later; these Acts are, however, not to be trusted as an infallible guide to the original order of the Acts of Paul. (See M. R. James, 'The Acts of Titus and the Acts of Paul', *JTS* 6 (1905), 549–56 (cf. id., 'A Note on the *Acta Pauli*', ibid. 244–6).)

(c) Syriac History of the Holy Apostle Paul

P. Bedjan, *Acta Martyrum et Sanctorum*, i (Paris, 1890), 33–6.

This text is possibly linked to the canonical Acts, rather than the Acta Pauli.

(d) Acts of Andrew and Paul (Coptic)

See under Acts of Andrew, F.

(e) Pseudo-Abdias, book 2

See under Other Apocryphal Acts, 6.

For other secondary acts relating details about Paul, see the Acts of Peter: Secondary Acts 2a, 2b, and 3; and cf. Hennecke[5], ii. 394–9 (A. de Santos Otero); Eng. trans. ii. 440–3.

The Acts of Peter

The figure of Peter gave rise to much apocryphal literature. The Acts and Passion of Peter appear in various forms and in various languages. The cycle of Pseudo-Clementine literature and the Preaching of Peter represent other traditions concerning Peter (and these are dealt with elsewhere in this volume).

Ancient testimony to the existence of episodes known from the Acts of Peter includes possible references in Clement of Alexandria, Origen, and the Didascalia, but these make no concrete reference to the written Acts, only to traditions about Peter. Literary references are therefore not certain before the time of Eusebius who in *HE* 3. 3. 2 declares the Acts of Peter to be heretical (Schwartz, *GCS* 9.1, pp. 188 f.). By the end of the fourth century Philaster of Brescia, *haer*. 88, speaks of the use of these Acts among Manichaeans and other heretics (ed. F. Marx *CSEL* 38 (Vienna, Prague, Leipzig, 1898), pp. 47 f.). The Gelasian Decree condemns the Acts.

The apparent use of the Acts of Peter by the Acts of Paul (as argued by C. Schmidt, ΠΡΑΞΕΙΣ ΠΑΥΛΟΥ (Glückstadt and Hamburg, 1936), pp. 127–30, *pace* James, *ANT* 306, or Michaelis, pp. 327 f.) may be seen especially in the famous Quo Vadis scene (which is out of place in the Acts of Paul). This would be the earliest evidence for the existence of the Acts of Peter and would of course prove its priority over the Acts of Paul. However, the interrelationship of these two Acts has not been satisfactorily resolved.

The relationship of the Acts of Peter and the Acts of John is another issue on which it is difficult to make a firm decision. Older editions of these apocrypha tended to argue that the Acts of Peter used the Acts of John, but the recent dating of the two works does not now allow this conclusion. There is indeed a certain affinity between the two works, but this is likely to be due to their shared similar common origins.

James, *Apoc. Anec.* i. xxiv f., claims that the author of the Acts of Peter is the same as that of the Acts of John, and identifies him as Leucius. The whole question of Leucian authorship is discussed at length by Schmidt in *Die alten Petrusakten*, and he concludes that only the Acts of John may legitimately be attributed to Leucius: because Leucius was identified with this type of literature his name was used as author of books for which he was not responsible. (See K. Schäferdiek, in Hennecke[3], ii. pp. 117–25 (Eng. trans. 178–88) and Hennecke[5], ii. pp. 81–93 (Eng. trans. ii. 87–100).)

The interrelationship of the Acts of Peter and the Pseudo-Clementine literature is problematic, but it is generally agreed that the latter (normally dated about 260) is later.

The original Greek of the Acts of Peter has survived only in the Martyrdom and in a small Oxyrhynchus fragment (P. Oxy. 849) outside the Martyrdom. There is, however, a long Latin text found in a Vercelli manuscript which contains some of the Acts of Peter.[1] This Latin manuscript (Codex Vercellensis 158) dates from the sixth–seventh century, but its text is likely to be a fourth–fifth century translation of the original Greek Acts. Codex Berol. 8502.4 (Coptic), which is plainly from a larger work, insofar as it tells of Peter's doings also very probably came from the Acts of Peter. The manuscript is fourth–fifth century and contains an episode (the healing of Peter's daughter) that was known to Augustine (*c. Adimantum* 17. 5 (Zycha, p. 170)).

Augustine also refers in this context to a healing of a gardener's daughter. Such an episode is to be found in the Epistle of Pseudo-Titus. That text survives in an eighth-century manuscript edited in its entirety by D. de Bruyne in *Rev. Bén.* 37 (1925), 47–72. The relevant portion is translated below (from de Bruyne, *Rev. Bén.* 25 (1908), 151 f.).

The Stichometry of Nicephorus indicates that the original Acts contained 2750 stichoi. This means that only about two-thirds has survived. It has been suggested that stories about Peter and Paul in Jerusalem would have made up much of the missing third. Vercelli chapter 23 refers to earlier contact between Simon and Paul, but Vouaux doubted if this chapter belonged to the original Acts. The healings of Peter's daughter and of the gardener's daughter which have survived are likely to have belonged to the Jerusalem cycle of stories.

Vouaux argued that some other portions of the Vercelli Acts did not derive from the original Acts. James agreed with him that Vercelli 1–3 could have been added to the original Acts by the writer of the Greek underlying the Vercelli manuscript to explain how there was a congregation in Rome before Peter reached it. (It is another question whether these chapters originated in the Acts of Paul.) Likewise Vouaux, followed by James, considered Vercelli 17 to have been inserted by the writer of the underlying Greek from the earlier, Jerusalem, section of the original Acts. The awkward sentences in the first paragraph and the sudden change to the third person suggest the chapter has been transplanted. The final sentence of 40 and the whole of 41 were also considered by Vouaux to have been added. Poupon in his *ANRW* article has argued that editorial activity may also be seen in Vercelli 4, 6, 10, 30, and elsewhere.

Although only the Martyrdom has survived in its entirety in Greek, the discovery of a portion of the Acts (corresponding to Vercelli 25–6) in P. Oxy. 849 proves that the original did exist in Greek. The Latin of the Vercelli manuscript betrays itself as a translation from Greek, as too does the more

---

[1] My translation is based on the Latin (and Coptic) for the Acts proper, and on the Greek for the Martyrdom.

literal translation found in the *Vita Abercii* of the fourth century (which contains speeches of Peter and of Paul found in the Vercelli Acts transferred to the life of St Abercius of Hierapolis).[2]

As so often in this type of literature the account of the Martyrdom circulated as a separate work (i.e. from Vercelli 30 in the case of the Athos Greek manuscript, or in the case of the Patmos Greek manuscript and the versions 33–41). It is to be found in Syriac, Armenian, Arabic, Ethiopic, Georgian, and Slavonic. The Coptic Martyrdom survives in a version edited by Guidi that commences at Vercelli 33. The other Coptic version edited by von Lemm commences near the middle of Vercelli 36.

The pioneering work of Lipsius in e.g. *Die Quellen*..., (below, bibliography under *Peter and Rome*) tended to emphasize the Gnostic character of these Acts. It is, however, now generally accepted that the Acts of Peter is not a Gnostic work although Gnostic and Encratite ideas, especially regarding marriage, are to be found in it. As with many of the other apocryphal Acts it is the product of popular piety. Such literature seems to have been influenced to a greater or lesser extent by the unorthodox teachings of the day (e.g. in Acts of Peter 38 about the significance of the cross), and this influence was responsible for prejudicing the early fathers against the work. More significant perhaps is that the use of these Acts by heretics ensured its removal from official church lists.

There is no detailed discussion in the Acts of Peter of the teaching of Simonian Gnosis. Simon Magus is here virtually a personification of evil, and the contests between him and Peter are in effect a classical battle between God and sin. The author has only limited theological competence or concerns.

The provenance of the composition must remain an open question, although Rome or Asia Minor remain the likeliest. A date in the closing decades of the second century is probable for the original Greek Acts.

EDITIONS

Greek

Lipsius–Bonnet, i. 78–103 (Martyrdom based on a 9th-cent. Patmos MS (no. 48) that corresponds to Vercelli 33–41, and a 10th–11th cent. Athos MS (Vatopedi 84) corresponding to Vercelli 30–41).

B. P. Grenfell and A. S. Hunt (eds.), 'No. 849, Acts of Peter', in *OP* 6 (London, 1908), 6–12 (Greek text corresponding to Vercelli 25.3–26.1).

---

[2] *Vita Abercii* 13, 15, 24, 26 contain passages taken from the Acts of Peter (Vercelli 2, 7, 20, 21); cf. edn. by T. Nissen, *S. Abercii Vita* (Leipzig, 1912).

Latin

Lipsius-Bonnet, i. 45-103 (= Codex Vercellensis 158; the MS lacks most of chs. 36-7).

Coptic

Episode of the healing of Peter's daughter = Codex Berol. 8502.4:
> See 'The Act of Peter', in D. M. Parrott (ed.), *Nag Hammadi Codices V, 2-5 and VI with Papyrus Berolinensis 8502, 1 and 4* (Leiden, 1979), 473-93 (= *Nag Hammadi Studies* 11).

Version of martyrdom based on 3 MSS in the Borgiana Library (128, 129, 130)—close to Athos Greek manuscript from end of ch. 4 (= Vercelli 33) to end of Martyrdom:
> Guidi, *AAL.R* 4, 3.2 (1887); 23-34; Italian trans., *Giornale*, 29-35.

Smaller fragment of Martyrdom:
> O. von Lemm, 'Koptische apokryphe Apostelacten', *Mélanges Asiatiques* 10 (St Petersburg, 1892), 300-42.

Syriac (See Secondary Acts of Peter below, no. 6)

F. Nau, 'La version syriaque inédite des martyres de S. Pierre, S. Paul et S. Luc d'après un manuscrit du dixième siècle', *Revue de l'orient chrétien* 3 (1898), 39-57, esp. 43-50, and 151-6 (French trans. of a 10th-cent. Syriac text close to Patmos Greek MS of the Martyrdom).

P. Bedjan, *Acta Martyrum et Sanctorum*, i (Paris and Leipzig, 1890; repr. Hildesheim, 1968), 1-33.

I. Guidi, *Zeitschrift der deutschen morgenländischen Gesellschaft* 46 (1892), 744-7 (text completed).

Arabic

Vat. Syr. 199, not edited. (The unedited Arabic MS and the Syriac of Bedjan's text contain résumés of episodes paralleled in the Vercelli Acts.)

Armenian

P. Vetter, 'Die armenische apokryphen Apostelakten, i. Das gnostische Martyrium Petri', *Or. Chr.* 1 (1901), 217-39. [See id., *ThQ* 3 (1903), 16-58, 324-83 (with Greek retroversion), and ibid. 88 (1906), 161-86 (for German trans. of the Acts of Peter and Paul).]

Leloir, *CCA* 3, 64-76.

Ethiopic

Malan, 1-10.

Wallis Budge, *Contendings*, i. 7–46 (and see also 382–436); ii. (Eng. trans.), 7–42 (and see also 466–526). [Most of this is a new story with frequent references to the revelations delivered by Peter to Clement.]

Georgian

N. Marr, 'Le synaxaire géorgien VII, Le martyre de Pierre à Rome', *PO* 19 (1926), .715–25.

Slavonic

Bibliography in de Santos Otero, *Altslav. Apok.* i. 52–9.

MODERN TRANSLATIONS

English

Pick, 50–122 (Cod. Berol.; Vercelli 1–29; Greek Martyrdom).
James, 300–36 (Cod. Berol.; Gardener's Daughter; fragment of speech; Vercelli 1–29; Greek Martyrdom).
Hennecke[3], ii. 259–322 (for contents see Hennecke[3] (German)).
Hennecke[5], ii. 271–321 (for contents see Hennecke[5] (German)).

French

Vouaux, *Les Actes de Pierre* (see below under *Twentieth-century studies*), 221–469 (Cod. Berol.; Vercelli 1–29; Greek Martyrdom; Oxyrhynchus fragment).
Amiot 185–225 (Cod. Berol. and Vercelli, repeating Vouaux).
Éac, 1041–114 (Cod. Berol.; Gardener's Daughter; Vercelli 1–29; Greek Martyrdom).

German

Michaelis, 317–79 (selections from Vercelli).
Hennecke[1], 383–423 (G. Ficker); cf. *Handbuch*, 395–491.
Hennecke[3], ii. 177–221 (W. Schneemelcher) (Cod. Berol.; Gardener's Daughter; fragment of speech from Codex Cambrai 254; Vercelli 1–29, with fns. showing Turner's suggested emendations, the alternatives found in the Vita Abercii, and also variants in P. Oxy. 849; Greek Martyrdom).
Hennecke[5], ii. 243–89 (Schneemelcher) (contents as in Hennecke[3]).

Italian

Erbetta, ii. 135–210 (Cod. Berol.; Gardener's Daughter; Vercelli; Martyrdom; and some secondary Acts (see below)).
Moraldi, ii. 963–1059;[2] ii. 41–135 (Borgiana Coptic fragments; Cod. Berol.; Gardener's Daughter; Vercelli; Martyrdom; and some secondary Acts (see below)).

GENERAL

For older studies see:

Lipsius, i. 34–5 (for bibliographical references); ii.1, 1–423; Ergänzungsheft, 32–61.
Zahn. *Kanon*, ii. 832–55.
Harnack, i. 131–6; ii.1, 549–60.

Twentieth-century studies

P. Peeters, 'Notes sur la légende des apôtres S. Pierre et S. Paul dans la littérature syrienne', *Anal. Boll.* 21 (1902), 121–40.
A. Baumstark, *Die Petrus- und Paulusacten in der litterarischen Ueberlieferung der syrischen Kirche* (Leipzig, 1902).
G. Ficker, *Die Petrusakten: Beiträge zu ihrem Verständnis* (Leipzig, 1903).
C. Schmidt, *Die alten Petrusakten im Zusammenhang der apokryphen Apostellitteratur nebst einem neuentdeckten Fragment* (Leipzig, 1903) (= *TU* 24.1 = *NF* 9.1) (Coptic text on pp. 3–7).[3]
D. de Bruyne, 'Nouveaux fragments des Actes de Pierre, de Paul, de Jean, d'André et de l'Apocalypse d'Élie', *Rev. Bén.* 25 (1908), 149–60, esp. 151–3.
T. Nissen, 'Die Petrusakten und ein bardesanistischer Dialog in der Aberkiosvita', *ZNW* 9 (1908), 190–203, 315–28.
J. Flamion, 'Les Actes apocryphes de Pierre', *Revue d'histoire ecclésiastique* 9 (1908), 233–54, 465–90; 10 (1909), 5–29, 245–77; 11 (1910), 5–28, 223–256, 447–470, 675–692; 12 (1911), 209–230, 437–50.
C. Erbes, 'Ursprung und Umfang der Petrusakten', *ZKG* 32 (1911), 161–85, 353–77, 497–530.
H. J. Bardsley, 'The Derivation of the Acta from Early Acts of Peter', *JTS* 16 (1915), 495–509.
L. Vouaux, *Les Actes de Pierre* (Paris, 1922) (= *Les apocryphes du Nouveau Testament*, ed. J. Bousquet and E. Amann).
C. Schmidt, 'Studien zu den alten Petrusakten', *ZKG* 43 (1924), 321–48; 45 (1927), 481–513.
——'Zur Datierung der alten Petrusakten', *ZNW* 29 (1930), 150–5.
C. H. Turner, 'The Latin Acts of Peter', *JTS* 32 (1931), 119–33 (attempts to improve on the text of Codex Vercellensis as published by Lipsius–Bonnet).
M. Blumenthal, *Formen und Motive in der apokryphen Apostelgeschichten* (Leipzig, 1933), esp. 10–26, 109–112 (= *TU* 48.1).
G. Quispel and R. M. Grant, 'Note on the Petrine Apocrypha', *VC* 6 (1952), 31–2.
Bauer, 64–71.
Vielhauer, 696–9.
Plümacher, cols. 19–24.
B. McNeil, 'A Liturgical Source in Acts of Peter 38', *VC* 33 (1979), 342–6.
G. Poupon, 'Les "Actes de Pierre" et leur remaniement', *ANRW* 2. 25. 6, 4363–83.
J. N. Bremmer (ed.), *The Apocryphal Acts of Peter: Magic, Miracles and Gnosticism* (Leuven, 1998) (= *Studies on the Apocryphal Acts of the Apostles* 3).

---

[3] Review by M. R. James, *JTS* 5 (1904), 293–6.

Peter and Rome

The traditions of Peter's sojourn in Rome and his death there have given rise to a good deal of literature, not least the ancient Pseudo-Clementines. A. A. de Marco, *The Tomb of St Peter* (Leiden, 1964) (= Supplements to *Novum Testamentum* 8), provides a detailed bibliography on these traditions. O. Cullmann, *Peter: Disciple, Apostle, Martyr: A Historical and Theological Study* (Eng. trans. London, 1953) discusses the tradition in patristic testimony and from archaeological evidence. The following may also be consulted:

R. A. Lipsius, *Die Quellen der römischen Petrus-sage kritisch untersucht* (Kiel, 1872).

A. Penna, *S. Pietro* (Brescia, 1954) (French trans. by E. Viale and Y. del Pozzo, *Saint Pierre* (Paris, 1958)). [See especially the Appendix for an analysis of Peter in the apocryphal literature.]

E. Dinkler, 'Die Petrus-Rom-Frage', *Theologische Rundschau* 25 (1959), 189–230, 289–335; ibid. 27 (1961), 33–64.

THE ACTS OF PETER

SUMMARY OF CONTENTS

The Acts of Peter

   (*a*) Peter's Daughter (Cod. Berol.).

   (*b*) The Gardener's Daughter (Pseudo-Titus).

Acts of Peter (Vercelli)

   1–3 Paul's Departure from Rome.

   4–6 Simon arrives in Rome and succeeds in drawing many Christians away from their faith. Peter is sent by God to Rome. An account of his journey from Caesarea.

   7 Peter preaches in Rome.

   8–11 The reconversion of Marcellus and the first signs of Peter's successes in Rome. The miracle of the talking dog.

   12–15 Peter's first assault on Simon. The miracle of the smoked fish. The miracle of the speaking infant.

   16–18 Peter's vision of Jesus. The account of how Peter drove Simon from Judaea after having exposed his thieving from Eubula.

   19–22 Peter's healing miracles.

   23–9 The contest with Simon in the Forum concerning the raising of a young man from death. Two further raisings (of the widow's son, and of the wealthy senator's son).

Martyrdom of the Holy Apostle Peter (Vercelli and Greek, Athos MS)

   30–2 (Greek 1–3) The death of Simon.

   33–40 (Greek 4–12) The martyrdom proper. The final words and death of Peter. Nero's vision.

TWO ACTS OF PETER

(a) Peter's Daughter[1]

But on the first day of the week, which is the Lord's Day, a multitude gathered together, and they brought many sick people to Peter for him to cure them. And one of the multitude was bold enough to say to Peter, 'Peter, behold, before our eyes you made many blind see and deaf hear and the lame walk, and you have helped the weak and given them strength; why have you not helped your virgin daughter, who has grown up beautiful and believed in the name of God? For behold, one of her sides is completely paralysed, and there she is helpless in the corner. We can see those whom you have cured, but you have neglected your own daughter.'

But Peter smiled and said to him, 'My son, God alone knows why her body is sick. Know that God is not unable or powerless to give his gift to my daughter. But in order that your soul may be convinced and those present believe the more'—he looked at his daughter and said to her, 'Arise from your place with the help of none except Jesus, and walk naturally before those present and come to me.' And she arose and came to him. The multitude rejoiced at what had taken place. And Peter said to them, 'Behold, your hearts are convinced that God is not powerless concerning the things which we ask of him.' They rejoiced the more and glorified God. Then Peter said to his daughter, 'Return to your place, sit down there and be helpless again, for it is good for me and you.' And the girl went back, lay down in her place and became as before. The whole multitude wept and besought Peter to make her well.

Peter said to them, 'As the Lord lives, this is good for her and for me. For on the day on which she was born to me I saw a vision and the Lord said to me, "Peter, this day has been born for you a great affliction, for this daughter will harm many souls, if her body remains well!" I, however, thought that the vision mocked me.

'When the girl was ten years old she became a stumbling-block to many. And a very rich man, Ptolemy by name, when he saw the girl bathing with her mother, sent for her to take her for his wife, but her mother did not consent. He often sent for her, for he could not wait ... [2]

'Ptolemy brought the girl, and leaving her before the door of the house went away.

'When I saw this, I and her mother went downstairs and found the girl with one side of her body paralysed from head to foot and dried up. We carried her away, praising the Lord that he had kept his servant from defilement and violation and ... This is the reason why the girl remains thus to this day. But

---
[1] From Cod. Berol. 8502.4, pp. 128–132, 135–141.
[2] Two pages of the manuscript are missing here.

now you shall hear what happened to Ptolemy. He repented and lamented night and day over that which had happened to him, and because of the many tears which he shed he became blind. Having decided to hang himself, behold, about the ninth hour of that day, whilst alone in his bedroom, he saw a great light which illuminated the whole house, and he heard a voice saying to him, "Ptolemy, God has not given the vessels for corruption and shame; it is not right for you, as a believer in me, to violate my virgin, whom you are to know as your sister, as if I had become one spirit to both of you—but arise, and speedily go to the house of the apostle Peter and you shall see my glory. He will explain the matter to you." And Ptolemy did not delay, but ordered his servants to show him the way and bring him to me. When he had come to me, he told all that had happened to him in the power of Jesus Christ, our Lord. And he saw with the eyes of his flesh and with the eyes of his soul, and many people set their hope on Christ; he did good to them and gave them the gift of God.

'After this Ptolemy died; he departed and went to his Lord. When he made his will, he left a piece of land in the name of my daughter because through her he became a believer in God and was made whole. I, however, who was appointed trustee, have acted carefully. I sold the acre, and God alone knows that neither I nor my daughter have kept anything from the money of the acre, but I sent the whole sum to the poor. Know, therefore, O servant of Christ Jesus, that God cares for his people and prepares for each what is good—even when we think that God has forgotten us. Now then, brethren, let us mourn, be watchful, and pray, and God's goodness will look upon us, and we hope for it.'

And Peter delivered other speeches before them, and glorifying the name of the Lord Christ he gave of the bread to all of them, and after distributing it he rose and went into the house.

(b) *The Gardener's Daughter*[3]

Consider and take note of the event about which the following account informs us:

A peasant had a girl who was a virgin. She was also his only daughter, and therefore he besought Peter to offer a prayer for her. After he had prayed, the apostle said to the father that the Lord would bestow upon her what was expedient for her soul. Immediately the girl fell down dead.

O reward worthy and ever pleasing to God, to escape the shamelessness of the flesh and to destroy the pride of the blood!

But this distrustful old man, failing to recognize the worth of the heavenly grace, the divine blessing, besought Peter again that his only daughter be

---

[3] From Pseudo-Titus, *De dispositione sanctimonii*, ed. D. de Bruyne, *Rev. Bén.* 37 (1925) 47–72.

raised from the dead. And some days later, after she had been raised, a man who passed himself off as a believer came into the house of the old man to stay with him and seduced the girl, and the two of them never appeared again.

ACTS OF PETER[4]

1. When Paul was at Rome confirming many in the faith, it also happened that a certain woman named Candida, wife of Quartus the prison warder, heard Paul and listened to his words and became a believer. And when she had instructed her husband he became a believer. Quartus persuaded Paul to leave the city and to go wherever he pleased. Paul said to him, 'If such be the will of God, he will reveal it to me.' And Paul fasted three days and besought the Lord to grant what was good for him, and in a vision he saw the Lord who said to him, 'Paul, arise, and be a physician to the Spaniards!' At this he related to the brethren what God had commanded him, and without hesitation he made ready to leave the city. When Paul was preparing to leave, there was a great lamentation among the brethren because they thought they would never see Paul again; they even tore their garments, bearing in mind that Paul often quarrelled with the teachers of the Jews and had confounded them by saying, 'Christ, on whom your fathers laid their hands, abrogated their Sabbath and their fasting and festivals and circumcision and abolished the teaching of men and other traditions.' And the brethren adjured Paul, by the coming of our Lord Jesus Christ, not to stay away more than a year saying, 'We know your love for your brethren; forget us not when you come to Spain and do not desert us like children without a mother.' And while they were beseeching him with tears a sound was heard from heaven and a very loud voice, saying, 'Paul, the servant of God, is chosen to the ministry for the rest of his life; under the hands of Nero, the wicked and bad man, he will be perfected before your eyes.' And there was a great fear among the brethren because of the voice, which had come from heaven, and they were the more confirmed in the faith.

2. And they brought bread and water to Paul for the sacrifice that he might offer prayer and distribute it among them. Among those present was a woman named Rufina, who also wished to receive the eucharist from the hands of Paul. And when she came forward, Paul, filled by the Spirit of God, said to her, 'Rufina, you do not approach the altar of God as a believer, since you rise from the side not of a husband but of an adulterer, and yet you endeavour to receive God's eucharist. Behold, Satan will trample down your heart and expose you before the eyes of all who believe in the Lord, so that they may see and believe and know that they have believed in the living God, the searcher of hearts. But if you repent of your deed, he is faithful to forgive your sins and

[4] From Cod. Vercellensis 158.

can free you from this sin. But if you do not repent while you are still in the body, the devouring fire and the outer darkness will receive you for ever.'

And at once Rufina collapsed, being paralysed on the left side from head to foot. Nor could she speak any more, for her tongue was tied. When the believers and neophytes saw this they beat their breasts, remembering their former sins, lamented, and said, 'We do not know whether God forgives us the former sins, which we have committed.'

And Paul asked for silence and said, 'Men and brethren, you who have now begun to believe in Christ, if you do not continue in your former works committed according to the tradition of your fathers, but abstain from every deceit and wrath, from all cruelty and fornication and pollution and pride and jealousy and insolence and enmity, Jesus the living God will forgive you what you have done in ignorance. Therefore, you servants of God, let every one of you put on peace, serenity, mildness, faith, love, knowledge, wisdom, love for the brotherhood, hospitality, mercy, moderation, chastity, goodness, righteousness. Then you will always have for your guide the first-born of all creation and have power in peace with our Lord.' When Paul had spoken they asked him to pray for them. And Paul lifted up his voice and said, 'Eternal God, God of heavens, God of unspeakable majesty, who has established all things by your word, who has broken the bond fixed to man, who brought the light of grace to all the world, Father of your holy Son Jesus Christ, we jointly beseech you through your Son Jesus Christ to strengthen the souls who were once unbelieving but now believe. Once I was a blasphemer, but now I am blasphemed; once I was a persecutor, now I suffer persecution from others; once I was an enemy of Christ, now I pray to be his friend. For I trust in his mercy and promise; for I believe that I am faithful and have received remission of my former sins. Therefore, I also exhort you, brethren, to believe in God the Father Almighty and put all your trust in our Lord Jesus Christ, his Son. If you believe in him, no man will be able to uproot you from his promise. Likewise you must bend your knees and commend me to the Lord, who am about to go to another nation, that his grace may go before me and my journey be prosperous, that it may receive his holy vessels and that the believers, thanking me, who proclaimed to them the word of the Lord, may become firmly established in the faith.' And the brethren wept for a long time and with Paul they implored God and said, 'O Lord Jesus Christ, be with Paul, and bring him safely back to us, for we know our weakness which is still in us.'

3. And a great multitude of women fervently implored the blessed Paul on their knees, and kissed his feet and conducted him to the harbour. And Dionysius and Balbus from Asia, who were Roman knights and illustrious men, together with a senator named Demetrius, took hold of Paul's right hand and said, 'Paul, I should like to leave the city and always be with you if I were not a magistrate.' In like manner spoke Cleobius and Iphitus and

Lysimachus and Aristeus of the house of Caesar, and two matrons, Berenice and Philostrate, together with the presbyter Narcissus, after they had conducted him to the harbour. As a storm was threatening, he sent the brethren back to Rome to announce that everyone who wished to hear Paul before he left might come out. When the brethren heard it they went up to the city. They communicated it to the brethren who had remained in the city, and the news soon spread. Some came on horses, others walked, others came down the Tiber to the harbour, and for three days he strengthened them in the faith, and on the fourth day to the fifth hour they each prayed with Paul, offered him their gifts, and put everything that was necessary into the ship, and gave him also two young men, who were believers, as companions, and bidding him farewell in the Lord they returned to Rome.

4. After a few days there was a great commotion in the congregation, for some said that they had seen strange things done by a man named Simon, who was at Aricia. They also added, 'He claims to be the great power of God, doing nothing without God. Is he then Christ? We, however, believe in him whom Paul has preached to us. For through him we saw the dead raised and some healed from various diseases. This power seeks conflicts, we know. For it is no small disturbance that has come upon us. Perhaps he has already come to Rome. For yesterday he was invited with great acclamation to do so, being told, "You are God in Italy, you are the saviour of the Romans; hasten to Rome as quickly as possible." And Simon addressed the people and said with a shrill voice, "On the following day about the seventh hour you shall see me fly over the gate of the city in the same form in which I now speak to you." Wherefore, brethren, if you agree, let us go and diligently await the end of the matter.' And they all went out and came to the gate. About the seventh hour there suddenly appeared afar off a dust-cloud in the sky, looking like smoke shining with a glare of fire. And when it reached the gate it suddenly disappeared. Then he appeared standing in the midst of the people. They all worshipped him and knew that it was he whom they had seen the day before. And the brethren were exceedingly disturbed, especially as Paul was not at Rome, nor Timothy and Barnabas, whom Paul had sent to Macedonia, nor anyone who could strengthen us (*sic*) in the faith, especially the neophytes. As Simon's authority grew more and more, some of those among whom he worked in their daily conversations called Paul a sorcerer and a deceiver and all of the great multitude which had been confirmed in the faith were led astray, excepting the presbyter Narcissus, and two women in the hospice of the Bithynians, and four others who could not leave their house; and day and night they entreated the Lord either that Paul might return as soon as possible or that some one else might come to care for his servants, whom the devil by his wickedness had perverted.

5. While they were grieving and fasting God was already preparing Peter at Jerusalem for the future. After the twelve years had passed, according to the

direction of the Lord to Peter, Christ showed to him the following vision, saying, 'Peter, Simon, whom you expelled from Judaea after having exposed him as a magician, has forestalled you at Rome. And in short, all who believed in me he has perverted by the cunning and power of Satan, whose agent he proves to be. But do not delay. Go tomorrow to Caesarea, and there you will find a ship ready to sail to Italy. And within a few days I will show you my grace which is boundless.' Instructed by this vision, Peter did not delay to mention it to the brethren and said, 'I must go up to Rome to subdue the enemy and opponent of the Lord and of our brethren.' And he went down to Caesarea and at once boarded the ship, which was ready to sail, without having obtained for himself any provisions. But the steersman, named Theon, looked at Peter and said, 'What we have belongs to you. For what grace is it for us in receiving a man like ourselves in difficult circumstances, without sharing with him what we have? Let us have a safe journey.' Peter thanked him for his offer. And he fasted in the ship, being dejected, and yet again comforted because God regarded him as a servant worthy of his service. A few days later the captain got up at meal time and asked Peter to eat with him, saying to him, 'Whoever you are, I hardly know you. You are either a God or a man. But as far as I can see, I think that you are a servant of God. As I was steering my ship in the middle of the night I fell asleep. It seemed to me as if a human voice from heaven said to me, "Theon, Theon!" Twice it called me by name and said to me, "Amongst all the passengers treat Peter in the most honourable way. For, with his help, you and the rest will escape safe from an unexpected incident."' Peter, however, thinking that God wished to show his providence to all those who were in the ship, began at once to speak to Theon of the great deeds of God, and how the Lord had chosen him among the apostles and for what cause he was sailing to Italy. Daily he spoke to him the word of God. After they had become better acquainted Peter found out that Theon was one with him in the faith and a worthy servant. When the ship was detained by the calm of the Adriatic Sea, Theon remarked on the calm to Peter and said, 'If you think me worthy to be baptized with the sign of the Lord, you have the chance now.' All the others in the ship were in a drunken stupor. Peter let himself down by a rope and baptized Theon in the name of the Father and of the Son and of the Holy Ghost. He came up out of the water rejoicing with great joy. Peter also had become more cheerful because God had deemed Theon worthy of his name. And it happened that in the same place where Theon was baptized, a young man, radiant in splendour, appeared and said to them, 'Peace be with you.'[5] And both Peter and Theon immediately went up and entered the cabin; and Peter took bread and gave thanks to the Lord, who had deemed him worthy of his holy service, and because a young man had appeared to them saying, 'Peace be with you.' Peter

---

[5] John 20: 19.

said, 'Most excellent and the only Holy One, for you appeared to us, O God Jesus Christ. In your name I have spoken, and he was signed with your holy sign. Therefore also I give to him, in your name, your eucharist, that he may for ever be your servant, perfect and without blemish.' When they were eating and rejoicing in the Lord, suddenly a moderate wind, not a violent one, arose at the prow of the ship and lasted six days and six nights till they came to Puteoli.

6. Having landed at Puteoli, Theon left the ship and went to the inn where he usually stayed, to make preparations for the reception of Peter. The inn-keeper's name was Ariston, a God-fearing man, and to him he went for the sake of the Name. And when he had come to the inn and found Ariston, Theon said to him, 'God, who counted you worthy to serve him, has also made known to me his grace through his holy servant Peter, who has just arrived with me from Judaea, being bidden by our Lord to go to Italy.' When Ariston heard this, he fell upon Theon's neck, embraced him and asked him to bring him to the ship and show Peter to him. For Ariston said, 'Since Paul has gone to Spain there was not one of the brethren who could strengthen me. Besides, a certain Jew named Simon has invaded the city. By means of his magical sayings and his wickedness he has completely perverted the entire fraternity, so that I have fled from Rome hoping for the arrival of Peter. For Paul had spoken of him, and I saw many things in a vision. Now I believe in my Lord, that he will again establish his ministry, that all deception be extinguished from his servants. For our Lord Jesus Christ is faithful, and he can renew our thoughts.' When Theon heard this from the weeping Ariston, his confidence was restored, and he was even more strengthened in his faith, knowing that he believed in the living God. When they came to the ship, Peter saw them and, filled with the Spirit, he smiled, so that Ariston fell upon his face to the feet of Peter and said, 'Brother and Lord, who makes known the sacred mysteries and teaches the right way, which is in the Lord Jesus Christ, our God, through you he has shown us his coming. All whom Paul entrusted to us we have lost through the power of Satan. But now I trust in the Lord, who sent his messenger and told you to hasten to us, that he has deemed us worthy to see his great and wonderful deeds done by your hands. I therefore beg you, come quickly to the city. For I left the brethren who had stumbled, whom I saw fall into the snares of the devil, and fled here saying to them, "Brethren, stand firm in the faith;[6] for it is to be that within the next two months the mercy of our Lord will bring you his servant." I saw a vision of Paul speaking to me and saying, "Ariston, flee from the city." Having heard this, I believed without wavering, departed from the city in the Lord, and though the flesh which I bear is weak, yet I came here, stood daily by the shore, and asked the sailors, "Has Peter come with you?" And now that the

---

[6] 1 Cor. 16: 13.

grace of the Lord abounds, I beseech you to go up to Rome without delay, lest the teaching of the wicked man increases still more.' When Ariston had spoken amidst tears Peter gave him his hand and lifted him up from the ground, and said with tears and sighs, 'He who tempts the world by his angels forestalled us; but he who has the power to deliver his servants from all temptation will destroy his deceits and put them under the feet of those who believe in Christ, whom we preach.' And when they entered by the gate Theon entreated Peter and said, 'During the long sea voyage you never refreshed yourself on the ship, and now will you go from the ship on such a rough road? No, stay, refresh yourself and then go. From here to Rome the road is rocky, and I fear you might hurt yourself with the shaking.' But Peter answered and said to them, 'But what would have happened if about my neck and that of the enemy of the Lord a millstone were hanged (as my Lord said to us,[7] if any one should offend one of the brethren), and we be drowned in the depths of the sea? Not only would it be a millstone, but what is worse, I the opponent of this persecutor of his servants would die far away from those who have believed in the Lord Jesus Christ.[8] In no way could Theon persuade him to remain a day longer. Whereupon Theon gave everything that was in the ship to be sold at a fair price, and followed Peter to Rome, and accompanied Ariston to the house of the presbyter Narcissus.

7. Soon it became known among the scattered brethren of the city that Peter had come to Rome[9] on account of Simon, to prove that he was a seducer and persecutor of the good. And the whole multitude came together to see the apostle of the Lord, confirming the congregation in Christ. When they gathered on the first day of the week to meet Peter he began to speak with a loud voice, 'You men who are here, hoping in Christ, you who suffered a brief temptation, learn why God sent his Son into the world, or why he begot him by the Virgin Mary, if it were not to dispense some mercy or means of salvation. For he meant to annul every offence and every ignorance and every activity of the devil, his instigations and powers, by means of which he once had the upper hand, before our God shone forth in the world. Since with their many and manifold weaknesses they fell to death by their ignorance, Almighty God had compassion and sent his Son into the world, and I was with him. And I walked on the water and survive as a witness; I confess I was there when he was at work in the world performing signs and wonders. Dearest brethren, I denied our Lord Jesus Christ, not once, but thrice; for those who ensnared me were wicked dogs, just as the prophet of the Lord said. But the Lord did not lay it to my charge; he turned to me and had mercy on the weakness of my flesh, so that I wept bitterly; and I mourned for my little faith, having been deceived by the devil and disobeyed the word of my

---

[7] Matt. 18: 6 and parallel.
[8] Text corrupt.
[9] Text corrupt.

Lord. And now I tell you, men and brethren, who are convened in the name of Jesus Christ, Satan the deceiver sends his arrows upon you too, to make you leave the way. But do not be disloyal, brethren, nor fail in your mind, but strengthen yourselves, stand fast, and doubt not. For if Satan has subverted me, whom the Lord esteemed so highly, so that I denied the light of my hope, causing me to fall and persuading me to flee as if I believed in a man, what do you think will happen to you, who have just become converted? Do you imagine that he will not subvert you to make you enemies of the Kingdom of God and to bring you by the worst error into perdition? For every one whom he deprives of the hope in our Lord Jesus Christ is a child of perdition for all eternity. Repent, therefore, brethren whom the Lord has chosen, and be firmly established in the Almighty Lord, the Father of our Lord Jesus Christ, whom no one has ever seen nor can see except he who believes in him. Understand whence the temptation has come for you. For I came not only for the sake of convincing you with words that he whom I preach is the Christ, but by reason of miraculous deeds and powers I exhort you by faith in Jesus Christ. Let no one wait for another saviour besides him who was despised and whom the Jews reviled, this crucified Nazarene, who died and rose again on the third day.'

8. The brethren repented and asked Peter to overcome Simon's claim that he was the power of God. Simon was staying at the house of the senator Marcellus whom he had won over by his magic. 'Believe us, brother Peter', they said, 'none among men was so wise as this Marcellus. All the widows who hoped in Christ took their refuge in him; all the orphans were fed by him. Will you know more, brother? All the poor called Marcellus their patron; his house was called the house of the pilgrims and poor. To him the emperor said, "I will give you no office, lest you rob the provinces to benefit the Christians." To this Marcellus replied, "Yet everything that is mine is yours." Caesar said to him, "It would be mine if you kept it for me, but now it is not mine, since you give it to whom you please, and who knows to what low people?" This, brother Peter, we know and report to you, now that the great benevolence of the man has been turned into blasphemy. For had he not been changed we certainly should not have left the holy faith in God our Lord. Now this Marcellus is enraged and repents of his good deeds and says, "So much wealth have I spent for such a long time in the foolish belief that I spent it for the knowledge of God." In his rage he even goes so far that when a pilgrim comes to the door of his house he beats him with a stick or has him driven off and says, "If only I had not spent so much money on those imposters!" And he utters many more blasphemies. But if you have something of the compassion of our Lord in you and the goodness of his commandments, help this man in his error for he has shown goodness to a great many of God's servants.' When Peter learned this he was very greatly moved and said, 'Oh, the manifold arts and temptations of the devil! Oh, the

cunnings and devices of the evil one, treasuring up to himself the great fire in the day of wrath, destruction of simple men, a ravening wolf devouring and destroying eternal life! You enticed the first man to evil lust and by your former wickedness and bodily bond bound him to you. You are the fruit of bitterness, which is entirely bitter, inducing various desires. You have forced my fellow disciple and co-apostle Judas to act wickedly and betray our Lord Jesus Christ; you must be punished. You hardened the heart of Herod and kindled Pharaoh and made him fight against Moses, the holy servant of God; you emboldened Caiaphas to deliver our Lord Jesus Christ to the cruel multitude; and now you are still firing your poisonous arrows at innocent souls. You wicked foe of all, you shall be cursed from the Church of the Son of the holy, almighty God and extinguished like a firebrand thrown from the fireplace by the servants of our Lord Jesus Christ. Let your blackness turn against you and against your sons, the wicked seed; let your wickedness turn against you, also your threats, and let your temptations turn against you and your angels, you beginning of iniquity, abyss of darkness! Let the darkness which you have be with you and your vessels which you own. Depart, therefore, from those who shall believe in God; depart from the servants of Christ and from those who will serve in his army. Keep for yourself your garments of darkness; without cause you knock at strange doors which belong not to you but to Christ Jesus who keeps them. For you, ravening wolf, will carry off the sheep which do not belong to you but to Christ Jesus, who keeps them with the greatest diligence.'

9. When Peter had spoken with great sorrow of soul many more believers were added to the congregation. And the brethren entreated Peter to fight with Simon and not allow him to disturb the people any longer. And without delay Peter left the meeting and went to the house of Marcellus where Simon was staying. And a great multitude followed him. When he came to the door he summoned the keeper and said to him, 'Go and tell Simon, "Peter, on whose account you left Judaea, awaits you at the door!"' The door-keeper answered and said to Peter, 'I do not know, sir, if you are Peter. But I have instructions. Knowing that you arrived yesterday in the city, he said to me, "Whether he comes in the day or at night or at whatever hour, say that I am not at home."' But Peter said to the young man, 'You were right to tell me this, although you have been forced by him not to tell me.' And Peter, turning around to the people, who followed him, said, 'You are about to see a great and wonderful sign.' And Peter saw a big dog, tied by a big chain, and he went and loosened him. The dog, being loosed, became endowed with a human voice and said to Peter, 'What will you have me do, servant of the ineffable living God?' to which Peter said, 'Go inside and tell Simon in the presence of the people, "Peter sends word to you to come outside. For on your account I have come to Rome, you wicked man and destroyer of simple souls."' And the dog ran away at once and went into the midst of the people

who were with Simon, and lifting his front legs he said with a very loud voice, 'Simon, Peter, who stands at the door, bids you to come outside in public; for he says "On your account have I come to Rome, you wicked man and destroyer of simple souls."' When Simon heard this and saw the incredible occurrence he lost the words with which he was deceiving the onlookers, and all were amazed.

10. When Marcellus saw this he ran outside and fell down before Peter and said, 'Peter, holy servant of the holy God, I embrace your feet. I have committed many sins; do not punish my sins if you have some true faith in Christ, whom you preach. If you remember the commandments, to hate none, to do no evil to anyone, as I have learned from your fellow-apostle Paul, do not consider my sins but pray for me to the Lord, the holy Son of God, whom I angered by persecuting his servants. Pray, therefore, for me, like a good advocate of God, that I may not be given over with the sins of Simon to the everlasting fire. For by his persuasion it came about that I erected a statue to him with the following inscription: "To Simon, the young god." If I knew, Peter, that you could be won over with money I would give you all my property. I would give it to you, to save my soul. If I had sons I would esteem them for nothing if only I could believe in the living God. I confess, however, that he seduced me only because he said that he was the power of God. Nevertheless I will tell you, dearest Peter: I was not worthy to hear you, servant of God, and I was not firmly established in the belief in God which is in Christ: for this reason I was made to stumble. I pray you, therefore, be not angry at what I am about to say. Christ our Lord, whom you preach in truth, said to your fellow-apostles in your presence "If you have faith like a grain of mustard-seed, you will say to this mountain: Remove yourself and at once it shall move."[10] But this Simon called you, Peter, an unbeliever, because you lost faith on the water. And I heard that he also said, "Those who are with me understood me not." If, therefore, you, upon whom he laid his hands, whom he has also chosen, with whom he even performed miraculous deeds—if you doubted, therefore I also repent, and relying upon his testimony I resort to your intercession. Receive me, who have fallen away from our Lord and his promise. But I believe that by repenting he will have mercy on me. For the Almighty is faithful to forgive my sins.' And Peter said with a loud voice, 'Glory and praise be unto our Lord, Almighty God, Father of our Lord Jesus Christ. To you be praise and honour for ever and ever. Amen. Since you have now fully strengthened us and fully established us in you in the sight of all who see it, holy Lord, confirm Marcellus and give him and his house your peace today. But all who are lost or erring, you alone can restore. We worship you, O Lord, the Shepherd of the sheep which once were scattered, but now will be brought together through you. So receive Marcellus also as one of your

---

[10] Matt. 17: 20; 21: 21.

sheep, and do not permit him to walk about any longer in error or in ignorance but receive him among the number of your sheep. Yes, Lord, receive him, since he beseeches you with sorrow and with tears.'

11. Having thus spoken, and having embraced Marcellus, Peter turned to the multitude who stood beside him, when he saw one man laughing, in whom was a very bad devil. Peter said to him, 'Whoever you are who have been laughing, show yourself in public.' When the young man heard this he ran into the courtyard of the house, cried with a loud voice, threw himself against the wall, and said, 'Peter, there is a mighty contest between Simon and the dog, which you sent inside. For Simon says to the dog, "Say I am not here." But the dog tells him more things than you commanded. And when he has fulfilled your wish he will die at your feet.' And Peter said, 'Demon, whoever you are, in the name of our Lord Jesus Christ depart from this young man without hurting him. Show yourself to all present.' When the young man heard this he rushed forward, took hold of a large marble statue, which stood in the courtyard of the house, and kicked it to pieces. It was a statue of Caesar. When Marcellus saw this he beat his forehead and said to Peter, 'A great crime has been committed, for should Caesar hear of it through one of his spies he will greatly punish us.' Peter answered, 'I see that you are not the man you were a short time ago when you said you were ready to spend everything for the salvation of your soul. But if you are truly repentant and believe in Christ with all your heart, take running water into your hands and, beseeching the Lord, sprinkle it in his name on the pieces of the statue and it shall be whole as before.' Marcellus did not doubt, but believed with his whole heart, and before taking the water he lifted up his hands and said, 'I believe in you, Lord Jesus Christ. For your apostle Peter has examined me whether I truly believe in your holy name. Therefore I take water in my hands and sprinkle these stones in your name that the statue become whole again as before. If it is your will, O Lord, that I live and receive no punishment from Caesar, let this statue be whole as before.' And he sprinkled water on the stones, and the statue became whole. Peter, therefore, exulted that he had not hesitated to petition the Lord, and Marcellus also rejoiced in the Spirit, that this first miracle took place by his hands. He believed therefore, with all his heart in the name of Jesus Christ, the Son of God, by whom all things impossible become possible.

12. And Simon, being inside, spoke thus to the dog, 'Tell Peter that I am not in.' But the dog said to him in the presence of Marcellus, 'You most wicked and shameless man, worst enemy of all who live and believe in Christ Jesus. A dumb animal, which received a human voice, has been sent to you to convict you and to prove that you are a cheat and deceiver. Did it require so many hours for you to say, "Say I am not here!" You have not been ashamed to lift up your weak and useless voice against Peter, the servant and apostle of Christ, as if you could be hidden from him who told me to speak to your face.

And this is not for your sake, but on account of those whom you deceived and brought to perdition. You shall therefore be accursed, enemy and destroyer of the way of Christ's truth. He shall punish your iniquities, which you have done, with imperishable fire and you shall be in outer darkness.' Having spoken these words the dog ran away. And the multitude followed so that Simon remained alone. And the dog came to Peter who was with the crowd who had come to see the face of Peter; and the dog reported what had happened with Simon. To the messenger and apostle of the true God the dog said as follows, 'Peter, you shall have a hard fight with Simon, the enemy of Christ, and with his adherents, but many whom he deceived you shall convert to the faith. For this you shall receive a reward for your work from God.' Having thus spoken the dog fell at the feet of Peter and expired. When the multitude with great astonishment saw the talking dog, many fell down at the feet of Peter, but others said, 'Show us another miracle that we may believe in you as a servant of the living God, for Simon too did many wonders in our presence, and on that account we followed him.'

13. And Peter turning around saw a smoked tunny fish hanging in a window. He took it, saying to the people, 'When you see this swimming in the water like a fish, will you be able to believe in him whom I preach?' And all said with one voice, 'Indeed we shall believe you.' So he went to the pond near by, saying, 'In your name, O Jesus Christ, in whom they do not yet believe, I say, "Tunny, in the presence of all these, live and swim like a fish."' And he cast the tunny into the pond, and it became alive and began to swim. The multitude saw the swimming fish and he made it swim not only for that hour but, lest they said that it was a deception, he made it swim longer, thereby attracting crowds from all parts and showing that the smoked tunny had again become a living fish. The success was such that many, seeing that the fish was alive, threw pieces of bread into the water. Very many who had witnessed this followed Peter and believed in the Lord, and met day and night in the house of Narcissus the presbyter. And Peter spoke to them of the prophetical writings and of the things done by our Lord Jesus Christ in word and deed.

14. Marcellus was more firmly established in the faith, seeing the signs which Peter did by the grace of Jesus Christ, which was given to him. And Marcellus attacked Simon, who sat in the dining-room of his house. Cursing him, he said to him, 'O you most malevolent and most pestilential of men, destroyer of my soul and of my house, who intended to lead me away from Christ, my Lord and Saviour.' And he laid his hand on him and ordered that he be thrown out of his house. And the servants, having obtained permission, treated him in the most shameful way; some struck him in the face, some beat him with a rod, some flung stones at him, some emptied vessels containing filth over his head. Those who, for his sake, had left their master and were imprisoned, and other servants whom he had maligned to their master, reviled

him and said to him, 'Now we repay to you the worthy reward, according to the will of God, who had mercy upon us and upon our master.' And Simon, thus treated, left the house and went to the house in which Peter was staying. Standing at the door of the house of the presbyter Narcissus, he cried, 'Behold, here am I, Simon. Come down, Peter, and I will prove that you believed in a Jewish man and the son of a carpenter.'

15. When Peter heard these things he sent to him a woman with her suckling child and said to her, 'Go down quickly and you shall see someone seeking me. As for you, do not speak, but keep silent and listen to what the child which you hold will say to him.' And the woman went down. And her baby was seven months old. Assuming a manly voice it said to Simon, 'You abomination before God and men, O destroyer of truth and most wicked seed of corruption, O unfaithful fruit of nature! After only a little while an everlasting punishment awaits you. Son of a shameless father, never taking root in good soil but in poison; unfaithful creature, destitute of all hope: when the dog accused you, you were not ashamed. I, a child, am forced by God to speak and still you do not blush. But against your will, on the coming Sabbath day, another shall lead you to the forum of Julius that you may be shown what you are. Leave by the doorway at which the saints enter. For no more shall you corrupt innocent souls whom you perverted and led away from Christ. Your whole evil nature will therefore be manifested, and your machinations will be spoiled. Now I say to you a last word: Jesus Christ says to you, "Be speechless by the power of my name and leave Rome till the coming Sabbath."'

At once he became speechless, and being constrained he left Rome till the next Sabbath and lodged in a stable. The woman returned to Peter with the baby and told Peter and the other brethren what the child had said to Simon. And they praised the Lord who had shown these things to men.

16. When night came Peter, still awake, saw Jesus clothed with a shining garment, smiling and saying to him, 'The greatest part of the brethren has already come back through me and through the signs which you have made in my name. But on the coming Sabbath you shall have a contest of faith, and many more Gentiles and Jews shall be converted in my name to me who was reviled, despised, and spat upon. For I shall show myself to you when you shall ask for signs and wonders and you shall convert many, but you will have Simon opposing you through the works of his father. But all his doings shall be manifested as sorcery and magical deception. And do not delay and you shall confirm in my name all those whom I shall send to you.' When it was day he told the brethren how the Lord had appeared to him and what he had commanded him.

17. 'Believe me, men and brethren, I have driven this Simon from Judaea where by means of his incantations he did much harm. In Judaea he stayed in the house of a woman called Eubola, highly esteemed in this world, possessing

much gold and valuable pearls. With two others like him Simon sneaked in; none of the servants saw the two but only Simon; they used their magic art, carried off all the woman's gold, and were not seen. When Eubola had found out what had taken place, she had the servants tortured, and said, "You made use of the opportunity when this godly man came to me and robbed me, because you saw that he came to honour a simple woman; his name is the name of the Lord." And I fasted three days and prayed that this event should become known, and in a vision I saw Italicus and Antulus, whom I had instructed in the name of the Lord, and a boy naked and bound, giving to me a wheaten bread and saying, "Peter, hold out for a further two days and you shall see the great deeds of God. By means of magical art and trickery Simon and his two fellows stole the things from the house of Eubola. At the ninth hour of the third day you shall see them at the gate which leads to Neapolis, trying to sell to a goldsmith, Agrippinus by name, a gold satyr weighing two pounds inset with a precious stone. But you must not touch him, in order not to pollute yourself; but let some of the lady's servants accompany you, and after showing them the shop of the goldsmith leave them. This event will make many believe in the Lord. For what they stole by their cunning and wickedness shall be made manifest."

'Upon hearing this I went to Eubola, whom I found sitting in grief wearing a torn garment with dishevelled hair. I said to her, "Eubola, rise from grief: compose your face, arrange your hair and put on a dress which befits you, and pray to the Lord Jesus Christ who judges every soul. For he is the Son of the invisible God, in whom you must be saved, if you will only repent with all your heart of your former sins. Receive strength from him. For the Lord wishes to inform you through me that you shall get back all that you have lost. And having received it all, see to it that he may find you as one who renounces the present world and seeks an everlasting comfort. Listen, let some of your servants keep watch at the gate which leads to Neapolis. On the day after tomorrow, about the ninth hour, they shall notice two young men with a golden satyr set with stones and weighing two pounds—for thus I was shown in a vision—and they will offer it for sale to a certain Agrippinus, a man of piety believing in the Lord Jesus Christ. Through him it will be shown to you must believe in the living God and not in Simon the magician, the deceitful demon who would keep you sorrowing and get your innocent servants tortured, and who deceived you with flattering words, but only with words, and spoke of piety with his lips alone whereas he is wholly impious. For when you celebrated a holy day and erected an idol and adorned it, and exhibited all your ornaments on a table, he came with two young men whom none of you saw; they uttered their incantation, robbed your jewels, and were not seen. But this trickery cannot last. For my God has revealed it to me that you should not be deceived and perish in hell, and whatever be the impeity and opposition you have shown toward God, who is all truth and a righteous judge of the living and the dead, he will pardon you. Men have no other hope of life except by him, through whom that which you have lost has been saved for you. And now save your soul." And she fell down at my feet and said, "Sir, who you are I know not. It is true that I received that man as a servant of God, and whatever he asked of me for the care of the poor I gave him, besides large presents. But what have I done to him that he brought such great misery over my house?" Peter[11] said to her, "We must not believe in words, but in works and deeds. Therefore let us go on with what we have begun." Thus I left her, and with two stewards of Eubola I went to Agrippinus and said to him, "Take note of these men. For tomorrow two young men shall come to you, offering for sale a golden satyr set in stones which belongs to these men's mistress. Receive them under the pretence of examining it and praising the work of the artist. These men will come in—and the rest God will bring about for a proof." On the following day the lady's stewards arrived about the ninth hour, and those young men wishing to sell to Agrippinus the golden satyr. They were seized at once, and the matter was reported to the lady. And she went to the magistrate, her mind being troubled, and with a very loud voice she told him of what had happened. When the governor, Pompey, saw her, a person who had never appeared in public before, and perceived how troubled she was in her mind, he arose from his judgement seat and went to the praetorium and had them brought before him and tortured. Under torture they confessed that they were in the service of Simon who had induced them with money. When tortured further they also confessed that all that belonged to Eubola was hidden in a cave under the ground outside the gate, together with many other things. When Pompey heard this he got up to go to the gate, the two men having been bound with double bonds. And behold, Simon came to the gate to seek them because they were so slow, and beheld the great multitude and the two men in bonds. He at once understood what had happened, took to flight, and was never again seen in Judaea. Eubola, after recovering her property, gave it for the service of the poor; she believed in the Lord Jesus Christ and was strengthened; she despised and renounced this world, supported the widows and orphans, clothed the poor, and after a long time fell asleep. This, most beloved brethren, took place in Judaea, and he who was called the messenger of Satan was driven away thence.

18. 'Dearest and most beloved brethren, let us fast and pray to the Lord. He who drove him away thence is powerful enough to extirpate him here. May he give us his power to oppose him and his incantations and to demonstrate that he is the messenger of Satan. For on the Sabbath our Lord will bring him against his will to the forum of Julius. Let us therefore bend our knees before Christ, who hears us though we have not called upon him; who sees us though he is not seen with these eyes, but is within us; if we are

---

[11] Better 'I'.

willing he will not forsake us. Let us therefore purify our souls from every evil temptation, and God will not leave us; and if we only beckon him with our eyes, he is with us.'

19. When Peter had spoken Marcellus came in and said, 'Peter, I have purified my whole house for you from every vestige of Simon and have removed all trace of his shameful dust. I took water and with other servants of mine, who belong to him, I called upon the holy name of Jesus Christ and sprinkled my whole house, all the dining-rooms and every colonnade as far as the door and said, "I know, O Lord Jesus Christ, that you are pure and undefiled from every impurity, so let my enemy and opponent be driven away from before your face." And now, most blessed man, I have invited to my purified house the widows and elders to come to you that they may pray with us. And each will receive for the sake of their ministry a piece of gold, that in truth they may be called servants of Christ. Everything else is already prepared for the service. Now I pray, most blessed Peter, that you will endorse their requests and grace their prayers for me. Let us therefore go. We will also take along Narcissus and all the brethren who are here.' Peter consented to his request and in order to fulfil his will he went with him and the other brethren.

20. When Peter had entered he saw one of the old women who was blind and her daughter led her by the hand and conducted her into the house of Marcellus. And Peter said to her, 'Come here, mother; from this day Jesus gives you his right hand; through him we have light unapproachable which darkness cannot hide. Through me he says to you, "Open your eyes, see and walk on your own."' And the widow at once saw Peter put his hand upon her. When Peter came into the dining-room he saw that the gospel was being read. And rolling it up he said, 'Men, who believe in Christ and hope in him, you shall know how the holy scriptures of our Lord must be explained. What we have written down according to his grace, though it may seem to you as yet so little, contains what is endurable to be understood by humanity. It is necessary that we first know God's will or his goodness; for when deceit was spread and many thousands of men were plunging into perdition the Lord was moved by compassion to show himself in another form and to appear in the image of man, by whom neither the Jews nor we are worthy to be enlightened. For each of us saw him as his capacity permitted. Now, however, I will explain to you that which has been read to you. Our Lord wished to let me see his majesty on the holy mountain; but when I with the sons of Zebedee saw his brightness I fell at his feet as dead, closed my eyes, and heard his voice in a manner which I cannot describe. I imagined I had been deprived of my eyesight by his splendour. I recovered a little and said to myself, "Perhaps the Lord has brought me here to deprive me of my eyesight." And I said, "If such is your will, O Lord, I shall not resist." And he took me by the hand and lifted me up. And when I arose I saw him again in a form which I could not

comprehend. So the merciful God, most beloved brethren, has borne our infirmities and carried our transgressions, as the prophet says, "He bears our griefs; and is afflicted for us; yet we did esteem him stricken and afflicted".[12] For he is in the Father and the Father in him;[13] in him also is the fullness of all majesty, who has shown us all his benefits. He ate and drank on our account though he was neither hungry nor thirsty; he suffered and bore reproaches for us, he died and rose for us. He also defended and strengthened me through his greatness when I sinned; he will also comfort you, so that you may love him, this Great and Small One, this Beautiful and Ugly One, this Young Man and Old Man, appearing in time, yet utterly invisible in eternity; whom a human hand has not grasped, yet is held by his servants; whom flesh has not seen and now sees; who has not been heard, but is known now as the word which is heard;[14] never chastised, but now chastised; who was before the world and is now perceived in time, beginning greater than all dominion, yet delivered to the princes; glorious, but lowly among us; ugly, yet foreseeing. This Jesus you have, brethren, the door, the light, the way, the bread, the water, the life, the resurrection, the refreshment, the pearl, the treasure, the seed, the abundance, the grain of mustard seed, the vine, the plough, the grace, the faith, the word: he is everything, and there is none greater than he; to him be praise in all eternity. Amen.'

21. When the ninth hour had passed they arose to pray. And behold, blind widows, from the company of the old women, who were present without Peter knowing it and had not stood up,[15] cried out suddenly and said to Peter, 'We sit together, O Peter, hoping and believing in Jesus Christ. As you gave eyesight to one of our company, we ask, Peter, give us also of his compassion and love.' But Peter said to them, 'If you believe in Christ, if he is confirmed in you, see with the mind what you cannot see with the eyes; and though your ears be closed, yet within your mind they may be opened. These eyes will be closed again, which see nothing else than men and cattle, and dumb animals and stone and wood; but not all eyes[16] see Jesus Christ. But now, O Lord, let your sweet and holy name help them; touch their eyes, for you are mighty, that they may see with their eyes.' After they had prayed, the dining-room in which they were became as bright as lightning, such as is in the clouds. And it was not such a light as is seen by day, but inexpressible, incomprehensible, such as no man can describe, a sight which illuminated us so brightly that we were dazzled with bewilderment, and we cried to the Lord and said, 'Lord, have mercy upon your servants! What we can endure, O Lord, grant to us; for this we can neither see nor endure.' While we were prostrated, only those

---

[12] Isa. 53: 4.
[13] John 10: 38.
[14] Text obscure.
[15] Text 'disbelieving'.
[16] Possibly 'only the inner eyes' is meant by 'but not all eyes'.

widows who were blind stood up. The bright light, however, which appeared to us, entered into their eyes and they regained their sight. Peter said to them, 'Tell us what you have seen.' They said, 'We saw an old man whose appearance we cannot describe to you.' Some, however, said, 'We saw a young man.' Others said, 'We saw a boy tenderly touching our eyes; thus our eyes were opened.' So Peter praised the Lord and said, 'You alone are the Lord God, to praise whom we need many lips able to thank you for your mercy. Therefore, brethren, as I told you briefly before, God is greater than our thoughts, as we have learned from the old widows, how they saw the Lord in different forms.'

22. And he exhorted all to understand the Lord with all their strength, and with Marcellus and the other brethren he began to minister to the virgins of the Lord, and to rest till morning. Marcellus said to them, 'You holy undefiled virgins of the Lord, hearken. You know where you may abide. For that which is mine, is it not yours? Do not depart, but refresh yourselves, for on the Sabbath which begins tomorrow Simon will contend with Peter, the holy one of God. As the Lord has always been with him, may the Lord Christ be on his side as his apostle. For Peter has refused to eat anything, but fasted continually to be enabled to overcome the wicked enemy and persecutor of the truth of the Lord. For my servants have come and reported how they saw platforms erected in the forum and heard the multitude say, "Tomorrow at break of day two Jews must contend here concerning the discourses[17] of God." Therefore let us watch till tomorrow morning and beseechingly ask our Lord Jesus Christ to hear our prayers on behalf of Peter.' And Marcellus slept for a little while, and on waking said to Peter, 'O Peter, apostle of Christ, let us boldly carry out our resolution. In my sleep I saw you sitting in an elevated place and before you a great multitude and a very ugly woman in appearance an Ethiopian, not an Egyptian, but very black, clad in filthy rags, who danced with an iron chain about the neck and a chain on her hands and feet. When you saw her you said to me with a loud voice, "Marcellus, this dancer is the whole power of Simon and of his god; behead her." And I said to you, "Brother Peter, I am a senator of a noble family and I have never stained my hands; I have not even killed a sparrow." Upon hearing this you cried even more loudly, "Come, our true sword, Jesus Christ, and not only cut off the head of this demon, but break all her limbs in the presence of all these whom I have tested in your service." And at once a man who looked like you, Peter, came with a sword in his hand and cut her into pieces. And I looked at both of you, at you and at him who cut up that demon, and to my astonishment you were both alike. Now I am awake I communicate to you these signs of Christ.' Upon hearing this, Peter was the more encouraged because Marcellus had seen these things, for the Lord always takes care of his own. Rejoicing and strengthened by these words, he rose to go to the forum.

[17] Possibly 'worship'.

23. The brethren and all who were in Rome came together, and on payment of a piece of gold each occupied a seat. Senators and prefects and officers also assembled. But when Peter came in he stood in the centre. All cried aloud, 'Show us, Peter, who your God is or which majesty it is which gave you such confidence. Be not disaffected to the Romans; they are lovers of the gods. We have had evidence from Simon, let us have yours also; show us, both of you, whom we must believe.' And when they had spoken Simon also came. Dismayed, he stood by the side of Peter gazing closely at him. After a long silence Peter said, 'Roman men, you shall be our true judges. I say that I believe in the living and true God, of whom I will give you proof already known to me, and to which many among you testify. You see that this man is silent because he has been refuted and because I have driven him from Judaea on account of the frauds perpetrated upon Eubola, a highly respected but simple woman, by means of his magic. Having been expelled by me from there, he has come here believing that he could remain hidden among you; and now here he stands face to face with me. Tell me, Simon, did you not fall at my feet and those of Paul, when in Jerusalem you saw the miraculous cures which took place by our hands, and say, "I pray you, take as much money from me as you wish, that I too by laying on of hands may perform such deeds"? And when we heard this from you, we cursed you: do you think that we try to possess money? And now are you not afraid? My name is Peter, because the Lord Christ had the grace to call me to be ready for every cause.[18] For I believe in the living God, through whom I shall destroy your magic arts. Let Simon perform in your presence the wonderful things which he used to do. And will you not believe me what I just told you about him?' And Simon said, 'You have the impudence to speak of Jesus the Nazarene, the son of a carpenter, himself a carpenter, whose family is from Judaea. Listen Peter. The Romans have understanding, they are no fools.' And turning to the people he said, 'Men of Rome, is a God born? Is he crucified? Whoever has a master is no God.' And when he spoke, many said, 'You are right, Simon.'

24. And Peter said, 'Cursed be your words against Christ. You spoke in these terms whereas the prophet says of him, "Who shall declare his generation?"[19] And another prophet says, "And we have seen him, and he had no form nor beauty."[20] And "In the last days a child shall be born of the Holy Spirit; his mother knows not a man and no one claims that he is his father."[21] And again he says, "She has given birth and has not given birth."[22] And again, "Is it a very little thing for you to go to battle? Behold, in the womb a

---

[18] Latin 'paratus'—a word play on Petrus; cf. Matt. 16: 17–19.
[19] Isa. 53: 8.
[20] Isa. 53: 2.
[21] Unknown quotation.
[22] Apocryphon of Ezekiel frag. 3.

The Acts of Peter

virgin shall conceive."[23] And another prophet says in honour of the Father, "We neither heard her voice, nor did a midwife come."[24] Another prophet says, "He came not out of the womb of a woman but descended from a heavenly place",[25] and "A stone was cut out without hands and has broken all kingdoms",[26] and "The stone which the builders rejected has become the headstone of the corner",[27] and he calls him "the tried, precious" stone.[28] And again the prophet says of him, "I saw him come on a cloud like the Son of man."[29] And what more shall I say? Men of Rome, if you knew the prophetical writings I would explain everything to you. It was necessary that through them it should be a mystery and the Kingdom of God be completed. But these things shall be revealed to you afterwards. Now I turn to you, Simon: do one of the signs whereby you deceived them before and I shall frustrate it through my Lord Jesus Christ.' Simon took courage and said, 'If the prefect permits.'

25. The prefect wished to show his impartiality to both, so that he might not appear to be acting unjustly. And the prefect summoned one of his slaves and spoke to Simon, 'Take him and kill him.' To Peter he said, 'And you revive him.' And to the people the prefect said, 'It is for you to decide which of these is accepted before God, he who kills, or he who revives.' And Simon whispered something into the ear of the slave and made him speechless, and he died. But when the people began to murmur, one of the widows who had been cared for by Marcellus cried out, 'Peter, servant of God, my son also is dead, the only one I had.' The people made room for her, and they brought her to Peter. And she fell down at his feet and said, 'I had only one son; by the labour of his hands he provided for me; he lifted me up, he carried me. Now he is dead, who will give me a hand?' Peter said to her, 'In the presence of these witnesses go and bring your son, that they may be able to see and believe that he was raised up by the power of God; the other shall see it and perish.' And Peter said to the young men, 'We need young men such as shall believe.' And at once thirty young men offered themselves to carry the widow and to fetch her dead son. When the widow had recovered the young men lifted her up. But she cried and said, 'Behold my son, the servant of Christ has sent for you', and she tore her hair and scratched her face. And the young men who had come examined the nose[30] of the boy to see if he were really dead. When they perceived that he was dead they comforted his mother and

---

[23] Isa. 7: 13–14.
[24] Ascension of Isaiah 11: 13.
[25] Unknown quotation.
[26] Dan. 2: 34.
[27] Ps. 118: 22; Mark 12: 10 and parallels.
[28] Isa. 28: 16.
[29] Dan. 7: 13; cf. Mark 13: 26 and parallels.
[30] P. Oxy. 849 begins here.

said, 'If you really believe in the God of Peter, we will lift him up and bring him to Peter, that he may revive him and restore him to you.'

26. While the young men were saying this the prefect in the forum looked at Peter and said, 'What do you say, Peter? Behold, the lad is dead; the emperor liked him, and I spared him not. I had indeed many other young men; but I trusted in you and in your Lord whom you proclaim, if indeed you are sure and truthful: therefore I allowed him to die.' And Peter said, 'God is neither tempted nor weighed in the balance. But he is to be worshipped with the whole heart by those whom he loves and he will hear those who are worthy. Since,[31] however, my God and Lord Jesus Christ is now tempted among you, he is doing many signs and miracles through me to turn you from your sins. In your power, revive now through my voice, O Lord, in the presence of all, him whom Simon killed by his touch.' And Peter said to the master of the lad, 'Come, take hold of him by the right hand and you shall have him alive and walking with you.' And the prefect Agrippa ran and came to the lad, took his hand, and restored him to life. And when the multitude saw this they cried, 'There is only one God, the God of Peter.'

27. Meanwhile the widow's son was brought in on a bier by the young men. The people made room, and they brought him to Peter. Peter, however, lifted up his eyes toward heaven, stretched forth his hands, and said, 'Holy Father of your Son Jesus Christ who has given us power to ask and to obtain through you and to despise everything that is in this world and follow you only, who are seen by few and wish to be known by many; shine round, O Lord, enlighten, appear, revive the son of the aged widow, who is helpless without him. And I take the word of my Lord Christ and say to you, "Young man, arise and walk[32] with your mother as long as you can be of use to her. Afterward you shall be called to a higher ministry and serve as deacon and bishop."' And the dead man rose immediately, and the multitude saw and were amazed, and the people cried, 'You, God the Saviour, you, God of Peter, invisible God and Saviour.' And they spoke with one another and wondered at the power of a man who with his word called upon his Lord, and they accepted what had taken place for their sanctification.

28. When the news had spread through the entire city, the mother of a senator came, and making her way through the multitude she threw herself at Peter's feet and said, 'I heard many people say that you are a minister of the merciful God and that you impart his mercy to all who desire this light. Bestow, therefore, also to my son this light, since I have learned that you are not ungenerous towards any one; do not turn away from a lady, who entreats you.' Peter said to her, 'Do you believe in my God through whom your son shall rise?' And the mother, weeping, said with a loud voice, 'I believe, Peter, I

---

[31] P. Oxy. 849 ends here.
[32] Luke 7: 14.

believe.' The whole multitude cried out, 'Give the mother her son.' And Peter said, 'Let him be brought here into the presence of all.' And Peter, turning to the people, said, 'Men of Rome, I, too, am one of you! I have human flesh and I am a sinner, but I have obtained mercy. Do not imagine that what I do, I do in my own power; I do it in the power of my Lord Jesus Christ who is the judge of the living and the dead. I believe in him, I have been sent by him, and I dare to call upon him to raise the dead. Go, therefore, woman, and have your son brought here and have him raised.' And the woman made her way through the multitude, ran into the street with great joy, and believed with her heart; coming to the house she made her slaves carry him and came back to the forum. And she told the young men to cover their heads and go before the bier and carry everything that she intended to spend on the body of her son in front of the bier, so that Peter, seeing this, might have pity on the body and on her. With them all as mourners she came to the assembly, followed by a multitude of senators and ladies who came to see God's wonderful deeds. And Nicostratus (the man who had died) was very noble and respected in the senate. They brought him and placed him before Peter. And Peter asked them to be silent and said with a very loud voice, 'Romans, let a righteous judgement now take place between me and Simon, and judge which of us believes in the living God, he or I. Let him revive the body which is before us, and believe in him as an angel of God. If he is not able I will call upon my God. I will restore the son alive to his mother and then you shall believe that he is a sorcerer and deceiver, this man who enjoys your hospitality.' When they heard this, it seemed right to them what Peter had said. They encouraged Simon saying, 'Show yourself publicly what you can do; either you convince us or you shall be convicted. Why do you stand still? Commence.'

When Simon perceived that they all pushed him, he stood in silence. When the people had become quiet and were looking at him, Simon cried out and said, 'Romans, when you see that the dead man is raised, will you cast Peter out of the city?' And the whole multitude said, 'We shall not only cast him out but also burn him at once.' Simon came to the head of the dead man, bowed three times, and he showed the people how the dead man had lifted up his head and moved it, and opened his eyes and lightly bowed to Simon.[33] And immediately they began to gather wood to burn Peter. But Peter, having received the power of Christ, lifted up his voice and said to those who were shouting against him, 'Now I see, Romans, that I must not call you foolish and silly so long as your eyes and your ears and your senses are blinded. So long as your mind is darkened you do not perceive that you are bewitched, since you seemingly believe that a dead man rose who has not risen. I would have been content, Romans, to keep silent and to die in silence and to leave you among the illusions of this world. But the punishment of the unquenchable

---

[33] Sentence obscure.

fire is before my eyes. If you agree, let the dead man speak, let him rise; if he is alive, let him untie the band from his chin, let him call his mother and say to you, "Bawlers, why are you crying?" Let him beckon to you with his hand. If, therefore, you wish to see that he is dead and you are spellbound, let this man step back from the bier, this one who persuaded you to withdraw from Christ, and you shall see the dead man as you saw him when you brought him in.' And the prefect Agrippa could no longer restrain himself but rose and with his own hand pushed Simon away. And the dead man looked as he had before. And the people were enraged and, converted from the magical spell of Simon, began to cry, 'Hear, O Caesar, should the dead not rise let Simon be burned instead of Peter, because he has really deceived us.' But Peter stretched forth his hand and said, 'Romans, be patient. I do not say that Simon should be burned if the boy is restored; it is only when I tell you to do it, that you will.' And the people cried, 'Even if you should not wish it, Peter, we shall do it.' Peter said to them, 'If you continue, the boy shall not rise. We have learned not to recompense evil for evil, but we have learned to love our enemies and to pray for those who persecute us. For should even he repent, it is better. For God will not remember the evil. Let him, therefore, come to the light of Christ. But if he cannot, let him inherit the portion of his father, the devil. But do not let your hands be contaminated.' Having thus spoken to the people he came to the boy, and before raising him he said to his mother, 'These young men, whom you set free in honour of your son, can as free men obey their living master. For I know that the souls of some among them will be wounded when they see your risen son and serve again as slaves. But let them all be free and receive their subsistence as before—for your son shall rise again—and let them be with him.' And Peter looked at her for some time awaiting the answer. And the mother of the boy said, 'How can I do otherwise? Therefore I declare before the prefect that they should possess all that which I had to spend on the corpse of my son.' Peter said to her, 'Let the rest be divided among the widows.' And Peter rejoiced in his soul and said in the spirit, 'O Lord, who are merciful, Jesus Christ, manifest yourself to your servant Peter who calls upon you, as you always show mercy and goodness. In the presence of all these who have been set free, that they may be able to serve, let Nicostratus now arise.' And Peter touched the side of the lad and said, 'Arise.' And the lad arose, took up his garment and sat and untied his chin, asked for other garments, came down from the bier, and said to Peter, 'I beg you, man, let us go to our Lord Christ, whom I heard speak to you; he said to you, pointing at me, "Bring him here, for he belongs to me."'' When Peter heard this he was still more strengthened in the spirit by the help of the Lord and said to the people, 'Romans, thus the dead are awakened, thus they speak, thus they walk when they are raised; they live for so long as it pleases God. But now I turn to you who came to see the spectacle. If you repent now from your sins and from all your man-made gods and from all uncleanness and lust, you shall receive the communion of Christ in faith so that you may obtain life for eternity.'

29. From that hour on they worshipped him like a god, and the sick, whom they had at home, they brought to his feet to be cured by him. And when the prefect perceived that such a great multitude adhered to Peter he asked him to depart. And Peter bade the people come into the house of Marcellus. And the mother of the lad asked Peter to come to her house. But Peter had arranged to go to Marcellus on Sunday to see the widows, as Marcellus had promised, so that he might minister to them with his own hand. And the lad who had been raised said, 'I shall not leave Peter.' And his mother returned joyfully and cheerfully to her house. And on the day after the Sabbath she came into the house of Marcellus and brought two thousand pieces of gold and said to Peter, 'Divide these among the virgins of Christ who minister to him.' But the lad who had been raised, perceiving that he had not yet given anything to anyone, ran to his house, opened a chest, and brought four thousand pieces of gold, and said to Peter, 'See, I also, who have been raised, offer the double gift and present myself from now on as a living sacrifice to God.'

MARTYRDOM OF THE HOLY APOSTLE PETER[34]

30(1). And on Sunday Peter spoke to the brethren and encouraged them in the faith of Christ. And many senators and knights and wealthy women and matrons were present, and they were strengthened in the faith. There was also present a very rich woman, named Chryse, because all her vessels were of gold—since her birth she had never used a vessel of silver or of glass, but only of gold. She said to Peter, 'Peter, servant of God, in a dream the one whom you call God came and said to me, "Chryse, bring ten thousand pieces of gold to my servant Peter; you owe them to him." So I have brought them, fearing that some evil may come from him whom I saw and who has gone to heaven.' And having said this she laid down the money and went away. And Peter seeing this praised God that the poor could now be provided for. Some of those present said to him, 'Peter, is it not wrong to have accepted this money from her? All Rome knows of her fornication, and it is reported that she is not satisfied with one husband; she uses even her own slaves. Therefore have nothing to do with the Chryse's table, but let everything be sent back to her that came from her.' When Peter heard this he laughed and said to the brethren, 'As to her conduct, I know nothing of it; since I have received this money I received it not without reason; she brought it to me as a debtor to Christ and gives it to the servants of Christ. For he himself has provided for them.'

[34] Translated from the Greek of Lipsius–Bonnet (Athos manuscript), the number of the Greek text being given in brackets.

31(2). And they also brought the sick to him on the Sabbath and asked him to treat them. And many paralytics and podagrous were healed, and those who had two- and four-day fevers and other diseases, and believed in the name of Jesus Christ, and very many were added every day to the grace of the Lord. When some days had passed Simon the magician promised the people that he could persuade Peter not to believe in the true God but in a fallacious one. As he performed many tricks those among the disciples who were steadfast laughed him to scorn. In the dining halls he made some spirits appear which had the semblance of life, but in reality did not exist. And what more shall I say? Having spoken a great deal about magic[35] he seemingly cured the lame and blind for a time, and many dead persons, too, he made alive and made them move about, as well as Stratonicus.[36] In all this Peter followed him and refuted him before those who saw it. And as he was always out of favour, and was ridiculed by the Romans and lost their confidence since he promised to do something which he could not do, it came about that he said to them, 'Romans, you now think that Peter has overcome me as if he were mightier than I, and you now pay more attention to him. You are mistaken. For tomorrow I shall leave you godless and impious ones and take refuge with God above, whose power I am, though enfeebled. If, therefore, you have fallen, behold I stand. I ascend to the father, and shall say to him, "Me, your son who stands, they desired to bring low; however, I had no deal with them, but returned to myself."'

32(3). And on the following day a still larger multitude gathered on the *via sacra* to see him fly. And Peter also went to the place to see the spectacle and to refute him. For when he came to Rome he astonished the people by his flying. But Peter, who rebuked him, was not yet at Rome, which he so misled and deceived that some were driven out of their senses. And standing on an elevated place, upon seeing Peter he began to speak. 'Peter, now, as I am about to ascend in the presence of all the onlookers, I say to you, if your God is almighty, (he whom the Jews killed, and they stoned you who were chosen by him), let him show that faith in him is of God; let it be manifested by this event, whether it is worthy of God. For I ascend and will show myself to this people what kind of being I am.' And, behold, he was lifted up and they saw him ascending over Rome and over its temples and hills. And the believers looked at Peter. And beholding the incredible spectacle Peter cried to the Lord Jesus Christ, 'If you allow him to do what he has undertaken, all who believed in you shall be overthrown, and the signs and wonders, which you have shown to them through me, will not be believed. Make haste, O Lord, show your mercy and let him fall down and become crippled but not die; let him be disabled and break his leg in three places.' And he fell down and

---

[35] Greek unclear. Possibly the phrase should be: 'Although he had often been refuted for his magic art'.
[36] Latin reads 'Nicostratus'.

broke his leg in three places. And they cast stones upon him, and each went to his home having faith in Peter. And one of Simon's friends, Gemellus by name, from whom Simon had received much money and who had a Greek wife, quickly ran along the street, and seeing him with his leg broken said, 'Simon, if God's power is broken, shall not that God, whose power you are, be darkened?' And Gemellus ran and followed Peter and said to him, 'I also wish to be one of those who believe in Christ.' And Peter said, 'How could I object, my brother? Come and stay with us.' And Simon, being in misery, found some helpers who carried him by night on a stretcher from Rome to Aricia. There he remained and stayed with a man named Castor who on account of sorcery had been driven from Rome to Terracina. Following an operation Simon, the messenger of the devil, ended his life.

33[37](4). Now Peter remained in Rome and rejoiced with the brethren in the Lord, returning thanks day and night for the multitude who were daily added to the holy name by the grace of the Lord. And the four concubines of the prefect Agrippa also came to Peter, Agrippina, Nicaria, Euphemia, and Doris. And they heard preaching concerning chastity and all the words of the Lord, and repented and agreed among themselves to abstain from cohabitation with Agrippa, but were molested by him. When Agrippa became perplexed and distressed—for he loved them very much—he had them secretly observed where they went, and he found out that they went to Peter. When they came back he said to them, 'That Christian has taught you not to consort with me. I tell you that I will destroy you and burn him alive.' But they were ready to endure anything by the hand of Agrippa but would no longer allow themselves to satisfy his lust; they had become strong in the power of Jesus.

34(5). And a very beautiful women named Xanthippe, the wife of Albinus, a friend of the emperor, also came to Peter with the other ladies and kept away from Albinus. Being in love with Xanthippe, he became enraged and wondered why she no longer slept with him, and raging like a beast he intended to kill Peter, for he perceived that he was the cause of her leaving his bed. And many other women delighted in the preaching concerning chastity and separated from their husbands, and men too ceased to sleep with their wives, because they wished to serve God in chastity and purity. And there was a great commotion in Rome, and Albinus told Agrippa what had happened to him and said, 'Either you avenge me of Peter, who has alienated my wife from me, or I shall do it myself.' And Agrippa said, 'I suffered the same, for he has alienated my concubines.' And Albinus said to him, 'Why are you waiting, Agrippa? Let us seize him and kill him as a trouble-maker, so that we may get our wives back and avenge those who cannot kill him but whose wives he has also alienated.'

35(6). And as they made plans together, Xanthippe heard of the conspiracy

---

[37] From here onwards translated from the Athos and Patmos Greek manuscripts.

which her husband had with Agrippa, and she sent word to Peter and asked him to leave Rome. And the other brethren, together with Marcellus, requested him to leave. But Peter said to them, 'Shall we act like deserters, brethren?' And they said, 'No; but by going you can still serve the Lord.' He obeyed the brethren, and went away alone, saying, 'Let none of you go with me, I will go alone in disguise.' When he went out of the gate he saw the Lord come into Rome. And when he saw him he said, 'Lord, where are you going?' And the Lord said to him, 'I go to Rome to be crucified.' And Peter said to him, 'Lord, are you being crucified again?' And he said, 'Yes, Peter, again I shall be crucified.' And Peter came to himself; and he saw the Lord ascending to heaven. Then he returned to Rome, rejoicing and praising the Lord because he had said, 'I am being crucified.' This was to happen to Peter.

36(7). He went again to the brethren and told them of the vision which he had. And their souls were sorrowing, and they wept and said, 'We entreat you, Peter, have regard for us, the young ones.' And Peter said, 'If it be the Lord's wish it will be, even if we would not have it so. The Lord is able to strengthen you in his faith, and he will establish you in it and increase it in you whom he has planted, so that you may also plant others through him. I will not object so long as the Lord will keep me alive; and again if he will take me away I shall be glad and rejoice.'

While Peter was speaking the brethren wept and four soldiers arrested him and brought him to Agrippa. And being enraged he ordered that he be crucified for godlessness. And the whole multitude of the brethren came together, rich and poor, widows and orphans, able-bodied and disabled alike; they wished to see Peter and rescue him. And the people cried unceasingly with one voice, 'What harm has Peter done, Agrippa? What evil has he done to you? Tell the Romans.' And others said, 'We must be afraid lest the Lord destroy us also, should he die.' And when Peter came to the place he appeased the multitude and said, 'You men who are in the service of Christ, men who hope in Christ, remember the signs and wonders which you saw through me; think of the compassion of God, how he performed healings for your sakes. Wait for him, till he comes and rewards every man according to his works. And now, do not be angry with Agrippa, for he is a servant of the power of his father. And that which happens takes place as the Lord has told me that it should happen. And why do I delay and not go to the cross?'

37(8). And when he had come to the cross he began to say, 'O name of the cross, hidden mystery; O unspeakable mercy, which is expressed in the name of the cross; O nature of man, which cannot be separated from God; O ineffable and inseparable love, which cannot be shown by impure lips; I seize you now I am standing at the end of my earthly career. I will make known what you are. I will not conceal the mystery of the cross once closed and hidden to my soul. You who hope in Christ, think not this to be a cross which is visible; for my passion, like that of Christ, is entirely different from that which is visible. And now especially, since you who can hear can hear it from me who am in the last and parting hour of life, listen. Keep your souls from everything which you can perceive with the senses, from all that seems to be, and is not truly real. Close these your eyes, shut these your ears; withdraw from actions which are seen outwardly and you shall perceive the facts about Christ and the whole mystery of your salvation. But the hour has come for you, Peter, to deliver your body to those who are taking it. Take it, whose business it is. Of you, executioners, I ask to crucify me with head downwards, and not otherwise. And the reason I shall explain to those who listen.'

38(9). After they had hanged him up as he wished he began to speak again, 'Men, whose calling it is to hear, listen to what I, being hanged, am about to tell you now. Understand the mystery of the whole creation and the beginning of all things, how it was. For the first man, whose image I bear, in falling head downward showed a manner of birth which did not formerly exist, for it was dead, having no motion. He, having been drawn down, he who cast his origin upon the earth, established the whole of the cosmic system, suspended after the manner of his calling, whereby he showed the right as the left and the left as the right and changed all signs of nature, to behold the ugly as beautiful and the really evil as good. Concerning this the Lord says in a mystery, "Unless you make the right as the left and the left as the right, and the top as the bottom and the front as the back, you shall not know the Kingdom."[38] I explain this information to you, and the manner of my suspension is symbolic of that man who was first made. You, my beloved, who now hear, and those who shall hear it, must renounce the first error and turn again. For you ought to come to the cross of Christ, who is the extended Word, the one and only, concerning whom the Spirit says, "For what else is Christ than the Word, the sound of God?" The Word is this upright tree on which I am crucified; the sound, however, is the crossbeam, namely the nature of man; and the nail which holds the crossbeam to the upright in the middle is the conversion and repentance of man.

39(10). 'Since you have made this known and revealed these things to me, O Word of life, which is now called tree, I thank you, not with these lips which are nailed, neither with this tongue, through which comes forth truth and falsehood, nor with this word, which is produced by the skill of earthly nature, but I thank you, O King, with that voice which is heard through silence, which is not heard by all, which does not come through the organs of the body, which does not enter the ears of flesh nor is heard by corruptible substance, which is not in the world or sounds upon earth, which is also not written in books, nor belongs to one, nor to another, but with this voice, Jesus Christ, I thank you: with the silence of the voice with which the Spirit within me intercedes, who loves you, speaks with you, and sees you. You are known

---

[38] Cf. Acts of Philip 140; Gospel of Thomas 22.

only to the Spirit. You are to me, father, mother, brother, friend, servant, steward. You are all, and all is in you; and you are Being, and there is nothing that is except you. To him, brethren, you also take refuge and learn that your existence is in him alone, and you shall then obtain that of which he said to you, "Eye has not seen, nor ear heard, neither has it entered into the heart of man."[39] We now ask undefiled Jesus for that which you promised to give us; we praise you, we thank you, we confess you in glorifying you, though we are weak, because you alone are God and no other, to whom be glory now and for ever, Amen.'

40(11). When the multitude surrounding him cried Amen, Peter, during this Amen, gave up his spirit to the Lord. When Marcellus saw that the blessed Peter had given up the ghost, without communicating with anyone, since it was not allowed, he took him down from the cross with his own hands and bathed him in milk and wine. And he ground seven pounds of mastic and also fifty pounds of myrrh and aloes and spice and anointed his body, and filled a very costly marble coffin with Attic honey and buried him in his own tomb. And Peter came to Marcellus by night and said, 'Marcellus did you not hear the Lord say, "Let the dead be buried by their own dead"?'[40] When Marcellus said, 'Yes', Peter said to him, 'What you spent on the dead is lost. For though alive you were like a dead man caring for the dead.' When Marcellus awoke he told of the appearance of Peter to the brethren, and he remained with those who had been strengthened by Peter in the faith of Christ, strengthening himself even more till the arrival of Paul at Rome.

41(12). When Nero heard that Peter had departed this life, he blamed the prefect Agrippa for having him killed without his knowledge; he had intended to punish him the more cruelly and severely because Peter had made disciples of some of his servants and alienated them from him. Therefore he was angry, and for a long time he would not speak with Agrippa. He sought how to destroy all those brethren whom Peter had instructed. And one night he saw a person striking him and saying, 'Nero, you cannot now persecute or destroy the servants of Christ. Keep your hands from them.' And in consequence of this vision Nero became greatly afraid and left the disciples alone from that time in which Peter had died. Thereafter the brethren continued with one accord, rejoicing and glorying in the Lord, and praised the God and Saviour of our Lord Jesus Christ with the Holy Spirit, to whom be glory for ever and ever. Amen.

---

[39] 1 Cor. 2: 9; cf. Gospel of Thomas 17.
[40] Matt. 8: 22 and parallel.

SECONDARY ACTS OF PETER[1]

Various late Acts and Passions of Peter were widely diffused:

1. *Martyrium beati Petri Apostoli*

Attributed to Linus, Peter's successor as bishop of Rome. It is written in Latin and follows the course of the original Martyrdom with some additions (e.g. the names of Peter's gaolers). It dates from about fourth–sixth century.[2]

EDITIONS

Lipsius–Bonnet, i. 1–22.
A. H. Salonius, *Martyrium beati Petri apostoli a Lino episcopo Conscriptum* (Helsinki, 1926) (= *Finska vetenskaps—societeten Commentationes Humanorum Litterarum* 1.6).
Fabricius, ii. 775 f.
Lipsius, ii. 85–96 (summary of contents). [His evaluation of Ps.-Linus as the original form of the Acts of Peter is now no longer accepted. Most scholars would now agree that Ps.-Linus', and Ps.-Marcellus' (below), versions are derived from, and are an elaboration of, an earlier Acts of Peter that approximates to, but is not necessarily identical with, that found in Codex Vercellensis 158.]

MODERN TRANSLATIONS

English

Hennecke[5], ii. 436–7 (introduction).

French

Migne, *Dictionnaire*, ii, cols. 459–70.

German

Hennecke[5], ii. 392 (introduction).

Italian

Erbetta, ii. 169–77.
Moraldi, ii. 1021–8; [2] ii. 97–104.

---

[1] Not translated.
[2] *The Acts of Nereus and Achilleus*, ed. H. Achelis (Leipzig, 1893) (= *TU* 11.2), contains portions taken from the Acts of Peter and includes details known elsewhere only in the Coptic fragments. The author seems to have used Ps.-Linus' Passion of Peter and Passion of Paul. The book tells the story of Petronilla, Peter's daughter. Cf. Lipsius, ii.1, 200–6.

2 (a) Passio sanctorum apostolorum Petri et Pauli

This text is attributed to Pseudo-Marcellus and survives in Latin and Greek, the Latin being the better known. Much of the account is devoted to the magical skills of Simon. Pilate's Letter to Claudius (see above, under The Gospel of Nicodemus) is incorporated in this text at §19. It is edited by Lipsius–Bonnet, i. 118–77.

2 (b). Acta Petri et Pauli

This Greek text (edited by Lipsius–Bonnet, i. 178–222) is based on 2(a), but in chs. 1–21, dating from the ninth century, a description of Paul's journey from Malta to Rome has been added. The date of the origin of the later chapters or of the form in 2(a) is not certain—perhaps these come from the fifth century.

EDITIONS

J. C. Thilo, *Acta Petri et Pauli* (Leipzig, 1837–8).
Fabricius, ii. 778–80.
Lipsius, ii.1, 284–366.

MODERN TRANSLATIONS

English

Walker, 256–76.
Hennecke[5], ii. 440–2 (introduction).

French

Migne, *Dictionnaire*, ii. cols. 714–32.
See Vouaux, 160–78.

German

Hennecke[5], ii. 395–8 (introduction).

Italian

Erbetta, ii. 178–92.
Moraldi, ii. 1041–59; [2] ii. 117–35.

Irish

See M. McNamara, *The Apocrypha in the Irish Church* (Dublin, 1975), 99–101.

ADAPTATIONS IN VERSIONS

Arabic

Smith Lewis, *Acta Myth.* 165–78; *Myth. Acts*, 193–209.

Ethiopic

Cf. H. Engberding, 'Bemerkungen zu den äthiopischen "Acta Petri et Pauli"', *Or. Chr.* 41 (1957), 65–6.

A. van Lantschoot, 'Contributions aux Actes de S. Pierre et de S. Paul', *Le Muséon* 68 (1955), 17–46, 219–33 (new Ethiopic fragments, with Garshuni text and French trans.).

Armenian

Leloir, *CCA* 3, 'Acts of Peter and Paul (Ps.-Marcellus)', 1–34 and 35–54 (summary of preceding text); 'Martyrdom of Peter and Paul', 55–63 (based on Greek for the Acts of Peter and Paul, but the Martyrdom of Peter and Paul is likely to be an Armenian product).

Slavonic

de Santos Otero, *Altslav. Apok.* i. 60–6.

3. *Passio Apostolorum Petri et Pauli*

Lipsius–Bonnet, i. 223–34, edits this Latin text which is largely based on Pseudo-Hegesippus (see Pseudo-Abdias below, 4). It is dated sixth century. It is a catholicized version of the Martyrdom.

Italian trans. in Erbetta, ii. 193–8. See also Lipsius, ii.1, 194–200, and cf. 366–80.

4. *Pseudo-Abdias, i. 16–end*

This tells of the conflict of Peter and Simon; the material is taken from Ps.-Hegesippus, *de excidis Hierosolymae* 3.

EDITION

Fabricius, ii. 402–41.

430   *The Acts of Peter*

MODERN TRANSLATIONS

Italian

Erbetta, ii. 199–210.
Moraldi, ii. 1453–59; ² ii. 517–35.

5. *Slavonic*

Accounts of the life of Peter that have survived in Slavonic are referred to in de Santos Otero, *Altslav. Apok.* i. 60–6. A 'Vita Petri' in Slavonic but apparently translated from a Greek original also exists. In part it shows the influence of the apocryphal gospels and is summarized by James, 474. See de Santos Otero in Hennecke[3] ii. 400–2 (Eng. trans. ii. 573–5); Hennecke[5], ii. 393–4 (Eng. trans. ii. 438–9). These texts differ from the Slavonic translations of the Greek Acts of Peter, but may indeed go back to a Greek original.

MODERN TRANSLATIONS

Italian

Erbetta, ii. 535–6 (summary).
Moraldi, ii. 1639 (summary).

6. *Syriac*

Versions of the Acts and Passion of Peter occur in such texts as *The Preaching of Simon Cephas in the City of Rome* (ed. W. Cureton, *Ancient Syriac Documents* (London, 1863), 35–41, and *The History of Simon Cephas the Chief of the Apostles* (ed. P. Bedjan, *Acta Martyrum et Sanctorum* i (Paris, 1890), 1–33.

7. *Arabic Acts*

Smith Lewis, *Acta Myth.* 156–64, *Myth. Acts*, 175–9, 'Story of Peter and Paul', and *Acta Myth.* 178–84, *Myth. Acts*, 210–16, 'Martyrdom of Peter', are very late adaptations of the tradition (cf. Moraldi, ii. 1640–4).

(The Nag Hammadi Codex 6, 'The Acts of Peter and the Twelve Apostles',[3] has nothing to do with the apocryphal Acts and is therefore not considered here among the derivative literature, although it is included as Section XVI in Hennecke[5], ii. 368–80; Eng. trans. ii. 412–25.)

---

[3] R. McL Wilson and D. M. Parrott, 'The Acts of Peter and the Twelve Apostles', in D. M. Parrott (ed.), *Nag Hammadi: Codices V, 2–5 and VI with Papyrus Berolinensis 8502, 1 and 4* (Leiden, 1979), 197–229 (= *Nag Hammadi Studies* 11); and see J. M. Robinson (ed.), *The Nag Hammadi Library in English* (Leiden, ³1988), 287–94; cf. M. Krause, 'Die Petrusakten in Codex VI von Nag Hammadi', in M. Krause (ed.), *Essays on the Nag Hammadi Texts in Honour of Alexander Böhlig* (Leiden, 1972), 36–58 (= *Nag Hammadi Studies* 3).

The Pseudo-Clementine Literature

Among the literature that circulated in the Early Church under the name of Clement of Rome are the *Homilies* and the *Recognitions*. The *Homilies* is a philosophical romance arranged in 20 discourses supposedly delivered by Clement in Rome and addressed to James, Jesus' brother, in Jerusalem. These are preceded by two letters addressed to James, one from Peter (the *Epistula Petri*) and the other by Clement. The *Homilies* describes Clement's travels to the East, his meeting with Peter, and his witnessing of Peter's conflicts with Simon Magus. The *Recognitions* probably represents a somewhat catholicized version of the *Homilies* translated into Latin by Rufinus in the fourth century (later epitomes also exist). The survival of the work may have been due to its popularity among Ebionites. (Vegetarianism is preached; water alone is permitted in the Eucharist.) The narrative is an introduction to missionary speeches attributed to Peter, and the purpose is thus to provide arguments and apologies for defending Christianity.

The interrelationship of these two works is likely to be due to their origin in a common *Grundschrift*. Attempts have been made to identify some of the sources behind this basic writing: one is usually referred to as the Kerygmata Petrou, and reconstructions of its likely contents have been proposed. The original *Grundschrift* is likely to go back to the third century, although the version of the *Homilies* and of the *Recognitions* known today is likely to date from the fourth century. The development of the material, its editing, and the nature and character of the various rewritings are the subject of much scholarly debate. Parts of both the *Recognitions* and the *Homilies* were translated into Syriac.

In the *Homilies* the following passages contain preaching attributed to Peter (including topics such as female prophecy, polemic against Paul, and the doctrine of Baptism): 2. (15), 16–17, 38, 43–4; 3. 17–26, 47–52; 11. 19, 25–33; 17. 13–19. None of these is included here.

The source for this material may have been an account of Peter's preaching (the Kerygmata Petrou). Another major source seems to have been an account of Peter's missionary activities. This includes details about his contacts with Simon (including Simon's former life), his appointment of, and instruction to, Zacchaeus as his successor, and his missionary journeys. These are to be found in *Homilies* 2. 22–6, 35; 3. 29–30, 38–43, 58–72; 4. 1, 6–22; 7. 1–2, 4, 5–9, 12; 8. 1, 4–7; *Recognitions* 10. 66–8.

As a sample of these acts of Peter the following are given in the translation below:

A. Peter and Simon at Caesarea (*Hom.* 2. 35; 3. 29–30, 38–43, 58).
B. Peter's missionary journeys to Tyre, Sidon, Berytus, Byblus, and Tripolis (*Hom.* 7. 1–2, 5–6, 8–10, 12; 8. 1, 4).

EDITIONS

Greek and Latin

A. R. Dressel, *PG* 2, cols. 19–468 (*Homilies*).
E. G. Gersdorf, *PG* 1, cols. 1158–1478 (*Recognitions*).

MODERN CRITICAL EDITIONS

B. Rehm, *Die Pseudoklmentinen*, i. *Homilien* (Berlin, 1953; rev. F Paschke, 1969, 3rd ed. by Georg Strecker, 1992) (= *GCS* 42); B. Rehm and F. Paschke, ii. *Rekognitionen* (Berlin, 1965, 2nd. ed by Georg Strecker, 1994) (= *GCS* 51); G. Strecker, iii.1. *Konkordanz* (Berlin, 1986) (= *GCS*); id. iii.2 (Berlin 1989) (= *GCS*).
F. Paschke, *Die beiden griechischen Klementinen-Epitomen und ihre Anhänge* (Berlin, 1966) (= *TU* 90).

Syriac

W. Frankenberg, *Die syrischen Clementinen mit griechischem Paralleltext* (Leipzig, 1937) (= *TU* 48.3).

Ethiopic

S. Grébaut, 'Littérature éthiopienne pseudo-Clémentine', *Revue de l'Orient Chrétien* (Paris), 12 (1907), 139–51; 15 (1910), 198–214, 307–23, 425–39; 16 (1911), 72–81, 167–75, 225–33; 17 (1912), 16–31, 133–44, 244–52, 337–46; 18 (1913), 68–79; 19 (1914), 324–30; 20 (1915–17), 33–7, 424–30; 21 (1918–19), 246–52; 22 (1920–1), 22–8, 113–17, 395–400; 26 (1927–8), 22–31.
[The texts discussed here belong to a different tradition; cf. E. A. Wallis Budge in bibliography to the Acts of Peter above.]

Slavonic

de Santos Otero, *Altslav. Apok.* i. 140–6.

MODERN TRANSLATIONS

English

Hennecke[3], ii. 94–127, 532–70.
Hennecke[5], ii. 483–541 (for contents see German below).

H.-D. Betz, *Galatians (Hermeneia Series)* (Philadelphia 1979), 331–3 (Epistula Petri and two extracts from the Homilies).
The Ante-Nicene Christian Library 17: *Homilies*, ed. T. Smith et al. (Edinburgh, 1870); ibid. 3: *Recognitions*, ed. T. Smith (Edinburgh, 1868).

German

Hennecke[3], ii. 63–80 (G. Strecker), 373–99 (J. Irmscher).
Hennecke[5], ii. 439–88 (G. Strecker and J. Irmscher) (Epistula Petri, Contestatio, Epistula Clementis, parts of the Clementine Romance, Kerygmata Petrou, Epitome II).

Italian

Erbetta, ii. 211–36 (Kerygmata Petrou and those acts of Peter allegedly behind the Pseudo-Clementine literature).

GENERAL

A. Hilgenfeld, *Die Klementinischen Recognitionen und Homilien nach ihrem Ursprung dargestellt* (Jena, 1848).
C. Bigg, *The Clementine Homilies* (Oxford 1890) (= *Studia Biblica et Ecclesiastica* 2).
A. C. Headlam, 'The Clementine Literature', *JTS* 3 (1902), 41–58.
H. Waitz, *Die Pseudoklementinen* (Leipzig, 1904) (= *TU* (10) 25.4).
B. Rehm, 'Zur Entstehung der pseudoclementinischen Schriften', *ZNW* 37 (1938), 77–184.
A. Salles, 'La diatribe anti-paulienne dans le "le roman pseudo-clémentin" et l'origine des "Kérygmes de Pierre"', *Rev. Bib.* 64 (1957), 516–51.
G. Strecker, *Das Judenchristentum in der Pseudoklementinen* (Berlin, 1958,[2] 1981) (= *TU* 70).
G. Quispel, 'L'Évangile selon Thomas et les Clémentines', *VC* 12 (1958), 181–96.
A. Salles, 'Simon le Magicien ou Marcion?', *VC* 12 (1958), 197–224.
L. L. Kline, *The Sayings of Jesus in the Pseudo-Clementine Homilies* (Missoula, 1975) (= *SBL Dissertation Series* 14).
André Schneider and Luigi Cirillo, *Les Reconnaissances du pseudo Clément* (Turnhout, 1999) (= *Apocryphes* 10).
F. Stanley Jones, 'Eros and Astrology in the Περίοδοι Πέτρου: the Sense of the Pseudo-Clementine Novel', *Apocrypha* 12 (2001), 53–78.

A. PETER AND SIMON IN CAESAREA

Hom. 2.35:

Towards morning Zacchaeus came in and greeted us. He said to Peter, 'Simon is postponing the disputation until tomorrow, for today is his sabbath, which occurs at eleven day intervals.' To that Peter answered, 'Say to Simon, "You may use your discretion, in the knowledge that we are ready to meet you whenever you wish in accordance with God's will."' When Zacchaeus heard this he went off to deliver the reply . . .

Hom. 3:

29. While Peter was about to explain fully to us this mystic word Zaccheus came, saying, 'Now indeed, Peter, is the time for you to go out and engage in the discussion; for a great crowd awaits you, packed together in the court; and in the midst of them stands Simon, like a war-chieftain attended by his spearmen.' And Peter, hearing this, ordered me to withdraw while he prayed, because I had not yet received baptism for salvation, and then he said to those who were already perfected, 'Let us rise and pray that God, by his unfailing mercies, may help me as I strive for the salvation of the men whom he has made.' And having thus spoken, and having prayed, he went out into the great open court; and there were many assembled for the purpose of seeing him, the forthcoming debate having made them more eager to listen.

30. Then, standing and seeing all the people gazing upon him in profound silence, and Simon the magician standing in the midst, he began to speak thus, 'Peace be to all you who are in readiness to give your right hands to the truth of God, which is his great and incomparable gift in the present world. He who sent us, being an infallible prophet of that which is supremely profitable, commissioned us, by way of salutation before our words of instruction, to announce to you this truth, in order that if there be any son of peace among you peace may take hold of him through our teaching; but if any of you will not receive it, then we shall shake off the dust from our feet, which we have borne through our toils and brought to you that you may be saved, and will go to the houses and the cities of others...'[1]

38. When Peter had thus spoken Simon, at the edge of the crowd, cried aloud, 'Why would you lie, and deceive the unlearned multitude standing around you, persuading them that it is unlawful to think that there are gods, and to call them so, when the books that are current among the Jews say that there are many gods? And now I wish, in the presence of all, to discuss with you from these books the necessity of thinking that there are gods; first respecting him whom you call God, that he is not the supreme and omnipotent, inasmuch as he is without foreknowledge, imperfect, in need, not good, and subject to many grievous passions. Wherefore, when this has been shown from the Scriptures, as I will prove, it follows that there is another, not written of, foreknowing, perfect, without want, good, removed from all grievous passions. But he whom you call the Demiurge is subject to the opposite evils.

39. 'Therefore Adam, being made at first after his likeness, is created blind, and is said not to have knowledge of good or evil, and is found a transgressor, and is driven out of paradise and is punished with death. In like manner also, he who made him, because he is not able to see in all places, says with reference to the overthrow of Sodom, "Come, and let us go down,

---

[1] Matt. 10: 12; Mark 6: 11; Luke 10: 5.

and see whether their deeds warrant the outcry which comes to me, that I may know".[2] Thus he shows himself ignorant. And in his saying respecting Adam, "Let us drive him out, lest he put forth his hand and touch the tree of life, and eat, and live for ever",[3] the *lest* shows he is ignorant; and in driving him out lest he should eat and live for ever, he is also envious. And when it is written that "God repented that he had made man",[4] this implies both repentance and ignorance. For this reflection is a view by which one, through ignorance, wishes to inquire into the result of the things which he wills, or it is the act of one repenting on account of the event not being according to his expectation. And when it is written, "And the Lord smelled a scent of sweetness",[5] it is the sign of one in need; and his being pleased with the smell of the flesh of the sacrifice is the sign of one who is not good. But his tempting, as it is written, "And God did tempt Abraham",[6] indicates one who is wicked, and who is ignorant of the result of his endurance.'

40. In such a manner Simon, by taking many passages from the Scriptures, seemed to show that God is subject to every infirmity. And to this Peter said, 'Does he who is evil, and wholly wicked, love to accuse himself in the things in which he sins? Answer me this.' Then Simon said, 'He does not.' Then Peter said, 'How, then, can God be evil and wicked, seeing that those evil things which have been commonly written regarding him, have been added by his own will?' Then Simon said, 'It may be that the charge against him is written by another power, and not according to his choice.' Then Peter said, 'Let us first inquire into this. If indeed he has of his own will accused himself, as you have just acknowledged, then he is not wicked; but if it is done by another power, we must ask and investigate with all energy who has subjected him who alone is good to all these evils.'

41. Then Simon said, 'You are manifestly avoiding the hearing of the charge from the Scriptures against your God.' Then Peter said, 'You yourself appear to me to be doing this; for he who avoids the order of inquiry, does not wish a true investigation to be made. Hence I, who proceed in an orderly manner and wish that the author should first be considered, am clearly desirous to walk in a straight path.' Then Simon said, 'First confess that if the things written against the Creator are true he is not above all, since, according to the Scriptures, he is subject to all evil; then afterwards we shall inquire as to the author.' Then Peter said, '...[7] I answer you. I say that if the things written against God are true they do not show that God is wicked.' Then Simon said, 'How can you maintain that?'

[2] Gen. 18: 21.
[3] Gen. 3: 22.
[4] Gen. 6: 6.
[5] Gen. 8: 21.
[6] Gen. 22: 1.
[7] The text of this passage is obscure.

42. Then Peter said, 'Because opposite things are written to those sayings which speak evil of him; wherefore neither the one nor the other can be confirmed.' Then Simon said, 'How, then, is the truth to be ascertained if some Scriptures say he is evil and others say he is good?' Then Peter said, 'Whatever sayings of the Scriptures are in harmony with the creation that was made by him are true, but whatever are contrary to it are false.' Then Simon said, 'How can you show that the Scriptures contradict themselves?' And Peter said, 'You say that Adam was created blind, which was not so; for he would not have pointed out the tree of the knowledge of good and evil to a blind man and commanded him not to taste of it.' Then Simon said, 'He meant that his mind was blind.' Then Peter said, 'How could he be blind in respect of his mind, who, before tasting of the tree with the agreement of him who made him, gave appropriate names to all the animals?' Then Simon said, 'If Adam had foreknowledge, how did he not foreknow that the serpent would deceive his wife?' Then Peter said, 'If Adam had not foreknowledge, how could he give names to his sons at their births with reference to their future doings, calling the first Cain (which is interpreted "envy"), who through envy killed his brother Abel (which is interpreted "grief", for his parents grieved over him), the first to be slain?

43. 'But if Adam, being the work of God, had foreknowledge, much more the God who created him. And it is false when it is written that God reflected, as if he had to reflect on account of ignorance; and likewise the statement that the Lord tempted Abraham, that he might know if he would endure it; and that which is written, "Let us go down, and see if their deeds warrant the outcry which comes to me, that I may know." And, not to extend my discourse too far, whatever sayings ascribe ignorance to him, or anything else that is evil, are proved to be false, being overturned by other sayings which affirm the contrary.'

58. Therefore Simon, perceiving that Peter was driving him to use the Scriptures as Jesus taught, was unwilling that the discussion should go into the doctrine concerning God, even although Peter had changed the discussion into question and answer, as Simon himself asked. However, the discussion occupied three days. And while the fourth was dawning he set off in the dark as far as Tyre of Phoenicia. And a few days after, some of those who had gone ahead came and said to Peter, 'Simon is doing great miracles in Tyre, and disturbing many of the people there; and by many slanders he has made you to be hated.'

B. PETER'S MISSIONARY JOURNEYS

Hom. 7:

1. And on the fourth day of our stay in Tyre, Peter went out about daybreak, and there met him not a few of the neighbouring people as well as very many

of the inhabitants of Tyre itself, who cried out and said, 'May God have mercy upon us through you and through you heal us!' And Peter stood on a high stone that all might see him, and having greeted them in a godly manner thus began,

2. 'God, who created the heavens and the whole universe, does not lack power for the salvation of those who would be saved...'

5. After Peter had spent a few days in teaching them in this way, and in healing them, they were baptized. At the time of his other wondrous deeds they all sat down together in the market-places in sackcloth and ashes, grieving because of their former sins. And when the people of Sidon heard it, they did likewise, and sent to beseech Peter, since they could not come themselves because of their diseases. And Peter did not spend many days in Tyre; but when he had instructed all its inhabitants, and freed them from all kinds of diseases, he founded a church, and set over it as bishop one of the elders who were with him, and departed for Sidon. But when Simon heard that Peter was coming, he straightway fled to Berytus with Appion and his friends.

6. And as Peter entered Sidon they brought many on couches, and laid them before him. And he said to them, 'Do not, I pray you, believe that I can do anything to heal you. I am a mortal man, myself subject to many evils. But I shall not refuse to show you the way in which you must be saved...'

8. ... Such was Peter's counsel to the men of Sidon. And in a few days many repented and believed, and were healed. And Peter, having founded a church, set over it as bishop one of the elders who were with him, and left Sidon.

9. No sooner had he reached Berytus than an earthquake took place; and the multitude, running to Peter, said, 'Help us, for we are afraid we shall all utterly perish.' Then Simon, along with Appion and Anubion and Athenodorus and the rest of his companions, tried to cry out to the people against Peter in public, 'Flee, friends, from this man: he is a magician; trust us, he it was who caused this earthquake; he sent us these diseases to terrify us, as if he were a god himself.' And many such false charges did Simon and his friends bring against Peter, as if he were somebody above human power. But as soon as the people gave him a moment's quiet, Peter with surprising boldness smiled and said, 'Friends, I admit that I can do, God willing, what these men say; and more than that, I am ready, if you do not believe what I say, to overturn your city from top to bottom.'

10. And the people were afraid, and promised to do whatever he should command. 'Let none of you', said Peter, 'either associate with these sorcerers, or have anything to do with them.' And as soon as the people heard this concise command they took up sticks and pursued them till they had driven them completely out of the town. And those who were sick and possessed with devils came and cast themselves at Peter's feet...

12. As he said these things they all fell on their knees before his feet. And he, lifting up his hands to heaven, prayed to God, and healed them all by his simple prayer alone. And he did not remain for long in Berytus; but after he had accustomed many to the service of the one God, and had baptized them, and had set over them a bishop from the elders who were him, he went to Byblus. And when he came there he learned that Simon had not waited for them for even a day, but had gone straightway to Tripolis. He remained there only a few days; and after he had healed not a few, and instructed them in the Scriptures, he followed in Simon's track to Tripolis, preferring to pursue him rather than flee from him.

Hom. 8:

1. Now as Peter was entering Tripolis the people from Tyre and Sidon, Berytus and Byblus, and many from the neighbourhood who were eager to get instruction, entered along with him; and not least were there gatherings of the multitudes from the city itself wishing to see him...

4. Then Peter, wondering at the eagerness of the multitudes, answered, 'You see, brethren, how the words of our Lord are manifestly fulfilled. For I remember his saying, "Many shall come from the east and from the west, the north and the south, and shall recline on the bosoms of Abraham, and Isaac, and Jacob".[8] But he also said, "Many are called but few chosen".[9] In their coming in response to the call, much is fulfilled. But inasmuch as it is not of themselves, but of God, who has called them and caused them to come, on this account alone they have no reward, since it is not of themselves, but of him who has wrought it in them. But if, after being called, they do things that are excellent, then this is of themselves and for this they shall have a reward.'

[8] Matt. 8: 11; Luke 13: 29.
[9] Matt. 22: 14.

The Acts of Thomas

Ancient testimony to the existence of the Acts of Thomas is late and may be seen in Epiphanius, *adv. Haer.* 2. 47. 1 and 2. 61. 1. (Holl, *GCS* 31, pp. 216, 380–2); Augustine *de Sermone Domini in monte* i. 20, 65 (*PL* 34, cols. 1262–3); *c. Adimant.* 17. 2. 5. (Zycha, pp. 164–72, esp. 170); *c. Faust.* 22. 79 (Zycha, pp. 680–2); Turribius of Astorga, *epist. ad Idacium et Ceponium* 5 (*PL* 54, cols. 693–5).

These warn against the heterodoxy of the Acts. Epiphanius refers to their Encratite character, Augustine to their Manichaean nature. Turribius' testimony informs us that Priscillianists in Spain were using these Acts, presumably in a Latin version, in the fifth century. We do not know in what form these fathers knew the writing, since the text was subjected to continuous alteration. Later catholicized versions, expunged of unacceptable ideas, became very popular in orthodox circles. The proliferation of censored texts and the creation of Syriac, Arabic, Georgian, Latin, Armenian, and Ethiopic adaptations show the varying form of the Acts.

The Stichometry of Nicephorus allocates only 1600 (or 1700) lines, so this must refer to only a portion of the total as this is less than the length of the text of the one complete Greek manuscript. The Acts of Thomas is the only one of the five primary Acts to have survived in its entirety.

The Syriac of the complete Acts was first published from a British Museum manuscript by Wright in 1871. This manuscript dates from the seventh century. Fragments of a fifth–sixth century Syriac palimpsest found on Mount Sinai were published by Burkitt and later, more thoroughly, by Smith Lewis. These forms in Syriac represent a later development of the text found in Greek (e.g. the prayer in ch. 27 is more orthodox in Syriac than Greek).

Bonnet's Greek is based on twenty-one manuscripts; Klijn's monograph (bibliography below, under Modern Translations) sets out clearly the extent of each of these manuscripts.[1] Only one eleventh-century manuscript (U) contains the Acts in its entirety, but another (P) of the tenth century is complete except for the Hymn of the Pearl (chs. 108–13). There are some eighty-five Greek manuscripts extant, the oldest being of the ninth century. In some Greek manuscripts the Martyrdom includes the great prayer of Thomas after 167 whereas the Syriac places it in 144 f. The later position seems preferable and is adopted in the translation below.

The original language is likely to have been Syriac,[2] although it is now

---

[1] Correct Klijn, p. 4, as follows: D ends at ch. 61; F has 144–9, 163–end.
[2] Several of the Gospel passages cited in the Acts of Thomas seem to be either from a form of the Diatessaron or from the Old Syriac (rather than the Peshitta).

generally agreed that (with the exception of the Hymn of the Pearl) the existing Syriac texts are later catholicized versions and that the existing Greek texts, albeit translations of the Syriac, have in general preserved the primitive form of the original Acts. There are many instances of the Greek translators' having misunderstood Syriac. The Hymn of the Pearl, which is discussed below (p. 441), has survived in Syriac and Greek, but most scholars accept that here the Syriac is more faithful than the Greek. Armenian and Latin translations of parts of the Acts survive, but for interpreting the original form of the Acts only the Greek and Syriac are relevant, other versions being secondary in importance. The Armenian is likely to have developed from the Syriac. The Martyrdom, as so often, circulated separately in the oriental versions and represents a different tradition. The Arabic (ninth-century) is likely to be developed from Coptic. The Ethiopic (fourteenth-century) is a translation of the Arabic. Few remains of the Coptic have survived.

Much literature on these Acts has concentrated on the supposed religious background. The *religionsgeschichtliche* school tended to see Manichaean influences (Bousset, Bornkamm, Widengren), others pre-Christian thought (e.g. A. Adam), others distinctive Syrian teaching (Klijn, Quispel).

Some of the Acts are strongly Encratite, but such teaching may well have been characteristic of third-century Christianity in Syria in so far as this is known from Ephraem, who betrays its richly syncretistic background, and in the Odes of Solomon, in Aphrahat's writing, and in some of the Pseudo-Clementine literature. If seen as basically orthodox rather than as Gnostic, the whole may be read as a kind of early 'Pilgrim's Progress', being a fictional romance of conversion. Chapters 79, 80, 143 reflect orthodox views of incarnation, ch. 72 teaches redemption through Christ's suffering. Unworldliness and abstinence as Christian virtues and true marriage seen only as marriage to the heavenly bridegroom are pushed to the extreme, but the idea that the redeemed life begins in this world is orthodox. The stress on the sacraments, especially anointing, eucharist, and baptism, has been the subject of critical comment. The hymns and prayers are of special significance.

Another dominant theme in much of the literature written on these Acts is that of the historicity of the tradition that Thomas brought Christianity to India. Those who wish to accept the tradition have put much weight on the actual existence of one of the main characters in the Acts, the Parthian-Indian king Gundaphorus, whose reign in the first century is attested from coins. The characters Gad and possibly Abban also are likely to have been historical figures. Because of these clues and because of allegedly authentic touches some, such as Medlycott and Dahlmann, accepted the historicity of the basic story in these Acts. Others, such as Farquhar, while recognizing their fictional character, were prepared to accept that the Acts were based on fact and reflected an actual evangelization of India by Thomas. The consensus of modern scholarly opinion is sceptical about the historicity of the Thomas story, and in any case the local references are perfunctory. As is usual in this type of literature the eponymous hero and the milieu of the separate episodes are colourless and stylized. It is not impossible that at the time of the original composition of the Acts Christianity had been established in India. The convention that apostolic activity was behind the establishment of a new Christian community encouraged the church in Edessa to magnify its own involvement in such a development by giving prominence to the pioneering work of Thomas.

Hymn of the Pearl
Much of the interest in the Acts lies in the prayers and sermons; above all it is the splendid oriental hymn now numbered chs. 108–13 that has been responsible for a vast secondary literature. This is the hymn conventionally referred to as the 'Hymn of the Pearl' or 'The Hymn of the Soul'.

The text is found in only one of the existing manuscripts of the Syriac Acts[3] and in only one of the Greek (as well as in an eleventh-century epitome by Nicetas of Thessalonica). The Syriac manuscript is of the tenth century, the Greek of the eleventh.

Scholars are divided about the origin of the hymn, but most accept that it was in existence prior to its incorporation in the Acts. The wording of the two editions suggests that there were two separate transmissions of the text. The original language seems to have been Syriac, but the Greek has been translated below (although with an eye to the Syriac). The Parthian origin of the hymn has been discussed by those who identify Iranian words in the Syriac text.

Like the Acts into which it has been incorporated, the hymn may be seen more as representative of popular piety and folkloristic story-telling. The interpretations given to the allegory differ. The identity of the elements and characters in the poem is not clear. A consistent picture emerges if the child in the poem is the soul which, when on earth, forgets its heavenly origin until reawakened by a divine revelation that results in its being reunited with its heavenly robe. If it is a myth of the soul's human incarnation, its eventual disengagement with the body, and ultimate reunion with God, then there is a homiletic appeal for conversion (and this may be seen at the end of 110). Those who wish to see it as a Gnostic myth emphasize the detail of the prince's putting on of a garment as an allegory for the acquiring of self-knowledge. Others interpret it as a redeemer myth: the allegory now requiring Christ to be the son in the poem. Ménard tries to unravel layers of redaction in the poem, seeing it finally as a Manichaean version based on a Gnostic reworking of an original more orthodox, Jewish-Christian work. This complexity merely serves to underline the ambiguous nature of the material.

[3] It is not in the Sachau MS edited by Bedjan. He reproduced Wright's text at this point.

Author, Date, Provenance

Judas Thomas is said to be the author. He is the twin of Jesus, having a similar appearance to Jesus (ch. 11) and sharing Jesus' redeeming work (31, 39). He is the recipient of secret knowledge and in that sense is comparable to the Thomas figure in the Gospel of Thomas. There is, however, no obvious literary interdependence between the Gospel of Thomas and the Acts of Thomas despite a shared theological background.

Edessa is likely to have been the place of origin of the Acts of Thomas. The date of the original Acts is third century. If this is correct then the Acts of Thomas is the oldest non-Biblical monument of the Syrian Church's literature.

My translation is based on Lipsius–Bonnet's text with some adjustment in chs. 144–8 and in the martyrdom.

EDITIONS

Greek

C. Thilo, *Acta S. Thomae Apostoli* (Leipzig, 1823) (based on four MSS).

C. Tischendorf, *Acta Apostolorum Apocrypha* (Leipzig, 1851), 190–230 (based on five MSS). Additions from two further MSS in id., *Apocalypses Apocryphae*, 156–61.

K. Lake, 'A Fragment of the Acta Thomae', in *Texts from Mount Athos* (Oxford, 1903), 164–9 (= *Studia Biblica et Ecclesiastica* 5) (edits 14th-cent. paper MS, Iveron 476).

Lipsius–Bonnet, ii.2, 99–291.

Syriac

Wright, *Apoc. Acts*, i. 171–333; ii (Eng. trans.), 146–298.

P. Bedjan, *Acta Martyrum et Sanctorum*, iii (Paris and Leipzig, 1892; repr. Hildesheim, 1968), 1–175 (publishes Sachau MS and modifies Wright's edition).

F. C. Burkitt, 'Fragments of the Acts of Judas Thomas from the Sinaitic Palimpsest', in A. Smith Lewis (ed.), *Select Narratives of Holy Women* (London, 1900), Appendix VII, 23–44 (= *Studia Sinaitica* 9).

Smith Lewis, *Acta Myth.* 190 ff.; *Myth. Acts*, 223–4.

Portions from Wright and Lewis are to be found in T. Jansma, *A Selection from the Acts of Judas Thomas* (Brill, 1952) (= *Semitic Study Series* 1).

For details of text and studies see I. Ortiz de Urbana, *Patrologia Syriaca* (Rome, ²1965), 37–41.

Latin

Fabricius, ii. 687–736 (cf. 819–28 (= Pseudo-Abdias)).

M. Bonnet, *Acta Thomae Graece partim cum novis codicis contulit*... (Leipzig, 1883), 96–160.

For 6th-cent. free reworkings of original Acts (De miraculis beati Thomae apostoli, an abridgement attributed to Gregory of Tours, and Passio sancti Thomae apostoli) see:

K. Zelzer, 'Zu Datierung und Verfasserfrage der lateinischen Thomasakten', in E. Livingstone (ed.), *Studia Patristica* 12 (Berlin, 1975) (= *TU* 115).

—— *Die alten lateinischen Thomasakten* (Berlin, 1977) (= *TU* 122).

—— 'Zu den lateinischen Fassungen der Thomasakten', *Wiener Studien* 84 (NS 5) (1971), 161–78; 85 (NS 6) (1972), 185–212.

Armenian

Mechitarists' edition [*Acta Apocrypha Armenica*] (Venice, 1904), 369–427.
Leloir, *CCA* 4, 548–69, 577–91, 597–615, 622–31.

The oriental versions of the Acts differ from the tradition in the languages noted above[4] and are to be found in Coptic, Ethiopic, Arabic, Slavonic, and Georgian. See Hennecke[5], ii. 412–14 (A. de Santos Otero); Eng. trans. ii. 457–8.

Coptic

P.-H. Poirier, *La version copte de la prédiction et du martyre du Thomas* (Brussels, 1984) (= *Subsidia Hagiographica* 67).

Ethiopic

Malan, 187–220 (repeated in James, *Apoc. Anec.* ii. 46–63).
Wallis Budge, *Contendings*, i. 265–95, 336–81; ii (Eng. trans.), 319–56, 404–65. [A revision of Malan based on more reliable manuscripts.]

Arabic

Smith Lewis, *Acta Myth.* 67–78 (cf. 79–83); *Myth. Acts*, 80–93 (cf. 94–9).
M. van Esbroeck, 'Les Actes apocryphes de Thomas en version arabe', *Parole de l'Orient* 14 (1987), 11–77.

Slavonic

A. de Santos Otero, *Altslav. Apok.* i. 84–96.

Georgian

G. Garitte, 'Le Martyre géorgien de l'apôtre Thomas', *Le Muséon* 83 (1970), 497–532.

---

[4] James, *Apoc. Anec.* ii, pp. xxxii–xliv, 27–45 gives the text of Greek MS Brit. Mus. 10073 f128–f153 with Eng. trans. This MS is close to the Coptic and Ethiopic tradition. Other divergent Greek traditions may be seen in Amphilohij, *Paleograficeskoe opisanie greceskih rukopisej*, ii (Moscow, 1880), 22–8, and D. Tamilia, 'Acta Thomae Apocrypha', in *Atti della Reale Accademia dei Lincei. Rendiconti. Classe di scienze morali, storiche e filologiche* 5, 12 (Rome, 1903), 385–408.

MODERN TRANSLATIONS

English

Pick, 222–362.
Walker, 389–422.
James, 364–438.
Hennecke[3], ii. 425–531.
Hennecke[5], ii. 322–411, 453–7.
A. F. T. Klijn, *The Acts of Thomas: Introduction, Text, Commentary* (Leiden, 1962) (= *Supplements to Novum Testamentum* 5) (includes Eng. trans. of Wright's Syriac), second ed. (Leiden, 2003) (= *Supplements to Novum Testamentum* 108).
Cartlidge and Dungan, 36–54 (selection).

French

Amiot, 262–74 (selection)
A. J. Festugière, 'Actes de Thomas', in *Les Actes apocryphes de Jean et de Thomas* (Geneva, 1983) (= *Cahiers d'orientalisme* 6).
Éac, 1323–470.

German

Hennecke[1], 473—544 (R. Raabe; introduction by E. Preuschen); cf. *Handbuch*, 562–602 (E. Preuschen).
Hennecke[3], ii. 297–372 (G- Bornkamm).
Hennecke[5], ii. 289–367 (H. J. W. Drijvers), 408–12 (A. de Santos Otero).
Michaelis, 402–38 (selections).

Italian

Moraldi, ii. 1225–1350, 1577–1603; 2 ii. 303–428. 653–79 (Pseudo-Abdias).
Erbetta, ii. 307–74, 375–91 (Pseudo-Abdias).

GENERAL

Lipsius, i. 225–347 (including German trans. of the Hymn of the Pearl (pp. 292–300) with copious explanatory remarks).
F. C. Burkitt, 'The Original Language of the Acts of Judas Thomas', *JTS* 1 (1900), 280–90 (cf. postscript *JTS* 2 (1901), 429, and 3 (1902), 94–5).
C. H. Turner, 'Priscillian and the Acts of Judas Thomas', *JTS* 7 (1906), 603–5.
R. H. Connolly, 'The Original Language of the Syriac Acts of Thomas', *JTS* 8 (1907), 249–61
W. Bousset, *Hauptprobleme der Gnosis* (Göttingen, 1907), esp. 276–319 (= *Forschungen zur Religion und Literatur des Alten und Neuen Testaments* 10).
—— 'Manichäisches in der Thomasakten', *ZNW* 18 (1917–18), 1–39.
G. Bornkamm, *Mythos und Legende in den apokryphen Thomas-Akten: Beiträge zur Geschichte der Gnosis und zur Vorgeschichte des Manichäismus* (Göttingen, 1933) (= *Forschungen zur Religion und Literatur des Alten und Neuen Testaments* 49 (NS 31)).

D. S. Margoliouth, 'Some Problems in the "Acta Judae Thomae"', in *Essays in Honour of Gilbert Murray* (London, 1936), 249–59.

G. Widengren, *Mesopotamian Elements in Manichaeism* (Uppsala, 1946) (= *Uppsala Universitet Aarsskrift* 3).

P. Devos, 'Actes de Thomas et Actes de Paul', *Anal. Boll.* 69 (1951), 119–30.

A. Hamman, 'Le "Sitz im Leben" des Actes de Thomas', in F. L. Cross (ed.), *Studia Evangelica* 3 (Berlin, 1964), part 2, 383–9 (= *TU* 88).

Vielhauer, 710–13

H. Conzelmann, 'Zu Mythos, Mythologie und Formgeschichte, geprüft an der dritten Praxis der Thomasakten', *ZNW* 67 (1976), 111–22.

Plümacher, cols. 34–43.

Y. Tissot, 'Les Actes de Thomas, exemple de recueil composite', in F. Bovon (ed.), *Les Actes apocryphes des apôtres: Christianisme et monde païen* (Geneva, 1981), 223–32 (= *Publications de la Faculté de Théologie de l'Université de Genève* 4).

—— 'L'encratisme des Actes de Thomas', *ANRW* 2.25.6, 4415–30.

M. Lipinski, *Konkordanz zu den Thomasakten* (Frankfurt, 1988) (= *Bonner Biblische Beiträge* 67) (*Anhang* gives text divided into chapters and verses).

R. J. Bauckham, 'The Parable of the Vine: Rediscovering a Lost Parable of Jesus', *NTS* 33 (1987), 84–101; and cf. M. Franzmann, 'The Parable of the Vine in Odes of Solomon 38: 17–19? A Response to Richard Bauckham', *NTS* 35 (1989), 604–8.

J. N. Bremmer (ed.), *The Apocryphal Acts of Thomas* (Leuven, 2001) (= *Studies on Early Christian Apocrypha* 6).

Aspects of the historicity of the Acts of Thomas or of apostolic activity in India are discussed in the following:

F. C. Burkitt, *Early Christianity outside the Roman Empire* (Cambridge, 1899), esp. 63–99.

A. E. Medlycott, *India and the Apostle Thomas: An Inquiry, with a Critical Analysis of the Acta Thomae* (London, 1905).

J. Dahlmann, *Die Thomas-Legende und die ältesten historischen Beziehungen des Christentums zum fernen Osten* (Freiburg, 1912) (= *Stimmen aus Maria Laach: Ergänzungsheft* 107).

J. N. Farquhar, 'The Apostle Thomas in North India', *BJRL* 10 (1926), 80–111.

—— 'The Apostle Thomas in South India', *BJRL* 11 (1927), 20–50.

A. Mingana, 'The Early Spread of Christianity in India', *BJRL* 10 (1926), 435–514.

L. W. Brown, *The Indian Christians of St. Thomas* (Cambridge, 1956).

G. Huxley, 'Geography in the Acts of Thomas', *Greek, Roman and Byzantine Studies* 24 (1983), 71–80.

Works specifically on the Hymn of the Pearl:

EDITIONS

Syriac

A. A. Bevan, *The Hymn of the Soul* (Cambridge, 1897) (= *Texts and Studies* 5.3) (with Eng. trans. and notes).

G. Hoffmann, 'Zwei Hymnen der Thomasakten', *ZNW* 4 (1903), 273–309 (important reconstruction of Syriac, with German trans.).
E. Preuschen, *Zwei Gnostische Hymnen* (Giessen, 1904) (with German trans. and discussion of text).
Johan Ferreira, *The Hymn of the Pearl* (Sydney, 2002) (= *Early Christian Studies* 3) (with English translation).

Greek

M. Bonnet, 'Actes de S. Thomas Apôtre. Le poème de l'âme. Version grecque remaniée par Nicétas de Thessalonique', *Anal. Boll.* 20 (1901), 159–64 (adaptation of part of the Greek Acts including a summary of the 'Hymn of the Pearl (Soul)')

MODERN TRANSLATIONS

English

F. C. Burkitt, *Early Eastern Christianity* (London, 1904), 218–23.
'The Hymn of the Pearl', in B. Layton (ed.), *The Gnostic Scriptures* (London, 1987), 366–75.

French

J. É. Ménard, 'Le Chant de la perle', *RSR* 42 (1968), 289–325.
P.-H. Poirier, '*L'Hymne de la perle des Actes de Thomas*': *Introduction, texte, traduction, commentaire* (Louvain-la-Neuve, 1981) (= *Homo Religiosus* 8) (includes trans. of the Greek and Syriac, and Nicetas' epitome).

GENERAL

F. C. Conybeare, 'The Idea of Sleep in the "Hymn of the Soul"', *JTS* 6 (1905), 609–10.
V. Burch, 'A Commentary on the Syriac Hymn of the Soul', *JTS* 19 (1918), 145–61.
A. Adam, *Die Psalmen des Thomas und das Perlenlied als Zeugnisse vorchristlicher Gnosis* (Berlin, 1959) (= Beihefte zur *ZNW* 24) (includes German translation).
A. F. J. Klijn, 'The so-called Hymn of the Pearl', *VC* 14 (1960), 154–64.
G. Quispel, *Makarius, Das Thomasevangelium und das Lied von der Perle* (Leiden, 1967), esp. ch. 6.[5]
I. P. Culianu, 'Erzählung und Mythos im "Lied von der Perle"', *Kairos* 21 (1979), 60–71.
H. Kruse, 'The Return of the Prodigal', *Orientalia* 47 (1978), 177–84 (Eng. trans. and commentary).
P. H. Poirier, 'L'Hymne de la perle des Actes de Thomas: Étude de la tradition manuscrite', *Orientalia Christiana Analecta* 205 (Rome, 1979), 17–29; id., 'L'Hymne de la perle et le manichéisme à la lumière de *Codex Manichéen* de Cologne', in L. Cirillo and A. Roselle (eds.), *Codex Manichaeus Coloniensis* (Cosenza, 1986), 235–48.

[5] Review by J. E. Ménard, *RSR* 42 (1968), 358–61.

THE ACTS OF THE HOLY APOSTLE THOMAS

SUMMARY OF CONTENTS

I. Judas Thomas is sold to the merchant Abban and taken to India. The royal wedding party. Thomas succeeds in urging celibacy on the bridal couple (1–16).
II. Thomas meets King Gundaphorus, who commissions him to build a royal palace (17–29).
III. Raising of a man killed by a serpent (30–8).
IV. The speaking colt (39–41).
V. Exorcism of the woman possessed by a demon (42–50).
VI. Raising the woman murdered by her lover. Her vision of hell (51–61).
VII. Siphor the captain of King Misdaeus finds Thomas to ask him to exorcize his wife and daughter. Thomas agrees to visit them (62–7).
VIII. The wild asses deliver Thomas and the captain to his family. Thomas addresses and exorcizes the demon(s) (68–81).
IX. Mygdonia, the wife of Charisius a kinsman of the king, is converted by Thomas. Charisius reacts by having the king agree to kill Thomas. Siphor testifies on Thomas' behalf to the king. The Hymn of the Pearl is sung by Thomas in prison (82–118).
X. Mygdonia is baptized (119–33).
XI. King Misdaeus' wife, Tertia, is also converted. Misdaeus has Thomas arrested again (134–8).
XII. Misdaeus' son Vazan is converted by Thomas in prison (139–49).
XIII. Vazan is baptized (150–8).
XIV. Martyrdom of Thomas. Conversion of Misdaeus as a result of the healing of one of his sons after an appearance by Thomas (159–70/1).

FIRST ACT OF THE APOSTLE JUDAS THOMAS.
HOW THE LORD SOLD HIM TO THE MERCHANT ABBAN,
THAT HE SHOULD GO DOWN AND CONVERT INDIA[1]

1. At that time we apostles were all in Jerusalem—Simon called Peter, and Andrew his brother, James the son of Zebedee, and John his brother, Philip and Bartholomew, Thomas and Matthew the taxgatherer, James the son of Alphaeus and Simon the Cananaean, and Judas the son[2] of James—and we portioned out the regions of the world, in order that each one of us might go into the region that fell to him by lot, and to the nation to which the Lord had sent him. By lot India fell to Judas Thomas, also called Didymus. And he did not wish to go, saying that he was not able to travel on account of the weakness of his body. He said, 'How can I, being a Hebrew, go among

---

[1] This title comes from the Syriac.
[2] Brother?

the Indians to proclaim the truth?' And while he was considering this and speaking, the Saviour appeared to him during the night and said to him, 'Fear not, Thomas, go away to India and preach the word there, for my grace is with you.' But he would not obey saying, 'Wherever you wish to send me, send me, but elsewhere. For I am not going to the Indians.'

2. And as he was thus speaking and considering, it happened that a merchant named Abban, who had come from India, was there, sent from King Gundaphorus, having received an order from him to buy a carpenter and bring him to him. And the Lord, having seen him walking about in the market at noon, said to him, 'Do you wish to buy a carpenter?' He replied, 'Yes.' And the Lord said to him, 'I have a slave who is a carpenter, and I wish to sell him.' And having said this he showed him Thomas from a distance and agreed with him for three pounds of uncoined silver, and wrote a bill of sale saying, 'I, Jesus, son of the carpenter Joseph, declare that I have sold my slave, Judas by name, to you, Abban, a merchant of Gundaphorus, king of the Indians.' When the purchase was completed the Saviour took Judas, also called Thomas, and led him to Abban, the merchant. When Abban saw him he said to him, 'Is this your master?' The apostle answered and said, 'Yes, he is my Lord.' And he said, 'I have bought you from him.' And the apostle held his peace.

3. On the following morning the apostle prayed and entreated the Lord, saying, 'I go wherever you wish, O Lord Jesus, your will be done.'[3] And he went to the merchant Abban, carrying nothing at all with him, but only his price. For the Lord had given it to him, saying, 'Let your worth also be with you along with my grace, wherever you may go.' And the apostle came up with Abban, who was carrying his luggage into the boat. He too began to carry it along with him. And when they had gone on board and sat down, Abban questioned the apostle, saying, 'What kind of work do you know?' And he said, 'In wood, ploughs and yokes and balances and ships and boats' oars and masts and small blocks; in stone, pillars and temples and royal palaces.' And Abban the merchant said to him, 'We need such a workman.' They began their voyage. And they had a fair wind; and they sailed cheerfully till they came to Andrapolis, a royal city.

4. And leaving the boat they went into the city. And behold, the sounds of flute-players and water-organs and trumpets echoed round them. And the apostle inquired saying, 'What festival is it in this city?' And the inhabitants there answered, 'The gods have brought you to keep festival in this city. For the king has an only daughter and now he is going to give her to a husband in marriage. This festival, then, which you see to-day, is the rejoicing and public assembly for the marriage. And the king has sent forth heralds to proclaim everywhere that all are to come to the marriage, rich and poor, bond and free,

---

[3] Matt. 6: 10; Luke 22: 42.

strangers and citizens. But if anyone should refuse and not come to the marriage, he is answerable to the king. And Abban, having heard this, said to the apostle, 'Let us also go so that we give no offence to the king, especially as we are strangers.' And he said, 'Let us go.' And having obtained lodgings at the inn and rested a little they went to the wedding. And the apostle, seeing them all reclining, reclined also in their midst. And they all looked at him as at a stranger, a man coming from a foreign land. And Abban the merchant, being the master, reclined in another place.

5. And whilst they were eating and drinking, the apostle tasted nothing. Those about him said to him, 'Why have you come here, neither eating nor drinking?' And he answered and said to them, 'For something greater than food or even drink have I come here, that I might accomplish the will of the king. For the heralds proclaim the wishes of the king, and whoever will not hear the heralds will be liable to the judgement of the king.' When they had dined and drunk, and crowns and perfumes had been brought, each took perfume, and one anointed his face, another his beard, and others different parts of the body. And the apostle anointed the crown of his head, and put a little of the ointment in his nostrils, and dropped it also in his ears, and applied it also to his teeth, and carefully anointed the parts round about his heart; but the crown that was brought to him, wreathed with myrtle and other flowers, he put on his head, and he took a branch of reed in his hand and held it. And the flute-girl, holding her flute in her hand, went round them all; and when she came to the place where the apostle was she stood over him, playing the flute over his head a long time. And that flute-girl was a Hebrew by race.

6. And as the apostle looked to the ground, one of the cupbearers stretched forth his hand and struck him. And the apostle, having raised his eyes, looked at the man who had struck him, saying, 'My God will forgive you for this wrong in the world to come, but in this world he will show his wonders, and I shall soon see that hand that struck me dragged along by dogs.' And having spoken he began to sing this song:

> 'The maiden is the daughter of the light,
> On whom rests the majestic splendour of kings;
> Delightful is the sight of her,
> Resplendent with brilliant beauty.
> Her garments are like spring flowers
> Sending forth sweet fragrance.
> On the crown of her head the king is seated
> Feeding with his own ambrosia those who live under him.
> Truth rests upon her head,
> Joy she shows forth with her feet.
> Her mouth is opened, and becomingly.[4]

[4] Syriac adds 'She sings loud songs of praise'.

Thirty-and-two are they who praise her.
Her tongue is like a door-curtain,
Drawn back for those who go in.[5]
Made by the first creator.
Her two hands point and make secret signs predicting the chorus of the blessed ages,
Her fingers show the gates of the city.
Her chamber is bright,
Breathing forth scent from balsam and every perfume,
Sending forth a sweet smell of myrrh and herbs.
Within are strewn myrtle-branches and all manner of sweet-smelling flowers,
The portal is adorned with reeds.

7. She is surrounded by her groomsmen, seven in number,
Chosen by herself;
Her bridesmaids are seven,
Who dance before her.
Twelve in number are they who minister before her
And are at her bidding.
Their gaze is attentively directed at the bridegroom,
That they be enlightened by his sight,
And be for ever with him in that everlasting joy,
And sit down at that wedding to which the princes assemble,
And abide at the supper, of which the eternal ones are deemed worthy,
And put on royal garments, and be dressed in splendid robes
That both may rejoice and exult
And praise the Father of all,
Whose majestic light they have received
And have been enlightened by the sight of their Lord,
Whose ambrosial food they received,
Of which there is no deficiency,
And drank also of his wine,
Which brings to them neither thirst nor desire,
And they praised and glorified with the living spirit
The Father of truth and the mother of wisdom.'

8. And when he had finished this song all who were present looked at him. He kept silence. They also saw his form changed, but they did not understand his words, as he was a Hebrew and his words were spoken in Hebrew. Only the flute-girl understood him, being of the Hebrew race; and leaving him she played the flute to the others, but repeatedly looked back and gazed at him.

---

[5] Syriac adds 'Her neck ascends like steps'.

For she loved him as one belonging to her race, and he was also beautiful in appearance above all who were there. And when the flute-girl had finished her flute-playing, she sat down opposite him, and looked steadily at him. But he looked at no one at all, neither did he pay attention to any one, but kept his eyes only on the ground, waiting until he could depart. And the cupbearer that struck him came down to the fountain to draw water. And there happened to be a lion there which killed him and left him lying in the place, after tearing his limbs asunder. And dogs immediately seized his limbs, among them a black dog, which grasped his right hand in his mouth and brought it to the place of the banquet.

9. When they all saw it they were frightened and inquired who was absent. And when it became known that it was the hand of the cupbearer that struck the apostle, the flute-girl broke her flute and threw it away, and went and sat at the feet of the apostle, saying, 'This man is either God or God's apostle. For I heard him say in Hebrew to the cupbearer, "I shall soon see the hand that struck me dragged about by dogs." This you have now seen. For just as he said, so also it has come to pass.' Some believed her, and some not. And when the king heard of it he came and said to the apostle, 'Rise up and go with me, and pray for my daughter. For she is my only child and to-day I give her away in marriage.' And the apostle would not go with him, for the Lord had not yet been revealed to him there. But the king took him away against his will to the bridal chamber, that he might pray for them.

10. And the apostle stood and began to pray and speak thus: 'My Lord and my God,[6] who accompanies his servants, guide and leader of those who believe in him, refuge and repose of the afflicted, hope of the poor and deliverer of the captives, physician of the souls laid low by disease, and saviour of every creature, who gives life to the world and strengthens the souls, you know the future and accomplish it through us; you, Lord, who reveal hidden mysteries and declare secret words; you, Lord, are the planter of the good tree and by your hand all good works are produced; you, Lord, are in all, and come through all, and exist in all your works and make yourself manifest through the working of them all; Jesus Christ, the Son of compassion and perfect Saviour; Christ, Son of the living God, the undaunted power which has overthrown the enemy; the voice, heard by the rulers, which shook all their powers; messenger, sent from on high, who went down even to Hades; who also, having opened the doors, brought out from there those who had been shut in for many ages in the treasuries of darkness, and showed them the way that leads up on high—I beseech you, Lord Jesus, offering you supplication for these young persons, that you may do to them what helps, benefits, and is profitable for them.' And having laid his hands on them and said, 'The Lord be with you', he left them in that place and went away.

[6] John 20: 28.

11. The king requested the groomsmen to leave the bridal chamber. When all had left, and the doors were shut, the bridegroom raised the curtain of the bridal chamber, that he might bring the bride to himself. And he saw the Lord Jesus talking with the bride. He had the appearance of Judas Thomas, the apostle, who shortly before had blessed them and departed; and he said to him, 'Did you not go out before them all? And how is it that you are here now?' And the Lord said to him, 'I am not Judas Thomas, I am his brother.' And the Lord sat down on the bed and ordered them to sit down on couches, and he began to speak to them.

12. 'Remember, my children, what my brother said to you, and to whom he commended you; and know that if you refrain from this filthy intercourse you become temples holy and pure, being released from afflictions and troubles, known and unknown, and you will not be involved in the cares of life and of children, whose end is destruction. But if you get many children, for their sakes you become grasping and avaricious, plundering orphans and deceiving widows, and by doing this you subject yourselves to most grievous punishments. For most children become unprofitable, being possessed by demons, some openly and some secretly. For they become either lunatics or half-withered or crippled or deaf or dumb or paralytics or idiots. And though they be healthy, they will be again good-for-nothing, doing unprofitable and abominable works. For they will be detected either in adultery or in murder or in theft or in unchastity, and by all these you will be afflicted. But if you obey and preserve your souls pure to God, there will be born to you living children, untouched by these hurtful things, and you will be without care, spending an untroubled life, free from grief and care, looking forward to receive that incorruptible and true marriage, and you will enter as groomsmen into that bridal chamber full of immortality and light.'

13. And when the young people heard this, they believed the Lord and gave themselves over to him and refrained from filthy lust, and remained thus spending the night in the place. And the Lord went away from them saying, 'The grace of the Lord be with you!'[7] And when dawn came the king arrived, and having furnished the table brought it in before the bridegroom and the bride. And he found them sitting opposite each other, and he found the face of the bride uncovered, and the bridegroom was very cheerful. And the mother came in and said to the bride, 'Why do you sit thus, child, and are not ashamed, but act as if you had lived for a long time with your own husband?' And her father said, 'Is it because of your great love to your husband that you are unveiled?'

14. The bride answered and said, 'Truly, father, I am in great love, and I

---

[7] 1 Cor. 16: 23.

pray to my Lord that the love which I have experienced this night may remain, and that I obtain that man whom I have experienced today. That I do not veil myself is because the mirror of shame has been taken away from me; I am no longer ashamed or abashed, since the work of shame and bashfulness has been removed far from me. And that I am not frightened is because alarm did not abide in me. And that I am cheerful and glad is because the day of joy has not been disturbed. And that I have set at naught this husband and these nuptials which have passed away from before my eyes is because I have been joined in a different marriage. And that I had no conjugal intercourse with a temporary husband, whose end is repentance and bitterness of soul, is because I have been united to the true husband.'

15. And when the bride was saying even more, the bridegroom answered and said, 'I thank you, Lord, who have been proclaimed by the stranger and found in us; who have put corruption far from me, and have sown life in me, who have delivered me from this disease, hard to heal, hard to cure and abiding for ever, and established in me sound health; who have shown yourself to me, and have revealed to me my condition, in which I am; who have redeemed me from falling, and have led me to something better, and who have released me from things temporary, but have deemed me worthy of things immortal and everlasting; who have humbled yourself to me and my weakness, to place me beside your greatness and to unite with you; who have not kept your compassion from me, who was lost, but have shown me how to seek myself, and to know who I was and who and how I now am, that I may become again what I was; whom I did not know, but you have sought me out; of whom I did not know, but you stood by me; whom I have experienced and am not able to forget; whose love is fervent in me and of whom I cannot speak as I ought. But what I have to say about him is short and very little, and is not in proportion to his glory; but he does not find fault with me if I dare to tell him even what I know not; for it is out of love to him I say this.'

16. And when the king heard these things from the bridegroom and the bride, he rent his garments and said to those standing near him, 'Go out quickly, and search the whole city, and seize and bring that man, the sorcerer, who has come by evil chance into this city. For I led him with my own hands into my house, and I told him to pray for my most unfortunate daughter. Whoever shall find him and bring him to me, I give him whatever he shall ask of me.' They departed, therefore, and went round seeking him, and did not find him; for he had set sail. They also went into the inn where he had stayed, and found there the flute-girl weeping and in distress, because he had not taken her with him. And when they told her what had taken place with the young people, she rejoiced greatly upon hearing it, setting aside her grief, and said, 'Now I also have found repose here!' And she arose and went to them, and was with them a long time, until they had instructed the king also. And

many of the brethren also met there, until the rumour had spread that the apostle had gone to the cities of India, and was teaching there. And they went away and joined him.

SECOND ACT OF THE APOSTLE THOMAS CONCERNING HIS APPEARANCE BEFORE KING GUNDAPHORUS

17. When the apostle came into the cities of India with Abban the merchant, Abban went away to greet King Gundaphorus and told him about the carpenter whom he had brought with him. And the king was glad and ordered him to appear before him. When he had come in the king said to him, 'What trade do you know?' The apostle said to him, 'That of the carpenter and the house-builder.' The king said to him, 'What work in wood do you know and what in stone?' The apostle said, 'In wood, ploughs, yokes, balances, pulleys, and ships and oars and masts; in stone, monuments, temples, and royal palaces.' And the king said, 'Will you build me a palace?' And he answered, 'Yes, I shall build it and finish it; for because of this I have come, to build and to do carpenter's work.'

18. And the king, having accepted him, took him out of the gates of the city, and on the way began to discuss with him the building of the palace, and how the foundations should be laid, till they came to the place where the work was to be carried out. And he said, 'Here is where I wish the building to be!' And the apostle said, 'Yes, this place is suitable for the building.' For the place was wooded and there was water there. And the king said, 'Begin at once!' And he answered, 'I cannot commence now.' The king said, 'When can you?' He said, 'I shall begin in November and finish in April.' And the king was surprised, and said, 'Every building is built in the summer, but can you build and finish a palace in the winter?' And the apostle replied 'Thus it must be done; it is impossible any other way.' And the king said, 'If you have resolved upon this, draw a plan for me how the work is to be done, since I shall come here after some time.' And the apostle took a reed, measured the place, and marked it out: the doors to be set towards the rising of the sun, to face the light; the windows toward the west, to the winds; the bakehouse he made toward the south; and the water-pipes necessary for the supply toward the north. When the king saw this, he said to the apostle, 'You are truly a craftsman, and it is fitting that you should serve kings.' And having left a lot of money with him, he went away.

19. And at the appointed times the king sent coined silver and the necessities for his and the workmen's living. And the apostle took everything and divided it, going about in the cities and surrounding villages, distributing to the poor and needy, and bestowing alms, and gave them relief, saying, 'The king knows that he will receive royal recompense, but the poor must be

refreshed, as their condition requires it.' After this the king sent a messenger to the apostle, having written the following: 'Let me know what you have done or what I should send to you or what you need.' The apostle sent word to him saying, 'The palace is built, and only the roof remains to be done.' Upon hearing this the king sent him again gold and uncoined silver and wrote, 'If the palace is built, let it be roofed.' And the apostle said to the Lord, 'I thank you, Lord, in every respect, that you died for a short time, that I may live in you for ever, and that you have sold me, to deliver many through me.' And he did not cease to teach and refresh the afflicted, saying, 'The Lord has dispensed this to you and he gives to each his food. For he is the support of the orphans and the nourisher of the widows, and rest and repose to all who are afflicted.'

20. When the king came to the city he inquired of his friends concerning the palace which Judas, surnamed Thomas, had built for him. And they said to him, 'He has neither built a palace, nor did he do anything of that which he promised to do, but he goes about in the cities and villages, and if he has anything he gives it to the poor, and teaches a new God, heals the sick, drives out demons, and performs many miracles. And we believe that he is a magician. But his acts of compassion and the cures done by him as a free gift, still more his simplicity and gentleness and fidelity, show that he is a just man, or an apostle of the new God, whom he preaches. For he continually fasts and prays and eats only bread with salt, and his drink is water, and he wears one coat, whether in warm weather or in cold, and he takes nothing from anyone but gives to others what he has.' Upon hearing this the king hit his face with his hands, shaking his head for a long time.

21. And he sent for the merchant who had brought him, and for the apostle, and said to him, 'Have you built the palace?' And he said, 'Yes, I have built it.' The king said, 'When shall we go to inspect it?' And he answered and said, 'Now you cannot see it, but you shall see it when you depart this life.' And the king was very angry and ordered both the merchant and Judas Thomas to be bound and cast into prison, until he should find out to whom the property of the king had been given, and so destroy him and the merchant. And the apostle went to prison rejoicing and said to the merchant, 'Fear nothing, believe only in the God who is preached by me, and you shall be freed from this world, and obtain life in the world to come.'

And the king considered by what death he should kill them. He decided to flog them and burn them with fire. On that very night Gad, the king's brother, fell ill; and through the grief and disappointment which the king had suffered he was grievously depressed. And having sent for the king he said to him, 'Brother and king, I commend to you my house and my children. For I have been grieved on account of the insult that has befallen you, and lo, I am dying, and if you do not proceed against the life of that magician you will give my soul no rest in Hades.' And the king said to his brother, 'I considered the whole night by what death I should kill him, and I have decided to flog him and burn him with fire, together with the merchant who brought him.'

22. While they were talking, the soul of Gad, his brother, departed, and the king mourned for Gad exceedingly, because he loved him, and ordered him to be prepared for burial in a royal and costly robe. While this was going on, angels received the soul of Gad, the king's brother, and took it up into heaven, showing him the places and mansions there, asking him, 'In what place do you wish to dwell?' And when they came near the edifice of the apostle Thomas, which he had erected for the king, Gad, upon beholding it, said to the angels, 'I entreat you, my lords, let me dwell in one of these lower chambers.' But they said to him, 'In this building you cannot dwell.' And he said, 'Why not?' They answered, 'This palace is the one which that Christian has built for your brother.' But he said, 'I entreat you, my lords, allow me to go to my brother to buy this palace from him. For my brother does not know what it is like, and he will sell it to me.'

23. And the angels let the soul of Gad go. And as they were putting on him the burial robe his soul came into him. And he said to those standing round him, 'Call my brother to me, that I may beg of him a request.' Straightway they sent the good news to their king, saying, 'Your brother has become alive again!' And the king arose and with a great multitude went to his brother. And coming in he went to the bed as if stupefied, unable to speak to him. And his brother said, 'I know and I am convinced, brother, that if anyone had asked of you the half of your kingdom, you would give it for my sake. Wherefore I entreat you to grant one favour, which I beg of you to do: that you sell to me that which I ask from you.' And the king answered and said, 'And what is it that you wish me to sell to you?' And he said, 'Assure me by an oath that you will grant it to me.' And the king swore to him, 'Whatever of my possession you ask, I will give you.' And he said to him, 'Sell me the palace which you have in heaven.' And the king said, 'A palace in heaven—where does this come to me from?' And he said, 'It is the one that Christian built for you, the man who is now in prison, whom the merchant brought, having bought him from a certain Jesus. I mean that Hebrew slave whom you wished to punish, having suffered some deception from him, on account of whom I also was grieved and died, and now have come alive again.'

24. Then the king heard and understood his words about the eternal benefits that were conferred upon him and destined for him, and said, 'That palace I cannot sell you, but I pray to be permitted to enter into it and to dwell there, being deemed worthy to belong to its inhabitants. And if you really wish to buy such a palace, behold, the man is alive, and will build you a better one than that.' And immediately he sent and brought the apostle out of prison, and the merchant who had been shut up along with him, saying, 'I entreat you, as a man entreating the servant of God, pray for me, and ask him, whose servant you are, to pardon me and to overlook what I have done to you or intended to

do, and that I may become worthy to be an inhabitant of that house for which indeed I have done nothing, but which you, labouring alone, have built for me with the help of the grace of your God, and that I may also become a servant and serve this God, whom you preach'. His brother also fell down before the apostle and said, 'I entreat you and supplicate before your God that I may become worthy of this service and become partaker of that which was shown to me by his angels.'

25. And the apostle, seized with joy, said, 'I give thanks to you, Lord Jesus, that you have revealed your truth in these men. For you alone are the God of truth and not another; and you are he who knows all things that are unknown to many; you, O Lord, are he who in all things shows mercy and compassion to men. For men, through the error that is in them, have overlooked you, but you have not forsaken them. And now, because I entreat you and supplicate you, accept the king and his brother and unite them with your flock, cleanse them by your baptism and anoint them with your oil from the error which encompasses them. Protect them also from the wolves and bring them into your meadows. Give them to drink of your ambrosial fountain, which is never fouled and never dries up. For they entreat and supplicate you and wish to become your servants, and on this account they have also resolved to be persecuted by your enemies and to endure for your sake hatred, insult, and death, as you also have suffered all this for our sakes, in order to gain us. You are Lord and truly a good shepherd. Grant to them that they put their trust in you alone, and obtain the help coming from you and hope of their salvation, which they expect from you alone, and that they may be confirmed in your mysteries and receive the perfect benefits of your graces and gifts, and flourish in your service and bear fruit to perfection in your Father.'

26. Being well disposed now toward the apostle, King Gundaphorus and his brother Gad followed him, never leaving him, providing for the poor, giving to all, and relieving all. And they entreated him that they might also receive the seal of the word, saying to him, 'Since our souls are at ease, and as we are earnest about God, give us the seal. For we heard you say that the Lord whom you preach knows his own sheep through his seal.' And the apostle said to them, 'I am glad and entreat you also to receive this seal, and to take part with me in this eucharist and blessed meal of the Lord, and to be made perfect by it. For he is the Lord and God of all, Jesus Christ, whom I preach, and he is the Father of truth, in whom I have taught you to believe.' And he ordered them to bring oil, that through the oil they might receive the seal. And they brought oil and lighted many lamps. For it was night.

27. And the apostle arose and sealed them. And the Lord was revealed to them through a voice saying, 'Peace be with you,[8] brethren!' And they heard his voice only, but his form they did not see, for they had not yet received the

---

[8] John 20: 19, 21, 26.

further sealing of the seal. And the apostle took the oil, poured it over their heads, anointed and chrismed them, and began to say:

'Come, holy name of Christ, which is above every name;[9]
Come, power of the Most High, and perfect compassion;
Come, gift most high;
Come, compassionate mother;
Come, fellowship of the male;
Come, revealer of secret mysteries;
Come, mother of the seven houses, that there may be rest for you in the eighth house.
Come, elder of the five members: intelligence, thought, prudence, reflection, reasoning,[10]
Communicate with these young men!
Come, Holy Spirit, and purify their loins and their hearts,
And seal them in the name of the Father and of the Son and of the Holy Ghost.'

And when they had been sealed, there appeared to them a young man holding a blazing lamp, so that the other lamps were darkened by the emanation of its light. And he went out and disappeared from their sight. And the apostle said to the Lord, 'Your light is too great for us, Lord, and we cannot bear it. For it is too much for our sight.' And when dawn came and it was light, he broke bread, and made them partakers of the eucharist of Christ. And they rejoiced and exulted. And many others also believed and were added to the faithful, and came to the refuge of the Saviour.

28. And the apostle did not cease preaching and saying to them, 'Men and women, boys and girls, young men and maidens, vigorous and aged, both bond and free, withhold yourselves from fornication, covetousness, and gluttony. For under these three heads all wickedness comes. For fornication destroys the mind and darkens the eyes of the soul and becomes a hindrance to the right regulation of the body, changing the whole man into feebleness and throwing the whole body into disease. Greediness brings the soul into fear and shame, being inside the body, and robs what belongs to another, and suspects that, in returning to the owners their property, it will be put to shame. Gluttony plunges the soul into cares, troubles, and sorrows, fearing that it will be wanting, and reaches out for that which is far away. In refraining from these things, you are without care, without grief, and without fear, and there remains to you that which was said by the Saviour: "Take no care for the morrow, for the morrow will take care of itself."[11] Remember also the word spoken before: "Look at the ravens, and behold the fowls of the

---

[9] Phil. 2: 9.
[10] James (*ANT* 378) includes a note by F. C. Burkitt on these five words for 'mind' in Syriac.
[11] Matt. 6: 34.

heaven, that they neither sow nor reap, nor gather into barns, and God takes care of them. How much more for you,[12] O you of little faith!" But look for his coming, set your hope in him, and believe in his name. For he is the judge of the living and of the dead,[13] and he gives to each one according to his works.[14] And at his coming and appearance at the end time, no one who is about to be judged by him has a word of excuse, as if he had not heard. For his heralds preach in the four quarters of the globe. Repent, therefore, and believe the preaching and take upon you an easy yoke and a light burden,[15] that you may live and not die. These things lay hold of, these things keep; come forth from the darkness, that the light may receive you! Come to him who is truly good, that from him you may receive grace and place his sign upon your souls!'

29. When he had said this, some of the bystanders said to him, 'It is time for the creditor to receive his debt.' And he said to them, 'The creditor, indeed, always wishes to receive more, but let us give him what is proper.' And having blessed them he took and blessed bread, oil, herbs, and salt, and gave to them. But he continued in his fastings, for the Lord's day was about to dawn. And as night fell, while he was asleep, the Lord came and stood by his head and said, 'Thomas, rise up early and bless them all; and after the prayer and service go along the eastern road two miles, and there I will show my glory in you. For because of the work, for which you go away, many will take refuge in me, and you shall reprove the nature and power of the enemy.' And he rose from his sleep and said to the brethren who were with him, 'Children and brethren, the Lord wishes to perform something through me today. Let us, however, pray and entreat him that nothing may be a hindrance for us toward him, but that as at all times let it now also be done to us according to his purpose and will.' And having thus spoken he laid his hands upon them and blessed them. And having broken the bread of the eucharist, he gave it to them, saying, 'May this eucharist be to you for compassion and mercy, and not for judgement and retribution!' And they said, 'Amen.'

THIRD ACT
CONCERNING THE SERPENT

30. And the apostle went out to go where the Lord had commanded him. And when he was near the second milestone he turned a little out of the way and saw the body of a beautiful youth lying there, and he said, 'Lord, was it for this that you brought me out to come here, that I might see this temptation? Your will, therefore, be done, as you intend!' And he began to

---

[12] Matt. 6: 26.
[13] Acts 10: 42.
[14] Matt. 16: 27.
[15] Matt. 11: 29–30.

pray, and to say, 'Lord, judge of the living and the dead, of the living who stand here, and of the dead who are lying here, Lord of all and Father—Father not of the souls that are still in bodies, but of those who have left them, because you are Lord and judge of the souls still in the bodies[16]—come in this hour in which I call upon you, and show your glory to him who is lying here.' And he turned to his companions and said, 'This work has happened for a purpose, but the enemy has wrought and effected this to make an assault, and you see that he has availed himself of no other form, and has wrought through no other living being than that which is his subject.'

31. And when he had said this, behold, a great serpent came from his den, beating his head and brandishing his tail on the ground, and said with a loud voice to the apostle, 'I will say before you why I have killed him, since you have come here to reprove my works.' The apostle said, 'Yes, say on.' And the serpent said, 'There is a certain woman in this place who is exceedingly beautiful. And as she was passing by I saw her and fell in love with her, followed her, and watched her. And I found this young man kissing her, and he had intercourse with her and did other shameful things with her. And it would be an easy matter for me to tell you this, but I dare not. For I know that you are the twin brother of Christ and always bring our race to naught. Not wishing to harass her, I did not kill him in that hour, but I watched him passing by in the evening, struck him, and killed him, especially as he had dared to do this on the Lord's day.' And the apostle enquired of him, saying, 'Tell me, of what seed and of what race are you?'

32. And he said to him, 'I am the offspring of the serpent, and the baleful son of a baleful father; I am a son of him who hurt and struck the four standing brothers. I am a son of him who sits on the throne which is under heaven, who takes his own from those who borrow; I am the son of him who encircles the globe; I am kinsman to him who is outside the ocean, whose tail lies in his mouth; I am he who went into Paradise through the fence, and said to Eve what my father bade me speak to her; I am he who inflamed and fired Cain to kill his own brother, and through me thorns and thistles sprang up in the ground; I am he who cast down the angels from above, and bound them by the desire of women, that earthborn children might be produced by them, and that I might fulfil my will in them; I am he who hardened Pharoah's heart, that he might kill the children of Israel and subjugate them through hard servitude; I am he who deceived the multitude astray in the desert, when they had made the calf; I am he who kindled Herod and inflamed Caiaphas to the lying accusation before Pilate, for this was fitting for me; I am he who inflamed Judas and bribed him to deliver the Messiah to death; I am he who inhabits and holds the abyss of Tartarus, but the Son of God has wronged me against my will and selected his own out of me; I am a kinsman of him who is

---

[16] Literally 'pollutions'.

to come from the east, to whom also power is given to do whatever he will upon earth.'

33. When the serpent had spoken these things in the hearing of the multitude, the apostle lifted up his voice and said, 'Stop now, O you most shameless one, and be ashamed that you are wholly powerless. For your end, destruction, has come. And do not dare to say what you have done through your dependants. But I command you in the name of that Jesus who even until now contends with you for the sake of those who are his own, to suck out the poison which you put into this man, and to draw it forth and take it out of him!' And the serpent said, 'The time of our destruction has not yet come as you have said. Why do you force me to take out what I have put in him, and to die before the time? For my father shall also find his end when he draws forth and sucks out what he has put into the creation.' And the apostle said to him, 'Show now the nature of your father!' And the serpent came, put his mouth upon the wound of the young man, and sucked the gall out of it. And in a short time the colour of the young man, which was like purple, grew white, but the serpent swelled up. And when the serpent had drawn up all the gall into himself, the young man sprang up and stood, and ran and fell at the apostle's feet. And the serpent, being swollen up, burst and died, and his poison and gall poured out. And in the place where his poison was poured out there was a great chasm, and the serpent was swallowed up. And the apostle said to the king and to his brother, 'Take workmen, and fill up the place and lay foundations and build houses above it, that there be a dwelling place for strangers.'

34. And the young man said to the apostle with many tears, 'In what way have I sinned against you? For you are a man having two forms, and wherever you wish, you are found, and are not prevented by anyone, as I see. For I saw how that man standing beside you said to you, "I have many wonders to show through you, and I have to accomplish great works through you, for which you shall obtain a reward, and you shall make many live, and they shall be in repose in eternal life, as the children of God. Therefore", said he, "raise this young man—whereby he meant me—stricken by the enemy and become his guardian for all time." You have done well to come here, and again you shall do well to depart to go to him, for indeed he never forsakes you. I have been released from care and reproach; he has enlightened me from the care of the night and from daily work. I was also released from him who urged me to do these things. I sinned against him who taught me the contrary, and I have destroyed that kinsman of the night, who forced me to sin by his own practices; but I found, however, that kinsman of mine who is the light. I have destroyed him who darkens and obscures his subjects, that they know not what they do, and being ashamed of their works they abandon them, and their deeds have an end. But I found him whose works are light and whose deeds are truth, of which no one repents, whoever does them. I was released from

him in whom falsehood abides, before whom darkness goes as a veil, and behind whom is shame, impudent in idleness. But I found him who revealed to me what is beautiful to lay hold of, the Son of truth, the kinsman of concord, who, driving away the mist, enlightens his creation, heals its wounds, and overthrows its enemies. But I entreat you, man of God, make me again to behold and see him who is now hidden from me, that I may also hear his voice, whose wonder I cannot express. For it is not of the nature of this bodily organ.'

35. And the apostle answered and said to him, 'If you are freed from those things whose nature, as you have said, you have known, and know who he is who has wrought these things in you, and have learned and become a follower of him after whom you now seek in your ardent love, you shall see him and be with him for ever in his repose and in his joy. But if you are rather carelessly disposed toward him, and return to your former deeds, and let go that beauty and that radiant countenance which has now been displayed to you, and if the splendour of his light, which you now desire, is entirely hidden from you, you shall be deprived not only of this life, but also of the future, and you shall go to him whom you said that you had lost, and you shall see no more him whom you said you had found.'

36. And when the apostle had said this he went to the city, holding the young man by the hand and saying, 'What you have seen, child, is only a little of the many things which God has. For it is not concerning these visible things that he preaches the gospel to us, but greater things than these he promises. So long as we are in the body we cannot tell and say what he will give to our souls in the future. For if we say that he gives us light, this is something visible and we have it already. But if we say that he will give us riches, they exist and appear already in this world, and we name them and we do not long for them, since it has been said: "With difficulty will a rich man enter into the kingdom of heaven."[17] And if we speak of fine cloaks, which the luxurious in this life put on, we name them, and it has been said, "Those who wear soft raiment are in kings' houses."[18] And when we speak of costly dinners, we mention things that exist, and concerning these we have received a commandment to beware of them, lest at any time our hearts be weighed down with surfeiting and drunkenness and cares of this life;[19] and it has been said, "Take no thought for your life, what you shall eat or what you shall drink; nor for your body, what you shall put on. For life is more than meat and body more than raiment."[20] And if we speak of this temporary rest, judgement has been appointed for it. We speak about the world above, about

---

[17] Matt. 19: 23.
[18] Matt. 11: 8.
[19] Luke 21: 34.
[20] Matt. 6: 25.

God and angels, about watchmen and saints, about the ambrosial food and the drink of the true wine, about enduring and not obsolescent garments, about things "which eye has not seen, nor ear heard, neither have they entered into the heart of sinful men, which God has prepared for those who love him."[21] Of these things we speak, and concerning these things we preach the gospel. You also, therefore, believe in him, that you may live; put your trust in him, and you shall not die. For he is not persuaded by gifts, that you should offer them to him; nor does he need sacrifice, that you should sacrifice to him. But look to him, and he will not disregard you; turn to him, and he will not forsake you. For his comeliness and beauty will make you love him, but it does not allow you to turn away from him.'

37. And after the apostle had said this, many people joined the young man. And looking about the apostle noticed how they lifted themselves up to see him, and they went up to elevated places. And the apostle said to them, 'Men who have come to the assembly of Christ, and who wish to believe in Jesus, learn from this, and see that if you do not get high up you cannot see me, who am small, and cannot look at me, who am like yourselves. Now if you cannot see me, who am like yourselves, unless you raise yourselves a little from the earth, how can you see him who lives above and now is found below, unless you first raise yourselves out of your former condition and unprofitable deeds and desires, which do not endure, and your riches, which must be left behind, and the possession which is of the earth and grows old, and garments which deteriorate, and beauty which ages and vanishes, indeed the whole body, in which all this is kept, grows old and becomes dust, returning to its own nature? For all these things support the body. But, rather, believe in our Lord Jesus Christ, whom we proclaim, that your hope may be upon him and you may have in him eternal life, that he may be your companion in this land of error, a haven in this troubled sea and an overflowing fountain in this thirsty land[22] and a chamber full of food in the place of the hungry, and rest for your souls, and also a physician of your bodies.'

38. When the multitude of those assembled heard these things, they wept and said to the apostle, 'Man of God, we dare not say that we belong to that God whom you preach, because our works which we have done are alien to him, not pleasing to him. But if he has compassion upon us and pities us and delivers us, overlooking our former deeds, and frees us from the evil which we have done when we were in error, and takes not into account nor recollects our former sins, we shall become his servants and we shall do his will to the end.' And the apostle answered and said to them, 'He neither condemns you nor does he count against you the sins done by you, being in error, but he overlooks your transgressions which you have done in ignorance.'

---

[21] 1 Cor. 2: 9.
[22] Cf. Gospel of Thomas 13.

FOURTH ACT
CONCERNING THE COLT

39. Whilst the apostle was still standing in the road speaking to the multitude, a colt of an ass came up to him and, opening its mouth, said, 'Twin brother of Christ, apostle of the Most High and initiated into the hidden word of Christ, who receives his secret utterances, fellow worker of the Son of God, who, though free, has been a servant, and, being sold, has brought many to freedom, kinsman of the great race which condemned the enemy and redeemed his own, who to many in the land of the Indians became a cause of life—because you came to erring men, and through your appearance and your divine words they now turn to the God of truth who sent you—mount, sit on me, and rest, until you come to the city.' And the apostle answered, 'O Jesus Christ, Son of the perfect mercy, O rest and calmness, and you of whom even the unreasoning animals speak; O hidden rest, and you who are manifest by your working as our Saviour and nourisher, keeping us and making us rest in strange bodies, Saviour of our souls, sweet and inexhaustible spring, secure, pure fountain which is never troubled,[23] helper and defender of your servants in the struggle, who turn aside and drive away from us the enemy, who fight for us in many battles, and make us victorious in all, our true and invincible champion, our holy and victorious general, most glorious, who give to your people imperishable joy and rest which knows of no affliction, good shepherd, who offered yourself for your sheep, overcame the wolf, and redeemed your sheep and led them to good pastures—we praise and glorify you and your invisible Father and your Holy Spirit and the mother of all creation.'

40. When the apostle said this, the whole multitude looked at him, waiting to hear what he would answer the colt. And after the apostle remained silent for a time, as if in a trance, and looking toward heaven, he said to the colt, 'Who are you, and to whom do you belong? For surprising and strange is that which was spoken by you. These things are also hidden from many.' And the colt answered and said, 'I am of that family which served Balaam, and to which also belonged that colt on which sat your Lord and your Master. And now I have been sent to give you rest as you sit on me, that these may believe and I may obtain that portion which I am about to receive through the service now offered to you, and which shall be taken from me if I do not serve you.' And the apostle answered, 'He who gave you this gift of speech can give it to you and to those belonging to your race until the end. Compared to this mystery I am powerless and weak.' And he would not mount. But the colt entreated him that by riding on it he might bless it. And the apostle mounted and sat down and everyone went with him, some going before, others following him, and they all ran, anxious to see how he would dismiss the colt.

41. And when he came near the gates of the city, he dismounted and said,

---

[23] Cf. Gospel of Thomas 13.

'Go and be kept safe where you were.' And immediately the colt fell to the ground at the feet of the apostle and died. All of those who were present were sorrowing and said to the apostle, 'Make it alive.' And he answered and said to them, 'I could do it indeed through the name of Jesus. But this would not help it. For he who gave it the speech that it spoke could also make it not die. I shall not raise it, not because I could not do it, but because this is the best for it.' And he ordered those present to dig a hole and bury the carcass. And they did as he commanded.

FIFTH ACT
CONCERNING THE DEMON THAT DWELT IN THE WOMAN

42. And the apostle went into the city followed by all the multitude. And he thought of going to the parents of the young man whom he had revived after he had been killed by the serpent, because they entreated him very much to come and to enter their house. Suddenly an exceedingly beautiful woman cried out, 'Apostle of the new God, who have come to India, and servant of that holy and only good God—for by you he is proclaimed the Saviour of the souls of those who come to him, and by you the bodies of those are healed who are punished by the enemy, and you have become the cause of life of all who turn to him—command that I be brought to you, that I may tell you what happened to me, and perhaps there may be hope for me and for those who stand beside you to be more confident in the God whom you preach. For not a little have I already been tormented by the enemy for five years. As a woman I formerly had rest, surrounded everywhere by peace, and I had anxiety for nothing. I had none to care for.

43. 'And one day when I left the bath, it happened that I met a man who looked troubled and disturbed. And his voice and answer seemed to be very faint and thin. And coming up to me he said, "Let us unite in love and have intercourse with each other as a man with his wife." And I answered and said, "I had no intercourse with my betrothed, as I refused to be married—how should I give myself up to you, who wish to have intercourse with me in adultery?" And having said this I passed on. And to my maid I said, "Did you see the young man and his impudence, how shamelessly and boldly he talked to me?" And she said, "I saw an old man talking with you." When I had come to my house and dined, my mind suggested to me a certain suspicion, especially as he appeared to me in two forms. And with this in my thoughts, I fell asleep. In that night he came in to me and made me share in his foul intercourse. I saw him also when it was day, and fled from him. According to his wont, he came at night and abused me. And now as you see me, I have been tormented by him five years, and he has not departed from me. But I know and am persuaded that even demons and spirits and monsters are subject to you and tremble at your prayer. Pray, then, for me, and drive away

from me the demon which torments me continually, that I also may become free, and may be brought to my original nature and receive the gift which has been granted to my kind.'

44. And the apostle said, 'O irrepressible wickedness! O shamelessness of the enemy! O jealous one that is never at rest! O hideous one who subjects the beautiful ones! O many-formed one—he appears as he wishes, but his nature cannot be changed! O crafty and perfidious one! O bitter tree, whose fruits are like it! O traducer, fighting over that which is not his! O deceit which uses shamelessness! O wickedness that creeps like a serpent and is related to it!' And when the apostle had spoken the enemy stood before him, no one seeing him except the apostle and the woman, and said in the hearing of all with a very loud voice:

45. 'What have we to do with you, apostle of the Most High?[24] What have we to do with you, servant of Jesus Christ? What have we to do with you, counsellor of the Holy Son of God? Why will you destroy us before our time? Why will you take our power? For until the present hour we had hope and time left to us. What have we to do with you? You are powerful in your own, and we in our own. Why will you use tyranny against us, since you teach others not to use violence? Why do you covet that which is not your own like one who is not satisfied with what he has? Why do you liken yourself to the Son of God, who wronged us? For you are altogether like him, as if you had him for a father. For we thought to bring him also under the yoke, like the rest. But he turned and left us under his power, because we knew him not. He deceived us by his unattractive form and his poverty and want. For when we saw him like this, we thought him to be a man clothed with flesh, not knowing that it was he who makes men live. And he gave us power over our own, and for the time being not to abandon our own, but to abide in them. But you wished to get more than is due and has been given you and to do violence to us!'

46. And having thus spoken the demon wept and said, 'I leave you, my most beautiful consort, whom I found long ago and with whom I was at rest. I leave you, my beloved, trusty sister, in whom I was well pleased. What I shall do or whom I shall call upon to hear me and protect me, I know not. I know what I shall do: I shall go to places where the fame of this man has not been heard; and in your stead, my beloved, I may perhaps find one with another name.' And lifting up his voice he said, 'Remain in peace since you have taken refuge with one greater than I. I will go away, and seek one like you; and if I find her not, I shall return again to you. For I know that when you are near this man you have a place of refuge in him; but when he has gone away you shall be as you were before he appeared; and you will forget him, but for me there will be again opportunity and boldness. But now I fear the name of him

---

[24] Cf. Mark 5: 7.

who has protected you.' And having thus spoken the demon disappeared. And after he had gone, fire and smoke were seen, and all present were struck with amazement.

47. And the apostle, seeing this, said to them, 'Nothing strange or unusual has the demon shown, but the element by which he shall be burned. For the fire shall consume him, and the smoke shall be scattered abroad.' And he began to say, 'Jesus, hidden mystery which has been revealed to us; you are he who made known to us many secrets, who separated me from all my companions and told me three words with which I am inflamed, but which I cannot communicate to others; Jesus, man, slain, dead, buried; Jesus, God of God and Saviour, who enlivens the dead, and heals the sick; Jesus, who appears to be in want, and saves as if in want of nothing, catching the fishes for the morning and evening meal, and satisfying all with a little bread; Jesus, who rests from the toil of the journey like a man, and walks upon the waves like a God; (48.) Jesus Most High, voice arising from perfect compassion, Saviour of all, right hand of the light, prostrating the wicked through his own nature, and bringing all his kind into one place; polymorphous, who are the only-begotten, the first-born among many brethren;[25] God of God Most High and man, despised until now; Jesus Christ, who do not neglect us when we call upon you; who have become the cause of life to the whole human race; you who were judged for our sakes and kept in prison, whereas you free all who are in bonds; you who were called a deceiver, whereas you deliver your own from deception—I pray you for these present and who believe in you. They wish to obtain your gifts, having a joyous hope in your help and taking refuge in your majesty. Their ears are open to hear the words which are spoken to them. May your peace come and dwell in them, and renew them by cleansing them from their former deeds, and let them put off the old man with his deeds and put on the new man now declared to them by me!'[26]

49. And he laid his hands on them and blessed them saying, 'The grace of our Lord Jesus be upon you for ever!'[27] And they said, 'Amen.'

And the woman begged him and said, 'Apostle of the Most High, give me the seal, that that foe may not come back to me again.' And he made her come near to him, laid his hands on her, and sealed her in the name of the Father and of the Son and of the Holy Ghost. And many others were also sealed with her. And the apostle ordered his deacon to set out a table. And they set out a stool which they found there. And having spread a linen cloth upon it, he put on it the bread of blessing. And the apostle stood by it and said, 'Jesus, who have deemed us worthy to partake of the eucharist of your holy body and blood, behold, we are emboldened to come to your eucharist and to invoke your holy name; come and commune with us.'

---

[25] Rom. 8: 29.
[26] Col. 3: 9–10.
[27] Rom. 16: 20.

50. And he began to say:

'Come, perfect compassion;
Come, fellowship with the male;
Come, you who know the mysteries of the Chosen One;
Come, you who have partaken in all the combats of the noble combatant;
Come, rest, that reveals the great deeds of the whole greatness;
Come, you who disclose secrets
And make manifest the mysteries;
Come, holy dove,
Who bear the twin young;
Come, secret mother;
Come, you who are manifest in your deeds;
Come, giver of joy
And of rest to those who are united to you;
Come and commune with us in this eucharist,
Which we celebrate in your name,
And in the agape
In which we are united at your calling.'

And having thus spoken he made the sign of the cross upon the bread, broke it, and began to distribute it. And first he gave it to the woman and said, 'This shall be to you for remission of sins and everlasting transgressions.' And after her he gave also to all the others who had received the seal.

SIXTH ACT
CONCERNING THE YOUNG MAN WHO KILLED THE MAIDEN

51. Now there was a certain young man, who had committed a nefarious deed. He came and partook of the eucharist. And his two hands withered, so that he could no longer put them to his mouth. When those present saw him, they told the apostle what had happened. And the apostle called him and said, 'Tell me, my son, and be not afraid of what you have done before you came here. For the eucharist of the Lord has convicted you. For this gift, by entering many, brings healing, especially to those who come in faith and love; but you it has withered away, and what has happened has happened not without some justification.' And the young man convicted by the eucharist of the Lord came up, fell at the apostle's feet, and besought him and said, 'An evil deed has been done by me, whilst I thought to do something good. I loved a woman who lived in an inn outside the city, and she loved me also. And when I heard about you, believing that you proclaim the living God, I came and received the seal from you along with the others. And you said, "Whoever shall indulge in impure intercourse, especially in adultery, shall not have life with the God whom I preach." As I loved her very much, I entreated her and

tried to persuade her to live with me in chaste and pure conduct, as you teach. And she would not. Since she would not, I took a sword and killed her. For I could not see her commit adultery with another.'

52. When the apostle heard this he said, 'O insane intercourse, how you lead to shamelessness! O unrestrained lust, how have you excited this man to do this! O work of the serpent, how you rage in your own!' And the apostle ordered some water to be brought in a dish. And when the water had been brought he said, 'Come, waters from the living waters; everlasting, sent to us from the everlasting; rest, sent to us from the one who gives rest; power of salvation, proceeding from that power which overcomes all and subjects it to its will—come and dwell in these waters, that the gift of the Holy Spirit may be completely fulfilled in them!' And to the young man he said, 'Go, wash your hands in these waters.' And when he had washed them they were restored. And the apostle said to him, 'Do you believe in our Lord Jesus Christ, that he can do all things?' And he said, 'Though I am the least, yet I believe. But I did this in the hope of doing something good. For I entreated her, as I told you already, but she would not be persuaded by me to keep herself chaste.'

53. And the apostle said to him, 'Come, let us go to the inn where you committed the deed, and let us see what happened.' And the young man went before the apostle on the road. When they had come to the inn they found her lying there. And when the apostle saw her he was sad, for she was a beautiful girl. And he ordered her to be brought into the middle of the inn. And putting her on a couch they carried it out and set it in the midst of the courtyard of the inn. And the apostle laid his hand on her and began to say, 'Jesus, who appear to us at all times—for this is your will, that we should always seek you, and you have given us the right to ask and to receive, and have not only permitted us this, but have also taught us how to pray—who are not seen by us with the bodily eyes, but who are never hidden from those of our soul, and who are hidden in form, but manifested to us by your works; by your many deeds we have recognized you as much as we are able, and you have given us your gifts without measure saying, "Ask, and it shall be given you; seek, and you shall find; knock, and it shall be opened unto you."[28] We pray, therefore, being afraid of our sins. And we ask you not for riches or gold or silver or possessions or any of those things that come from earth and go into the earth again; but we beg of you and entreat that in your holy name you raise this woman lying here by your power, to your glory and to an awakening of faith in those who stand by.'

54. And he said to the young man, after sealing him, 'Go and take her hand and say to her, "With iron I killed you with my hands, and with my hands I raise you because of faith in Jesus."' And the young man went and

---

[28] Matt. 7: 7.

stood by her, saying, 'I have believed in you, O Christ Jesus.' And looking upon Judas Thomas the apostle, he said to him, 'Pray for me, that my Lord, upon whom I call, may come to my help.' And laying his hand on her hand he said, 'Come, Lord Jesus Christ, give her life and me the reality of your faith.' And he drew her by the hand, and she sprang up and sat looking at the great multitude standing around. And she also saw the apostle standing opposite her, and leaving her couch she sprang up and fell at his feet and took hold of his garments, saying, 'I pray, Lord, where is your companion who has not left me to remain in that fearful and grievous place, but has given me up to you, saying, "Take this one, that she may be made perfect, and thereafter be brought into her own place"?'

55. And the apostle said to her, 'Tell us where you have been.' And she answered, 'Do you, who were with me, to whom also I was entrusted, wish to hear?' And she commenced thus: 'An ugly-looking man, entirely black, received me; and his clothing was exceedingly filthy. And he took me to a place where there were many chasms, and a great stench and most hateful vapour were given forth thence. And he made me look into each chasm, and in the first I saw blazing fire, and fiery wheels running, and souls were hung upon these wheels, dashing against each other. And there was crying and great lamentation and no Saviour was there. And that man said to me, "These souls are akin to you, and in the days of reckoning they were delivered to punishment and destruction. And then others are brought in their stead; in like manner all these are again succeeded by others. These are they who perverted the intercourse of man and wife." And again I looked down, and saw infants heaped upon each other, struggling and lying upon each other. And he said to me, "These are their children, and for this they are placed here for a testimony against them."

56. 'And he brought me to another chasm, and as I looked into it I saw mud and worms spouting forth, and souls wallowing there; and I heard a great gnashing of teeth come from them. And that man said to me, "These are the souls of women who left their husbands and committed adultery with others, and they have been brought to this torment." And he showed me another chasm, and looking into it I saw souls hung up, some by the tongue, some by the hair, some by the hands, others by the feet, head downward, and reeking with smoke and sulphur. Concerning these the man who accompanied me said the following: "The souls hung up by the tongue are slanderers and such as have spoken false and disgraceful words and are not ashamed. Those hung up by their hair are the shameless, who are not ashamed at all and go about with uncovered heads in the world. Those hung up by the hands are they who took that which did not belong to them and have stolen, and who never gave anything to the poor, nor helped the afflicted; but they did so because they wished to get everything, and cared neither for law nor right. And these hung up by the feet are those who lightly and eagerly walked in wicked ways and

disorderly paths, not visiting the sick nor escorting those who depart this life. On this account each soul receives what it has done."

57. 'And again he led me forth and showed me a very dark cavern, exhaling a very bad stench. Many souls were peeping out thence, wishing to get some share of the air. And their keepers would not let them look out. And my companion said to me, "This is the prison of those souls which you saw. For when they have fully received their punishment for that which each has done, others succeed them. Some are fully consumed, others are given up to other punishments." And the keepers of the souls in the dark cavern said to the man that had charge of me, "Give her to us, that we may bring her to the others till the time comes when she is handed over to punishment." But he said to them, "I will not give her to you, because I am afraid of him who delivered her to me. For I was not told to leave her here; I shall take her back with me, till I get an injunction about her." And he took me and brought me to another place, where there were men who were cruelly tortured. He who is like you took me and gave me up to you, saying to you, "Take her, for she is one of the sheep which have wandered away." And received by you, I now stand before you;. I beg, therefore, and supplicate you that I may not come to those places of punishment which I have seen.'

58. And the apostle said, 'You have heard what this woman has recounted. And these are not the only punishments, but there are others worse than these. And you too, unless you turn to the God whom I preach, and abstain from your former works and from the deeds which you did in ignorance, shall find your end in these punishments. Believe, therefore, in Christ Jesus, and he will forgive you the former sins and will cleanse you from all your bodily desires that remain on the earth, and will heal you from the faults that follow after you and go along with you and are found before you. Let every one of you put off the old man and put on the new,[29] and leave your former course of conduct and behaviour. Those who steal, let them steal no more, but let them live, labouring and working.[30] The adulterers are no more to commit adultery, lest they give themselves up to everlasting punishment. For with God adultery is an evil exceedingly wicked above all other evils. Put away also covetousness and lying and drunkenness and slandering, and do not return evil for evil![31] For all these are alien and strange to the God whom I preach. But walk rather in faith and meekness and holiness and hope, in which God rejoices, that you may become his kinsmen, expecting from him those gifts which only a few receive.'

59. The whole people therefore believed and presented obedient souls to the living God and Christ Jesus, rejoicing in the blessed works of the Most High and in his holy service. And they brought money for the service of the

---

[29] Cf. Col. 3: 9.
[30] Cf. Eph. 4: 28.
[31] Cf. 1 Pet. 3: 9.

widows. For he had them gathered together in the cities, and he sent to all of them by his deacons what was necessary, both clothing as well as food. He himself did not cease to preach and to speak to them and to show that this Jesus is the Messiah of whom the Scriptures have spoken that he should be crucified and be raised after three days from the dead. He also showed to them and explained, beginning from the prophets, what was said concerning the Messiah, that it was necessary for him to come, and that everything had to be accomplished which had been prophesied of him. And the fame of him spread over all the cities and villages, and all who had sick persons or such as were troubled by unclean spirits brought them to him; and some they laid on the road by which he was to pass, and he healed all by the power of the Lord. And those who were healed by him said with one accord and one voice, 'Glory to you, Jesus, who in like manner has given healing to all through your servant and apostle Thomas! And being in good health and rejoicing, we pray that we may become members of your flock and be counted among your sheep. Receive us, therefore, O Lord, and consider not our trespasses and our former transgressions, which we did while we were in ignorance!'

60. And the apostle said, 'Glory be to the only-begotten of the Father,[32] glory to the first-born of many brethren;[33] glory to you, the helper and defender of those who come to your refuge. You are the sleepless one who awaken those who sleep, and who live and bring to life those lying in death; O God Jesus Christ, Son of the living God, redeemer and helper, refuge and rest of all those that labour in your work, who heal those who for your name's sake bear the burden and heat of the day,[34] we give thanks for the gifts given to us by you, and for the help from you bestowed upon us, and your providential care that has come upon us from you.

61. 'Perfect these things upon us to the end, that we may have confidence in you. Look upon us because for your sake we have left our houses and our patrimony, and for your sake we have gladly and willingly become strangers. Look upon us, O Lord, because for your sake we have given up our own possessions, that we might obtain you for a possession that shall not be taken away. Look upon us, O Lord, because we have left those related to us by ties of kindred, in order that we may be united in relationship to you. Look upon us, O Lord, who have left our fathers and mothers and guardians, that we may behold your father and be satisfied with his divine nourishment. Look upon us, O Lord, because for your sake we have left our bodily consorts and our earthly fruit, in order that we may share in that true and lasting communion and bring forth true fruits, whose nature is from above, which no one can take from us, in which we abide and they abide with us.'

---

[32] John 1: 14.
[33] Rom. 8: 29.
[34] Matt. 20: 12.

SEVENTH ACT
CONCERNING THE CAPTAIN

62. While the apostle Judas Thomas was preaching the word of God in India, a captain of King Misdaeus came to him and said to him, 'I have heard that you do not take a reward but give to the poor what you have. For if you did take a reward I should have sent you a large sum of money, and I would not have come myself, since the king does nothing without me. For my possessions are great and I am rich, one of the wealthiest in India. But I never did anything wrong to anyone. But the reverse I have experienced. I have a wife, and I had a daughter by her, and I love her very much, as nature demands, and I had no intercourse with another woman. And it happened that there was a wedding in our city, and those who made the wedding were good friends of mine. So they came and asked me, also inviting my wife and daughter. As they were my friends I could not refuse. So I sent her, though she did not wish to go, and I also sent many slaves with them. So they went away, decked with much jewellery, she and her daughter.

63. 'And when it was evening and the time had come to leave the wedding, I sent lamps and torches to meet them, and I stood looking out when they should come, and I could see her and my daughter. And as I stood I heard a lamentation. "Woe to her!" was heard from every mouth. And the slaves returned with torn garments and told me what had happened. "We saw", they said, "a man and a boy with him; the man had his hand upon your wife, the boy upon your daughter. But they ran away from them. And we wounded them with swords, but the swords fell to the ground and the women also fell, gnashing their teeth and knocking their heads against the ground. And when we saw this, we came to tell you." Upon hearing this I tore my garment and struck my face with my hands, and ran like a madman all the way. And having gone I found them prostrate in the market. And I took them and brought them into my house, and having regained their senses they eventually calmed down and rested.

64. 'I now began to ask my wife, "What happened to you?" And she said, "Do you not know what happened to me? I asked you not to let me go to the wedding, since I did not feel very well. And as I walked along the street and came to the aqueduct, I saw a black man before me, his head shaking a little, and a boy like him, standing by his side. And I said to my daughter, "Look at these two ugly men, whose teeth are like milk and whose lips are like soot." And we left them at the aqueduct and went on. After sunset, when we had come away from the wedding and were going with the slaves through the city, near the aqueduct my daughter noticed them first, and she came to me. And afterwards I saw them also, coming towards us, and we ran away from them. And the slaves who were with us ran away. And the men beat us and threw us down." And as she told me this the demons came near again and threw them

down. And since that hour they can go out no more, being locked up in one room or another. And on their account I suffer much and am troubled. For wherever they are the demons throw them down and strip them naked. I ask you, therefore, to pray to God: help me and have mercy upon me! For three years no table has been set in my house, and my wife and my daughter have not sat at table. Especially I ask you for my unhappy daughter, who has not seen anything good in this world.'

65. When the apostle heard this from the captain he felt very sorry for him. And he said to him, 'Do you believe that Jesus can heal?' And the captain said, 'Yes.' And the apostle said, 'Commit yourself to Jesus, and he will heal and help them.' The captain said, 'Show him to me, that I may ask him and believe in him.' And the apostle said, 'He appears not to these bodily eyes, but is only found with the eyes of the mind.' And the captain lifted up his voice and said, 'I believe in you, Jesus, and I beseech and ask of you, help my little faith, which I have toward you.' The apostle commanded the deacon Xenophon to bring everybody together in one place. And when the multitude was assembled, the apostle spoke, standing in the midst:

66. 'My children and brethren, who believe in the Lord, remain in this faith by preaching Jesus, who has been preached to you by me and by putting your hope in him. Forsake him not, and he shall not forsake you. When you sleep in this slumber weighing down the sleepers, he sleeps not and watches. And when you travel by sea and are in danger and there is no one to help, he walks upon the waters and helps. I am now about to go from you, and it is uncertain whether I shall see you again in my body. Be not like the people of Israel who fell, when left alone for a short time by their shepherd. I leave with you in my place deacon Xenophon, for he also preaches Jesus like myself. I am nothing; neither is he. Only Jesus is something. For I also am a man, clothed with a body, a son of man, like one of you. I have no riches, unlike some of you; these convict their possessors as they are entirely useless, since they are left behind on earth, whence they came. But the trespasses which come upon men on their own account and the filth of sin they take with them. The rich are seldom found in the practice of mercy. But the merciful and the meek of heart shall inherit the Kingdom of God. Even beauty does not remain with man. For those who rely on it shall suddenly be confounded when old age comes. Everything has its time. There is a time to love, a time to hate.[35] Let the hope, therefore, be in Jesus Christ, the Son of God, who is always loved and desired, and remember us, as we remember you. For we also, unless we carry the burden of the commandments, are not worthy to be preachers of that name and shall be punished there afterward.'

67. And having prayed with them, he remained a long time in prayer and supplication, and commended them to the Lord, and said, 'Lord, the Lord of

---

[35] Eccles. 3: 8.

each soul, which is in a body; Lord, Father of the souls who hope in you and wait for your mercy, you who redeem your men from error, and free from servitude and corruption those who are subject to you and take refuge with you, come to the flock of Xenophon, anoint them with holy oil, heal their wounds and keep them from the grievous wolves.' And he laid his hands upon them and said, 'The peace of the Lord come upon you and go also with us!'

EIGHTH ACT
CONCERNING THE WILD ASSES

68. And the apostle went forth to go on his way. And they all accompanied him with tears and adjured him to remember them in his prayers and not to forget them. And when he had mounted the wagon and all the brethren were left behind, the captain came, ordered the driver to rise, and said, 'I pray and supplicate to be deemed worthy to sit under his feet and to become his driver on this road, that he may become my companion on that way, by which only a few travel.'

69. And having gone about two miles the apostle bade the captain to rise and sit beside him, allowing the driver to take his own seat. And as they went off it happened that on account of the great heat the beasts became tired and could move no more. And the captain became very vexed and discouraged, and thought of running by foot to fetch other animals for the wagon. But the apostle said, 'Let not your heart be troubled, neither let it be afraid; but believe in Jesus Christ, whom I have preached to you, and you shall see great wonders.' And looking about he saw a herd of wild asses grazing by the way. And he said to the captain, 'If you believe in Jesus Christ, go to the herd of wild asses and say, "Judas Thomas, the apostle of Christ, the new God, says: Let four of you come, because we need you!"'

70. And the captain went, seized by fear because they were so many. And as he went, they came to meet him. And coming near he said to them, 'Judas Thomas, the apostle of the new God, commands you that four of you should come, because I need them!' And the wild asses, upon hearing this, came to him running with one accord; and having come, they fell upon their knees.[36] And the apostle said to them, 'Peace be with you! Yoke four in place of these beasts who are at a standstill!' And every one of them came and crowded to be yoked. But there were four stronger than the rest, and these were yoked. Of the others, some went before, some followed. And having gone a short distance he dismissed them, saying, 'To you, the inhabitants of the desert, I say, go to your pastures! For if I needed all, you would all go with me. But now go to your place where you were.' And they quietly went away till they were out of sight.

---

[36] The Syriac inserts here a hymn.

71. While the apostle, the captain, and the driver went on, the wild asses walked quietly and evenly, in order not to disturb the apostle of God. And when they had come near the gate of the city, they turned aside and stopped before the house of the captain. And the captain said, 'It is not possible to tell what happened, but I will await the end and then I will speak.' And the whole city came, having seen the wild asses yoked. And the rumour also spread that the apostle intended to remain there. The apostle asked the captain, 'Where is your house and where are you bringing us?' And he said to him, 'You yourself know that we are at the door, and these which have come along at your behest know it better than I.'

72. Having said this, they alighted from the wagon. And the apostle began to say, 'Jesus Christ, whose knowledge is despised in this country; Jesus Christ, of whom nothing has been heard in this country; Jesus, who receive all apostles in every country and every city, and by whom all worthy of you are glorified; Jesus, who have taken a form and become like a man and appeared to all of us in order not to separate us from your love; Lord, you are he who has given himself for us and has bought us with a price by his blood, as a precious possession. But what have we, Lord, to offer in exchange for your life which you have given for us? For what we have is your gift. We entreat you and thereby have life.'

73. And when he had spoken thus many came from all sides to see the apostle of the new God. And the apostle said again, 'Why do we stand idle? Lord Jesus, the hour has come. What do you wish that should be done? Command, therefore, that what must come to pass be accomplished.' And the wife and daughter of the captain were very troubled by the demons, in such a way that the inmates of the house thought that they would rise no more. For the demons would not allow them to eat anything at all, but threw them on their beds, and they recognized no one till the day on which the apostle came. The apostle said to one of the wild asses, which were yoked on the right side, 'Go into the court and, standing there, call the demons, and say to them, "Judas Thomas, the apostle and disciple of Jesus Christ says: Come out here! For for your sakes and against your race I have been sent to destroy you and to persecute you to your place, till the time of consummation comes and you go down into your depth of darkness."'

74. The wild ass, accompanied by many people, went in and said, 'I speak to you, the enemies of Jesus the Christ, I speak to you who close your eyes not to see the light—since the worst nature cannot be changed for good—to you I say, the children of hell and destruction, the children of him who unceasingly does evil, who always renews his operations and those things which belong to his nature, to you I speak, most shameless, who shall be destroyed by yourselves—but what I should say concerning your destruction and end and what I should advise, I know not. For there are innumerable things to hear. But your trespasses are greater than the punishment which is reserved for

you. But to you, demon, and your son, who follows you, I speak—for now I have been sent against you—but why make many words about your nature and origin, which you know yourselves and of which you are nevertheless unashamed? Judas Thomas, the apostle of Jesus Christ, who has been sent here out of much love and kindness, commands you, "Go out in the presence of all the people here and tell me of what race you are!"'

75. And immediately the woman and her daughter came forth, like people dead and dishonoured. And when the apostle saw them he was sad, especially on account of the girl, and said to the demons, 'Let no forgiveness and forbearance fall to your lot, for you know no forbearance or compassion! But, in the name of Jesus, leave them and stand aside!' When the apostle had said this, the women fell down and died. For they neither had breath nor did they speak. And the demon answered with a loud voice, 'Have you come again, mocker of our nature and kindred? Have you come again to thwart our plans? And I think you will not suffer us to remain upon earth. But this you cannot do at this time.' The apostle, however, recognized that this was the same demon that had been driven out from that woman.

76. And the demon said, 'I beseech you, let me go and dwell where you wish, and command me for that purpose, then I shall not fear the mighty one who has power over me. For as you have come to preach, so have I come to destroy. As he who sent you punishes you for not fulfilling his will, so, unless I do the will of him who has sent me, I am sent before the time and season appointed to my nature. And as Christ helps you in your work, so my father helps me in that which I do. And as he prepares for you the vessels worthy for your habitation, so my father selects vessels by which I accomplish his deeds. And as he nourishes and provides for his subjects, so my father prepares for me and those in whom I dwell punishments and torments. And as he gives you eternal life as reward for your work, so my father offers me as recompense for my works everlasting destruction. And as you enjoy your prayer and good works and spiritual hymns, so I enjoy murders and adulteries and the sacrifices offered with wine upon the altars. And as you turn men over to everlasting life, I turn those who obey me to everlasting damnation and punishment. You receive your reward, I mine.'

77. When the demon had spoken this and much more, the apostle said, 'Jesus commands you and your son through me, that you no more enter into a human dwelling, but go out and depart and dwell completely outside the dwelling of men!' And the demons said to him, 'You have given us a hard order. But what will you do to those now hidden from you? For the makers of idols rejoice in them more than you, and the multitude worships them and does their will, bringing sacrifices to them and offering wine and water libations as food and presenting gifts.' And the apostle said, 'They shall now be destroyed with their deeds.' And suddenly the demons became invisible. But the women lay like dead people upon the ground, making no sound.

78. And the wild asses stood together and did not leave. But the wild ass which by the power of God was able to speak said to the apostle, whilst all were silent and looked on to see what they would do, 'Why do you stand idle, apostle of the Most High, who waits for you to beseech him for the greatest knowledge? Why do you delay? For your teacher wishes to show his great deeds by your hands. Why do you tarry, herald of the hidden One? For your Master will make known through you secrets, reserving them for those whom he deems worthy to hear them. Why do you rest, who perform great deeds in the name of the Lord? For your Lord encourages you, by giving you courage. Be not afraid. For he will forsake no soul which according to race belongs to you. Begin, therefore, to call upon him, and he shall willingly hear you. Why do you stand and admire all his deeds and effects? For these things are small which he has shown through you. And what will you say of his great gifts? For you shall not be able to tell them fully. Why do you wonder at his bodily cures, which are transient, especially when you know the true and lasting healing which he gives to those who belong to him? And why do you look at this temporal life, and give no thought of the eternal?'

79. 'And to you, multitudes standing here expecting that the prostrated women shall be raised, I say: Believe the apostle of Jesus Christ; believe the teacher of truth; believe him who shows you the truth; believe in Jesus; believe in the Messiah who was born, that the born might have life through his life; who also became a child and was educated, that perfect humanity might appear through him. He taught his own teacher, because he is the teacher of truth[37] and the wisest of the wise; he offered sacrifice in the temple, to show that every offering is hallowed. This man is his apostle, the revealer of truth. It is he who does the will of him who sent him. But false apostles and prophets of lawlessness shall come, whose end shall be according to their deeds, who indeed preach and give laws that one should flee lawlessness, but they are found at all times in sins. They are clothed indeed in sheep's clothing, but inwardly they are ravening wolves,[38] they are not satisfied with one wife, but corrupt many women; they say that they despise children, yet ruin many children and suffer for them; they are not satisfied with what they possess, but wish that everything should serve them alone, whereas they pretend to be his disciples; they say one thing with their mouth, but in their heart they think otherwise; they command others to refrain from wickedness, but they themselves do nothing good; they are regarded as temperate and command others to abstain from fornication, theft, and avarice, but in secret they do all these things themselves, while teaching others not to do these things.'

80. While the wild ass was talking, everybody looked at it. And when it was

---

[37] Infancy Gospel of Thomas 6–8, 14, 15.
[38] Matt. 7: 15.

silent, the apostle said, 'What I am to think of your beauty, O Jesus, and what I am to say about you, I know not; rather, I cannot. For I am not able, O Christ, to declare it, O you who are at rest and alone are wise, who alone know what is in the heart and the contents of thought—glory be to you, merciful and tranquil; glory be to you, wise word; glory to your mercy, which is shed over us; glory to your compassion which is spread over us; glory to your majesty, who came down for our sakes; glory to your most exalted kingship, which humbled itself for our sakes; glory to your strength, which became weak for our sakes; glory to your Godhead, which for our sakes appeared in the image of man; glory to your humanity, which died for our sakes, to make us alive; glory to your resurrection from the dead, for by it our souls shall share in the resurrection and rest; glory and praise to your ascension into heaven, for by it you showed us the way to the highest, having promised that we shall sit on your right hand and judge with you the twelve tribes of Israel. You are the heavenly word of the Father; you are the hidden light of the mind; you are he who shows the way of truth, persecutor of darkness and destroyer of error.'

81. When the apostle had spoken he went to the women and said, 'My Lord and my God, I doubt not in you, nor do I call upon you in unbelief. You are always our helper and assistance and restorer who give us your strength, encourage us, and give your servants freedom in love. I beseech you, let these women rise up healed, and become again as they were before the demons struck them.' When he had thus spoken the women turned and sat up. And the apostle ordered the captain that his servants should take them and bring them indoors. And when they had gone in, the apostle said to the wild asses, 'Follow me.' And they followed him till they were outside the gates. And when they came out, he told them, 'Go in peace to your pastures!' And the wild asses went away willingly, the apostle standing and seeing to it that no harm was done to them by anyone, till they were far off and out of sight. And the apostle returned with the people into the house of the captain.

NINTH ACT
ABOUT THE WIFE OF CHARISIUS

82. It came to pass that a woman named Mygdonia, the wife of Charisius, the near relative of the king, came to see and to behold the new appearance of the new God, who was being preached, and the new apostle, who abode in their country. And she was carried by her slaves, but could not be brought to him on account of the great crowd and the narrow space. So she sent to her husband for more servants. They came and went before her, pushing and beating the people. When the apostle perceived this he said to them, 'Why do you make those go away who come to hear the word and show willingness for it? You wish to be near me, whereas you are far off—as it has been said of the

people who came to the Lord: "Having eyes you see not, and having ears you hear not."[39] And to the multitudes he said, "He who has ears to hear, let him hear;"[40] and "Come to me all who labour and are heavy laden, and I will give you rest."[41]

83. And looking at her carriers, he said to them, 'This beatitude, which was given to them, is now also given to you who are heavy laden. You are those who carry burdens grievous to be borne, and are driven onward by her behest. And although you are men they lay burdens upon you, as upon the irrational beasts, because your lords think that you are not men like themselves.... whether they be bond or free. For neither shall riches help the rich, nor will poverty save the poor from judgement. For we did not receive a commandment which we cannot fulfil, nor did he put upon us heavy burdens grievous to be borne, which we cannot carry. Nor did he put upon us such a building as men build, nor stones to be hewn and houses to be established, as your craftsmen prepare by their intelligence, but we received the commandment from the Lord, that what is displeasing to us when done to us by another we should not do to another man.

84.[42] 'First of all abstain from adultery, for it is the cause of every evil... also from theft, which ensnared Judas Iscariot and caused him to hang himself... for those who are given to avarice see not what they do; and from ostentation and all disgraceful deeds, especially the carnal...[43] the end of which is eternal damnation. For this uncleanliness is the starting point of every evil. In like manner, it also leads those who are proud into servitude, drawing them down to the depth and subjecting them under its hands, that they see not what they do, so that their deeds are unknown to them.

85. 'You, however,...[44] and become thereby well-pleasing to God... and gives life eternal and despises death. And walk in kindness, for it overcomes the enemy and alone obtains the crown of victory. And walk in gentleness, helping the poor and satisfying the want of the needy, by bringing your possessions and distributing them to the needy, especially to those who walk in holiness, for this is chosen by God and leads to eternal life. Before God this is the chief city of all good. Those who do not contend in the stadium of Christ shall not obtain holiness. Holiness is of God, destroying fornication, overcoming the foe, well-pleasing to God. It is an invincible athlete, it is highly esteemed of God and is glorified by many. It is the messenger of peace, preaching peace. If any one acquires temperance, he is without cares because he pleases the Lord and waits for the time of redemption. For it does nothing which is wrong, and gives life and rest and joy to all who obtain it.

[39] Mark 8: 18.
[40] Matt. 11: 15 and elsewhere.
[41] Matt. 11: 28.
[42] I follow the Rome manuscript U for chs. 84–5. The text is corrupt but is longer than that in the Paris manuscript P.
[43] The Syriac refers to sexual intercourse here.
[44] The Syriac includes 'walk in holiness'.

86. 'But meekness has subdued death, bringing it under authority. Meekness has overcome the enemy. Meekness is a good yoke. Meekness fears none and resists not. Meekness is peace and joy and enjoyment of rest. Remain, therefore, in holiness and take freedom from care and approve meekness. For in these three main parts the Messiah is portrayed, whom I preach to you. Holiness is a temple of the Messiah, and whoever lives in it obtains him as an inhabitant. For he fasted forty days and forty nights, without tasting anything. And whoever observes temperance shall live in it as upon a mountain. Meekness, however, is his glory, for he said to our fellow-apostle Peter, "Replace your sword and put it again into its sheath. For if I wanted to do this could I not have brought more than twelve legions of angels from my Father on my side?"'[45]

87. When the apostle spoke this and the whole multitude heard it, they crowded and came near. But the wife of Charisius, the relative of the king, sprang up from the palanquin, threw herself to the ground before the apostle, took hold of his feet, beseeching him and saying, 'Disciple of the living God, you have come into a desert country. For we live in a desert, because by our life we are like the unreasoning animals; but now we shall be saved through your hands. I beseech you, therefore, care for me and pray for me, that the mercy of God, whom you preach, may come upon me and I become his dwelling place and be joined in the prayer and in the hope and in the faith in him, and receive also the seal and become a holy temple and he dwell in me.'

88. And the apostle said, 'I pray and ask for all you brethren who believe in the Lord, and for you, sisters, who hope in Christ, that the word of God may rest on you all and dwell in you; for we have no power over you.' And he began to speak to the woman, Mygdonia, 'Rise up from the ground and remove your adornments. For this ornament which you have on will not help you at all, nor the beauty of your body nor your garments. Neither the fame of the authority which surrounds you nor the power of this world nor this filthy intercourse with your husband will be of use to you if you are deprived of the true intercourse. For the exhibition of jewellery is destroyed, and the body ages and changes, and garments wear out, and power and dominion pass away...[46] And the communion of begetting children also passes away, since it is an object of contempt. Jesus alone remains for ever and they who hope in him.' When he had spoken this, he said to the woman, 'Go in peace, and the Lord will make you worthy of his mysteries.' And she said, 'I am afraid to go away, fearing lest you leave me and go to another people.' And the apostle said to her, 'Even if I go away, I shall not leave you alone, but Jesus will be with you because of his compassion.' And she fell down, worshipped him, and went to her house.

89. And Charisius, the relative of King Misdaeus, after having bathed,

---

[45] Matt. 26: 52-3.
[46] Greek corrupt.

went up to recline at dinner. And he inquired after his wife, where she was. For she had not come as usual from her chamber to meet him. And her servants said to him, 'She is unwell.' And he quickly went to the chamber and found her on the couch and veiled. And he unveiled her, kissed her, and said to her, 'Why are you so sad?' And she said, 'I am unwell.' He said to her, 'Why did you not observe the decency becoming a free woman and stay at home, but went to listen to idle words and look at works of sorcery? But rise, dine with me, for I cannot eat without you.' But she said to him, 'Excuse me for today, for I am very much afraid.'

90. Upon hearing this from Mygdonia, Charisius would not partake of the meal, but ordered his servants to bring her to eat with him. And when they brought her he demanded that she should eat with him. And she excused herself. As she would not, he ate alone, saying to her, 'On your account I refused to eat with King Misdaeus and why would you not eat with me?' And she said, 'Because I am unwell.' Having risen up, Charisius intended to sleep with her as usual. But she said, 'Have I not told you that I refused for today?'

91. Upon hearing this he went away to sleep on another couch. When he awoke from his sleep he said, 'My mistress Mygdonia, hear the dream which I have seen. I saw myself at a meal near King Misdaeus, and beside us stood a table fully laden. And I saw an eagle coming down from heaven taking away two partridges from the place before me and the king, which he carried into his nest.[47] And he came near again fluttering about us. And the king ordered a bow to be brought to him. The eagle took a dove and a pigeon from the place before us. The king shot an arrow at him which passed through him from one side to the other without hurting him. And he flew to his nest unscathed. And now that I am awake, I am frightened and very sad because I had tasted the partridge and he would not allow me to put it to my mouth again.' And Mygdonia said to him, 'Your dream is good, for you eat partridges daily, whereas this eagle has not till now tasted a partridge.'

92. When it was morning, Charisius went and dressed and put the left shoe on the right foot.[48] And pausing, he said to Mygdonia, 'What does this mean? For behold the dream and this act!' Mygdonia said to him, 'This also is not bad, but seems to me very good: from a bad thing comes the better.' Having washed his hands, he went to greet King Misdaeus.

93. Likewise also Mygdonia went early in the morning to greet the apostle Judas Thomas. She met him talking to the captain and the multitude. And he exhorted them by speaking of the woman who had received the Lord into her soul, and asked whose wife she was. The captain said, 'She is the wife of Charisius, the relative of King Misdaeus. And her husband is very severe, and the king obeys him in everything which he says. And he will not allow her to remain in the opinion which she professes. He has also often praised her in

---

[47] Greek 'heart'.
[48] Cf. Gospel of Thomas 22.

the presence of the king by saying none were so good for love as she. Everything of which you speak to her is strange to her.' And the apostle said, 'If the Lord has truly and indeed risen in her soul and she has received the sown seed, she will neither care for this earthly life nor fear death, nor will Charisius be able to harm her in any way. For he whom she has received into her soul is greater, if indeed she has truly received him.'

94. When Mygdonia heard this she said to the apostle, 'In truth, my lord, I have received the seed of your words and shall bring forth fruits from such seed.' The apostle said, 'Lord, these souls which are yours praise and thank you; the bodies which you deemed worthy to be habitations of your heavenly gift thank you.' And he also said to those about him, 'Blessed are the saints, whose souls have never condemned them; because they have gained them, they doubt not in themselves. Blessed are the spirits of the saints who have safely received the heavenly crown intact from the aeon appointed to them. Blessed are the bodies of the saints, because they were deemed worthy to become temples of God, that Christ might dwell in them. Blessed are you, because you have power to remit sins. Blessed are you, if you lose not that which is committed to you but take it with you with joy and gladness. Blessed are you saints, because it is given to you to ask and to receive. Blessed are you meek,[49] because God has deemed you worthy to become heirs of the heavenly kingdom. Blessed are you meek, for you have overcome the wicked one. Blessed are you meek, because you shall see the face of the Lord. Blessed are you who hunger for the Lord's sake, for rest is preserved for you and your souls rejoice from now on. Blessed are you quiet ones, because you were found worthy to be delivered from sin.' When the apostle had said this in the hearing of the whole multitude Mygdonia was more strengthened in the faith and in the glory and majesty of Christ.

95. But Charisius, the king's relative and friend, came to the breakfast and did not find his wife at home. And he asked all in his house, 'Where has your mistress gone?' And one of them said, 'She went to that stranger.' Upon hearing this from his servant he was angry at the others because they did not report to him at once what had happened. And he sat down and waited for her. And when it was evening and she entered the house, he said to her, 'Where have you been?' She answered and said, 'To the physician.' He said, 'Is the stranger a physician?' She said, 'Yes, a physician of souls. Most physicians heal bodies, which decay; but he heals souls, which do not perish.' When Charisius heard this he was angry at heart at Mygdonia on account of the apostle. But he answered nothing, for he was afraid, as she was superior to him in riches and intelligence. He went to dinner, but she went to her chamber. And he said to his servants, 'Call her to dinner.' But she would not come.

96. When he heard that she would not leave her chamber, he went in and

[49] Matt. 5: 5–8.

said to her, 'Why will you not eat with me? And will you not also have intercourse with me according to custom? And in this respect I am more suspicious, for I heard that this sorcerer and deceiver teaches that no man should cohabit with his wife, and he reverses what nature demands and the deity has ordered.' When Charisius said this Mygdonia held her peace. Again he said to her, 'My lady and wife Mygdonia, be not led astray by deceitful and foolish words, nor by the works of sorcery which this man, as I heard, does in the name of the Father, the Son, and the Holy Ghost. In this world it has never been heard that anyone has raised the dead. But, as I hear, he is reported to raise the dead. And as he neither eats nor drinks, do not assume that he neither eats nor drinks for righteousness' sake. He rather does it because he has nothing. For what should he do who has not even his daily bread? And he has only one garment because he is poor. And as for his not receiving anything from anyone, he does it because he is aware that no one has been healed by him.'

97. When Charisius said this, Mygdonia was silent like a stone. She prayed, however, for daylight, that she might go to the apostle of Christ. He left her and sadly partook of his meal, for he was anxious to have intercourse with her. When he had left, she bent her knees and prayed thus: 'Lord God, merciful Father, and Redeemer Christ, give me strength that I overcome Charisius' shamelessness, and grant me to keep the holiness which is well-pleasing to you, that through it I too may find eternal life.' Having thus prayed she betook herself, veiled, to her bed.

98. Having eaten, Charisius came near her. And she cried, 'Henceforth you have no place beside me, for my Lord Jesus, who is with me and rests in me, is better than you.' And laughingly he said, 'Well do you mock saying these words about that sorcerer, and well do you laugh at him who says, "You have no life with God unless you sanctify yourselves!"' Having said this, he tried to sleep with her. But she would not allow it and cried out with a piercing voice, 'I call upon you, Lord Jesus, forsake me not! I have taken refuge in you! As I have perceived that it is you who seek those who are imprisoned in ignorance and save those who are kept in error, so now I pray to you whose report I heard and in whom I believed. Come to my assistance and save me from Charisius' shamelessness, that his impurity have no power over me.' And she put her hands to her face and ran away naked. And upon leaving she tore down the curtain of her chamber, put it around her, went to the nurse, and slept there with her.

99. And Charisius spent the whole night in sadness, beating his face with his hands. And he thought of going immediately to the king to report to him about the power which had come upon him. But on reflection he said within himself, 'If the great sadness which now fills my heart obliges me to go to the king, who will introduce me to him? For I know that an evil report has thrown me down from my pride and vainglory and greatness and brought me to this

pettiness and separated my sister Mygdonia from me. Even if the king stood at the door I could not have come out at this time and given him an answer. But I shall wait till it is day. I know that the king will grant what I ask of him. And I will speak of the madness of the stranger, whose tyranny throws the great and illustrious into the abyss. For it pains me not that I am deprived of her intercourse, but I sorrow for her because her noble soul has been humbled. She, a woman of nobility, in whom none of the servants has ever detected a fault, ran uncovered from her chamber, and I do not know where she went. But it is possible that having been made mad by that sorcerer she went in her frenzy to the market to seek him. For nothing seems lovable to her except that man and his words.'

100. Having spoken thus, he began to lament and say, 'Woe to me, wife, and woe to you also! For too soon have I been deprived of you! Woe to me, most beloved, for you are better than my whole kindred. For I have neither a son nor a daughter from you that I could enjoy them. You have not even lived with me a year, and an evil eye has snatched you from me. Would that the power of death had taken you away, then I should have counted myself a king and leader! But that I should suffer this at the hand of a stranger! And possibly he is a runaway slave, to my harm and to that of my most unhappy soul. But let nothing come in my way till I have destroyed him and avenged this night. And let King Misdaeus not find pleasure in me unless he gives me revenge with the head of the stranger, and I will also tell him of captain Siphor, who was the cause of this destruction. For through him he came here and lodges with him. And many come into contact with him who teaches a new doctrine by saying that none can live unless he free himself from all his possessions and like himself become an abstainer. And he endeavours to make many converts.'

101. As Charisius was considering this, day broke. And having passed the night waking, he put on a cheap garment, and shoes on his feet, and looking sad and dejected he went to greet the king. Upon seeing him the king said, 'Why are you so sad, and why did you come in such attire? And your face is also changed.' Charisius answered and said to the king, 'I have to tell you of something new, and of a new devastation which captain Siphor has brought to India: a Hebrew magician whom he has in his house and who does not leave him. Many go to him and he teaches a new God and gives them new laws, of which no one has ever heard, by saying, "It is impossible that you enter into the eternal life which I preach to you unless you give up your wives and the wives also give up their husbands." It happened that my ill-fated wife also went to him and heard his words. And she believed them, left me during the night, and ran to the stranger. But let Siphor and the sorcerer hidden in his house be brought to you, and punish them, that all of our people do not perish.'

102. When his friend Misdaeus heard this he said to him, 'Be not sad and

discouraged! I will have him brought here, and I will avenge you, and you shall have your wife again. For if I avenge others who cannot avenge themselves, I will avenge you above all.' And the king went out and sat upon the seat of judgement. Being seated, he ordered Siphor, the captain, to be called. And having come into his house, they found him at the right hand of the apostle, and Mygdonia at his feet, listening to him with the whole people. And the king's messengers came to Siphor and said, 'You are sitting here listening to foolish words, and King Misdaeus is enraged thinking how to destroy you because of this sorcerer and deceiver, whom you have brought into your house!' Upon hearing this, Siphor was dismayed, not because of the king's threat against him, but on account of the apostle, because the king was opposed to him. And he said to the apostle. 'I am distressed about you. For I told you from the beginning that that woman is the wife of Charisius, the relative and friend of the king, and he does not allow her to do what she has promised, and the king grants him everything which he asks.' And the apostle said to Siphor, 'Fear nothing, but believe in Jesus, who comes to our defence. For we have been gathered to his place of refuge.' Upon hearing this, Siphor put on his cloak and went to King Misdaeus.

103. And the apostle inquired of Mygdonia, 'What is the cause that your husband is so enraged and has prepared these devices against us?' She said, 'Because I did not yield to his desire. In the evening he wanted to force me and to subject me to that lust which he indulges. But he to whom I commended my soul delivered me from his hands. And I ran away naked and slept with my nurse. But what happened to him that he made these cunning devices, I know not.' The apostle said, 'These things will not hurt us. Believe in Jesus, and he will destroy Charisius' wrath and madness and passion, and he will be your companion on the dangerous road and guide you into his kingdom; and he shall bring you to eternal life by giving you a sure hope which does not pass away nor change.'

104. And Siphor stood before the king, who asked him, 'Who is he and where is he from and what does that magician teach whom you have in your house?' And Siphor answered the king, 'O king, you are not ignorant of the trouble and sadness which I and my friends suffered because of my wife, whom you know and others remember, and because of my daughter, whom I regard more than all my possessions, what a time of trial I had to undergo. For I became an object of derision and curse for our whole country. But I heard of that man, went to him, besought him, and took him and brought him here. And on the way I perceived wonderful and surprising things, and many here heard of the wild ass and of the demon which he drove out; and he healed my wife and daughter, and now they are well. He asks no reward, but demands faith and holiness that men become fellow workers in his labours. He teaches men to worship and fear one God, the Lord of all, and Jesus

Christ, his Son, that they may have life eternal. He eats only bread and salt, and drinks water from evening to evening; and he prays a great deal, and whatever he asks of God is given to him. And he teaches that this God is holy and mighty, and that Christ is life and makes alive. Therefore he exhorts those who are with him to come to God in holiness, purity, love, and faith.'

105. When Siphor had spoken thus, King Misdaeus sent many soldiers into the house of Siphor, the captain, to bring Thomas and all those who should be found there. And when the messengers came into the house, they found him teaching a great multitude, and Mygdonia sitting at his feet. And when the messengers saw the multitude they were afraid, went to the king and said, 'We did not dare to say anything to him on account of the many people around him; Mygdonia also was listening to his words, sitting at his feet.' When King Misdaeus and Charisius heard these things, Charisius sprang up, took many people with him, and said, 'I shall bring him, O king, and Mygdonia, whose mind he has disturbed.' And greatly perplexed, he came into the house of Siphor. And he found him teaching; but Mygdonia he found not, because she had returned to her house, having perceived that her husband knew of her presence there.

106. And Charisius said to the apostle, 'Rise, wicked man and destroyer and enemy of my house, for your sorcery harms me not; and I shall visit your sorcery upon your head.' When he had said this, the apostle looked at him and said, 'Your threats shall turn against you, for you shall not harm me. For greater than you and your king and your whole army is the Lord Jesus Christ, in whom I put my hope.' And Charisius took a kerchief from one of his servants, put it on the neck of the apostle, and said, 'Drag him off and take him away; I shall see whether God can save him from my hands.' And they dragged him off and took him to King Misdaeus. When the apostle came into the presence of the king, the king said to him, 'Tell me who you are and by what power you do these things'. But the apostle held his peace. And the king ordered his subjects to scourge him with one hundred and twenty-eight lashes and cast him bound into the prison. And they bound him in chains and led him away. And the king and Charisius considered how to kill him, but the multitude worshipped him upon their knees like a God. And they had it in their mind to say this: 'The stranger acted wickedly against the king, and is a deceiver.'

107. And when the apostle went to the prison, he said with gladness and rejoicing, 'I praise you, Jesus, that you have not only deemed me worthy to believe in you, but also to suffer much for you. I thank you, Lord, that you have cared for me and have given me patience. I thank you, Lord, that on your account I have been called a sorcerer and magician. May I also receive of the blessings of the lowly, and of the rest of the weary, and of the blessings of those whom men hate and persecute and revile by speaking evil against

The Acts of Thomas

them.[50] For, behold, on your account I am hated; behold, on your account I am avoided by the multitude, and on your account they call me what I am not.'

108. And all the prisoners saw him pray and asked him to pray for them. And when he had sat down he began to utter the following psalm:

108.
1.[51] When I was a little child, in my father's palace,
2. And enjoyed the wealth and luxury of those who nurtured me,
3. My parents equipped me with provisions and sent me out from the East, our homeland.
4. From the wealth of our treasury they gave me a great burden,
5. Which was light so that I could carry it by myself:
6. Gold from the land above, silver from great treasuries,
7. And stones, chalcedonies of India and agates from Kushan.
8. And they girded me with steel,
9. And they took away from me the garment set with gems and spangled with gold
Which they had made out of love for me
10. And the yellow robe which was made for my size,
11. And they made a covenant with me
And wrote it in my mind that I might not forget:
12. 'If you go down to Egypt and bring the one pearl
13. Which is in the land of the devouring serpent,
14. You shall put on again that garment set with stones and the robe which lies over it,
15. And with your brother, our next in command, you shall be a herald for our kingdom.'

109.
16. So I departed from the East on a difficult and frightening road led by two guides,
17. And I was very young to travel on it.
18. I passed over the borders of the Mosani, where there is the meeting-place of the merchants of the East,
19. And reached the land of the Babylonians.
20. I went down to Egypt, and my companions parted from me.
21. I went straight to the serpent and stayed near his den
22. Until he should slumber and sleep, so that I might take the pearl from him.
23. Being alone I altered my appearance and seemed an alien even to my own people,
24. But I saw one of my kinsmen there, a free-born man from the East,
25. A youth fair and beautiful, the son of courtiers.

---

[50] Cf. Matt. 5: 11.
[51] Line numbers follow the Syriac.

26 He came and kept me company.
27 And I made him my intimate friend, a comrade with whom I communicated my business.
28 Being exhorted to guard against the Egyptians and against partaking of unclean things,
29 I clothed myself in garments like theirs, so that I would not be seen as a stranger
30 And as one who had come from abroad to take the pearl,
   Lest the Egyptians might arouse the serpent against me.
31 But somehow they learned that I was not their countryman.
32 They dealt with me treacherously, and I tasted their food.
33 I no longer recognized that I was a king's son, and I served their king.
34 I forgot the pearl for which my parents had sent me.
35 And I fell into a deep sleep because of the heaviness of their food.
36 While I was suffering these things my parents were aware of it and grieved over me.
37 And a proclamation was heralded in our kingdom that all should present themselves at our doors.
38 The kings of Parthia and those in office, and the great men of the East
39 Resolved that I should not be left in Egypt.
40 So the courtiers wrote me a letter:
41 'From your father the king of kings and your mother, the mistress of the East
42 And their brothers, who are second to us,
   To our son in Egypt, greetings!
43 Awake, and rise from your sleep.
44 Listen to the words in this letter,
   Remember you are the son of kings,
   You have fallen beneath the yoke of slavery.
45 Remember your gold-spangled garment,
46 Recall the pearl for which you were sent to Egypt,
47 Your name has been called to the book of life,
48 Together with that of your brother whom you have received in our kingdom.'
49 And the king sealed it to make it an ambassador,
50 Because of the wicked Babylonian children and the tyrannical demons of the Labyrinth.
53 [52] I rose from sleep when I recognized its voice,[53]
54 I took it up and kissed it and I read.
55 And what was written concerned that which was engraved on my heart.

---

[52] In Syriac are found vv. 51–2: (51) 'It flew in the form of an eagle, the king of birds, (52) It flew and alighted beside me and became all speech.'
[53] Literally '... at its voice and perception'.

56 And I immediately remembered that I was a son of kings and that my freedom demanded my people.[54]
57 I remembered the pearl for which I had been sent to Egypt,
58 And the fact that I had come to snatch it from the terrifying serpent.
59 I subdued it by calling out my father's name,
61[55] And I snatched the pearl and turned about to go to my parents.
62 And I took off the dirty clothing and left it behind in their land.
63 And directed my way forthwith to the light of our Eastern home.
64 And on the road I found a female[56] who lifted me up.
65 She awakened me, giving me an oracle with her voice, and guided me to the light.
66 The Royal silken garment shone before my eyes.
68[57] And with familial love leading me and drawing me on
69 I passed by the Labyrinth,
And leaving Babylon behind on the left,
70 I reached Meson which is a great coast.

112. 75[58] But I could not recall my splendour,
For it had been when I was still a child and quite young that I had left it behind in my father's palace.
76 But, when suddenly I saw my garment reflected as in a mirror,
77 I perceived in it my whole self as well
And through it I knew and saw myself.
78 For though we originated from the one and the same we were partially divided,
Then again we were one, with a single form.
79 The treasurers too who had brought the garment
80 I saw as two beings, but there existed a single form in both,
One royal symbol consisting of two halves.
81 And they had my money and wealth in their hands and gave me my reward:
82 The fine garment of glorious colours,
83 Which was embroidered with gold, precious stones, and pearls to give a good appearance.
84 It was fastened at the collar
86[59] And the image of the King of Kings was all over it.

---

[54] Greek obscure. Syriac has 'My noble birth asserted itself'.
[55] Syriac adds v. 60: 'And the name of our second in rank and of my mother, the Queen of the East'.
[56] Syriac: 'my letter'.
[57] Syriac adds v. 67: 'And with its voice and its guidance encouraging me to speed'.
[58] Syriac adds vv. 71–4: 'And my splendid robe which I had taken off | And my toga with which it was wrapped about | From the heights of Hyrcania | My parents sent there | By the hand of their treasurers, | Who for their faithfulness were so entrusted.'
[59] Syriac adds v. 85: 'And with stones of adamant all its seams were fastened.'

87 Stones of lapis lazuli had been skilfully fixed to the collar,
88 And I saw in turn that motions of knowledge were stirring throughout it,
89 And that it was prepared to speak.
90 Then I heard it speak:
91 'It is I who belong to the one who is stronger than all men and for whose sake I was written about by the father himself.'
92 And I took note of my stature,
93 And all the royal feelings rested on me as its energy increased.
94 Thrust out by his hand the garment hastened to me as I went to receive it,
95 And a longing aroused me to rush and meet it and to receive it.
96[60]
97 And I covered myself completely with my royal robe over it.
98 When I had put it on I ascended to the land of peace and homage.
99 And I lowered my head and prostrated myself before the splendour of the father who had sent it to me.
100 For it was I who had obeyed his commands
And it was I who had also kept the promise,
101 And I mingled at the doors of his ancient royal building.
102 He took delight in me and received me in his palace.
103 All his subjects were singing hymns with harmonious voices.
104 He allowed me also to be admitted to the doors of the king himself,
105 So that with my gifts and the pearl I might appear before the king himself.

113.

114. Charisius went home rejoicing, believing that his wife would live with him again and be as she was before she heard the divine word and believed in Jesus. Coming back, he found her hair cut off and her garment rent. Seeing her, he said to her, 'My lady Mygdonia, why does this nauseous disease take possession of you? And why have you done this? I am your husband since the time of your virginity, and the gods as well as the laws give me the right to rule over you. What is this great madness of yours that makes you ridiculous in the eyes of all the people? Put away the anxiety which comes from that sorcerer. I shall remove him from sight, so that you may see him no more.'

115. When Mygdonia heard these words, she gave vent to her feelings and sighed and lamented. And Charisius said again, 'I must have greatly sinned against the gods, that they have afflicted me with such a disease. I pray you, Mygdonia, torment not my soul by this your lamentable sight and humble appearance, and do not make my heart heavy through care over you. I am your husband Charisius, whom all the people honour and fear. What shall I do? I know not how to act. What shall I think? Shall I keep silence and endure?

---

[60] Greek corrupt. Syriac has: 'And I stretched out and took it and adorned myself with the beauty of its colours.'

Who can bear it when his treasure is taken from him? And who could tolerate to be deprived of your delightful ways? Your fragrance is in my nostrils, and your cheerful face is in my eyes. They take away my soul, and they destroy the beautiful body which I enjoyed when I saw it. They blind the sharpest eye and cut off my right hand. My joy is turned into sadness, and my life into death; the light is plunged into darkness. None of my relatives shall see me any more, none of whom have helped me, and the gods of the East I shall worship no more, who have surrounded me with such great misfortune. And indeed I shall no more pray to them nor sacrifice to them, having been deprived of my wife. What else shall I ask of them? All my glory has been taken away. And I am a prince, second in authority to the king. All this Mygdonia has taken from me by rejecting me. Would that they pluck my eyes out, if only you turn your eyes upon me as of old!'

116. While Charisius was speaking with tears, Mygdonia sat silent and looked on the ground. He came near and said, 'My most beloved lady Mygdonia, remember that of all the women in India I selected you as the most beautiful and took you, although I could have married others, more beautiful than you. But no, I lie, Mygdonia. For by the gods it is impossible to find one like you in the land of the Indians. Woe to me for ever, that you do not even answer me! Abuse me, if it pleases you, but speak. Look at me. I am far more handsome than that sorcerer. I have riches and honour, and everybody knows that none has such a family as mine. But you are my riches and honour, you are my family and kindred. And behold, he separates you from me.'

117. When Charisius had said this, Mygdonia said to him, 'He whom I love is better than you and your possessions. For your possessions, being earthly, return to earth. But he whom I love is heavenly and shall bring me also into heaven. Your riches shall pass away, and your beauty shall be destroyed, so likewise your garments and your many works. And you will remain alone with your trespasses. But do not remind me of your actions to me. For I pray to the Lord that you would forget and think no more of the former pleasures and the bodily intercourse, which shall pass like a shadow. Jesus alone remains forever, and the souls which trust in him. Jesus himself shall free me from the shameful deeds which I did before with you.'

Upon hearing this, Charisius, broken in his soul, turned to sleep, saying to her, 'Think the matter over during the night! If you will be with me as you were before you saw that sorcerer, I will fulfil all your wishes, and if it pleases you on account of your kind disposition toward him, I shall release him from the prison and set him free and let him go to another country. And I shall not trouble you, for I know how much you think of the stranger. He did not begin with you, but along with you he also deceived many other women. These have come to their senses and think differently. Now consider my words and make me not a reproach among the Indians.'

118. Thus speaking, he fell asleep. And she took ten denarii, and went

secretly away to give them to the jailers in order to be permitted to go to the apostle. On the way Judas Thomas met her and went to her. Upon seeing him, she was afraid, because she took him for one of the princes, for a great light went before him. And running away, she said within herself, 'I have ruined you, poor soul, for you shall not again see Judas, the apostle of the living God, and you have not received the holy seal.' And as she fled she went to a narrow place and hid herself there, saying, 'It is better to be caught by poorer people whom one can persuade, than to meet this powerful prince, who despises gifts.'

TENTH ACT
HOW MYGDONIA RECEIVES BAPTISM

119. As Mygdonia was considering this within herself, Judas came and stood over her. And seeing him, she was afraid, and fell down as if dead. He came to her, took her by the hand, and said to her, 'Fear not, Mygdonia; Jesus will not forsake you and your Lord will not neglect you, to whom you have given yourself; his merciful rest will not fail you; he who is kind will not forsake you on account of his great kindness, and he who is good because of his goodness. Arise from the ground, since you are raised above it. Behold the light, for the Lord does not allow those who love him to walk in darkness. Look at the companion of his servants, because he is their ally in dangers.' And Mygdonia stood up, looked at him, and said, 'Where did you go, my lord? And who is it who brought you out from prison to see the sun?' Judas Thomas said to her, 'My Lord Jesus is more powerful than all powers and kings and princes.'

120. And Mygdonia said, 'Give me the seal of Jesus Christ, and let me receive a gift from your hands before you depart from life!' And she took him, went into the court, awoke the nurse, and said to her, 'My mother and nurse Marcia, all the services and joys which you have given me from childhood were vain, and I owe you only temporal thanks. And now do me a favour, that you may for ever receive recompense from him who gives the great gifts.' At this Marcia said, 'What is your wish, my daughter Mygdonia, and what can be done for your pleasure? The honours which you promised to me before, the stranger did not allow you to fulfil, and you have made me a reproach among the whole people. And now, what is the new thing you ask of me?' Mygdonia said, 'Be my partner for eternal life, that I may receive from you perfect nourishment. Take a loaf and bring it to me, also a very small measure of water, having regard for my free birth.' And the nurse said, 'I will bring you many loaves, and instead of water I will bring gallons of wine and fulfil your wish.' And she said to the nurse, 'I need no gallons, nor the many loaves, but bring only this: a small measure of water, a loaf, and oil.'

121. When Marcia had brought these things, Mygdonia stood before the apostle with uncovered head. And he took the oil, poured it upon her head,

and said, 'Holy oil, given to us for sanctification; hidden mystery, in which the cross was shown to us; you are the straightener of bent limbs; you are the humbler of hard works; you point out the hidden treasures; you are the sprout of goodness. Let your power come and rest on your servant Mygdonia, and heal her by this liberty.' Having poured out the oil, he bade the nurse undress her and put around her a linen dress. And there was in that place a spring to which the apostle went and he baptized Mygdonia in the name of the Father and of the Son and of the Holy Ghost. And when she was baptized and had dressed herself, he broke bread, took a cup of water, and made her partake of the body of Christ and of the cup of the Son of God, saying, 'You have received your seal and obtained eternal life!' And instantly a voice was heard from above saying, 'Yea, Amen!' When Marcia heard this voice, she was afraid, and asked the apostle to give her the seal also, and the apostle did so and said, 'May the zeal of the Lord encompass you like the others!'

122. When the apostle had done this, he returned to the prison, but found the doors open and the keepers sleeping. And Thomas said, 'Who is like you, God, who withhold your tender love and your zeal from none; who is like you, merciful, who have delivered your creatures from evil? Life, which has overcome death; rest, which has ended toil! Glory be to the only-begotten of the Father,[61] glory to the Merciful, who was sent out of his heart!' When he had said this, the keepers woke up and saw all the doors opened, but the prisoners within. And they said among themselves, 'Have we not secured the doors? How are they now opened and the prisoners within?'

123. When it was day Charisius went to Mygdonia. And he found the women praying and saying, 'New God who has come to us through the stranger; God, hidden from the inhabitants of India; God, who have shown your glory through your apostle Thomas; God, of whom we heard and in whom we believe; God, to whom we have come to be saved; God, who out of kindness and compassion descended to our weakness; God, who sought us when we did not know you; God, who dwells in the heights and is not hidden from the depths, take from us the madness of Charisius.' Upon hearing this, Charisius said to Mygdonia, 'Justly you call me evil and ugly and mad! For had I not tolerated your disobedience and given you freedom, you would not have called out against me and mentioned my name before God. But believe me, Mygdonia, that nothing is to be gained from the sorcerer, and he cannot do what he promises. But I do everything that I promise before your eyes, that you may believe and endure my words and be toward me as before.'

124. And coming near, he asked her again, and said, 'If you obey me, I shall have no more grief. Remember that day on which we first met. Tell the truth: did I not appear to you then more beautiful than Jesus now?' And Mygdonia said, 'That time required its own, and this time requires its own.

---

[61] Cf. John 1: 14.

That time was of the beginning, but this is of the end. That time was of the earthly life, this of the everlasting. That was of a transient pleasure, this of an everlasting. That was of the day and of the night, this of the day without night. You have seen the wedding which passed over and remains here. This wedding remains in eternity. That communion was of destruction, this is of eternal life. Those groomsmen and bridesmaids are temporary men and women; but these now remain to the end. That wedding... That bride chamber passes away, but this remains for ever. That bed was covered with mantles, but this with charity and faith. You are a bridegroom who pass away and are destroyed, but Jesus is the true bridegroom, remaining immortal in eternity. That bridal gift was treasures and garments which grow old; this, however, is living words which never pass away.'

125. Having heard this, Charisius went to the king, and told him all. And the king ordered Judas to be brought that he might judge him and kill him. But Charisius said, 'Have a little patience, O king; frighten the man first by words, and persuade him to induce Mygdonia that she behave towards me as before.' And Misdaeus sent for the apostle of Christ and had him brought from the prison. And all the prisoners were sad because the apostle went away from them, for they all loved him very much and said, 'Even this consolation which we had is taken from us!'

126. And Misdaeus said to the apostle, 'Why do you teach this new doctrine, which gods and men hate and in which there is no profit?' And Judas said, 'What evil do I teach?' Misdaeus said, 'You teach that it is impossible for men to live well unless they keep pure for the God whom you preach.' Judas said, 'You speak true, O king; this I teach indeed. For tell me: are you not indignant when your soldiers accompany you in filthy garments? Now, if you, who are an earthly king and return to earth, demand that your subjects are decent in their exterior, how could you be angry and say that I teach evil by saying: Those who serve my king must be holy and pure and free from grief and care for children and unnecessary riches and transitory troubles? You require your subjects to follow your behaviour and manners, and when they despise your commandments you punish them; how much more ought they who believe in my God to serve him with great holiness, purity and chastity, free from all fleshly pleasures, from adultery and dissipation, theft, drunkenness, gluttony and other dishonourable acts!'

127. When Misdaeus heard these things he said, 'Behold, I set you free. Go and persuade Mygdonia, Charisius' wife, that she separate not from him.' Judas said to him, 'Delay not, if you have to do something. For if she has correctly received what she has learned, neither iron, nor fire, nor anything else which is stronger than these things will be able to harm her nor to separate him whom she retains in her soul.' Misdaeus said to Judas, 'Some remedies nullify others and a theriac makes the viper's bites ineffective. And if you wish you can make poisons ineffective and bring peace and concord to

this marriage. For by doing so you can save yourself. For you have not yet lived your life to the full. But know, if you do not persuade her I shall remove you from this life desirable to all.' And Judas said, 'This life is given to us as a loan, and this time changes. The life which I teach is imperishable, whereas beauty and conspicuous youth shall be no more after a short time.' And the king said, 'I advised you what is expedient, but you make your position worse.'

128. When the apostle was leaving the king Charisius came and said to him beseechingly, 'I pray you, O man—for I never did anything wrong to you or anybody else nor against the gods—why have you brought such great misery upon me? Why have you incited such sedition against my house? And what profit do you have from it? But if you think to profit by it, tell me what kind of profit it is, and I will obtain it for you without trouble. Why make me mad and destroy yourself? For if you persuade her not I shall slay you and finally kill myself. But if, as you say, there is life and death after this life, and also condemnation and victory and a judgement, I shall appear there also and be judged with you, and if God, whom you preach, is just and judges justly, I know that I shall be vindicated. For you harmed me, without your ever having been harmed by me. Here I can avenge myself for everything that you did against me. Obey me, therefore, and go into my house and persuade Mygdonia to behave toward me as she did before she saw you.' Judas said to him, 'Believe me, my son, if men loved God as much as one another they would receive from him everything that they ask, without being forced by anyone.'

129. While Thomas was saying this they came into the house of Charisius and found Mygdonia sitting, and Marcia standing by her, with her hand on Mygdonia's cheek. And she said, 'Mother, may the remaining days of my life be shortened and all the hours be like one hour, and I could leave this life to depart more quickly and see that beautiful one of whom I heard, that living one who gives life to all who believe in him, where there is neither day and night nor light and darkness, neither good and bad nor poor and rich, male and female, free or bond, no proud one subduing the meek.' And while she was speaking, the apostle came to her. And immediately she rose up and fell down before him. And Charisius said to him, 'Do you see how she fears and honours you and willingly does what you command?'

130. As he said this, Judas said to Mygdonia, 'My daughter Mygdonia, obey what brother Charisius says.' And Mygdonia said, 'If you could not express the thing by a word, how will you force me to suffer the deed? For I heard you say that this life is only a loan, and that this rest is only temporary and these possessions transient. And again you said that he who renounces this life shall receive the everlasting life, and whoever hates the light of the day and of the night shall see light which is not extinguished, and he who despises these treasures shall find other everlasting treasures. And now you say this because you are afraid. Who changes a work which he has executed and in which he

has been praised? Who builds a tower and destroys it again? Who fills in again a well which he dug in a dry place? Who finds a treasure and does not use it?' Upon hearing this Charisius said, 'I shall not imitate you nor hasten to destroy you. Since I have the power, I will put you in fetters and not permit you to speak with the sorcerer. And if you do not obey me, I know what I have to do.'

131. Judas left the house of Charisius and went to the house of Siphor and lodged with him. And Siphor said, 'I will prepare for him a dining-room in which he shall teach.' And he did so. And Siphor said, 'I and my wife and my daughter shall from now on live in holiness, in purity, and in one mind. I pray, give us the seal that we may become servants of the true God and be counted among his sheep and lambs.' And Judas said, 'I fear to say what I think. I know something, and what I know I cannot express.'

132. And he began to speak of baptism: 'This baptism is forgiveness of sins. It is a light shed abroad everywhere. It generates the new man, establishes the new man in a threefold manner, and is partaker in forgiveness of sins. Praise be to you, hidden power, which is united with us by baptism! Praise be to you, invisible power, which is in the baptism! Praise be to you, renovation, by which those baptized are renewed, taking hold of you with love.' And having said this, he poured oil upon their heads and said, 'Praise be to you, love of mercy! Praise be to you, name of Christ! Praise be to you, power that dwells in Christ!' And he had a basin brought and baptized them in the name of the Father and of the Son and of the Holy Ghost.

133. And when they were baptized and had dressed, he put bread on the table, and blessing it said, 'Bread of life, those who eat of which shall be imperishable; bread which satisfies hungry souls with its blessedness—you have been deemed worthy to receive a gift, that you may become to us a forgiveness of sins, and those who eat you immortal; we name over you the name of the mother, the hidden mystery of the hidden dominions and powers, we name over you the name of Jesus.' And he said, 'Let the power of blessing rest upon the bread, that all souls who partake of it be delivered from their sins.' And he broke the bread and gave it to Siphor and to his wife and daughter.

ELEVENTH ACT
CONCERNING THE WIFE OF MISDAEUS

134. After King Misdaeus had dismissed Judas he went to his house to dine and told his wife what had happened to their relative Charisius, saying, 'See what happened to that unfortunate man! You yourself know, my sister Tertia, that a man has nothing more beautiful than his wife, whom he enjoys. Now it happened that his wife went to the sorcerer of whom you have heard that he came as a stranger into the land of the Indians, and she became enticed by his sorceries and separated from her husband. And he does not know what to do.

And as I was about to destroy the malefactor he would not allow it. But go and advise her to turn again to her husband, and to keep away from the foolish words of the sorcerer.'

135. And Tertia rose up immediately and went to the house of Charisius, the relative of her husband. And she found Mygdonia prostrated upon the ground resting on sackcloth and ashes. And she was praying that the Lord would pardon her her former sins and quickly take her from this life. And Tertia said to her, 'Mygdonia, most beloved sister and companion, what disease has taken hold of you? Why do you do the deeds of madmen? Know yourself and return to your own ways. Draw near to your numerous family, and save your husband Charisius, and do not do what is alien to your free birth!' Mygdonia said to her, 'O Tertia, you have not yet heard the preacher of life! His voice has not yet come to your ears, neither have you tasted the medicine of life, nor have you been delivered from destructive sighs. Since you stand in the temporary life, you know not the life eternal and the redemption, and without perceiving the imperishable communion...[62] You stand here clad in garments which grow old, and do not desire the eternal. You are proud of your beauty which shall be destroyed, and consider not the ugliness of the soul. You are rich in slaves. You are proud of the glory of the multitude, but do not free yourself from the condemnation of death.'

136. When Mygdonia had spoken thus, Tertia said, 'I pray you, sister, bring me to the stranger who teaches these great things, that I may also go and hear him and be taught to worship the God whom he preaches and take part in his prayers and in that of which you have spoken to me.' Mygdonia said to her, 'He is in the house of Siphor the captain, who became the cause of life for all who are being saved in India.' Upon hearing this Tertia went hastily to the house of Siphor to see the new apostle who had come into the land. When she entered, Judas said to her, 'What have you come to see? A stranger, poor and despised and beggarly, who has neither riches nor possession? But one possession I have which neither a king nor a prince can take away, which is neither destroyed nor does it come to an end, which is Jesus, the redeemer of mankind, the Son of the living God, who gave life to all who believe in him and take refuge in him, and who is known by the number of his servants.' Tertia said to him, 'Let me have part in this life which, as you promise, all shall receive who come to the hostelry of God.' And the apostle said, 'The treasury of the holy king is open, and they who worthily take part of the treasures deposited there rest, and by resting they reign.[63] But firstly, no unclean and bad man comes to him. For he knows our hearts and the depths of our thoughts, and none can be hidden from him. You too, if you truly believe in him shall be deemed worthy of his mysteries, and he will make you great and rich and an heir of his Kingdom.'[64]

---

[62] Syriac adds: 'You are afflicted by corruptible communion'.
[63] Cf. Gospel of Thomas 2.
[64] Cf. Gospel of Thomas 2.

137. Having heard this, Tertia returned to her house rejoicing. And she found her husband, who, without having breakfasted, had waited for her. When Misdaeus saw her he said, 'Why is your coming in so much more beautiful to-day? And why did you come on foot, which is unbecoming a person like you?' Tertia said to him, 'I am under great obligation to you for having sent me to Mygdonia. For by going there I heard of the new life and saw the apostle of the new God, who gives life to those who believe in him and fulfil his commandments. I ought to recompense you for this grace with good advice. For you shall be a great king in heaven if you obey me and fear the God preached by the stranger and keep yourself holy to the living God. For this kingdom passes away, and your comfort will be turned into sadness. But go to that man and believe him, and you shall live unto the end.' When Misdaeus heard this from his wife he struck his face with his hands, tore his garments, and said, 'Let the soul of Charisius have no rest, because he has struck me at the soul, and let him have no hope, because he has taken away my hope.' And he went away troubled.

138. In the market-place he found his friend Charisius and said, 'Why did you throw me as your companion into Hell? Why have you robbed me and caused loss to me without having profited anything yourself? Why have you hurt me without having any benefit? Why have you killed me without having life yourself? Why have you wronged me without having obtained the right yourself? Why did you not allow me to kill the sorcerer before he destroyed my house by his sorcery?' And he quarrelled with Charisius, and Charisius said, 'What has happened to you?' And Misdaeus said, 'He has bewitched Tertia!' And both went to the house of the captain Siphor. And they found Judas sitting and teaching. And those present rose up before the king, but he did not get up. And Misdaeus knew that it was he, and taking the seat upturned it, and lifting up the chair with both hands, he struck him so hard on the head that he wounded him. And he delivered him to his soldiers with the words, 'Drag him along by force without restraint, that his insolence may become known to all.' And they dragged him to a place where Misdaeus used to sit in judgement. There he stood, held by the soldiers of Misdaeus.

TWELFTH ACT
CONCERNING VAZAN, THE SON OF MISDAEUS

139. Now Vazan, Misdaeus' son, went to the soldiers and said, 'Give him to me that I may speak to him till the king comes.' And they handed him over. And he led him to the place where the king used to sit in judgement. And Vazan said, 'Do you know that I am the son of Misdaeus the king, and that I am at liberty to say to the king what I will, and that if I tell him he will spare your life? Tell me, therefore, who your God is, and on whose power you rely and glory in. For if it is a power of magic and of sorcery, tell it and teach me, and I will set you free.' Judas said to him, 'You are the son of King Misdaeus,

who is a temporal king. I am, however, the servant of Jesus Christ, the eternal king. You are at liberty to ask your father to spare those whom you wish in this temporal life, in which men do not remain, though you and your father give it to them. I, however, beseech my Lord and implore him for men, and he gives them new life, which abides forever. You glory in possessions, slaves, garments, revelry, and unclean beds; but I glory in poverty, love of wisdom, humility, fasting, and prayer, and communion with the Holy Spirit and with my brethren, who are worthy of God, and I boast in an eternal life. You have sought refuge with a man like you, who is unable to save his own soul from judgement and from death; but I have taken refuge in the living God, in the redeemer of kings and princes, the judge of all. To-day you may live, but not to-morrow; but I have taken refuge in him who remains in eternity, who knows all our times and circumstances. But if you would become a servant of this God, you can become it soon. And if you are a servant of him, you will show it in the following things: first in sanctification, which is the principal part of all good things; then in the communion with this God whom I preach, and in the love of wisdom, in simplicity, in love, in faith, by the hope in him and by the unity of pure life.'[65]

140. And the young man, convinced by the Lord, sought an opportunity how he could help Judas escape. While he was considering it, the king came. And the soldiers took Judas and led him out. And Vazan also went with him and stood beside him. And the king took his seat and had Judas brought in with his hands tied behind him. Being led into the midst, he stood still. And the king said, 'Tell me who you are and by whose power you do these things.' Judas said to him, 'I am a man like yourself, and do these things by the power of Jesus Christ.' And Misdaeus said, 'Tell the truth before I destroy you.' Judas said, 'You have no power over me, as you think, and will hurt me in nothing.' Indignant at the words, the king ordered (the soldiers) to heat iron plates and to put him barefoot on them. And when the soldiers removed his shoes he said, 'The wisdom of God is better than the wisdom of men. You, Lord and King, let your goodness oppose his wrath!' And they brought the plates which were like fire and put the apostle on them. And straightway water gushed forth from the ground and the plates were swallowed up. And those who held him let him go and fell back.

141. When the king saw the great amount of water he said to Judas, 'Pray your God that he deliver me from this death, that I perish not by the flood.' And the apostle prayed and said, 'You who have bound this nature and united it in one place and send it out to different countries; who have brought order out of disorder, who do mighty deeds and great miracles by the hands of your servant Judas; who have pity on my soul, that I may always receive your light; who give reward to the weary; who save my soul and bring it again to its own

---

[65] Greek: 'food'.

nature, not to unite with those who do harm; who are always author of life—calm this element that it rise not and destroy. For there are some here among those present who shall live,[66] because they have believed in you.' When he had prayed, the water was soon absorbed, and the place was dry. And when Misdaeus saw this he ordered him to be led to prison, 'Till I have decided what to do with him.'

142. When Judas was taken to the prison, Vazan, the king's son, walked at his right, and Siphor at his left. Having entered the prison he sat down with Vazan and Siphor, and the latter persuaded his wife and his daughter to sit down. For they too had come to hear the word of life. For they knew that Misdaeus would kill him because of his extreme wrath. And Judas began to say, 'Deliverer of my soul from the servitude of the multitude, because I gave myself to be sold, behold, I rejoice and am glad, since I know that the times are fulfilled that I go in and receive you. See, I am freed from earthly cares. Behold, I fulfil my hope and receive truth. Behold, I am delivered from sadness and have only joy. Behold, I am free from care and pain and live in rest. Behold, I am free from servitude and I am called to liberty. Behold, I have served times and seasons and have been lifted up above times and seasons. Behold, I receive my reward from the rewarder, who gives without counting, because his riches are sufficient for his gifts. Behold, I undress myself and I dress myself, and shall not again be undressed. Behold, I sleep and wake up and shall not sleep again. Behold, I die and return to life and shall not taste death again. Behold, with gladness they wait until I come and am united with their kindred. I shall be put as a flower into their wreath. Behold, I reign in the Kingdom for which I have set my hope here. Behold, the disobedient fall before me, because I have escaped them. Behold, it is peace to which all come.'

143. As the apostle spoke this, all those present listened, believing that he was to depart his life in this hour. And he continued, saying, 'Believe in the physician of everything visible and invisible and in the redeemer of souls who need his help. He is free, son of kings. He is the physician of his creatures. It is he who is reviled by his own servants. He is the Father of the height and the Lord and judge of nature. He became the highest from the greatest, the only-begotten Son of the depth. And he was called son of the virgin Mary and son of the carpenter Joseph; he whose lowliness we beheld with our bodily eyes, whose majesty, however, we have received by faith and seen in his works; whose human body we handled with our hands, whose transfigured appearance we saw with our eyes, whose heavenly form, however, we could not see on the mountain; he who baffled the princes and overcame death; he who is infallible truth and paid tribute at the end for himself and his disciples; he at whose sight the archon became afraid and the powers with him were

---

[66] Cf. Mark 9: 1 and parallels.

confounded. And the archon asked who and whence he was, and he did not tell him the truth, since he is a stranger to truth;[67] though having power over the world and its pleasures, treasures, and enjoyments, he abstains from all these things and urges his subjects to make no use thereof.'

144. Having finished his address, he rose and prayed thus: 'Our Father in heaven, hallowed be your name; your kingdom come; your will be done as in heaven, so also on earth;[68] forgive us our trespasses as we have forgiven our debtors; and lead us not into temptation, but deliver us from evil.'[69,70]

149.[71] And turning to those who were in the prison with him he said, 'Believe, my children, in this God whom I preach; believe in Jesus Christ, whom I proclaim; believe in him who makes alive and helps his servants; believe in the redeemer of those who toiled in his service. For my soul already rejoices, because my time is at hand to receive him. Being beautiful, he always makes me speak of his beauty, of what manner it is, although I cannot speak of it as I wish and ought. You who are the light of my poverty, and the supplier of my want and the provider of my need—be with me till I come and receive you in eternity.'

THIRTEENTH ACT
HOW VAZAN AND THE OTHERS WERE BAPTIZED

150. And the young man Vazan made a request to the apostle and said, 'I pray you, man, apostle of God, allow me to go out, and I shall persuade the jailer to let you go to my house so that from you I may receive the seal and become your servant and one who keeps the commandment of God whom you preach. For previously I walked in accordance with your preaching till my father forced me and bound me to a woman named Mnesara. Being twenty-one years of age, I have been married to her seven years. Before she became my wife I knew no other woman. On this account my father considered me as useless. And neither son nor daughter has ever been born to me by this wife. But my wife also lived all this time in chastity with me, and to-day I know that if she were well and heard your words, I should have rest and she would receive eternal life. But danger and many sufferings try her. I will therefore persuade the keeper, provided you will come with me. For I live all alone. At the same time you shall heal the unfortunate one.' Upon hearing this, Judas, the apostle of the Most High, said to Vazan, 'If you believe, you shall see the wonders of God and how he saves his servants.'

151. And as they were thus conversing, Tertia and Mygdonia and Marcia

---

[67] Cf. John 8: 44.
[68] Syriac adds 'give us the constant bread of the day'.
[69] Matt. 6: 9 ff.
[70] The section from here to 148 follows 167, as in manuscript P. See James, *ANT* 428, 436.
[71] MSS U and S contain 149. The first three verses of the speech are from the Syriac.

stood in the door of the prison, and after giving three hundred and sixty-three silver pieces to the jailer they went in to Judas. And they found Vazan and Siphor and his wife and his daughter and all the prisoners, sitting and listening to the word. And as they came to him, he said to them, 'Who allowed you to come to us, and who opened the sealed door to go out?' Tertia said to him, 'Did you not open the door and bid us to go to the prison, so that we should find our brethren there and then the Lord might show his glory in us? And as we came near the door you were separated from us—I know not how—and, being hidden from us, you came here first, where we heard the noise of the door as you shut us out. We gave money to the keepers and thus we got in, and now we are here and beseech you to let us help you to get away from here, till the anger of the king against you ceases.' And Judas said to her, 'Tell us first how you were locked up.'

152. And she said to him, 'You were with us and did not leave us even for an hour, and can you ask how we were locked up? But if you desire to hear, listen. King Misdaeus sent for me and said, "The magician has not yet become master over you, because, as I hear, he enchants the people by oil, water, and bread, but he has not yet enchanted you. Now obey me, otherwise I shall lock you up and strike you, but destroy him. For I know that if he has not yet given you oil, water, and bread, he has not been able to have power over you." And I said to him, "You have power over my body; do to it as you please, but my soul I will not destroy with you." Upon hearing this he locked me up in a room. And Charisius also brought Mygdonia and locked her up with me. And you have taken us out and brought us hither to this assembly. Now give us the seal so that the hopes of Misdaeus, who is plotting, be destroyed.'

153. Upon hearing this, the apostle said, 'Glory to you, polymorphous Jesus; praise to you, who appear like our poor humanity! Praise to you, who give us courage and strength and joy, and comfort and help in all dangers, and strength in our weakness.' When he had said this, the jailer came in and said, 'Put your lamps away, lest we be reported to the king.' Having extinguished the lamps, they turned to sleep. And the apostle spoke with the Lord, 'Now, Jesus, is the time for you to hasten, for behold, the children of darkness put us into their darkness. Illuminate us by the light of your nature!' And suddenly the whole prison was as light as the day. And while all those who were in the prison were asleep, only those who believed in the Lord were awake.

154. And Judas said to Vazan, 'Go ahead and prepare everything necessary.' Vazan said, 'And who shall open the prison gates? For the keepers have closed them and are asleep.' And Judas said, 'Believe in Jesus, and you shall find the gates open.' When he left them to go out, the others followed him. And as Vazan went ahead he met his wife Mnesara, who was going to the prison. And as she recognized him she said to him, 'My brother Vazan, is it you?' He said, 'Yes. And are you Mnesara?' She said, 'Yes.' And Vazan said to her, 'Where are you going at this time? And how did you get up?' And she

said, 'This young man put his hand upon me and raised me up, and in my sleep I saw that I should go where the stranger was, in order to recover fully.' Vazan said to her, 'What young man is with you?' She said, 'Do you not see who leads me by the right hand?'

155. And as they were thus conversing, Judas came with Siphor and his wife and his daughter and Tertia and Mygdonia and Marcia into the house of Vazan. And when Mnesara, Vazan's wife, saw him, she fell upon her knees and said, 'Have you come to save us from the dreadful disease? You are he whom I saw in the night as he gave me this young man to bring me to the prison. But your goodness would not allow me to become weary, but you yourself came to me.' And when she said this and turned around, she saw the young man no more. And not finding him, she said to the apostle, 'I cannot walk alone. The young man is not here, whom you gave me.' And Judas said, 'Jesus shall lead you.' And she went before them. And when they had come into the house of Vazan, the son of King Misdaeus, a great light shone, which was spread around them, although it was still night.

156. And Judas began to pray and to say, 'Companion and associate, hope of the weak and trust of the poor, refuge and shelter of the weary, voice which came forth from on high, comforter who dwells among us, shelter and haven of those who travel through dark countries, physician who heals without money, who was crucified among men for many, who descended into Hades with great might, whose sight the princes of death could not bear, and you ascended with much glory, and gathered all who take refuge with you and prepared the way, and in your steps all journeyed whom you redeemed and you brought them to your own flock and united with them your sheep; Son of mercy, Son sent to us out of philanthropy from the perfect fatherland above; Lord of undefiled possessions; who minister to your servants that they live; who have filled the creation with your riches; poor one, who was in need and hungered forty days; who satisfies thirsty souls with your goods—be with Vazan, Misdaeus' son, and Tertia and Mnesara, and gather them into your fold and unite them with your number; be their guide in the land of error, their physician in the land of sickness, their rest in the land of the weary; sanctify them in the impure country, be the physician of their bodies and souls, make them your holy temples, and let your Holy Spirit dwell in them!'

157. Having thus prayed for them, the apostle said to Mygdonia, 'Undress your sisters!' She undressed them and put aprons about them and brought them forward. Vazan had gone first, and they followed. And Judas took oil in a silver cup and spoke thus: 'Fruit, more beautiful than the other fruits, with which no other can be compared; most compassionate; you who burn with the power of the word; power of the wood, which if men put on they overcome their enemies; you who crown the victors; symbol and joy of the weary; who have brought to men the good news of their salvation; who show light to those in darkness; whose leaves are bitter but whose fruit is most sweet; who are

rough in appearance, but tender to use; who seem weak, but carry the all-seeing power by the extraordinariness of your power... Jesus, let your victorious power come and rest upon this oil as it once rested upon the wood related to it—and your crucifiers could not endure its word; let also the gift come by which you breathed upon your enemies and thereby made them retreat and fall headlong, and may it dwell in this oil over which we name your holy name!' And after the apostle had said this he poured it first upon the head of Vazan, then upon the heads of the women, saying, 'In your name, Jesus Christ, let it be to these souls for forgiveness of sins and for keeping away of the enemy and for the salvation of their souls!' And he ordered Mygdonia to anoint the women while he himself anointed Vazan. And having anointed them he made them go down into the water in the name of the Father and of the Son and of the Holy Ghost.

158. When they came out of the water, he took bread and a cup, blessed, and said, 'We eat your holy body, crucified for us; and we drink your blood, shed for us for redemption. May your body be redemption for us, and your blood be for the forgiveness of sins! For the gall which you drank for our sakes, may the gall of the devil around us be taken away; and for the vinegar which you drank for us, may our weakness be strengthened; for the spittle which you received for our sakes, may we receive the dew of your goodness, and for the reed with which they struck you for our sakes, may we receive the perfect house! Because you received a crown of thorns for our sakes, may we who have loved you crown ourselves with an imperishable crown! And for the linen, in which you were wrapped, let us be clothed with your invincible power; for the new tomb and burial let our souls receive renewal of soul and body.[72] Because you rose again and came to life, let us rise again and live and stand before you in righteous judgement!' And he broke the bread of the eucharist and gave it to Vazan, Tertia, and Mnesara, and to the wife and daughter of Siphor, and said, 'May this eucharist be to your salvation and joy and to the healing of your souls!' And they said, 'Amen.' And a voice was heard saying, 'Amen. Be not afraid, only believe!'

MARTYRDOM OF THE HOLY AND FAMOUS APOSTLE THOMAS[73]

159. In those days the apostle departed to be imprisoned. And Tertia with Mygdonia and Marcia also went to be imprisoned. And the apostle Thomas said to the multitude of believers, 'Daughters and sisters and fellow-servants who have believed in my Lord and God, ministers of my Jesus, hearken to me this day: for I deliver my word to you, and I shall no more speak with you in this flesh nor in this world; for I go up to my Lord and God Jesus Christ, to

---

[72] Note allusions to Matt. 27.
[73] The translation follows MS P and its allies (with James). U has a different text.

him who sold me, to that Lord who humbled himself even to me the little, and brought me up to eternal greatness, who vouchsafed to me to become his servant in truth and steadfastness: to him do I depart, knowing that the time is fulfilled, and the day appointed has drawn near for me to go and receive my recompense from my Lord and God: for my recompenser is righteous; he knows how I ought to receive my reward; for he is not grudging nor envious, but is rich in his gifts; he is not a lover of craft in what he gives, for he has confidence in his possessions which cannot fail.

160. 'I am not Jesus, but I am his servant: I am not Christ, but I am his minister: I am not the Son of God, but I pray to become worthy of God. Continue in the faith of Christ; continue in the hope of the Son of God; faint not at affliction, neither be divided in mind if you see me mocked or shut up in prison; for I do accomplish his will. For if I had willed not to die, I know in Christ that I am able; but this which is called death is not death, but a setting free from the body; wherefore I receive gladly this setting free from the body, that I may depart and see him who is beautiful and full of mercy, him who is to be loved; for I have endured much toil in his service, and have laboured for his grace that is come upon me and does not depart from me. Let not Satan, then, enter you by stealth and catch away your thoughts; let there be in you no place for him; for he is mighty whom you have received. Look for the coming of Christ, for he shall come and receive you, and this is he whom you shall see when he comes.'

161. When the apostle had ended these sayings, they went into the house, and the apostle Thomas said, 'Saviour who suffered many things for us, let these doors be as they were and let seals be set on them.' And he left them and went to be imprisoned, and they wept and were in heaviness, not knowing that Misdaeus would release him.

162. And the apostle found the keepers wrangling and saying, 'Wherein have we sinned against this magician, for by his magic art he has opened the doors and would have had all the prisoners escape? But let us go and report it to the king, and tell him about his wife and his son.' And as they disputed, Thomas held his peace. They rose up early, therefore, and went to the king and said to him, 'Our lord and king, take away that sorcerer and cause him to be shut up elsewhere, for we are not able to keep him; for only your good fortune kept the prison, otherwise all the condemned persons would have escaped; this is the second time that we found the doors open; and also your wife, O king, and your son and the rest never leave him.' And the king, hearing that, went and found the seals that were set on the doors whole; and he took note of the doors also and said to the keepers, 'Why do you lie, for the seals are whole? Why did you say that Tertia and Mygdonia came to him in the prison?' And the keepers said, 'We have told you the truth.'

163. And Misdaeus went to the prison and took his seat, and sent for the apostle Thomas and stripped him and set him before him and said to him,

'Are you bond or free?' Thomas said, 'I am the bondsman of one only, over whom you have no authority.' And Misdaeus said to him, 'How did you run away and come to this country?' And Thomas said, 'I was sold hither by my master, that I might save many, and by your hands depart out of this world.' And Misdaeus said, 'Who is your lord, and what is his name, and of what country is he?' And Thomas said, 'My Lord is your master, and he is Lord of heaven and earth.' And Misdaeus said, 'What is his name?' Thomas said, 'You can not hear his true name at this time; but the name that was given to him is Jesus Christ.' And Misdaeus said to him, 'I have not made haste to destroy you, but have had long patience with you; but you have added to your evil deeds, and your sorceries are dispersed abroad and heard of throughout all the country; but this I do that your sorceries may depart with you, and our land be cleansed from them.' Thomas said to him, 'These sorceries depart with me when I set forth hence, and know this that I shall never forsake those who are here.'

164. When the apostle had said these things, Misdaeus considered how he should put him to death; he was afraid because of the many people who were subject to him, for many of the nobles and of those in authority believed in him. He therefore took him and went out of the city, and armed soldiers also went with him. And the people supposed that the king desired to learn something from him, and they stood still and gave heed. And when they had walked one mile, he delivered him to four soldiers and an officer, and commanded them to take him into the mountain and there pierce him with spears and put an end to him, and return again to the city. And having said this to the soldiers he himself returned to the city.

165. But the men ran after Thomas, desiring to deliver him from death. And two soldiers went at the right hand of the apostle and two on his left, holding spears, and the officer held his hand and supported him. And the apostle Thomas said, 'O the hidden mysteries which even until our departure are accomplished in us! O riches of his glory, who will not suffer us to be swallowed up in this passion of the body! Four are they that cast me down, for of four am I made; and one is he who draws me, for of one I am, and to him I go. And this I now understand, that my Lord and God Jesus Christ, being of one, was pierced by one, but I, who am of four, am pierced by four.'

166. And having come up into the mountain to the place where he was to be slain, he said to those who held him and to the rest, 'Brethren, hearken to me now at the last; for I am come to my departure out of the body. Let not then the eyes of your heart be blinded nor your ears be made deaf. Believe in the God whom I preach, and be not guides to yourselves in the hardness of your heart, but walk in all your liberty, and in the glory that is toward men and the life that is toward God.'

167. And he said to Vazan, 'You, son of King Misdaeus and minister of our Lord Jesus Christ: give to the servants of Misdaeus their price that they

may allow me to go and pray.' And Vazan persuaded the soldiers to let him pray. And the blessed Thomas went to pray and kneeled down, and rose up and stretched forth his hands to heaven and spoke thus:[74]

144. 'My Lord and God, my hope and my confidence and my teacher, you have implanted courage in me, you taught me to pray thus; behold, I pray your prayer and bring your will to fulfilment; be with me to the end. You are he who from my youth gave me patience in temptation and sowed in me life and preserved me from corruption; you are he who brought me into the poverty of this world and filled me with the true riches; you are he who showed me that I was yours: wherefore I was never joined to a wife, that the temple worthy of you might not be found in pollution.

145. 'My mouth is insufficient to praise you, neither am I able to conceive the care and providence which you have had for me. For I desired to gain riches, but you by a vision showed me that they are full of loss and injury to those who gain them; and I believed your showing, and continued in the poverty of the world until you, the true riches, were revealed to me, who filled both me and the rest who were worthy of you with your own riches and set free your own from care and anxiety. I have therefore fulfilled your commandments, O Lord, and accomplished your will, and become poor and needy and a stranger and a bondman and set at nought and a prisoner and hungry and thirsty and naked and unshod, and I have toiled for your sake, that my confidence might not perish, and my hope that is in you might not be confounded, and my labour might not be in vain, and my weariness not be counted for nought: let not my prayers and my continual fastings perish, and my great zeal toward you; let not my seed of wheat be changed for tares on your land; let not the enemy carry it away and mingle his own tares with it; for your land can truly not receive his tares, neither indeed can they be laid up in your houses.

146. 'I have planted your vine in the earth; it has sent down its roots to the depth, and its growth is spread out in the height, and the fruits of it are stretched forth upon the earth, and they who are worthy of you are made glad by them, whom also you have gained. The money which you have from me I laid down upon the table; this, when you require it, restore to me with usury, as you have promised. With your one mina have I traded and have made ten; you have added more to me beside that which I had, as you covenanted. I have

---

[74] Here P and the rest give—rightly—the prayer of chs. 144–8. U and its companions give the following: 'He turned to his prayer; and it was this, "My Lord and my God [John 20: 28], and hope and redeemer and leader and guide in all countries, be with all those who serve you, and guide me this day as I come to you. Let no one take my soul which I have committed to you; let not the publicans see me, and let not the tax-gatherers accuse me falsely. Let not the serpent see me, and let not the children of the dragon hiss at me. Behold, Lord, I have accomplished your work and perfected your commandment. I have become a bondman; therefore to-day I receive freedom. Therefore give me this and perfect me: and this I say, not that I doubt, but that they may hear for whom it is needful to hear."'

forgiven my debtor the mina, require it not at my hands. I was bidden to the supper, and I came; and I refused the land and the yoke of oxen and the wife, that I might not for their sake be rejected. I was bidden to the wedding, and I put on white raiment, that I might be worthy of it and not be bound hand and foot and cast into the outer darkness. My lamp with its bright light expects the master coming from the marriage, that it may receive him, and I may not see it dimmed because the oil is spent. My eyes, O Christ, look upon you, and my heart exults with joy because I have fulfilled your will and perfected your commandments that I may be likened to that watchful and careful servant who in his eagerness neglects not to keep vigil. All the night have I laboured to keep my house from robbers, lest it be broken through.

147. 'My loins have I girt with truth[75] and bound my shoes on my feet, that I may never see them gaping: my hands have I put to the yoked plough and have not turned back, lest my furrows go crooked. The plough-land is white and the harvest is come, that I may receive my wages. My garment that grows old I have worn out, and the labour that has brought me to rest have I accomplished. I have kept the first watch and the second and the third, that I may behold your face and adore your holy brightness. I have rooted out my storehouses and left them desolate on earth, that I may be filled full from your treasures. The moist spring that was in me have I dried up, that I may live and rest beside your inexhaustible spring.[76] The captive whom you committed to me I have slain, that he who is set free in me may not fall from his confidence. The inward I have made the outward and the outward the inward,[77] and all your fullness has been fulfilled in me. I have not returned to the things that are behind, but have gone forward to the things that are before, that I do not become a reproach. The dead man have I quickened, and the living one have I overcome, and that which was lacking I have filled up, that I may receive the crown of victory, and the power of Christ may be accomplished in me. I have received reproach upon earth, but give me the return and the recompense in the heavens.

148. 'Let not the powers and the officers perceive me, and let them not have any thought concerning me; let not the publicans and tax-gatherers ply their calling upon me; let not the weak and the evil cry out against me who am valiant and humble; and when I am borne upward let them not rise up to stand before me, by your power, O Jesus, which surrounds me as a crown: for they flee and hide themselves, they cannot look on you; but suddenly they fall upon those who are subject to them, and the portion of the sons of the evil one itself cries out and convicts them; and it is not hid from them, for their nature is made known; the children of the evil one are separated off. Grant me, Lord, that I may pass by in quietness and joy and peace, and pass over

[75] Eph. 6: 14.
[76] Cf. Gospel of Thomas 13.
[77] Cf. Gospel of Thomas 22, and Gospel of the Egyptians.

and stand before the judge; and let not the devil look upon me; let his eyes be blinded by your light which you have made to dwell in me; muzzle his mouth for he has found nothing against me'.

168. And when he had thus prayed he said to the soldiers, 'Come here and accomplish the commandments of him who sent you.' And the four came and pierced him with their spears, and he fell down and died.

And all the brethren wept; and they brought beautiful robes and much fair linen, and buried him in a royal sepulchre wherein the earlier kings were laid.

169. But Siphor and Vazan would not go down to the city, but continued sitting by him all the day. And the apostle Thomas appeared to them and said, 'Why do you sit here and keep watch over me? I am not here but I have gone up and received all that I was promised. But rise up and go down hence; for after a little time you also shall be gathered to me.'

But Misdaeus and Charisius took away Mygdonia and Tertia and afflicted them, but they did not consent to their will. And the apostle appeared to them and said, 'Do not be deceived: Jesus the holy, the living one, shall quickly send help to you.' And Misdaeus and Charisius, when they perceived that Mygdonia and Tertia did not obey them, allowed them to live according to their own desire.

And the brethren gathered together and rejoiced in the grace of the Holy Ghost. Now the apostle Thomas when he departed out of the world made Siphor a presbyter and Vazan a deacon, when he went up into the mountain to die. And the Lord worked through them, and many were added to the faith.

170. Now it came to pass after a long time that one of the children of Misdaeus the king was a demoniac and no one could cure him, for the devil was extremely fierce. And Misdaeus the king took thought and said, 'I will go and open the sepulchre, and take a bone of the apostle of God and hang it upon my son, and he shall be healed.' But while Misdaeus thought about this, the apostle Thomas appeared to him and said to him, 'You did not believe in a living man,[78] and will you believe in the dead? Yet fear not, for my Lord Jesus Christ has compassion on you and pities you of his goodness.'

And he went and opened the sepulchre, but did not find the apostle there, for one of the brethren had stolen him away and taken him to Mesopotamia; but from that place where the bones of the apostle had lain Misdaeus took dust and put it about his son's neck, saying, 'I believe in you, Jesu Christ, now that he has left me who troubles men and opposes them lest they should see you.' And when he had hung it upon his son, the boy became whole.

Misdaeus the king therefore was also included among the brethren, and bowed his head under the hands of Siphor the priest; and Siphor said to the brethren, 'Pray for Misdaeus the king, that he may obtain mercy of Jesus Christ and that he may no more remember evil against him.' Therefore, they

---

[78] Cf. Gospel of Thomas 52.

all with one accord rejoiced, and made prayer for him; and the Lord who loves men, the King of Kings and Lord of Lords, granted Misdaeus also to have hope in him; and he was gathered with the multitude of those who had believed in Christ, glorifying the Father and the Son and the Holy Ghost; theirs is the power and adoration, now and for ever and world without end. Amen.[79]

[79] Some manuscripts include an extra section, numbered ch. 171 in Bonnet's edition.

Other Apocryphal Acts

The minor Acts, especially those known from the oriental tradition, show the development from rather dim historical reminiscences used as a framework for doctrinal teaching to thaumaturgy plus doctrine and then to pure thaumaturgy. In these Acts the teaching is conventional, and becomes increasingly perfunctory, while the miracles become increasingly sensational, with an obvious borrowing from pagan romances as is evidenced in the Clementine literature (*q.v.*) and in the Acts of Xanthippe and Polyxena (below, 5).

From a theological point of view these texts are of little significance, but as depositories of legend and art they have considerable interest.

The texts included below are:

1. The Acts of Philip (translation or summaries of extracts)
2. The Passion of Bartholomew (summary of extract)
3. The Passion of Matthew (summary of extracts)
4. The Acts of Barnabas (introduction)
5. The Acts of Xanthippe and Polyxena (introduction)
6. Pseudo-Abdias (summaries of extracts)
7. Oriental Acts (introduction)
8. The Epistle of Pseudo-Titus (introduction)

1. THE ACTS OF PHILIP

M. R. James described this work as 'grotesque' but 'yet a catholic novel'. Like the Acts of Thomas, the original was divided into separate acts, of which there were apparently fifteen. Chapters 1–7 seem to have been a separate composition from chapter 8-the Martyrdom. The Martyrdom, itself a homogeneous work, also circulated as a separate work: it occurs in various recensions, three of which are set out in Bonnet's text. The complete work is no longer extant. Even with the additions to Bonnet's Greek text to be published by Bovon from the Athos manuscript Xenophontos 32 Act X is still wanting, and parts of XI and fragments of XIV and XV are also missing.[1] The separate act found only in Syriac and summarized by James, *ANT* 450–2, cannot easily be fitted into the Greek text. The Greek text itself combines separate episodes, some-

---

[1] A sample of the first acts appears in B. Bouvier and F. Bovon, 'Actes de Philippe I, d'après un manuscrit inédit' in D. Papandreou, W. A. Bienert, and K. Schäferdiek (eds.), *Oecumenica et Patristica* (Festschrift for W. Schneemelcher) (Geneva, 1989), 367–94.

times in a rough and abrupt manner, into a sequence of acts preceding the Martyrdom. The Latin Acts of Philip that forms Pseudo-Abdias, book 10, diverges from the Greek account.

The work probably originated in the fourth–fifth century, and seems to have drawn inspiration from the major apocryphal Acts. The titles of the individual acts are:

I. When he came out of Galilee and raised the dead man.
II. When he entered Greece of Athens (or upper Greece).
III. In the land of the Parthians.
IV. The daughter of Nicocleides, whom he healed at Azotus.
V. Done in the city of Nicatera, and concerning Ireus.
VI. In the city of Nicatera, a city of Greece.
VII. Of Nerkela, the wife of Ireus in Nicatera.
VIII. The kid and the leopard in the wilderness become believers (see translation below).
IX. Concerning the dragon that was slain.
X. Not extant.
XI. The conclusion of XI survives and includes a prayer based on the Acts of John 94–6.
XII. The leopard and the kid ask for communion.
XIII. Arrival in Hierapolis.
XIV. Performed on Stachys the blind.
XV. Concerning Nicanora, the governor's wife. The martyrdom of Philip (summary below).

A translation of Act VIII is given below because it includes a popular theme in apocryphal literature, namely that of animals who are believers (Act XII has the animals asking for communion), and because its introduction has an interesting link with the beginning of the Acts of Thomas, the Martyrium Prius (a Greek martyrdom of Andrew), and the Acts of Andrew and Matthias with the dispersal of the apostles by lot. This is followed by a summary of the Martyrdom.

EDITIONS

Greek

Tischendorf, *Apoc. Apoc.* 141–56.
Lipsius–Bonnet, ii.2, 1–90 (with a later digest, 91–8).
James, *Apoc. Anec.* i. 158–63.
François Bovon, Bertrand Bouvier, Frédéric Amsler, *Acta Philippi* 2 vols. (Turnhout 1999) (= *CCSA* 11 and 12).

Syriac

Wright, i. 73–99; ii (Eng. trans.), 69–92.

Slavonic

de Santos Otero *Altslav. Apok.* i. 124–9 (martyrdom).
Armenian,[2] Georgian, and Irish versions also exist.

The preaching and martyrdom are found in Coptic, and through Coptic, in Arabic and Ethiopic:

Coptic

Guidi, *AAL. R* 4, 3.2 (1887), 20–3; Italian trans., *Giornale*, 27–9.
O. von Lemm, 'Koptische apokryphe Apostelacten, I', in *Mélanges Asiatiques* 10 (St Petersburg, 1892), 110–47.

Arabic

Smith Lewis, *Acta Myth.* 51–8; *Myth. Acts*, 60–9.

Ethiopic

Malan, 66–72.
Wallis Budge, *Contendings*, i. 126–39; ii (Eng. trans.), 146–62.

MODERN TRANSLATIONS

English

Walker, 429–39 (summary).
James, 439–53 (summary), 469 (summary of Ps.-Abdias 10).

French

Migne, *Dictionnaire*, ii, cols. 679–88 (including part of Ps.-Abdias 10).
Éac, 1181–320.
F. Amsler, F. Bovon, B. Bouvier, *Actes de L'apôtre Philippe* (Turnhout, 1996) (= *Apocryphes* 8).

Italian

Erbetta, ii. 451–87, 488–90 (from Ps.-Abdias 10).
Moraldi, ii. 1625–32; [2] ii. 680–2 (summary), 1604–6; [2] ii. 700–6 (trans. of part of Ps.-Abdias 10).

[2] A French translation of the Armenian martyrdom appears in Leloir, *CCA* 4, 448–59.

GENERAL

Lipsius, ii.2, 1–53; *Ergänzungsband*, 64–73.

J. Flamion, 'Les trois recensions grecques du martyre de l'apôtre Philippe', in *Mélanges d'histoire offerts a Ch. Moeller*, i (Louvain and Paris, 1914), 215–25 (= *Recueil de travaux publiés par les membres des conférences d'histoire et de philologie* 40).

E. Peterson, 'Die Häretiker der Philippus-Akte', *ZNW* 31 (1932), 97–111.

—— 'Zum Messalianismus der Philippus-Akten', *Oriens Christianus* NS 7 (1932), 172–9.

—— 'Die Philippus-Akten in Armenischen Synaxar', *ThQ* 113 (1933), 289–98.

A. Kurfess, 'Zu den Philippus-Akten', *ZNW* 44 (1952–3), 145–51.

F. Bovon, 'Les Actes de Philippe', *ANRW* 2.25.6, 4431–4527.

Hennecke[5], ii. 424–30 (A. de Santos Otero); Eng. trans. ii. 468–73.

Translation

VIII. *The kid and the leopard in the wilderness become believers*

It came to pass when the Saviour divided the apostles and each went forth according to his lot, that it fell to Philip to go to the country of the Greeks: and he thought about it hard, and wept. And Mariamne his sister (it was she who made ready the bread and salt at the breaking of bread, but Martha was the one who ministered to the multitudes and laboured much), seeing it, went to Jesus and said, 'Lord, do you not see how my brother is vexed?' And he said, 'I know, you chosen among women; but go with him and encourage him, for I know that he is a wrathful and rash man, and if we let him go alone he will bring many retributions on men. But lo, I will send Bartholomew and John to suffer hardships in the same city, because of the great wickedness of those who dwell there; for they worship the viper, the mother of snakes. You change your woman's aspect and go with Philip.' And to Philip he said, 'Why are you fearful? for I am always with you.'

So they all set out for the land of the Ophiani; and when they came to the wilderness of dragons, behold, a great leopard came out of a wood on the hill, and ran and cast himself at their feet and spoke with human voice, 'I worship you, servants of the divine greatness and apostles of the only-begotten Son of God; command me to speak perfectly.' And Philip said, 'In the name of Jesus Christ, speak.' And the leopard adopted perfect speech and said, 'Hear me Philip, groomsman of the divine word. Last night I passed through the flocks of goats near the mount of the she-dragon, the mother of snakes, and seized a kid; and when I went into the wood to eat, after I had wounded it, it took a human voice and wept like a little child, saying to me, "O leopard, put off your fierce heart and the beastlike part of your nature, and put on mildness, for the apostles of the divine greatness are about to pass through this desert, to accomplish perfectly the promise of the glory of the only-begotten Son of God." At these words of the kid I was perplexed, and gradually my heart was changed, and my fierceness turned to mildness, and I did not eat it. And as I listened to its words I lifted up my eyes and saw you coming, and knew that you were the servants of the good God. So I left the kid and came to worship you. And now I beseech you to give me liberty to go with you everywhere and put off my beastlike nature.'

And Philip said, 'Where is the kid?' And he said, 'It is cast down under the oak opposite.' Philip said to Bartholomew, 'Let us go and see him that was smitten, healed, and healing the smiter.' And at Philip's bidding the leopard guided them to where the kid lay. Philip and Bartholomew said, 'Now know we of a truth that there is none that surpasses your compassion, O Jesu, lover of man; for you protect us and convince us by these creatures to believe more and earnestly fulfil our trust. Now therefore, Lord Jesus Christ, come and grant life and breath and secure existence to these creatures, that they may forsake their nature of beast and cattle and come to tameness, and no longer eat flesh, nor the kid the food of cattle; but that men's hearts may be given them, and they may follow us wherever we go, and eat what we eat, to your glory, and speak after the manner of men, glorifying your name.'

And in that hour the leopard and kid rose up and lifted up their fore-feet and said, 'We glorify and bless you who have visited and remembered us in this desert, and changed our beastlike and wild nature into tameness, and granted us the divine word, and put in us a tongue and sense to speak and praise your name, for great is your glory.' And they fell and worshipped Philip and Bartholomew and Mariamne; and all set out together, praising God.

Summary
In the days of Trajan, after the Martyrdom of Simon, son of Clopas, bishop of Jerusalem, successor to James, Philip the apostle was preaching through all the cities of Lydia and Asia. And he came to the city of Ophioryme, which is called Hierapolis of Asia, and was received by Stachys, a believer. And with him were Bartholomew, one of the Seventy, and his sister Mariamne, and their disciples. And they assembled at Stachys' house. And Mariamne sat and listened to Philip discoursing. He spoke of the snares of the dragon, who has no shape in creation, and is recognized and shunned by beasts and birds. For the men of the place worshipped the snake and had images of it; and called Hierapolis Ophioryme. And many were converted. And Nicanora the proconsul's wife believed; she was diseased, especially in her eyes, and had been healed. She now came in a silver litter. And Mariamne said in Hebrew, 'Alikaman, ikasame, marmari, iachaman, mastranan, achaman', which means: O daughter of the father, my lady, who was given as a pledge to the serpent, Christ is come to you. And Nicanora said, 'I am a Hebrew, speak to me in my fathers' tongue. I heard of your preaching and was healed.' And they prayed for her. But her tyrant husband came and said, 'How is this? who has healed you?' And she said, 'Depart from me, and lead a chaste and sober life.' And he dragged her by the hair and threatened to kill her. And the apostles were

arrested, and scourged and dragged to the temple, and shut up in it with the leopard and the kid.[1] The people and priests came and demanded vengeance on the sorcerers. The proconsul was afraid of his wife, for he had been almost blinded by a wonderful light when he looked through the window at her when praying. They stripped and searched the apostles for charms, and pierced Philip's ankles and thighs and hung him head downward, and Bartholomew they hung naked by the hair. And they smiled on each other, as if they were not being tormented. But Mariamne on being stripped became like an ark of glass full of light and fire, and everyone ran away. And Philip and Bartholomew talked in Hebrew, and Philip said, 'Shall we call down fire from heaven?' And now John arrived, and asked what was happening, and the people told him. And he was taken to the place. Philip said to Bartholomew in Hebrew, 'Here is John the son of Barega (*or*, he that is in Barek), that is (*or*, where is) the living water.' And John said, 'The mystery of him who hanged between the heaven and the earth be with you.'

Then John addressed the people, warning them against the serpent. When all matter was wrought and spread out throughout the system of heaven, the works of God entreated God that they might see his glory; and when they saw it, their desire became gall and bitterness, and the earth became the storehouse of that which went astray, and the result and the superfluity of the creation was gathered together and became like an egg; and the serpent was born.

The people said, 'We took you for a fellow citizen, but you are in league with these men. The priests are going to wring out your blood and mix it with wine and give it to the viper.' When they came to take John their hands were paralysed. John said to Philip, 'Let us not render evil for evil.' Philip said, 'I shall endure it no longer.' The three others dissuaded him; but he said, 'Abalo, arimouni, douthael, tharseleën, nachaoth, aeidounaph, teleteloein', which is (after many invocations descriptive of God): 'Let the deep open and swallow these men: yea, Sabaoth.' It opened and the whole place was swallowed, about seven thousand men, except where the apostles were. And their voices came up, crying for mercy and saying, 'Lo, the cross enlightens us.' And a voice was heard: 'I will have mercy on you in my cross of light.' But Stachys and his house, and Nicanora, and fifty others, and one hundred virgins remained safe. Jesus appeared and rebuked Philip. But he defended himself. And the Lord said, 'Since you have been unforgiving and wrathful, you shall indeed die in glory and be taken by angels to paradise, but shall remain outside it forty days, in fear of the flaming sword, and then I will send Michael and he shall let you in. And Bartholomew shall go to Lycaonia and be crucified there, and Mariamne's body shall be laid up in the river Jordan. And

---

[1] Some MSS omit 'with the leopard and the kid'.

I shall bring back those who have been swallowed up.' And he drew a cross in the air, reaching down into the abyss, and it was filled with light, and the cross was like a ladder. And Jesus called the people, and they all came up, save the proconsul and the viper. And seeing the apostles they mourned and repented. And Philip, still hanging, spoke to them and told them of his offence. And some ran to take him down, but he refused and spoke to them.... 'Be not grieved that I hang thus, for I bear the form of the first man, who was brought upon earth head downwards, and again by the tree of the cross made alive from the death of his transgression. And now I fulfil the precept. For the Lord said to me, "Unless you make that which is beneath to be above, and the left to be right (and the right left), you shall not enter into my kingdom." Be like me in this: for all the world is turned the wrong way, and every soul that is in it.' Further he spoke to them of the incarnation, and bade them loose Bartholomew, and told him and Mariamne of their destiny. 'Build a church in the place where I die, and let the leopard and kid be there, and let Nicanora look after them till they die, and then bury them at the church gate: and let your peace be in the house of Stachys': and he exhorted them to purity. 'Therefore our brother Peter fled from every place where a woman was: and further, he had offence given by reason of his own daughter. And he prayed the Lord, and she had a palsy of the side that she might not be led astray.' Bury me not in linen like the Lord, but in papyrus, and pray for me forty days. Where my blood is dropping a vine will grow, and you shall use the wine of it for the cup, and partake of it on the third day. And he prayed the Lord to receive him, and protect him against all enemies: 'Let not their dark air cover me, that I may pass the waters of fire and all the abyss. Clothe me in your glorious robe and your seal of light that always shines, until I have passed by all the rulers of the world and the evil dragon that oppose us.' And he died. And they buried him as he directed. And a heavenly voice said he had received the crown.

After three days the vine grew up. And they made the offering daily for forty days, and built the church and made Stachys bishop. And all the city believed. And at the end of forty days the Saviour appeared in the form of Philip and told Bartholomew and Mariamne that he had entered paradise, and bade them go their ways. And Bartholomew went to Lycaonia and Mariamne to Jordan, and Stachys and the brethren abode where they were.

2. THE PASSION OF BARTHOLOMEW

This text, preserved in Greek, Latin, and Armenian, may have originated in the fifth–sixth century. Modern scholarship generally considers the Greek to be a translation from the Latin possibly used by Pseudo-Abdias 8 (cf. M. Bonnet, 'La Passion de S. Barthélemy: en quelle langue a-t-elle été écrite?',

Anal. Boll. 14 (1895), 353–66). James's summary (*ANT* 467–9) from Pseudo-Abdias is given below.

EDITIONS

Greek and Latin

Lipsius–Bonnet, ii.1, 128–50.

Armenian

Leloir, *CCA* 4, 479–524 (French trans.).

Ethiopic

Malan, 29–42.
Wallis Budge, *Contendings*, i. 93–100; ii (Eng. trans.), 104–10.

Arabic

Smith Lewis, *Acta Myth.* 64–6; *Myth. Acts*, 76–9.

MODERN TRANSLATIONS

English

Walker, 429–39.
James, 467–9 (summary).

Italian

Erbetta, ii. 589–91 (summary of Armenian); ii. 581–8 (Ps.-Abdias 8).
Moraldi, ii. 1623–4; ² 644–52 (summary of Armenian); ii. 1568–76; ² 698–9 (Ps.-Abdias 8).

Irish

M. McNamara, *The Apocrypha in the Irish Church* (Dublin, 1975), 93–4 (summary).

GENERAL

Lipsius, ii.2, 54–108.
Hennecke[5], ii. 407–8 (A. de Santos Otero); Eng. trans. ii. 452–3.

India is divided into three parts: Bartholomew went there to a temple of Astaroth, who ceased to answer his worshippers. So they went to another city; and inquired of Berith, who said Bartholomew was the cause. What is he like?

they asked. 'He has black curly hair, white skin, large eyes, straight nose, his hair covers his ears, his beard long and grizzled, middle height: he wears a white *colobium* with a purple stripe, and a white cloak with four purple "gems" at the corners; for twenty-six years he has worn these and they never grow old; his shoes have lasted twenty-six years; he prays one hundred times a day and one hundred times a night: his voice is like a trumpet; angels wait on him; he is always cheerful and knows all languages.' For two days they could not find him, but then he cast a devil out of a man. King Polymius heard of it and sent for him to heal his lunatic daughter who bit every one. She was loosed—the apostle having reassured her keepers—and cured. The king sent camels laden with riches, but the apostle could not be found. Next day, however, he came to the king and expounded the Christian faith, and offered to show him the devil who inhabited his idol. There was a dialogue, in which the demon explained his doings. Bartholomew made the people try to pull the statue down, but they could not. The ropes were removed and he bade the demon leave the statue, which was instantly broken. After a prayer of the apostle, an angel appeared and signed the four corners of the temple with the cross; and then showed them the devil: black, sharp-faced, with long beard, hair to the feet, fiery eyes, breathing flame, spiky wings like a hedgehog, bound with fiery chains; and then the angel sent him away howling. The king and the rest were baptized. But the heathen priests went and complained to his brother Astriges, who had Bartholomew brought bound, and questioned him. It was told him that his idol Vualdath had fallen and was broken to pieces, and in anger he had Bartholomew beaten with clubs and beheaded. And the people buried him honourably, and built a basilica over him. After twenty days Astriges was seized by a devil, and he and all the priests died. And there was great fear, and all believed: King Polymius became bishop and presided twenty years.

3. THE PASSION OF MATTHEW

This martyrdom, together with allied stories in Coptic and Ethiopic, was probably based on a lost Acts of Andrew, itself apparently based on the apocryphal Acts of Andrew and Matthias: it exists in Greek and Latin versions. There is also an abbreviated Coptic form, and Arabic and Ethiopic versions, originally from Coptic. An adapted form of James's summary (*ANT* 460–2) is given here. The story is late.

EDITIONS

Greek and Latin

Lipsius–Bonnet ii.1, 217–62.

Ethiopic

Malan, 43-59.
Wallis Budge, *Contendings*, i. 101-18; ii (Eng. trans.), 111-35.

Arabic

Smith Lewis, *Acta Myth.* 83-94; *Myth. Acts*, 100-12.

Armenian

Leloir, *CCA* 4, 655-65.

Slavonic

de Santos Otero, *Altslav. Apok.* ii. 130-5.

MODERN TRANSLATIONS

English

Walker, 429-39.
James, 460-2 (summary).

Italian

Erbetta, ii. 506-17 (Greek/Latin martyrdom; summary of Ethiopic).
Moraldi, ii. 1635-8; [2] ii. 709-12 (summary of Greek/Latin martyrdom and of Ethiopic).

GENERAL

Lipsius, ii.2, 109-41.
T. Atenolfi, *I testi meridionali degli Atti di S. Matteo l'Evangelista* (Rome, 1958).
Hennecke[5], ii. 414-17 (A. de Santos Otero); Eng. trans. ii. 458-61.

The holy Matthew remained alone on the Mount praying, in the apostolic robe, barefoot, and Jesus appeared to him in the form of one of the children that were singing in Paradise. A dialogue. Matthew said. 'I know that I saw you in Paradise singing with the other children that were slain at Bethlehem; but how you came so quickly, I marvel at. But tell me, where is that ungodly Herod?' 'He dwells in hell, and there is prepared for him fire unquenchable, unending gehenna, boiling mire, the worm that sleeps not, because he killed three thousand children. Now take my staff and go to Myrna the city of the man-eaters, and plant it at the gate of the church which you and Andrew founded. It will become a tree, and a spring will rise at its foot, and the man-eaters will eat of the tree and wash in the spring, and their bodies will be changed and they will be ashamed of their nakedness, and use fire to cook their food, and learn to know me.' At the city gate he was met by Phulbana the king's wife, Phulbanos his son, and Erba his wife, all possessed by devils—and the devils cried out and threatened Matthew that they would rouse the king against him. He cast them out. The bishop Plato heard and came out to meet him with the clergy. And Matthew preached to the people, and planted the staff. And the people became humanized. He baptized the queen and the rest. At dawn the staff was become a tree. Phulbanus the king was pleased with all this at first, but when they refused to quit Matthew he resolved to burn him. Matthew had a consoling vision, and warned the people of his death. The devil whom he had cast out disguised himself as a soldier and went to the king, and advised him to seize Matthew. He sent four soldiers, who could hear only two men talking (Matthew and Plato), and then ten, who were routed by seeing a child with a torch. The devil described to the king the difficulty of seizing Matthew, and all that he could do. The king said, 'Take him yourself.' 'I cannot, for he has destroyed all our race.' 'Who, then, are you?', said the king. 'I am the demon Asmodaeus who was in your wife.' The king adjured him to depart without harming anyone, and he vanished as smoke. That day the king remained quiet, but next day took two soldiers and went to the church and sent for Matthew. He came out with Plato, but the king could not see him. Matthew opened his eyes. The king treacherously led him to the palace. They pinned him hand and foot to the earth and covered him with papyrus soaked in dolphin oil, and poured brimstone, asphalt, and pitch on him, and heaped up tow and wood. And the fire turned to dew, and all the people praised God. A good deal of charcoal from the royal baths was brought, and the twelve gods of gold and silver were set round the fire. Matthew looking up to heaven, cried, 'Adonai Eloï Sabaoth marmari marmounth.' The fire blazed up, and the king said, 'Where is now your magic?' But all the fire flew out about the idols and melted them—whose weight was one thousand talents of gold. And the king lamented that gods of stone and clay were superior. The fire burnt up many soldiers, and then took the form of a dragon and chased the king to the palace, and curled round so that he could not go in and made him come back to Matthew, crying for help. Matthew rebuked the fire and prayed, and gave up the ghost.

The king had him borne in state to the palace. The body and robes were intact, and sometimes he was seen on the bier, sometimes following or preceding it, and laying his hand on Plato's head. And many sick were healed.

When they reached the palace Matthew was seen to rise from the bier and ascend to heaven, led by a beautiful child, and twelve men in crowns, and we saw the child crown him. The king had a coffin made of iron and sealed it with lead, and privately put it on a ship at midnight and sank it in the sea.

All night the brethren watched at the palace gate, and at dawn a voice came, 'Plato, take the Gospel and the Psalter and go to the east of the palace and sing Alleluia, and read the Gospel, and offer of the bread and the vine, pressing three clusters into the cup, and communicate with me, as the Lord Jesus showed us the offering that is above, on the third day after he rose.' So it was done, and the cantor went up on a great stone and sang: 'Precious in the sight of the Lord.... I slept and rose up again...' And they answered, 'Shall not the sleeper awake?'... 'Now will I arise, says the Lord.' 'Alleluia.' They read the Gospel and made the offering.

It was about the sixth hour, and Plato looked out to sea seven stadia away, and behold, Matthew standing on the sea between two men in bright apparel, and the beautiful child before them. And they said, 'Amen, Alleluia.' And the sea was like a crystal stone, and before the child a cross came up out of the deep, and at the lower end of it the coffin of Matthew; and in a moment it was set on the land where they were.

The king beheld all from a window, and came down and fell at their feet and confessed his sin and his belief. He would give them the palace for a sanctuary, and the coffin should be laid on his golden couch in the great hall. Plato baptized and communicated him. The apostle appeared and said, 'Your name shall no more be Bulphamnus but Matthew; your son not Bulphandrus but also Matthew; your wife Ziphagia, Sophia; and his wife Orba, Synesis.' He ordained the king a priest, being thirty-seven, his son a deacon, being seventeen: his wife a presbytis, and his son's wife a deaconess, being seventeen. The king destroyed his idols, and issued a decree establishing the new faith[4]. Matthew bade them offer the offering daily for forty-nine days and repeat it yearly, and told Plato he should join him in three years, and be succeeded by the king, and he by his son. Then with two angels he departed to heaven. And a voice came, promising peace and safety to the city.

4. THE ACTS OF BARNABAS

The story tells of John Mark's account of the activities and death of Barnabas in Cyprus; the date of the composition is probably fifth to sixth century. No summary is provided here.

EDITIONS

Greek

Lipsius–Bonnet, ii.2, 292–302.

Slavonic

de Santos Otero, *Altslav. Apok.* i. 136–7.

---

[4] This chapter is in one recension only.

MODERN TRANSLATIONS

English

Walker, 293–300.

French

Migne, *Dictionnaire*, ii, cols. 139–50.

Italian

Erbetta, ii. 595–600.
Moraldi, ii. 1620–2; [2] ii. 695–7 (summary).

GENERAL

Lipsius, ii. 2, 270–320.
Hennecke[5], ii. 421–2 (A. de Santos Otero); Eng trans. ii. 465–6.

5. THE ACTS OF XANTHIPPE AND POLYXENA

Material here has been borrowed from, among other places, the Acts of Peter, the Acts of Paul, the Acts of Andrew, and the Acts of Thomas. The text was published by M. R. James from an eleventh-century manuscript.

James argued (*Apoc. Anec.* 54) for a third-century date for the origin of this apocryphon. He stated that it is a good example of a Christian substitute for the conventional pagan literature of the day. The aim of the author (as of the authors of other apocryphal acts) is to blend instruction with entertainment. It contains the belief that Paul visited Spain. In the first half, based on Xanthippe, there are numerous speeches and prayers; in the second part (from ch. 22) there is a change of pace, with many incidents and a variety of characters; here the episodes relate to Polyxena.

No translation is given here.

EDITION

James, *Apoc. Anec.* i. 43–85 (introduction and Greek text).

MODERN TRANSLATIONS

English

W. A. Craigie, 'The Acts of Xanthippe and Polyxena', in A. Menzies (ed.), *Ante-Nicene Christian Library*, Additional Volume 9 (Edinburgh, 1897), 203–17.

GENERAL

Lipsius, ii.1, 217-27.
E. Peterson, 'Die Acta Xanthippae et Polyxenae und die Paulusakten', *Anal. Boll.* 65 (1947), 57-60.
E. Junod, 'Vie et conduite des saintes femmes Xanthippe, Polyxène et Rébecca (BHG 1877)', in D. Papandreou, W. A. Bienert, and K. Schäferdiek (eds.), *Oecumenica et Patristica* (Festschrift for W. Schneemelcher) (Geneva, 1989), 83-106.

6. LATIN: PSEUDO-ABDIAS

Mention has already been made above (pp. 304, 338-45) of the Apostolic History attributed to Abdias, bishop of Babylon. M. R. James (*ANT* 462-9) provided summaries of the books that do not occur elsewhere in his collection. This apostolic history was probably put together, perhaps in France, in the sixth-seventh century.

The subjects of the ten books are as follows (for those marked with an asterisk James's summaries are given below):

1. Peter (see Acts of Peter).
2. Paul (see Acts of Paul).
3. Gregory of Tours' version of the Acts of Andrew, together with a version of the Passion taken from Conversante et Docente (see Acts of Andrew).
4. *James the Great, taken probably from a Greek original (not to be confused with the Acts of James the Great referred to in Lipsius, ii.2, 201-28 and dismissed by James, *ANT* 470, as 'without interest'. It is this text that is related to the Armenian translated by Leloir *CCA* 3, 270-88).
5. John (see Acts of John).
6. *James the Less. This includes the Acts of Simon and Jude, taken from a larger work that presumably dealt with their activities in Babylonia and Persia. See Lipsius, ii.2, 142-200, esp. 164-8.
7. *Matthew. This differed from the Passion of Matthew (above 3).
8. Bartholomew (see above 2).
9. Thomas (see Acts of Thomas).
10. *Philip. This account differs from the Greek Acts of Philip.[5]

EDITIONS

[F. Nausea], *Anonymi Philalethi Eusebiani in vitas, miracula passionesque apostolorum rhapsodiae* (Cologne, 1531).

[5] According to M. McNamara, *Irish Biblical Apocrypha* (Edinburgh, 1989), 182, the Passion of the Apostle Philip in the Irish tradition is close to Pseudo-Abdias 10 (cf. also F. Bovon *ANRW* 2.25.6, 4443).

Most conveniently to be found in

Fabricius, ii. 387–742, which includes Lazius' expansions (W. Lazius, *Abdiae Babyloniae episcopi et apostolorum discipuli de historia certaminis apostolici libri decem* (Basle, 1552)).

MODERN TRANSLATIONS

English

James, 462–9 (summaries of certain books).

French

Migne, *Dictionnaire*, ii:
Book		
1	cols.	695–716
2		657–64
3		57–93
4		265–76
5		327–56
6		275–382, 939–54
7		549–64
8		149–59
9		987–1016
10		687–90.

Italian

Moraldi, ii. 1431–1606; [2] ii. 511–687.
Erbetta, ii:
Book		
1	pp.	199–210
2		297–301
3		408–28
4		543–8
5		111–29
6		549–71
7		518–26
8		581–8
9		375–91
10		488–90.

GENERAL

Lipsius, i. 117–78.

(a) James the Great

1. Describes James's preaching. 2. In the course of it he was opposed by Hermogenes and Philetus. Philetus was converted by James, and told Hermogenes he should leave him. Hermogenes in anger bound him by magical incantations and said, 'We will see if James can free you.' Philetus found means to send a servant to James, who sent back his kerchief, and by it Philetus was freed and came to James.

3. Hermogenes in anger sent devils to fetch both James and Philetus to him, but when they got there they began to howl in the air and complain that an angel had bound them with fiery chains. James sent them to bring Hermogenes bound. They tied his arms with ropes and brought him, mocking him. 'You are a foolish man,' said James, 'but they shall not hurt you.' The devils clamoured for leave to avenge themselves on him. 'Why do you not seize Philetus?', said James. 'We dare not touch so much as an ant in your chamber', they said. James bade Philetus loose Hermogenes, and he stood confounded. 'Go free,' said James, 'for we do not render evil for evil.' 'I fear the demons', he said. And James gave him his staff to protect him.

4. Armed with this, he went home and filled baskets with magical books and began to burn them. 'Not so', said James, 'lest the smoke vex the unwary; cast them into the sea.' He did so, and returned and begged for pardon. James sent him to undo his former work on those he had deceived, and spend in charity what he had gained by his art. He obeyed, and grew in faith so much that he even performed miracles.

5. The Jews bribed two centurions, Lysias and Theocritus, to seize James. And while he was being taken away, there was a dispute between him and the Pharisees. He spoke to them first of Abraham, 6. and went on to cite prophecies. Isaiah: Behold a virgin... Jeremiah: Behold, your redeemer shall come, O Jerusalem, and this shall be the sign of him: he shall open the eyes of the blind, restore hearing to the deaf, and raise the dead with his voice. Ezekiel: your king shall come, O Zion, he shall come humbly, and restore you. Daniel: As the son of man, so shall he come and receive princedoms and powers. David: The Lord said to my Lord... Again: He shall call me, you are my Father... I will make him my first-born. Of the fruit of your body... Isaiah again: Like a sheep to the slaughter. David: They pierced my hands... They gave me gall... My flesh shall rest... I will arise and be with you... For the comfortless trouble's sake... He is gone up on high... God is gone up. He rode on the cherubim... The Lord shall come, and shall not keep silence,... 7. Isaiah: The dead shall rise. David: God spoke once... They rewarded me evil for good... He that did eat my bread... The earth opened and swallowed up Dathan. 8. The people cried out, 'We have sinned.' Abiathar the high priest stirred up a tumult, and a scribe cast a rope about James's neck and dragged him before Herod, who sentenced him to be beheaded. On the way he healed a paralytic.

9. The scribe, named Josias, was converted, and prayed for pardon. And Abiathar procured that he should be beheaded with James. Water was brought, James baptized him, they exchanged the kiss of peace, and were beheaded.

(b) James the Less

The first six chapters are from the canonical Gospels and Acts and from Hegesippus as quoted by Eusebius (Rufinus).

7. Simon and Jude, going to Persia, found there two magicians, Zaroës and Arfaxat, whom Matthew had driven out of Ethiopia. Their doctrines were that the God of the Old Testament was the god of darkness, Moses and the Prophets deceivers, the soul the work of the good God, the body the work of the god of darkness, so that soul and body are contrary to each other; that the sun and moon are gods, and also water; that the incarnation of Christ was in appearance only.

8. On entering the country they met Varardach, the general of King Xerxes, with an army preparing to repel an invasion of India. He had many priests and diviners with him; their gods explained that they could give no answers because of the presence of Simon and Jude. Varardach sent for them and they offered to expound their teaching: he said he would hear them after the campaign. Jude urged him to hear now. He asked them to foretell his success or failure.

9. Simon said, 'We will allow your gods to answer your diviners.' So they prayed, and the prophets said, 'There will be a great battle, and many will fall on either side.' The apostles laughed, though Varardach was impressed; and they said, 'The truth is that to-morrow the Indians will send and offer you peace and become tributaries to Persia.' After some dispute with the priests it was agreed (10) that both parties should be kept in custody till the morrow— (11) when the apostles' prediction was fulfilled. But they interceded for the priests, whom Varardach would have killed. 'At least', said he, 'you will receive their goods.' Their pay was reckoned up: one-hundred and twenty talents in all, besides the chief priest's, who had four pounds of gold a month: and a lot of clothing. 12-13. On his return, Varardach reported all this to the king; but Zaroës and Arfaxat made light of it, and proposed a test before the apostles came. The lawyers of the land were to be summoned to dispute with them. And first they made them unable to speak, then restored their speech but took away their power of motion, and then made them unable to see. The lawyers retired in confusion. 14. Varardach told the apostles, and they asked him to send for the lawyers, and proposed a second trial. If the lawyers would believe in their God, they would sign them with the cross and enable them to overcome the wizards. The lawyers were at first inclined to despise them for their mean appearance; but, convinced by Simon's words, they believed.

15. The apostles prayed over them, 'O God of Israel, who confounded the magic illusions of Jannes and Mambres and gave them over to confusion and sores and caused them to perish: let your hand be also on these magicians Zaroës and Arfaxat.' The contest took place and the magicians were powerless. One of the lawyers, Zebeus, explained to the king how they were the instruments of the evil angel, and defied them to do as they had done the day before. 16. They were enraged and called in a host of snakes. The apostles were hastily summoned, and made the snakes all turn on the magicians and bite them; they howled like wolves. 'Kill them outright', said the king; but the apostles refused, and instead made the serpents suck out all their venom, which hurt still more. 17. And for three days, in the hospital, the wizards continued screaming. When they were on the point of death, the apostles healed them, saying, 'Our God does not ask for forced service; if you will not believe, you may go free.' They wandered about Persia, slandering the apostles and telling the people to kill them when they came.

18. The apostles stayed in Babylon, healing the sick and ordaining clergy. A deacon, Euphrosinus, was accused of incontinence by the daughter of a satrap who had been seduced by another. The parents clamoured against the deacon. The apostles sent for the infant who had been born that day, and on their bidding it spoke and cleared Euphrosinus: but the apostles refused to question it about the guilty man.

19. Two fierce tigers had escaped from their cages and were devouring everybody they met. The apostles, appealed to, made the beasts follow them home, where they stayed three days. Then the apostles called the people together, and announced that they were going to leave them, to visit the rest of Persia. On the urgent prayer of the people they stayed fifteen months longer, baptized sixty thousand people, (20) ordained Abdias bishop and set out, accompanied by many disciples. For thirteen years they travelled, and Craton their disciple recorded their acts in ten books, which Africanus the historian translated into Latin, and from which we have here made extracts.

Zaroës and Arfaxat always went before the apostles and warned people against them, but were as regularly confuted.

At Suanir there were seventy priests, who received a pound of gold apiece from the king at each of the feasts of the sun (at the beginning of each of the four seasons). The magicians warned these men that two Hebrews were coming, who would deprive them of all their gains: they should be compelled to sacrifice immediately on their arrival.

21. After travelling through all the twelve provinces the apostles came to Suanir and lodged with a chief citizen, Sennes. The priests and mob flocked thither, crying out, 'Bring out the enemies of our gods.' So they were taken to the temple of the sun; and as they entered, the devils began to cry out that they were being burned. In the east, in the temple, was a four-horse chariot of the sun in silver, and on the other side a four-oxed chariot of the moon, also

silver. 22. The priests would now compel the apostles to sacrifice. Jude said to Simon, 'I see the Lord calling us.' Simon said, 'I see him also among the angels; moreover, an angel has said to me, "Go out hence and the temple shall fall", but I said, "No, for some here may be converted"' As they spoke (in Hebrew) an angel came and said, 'Choose either the death of all here or the palm of martyrdom.' They chose the palm. As the priests pressed on them they demanded silence. After a few words Simon commanded the devil to leave the chariot of the sun and break it, and Jude spoke likewise of the moon. Two hideous black men appeared and fled howling. The priests and people attacked the apostles and slew them. 23. This was on the first of July. Sennes suffered with them. Lightning struck the temple and split it into three pieces and burnt Zaroës and Arfaxat to coal. After three months Xerxes sent and confiscated the priests' goods and translated the bodies to his city, and built a marble basilica, octagonal, and eight times eighty feet in circumference and one hundred and twenty feet high, plated with gold inside, and the sarcophagus of silver in the middle. It took three years to build.

(c) *Matthew*

1. Matthew came to Naddaver in Ethiopia, where King Aeglippus reigned. There were two magicians, Zaroës and Arfaxat, who could make men immovable, blind, or deaf, as they pleased, and also charmed serpents, like the Marsi. 2. Matthew counteracted all these acts, sent the snakes to sleep, and cured their bites with the cross. A eunuch named Candacis, whom Philip had baptized, took the apostle in, and he did many cures. 3. Candacis asked him how he, a Hebrew, could speak other tongues. Matthew told him the stories of Babel and of Pentecost. 4. One came and announced that the magicians were coming with two crested dragons breathing fire and brimstone. Matthew crossed himself and rose to meet them. 'Speak from the window', said Candacis. 'You can be at the window; I will go out.' When the dragons approached, both fell asleep at Matthew's feet, and he challenged the magicians to rouse them. They could not. Then he adjured them to go quietly and hurt no man, and so they did. 5. The apostle then spoke, describing Paradise at length, and (6) the Fall. 7. It was now announced that Euphranor the king's son was dead. The magicians, who could not raise him, said he had been taken up among the gods, and an image and temple ought to be built. Candacis said, 'Keep these men till Matthew comes.' He came; the queen Euphenissa fell at his feet. He consoled her and raised Euphranor. 8. The people came to sacrifice to him as a god. He persuaded them to build a church; eleven thousand men did it in thirty days; it was called the Resurrection. Matthew presided there twenty-three years, ordained clergy, and founded churches; baptized the king, queen, prince, and princess Ephigenia, who vowed chastity. Zaroës and Arfaxat fled the country. It would

be long to tell of all Matthew's cures and miracles: I will proceed to his martyrdom. 9. Aeglippus was succeeded by his brother Hyrtacus, who wished to marry Ephigenia, now presiding over more than two hundred sacred virgins. He offered Matthew half his kingdom to persuade her. Matthew said, 'Assemble all the virgins tomorrow, and you shall hear what good things I will speak of marriage.' 10. His address on the divine institution and merits of matrimony. 11. Loudly applauded by Hyrtacus and his followers; he then pointed out that it would be sacrilege to marry Ephigenia. Hyrtacus went away in a rage. 12. But Matthew exhorted them not to fear man. 13. Ephigenia prayed for him to consecrate her and the other virgins. And he veiled them (with a long prayer). 14. And as he stood at the altar praying, a soldier sent by Hyrtacus pierced him in the back and he died. The people threatened to burn the palace, but the clergy restrained them. 15. Ephigenia gave all her wealth to the church. Hyrtacus sent the nobles' wives to her, then tried to send demons to carry her off, then surrounded her house with fire. But an angel, and Matthew, appeared and encouraged her. And a great wind rose and drove all the fire on the palace, and only Hyrtacus and his son escaped. The son was seized by a devil, and rushed to Matthew's tomb and confessed his father's crimes. Hyrtacus was attacked with elephantiasis, and stabbed himself. Beor, the brother of Ephigenia, a Christian, succeeded and reigned twenty-five years, dying at eighty-eight, and appointing successors in his lifetime, and he had peace with the Romans and Persians, and all Ethiopia was filled with churches, unto this day.

(d) Philip

1. He goes to Scythia twenty years after the Ascension. 2. Before a statue of Mars: a great dragon comes out from beneath the statue and kills the priest's son and two tribunes, and makes many ill with its venomous breath. Philip banishes the dragon and raises and heals the dead and sick. 3. He teaches them for a year; they break the image, and many thousands are baptized. After ordaining bishop and clergy he returns to Asia, to Hierapolis, where he extinguishes the malignant heresy of the Ebionites, who said that the Son of God was not born as a man, but took his humanity from the Virgin. 4. And he had two daughters who converted many. Seven days before his death he calls the clergy together, exhorts them, and dies, aged eighty-seven, and is buried at Hierapolis, and his two daughters after a few years are laid at his right and left. Many miracles are done there by his intercession.

7. ORIENTAL ACTS

There are many apocryphal Acts containing the preaching and martyrdoms of the apostles in Ethiopic, Arabic and Coptic. Many in Ethiopic may be read in

Malan, or in Wallis Budge, *Contendings*. Arabic texts may be seen in Smith Lewis, *Acta Myth./Myth. Acts*. The Arabic and Ethiopic collections are likely to derive from Coptic. Existing Coptic texts are very fragmentary, although some of the older martyrdoms have survived fairly complete in Coptic.[6] There are also some stories that are known only in Coptic. These include the Acts of Andrew and Paul (see under Acts of Andrew above).

8. THE EPISTLE OF PSEUDO-TITUS

Written in barbarous Latin this apocryphon is mainly a declamation about virginity. Such was M. R. James's judgement on the epistle. This text survives in an eighth-century manuscript in Würzburg. D. de Bruyne published the quotations from apocryphal Acts found in the epistle in 1908, but it was not until 1925 that the complete text was published.

The epistle may have originated in the fifth century in Spain and was used in the Priscillianist movement, which was rigorously ascetic.

The text is not translated or summarized here, but the relevant extracts possibly originating from the apocryphal Acts of Peter and of John and of Andrew are included above (ad loc.).

EDITIONS

D. de Bruyne, 'Epistula Titi Discipuli Pauli, de Dispositione Sanctimonii', *Rev. Bén.* 37 (1925), 47–72; cf. id., 'Nouveaux fragments des Actes de Pierre, de Paul, de Jean, d'André et de l'Apocalypse d'Élie', *Rev. Bén.* 25 (1908), 149–60. [Corrigenda in V. Bulhart, 'Nochmals Textkritisches', *Rev. Bén.* 62 (1952), 297–9.]

A. Hamman, 'Epistula in Titi de Dispositione Sanctimonii', in Migne, *PL* Suppl. 2.4, cols. 1522–42.

MODERN TRANSLATIONS

English

Hennecke[3], ii. 141–66.
Hennecke[5], ii. 53–74.

German

Hennecke[3], ii. 90–109 (A. de Santos Otero).
Hennecke[5], ii. 50–70 (A. de Santos Otero).

---

[6] See F. Morard, 'Notes sur le recueil copte des actes apocryphes des apôtres', *RThPh* 113 (1981), 403–13; and I. Guidi, 'Frammenti copti', in *AAL. R* (1887).

Italian

Erbetta, iii. 93–110.
Moraldi, ii. 1757–88 (cf. ii. 1211–12); ² iii. 115–46 (cf. ii. 290–1).

GENERAL

A. von Harnack, 'Der apokryphe Brief des Paulusschülers Titus "de dispositione sanctimonii"', *SPAW* 17 (1925), 180–213. [A major investigation into the text and contents.]

See also G. Sfameni Gasparro 'L'Epistula Titi discipuli Pauli de dispositione sanctimonii e la tradizione dell'enkrateia', *ANRW* 2.25.6, 4551–64. [This includes a full bibliography.]

III

APOCRYPHAL EPISTLES

Introduction

This form was not generally used: writers preferred narrative or an apocalypse as a vehicle for their material. Our apocryphal epistles are few and not impressive. In this category, however, comes the important Epistle of the Apostles, conventionally included among the epistles but more properly assigned to a different category, being a dialogue. The latest edition of the Hennecke collection assigns the Epistle of the Apostles and other texts to a chapter entitled 'Dialogues of The Redeemer'.

The texts included here are:

Shorter Epistles
 1. The Letters of Christ and Abgar.
 2. The Letter of Lentulus.
 3. The Epistle to the Laodiceans.
 4. The Correspondence of Paul and Seneca.
 5. The Epistle to the Alexandrians (description).

The Epistle of the Apostles (Epistula Apostolorum).

The Third Epistle to the Corinthians is included above, within the Acts of Paul. The so-called Epistle of Pseudo-Titus is dealt with in the section of Apocryphal Acts (and also see Acts of John, Acts of Peter, Acts of Andrew); although called a letter it is in fact a theological treatise in the style of a homily on the theme of celibacy.

Shorter Epistles

1. THE LETTERS OF CHRIST AND ABGAR

The basic sources for the legend of the conversion of Edessa to Christianity are the Doctrina Addai (as edited by Phillips) and a shorter version found in Eusebius, *HE* 1. 13 (cf. 2. 1. 6–8) (Schwartz, *GCS* 9.1 pp. 82–97 (letters in Greek with Rufinus' Latin translation, pp. 86–9)). The latter is the earliest Greek text; Eusebius claims that it was extracted by him from the archives of Edessa and translated from Syriac word for word.

According to Eusebius, Abgar, who was king of Edessa from 4 BC to AD 7 and again from AD 13 to 50, sent a letter to Jesus asking him to come and heal his malady. Jesus did not accede to this request, but in a letter said he would send a disciple to Edessa after his resurrection. After Jesus' death Thomas sent Thaddaeus (Addai in the Syriac tradition) to visit the king. Thaddaeus healed Abgar and converted Edessa to Christianity. According to the Pilgrimage of Etheria 17.1, 19.6 (ed. P. Geyer, *CSEL* 39 (Prague, Vienna, Leipzig, 1898), pp. 60, 62), a letter of Christ's was preserved and copied and miraculous powers ascribed to it. Other evidence exists, stating that the letter by Christ enjoyed wide circulation as an amulet affixed to doorposts and walls.

The Syriac Doctrina Addai represents a different form of the tradition from that found in Eusebius, but the precise history and interrelationship of the two traditions are disputed. Despite the verdict of Augustine (*c. Faust.* 28.4 (Zycha, p. 741)) and Jerome (*on Ezech.* 44. 29, ed. F. Glorie, *CCL* 75 (Turnhout, 1964), p. 669) that Jesus left nothing in writing, a judgement that probably influenced the Gelasian Decree in branding the letters as apocryphal, the correspondence and the Thaddaeus tradition were widespread, with versions in Syriac, Greek, Latin, Armenian, Arabic, Coptic, and Slavonic. The popularity of the tradition in the West was due to Rufinus' Latin translation of Eusebius' *History*.

In the Doctrina Addai is found the tradition that Ananias, who carries Abgar's letter to Jesus, paints a portrait of Jesus which he then gives to Abgar. There is no mention of Jesus' letter to Abgar in this version of the story.

The general consensus of scholarly opinion is that the original tradition developed towards the end of the second century.

The translation below is made from the Greek text of Eusebius.

EDITIONS[1]

Greek and Latin

Eusebius (see introduction above).
Fabricius, ii. 279–321.
Jones (²1798), ii. 1–4. [Cf. Lipsius–Bonnet, i. 279–83.]
L. Casson and L. E. Hettich. *Excavations at Nessana*, ii (Princeton, 1950), 143–7 (Greek text).
OP 65 (London, 1998) 122–9, plate xiv.

Coptic

A. M. Kropp, *Ausgewählte koptische Zaubertexte*, ii (Brussels, 1931), 72–89 (German trans.).
H. C. Youtie, 'A Gothenburg Papyrus and the Letter to Abgar', *HTR* 23 (1930), 299–302.
—— 'Gothenburg Papyrus 21 and the Coptic Version of the Letter to Abgar', *HTR* 24 (1931), 61–5.
[Both are reproduced with addenda and corrigenda in id., *Scriptiunculae*, i (1973), 455–9, 461–6.]
Yassa 'abd al-Masīḥ, 'An Unedited Bohairic Letter of Abgar', *Bulletin de l'institut français d'archéologie orientale* 45 (1946), 65–80, and 54 (1954), 13–43. [The second article covers texts, including the letters themselves, and allied stories in Coptic, Greek, Syriac and Arabic, with full bibliographies.]

Ethiopic

S. Grébaut, 'Les relations entre Abgar et Jésus', *Revue de l'Orient Chrétien* 3 (1918–19), 73–91, 190–203, 353–60.

Arabic

Graf, i. 237–8.

Slavonic

de Santos Otero, *Altslav. Apok.* i. 149–57.

MODERN TRANSLATIONS

English

Hone, 62–3.
James, 476–7 (letters).
Cowper, 217–20.

---

[1] For the *Doctrina Addai* see separate bibliography below (p. 541).

J. Quasten, *Patrology*, i (Utrecht, Brussels, 1950), 141–3 (text of letters in Eusebius).
Hennecke[3], i. 437–44.
Hennecke[5], i. 492–500.
Cartlidge and Dungan, 91–2.

French

Amiot, 46.
Migne, *Dictionnaire*, ii, cols. 19–26.

German

Hennecke[1], 76–9 (A. Stülcken); cf. *Handbuch*, 153–65.
Hennecke[3], i. 325–9 (W. Bauer).
Hennecke[5], i. 389–95 (H. J. W. Drijvers).
Michaelis, 452–61.

Italian

Erbetta, iii. 77–84.
Moraldi, ii. 1657–68; [2] iii. 17–26.

Spanish

González-Blanco, iii. 62–5.
de Santos Otero, 662–9 (with Greek text).

Irish

M. McNamara, *The Apocrypha in the Irish Church* (Dublin, 1975), 58–9. [Cf. P. Considine, 'Irish Versions of the Abgar Legend', *Celtica* 10 (1973), 237–57.]

GENERAL

For a fuller bibliography see de Santos Otero, 666–7.

R. A. Lipsius, *Die edessenische Abgarsage kritisch untersucht* (Brunswick, 1880).
L. J. Tixeront, *Les origines de l'église d'Édesse et la légende d'Abgar: Étude critique suivie de deux textes orientaux inédits* (Paris, 1888).
J. P. Martin, *Les origines de l'église d'Édesse et des églises syriennes* (Paris, 1889).
E. von Dobschütz, *Christusbilder* (Leipzig, 1899), 102–96, 158*–249*, 130**–156** (= *TU* 18 (3)).
—— 'Der Briefwechsel zwischen Abgar und Jesus', *ZWT* 43 (1900), 422–86.
E. Schwartz, 'Zur Abgarlegende', *ZNW* (1903), 61–6.
Bauer, 79–81.

DOCTRINA ADDAI (ACTS OF THADDAEUS)

EDITIONS

Syriac

W. Cureton, *Ancient Syriac Documents* (London, 1864), 5-23 (with Eng. trans.).
G. Phillips, *The Doctrine of Addai the Apostle Now First Edited in a Complete Form in the Original Syriac with an English Translation and Notes* (London, 1876; repr. G. Howard (ed.), *The Teaching of Addai* (Chico, 1981)).

Armenian

L. Alischan, *Laboubnia, Lettre d'Abgar ou Histoire de la conversion des Édesséens par Laboubnia, écrivain contemporain des apôtres* (Venice, 1868) (French trans.).
B. Outtier, 'Une forme enrichie de la Légende d'Abgar en arménien' in V. Calzolari Bouvier, J.-D. Kaestli and B. Outtier (eds.), *Apocryphes arméniens* (Lausanne, 1999), 129-45 (= *Publications de l'Institut romand des sciences bibliques* 1).

Greek

Lipsius-Bonnet, i. 273-8.
R. Peppermüller, 'Griechische Papyrusfragmente der Doctrina Addai', *VC* 25 (1971), 289-301.

MODERN TRANSLATIONS

French

Éac, 1473-525.
A. Desreumaux, *Histoire du roi Abgar et de Jésus* (Turnhout, 1993) (= *Apocryphes. Collection de poche de l'AELAC* 1).

Italian

Erbetta, ii. 575-8. Moraldi, ii. 1645-8;[2] ii. 719-22.

GENERAL

Lipsius, ii. 2, 142-200.
H. J. W. Drijvers, 'Addai und Mani, Christentum und Manichäismus im dritten Jahrhundert in Syrien', *Orientalia Christiana Analecta* 221 (1983), 171-85.

Copy of a letter written by Abgar the Toparch to Jesus and sent to him by the hand of Ananias the courier in Jerusalem

Abgar Ouchama, the Toparch, to Jesus, the good Saviour who has appeared in the area of Jerusalem, greeting. I have heard about you and your healings which you do without medicines and herbs. According to the report, you make the blind see, the lame walk; you cleanse those with leprosy, you exorcize unclean spirits and demons, you heal those tormented by chronic disease, and you raise the dead.

When I heard these things about you I decided you are one of two things: either you are God and you came down from Heaven to do these things, or you do them because you are a son of God. I, therefore, have written to beg you to take the trouble to come to me and to heal the suffering I have. I also heard that the Jews are spreading evil rumours about you and wish to hurt you. My city is small and holy, and there is room for both of us.

Copy of the things written by Jesus by the hand of Ananias the courier to Abgar the Toparch

You are blessed; you believe in me, and you have not seen me. It is written concerning me, 'Those who have seen me will not believe in me',[1] and 'Those who have not seen me will believe and will be saved.'[2] Regarding what you wrote to me that I should come to you, I have to complete here everything I was sent to do and, after I have accomplished it, to be taken up to him who sent me. After I have been taken up, I will send to you one of my disciples to heal your suffering and to provide life for you and those with you.

2. THE LETTER OF LENTULUS

This thirteenth-century text is given the form of a letter purporting to have been written by a Roman official, Lentulus, at the time of Tiberius Caesar. This detail is found in some (but not in the oldest) of the manuscripts. The original language is Latin, but a Syriac Letter of Lentulus was found in the Mingana collection (Syr. 47). Persian and Armenian translations also exist.

The text became famous because of its description of Christ's physical appearance, which probably had a direct influence on later iconography.

The translation below is from von Dobschütz's edition of the Latin with adaptations.

EDITIONS

Latin

E. von Dobschütz, *Christusbilder* (Leipzig, 1899), 308**–30**, esp. 318** f. (= *TU* 18 (3)).

Syriac

S. P. Brock, 'A Syriac Version of the Letters of Lentulus and Pilate', *Orientalia Christiana Periodica* 35 (1969), 45–62.

---

[1] Isa. 6: 10.
[2] John 9: 39.

MODERN TRANSLATIONS

English

Cowper, 221–2.
James, 477–8.

French

Migne, *Dictionnaire*, ii, cols. 453–6.

Italian

Erbetta, iii. 137–8.
Moraldi, ii. 1651–6; [2] iii. 11–16.

In these days there appeared, and there still is, a man of great power named Jesus Christ, who is called by the Gentiles the prophet of truth, whom his disciples call the Son of God, raising the dead and healing diseases—a man in stature middling tall, and comely, having a reverend countenance, which those who look upon may love and fear; having hair of the hue of an unripe hazel-nut and smooth almost down to his ears, but from the ears in curling locks somewhat darker and more shining, flowing over his shoulders; having a parting at the middle of the head according to the fashion of the Nazareans; a brow smooth and very calm, with a face without wrinkle or any blemish, which a moderate red colour makes beautiful; with the nose and mouth no fault at all can be found; having a full beard of the colour of his hair, not long, but a little forked at the chin; having an expression simple and mature, the eyes grey, flashing, and clear; in rebuke terrible, in admonition kind and lovable, cheerful yet keeping gravity; sometimes he has wept, but never laughed; in stature of body tall and straight, with hands and arms fair to look upon; in talk grave, reserved and modest, fairer than the children of men.

3. THE EPISTLE TO THE LAODICEANS

Paul in Col. 4: 16 probably refers to a letter he wrote to the Laodiceans. That letter did not survive. The cue for much writing now labelled 'New Testament Apocrypha' is to be found within the canonical New Testament. So it is in this case. The apocryphal letter to the Laodiceans has been written to create an epistle intended to be accepted as that referred to by Paul.

As a document it is a harmless theological forgery, being a cento of Pauline phrases taken mainly from Philippians and Galatians.[1] There is no obvious doctrinal motive behind its composition.

---

[1] e.g. Phil. 1: 2, 3, 12, 13, 18, 19–20, 21; 2: 2, 12, 13, 14; 3: 1; 4: 6, 8, 9, 22, 23; Gal. 1: 3, 11; 6: 18.

Although it has survived only in Latin (and in modern vernacular translations from the Latin) the language of the original is likely to have been Greek. The Latin reflects Greek idiom, and the Pauline language does not follow known Latin versions of the canonical epistles. Some early Greek Fathers (Theodore, Theodoret for example) seem to have known this work (or at least an epistle to the Laodiceans) although there are no extant examples of the text in Greek.

The epistle is found in several Latin manuscripts of the New Testament, including Fuldensis, Cavensis, and Ardmachanus, usually placed at the end of the New Testament, and although it was never included in the canon was favourably received by the Church in the West.

The date of composition is a vexed question because although a Letter to the Laodiceans is listed in the Muratorian Fragment (line 64) it is not certain that our apocryphon was meant. Tertullian, *adversus Marcionem*. 5. 11 and 5. 17 (ed. E. Kroymann, *CSEL* 47 (Vienna, Leipzig, 1906), pp. 614, 632), suggested that Marcion named the canonical Ephesians as Laodiceans, and it may be that the Muratorian Fragment means the former, although that seems unlikely in so far as Ephesians is also included in the list; and as that canonical epistle does not qualify for the Marcionite character given to the epistle in the Fragment, possibly the Muratorian list knew of another forgery. The words of Col. 4: 16 would doubtless have offered a temptation to more than one forger. The suggestion, originally proposed by Harnack, that Marcion was responsible for the authorship of the letter now finds little favour. It is unlikely that either Marcion or one of his followers wrote it.

Much early patristic evidence about the letter is unclear, but the mention of it in Latin fathers of the fourth century means that the date of the composition is between the second and fourth centuries. Jerome denounced it (*de Vir. Ill.* 5 (Richardson, pp. 10–11)), but Gregory the Great favoured its canonicity, stating that the Church had restricted the number of Paul's letters to create the significant number of fourteen. Later writers were influenced by Gregory's judgement that Paul had actually written fifteen letters.

The translation below is from Harnack's edition of the Latin (*Kleine Texte* 12).

EDITIONS

Latin

Biblia Sacra Vulgata, ed. R. Weber *et al.* (Stuttgart, ³1983), Appendix, p. 1976.
R. Anger, *Über den Laodicinerbrief: eine biblische-kritische Untersuchung* (Leipzig, 1843), 155–65 (= *Beiträge zur historisch-kritischen Einleitung in das Alte und Neue Testament*).
J. B. Lightfoot, *Saint Paul's Epistles to the Colossians and to Philemon* (London and New York, ³1879), 272–99 (with Greek retroversion).

A. von Harnack, *Apocrypha*, iv. *Die apokryphen Briefe des Paulus an die Laodicener und Korinther* (Bonn 1905, ²1912; Berlin, ³1931), 2–6 (= *Kleine Texte* 12 ed. H. Lietzmann).
—— *Marcion, das Evangelium vom fremden Gott* (Leipzig, ²1924; repr. Darmstadt, 1985, 134*–49* (= *TU* 15 (= 45)) (Latin and Lightfoot's Greek retroversion).

See also:

Fabricius, ii. 873–9.
E. J. Goodspeed, 'The Madrid MS. of Laodiceans', *AJT* 8 (1904), 536–8.
—— 'A Toledo Manuscript of Laodiceans', *JBL* 23 (1904), 76–8.
R. Y. Ebied, 'A Triglot Volume of the Epistle to the Laodiceans, Psalm 151 and other Biblical Materials', *Biblica* 47 (1966), 343–54, esp. 348–51 (Hebrew text). [The manuscript contains Epistle in Hebrew, Greek[2], and Latin.]

Arabic (translated from Latin)

B. Carra de Vaux, 'L'Épitre aux Laodiceans en arabe', *Rev. Bib.* 5 (1896), 221–6 (with Arabic text).

Slavonic

de Santos Otero, *Altslav. Apok.* i. 147–8.

MODERN TRANSLATIONS

English

Hone², 94.
James, 478–9.
Hennecke³, ii. 128–32.
Hennecke⁵, ii. 42–6.

French

Vouaux, 315–26 (with Latin text).
Migne, *Dictionnaire*, i, cols. 1285–90.

German

Hennecke¹, 138–40 (R. Knopf); cf. *Handbuch*, 204.
Hennecke³, ii. 80–4 (W. Schneemelcher).
Hennecke⁵, ii. 41–4 (W. Schneemelcher).

---

[2] The Greek seems to be based on Elias Hutter's polyglot New Testament of 1599–1600.

Italian

Moraldi, ii. 1720–3, 1733–4, 1737–8; iii. 78–80, 90, 95–6.
Erbetta, iii. 63–7.

GENERAL

Zahn, *Kanon*, ii. 566–85 (with Latin text, 586–7).
E. Jacquier, *Le Nouveau Testament dans l'Église chrétienne*, i (Paris, 1911), 345–51.
K. Pink, 'Die Pseudo-Paulinischen Briefe, ii: (2) Der Laodizinerbrief,' *Biblica* 6 (1925), 179–92.

To the Laodiceans

1. Paul, an apostle not of men and not through man, but through Jesus Christ, to the brethren who are in Laodicea: 2. Grace to you and peace from God the Father and the Lord Jesus Christ.

3. I thank Christ in all my prayer that you continue in him and persevere in his works, in expectation of the promise at the day of judgement. 4. And may you not be deceived by the vain talk of some people who tell tales that they may lead you away from the truth of the gospel which is proclaimed by me. 5. And now may God grant that those who come from me for the furtherance of the truth of the gospel (...) may be able to serve and to do good works for the well-being of eternal life.

6. And now my bonds are manifest, which I suffer in Christ, on account of which I am glad and rejoice. 7. This to me leads to eternal salvation, which itself is brought about through your prayers and by the help of the Holy Spirit, whether it be through life or through death. 8. For my life is in Christ and to die is joy.

9. And his mercy will work in you, that you may have the same love and be of one mind. 10. Therefore, beloved, as you have heard in my presence, so hold fast and work in the fear of God, and eternal life will be yours. 11. For it is God who works in you. 12. And do without hesitation what you do. 13. And for the rest, beloved, rejoice in Christ and beware of those who are out for sordid gain. 14. May all your requests be manifest before God, and be steadfast in the mind of Christ. 15. And do what is pure, true, proper, just and lovely. 16. And what you have heard and received, hold in your heart, and peace will be with you.

17.[1] Salute all the brethren with the holy kiss. 18. The saints salute you. 19. The grace of the Lord Jesus Christ be with your spirit. 20. And see that (this epistle) is read to the Colossians[2] and that of the Colossians to you.

---

[1] V. 17 is absent in some manuscripts.
[2] Some MSS omit 'to the Colossians'.

4. THE CORRESPONDENCE OF PAUL AND SENECA

Fourteen letters, eight by Seneca (the first-century Roman moralist) and six by Paul, are translated below. Their style shows that they cannot be the work either of Seneca or of Paul. They are probably the same letters known (*a*) to Jerome (*de Vir. Ill.* 12 (Richardson, p. 15)) where it is said they are 'read by many' and (*b*) to Augustine (*ep.* 153. 14 ed., A. Goldbacher, *CSEL* 44 (Vienna, Leipzig, 1904)), pp. 461–2. Pseudo-Linus on the Passio Pauli i (Lipsius–Bonnet, i. 23 f.) knew of the letters in the seventh century.

Some scholars have suggested the present letters are late, written up on the basis of Jerome's testimony, and that the correspondence known to Jerome is lost. Such a view is not generally accepted. However, not all the letters may belong to the same period. The unity of the correspondence is open to question. Epistle 11 (Barlow's numeration) seems not to belong with the other letters, and is written in a different style of Latin. Epistle 14 has a more Christian and even Pauline ring to it. The language and style of 14 suggests a later composition than the other letters. Letter 13 is also likely to have been added later.

The motive for the writing was obviously to show the superiority of Christianity over pagan philosophy. Christian tradition believed that Seneca had been influenced by Paul and was indeed converted to Christianity. However, there is nothing in the authentic writings of Seneca that proves he had ever been influenced by Christian doctrines. There is likewise no evidence that these two contemporaries ever met. A fourth-century date for most of the correspondence is quite appropriate, as Liénard has demonstrated.

The history of the tradition from the time of Jerome is unclear. The surviving manuscripts (of which there are many) are very corrupt. The oldest is ninth century.

The translation below, based on Barlow's Latin, follows the sequence of Barlow in which Erasmus' order of epistles 11 and 12 is reversed.[1] Barlow's monograph covers the Latinity of the correspondence, the extant manuscripts, and the history of modern editions.

(For titles written between 1883 and 1938 see J. Haussleiter, 'Literatur zu der Frage "Seneca und das Christentum"', *Jahresberichte über die Fortschritte der klassischen Altertumswissenschaft* 281 (1943), 172–5.)

EDITIONS

C. W. Barlow, *Epistolae Senecae ad Paulum et Pauli ad Senecam 'quae vocantur'* (Rome 1938) (= *Papers and Monographs of the American Academy in Rome* 10) (with full

---

[1] L. Bocciolini Palagi, *Il carteggio apocrifo di Seneca e San Paolo* (Florence, 1978) suggests that the sequence should be . . . 10, 14, 11, 13, 12 . . .; Hennecke[5] raises the possibility of the order . . . 10, 12, 14, 13, 11 . . .

bibliography and with English translation). [Latin text printed in *PL*, Supplementum i, cols. 673-8.]
Fabricius, ii. 892-904.

MODERN TRANSLATIONS

English

Hone, 95-9.
Hennecke[3], ii. 133-41.
Hennecke[5], ii. 46-53.
James, 480-4.

French

Migne, *Dictionnaire*, ii, cols. 922-30, 1318-19.
Vouaux, 332-69 (with Latin text of MS M and full introduction).
Éac, 1581-94 (with text of Bocciolini Palagi).

German

Hennecke[3], ii. 84-9 (A. Kurfess).
Hennecke[5], ii. 44-50 (C. Römer).

Italian

Erbetta, iii. 85-92.
Moraldi, ii. 1730-2, 1735-6, 1749-55; [2] iii. 87-9, 92-3, 107-13.

GENERAL

E. Westerburg, *Der Ursprung der Sage, daß Seneca Christ gewesen sei: Eine kritische Untersuchung nebst einer Rezension des apokryphen Briefwechsels des Apostels Paulus mit Seneca* (Berlin, 1881).[2]

K. Pink, 'Die Pseudopaulinische Briefe, ii: (4) Der Briefwechsel zwischen Paulus und Seneca', *Biblica* 6 (1925), 193-200.

E. Liénard, 'Sur la correspondance apocryphe de Sénèque et de Saint-Paul', *Revue belge de philologie et d'histoire* 11 (1932), 5-23.

A. Kurfess, 'Zum apokryphen Briefwechsel zwischen Seneca und Paulus', *Theologie und Glaube* 29 (1937), 317-22.

—— 'Zum apokryphen Briefwechsel zwischen Seneca und Paulus', *ThQ* 119 (1938), 318-31.

Cf. also: Zahn, *Kanon*, ii. 612-21.
Harnack, i. 763-5; ii. 458-9.
Bauer, 90-3.

---

[2] Reviewed by A. von Harnack, *TLZ* 6 (1881), cols. 444-9.

Paul's relationship with Seneca

J. B. Lightfoot, *St. Paul's Epistle to the Philippians* (London, ⁴1878), 270–333, esp. 329–31.

J. N. Sevenster, *Paul and Seneca* (Leiden, 1961) (= *NovT* Supplements 4). [On the correspondence, see 11–14.]

1. Seneca to Paul greeting

I believe that you have been informed, Paul, of the discussion which my friend Lucilius and I held yesterday concerning the apocrypha and other matters: for some of the followers of your teachings were with me. We had retired to the gardens of Sallust, and it was our good fortune that these disciples whom I have mentioned saw us there and joined us, although they were on their way elsewhere. You may be sure that we wished that you, too, had been present, and I also want you to know this: when we had read your book, that is to say one of the many letters of admirable exhortation to an upright life which you have sent to some city or to the capital of a province, we were completely refreshed. These thoughts, I believe, were expressed not by you, but through you; though sometimes they were expressed both by you and through you; for they are so lofty and so brilliant with noble sentiments that in my opinion generations of men could hardly be enough to become established and perfected in them. I wish you good health, brother.

2. To Annaeus Seneca Paul greeting

I was extremely glad to receive your letter yesterday, and I could have answered it immediately if I had had with me the young man whom I intended to send to you. You know when and by whom and at what time and to whom a thing should be given or entrusted. Therefore I ask you not to think yourself neglected, while I pay attention to the qualities of the messenger. But you write somewhere that you are pleased with my letter, and I count myself fortunate in the approval of a man who is so great. For you, a critic, a philosopher, the teacher of so great a ruler, nay even of everyone, would not say this unless you speak the truth. I hope that you may long be in good health.

3. Seneca to Paul greeting

I have arranged some of my works and set them in order according to their proper divisions. I also intend to read them to Caesar. If only fate is kind enough to cause him to show renewed interest, perhaps you will be there also; if not, I will at some other time set a day on which we may examine this work together. I could not show him this writing without first conferring with you, if only it were possible to do so without risk, so that you may know that you are not being forgotten. Farewell, dearest Paul.

4. To Annaeus Seneca Paul greeting

Whenever I hear your letters, I think that you are present and I imagine nothing else than that you are continually with us. As soon, therefore, as you begin to come, we shall see each other face to face. I hope that you are in good health.

5. Seneca to Paul greeting

We are distressed at your exceedingly long retirement. What is the matter? What makes you stay away? If it is the displeasure of our empress because you have withdrawn from your old rite and creed and are a convert, then you will be given an opportunity of asking her to believe that you acted reasonably, not lightly. A kind farewell.

6. To Seneca and Lucilius Paul greeting

I may not speak with pen and ink concerning what you have written to me, for the one marks a thing down and defines it, while the other makes it all too clear—especially since I am certain that there are some among your number, with you and in your midst, who are able to understand me. We must show respect to everyone, the more so as they are apt to find cause for offence. If we are patient with them we shall overcome them in every way and on every side—that is, if only they are the kind of people who can be sorry for what they have done. A kind farewell.

7. Annaeus Seneca to Paul and Theophilus greeting

I admit that I enjoyed reading your letters to the Galatians, to the Corinthians, and to the Achaeans, and may our relations be like that religious awe which you manifest in these letters. For the holy spirit that is in you and high above you expresses with lofty speech thoughts worthy of reverence. Therefore since you have such excellent matters to propose I wish that refinement of language might not be lacking to the majesty of your theme. And in order that I may not keep anything secret from you, brother, and burden my conscience, I confess that Augustus was affected by your sentiments. When your treatise on the power that is in you was read to him, this was his reply: he was amazed that one whose education had not been normal could have such ideas. I answered him that the gods are accustomed to speak through the mouths of the innocent and not through those who pride themselves on their learning. When I gave him the example of Vatienus, a farmer to whom appeared in the territory of Reate two men who later were found to be Castor and Pollux, he seemed thoroughly enlightened. Farewell.

8. To Seneca Paul greeting

Even though I am not unaware that our Caesar is now fond of wonders, although he may sometimes lapse, still he allows himself not to be rebuked, but to be informed. I think that it was a very serious mistake on your part to wish to bring to his notice what is against his practice and training. Inasmuch as he worships the gods of the heathen, I do not see what you had in mind wishing him to know this, unless I am to think that you are doing this from your great love for me. I beg you not to do this in the future. You must also be careful not to offend our empress while showing affection for me. Her displeasure, to be sure, cannot harm us if it lasts, nor can we be helped if it never happens. As a queen she will not be insulted; as a woman she will be angry. A kind farewell.

9. Seneca to Paul greeting

I know that it was not so much for your own sake that you were disturbed when I wrote to you that I had read your letters to Caesar as by the nature of things, which withholds the minds of men from all upright pursuits and practices,—so that I am not astonished today, particularly because I have learned this well from many clear proofs. Therefore let us begin anew, and if in the past I have been negligent in any way, you will grant pardon. I have sent you a book on elegance of expression. Farewell, dearest Paul.

10. To Seneca Paul greeting

Whenever I write to you and place my name after yours, I commit a serious fault and one incompatible with my status. For I ought, as I have often claimed, to be all things to all men and to observe towards you what the

Roman law has granted for the honour of the senate—namely, to choose the last place when I have finished my letter, lest I desire to perform in an inadequate and disgraceful manner what is my own will. Farewell, most devoted of teachers. Written 27 June in the consulship of Nero III and Messala [= AD 58].

11. Seneca to Paul greeting

Greetings, my dearly beloved Paul. Do you think I am not saddened and grieved because you innocent people are repeatedly punished? Or because the whole populace believes you so implacable and so liable to guilt, thinking that every misfortune in the city is due to you? But let us endure it calmly and take advantage of whatever opportunity fortune allots to us, until invincible happiness gives us release from our troubles. Earlier ages endured the Macedonian, the son of Philip, the Cyruses, Darius, Dionysius; our own age endured Gaius Caesar; all of them were free to do whatever they pleased. The source of the frequent fires which the city of Rome suffers is plain. But if lowly people had been allowed to tell the reason, and if it were permitted to speak safely in these times of ill-fortune, everyone would now understand everything. Christians and Jews, charged with responsibility for the fire—alas!—are being put to death, as is usually the case. That ruffian, whoever he is, whose pleasure is murdering and whose refuge is lying, is destined for his time of reckoning, and just as the best is sacrificed as one life for many, so he shall be sacrificed for all and burned by fire. One hundred and thirty-two private houses and four thousand apartment-houses burned in six days; the seventh day gave respite. I hope that you are in good health, brother. Written 28 March in the consulship of Frugi and Bassus [= AD 64].

12. Seneca to Paul greeting

Greetings, my dearly beloved Paul. If such a great man as you and one who is beloved of God is to be, I do not say joined, but intimately associated in all respects with me and my name, then your Seneca will be wholly satisfied. Since, therefore, you are the peak and crest of all the most lofty mountains, do you not, then, wish me to rejoice if I am so close to you as to be considered a second self of yours? Therefore do not think that you are unworthy of having your name in first place in your letters, or else you may seem to be tempting me rather than praising me, especially since you know that you are a Roman citizen. For I wish that my position were yours, and that yours were as mine. Farewell, my dearly beloved Paul. Written 23 March in the consulship of Apronianus and Capito [= AD 59].

The Epistle to the Alexandrians 553

13. Seneca to Paul greeting

Many writings composed by you are throughout allegorical and enigmatic, and for that reason you must adorn that powerful gift of truth and talent which has been bestowed upon you not so much with embellishment of words as with a certain amount of refinement. And do not fear, as I remember I have frequently said, that many who affect such things spoil the thoughts and emasculate the force of their subject-matter. I do wish you would obey me and comply with the pure Latin style, giving a good appearance to your noble utterances, in order that the granting of this excellent gift may be worthily performed by you. A kind farewell. Written 6 July in the consulship of Lurco and Sabinus [= AD 58].

14. Paul to Seneca greeting

Things have been revealed to you in your reflections which the Godhead has granted to few. Therefore I am certain that I am sowing a rich seed in a fertile field, not a corruptible matter, but the abiding word of God, derived from him who is ever-increasing and ever-abiding. The determination which your good sense has attained must never fail—namely, to avoid the outward manifestations of the heathens and the Israelites. You must make yourself a new herald of Jesus Christ by displaying with the praises of rhetoric that blameless wisdom which you have almost achieved and which you will present to the temporal king and to the members of his household and to his trusted friends, whom you will find it difficult or nearly impossible to persuade, since many of them are not at all influenced by your presentations. Once the word of God has inspired the blessing of life within them it will create a new man, without corruption, an abiding being, hastening thence to God. Farewell, Seneca, most dear to us. Written 1 August in the consulship of Lurco and Sabinus [= AD 58].

5. THE EPISTLE TO THE ALEXANDRIANS

This is a now lost epistle, the existence of which is known only from a reference in the Muratorian Fragment (line 64) where it is rejected as Marcionite.

James (*ANT* 479-80) includes a liturgical epistle, which Zahn[1] had considered to be part of the lost epistle to the Alexandrians. It forms part of the

---

[1] *Kanon*, ii. 586-92 (Latin text). The text is also in French in Vouaux, 327-32. Italian trans.: Erbetta, iii. 69-70; Moraldi, ii. 1723, 1733-4, 173; [2] iii. 81, 90, 97.

seventh–eighth century Sacramentary and Lectionary of Bobbio (Paris Bib. Nat. Lat. 13246) and is headed 'Epistle of Paul the Apostle to the Colossians', but it is not from that letter or any other Pauline epistle. James judged it not to be an apocryphon at all. There are many other similar pieces scattered about in manuscripts called 'preachings' of Paul or the like, which are just centos of texts and precepts. James suggested an Irish provenance for such a text; M. McNamara, *The Apocrypha in the Irish Church* (Dublin, 1975, [2]1984) includes a mention of it (p. 104).

The Epistle of the Apostles (Epistula Apostolorum)

The original title has not been transmitted, but Guerrier's title, 'Le Testament de Notre Seigneur...', is unsatisfactory in so far as it may encourage identification of this document with the Testamentum Domini (the short early Christian treatise on matters of ecclesiastical order, which also contains a complete liturgy). Generally the work is known as the Epistula (or Epistola) Apostolorum.

Although the document is included here under 'Epistles', following M. R. James's example, it cannot really be described accurately as a letter. After only a few pages the work changes from the form of a letter to that of an apocalypse. It begins with the eleven disciples confessing Christ and a description of Jesus' miracles. There then follows an account of the resurrection. This leads on to a series of revelations of the risen Christ in reply to questionings from the disciples. Other such dialogues of the redeemer (to borrow the preferred description of this *Gattung* from Hennecke-Schneemelcher) are the Letter of James from Nag Hammadi (below, pp. 673–81), the two apocalypses of James, the Letter of Peter to Philip, and the Book of Thomas the Contender. To these we could perhaps add the Questions of Bartholomew (below, pp. 652–72).

In the Epistle of the Apostles the risen Jesus pronounces on the second coming, the resurrection of the body, the Last Judgement, the signs of the end of the world, the fate of the damned, the incarnation, the redemption, the *descensus ad inferos*, missionary activity of the apostles, Paul's mission, and Simon (Magus) and Cerinthus. The work ends with a description of the ascension.

Much of the teaching, especially on resurrection and incarnation, is deliberately anti-Gnostic, and this may explain the motive for the composition. Direct condemnation of Simon and Cerinthus as heretics is evident.

Interest in this epistle usually centres on the liturgical contents, especially the eucharist (called here the Pascha), teaching on which gives an insight into the quartodeciman controversy. Such teaching has a bearing on the date and provenance of the document. An early dating is also encouraged by the document's concern with the imminence of the Parousia.

Links between the Epistle and the Ascension of Isaiah (text in H. F. D. Sparks (ed.), *The Apocryphal Old Testament* (Oxford, 1984), 775–812 (R. H. Charles, rev. J. M. T. Barton)) may be seen in the account of Christ's descent, during which he is said in both documents to have taken on the form of the angel in each of the heavenly spheres he passes through in order to reach earth unrecognized. (Cf. Ep. Ap. 13 and Ascension of Isaiah 10. 7 ff.)

Although various scholarly authorities offer differing dates for the composition of the work, the consensus of opinion puts it in the third quarter of the second century. There is less consensus on its provenance, Asia Minor and Egypt being the two places most frequently favoured.

The document, surprisingly, seems not to be referred to in any of the ancient Christian writings, which possibly suggests a limited circulation chronologically and geographically. Its existence in recent times was known only towards the end of the last century when Schmidt discovered a Coptic version in 1895 in Cairo. This dates from the fourth–fifth century. A more complete version of the same text is found in Ethiopic. A small Latin fragment survives. Greek is likely to have been the original language. The author seems to have had access to the canonical Gospels, the Apocalypse of Peter, the Epistle of Barnabas, and the Shepherd of Hermas.

Schmidt's text was created from all three surviving versions. The translation below is taken with permission from the English version, originally by R. E. Taylor, in Hennecke[5], i. 249–84 (slightly modified). James's English translation needs treating with caution because he conflated the Coptic and Ethiopic.

EDITIONS

Coptic

C. Schmidt, *Gespräche Jesu mit seinen Jüngern nach der Auferstehung* (Leipzig, 1919, repr. Hildesheim, 1967) (= *TU* 43 (= III 13)) (includes Ethiopic text trans. I. Wainberg).[1]

Ethiopic

L. Guerrier and S. Grébaut, *Le Testament en Galilée de Notre-Seigneur Jésus-Christ* (Paris, 1913; Turnhout, [2]1982), 141–236 (= *PO* 9.3) (with French translation). [Cf. the earlier announcement by L. Guerrier, 'Un "Testament de Notre-Seigneur et Sauveur Jésus-Christ" en Galilée', *Revue de l'Orient Chrétien* 12 (1907), 1–8, concerning which James altered readers of *JTS* 12 (1911) to the Ethiopic being a version of the Epistola Apostolorum.]

Latin

J. Bick, '*Wiener Palimpseste, I. Teil. Codex Palat. Vindobodensis 16 olim Bobbiensis*', *VII Abhandlungen der Sitzungsberichte der K. Akademie der Wissenschaften in Wien: Phil.-hist. Klasse* 159 (1908), 97–9 and plate IV. [Cf. E. Hauler, 'Zu den neuen lateinischen Bruchstücken der Thomas-Apokalypse und eines apostolischen Sendschreibens in Codex Vindob. Nr 16', *Wiener Studien* 30 (1908), 308–40.]

---

[1] Reviewed by H. Duensing, *Göttingische Gelehrte Anzeigen* 184 (1922), 241–52, and G. Bardy, *Rev. Bib.* 30 (1921), 110–34.

Slavonic

de Santos Otero, *Altslav. Apok.* 210–11 (references only).

MODERN TRANSLATIONS

English

James, 485–503.
Hennecke[3], i. 189–227. Hennecke[5], i. 252–84.

German

H. Duensing, *Epistula Apostolorum* (Bonn, 1925) (= *Kleine Texte* 152).
Hennecke[2], 146–50 (E. Hennecke).
Hennecke[3], i. 126–55 (H. Duensing).
Hennecke[5], i. 205–33 (C. Detlef G. Müller).
Michaelis, 440–6.

French

Amiot, 275–85 (selection based on Guerrier).
Éac, 359–92.
J. N. Pérès, *L'Épître des apôtres* (Turnhout, 1994) (= *Apocryphes. Collection de poche de l'AELAC* 5).

Italian

Erbetta, iii. 37–62.
Moraldi, ii. 1669–1702; [2] iii. 27–60.

GENERAL

M. R. James, 'The Epistula Apostolorum in a New Text', *JTS* 12 (1911), 55–6.
—— 'Epistola Apostolorum: a Possible Quotation', *JTS* 23 (1922), 56.
H. J. Cladder, 'Zur neuen "Epistola Apostolorum"', *ThR* 18 (1919), 452–3.
H. Lietzmann, 'Die Epistula Apostolorum', *ZNW* 20 (1921), 173–6.
K. Lake, 'The Epistola Apostolorum', *HTR* 14 (1921), 15–29.
F. J. Dolger, ΙΧΘΥΣ (Münster, 1922), ii. 552–5.
J. de Zwaan, 'Date and Origin of the Epistle of the Eleven Apostles', in H. G. Wood (ed.), *Amicitiae Corolla* (London, 1922), 344–55.
T. Schneider, 'Das prophetische "Agraphon" der Epistola Apostolorum', *ZNW* 24 (1925), 151–4.
Bauer, 87–8.
L. Gry, 'La date de la parousie d'après l'Epistula Apostolorum', *Rev. Bib.* 49 (1940), 86–97.
A. A. T. Ehrhardt, 'Judaeo-Christians in Egypt, the Epistula Apostolorum and the Gospel to the Hebrews', in F. L. Cross (ed.), *Studia Evangelica* iii (Berlin, 1964) part 2, 360–82 (= *TU* 88).

M. Hornschuh, *Studien zur Epistola Apostolorun* (Berlin, 1965) (= *Patristische Texte und Studien* 5) (with full bibliography).

—— 'Das Gleichnis von den zehn Jungfrauen in der Epistula Apostolorum', *Zeitschrift für Kirchengeschichte* 73 (1962), 1–8. [Cf. R. Bauckham, 'Synoptic Parousia Parables Again', *NTS* 29 (1983), 129–34.]

A. H. C. van Eijk, ' "Only That Can Rise which has Previously Fallen": The History of a Formula', *JTS* 22 (1971), 517–29.

I. Frank, 'Epistula Apostolorum', in id., *Der Sinn der Kanonbildung* (Freiburg, 1971), 110–11 (= *Freiburger Theologische Studien* 9),

J. Hills, 'Proverbs as Sayings of Jesus in the Epistula Apostolorum' in R. Cameron (ed.), *The Apocryphal Jesus and Christian Origins* (Decatur, Ga., 1990), 7–34 (= *Semeia* 49).

—— *Tradition and Composition in the Epistula Apostolorum* (Minneapolis, 1990) (= HDR 24).

Klauck, 198–207: ET 152–60.

The Epistle of the Apostles[1]

1. (*Chs. 1–6 in Eth. only.*) What Jesus Christ revealed to his disciples as a letter, and how Jesus Christ revealed the letter of the council of the apostles, the disciples of Jesus Christ, to the Catholics; which was written because of the false apostles Simon and Cerinthus, that no one should follow them—for in them is deceit with which they kill men—that you may be established and not waver, not be shaken and not turn away from the word of the Gospel[2] that you have heard. As we have heard (it),[3] kept (it), and have written (it) for the whole world, so we entrust (it) to you, our sons and daughters, in joy and in the name of God the Father, the ruler of the world, and in Jesus Christ. May Grace increase upon you.

2. (We,) John and Thomas and Peter and Andrew and James and Philip and Bartholomew and Matthew and Nathanael and Judas Zelotes and Cephas,[4] we have written (*or*, write) to the churches of the East and West, towards North and South, recounting and proclaiming to you concerning our Lord Jesus Christ, as we have written; and we have heard and felt him after he had risen from the dead;[5] and how he has revealed to us things great, astonishing, real.

3. We know this: our Lord and Saviour Jesus Christ (is) God and Son of God, who was sent from God, the ruler of the entire world, the maker and

---

[1] The translation rests on a careful revision of that prepared by Hugo Duensing. So far as they are not specially marked, words in brackets in the Ethiopic part are to facilitate understanding. In the Coptic part, restorations which are not quite certain have been placed in brackets. Where restorations of the lacunae are certain, they are not marked as such. Certain roughnesses in the original text have been retained in the translation.

[2] Acts 15: 7.

[3] Cf. 1 John 1: 1.

[4] On the list of apostles, cf. the *Apostolic Church Order*, where Peter and Cephas are regarded as different disciples.

[5] 1 John 1: 1; John 20: 27.

The Epistle of the Apostles

creator of what is named with every name,[6] who is over all authority (as) Lord of lords and King of kings,[7] the ruler of the rulers, the heavenly one who is over the Cherubim[8] and Seraphim and sits at the right hand of the throne of the Father,[9] who by his word commanded the heavens and built the earth and all that is in it and bounded the sea that it should not go beyond its boundaries,[10] and (caused) deeps and springs to bubble up and flow over the earth day and night; who established the sun, moon, and stars in heaven, who separated light from darkness;[11] who commanded hell, and in the twinkling of an eye summons the rain for the winter-time, and fog, frost, and hail, and the days in their time; who shakes and makes firm; who has created man according to his image and likeness;[12] who spoke in parables through the patriarchs and prophets and in truth through him whom the apostles declared and the disciples touched.[13] And God, the Lord (= the Father), and the Son of God, we believe: the word which became flesh[14] through the holy virgin Mary, was hidden in her birthpangs by the Holy Spirit, and was born not by the lust of the flesh but by the will of God,[15] and was wrapped (in swaddling clothes)[16] and made known at Bethlehem; and that he was reared and grew up as we saw.

4. This is what our Lord Jesus Christ did, who was delivered by Joseph and Mary his mother to where he might learn letters. And he who taught him said to him as he taught him, 'Say Alpha.' He answered and said to him, 'First you tell me what Beta is.'[17] And truly (it was) a real thing which was done.

5. Then there was a marriage in Cana of Galilee.[18] And he was invited with his mother and his brothers.[19] And he made water into wine and awakened the dead and made the lame to walk;[20] for him whose hand was withered, he stretched it out again,[21] and the woman who suffered twelve years from a haemorrhage touched the edge of his garment and was immediately whole; and while we reflected and wondered concerning the miracle he performed, he said to us, 'Who touched me?' And we said to him, 'O Lord, the crowd of people touched you.' And he answered and said to us,

---

[6] Eph. 1: 21.
[7] 1 Tim. 6: 15; Rev. 17: 14; 19: 16.
[8] Dan. 3: 54 LXX.
[9] Cf. Matt. 22: 24; 26: 64; Mark 16: 19; Acts 2: 33; Heb. 1: 3; 8: 1; 12: 2.
[10] Job 38: 10f.; 1 Clem. 20.6f.
[11] Gen. 1: 14; 1 Clem. 20.2f.
[12] Gen. 1: 26f.
[13] Cf. Hebr. 1: 1.
[14] John 1: 14.
[15] Cf. John 1: 13.
[16] Luke 2: 7.
[17] Infancy Gospel of Thomas 6. 3; 14. 2; Pseudo-Matt., Infancy Gospel 38. 1.
[18] John 2: 1 ff.
[19] Brothers: cf. John 2: 12.
[20] Luke 7: 14f.; 8: 49ff.; Mark 5: 35ff.; John 11: 39ff.; Mark 2: 3ff.; Matt. 9: 2ff.
[21] Matt. 12: 10ff.; Mark 3: 3ff.

'I noticed that a power went out from me.' Immediately that woman came before him, answered, and said to him, 'Lord, I touched you.' And he answered and said to her, 'Go, your faith has made you whole.'[22] Then he made the deaf to hear and the blind to see, and he exorcized those who were possessed,[23] and he cleansed the lepers.[24] And the demon Legion, that a man had, met with Jesus, cried and said, 'Before the day of our destruction has come you have come to turn us out.' But the Lord Jesus rebuked him and said to him, 'Go out of this man without doing anything to him.' And he went into the swine and drowned them in the sea, and they were choked.[25] Then he walked on the sea, and the winds blew, and he rebuked them, and the waves of the sea became calm.[26] And when we, his disciples, had no denarii, we said to him, 'Master, what should we do about the tax-collector?' And he answered and said to us, 'One of you cast the hook, the net, into the deep and draw out a fish, and he will find a denarius in it. Give that to the tax-collector for me and for you.'[27] Then when we had no bread except five loaves and two fish, he commanded the people to lie down, and their number amounted to 5000 besides children and women, whom we served with pieces of bread; and they were filled, and there was (some) left over, and we carried away twelve baskets full of pieces,[28] asking and saying, 'What meaning is there in these five loaves?' They are a picture of our faith concerning the great Christianity, and that is in the Father, the ruler of the entire world, and in Jesus Christ our Saviour, and in the Holy Spirit, the Paraclete, and in the holy Church and in the forgiveness of sins.

6. And these things our Lord and Saviour revealed and showed to us, and likewise we to you, that you, reflecting upon eternal life, may be associates in the grace of the Lord and in our service and in our glory. Be firm, without wavering, in the knowledge and investigation of our Lord Jesus Christ, and he will prove gracious and will save always in all never-ending eternity.

7. (*Here begins the Coptic.*) Cerinthus and Simon have come to go through the world. But they are enemies of our Lord Jesus Christ,

Ethiopic	Coptic
who in reality alienate those who believe in the true word and deed, namely Jesus Christ. Therefore take care and beware of them,[29] for in	for they pervert the words and the object, which is Jesus Christ. Now keep yourselves away from them,[29] for death is in them and a great stain

---

[22] Matt. 9: 20 ff.; Mark 5: 25 ff.; Luke 8: 43 ff.
[23] Matt. 11: 4 f.; 15: 30; Luke 7: 22; Matt. 9: 32 f.; Mark 7: 32 ff.; 8: 22 ff.; John 9: 1 ff.; Matt. 4: 24; 8: 16; Mark 1: 34.
[24] Matt. 8: 2 f.; Mark 1: 40 ff.; Luke 5: 12 ff.
[25] Mark 5: 1–20; Luke 8: 26–39.
[26] Matt. 14: 23 ff.; Mark 6: 47 ff. in connection with Mark 4: 35 ff. and parallels.
[27] Matt. 17: 24 ff.
[28] Matt. 14: 17 ff.; Mark 6: 38 ff.; John 6: 9 ff.
[29] Cf. Ignatius, *ad Trall.* 7. 1; *ad Smyrn.* 7. 2; *ad Trall.* 11. 1.

The Epistle of the Apostles

them is affliction and contamination and death, the end of which will be destruction and judgement.

of corruption—these to whom shall be judgement and the end and eternal perdition.

8. Because of that we have not hesitated

with the true testimony of our Lord and Saviour Jesus Christ, how he acted while we saw him, and how he constantly both explained and caused our thoughts within us.

to write to you concerning the testimony of our Saviour Christ, what he did when we were behind him watching and yet again in thoughts and deeds.

9. He of whom we are witnesses we know as the one crucified in the days of Pontius Pilate and of the prince Archelaus, who was crucified between two thieves;[30] and was taken down from the wood of the cross together with them; and he was buried in a place which is called the place of the skull,[31] to which three women came, Sarah, Martha and Mary Magdalene. They carried ointment to pour out

He concerning whom we bear witness that this is the Lord who was crucified by Pontius Pilate and Archelaus between the two thieves[30]

and who was buried in a place called the place of the skull.[31] There went to that place three women: Mary, the daughter of Martha and Mary Magdalene. They took ointment to pour

upon his body,[32] weeping and mourning[33] over what had happened.

And they approached the tomb and found the stone where it had been rolled away from the tomb,[35] and they opened the door

But when they had approached the tomb they looked inside[34]

and did not find his (*Coptic*: the) body.[36]

10. And (*Copt.*: But) as they were mourning and weeping, the Lord appeared to them and said to them, '(*Copt.*: For whom are you weeping? Now) do not weep;[37] I am he whom you seek.[38] But let one of you go to your brothers and say (*Eth.*: to them),[39] "Come, our (*Copt.*: the) Master has risen from the dead."'[40]

---

[30] Matt. 27: 38; Mark 15: 27; John 19: 18.
[31] Matt. 27: 33; Mark 15: 22; Luke 23: 33; John 19: 17.
[32] Mark 16: 1; Luke 24: 1.
[33] Mark 16: 10.
[34] John 20: 11; Gospel of Peter 55.
[35] Luke 24: 2; Mark 16: 4.
[36] Luke 24: 3.
[37] John 20: 14 f.; Mark 16: 6.
[38] Cf. John 20: 15 (18: 4).
[39] Matt. 28: 7.
[40] Matt. 28: 10; John 20: 17.

And Mary came to us and told us. And we said to her, 'What have we to do with you, O woman? He that is dead and buried, can he then live?' And we did not believe her,[41] that our Saviour had risen from the dead.	Martha came and told it to us. We said to her, 'What do you want with us, O woman? He who has died is buried, and could it be possible for him to live?' We did not believe her,[41] that the Saviour had risen from the dead.

Then she went back to our (*Copt.*: the) Lord and said to him, 'None of them believed me

concerning your resurrection'. And he said to her,	that you are alive.' He said,

Let another one of you go (*Copt.*: to them) saying this again to them.'

And Sarah came and gave us the same news, and we accused her of lying. And she returned to our Lord and spoke to him as Mary had.	Mary came and told us again, and we did not believe her. She returned to the Lord and she also told it to him.

11. Then (*Eth.*: And then) the Lord said to Mary and (*Copt.*: and also) to her sisters, 'Let us go to them.' And he came[42] and found us inside, veiled.

And we doubted and did not believe. He came before us like a ghost[43] and we did not believe that it was he. But it was he. And thus he said to us, 'Come, and	He called us out. But we thought it was a ghost,[43] and we did not believe it was the Lord. Then he said to us, 'Come,

do not be afraid.[44] I am your teacher (*Copt.*; ⟨master⟩) whom you, Peter, denied three times (*Eth.*: before the cock crowed);[45] and now do you deny again?'

And we went to him, thinking and doubting[46] whether it was he. And he said to us,	But we went to him, doubting[46] in our hearts whether it was possibly he. Then he said to us,

'Why do you (*Copt.*: still) doubt and (*Eth.*: why) do you not believe?[47] (*Eth.*: believe that) I am he who spoke to you concerning my flesh, my death, and my resurrection.

And that you may know that it is I, lay your hand, Peter, (and your finger) in the nail-print of my hands;	That you may know that it is I, put your finger, Peter, in the nail-prints of my hands; and you, Thomas, put

---

[41] Mark 16: 11 ff.; Luke 24: 11–41.
[42] John 20: 19, 26; Mark 16: 14.
[43] Cf. Luke 24: 37, 39.
[44] Matt. 28: 10.
[45] Matt. 26: 34, 69 ff. and parallels.
[46] Matt. 28: 17 (14: 31).
[47] John 20: 27; Mark 16: 14.

The Epistle of the Apostles

and you, Thomas, in my side;[48] and also you, Andrew, see whether my foot steps on the ground and leaves a footprint. "But a ghost, a demon, leaves no print on the ground."[49]

12. But now we felt him,[50] that he had truly risen in the flesh. And then we fell on our faces before him, asked him for pardon and entreated him because we had not believed him. Then our Lord and Saviour said to us, 'Stand up and I will reveal to you what is on earth, and what is above heaven, and your resurrection that is in the kingdom of heaven, concerning which my Father has sent me, that I may take up[52] you and those who believe in me.'

13. And what he revealed is this, as he said to us,[53] 'While I was coming from the Father of all, passing by the heavens, wherein I put on the wisdom of the Father and by his power clothed myself in his power, I was like the heavens. And passing by the angels and archangels in their form and as one of them, I passed by the orders, dominions, and princes, possessing the measure of the wisdom of the Father who sent me. And the archangels Michael

your finger in the spear-wounds of my side;[48] but you, Andrew, look at my feet and see if they do not touch the ground. For it is written in the prophet, "The foot of a ghost or a demon does not join to the ground."[49]

But we touched him[50] that we might truly know whether he had risen in the flesh, and we fell on our faces confessing our sin, that we had been unbelieving. Then the Lord our redeemer said, 'Rise up, and I will reveal to you what is above heaven and what is in heaven, and your rest that is in the kingdom of heaven.[51] For my Father has given me the power to take up[52] you and those who believe in me.'

But what he revealed is this that he said,[53] 'But it happened, as I was about to come down from the Father of all, I passed by the heavens; I put on the wisdom of the Father and the power of his might.

I was in the heavens, and I passed by the angels and archangels in their form, as if I were one of them among the dominions and powers. I passed through them, possessing the wisdom of him who sent me. But the chief leader of the angels is Michael,

---

[48] Cf. John 20: 20, 27.
[49] Cf. Commodian (probably 3rd-cent.). *Carmen apologeticum* 5. 564, ed. B. Dombart, *CSEL* 15 (Vienna, 1887), p. 152: 'Vestigium umbra non facit' (a shadow does not make a mark); cf. also Acts of John 93.
[50] Luke 24: 39; 1 John 1: 1; Ignatius, *ad Smyrn.* 3. 2.
[51] 2 Clem. 5.5; 6.7.
[52] John 12: 32.
[53] On the following cf. Ascension of Isaiah 10. 7 ff. (H. F. D. Sparks, *The Apocryphal Old Testament* (Oxford, 1984), pp. 775–812 (R. H. Charles, rev. J. M. T. Barton).

and Gabriel, Raphael and Uriel followed me (*Lat. adds*: secretly) until the fifth firmament of heaven, while I appeared as one of them. This kind of power was given me by the Father. Then I made the archangels to become distracted with the voice and go up to the altar[54] of the Father and serve the Father in their work until I should return to him. I did this thus in the likeness[55] of his wisdom. For I became all in all with them, that I, fulfilling the will of the mercy of the Father and the glory of him who sent me, might return to him.[57]

14. Do you know that the angel Gabriel came and brought the message to Mary?'[58] And we said to him, 'Yes, O Lord.' And he answered and said to us, 'Do you not remember that I previously said to you that I became like an angel to the angels?' And we said to him, 'Yes, O Lord.' And he said to us, 'At that time I appeared in the form of the archangel Gabriel to (the virgin: *not in all MSS*) Mary[59] and spoke with her, and her heart received (me); she believed and laughed;[60] and I, the Word, went into her and became flesh;[61] and I myself was servant[62] for myself; and in the like-

and Gabriel and Uriel and Raphael, but they followed me to the fifth firmament, thinking in their hearts that I was one of them. But the Father gave me power of this nature.

And in that day I adorned the archangels with a wondrous voice that they might go up to the altar[54] of the Father and serve and complete the service until I should go to him. Thus I did it through the wisdom of the likeness. For I became all things in everything that I might fulfil the plan[56] of the Father of glory who sent me, and might return to him.[57]

For you know that the angel Gabriel brought the message to Mary.'[58] We answered, 'Yes, O Lord.' Then he answered and said to us, 'Do you not then remember that a little while ago I told you: I became an angel among the angels. I became all things in everything?' We said to him, 'Yes, O Lord.' Then he answered and said to us, 'On that day, when I took the form of the angel Gabriel, I appeared to Mary[59] and spoke with her. Her heart received me and she believed; I formed myself and entered into her womb; I became flesh,[61] for I alone was servant[62] to myself with respect to Mary in an

---

[54] Rev. 8: 3 f.
[55] Gen. 1: 11, 26/27 is echoed here.
[56] Col. 1: 25; Eph. 1: 10.
[57] John 14: 12, 28.
[58] Luke 1: 26 ff.
[59] Cf. R. Reitzenstein, *Zwei religionsgeschichtliche Fragen*, 119 ff.
[60] Laughed: Sibylline Oracles 8. 466 ff. in J. H. Charlesworth (ed.), *The Old Testament Pseudepigrapha*, i (London 1983), 317–472 (J. J. Collins).
[61] John 1:14.
[62] Servant: *Pistis Sophia* 344. 24 and 403 s.v. (Schmidt-Till, *Koptisch-gnostische Schriften*, i. (Berlin, 1959) (= GCS 45 (13)) Eng. trans. G. Horner (London 1924), 61, 4 lines from bottom).

The Epistle of the Apostles

ness of an angel, like him will I do, and after it I will go to my Father.

15. And you therefore celebrate the remembrance of my death,[63] which is the Passover;

appearance of the form of an angel. So will I do, after I have gone to the Father.

And you remember my death.[63] If now the passover takes place,

then will one of you (*Eth.*: who stands beside me) be thrown into prison for my name's sake,[64] and he will

be very grieved and sorrowful, for while you celebrate the passover he who is in custody did not celebrate it with you. And I will send my power in the form of (my) angel, and the door of the prison will open, and he will come out and come to you to watch with you and to rest. And when you complete my Agape and my remembrance[65] at the crowing of the cock,[66] he will again be taken and thrown in prison for a testimony,[67] until he comes out to preach, as I have commanded you.' And we said to him, 'O Lord, have you then not completed the drinking of the passover?[68] Must we, then, do it again?' And he said to us, 'Yes, until I come from the Father with my wounds.'

be in sorrow and care that you celebrate the passover while he is in prison and far from you; for he will sorrow that he does not celebrate the passover with you. I will send my power in the form of the angel Gabriel, and the doors of the prison will be opened. He will go out and come to you; he will spend a night of the watch with you and stay with you until the cock crows.[66] But when you complete the remembrance[65] that is for me, and the Agape, he will again be thrown into prison for a testimony,[67] until he comes out from there and preaches what I have delivered to you.' And we said to him, 'O Lord, is it perhaps necessary again that we take the cup and drink?' He said to us, 'Yes, it is necessary until the day when I come with those who were killed for my sake.'[69]

16. And we said to him, 'O Lord, great is this that you say and reveal to us. In what kind of power and form are you about to come?' And

We said to him, 'O Lord, what you have revealed to us beforehand is great. In a power of what sort or in an appearance of what order will

---

[63] 1 Cor. 11: 26.
[64] Acts. 12: 3 ff.; Luke 21: 12; Rev. 2: 3; cf. John 15: 21.
[65] Luke 22: 19; 1 Cor. 11: 24 f.
[66] Mark 13: 35.
[67] Testimony: Mark 13: 9.
[68] Matt. 26: 27 f.; Mark 14: 23; 1 Cor. 11: 25.
[69] Rev. 6: 9; 20: 4; *Didache* 16: 7; Apocalypse of Elias 43: 10, ed. G. Steindorff (Berlin, 1899) (= TU 2.3a) 105.

he said to us, 'Truly I say to you, I will come as the sun which bursts forth; thus will I, shining seven times brighter than it in glory,[70] while I am carried on the wings of the clouds in splendour with my cross going on before me,[71] come to the earth to judge the living and the dead.'[72]

17. And we said to him, 'O Lord, how many years yet?' And he said to us, 'When the hundred and fiftieth year is completed, between pentecost and passover will the coming of my Father take place.' And we said to him, 'O Lord, now you said to us, "I will come", and then you said, "he who sent me will come."' And he said to us, 'I am wholly in the Father and the Father in me.'[73] Then we said to him, 'Will you really leave us until your coming? Where will we find a teacher?' And he answered and said to us, 'Do you not know that until now I am both here and there with him who sent me?' And we said to him, 'O Lord, is it possible that you should be both here and there?' And he said to us, 'I am wholly in the Father and the Father in me after his image and after his likeness[74] and after his power and after his perfection and after his light, and I am his perfect word.'[75]

18. This is, when he was crucified, had died and risen again,

you come?' But he answered, saying, 'Truly I say to you, I will come as does the sun that shines, and shining seven times brighter than it[70] in my brightness; with the wings of the clouds carrying me in splendour and the sign of the cross before me,[71] I will come down to the earth to judge the living and the dead.'[72]

But we said to him, 'O Lord, after how many years yet will this happen?' He said to us, 'When the hundredth part and the twentieth part is completed, between pentecost and the feast of unleavened bread, will the coming of the Father take place.' But we said to him, 'Here now, what have you said to us, "I will come", and how do you say, "It is he who sent me who will come"?' Then he said to us, 'I am wholly in my Father and my Father is in me[73]

with regard to the resemblance[74] of form and of power and of perfection and of light and (with regard to) the full measure and the voice. I am the word.[75]

'I have become to him a thing, which is this. I am the perfect

---

[70] Apocalypse of Peter 1.
[71] Apocalypse of Elias 87. 32 ed. Steindorff (n. 69 above); Apocalypse of Peter 1; cf. Gospel of Peter 10 (39).
[72] Acts 10: 42; 1 Pet. 4: 5; 2 Tim. 4: 1.
[73] John 10: 38; 14: 10, 11–20; 17: 21, 22, 23; Cf. Acts of John 100.
[74] Cf. Gen. 1: 11, 26/27.
[75] John 1: 1.

The Epistle of the Apostles

as he said this, and the work that was thus accomplished in the flesh, that he was crucified, and his ascension—this is the fulfilling of the number. 'And the wonders and his image and everything perfect you will see in me with respect to redemption which takes place through me, and while I go to the Father and into heaven.[77] But look, a new commandment I give you, that you love one another[78]	thought in the type. I came into being on the eighth day, which is the day of the Lord.[76] But the whole completion of the completion you will see through the redemption that has happened to me, and you will see me, while I go to heaven to my Father who is in heaven.[77] But look now, I give you a new commandment; love one another[78] and [*One leaf missing in the Coptic.*]

and obey each other and (that) continual peace reign among you. Love your enemies, and what you do not want done to you, that do to no one else.[79]

19. 'And both preach and teach this to those who believe in me, and preach concerning the (heavenly[80]) kingdom of my Father,[81] and as my Father has given me the power (*addition in Paris No. 199:* so I give it to you) that you may bring near the children of the heavenly Father. Preach, and they will believe. You (it is) whose duty is to lead his children into heaven.' And we said to him, 'O Lord, it is possible for you to do what you have told us; but how will we be able to do (it)?' And he said to us, 'Truly I say to you, preach and teach, as I will be with you.[82] For I am well pleased to be with you, that you may become joint heirs with me[83] of the kingdom of heaven of him who sent me. Truly I say to you, you will be my brothers and companions, for my Father has delighted in you and in those who will believe in me through you. Truly I say to you, such and so great a joy has my Father prepared (for you) that angels and powers desired and will desire to view and to see it, but they will not be allowed to see the greatness of my Father.'[84] And we said to him, 'O Lord, what kind (of thing) is this that you tell us?'

And he said to us, 'You will see a light brighter than light and more perfect than perfection. And the Son will be perfected through the	He said to us, 'You will see a light..., in that it is more exalted than that which shines... [*restored after the Ethiopic text*] the perfection

---

[76] Barn. 15. 8; Justin, *Dialogue with Trypho* 24, 41, 138; Clement of Alexandria, *Exc. ex Theod.* 63. 1; *Strom.* 7. 57. 5 and 5. 106. 2–4.
[77] Matt. 7: 21 *et passim*.
[78] John 13: 34.
[79] Matt. 5: 44; Luke 6: 27, 35; Tob. 4: 15; Acts 15: 20, 29 Cod. D; *Didache* 1: 2; *Apostolic Constitutions* 7.1.
[80] 'Heavenly' not in all MSS.
[81] Luke 9: 2.
[82] Matt. 28: 18 ff.
[83] Cf. Rom. 8: 17.
[84] Cf. 1 Pet. 1: 12.

Father, the light—for the Father is perfect—(the Son) whom death and resurrection make perfect, and the one accomplishment surpasses the other. And I am fully the right hand of the Father; I am in him who accomplishes.' And we twelve said to him, 'O Lord, in all things you have become to us salvation and life. Do you speak (*or*, while you speak) to us of such a hope?' And he said to us, 'Have confidence and be of good courage. Truly I say to you,[85] such a rest will be yours where there is no eating and drinking and no mourning and singing (*or* care) and neither earthly garment nor perishing. And you will not have part in the creation of below, but will belong to the incorruptibility of my Father, you who will not perish. As I am continually in the Father, so also you (are) in me.'[86] And we said again to him, 'In what form?[87] Of an angel or that of flesh?' And for this he answered and said to us, 'I have put on your flesh, in which I was born and died and was buried and rose again through my heavenly Father, that it might be fulfilled that was said by the prophet David[88] concerning my death and resurrection: "O Lord, how numerous have they become that oppress me; many have risen up against me. Many say to my soul, 'He has no salvation by his God.' But you, O Lord, are my refuge, my glory, and he who lifts up my head. With my voice I

that is perfected in... I am fully the right hand of the Father... me, which is the fullness.' But we said to him, 'O Lord, in all things you have become to us salvation and life. You have proclaimed to us these words of this kind.' He said to us, 'Have confidence and be of a peaceful heart. Truly I say to you,[85] your rest will be in heaven (?) in the place where there is neither eating nor drinking, neither rejoicing nor mourning nor perishing of those who are in it. You have no part in..., but you (*restored*) will receive of the incorruptibility of my Father. As I (*restored from first 'of'*) am in him, so you will rest yourselves (?) in me.'[86]

Again we said to him, 'In what form?[87] In the manner of angels, or in flesh?' [*restored after the Ethiopic text*] He answered and said to us, 'Look. I have put on (your) flesh, in which I was born and crucified and rose again through my Father who is (in heaven), that the prophecy of the prophet David might be fulfilled[88] concerning what he foretold about me and my death and my resurrection, saying, "O Lord, numerous have they become that strive with me, and many have risen up against me. Many say to my soul, 'There is no deliverance for you with God'.

---

[85] Synoptic introductory formula.
[86] Cf. John 14: 20; 15: 4f.
[87] Cf. Gen. 1: 11, 26/27.
[88] Cf. Luke 24: 44f.

cried to God, and he heard me from the mount of his sanctuary. I lay down and fell asleep; and I rose up, for God raised me up. I was not afraid of thousands of people who surrounded me and rose up against me. Arise, O Lord my God, and save me. For you have smitten (and trodden down: *only in Stuttgart Cod. Orient. fol. no. 49*) all who show me enmity without cause; and you have shattered the teeth of sinners. Deliverance is of God, and your blessing (be) upon your people."[89]

'All that was said by the prophets was thus performed and has taken place and is completed in me, for I spoke in (or, by) them;[90] how much more will what I myself have made known to you really happen, that he who sent me may be glorified[91] by you and by those who believe in me.'

But you, O Lord, are my protector; you are my glory and he who lifts up my head. With my voice I cried out to the Lord, and he heard me. I lay down and fell asleep; I rose up, for you, O Lord, are my protector. I will not be afraid of tens of thousands of people who set themselves against me round about. Rise up, O Lord; save me, my God. For you have cast down all who are my enemies without cause; the teeth of sinners you have broken. To the Lord is salvation and his delight in his people."[89]

'But if all the words that were spoken by the prophets are fulfilled in me—for I was in them[90]—how much more will what I say to you truly [what I say to you (*dittography*)] happen, that he who sent me may be glorified[91] by you and by those who believe in me.'

20. (*Copt.*: But) After he had said this to us, we said to him, 'O Lord, in all things you have shown yourself merciful to us and have saved us; you have revealed all (*Eth.*: all this) to us. Yet (*Eth.*: Yet one thing) might we ask you, if you permit us.' (*Eth.*: And) He answered and said to us, 'I know

that you are listening and long to listen; concerning what you wish, ask me. Look; ask me and keep in mind what you hear, and it will be agreeable with me to speak with you.

that you will endure and that your heart is pleased when you hear me. But ask me concerning what you wish, and I will speak well with you.

21. '(*Copt.*: For) Truly I say to you, as the (*Copt.*: my) Father awakened me from the dead, in the same manner you also will arise[92]

in the flesh, and he will cause you to rise up above the heavens to the place of which I have spoken to you from the beginning (*or*, already), which he who sent me has prepared

and be taken up above the heavens to the place of which I have spoken to you from the beginning (before), to the place which he who sent me has prepared for you. And thus will

---

[89] Ps. 3: 1–8.
[90] Cf. Hebr. 1: 1 and 1 Pet. 1: 10 f.
[91] Cf. John 13: 31 f.
[92] Cf. John 5: 21; 2 Clem. 9.5.

for you. And for this cause have I perfected all mercy: without being begotten I was born (*or*, begotten) of man, and without having flesh I put on flesh and grew up, that (I might regenerate) you who were begotten in the flesh, and

I complete all arrangements (for salvation): being unbegotten and (yet) begotten of man, being without flesh (and yet) I have worn flesh,[93] for on that account have I come, that you ... (*from here the Coptic is defective and fragmentary*)

in regeneration you obtain the resurrection in your flesh,[94] a garment that will not pass away, with all who hope and believe in him who sent me;[95] for my Father has found pleasure in you; and to whoever I will I give the hope of the kingdom.' Then we said to him, 'It is great, how you cause to hope, and how you speak.' He answered and said to us, 'Believe (*must mean*, Do you believe) that everything I say to you will happen.' And we answered him and said to him, 'Yes, O Lord.' And he said to us, 'Truly I say to you that I have received all power[96] from my Father that I may bring back those in darkness into light[97] and those in corruptibility into incorruptibility and those in error into righteousness and those in death into life, and that those in captivity may be loosed, as what is impossible on the part of men is possible on the part of the Father.[98] I am the hope of the hopeless, the helper of those who have no helper, the treasure of those in need, the physician of the sick, the resurrection of the dead.'[99]

22. After he had said this to us, we said to him, 'O Lord, is it really in store for the flesh to be judged (together) with the soul and spirit,[100] and will (one of these) (*Cop*.: really) rest in heaven and the other (*Copt*.: however) be punished eternally while it is (still) alive?'[101] And (*Copt*.: But) he said to us, 'How long do you still ask and inquire?'

23. And (*not in Copt*.) we said again to him, 'O Lord,

but it is necessary, since you have commanded us to preach, prophesy, and teach, that we, having heard accurately from you, may be good preachers and may teach them, that

there is a necessity upon us to inquire through you, for you command us to preach, that we ourselves may learn with certainty through you and be profitable preachers, and

---

[93] Ignatius, *ad Eph.* 7. 2.
[94] 2 Clem. 9.5.
[95] John 5: 24.
[96] Cf. Matt. 28: 18.
[97] 1 Pet. 2: 9; Cf. Odes of Solomon 21: 3 and 42. 16, ed. Michael Lattke (= *Orbis Biblicus et Orientalis* 25 (Freiburg and Göttingen (1979–80)); Sparks (n. 53 above), 683–73 (J. A. Emerton).
[98] Matt. 19: 26 and parallels.
[99] Acts of Paul and Thecla 37; Liturgy of Mark (in F. E. Brightman, *Liturgies Eastern and Western*, i (Oxford, 1896), p. 124, lines 2 ff.).
[100] Cf. 1 Thess. 5: 23.
[101] Cf. 2 Clem. 9.1.

The Epistle of the Apostles

they may believe in you. Therefore we question you.'

24. He answered and said to us, 'Truly I say to you, the flesh of every man will rise with his soul alive (*Paris No. 51 omits 'alive'*) and his spirit.'

(that) those who will be instructed by us may believe in you. Therefore we question you frequently.'

He answered us, saying, 'Truly I say to you, the resurrection of the flesh will happen while the soul and the spirit are in it.'

And we said to him, 'O Lord, then can what is departed and scattered become alive? Not as if we deny it do we ask; rather we believe that what you say has happened and will happen.' And he said to us, being angry, 'You of little faith,[102] how long yet do you ask me? And inquire (only) without anguish after what you wish to hear.

is it then possible that what is dissolved and destroyed should be whole? Not as unbelieving do we ask you—nor is it impossible for you—rather we really believe that what you say will happen.' And he was angry with us, saying to us, 'O you of little faith,[103] until what day do you ask? But what you wish, say to me, and I will tell it to you without grudging. Only

Keep my commandments,[104] and do what I tell you,

without delay and without reserve and without respect of persons;[105] serve in the strait, direct, and narrow way.[106] And thereby will the Father in every respect rejoice concerning you.'

and do not turn away your face from anyone, that I also may not turn my face away from you; rather without delay and without reserve...(and) without respect of persons[105] serve in the way that is direct and strait and oppressed (narrow).[106] So it is also with my Father. He will rejoice concerning you.'

25. And we said again to him, 'O Lord, look; we are mocking you with so many questions.' And he said to us,

Again we said to him, 'O Lord, already we are ashamed that we repeatedly question and trouble you.' Then he answered and said to us,

'I know that in faith and with (*Copt.*: from) your whole heart you question me. Therefore (*Eth.*: And) I am glad because of you. (*Copt.*: For) Truly I say to you

---

[102] Cf. Matt. 6: 30; 8: 26; 14: 31; 16:8.
[103] Ibid.
[104] John 14: 15; 21; 15: 10.
[105] Cf. Rom. 2: 11; Eph. 6: 9; Col. 3: 25; Jas. 2: 1; Luke 20: 21.
[106] Matt. 7: 14; Luke 13: 24.

572   *Apocryphal Epistles*

I am pleased, and my Father in me[107] rejoices, that you thus inquire and ask. Your boldness makes me rejoice, and it affords yourselves life.' And when he had said this to us, we were glad, for he had spoken to us in gentleness. And we said again to him, 'Our Lord, in all things you have shown yourself gracious toward us and grant us life; for all we have asked you you have told us.' Then he said to us, 'Does the flesh or the spirit fall away?' And we said to him, 'The flesh'. And he said to us, 'Now what has fallen will arise, and what is ill will be sound, that my Father may be praised therein; as he has done to me, so I (will do) to you and to all who believe in me.

I am glad, and my Father who is in me,[107] that you question me. For your boldness affords me rejoicing and gives yourselves (life).' But when he had said this to us we were glad that we asked him. And we said to him, 'O Lord, in all things you make us alive and pity us. Only now will you make known to us what we will ask you?' Then he said to us, 'What is it then that passes away? Is it the flesh (or) the spirit?' We said to him, 'The flesh is perishable.' Then he said to us, 'What has fallen will arise, and what is lost will be found and what is weak will recover, that in what is thus done may be revealed the glory of my Father. As he has done to me, so will I do to all of you who believe.

26. '(*Copt*.: But) Truly I say to you, the flesh will rise alive with the soul, that

they may confess and be judged with the work

their accounting may take place on that day, concerning what

they have done, whether it is good or bad,[108] in order that

there may be a selection[109] and exhibition for those who have believed and have done the commandment of my Father who sent me. Then will the righteous judgement take place; for thus my Father wills, and he said to me, "My son, on the day of judgement[110] you will not fear the rich and not spare (*Paris Nos. 90 and 199:* pity) the poor; rather deliver each one to eternal punishment[111] according to his sins." But to those who have loved me and do love me

a selection[109] may take place of believers who have done the commandments of my Father who sent me. And thus will the judgement take place in severity. For my Father said to me, 'My son, on the day of judgement[110] you will neither fear the rich nor will you have pity on the poor; rather according to the sin of each one will you deliver him to eternal punishment.'[111] But to my beloved ones who have done the commandments of my Father who

---

[107] Cf. John 14: 10.
[108] Cf. 2 Cor. 5: 10.
[109] Cf. 1 Thess. 1: 4; 2 Pet. 1: 10.
[110] Matt. 10: 15; 11: 22, 24; 2 Pet. 2: 9; 3: 7; 1 John 4: 17; Jude 6.
[111] Cf. Matt. 25: 46.

and who have done my commandment I will grant rest in life in the kingdom of my heavenly Father.[112] Look, see what kind of power he has granted me, and he has given me, that...what I want and as I have wanted...and in whom I have awakened hope.[113]

27. And on that account I have descended and have spoken with Abraham and Isaac and Jacob, to your fathers the prophets, and have brought to them news[115] that they may come from the rest which is below into heaven, and have given them the right hand of the baptism of life and forgiveness[116] and pardon for all wickedness as to you, so from now on also to those who believe in me. But whoever believes in me and does not do my commandment[117] receives, although he believes in my name, no benefit from it. He has run a course in vain.[118] His end is determined for ruin and for punishment of great pain, for he has sinned against my commandment.

28. But to you I have given that you should be children of the light in God and should be pure from all wickedness and from all power of the judgement (*probably should be*: rulers, *or* archons); and to those who believe in me through you I will do the same, and as I have said and promised to you, that he should go

sent me I will grant rest of life in the kingdom of my Father who is in heaven,[112] and they will see what he has granted me; and he has given me power that I may do what I wish, and that I may give to...and to those whom I have determined to give and to grant.[113]

On that account I have descended to the place of Lazarus,[114] and have preached to the righteous and to the prophets,[115] that they may come forth from the rest which is below and go up to what is (above)...(; in that I stretch out) my right hand over them...of life and forgiveness and deliverance from all evil, as I have done to you and to those who believe in me. But if someone believes in me and does not do my commandments,[117] although he has acknowledged my name he receives no benefit from it. He has run a futile course.[118] For such will be in error and in (ruin), since they have disregarded my commandments.

(But so much more) you, the children of life, I have redeemed from all evil and from (the power of) the archons,[119] and all who through you will believe in me. For what I have promised you I will also give to them, that they may come out of the prison and the chains of the archons and the powerful fire.'[120]

---

[112] Cf. 2 Clem. 5. 5; 6. 7.
[113] In this sentence the text has fallen into disorder. Something has evidently dropped out.
[114] Cf. Luke 16: 23.
[115] Cf. 1 Pet. 3: 19.
[116] Cf. Barnabas 11. 1.
[117] Cf. 1 John 2: 4.
[118] Cf. Gal. 2: 2; Phil. 2: 16.
[119] Archons: cf. 1 Cor. 2: 6, 8.

out of prison and should be rescued from the chains and the spears (*probably should be*: archons) and the terrible fire.'[120] And we said to him, 'O Lord, in every respect you have made us rejoice and have given us rest; for in faithfulness and truthfulness you have preached to our fathers and to the prophets, and even so to us and to every man.' And he said to us, 'Truly I say to you, you and all who believe and also they who yet will believe in him who sent me[121] I will cause to rise up into heaven, to the place which the Father has prepared for the elect[122] and most elect, (the Father) who will give the rest[123] that he has promised, and eternal life.[124]

29. But those who have sinned against my commandment, who teach something else, subtract from and add to and work for their own glory, alienating those who rightly believe in me (I will deliver them to ruin: *only Stuttgart Cod. Orient. fol. No. 49*).'[125] And we said to him, 'O Lord, will there exist another teaching and grievance (?)?' And he said to us, 'As those who fulfil what is good and beautiful, so (also) the wicked shall be manifest.[126] And then a righteous judgement will take place according to their work, how they have acted;[127] and they will be delivered to ruin.' And we said to

We answered and said to him, 'O Lord, you have given rest of (life to us?) and have given... in wonders (for the strengthening?) of faith; will you now yourself preach this (to us)? You have preached to the (fathers) and to the prophets.' Then he said to us, 'Truly I say to you, all who have believed in me and who will believe in him who sent me[121] I will (lead) up to heaven, to the place which my Father has (prepared) for the elect,[122] and I will give you the chosen kingdom in rest,[123] and eternal life.[124]

But those who have transgressed (my) commandments and have taught another teaching, (in that they dissolve) the written (teaching) and add... their own, teaching with other words (those who believe) in me rightly, if they are brought to ruin by such things (they will receive) eternal punishment.' But we said to him, 'O Lord, then will there exist teaching from others, besides what you have told us?' He said to us, 'It is necessary that they exist, that what is evil and what is good should be manifest.[126] And thus will the judgement to those who do these works be revealed, and according to

---

[120] Matt. 3: 10; Luke 3: 17 and often elsewhere.
[121] Cf. John 5: 24; 12: 44.
[122] Matt. 24: 22, 24, 31; Mark 13: 20.
[123] Cf. 2 Clem. 5. 5; 6. 7.
[124] John 10: 28; 17: 2.
[125] Matt. 25: 46.
[126] 1 Cor. 11: 19; 1 John 2: 19; Luke 17: 1.

him, 'Blessed are we, for we see and hear you as you speak to us, and our eyes have seen such mighty deeds that you have done.'[128] And he answered and said to us, 'But much more blessed will they be who do not see me and (yet) believe in me,[129] for they will be called children of the kingdom[130] and (will be) perfect in the perfect one;[131] to these I will become eternal life in the kingdom of my Father.'[132] And we said again to him, 'O Lord, how will it be possible to believe that you will leave us, as you said: "There is coming a time and an hour[133] when it is in store for you to go to your Father"?'[135]

30. He answered and said to us, 'Go and preach[136] to the twelve tribes of Israel[137] and to the gentiles and Israel and to the land of Israel towards East and West, North and South;[138] and many will believe in me, the son of God.'[139] And we said to him, 'O Lord, who will believe us and who will listen to us and how can we do and teach and tell the wonders and signs and mighty

their works[127] will they be judged and delivered to death.' We said again to him, 'O Lord, blessed are we, who see you and hear you as you (speak) such (words), for our eyes have seen these great wonders that you have done.'[128] He answered and said to us, 'Much more blessed are they who have not seen and (yet) have believed,[129] for such will be called children of the kingdom,[130] and they will be perfect (in) the perfect one[131] and I will be life (to them) in the kingdom of my Father.'[132] Again we said to him, 'O Lord, in what way will one be able to believe that you will go and leave us, as you said to us, "A day will come and an hour[134] when I shall go up to my Father"?'[135]

But he said to us, 'Go you and preach[136] to the twelve tribes[137] and preach also to the gentiles and to the whole land of Israel from sunrise to sunset and from South to North,[138] and many will believe in the son of God.'[139] But we said to him, 'O Lord, who will believe us or who will listen to us (while we do, teach and tell) the powers and the signs that you have done, and the

---

[127] Rom. 2: 6.
[128] Matt. 13: 16 f.
[129] Cf. John 20: 29.
[130] Cf. Matt. 13: 38.
[131] Cf. Matt. 5: 48.
[132] Matt. 26: 29.
[133] Cf. John 5: 25, 28; 16: 25, 32.
[134] Ibid.
[135] John 16: 10, 17, etc.
[136] Cf. Matt. 28: 19; Mark 16: 15.
[137] Matt. 19: 28; Luke 22: 30; Acts 26: 7; Jas. 1: 1; Rev. 21: 12.
[138] Luke 13: 29; Mark 16 (shorter ending).
[139] Cf. John 9: 35; 12: 37.

deeds,[140] as you have done?' And he answered and said to us, 'Go and preach (and teach: *addition in Paris No. 90*) concerning (the coming and: *addition in Paris No. 90*) the mercy of my Father. As my Father has done through me, I will also do through you in that I am with you, and I will give you my peace and my spirit[141] and my power, (that it may happen to you; *not in all MSS*) that they believe. Also to them will this power be given and transmitted that they may give it to the gentiles.

(wonders)?'[140] Then he answered and said to us, 'Go and preach the mercy of my Father; and what he has done through me will I myself do through you in that I am in you, and I will give you my peace, and from my spirit I will give you a power that you may prophesy to them to eternal life. But to the others will I myself also give my power, that they may teach the other nations.
(*In the Coptic there follows a gap of four pages*)

31. And look, you will meet a man whose name is Saul, which being interpreted means Paul.[142] He is a Jew,[143] circumcised according to the command of the law,[144] and he will hear my voice from heaven[145] with terror, fear, and trembling; and his eyes will be darkened[146] and by your hand be crossed with spittle. And do all to him as I have done to you. Deliver him to others![147] And this man—immediately his eyes will be opened,[148] and he will praise God, my heavenly Father. And he will become strong among the nations and will preach and teach, and many will be delighted when they hear and will be saved. Then will he be hated and delivered into the hand of his enemy, and he will testify before (mortal and perishable: *the bracketed adjectives are not uniformly in all MSS*) kings,[149] and upon him will come the completion of the testimony to me; because he had persecuted[150] and hated me, he will be converted to me and preach and teach, and he will be among my elect, a chosen vessel and a wall that does not fall.[151] The last of the last will become a preacher to the gentiles,[152] perfect in (*or*, through) the will of my Father. As you have learned from the scriptures that your fathers the prophets spoke

---

[140] Acts 2: 22; 2 Cor. 12: 12; 2 Thess 2: 9; Hebr. 2: 4.
[141] John 14: 27; 20: 21, 22; Acts 1: 8; 2: 17 f.
[142] Acts 13: 9.
[143] Acts 21: 39; 22: 3.
[144] Phil. 3: 5.
[145] Acts 9: 4; 22: 7; 26: 14.
[146] Acts 9: 8 f.; 22: 11.
[147] Here the thought is probably of the blinded Paul's journey to Damascus; Acts 9: 6, 8.
[148] Acts 9: 18.
[149] Acts 9: 15; 1 Clem 5. 7.
[150] Acts 9: 5; 22: 7 f.; 26: 14 f.; Gal. 1: 13; 1 Cor. 15: 9.
[151] Acts 9: 15. Cf. A. von Harnack, 'Der apokryphe Brief des Paulusschülers Titus "De dispositione sanctimonii"', *SPAW* 17 (1925), 198: 'vas electionis—inexpugnabilis murus'. Cf. Jer. 1: 18; 15: 20.
[152] Gal. 1: 16; 2: 8 f.; Acts 26: 17.

concerning me, and it is fulfilled in me'—this certain thing he said—'so you must become a leader to them. And every word which I have spoken to you and which you have written concerning me, that I am the word of the Father[153] and the Father is in me,[154] so you must become also to that man, as it befits you. Teach and remind (him) what has been said in the scriptures and fulfilled concerning me, and then he will be for the salvation of the gentiles.'[155]

32. And we said to him, 'O master, do we have together with them one hope of the inheritance?'[156] He answered and said to us, 'Are the fingers of the hand alike or the ears of corn in the field? Or do the fruit-bearing trees give the same fruit? Do they not bring forth fruit according to their nature?' And we said to him, 'O Lord, are you speaking again in parables to us?' And he said to us, 'Do not be grieved. Truly I say to you, you are my brothers, companions in the kingdom of heaven with my Father, for so has it pleased him. Truly I say to you, also to those whom you shall have taught and who have become believers in me will I give this hope.'

33. And we said again to him, 'When, Lord, will we meet that man, and when will you go to your Father and to our God and Lord?' And he answered and said to us, 'That man will set out from the land of Cilicia[157] to Damascus in Syria[158] to tear asunder the Church[159] which you must create. It is I who will speak (to him) through you, and he will come quickly. He will be (strong: *only Paris No. 199*) in this faith, that the word of the prophet may be fulfilled[160] where it says,[161] "Behold, out of the land of Syria I will begin to call a new Jerusalem, and I will subdue Zion and it will be captured; and the barren one who has no children will be fruitful[162] and will be called the daughter of my Father, but to me, my bride; for so has it pleased him who sent me." But that man will I turn aside, that he may not go there and complete his evil plan. And glory of my Father will come in through him. For after I have gone away and remain with my Father, I will speak with him from heaven,[163] and it will all happen as I have predicted to you concerning him.'

34. And we said again to him, 'O Lord, such meaningful things you have spoken and preached to us and have revealed to us great things never yet spoken, and in every respect you have comforted us and have shown yourself gracious to us. For after your resurrection you revealed all this to us that we

---

[153] 1 John 1: 1.
[154] John 10: 38; 14: 20.
[155] Acts 13: 47; 26: 18; 28: 28.
[156] Cf. Eph. 3: 6; Acts 26: 6.
[157] Acts 21: 39; 22: 3; 23: 34.
[158] Acts 9: 2; 22: 5; 26: 12 and often elsewhere.
[159] Gal. 1: 13, 23.
[160] John 12: 38 and often elsewhere.
[161] Source unknown. Cf. Rev. 3: 12; 21: 2–10; Heb. 12: 22; Gal. 4: 26 (probably very free).
[162] Cf. Gal. 4: 27; Isa. 54: 1.
[163] Acts 9: 4; 22: 6 f.; 26: 14.

might be really saved. But you told us only that signs and wonders would happen in heaven and upon earth before the end of the world comes.[164] Teach us, that we thus may recognize it.' And he said to us, 'I will teach you, and not only what will happen to you, but (also) to those whom you shall teach and who shall believe,[165] and there are such as will hear this man and will believe in me. In those years and in those days this will happen.' And we said to him again, 'O Lord, what is it then that will happen?' And he said to us, 'Then will the believers and also they who do not believe see a trumpet in heaven, and the sight of great stars that are visible while it is day, and a dragon (*only Paris No. 51 and Stuttgart Cod. Orient. fol. No. 49; British Museum Or. 793 and Paris No. 90*: stars and wonders; *Paris No. 199 has a scribal error*) reaching from heaven to earth, and stars that are like fire falling down[166] and great hailstones of severe fire,[167] and how sun and moon fight against each other, and constantly the frightening of thunder and lightning, thunderclaps and earthquakes,[168] how cities fall down and in their ruin men die,[169] constant drought from the failing of the rain, a great plague and an extensive and often quick death, so that those who die will lack a grave; and the going out (*or*, carrying out) of children and relatives will be on one bed (*or*, bier). And the relative will not turn toward his child, nor the child to his relative; and a man will not turn toward his neighbour. But those forsaken who were left behind will rise up and see those who forsook them, in that they did (not)[170] bring them out because (there was) plague. Everything is hatred and affliction and jealousy, and they will take from the one and give to another; and what comes after this will be worse than this. (Mourn those who have not listened to his commandment.)[171]

35. Then my Father will become angry because of the wickedness of men; for their offences are many and the horror of their impurity is much against them in the corruption of their life.' And we said to him, 'What, Lord, what (is allotted) to those who hope in you?' And he answered and said to us, 'How long are you still slow of heart?[172] Truly I say to you, as the prophet David has spoken concerning me and my people, so will it also be concerning those who shall believe in me. But there will be in the world deceivers and enemies (*Paris Nos. 90 and 199*: blasphemers) of righteousness,[173] and they will meet the prophecy of David who said, 'Their feet are quick to shed blood[174] and

---

[164] Cf. Matt. 24; Mark 13; Luke 21.
[165] Cf. John 17: 20.
[166] Cf. Rev. 6: 13; 8: 10; 9: 1.
[167] Cf. Rev. 8: 7; 11: 19; 16: 21.
[168] Cf. Rev. 8: 5; 11: 19; 16: 18.
[169] Rev. 11: 13; 16: 19.
[170] *Testament*, ed. Guerrier, *PO* 9.3, 40.
[171] Ibid.
[172] Cf. Luke 24: 25.
[173] Cf. Acts 13: 10.
[174] Ps. 13: 3 LXX.

their tongue weaves deceit[175] and the venom of serpents is under their lips.[174] And I see you as you wander with a thief and your share is with a fornicator.[176] While you sit there furthermore you slander your brother, and set a trap for the son of your mother.[177] What do you think? Should I be like you?[178] And now see how the prophet of God has spoken concerning everything, that all may be fulfilled that was said before.'

36. And we said to him again, 'O Lord, will the Gentiles then not say, "Where is their God?"'[179] He answered and said to us, 'Thus will the elect be revealed, in that they go out after they have been afflicted by such a distress.' And we said to him, 'Will their exit[180] from the world (take place) through a plague that has tormented them?' And he said to us, 'No, but if they suffer torment, such suffering will be a test for them, whether they have faith[181] and whether they keep in mind these words of mine and obey my commandment.[182] They will rise up, and their waiting will last (only a) few days, that he who sent me may be glorified, and I with him.[183] For he has sent me to you. I tell you this. But you tell (it) to Israel and to the gentiles, that they may hear; they also are to be saved and believe in me and escape the distress of the plague. And whoever has escaped the distress of death, such a one will be taken and kept in prison, under torture like that of a thief.' And we said to him, 'O Lord, will they be like unto the unbelievers, and will you likewise punish those who have escaped the plague?' And he said to us, 'Believing in my name they have done the work of sinners; they have acted like unbelievers.'[184] And we said again to him, 'O Lord, have they who have escaped this destiny no life?' He answered and said to us, 'Whoever has done the glorification of my Father, he is the dwelling-place of my Father.'[185]

37. And we said to him, 'O Lord, teach us what will happen after this.' And he said to us, 'In those years and days there shall be war upon war, and the four corners of the world will be shaken and will make war upon each other. And then a disturbance of the clouds (will cause?) darkness and drought[186] and persecution of those who believe in me, and of the elect. Then dissension, conflict, and evil of action against each other. Among them there are some who believe in my name and (yet) follow evil and teach vain teaching. And men will follow them and will submit themselves to their riches,

---

[175] Ps. 49: 19b LXX.
[176] Ps. 49: 18 LXX.
[177] Ps. 49: 20 LXX.
[178] Ps. 49: 21b LXX.
[179] Ps. 78: 10 LXX.
[180] Exit: cf. Wisd. 3: 2.
[181] Cf. Jas. 1: 3; 1 Pet. 1: 7.
[182] John 14: 15; 15: 10.
[183] Cf. John 13: 31 f.; 14: 13.
[184] Cf. 1 John 2: 4.
[185] Cf. John 14: 23.
[186] Cf. Luke 21: 10 f.

their depravity, their mania for drinking, and their gifts of bribery; and respect of persons will rule among them.

38. But those who desire to see the face of God and who do not regard the person of the sinful rich and who do not fear the men who lead them astray, but reprove them, they will be crowned in the presence of the Father, as also those who reprove their neighbours will be saved. This is a son of wisdom and of faith. But if he does not become a son of wisdom, then he will hate and persecute and not turn towards

his brother, and will despise (him) and cast him away.	his neighbour, will turn against him and ... him.

But those who walk in truth and in the knowledge of faith[187]

in me, and have the knowledge of wisdom and perseverance for righteousness' sake, in that men despise those who strive for poverty and they (nevertheless) endure—great is their reward. Those who are reviled, tormented, persecuted,[188] since they are destitute and men are arrogant against them and they hunger and thirst and because they have persevered—blessed will they be in heaven, and they will be there with me always.[189] Woe to those who hate and despise them! And their end is for destruction.'[190]	possessing love for me—for they have endured abuse—they will be proud, walking in poverty and tolerating those who hate them and revile them.[188] They have been tormented, being destitute, since men were arrogant against them while they walk in hunger and thirst; but because they have persevered for the blessedness of heaven, they also will be with me eternally.[189] But woe to those who walk in pride and boasting, for their end is destruction.'[190]
39. And we said to him, 'O Lord, will all this happen?' And he said to us, 'How will the judgement of righteousness take place for the sinners and the righteous?'[191] And we said to him, 'Will they not in that day say to you, "You caused to lead toward righteousness and sin and have separated (*British Museum Or. 793*: created) darkness and light, evil and good"?' And he said to us,	But we said to him, 'O Lord, what is yours is this, that you do not let us come upon them.' But he answered and said to us, 'How will the judgement come about? Either of the righteous or of the unrighteous?'[191] But we said to him, 'O Lord, in that day they will say to you, "You did not pursue righteousness and unrighteousness, light and darkness, evil and good,"' Then he said, 'I

[187] Cf. Acts 23: 1; Phil. 1: 27; 2 John 4; 3 John 4; 1 Tim. 2: 7.
[188] Luke 6: 22–7; John 15: 18; 1 John 3: 13; Matt. 5: 11.
[189] Cf. 1 Thess. 4: 17.
[190] Cf. Phil. 3: 19.
[191] Cf. Acts 24: 15.

'Adam was given the power that he might choose what he wanted from the two;[192] and he chose the light and stretched out his hand and took (it) and left the darkness and withdrew from it (*according to Duensing, perhaps should be*: put it away from himself). Likewise every man is given the ability to believe in the light;[193] this is the life[194] of the Father who sent me. And whoever has believed in me will live,[196] if he has done the work of light. But if he does not acknowledge (*Paris Nos. 51 and 199 without* 'not') that there is the light and does what is (characteristic) of darkness, then he has neither anything that he can say in defence nor will he be able to raise his face and look at the son, which (Son) I am. And I will say to him, "You have sought and found, have asked and received.[199] What do you blame us for? (*Other MSS*: Why do you not understand us?). Why did you withdraw (from me and) from my kingdom? You have acknowledged me and (yet) denied."[200] Now therefore see that each one is able to live as well as to die (*Other MSS*: to believe). And whoever does my commandment and keeps it[201] will be a son of the light,[202] that is, of will answer them saying, "Adam was given the power to choose one of the two.[192] He chose the light and put his hand upon it; but he forsook the darkness and cast it from him. So have all men the power to believe in the light[193] which is life[194] and which is the Father[195] who sent me." But everyone who believes (and) does the works of light will live in them.[196] But if there is someone who acknowledges that he is reckoned to the light, while he does the works of darkness[197]—such a one has no defence to make, nor will he be able to lift up his face to (look at the) son of God, which (Son) I am.[198] I will say to him, "As you sought you have found, and as you asked you have received.[199] In what do you condemn me, O man? Why did you leave me and deny me? Why did you acknowledge me and (yet) deny me?[200] Does not every man have the power to live or to die?" Now whoever has kept my commandments[201] will be a son of light,[202] that is of the Father who is in me.[203] But on account of those who pervert my words I have come down from heaven. I am the Logos; I became flesh,[204] labouring and teaching that those who are called

---

[192] Cf. Ecclus. 15: 16 ff.
[193] John 12: 36.
[194] Cf. John 1: 4.
[195] Cf. 1 John 1: 5.
[196] Cf. Gal. 3: 12; Rom. 10: 5.
[197] Cf. Rom. 13: 12; Eph. 5: 11.
[198] Cf. John 10: 36.
[199] Cf. Matt. 7: 7; Luke 11: 9 f.
[200] Cf. Tit. 1: 16.
[201] Cf. John 14: 15 and frequently.
[202] Luke 16: 8; John 12: 36; Eph. 5: 8; 1 Thess. 5: 5.
[203] John 10: 38; 14: 10, 11, 20; 17: 21, 22, 23; cf. Acts of John 100.

my Father. And for those who keep and do (it), for their sake I came down from heaven; I, the Word, became flesh[204] and died, teaching and guiding, that some shall be saved, but the others eternally ruined, being punished by fire in flesh and spirit.'

40. And we said to him, 'O Lord, we are truly troubled on their account.' And he said to us, 'You do well, for so are the righteous anxious about the sinners, and they pray and implore God and ask him.' And we said to him, 'O Lord, does no one entreat you?' And he said to us, 'Yes, I will hear the requests of the righteous concerning them.'[206] And we said to him, 'O Lord, all this you have taught us, and have stimulated us and have proved gracious toward us. And we will preach it to those to whom it is fitting. But will there be for us a reward with you?'[207]

41. And he said to us, 'Go and preach and be good ministers and servants.' And we said to him, 'O Lord, you are our father.'[209] And he said to us, 'Are all fathers and all servants, all teachers?' And we said to him, 'O Lord did you not say, "Do not call (anyone) on earth father and master, for one is your father and teacher, he who is in heaven"?[210] Now you say to us that we should like you become fathers to

will be saved,[205] and the lost will be lost eternally. They will be tormented alive and will be scourged in their flesh and in their soul.'

But we said to him, 'O Lord, truly we are anxious on their account.' But he said to us, 'You do well, for the righteous are anxious about the sinners, and pray for them, asking my Father.' Again we said to him, 'O Lord, now why is no one afraid of you?' But he said to us, 'Yes, I will hear the prayer of the righteous that they make for them.'[206] But when he had said this to us, we said to him, 'O Lord, in all things you have taught us [...] and pitied us and saved us, that we may preach to those who are worthy to be saved, and shall we earn a reward with you?'[207]

But he answered and said to us, 'Go, and preach; thus you will become workers[208] ... and servants.' But we said to him, 'You it is who will preach through us.' Then he answered us saying, 'Do not be all fathers nor all masters.' We said to him, 'O Lord, it is you who said, "Do not call (anyone) father upon earth, for one is your father who is in heaven[210] and your master." Why do you now say to us, "You will

---

[204] Cf. John 1: 14.
[205] Matt. 22: 8; Luke 14: 24; Rev. 17: 14.
[206] Cf. Jas. 5: 16.
[207] Cf. Matt. 5: 12 and frequently.
[208] Matt. 9: 37 and frequently.
[209] Cf. John 12: 26.
[210] Matt. 23: 8 f.

many children[211] and also teachers and servants.' And he answered and said to us. 'You have rightly said. Truly I say to you, all who have listened to you and have believed in me will receive the light of the seal that is in my hand, and through me you will become fathers and teachers.'

42. And we said to him, 'O Lord, how is it possible for these three to be in one?' And he answered and said to us, 'Truly, truly I say to you, you will be called fathers, for you, full of love and compassion, have revealed to them what (is) in heaven (... for) by my hand they will receive the baptism of life and forgiveness of sin.[212] And teachers, for you have delivered to them my word without anguish and have warned them and they have turned back in the things for which you rebuked them. And you were not afraid of their riches and did not respect the face (or, the person), but you kept the commandment of the Father and did it. And you have a reward with my heavenly Father;[213] and they shall have forgiveness of sins and eternal life and a share of the kingdom.' And we said to him, 'O Lord, if they had a ten-thousandfold mouth[214] they would not be able to give thanks to you as it is fitting.' And he answered and said to us, 'I say this to you that you may do as I have done to you;[215]

be fathers of many children[211] and servants and masters"?' But he answered and said to us, 'As you have said. For truly I say to you, whoever will hear you and believe in me, he will receive from you the light of the seal through (me) and baptism through me; you will become fathers and servants and also masters.'

But we said to him, 'O Lord, how now (is it possible) that each one of us should become these three?' But he said to us, 'Truly I say to you, you will first of all be called fathers, for you have revealed to them with seemly hearts and in love the things of the kingdom of heaven. And you will be called servants, for they will receive by my hand through you the baptism of life and the forgiveness of their sins.[212] And you will be called masters, for you have given them the word (*logos*) without grudging. You have warned them, and when you warned them they turned back. You were not afraid of their riches and of their face, but you kept the commandments of my Father and performed them. And you will have a great reward with my Father[213] who is in heaven, and they shall have forgiveness of sins and eternal life, and will have a part in the kingdom of heaven.' But we said to him, 'O Lord, even if each one of us had ten thousand tongues[214] to speak with, we would not be able to give thanks

---

[211] Cf. 1 Cor. 4: 15.
[212] Cf. Barn. 11. 1.
[213] Cf. Matt. 5: 12; Luke. 6: 23; Matt. 10: 41 f.
[214] Cf. Theoph. *ad Autol.* 2. 12 (ed. G. Bardy, *SC* 20 (Paris, 1948)).
[215] Cf. John 13: 15.

43. and be as the wise virgins who kindled the light and did not slumber and who went with their lamps to meet the lord, the bridegroom, and have gone in with him into the bridegroom's chamber. But the foolish ones who talked with them were not able to watch, but fell asleep.'[216] And we said to him, 'O Lord, who are the wise and who the foolish?' And he said to us, 'The wise are these five, who are called by the prophet daughters of God,[217] whose names let men hear.' But we were sad and troubled and wept for those who had been shut out. And he said to us, 'The five wise are these: Faith, Love, Joy, Peace, Hope. As soon as they who believe in me have these, they will be leaders[218] to those who believe in me and in him who sent me. I am the Lord and I am the bridegroom; they have received me and have gone with me into the house of the bridegroom, and laid themselves down (at table) with the bridegroom and rejoiced. But the five foolish slept, and when they awoke they came to the house of the bridegroom and knocked at the doors, for they had been shut; and they wept, because they were shut.'[219] And we said to him, 'O Lord, now these their wise sisters who (are) in the house—do they not open to them and are they not sorrowful on their account?' And he said to us, 'Yes they are sorrowful and concerned on

to you, for you promise us such things'. Then he answered saying, 'Only do what I say to you, as I myself have also done, and you will be like the wise virgins who watched and did not sleep, but (went) out to the lord into the bride-chamber. But the foolish were not able to watch, but fell asleep'.[216] But we said to him, 'O Lord, who are the wise and who are the foolish?' He said to us, 'Five wise and five foolish, these with respect to whom the prophet said, "They are children of God."'[217] Now hear their names.' But we wept and were sad about those who had fallen asleep. He said to us, 'The five wise are Faith and Love and Grace, Peace, and Hope. Among those who believe they who have these will be guides[218] to those who have believed in me and in him who sent me. I am the Lord and I am the bridegroom whom they have received, and they have gone into the house of the bridegroom and have laid themselves down with me in my bride-chamber (and rejoiced). But the five foolish slept, they awoke, came to the door of the bride-chamber and knocked, for it had been shut.[219] Then they wept and grieved that it was not opened for them.' But we said to him, 'O Lord, and their wise sisters who were within in the house of the bridegroom, did they remain in there without opening to them, and did they not grieve on their account or

---

[216] Matt. 25: 1 ff.
[217] Cf. Ps. 81: 6 LXX.
[218] Cf. Matt. 15: 14; 23: 24.
[219] Matt. 25: 10.

The Epistle of the Apostles

their account and entreat the bridegroom and yet are not able to obtain (anything) on their account.' And we said to him, 'O Lord, when will they go in for their sisters' sakes?' And he said to us, 'Whoever is shut out is shut out.' And we said to him, 'O Lord, is this thing definite? Who now are these foolish ones?' And he said to us, 'Listen: Insight, Knowledge, Obedience, Endurance, Mercy. These have slept in those who have believed and acknowledged me.

44. 'And since those who slept did not fulfil my commandment, they will be outside the kingdom and the fold of the shepherd;[220] and whoever remains outside the fold will the wolf eat.[221] And although he hears he will be judged (*only in Paris No. 199*) and will die, and much suffering and distress and endurance will come upon him; and although he is badly pained, and although he is cut into pieces and lacerated with long and painful punishment, yet he will not be able to die quickly.'

45. And we said to him, 'O Lord, you have revealed everything to us well.' And he said to us, 'Understand and apprehend these words.'[223] And we said to him, 'O Lord, these five it is through which they (*fem.*) have the expectation of going into your kingdom; and five who are shut out, through which they will be out-

did they not pray the bridegroom to open to them?' He answered saying, 'They were not yet able to find grace on their behalf.' We said to him, 'O Lord, on what day will they go in for their sisters' sakes?' Then he said to us, 'Whoever is shut out is shut out.' But we said to him, 'O Lord, (we have understood this word.) Now who are the foolish?' He said to us, 'Hear their names. They are Knowledge (Gnosis) and Wisdom, Obedience, Forbearance, and Mercy. These are they which slept in those who have believed and acknowledged me.

But my commandments were not fulfilled by those who slept. Consequently they will remain outside the kingdom and the fold of the shepherd and his sheep.[220] But whoever remains outside the fold of the sheep will the wolves eat,[221] and he will (be judged?), dying in much suffering. Rest (?) and perseverance will not be in him, and he will be (badly?) tormented that he . . . ; and he will be punished (?) in great punishment (?), and he will be under tortures.'[222]

But we said to him, 'O Lord, you have revealed everything to us well.' Then he answered saying to us, 'Do you not apprehend these words?' We said to him, 'Yes, O Lord; through the five will they come into your kingdom.

Yet they who watched and were with

---

[220] John 10: 1 f.
[221] Cf. Matt. 7: 15; 10: 16; John 10: 12; Acts 20: 29.
[222] Cf. Rev. 14: 10 f.
[223] Cf. Mark 8: 17.

side your kingdom. Yet they who have watched and who have gone in with the Lord, the bridegroom, will not rejoice because of those who slept'. And he said to us, 'They will rejoice that they have gone in with the Lord, and will be grieved on account of those who slept; for they are their sisters. And these daughters of God are ten.' And we said to him, 'O Lord, it suits your greatness that you show grace to their sisters.' And he said to us, 'This thing is not yours, but his who sent me, and I also agree with him.

46. 'But you, as you go, preach and teach truly and rightly, respecting and fearing the person of no one, but especially (not) that of the rich, of whom it will be found, that they do not do my commandment,[224] who revel in their riches.'[225] And we said to him, 'O Lord, do you speak to us only of the rich?' And he said to us, 'Also of him who is not rich; as soon as he gives and does not deny to him who has nothing, of such a one (I say this:) he will be called by men a doer.

47. 'But if someone should fall bearing his burden, that is, the sin he has committed against the person of his neighbour, then his neighbour should admonish him because of what he has done to his neighbour. And when his neighbour has admonished him and he has returned, then he will be saved,[226] and he who has admonished him will obtain

you, the Lord and bridegroom, will nevertheless not rejoice because of those who slept.' He said to us, 'They (will rejoice) that they have gone in with the bridegroom, the Lord; and they are troubled on account of those who slept, for they are their sisters. The ten are the daughters of God the Father.' We then said to him, 'O Lord, it is yours that you . . .' He said to us, '. . . , but his who sent me, and I agree with him.

But you preach and teach in uprightness (and) well, hesitating before no one and fearing no one, but especially (not) the rich, for they do not do my commandments,[224] but flourish in their riches.'[225] But we said to him, 'O Lord, if (it) is the rich (alone)?' He answered saying ('If) anyone who is not rich and possesses a (little) property gives to the needy (and to the poor), then men will call him a benefactor.

'But if someone should fall under the load because of the sins he has committed, (then let) his neighbour admonish him for (the good) that he has done to his neighbour. Now if his neighbour has admonished him and he returns he will be saved;[226] (and) he who admonished him will receive a reward and live for ever. For a needy man, if he sees someone

---

[224] Cf. Matt. 19: 23 f. and parallels; Luke 6: 24; 18: 24; 12: 15 f.; Jas. 1: 10 f.; 2: 1 f.; Hermas, *Sim.* 9. 20.
[225] Cf. Hermas, *Vis.* 1. 1. 8; 3. 9. 6.
[226] Cf. Jas. 5: 19 f.

eternal life. But if (he sees) how this one who renders him (something) sins, and encourages him, such a one will be judged in a great judgement. For a blind man who leads a blind man, both will fall into a ditch.[227] Even so the one who encourages, who respects the person, and also the one whom he encourages and whose person he respects, will both be punished with one punishment, as the prophet said, "Woe to those who encourage, who speak fair to the sinner for the sake of a bribe,[228] whose God is their belly."[229] You see how the judgement is? Truly I say to you, in that day I will not fear the rich and will have no pity for the poor.

sinning who has done him good, and does not admonish him, then he will be judged in an evil judgement. But a blind man who leads a blind man, both are wont to fall into a ditch.[227] And whoever regards the person for (their) sake, (he will be like) the two, as the prophet said, "Woe to those who regard the person and (justify the ungodly) for the sake of gifts,[228] whose (God is) their belly."[229] See now that a judgement (is appointed for them.) For truly I say to you, in that day I will neither fear the rich nor have sympathy with the poor.

48. 'If you have seen with your eyes how (someone) sins, then correct him, you alone (*or*, under four eyes). If he listens to you, then you have won him. But if he does not listen to you, then come out with one or at the most two others; correct your brother. But if he (even then) does not listen to you, so shall he be to you as a gentile and a tax-collector.[230]

'If you see a sinner, then admonish him between yourself and him. But if he does not listen to you, then take with you another up to three and instruct your brother. If he will not listen to you again, then set him before you as...'[230]
(*Here the Coptic text breaks off.*)

49. 'If you hear something, then do not give any belief against your brother and do not slander and do not love to listen to slander. For it is written, "Let your ear listen to nothing against your brother, but (only) if you have seen, censure, correct, and convert him."' And we said to him, 'Lord, you have taught and exhorted us in everything. But, Lord, among the believers who believe in the preaching of your name should there be dissension and dispute and envy and confusion and hatred and distress? For you have nevertheless said, "They will find fault with one another and have not regarded the person (*or*, without regarding the person)." Do these sin who hate the one who has

---

[227] Matt. 15: 14; Luke 6: 39.
[228] Cf. Isa. 5: 23.
[229] Phil. 3: 19.
[230] Matt. 18: 15 f.

corrected them?' And he answered and said to us, 'Now why will the judgement take place? That the wheat may be put in its barn and its chaff thrown into the fire.[231]

50. '...who thus hate, and he who loves me and finds fault with those who do not do my commandments,[232] these will thus be hated and persecuted, and men will despise and mock (them). They will also deliberately say what is not (true), and there will come a conspiracy against those who love me. But these will rebuke them that they may be saved. And those who will find fault with them and correct and exhort them will be hated and set apart and despised; and those who wish (to) do good to them will be prevented (from it). But those who have endured this will rank as martyrs with the Father, for they were zealous concerning righteousness and were not zealous with corruptible zeal.' And we said to him, 'Will such, Lord, also happen in our midst?' And he said to us, 'Do not fear what will happen not with many but (only) with few.' And we said to him, 'Tell us in what way.' And he said to us, 'There will come another teaching and a conflict;[233] and in that they seek their own glory[234] and produce worthless teaching an offence of death will come thereby, and they will teach and turn away from my commandment even those who believe in me and bring them out of eternal life. But woe to those who use my word and my commandment for a pretext,[235] and also to those who listen to them and to those who turn away from the life of the teaching, to those who turn away from the commandment of life (*this last clause not in Paris Nos. 51, 90 and 199*), they will be eternally punished with them.'

51. And after he had said this and had ended the discourse with us, he said again to us, 'Look. After three days and three hours he who sent me will come that I may go with him.' And as he spoke there was thunder and lightning and an earthquake, and the heavens divided and a bright cloud came and took him away.[236] And (we heard; *only in Paris No. 199*) the voice of many angels as they rejoiced and praised and said, 'Assemble us, O priest,[237] in the light of glory.' And when he (*Paris No. 51, 199 and Stuttgart Cod. Orient. fol. No. 49:* they) had come near to the firmament of heaven, we heard him say, 'Go in peace.'[238]

[231] Cf. Luke. 3: 17; Matt. 3: 12; 13: 30.
[232] Cf. Matt. 5: 11; 10: 22.
[233] Cf. Rom. 16: 17.
[234] Cf. John 7: 18.
[235] Matt. 24: 5 ff.; Rom 16: 18.
[236] Acts 1: 9.
[237] Cf. Heb. 8: 1; 10: 11–12; 1 Clem. 36. 1.
[238] Mark 5: 34; Acts 16: 36; Jas. 2: 16.

IV

APOCRYPHAL APOCALYPSES

Introduction

Although apocalyptic passages within the New Testament Gospels and Epistles and the Book of Revelation in the canon may be considered to have been a model that inspired later Christian apocalyptic literature much of it seems rather to be based on Jewish models. To follow a definition adopted by A. Y. Collins in her *ANRW* article:

> Apocalypse is a genre of revelatory literature with a narrative framework in which a revelation is mediated by an otherworldly being to a human recipient, disclosing a transcendent reality which is both temporal, insofar as it envisages eschatological salvation, and spatial insofar as it involves another, supernatural world. (p. 4670)

Such a definition would of course apply to Jewish apocalypses as well. An apocalypse was obviously not a literary genre that was the original creation of Christians. In any case, it is difficult to see the apocalypses following one pattern. Within this category come dialogues of the saviour usually in a question and answer form, otherworldly journeys, oracles, and (if we include 5 and 6 Ezra and the Sibyllines) apocalyptic prophecy. The Apocalypse of Peter and the Apocalypse of Paul, included here, give visions of the next world; the Apocalypse of Thomas is a prophecy about the end of this one.

GENERAL AND BACKGROUND

A. Y. Collins, 'Early Christian Apocalyptic Literature', *ANRW* 2.25.6, 4665–4711.
C. Rowland, *The Open Heaven: A Study of Apocalyptic in Judaism and Christianity* (London, [2]1985).
P. Vielhauer and G. Strecker, 'Apokalypsen und Verwandtes: Einleitung', in Hennecke[5], ii. 493–547; Eng. trans. ii. 569–602. [Cf. Vielhauer's essays in Hennecke[3], ii. 407–53; Eng. trans. ii. 581–642.]
Richard Bauckham, *The Fate of the Dead Studies on the Jewish and Christian Apocalypses* (Leiden, 1998) (= *Novum Testamentum Supplements* 93).

OLD TESTAMENT APOCALYPTIC

H. F. D. Sparks (ed.), *The Apocryphal Old Testament* (Oxford, 1984).
J. H. Charlesworth (ed.), *The Old Testament Pseudepigrapha*, i. *Apocalyptic Literature and Testaments* (London, 1983).

The following apocalypses are included with translations:

1. Apocalypse of Peter, with appendix from the Sibylline Oracles.
2. Apocalypse of Paul (Visio Pauli).
3. Apocalypse of Thomas.

4.(*a*) The Questions of Bartholomew, and
  (*b*) The Book of the Resurrection of Jesus Christ by Bartholomew the Apostle.
5.　The Letter of James (Epistula Iacobi apocrypha).

Other apocalypses (with only short introductory notes) follow the above texts. (The Epistle of the Apostles could qualify for inclusion in this category as a revelatory document but is included by convention with other epistles.)

The Apocalypse of Peter[1]

The existence of this apocalypse was known in antiquity. The Muratorian Fragment and the Stichometry of Nicephorus include it among their 'disputed' texts. The catalogue of Biblical writings in Codex Claromontanus (Paris gr. 107) includes the Shepherd of Hermas, the Acts of Paul, and the Apocalypse of Peter among its canonical writings, but Eusebius, *HE* 6. 14. 1 and especially 3. 3. 2 and 3. 25. 4 (Schwartz, *GCS* 9.2, pp. 548–60, 188, 252), classes it as 'spurious' (cf. also Origen, *on John* 13. 7 (Preuschen, pp. 231–2)). Sozomen in the fifth century, *HE* 7. 19 (ed. J. Bidez and G. C. Hansen, *GCS* 50 (Berlin, 1960), p. 331), refers to its being used in public worship on Good Friday. (It is not listed in the Gelasian Decree.) Thus it is clear that the book was popular and widespread in use in the early centuries of Christianity and hovered on the edges of canonical scripture. The Akhmim manuscript (see below) testifies to the popularity of the text up to the eighth or ninth century, when that manuscript was copied.

Citations from the ancient apocalypse have been identified in Clement of Alexandria, Methodius, Macarius, and possibly in Theophilus of Antioch (and these are set out below): Macarius and Clement name the source. A fourth-century Latin homily cited below (A 7) also gives the source of a quotation as the Apocalypse of Peter. The citations have been verified by the discovery and publication of the text. A portion of the Apocalypse of Peter in Greek (comprising about one half of the original length) was discovered at the end of the nineteenth century in Akhmim in a manuscript that also contains a fragment of the Gospel of Peter (*q.v.*) and 1 Enoch. Further portions in Greek are to be found in the Bodleian and Rainer texts (originally from one manuscript); these are likely to be closer to the original Greek than the Akhmim text is. The complete work is to be found in an Ethiopic text of Pseudo-Clementine literature published in 1907–10 by S. Grébaut from which M. R. James identified the Apocalypse of Peter. The length agrees with the 300 lines in the Stichometry of Nicephorus. The existence of one further Ethiopic text (apparently the ancestor of the text published by Grébaut) has been reported by Cowley.

The interrelationship of the Greek and Ethiopic versions of the apocalypse has exercised scholars working on those texts even though few have given the

---

[1] This Apocalypse of Peter has no connection with the Gnostic Apocalypse of Peter from Nag Hammadi (now included in Hennecke[5], ii. 633–43; Eng. trans. ii. 700–12).

Ethiopic text the thorough study it deserves. The Akhmim portion agrees with Ethiopic chs. 7–10, 15–16a. The general opinion seems to be that the Ethiopic, despite its shortcomings and in some places its obscurities, nevertheless represents the original apocalypse better than the Akhmim fragment. The Sibylline Oracles seem to have been dependent on the text represented by the Ethiopic; the patristic citations also are closer to the Ethiopic than the Greek tradition. James concluded that the Akhmim fragment was an adaptation made by the author of the Gospel of Peter to make it fit his Gospel. The juxtaposition of the Gospel and Apocalypse in the Akhmim manuscript is suggestive of this, and the editorial additions to the Akhmim apocalypse are in agreement with the language and style of the Gospel of Peter. The Apocalypse seems to be older than the Gospel and may well have been one of the sources used by the author of the Gospel: he had used the synoptic Gospels in composing the Gospel of Peter, so to have incorporated an existing apocalypse into that Gospel is not unlikely, especially as we may find precedents for such adaptations (especially of apocalyptic discourses) in the composition of the canonical Gospels themselves. Many of the extant apocryphal writings seem to have been built up by combining and incorporating many previously separate stories, poems, or sayings. In fact it is a characteristic of much Christian literature (canonical and apocryphal) that texts increase in length (although of course for liturgical purposes extracts were removed from larger works, and in the case of the apocryphal Acts stories of martyrdom circulated separately for the commemoration of the saint's day).

Differences between the Akhmim and Ethiopic texts may be seen in the translation below. These are set out in parallel columns for the portions in common. I follow the sequence of the Ethiopic, where the revelation of Paradise follows the revelation of Hell. Another major difference between the two texts is the punishments at the end—these are set in the future in the Ethiopic, whereas they are set within a revelation to Peter in the Akhmim text.

M. R. James claimed that the influence of the Apocalypse of Peter was very great, and many subsequent descriptions of Heaven and Hell throughout Christian literature down to the time of Dante were said to be due directly to the influence of this apocryphon. Although some scholars have been sceptical about the high claims made by James in regard to the influence of this Apocalypse, preferring to attribute some of the later descriptions of Heaven and Hell to traditional material to be found in Jewish and Graeco-Roman literature, nevertheless it is not improbable that the Apocalypse of Paul (q.v.) and the descriptions of Hell in the Acts of Thomas (chs. 55–7, q.v.) were dependent on the Apocalypse of Peter. The second book of Sibylline Oracles paraphrases part of this apocalypse.[2] In any case, the Apocalypse of Peter is

---

[2] Details of similarities between the Apocalypse and these three allegedly dependent texts may be seen in Robinson and James (bibliography below, under General, 63–5, 65–7, 56–63 respectively).

our earliest extant Christian document that describes Heaven and Hell. A thorough investigation of the origin of much of this imagery is still awaited; the earlier and influential study by Dieterich which claimed an Orphic origin for such ideas is now not so readily accepted. The influence of a whole range of oriental mythology and of Jewish writings such as Enoch is as probable as Greek. The whole problem of Jewish apocalyptic and its sources remains obscure. Among other apparent influences on the author of this Apocalypse are 2 Peter, especially for the accounts of the transfiguration, and 4 Ezra (especially 8, 44, 47 (and perhaps 5, 33)) on Ethiopic ch. 3. The influence of Matthew (and to a lesser extent other New Testament writings) on the Apocalypse of Peter is shown by E. Massaux in his *Influence de l'Évangile de saint Matthieu sur la littérature chrétienne avant saint Irenée* (Louvain and Gembloux, 1950; ²Leuven, 1986) (= *BETL* 75).

The date of the original composition of the Apocalypse is early. If it was used by Clement of Alexandria and by the author of the Sibylline Oracles then it must have been in existence before AD 150. If it made use of 4 Ezra then a *terminus a quo* seems to be fixed about AD 100. Bauckham has tried to identify the anti-Christ figure in the Apocalypse with Bar Kokhba and is therefore prepared to date the composition more precisely (AD 132–5) at the time of the Bar Kokhba revolt. In any case, a date in the first half of the second century is generally agreed upon.

The provenance of the composition is not known. If indeed the Apocalypse refers to the Bar Kokhba revolt, then a Palestinian origin seems likeliest, but, as such a suggestion is not universally accepted, the question of the provenance of this Apocalypse must remain open.

The main interest in this text is in the early pictures of Heaven and Hell. The eclipse of the Apocalypse of Peter in antiquity may have been due to the greater popularity of its views disseminated in the West in the context of the Apocalypse of Paul. (In the East apocalypses of the virgin probably satisfied this curiosity.) M. R. James suggested that the Apocalypse of Peter originally contained the controversial idea of the ultimate salvation of all sinners, which is to be found in the derivative Sibylline Oracles but which was subsequently removed from the Apocalypse of Peter itself and which may have resulted in the suppression of the Apocalypse of Peter in its entirety.

EDITIONS

Greek

Akhmim Text:

U. Bouriant, 'Fragments du texte grec du livre d'Énoch et de quelques écrits attribués à Saint Pierre' (Paris, 1892), 142–7 (= *Mémoires publiés par les membres de la mission archéologique française au Caire* 9.1) (*editio princeps*).
A. Lods, *L'Évangile et l'Apocalypse de Pierre* (Paris, 1893) (= *Mémoires* ... 9.3, 224–8) (facsimile edition).

O. von Gebhardt, *Das Evangelium und die Apokalypse des Petrus* (Leipzig, 1893) (facsimile edition with German trans.).

A. Lods, *Evangelii secundum Petrum et Petri Apocalypseos quae supersunt* . . . (Paris, 1892), 29–35, 52–9 (French edn. *L'Évangile et l'Apocalypse de Pierre* . . . (Paris, 1893), 25–31, 85–109 (including French trans.)).

Klostermann, *Apocrypha*, i. 8–12.

Preuschen, 84–8, 188–92 (with German trans.).

Thomas J. Kraus and Tobias Nicklas, *Das Petrusevangelium und die Petrusapokalypse* (Berlin and New York, 2004) (= GCS 11: *Neutestamentliche Apokryphen* 1)

Rainer Fragment:

M. R. James, 'The Rainer Fragment of the Apocalypse of Peter', *JTS* 32 (1931), 270–9.

(For Bodleian Fragment see 'General' below, under James, *JTS* 1911.)

Ethiopic Text

S. Grébaut 'Littérature éthiopienne pseudo-Clémentine', *Revue tie l'Onent chrétien* 12 (1907), 139–51; 13 (1908), 285–7; 15 (1910), 198–214, 307–23, 425–39 (with French trans.).

H. Duensing, 'Ein Stück der urchristlichen Petrusapokalypse enthaltender Traktat der äthiopischen pseudoclementinischen Literatur', *ZNW* 14 (1913), 65–78 (with German trans.).

D. D. Buchholz, *Your Eyes Will Be Opened: A Study of the Greek (Ethiopic) Apocalypse of Peter* (Atlanta 1988) (= *SBL Dissertation Series* 97). [This includes an edition of the Ethiopic text based (for the first time) on both the known manuscripts, as well as English trans. and commentary.]

Arabic (this text differs from the Greek and Ethiopic Apocalypse)

J. R. Harris, 'The Odes of Solomon and the Apocalypse of Peter', *ExpT* 42 (1930), 21–3.

A. Mingana, 'Apocalypse of Peter', *BJRL* 14 (1930), 182–297, 423–562; 15 (1931), 179–279; repr. *Woodbrooke Studies* 3 (Cambridge, 1931), 93–450.[3]

Cf. *Coptic* (an otherwise unknown apocalypse)

O. von Lemm, 'Bruchstück einer Petrusapokalypse', P. Nagel (ed.), *Koptische Miscellen* (repr. Leipzig, 1972), 107–12 (= *Studia Byzantina* 10, 11.)

Slavonic

de Santos Otero, *Altslav. Apok.* i. 212–13.

MODERN TRANSLATIONS

English

A. Rutherfurd, in A. Menzies (ed.), *Ante-Nicene Christian Library*: Additional Volume 9 (Edinburgh, 1897), 41–8 (Akhmim Fragment).

---

[3] Review by M. R. James, *JTS* 33 (1932), 311–13.

B. Pick, *Paralipomena: Remains of Gospels and Sayings of Christ* (Chicago, 1908), 118–23 (Akhmim Fragment).
James, 505–24 (including part of Second Book of Sibylline Oracles).
Hennecke[3], ii. 663–83.
Hennecke[5], ii. 620–38.

French

Amiot, 287–94 (selections).
Éac, 747–74.

German

Hennecke[1], 211–17 (H. Weinel); cf. *Handbuch*, 285–90.
Hennecke[3], ii. 468–83 (C. Maurer and H. Duensing).
Hennecke[5], ii. 562–78 (C. Detlef G. Müller).
Michaelis, 469–81.
Bauer (main bibliography, under Reference and General), 102–5.

Italian

Erbetta, iii. 209–33.
Moraldi, ii. 1803–54;[2] iii. 319–68 (includes part of Second Book of Sibylline Oracles).

GENERAL

Zahn, 'Die Apokalypse des Petrus', in *Kanon*, ii. 810–20. [Cf. i. 307–10.]
A. Robinson and M. R. James, *The Gospel according to Peter and the Revelation of Peter* (London, ²1892), 39–82, 89–93 (with Greek text; trans. in 20 verses, 48–51).
A. von Harnack, *Bruchstücke des Evangeliums und der Apokalypse des Petrus* (Leipzig, ²1893), esp. 16–22, 80–7 (= *TU* 9.2).
—— *Die Petrusapokalypse in der abendländischen Kirche* (Leipzig, 1895), 71–3 (= *TU* 13.1).
A. Marmorstein, 'Jüdische Parallelen zur Petrusapokalypse', *ZNW* 10 (1909), 297–300.
F. Spitta, 'Die Petrusapokalypse und der zweite Petrusbrief', *ZNW* 12 (1911), 237–42.
M. R. James, 'A New Text of the Apocalypse of Peter', *JTS* 12 (1911), 36–54, 362–83 (367–9 = Bodleian Fragment), 573–83.
—— 'Additional Notes on the Apocalypse of Peter', *JTS* ibid. 157.
A. Dieterich, *Nekyia: Beiträge zur Erklärung der neuentdeckten Petrusapokalypse* (Leipzig, ²1913).
M. R. James, 'The Recovery of the Apocalypse of Peter', *Church Quarterly Review* (1915), 1–36, 248. [Very little innovative writing seems to have been published on the Apocalypse of Peter for many years after this.]
G. Quispel and R. M. Grant, 'Note on the Petrine Apocrypha', *VC* 6 (1952), 31–2.
E. Peterson, 'Das Martyrium des Hl-Petrus nach der Petrus-Apokalypse', in id.,

Frühkirche, Judentum und Gnosis (Rome, Freiburg, Vienna, 1959), 88–91; and 'Die Taufe im Acherusischen See', ibid. 310–32.

Vielhauer, 507–11.

R. W. Cowley, 'The Identification of the Ethiopian Octateuch of Clement and its Relationship to the other Christian Literature', *Ostkirchliche Studien* 27 (1978), 37–45.

D. D. Fiensey, 'Lex Talionis in the Apocalypse of Peter', *HTR* 76 (1983), 255–8.

M. Himmelfarb, *Tours of Hell: An Apocalyptic Form in Jewish and Christian Literature* (Philadelphia, 1983).

R. W. Cowley, 'The Ethiopic Work which is Believed to Contain the Material of the Ancient Greek Apocalypse of Peter', *JTS* 36 (1985), 151–3.

R. J. Bauckham, 'The Two Fig Tree Parables in the Apocalypse of Peter', *JBL* 104 (1985), 269–87.

—— 'The Apocalypse of Peter: An Account of Research', ANRW 2.25.6, 4712–49.

—— 'Early Jewish Visions of Hell', *JTS* 41 (1990), 355–85.

J. V. Hills, 'Parables, Pretenders and Prophecies: Translation and Interpretation in the *Apocalypse of Peter* 2', RB 98 (1991), 560–73.

J. N. Bremmer and I. Czachesz (eds.), *The Apocalypse of Peter* (Leuven, 2003) (= *Studies on Early Christian Apocrypha* 7).

A. PATRISTIC AND OTHER CITATIONS

Clement of Alexandria, *Eclogae*[1] 41. 1–2 (Stählin, *GCS* 17.2, p. 149):

1 The Scripture says that the children who have been exposed by their parents are delivered to a care-taking angel by whom they are educated, and made to grow up; and they shall be, it says, as the faithful of a hundred years old are here in this life.[2] (41. 2) Wherefore Peter in the Apocalypse says: And a flash of fire leaping from those children and smiting the eyes of the women.[3]

Ibid. 48. 1 (Stählin, *GCS* 17.2, p. 150):

2 The providence of God does not alight only on those in the flesh. For example, Peter in the Apocalypse says that the children born out of due time receive the better part (i.e. would have been saved if they had lived)—these are delivered to a care-taking angel, that they may partake of knowledge and obtain the better abode, as if they had suffered what they would have suffered had they been in the body. But the others (i.e. those who would not have been saved, had they lived) shall obtain salvation only as beings who have been injured and had mercy shown to them and shall continue without torment, receiving that as a reward.

---

[1] A series of detached sentences excerpted from some longer work, generally supposed to be his *Hypotyposes* or *Outlines*.
[2] See Ethiopic 8 below.
[3] See Ethiopic 8 below.

The Apocalypse of Peter 599

But the milk of the mothers, flowing from their breasts and congealing, says Peter in the Apocalypse, shall engender small beasts devouring the flesh and these running upon them devour them; teaching that the torments come to pass because of the sins.[4]

Methodius of Olympus, *Symposium* 2. 6 (ed. G. Bonwetsch, GCS 27 (Leipzig, 1917), p. 23):

3 Whence also we have received in inspired writings that children born untimely—even if they be the offspring of adultery—are delivered to care-taking angels. For if they had come into being contrary to the will and ordinance of that blessed nature of God, how could they have been delivered to angels to be nourished in all repose and tranquillity? And how could they have confidently summoned their parents before the judgement-seat of Christ to accuse them saying, 'You, O Lord, did not begrudge us this light that is common to all, but these exposed us to death, despising your commandment.'[5]

Macarius Magnes, *Apocritica* 4. 6. 7 (ed. G. Blondel (Paris, 1876), pp. 164–5):[6]

4 And by way of superfluity let this also be cited which is said in the Apocalypse of Peter. He introduces the heaven, to be judged along with the earth, thus: The earth, he says, shall present all men to God to be judged on the day of judgement, itself also being judged along with the heaven that encompasses it.[7]

Ibid.:

5 And this again he says, which is a statement full of impiety: And every power of heaven shall burn, and the heaven shall be rolled up like a book, and all the stars shall fall like leaves from the vine, and as the leaves from the fig-tree.[8]

Theophilus of Antioch, *ad Autolycum* 2. 19 (ed. R. M. Grant (Oxford, 1970), pp. 57–8):

6 God chose for Adam as paradise a place in the eastern region marked out by light illuminated by shining air, with plants of wondrous beauty.[9]

---

[4] See Ethiopic 8 below.
[5] See Ethiopic 8 below.
[6] This work consists of extracts from a heathen opponent's attack on Christianity (Porphyry and Hierocles are named as possible authors of it) and Macarius' own answers. In these passages the heathen writer is quoted.
[7] See Ethiopic 4 below.
[8] See Ethiopic 5 below.
[9] See Ethiopic 16 below.

Latin Homily on the Ten Virgins preserved in an Épinal manuscript and considered to be fourth century:[10]

7 The closed door is the river of fire by which the ungodly will be kept out of the kingdom of God, as it is written in Daniel and by Peter in his Apocalypse.[11]

B. THE ETHIOPIC AND AKHMIM TEXTS

Ethiopic

1. The Second Coming of Christ and Resurrection of the Dead which Christ revealed through Peter to those who died for their sins, because they did not keep the commandment of God, their creator.

And he (Peter) pondered thereon, that he might perceive the mystery of the Son of God, the merciful and lover of mercy.

And when the Lord was seated upon the Mount of Olives, his disciples came to him.

And we besought and entreated him severally and implored him, saying to him, 'Declare to us what are the signs of your coming and of the end of the world,[12] that we may perceive and mark the time of your coming and instruct those who come after us, to whom we preach the word of your gospel, and whom we install in your church, that they, when they hear it, may take heed to themselves and mark the time of your coming.'

And our Lord answered us saying, 'Take heed that no man deceive you[13] and that you be not doubters and serve other gods. Many shall come in my name saying, "I am the Christ."[14] Believe them not, neither draw near to them.[15] For the coming of the Son of God shall not be plain; but as the lightning that shines from the east to the west,[16] so will I come upon the clouds of heaven with a great host in my majesty;[17] with my cross going before my face will I come in my majesty; shining seven times brighter than the sun will I come in my majesty with all my saints, my angels.[18] And my Father shall set a crown upon my head, that I may judge the quick and the dead and recompense every man according to his works.[19]

2. 'And you learn a parable from the fig-tree: as soon as its shoots have come forth and the twigs grown, the end of the world shall come.'[20]

---

[10] Cf. M. R. James, 'A New Text of the Apocalypse of Peter, 2', *JTS* 12 (1911), 362–83, esp. 383.
[11] See Ethiopic 12 below.
[12] Matt. 24: 3.
[13] Matt. 24: 4.
[14] Matt. 24: 5.
[15] Matt. 24: 26; Luke 17: 23.
[16] Matt. 24: 27; Luke 17: 20.
[17] Matt. 24: 30 and parallels.
[18] Matt. 16: 27.
[19] Matt. 16: 27.
[20] Matt. 24: 32 f.

And I, Peter, answered and said to him, 'Interpret the fig-tree to me: how can we understand it? For throughout all its days the fig-tree sends forth shoots and every year it brings forth its fruit for its master? What then does the parable of the fig-tree mean? We do not know.'

And the Master answered and said to me, 'Do you not understand that the fig-tree is the house of Israel? It is like a man who planted a fig-tree in his garden and it brought forth no fruit. And he sought the fruit many years, and when he did not find it he said to the keeper of his garden, "Uproot this fig-tree so that it does not make our ground unfruitful." And the gardener said to his master, "Let us rid it of weeds and dig the ground round about it and water it. If then it does not bear fruit, we will straightway uproot it from the garden and plant another in place of it." Have you not understood that the fig-tree is the house of Israel? Verily I say to you, when its twigs have sprouted forth in the last days, then shall false Christs come and awake expectation, saying, "I am the Christ who has now come into the world."[21] And when they perceive the wickedness of their deeds they shall turn away and deny him whom our fathers praised, the first Christ whom they crucified and therein sinned a great sin. But this deceiver is not the Christ. And when they reject him, he shall slay them with the sword, and there shall be many martyrs. Then shall the twigs of the fig-tree, that is, the house of Israel, shoot forth: many shall become martyrs at his hand. Enoch and Elijah shall be sent to teach them that this is the deceiver who must come into the world and do signs and wonders in order to deceive. And therefore those who die by his hand shall be martyrs, and shall be reckoned among the good and righteous martyrs who have pleased God in their life.'

3. And he showed me in his right hand the souls of all men. And on the palm of his right hand the image of that which shall be accomplished at the last day; and how the righteous and the sinners shall be separated, and how those who are upright in heart will fare, and how the evil-doers shall be rooted out to all eternity. We beheld how the sinners wept in great affliction and sorrow, until all who saw it with their eyes wept, whether righteous or angels, and he himself also.

And I asked him and said to him, 'Lord, allow me to speak your word concerning the sinners, "It were better for them if they had not been created."'[22] And the Saviour answered and said to me, 'Peter, why do you say that not to have been created were better for them?[23] You resist God. You would not have more compassion than he for his image: for he has created them and brought them forth out of not-being. Now because you have seen the lamentation which shall come upon the sinners in the last days, therefore your heart is troubled; but I will show you their works, whereby they have sinned against the Most High.

---

[21] Matt. 24: 24.
[22] Matt. 26: 24 and parallels.
[23] Rev. 20: 13.

4. 'Behold now what shall come upon them in the last days, when the day of God and the day of the decision of the judgement of God comes. From the east to the west shall all the children of men be gathered together before my Father who lives for ever. And he shall command hell to open its bars of adamant and give up all that is therein.

'And the wild beasts and the fowls shall he command to restore all the flesh that they have devoured, because he wills that men should appear; for nothing perishes before God and nothing is impossible with him, because all things are his.

'For all things come to pass on the day of decision, on the day of judgement, at the word of God: and as all things were done when he created the world and commanded all that is therein and it was done, even so shall it be in the last days; for all things are possible with God. And therefore he said in the scripture,[24] "Son of man, prophesy upon the several bones and say to the bones: bone unto bone in joints, sinew, nerves, flesh, and skin and hair thereon."

'And soul and spirit shall the great Uriel give them at the commandment of God; for God has set him over the resurrection of the dead at the day of judgement.

'Behold and consider the corns of wheat that are sown in the earth. As something dry and without soul do men sow them in the earth: and they live again and bear fruit, and the earth restores them as a pledge entrusted to it.

'And this which dies, that is sown as seed in the earth, and shall become alive and be restored to life, is man.

'How much more shall God raise up on the day of decision those who believe in him and are chosen of him, for whose sake he made the world? And all things shall the earth restore on the day of decision, for it also shall be judged with them, and the heaven with it.[25]

5. 'And this shall come at the day of judgement upon those who have fallen away from faith in God and have committed sin. Cataracts of fire shall be let loose; and darkness and obscurity shall come up and clothe and veil the whole world; and the waters shall be changed and turned into coals of fire, and all that is in them shall burn, and the sea shall become fire. Under the heaven there shall be a sharp fire that cannot be quenched, and it flows to fulfil the judgement of wrath. And the stars shall be melted by flames of fire,[26] as if they had not been created, and the firmaments of the heaven shall pass away for lack of water and shall be as though they had not been. And the lightnings of heaven shall be no more, and by their enchantment they shall affright the world. The spirits of the dead bodies shall be like them and shall become fire at the commandment of God.

[24] Ezek. 37: 4 ff.
[25] Cf. Macarius, A4 above.
[26] Cf. Macarius, A4 above.

The Apocalypse of Peter

'And as soon as the whole creation dissolves, the men who are in the east shall flee to the west, ⟨and those who are in the west⟩ to the east; those in the south shall flee to the north, and those who are in the north to the south. And in all places shall the wrath of a fearful fire overtake them; and an unquenchable flame driving them shall bring them to the judgement of wrath, to the stream of unquenchable fire which flows, flaming with fire, and when the waves thereof part themselves one from another, burning, there shall be a great gnashing of teeth among the children of men.

6. 'Then shall they all behold me coming upon an eternal cloud of brightness; and the angels of God who are with me shall sit upon the throne of my glory at the right hand of my heavenly Father; and he shall set a crown upon my head. And when the nations behold it, they shall weep,[27] every nation for itself.

'Then shall he command them to enter into the river of fire while the works of every one of them shall stand before them. ⟨Rewards shall be given⟩ to every man according to his deeds.[28] As for the elect who have done good, they shall come to me and not see death by the devouring fire. But the unrighteous, the sinners, and the hypocrites shall stand in the depths of darkness that shall not pass away, and their chastisement is the fire, and angels bring forward their sins and prepare for them a place wherein they shall be punished for ever, every one according to his transgression.

'Uriel the angel of God shall bring forth the souls of those sinners who perished in the flood, and of all who dwelt in all idols, in every molten image, in every object of love, and in pictures, and of those who dwelt on all hills and in stones and by the wayside, whom men called gods: they shall be burned with them in everlasting fire; and after all of them with their dwelling-places are destroyed, they shall be punished eternally.

Ethiopic

7. 'Then shall men and women come to the place prepared for them. By their tongues wherewith they have blasphemed the way of

Akhmim

21. And I saw also another place opposite that one, very squalid; and it was a place of punishment, and those who were punished and the angels that punished them had dark raiment in accordance with the air of the place.

22. And some there were hanging by their tongues; and these were the ones who blasphemed the way of righteousness, and under them was

---

[27] Matt. 26: 64, 16: 27 and parallels.
[28] Matt. 16: 27; Ps. 62: 12.

righteousness shall they be hanged up. There is spread under them unquenchable fire so that they do not escape it.

'Behold another place: there is a pit, great and full. In it are those who have denied righteousness: and angels of punishment chastise them and there they kindle upon them the fire of their torment.

'And again behold two women: they hang them up by their neck and by their hair; they shall cast them into the pit. These are those who plaited their hair, not to make themselves beautiful but to turn them to fornication, that they might ensnare the souls of men to perdition. And the men who lay with them in fornication shall be hung by their loins in that place of fire; and they shall say one to another, "We did not know that we should come to everlasting punishment."

'And the murderers and those who have made common cause with them shall they cast into the fire, in a place full of venomous beasts, and they shall be tormented without rest, feeling their pains; and their worms shall be as many in number as a dark cloud. And the angel Ezrael shall bring forth the souls of those who have been slain, and they shall behold the torment of those who slew them and say one to another, "Righteousness and justice is the judgement of God.[29] For we heard, but we believed not, that we should come into this place of eternal judgement."

laid fire flaming and tormenting them.

23. And there was a great lake full of flaming mire, wherein were certain men who had turned away from righteousness; and angels, tormentors, were set over them.

24. And there were also others, women, hanged by their hair over that mire which boiled up; and these were the ones who adorned themselves for adultery.

And the men who were joined with them in the defilement of adultery were hanging by their feet, and had their heads hidden in the mire and said, 'We did not believe that we should come to this place.'

25. And I saw the murderers and those who were accomplices cast into a gorge full of evil, creeping things, and smitten by those beasts, writhing about in that torment. And upon them were set worms like clouds of darkness. And the souls of those who were murdered stood and looked upon the torment of those murderers and said, 'O God, righteous is your judgement.'[30]

---

[29] Rev. 16: 7, 19: 2.
[30] Rev. 16: 7, 19: 2.

The Apocalypse of Peter

8. 'And near this flame there is a pit, great and very deep, and into it flows from above all manner of torment, foulness, and excrement. And women are swallowed up therein up to their necks and tormented with great pain. These are they who have caused their children to be born untimely and have corrupted the work of God who created them. Opposite them shall be another place where their children sit alive and cry to God. And flashes of lightning go forth from those children and pierce the eyes of those who for fornication's sake have caused their destruction.[31]

'Other men and women shall stand above them, naked; and their children stand opposite them in a place of delight, and sigh and cry to God because of their parents saying, "These are they who despised and cursed and transgressed your commandments and delivered us to death: they have cursed the angel that formed us and have hanged us up and begrudged us the light which you have given to all creatures. And the milk of their mothers flowing from their breasts shall congeal and from it shall come beasts devouring flesh, which shall come forth and turn and torment them for ever with their husbands because they forsook the commandments of God and slew their children. As for their children, they shall be delivered to the angel Temlakos.[32] And those who slew them shall be tormented eternally, for God wills it so.

26. And near that place I saw another gorge wherein the discharge and excrement of those who were in torment ran down, and became like a lake there. And women sat there up to their necks in that filth, and over against them many children born out of due time sat crying; and from them went forth rays of fire and smote the women in the eyes; and these were those who conceived out of wedlock and caused abortion.

[31] Cf. Clement of Alexandria, A1 above.
[32] Cf. Clement of Alexandria and Methodius, A2 and A3 above. Temlakos is taken to be a proper name of an angel: it is in fact the rare Greek word temeloukhos, 'care-taking'.

9. 'Ezrael the angel of wrath shall bring men and women, with half of their bodies burning, and cast them into a place of darkness, the hell of men; and a spirit of wrath shall chastise them with all manner of torment, and a worm that never sleeps shall devour their entrails; and these are the persecutors and betrayers of my righteous ones.

'And beside those who are there, shall be other men and women, gnawing their tongues; and they shall torment them with red-hot irons and burn their eyes. These are they who slander and doubt my righteousness.

'Other men and women whose works were done in deceitfulness shall have their lips cut off; and fire enters into their mouth and their entrails. These are they who caused the martyrs to die by their lying.

'And beside them, in a place near at hand, upon the stone shall be a pillar of fire, and the pillar is sharper than swords. And there shall be men and women clad in rags and filthy garments, and they shall be cast thereon to suffer the judgement of an unceasing torment; these are the ones who trusted in their riches and despised the widows and the women with fatherless children... before God.

10. 'And into another place nearby, full of filth, they cast men and women up to the knees. These are they who lent money and took usury.

'And other men and women cast themselves down from a high place

27. And other men and women were being burned up to their middle and were cast down in a dark place and were scourged by evil spirits, having their entrails devoured by worms that never rested. And these were the ones who had persecuted the righteous and delivered them up.

28. And near to them were women and men gnawing their lips and in torment having heated iron in their eyes. And these were the ones who did blaspheme and speak evil of the way of righteousness.

29. And over against these were yet others, men and women, gnawing their tongues and having flaming fire in their mouths. And these were the false witnesses.

30. And in another place were gravel-stones sharper than swords or any spit, heated with fire, and men and women clad in filthy rags rolled upon them in torment. And these were they who were rich and trusted in their riches, and had no pity upon orphans and widows but neglected the commandments of God.

31. And in another great lake full of foul pus and blood and boiling mire stood men and women up to their knees. And these were the ones who lent money and demanded usury upon usury.

32. And other men and women being cast down from a great

and return again and run, and devils drive them. These are the worshippers of idols, and they drive them up to the top of the height and they cast themselves down. And this they do continually and are tormented for ever. These are they who have cut their flesh as apostles of a man: and the women with them... and these are the men who defiled themselves together as women.

'And beside them... and beneath them shall the angel Ezrael prepare a place of much fire: and all the idols of gold and silver, all idols, the work of men's hands, and the semblances of images of cats and lions, of creeping things and wild beasts, and the men and women that have prepared the images thereof, shall be in chains of fire and shall be chastised because of their error before the idols, and this is their judgement for ever.

'And beside them shall be other men and women, burning in the fire of the judgement, and their torment is everlasting. These are they who have forsaken the commandment of God and followed the (persuasions?) of devils.

precipice fell to the bottom and again were driven by those who were set over them to go up upon the rock and thence were cast down again to the bottom and thus they had no rest from this torment. And these were the ones who defiled their bodies, behaving as women: and the women who were with them were those who lay with one another as a man with a woman.

33. And beside that rock was a place full of fire, and there stood men which with their own hands had made images for themselves instead of God, [And beside them other men and women][33] having rods of fire and smiting one another and never resting from this manner of torment...

34. And yet others near to them, men and women, were burned and turned in the fire and were roasted. And these were those who forsook the way of God.[34]

Ethiopic
11. 'And there shall be another place, very high... The men and women whose feet slip shall go rolling down into a place where is fear. And again while the fire that is prepared flows, they mount up and fall down again and continue to roll down. Thus shall they be tormented for ever. These are they

---

[33] The bracketed words are intrusive.

[34] Bodleian fragment: '[Recto] Women holding chains and scourging themselves before those idols of deceit. And they shall unceasingly experience the torment, and near [verso] them other men and women burning in the fire of them who were mad after idols. And these are the ones who forsook entirely the way of God.'

who honoured not their father and mother and of their own accord withheld themselves from them. Therefore shall they be chastised eternally.

'Furthermore the angel Ezrael shall bring children and maidens, to show them those who are tormented. They shall be chastised with pains, with hanging up(?) and with a multitude of wounds which flesh-devouring birds shall inflict upon them. These are they who trust in their sins and do not obey their parents and do not follow the instruction of their fathers and do not honour those more aged than they.

'Beside them shall be girls clad in darkness for a garment, and they shall be seriously punished and their flesh shall be torn in pieces. These are they who did not preserve their virginity until they were given in marriage and with these torments shall they be punished and shall feel them.

'And again, other men and women, gnawing their tongues without ceasing, and being tormented with everlasting fire. These are the servants who were not obedient to their masters; and this then is their judgement for ever.

12. 'And near by this place of torment shall be men and women who are dumb and blind and whose raiment is white. They shall crowd one upon another, and fall upon coals of unquenchable fire. These are they who give alms and say, "We are righteous before God", whereas they have not sought after righteousness.

'Ezrael the angel of God shall bring them forth out of this fire and establish a judgement of decision (?). This then is their judgement. A river of fire shall flow, and all those judged shall be drawn down into the middle of the river.[35] And Uriel shall set them there.

'And there are wheels of fire, and men and women hung thereon by the force of the whirling. And those in the pit shall burn; now these are the sorcerers and sorceresses. Those wheels shall be in all decision by fire without number.[36]

13. 'Thereafter shall the angels bring my elect and righteous who are perfect in all uprightness and bear them in their hands and clothe them with the raiment of the life that is above. They shall see their desire on those who hated them,[37] when he punishes them and the torment of every one shall be for ever according to his works.

'And all those in torment shall say with one voice, "Have mercy upon us, for now we know the judgement of God, which he declared to us beforetime and we did not believe." And the angel Tatirokos[38] shall come and chastise them with even greater torment, and say to them, "Now do you repent, when it is no longer the time for repentance, and nothing of life remains." And they

---

[35] Homily on the Ten Virgins, A7 above.
[36] Text obscure.
[37] Ps. 54: 7, 59: 10.
[38] The keeper of hell (Tartaros), a word corresponding in formation to Temeloukhos (see above).

shall say, "Righteous is the judgement of God, for we have heard and perceived that his judgement is good,[39] for we are recompensed according to our deeds."

14. 'Then will I give to my elect and righteous the baptism and the salvation for which they have besought me, in the field of Akrosja (Acherusia) which is called Aneslasleja (Elysium). They shall adorn with flowers the portion of the righteous, and I shall go . . . I shall rejoice with them. I will cause the peoples to enter into my everlasting kingdom, and show them eternal good things to which I have made them set their hope, I and my Father in heaven.

'I have spoken this to you, Peter, and declared it to you. Go forth therefore and go to the city of the west and enter into the vineyard which I shall tell you of, in order that by the sufferings of the Son who is without sin the deeds of corruption may be sanctified. As for you, you are chosen according to the promise which I have given you. Spread my gospel throughout all the world in peace. Verily men shall rejoice; my words shall be the source of hope and of life, and suddenly shall the world be ravished.'[40]

Ethiopic

15. And my Lord Jesus Christ, our King, said to me, 'Let us go to the holy mountain.' And his disciples went with him, praying.

Akhmim

1. Many of them shall be false prophets, and shall teach ways and diverse doctrines of perdition. 2. And they shall become sons of perdition. 3. And then God shall come to my faithful ones who hunger and thirst and are afflicted and prove their souls in this life, and shall judge the sons of iniquity.'

4. And the Lord continued and said, 'Let us go to the mountain and pray.' 5. And going with him, we the twelve disciples besought him that he would show us one of our righteous brethren who had departed

---

[39] Rev. 16: 7, 19: 2.
[40] An adapted version of James's translation of the Rainer fragment (in *JTS* 32 (1931), 270-9) is as follows: 'Then will I give to my called and my chosen whomsoever they shall ask me for, out of torment, and will give them a fair baptism to salvation from the Acherusian lake which men so call in the Elysian field even a portion of righteousness with my holy ones. And I will depart, I and my chosen, rejoicing, with the patriarchs, to my eternal kingdom, and I will fulfil for them the promises which I promised them, I and my Father in heaven. Lo, I have manifested to you, Peter, and have expounded all this. And go into a city that rules over the west, and drink the cup which I promised you, at the hands of the son of him who is in Hades, that his destruction may have a beginning; and you may be acceptable of the promise . . . (Cf. *Sibylline Oracles* 2. 330-9.)

And behold there were two men there, and we could not look upon their faces, for a light came from them, shining more than the sun, and their raiment also was shining and cannot be described and nothing is sufficient to be compared to them in this world. And the sweetness of them... that no mouth is able to utter the beauty of their appearance, for their aspect was astonishing and wonderful. And the other, great, I say, shines in his aspect above crystal. Like the flower of roses is the appearance of the colour of his aspect and of his body... his head. And upon his shoulders... and on their foreheads was a crown of nard woven from fair flowers. As the rainbow in the water, so was their hair. And such was the comeliness of their countenance, adorned with all manner of ornament.

16. And when we suddenly saw them, we marvelled. And I drew near to God, Jesus Christ, and said to him, 'O my Lord, who are these?' And he said to me, 'They are Moses and Elijah.' And I said to him, 'Where then are Abraham and Isaac and Jacob and the rest of the righteous fathers?' And he showed us a great garden, open, full of fair trees and blessed fruits and of the odour of perfumes.[41] The fragrance was pleasant and reached us. And of

out of the world, that we might see of what form they are, and take courage and encourage the men who hear us.

6. And as we prayed, suddenly there appeared two men standing before the Lord upon whom we were not able to look. 7. For there issued from their countenance a ray as of the sun and their raiment was shining such as the eye of a man never saw the like; for no mouth is able to declare nor heart to conceive the glory wherewith they were clad and the beauty of their countenance.

8. When we saw them we were astonished, for their bodies were whiter than any snow and redder than any rose. 9. And the redness of them was mingled with the whiteness and I am simply not able to declare their beauty. 10. For their hair was curling and flourishing and fell comely about their countenance and their shoulders like a garland woven of nard and various flowers or like a rainbow in the air: such was their comeliness.

11. Seeing the beauty of them we were astonished at them, for they appeared suddenly.

12. And I drew near to the Lord and said, 'Who are these?' 13. He said to me, 'These are your righteous brethren whose appearance you wished to see.'

14. And I said to him, 'And where are all the righteous? What is the world of those who possess this glory?' 15. And the Lord showed me a very great region outside this world

---

[41] Cf. Theophilus of Antioch, A6 above.

that tree... I saw many fruits. And my Lord and God Jesus Christ said to me, 'Have you seen the companies of the fathers?'

exceedingly bright with light, and the air of that place illuminated with the rays of the sun, and the earth itself flowering with blossoms that do not fade, and full of spices and plants, fair-flowering and incorruptible, and bearing blessed fruit.

16. And so great was the blossom that the odour thereof was borne from there to where we were.

17. And the inhabitants in that place were clad with the raiment of shining angels, and their raiment was like their land.

18. And angels ran round about them there. 19. And the glory of those who dwelt there was equal, and with one voice they praised the Lord God, rejoicing in that place.

20. The Lord said to us, 'This is the place of your leaders, the righteous men.'

Ethiopic
'As is their rest, such also is the honour and the glory of those who are persecuted for my righteousness' sake.'[42] And I rejoiced and believed and understood that which is written in the book of my Lord Jesus Christ. And I said to him, 'O my Lord, do you wish that I make here three tabernacles, one for you, and one for Moses, and one for Elijah?'.[43] And he said to me in wrath, 'Satan makes war against you, and has veiled your understanding; and the good things of this world prevail against you. Your eyes therefore must be opened and your ears unstopped that you may see a tabernacle, not made with men's hands, which my heavenly Father has made for me and for the elect.' And we beheld it and were full of gladness.

17. And behold, suddenly there came a voice from heaven, saying, 'This is my beloved Son in whom I am well pleased:[44] ⟨he has kept⟩ my commandments.' And then came a great and exceedingly white cloud over our heads and bore away our Lord and Moses and Elijah. And I trembled and was afraid; and we looked up, and the heaven opened and we beheld men in the flesh and they came and greeted our Lord and Moses and Elijah and went to

---

[42] Matt. 5: 10.
[43] Matt. 17: 4 and parallels.
[44] Matt. 17: 5 and parallels.

another heaven. And the word of the scripture was fulfilled: 'This is the generation that seeks him and seeks the face of the God of Jacob'.[45] And great fear and commotion took place in heaven, and the angels pressed one upon another that the word of the scripture might be fulfilled which says, 'Open the gates, you princes.'[46]

Thereafter was the heaven shut, that had been open.

And we prayed and went down from the mountain, glorifying God, who has written the names of the righteous in heaven in the book of life.

There is a great deal more of the Ethiopic text. James gives a résumé of its contents (ANT 520 f.). This may be adapted as follows:

Peter opened his mouth and said to me, 'Hearken, my son Clement; God created all things for his glory', and this proposition is dwelt upon. The glory of those who duly praise God is described in terms borrowed from the Apocalypse: 'The Son at his coming will raise the dead ... and will make my righteous ones shine seven times more than the sun, and will make their crowns shine like crystal and like the rainbow in the time of rain, (crowns) which are perfumed with nard and cannot be contemplated, (adorned) with rubies, with the colour of emeralds shining brightly, with topazes, gems, and yellow pearls that shine like the stars of heaven, and like the rays of the sun, sparkling, which cannot be gazed upon.' Again, of the angels: 'Their faces shine more than the sun; their crowns are as the rainbow in the time of rain. (They are perfumed) with nard. Their eyes shine like the morning star. The beauty of their appearance cannot be expressed ... Their raiment is not woven, but white as that of the fuller, just as I saw on the mountain where Moses and Elijah were. Our Lord showed at the transfiguration the apparel of the last days, of the day of resurrection, to Peter, James and John the sons of Zebedee, and a bright cloud overshadowed us, and we heard the voice of the Father saying to us, 'This is my Son whom I love and in whom I am well pleased: hear him.' And being afraid we forgot all the things of this life and of the flesh and knew not what we said because of the greatness of the wonder of that day and of the mountain whereon he showed us the second coming in the kingdom that does not pass away.

Next: 'The Father has committed all judgement to the Son.' The destiny of sinners—their eternal doom—is more than Peter can endure; he appeals to Christ to have pity on them.

And my Lord answered me and said to me, 'Have you understood that which I said to you before? It is permitted to you to know that concerning which you ask, but you must not tell that which you hear to the sinners lest they transgress the more and sin.' Peter weeps many hours and is at last consoled by an answer which, though exceedingly diffuse and vague, does seem to promise ultimate pardon for all: 'My Father will give to them all the life, the glory, and the kingdom that passes not away ... It is because of those who have believed in me that I come. It is also because of those who have believed in me, that, at their word, I shall have pity on men.'

Ultimately Peter orders Clement to hide this revelation in a box so that foolish men may not see it.

[45] Ps. 24: 6.
[46] Ps. 24: 7-9.

APPENDIX: THE SIBYLLINE ORACLES

Books 1 and 2 of the Sibylline Oracles contain Christian redaction and may be from the second or third century. Following M. R. James's example (*ANT* 521–4) I include a translation of lines 190–338 of the second book. This section seems to have been taken from the Apocalypse of Peter. The final lines of the extract seem to point to the ultimate salvation of all sinners, an idea to be found in the Appendix of the Ethiopic text of the Apocalypse of Peter (see above, at end of text). The Coptic Apocalypse of Elias (Elijah) also contains this conclusion:

> The righteous will behold the sinners in their punishment, both those who have persecuted them and those who have handed them over to death. Then the sinners will see the place of the righteous and be partakers of grace. In that day that for which the righteous often pray will be granted to them.[1]

See also the Epistula Apostolorum 40.

The oracles, written in hexameters, are a collection of fifteen books in Greek, worked up by Jewish and Christian authors in imitation of the pagan Sibylline texts. Not all these fifteen books survive but those with the strongest Christian elements are books 1, 2, 6, 7, 8. The motive for the composition is likely to have been to win pagans to Jewish or Christian doctrines. The Christian additions seem to date from the late second century onwards.

TEXTS AND TRANSLATIONS

J. Geffcken, *Die Oracula Sibyllina* (Leipzig, 1902; repr. Berlin, 1967) (= *GCS* 8).
J. J. Collins, 'Sibylline Oracles', in J. H. Charlesworth, *The Old Testament Pseudepigrapha*, i (London, 1983), 317–472 (with introduction and full bibliography).
Portions of the text translated in Hennecke, (German) ³ii. 502–28 (A. Kurfess), ⁵ii. 591–619 (U. Treu); (English) ³ii. 703–45, ⁵ ii. 652–85.
Italian translation of the Christian Sibyllines in Erbetta, iii. 486–540.

SIBYLLINE ORACLES 2, LINES 190–338

After saying (l. 187) that Elijah will descend and display three great signs, the text proceeds:
Woe to all those who are found great with child in that day, and to those who give suck to infant children, and to those who dwell on the wave. Woe to those who shall behold that day. For a dark mist shall cover the boundless world, from east and west, south and north. And then shall a great river of flaming fire flow from heaven and consume all places, the earth and the great ocean and the gleaming sea, lakes and rivers and fountains, and merciless Hades and the vault of heaven; but the lights of heaven shall melt together in one into a desolate shape. For the stars shall all fall from heaven into the sea, and all the souls of men shall gnash their teeth as they burn in the river of

---

[1] See K. H. Kuhn, 'The Apocalypse of Elijah', in H. F. D. Sparks (ed.), *The Apocryphal Old Testament* (Oxford, 1984), 753–73, esp. 772–3.

brimstone and the raging fire in the blazing plain, and ashes shall cover all things. And then shall all the elements of the world be laid waste, air, earth, sea, light, heaven, days and nights, and no more shall the multitudes of birds fly in the air nor swimming creatures any more swim the sea; no ship shall sail with its cargo over the waves; no guided oxen shall plough the tilled land; there shall be no more sound of swift winds, but he shall fuse all things together into one, and purge them clean.

Now when the immortal angels of the undying God, Barakiel, Ramiel, Uriel, Samiel, and Azael, knowing all the evil deeds that anyone has previously done shall come, then out of the misty darkness they shall bring all the souls of men to judgement, to the seat of God the immortal, the great. For he only is incorruptible, himself the Almighty, who shall be the judge of mortal men. And then to those of the underworld shall the heavenly one give souls and spirit and speech, and their bones joined together, with all the joints and the flesh and sinews and veins, and skin over the flesh, and hair as before, and the bodies of earthly men shall be moved and arise in one day, joined together in immortal fashion and breathing.

Then shall the great angel Uriel break the monstrous bars of unyielding and unbreakable steel, of the brazen gates of Hades, and cast them down, and bring forth to judgement all the sorrowful forms, the ghosts of the ancient Titans, and of the giants, and all whom the flood overtook. And all whom the wave of the sea has destroyed in the waters, and all whom beasts and creeping things and fowls have feasted on: all these shall he bring to the judgement seat; and again those whom flesh-devouring fire has consumed in the flames, these also shall he gather and set before God's seat.

And when he has overcome Fate and raised the dead, then shall Adonai Sabaoth, the high thunderer, sit on his heavenly throne and set up a great pillar, and Christ himself, the undying, shall come to the eternal in the clouds in glory with the pure angels, and shall sit on the seat on the right of the Great One, judging the life and character of godly and ungodly men.

And the great Moses, friend of the Most High, shall come, clad in flesh, and the great Abraham himself shall come, and Isaac and Jacob, Joshua, Daniel, Elijah, Habakkuk, and Jonah, and those whom the Hebrews slew; and all the Hebrews who were after Jeremiah shall be judged at the judgement seat, and he shall destroy them, so that they may receive a due reward and expiate all that they did in their mortal life.

And then shall all men pass through a blazing river and unquenchable flame, and all the righteous shall be saved whole, but all the ungodly shall perish for all ages, as many as formerly did evil, and committed murders, and all who were privy thereto, liars, thieves, deceivers, cruel destroyers of houses, gluttons, adulterers, slanderers, insolent, lawless, idolaters, and all that forsook the great immortal God and became blasphemers and ravagers of the godly, breakers of faith and destroyers of righteous men. And all who look with guileful and shameless face—reverend priests and deacons[1] and judge unjustly, dealing perversely, obeying false rumours ... more deadly than leopards and wolves, and very evil; and all who are arrogant, and usurers that heap up in their houses usury out of usury and injure orphans and widows continually; and they who give alms from ill-gotten gains to widows and orphans, and they who, when they give alms of their own toil, reproach them; and they who have forsaken their

---

[1] Something is lost or corrupt here.

parents in their old age and not repaid them at all, nor recompensed them for their nurture; and they who have disobeyed and spoken hard words against their parents; they also who have received pledges and denied them, and servants who have turned against their masters; and again they who have defiled their flesh in lasciviousness, and have loosed the girdle of virginity in secret union, and they who make the child in the womb miscarry, and who cast out their offspring unlawfully; sorcerers also and sorceresses with these shall the wrath of the heavenly and immortal God bring near to the pillar, around which the untiring river of fire shall flow. And all of them shall the undying angels of the immortal everlasting God chastise terribly from above with flaming scourges, and shall bind them fast in fiery chains and unbreakable bonds. And then shall they cast them down in the darkness of night into Gehenna among the beasts of hell, many and frightful, where there is darkness without measure.

And when they have dealt out many torments to all whose heart was evil, later out of the great river shall a wheel of fire encompass them, because they devised wicked works. And then shall they lament, one here, one there, in miserable fate, fathers and infant children, mothers and sucklings weeping, nor shall they be sated with tears, nor shall the voice of those who mourn piteously here and there be heard; but far under dark and squalid Tartarus shall they cry in torment, and in unhallowed places shall they abide and expiate threefold every evil deed that they have done, burning in a great flame; and shall gnash their teeth, all of them wasting away with fierce thirst and violence, and shall call death lovely and it shall evade them; for no more shall death nor night give them rest, and often shall they beseech in vain the Almighty God, and then shall he openly turn away his face from them. For he has granted the limit of seven ages for repentance to men who err, by the hand of a pure virgin.

But the residue who have cared for justice and good deeds, and godliness and righteous thoughts, shall angels bear up and carry through the flaming river to light, and life without care, where the immortal path of the great God is found, and three fountains, of wine and honey and milk. And the earth, common to all, not divided with walls or fences, shall then bring forth of her own accord much fruit, and life and wealth shall be common and undistributed. For there shall be no poor man, nor rich, nor tyrant, nor slave, none great nor small any longer, no kings, no princes; but all men shall be on a par together. And no more shall any man say 'night is come', nor 'the morrow', nor 'it was yesterday'. He is no longer concerned with days, nor spring, nor winter, nor summer, nor autumn, neither marriage, nor death, nor selling, nor buying, nor sunset, nor sunrise. For God shall make one long day.

And to the godly, shall the almighty and immortal God grant another boon, when they shall ask it of him. He shall grant them to save men out of the fierce fire and the eternal torments; and this will he do, for he will gather them again out of the everlasting flame and remove them elsewhere, sending them for the sake of his people to another life eternal and immortal, in the Elysian plain where are the long waves of the Acherusian lake exhaustless and deep bosomed.

The Apocalypse of Paul (Visio Pauli)

Paul's description of his being caught up into Paradise (2 Cor 12) gave the cue for creating this Apocalypse which includes his vision of the afterlife. The prefaced introductory chapters (to be found at the end in the Syriac version) explain how and why his vision remained hidden until the time of the consulate of Theodosius and Cynegius. This introductory matter gives a valuable clue to the date of the composition: the consuls were in office about AD 388, and it is likely that the author of the Apocalypse launched it around that time as a recently discovered work. The original composition is likely to be earlier. In any case, in his compilation the author has made use of earlier material (the Apocalypse of Peter (for the descriptions of punishments—especially for those guilty of abortions), the Apocalypse of Elias (Elijah), the Apocalypse of Zephaniah). The theology is orthodox, although the author has ascetic interests.

The Apocalypse of Paul more than any other of the apocryphal apocalypses was responsible for the spread of many of the popular ideas of Heaven and Hell throughout Christianity and especially in the Western church of the Middle Ages. Dante's *Inferno* seems to owe its inspiration to some of the vivid descriptions of afterlife found here.

The first form of the work is likely to have been written in Greek about the mid-third century and was translated into Latin, Coptic, Syriac, and other languages. It probably originated in Egypt. It is a rambling, repetitive, and poorly constructed work, the developed and best form of which seems to be represented in a long Latin version of the fifth–sixth century now found in Paris MS 1631 of the eighth century. This text, originally published by M. R. James, forms the basis of the translation offered below. Because of the nature of the work, shorter recensions were produced, and at least eight Latin versions have been identified. A motive for these recensions was to provide admonitory sermons in which the revisers concentrated on the torments of Hell to the exclusion of the visions of Paradise.

Much of the research into these recensions was done by Brandes and later by Silverstein, and a useful family tree of the interrelationship of these recensions is to be found in Erbetta, iii. 355. The fourth recension seems to be the one that became the most popular. The full story of the history of the text in Latin and in other versions is, however, still not known, and much work needs to be done. Work on the rich Slavonic material is still to be undertaken. The only Greek manuscripts extant are the ones published by Tischendorf, a fifteenth-century text in Milan and a thirteenth-century text in Munich; this Greek text is only a summary of the original.

Patristic citations are few. Epiphanius, *adv. Haer.* 38. 2 (Holl, *GCS* 31, pp. 64–5), refers to a Gnostic Ascent of Paul but this is not our work. There are other ancient works of the same or similar title including the Coptic Apocalypse of Paul found at Nag Hammadi (now included in Hennecke[5], ii. 628–33; Eng. trans. ii. 695–700). Origen, *hom. V in Psalmos* 36 (ed. C. H. U. Lommatzsch (Berlin, 1841), p. 233), describes the fate of souls after death and this seems to be drawn from the Apocalypse of Paul 13 ff.: if so, the early date of the original composition is fixed. Prudentius, *Cathemerinon* 5. 125 ff., of *c*.400, seems to know of the work (ed. J. Bergman, *CSEL* 61 (Vienna, Leipzig, 1926), p. 30). Augustine's *Tractate on John* 98. 8 of the early fifth century (ed. R. Willems, *CC* 36 (Turnhout, 1954), p. 581) refers to the Apocalypse of Paul not being accepted by the church. Sozomen at the end of the fourth century also refers to the work in his *Historia Ecclesiastica* 7. 19 (ed. J. Bidez and G. C. Hansen, *GCS* 50 (Berlin, 1960), p. 331). The Gelasian Decree and the List of Sixty Books include this apocalypse among the condemned writings.

EDITIONS

Greek

Tischendorf, *Apoc. Apoc.*, pp. xiv–xviii, 34–69.

Latin

T. Silverstein, *Visio Sancti Pauli: The History of the Apocalypse in Latin together with Nine Texts* (London, 1935) (= *Studies and Documents* 4) (with extensive bibliography of texts, manuscripts, and general studies (pp. 219–29)).

James, *Apoc. Anec.* i. 1–42 (oldest Latin text, Paris 1631, pp. 11–42; comparison of the contents of the Greek, Syriac, and Latin on pp. 4–7).

C. Kappler, 'L'Apocalypse latine de Paul', in id. (ed.), *Apocalypses et voyages dans l'Au-delà* (Paris, 1987), 237–66.

T. Silverstein, *Visiones et revelaciones Sancti Pauli: Una nuova tradizione di testi latini nel Medio Evo* (Rome: Accademia nazionale dei Lincei, 1974) (= *Problemi attuali di scienza e di cultura* 188).

J. Silverstein and A. Hilhorst, *Apocalypse of Paul* (Geneva, 1997) (= *Cahiers d'orientalisme* 21).

Syriac

G. Ricciotti, 'Apocalypsis Pauli Syriace iuxta codices vaticanos', *Orientalia* ii. 1, 2 (1933), 1–24, 120–49 (with Latin trans.).

J. Perkins, 'The Revelation of the Blessed Apostle Paul. Translated from an Ancient Syriac Manuscript', *Journal of the American Oriental Society* 8 (1864), 183–212 (English trans. of a Nestorian MS from Urûmiah) (repr. *Journal of Sacred Literature and Biblical Record* 6 (1865), 372–401, and also to be found in the apparatus to Tischendorf's Greek text).

Coptic

E. A. Wallis Budge, *Miscellaneous Coptic Texts* (London, 1915), 534–74, 1043–84 (with Eng. trans.—begins at Apocalypse of Paul 16 with frequent expansions of the original).

Armenian

P. Vetter, 'Die armenische Paulusapokalypse', *TQ* 88 (1906), 508–95; 89 (1907), 58–75.
Leloir, *CCA* 3, 87–172.

Slavonic

de Santos Otero, *Altslav. Apok.* i. 170–87.
E. Turdeanu, 'La vision de saint Paul', *Die Welt der Slaven* 1 (1956), 406–30.

Ethiopic

A seventh-century adaptation of the Apocalypse of Paul 13–44 (and also of the Apocalypse of Peter) ed. M. Chaîne, 'Apocalypsis seu Visio Mariae Virginis', in *Apocrypha de Beata Maria Virgine: (Scriptores Aethiopici*, series i, vol. vii; Rome, 1909; repr. Louvain, 1955) (= *CSCO* 39, Aeth 22, 51–80. Latin trans. in *CSCO* 40 = Aeth 23, 43–68).
Italian trans. Erbetta, iii. 455–70, and Moraldi, i. 901–26; Eng. summary in James, *ANT* 563–4.

MODERN TRANSLATIONS

English

A. Walker, *Ante-Nicene Christian Library* 16 (Edinburgh, 1870), 477–92 (trans. of Tischendorf's Greek).
A. Rutherfurd, in A. Menzies (ed.), *Ante-Nicene Christian Library*: Additional Volume 9 (Edinburgh, 1897), 151–66 (trans. of James's edn. of the Latin from the Paris MS).
James, 526–55.
Hennecke[3], ii. 755–98.
Hennecke[5], ii. 712–48.

Anglo-Saxon

A. di P. Healey, *The Old English Vision of St Paul* (Cambridge, Mass., 1978) (= *Speculum Anniversary Monographs* 2).

French

Amiot, 295–331.
Éac, 777–824.

German

Hennecke[3], ii. 536–67 (H. Duensing).
Hennecke[5], ii. 644–75 (H. Duensing and A. de Santos Otero).

Italian

G. Ricciotti, *L'Apocalisse di Paoli siriaca* (Brescia, 1932).
Erbetta, iii. 353–86.
Moraldi, ii. 1855–1911.

Irish

St J. D. Seymour, 'Irish Versions of the Visions of St Paul', *JTS* 24 (1922–3), 54–9.
M. McNamara, *The Apocrypha in the Irish Church* (Dublin, 1975), 135–8.
M. Herbert and M. McNamara, *Irish Biblical Apocrypha* (Edinburgh, 1989), 132–6.

GENERAL

C. H. Kraeling, 'The Apocalypse of Paul and the "Iranische Erlösungsmysterium"', *HTR* 24 (1931), 209–44.
R. P. Casey, 'The Apocalypse of Paul', *JTS* 34 (1933), 1–32.
T. Silverstein, 'Did Dante know of the Vision of St Paul?', *Harvard Studies and Notes in Philology and Literature* 19 (1937), 231–47.
—— 'The Date of the Apocalypse of Paul', *Mediaeval Studies* 24 (1962), 335–48.
D. D. R. Owen, 'The "Vision of St Paul"', *Romance Philology* 12 (1958), 33–51.
—— *The Vision of Hell* (Edinburgh and London, 1970).
M. Himmelfarb, *Tours of Hell: An Apocalyptic Form in Jewish and Christian Literature* (Philadelphia, 1983).
—— 'The Experience of the Visionary and Genre in the Ascension of Isaiah 6–11 and the Apocalypse of Paul', *Semeia* 26 (1986), 97–111.
R. Bauckham, 'Early Jewish Visions of Hell', *JTS* 41 (1090), 355–85.
—— 'The Conflict of Justice and Mercy: Attitudes to the Damned in Apocalyptic Literature', in *La Fable apocryphe: Actes du colloque du centenaire de l'école pratique des hautes études*, v (Turnhout, 1990), 181–96 (= *Apocrypha. Le champ des apocryphes* 1).
C. Carozzi, *Escatologie et Au-delà. Recherches sur l'Apocalypse de Paul* (Aix-en-Provence, 1994). [Review: *VC* 50 (1996) 94–9.]
J. N. Bremmer and I. Czachesz (eds.), *The Apocalypse of Paul* (Leuven, 2004) (= *Studies on Early Christian Apocrypha* 9).

THE APOCALYPSE OF PAUL

SUMMARY OF CONTENT

1–2 Discovery of the Vision
3–6 Appeal of Creation to God against sinful man
7–10 Reports of the angels to God about man
11–18 Death and judgement of the righteous and the wicked

19–30 Paul's vision of Paradise
31–44 Paul's vision of Hell.
   Rest on Sundays for the damned is obtained by Paul.
   (None of the shorter Latin recensions goes beyond chapter 44)
45–51 Second vision of Paradise.

The Coptic has a continuation beyond the abrupt ending of the Greek, Latin, and Syriac, containing a third visit to Paradise. Part of this Coptic conclusion is used in the translation below.

'But I will come to visions and revelations of the Lord: I know a man in Christ fourteen years ago (whether in the body, I know not; or out of the body, I know not, God knows) snatched up to the third heaven; and I know such a man, whether in the body or out of the body I know not, God knows; how he was snatched up into Paradise and heard secret words which it is not lawful for men to speak; on behalf of such a man I will glory; but on my own behalf I will not glory, save in my infirmities.'[1]

1. At what time was this revelation made? In the consulship of Theodosius Augustus the Younger and Cynegius, a certain nobleman was then living in Tarsus, in the house which was that of Saint Paul; an angel appeared in the night and revealed it to him, saying that he should open the foundations of the house and should publish what he found, but he thought that these things were dreams.

2. But the angel coming for the third time beat him and forced him to open the foundation. And digging he found a marble box, inscribed on the sides; there was the revelation of Saint Paul, and his shoes in which he walked teaching the word of God. But he feared to open that box and brought it to the judge; when he had received it, the judge, because it was sealed with lead, sent it to the emperor Theodosius, fearing lest it might be something else; when the emperor had received it he opened it, and found the revelation of Saint Paul, a copy of which he sent to Jerusalem, and retained the original himself.[2]

3. While I was in the body in which I was snatched up to the third heaven, the word of the Lord came to me, saying, 'Speak to the people, "How long will you transgress, and heap sin upon sin, and tempt the Lord who made you?[3] You are the sons of God, doing the works of the devil in the faith of Christ, on account of the impediments of the world. Remember therefore and know that, while every creature serves God, the human race alone sins. It reigns over every creature and sins more than all nature"'.

4. For indeed the sun, the great light, often addressed the Lord saying, 'Lord God Almighty, I look out upon the impieties and injustices of men;

[1] 2 Cor. 12: 1–5.
[2] The Syriac places the story of the discovery at the end.
[3] Isa. 30: 1.

permit me and I shall do to them what are my powers, that they may know that you are God alone.' And there came a voice saying to him, 'I know all these things, for my eye sees and my ear hears, but my patience bears with them until they be converted and repent. But if they do not return to me I will judge them all.'

5. Sometimes the moon and stars addressed the Lord saying, 'Lord God Almighty, to us you have given the power of the night;[4] how long shall we look down upon the impieties and fornications and homicides done by the sons of men? Permit us to deal with them according to our powers, that they may know that you are God alone.' And there came a voice to them, saying, 'I know all these things, and my eye sees and my ear hears, but my patience bears with them until they be converted and repent. But if they do not return to me I will judge them.'

6. And frequently the sea exclaimed, saying, 'Lord God Almighty, men have defiled your holy name in me; permit me to arise and cover every wood and orchard and the whole world, until I blot out all the sons of men from before your face, that they may know that you are God alone.' And the voice came again and said, 'I know all these things; my eye sees everything, and my ear hears, but my patience bears with them until they be converted and repent. But if they do not return to me I will judge them.' Sometimes the waters also spoke against the sons of men saying, 'Lord God Almighty, all the sons of men have defiled your holy name.' And there came a voice saying, 'I know all things before they come to pass, for my eye sees and my ear hears all things, but my patience bears with them until they be converted. But if not, I will judge them.' Frequently also the earth too exclaimed to the Lord against the sons of men, saying, 'Lord God Almighty, I above every other creature am harmed, supporting the fornications, adulteries, homicides, thefts, perjuries, and magic and ill-doings of men and all the evil they do, so that the father rises up against the son, and the son upon the father, the alien against the alien, and each one defiles his neighbour's wife. The father mounts the bed of his own son, and the son likewise ascends the couch of his own father; and in all these evils, they who offer the sacrifice to your name have defiled your holy place. Therefore I am injured above every creature, not desiring to show my power to myself, and my fruits to the sons of men. Permit me and I will destroy the virtue of my fruits.' And there came a voice and said, 'I know all things, and there is none who can hide himself from his sin. Moreover I know their impieties, but my holiness endures them until they be converted and repent. But if they do not return to me I will judge them.'

7. Behold, you sons of men, the creature is subject to God, but the human race alone sins. For this reason, therefore, you sons of men, bless the Lord God unceasingly, every hour and every day, but more especially when the sun

---

[4] Cf. Jer. 31: 35.

has set: for at that hour all the angels proceed to the Lord to worship him and to present the works of men, which every man has wrought from the morning till the evening, whether good or evil. And there is a certain angel who proceeds rejoicing from the man in whom he dwells.[5] When the sun has set in the first hour of the night, in the same hour comes the angel of every people and every man and woman, who protects and preserves them, because man is the image of God; similarly also in the hour of morning which is the twelfth of the night, all the angels of men and women go up to God to worship God, and present every work which each man has wrought, whether good or evil. Moreover every day and night the angels show to God an account of all the acts of the human race. To you, therefore, I say, you sons of men, bless the Lord God without fail all the days of your life.

8. Therefore at the appointed hour all the angels, rejoicing at once together, proceeded before God that they might meet to worship at the hour determined. And behold suddenly it became the hour of meeting,[6] and the angels came to worship in the presence of God, and the spirit proceeded to meet them; and there came a voice and said, 'Whence come you, our angels, bearing the burdens of tidings?'

9. They answered and said, 'We come from those who have renounced this world for the sake of your holy name, wandering as pilgrims in the caves of the rocks, and weeping every hour in which they inhabit the earth, and hungering and thirsting because of your name, with their loins girded, having in their hands the incense of their hearts, and praying and blessing every hour, and restraining and overcoming themselves, weeping and wailing above the rest that inhabit the earth. And we indeed, their angels, mourn along with them; therefore, wherever it shall please you, command us to go and minister, lest others also do it, but the destitute above the rest who are on earth.'[7] And there came the voice of God to them saying, 'Know that now and henceforward my grace is appointed to you, and my help, who is my well-beloved Son, shall be present with them, guiding them every hour; ministering also to them, never deserting them, since their place is his habitation.'

10. When these angels had retired, behold, other angels came weeping in the assembly to adore in the presence of honour; and the spirit of God proceeded to meet them, and there came the voice of God and said, 'Whence come you, our angels, bearing the burdens of the ministry of the tidings of the world?' They answered and said in the presence of God, 'We have arrived from those who called upon your name, and the impediments of the world made them wretched, devising many occasions every hour, not even making one pure prayer, not even out of their whole heart, in all the time of their life; what need, therefore, is there to be present with men who are sinners?' And

---

[5] Greek adds: 'and another goes with a sad face'.
[6] Text corrupt.
[7] Text corrupt. Greek has the angels ask that these good men may continue in goodness.

there came the voice of God to them, 'It is necessary that you should minister to them until they be converted and repent,[8] but if they do not return to me I will judge them. Know therefore, sons of men, that whatever things are wrought by you, these angels report to God, whether it is good or evil.'

11.[9] And the angel answered and said to me, 'Follow me, and I will show you the place of the just where they are led when they are deceased, and after these things I will take you into the abyss and I will show you the souls of sinners and what sort of place they are led into when they are deceased.' And I followed the angel, and he led me into heaven, and I looked back upon the firmament, and I saw in the same place power, and there was there oblivion which deceives and draws down to itself the hearts of men, and the spirit of detraction, and the spirit of fornication, and the spirit of madness, and the spirit of insolence, and there were there the princes of vices: these I saw under the firmament of heaven; and again I looked back, and I saw angels without mercy, having no pity, whose countenance was full of madness, and their teeth sticking out beyond the mouth; their eyes shone like the morning star of the east, and from the hairs of their head or from their mouth sparks of fire went out. And I asked the angel saying. 'Sir, who are those?' And the angel answered and said to me, 'These are those who are destined to the souls of the impious in the hour of need, who did not believe that they had the Lord for their helper, nor hoped in him.'

12. And I looked on high, and I saw other angels whose countenance shone as the sun, their loins girded with golden girdles, having palms in their hands, and the sign of God, clothed with garments in which was written the name of the Son of God, filled with all meekness and pity; and I asked the angel, saying, 'Who are these, sir, in so great beauty and pity?' And the angel answered and said to me, 'These are the angels of justice who are sent to lead up the souls of the just in the hour of need, who believed that they had the Lord for their helper.' And I said to him, 'Do the just and sinners of necessity meet witnesses when they have died?' And the angel answered and said to me, 'There is one way by which all pass over to God, but the just having their helper with them are not confounded when they go to appear in the sight of God.'

13. And I said to the angel, 'I wish to see the souls of the just and of sinners going out of the world.' And the angel answered and said to me, 'Look down upon the earth.' And I looked down from heaven upon the earth, and saw the whole world, and it was as nothing in my sight and I saw the sons of men as though they were naught and growing weak, and I wondered and said to the angel, 'Is this the greatness of men?' And the angel answered and said to me, 'It is, and these are they who do evil from morning till evening.' And I

---

[8] Heb. 1: 14.
[9] Syriac adds that he saw one of the angels who carried him up in the spirit to the third heaven.

looked and saw a great cloud of fire spread over the whole world, and I said to the angel, 'What is this, my lord?', and he said to me, 'This is injustice stirred up by the princes of sinners.'

14. When I had heard this I sighed and wept, and said to the angel, 'I wish to see the souls of the just and of sinners, and to see in what manner they go out of the body.' And the angel answered and said to me, 'Look again upon the earth.' And I looked and saw all the world, and men were as naught and growing weak; and I looked carefully and saw a certain man about to die, and the angel said to me, 'This one whom you see is a just man.' And I looked again and saw all his works, whatever he had done for the sake of God's name, and all his desires, both what he remembered, and what he did not remember; they all stood in his sight in the hour of need; and I saw the just man advance and find refreshment and confidence, and before he went out of the world the holy and the impious angels both attended; and I saw them all, but the impious found no place of habitation in him, but the holy angels took possession of his soul, guiding it till it went out of the body; and they roused the soul saying, 'Soul, know the body you leave, for it is necessary that you should return to the same body on the day of the resurrection, that you may receive the things promised to all the just.' Receiving therefore the soul from the body, they immediately kissed it as if it were familiar to them, saying to it, 'Be of good courage, for you have done the will of God while placed on earth.' And there came to meet it the angel who watched it every day, and said to it, 'Be of good courage, soul; I rejoice in you, because you have done the will of God on earth; for I related to God all your works just as they were.' Similarly also the spirit proceeded to meet it and said, 'Soul, fear not, nor be disturbed, until you come to a place which you have never known, but I will be a helper to you: for I found in you a place of refreshment in the time when I dwelt in you, while I was on earth.' And his spirit strengthened it, and his angel received it, and led it into heaven; and an angel said, 'Where are you running to, O soul, and do you dare to enter heaven? Wait and let us see if there is anything of ours in you; and behold we find nothing in you. I see also your divine helper and angel, and the spirit is rejoicing along with you, because you have done the will of God on earth.'[10] And they led it along till it should worship in the sight of God. And when it[11] had ceased, immediately Michael and all the army of angels, with one voice, adored the footstool of his feet and his doors, saying at the same time to the soul, 'This is your God of all things, who made you in his own image and likeness.' Moreover the angel ran on ahead and pointed him out, saying, 'God, remember his labours; for this is the soul, whose works I related to you, acting according to your judgement.' And the spirit said likewise, 'I am the spirit of vivification inspiring it; for I had

---

[10] Syriac differs here, and includes a conflict between good and evil angels.
[11] Literally 'they'.

refreshment in it, in the time when I dwelt in it, acting according to your judgement.' And there came the voice of God and said, 'In as much as this man did not grieve me, neither will I grieve him; as he had pity, I also will have pity. Let it therefore be handed over to Michael, the angel of the Covenant, and let him lead it into the Paradise of joy, that it may become coheir with all the saints.' And after these things I heard the voices of a thousand thousand angels and archangels and cherubim and twenty-four elders, saying hymns and glorifying the Lord and crying, 'You are just, O Lord, and just are your judgements, and there is no respect of persons with you, but you reward every man according to your judgement.' And the angel answered and said to me, 'Have you believed and known that whatever each man of you has done he sees in the hour of need?' And I said, 'Yes, sir.'

15. And he said to me, 'Look again down on the earth, and watch the soul of an impious man going out of the body, which grieved the Lord day and night, saying, "I know nothing else in this world, I eat and drink, and enjoy what is in the world; for who is there who has descended into hell and, ascending, has declared to us that there is judgement there!"' And again I looked carefully, and saw all the scorn of the sinner, and all that he did, and they stood together before him in the hour of need; and it was done to him in that hour, when he was led out of his body at the judgement, and he said, 'It were better for me if I had not been born.' And after these things, there came at the same time the holy angels and the evil angels, and the soul of the sinner saw both and the holy angels did not find a place in it. Moreover the evil angels cursed it; and when they had drawn it out of the body the angels admonished it a third time, saying, 'O wretched soul, look upon your flesh from which you have come out; for it is necessary that you should return to your flesh in the day of resurrection, that you may receive what is the due for your sins and your impieties.'

16. And when they had led it forth the guardian angel preceded it, and said to it, 'O wretched soul, I am the angel belonging to you, relating daily to the Lord your evil works, whatever you did by night or day; and if it were in my power, not for one day would I minister to you, but none of these things was I able to do: the judge is full of pity and just, and he himself commanded us that we should not cease to minister to the soul till you should repent, but you have lost the time of repentance. I have become a stranger to you and you to me. Let us go on then to the just judge; I will not dismiss you before I know from today I am to be a stranger to you.' And the spirit afflicted it, and the angel troubled it. When they had arrived at the powers, when it started to enter heaven, a burden was imposed upon it, above all other burden: error and oblivion and murmuring met it, and the spirit of fornication, and the rest of the powers, and said to it, 'Where are you going, wretched soul, and do you dare to rush into heaven? Hold, that we may see if we have our qualities in you, since we do not see that you have a holy helper.' And after that I heard

voices in the height of heaven saying, 'Present that wretched soul to God, so it may know that it is God whom it despised.' When, therefore, it had entered heaven all the angels saw it; a thousand thousand exclaimed with one voice, all saying, 'Woe to you, wretched soul, for the sake of your works which you did on earth; what answer are you about to give to God when you have approached to adore him?' The angel who was with it answered and said, 'Weep with me, my beloved, for I have not found rest in this soul.' And the angels answered him and said, 'Let such a soul be taken away from our midst, for from the time it entered the stink of it crosses to us angels.' And after these things it was presented, that it might worship in the sight of God, and an angel of God showed it God who made it after his own image and likeness. Moreover its angel ran before it saying, 'Lord God Almighty, I am the angel of this soul, whose works I presented to you day and night, not acting in accordance with your judgement. And the spirit likewise said, 'I am the spirit who dwelt in it from the time it was made; in itself I know it, and it has not followed my will; judge it, Lord, according to your judgement.' And there came the voice of God to it and said, 'Where is your fruit which you have made worthy of the goods which you have received? Have I put a distance of one day between you and the just man? Did I not make the sun to arise upon you as upon the just?' But the soul was silent, having nothing to answer, and again there came a voice saying, 'Just is the judgement of God, and there is no respect of persons with God, for whoever shall have done mercy, on him shall he have mercy, and whoever shall not have been merciful, neither shall God pity him. Let it therefore be handed over to the angel Tartaruchus,[12] who is set over the punishments, and let him cast it into outer darkness, where there is weeping and gnashing of teeth, and let it be there till the great day of judgement.' And after these things I heard the voice of angels and archangels saying, 'You are just, Lord, and your judgement is just.'

17. And again I saw and, behold, a soul which was led forward by two angels, weeping and saying, 'Have pity on me, just God, God the judge, for to-day it is seven days since I went out of my body, and I was handed over to these two angels, and they brought me to those places which I had never seen.' And God, the just judge, said to it, 'What have you done? For you never showed mercy, therefore you were handed over to such angels as have no mercy, and because you did not do right, so neither did they act compassionately with you in your hour of need. Confess your sins which you committed when placed in the world.' And it answered and said, 'Lord, I did not sin.' And the Lord, the just Lord, was angered in fury when it said, 'I did not sin', because it lied; and God said, 'Do you think you are still in the world where any one of you, sinning, may conceal and hide his sin from his

---

[12] See J. M. Rosenstiehl, 'Tartarouchos—Temelouchos. Contribution à l'étude de Apocalypse apocryphe de Paul', in *Deuxième Journée d'études coptes*, Strasbourg 25 May 1984 (Louvain, 1986), 29–56 (= *Cahiers de la Bibliothèque copte* 3).

neighbour? Here nothing whatever shall be hidden, for when the souls come to worship in sight of the throne both the good works and the sins of each one are made manifest.' And hearing these things the soul was silent, having no answer. And I heard the Lord God, the just judge, again saying, 'Come, angel of this soul, and stand in the midst.' And the angel of the sinful soul came, having in his hands a document, and said, 'These, Lord, in my hands, are all the sins of this soul from its youth till to-day, from the tenth year of its birth; and if you command, Lord, I will also relate its acts from the beginning of its fifteenth year.' And the Lord God, the just judge, said, 'I say to you, angel, I do not expect of you an account of it since it began to be fifteen years old, but state its sins for five years before it died and before it came hither.' And again God, the just judge, said, 'For by myself I swear, and by my holy angels, and by my virtue, that if it had repented five years before it died, on account of a conversion one year old, oblivion would now be thrown over all the evils which it sinned before, and it would have indulgence and remission of sins: now indeed it shall perish.' And the angel of the sinful soul answered and said, 'Lord, command that angel to exhibit those souls.'

18. And in that same hour the souls were exhibited in the midst, and the soul of the sinner knew them; and the Lord said to the soul of the sinner, 'I say to you, soul, confess your work which you wrought in these souls whom you see, when they were in the world.' And it answered and said, 'Lord, it is not yet a full year since I slew this one and poured his blood upon the ground, and with another I committed fornication; not only this, but I also greatly harmed her in taking away her goods.' And the Lord God, the just judge, said, 'Did you not know that if someone does violence to another and the person who sustains the violence dies first, he is kept in this place until the one who has committed the offence dies, and then both stand in the presence of the judge, and now each receives according to his deed.' And I heard a voice of one saying, 'Let that soul be delivered into the hands of Tartarus, and led down into hell; he shall lead it into the lower prison, and it shall be put in torments and left there till the great day of judgement.' And again I heard a thousand thousand angels saying hymns to the Lord, and crying, 'You are just, O Lord, and just are your judgements.'

19. The angel answered and said to me, 'Have you perceived all these things?' And I said, 'Yes, sir.' And he said to me, 'Follow me again, and I will take you, and show you the places of the just.' And I followed the angel, and he raised me to the third heaven and placed me at the entry of the door; and looking, I saw that the door was of gold, and two columns of gold above it full of golden letters, and the angel turned again to me and said, 'Blessed are you if you enter through these doors, for it is not permitted for any to enter except those who have goodness and purity of body in all things.' And I asked the angel about everything and said, 'Sir, tell me on what account these letters are set upon those tables?' The angel answered and said to me, 'These are the

names of the just who dwell on the earth and serve God with their whole heart.' And again I said, 'Sir, are their names written in heaven while they are still on the earth?' And he said, 'Not only their names,[13] but also their countenance and the likeness of those who serve God are in heaven and are known to the angels; for they know who are the servants of God with all their heart, before they go out of the world.'

20. And when I had entered within the gate of Paradise, there came out to meet me an old man whose countenance shone as the sun; and when he had embraced me he said, 'Hail, Paul, beloved of God.' And he kissed me with a cheerful countenance. He wept, and I said to him, 'Brother, why do you weep?' And again sighing and lamenting he said, 'We are hurt by men, and they grieve us greatly; for many are the good things which the Lord has prepared, and great is his promise, but many do not perceive them.' And I asked the angel and said, 'Sir, who is this?' And he said to me, 'This is Enoch, the scribe of righteousness.' And I entered into that place, and immediately I saw Elijah,[14] and he came and greeted me, laughing and rejoicing. And when he had seen me, he turned away and wept, and said to me, 'Paul, would that you should receive the rewards of your labours which you have done for the human race. As for me, I have seen great and many good things which God has prepared for the just, and the promises of God are great, but many do not perceive them; but even after many labours scarcely one or two enters into these places.'

21. And the angel answered and said to me, 'Whatever I now show you here, and whatever you shall hear, tell no one on earth.' And he led me and showed me; and there I heard words which it is not lawful for a man to speak.[15] And again he said, 'Follow me, and I will show you what you ought to report in public and relate.'

And he took me down from the third heaven, and led me into the second heaven, and again he led me on to the firmament, and from the firmament he led me over the gates of heaven; the beginning of its foundation was on the river which waters all the earth. And I asked the angel and said, 'Lord, what is this river of water?' And he said to me, 'This is the ocean!' And suddenly I went out of heaven, and I understood that it is the light of heaven which lightens all the earth. For the land there is seven times brighter than silver. And I said, 'Lord, what is this place?' And he said to me, 'This is the land of promise. Have you never heard what is written: Blessed are the meek for they shall inherit the earth?[16] The souls of the just, when they have gone out of the body, are dismissed to this place for a while.' And I said to the angel, 'Then this land will be manifested before the time?' The angel answered and said to

---

[13] 'Written...names' omitted in Latin by homoioteleuton: words supplied from Coptic.
[14] Reading 'Helios' as 'Helias'.
[15] 2 Cor. 12: 4.
[16] Matt. 5: 5.

me, 'When Christ, whom you preach, shall come to reign, then, by the sentence of God, the first earth will be dissolved and this land of promise will then be revealed, and it will be like dew or cloud, and then the Lord Jesus Christ, the King Eternal, will be manifested and will come with all his saints to dwell in it, and he will reign over them a thousand years,[17] and they will eat of the good things which I shall now show you.'

22. And I looked around upon that land, and I saw a river flowing with milk and honey, and there were trees planted by the bank of that river, full of fruit; moreover, each single tree bore twelve fruits in the year, having various and diverse fruits; and I saw the created things which are in that place and all the work of God, and I saw there palms of twenty cubits, but others of ten cubits; and that land was seven times brighter than silver. And there were trees full of fruits from the roots to the highest branches, of ten thousand fruits of palms upon ten thousand fruits. The grape-vines had ten thousand plants. Moreover in the single vines there were ten thousand thousand bunches and in each of these a thousand single grapes; moreover these single trees bore a thousand fruits. And I said to the angel, 'Why does each tree bear a thousand fruits?' The angel answered and said to me, 'Because the Lord God gives an abounding profusion of gifts to the worthy and because they of their own will afflicted themselves when they were placed in the world doing all things on account of his holy name.' And again I said to the angel, 'Sir, are these the only promises which the Most Holy God makes?' And he answered and said to me, 'No! There are seven times greater than these. But I say to you that when the just go out of the body they shall see the promises and the good things which God has prepared for them. Till then, they shall sigh and lament, saying, "Have we uttered any word from our mouth to grieve our neighbour even on one day?"' I asked and said again, 'Are these alone the promises of God?' And the angel answered and said to me, 'These whom you now see are the souls of the married and those who kept the chastity of their nuptials, controlling themselves. But to the virgins and those who hunger and thirst after righteousness[18] and those who afflicted themselves for the sake of the name of God, God will give seven times greater than these, which I shall now show you.'

And then he took me up from that place where I saw these things and behold, a river, and its waters were much whiter than milk, and I said to the angel, 'What is this?' And he said to me, 'This is the Acherusian Lake where is the City of Christ, but not every man is permitted to enter that city; for this is the journey which leads to God, and if anyone is a fornicator and impious, and is converted and shall repent and bear fruits worthy of repentance, at first when he has gone out of the body, he is brought and worships God, and

---

[17] Cf. Rev. 20: 2.
[18] Matt. 5: 6.

thence by command of the Lord he is delivered to the angel Michael and he baptizes him in the Acherusian Lake—then he leads him into the City of Christ alongside those who have never sinned.' But I marvelled and blessed the Lord God for all the things which I saw.

23. And the angel answered and said to me, 'Follow me, and I will lead you into the City of Christ.' And he was standing on the Acherusian Lake and he put me into a golden ship and about three thousand angels were singing a hymn before me till I arrived at the City of Christ. Those who inhabited the City of Christ greatly rejoiced over me as I went to them, and I entered and saw the City of Christ, and it was all of gold, and twelve walls encircled it, and twelve interior towers, and there was a stade between each of the encircling walls. And I said to the angel, 'Sir, how much is a stadium?' The angel answered and said to me, 'As much as there is between the Lord God and the men who are on the earth, for the City of Christ alone is great.' And there were twelve gates in the circuit of the city, of great beauty, and four rivers which encircled it. There was a river of honey, and a river of milk, and a river of wine, and a river of oil. And I said to the angel, 'What are these rivers surrounding that city?' And he said to me, 'These are the four rivers which flow abundantly for those who are in this land of promise; the names are these: the river of honey is called Pison, and the river of milk Euphrates, and the river of oil Gion, and the river of wine Tigris. When they were in the world they did not use their power over these things, but they hungered and afflicted themselves for the sake of the Lord God, so that when they enter this city the Lord will assign them these things above all measure.'

24. When I entered the gate I saw trees great and very high before the doors of the city, having no fruit but leaves only, and I saw a few men scattered in the midst of the trees, and they lamented greatly when they saw anyone enter the city. And those trees were sorry for them and humbled themselves and bowed down and again erected themselves. And I saw it and wept with them, and I asked the angel and said, 'Sir, who are these who are not admitted to enter into the City of Christ?' And he said to me, 'These are they who zealously abstained day and night in fasts, but they had a proud heart above other men, glorifying and praising themselves and doing nothing for their neighbours. They gave some people friendly greeting, but to others they did not even say "Hail!" And, indeed, they showed hospitality only to those whom they wished, and if they did anything whatever for their neighbour they were immoderately puffed up.' And I said, 'What then, sir? Did their pride prevent them from entering into the City of Christ?' And the angel answered and said to me, 'Pride is the root of all evils. Are they better than the Son of God who came to the Jews with much humility?' And I asked him and said, 'Why is it that the trees humble themselves and erect themselves again?' And the angel answered and said to me, 'The whole time which these men passed on earth, they zealously served God, but on account of the shame and reproaches of men for a time they blushed and humbled themselves, but

they were not saddened, nor did they repent that they should desist from the pride which was in them. This is why the trees humble themselves, and again are raised up.' And I asked and said, 'For what reason were they admitted to the doors of the city?' The angel answered and said to me, 'Because of the great goodness of God, and because this is the entrance of his saints entering this city: for this reason they are left in this place, but when Christ the King Eternal enters with his saints, all the righteous may pray for them, and then they may enter into the city along with them; yet none of them is able to have the same confidence as those who humbled themselves, serving the Lord God all their lives.'

25. But I went on with the angel leading me, and he brought me to the river of honey, and I saw there Isaiah and Jeremiah and Ezekiel and Amos and Micah and Zechariah, the minor and major prophets, and they greeted me in the city. I said to the angel, 'What is this way?' And he said to me, 'This is the way of the prophets; every one who shall have afflicted his soul and not done his own will because of God, when he has come out of the world and has been led to the Lord God and adored him, then by the command of God he is handed over to Michael, and he leads him into the city to this place of the prophets, and they greet him as their friend and neighbour because he did the will of God.'

26. Again he led me where there is a river of milk, and I saw in that place all the infants whom Herod slew because of the name of Christ, and they greeted me, and the angel said to me, 'All who keep their chastity and purity, when they have come out of the body, after they adore the Lord God are delivered to Michael and are led to the infants, and they greet them, saying that they are our brothers and friends and members; among them they shall inherit the promises of God.'

27. Again he took me up and brought me to the north of the city and led me where there was a river of wine, and there I saw Abraham and Isaac and Jacob, Lot and Job and other saints, and they greeted me; and I asked and said, 'What is this place, my lord?' The angel answered and said to me, 'All who have given hospitality to strangers when they go out of the world first adore the Lord God, and are delivered to Michael and by this route are led into the city, and all the just greet them as son and brother, and say to them, "Because you have observed humanity and helped pilgrims, come, have an inheritance in the city of the Lord our God: every righteous man shall receive good things of God in the city, according to his own action."'

28. And again he carried me near the river of oil on the east of the city. And I saw there men rejoicing and singing psalms, and I said, 'Who are those, my lord?' And the angel said to me, 'These are they who devoted themselves to God with their whole heart and had no pride in themselves. For all those who rejoice in the Lord God and sing psalms to the Lord with their whole heart are here led into this city.'

29. And he carried me into the midst of the city near the twelve walls. But

there was in this place a higher wall, and I asked and said, 'Is there in the City of Christ a wall which exceeds this place in honour?' And the angel answered and said to me, 'There is a second better than the first, and similarly a third better than the second, as each exceeds the other up to the twelfth wall.' And I said, 'Tell me, sir, why one exceeds another in glory.' And the angel answered and said to me, 'All who have in themselves even a little slander or zeal or pride, something of his glory would be made void even if they were in the City of Christ: look behind you.'

And turning round I saw golden thrones placed in each gate, and on them men having golden diadems and gems; and I looked and I saw inside between the twelve men thrones placed in another rank which appeared to be of greater glory, so that no one is able to recount their praise. And I asked the angel and said, 'My lord, who is on the throne?' And the angel answered and said to me, 'Those thrones belong to those who had goodness and understanding of heart, yet made themselves fools for the sake of the Lord God, as they knew neither Scripture nor psalms, but mindful of one chapter of the commands of God, and hearing what it contained, they acted with much diligence and had a true zeal before the Lord God, and the admiration of them will seize all the saints in the presence of the Lord God, for talking with one another they say, "Wait and see how these unlearned men who know nothing more have merited so great and beautiful a garment and so great glory on account of their innocence."'

And I saw in the midst of this city a great altar, very high, and there was someone standing near the altar whose countenance shone as the sun, and he held in his hands a psaltery and harp, and he sang saying, 'Alleluia!' And his voice filled the whole city; at the same time, when all they who were on the towers and gates heard him, they responded, 'Alleluia!' so that the foundations of the city were shaken; and I asked the angel and said, 'Sir, who is this of so great power?' And the angel said to me, 'This is David; this is the city of Jerusalem, for when Christ the King of Eternity shall come with the assurance of his kingdom, he again shall go before him that he may sing psalms, and all the righteous at the same time shall sing responding "Alleluia!"' And I said, 'Sir, how did David alone above the other saints make a beginning of psalm-singing?' And the angel answered and said to me, 'Because Christ the Son of God sits at the right hand of his Father, and this David sings psalms before him in the seventh heaven, and as it is done in the heavens so also below, because a sacrifice may not be offered to God without David, but it is necessary that David should sing psalms in the hour of the oblation of the body and blood of Christ: as it is performed in heaven, so also on earth.'

30. And I said to the angel, 'Sir, what is Alleluia?' And the angel answered and said to me, 'You ask questions about everything.' And he said to me, 'Alleluia is Hebrew, the language of God and angels, for the meaning of Alleluia is this: *tecel cat marith macha*.' And I said, 'Sir, what is *tecel cat marith*

macha?' And the angel answered and said to me, '*Tecel cat marith macha* is: Let us all bless him together.' I asked the angel and said, 'Sir, do all who say Alleluia bless the Lord?' And the angel answered and said to me, 'It is so, and if any one sing Alleluia and those who are present do not sing at the same time, they commit sin because they do not sing along with him.' And I said, 'My lord, does he also sin if he be hesitating or very old?' And the angel answered and said to me, 'Not so, but he who is able and does not join in the singing you know as a despiser of the Word, and it would be proud and unworthy that he should not bless the Lord God his maker.'

31. When he had ceased speaking to me, he led me outside the city through the midst of the trees and far from the places of the land of the good, and put me across the river of milk and honey; and after that he led me over the ocean which supports the foundations of heaven.

The angel answered and said to me, 'Do you understand why you go hence?' And I said, 'Yes, sir.' And he said to me, 'Come and follow me, and I will show you the souls of the godless and sinners, that you may know what manner of place it is.' And I went with the angel, and he carried me towards the setting of the sun, and I saw the beginning of heaven founded on a great river of water, and I asked, 'What is this river of water?' And he said to me, 'This is the ocean which surrounds all the earth.' And when I was at the outer limit of the ocean I looked, and there was no light in that place, but darkness and sorrow and sadness; and I sighed.

And I saw there a river boiling with fire, and in it a multitude of men and women immersed up to the knees, and other men up to the navel, others even up to the lips, others up to the hair. And I asked the angel and said, 'Sir, who are those in the fiery river?' And the angel answered and said to me, 'They are neither hot nor cold, because they were found neither in the number of the just nor in the number of the godless. For those spent the time of their life on earth passing some days in prayer, but others in sins and fornications, until their death.' And I asked him and said, 'Who are these, sir, immersed up to their knees in fire?' He answered and said to me, 'These are they who when they have gone out of church occupy themselves with idle disputes. Those who are immersed up to the navel are those who, when they have taken the body and blood of Christ, go and fornicate and do not cease from their sins till they die. Those who are immersed up to the lips are those who slander each other when they assemble in the church of God; those up to the eyebrows are those who nod to each other and plot spite against their neighbour.'

32. And I saw to the north a place of various and diverse punishments full of men and women, and a river of fire ran down into it. I observed and I saw very deep pits and in them several souls together, and the depth of that place was about three thousand cubits, and I saw them groaning and weeping and saying, 'Have pity on us, O Lord!', and no one had pity on them. And I asked

the angel and said, 'Who are these, sir?' And the angel answered and said to me, 'These are they who did not hope in the Lord, that they would be able to have him as their helper.' And I asked and said, 'Sir, if these souls remain for thirty or forty generations thus one upon another, I believe the pits would not hold them unless they were dug deeper.' And he said to me, 'The Abyss has no measure, for beneath it there stretches down below that which is below it; and so it is that if perchance anyone should take a stone and throw it into a very deep well after many hours it would reach the bottom, such is the abyss. For when the souls are thrown in there, they hardly reach the bottom in fifty years.'

33. When I heard this, I wept and groaned over the human race. The angel answered and said to me, 'Why do you weep? Are you more merciful than God? For though God is good, he knows that there are punishments, and he patiently bears with the human race, allowing each one to do his own will in the time in which he dwells on the earth.'

34. I observed the fiery river and saw there a man being tortured by Tartaruchian angels having in their hands an iron instrument with three hooks with which they pierced the bowels of that old man; and I asked the angel and said, 'Sir, who is that old man on whom such torments are imposed?' And the angel answered and said to me, 'He whom you see was a presbyter who did not perform his ministry well: when he had been eating and drinking and committing fornication he offered the host to the Lord at his holy altar.'

35. And I saw not far away another old man led on by evil angels running with speed, and they pushed him into the fire up to his knees, and they struck him with stones and wounded his face like a storm, and did not allow him to say, 'Have pity on me!' And I asked the angel, and he said to me, 'He whom you see was a bishop and did not perform his episcopate well, who indeed accepted the great name but did not enter into the witness of him who gave him the name all his life, seeing that he did not give just judgement and did not pity widows and orphans, but now he receives retribution according to his iniquity and his works.'

36. And I saw another man in the fiery river up to his knees. His hands were stretched out and bloody, and worms proceeded from his mouth and nostrils, and he was groaning and weeping, and crying he said, 'Have pity on me! For I am hurt more than the rest who are in this punishment.' And I asked, 'Sir, who is this?' And he said to me, 'This man whom you see was a deacon who devoured the oblations and committed fornication and did not do right in the sight of God; for this cause he unceasingly pays this penalty.'

And I looked closely and saw alongside of him another man, whom they delivered up with haste and cast into the fiery river, and he was in it up to the knees; and the angel who was set over the punishments came with a great fiery razor, and with it he cut the lips of that man and the tongue likewise. And sighing, I lamented and asked, 'Who is that, sir?' And he said to me, 'He whom you see was a reader and read to the people, but he himself did not keep the precepts of God; now he also pays the proper penalty.'

37. And I saw another multitude of pits in the same place, and in the midst of it a river full with a multitude of men and women, and worms consumed them. But I lamented, and sighing asked the angel and said, 'Sir, who are these?' And he said to me, 'These are those who exacted interest on interest and trusted in their riches and did not hope in God that he was their helper.'

And after that I looked and saw another place, very narrow, and it was like a wall, and fire round about it. And I saw inside men and women gnawing their tongues, and I asked, 'Sir, who are these?' And he said to me, 'These are they who in church disparage the Word of God, not attending to it, but as it were making naught of God and his angels; for that reason they now likewise pay the proper penalty.'

38. And I observed and saw another pool[19] in the pit and its appearance was like blood, and I asked and said, 'Sir, what is this place?' And he said to me, 'Into that pit stream all the punishments.' And I saw men and women immersed up to the lips, and I asked, 'Sir, who are these?' And he said to me, 'These are the magicians who prepared for men and women evil magic arts and did not cease till they died.'

And again I saw men and women with very black faces in a pit of fire, and I sighed and lamented and asked, 'Sir, who are these?' And he said to me, 'These are fornicators and adulterers who committed adultery, having wives of their own; likewise also the women committed adultery, having husbands of their own; therefore they unceasingly suffer penalties.'

39. And I saw there girls in black raiment, and four terrifying angels having in their hands burning chains, and they put them on the necks of the girls and led them into darkness; and I, again weeping, asked the angel, 'Who are these, sir?' And he said to me, 'These are they who, when they were virgins, defiled their virginity unknown to their parents; for which cause they unceasingly pay the proper penalties.'

And again I observed there men and women with hands cut and their feet placed naked in a place of ice and snow, and worms devoured them. Seeing them I lamented and asked, 'Sir, who are these?' And he said to me, 'These are they who harmed orphans and widows and the poor, and did not hope in the Lord, for which cause they unceasingly pay the proper penalties.'

And I observed and saw others hanging over a channel of water, and their tongues were very dry, and many fruits were placed in their sight, and they were not permitted to take of them, and I asked, 'Sir, who are these?' And he said to me, 'These are they who broke their fast before the appointed hour; for this cause they unceasingly pay these penalties.'

And I saw other men and women hanging by their eyebrows and their hair,

---

[19] Latin 'senem'!

and a fiery river drew them, and I said, 'Who are these, sir?' And he said to me, 'These are they who join themselves not to their own husbands and wives but to whores, and therefore they unceasingly pay the proper penalties.'

And I saw other men and women covered with dust, and their countenance was like blood, and they were in a pit of pitch and sulphur running in a fiery river, and I asked, 'Sir, who are these?' And he said to me, 'These are they who committed the iniquity of Sodom and Gomorrah, the male with the male, for which reason they unceasingly pay the penalties.'

40. And I observed and saw men and women clothed in bright garments, but with their eyes blind, and they were placed in a pit, and I asked, 'Sir, who are these?' And he said to me, 'These are heathen who gave alms, and knew not the Lord God, for which reason they unceasingly pay the proper penalties.' And I observed and saw other men and women on a pillar of fire, and beasts were tearing them in pieces, and they were not allowed to say, 'Lord have pity on us!' And I saw the angel of torments[20] putting heavy punishments on them and saying, 'Acknowledge the Son of God; for this was prophesied to you when the divine Scriptures were read to you, and you did not attend; for which cause God's judgement is just, because your actions have apprehended you and led you into these punishments.' But I sighed and wept, and I asked and said, 'Who are these men and women who are strangled in the fire and pay their penalties?' And he answered me, 'These are women who defiled the image of God by bringing forth infants out of the womb, and these are the men who lay with them. And their infants addressed the Lord God and the angels who were set over the punishments, saying, "Avenge us of our parents, for they defiled the image of God, having the name of God but not observing his precepts; they gave us for food to dogs and to be trodden on by swine; others they threw into the river." But the infants were handed over to the angels of Tartarus who were set over the punishments, that they might lead them to a spacious place of mercy; but their fathers and mothers were tortured in a perpetual punishment.'

And after that I saw men and women clothed with rags full of pitch and fiery sulphur, and dragons were coiled about their necks and shoulders and feet, and angels with fiery horns restrained them and smote them, and closed their nostrils, saying to them, 'Why did you not know the time in which it was right to repent and serve God, and did not do it?' And I asked, 'Sir, who are these?' And he said to me, 'These are they who seemed to renounce the world, putting on our garb, but the impediments of the world made them wretched, so that they did not maintain a single Agape, and they did not pity widows and orphans; they did not receive the stranger and the pilgrim, nor did they offer an oblation and they did not show mercy to their neighbour. Moreover not even on one day did their prayer ascend pure to the Lord God,

---

[20] Coptic: 'Aftemeloukos'.

but many impediments of the world detained them, and they were not able to do right in the sight of God, and the angels enclosed them in the place of punishments. And those who were in punishments saw them and said to them, "We indeed neglected God when we lived in the world and you also did likewise; when we were in the world we indeed knew that we were sinners, but of you it was said, 'These are just and servants of God.' Now we know that in vain you were called by the name of the Lord, for which cause you pay the penalties."'

And sighing I wept and said, 'Woe unto men, woe unto sinners! Why were they born?' And the angel answered and said to me, 'Why do you lament? Are you more merciful than the Lord God who is blessed forever, who established judgement and sent forth every man to choose good and evil in his own will and do what pleases him?' Then I lamented again very greatly, and he said to me, 'Do you lament when as yet you have not seen greater punishments? Follow me and you shall see seven times greater than these.'

41. And he carried me to the north and placed me above a well, and I found it sealed with seven seals; and the angel who was with me said to the angel of that place, 'Open the mouth of the well that Paul, the well-beloved of God, may see, for authority is given him that he may see all the torments of hell.' And the angel said to me, 'Stand far off that you may be able to bear the stench of this place.' When the well was opened, immediately there arose from it a disagreeable and evil stench, which surpasses all punishments; and I looked into the well, and I saw fiery masses glowing on all sides and anguish, and the mouth of the well was narrow so as to admit one man only. And the angel answered and said to me, 'If any man has been put into this well of the abyss and it has been sealed over him, no remembrance of him shall ever be made in the sight of the Father and his Son and the holy angels.' And I said, 'Who are these, sir, who are put into this well?' And he said to me, 'They are those who do not confess that Christ has come in the flesh and that the Virgin Mary brought him forth, and those who say that the bread and cup of the Eucharist of blessing are not the body and blood of Christ.'

42. And I looked from the north to the west and I saw there the worm that never rests,[21] and in that place there was gnashing of teeth; and the worms were one cubit long, and had two heads, and there I saw men and women in the cold gnashing their teeth. And I asked and said, 'Sir, who are these in this place?' And he said to me, 'These are they who say that Christ did not rise from the dead and that this flesh will not rise again.' And I asked and said, 'Sir, is there no fire nor heat in this place?' And he said to me, 'In this place there is nothing else but cold and snow.' And again he said to me, 'Even if the sun should rise upon them, they do not become warm on account of the excessive coldness of that place and the snow.'

---

[21] Mark 9: 44, 46, 48.

But hearing these things I stretched out my hands and wept, and sighing again I said, 'It were better for us if we had not been born, all of us who are sinners.'

43. But when those who were in that place saw me weeping with the angel, they cried out and wept saying, 'Lord God have mercy upon us!' And after these things I saw the heavens open, and Michael the archangel descending from heaven, and with him was the whole army of angels, and they came to those who were placed in punishment, and seeing him, again weeping, they cried out and said, 'Have pity on us! Michael the archangel, have pity on us and on the human race for because of your prayers the earth continues. We now see the judgement and acknowledge the Son of God! It was impossible for us before these things to pray for this, before we entered into this place; for we heard that there was a judgement before we went out of the world, but impediments and the life of the world did not allow us to repent.' And Michael answered and said, 'Hear Michael speaking! I am he who stands in the sight of God every hour. As the Lord lives, in whose sight I stand, I do not stop one day or one night praying incessantly for the human race, and I indeed pray for those who are on the earth; but they do not cease committing iniquity and fornications, and they do not do any good while they are placed on earth; and you have consumed in vanity the time in which you ought to have repented. But I have always prayed thus, and I now beseech that God may send dew and send forth rains upon the earth, and now I continue to pray until the earth produce its fruits, and I say that if anyone has done but a little good I will strive for him, protecting him till he escapes the judgement of punishments. Where are your prayers? Where are your penances? You have lost your time contemptibly. But now weep, and I will weep with you and the angels who are with me with the well-beloved Paul, if by chance the merciful God will have pity and give you refreshment.' But hearing these words they cried out and wept greatly, and all said with one voice, 'Have pity on us, Son of God!' And I, Paul, sighed and said, 'O Lord God! Have pity on your creation, have pity on the sons of men, have pity on your own image.'

44. And I looked and saw the heaven move like a tree shaken by the wind. Suddenly, they threw themselves on their faces before the throne. And I saw twenty-four elders and the four beasts[22] adoring God, and I saw an altar and veil and throne, and all were rejoicing; and the smoke of a good odour rose near the altar of the throne of God, and I heard the voice of one saying, 'For what reason do our angels and ministers intercede?' And they cried out, saying, 'We intercede seeing your many kindnesses to the human race.' And after these things I saw the Son of God descending from heaven, and a diadem was on his head. And seeing him, all those who were placed in punishment exclaimed with one voice saying, 'Have pity, Son of the High

---

[22] Reading 'animalia' for 'milia'.

God! It is you who have granted rest for all in the heavens and on earth, and on us likewise have mercy, for since we have seen you we have refreshment.' And a voice went out from the Son of God through all the punishments, saying, 'And what work have you done that you demand refreshment from me? My blood was poured out for your sakes, and even so you did not repent; for your sakes I wore the crown of thorns on my head; for you I received buffets on my cheeks, and you did not repent. I asked for water when hanging on the cross, and they gave me vinegar mixed with gall, with a spear they opened my right side, for my name's sake they slew my prophets and just men, and in all these things I gave you the chance for repentance and you would not. Now, however, for the sake of Michael the archangel of my covenant and the angels who are with him, and because of Paul the well-beloved, whom I would not grieve, for the sake of your brethren who are in the world and offer oblations, and for the sake of your sons, because my commandments are in them, and more for the sake of my own kindness, on the day on which I rose from the dead, I give to you all who are in punishment a night and a day of refreshment forever.' And they all cried out and said, 'We bless you, Son of God, that you have given us a night and a day of respite. For a refreshment of one day is better for us than all the time of our life which we were on earth, and if we had plainly known that this place was intended for those who sin, we would have worked no other work, we would have done no business, and we would have done no iniquity: what need had we to be born[23] in the world? For here our pride is captured which ascended from our mouth against our neighbour; our plagues and excessive anguish and the tears and the worms which are under us, these are much worse for us than the pains which we have left behind us.'[24] When they had said this, the evil angels of torment were angered with them, saying, 'How long do you lament and sigh? For you had no mercy. For this is the judgement of God who had no mercy. But you received this great grace of a day and a night's refreshment on the Lord's Day for the sake of Paul the well-beloved of God who descended to you.'

45. And after that the angel said to me, 'Have you seen all these things?' And I said, 'Yes, sir.' And he said to me, 'Follow me, and I will lead you into Paradise, that the just who are there may see you, for lo, they hope to see you, and they are ready to come to meet you in joy and gladness!' And I followed the angel by the swiftness of the Holy Spirit, and he placed me in Paradise and said to me, 'This is Paradise in which Adam and his wife erred.' I entered Paradise and saw the beginning of waters, and there was an angel making a sign to me, and he said to me, 'Observe the waters, for this is the river of Pison which surrounds all the land of Evila, and the second is Gion which

---

[23] Reading 'natum esse' for 'nasum'.
[24] Text corrupt.

surrounds all the land of Egypt and Ethiopia, and the third is Tigris which is over against the Assyrians, and another is Euphrates which waters all the land of Mesopotamia.' And when I had gone inside I saw a tree planted from whose roots water flowed out, and from this beginning there were four rivers. And the Spirit of God rested on that tree, and when the Spirit blew, the waters flowed forth, and I said, 'My lord, is it this tree itself which makes the waters flow?' And he said to me, 'From the beginning, before the heavens and earth were manifested, all things were invisible and the Spirit of God hovered upon the waters, but from the time when the command of God made the heavens and earth to appear, the Spirit rested upon this tree; wherefore, whenever the Spirit blows, the waters flow forth from the tree.' And he held me by the hand and led me near the tree of knowledge of good and evil, and he said, 'This is the tree by which death entered into the world, and Adam, receiving of it through his wife, ate, and death entered into the world.' And he showed me another tree in the midst of Paradise and said to me, 'This is the tree of life.'

46. While I was still looking upon the tree, I saw a virgin coming from afar and two hundred angels before her singing hymns, and I asked and said, 'Sir, who is she who comes in so great glory?' And he said to me, 'This is Mary the Virgin, the Mother of the Lord.' And coming near, she greeted me and said, 'Hail, Paul, well-beloved of God and angels and men! For all the saints prayed to my Son Jesus who is my Lord that you might come here in the body that they might see you before you go out of the world. And the Lord said to them, "Wait and be patient: in a little while you shall see him and he shall be with you for ever", and again they all said to him together, "Do not grieve us, for we desire to see him in the flesh, for by him your name was greatly glorified in the world, and we have seen that he endured all the works whether of the great or of the less. This we learn from those who come here. For when we say, 'Who is he who directed you in the world?', they reply to us, 'There is one in the world whose name is Paul; he preaches and announces Christ', and we believe that many have entered into the kingdom through the power and sweetness of his speeches." Behold all the righteous men are behind me coming to meet you. But I say to you, Paul, that I come first to meet those who did the will of my Son and my Lord Jesus Christ, I advance first to meet them and do not send them away to be as wanderers until they meet in peace.'

47. When she had thus spoken, I saw three men coming from afar, very beautiful in the likeness of Christ, and their forms were shining, and their angels, and I asked, 'Sir, who are these?' And he said to me, 'Do you not know those?' And I said, 'No, sir.' And he answered, 'These are the fathers of the people, Abraham, Isaac, and Jacob.' And coming near, they greeted me and said, 'Hail, Paul, well-beloved of God and men; blessed is he who suffers violence for the Lord's sake.' And Abraham answered me and said, 'This is my son Isaac, and Jacob my well-beloved, and we have known the Lord and followed him; blessed are all those who believed in your word, that they may

be able to inherit the Kingdom of God by labour, by renunciation and sanctification, and humility, and charity, and meekness, and right faith in the Lord; and we also have had devotion to the Lord whom you preach, covenanting that we might assist all those who believe in him and might minister to them as fathers minister to their children.'

When they had spoken, I saw twelve others coming from afar in honour, and I asked, 'Sir, who are these?' And he said, 'These are the patriarchs.' And coming near, they greeted me and said, 'Hail, Paul, well-beloved of God and men; the Lord did not grieve us, that we might see you still in the body, before you go out of the world.' And each one of them reminded me of his name in order, from Reuben to Benjamin; and Joseph said to me, 'I am he who was sold; but I say to you, Paul, that all the things that my brothers did to me, in nothing did I act maliciously against them, nor in all the labour which they imposed on me, nor in any point was I hurt by them on that account from morning till evening: blessed is he who receives some injury on account of the Lord, and bears it, for the Lord will repay him many times when he shall have gone out of the world.'

48. When he had spoken, I saw another beautiful one coming from afar, and his angels were singing hymns, and I asked, 'Sir, who is this that is beautiful of countenance?' And he said to me, 'Do you not know him?' And I said, 'No, Sir.' And he said to me, 'This is Moses the law-giver, to whom God gave the law.' And when he had come near me, he immediately wept, and after that he greeted me, and I said to him, 'Why do you lament, for I have heard that you excel every man in meekness?' And he answered, saying, 'I weep for those whom I planted with toil, because they did not bear fruit, nor did any profit by them; and I saw all the sheep whom I fed were scattered and become as if they had no shepherd,[25] and because all the toils which I endured for the sake of the sons of Israel were accounted as nothing, and how many virtues I did in the midst of them they did not understand, and I am amazed that strangers and uncircumcised and idol-worshippers have been converted and have entered into the promises of God, but Israel has not entered; and now I say to you, brother Paul, that in that hour when the people hanged Jesus whom you preach, the Father, the God of all, who gave me the law, and Michael and all the angels and archangels, and Abraham and Isaac, and Jacob, and all the righteous wept over the Son of God hanging on the cross. In that hour all the saints attended on me looking at me, and they said to me, "See, Moses, what your people have done to the Son of God." Therefore you are blessed, Paul, and blessed be the generation and race which believed in your word.'

49. When he had spoken there came another twelve, who seeing me said, 'Are you Paul, the one who is glorified in heaven and on earth?' And I

---

[25] Cf. Matt. 9: 36.

answered and said, 'Who are you?' The first answered and said, 'I am Isaiah whom Manasses cut asunder with a wooden saw.' And the second said likewise, 'I am Jeremiah who was stoned by the children of Israel and slain.' And the third said, 'I am Ezekiel whom the children of Israel dragged by the feet over the rocks on a mountain till they dashed out my brains, and we endured all these toils, wishing to save the children of Israel; and I say to you that after the toils which they laid upon me I threw myself on my face in the sight of the Lord, praying for them, bending my knees until the second hour of the Lord's day, till Michael came and lifted me up from the earth. Blessed are you, Paul, and blessed the nation which believed through you.'

And as these passed by, I saw another, beautiful of countenance, and I asked, 'Sir, who is this?' When he had seen me he rejoiced,[26] and he said to me, 'This is Lot who was found in Sodom.' And approaching, he greeted me and said, 'Blessed are you, Paul, and blessed the generation to which you did minister.' And I answered and said to him, 'Are you Lot who was found righteous in Sodom?' And he said, 'I entertained angels, as travellers, and when the men of the city wished to violate them, I offered them my two virgin daughters who had not yet known men, and gave them to them saying, "Use them as you will, but to these men do no evil"; for this reason they entered under the roof of my house. For this reason, therefore, we ought to be confident and know that if anyone shall have done anything, God shall repay him many times when they shall come to him. Blessed are you, Paul, and blessed the nation which believed in your word.'

When he had ceased talking to me, I saw another coming from a distance, very beautiful of countenance, and smiling, and his angels singing hymns; and I said to the angel who was with me, 'Has then each of the righteous an angel for companion?' And he said to me, 'Each one of the saints has his own angel assisting him and singing a hymn, and the one does not depart from the other.' And I said, 'Who is this, sir?' And he said. 'This is Job.' And approaching, he greeted me and said, 'Brother Paul, you have great praise with God and men. And I am Job, who laboured much for a period of thirty years from a suppurating wound; and in the beginning the wounds which came from my body were like grains of wheat. But on the third day they became as the foot of an ass; worms moreover, which fell four digits in length; and the devil appeared three times and said to me, "Say something against God and die." I said to him, "If such be the will of God that I should remain under a plague all my life till I die, I shall not cease from blessing the Lord, and I shall receive more reward." For I know that the labours of that world are nothing to the refreshment which is afterwards; for which cause blessed are you, Paul, and blessed the nation which believed through you.'

50. When he had spoken, another came calling from afar and saying, 'Blessed are you, Paul, and blessed am I because I saw you, the beloved of the

---

[26] These words probably belong to the beginning of the following sentence.

Lord.' And I asked the angel, 'Sir, who is this?' And he answered and said to me, 'This is Noah in the time of the flood.' And immediately we greeted each other; and greatly rejoicing, he said to me, 'You are Paul the most beloved of God.' And I asked him, 'Who are you?' And he said, 'I am Noah who lived in the time of the flood. And I say to you, Paul, that working for a hundred years, I made the ark, not removing the tunic with which I was clad, nor did I cut the hair of my head. Till then also I cherished continence, not approaching my own wife; in those hundred years not a hair of my head grew in length, nor did my garments become soiled; and I besought men at all times saying, "Repent, for a flood of waters will come upon you." But they laughed at me, and mocked my words; and again they said to me, "But this is the time for people to play and sin freely, desiring her with whom it is possible to commit fornication frequently,[27] for God does not regard this and does not know what things are done by us men, and there is no flood of waters coming upon this world." And they did not cease from their sins till God destroyed all flesh which had the breath of life in it. Know then that God loves one righteous man more than all the world of the impious. Therefore, blessed are you, Paul, and blessed is the nation which believes through you.'

51. And turning round, I saw other just ones coming from afar, and I asked the angel, 'Sir, who are those?' And he answered me, 'These are Elijah and Elisha.' And they greeted me; and I said to them, 'Who are you?' And one of them answered and said, 'I am Elijah, the prophet of God; I am Elijah who prayed, and because of my word the heaven did not rain for three years and six months, on account of the unrighteousness of men. God is righteous and true, who does the will of his servants; for the angels often besought the Lord for rain, and he said, "Be patient till my servant Elijah shall pray and petition for this and I will send rain on the earth."'

The Latin version here breaks off abruptly, as does also the Greek. In the Syriac as translated by J. Perkins, the narrative runs as follows:

And often the angels asked that he would give them rain, and he did not give it, until I called upon him again; then he gave it to them. But blessed are you, O Paul, that your generation, and those you teach, are the sons of the kingdom. And know you, O Paul, that every man who believes through you has a great blessing, and a blessing is reserved for him.' Then he departed from me.

And the angel who was with me led me forth, and said to me, 'Lo, to you is given this mystery and revelation; as you please make it known to the sons of men.' And I, Paul, returned to myself, and I knew all that I had seen; and in life I had no rest that I might reveal this mystery. But I wrote it and deposited it under the ground and the foundation of a certain faithful man with whom I used to be, in Tarsus, a city of Cilicia. And when I was released from this life of time and stood before my Lord, thus he said to me, 'Paul, have we shown all these things to you that you should deposit them under the foundation of a house? Then send, and disclose this revelation that men

---

[27] Text confused.

may read it, and turn to the way of truth, that they also may not come to these bitter torments.'

Then follows the story of the discovery of the revelation at Tarsus in the reign of Theodosius as given at the beginning of the Greek and Latin versions. The Coptic continues as follows:

'The suffering which each endures for God's sake God will repay him twofold. Blessed are you, Paul, and blessed is the people who will believe through you.' And as he was speaking another, Enoch, came and greeted me and said to me, 'The sufferings which a man endures for the sake of God God does not afflict him with when he leaves the world.'

As he was speaking, behold, two other men came up together and another was coming after them crying out to them, 'Wait for me, that I may come to see Paul the beloved of God; there will be deliverance for us if we see him while he is still in the body.' I said to the angel, 'My lord, who are these?' He said to me, 'This is Zacharias and John his son.' I said to the angel, 'And who is the other who runs after them?' He said, 'This is Abel whom Cain killed.' They greeted me and said to me, 'Blessed are you, Paul, you who are righteous in all your works.' John said, 'I am he whose head they took off in prison for the sake of a woman who danced at a feast.' Zacharias said, 'I am he whom they killed while I was presenting the offering to God; and when the angels came for the offering, they carried up my body to God, and no man found where my body was taken.' Abel said, 'I am he whom Cain killed while I was presenting a sacrifice to God. The sufferings which we endured for the sake of God are nothing; what we have done for the sake of God we have forgotten.' And the righteous and all the angels surrounded me, and they rejoiced with me because they had seen me in the flesh.

And I looked and saw another taller than them all and very beautiful. And I said to the angel, 'Who is this, my lord?' He said to me, 'This is Adam, the father of you all.' When he came up to me, he greeted me with joy. He said to me, 'Take courage, Paul, beloved of God, you have brought a multitude to faith in God and to repentance. I myself have repented and received my praise from the compassionate and merciful one.'

After this Paul is carried into the third heaven. The angel who is with him changes in appearance and bursts into flames of fire, and a voice forbids Paul to reveal what he has seen.

There is a description of a mysterious vision of an altar with seven eagles of light on the right and seven on the left. And this is followed by more descriptions of Paradise. The meek, the prophets, David, all figure again in this episode: last are the martyrs. The conclusion runs thus (in substance):

The angel of the Lord took me up and brought me to the Mount of Olives. I found the apostles assembled and told them all I had seen. They praised God and commanded us, that is me, Mark, and Timothy, to write the revelation. And while they were talking, Christ appeared from the chariot of the cherubim and spoke greetings to Peter, John, and especially Paul. He promised blessings to those who should write or read the Apocalypse, and curses on those who should deride it. Peter and Paul should end their course on the fifth of Epiphi (29 June). He then bade a cloud take the apostles to the various countries allotted to them, and commanded them to preach the Gospel of the Kingdom. And a doxology follows.

The Apocalypse of Thomas

The Gelasian Decree condemns the Revelation of Thomas, but knowledge of the text in modern times dates only from the beginning of the twentieth century. Wilhelm's edition of the text in a ninth-century Munich manuscript and Hauler's fragment in a fifth-century Vienna palimpsest were published in 1907–8. M. R. James published the beginning of this apocalypse from an eighth-century Verona manuscript. Other texts came to light soon afterwards. The original language seems to have been Latin, but the various Latin manuscripts betray numerous variants among themselves: a definitive critical edition is still wanting.

There are two versions of the Apocalypse: the longer includes matter interpolated from other sources and concerns the signs predicting the End. Historical allusions in that section suggest a date in the second half of the fifth century. The shorter text does not include this material and is likely to have originated prior to the fifth century: it seems to have found favour in Priscillianist circles.

Patristic citation seems to be restricted to a reference to the Apocalypse of Thomas in the Chronicle of Jerome found in an eighth–ninth century Berlin manuscript and published by C. Frick, *ZNW* 9 (1908), 172–3.

The translation below follows James for both the longer and shorter texts—Hennecke[3] and Hennecke[5] give only the shorter text.

EDITIONS

Longer Text

F. Wilhelm, *Deutsche Legenden und Legendare* (Leipzig, 1907), 40*–2* (= Munich Clm. 4585).

M. R. James, 'Notes on Apocrypha, 1: Revelatio Thomae', *JTS* 11 (1910), 288–90, 569 (= Verona MS).

Shorter Text

E. Hauler, 'Zu den neuen lateinischen Bruchstücken der Thomasapokalypse und eines apostolischen Sendschreibens in Cod. Vindob. Nr. 16', *Wiener Studien* 30 (1908), 308–40 (= Vindob. Palatinus 16 of the fifth century).

P. Bihlmeyer, 'Un texte non interpolé de l'Apocalypse de Thomas', *Rev. Bén.* 28 (1911), 270–82 (= Munich Clm. 4563 of the eleventh–twelfth century).

Old English Version

Sermon 15 in the Vercelli Anglo-Saxon version comes from this Apocalypse:

M. Förster, 'Der Vercelli-Codex CXVII nebst Abdruck einiger altenglischer Homilien der Handschrift' (*Festgabe* Morsbach), *Studien zur englischen Philologie* 50 (1913), esp. 116–37.

Charles D. Wright, 'The Apocalypse of Thomas. Some New Latin Texts and their Significance for the Old English Version' in Kathryn Powell and Donald Scrogg (eds.), *Apocryphal Texts and Traditions in Anglo-Saxon England* (Cambridge, 2003), 27–64.

Mary Swan, 'The Apocalypse of Thomas in Old English' *Leeds Studies in English* 29 (1998) 333–46.

MODERN TRANSLATIONS

English

James, 555–62.
Hennecke[3], ii. 798–803.
Hennecke[5], ii. 748–52.

German

Hennecke[3], ii. 568–72 (A. de Santos Otero).
Hennecke[5], ii. 675–9 (A. de Santos Otero).

Italian

Erbetta, iii. 387–95 (longer and shorter texts).
Moraldi, ii. 1939–50 (longer and shorter texts); iii. 453–64.

GENERAL

M. Dando, 'L'Apocalypse de Thomas', *Cahiers d'études cathares* 28/37 (1977), 3–58 (with Italian trans., 13–19).

M. Herbert and M. McNamara, *Irish Biblical Apocrypha* (Edinburgh, 1989), Section 29 'The Signs Before Doomsday', 153–9 and Notes.

Armenian and Hebrew versions of The Signs of the Judgement (edn. and trans.) in M. E. Stone, *Signs of the Judgement, Onomastica Sacra and The Generations from Adam* (Chico, Calif., 1981) (= *University of Pennsylvania Armenian Texts and Studies* 3).

W. W. Heist, *The Fifteen Signs before Doomsday* (East Lansing: Michigan State College, 1952): important study of the complicated European history of the Apocalypse of Thomas and the Signs of the Judgement, though his conclusions now need modifying in light of the Armenian version and Stone's introduction.

A. Verona fragment (eighth century), and Wilhelm's text (Munich 4585, ninth century)

Hear, Thomas, the things which must come to pass in the last times: there shall be famine and war and earthquakes in divers places, snow and ice and great drought and many dissensions among the peoples, blasphemy, iniquity, envy and villainy, indolence, pride, and intemperance, so that every man shall speak that which pleases him. And my priests shall not have peace among themselves, but shall sacrifice to me with deceitful mind; therefore I will not look on them. Then shall the priests behold the people departing from the house of the Lord and turning to the world and setting up landmarks in the house of God. And they shall claim for themselves many things and places that were lost and that shall be subject to Caesar as they were before, exacting poll-taxes of the cities, gold and silver; and the chief men of the cities shall be condemned,[1] and their substance brought into the treasury of the kings, and they shall be filled.

For there shall be great disturbance throughout all the people, and death. The house of the Lord shall be desolate, and their altars shall be abhorred, so that spiders weave their webs therein.

The place of holiness shall be corrupted, the priesthood polluted, distress shall increase, virtue shall be overcome, joy perish, and gladness depart. In those days evil shall abound; there shall be respect for no one, hymns shall cease in the house of the Lord, truth shall be no more, covetousness shall abound among the priests, an upright man shall not be found.

Suddenly there shall arise near the last time a king, a lover of the law, who shall not rule for long; he shall leave two sons. The first is named after the first letter, the second after the eighth. The first shall die before the second.[2]

Thereafter shall arise two princes to oppress the nations, under whose hands there shall be a very great famine in the right-hand part of the east, so that nation shall rise up against nation and be driven out from their own borders.

Again another king shall arise, an astute man, and shall command a golden image of Caesar to be made, and martyrdoms shall abound. Then shall faith return to the servants of the Lord, and holiness shall be multiplied and distress increase. The mountains shall be comforted and shall drop down sweetness of fire from the face, that the number of the saints may be accomplished.[3]

After a little space there shall arise a king out of the east, a lover of the law, who shall cause all necessary and good things to abound in the house of the Lord; he shall show mercy to widows and to the needy and command a royal gift to be given to the priests. In his days there shall be abundance of all things.

And after that again a king shall arise in the south part of the world and shall hold rule a little space. In his days the treasury shall fail because of the

---

[1] Verona fragment ends here.
[2] Theodosius had two sons: Arcadius († 408), Honorius († 423).
[3] Text obscure.

wages of the Roman soldiers, so that the patrimony of all the aged shall be commanded to be taken and given to the king to distribute.

Thereafter there shall be plenty of corn and wine and oil, but great inflation, so that gold and silver shall be given for corn, and there shall be great dearth.

At that time there shall be a very great rising of the sea, so that no man shall tell news to any man. The kings of the earth and the princes and the captains shall be troubled, and no man shall speak freely. Grey hairs shall be seen upon boys, and the young shall not give place to the aged.

After that shall arise another king, an astute man, who shall rule for a short space: in his days there shall be all manner of evils, even the death of the race of men from the east up to Babylon. And thereafter death and famine and sword in the land of Canaan as far as Rome.[4] Then shall all the fountains of waters and wells boil over and be turned into blood. The heaven shall be moved, the stars shall fall upon the earth, the sun shall be cut in half like the moon, and the moon shall not give her light. There shall be great signs and wonders in those days when Antichrist draws near. These are the signs to those who dwell on earth. In those days the pains of great travail shall come upon them. Woe to those who build, for they shall not inhabit. Woe to those who break up the fallow, for they shall labour without cause. Woe to those who make marriages, for to famine and need shall they beget sons. Woe to those who join house to house or field to field, for all things shall be consumed with fire. Woe to those who do not look to themselves while there is time, for hereafter shall they be condemned for ever. Woe to those who turn away from the poor man when he asks.[5]

These are the seven signs before the ending of this world. There shall be in all the earth famine and great pestilence and much distress: then shall all men be led captive among all nations and shall fall by the edge of the sword.

On the first day of the judgement there will be a great marvel. At the third hour of the day there shall be a great and mighty voice in the firmament of the heaven, and a great cloud of blood coming down out of the north, and great peals of thunder and mighty flashes of lightning shall follow that cloud, and there shall be a rain of blood upon all the earth. These are the signs of the first day.

And on the second day there shall be a great voice in the firmament of the heaven, and the earth shall be moved out of its place, and the gates of heaven shall be opened in the firmament of heaven toward the east, and a great power shall be belched forth by the gates of heaven and shall cover all the heaven until evening. These are the signs of the second day.

And on the third day, about the second hour, there shall be a voice in

---

[4] The MS has 'nona', ninth.

[5] Here is a break. The text goes on: 'For I am ⟨the Son⟩ of the high and powerful: I am the Father of all.' Cf. the beginning of the older (?) and shorter text.

heaven, and the abysses of the earth shall utter their voice from the four corners of the world. The first heaven shall be rolled up like a book and shall straightway vanish. And because of the smoke and stench of the brimstone of the abyss the days shall be darkened unto the tenth hour. Then shall all men say, 'I think that the end draws near, that we shall perish.' These are the signs of the third day.

And on the fourth day, at the first hour, the earth in the east shall speak, the abyss shall roar, then shall all the earth be moved by the strength of an earthquake. In that day shall all the idols of the heathen fall and all the buildings of the earth. These are the signs of the fourth day.

And on the fifth day, at the sixth hour, there shall suddenly be great thunderings in the heaven, and the power of light and the wheel of the sun shall be caught away, and there shall be great darkness over the world until evening, and the stars shall be turned away from their ministry. In that day all nations shall hate the world and despise the life of this world. These are the signs of the fifth day.

And on the sixth day there shall be signs in heaven. At the fourth hour the firmament of heaven shall be split from the east unto the west. And the angels of the heavens shall be looking forth upon the earth through the opening of the heavens. And all men shall see above the earth the host of the angels looking forth out of heaven. Then shall all men flee.[6]

B. Bihlmeyer's text, from Munich 4563 (eleventh to twelfth century, from Benediktbeuern); and the Vienna fragment

Hear, O Thomas, for I am the Son of God the Father, and I am the father of all spirits. Hear from me the signs which shall come to pass at the end of this world, when the end of the world shall be fulfilled before my elect depart out of the world. I will tell you that which shall come to pass openly (or, will tell you openly, etc.): but when these things shall be the princes of the angels do not know, for they are now hidden from them.

Then shall there be in the world sharings between king and king, and in all the earth there shall be great famine, great pestilences, and much distress, and the sons of men shall be led captive in every nation and shall fall by the edge of the sword and there shall be great commotion in the world.[7] Then after that, when the hour of the end draws near, there shall be for seven days great signs in heaven, and the powers of the heavens shall be moved.

Then shall there be on the first day the beginning: at the third hour of the day a great and mighty voice in the firmament of heaven and a cloud of blood

---

[6] Here Wilhelm's text ends abruptly.
[7] Vienna fragment omits this last clause.

coming up out of the north, and great peals of thunder and mighty flashes of lightning shall follow it, and it shall cover the whole heaven, and it will rain blood upon all the earth. These are the signs of the first day.

And on the second day there shall be a great voice in the firmament of heaven, and the earth shall be moved out of its place, and the gates of heaven shall be opened in the firmament of heaven toward the east, and the smoke of a great fire shall break forth through the gates of heaven and shall cover all the heaven until evening. In that day there shall be fear and great terror in the world. These are the signs of the second day.

But on the third day, about the third hour, there shall be a great voice in heaven, and the depths of the earth[8] shall roar from the four corners of the world; the pinnacles of the firmament of heaven shall be opened, and all the air shall be filled with pillars of smoke. There shall be an exceedingly evil stench of brimstone, until the tenth hour, and men shall say, 'We think the time draws near that we perish.' These are the signs of the third day.

And on the fourth day, at the first hour, from the land of the east the abyss shall melt and roar. Then shall all the earth be shaken by the might of an earthquake. In that day shall the ornaments of the heathen fall, and all the buildings of the earth, before the might of the earthquake. These are the signs of the fourth day.

But on the fifth day, at the sixth hour, suddenly there shall be a great thunder in heaven, and the powers of light and the wheel of the sun shall be caught away,[9] and there shall be great darkness in the world until evening, and the air shall be sorrowful without sun or moon, and the stars shall cease from their ministry. In that day shall all nations behold as in a sack[10] and shall despise the life of this world. These are the signs of the fifth day.

And on the sixth day, at the fourth hour, there shall be a great voice in heaven, and the firmament of the heaven shall be split from the east to the west, and the angels of the heavens shall be looking out upon the earth through the gaps in the heavens, and all those on the earth shall behold the host of the angels looking forth out of heaven. Then shall all men flee to the tombs and hide themselves from the face of the righteous angels and say, 'Would that the earth would open and swallow us up!' And such things shall happen as never happened since this world was created.

Then shall they behold me coming from above in the light of my Father with the power and honour of the holy angels.[11] Then at my coming shall the fence of fire of paradise be loosed—because paradise is girt round about with fire. And this is the perpetual fire that shall consume the earth and all the elements of the world.

[8] Vienna fragment ends.
[9] Reading 'aperietur' as 'operietur'.
[10] Text obscure. Possibly 'speculo' (mirror) is intended, not 'sacculo'.
[11] Cf. Matt. 24: 30; Mark 13: 26 f.; Luke 21: 27; Dan. 7: 13.

Then shall the spirits and souls of all men come forth from paradise and shall come upon all the earth, and every one of them shall go to his own body, where it is laid up, and every one of them shall say, 'Here lies my body.' And when the great voice of those spirits shall be heard, then shall there be a great earthquake over all the world, and by its force the mountains shall be shattered above and the rocks beneath. Then shall every spirit return to his own vessel, and the bodies of the saints who have fallen asleep shall arise.

Then shall their bodies be changed into the image and likeness and the honour of the holy angels, and into the power of the image of my holy Father. Then shall they be clothed with the garment of life eternal, out of the cloud of light which has never been seen in this world; for that cloud comes down out of the highest realm of the heaven from the power of my Father. And that cloud shall invest with its beauty all the spirits who have believed in me.

Then shall they be clothed and shall be borne by the hands of the holy angels as I have told you before. Then they shall be lifted up into the air upon a cloud of light, and shall go with me rejoicing into heaven, and then shall they remain in the light and honour of my Father. Then shall there be great gladness for them with my Father and the holy angels. These are the signs of the sixth day.

And on the seventh day, at the eighth hour, there shall be voices in the four corners of the heaven. And all the air shall be shaken, and filled with holy angels, and they shall make war among themselves all the day long. And in that day shall my elect be sought out by the holy angels from the destruction of the world. Then shall all men see that the hour of their destruction draws near. These are the signs of the seventh day.

And when the seven days are passed by, on the eighth day, at the sixth hour, there shall be a sweet and tender voice in heaven from the east. Then shall that angel be revealed which has power over the holy angels, and all the angels shall go forth with him, sitting upon chariots of the clouds of my holy Father, rejoicing and flying in the air beneath the heaven to deliver the elect who have believed in me. And they shall rejoice that the destruction of this world has come.

The words of the Saviour to Thomas are ended, concerning the end of this world.

The Questions of Bartholomew

Although antiquity knew of a Gospel of Bartholomew through Jerome's prologue to his Commentary to Matthew and the Gelasian Decree (where 'evangelia' is used in the context, i.e. 'gospels under the name of Bartholomew') there is no evidence that what they knew is what has been commonly referred to recently (thanks largely to Wilmart and Tisserant) as the Gospel of Bartholomew. A better title for the texts that they and others have published is the Questions of Bartholomew, which is the title of the Slavonic versions and of one of the Latin versions (the Casanatensis). These 'questions' deal with various aspects of Christ's descent comparable to the Descensus in the Gospel of Nicodemus (q.v.), of the annunciation, of Satan's origin and power and also concern deadly sins. It is a suitable title, given the way in which the subject-matter is accorded question and answer treatment; it also serves to avoid linking this work with other gospels. It may equally well be classified as a gospel or an apocalypse, although, despite tradition, the present collection links it with the apocalypses.

The Questions were originally composed in Greek, possibly in Egypt, but the date of the work is not certain, being estimated between the second and sixth centuries. Latin and Slavonic versions exist, but the relationship between them all is not clear. James's translation is based predominantly on the Greek and Slavonic where they exist, but with some passages added from the Latin; it is repeated below with minor changes. James's presentation is commended by Kaestli (*Revue Biblique* 95 (1988), 20).

The Bartholomew literature seems to have originated in Egypt and had a changing and developing tradition prior to the composition of the extant texts. The presence of Gnostic ideas is a subject of debate: Beeston's short article (bibliography below) gives an example of how the text can be interpreted without recourse to Gnosticism.

The Questions of Bartholomew is to be distinguished from a Coptic text known as 'The Book of the Resurrection of Jesus Christ by Bartholomew the Apostle' (to be found in Wallis Budge, 1–48 (Eng. trans. 179–230), based on his London manuscript). Many other Coptic fragments in Paris and Strasbourg have also been assigned (by Revillout in particular) to the Gospel of Bartholomew, although his judgement has been questioned and some scholars (especially Baumstark and James) would prefer to assign some of the fragments to the Gospel of Gamaliel (q.v.); indeed one of Revillout's fragments (his no. 15) has a definite attribution to Gamaliel. The Coptic texts date from perhaps the fifth–sixth century. Most of the fragments which

Revillout published under the general title of 'The Gospel of the Twelve Apostles' (which is a misnomer) are not from an apocryphal gospel, either Bartholomew's or another's, but are from homiletical works, although some of Revillout's fragments (e.g. no. 12 and those on his pp. 185–94) may relate to a gospel of Bartholomew. Schneemelcher (in Hennecke³, i. 372–6; ⁵i. 437–40) and James (*ANT* 147–52) tried to bring order into the Coptic fragments, as too did Haase in his *ZNW* article. The Coptic fragments may be deemed to come from a different cycle of tradition from the Quaestiones Bartholomaei. Only three extracts are given below (B), a summary of Budge's London manuscript and Revillout nos. 6, and 12 (which has a stronger claim to be part of the same tradition as Budge's London manuscript).

TEXTS AND EDITIONS

THE QUESTIONS OF BARTHOLOMEW

Greek   Vindobonensis Gr. hist. 67
             Jerusalem. St. Saba 13
Latin   Casanetensis 1880 (= Latin 2 in the translation below)
             Vaticanus Reg. 1050 (= Latin 1 in the translation below)
Slavonic   Vindobonenis slav. 125
             St. Petersburg cod. Alex. Nevski

Greek and Latin

A. Wilmart and E. Tisserant, 'Fragments grecs et latins de l'Évangile de Barthélemy', *Rev. Bib.* 10 (1913), 161–90, 321–68 (= Jerusalem Greek, Vatican Latin).
V. Moricca, 'Un Nuovo Testo dell "Evangelo di Bartolemeo"', *Rev. Bib.* NS 18 (= 30) (1921), 481–516, and NS 19 (= 31) (1922), 20–30 (= Casanatensis Latin).

Slavonic

N. Bonwetsch, 'Die Apokryphen Fragen des Bartholomäus', *Gött. Gel. Nachr. Philol-hist. Kl* (1897), 1–42 (also includes Vienna Greek).

THE BOOK OF THE RESURRECTION OF JESUS CHRIST BY BARTHOLOMEW THE APOSTLE

P. Lacau, *Fragments d'apocryphes coptes* (Cairo, 1904), 23–37 ('Évangile (?) apocryphe'); 39–77 ('Apocalypse de Barthélemy') (with French trans.) (= *Mémoires publiés par les membres de l'institut français d'archéologie orientale du Caire* (9).[1]
A. Wilmart and E. Tisserant (as above), 352–68.
E. Revillout, 'Les apocryphes coptes, I. Les Évangiles des douze apôtres et de Saint Barthélemy', in *PO* 2.2, ed. R. Graffin (Paris, 1904; repr. 1946), 117–83, 184–98;

[1] Reviewed by M. R. James, *JTS* 6 (1905), 577–86.

cf. id. 'Supplément à l'évangile des XII apôtres', in *PO* 9.2, ed. R. Graffin and F. Nau (Paris, 1913), 133–9.[2]

E. A. Wallis Budge, *Coptic Apocrypha in the Dialect of Upper Egypt* (London, 1913), 1–48, 179–230.

A. M. Kropp, *Ausgewählte koptische Zaubertexte* (Brussels, 1931), i. 79–81; ii. 249–51.

A. von Harnack and C. Schmidt, 'Ein koptisches Fragment einer Moses-Adam Apokalypse', *SPAW* (1891), 1045–9.

MODERN TRANSLATIONS

English

James, 166–181 (Questions of Bartholomew); 181–6 (analysis of Coptic fragments of the Book of the Resurrection). [Cf. pp. 161–3 above for summary of Revillout's fragments of Coptic narratives of the Ministry and Passion.

Hennecke[3], i. 484–508 (Questions of Bartholomew and the Book of the Resurrection).
Hennecke[5], i. 537–57.

French

Éac, 257–95, 299–356 (Questions of Bartholomew and the Book of the Resurrection).
J.-D. Kaestli and P. Cherix, *L'évangile de Barthélemy* (Turnhout, 1993) (= *Apocryphes* 1).

German

Hennecke[3], i. 359–76 (Questions of Bartholomew and the Book of the Resurrection) (F. Scheidweiler and W. Schneemelcher).
Hennecke[5], i. 424–40 (Questions of Bartholomew and the Book of the Resurrection) (F. Scheidweiler and W. Schneemelcher).

Italian

Moraldi, i. 749–800 (Gospel of Bartholomew).
Moraldi, i. 801–5 (the Book of the Resurrection: summary).
Erbetta, i.2, 288–300 (Gospel of Bartholomew); 301–19 (the Book of the Resurrection).

Spanish

de Santos Otero, 536–72 (Questions of Bartholomew).

GENERAL

P. Ladeuze, 'Apocryphes évangéliques coptes: Pseudo-Gamaliel: Évangile de Barthélemy', *RHE* 7 (1906), 245–68.
F. H. Hallock, 'Coptic Apocrypha', *JBL* 52 (1933), 163–74.

---

[2] Reviewed by M. R. James, *JTS* 7 (1906), 633–4; P. Ladeuze, *RHE* 7 (1906), 245–68; A. Baumsrark, *Rev. Bib.* 3 (1906), 245–65.

A. F, L. Beeston, 'The Quaestiones Barrholomae', *JTS* 25 (1974), 124-'7.
J.-D. Kaestli, 'Où en est l'étude de l'"Évangile de Barthélemy"?' *Rev. Bib.* 95 (1988), 5–33.
Klauck, 131–9: ET 99–104.

A. THE QUESTIONS OF BARTHOLOMEW

I[1]

Greek. 1. After the resurrection from the dead of our Lord Jesus Christ, Bartholomew came to the Lord and questioned him, saying, 'Lord, reveal to me the mysteries of the heavens.'

2. Jesus answered and said to him, 'If I put (not) off the body of the flesh, I shall not be able to tell them to you.'

3. *Omit.*

Slavonic. 1. Before the resurrection of our Lord Jesus Christ from the dead, the apostles said, 'Let us question the Lord: Lord, reveal to us the wonders.'

2. And Jesus said to them, 'If I put (not) off the body of the flesh, I cannot tell them to you.'

3. But when he was buried and risen again, none of them dared question him, because it was not possible to look upon him, but the fullness of his Godhead was seen.

4. But Bartholomew, *etc.*

Latin 2. 1. At that time, before the Lord Jesus Christ suffered, all the disciples were gathered together, questioning him and saying, 'Lord, show us the mystery in the heavens.'

2. But Jesus answered and said to them, 'If I put not off the body of flesh I cannot tell you.'

3. But after he had suffered and risen again, all the apostles, looking upon him, did not dare to question him, because his countenance was not as it had been previously, but showed forth the fullness of power.

Greek. 4. Bartholomew therefore drew near to the Lord and said, 'I have a word to speak to you, Lord.'

5. And Jesus said to him, 'I know what you are about to say; say then what you will and I will answer you.'

6. And Bartholomew said, 'Lord, when you went to be hanged upon the cross, I followed you afar off and saw you hung upon the cross, and the angels coming down from heaven and worshipping you. And when there came darkness, (7) I looked and I saw that you vanished away from the cross, and I heard only a voice in the parts under the earth, and great wailing and gnashing of teeth all of a sudden. Tell me, Lord, where did you go to from the cross?'

8. And Jesus answered and said, 'Blessed are you, Bartholomew, my

---

[1] I give the opening verses in all three texts.

beloved, because you saw this mystery; and now I will tell you all things whatsoever you ask me. 9. For when I vanished from the cross, then I went down into Hades that I might bring up Adam and all those who were with him, according to the supplication of Michael the archangel.

10. Then Bartholomew said, 'Lord, what was the voice which was heard?'

11. Jesus said to him, 'Hades said to Beliar, "As I perceive, a God comes hither."'

Slavonic and Latin 2. 'And the angels cried to the powers saying, "Remove your gates, you princes, remove the everlasting doors for behold the King of Glory comes down." 12. Hades said, "Who is the King of Glory, who comes down from heaven to us?"[2]

13. 'And when I had descended five hundred steps, Hades was troubled saying, "I hear the breathing of the Most High, and I cannot endure it." [*Lat. 2*: He comes with great fragrance and I cannot bear it.] 14. But the devil answered and said, "Submit not yourself, O Hades, but be strong, for God himself has not descended upon the earth." 15. But when I had descended five hundred steps, the angels and the powers cried out, "Take hold, remove the doors, for behold the King of Glory comes down." And Hades said, "O, woe unto me, for I hear the breath of God."

Greek. 16–17. 'And Beliar said unto Hades, "Look carefully who it is who comes, for it is Elijah, or Enoch, or one of the prophets that this man seems to me to be." But Hades answered Death and said, "Not yet are six thousand years accomplished. And whence are these, O Beliar, for the sum of the number is in my hands?"

[*Slavonic.* 16. 'And the devil said unto Hades, "Why do you frighten me, Hades? It is a prophet, and he has made himself like God. This prophet will we take and bring him hither to those who think to ascend into heaven." 17. And Hades said, "Which of the prophets is it? Show me. Is it Enoch the scribe of righteousness? But God has not suffered him to come down upon the earth before the end of the six thousand years. Do you say that it is Elijah, the avenger? But before the end he does not come down. What shall I do, for the destruction is from God, for surely our end is at hand? For I have the number of the years in my hands."]

Greek. 18. 'And Beliar said unto Hades, "Be not troubled, make safe your gates and strengthen your bars. Consider, God comes not down upon the earth."

19. 'Hades said to him, "These are no good words that I hear from you; my belly is rent, and my inward parts are pained: it cannot be but that God comes hither. Alas, whither shall I flee before the face of the power of the great king? Suffer me to enter into myself [*Latin*: yourself]: for before [*Latin*: of] you was I formed."

[2] Cf. Ps. 24: 10.

20. 'Then did I enter in and scourged him and bound him with chains that cannot be loosed, and brought forth thence all the patriarchs and came again to the cross.'

21. Bartholomew said to him, [*Lat. 2*: 'I saw you again, hanging upon the cross, and all the dead arising and worshipping you, and going up again into their sepulchres.'] 'Tell me, Lord, who was he whom the angels carried up in their hands, that man who was very great of stature?' [*Slav., Lat. 2*: 'And what did you say to him that he sighed so deeply?']

22. Jesus answered and said to him, 'It was Adam the first-formed, for whose sake I came down from heaven upon earth. And I said to him, "I was hung upon the cross for you and for your children's sake." And he, when he heard it, groaned and said, "Such was your good pleasure, O Lord."'

23. Again Bartholomew said, 'Lord, I saw the angels ascending before Adam and singing praises. 24. But one of the angels who was very great, above the rest, would not ascend with them; and there was in his hand a sword of fire, and he was looking steadfastly upon you only.'

Slavonic. 25. 'And all the angels besought him that he would go up with them, but he would not. But when you commanded him to go up, I beheld a flame of fire issuing out of his hands and going even to the city of Jerusalem.' 26. And Jesus said to him, 'Blessed are you, Bartholomew my beloved, because you saw these mysteries. This was one of the angels of vengeance which stand before my Father's throne: and this angel he sent to me. 27. And for this cause he would not ascend, because he desired to destroy all the powers of the world. But when I commanded him to ascend, there went a flame out of his hand and rent asunder the veil of the temple, and parted it in two pieces for a witness to the children of Israel for my passion because they crucified me.' [*Lat. 1*: 'But the flame which you saw issuing out of his hands smote the house of the synagogue of the Jews, for a testimony of me, because they crucified me.']

Greek. 28. And when he had spoken he said to the apostles, 'Tarry for me in this place, for today a sacrifice is offered in paradise.' 29. And Bartholomew answered and said to Jesus, 'Lord, what is the sacrifice which is offered in paradise?' And Jesus said, 'There are souls of the righteous which today have departed out of the body and go to paradise, and unless I be present they cannot enter into paradise.'

30. And Bartholomew said, 'Lord, how many souls depart out of the world daily?' Jesus said to him, 'Thirty thousand.'

31. Bartholomew said to him, 'Lord, when you were with us teaching the word, did you receive the sacrifices in paradise?'[3] Jesus answered and said to him, 'Verily I say unto you, my beloved, that I both taught the word with you and continually sat with my Father and received the sacrifices in paradise every day.' 32. Bartholomew answered and said to him, 'Lord, if thirty

---

[3] In Lat. 2, 31 follows 29.

thousand souls depart out of the world every day, how many souls out of them are found righteous?' Jesus said to him, 'Hardly fifty-three[4], my beloved.' 33. Again Bartholomew said, 'And how do three only enter into paradise?' Jesus said to him, 'The fifty-three enter into paradise or are laid up in Abraham's bosom: but the others go into the place of the resurrection, for the three are not like the fifty.'

34. Bartholomew said to him, 'Lord, how many souls above the number are born into the world daily?' Jesus said to him, 'One soul only is born above the number of those who depart.'[5]

35. And when he had said this he gave them the peace, and vanished away from them.

II

1. Now the apostles were in the place Cherubim [*variants*: Cheltoura, Chritir] with Mary. 2. And Bartholomew came and said to Peter and Andrew and John, 'Let us ask her who is highly favoured how she conceived the incomprehensible, or how she bore him that cannot be carried, or how she brought forth so much greatness.' But they hesitated to ask her. 3. Bartholomew therefore said to Peter, 'You are the chief, and my teacher, draw near and ask her.' But Peter said to John, 'You are a virgin and undefiled and beloved and you must ask her.' 4. And as they all doubted and disputed, Bartholomew came near to her with a cheerful countenance and said to her, 'You who are highly favoured, the tabernacle of the Most High, unblemished, we, all the apostles, ask you (*or* All the apostles have sent me to ask you) to tell us how you conceived the incomprehensible, or how you bore him who cannot be carried, or how you brought forth so much greatness.'

5. But Mary said to them, 'Ask me not (*or* Do you indeed ask me) concerning this mystery. If I should begin to tell you, fire will issue forth out of my mouth and consume all the world.' 6. But they continued the more to ask her. And she, for she could not refuse to hear the apostles, said, 'Let us stand up in prayer.' 7. And the apostles stood behind Mary, but she said to Peter, 'Peter, you chief, you great pillar, do you stand behind us? Did not our Lord say, "The head of the man is Christ [*Slav., Lat.* 2 add but the head of the woman is the man]"? Now therefore stand before me and pray.' 8. But they said to her, 'In you did the Lord set his tabernacle, and it was his good

---

[4] The MSS are confused with this and the numbers in the next verse.

[5] *Lat. 1*, 30, etc.: Bartholomew said, 'How many are the souls which depart out of the body every day?' Jesus said, 'Verily I say unto you, twelve (thousand) eight hundred, four score and three souls depart out of the body every day.'

Lat. 2, 30–4: 'six thousand and seventy-four souls depart out of the body every day. Three go into paradise.' 33. 'How three only?' 'Fifty-three go into paradise, but only three into Abraham's bosom. The rest are in the place of repose, for they are not like the three. 34. One more soul departs every day than is born.'

pleasure that you should contain him, and you ought to be the leader in the prayer.' 9. But she said to them, 'You are shining stars and, as the prophet said, "I lift up my eyes to the hills: where is my help to come from?"[6] You, therefore, are the hills, and it behoves you to pray.' 10. The apostles said to her, 'You ought to pray, you are the mother of the heavenly king.' 11. Mary said to them, 'In your likeness did God form the sparrows,[7] and sent them forth into the four corners of the world.' 12. But they said to her, 'He who is hardly contained by the seven heavens was pleased to be contained in you.'

13. Then Mary stood up before them and spread out her hands toward the heaven and began to speak thus, 'Elphuë Zarethra Charboum Nemioth Melitho Thraboutha Mephnounos Chemiath Aroura Maridon Elison Marmiadon Seption Hesaboutha Ennouna Saktinos Athoor Belelam Opheoth Abo Chrasar,[8] which is in the Greek tongue [*Slav.*: Hebrew]: O God the exceeding great and all-wise and king of the worlds (ages), who are not to be described, the ineffable, who established the greatness of the heavens and all things by a word, that out of darkness constituted and fastened together the poles of heaven in harmony, brought into shape the matter that was in confusion, brought into order the things that were without order, parted the misty darkness from the light, established in one place the foundations of the waters, you who made the beings of the air tremble, and are the fear of those who are on the earth, who settled the earth and did not suffer it to perish, and filled it, which is the nourisher of all things, with showers of blessing: Son of the Father, whom the seven heavens hardly contained, but who were well-pleased to be contained without pain in me, you who are yourself the full word of the Father in whom all things came to be, give glory to your exceeding great name and bid me to speak before your holy apostles.'

14. And when she had ended the prayer she began to say to them, 'Let us sit down upon the ground; and come, Peter the chief, and sit on my right hand and put your left hand beneath my armpit; and you, Andrew, do so on my left hand; and you, John, the virgin, hold my bosom; and you, Bartholomew, set your knees against my back and hold my shoulders, lest when I begin to speak my bones be loosed one from another.'

15. And when they had so done she began to say, 'When I abode in the temple of God and received my food from an angel, on a certain day there appeared to me one in the likeness of an angel, but his face was incomprehensible, and he did not have in his hand bread or a cup, as did the angel

---

[6] Ps. 121: 1.
[7] See the Infancy Gospels, esp. the Infancy Gospel of Thomas 2.
[8] This is the reading of one Greek copy: the others and the Slavonic have many differences, as in all such cases; but as the original words—assuming them to have once had a meaning—are hopelessly corrupted, the matter is not of importance.

Lat. 2: Helfoith. Alaritha. Arbar. Neniotho. Melitho. Tarasunt. Chanebonos. Umia. Theirura. Marado. Seliso. Heliphomar. Mabon. Saruth. Gefutha. Enunnas. Sacinos. Thatis. Etelelam. Tetheo. Abocia. Rusar.

which came to me previously. 16. And straightway the veil of the temple was rent and there was a very great earthquake, and I fell upon the earth, for I was not able to endure the sight of him. 17. But he put his hand beneath me and raised me up, and I looked up into heaven and there came a cloud of dew and sprinkled me from the head to the feet, and he wiped me with his robe. 18. And he said to me, 'Hail, you who are highly favoured, the chosen vessel, grace inexhaustible.' And he smote his garment upon the right hand and there came a very great loaf, and he set it upon the altar of the temple and did eat of it first himself, and gave to me also. 19. And again he smote his garment upon the left hand and there came a very great cup full of wine, and he set it upon the altar of the temple and did drink of it first himself, and gave also to me. And I looked and saw the bread and the cup whole as before.

20. 'And he said to me, "In three years, I will send my word to you and you shall conceive my son, and through him shall the whole creation be saved. Peace be to you, my beloved, and my peace shall be with you continually." 21. And when he had spoken he vanished away from my eyes, and the temple was restored as it had been before.'

22. And as she was saying this, fire issued out of her mouth; and the world was at the point to come to an end. But Jesus appeared quickly [*Lat. 2*: and laid his hand upon her mouth] and said unto Mary, 'Utter not this mystery, or this day my whole creation will come to an end' [*Lat. 2*: and the flame from her mouth ceased]. And the apostles were taken with fear lest the Lord should be angry with them.

III

1. And he departed with them to mount Mauria [*Lat. 2*: Mambre], and sat in the midst of them. 2. But they hesitated to question him, being afraid. 3. And Jesus answered and said to them, 'Ask me what you will that I should teach you, and I will show it to you. For in seven days I ascend to my Father, and I shall no more be seen of you in this likeness.' 4. But they, still hesitating, said to him, 'Lord, show us the deep abyss according to your promise.' 5. And Jesus said to them, 'It is not good [*Lat. 2*: is good] for you to see the deep; notwithstanding, if you desire it, in accordance with my promise, come, follow me and behold.' 6. And he led them away into a place that is called Cherubim [*Slav.*: Cherukt; *Gr.*: Chairoudee; *Lat. 2 omits*], that is the place of truth. 7. And he beckoned to the angels of the west, and the earth was rolled up like a volume of a book and the deep was revealed to them. 8. And when the apostles saw it they fell on their faces upon the earth. 9. But Jesus raised them up saying, 'Did I not say to you, "It is not good for you to see the deep"?' And again he beckoned to the angels and the deep was covered up.

IV

1. And he took them and brought them again to the Mount of Olives.

2. And Peter said to Mary, 'You who are highly favoured, entreat the Lord to reveal to us the things that are in the heavens.'

3. And Mary said to Peter, 'O stone hewn out of the rock, did not the Lord build his church upon you? Go first and ask him.'

4. Peter said again, 'O tabernacle who are spread abroad, it behoves you to ask.' 5. Mary said, 'You are the image of Adam; was not he first formed and then Eve? Look upon the sun; according to the likeness of Adam it is bright, and upon the moon; because of the transgression of Eve it is full of clay. For God placed Adam in the east and Eve in the west, and appointed the lights—that the sun should shine on Adam in the east with its fiery chariots, and the moon in the west should give light to Eve with a light like milk. And she defiled the commandment of the Lord. Therefore the moon was stained with clay [*Lat. 2*: is cloudy] and her light is not bright. You, therefore, since you are the likeness of Adam, ought to ask him; but in me was he contained that I might recover the dignity of woman.'

6. Now when they came up to the top of the mount, and the master withdrew from them for a little while, Peter said to Mary, 'You are she who brought to nought the transgression of Eve, changing it from shame into joy; it is lawful, therefore, for you to ask.'

7. When Jesus appeared again, Bartholomew said to him, 'Lord, show us the adversary of men that we may behold him, of what fashion he is, and what is his work, and whence he comes forth, and what power he has that he spared not even you but caused you to be hanged upon the tree.' 8. But Jesus looked upon him and said, 'You bold heart! You ask for that which you are not able to look upon.' 9. But Bartholomew was troubled and fell at Jesus' feet and began to speak thus, 'O lamp that cannot be quenched, Lord Jesu Christ, maker of the eternal light, who have given to those who love you the grace that beautifies all, and have given us the eternal light by your coming into the world, who have ... the heavenly essence by a word ... have accomplished the work of the Father, have turned the shamefacedness of Adam into mirth, have done away the sorrow of Eve with a cheerful countenance by your birth from a virgin: remember not evil against me but grant me the work of my asking.' [*Lat. 2*: 'who came down into the world, who have confirmed the eternal word of the Father, who have called the sadness of Adam joy, who have made the shame of Eve glad, and restored her by willing to be contained in the womb.']

10. And as he spoke, Jesus raised him up and said to him, 'Bartholomew, will you see the adversary of men? I tell you that when you behold him not only you but the rest of the apostles and Mary will fall on your faces and become as dead corpses.'

11. But they all said unto him, 'Lord, let us behold him.'

12. And he led them down from the Mount of Olives and looked wrathfully upon the angels that keep hell (Tartarus), and beckoned to Michael to sound

the trumpet in the height of the heavens. And Michael sounded, and the earth shook, and Beliar came up, being held by six hundred and sixty [*Gk.*: five hundred and sixty; *Lat. 1*: six thousand and sixty-four; *Lat. 2*: six thousand and sixty] angels and bound with fiery chains. 13. And the length of him was one thousand six hundred cubits and his breadth forty [*Lat. 1*: three hundred; *Slav.*: seventeen] cubits [*Lat. 2*: his length one thousand nine hundred cubits, his breadth seven hundred, one wing of him eighty], and his face was like a lightning of fire and his eyes full of darkness [*Slav.*: like sparks]. And out of his nostrils came a stinking smoke; and his mouth was as the gulf of a precipice, and one of his wings was four-score cubits. 14. And straightway when the apostles saw him, they fell to the earth on their faces and became as dead. 15. But Jesus came near and raised the apostles and gave them a spirit of power, and he said to Bartholomew, 'Come near, Bartholomew, and trample your feet on his neck, and he will tell you his work, what it is, and how he deceives men.' 16. And Jesus stood afar off with the rest of the apostles. 17. And Bartholomew was afraid and raised his voice and said, 'Blessed be the name of your immortal Kingdom from henceforth even for ever.' And when he had spoken, Jesus ordered him, saying, 'Go and tread upon the neck of Beliar.' And Bartholomew ran quickly upon him and trod upon his neck, and Beliar trembled. [17. *Vienna Gk. Ms*: And Bartholomew raised his voice and said thus, 'O womb more spacious than a city, wider than the spreading of the heavens, that contained him whom the seven heavens contain not, but you without pain did contain, sanctified in your bosom' (evidently out of place); *Lat. 1*: Then did Antichrist tremble and was filled with fury.]

18. And Bartholomew was afraid and fled, and said to Jesus, 'Lord, give me a hem of your garments [*Lat. 2*: the kerchief (?) from your shoulders] that I may have courage to draw near to him.' 19. But Jesus said to him, 'You cannot take a hem of my garments, for these are not my garments which I wore before I was crucified.' 20. And Bartholomew said, 'Lord, I fear because, just as he did not spare your angels, he will swallow me up also.' [*Lat. 2 omits* 20.] 21. Jesus said to him, 'Were not all things made by my word, and by the will of my Father the spirits were made subject to Solomon? You, therefore, being commanded by my word, go in my name and ask him what you will.' 22.[9] [And Bartholomew made the sign of the cross and prayed to Jesus and went behind him. And Jesus said to him, 'Draw near.' And as Bartholomew drew near, the fire was kindled on every side, so that his garments appeared fiery. Jesus said to Bartholomew, 'As I said to you, tread upon his neck and ask him what is his power.'] And Bartholomew went and trod upon his neck, and pressed down his face into the earth as far as his ears. 23. And Bartholomew said to him, 'Tell me who you are and what is your

---

[9] Words enclosed by square brackets are from Jerusalem Gk. MS and Lat. 1.

name.' And he said to him, 'Lighten me a little, and I will tell you who I am and how I came hither, and what my work is and what my power is.' 24. And he eased him and said to him, 'Say all that you have done and all that you will do.' 25. And Beliar answered and said, 'If you will know my name, at the first I was called Satanael, which is interpreted a messenger of God, but when I rejected the image of God my name was called Satanas, that is, an angel that keeps hell (Tartarus).'[10] 26. And again Bartholomew said to him, 'Reveal to me all things and hide nothing from me.' 27. And he said to him, 'I swear to you by the power of the glory of God that even if I would hide anything I cannot, for he who would convict me is near. For if I were able I would have destroyed you like one of those who were before you. 28. For indeed I was formed the first angel; for when God made the heavens, he took a handful of fire and formed me first, Michael second [*Vienna Gk. MS adds* for he had his Son before the heavens and the earth and we were formed (for when he took thought to create all things, his Son spoke a word), so that we also were created by the will of the Son and the consent of the Father. He formed first me, next Michael the chief captain of the hosts that are above], Gabriel third, Uriel fourth, Raphael fifth, Nathanael sixth, and other angels of whom I cannot tell the names. [*Jerusalem Gk. MS*: Michael, Gabriel, Raphael, Uriel, Xathanael, and other six thousand angels; *Lat. 1*: Michael the honour of power, third Raphael, fourth Gabriel, and another seven; *Lat. 2*: Raphael third, Gabriel fourth, Uriel fifth, Zathael sixth, and another six.] For they are the rod-bearers of God, and they smite me with their rods and pursue me seven times in the night and seven times in the day, and leave me not at all and break in pieces all my power. These are the [*Lat. 2*: twelve] angels of vengeance who stand before the throne of God: these are the angels that were first formed. 30. And after them were formed all the angels. In the first heaven are a hundred myriads, and in the second a hundred myriads, and in the third a hundred myriads, and in the fourth a hundred myriads, and in the fifth a hundred myriads, and in the sixth a hundred myriads, and in the seventh [*Jerusalem Gk. MS*: a hundred myriads, and outside the seven heavens,] is the first firmament wherein are the powers which work upon men. 31. For there are four other angels set over the winds. The first angel is over the north, and he is called Chairoum [*Lat. 2*: angel of the north,[11] Mauch], and has in his hand a rod of fire and restrains the superfluity of moisture that the earth be not too wet. 32. And the angel that is over the north[12] is called Oertha [*Lat. 2*: Alfatha]: he has a torch of fire and puts it to his sides, and they warm his great coldness so that he may not freeze the world. 33. And the angel that is over the south is called Kerkoutha [*Lat. 2*: Cedar], and they break his fierceness so that he may not shake the earth. 34. And the angel

---

[10] Lat. 2 adds about seven lines descriptive of Satan's character.
[11] Boreas
[12] Aparktios.

that is over the south-west is called Naoutha, and he has a rod of snow in his hand and puts it into his mouth, and quenches the fire that comes out of his mouth. And if the angel did not quench it at his mouth it would set all the world on fire. 35. And there is another angel over the sea which makes it rough with the waves. 36. But the rest I will not tell you, for he who stands by does not permit it.'

37. Bartholomew said to him, 'How do you chastise the souls of men?' 38. Beliar said to him, 'Do you wish me to describe the punishment of the hypocrites, of the backbiters, of the jesters, of the idolaters, and the covetous, and the adulterers, and the wizards, and the diviners, and of those who believe in us, and of all whom I look upon (deceive?)?' 39. Bartholomew said to him, 'I wish you to be brief.' [*Lat. 2*: 38. When I will show any illusion by them. But those who do these things, and those who consent to them or follow them, perish with me.' 39. Bartholomew said to him, 'Declare quickly how you persuade men not to follow God, and your evil arts, that are slippery and dark, that they should leave the straight and shining paths of the Lord.'] 40. And he smote his teeth together, gnashing them, and there came up out of the bottomless pit a wheel having a sword flashing with fire, and in the sword were pipes. 41. And I (he) asked him, saying, 'What is this sword?' 42. And he said, 'This sword is the sword of the gluttonous, for into this pipe are sent those who through their gluttony devise all manner of sin; into the second pipe are sent the backbiters who slander their neighbours secretly; into the third pipe are sent the hypocrites and the rest whom I overthrow by my contrivance.' [*Lat. 2*: 40. And Antichrist said, 'I will tell you.' And a wheel came up out of the abyss, having seven fiery knives. The first knife has twelve pipes ... 42. Antichrist answered, 'The pipe of fire in the first knife; in it are put the casters of lots and diviners and enchanters, and those who believe in them or have sought them, because in the iniquity of their heart they have invented false divinations. In the second pipe of fire are first the blasphemers ... suicides ... idolaters ... In the rest are first perjurers ...' (*long enumeration*).] 43. And Bartholomew said, 'Do you then do these things by yourself alone?' 44. And Satan said, 'If I were able to go forth by myself I would have destroyed the whole world in three days, but neither I nor any of the six hundred go forth. For we have other swift ministers whom we command, and we furnish them with a hook of many points and send them forth to hunt, and they catch for us souls of men, enticing them with various tempting baits, that is, by drunkenness and laughter, by backbiting, hypocrisy, pleasures, fornication, and the rest of the trifles that come out of their treasures. [*Lat. 2 amplifies enormously.*]

45. 'And I will tell you also the rest of the names of the angels. The angel of the hail is called Mermeoth, and he holds the hail upon his head, and my ministers adjure him and send him whither they will. And other angels are there over the snow, and others over the thunder, and others over the

lightning, and when any spirit of ours wishes to go forth either by land or by sea, these angels send out fiery stones and set our limbs on fire.' [*Lat. 2 enumerates all the transgressions of Israel and all possible sins.*]

46. Bartholomew said, 'Be still, you dragon of the pit.' 47. And Beliar said, 'Many things will I tell you of the angels. Those who run together throughout the heavenly places and the earthly are these: Mermeoth, Onomatath, Douth, Melioth, Charouth, Graphathas, Oethra, Nephonos, Chalkatoura. With them fly (are administered?) the things that are in heaven and on earth and under the earth.'

48. Bartholomew said to him, 'Be still and be powerless, so that I may entreat my Lord.' 49. And Bartholomew fell upon his face and cast earth upon his head and began to say, 'O Lord Jesu Christ, the great and glorious name. All the choirs of the angels praise you, O Master, and I who am unworthy with my lips... do praise you, O Master. Hearken to me, your servant, and as you chose me from the receipt of custom and did not allow me to continue in my way of life to the end, O Lord Jesu Christ, hearken to me and have mercy upon the sinners.' 50. And when he had spoken, the Lord said to him, 'Rise up, permit the one who groans to arise; I will declare the rest to you.' 51. And Bartholomew raised up Satan and said to him, 'Go to your place with your angels; but the Lord has mercy upon all his world.' [*50, 51, again enormously amplified in Lat. 2. Satan complains that he has been tricked into telling his secrets before the time. 49 follows 51 in this text.*]

52. But the devil said, 'Permit me, and I will tell you how I was cast down into this place and how the Lord made man. 53. I was going to and fro in the world, and God said to Michael, "Bring me a clod from the four corners of the earth, and water out of the four rivers of paradise." And when Michael brought them, God formed Adam in the regions of the east, and shaped the clod which was shapeless, and stretched sinews and veins upon it and established it with joints; and he showed him reverence for his own sake because he was the image of God. Michael also worshipped him. 54. And when I came from the ends of the earth, Michael said, "Worship the image of God, which he has made according to his likeness." But I said, "I am fire of fire, I was the first angel formed, and shall I worship clay and matter?" 55. And Michael said to me, "Worship, lest God be angry with you." But I said to him, "God will not be angry with me; but I will set my throne over against his throne, and I will be as he is." Then God was angry with me and cast me down, having commanded the windows of heaven to be opened. 56. And when I was cast down, he also asked the six hundred that were under me if they would worship, but they said, "Just as we have seen the first angel do, neither will we worship him who is less than ourselves." Then the six hundred were also cast down by him with me. 57. And when we were cast down upon the earth we were senseless for forty years; and when the sun shone forth seven times brighter than fire, suddenly I awoke; and I looked

about and saw the six hundred that were under me senseless. 58. And I woke my son Salpsan and took counsel with him how I might deceive the man on whose account I was cast out of the heavens. 59. And thus did I contrive it. I took a vial in my hand and scraped the sweat from off my breast and the hair of my armpits, and washed myself [*Lat. 2*: I took fig-leaves in my hands and wiped the sweat from my bosom and below mine arms and cast it down beside the streams of waters. *59 is greatly prolonged in this text*] in the springs of the waters whence the four rivers flow out, and Eve drank of it and desire came upon her; for if she had not drunk of that water I should not have been able to deceive her.' 60. Then Bartholomew commanded him to go into hell.

61. And Bartholomew came and fell at Jesus' feet and began with tears to say, 'Abba, Father, you are incapable of being discovered by us. Word of the Father, whom the seven heavens hardly contained, but who were pleased to be contained easily and without pain within the body of the Virgin, whom the Virgin knew not that she bore; you by your thought have ordained all things to be; you give us that which we need before you are entreated. 62. You who wore a crown of thorns that you might prepare for us who repent the precious crown from heaven; you did hang upon the tree, that ... [*Lat. 2*: that you might turn from us the tree of lust and concupiscence. *The verse is prolonged for over forty lines*] (who did drink wine mingled with gall) that you might give us to drink of the wine of compunction, and were pierced in the side with a spear that you might fill us with your body and your blood; (63) you who gave names to the four rivers: to the first Pison, because of the faith which you appeared in the world to preach; to the second Geon, for that man was made of earth; to the third Tigris, because by you was revealed to us the consubstantial Trinity in the heavens; to the fourth Euphrates, because by your presence in the world you made every soul to rejoice through the word of immortality.

64.[13] 'My God, and Father, the greatest, my King: save, Lord, the sinners.' 65. When he had prayed, Jesus said to him, 'Bartholomew, my Father named me Christ, that I might come down upon earth and anoint every man who comes to me with the oil of life; and he called me Jesus that I might heal every sin of those who know not ... and give to men ... the truth of God.'

66. And again Bartholomew said to him, 'Lord, is it lawful for me to reveal these mysteries to every man?' 67. Jesus said to him, 'Bartholomew, my beloved, as many as are faithful and are able to keep them to themselves, to them you may entrust these things. For some there are who are worthy of them, but there are also others to whom it is not fit to entrust them; for they are vain drunkards, proud, unmerciful, partakers in idolatry, authors of fornication, slanderers, teachers of foolishness, and doing all works that are of

---

[13] In Lat. 2, vv. 64-71 occupy eighty-three lines, of which v. 65 fills nearly fifty. Jesus dwells on the words, 'I am the way, the truth, and the life', and speaks at some length of his benefits to the Jewish nation and of their blindness and ingratitude (recalling the Improperia and 2 Esdras 1); there are also many clauses from John 13-15.

the devil; and therefore they are not worthy that these should be entrusted to them. 68. And also they are secret, because of those who cannot contain them; for as many as can contain them shall have a part in them. Hitherto, therefore, my beloved, have I spoken to you, for blessed are you and all your kindred who have this word entrusted to them; for all those who can contain it shall receive whatsoever they will in the ⟨day?⟩ of my judgement.'

69. Then I, Bartholomew, who wrote these things in my heart, took hold of the hand of the Lord the lover of men and began to rejoice and to speak thus:

'Glory be to you, O Lord Jesus Christ, who gives unto all your grace which we have all perceived. Alleluia.

Glory be to you, O Lord, the life of sinners.

Glory be to you, O Lord, death is put to shame.

Glory be to you, O Lord, the treasure of righteousness.

For unto God do we sing.'

70. And as Bartholomew spoke, Jesus put off his mantle and took a kerchief from the neck of Bartholomew and began to rejoice and say, [*Lat. 2*: Then Jesus took a kerchief (?) and said, 'I am good: mild and gracious and merciful, strong and righteous, wonderful and holy'] 'I am good. Alleluia. I am meek and gentle. Alleluia. Glory be to you, O Lord: for I give gifts to all who desire me. Alleluia.

'Glory be to you, O Lord, world without end. Amen. Alleluia.'

71. And when he had ceased, the apostles kissed him, and he gave them the peace of love.

V[14]

1. Bartholomew said to him,[15] 'Declare to us, Lord, what sin is more grievous than all sins?' 2. Jesus said to him, 'Truly I say to you that hypocrisy and backbiting are more grievous than all sins: for because of them the prophet said in the psalm that "the ungodly shall not rise in judgement, neither sinners in the council of the righteous",[16] neither the ungodly in the judgement of my Father. Truly, truly, I say to you, that every sin shall be forgiven to every man, but the sin against the Holy Ghost shall not be forgiven.' 3. And Bartholomew said to him, 'What is the sin against the Holy Ghost?' 4. Jesus said to him, 'Whosoever shall decree against any man who has served my holy Father has blasphemed against the Holy Ghost. Every man who serves God with reverence is worthy of the Holy Ghost, and he who speaks anything evil against him shall not be forgiven.[17]

5. 'Woe to him who swears by the head of God, woe to him who swears falsely by him even when speaking the truth. For there are twelve heads of

---

[14] Possibly this section is a late addition.
[15] In Lat. 2, vv. 1–6 occupy fifty-eight lines.
[16] Ps. 1: 4.
[17] Lat. 2 enumerates seventeen other sins—chiefly forms of idolatry and wrong belief.

God the most high: for he is the truth, and in him is no lie, neither forswearing. 6. You, therefore, go and preach to all the world the word of truth, and you, Bartholomew, preach this word to every one who desires it; and as many as believe shall have eternal life.'

7. Bartholomew said,[18] 'O Lord, and if anyone sin with sin of the body, what is their reward?' 8. And Jesus said, 'It is good if he who is baptized preserve his baptism blameless: but the pleasure of the flesh will become an allurement. For a single marriage belongs to sobriety: for truly I say to you, he who sins after the third marriage is unworthy of God. [*Lat. 2 is to this effect*:... But if the lust of the flesh come upon him, he ought to be the husband of one wife. The married, if they are good and pay tithes, will receive a hundredfold. A second marriage is lawful, on condition of the diligent performance of good works, and due payment of tithes; but a third marriage is reprobated: and virginity is best.] 9. But preach to every man that they keep themselves from such things: for I depart not from you and I do supply you with the Holy Ghost.' [*Lat. 2*: at the end of 9, Jesus ascends in the clouds, and two angels appear and say. 'You men of Galilee...'] 10. And Bartholomew worshipped him with the apostles, and glorified God earnestly, saying, 'Glory be to you, Holy Father, Sun unquenchable, incomprehensible, full of light. To you be glory, to you honour and adoration, world without end. Amen.' (*Lat. 2 adds* End of the questioning of the most blessed Bartholomew and the other apostles with the Lord Jesus Christ.]

B. THE BOOK OF THE RESURRECTION OF JESUS CHRIST BY BARTHOLOMEW THE APOSTLE

1. *Summary, based on James, ANT 182–6, of the London manuscript published by Wallis Budge*

Five leaves are wanting at the beginning of the British Museum manuscript. The contents of these can be partly filled up from Lacau and Revillout. But in the first place a passage (p. 193, Budge) may be quoted which shows something of the setting of the book: 'Do not let this book come into the hand of any man who is an unbeliever and a heretic. Behold, this is the seventh time that I have commanded you, O my son Thaddaeus, concerning these mysteries. Do not reveal them to any impure man, but keep them safely.' We see that the book was addressed by Bartholomew to his son Thaddaeus, and this would no doubt have been the subject of some of the opening lines of the text.

Next we may place the two fragments, one about the child of Joseph of Arimathaea, the other about the cock raised to life (Revillout no. 6, below, p. 672).

---

[18] In Lat. 2, vv. 7–10 fill sixty-nine lines.

Then we have a piece which in Revillout is no. 12 (below, p. 672). There can be but little matter lost between this and the opening of the British Museum manuscript, in the first lines of which the taking of Ananias' soul to heaven is mentioned.

We now take up the British Museum manuscript as our basis. Certain passages of it are preserved in the Paris fragments which partly overlap each other, and so three different texts exist for some parts: but it will not be important for our purpose to note many of the variations.

Joseph of Arimathaea buried the body of Jesus. Death came into Amente (the underworld), asking who the new arrival was, for he detected a disturbance.

He came to the tomb of Jesus with his six sons in the form of serpents. Jesus lay there (it was the second day, i.e. the Saturday) with his face and head covered with napkins.

Death addressed his son the Pestilence, and described the commotion which had taken place in his domain. Then he spoke to the body of Jesus and asked, 'Who are you?' Jesus removed the napkin that was on his face and looked in the face of Death and laughed at him. Death and his sons fled. Then they approached again, and the same thing happened. He addressed Jesus again at some length, suspecting, but not certain, who he was.

Then Jesus rose and mounted into the chariot of the Cherubim. He wrought havoc in Hell, breaking the doors, binding the demons Beliar and Melkir and delivered Adam and the holy souls.

Then he turned to Judas Iscariot and uttered a long rebuke, and described the sufferings which he must endure. Thirty names of sins are given, which are the snakes that were sent to devour him.

Jesus rose from the dead, and Abbaton (Death) and Pestilence came back to Amente to protect it, but they found it wholly desolate, only three souls were left in it (those of Herod, Cain, and Judas, according to the Paris manuscript).

Meanwhile the angels were singing the hymn which the Seraphim sing at dawn on the Lord's day over his body and his blood.

Early in the morning of the Lord's day the women went to the tomb. They were Mary Magdalene, Mary the mother of James whom Jesus delivered out of the hand of Satan, Salome who tempted him, Mary who ministered to him and Martha her sister, Joanna the wife of Chuza who had renounced the marriage bed, Berenice who was healed of an issue of blood in Capernaum, Leah the widow whose son he raised at Nain, and the woman to whom he said, 'Your sins which are many are forgiven you.'

These were all in the garden of Philogenes, whose son, Simeon, Jesus healed when he came down from the Mount of Olives with the apostles.

Mary said to Philogenes, 'If you are indeed he, I know you.' Philogenes said, 'You are Mary the mother of Thalkamarimath, which means joy, blessing, and gladness.' Mary said, 'If you have borne him away, tell me where you have laid him and I will take him away: fear not.' Philogenes told how the Jews sought a safe tomb for Jesus that the body might not be stolen, and he offered to place it in a tomb in his own garden and watch over it; and they sealed it and departed. At midnight he rose and went out and found all the orders of angels: Cherubim, Seraphim, Powers, and Virgins. Heaven opened, and the Father raised Jesus. Peter, too, was there and supported Philogenes, or he would have died.

The Saviour then appeared to them on the chariot of the Father and said to Mary, 'Mari Khar Mariath (Mary the mother of the Son of God).' Mary answered, 'Rabbouni Kathiathari Mioth (The Son of God the Almighty, my Lord, and my Son).' A long address to Mary from Jesus follows, in the course of which he bids her tell his brethren, 'I ascend to my Father and your Father.' Mary says, 'If indeed I am not permitted to touch you, at least bless my body in which you deigned to dwell.'

Believe me, my brethren the holy apostles, I, Bartholomew, beheld the Son of God on the chariot of the Cherubim. All the heavenly hosts were about him. He blessed the body of Mary.

She went and gave the message to the apostles, and Peter blessed her, and they rejoiced.

Jesus and the redeemed souls ascended into heaven, and the Father crowned him. The glory of this scene Bartholomew could not describe. It is here that he enjoins his son Thaddaeus not to let this book fall into the hands of the impure.

Then follows a series of hymns sung in heaven, eight in all, which accompany the reception of Adam and the other holy souls into glory. Adam was eighty cubits high and Eve fifty. They were brought to the Father by Michael. Bartholomew had never seen anything to compare with the beauty and glory of Adam, save that of Jesus. Adam was forgiven, and all the angels and saints rejoiced and saluted him, and departed each to their place.

Adam was set at the gate of life to greet all the righteous as they enter, and Eve was set over all the women who had done the will of God, to greet them as they come into the city of Christ.

As for me, Bartholomew, I remained many days without food or drink, nourished by the glory of the vision.

The apostles thanked and blessed Bartholomew for what he had told them: he should be called the apostle of the mysteries of God. But he protested, 'I am the least of you all, a humble workman. Will not the people of the city say when they see me, "Is not this Bartholomew the man of Italy, the gardener, the dealer in vegetables? Is not this the man who lives in the garden of Hierocrates the governor of our city? How has he attained this greatness?"'

The next words introduce a new section.

At the time when Jesus took us up into the Mount of Olives he spoke to us in an unknown tongue, which he revealed to us, saying, 'Anetharath (*or*

Atharath Thaurath).' The heavens were opened and we all went up into the seventh heaven. (So the London manuscript; in the Paris copy only Jesus went up, and the apostles gazed after him.) He prayed to the Father to bless us. The Father, with the Son and the Holy Ghost, laid his hand on the head of Peter (and made him archbishop of the whole world: Paris B). All that is bound or loosed by him on earth shall be so in heaven; none who is not ordained by him shall be accepted. Each of the apostles was separately blessed (there are omissions of single names in one or other of the three texts). Andrew, James, John, Philip (the cross will precede him wherever he goes), Thomas, Bartholomew (he will be the depositary of the mysteries of the Son), Matthew (his shadow will heal the sick), James son of Alphaeus, Simon Zelotes, Judas of James, Thaddeus, Matthias (who was rich and left all to follow Jesus).

And now, my brethren the apostles, forgive me. I, Bartholomew, am not a man to be honoured.

The apostles kissed and blessed him. And then, with Mary, they offered the Eucharist.

The Father sent the Son down into Galilee to console the apostles and Mary: and he came and blessed them and showed them his wounds, and committed them to the care of Peter, and gave them their commission to preach. They kissed his side and sealed themselves with the blood that flowed thence. He went up to heaven.

Thomas was not with them, for he had departed to his city, hearing that his son Siophanes (Theophanes?) was dead. It was the seventh day since the death when he arrived. He went to the tomb and raised him in the name of Jesus.

Siophanes told him of the taking of his soul by Michael: how it sprang from his body and lighted on the hand of Michael, who wrapped it in a fine linen cloth; how he crossed the river of fire and it seemed to him as water, and was washed thrice in the Acherusian lake; how in heaven he saw the twelve splendid thrones of the apostles, and was not permitted to sit on his father's throne.[19]

Thomas and he went into the city to the consternation of all who saw them. He, Siophanes, addressed the people and told his story; and Thomas baptized twelve thousand of them, founded a church, and made Siophanes its bishop.

Then Thomas mounted on a cloud, and it took him to the Mount of Olives and to the apostles, who told him of the visit of Jesus and he would not believe. Bartholomew admonished him. Then Jesus appeared, and made Thomas touch his wounds and departed into heaven.

This is the second time that he showed himself to his disciples after he had risen from the dead.

---

[19] This vision resembles one inserted in the end of the Coptic version of the Apocalypse of Paul.

This is the Book of the Resurrection of Jesus the Christ, our Lord, in joy and gladness. In peace. Amen.

Peter said to the apostles, 'Let us offer the offering before we separate.' They prepared the bread, the cup, and incense.

Peter stood by the sacrifice and the others round the table. They waited (*break in the text*) table... their hearts rejoiced... worshipped the Son of God. He took his seat... his Father. His body was on the table around which they were assembled, and they divided it. They saw the blood of Jesus pouring out as living blood down into the cup. Peter said, 'God has loved us more than all, in letting us see these great honours; and our Lord Jesus Christ has allowed us to behold and has revealed to us the glory of his body and his divine blood.' They partook of the body and blood, and then they separated and preached the word.

2. *Summary of extracts from Revillout (bibliography above)*

Revillout 6 (= Lacau no. 3, pp. 33-4):

Jesus and the apostles at table. The table turned of itself after Jesus had partaken of a dish, to present it to each apostle.

Matthias set a dish on the table in which was a cock, and told Jesus how, when he was killing it, the Jews said, 'The blood of your master shall be shed like that of this cock.' Jesus smiled and answered that it was true; and after some more words bade the cock come to life and fly away and 'announce the day whereon they will deliver me up'. And it did so.

Revillout 12 (= Lacau no. 3, pp. 35-6) parallels an incident referred to in Budge's London manuscript:

Ananias hurries to the cross and tells the Jews to crucify him and not Jesus. A voice from the cross tells Ananias that his soul will not enter Amente nor his body decay. The priests unsuccessfully try to stone Ananias. He is thrown into a fire but stays there unharmed for three days and nights. He is finally killed with a spear-thrust but Jesus carries off his soul to heaven.

Revillout pp. 185-94 and 149-50 (= Lacau no. 4, pp. 39-77) closely parallel the London manuscript.

The Letter of James

The Letter (or Apocryphon) of James belongs to a type of literature increasingly being categorized as 'Dialogues of the Saviour'. The Epistula Apostolorum, included above for historical reasons among the apocryphal epistles, might really stand alongside this so-called Epistula Iacobi. The document begins by claiming to be a letter written by James to another person, whose name is not legible; it also claims to be a secret book (apocryphon) revealed to the author and to Peter by the Lord.

This apocryphon occupies the first pages of the Jung Codex of the Nag Hammadi collection (Codex I, 2: 1. 1–16. 30). Koester includes it among the formative gospels of early Christianity. Because of claims, such as his, that we have in our hands a document comparable in age and influence to Papyrus Egerton 2, to Q, and to the Coptic Gospel of Thomas, and also because of its links with the canonical Gospels, it seemed appropriate to provide a translation of it here.

Koester sees rather more links to the canonical and other gospels than are normally shown. He draws attention to links between the following:

Epistle of James	2 ll. 22–33	John 14: 2, 4, 6
	3 8–11	Coptic Gospel of Thomas, logion 28
	3 17–26	John 20: 29
	4 23–30	Mark 10: 28–30
	7 1–6	John 16: 29
	9 4–6	John 16: 26
	18–24	Coptic Thomas, logion 69a; Matt. 5:11
	10 32–4	John 16: 23b
	12 l. 31–13 l.1	John 12: 35–6

The parables listed in the Letter of James can be linked with parables known to the synoptic Gospels. The parable of the grain of wheat in the Letter of James 8 may be compared with that in Mark 4: 26–9.

The epistolary framework is perhaps of later date. The bulk of the text is a dialogue between the risen Christ and James and Peter. After Jesus' ascension, the apostles travel to heaven, thus linking the text here with other apocryphal apocalypses.

The date for the original contribution is usually put at third century, but some, like Koester, would give an earlier date. The provenance is likely to be

Egypt. The original language is likely to have been Greek, but is known now only in Coptic.

The contents have been variously described as Gnostic of Valentinian origin or an offshoot of early Christian literature without any connection with Gnosticism. It is comparable with the Epistula Apostolorum not only in form but in content—both lack a thoroughly heretical character.

The translation from the Coptic is based on the work of Ron Cameron, who has made a special study of this apocryphon, as can be seen in the bibliography below. I acknowledge with grateful thanks his contribution to this volume.

EDITIONS

M. Malinine, H.-C. Puech, G. Quispel, R. Kasser, R. McL. Wilson, J. Zandee (eds.), *Epistula Iacobi Apocrypha* (Zürich and Stuttgart, 1968).

F. E. Williams, 'The Apocryphon of James', in H. W. Attridge (ed.), *Nag Hammadi Codex I (The Jung Codex): Introduction, Texts, Translations, Notes*, 2 vols. (Leiden, 1985), i. 13–53; ii. 7–37 (= Nag Hammadi Studies 22–3).

The Facsimile Edition of the Nag Hammadi Codices: Codex I (Leiden, 1977).

MODERN TRANSLATIONS

English

J. M. Robinson (ed.), *The Nag Hammadi Library in English* (Leiden,[3] 1988), 29–36.
Cameron, 55–64.
Hennecke[3], i. 333–8 (not a full trans.).
Hennecke[5], i. 285–300.

German

Hennecke[3], i. 245–9 (H.-C. Puech) (not a full trans.).
Hennecke[5], i. 234–44 (D. Kirchner).

Italian

Moraldi [2] iii. 147–59.

GENERAL

H.-M. Schenke, 'Der Jacobusbrief aus dem Codex Jung', *Orientalische Literaturzeitung* 66 (1971), cols. 117–30 (with German trans.).

J. Heldermann, 'Anapausis in the Epistula Jacobi Apocrypha', in R. McL. Wilson (ed.), *Nag Hammadi and Gnosis* (Leiden, 1978), 34–43 (= Nag Hammadi Studies 14).

C. W. Hedrick, 'Kingdom Sayings and Parables of Jesus in the Apocryphon of James', *NTS* 29 (1983), 1–24.

G. Gianotto, 'La letteratura apocrifa attribuita a Giacomo a Nag Hammadi (NHC I, 2; V, 3; V, 4)', *Augustinianum* 23 (1983), 111–21.

R. Cameron, *Sayings Traditions in the Apocryphon of James* (Philadelphia, 1984) (= HTS 34).

—— *Parable and Interpretation in the Gospel of Thomas* (Sonoma, Calif., 1986) (= *Foundations and Facets Forum* 2.2).

B. Dehandschutter, 'L'Epistula Jacobi apocrypha de Nag Hammadi (CG I, 2) comme apocryphe néotestamentaire', *ANRW* 2.25.6, 4529–50.

D. Rouleau, *L'Épître apocryphe de Jacques* (NH I, 2) (Quebec, 1987) (= *Bibliothèque copte de Nag Hammadi, Section Textes* 18).

D. Kirchner, *Epistula Jacobi Apocrypha: Die zweite Schrift aus Nag-Hammadi-Codex* I (Berlin, 1989) (= *TU* 136).

H. Koester, *Ancient Christian Gospels* (London, 1990), esp. 187–200.

J. van der Vliet, 'Spirit and Prophecy in the Epistula Iacobi Apocrypha (NHC I. 2)', *Vigiliae Christianae* 44 (1990), 25–53.

(1.1) [James, writing] to [- - -]thos. Peace [to you (*sing.*) from] peace, [love from] love, (5) [grace from] grace, [faith] from faith, life from holy life!

Since you asked me to send (10) you a secret book which was revealed to Peter and me by the Lord, I could neither refuse you nor dissuade you; (15) so [I have written] it in Hebraic letters and have sent it to you—and to you alone. Nevertheless, you should do your best, as a minister of the salvation (20) of the saints, to take care not to disclose this book to many—this which the Saviour did not wish [to] disclose to all of us, his (25) twelve disciples. Still, blessed are they who will be saved through the trustworthiness of this text.

Ten months ago I sent you (30) another secret book which the Saviour revealed to me. However, that one you are to regard in this way, as revealed (35) to me, James. And this one (2.1) [... revealed ...] those who [...], therefore, and seek [...] (5) so it is [...] salvation [...].

Now the twelve disciples [used to] sit all together at the [same time], (10) remembering what the Saviour had said to each one of them, whether secretly or openly, and setting it down (15) in books. I was writing what went in [my book]—suddenly, the Saviour appeared, [after] he had departed from [us, and while we were watching] for him. And so, five hundred (20) and fifty days after he rose from the dead, we said to him, 'You went away and left us!'

'No', Jesus said, 'but I shall go to the place from which I have come. (25) If you (*pl.*) wish to come with me, come on!'

They all answered and said, 'If you bid us, we shall come.'

He said, 'Truly, I say to you, (30) no one ever will enter the kingdom of heaven if I bid him, but rather because you yourselves are full. Let me have James and Peter, (35) so that I may fill them.'

And when he called these two, he took them aside, and commanded the rest to carry on with what they had been doing.

The Saviour said, (40) 'You have received mercy (3.1) [...] become [...] they wrote [...] book, as [...] to you [...] (5) and just as [...] they [...] hear and [...] they [...] understand. So do you not desire to be filled? And is your heart drunk? (10) So do you not desire to be sober? You ought, then, to be ashamed! And now, waking or sleeping, remember that you have seen the Son of Man, and with him (15) have you spoken, and to him have you listened. Woe to those who have seen the Son [of] Man. Blessed are they who (20) have not seen the man, and who have not associated with him, and who have not spoken with him, and who have not listened to anything from him. Yours is (25) life! Know, therefore, that he treated you when you were sick, so that you might reign. Woe to those who have been relieved of their sickness, for they will (30) relapse again into sickness. Blessed are they who have not been sick, and have experienced relief before they became sick. Yours is the kingdom of God! Therefore, I (35) say to you, become full and leave no place within you empty, or else the one who is coming will be able to mock you.'

Then Peter responded, 'Look, three (40) times you have told us, (4.1) "Become [full", but] we are full.'

The [Lord answered and] said, 'This [is why I told] you, ["Become full", so] (5) that [you] might not [be lacking; those who are lacking] will not [be saved]. For fullness is good [and lacking], bad. Therefore, inasmuch as it is good for you (*sing.*) to lack but bad for you to be filled, so (10) whoever is full tends to be lacking. One who lacks is not filled in the same way as another who lacks is filled; but whoever is full receives his just deserts. Therefore, it is fitting to lack (15) while it is possible to fill yourselves, and to be filled while it is possible to lack, so that you (*pl.*) may be able [to fill] yourselves the more. Therefore, [become] full of the spirit (20) but lacking in reason. For reason is of the soul; indeed, it is soul.'

And I answered and said to him, 'Lord, we can obey you (25) if you wish, for we have forsaken our fathers and our mothers and our villages and have followed you. Give us the means, [then], not to be tempted (30) by the evil devil.'

The Lord answered and said, 'If you do the Father's will, what credit is that to you—unless he gives you, as (35) part of his gift, your being tempted by Satan? But if you are oppressed by Satan, and (40) are persecuted, and you do his (5.1) will, I [say] that he will love you, and will make you equal with me, and will regard [you] as having become (5) [beloved] through his providence according to your own choice. So will you not cease being lovers of the flesh and afraid of suffering? Or (10) do you not realize that you have not yet been abused and have not yet been accused unjustly, nor have you yet been locked up in prison, nor (15) have you yet been condemned unlawfully, nor have you yet been crucified ⟨without⟩ reason, nor have you yet been buried in the sand, as I myself was, (20) by the evil one? Do you dare to spare the flesh, you for whom the spirit acts as an encircling wall? If you think about the world, about how long it existed (25) ⟨before⟩ you and how long it will exist after you, you will discover that your life is but a single day, and your sufferings but a single hour. Accordingly, since what is good (30) will not enter this world, you should scorn death and be concerned about life. Remember my cross and my death, and you will (35) live!'

And I answered and said to him, 'Lord, do not proclaim the cross and death to us, for they are far (6.1) from you.'

The Lord answered and said, 'Truly, I say to you, none will be saved unless they believe in my cross; (5) [for] the kingdom of God belongs to those who have believed in my cross. Become seekers of death, therefore, like the dead who are seeking life, (10) for what they seek is manifest to them. So what can be of concern to them? When you enquire into the subject of death, it will teach you about election. In truth, (15) I say to you, none will be saved who are afraid of death; for the kingdom of ⟨God⟩ belongs to those who are dead. Become better than I; (20) be like the son of the Holy Spirit!'

Then I asked him, 'Lord, how shall we be able to prophesy to those who ask us to prophesy (25) to them? For there are many who enquire of us, and who look to us to hear an oracle from us.'

The Lord answered and said, (30) 'Do you not realize that the head of prophecy was severed with John?'

But I said, 'Lord, it is not possible to remove the head of prophecy, is it?'

The Lord said (35) to me, 'When you (*pl.*) comprehend what "head" means, and that prophecy issues from the head, understand what "Its head was removed" means. (7.1) I first spoke with you parabolically, and you did not understand. Now I am speaking with (5) you openly, and you do not perceive. Nevertheless, for me you were a parable among parables, and the disclosure (10) of openness.

'Be eager to be saved without being urged. Instead, become zealous on your own and, if possible, surpass (15) even me. For that is how the Father will love you.

'Become haters of hypocrisy and an evil disposition. For such a disposition (20) is what produces hypocrisy, and hypocrisy is far from the truth.

'Do not let the kingdom of heaven wither away. For it is like a date-palm shoot (25) whose fruit fell down around it. It put forth buds, and when they blossomed its productivity was caused to dry up. So it also is with the fruit that (30) came from this singular root: when it was picked, fruit was gathered by many. Truly, this was good. Is it not possible to produce such new growth now? (35) Cannot you (*sing.*) discover how?

'Since I was glorified in this way before now, why do you (*pl.*) detain me when I am eager to go? (8.1) For after my [labours] you have constrained me to stay with you eighteen more days for the sake of parables. It was enough (5) for some people ⟨to⟩ pay attention to the teaching and understand The Shepherds, and The Seed, and The Building, and The Lamps of the Virgins, and The Wage of the Workers, and The Silver Coins, and The (10) Woman.

'Become eager for instruction. For the first prerequisite for instruction is faith, the second is love, the third is works; (15) now from these comes life. For instruction is like a grain of wheat. When someone sowed it he had faith in it; and when it sprouted he loved it, because he envisioned (20) many grains in place of one; and when he worked he was sustained, because he prepared it for food, then kept the rest in reserve to be sown. So it is possible for you, too, to receive (25) for yourselves the kingdom of heaven: unless you receive it through knowledge, you will not be able to discover it.

'Therefore, I say to you, be sober; do not go astray. (30) Moreover, I have often said to you all together—and also to you alone, James, have I said—"Be saved". I have commanded you (*sing.*) to follow me, (35) and I have taught you how to respond in the presence of the rulers. Observe that I have descended, and have spoken, and have expended myself, and have won my crown, (9.1) so as to save you (*pl.*). For I descended to dwell with you so that you might also dwell with me. And (5) when I found your houses to be without roofs, I dwelt instead in houses that could receive me at the time of my descent.

'Therefore, rely (10) on me, my brothers; understand what the great light is. The Father does not need me. For a father does not need a son, but it is the son who needs (15) the father. To him do I go, for the Father of the Son is not in need of you.

'Pay attention to instruction, understand knowledge, love (20) life. And no one will persecute you, nor will any one oppress you, other than you yourselves.

'You wretches! You (25) unfortunates! You pretenders to the truth! You falsifiers of knowledge! You sinners against the spirit! Do you even now dare (30) to listen, when it behoved you to speak from the beginning? Do you even now dare to sleep, when it behoved you to be awake from the beginning, so that (35) the kingdom of heaven might receive you? (10.1) In truth, I say to you, it is easier for a holy one to descend into defilement, and for an enlightened person to descend into (5) darkness, than for you to reign—or even not to!

'I have remembered your tears and your grief and your sorrow; they are far from us. Now, then, you who are (10) outside the Father's inheritance, weep where it is called for, and grieve, and proclaim what is good: how the Son is ascending, as he should. (15) In truth, I say to you, were I sent to those who would listen to me, and were I to have spoken with them, I would never have come down (20) to earth. From now on, then, be ashamed for them.

'See, I shall leave you and go away; I do not wish to stay with you any longer—just as (25) you have not wished it either. Now, then, follow me eagerly. Therefore, I say to you, for your sake I descended. You are (30) the beloved; it is you who will become the cause of life for many. Invoke the Father, pray to God frequently, and he will give to you. Blessed (35) is whoever has envisioned you along with him when he is proclaimed among the angels and glorified among the saints. Yours is life! Rejoice and exult as (11.1) children of God. Keep [his] will, so that you may be saved. Accept reproof from me and save yourselves. I am pleading (5) for you with the Father, and he will forgive you much.'

When we heard these things, we became elated, for we had despaired over what we recounted earlier. (10) But when he saw us rejoicing, he said, 'Woe to you who require an intercessor. Woe to you who stand in need of grace. Blessed are (15) they who have spoken out fearlessly, and have obtained grace for themselves. Compare yourselves to foreigners: how are they regarded by your (20) city? Why be upset if you exile yourselves and leave your city? Why abandon your home (25) on your own, making it available for those who wish to live in it? You outcasts and runaways! Woe to you, for you will be caught. Or (30) perhaps you think that the Father is a lover of humanity? Or that he is persuaded by prayers? Or that he grants favours to one on behalf of another? Or that he bears with someone who seeks? (35) For he knows about desire, as well as what the flesh needs: does it not long for the soul? For without the soul the body does not sin, just as (12.1) the soul is not saved without the spirit. But if the soul could be saved from evil, and the spirit were also saved, then the body (5) would become sinless. For the spirit is what animates the soul, but the body is what kills it—in other words, it is the soul which kills itself. Truly, I say to you, (10) he will never forgive the sin of the soul, nor the guilt of the flesh; for none of those who have worn the flesh will be saved. Do you think, then, that many have (15) found the kingdom of heaven? Blessed is whoever has envisioned himself as the fourth one in heaven.'

When we heard these things, we became distressed. But when he saw that we were distressed, (20) he said, 'This is why I say this to you, that you may know yourselves. For the kingdom of heaven is like a head of grain which sprouted in a field. And (25) when it ripened, it scattered its fruit and, in turn, filled the field with heads of grain for another year. You also: be eager to reap for yourselves a head of the grain of life, so (30) that you may be filled with the kingdom.

'As long as I am with you, pay attention to me and obey me; but when I take leave of you, (35) remember me. Remember me because I was with you, though you did not know me. Blessed are they who have known me. Woe to those who have (40) heard and have not believed. Blessed are they (13.1) who have not seen [but] have [had faith].

'Once again do I [appeal] to you. For I reveal myself to you so that I may build a house of great value (5) to you, since you take shelter in it; likewise, it can support your neighbours' house when theirs is in danger [of] collapsing. In truth, I say to you, (10) woe to those for whose sake I was sent down here. Blessed are they who are on the way to the Father. Again I admonish you. You who exist, be (15) like those who do not exist, so that you may dwell with those who do not exist.

'Do not let the kingdom of heaven become desolate among you. Do not be arrogant (20) about the light that enlightens. Rather, behave toward yourselves in the way that I have toward you: I placed myself under a curse for you, so that you (25) might be saved.'

To this Peter answered and said, 'Sometimes you urge us on toward the kingdom of (30) heaven, yet other times you turn us away, Lord. Sometimes you make appeals, draw us toward faith, and promise us life, yet other times you drive (35) us away from the kingdom of heaven.'

The Lord answered and said to us, 'I have offered you faith many times; moreover, I have made myself known to you, (14.1) James, and you (*pl.*) have not understood me. On the other hand, now I see you rejoicing again and again. And even though you are elated (5) over [the] promise of life, you still despair and become distressed when you are taught about the kingdom. But you, through faith [and] knowledge, have received (10) life. Accordingly, disregard rejection when you hear [it], but when you hear about the promise, exult all the more. In truth, I say to you, (15) whoever receives life and believes in the kingdom will never leave it—not even if the Father wishes to banish him!

'This is all I shall tell (20) you at this time. Now I shall ascend to the place from which I have come. But you, when I was eager to go, have rebuffed me; and instead of accompanying me, (25) you have chased me away. Still, pay attention to the glory that awaits me and, having opened your hearts, listen to the hymns that await me up in heaven. (30) For today I must take my place at the right hand of my Father. I have spoken my last word to you; I shall part from you. For a chariot of spirit has lifted me up, (35) and from now on I shall strip myself so that I may clothe myself. So pay attention: blessed are they who proclaimed the Son before he descended, (40) so that, having come, I might ascend. Blessed three (15.1) times over are they who [were] proclaimed by the Son before they existed, so that you might have a share with (5) them.'

When he said this, he went away. So Peter and I knelt down, gave thanks, and sent our hearts up to heaven. We heard with (10) our ears and saw with our eyes the sound of battles and a trumpet's blast and utter turmoil.

And when we passed beyond (15) that place, we sent our minds up further. We saw with our eyes and heard with our ears hymns and angelic praises and (20) angelic rejoicing. Heavenly majesties were singing hymns, and we ourselves were rejoicing.

After this, we also desired to send our (25) spirits heavenward to the majesty. And when we went up, we were not permitted to see or hear a thing. For the rest of the disciples called to us and (30) asked us, 'What did you hear from the Teacher?', and, 'What did he tell you?', and, 'Where has he gone?'

We answered (35) them, 'He has ascended', and, 'He has given us a pledge, and promised all of us life, and disclosed to us children who are to come after us, having bidden (16.1) [us to] love them, since we shall [be saved] for their sake.'

And when they heard, they believed the revelation, yet were angry about (5) those who would be born. So, not wishing to give them an occasion to take offence, I sent each one to a different place. And I myself went up to

Jerusalem, praying that I might (10) obtain a share with the beloved who are to appear.

Now I pray that a beginning may take place with you (*sing.*). For this is how I can be saved—(15) since they will be enlightened through me, through my faith and through another's which is better than mine, for I wish for mine to be more lowly. (20) Do your best, therefore, to be like them, and pray that you may obtain a share with them. For, apart from what I have recounted, (25) the Saviour did not disclose revelation to us. For their sake do we proclaim a share with those for whom this has been proclaimed, those whom the Lord has made his (30) children.

Other Apocryphal Apocalypses

Among the many other apocalypses, prophecies and oracles are the following which are treated to only brief introductory notes:
1. The Apocalypse of Zephaniah
2. The Apocalypse of Elias (Elijah)
3. The Apocalypse of Stephen
4. The Apocalypses of John
5. The Apocalypse of Bartholemew
6. The Apocalypse of Zechariah
7. 5 and 6 Ezra
8. The Book of Elchasai
9. The Apocalypses of the Virgin

The Ascension of Isaiah and the Apocalypse of Esdras (the Greek Apocalypse of Ezra) which sometimes occur in collections of New Testament apocrypha are to be found in the companion volume, *The Apocryphal Old Testament* ed. H. F. D. Sparks (Oxford, 1984).

1. THE APOCALYPSE OF ZEPHANIAH

This is also known as the Apocalypse of Sophonias. It is rejected as apocryphal in the Stichometry of Nicephorus and in the Catalogue of the Sixty Books. The existing apocalypse is known only in Coptic. The Apocalypse of Paul may have made use of this apocryphon. The date of the original composition is likely to be between 100 BC and AD 175.

EDITION

G. Steindorff, *Die Apokalypse des Elias, eine unbekannte Apokalypse und Bruchstücke der Sophonias-Apokalypse* (Leipzig, 1899) (= *TU* 17, 3a).

ENGLISH TRANSLATIONS

J. H. Charlesworth (ed.), *The Old Testament Pseudepigrapha*, i (London, 1983), 497–515 (O. S. Wintermute).

H. F. D. Sparks (ed.), *The Apocryphal Old Testament* (Oxford, 1984), 915–25 (K. H. Kuhn).

GENERAL

B. J. Diebner, 'Literarkritische Probleme der Zephanja-Apokalypse', in R. McL. Wilson (ed.), *Nag Hammadi and Gnosis* (Leiden, 1978), 152-67 (= *NHS* 14).

2. THE APOCALYPSE OF ELIAS (ELIJAH)

This apocalypse is rejected as apocryphal in the Stichometry of Nicephorus and in the Catalogue of the Sixty Books. The text is known mainly in Coptic, although some fragments in Greek have been found. It is to be distinguished from an ancient Jewish Apocalypse of Elijah (of which a later Hebrew apocalypse survives), but the Coptic text may be a Christianized version of a Jewish original. It shows some dependence on the Apocalypse of Peter. Estimates of the date vary between the first and fourth centuries.

EDITIONS

G. Steindorff, *Die Apokalypse des Elias, eine unbekannte Apokalypse und Bruchstücke der Sophonias-Apokalypse* (Leipzig, 1899) (= *TU* 17, 3a).
J.-M. Rosenstiehl, *L'Apocalypse d'Élie: Introduction, Traduction et Notes* (Paris, 1972) (= *Textes et Études pour servir à l'histoire du Judaïsme intertestamentaire* 1).
M. E. Stone and J. Strugnell, *The Books of Elijah*, Parts 1-2 (Missoula, Mont., 1979) (= *SBL Texts and Translations* 18).
W. Schrage, 'Die Elia-Apokalypse', in *Jüdische Schriften aus hellenistisch-römischer Zeit*, V (Gütersloh, 1980), 183-288.
A. Pietersma and S. T. Comstock, with H. W. Attridge, *The Apocalypse of Elijah based on P. Chester Beatty 2018* (Chicago, 1981) (= *SBL Texts and Translations* 19: Pseudepigrapha Series 9)

ENGLISH TRANSLATIONS

Charlesworth (as above), 721-53 (O. S. Wintermute). Sparks (as above), 753-73 (K. H. Kuhn).

3. THE APOCALYPSE OF STEPHEN

The Gelasian Decree rejects a *Revelatio Sancti Stephani*, but nothing more is known of this apocalypse. Migne, *PL* 41, cols. 805-18, gives two accounts of the discovery of the relics of Stephen: this story may have given rise to the title in the Gelasian Decree. (James, *ANT* 564-8 gives a summary of a Slavonic story of Stephen's death.)

See Erbetta, iii. 397-408.

4. THE APOCALYPSES OF JOHN

(a) The Greek text given in Tischendorf, *Apoc. Apoc.* 70–94 is based on several manuscripts, but the text itself is considerably older (possibly fifth century). It is a typical question and answer account of the other world.

MODERN TRANSLATIONS

English

Walker, 493–503.

Italian

Erbetta, iii. 409–14.
Moraldi, ii. 1951–66; [2] iii. 465–78.
[For the Slavonic versions related to this see A. de Santos Otero, *Altslav. Apok.* ii. 197–209.]

(b) Another Greek apocalypse of John attributed to John Chrysostom was published by F. Nau, *Rev. Bib.* 11 (1914), 209–21, and is a sixth–eighth century text.

(c) A third apocalyptic text attributed to John is in an eleventh-century Coptic manuscript published by E. A. Wallis Budge, *Coptic Apocrypha in the Dialect of Upper Egypt* (London, 1913), 59–74; Eng. trans. 241–57.

ITALIAN TRANSLATION

Erbetta, iii. 417–24.

GENERAL

John Court, *The Book of Revelation and the Johannine Apocalyptic Tradition* (Sheffield, 2000).

5. THE APOCALYPSE OF BARTHOLOMEW

See The Questions of Bartholomew (above).

6. THE APOCALYPSE OF ZECHARIAH

See The Protevangelium of James (above), chs. 22–4.

7. 5 AND 6 EZRA

In many manuscripts of the Latin Bible 4 Ezra has two additional chapters at the beginning and two at the end. These are not present in other versions. Chs. 1–2 are usually described as a Christian apocalypse, possibly of the late second century and known as 5 Ezra; chs. 15–16 are apocalyptic prophecies known as 6 Ezra, and are probably a century later in origin. The Latin text of one recension can be found conveniently in the Appendix to the Stuttgart Vulgate (ed. R. Weber). (There is a small Greek portion of 6 Ezra in A. S. Hunt, *OP* 7 (London, 1910), 11 ff.)

EDITIONS

R. L. Bensly, *The Fourth Book of Ezra* (Cambridge, 1895) (= *Texts and Studies* 3.2).
T. A. Bergren, *Fifth Ezra: The Text, Origin and Early History* (Atlanta, 1990) (= Society of Biblical Literature Septuagint and Cognate Studies Series 25).
T. A. Bergren, *Sixth Ezra. The Text and Origin* (New York and Oxford, 1998).

See also:

J. M. Myers, *1 and 2 Esdras* (New York, 1974) (= *Anchor Bible* 42).
M. A. Knibb, 'The Second Book of Esdras', in R. J. Coggins and M. A. Knibb, *The First and Second Books of Esdras* (Cambridge, 1979).

MODERN TRANSLATIONS

English

Hennecke[3], ii. 689–703.
Hennecke[5], ii. 641–52.
Charlesworth (as above), 516–59 (B. M. Metzger).

French

Éac, 635–51, 655–70.

German

Hennecke[1], 390–4 (H. Weinel); cf. *Handbuch*, 331–6.
Hennecke[3], ii. 488–98 (H. Duensing).
Hennecke[5], ii. 581–90 (H. Duensing and A. de Santos Otero).

Italian

Erbetta, iii. 317–31.
Moraldi, ii. 1917–38; [2] iii. 431–51.

GENERAL

G. N. Stanton, '5 Ezra and Matthean Christianity in the Second Century', *JTS* 28 (1977), 67–83.

8. THE BOOK OF ELCHASAI

This work is extant only in fragments found in Hippolytus, *Haer.* 9. 13–17, 10. 29 (Wendland, pp. 251–5, 284); Epiphanius, *Haer.* 19 and 30 (Holl, *GCS*

25, pp. 299 f., 333 ff.); and Origen in Eusebius, *HE* 6. 38 (Schwartz, *GCS* 9.2, pp. 592–4). It seems to have been a Jewish work overlaid with Christian (or rather Christian-Gnostic) ideas. See G. P. Luttikhuizen, *The Revelation of Elchasai* (Tübingen, 1985) (= *Texte und Studien zum antiken Judentum*).

Fragments in:

A. Hilgenfeld, *Novum Testamentum extra canonum receptum*, iii. 2.2 (Leipzig, 1881), 227–40.

MODERN TRANSLATIONS

English

Hennecke[3], ii. 745–50. Hennecke[5], ii. 685–90.

French

Éac, 829–72.

German

Hennecke[3], ii. 529–32 (J. Irmscher). Hennecke[5], ii. 619–23 (J. Irmscher).

Italian

Erbetta, iii. 549–54.

9. THE APOCALYPSES OF THE VIRGIN

There are two apocalypses under the name of the Virgin Mary. One is in Greek, Armenian, Ethiopic, and Slavonic; the other is in Ethiopic.

(a) *The Greek Apocalypse*

Mary, during her Descensus ad Inferos, is shown the tortures of Hell, and begs pardon for the sufferers. Intercession for sinners is a theme found in the Apocalypse of Paul, and in other books of this genre (e.g. 4 Esdras, the Greek and Slavonic Apocalypse of Baruch (3 Baruch), Apocalypse of Esdras, etc). It is a ninth-century work and seems to have drawn on the Apocalypse of Paul and perhaps also on the Apocalypse of Peter.

EDITION

James, *Apoc. Anec.* i. 109–26.

MODERN TRANSLATIONS

English

R. Rutherfurd, in A. Menzies (ed.), *Ante-Nicene Christian Library*, Additional volume 9 (Edinburgh, 1897), 167–74.
James, 563 (summary).

Italian

Erbetta, iii. 447–54.

(*b*) *The Ethiopic Apocalypse*
See bibliography to The Apocalypse of Paul under 'Ethiopic' (above, p. 618).

GENERAL

R. Bauckham, 'Virgin, Apocalypses of the' in D. N. Freedman (ed.), *Anchor Bible Dictionary* (New York, 1992), vi. 854–6 (with a full bibliography).
For further details of these apocalypses of Mary see R. Bauckham, 'The Conflict of Justice and Mercy: Attitudes to the Damned in Apocalyptic Literature', in *La fable apocryphe: Actes du colloque de centenaire de l'école pratique des hautes études V^e section* (Turnhout, 1990), 181–96 (= *Apocrypha. Le champ des apocryphes* 1); and see further below—Appendix: *The Assumption of the Virgin*.

Appendix

The Assumption of the Virgin

The assumption (or dormition, or falling asleep, or passing away, or transitus, or obsequies) of Mary seems to have been a belief that originated in apocryphal literature from about the fourth century onwards and had a profound effect on Christian theology and practice in both East and West. The Gelasian Decree stigmatizes as apocryphal the 'Book called the home-going of the Holy Mary'.

There is a large number of accounts of the death and assumption of the Virgin Mary, published in various languages (including Greek, Latin, Coptic, Syriac, Ethiopic, Arabic). The history of this tradition is still largely unknown, and most editors of modern translations include only a sample. The largest collection is found in Erbetta's Italian edition. The traditions about Mary are normally considered under the different language groups, and this is the method applied by M. R. James. He was of the opinion that the legends about Mary's passing originated in Egypt, and so he gave prominence to the Coptic tradition.

The standard Greek text is the one attributed to St John the Theologian (Evangelist) and edited by Tischendorf. The standard Latin is that attributed to Melito of Sardis. Tischendorf published this as his Transitus Mariae B. (Tischendorf's Transitus A is a late Italian fiction attributed to Joseph of Arimathea.)

The Arabic is akin to the Syriac and is not included below. Neither are the various Ethiopic accounts included. These also are, in general, dependent on the Syriac. So too is the Armenian. The Irish tradition also seems to have close relationships with the Syriac.

The various accounts tell of the death of Mary in Jerusalem. In the Coptic tradition Mary's corporeal assumption is a feature: there is a long interval between her death and her assumption. This tradition includes nothing of the summoning of the apostles for missionary work. Only John and Peter are present. Mary is warned of her death by Jesus, and not by an angel. In the tradition represented by the Greek, Latin, and Syriac Mary's death is announced by an angel (who in the Latin brings her a palm branch); the apostles are summoned from all parts of the world; Mary's corporeal assumption occurs soon after her death.

Appendix

EDITIONS

Greek

Tischendorf, *Apoc. Apoc.*, pp. xxxiv–xlvi, 95–112.
A. Wenger, *L'Assomption de la T. S. Vierge dans la tradition byzantine de vi^e au xe siècle* (Paris, 1955) (= *Études et Documents: Archives de l'Orient Chrétien* 5).

Latin

Tischendorf, *Apoc. Apoc.*, pp. xxxiv–xlvi, 113–23 (Latin A); 124–36 (Latin B: Ps.-Melito).
A. Wilmart, 'Assumptio Sanctae Mariae' and 'L'ancien récit de l'Assomption', in id., *Analecta Reginensia* (Rome, 1933), 323–62 (= *Studi e Testi* 59).
B. Capelle, 'Vestiges grecs et latins d'un antique transitus de la Vierge', *Anal. Boll.* 67 (1949), 21–48 (Codex Colbertianus lat. 2672; Italian trans. by Moraldi, see below).
M. Haibach-Reinisch, *Ein Neuer 'Transitus Mariae' des Pseudo-Melito* (Rome, 1962) (= *Bibliotheca Assumptionis B.V.M.* 5).

Coptic

Forbes Robinson, *Coptic Apocryphal Gospels* (Cambridge, 1896) (= *Texts and Studies* 4.2) (Sahidic account in the Twentieth Discourse of Cyril of Jerusalem; Bohairic accounts of the falling asleep of Mary and Sahidic fragments).
E. Revillout, 'Les apocryphes coptes, i. Les Évangiles des douze apôtres et de Saint Barthélemy', in *PO* 2, ed. R. Graffin (Paris, 1904; repr. 1946), 174–83 (summary under D below).
E. A. Wallis Budge, *Miscellaneous Coptic Texts in the Dialect of Upper Egypt* (London, 1915), 49–73; Eng. trans. 626 ff. (Twentieth Discourse of Cyril of Jerusalem; cf. Robinson, 25–41).
M. Chaîne, 'Sermon de Théodose patriarche d'Alexandrie, sur la dormition et l'assomption de la Vierge', *Revue de l'orient chrétien* 29 (1933–4), 273–314 (re-edits text to be found in Forbes Robinson, 90–127).

Syriac

Wright, *Contributions*, 18–24 (History of the Virgin Mary); 24–41 (Transitus); 10–15, 42–51 (Obsequies).
—— 'The Departure of my Lady Mary from the World', *Journal of Sacred Literature* 6 (1865), 417–48; 7 (1865), 110–60 (text of BM Add. 14484 with variants of BM Add. 14732 and Eng. trans.). [Re-edited in A. Smith Lewis, *Apocrypha Syriaca. The Protevangelium Jacobi and Transitus Mariae* (London and Cambridge 1902), 12–69 (= *Studia Sinaitica* 11).]
E. A. Wallis Budge, *The History of the Blessed Virgin Mary* (London, 1899), 93–146; Eng. trans. ii. 97–153 (= *Luzac's Semitic Text and Translation Series* 4 and 5).

Armenian

P. I. Daietsi, *Ankanon Girkh' Nor Ktakaranac'* i (Venice, 1898), 452–78.
P. Vetter, 'Die armenische Dormitio Mariae', *TQ* 84 (1902), 421–49.

Ethiopic

M. Chaîne, 'Liber Iohannis Apostoli de Transitu b. Mariae Virginis', in *Apocrypha de Beata Maria Virgine* (*Scriptores Aethiopici* series 1, vol. 7; Rome, 1909; repr. Louvain, 1955) (= *CSCO* 39, Aeth. 22, and *CSCO* 40, Aeth. 23).
E. A. Wallis Budge, *Legends of our Lady Mary* (London, 1922), 152–67.
V. Arras, *De Transitu Mariae Apocrypha Aethiopice*, i (Louvain, 1973), *CSCO* 342, 343 (Aeth. 66 and 67) (cf. id., *CSCO* 351, Aeth. 68; *CSCO* 352, Aeth. 69).

Arabic

M. Enger, *Ioannis Apostoli de Transitu Beatae Virginis Liber* (Elberfeld, 1854) (with Latin trans.).
Cf. Graf, i. 246–57.

Slavonic

de Santos Otero, *Altslav. Apok.* ii. 161–95 ('Obdormatio Deiparae').

Georgian

M. van Esbroeck, 'Apocryphes géorgiens de la Dormition', *Anal. Boll.* 91 (1973), 55–75 (cf. 90 (1972), 363–9 and 92 (1974), 128–63).

MODERN TRANSLATIONS

English

Walker, 504–14 (Tischendorf's three texts).
James, 194–227.

French

Amiot, 112–34 (Ps.-Melito; Arabic (extracts)).
Migne, *Dictionnaire*, ii, cols. 503–42 (John); 587–98 (Ps.-Melito).
Éac, 165–88 (Discourse of John the Theologian).

Spanish

González-Blanco, iii. 5–61.
de Santos Otero, 574–659 (with good bibliography).

Italian

Erbetta, i.2. 407–632 (with full bibliography).
Moraldi, i. 807–95: ² iii, 163–282.
Bonaccorsi, i. 260–90 (Discourse of John the Theologian).
Cravieri, 449–63 (Discourse of John the Theologian); 465–74 (Narrative of Joseph of Arimathaea).

Irish

C. Donahue, *The Testament of Mary: The Gaelic Version of the Dormitio Mariae* (New York, 1942) (= *Fordham University Studies, Language Series* 1).
St. J. D. Seymour, 'Irish Versions of the Transitus Mariae', *JTS* 23 (1922), 36–43.
H. Willard, 'The Testament of Mary: The Irish Account of the Death of Mary', *Recherches de théologie ancienne el médievale* 9 (1937), 341–64.
M. McNamara, *The Apocrypha in the Irish Church* (Dublin, 1975); 122 f.
M. Herbert and M. McNamara, *Irish Biblical Apocrypha* (Edinburgh, 1989), 119–31 (Transitus Mariae from the Liber Flavus Fergusiorum).

GENERAL

M. Jugie, *La mort et l'Assomption de la sainte Vierge* (Vatican, 1044).
A. van Lantschoot, 'L'Assomption de la sainte Vierge chez les Coptes', *Gregorianum* 27 (1946), 493–525.
C. Balić, *Testimonia de Assumptione beatae Virginis Mariae* (Rome, 1948).
M. van Esbroeck, 'Les textes littéraires sur l'Assomption avant le xe siècle', in F. Bovon (ed.), *Les Actes apocryphes des Apôtres* (Geneva, 1981), 265–85 (= *Publications de la Faculté de Théologie de l'Université de Genève* 4).
E. Testa. 'L'origine e lo sviluppo della Dormitio Mariae', *Augustinianum* 23 (1983), 250–62.
S. C. Mimouni, *Dormition et Assomption de Marie. Histoire des traditions anciennes* (Paris, 1995).
Stephen J. Shoemaker, *Ancient Traditions of the Virgin Mary's Dormition and Assumption* (Oxford. 2002) (= *Oxford Early Christian Studies*).
Klauck, 247–60: ET 192–204.

THE ASSUMPTION OF THE VIRGIN
SUMMARY OF CONTENTS

The following texts are translated or summarized, following James, *ANT* 104–227:

1. Coptic

A. Summary of the Homily in Bohairic attributed to Evodius, Archbishop of Rome. Sahidic fragments also exist. From Forbes Robinson, 44–67 (but beginning at section V) and 66–89.
B. The Twentieth Discourse of Cyril of Jerusalem. In Sahidic. Summary taken from Wallis Budge, 642 ff; cf. Forbes Robinson, 24–41.
C. Summary of the Discourse of Theodosius, Archbishop of Alexandria (AD 536–68). In Bohairic. From Forbes Robinson, 98–127, and Chaîne, *ROC* 29.
D. Summary of a Sahidic fragment edited by Revillout as his 'Gospel of The Twelve Apostles', fr. 16.

2. Greek

The Discourse of St John the Divine, trans. from Tischendorf, *Apoc. Apoc.* 95–112.

3. Latin

A. The Narrative of Ps.-Melito, trans. from Tischendorf, *Apoc. Apoc.* 124–36.
B. Summary of the Narrative by Joseph of Arimathaea, taken from Tischendorf, *Apoc. Apoc.* 113–23.

4. Syriac

Summaries of:
A. Smith Lewis, *Apocrypha Syriaca*, 12–69. A congeries of documents divided into six books (actually only five appear, but six are promised).
B. Wright, *Contributions*, 18–24.
C. Wright, *Contributions*, 24–41.
D. Wallis Budge, *History of the Blessed Virgin Mary*, 97–153.
E. Four fragments (i–iv) from Wright, *Contributions*, 42–51; cf. his preface, 10–15. Final fragment (iv, pp. 50–1) translated in full.

I. COPTIC TEXTS

A. *The Homily attributed to Evodius, Archbishop of Rome*

The first four sections of the homily are panegyric. The narrative begins with V.

Evodius first tells of his calling by Jesus. He was with Peter and Andrew and Alexander and Rufus his kinsmen, and followed Jesus when Peter and Andrew did, and was of the seventy-two disciples.

They lived with Mary after the Passion, as did Salome and Joanna and the rest of the virgins who were with her, and Peter sanctified an altar in the house.

VI. On the twentieth of the month Tobi they were all gathered at the altar, and Jesus appeared and greeted them. He bade Peter prepare the altar, saying, 'I must needs take a great offering from your midst on the morrow, before each one of you goes to the place where you have been chosen by lot to preach.' He then ordained Peter archbishop, and others, including Evodius, presbyters, and also deacons, readers, psalmists, and doorkeepers; and departed to heaven. They remained, wondering what the offering was to be.

VII. On the twenty-first of Tobi Jesus returned, on the chariot of the cherubim, with thousands of angels, and David the sweet singer. We besought him to tell what the great offering was to be, and he told them that it was his mother whom he was to take to himself.[1]

---

[1] Parts of VII and VIII exist in Sahidic fragment I (Robinson, 66–9).

VIII. We all wept, and Peter asked if it was not possible that Mary should never die, and then if she might not be left to them for a few days. But the Lord said that her time was accomplished.

IX. The women, and also Mary, wept, but Jesus consoled her. She said, 'I have heard that Death has many terrible faces. How shall I bear to see them?' He said, 'Why do you fear his divine shape when the Life of all the world is with you?' And he kissed her, and blessed them all, and bade Peter look upon the altar for heavenly garments which the Father had sent to shroud Mary in.

X.[2] Mary arose and was arrayed in the garments, and turned to the east and uttered a prayer in the language of heaven, and then lay down, still facing eastward.

Jesus made us stand for the prayer, and the virgins also who used to minister in the temple and had come to wait on Mary after the Passion. We asked them why they left it. They said, 'When we saw the darkness at the crucifixion we fled into the holy of holies and shut the door. We saw a mighty angel come down with a sword, and he rent the veil in two; and we heard a great voice (*Sah.*: from the house of the altar) saying, "Woe to you, Jerusalem, who kill the prophets." The angel of the altar flew up into the canopy of the altar with the angel of the sword; and we knew that God had left his people, and we fled to his mother.'

XI. The virgins stood about Mary singing, and Jesus sat by her. She besought him to save her from the many terrors of the next world—the accusers of Amente, the dragon of the abyss, the river of fire that proves the righteous and the wicked. (All this *Sah.* omits.)

XII. He comforted her and said to the apostles, 'Let us withdraw for a little while, for Death cannot approach while I am here.' And they went out, and he sat on a stone and looked up to heaven and groaned and said, 'I have overcome you, O Death, who dwell in the storehouses of the south. Come, appear to my virgin mother but not in a fearful shape.' He appeared, and when she saw him her soul leaped into the bosom of her son—white as snow, and he wrapped it in garments of fine linen and gave it to Michael.

All the women wept; Salome ran to Jesus and said, 'Behold, she whom you love is dead.' David the singer rejoiced and said, 'Very dear in the sight of the Lord is the death of his saints.' (The Sahidic does not describe the moment of death, but says it took place at the ninth hour of the 21st of Tobi; and it omits David.)

XIII. They re-entered the house and found her lying dead, and Jesus blessed her.

XIV. Jesus shrouded the body in the heavenly garments, and they were fastened to it. He bade the apostles take up the body, Peter bearing the head and John the feet, and carry it to a new tomb in the field of Jehoshaphat, and watch it for three and a half days.

---

[2] At this point begins Sahidic fragment II (Robinson, 70–89) and continues into XVII; it has important differences, some of these being indicated ad loc. below.

David rejoiced, saying, 'She shall be brought to the king' (Ps. 45: 14), and, 'Arise, O Lord, into your resting place' (Ps. 132: 8).

(*Sah.* omits details: the order is merely to carry the body to the tomb, David again omitted.)

XV. Jesus ascended with Mary's soul in the chariot of the Cherubim. (*Sah.* merely: he hid himself from us.) We took up the body, and when we came to the field of Jehoshaphat, the Jews heard the singing and came out intending to burn the body. But a wall of fire encompassed us, and they were blinded; and the body was laid in the tomb and watched for three and a half days.

(*Sah.* omits everything after the blindness.)

XVI. The Jews were in terror and confessed their sin and asked pardon. Their eyes were opened and they sought but did not find the body; and they were amazed, and confessed themselves guilty.

(Here *Sah.* has a very confusing insertion. When the eyes of the Jews have been opened, 'there came a great choir of angels and caught away the body of the Virgin, and Peter and John and we looked on while she was carried to heaven, until we lost sight of it. And the Jews saw it also, and confessed themselves guilty.')

XVII. At midday on the fourth day all were gathered at the tomb. A great voice came, saying, 'Go every one to his place till the seventh month, for I have hardened the heart of the Jews, and they will not be able to find the tomb or the body till I take it up to heaven. Return on the 16th of Mesore.' We returned to the house.

In the seventh month after the death, on the 15th of Mesore, we reassembled at the tomb and spent the night in watching and singing.

(*Sah.* has only: We returned to the house.)

XVIII. At dawn on the 16th of Mesore, Jesus appeared. Peter said, 'We are grieved that we have not seen your mother since her death.' Jesus said, 'She shall now come.' The chariot of the Cherubim appeared with the Virgin seated in it. There were greetings. Jesus bade the apostles go and preach in all the world. He spent all that day with us and with his mother, and gave us the salutation of peace and went up to heaven in glory.

XIX. Such was the death of the Virgin on the 21st of Tobi, and her assumption on the 16th of Mesore. I, Evodius, saw it all. The sermon ends with a blessing.

(*Sah.* has: XVIII. At dawn on the eighth day after her death Jesus appeared (as in *Boh.*), and the fragment ends at his promise that the apostles shall now see the Virgin.)

B. *The Twentieth Discourse of Cyril of Jerusalem*

For ten (*Robinson*: fifteen) years after the resurrection, according to Josephus and Irenaeus(!), John and Mary lived together at Jerusalem. One day the Virgin bade John summon Peter and James; and they sat down before her, and she addressed them, reminding them of the life of Jesus (up to the Ascension and Pentecost). She went on to say that Jesus had come to her and warned her that her time was accomplished. 'I will hide your body in the earth', he had said; 'no man shall find it until the day when I raise it incorruptible. A great church shall be built over it. Now therefore summon the virgins'.

It was done. Mary took the hand of one of them, Mary Magdalene, now very old, and committed the others to her charge.

She bade Peter fetch from the house of his disciple Birrus the linen clothes she had committed to him: James was to buy for a stater (*Robinson*: shekel) spices and perfumes.

John lit the lamps. Mary spread the linen on the ground and poured the spices upon it and stood and prayed, facing east; she asked to be delivered from the terrors of the next world—the dragon and the river of fire. Then she lay down facing east.

Jesus appeared on the Cherubim and bade her not fear death. And said to Death, 'Come, you who are in the chambers of the south.' When Mary saw him her soul leaped into the bosom of her son, and he wrapped it in a garment of light.

She fell asleep on the night of the 20th day of Tobi (*Robinson*: early on the 21st).

The Lord bade the apostles take the body to the valley of Jehoshaphat and set down the bier, because of the Jews, and he would hide it.

In the morning they took it out. The Jews heard the singing, and took counsel and set out with fire to burn it. The apostles saw them coming, and dropped the bier and fled. The Jews found nothing but the bier, and that they burnt. A sweet odour came from the place where the body was laid, and a voice said, 'Let no man give himself the trouble of seeking it till the great day of the appearing of Christ.' The Jews were ashamed and fled, and told their neighbours, but bade them tell no one.

C. *The Discourse of Theodosius, Archbishop of Alexandria*

I. At the moment of the Ascension Jesus charged Peter, 'his bishop', and John to remain with Mary till her death.

II. She was living in Jerusalem with a number of virgins. We also, the apostles Peter and John were with her.

On the 20th of Tobi we came to her and found her amazed. She explained that that night, after she had finished the 'little office (*synaxis*)', she slumbered and saw a beautiful youth about thirty years of age, and Peter and John standing at his right hand, with garments in their hands. She perceived that it was Jesus, and he told her that the garments were her shroud; and he vanished.

Then Mary makes a long discourse on the horrors of death—the river of fire, the two powers of light and darkness, the avengers with diverse faces, the worm, the unquenchable fire which three tears will put out, the ruler of darkness.

On hearing this we wept.

III. There was a knocking at the door. It was the virgins who had come from the Mount of Olives, with censers and lamps. They had been warned by a voice in the night to come to Mary, who was to die next day.

Mary bade us withdraw a little, and uttered a long thanksgiving to her son, and a prayer to be delivered from the terrors of the next world.

IV. There were thunderings and lightnings. Jesus came on a chariot of light with Moses, David, the prophets, and the righteous kings, and addressed Mary. (There is a refrain to the speech, 'O my beloved Mother, arise, let us go hence'.)

Mary spoke words of comfort to the apostles. Jesus spoke of the necessity of death. He said that if she were translated, 'wicked men will think concerning you that you are a power which came down from heaven, and that the dispensation (the Incarnation) took place in appearance'.

V. He turned to the apostles—to me, Peter, and to John—and said that Mary should appear to them again. 'There are 206 days from her death to her holy assumption. I will bring her to you arrayed in this body.'

He bade them bring garments and perfumes from the altar, which were sent from heaven.

They spread them on the bed.

The Virgin arose and prayed him to receive her.

VI. She lay down on the garments, turned her face to him, and straightway commended her spirit into his hands.

He bade us prepare her for burial, and gave us three palms from paradise and three branches of the olive-tree which Noah's dove brought to Noah, and we laid them on her body. Peter was to bear the head, John the feet. The Jews would plot against her, but they should be blinded. The body was to be placed in the stone coffin and watched, and in 206 days he would bring the soul to it.

He went up to heaven and presented the soul to the Father and the Holy Ghost. And the voice of the Holy Trinity was heard welcoming the soul.

VII. We carried the body out to the field of Jehoshaphat. The Jews saw it and took counsel to come and burn it. The apostles set down the bier and fled.

Darkness came on the Jews, and they were blinded and smitten by their own fire. They cried out for mercy and were healed, and many were converted.

We returned to Jerusalem, and often came back to the tomb.

VIII. When the 206 days were over, on the evening of the 15th, that is the morning of the 16th of Mesore, we gathered at the tomb and watched all night.

At the tenth hour there were thunderings, and a choir of angels was heard, and David's harp. Jesus came on the chariots of the Cherubim with the soul of the Virgin seated in his bosom, and greeted us.

He called over the coffin and bade the body arise (a long address).

IX. The coffin, which had been shut like Noah's ark, opened. The body arose and embraced its own soul, just as two brothers who have come from a strange country, and they were united one with another. David said, 'Mercy and truth are met together.'

Jesus went up to heaven, blessing us, and we heard the voice of the powers singing. 'Bring to the Lord the honour due to his name. The virgins that are her fellows shall be her company.'

D. *Sahidic Fragment* (Revillout no. 16)

The high priest begs to be healed. Peter says that if he believes in Jesus Christ he can be healed.

The high priest acknowledges that he and his people crucified Jesus (knowing him to be the Son of God) because he drove the traders out of the temple.

Peter bids him, if he believes, to embrace the body of the Virgin and profess his belief.

He does so and takes his own cut-off hand and puts it to the stump and it adheres.

Peter bids him take the palm branch and go to the city and lay it on the eyes of those who are blind. He found many of them lamenting, and all who believed were healed.

Meanwhile the apostles laid the body in the tomb and remained there, to wait till the Lord should come and raise it up as he had said.

They bade the virgins go home in peace, but they wanted to stay there too. Peter and John reassured them. They asked to be blessed, and Peter blessed them.

At the third hour of the day the converted high priest came and told Peter that the Jews were still plotting to burn the body and the tomb.

Peter warned the disciples, but God sent forgetfulness upon the Jews. The apostles took courage. A voice from heaven came also promising safety.

On the 16th of Mesore we were gathered with the apostles at the tomb. We saw lightnings and were afraid. There was a sweet odour and a sound of trumpets. The door of the tomb opened; there was a great light within. A chariot descended in fire; Jesus was in it; he greeted us.

He called into the tomb, 'Mary, my mother, arise!' And we saw her in the body, as if she had never died. Jesus took her into the chariot. The angels went before them. A voice called, 'Peace be to you, my brethren.'

The miracle was even greater than that of the resurrection of Jesus, which no one saw except Mary and Mary Magdalene.

We, then, the apostles, are witnesses of these things, and have added or diminished nothing.

We went to the tomb and found the garments where the body had lain; we buried them.

2. GREEK NARRATIVE
THE DISCOURSE OF ST JOHN THE DIVINE CONCERNING THE FALLING ASLEEP OF THE HOLY MOTHER OF GOD

1. When the all-holy glorious mother of God and ever-virgin Mary, according to her custom, went to the holy sepulchre of our Lord to burn incense, and bowed her holy knees, she besought Christ our God who was born of her to come and abide with her.

2. And when the Jews saw her resorting to the holy sepulchre they came to the chief priests saying, 'Mary goes every day to the sepulchre.' And the chief priests called the watchmen who were charged by them not to allow anybody to pray at the holy sepulchre, and enquired of them if it were so in truth. But the watch answered and said that they saw no such thing; for God did not allow them to see her venerable presence.

3. Now on one day, which was Friday, the holy Mary came as usual to the sepulchre, and as she prayed the heavens were opened and the archangel Gabriel came down to her and said, 'Hail, you who bore Christ our God; your prayer has passed through the heavens to him who was born of you and has been accepted, and henceforth according to your petition you shall leave the world and come to the heavenly places to your Son, to the true life that has no successor.'

4. And when she heard that from the holy archangel she returned to Bethlehem the holy, having with her three virgins who ministered to her. And when she had rested a little she sat up and said to the virgins, 'Bring me a censer that I may pray.' And they brought it as it was commanded them.

5. And she prayed saying, 'My Lord Jesu Christ, who vouchsafed of your excellent goodness to be born of me, hear my voice and send to me your apostle John, that seeing him I may have the first fruits of joy; and send to me also the rest of your apostles, both those who have already come to dwell with you and those who are in this present world, in whatever land they may be, by your holy commandment, that I may behold them and bless your name that is greatly extolled, for I have confidence that you hear your handmaid in everything.'

6. And as she prayed I, John, came to her, for the Holy Ghost caught me up by a cloud from Ephesus and set me in the place where the mother of my Lord lay. And I entered and gave glory to him who was born of her and said, 'Hail, mother of my Lord, who bore Christ our God: rejoice, for you depart out of this life with great glory.'

7. And the holy mother of God glorified God that I, John, came to her, remembering the word of the Lord which he spoke, 'Behold your mother, and behold your son.' And the three virgins came and worshipped.

8. And the holy mother of God said to me, 'Pray and put on incense.' And I prayed thus, 'O Lord Jesus Christ who do marvellous things, do now marvellous things before her who bore you, and let your mother depart out of this life, and let those who crucified you and did not believe in you be troubled.'

9. And after I had finished the prayer the holy Mary said to me, 'Bring me the censer.' And she cast in incense and said, 'Glory be to you, my God and my Lord, because in me are fulfilled all things that you promised me before you ascended into the heavens, that whenever I should depart out of this world you would come to me in glory, you and the multitude of your angels.'

10. And I, John, said to her, 'Our Lord and our God Jesus Christ comes, and you behold him as he promised you.' And the holy mother of God answered and said to me, 'The Jews have sworn that when my end comes they will burn my body.' And I answered and said to her, 'Your holy and precious body shall not see corruption.' And she answered and said to me, 'Bring a censer and put incense in it and pray.' And there came a voice from heaven and said the Amen.

11. And I, John, listened to that voice, and the Holy Ghost said to me, 'John, did you hear this voice which was uttered in heaven after the ending of the prayer?' And I answered and said, 'Yes, I heard it.' And the Holy Ghost said to me, 'This voice which you heard signifies the coming of your brethren the apostles and of the holy powers, which is to be; for today they are coming here.'

12. And thereupon I, John, fell to prayer. And the Holy Ghost said to the apostles, 'All of you together mount up upon clouds from the ends of the world and gather at the same time at Bethlehem the holy because of the mother of our Lord Jesus Christ.' Peter came from Rome, Paul from Tiberia, Thomas out of the inmost Indies, James from Jerusalem.

13. Andrew the brother of Peter, and Philip, Luke, and Simon the Canaanite, and Thaddaeus, who had fallen asleep, were raised up by the Holy Ghost out of their sepulchres. The Holy Ghost said to them 'Do not think that the resurrection has occurred. The reason why you have been raised from your graves is so that you may go to greet with an honour and wonderful sign the mother of your Lord and Saviour Jesus Christ. For the day of her departure has arrived, and she is going to abide in heaven.'

14. And Mark, who was still alive, came from Alexandria with the rest, as has been said, from their several countries.

15. But Peter, when he was lifted up by the cloud, stood between the heaven and the earth, for the Holy Ghost sustained him, and looked while the rest of the apostles also were caught up in the clouds to be present with Peter. And so all came together by the means of the Holy Ghost, as has been said.

15.[3] And we approached the mother of our Lord and God and worshipped her and said, 'Fear not, neither be grieved; the Lord God who was born of you shall bring you out of this world with glory.' And she, rejoicing in God her Saviour, sat up in bed and said to the apostles, 'Now I believe that our teacher and our God comes from heaven, and I shall behold him, and so depart out of this life, just as I have seen you come to me. And I wish that you would tell me how you knew that I was departing and came to me, and from what lands and how far you have come hither, that you have been so quick to visit me; for neither has he who was born of me, our Lord Jesus Christ, hidden it from me. For I have believed now also that he is the Son of the Most High.'

16. And Peter answered and said to the apostles, 'Let each one certify to the mother of our Lord in what manner the Holy Ghost announced it to us and charged us.'

17. And I, John, answered and said, 'When I was entering the holy altar in Ephesus to minister, the Holy Ghost said to me, "The time of the departure of the mother of your Lord has come near; go to Bethlehem to greet her." And a cloud of light caught me up and set me at the door of the house where you lie.' 18. And Peter also answered, 'I was in Rome, and about dawn I heard a voice by the Holy Ghost saying to me, "The mother of your Lord must depart, for the time has come: go to Bethlehem to greet her", and lo, a cloud of light caught me up, and I beheld the rest of the apostles coming to me upon clouds, and a voice saying to me, "Go all of you to Bethlehem."' 19. Paul answered and said, 'I also was abiding in a city not very far off from Rome; and the place is called Tiberia. And I heard the Holy Ghost saying to me, "The mother of your Lord leaves this world to go to the heavenly places, and ends her course by departure: but go to Bethlehem to greet her." And lo, a cloud of light caught me up and set me where it set you also.' 20. Thomas also answered and said, 'I had passed through the land of the Indians, and my preaching was increased in strength by the grace of Christ, and the son of the king's sister, by name Labdanes, was about to be sealed by me in the palace, and suddenly the Holy Ghost said to me, "You also, Thomas, go to Bethlehem to greet the mother of your Lord, for she is departing to heaven." And a cloud of light caught me up and set me with you.' 21. And Mark also answered and said, 'As I was finishing the service of the third hour in the city of Alexandria, while I prayed, the Holy Ghost caught me up and brought me to you.'

22. And James also answered and said, 'While I was in Jerusalem the Holy Ghost admonished me, saying, "Be present at Bethlehem, for the mother of your Lord makes her departure." And lo, a cloud of light caught me up and brought me to you.'

23. And Matthew also answered and said, 'I glorified and do glorify God,

---

[3] The number 15 is, by an error, repeated in Tischendorf.

for as I was in a ship and it was tossed, the sea boisterous with waves, suddenly a cloud of light overshadowed us, and overcame the billows of the tempest and made them calm, and it caught me up and brought me to you.'

24. Likewise those who had departed this life before told how they came. And Bartholomew said, 'I was preaching the word in the country of Thebes, and lo, the Holy Ghost said to me, "The mother of your Lord makes her departure: go therefore to greet her at Bethlehem." And lo, a cloud of light caught me up and brought me to you.'

25. All these things the apostles said to the holy mother of God, telling how and in what fashion they came. And she spread forth her hands to heaven and prayed, saying, 'I worship and praise and glorify your name, which is greatly extolled, O Lord, because you have regarded the lowliness of your handmaiden, and you who are mighty have magnified me, and behold all generations shall call me blessed.' 26. And after the prayer she said to the apostles, 'Cast on incense and pray.' And when they had prayed there came a thunder from heaven and a terrible sound as of chariots, and lo, a multitude of the host of angels and powers, and a voice as of the Son of Man was heard, and the Seraphim came round about the house in which the holy and spotless mother of God, the virgin, lay; so that all who were in Bethlehem beheld the marvellous sights, and went to Jerusalem and declared all the wonderful things that had happened.

27. And it came to pass after that sound that the sun and the moon appeared about the house, and an assembly of the first-begotten saints came to the house where the mother of the Lord lay for her honour and glory. And I saw many signs come to pass, blind receiving sight, deaf hearing, lame walking, lepers cleansed, and those who were possessed of unclean spirits, healed. And every one with sickness or disease came and touched the wall where she lay, and cried, 'Holy Mary, you who bore Christ our God, have mercy on us.' And immediately they were cured.

28. And many multitudes who were dwelling in Jerusalem out of every country because of a vow, when they heard the signs that were being done in Bethlehem by means of the Lord's mother, came to the place, seeking to be healed of various diseases; and they obtained health. And there was unspeakable joy on that day among the multitude of those who were healed, and among the onlookers, glorifying Christ our God and his mother. And all Jerusalem returned from Bethlehem, keeping a holy day with singing of psalms and spiritual songs.

29. But the priests of the Jews, together with their people, were amazed at that which was done, and were taken with bitter envy, and with vain thoughts they gathered a council and decided to send men against the holy mother of God and the holy apostles who were there at Bethlehem. And when the multitude of the Jews was on its way to Bethlehem, about a mile away, it came to pass that they saw a terrible vision, and their feet were bound; and they

departed to their fellow-countrymen and declared the fearful vision to the chief priests. 30. But they, being yet more inflamed in the spirit, went to the governor, crying out and saying, 'The nation of the Jews is destroyed because of this woman; drive her away from Bethlehem and from the province of Jerusalem.' But the governor was astonished at the wonders and said to them, 'I will not drive her out from Bethlehem nor from any other place.' But the Jews continued crying out and urged him by the authority of Tiberius Caesar that he should lead the apostles out of Bethlehem, 'If you do not do it we will report it to Caesar.' And, being now compelled, he sent a captain of a thousand against the apostles to Bethlehem.

31. But the Holy Ghost said to the apostles and the mother of the Lord, 'Behold, the governor has sent a captain of a thousand against you, because the Jews have made a tumult. Go out therefore from Bethlehem, and fear not; for behold, I will bring you by a cloud to Jerusalem; for the power of the Father and of the Son and of the Holy Ghost is with you.'

32. The apostles therefore rose up straightaway and went out of the house, bearing the bed of their lady the mother of God, and went forward towards Jerusalem: and immediately, just as the Holy Ghost said, they were lifted up by a cloud and were found at Jerusalem in the house of their lady. And we stood up and for five days we sang praise without ceasing.

33. But when the captain came to Bethlehem and did not find there the mother of the Lord, nor the apostles, he laid hold upon the Bethlehemites, saying to them, 'Did you not come and tell the governor and the priests all the signs and wonders that happened, and how the apostles came out of every land? Where then are they? Come to Jerusalem to the governor.' For the captain did not know of the departure of the apostles and the mother of the Lord to Jerusalem. So the captain took the Bethlehemites and went to the governor, saying that he had found no man.

34. Now after five days it was made known to the governor and to the priests and to all the city that the mother of the Lord was in her own house in Jerusalem with the apostles, because of the signs and wondrous things that came to pass there; and a multitude of men and women were assembled, crying out, 'O holy virgin who bore Christ our God, forget not the race of men.' 35. And because of this the people of the Jews, moved even more with envy, together with the priests, took wood and fire and came, desiring to burn the house where the mother of the Lord lay, together with the apostles. But the governor stood observing the sight afar off. And when the people of the Jews had come to the door of the house, behold, suddenly a force of fire came from within it by means of an angel and burnt a great multitude of the Jews, and there was great fear throughout all the city and they glorified God who was born of her. 36. But when the governor saw what was done, he cried aloud before all the people saying, 'Of a truth he is the Son of God, who was born of the virgin whom you thought to drive out; for these signs are of a true

God.' And there was a division among the Jews, and many believed in the name of our Lord Jesus Christ because of the signs which came to pass.

37. Now after all these wonders occurred because of Mary the mother of God and ever-virgin, the mother of the Lord, while we, the apostles, were with her in Jerusalem, the Holy Ghost said to us, 'You know that on the Lord's day the good tidings were told to the Virgin Mary by the archangel Gabriel, and on the Lord's day the Saviour was born in Bethlehem, and on the Lord's day the children of Jerusalem went forth with palm-branches to meet him, saying, "Hosanna in the highest: blessed is he who comes in the name of the Lord." And on the Lord's day he rose from the dead, and on the Lord's day he shall come to judge the living and the dead, and on the Lord's day he shall come from heaven for the glory and honour of the departure of the holy and glorious virgin who bore him. 38. And upon the same Lord's day the mother of the Lord said to the apostles, "Cast on incense, for Christ comes with a host of angels: and, behold, Christ comes sitting upon the throne of the Cherubim."' And as we all prayed there appeared innumerable multitudes of angels, and the Lord riding upon the Cherubim in great power. And lo, an appearance of light going before him and lighting upon the holy virgin because of the coming of her only-begotten son; and all the powers of the heavens fell down and worshipped him. 39. And the Lord called to his mother and said, 'Mary.' And she answered and said, 'Behold, here am I, Lord.' And the Lord said to her, 'Be not grieved, but let your heart rejoice and be glad; for you have found grace to behold the glory of my Father that was given me.' And the holy mother of God looked up and saw in him glory which the mouth of man cannot utter nor comprehend. And the Lord stayed by her, saying, 'Behold, henceforth shall your precious body be translated to paradise, and your holy soul shall be in the heavens in the treasuries of my Father in surpassing brightness, where there is continual peace and rejoicing of the holy angels.' 40. And the mother of the Lord answered and said to him, 'Lay your right hand upon me, Lord, and bless me.' And the Lord spread out his unstained right hand and blessed her; and she, holding his unstained right hand, kissed it, saying, 'I worship this right hand which made the heaven and the earth; and I beseech your name which is greatly extolled, O Christ, God, King of the ages, only-begotten of the Father, receive your handmaid, you who vouchsafed to be born of me, the lowly one, to save mankind by your unutterable dispensation. To every man who calls on or entreats or names the name of your handmaid grant your help.' 41. And as she thus spoke, the apostles came near to her feet and worshipped the Lord and said, 'O mother of the Lord, leave to the world a blessing, for you depart out of it; for you blessed it and raised it up from destruction when you bore the light of the world.' And the mother of the Lord prayed, and thus she said in her prayer, 'O God, who of your great goodness sent your only-begotten Son to dwell in

my lowly body, who vouchsafed to be born of me, the lowly one, have mercy upon the world and upon every soul who calls upon your name.'

42. And again she prayed and said, 'O Lord, King of the heavens, son of the living God, accept every man who calls upon your name, that your birth may be glorified.' And again she prayed and said, 'O Lord Jesus Christ, who have all power in heaven and on earth, I entreat your holy name with this supplication: At every time and in every place where there is a memorial of my name, sanctify that place, and glorify those who glorify you through my name, accepting every offering and every supplication and every prayer.' 43. And when she had thus prayed, the Lord said to his own mother, 'Let your heart be glad and rejoice; for every grace and every gift has been given you of my Father who is in heaven and of me and of the Holy Ghost. Every soul who calls upon your name shall not be put to shame, but shall find mercy and consolation and succour and confidence, both in this world and in that which is to come, before my Father who is in heaven.' 44. And the Lord turned and said to Peter, 'The time has come to begin the song of praise.' And when Peter began the song of praise, all the powers of the heavens answered 'Alleluia.' And then the countenance of the mother of the Lord shone above the light. And she rose up and with her own hand blessed every one of the apostles, and all of them gave glory to God; and the Lord spread forth his unstained hands and received her holy and spotless soul. 45. And at the going forth of her spotless soul the place was filled with sweet odour and light unspeakable, and lo, a voice from heaven was heard, saying, 'Blessed are you among women.' And Peter ran, and I, John, and Paul, and Thomas, and embraced her precious feet to receive sanctification; and the twelve apostles laid her honourable and holy body upon a bed and carried it out.

46. And behold, as they carried her, a certain Hebrew named Jephonias, mighty of body, ran forth and attacked the bed as the apostles carried it, and lo, an angel of the Lord with invisible power struck his two hands from off his shoulders with a sword of fire and left them hanging in the air beside the bed. 47. And when this miracle came to pass, all the people of the Jews who beheld it cried out, 'Verily he is the true God who was born of you, Mary, mother of God, ever-virgin.' And Jephonias himself, being commanded by Peter that the wonderful works of God might be shown, stood up behind the bed and cried, 'Holy Mary, who bore Christ who is God, have mercy on me.' And Peter turned and said to him, 'In the name of him who was born of her your hands which were taken from you shall be joined back on.' And immediately at the word of Peter the hands that were hanging beside the bed of our lady went back and joined Jephonias; and he also believed and glorified Christ, the God, who was born of her.

48. And after this miracle the apostles carried the bed and laid her precious and holy body in Gethsemane in a new tomb. And lo, an odour of

sweet savour came out of the holy sepulchre of our lady the mother of God: and until three days were past the voices of invisible angels were heard glorifying Christ our God who was born of her. And when the third day was fulfilled the voices were no more heard, and thereafter we all perceived that her spotless and precious body was translated into paradise.

49. Now after it was translated, lo, we beheld Elizabeth, the mother of the holy John the Baptist, and Anna the mother of our lady, and Abraham and Isaac and Jacob, and David singing 'Alleluia', and all the choirs of the saints worshipping the precious body of the mother of the Lord, and we saw a place of light, than which light nothing is brighter, and a great fragrance came from that place to which her precious and holy body was translated in paradise, and a melody of those who praised him who was born of her; and to virgins only is it given to hear that sweet melody wherewith no man can be sated.

50. We, therefore, the apostles, while we beheld the sudden translation of her holy body, glorified God who had shown to us his wonders at the departure of the mother of our Lord Jesus Christ, by the prayer and intercession of whom may we all be accounted worthy to come into her protection and succour and guardianship, both in this world and in that which is to come; at all times and in all places glorifying her only-begotten Son, with the Father and the Holy Ghost, world without end. Amen.

3. LATIN

A. *The Narrative of Pseudo-Melito*

I. *Prologue.* Melito, servant of God, bishop of the church of Sardis, to the brethren who are established in peace at Laodicea, reverential to the Lord, greeting.

I remember that I have often written concerning a certain Leucius, who, after he had been a companion of the apostles with us, with alienated sense and rash mind departed from the way of righteousness and put into his books many things concerning the acts of the apostles, and spoke many and diverse things of their mighty deeds, but concerning their teaching lied much, affirming that they taught otherwise than they had, and establishing his own wicked position as if by their words. Nor did he account this sufficient, but also corrupted with an evil pen the departure of the blessed Mary ever-virgin, the mother of God, so that it is unlawful not only to read but even to hear it in the church of God. We therefore at your petition have written simply those things which we heard from the apostle John, and have sent them to your brotherhood, believing no alien doctrines which sprout out from heretics, but that the Father is in the Son, the Son in the Father, the triune person of godhead and undivided essence abiding; and that not two natures of man were created, a good and a bad, but that one good nature was created by a good

God, which by the fraud of the serpent was corrupted through sin, and restored by the grace of Christ.

II. When therefore the Lord and Saviour Jesus Christ for the life of the whole world hung on the tree of the cross pierced with nails, he saw standing beside the cross his mother and John the evangelist, whom he loved more than the other apostles because he alone of them was a virgin in body. To him therefore he committed the charge of the holy Mary saying to him, 'Behold your mother', and to her, 'Behold your son.'[4] From that hour the holy mother of God continued in the especial care of John as long as she endured the sojourn of this life. And when the apostles had divided the world by lot for their preaching, she abode in the house of his parents beside the Mount of Olivet.

III. 1. In the second year after Christ had overcome death and had ascended into heaven, on a certain day, Mary, fervent with desire of Christ, betook herself alone into the refuge of her dwelling to weep. And lo, an angel shining in a garment of great brightness stood before her and uttered words of greeting saying, 'Hail blessed of the Lord, receive the greeting of him who granted salvation to Jacob by his prophets. Behold this palm branch. I have brought it to you from the paradise of the Lord, and you shall cause it to be carried before your bier on the third day when you will be taken up out of the body. For behold, your Son with the thrones and the angels and all the powers of heaven awaits you.' 2. Then Mary said to the angel, 'I ask that all the apostles of the Lord Jesus Christ be gathered together to me.' And the angel said, 'Lo, this day by the power of my Lord Jesus Christ all the apostles shall come to you.' And Mary said to him, 'I ask that you would put your blessing upon me, that no power of hell may meet me in that hour in which my soul goes out of the body, and that I may not see the prince of darkness.' And the angel said, 'The power of hell shall not hurt you; but the Lord your God has given you an eternal blessing. I am his servant and messenger, but do not think that the power not to see the prince of darkness can be given by me, but only by him whom you bore in your womb, for his is all power, world without end.' And thus saying, the angel departed with a great light. 3. Now the palm-branch shone with exceeding brightness. Then Mary took off her garments and clothed herself in her best raiment, and taking the palm which she had received from the angel's hand she went out into the Mount of Olivet and began to pray and to say, 'I was not worthy to receive you, Lord, if you had not had mercy on me; nevertheless I kept the treasure which you committed to me. Therefore I pray you, O king of glory, that no power of hell may hurt me. For if the heavens and the angels quake before you every day, how much more a man created of the earth, in whom there is no good save what he has received of your bounty. You, Lord, are God, blessed for ever, world without end.' And having thus spoken, she returned to her dwelling.

[4] John 19: 26–7.

IV. 1. And behold, suddenly, while Saint John was preaching at Ephesus, on the Lord's day, at the third hour, there was a great earthquake, and a cloud raised him up and took him out of the sight of all and brought him before the door of the house where Mary was. And he knocked at the door and immediately went in. When Mary saw him she rejoiced greatly and said, 'I pray to you, my son John, remember the words of my Lord Jesus Christ wherewith he commended me to you. For behold, on the third day I am to depart out of the body and I have heard the counsels of the Jews who say, "Let us wait until the day when she who bore that deceiver shall die, and let us burn her body with fire."' 2. So she called Saint John and took him into the secret part of the house and showed him her grave-clothes and that palm of light which she had received from the angel, and charged him to cause it to be borne before her bier when she should go to the tomb.

V. And Saint John said to her, 'How shall I alone prepare your burial unless my brethren and fellow apostles of my Lord Jesus Christ come to pay honour to your body?'

And lo, suddenly, by the commandment of God, all the apostles were lifted up on a cloud and taken away from the places where they were preaching and set down before the door of the house where Mary dwelt. And they greeted each other and marvelled, saying, 'Why has the Lord gathered us together here?'

[*Other manuscripts read*: And Paul, who was turned from the circumcision and taken with Barnabas to minister to the Gentiles, came with them. And when there arose among them a godly contention, which of them should first pray to the Lord to show them the cause of their coming, Peter exhorted Paul to pray first. Paul answered, saying, 'It is your office to begin first, since you were chosen of God to be a pillar of the church, and you are before all in the apostleship; but it does not befit me at all, for I am the least of all of you, and Christ was seen by me as of one born out of due time, and I do not presume to count myself equal with you; yet by the grace of God I am what I am.']

VI. Then all the apostles, rejoicing with one mind, finished their prayer; and when they had said Amen, lo, suddenly the blessed John came and showed them all these things. And the apostles entered the house and found Mary and greeted her, saying, 'Blessed be you of the Lord who made heaven and earth.' And she said to them. 'Peace be to you my most beloved brethren. How did you come here?' And they told her how they had come, each one of them being lifted up on a cloud by the Spirit and set down in that place. And she said to them, 'God has not deprived me of the sight of you. Behold, I go the way of all the earth, and I doubt not that the Lord has now brought you hither to give me comfort in the anguish that is to come upon me. Now therefore I beseech you that we all keep watch together without ceasing, until the hour when the Lord shall come and I shall depart out of the body.'

VII. And they sat about her comforting her, and for three days gave themselves to the praises of God, then lo, on the third day, about the third hour of the day, sleep fell upon all who were in that house, and no one at all could keep awake, except the apostles and three virgins who were there. And behold, suddenly the Lord Jesus Christ came with a great multitude of angels, and a great light came down upon that place, and the angels were singing hymns and praising the Lord. Then the Saviour spoke saying, 'Come, you most precious pearl, enter into the receptacle of eternal life.'

VIII. 1. Then Mary fell on her face on the ground, worshipping God, and said, 'Blessed be the name of your glory, O Lord my God, who have vouchsafed to choose me, your handmaid, and to commit to me your secret mystery. Remember me, therefore, O king of glory; for you know that with all my heart I have loved you and have kept the treasure committed to me. Receive me, your servant, and deliver me from the power of darkness, and let not any assault of Satan meet me, neither let me see ugly spirits coming to meet me.' 2. And the Saviour answered her, 'When I was sent by the Father and for the salvation of the world was hung on the cross, the prince of darkness came to me; but as he was not able to find in me any sign of his work he departed vanquished and trodden down. When you see him, you shall see him according to the law of mankind whereby the end, even death, is allotted to you; but he cannot hurt you, for I am with you to help you. Come without fear, for the heavenly host awaits you to bring you into the joy of paradise.' 3. And as the Lord thus spoke, Mary arose from the ground and laid herself on her bed, and giving thanks to God she gave up the ghost. But the apostles saw her soul, and it was of such whiteness that no tongue of mortal men can worthily express it, for it excelled all whiteness of snow and of all metal and silver that shines with great brightness of light.

IX. 1. Then the Saviour spoke saying, 'Arise, Peter, and take the body of Mary and bear it to the right-hand side of the city toward the east, and you will find there a new sepulchre in which you shall place it, and wait till I come to you.'

2. And when the Lord had spoken, he delivered the soul of the holy Mary to Michael, who was set over paradise and is the prince of the people of the Jews; and Gabriel went with them. And immediately the Saviour was received into heaven with the angels.

X. Now the three virgins who were there on guard took the body of the blessed Mary to wash it after the custom of burials. And when they had stripped it of its apparel, that holy body shone with such brightness that it could indeed be touched as a rite, but the appearance could not be looked upon for the exceeding flashing of light; and a great splendour appeared in it, and nothing could be sensed when the body was washed, but it was most pure and not stained with any manner of defilement. And the body of the blessed Mary was like the flowers of the lily, and a great sweetness of fragrance issued from it: nothing like that sweetness could be found elsewhere.

XI. 1. Then the apostles laid the holy body upon a bier and said to one another, 'Who shall bear the palm before her bier?' Then John said to Peter, 'You who were before us in the apostleship ought to bear this palm before her bed.' And Peter answered him, 'You only of us are a virgin chosen of the Lord, and have found such favour that you lay on his breast; and he, when he hung for our salvation on the tree of the cross, committed her to you with his own mouth. You therefore ought to carry this palm; and let us take up the body to bear it to the place of the sepulchre.' 2. Afterwards Peter lifted up the head of the body and began to sing, saying, 'Israel has come out of Egypt. Alleluia.' And with him the other apostles bore the body of the blessed Mary, and John carried the palm of light before the bier. And the rest of the apostles sang with exceedingly sweet voices.

XII. 1. And behold a new miracle. There appeared a very great cloud over the bier like the great circle seen about the splendour of the moon; and a host of angels was in the cloud sending forth a song of sweetness, and the earth echoed with the sound of that great melody. Then the people came out of the city, about fifteen thousand, and marvelled and said, 'What is this sound of such sweetness?' 2. Then someone stood up and told them, 'Mary is gone out of the body, and the disciples of Jesus are singing praises about her.' And they looked and saw the bier crowned with great glory and the apostles singing with a loud voice. And behold, one of them who was a prince of the priests of the Jews was filled with fury and wrath and said to the rest, 'Behold the tabernacle of the man who troubled us and all our nation, what glory it has received.' And he came near and tried to overthrow the bier and cast the body on the earth. And forthwith his hands dried up from his elbows and stuck to the bier. And when the apostles lifted the bier, part of him was hanging loose and part stuck to the bier, and he was wrung with extreme torment as the apostles went on and sang. But the angels who were in the clouds smote the people with blindness.

XIII. 1. Then that prince cried out saying, 'I beseech you, holy Peter, despise me not in this so great necessity, for I am tormented with great pains. Remember when the damsel who kept the door knew you in the judgement hall and told the rest that they might challenge you, how then I spoke good on your behalf.' Then Peter answered and said, 'It is not for me to give you anything; but if you believe with your whole heart in the Lord Jesus Christ, whom this woman bore in her womb and continued a virgin after the birth, the mercy of the Lord, which by his great pity saves the unworthy, shall heal you.'

2. To this he answered, 'Do we not believe? What shall we do? The enemy of mankind has blinded our hearts, and shame has covered our faces that we should not confess the mighty works of God; especially when we cursed ourselves, crying out against Christ: "His blood be on us and on our children."' Then Peter said, 'See, that curse will hurt him who continues not to believe in him, but to those who turn to God mercy is not denied.' And he

said, 'I believe all that you say to me: only I beseech you, have mercy on me lest I die.'

XIV. 1. Then Peter made the bier stand still and said to him, 'If you believe with your whole heart in Jesus Christ, your hands shall be loosed from the bier.' And when he had said that he did, straightway his hands were loosed from the bier and he began to stand on his feet; but his arms were still withered, neither did the pain depart from him. 2. Then Peter said to him, 'Go near to the body and kiss the bed and say, "I believe in God and in the Son of God whom this woman bore, that is to say Jesus Christ, and I believe all the things that Peter the apostle of God has told me."' And he came near and kissed the bed, and forthwith all pain left him and his hands were made whole. 3. Then he began to bless God greatly and to speak from the books of Moses testimonies to the praise of Christ, so that even the apostles themselves marvelled and wept for gladness, praising the name of the Lord.

XV. 1. But Peter said to him, 'Take this palm at the hand of our brother John, and go into the city, and you will find people blinded; and declare to them the mighty works of God, and whosoever believes in the Lord Jesus Christ, lay this palm upon his eyes and he shall see; but whosoever does not believe shall continue to be blind.' 2. And when he had done so, he found many people blinded and lamenting thus, 'Woe unto us, for we are become like the men of Sodom who were stricken with blindness. Nothing remains for us now except to perish.' But when they had heard the words spoken by the prince who was healed, they believed in the Lord Jesus Christ, and when he laid the palm upon their eyes, they recovered sight; but whosoever continued in hardness of heart died. And the prince of the priests went to the apostles and gave back the palm and reported all that had come to pass.

XVI. 1. But the apostles carrying Mary came into the place of the valley of Josaphat which the Lord had showed them, and laid her in a new tomb and shut the sepulchre. They sat down at the door of the tomb as the Lord had charged them; and lo, suddenly the Lord Jesus Christ came with a great multitude of angels, and light flashing with great brightness, and said to the apostles, 'Peace be with you.' And they answered and said, 'Let your mercy, O Lord, be upon us, just as we have hoped in you.'

2. Then the Saviour spoke to them, saying, 'Before I ascended to my Father I gave you a promise, saying that you who have followed me, in the regeneration when the Son of man shall sit on the throne of his majesty, you also shall sit on twelve thrones, judging the twelve tribes of Israel. Now this woman I chose out of the twelve tribes of Israel by the commandment of my Father, to dwell in her. What then do you wish me to do to her?' 3. Then Peter and the other apostles said, 'Lord, you chose this your handmaid to become your immaculate chamber, and us your servants for your ministry. All things you foreknew before the worlds with your Father, with whom to you and the Holy Ghost there belong equal Godhead and infinite power. If

therefore the power of your grace can bring this about, it has appeared right to us your servants that, as you having overcome death reign in glory, so you should raise up the body of your mother and take her with you rejoicing into heaven.'

XVII. 1. Then the Saviour said, 'Be it done according to your will.' And he commanded Michael the archangel to bring the soul of the holy Mary. And behold, Michael the archangel rolled away the stone from the door of the sepulchre, and the Lord said, 'Rise up, my love and my kinswoman: you who did not suffer corruption by union of the flesh shall not suffer dissolution of the body in the sepulchre.' 2. And immediately Mary rose up from the grave and blessed the Lord, and fell at the Lord's feet and worshipped him, saying, 'I am not able to render you worthy thanks, O Lord, for your innumerable benefits which you have vouchsafed to grant to me, your handmaid. Let your name be blessed for ever, redeemer of the world, you God of Israel.'

XVIII. 1. And the Lord kissed her and departed, and delivered her to the angels to bear her into paradise. And he said to the apostles, 'Come near to me', and when they had come near he kissed them and said, 'Peace be to you; as I have been always with you, so will I be even to the end of the world.'

2. And as soon as the Lord had spoken he was lifted up in a cloud and received into heaven, and the angels with him, bearing the blessed Mary into the paradise of God.

But the apostles were taken up upon clouds and returned every one to the lot of his preaching, declaring the mighty works of God and praising the Lord Jesus Christ, who lives and reigns with the Father and the Holy Ghost in perfect unity and in one substance of the Godhead, world without end. Amen.

B. *Narrative by Joseph of Arimathaea*

1. Before the Passion the Virgin asked Jesus to certify her of her death on the third day before it, and to receive her with his angels. 2, 3. He promised that this should be so.

4. In the second year after the ascension she was constantly praying. On the third day before her death an angel[5] came and gave her a palm and told her of her departure.

5. She sent for Joseph of Arimathaea and other disciples, and told them, and then washed and arrayed herself as a queen. Three virgins were with her—Sepphora, Abigea, and Zael. The apostles were already dispersed about the world.

6. At the third hour, thunder, rain, earthquake. John was suddenly brought from Ephesus and entered the chamber and greeted her. She said, 'Dearest son, why have you left me for so long?'

---

[5] One MS reads Gabriel.

The Assumption of the Virgin

7. All the disciples except Thomas now arrived on clouds and greeted her.
8. They were John, James his brother, Peter, Paul, Andrew, Philip, Luke, Barnabas, Bartholomew, Matthew, Matthias surnamed Justus, Simon the Canaanite, Jude and his brother, Nicodemus, Maximianus.[6]
9. Mary asked, 'Why have you all come?' Peter said, 'It is for us to ask you. None of us knows. I was at Antioch, and now I am here.' And all told where they had been. 10. Mary told them the reason, that she was to depart on the morrow, and asked them to watch and pray with her. So they did, all night, with lights and psalmody.
11. On the Sunday at the third hour Christ came down with a host of angels and took the soul of his mother. Such was the light and fragrance that all fell on their faces and none could rise for an hour and a half. 12. As the light receded, the soul of Mary was taken up with it, with singing; and as the cloud went up, the earth shook, and all in Jerusalem saw the death of Mary in one instant.
13. Then Satan entered into them and they took arms to burn the body and kill the apostles; but they were struck blind, and smote their heads against walls, and hit one another.
14. The apostles took up the body to bear it from Mount Sion to the valley of Josaphat. As they went, a Jew named Reuben tried to upset the bier, but his hands withered at the elbow and he had to go on into the valley weeping and crying, for his hands stuck to the bier. 15. He began to ask the apostles to pray for him that he might be saved and become a Christian. They knelt and prayed, and his hands were loosed and he was healed. He was baptized at once, and began to proclaim Christ.
16. Then the apostles laid the body in the tomb with great honour, weeping and singing for pure love and sweetness. And suddenly a light from heaven shone round about them, and as they fell to the earth the holy body was taken up by angels into heaven (the apostles not knowing it).
17. Thomas was suddenly brought to the Mount of Olives and saw the holy body being taken up, and cried out to Mary, 'Make your servant glad by your mercy, for now you go to heaven.' And the girdle with which the apostles had girt the body was thrown down to him; he took it and went to the valley of Josaphat. 18. When he had greeted the apostles, Peter said, 'You were always unbelieving, and so the Lord has not suffered you to be at his mother's burial.' He smote his breast and said, 'I know it and I ask pardon of you all', and they all prayed for him. 19. Then he said, 'Where have you laid her body?', and they pointed to the sepulchre. But he said, 'The holy body is not there.' Peter said, 'Formerly you would not believe in the resurrection of the Lord before you touched him: how should you believe us?' Thomas went on

---

[6] This must be the legendary Maximin of Aix en Provence who figures in the late legend of Mary Magdalene's mission to Marseilles.

saying, 'It is not here.' Then in anger they went and took away the stone, and the body was not there; and they did not know what to say, being vanquished by Thomas's words. 20. Then Thomas told them how he had been saying mass in India (and he still had on his priestly vestments), and how he had been brought to the Mount of Olives and seen the ascension of Mary and she had given him her girdle; and he showed it. 21. They all rejoiced and asked his pardon, and he blessed them and said, 'Behold how good and pleasant a thing it is, brethren, to dwell together in unity.'

22. The same clouds which had brought them now carried them back, as we read in the Acts about Philip who baptized the eunuch, and as Habakkuk was brought to Daniel and taken back.

23. It is wonderful that Christ should do such things (miracles are enumerated).

24. I am that Joseph who laid the body of the Lord in my tomb and saw him rise again, and always watched over his most holy temple, even the blessed Mary, ever-virgin, before the ascension of the Lord and after it; and upon this page and in my heart have I written the things that came out of the mouth of God, and how the aforesaid matters came to pass, and I have made known to all the Jews and Gentiles what I saw with my eyes and heard with my ears, and as long as I live I shall not cease to proclaim them.

Her assumption is this day reverenced and honoured throughout all the world; let us constantly pray to her that she remember us before her most merciful son in heaven, to whom is praise and glory for infinite ages. Amen.[7]

4. THE SYRIAC NARRATIVES

A

Book I, after a panegyrical introduction, tells how the narrative was found. It was attested in autograph by James, bishop of Jerusalem. Two apostles wrote each of the six books, and they were entrusted to John.

His copy was found at Ephesus, attested by the Twelve and the Seventy-Two, and written in Hebrew, Greek, and Latin.

Book II. In the year 344 (of the era of the Greeks), on the third day of the latter Teshrin (September), being the third day of the week at the third hour, Mary went to the tomb.

The Jews immediately after the Passion had closed it with great stones and forbidden resort to it on pain of death. They also hid the cross, spear, sponge, robe, crown of thorns, and nails.

The priests told the guardians of the tomb to stone Mary if she came there again. They said, 'Do it yourselves.' On the Friday Mary burnt incense there;

---

[7] One MS has a statement that any Christian who has this writing in his house will be safe from various afflictions—lunacy, deafness, blindness, sudden death—and will have the protection of the Virgin at his end.

The Assumption of the Virgin

Gabriel came down and told her of her approaching death. (There is no mention of a palm.)

The guards informed the priests that Mary had come again. The priests asked the governor to forbid her.

At this time Abgar of Edessa (converted by Addai) wished to destroy Jerusalem because of Christ's death, and came as far as the river Euphrates, but hesitated to cross it. He wrote to the procurator Sabinus, who sent the letter to Tiberius, who was greatly moved against the Jews. The Jews were alarmed. They said to the governor, 'Forbid Mary to go to the tomb.' He said, 'Forbid her yourselves.' A long abusive speech of the Jews to Mary follows.

She left Jerusalem and went to Bethlehem with her three virgins, Calletha daughter of Nicodemus, Neshra daughter of Gamaliel, Tabitha daughter of Archelaus. (There is a description of the service which these did to Mary; Gabriel tells her to go to Bethlehem.)

On Friday Mary burnt incense and prayed that John might be sent to her. John was brought from Ephesus. His arrival and conversation with Mary.

The other apostles were brought.[8]

John received the apostles. They each told Mary how they had come. Mark was performing the service of the third hour. Matthew says, 'I have given and am giving glory to God', and so on. The Greek, however, does not give the speeches of those who had been raised from the grave to come, but the Syriac does for Philip, Simon, Luke, and Andrew. And after Andrew, Bartholomew (not already dead) follows, as in the Greek.

There was a great concourse of angels, and the Bethlehemites in fear went and told the governor and the priests.

Book III. All the great signs attracted people from many quarters. Before this many used to come to the Virgin to be healed. (Five instances are given of cures.)

There was now a festival at Jerusalem, and many sick went out to Bethlehem to be healed. 2,800 were cured (cf. Greek ch. 28).

On the 21st of Teshrin II in the night, men rose up to attack the house. Angels of fire descended from heaven (cf. Greek ch. 29).

The priests insisted on Mary's banishment by the governor. He sent a chiliarch to Bethlehem with thirty men. The Spirit told the apostles to take Mary to Jerusalem. They did so and held a five days' service.

Meanwhile the chiliarch found nothing at Bethlehem, and the priests said this was due to magic.[9]

After the five days, Mary's presence in Jerusalem was realized. The Jews wished the governor to burn the house; he told them to do so themselves, and watched from a distance. The attackers were scorched and burnt. The governor declared his belief in Christ (cf. Greek chs. 34–5). Here the Syriac

---

[8] Here we are following the Greek text pretty closely.
[9] This last is not in Greek chs. 31–3, which is otherwise represented well.

has a very long digression not represented in the Greek, and belonging properly, it seems, to the story of the Cross.

Caleb the Sadducee, who was a secret believer, whispered to the governor that he should adjure the Jews by the God of Israel to tell them their real opinion about Jesus.

So all Jerusalem was assembled; and there follows a long altercation between the believers and unbelievers before the governor. Eventually some of the latter are forced by scourging to tell how they had hidden the cross and the other items. The governor has the place obstructed with great stones.

He then goes to see Mary. He greets the apostles, and they tell him how they came there. Mary at his request tells him the story of the Annunciation. The governor left Jerusalem and went to Rome and told the emperor, and the account of all this was written down by disciples at Rome, who also wrote to the apostles telling them of various miracles (seven are told) which Mary had wrought.

The text then leaps to ch. 45 of the Greek, omitting (in this place) all notice of the death of the Virgin.

The Spirit told the apostles to bear her to a place where there were three caves, and to lay her on a bench there and await his bidding.

Jephonias, 'strong and tall, and handsome of figure', attacked them, and was smitten and healed (but Mary is not dead yet, for she speaks to him). Peter gave a dry rod to Jephonias and sent him to the Jews. The rod blossomed. He healed a man born blind, and many others (cf. Greek chs. 45–7, and Latin chs. XII–XV). The Greek does not have the healing of the Jews, and the Syriac has distorted it.

The apostles laid Mary in the eastern cave and held a service of three days and nights. Some Jews came to the cave; three ventured in, and were burnt and swallowed up. Many believed, but the priests threatened and bribed them.

This, which concludes Book III, is badly confused in the Syriac, which has made the great mistake of saying that the apostles bore the Virgin to the cave before she was dead.

Book IV. While the apostles were ministering to Mary in the cave the Spirit spoke to them and told the story of the Annunciation. He spoke also of the date of her death, and then told how Sunday is the day of the Annunciation, the Nativity, the Entry, Resurrection, Ascension, and Judgement (cf. Greek ch. 37).

Eve, Anna, Elizabeth, Adam, and other patriarchs now came and greeted Mary, and then the procession of heavenly chariots, and then Christ. His words to her, and her answer. Her kissing of his hand, and prayers and blessing and death, are as in Greek chs. 38–44, but the blessing is far longer.

Then the body was prepared for burial. Twelve chariots took up the apostles and bore them all to paradise; and they returned thence and ordained a commemoration of her three times a year (cf. Greek ch. 49).

The Assumption of the Virgin

After this is a very long disquisition on the rules which the apostles made about the commemoration.

When they had come back to the cave they agreed to write a book in Hebrew, Greek, and Latin, and commit it to John; and, with more unimportant matter following on this, the book ends.

Book V. This is a diffuse account of the Virgin's visit to paradise. One paragraph tells of her seeing Gehenna.

John and Peter were with her, and she revealed everything to John and told him to write it: it would be made public at the end of the world.

Christ then says he will tell her what is to happen at his second coming, but nothing is told. Mary answers with thanksgiving and prayer. Book V ends. Book VI does not appear.

B

A prefatory section declares the apostles to be the witnesses and authors of what follows.

The story then begins, and gives a shorter form of what we have had, in this order:

Mary goes to the tomb.

The Jews threaten to stone her.

She asks Jesus to take her out of the world.

The angel comes to tell her her prayer is heard.

The guards of the tomb report this.

The Jews ask Sabinus the governor to banish her.

He refers them to her. They come and abuse her.

She goes to Bethlehem with the three virgins (named as in A).

She prays that John may be sent. He comes.

The other apostles arrive.

They begin to tell how they came. The first fragment ends in John's narrative. It was left unfinished by the scribe.

C

This begins in the middle of the dispute between believers and unbelievers before the governor, and the story follows the course of A down to the point where the apostles lay Mary in the cave. Here the first fragment ends.

The second fragment does not seem to have an exact textual equivalent in A.

Chariots of light and saints arrive, and Mary is borne to paradise.

The apostles return to the Mount of Olives, and pray to be allowed to ordain a commemoration of Mary.

And so with rather a long doxology the book ends.

It is, so far as we have it, far more compact and coherent than A or D.

D[10]

Mary goes to the tomb.

The Jews plot to kill her, close the cave, set guards on it.

Gabriel comes.

The guards report it.

Mary goes to Bethlehem with the three virgins (as above).

The Jews hid the cross and the other items, and asserted that 'here are buried the Book of Moses and the box of manna and the rod of Aaron and the mantle of Elijah', so that if miracles did happen there, they could be attributed to those relics.

Abgar's letter. Sabinus is angry with the Jews. Mary prayed that the apostles might be sent.

John came.

Then the others. The statement that they came and the circumstances of their doing so are put into one narrative, not repeated as in A.

After the apostles had greeted Mary, Anna, Elizabeth, Adam, and others, came, and all the various orders of saints and angels; and Christ. This dialogue and her prayers are rather shortened, but essentially as in A.

Mary died and her soul was taken up.

Then we have a bad dislocation.

The believers in the city went to the governor and told him the truth about Jesus and the Jews. He was angry with the chiefs, and beat them and told them not to harm the Christians. This is a condensation into a few lines of the dispute before the governor. Yet this dispute occurs later on. Here, however, we have the sequel.

The governor visited Mary with his sick son (who was healed). The apostles told him of their miraculous coming. The governor went to Rome and told the emperor, and the believers there wrote down the wonderful record. This is a shorter form of A.

A paragraph on the age of Mary (52) follows.

The apostles said, 'Let us make a distinction between the burial of believers and non-believers, and make a beginning with Mary'. They prepared her body for burial, and set out in procession.

The Jews saw it and bribed the governor not to interfere with them. They also bribed a gigantic soldier of his, Yophana, to go with them and attack the bier.

Then we have the affliction and cure of Yophana, who goes back to the governor, and he laughs at the Jews.

The apostles laid the body in the cave.

Peter asked the multitude to set guards over it. He also spoke to the believers of the glory of Mary.

[10] This is mainly identical in content with A but has points of its own.

The Jews plotted and put a number of dead bodies in the cave, but in vain; and then tried to burn the body, but were burnt themselves.

Then the apostles brought out the body and laid it on a bier.

Then came all the chariots of light, and the body was put in a chariot of light, and it and all the apostles went up to Paradise.

And the cloud took them back to Jerusalem. And they wrote down all the triumphs of the Virgin and sent the books everywhere, and ordained three yearly commemorations; and were taken back to the places whence they had come.

Then a homiletical paragraph. It introduces the revelation of John about the Virgin in paradise—A, Book V.

The Jews thought the body was still in the cave, and they went in and did not find it. Many believed.

The unbelievers (again?) put dead bodies in the cave.

The believers told the governor, and he sent Yophana, who confiscated all the goods of the offenders.

Visions of angels, multitudes of sick healed: six miracles narrated, as in A. The healing of 2,800 people.

Plot to attack the house. Descent of angels of fire. All this is in A.

The priests insisted on the banishment of Mary. The chiliarch sent. The apostles bore Mary to Bethlehem (*read* Jerusalem). The five days' service. The house in Jerusalem attacked, the besiegers burnt, the governor's declaration of belief.

The dispute between believers and unbelievers before the governor. The hiding-place of the cross obstructed.

Afterwards the disciples of the apostles wrote (to various places) with an account of the departure of Mary, and took it with them to Byzantium.

And then a series of miracles is narrated, which are nearly all identical with those in A.

E

i. Wright, pp. 10–15. The appearance of the Lord to his mother: her last words and death. Her soul is delivered to Michael. Peter begins to speak to Christ.

The funeral procession. Jews are blinded, and he who tries to overset the bier has his arms fixed to it. They are restored. Peter gives him a staff with which he heals 5,000 blinded people.

ii. Wright, p. 42. First long fragment. Paul is speaking, and telling a long story about Solomon, who had been told by a demon that a certain young man would die. A form of this story occurs in the Testament of Solomon.

The apostles ask Paul to go on speaking. They say, 'Our Lord has sent you to gladden us during these three days'. Paul asks them what they will preach when they go forth, and is answered by Peter, John, and Andrew. He criticizes them as too severe, and recommends a gentler policy. They are angry.

And as they were all sitting disputing before the entrance to Mary's tomb, Jesus appeared and justified Paul's view, as against the others.

He summoned Michael and bade him bring forth the body of Mary into the clouds. They were all carried to paradise.

The apostles then asked the Lord to show them the place of torment, reminding him of his promise that on the day of the departure of Mary they should see it.

They were all taken on a cloud to the west. The Lord spoke to the angels of the pit, and the earth sprang upwards and they saw the pit.

The lost souls saw Michael and begged for respite. Mary and the apostles fell down and interceded for them. Michael spoke to them, telling them that at all the twelve hours of the day and of the night the angels intercede for creation. The angel of the waters intercedes for the waters. Here the fragment ends.

iii. Wright, p. 48. The next fragment is a story told by Michael to Mary about the concealing of the bones of Joseph in the Nile by Pharaoh and their discovery by Moses. It seems as if this must have been told in answer to some inquiry of Mary's about her own body, and therefore it should be placed earlier in order.

iv. Wright, p. 50.[11] ... them according to their wish. And he sent by the hand of the apostles to them (to ask) whether these things were not so?

And he said, 'These are the shepherds of the house of Israel, who are praying for the sheep, that they may be sanctified and made glorious before the sons of men; and themselves they are not able to sanctify, because they exalt themselves like the strong. Did I not give them many signs?'

And the apostles said, 'Lord, lo, they beseech and pray, and repent, and kneel upon their knees. Why do you not hear them?' Our Lord said to them, 'I too was willing to hear them, but there is deception in them (as) you too know.'

And when Jesus wished to show the apostles for what reason he did not hear them, he took them up into a mountain and let them become hungry. And when the apostles had gone, they asked him, saying to him, 'Lord we are hungry; what have we then to eat in this desert?' And Jesus told them to go to the trees which were before them. And he said to them, 'Go to those trees which are opposite us, whose branches are many and fair and beautiful at a distance, and from them you shall get food.' And when the apostles went, they did not find fruit on the trees.

And they returned to Jesus and said, 'Good Teacher, you sent us to those trees which are opposite us, and we went and found on them no fruit, but only branches which were fair and beautiful, but there was no fruit on them.'

---

[11] This last fragment, which may be part of an apocryphal gospel, is translated in full.

The Assumption of the Virgin

And Jesus said to them, 'You have not seen them, because the trees grow straight upwards. Go therefore at once, because the trees are bending themselves, and you shall find on them fruit, and get yourselves food.' And when they went, they found the trees bending down, but they did not find fruit upon them.

And they returned again to Jesus in great distress and said to him, 'What is this, Teacher, that we are mocked? For at first you said to us, "You shall find trees which are straight, and there is fruit on them", and we found none. Why are we mocked? But it is fitting that you should teach us what this is that has happened; for we think that what you wished to teach us is false; for by a visible power the trees were laid hold of and bent down. If this be a temptation, make known to us what it is.'

And Jesus said to them, 'Go and sit under them, and you shall see what it is that abides on them, but you shall not be able to bend them again.' And when the apostles went and sat under the trees, straightway the trees threw down stinking worms. And the apostles came again to Jesus and said to him, 'Teacher, do you wish to lead us astray or to turn us away from you . . . ?'

Indexes

1. Index of Apocryphal Writings with Detailed Lists of Contents
2. Index of Subjects and Proper Names
   (See also contents of individual works in the Index of Apocryphal Writings)
3. Index of Biblical and Other Citations
4. Index of Ancient Authorities

1. Index of Apocryphal Writings with Detailed Lists of Contents

Acts of Andrew 231–302, 524
  texts:
  Laudatio 233
  Martyrium Alterum 233
  Martyrium Prius 233, 240, 513
  Narratio 233
  Epistle of the Presbyters and Deacons
    of Achaea 233–4
  Conversante et Docente 234
  Epistle of Pseudo-Titus 234
  narrative 245–67
  conversion of Stratocles 245–7
  Maximilla personated by Euclia 250–1
  Aegeates' concern for Maximilla . . . 251–2
  Iphidama visits Andrew in Prison . . . 253–4
  Iphidama and Maximilla visit Andrew
    in prison 254–5, 256–61
  address to the cross 262
  final address and martyrdom 263–6
  suicide of Aegeates 266
Acts of Andrew: Bodleian Fragment . . 271–2
Acts of Andrew: Epitome by Gregory
  of Tours 272–83
  healing of blind man 273
  healing of Demetrius' boy 273
  saving Sòstratus from incest 273
  healing of Gratinus 273–4
  exorcism at Nicaea 274
  healing of boy at Nicomedia 274
  storm in the Hellespont 274
  resisting attack in Thrace 274
  conversion of ship's crew 274
  wedding at Philippi 274–5
  conversion of Exuos and incendiarism
    at Philippi 275
  healing of Adiamantus 275–6
  raising dead son 276
  healing of Philomedes 276
  healing of Nicolaus' daughter 276
  exorcism of a youth 276
  arrest of Virinus 277
  killing of a snake and healing of
    a boy 278
  Andrew's vision 278
  calming of storm at sea and rescue of man
    overboard 279
  conversion of pro-consul and of
    Trophima 279

  raising of Callisto 280
  Philopater and thirty-nine other drowned
    men raised 280
  Calliopa's pregnancy 281
  meeting with Philopater's father 281
  exorcisms at a bath-house 281
  conversion of Nicolaus 281–2
  exorcisms at Megara 282
  healing of Maximilla 282
  healing of a sick beggar 282
  healing of a blind family 282
  healing of sailor's son 282–3
  exorcism of slave and conversion of
    Stratocles 283
  Maximilla and Aegeates 283
  imprisonment and martyrdom of
    Andrew 283
Acts of Andrew: Utrecht Fragment . . 267–71
Acts of Andrew and Bartholomew 244
Acts of Andrew and Matthias 240–2, 513
  narrative 283–99
  Andrew's sea voyage 285–90
  speaking sphinx in the temple 288–90
  Andrew in Myrmidonia releases
    Matthias 290–2
  Andrew releases the cannibals'
    victims 293–4
  Andrew tortured and imprisoned . . . 295–6
  Andrew escapes from prison 297
  flooding of Myrmidonia 297–8
  conversion of the people of
    Myrmidonia 299
Acts of Andrew and Paul 243–4, 301–2,
                                    389, 532
Acts of Barnabas 523–4
Acts of James the Great 525
Acts of James the Great in Pseudo-
  Abdias 527–8
Acts of James the Less 525
Acts of James the Less in Pseudo-
  Abdias 528–30
Acts of John 235, 303–49, 390
  narrative 311–47
  Lycomedes and Cleopatra raised from the
    dead 311–13
  John's portrait painted 313–14
  John's sermon in the theatre 315–16
  the polymorphous nature of Christ 317–18

728 *Index of Apocryphal Writings*

Acts of John (*cont.*):
Hymn of Christ 318–20
revelation of the mystery of the
   cross 320–1
destruction of the temple of
   Artemis 322–3
raising the priest of Artemis 324
story of the parricide 324–6
John and the partridge 326–7
the sons of Antipatros 327
the obedient bedbugs 328
Drusiana and Callimachus 328–35
John's final act of worship......... 335–8
John's death 338
the broken gems 338–9
rods and stones changed to gold and
   jewels....................... 339–43
Dives and Lazarus story 340
raising of Stacteus 343
Aristodemus and the poisoned cup.. 343–5
John and the soldier 346
Acts of John by Prochorus 240, 303, 347
Acts of John in Rome 305, 347
Acts of Matthew in Pseudo-Abdias ... 530–1
Acts of Nereus and Achilleus 427
Acts of Paul 350–89, 390, 524
narrative...................... 364–88
journey from Damascus to Jerusalem . 364
baptism of a lion 364
raising of Panchares 364
Paul's appearance 364
Acts of Paul and Thecla 364–74
Paul preaches in the house of
   Onesiphorus 365
Thecla hears Paul 365
Thecla's fiancé 366
plot against Paul 366
Paul's defence to the pro-consul 367
Thecla visits Paul in gaol 367
Thecla sentenced to burning 367
Thecla finds Paul 368–9
Thecla and Alexander 369
Thecla exhibited to beasts 369–71
Thecla visits Paul at Myra 371–2
Thecla works and dies in Seleucia 372
Paul in Myra heals Hermocrates 374
Paul raises Dion 374–5
Paul in Sidon 375–6
Paul in Tyre 376
Paul and the lion in Ephesus 376–9
Paul in Philippi 379–82
Paul's correspondence with the
   Corinthians 380–2
raising of Frontina 382
Paul in Corinth 382–3
en route for Rome 383–5
Paul's sermon in Puteoli 384–5

Paul raises Nero's cup-bearer 385–6
Paul's martyrdom 385–8
Paul appears to Nero 388
Acts of Paul and Thecla, *see* Acts of Paul
Acts of Peter 34, 235, 390–430, 524
narrative...................... 397–426
story of Peter's daughter.......... 397–8
gardener's daughter 398–9
departure of Paul from Rome.... 399–401
Simon Magus in Rome............ 401
Peter prepares to go to Rome 401–2
Peter and Theon on board ship 402–3
Peter in Puteoli 403–4
arrival in Rome 404–5
reconversion of Marcellus 405–8
miracle of the talking dog 408–9
miracle of the statue 409
miracle of the tunny fish 409
miracle of the speaking infant......... 410
Peter's vision of Jesus 410
Simon and Eubola in Judaea 410–12
Peter's sermon and healing
   miracles..................... 413–14
Marcellus' vision................. 415
Simon and Peter's contest 416–21
two further raisings 418–19
Chryse's conversion 421
death of Simon 422–3
arrest of Peter 424
final words of Peter 424–5
death of Peter 426
Acts of Peter by Pseudo-Clement 433–8
Acts of Peter and Andrew .. 242–3, 299–301
Acts of Peter and Paul 428–9
Acts of Peter and the Twelve Apostles... 430
Acts of Philip 240, 512–18
narrative...................... 515–18
the kid and the leopard 515–16
healing of the pro-consul's wife 516
martyrdom of Philip 518
Acts of Philip in Pseudo-Abdias 531
Acts of Pilate (*Acta Pilati*), *see* Gospel of
   Nicodemus: Acts of Pilate
Acts of the Second Nicaean Council 305
Acts of Simon and Jude 525
Acts of Thomas........ 240, 439–511, 512,
                  513, 524, 594
narrative...................... 448–511
Judas Thomas sold to Abban 448
Thomas taken to India 448–9
royal wedding party............. 449–52
cup-bearer killed 451
Thomas urges celibacy of the bridal
   'couple 452–4
Thomas meets King Gundaphorus ... 454
royal palace commissioned 454–9
raising of man killed by a serpent .. 459–63

Index of Apocryphal Writings 729

the speaking colt 464–5
exorcism of woman 465–8
raising of woman killed by her
   lover 468–70
woman's vision of hell 470–1
Siphor begs Thomas to exorcize
   his wife and daughter 473–5
wild asses deliver Thomas and Siphor
   to the family 475–7
Thomas exorcizes the demons 477–9
conversion of Mygdonia 479–81
Charisius plots Thomas's death 482–6
Thomas imprisoned 487
Hymn of the Pearl 488–91
Mygdonia baptized 493–4
king's wife converted 497–9
king's son converted 499–505
martyrdom of Thomas 505–10
conversion of the king 510
Acts of Titus by Pseudo-Zenas 355, 389
Acts of Xanthippe and Polyxena.... 240, 512,
                           524–5
Agrapha......................... 26–30
Anaphora Pilati 206, 208, 211–13
Apocalypse of Bartholomew 684
Apocalypse of Elias (Elijah) 616, 683
Apocalypse of Elijah in Coptic 613
Apocalypse of Esdras 682
Apocalypse of Ezra, *see* Apocalypse of Esdras
Apocalypse of Paul 591, 594, 616–44
   narrative....................... 620–44
   discovery of the vision 620
   appeal of creation to God 620–2
   report of the angels to God 622–3
   death and judgement of the righteous
      and the wicked 624–8
   Paul's vision of paradise 628–33
   Paul's vision of hell 633–9
   second vision of paradise 639–43
Apocalypse of Paul in Coptic 617, 671
Apocalypse of Peter 591, 593–615, 616
   narrative...................... 598–612
   parable of the fig-tree 600–1
   endtime predicted................ 601–3
   vision of hell 603–9
   revelation of paradise 609–12
Apocalypse of Sophonias, *see* Apocalypse of
   Zephaniah
Apocalypse of Stephen 683
Apocalypse of Thomas 545–51, 591, 645
Apocalypse of Zechariah 684
Apocalypse of Zephaniah 610, 682–3
Apocalypses of John 684
Apocalypses of the Virgin 686–7
Apocryphon of James, *see* Letter of James
Apocryphon of Ezekiel 30
Arabic Infancy Gospel ... 48, 68, 100–7, 118

narrative....................... 102–7
exorcism of demoniac woman 104
healing dumb bride............... 104–5
leprous girl healed 105
two robbers 105
fountain at Matarea 105
sick child healed 105–6
Jesus and the dyer................. 106
children in the oven 106–7
Armenian Infancy Gospel 48, 68, 71,
                            100, 118–19
Arundel 404 .... 32, 71, 85, 108–10
Ascension of Isaiah 555, 682
Assumption of the Virgin 689–723
   texts 695–723
   Homily of Evodius of Rome 695–7
   Discourse of Cyril of Jerusalem 697–8
   Discourses of Theodosius of
      Alexandria.................. 698–700
   Sahidic Fragment 700–1
   Discourse of John the Divine 701–8
   Narrative of Pseudo-Melito 708–14
   Narrative of Joseph of Arimathaea 714–16
   Syriac fragments 716–23

narrative:
(a) apostles told by Jesus that Mary is to
   die 695–6
   Mary's death................... 696
   ascension of Mary's soul 697
   Mary's burial 697
   reappearance of the Virgin 697
   assumption 697
(b) John comes to Mary 701
   appearance to the disciples....... 701–4
   Jews chase Mary from Bethlehem 704–5
   death of Mary 707
   attack on Mary's bier and a miraculous
      healing 707
   assumption 708
(c) Mary receives the palm 709
   John appears 710
   appearance of all the disciples 710
   death of Mary 711
   attack on Mary's bier and the miraculous
      healing 712–13
   assumption 714

Berlin Payrus 8502.1 121
Berlin Papyrus 11710............... 42–3
Birth of Mary, *see* Protevangelium of James
Bodleian Fragment of the Acts of Andrew, *see*
   Acts of Andrew
Book of Elchasai 685–6
Book of Enoch 593
Book of Joseph Caiaphas, *see* Arabic Infancy
   Gospel

Index of Apocryphal Writings

Book of the Resurrection of Jesus Christ by
   Bartholomew 161
   narrative 668–72
   Jesus speaks to Mary and others 670
   ascension of Theophanes 671
   raising of the cock 672
   raising of Ananias 672

Cairo Papyrus 10735 36–7
Clementine literature, see Pseudo-Clementine literature
Conflict of Andrew 244
Conflict of Andrew and Bartholomew ... 244
Conflict of Andrew and Philemon 244
Coptic Infancy Stories 121
Coptic Narratives of the Ministry and Passion 161–3
correspondence of Paul with the Corinthians (3 Corinthians), see Acts of Paul
correspondence of Paul and Seneca .. 547–53

de Nativitate Mariae, see Gospel of the Birth of Mary
Descensus Christi ad Inferos 165
   see also Gospel of Nicodemus: Descent
Dialogue of the Redeemer 25

Egerton Papyrus 2 .... 37–40, 150
Epistle to the Achaeans 550
Epistle to the Alexandrians 553–4
Epistle of the Apostles 68, 555–88
   narrative 558–88
   Jesus in dialogue with the apostles 563–88
   Peter's imprisonment predicted 565
   date of last judgement 566
   Paul's conversion predicted 576
   signs of last judgement 577–82
   parable of the ten virgins 584–5
   ascension 588
Epistle to the Laodiceans 543–6
Epistle of Pseudo-Titus 305, 346, 391, 532–3
   see also Acts of Andrew: texts
Epistle of Titus, see Epistle of Pseudo-Titus
Epistula Apostolorum, see Epistle of the Apostles
Epistula Iacobi, see Letter of James
Epistula Petri 431
Ezra, 5th and 6th 684–5

Fayyum Fragment 43–5

Genna Marias 120
Gospel according to the Hebrews .. 5, 9–10, 32, 129
Gospel of the Adversaries of the Law and the Prophets 24
Gospel of Andrew 25

Gospel of Apelles 25
Gospel of Bartholomew 159
Gospel of Bartholomew, see Questions of Bartholomew
Gospel of the Birth of Mary 48, 84, 85, 108, 120–1
Gospel of Cerinthus 25
Gospel of the Ebionites 5–6, 14–16
Gospel of the Egyptians 16–19, 128
Gospel of Eve 25
Gospel of Gamaliel 159–60, 161
Gospel of Judas Iscariot 25
Gospel of Mary 34
Gospel of the Nazaraeans 5, 10–14
Gospel of Nicodemus 164–204, 224
   Acts of Pilate 169–85
   Jews accuse Jesus before Pilate 170–1
   ensigns pay homage to Jesus 171–2
   Pilate judges Jesus 173–4
   Nicodemus speaks on behalf of Jesus . 174
   Jesus sentenced to crucifixion 176
   Jesus' death 177
   Joseph buries Jesus 177–8
   announcement of the resurrection of Jesus 179
   Jesus sought on Mount Mamilch 180
   announcement of Jesus' ascension 181
   Joseph testifies about Jesus to the Jews 181–2
   eyewitness report about Jesus on mount Mamilch 183
   Descent (Greek) 185–90
   report of men raised from Hades 185
   meetings with Abraham and others ... 186
   Satan and Hades discuss Jesus' arrival 187
   Jesus at the gates of Hades 187–8
   Jesus enters Hades and binds Satan 188–9
   Jesus raises Adam 189
   Testimony of the good thief 189–90
   Descent (Latin A) 190–8
   Leucius and Karinus found 190–1
   their reports 191–7
   John the Baptist in Hades 191
   Adam in Hades 191–2
   Satan and Hades discuss Jesus' arrival 192–3
   Jesus at the gates of Hades 193–4
   Jesus enters Hades and binds Satan .. 194
   Hades addresses Jesus 194
   Jesus raises Adam 195
   testimony of the good thief 196
   Pilate investigates the date of the coming of Christ 197–8
   Descent (Latin B) 198–204
   the rabbis meet Karinus and Leucius 198–9

Index of Apocryphal Writings

the council meets Karinus and
   Leucius 199
arrival of Jesus at the gates of Hades .. 200
Satan and Hades discuss Jesus'
   arrival 200-1
report of Karinus and Leucius 200-4
Adam and others await Jesus 201-2
good thief enters Hades 202
Jesus enters Hades 203
Satan expelled to Tartarus 203
Adam and others led by Jesus from
   Hades 203
Gospel of Peter 32, 108, 150-8, 593
Gospel of Philip 25, 68
Gospel of Pseudo-Matthew 48, 68, 71,
                  84-99, 108, 109, 120
  narrative...................... 88-99
  journey to Bethlehem 92-3
  Jesus' birth in a cave and the
    midwives 92-3
  healing of Salome's hand 94
  adoration of Jesus by the ox and the ass . 94
  Jesus subdues the dragons 94
  animals accompany Jesus and his family 95
  miracle of the palm-tree 95-6
  miraculous journey to the coast 96
  Egyptian idols shattered 96
  conversion of Affrodosius.......... 96-7
  lions worship Jesus 97
  Joseph raises his namesake 98
  Jesus sanctifies his family 98-9
Gospel of Thomas 123-47
Gospel of Truth 25
Gospel of the Twelve Apostles........ 159
Gospel of Valentinus 25
Gregory of Tours' Epitome, *see* Acts of
   Andrew: Epitome

Historia de Nativitate Mariae et de Infantia
   Salvatoris, see Gospel of Pseudo-Matthew
History of Joseph the Carpenter 48, 68,
                           111-17
History of Simon Cephas the Chief of the
   Apostles..................... 430
Hymn of Christ, *see* Acts of John
Hymn of the Soul, *see* Acts of Thomas

Infancy Gospel of Thomas 48, 68-83,
                  84, 85, 100, 118, 124
  narrative...................... 75-83
  Greek A:
  Jesus and the pools 75-6
  Jesus and the sparrows 76
  Jesus and Annas' son 76
  Jesus kills a child 76
  Joseph admonishes Jesus 76-7
  Zacchaeus and the alphabet 76-7

  Jesus revives Zeno 78
  Jesus heals the neighbour's foot 78
  Jesus fetches water 78
  Jesus reaps a harvest 78
  Jesus stretches wood.............. 78-9
  Jesus learns the alphabet 79
  Jesus with another teacher 79
  Jesus and the viper 79
  Jesus revives a child 80
  Jesus revives a workman 80
  Jesus in the temple at the age of twelve . 80
  Greek B:
  Jesus and the pools 81
  Jesus and Annas' son 81
  Jesus and the sparrows 81
  Jesus kills a child................... 81
  Zacchaeus and the alphabet 81-2
  Jesus revives Zeno 82
  Jesus heals the neighbour's foot 82
  Jesus fetches water 82
  Jesus stretches wood............... 82
  Latin:
  flight to Egypt 82-3
  Jesus revives a fish 83
  teacher casts Jesus out of the city 83
  return to Nazareth 83

Jewish Christian Gospels 3-16
Jewish Gospel, *see* Judaikon
Judaikon 4, 5

Kergyma Petrou, *see* Preaching of Peter

Lament of Mary 159
  see also Gospel of Gamaliel
Latin infancy gospels 48
Letter of Cromatius and Heliodorus to
   Jerome.................. 91-2, 108
Letter to the Ephesians 544
Letter to the Galatians (canonical)...... 550
Letter of James 673-81
Letter of Jerome to Cromatius and
   Heliodorus 92, 108
Letter of Lentulus 542-3
Letter of Pilate to Claudius . 205-6, 211, 428
Letter of Pilate to Tiberius 206-8
Letter of Tiberius to Pilate.......... 224-5
Letters of Christ and Abgar 538-42
Letters to the Corinthians (canonical) ... 550
Letters of Pilate to Herod and of Herod to
   Pilate..................... 222-4
Liber Flavus Fergusiorum 305, 347
Liber de Infantia............... 48, 84, 108
  see also Gospel of Pseudo-Matthew
Liber de Infantia-Salvatoris 71, 108, 119
  see also Arundel 404

Index of Apocryphal Writings

lost gospels 3–25

Martyrdom of Andrew 244
Martyrdom of Andrew in Scythia 244
Martyrdom of Peter 430
Martyrium Beati Pauli Apostoli by Pseudo-Linus 388
Martyrium Beati Petri Apostoli by Pseudo-Linus 427
Memoria of the Apostles 24
Merton Fragment 45
Mors Pilati 216–17

Narrative of Joseph of Arimathaea 48, 217–22

Oxyrhynchus Papyrus 1 ...... 125, 128–30, 130–1
Oxyrhynchus Papyrus 654 .... 125, 128–30, 131–2, 135–6
Oxyrhynchus Papyrus 655 .... 125, 128–30, 132, 138, 140–1
Oxyrhynchus Papyrus 840 31–4
Oxyrhynchus Papyrus 850 ...... 305, 345–6
Oxyrhynchus Papyrus 1081 34–5
Oxyrhynchus Papyrus 1224 35–6
Oxyrhynchus Papyrus 3525 121

Paradosis Pilati 208–11, 222
Passio Apostolorum Petri et Pauli 429
Passio Iohannis by Pseudo-Melito 347
Passio Sanctorum Apostolorum Petri et Pauli by Pseudo-Marcellus 428–9
Passion of Bartholomew 518–20
Passion of Matthew 520–3
Peter's Missionary Journeys by Pseudo-Clement 436–8
Preaching of Andrew 244
Preaching of Matthias 244
Preaching of Peter 20–4, 30, 390
Preaching of Simon Cephas in the City of Rome 430
Protevangelium Iacobi, see Protevangelium of James
Protevangelium of James 48–67, 71, 84, 100, 108, 111, 118
  narrative 57–67
  Joachim's offering spurned 57
  Anna's childlessness 57–9
  announcement of Anna's pregnancy . 58–9
  birth and childhood of Mary 59–60
  Mary in the temple 60
  Joseph takes Mary as his ward 60–1
  annunciation to Mary 61
  Mary and Elizabeth 61–2
  Joseph discovers Mary's pregnancy .. 62–3
  journey to Bethlehem 63–4
  birth of Jesus in a cave 64–5
  adoration of the magi 65
  death of John the Baptist 65–6
Pseudo-Abdias 235, 429–30, 525–31
Pseudo-Clementine literature 390, 431–8, 512

Questions of Bartholomew 652–72
  narrative 655–68
  Jesus tells of his visit to Hades 656–7
  Jesus tells of the raising of Adam 657
  Bartholomew's questions about the righteous dead 657–8
  questioning the Virgin about the annunciation 658–60
  Jesus shows the abyss 660
  Bartholomew asks to see Beliar 661–2
  Beliar tells his history 663–6
  Bartholomew praises Christ 666–7
  Bartholomew asks about the unforgivable sin 667–8

Revelation of James, see Protevangelium of James
Revelation of Thomas, see Apocalypse of Thomas
Rylands Papyrus 463 121–2

Secret Gospel of Mark 148–9
Sibylline Oracles 613–15
  signs of the end 613–14
  judgement 614
  breaking into Hades 614
  torments for the sinful 614–15
  rewards for the just 615
Sophia Jesu Christi 25, 34
Story of Joseph of Arimathaea, see Narrative of Joseph of Arimathaea
Story of Peter and Paul 430
Strasbourg Fragment 41–2
Syriac Acts of John Son of Zebedee 347

Traditions of Matthias 19–20
Two Books of Jeu 25

Utrecht Fragment, see Acts of Andrew: Utrecht

Vengeance of the Saviour, see *Vindicta Salvatoris*
Vindicta Salvatoris 213–16
Virtutes by Pseudo-Abdias 389, 518, 519, 525–31
Visio Pauli, see Apocalypse of Paul
Vita Petri 430

2. Index of Subjects and Proper Names

Abban 440, 447–8
Abdias (bishop) 529
Abel 644
Abgar 538, 541–2, 717, 720
Abiathar 84, 88–9, 527
Abigea 89, 714
Abraham 186, 340, 573, 614, 631, 640, 708
Achaea (Achaia) 252, 264, 273, 284
Achar 84
Acherusia, field of (Elysium) 609
Acherusia, lake of 615, 629–30, 671
Adam 186, 189, 191, 194–5, 201, 202, 644, 657, 670, 718, 720
Adas 179, 183, 198
Addai, *see* Thaddaeus
Adimantus 276
Adonai Sabaoth 614
Aegeates 232, 245–9, 251–3, 255, 259, 261, 265–6, 282
Aeglippus 530
Affrodosius 96–7
Africanus 529
Aftemeloukos 636
Agrippa (a Jew) 172
Agrippa (prefect) 420, 423, 426
Agrippina 423
Agrippinus 411–12
Albinus 423
Albius 210
Alcman 248, 283
Alexander 299, 695
Alexander (a Jew) 170
Alexander (a Syrian) 369, 373
Alexandria 703
Alfatha 663
Aline 376
Alphaeus (husband of Mary daughter of Anna & Cleophas) 98
Amalech 199
Amente 301, 669, 672, 696
Amente (personified) 115
Amnes 172
Amos 631
Ananias (a messenger) 538, 541–2
Ananias (officer) 169
Ananias of Bethlehem 669, 672
Anchares, *see* Panchares
Andrapolis 448
Andrew 158, 162, 232, 245–302, 316, 447, 558, 563, 658, 695, 702, 715, 717, 722
Andronicus 315, 322, 324, 328, 331–5, 346
Angaeus 179, 183–4
Angaeus, *see also* Egias
angel 620–44
angel appears to Mary 93
angel appears to Salome 94
Anna (mother of virgin Mary) 57–60, 88, 98, 708, 718, 720
Anna (prophetess) 89
Annas (high priest) 62–3, 170, 172, 185, 190, 197, 199, 209, 212, 219, 225
Annas (scribe) 76
  son of 81, 89, 104
Anthimus 279
Antichrist 648
Antioch 364, 369
Antipatros 327
Antiphanes 249
Antiphanes of Megara 282
Antonius 172
Antulus 411
Anubion 437
Apollonius 302
Apollophanes 380
Appion 437
Aquila 379
Arcadius 647
Archelaus 209, 212, 214, 225
Arfaxat 528–9, 529–30
Aricia 401
Arimathaea 185, 190, 196
Aristeus 401
Aristippus 328
Aristobula 328
Aristocles 245
Aristodemus 313
Ariston 403
arrest and crucifixion of Jesus 219–21
Artemilla 377–8
Artemis 322, 373
Artemon 384
ascension 680
Asmodaeus 522
Assia 114
Astaroth, temple of 519
Asterius 172
Astriges 519
Athenodorus 437

Index of Subjects and Proper Names

Atticus 342
Azael 614
Azotus 513

Babylon 490
Babylonia 488
Bacharias 12
Balaam 464
Balbus 400
baptism 283, 370, 402, 497, 504–5
Barabbas 12, 175
Barakiel 614
Barnabas 401, 523, 710, 715
Barsabas Justus 386, 388
Bartholomew 103, 163, 447, 515–16, 518, 519, 558, 652, 655–68, 704, 715, 717
Beliar 656, 662, 669
Beor 531
Berenice (not Veronica) 401
Berenice (Veronica) 175, 669
  see also Veronica
Berith 519
Bernice, see Berenice
Berytus 437
Bethlehem 701, 705, 717, 719, 720
Birrus 698
birth of Jesus in cave 64, 93–4, 110
Bithynians, lodging of the 401
Bulphamnus 523
Bulphandrus 523
Burgidalla 214
Buthem 184
Byblus 438
Byzantium 274

Caesar 209, 213
Caesarea 402
Caiaphas 102, 170, 172, 178, 185, 190, 197, 199, 209, 212, 219, 225
Cain 644
Calaman 373
Caleb 718
Calletha (daughter of Nicodemus) 717
Callimachus 331–5
Calliopa 281
Callippus 311
Callisto 280
Callistus 274
camel passes through the eye of a needle 300–1
Candacis 530
Candida 399
Capernaum 98
Carius 162
Carpianus 276
Castellius 366
Castor 423

Cedar 663
Cephas (not Peter) 558
Cerinthus 555, 558, 560
Cestus 387, 388
Chairoum 663
Chalkatoura 665
Charisius 479, 481–7, 491–2, 494–7, 499, 503, 510
Charouth 665
Cheltoura 658
Cherubim 658
Chritir 658
Chrysa 376
Chryse 421
Chuza 669
Claudius 206, 384
Clement 612
Cleobius 311, 313, 328, 380, 383, 400
Cleon 376
Cleopatra 311, 312–13
Cleophas (Anna's second husband) 98
Cleophas (child) 103
Colossians (people) 546
conversion of many Jews 302
Corinth 281, 382–3
Craton 338, 529
Crispus 172
Cynegius 616
Cyprus 523

Dalmatia 385
Damascus 364
Daniel 614
Daphne 368
Daphnus 380
Dathaes 170
David 188, 193, 195, 202, 632, 695, 699–700, 708
Death (personified) 115
death of Jesus 155–6
death of Pilate 211, 217, 225
decline of Herod Antipas' family 224
Demas (Acts of Paul) 364, 366
Demas (thief) 218, 220; see also Dysmas
Demetrius 400
Demetrius of Amasea 273
Demonicus 313
destruction of idols 210
devil:
  described 520
  in the guise of an old man 294
  in the guise of a soldier 522
Didymus, see Thomas
Dion 374
Dionysius 400
Diophantes 377, 378
Doris 423

Index of Subjects and Proper Names

Douth 665
Drusiana 316, 322, 328–35
Dumachus 103, 105
Dyrus, *see* Verus
Dysmas 176–7
  see also Demas

Ebionites 3
Edessa 538
Egetes, *see* Aegeates
Egias 198
Egypt 83, 488
Eirusia 269
Elders 156, 180–1
Elijah 180, 182, 189, 196, 601, 610–12, 614, 628, 643
Elisha 180, 643
Elizabeth 37, 61–2, 66, 98, 708, 718, 720
Elysium (Elysian plain) 609, 615
Emerina 98
Enoch 189, 196, 601, 628
Ephesus 311, 322, 327, 328, 376–9, 703, 710
Ephigenia 530
Epiphanius 382
Erba 522
Ethiopia 528
Eubola 410–11, 412, 416
Eubula 377–9
Eubulus 380
Eucharist 279, 383, 398, 399, 458, 467–8, 497, 505, 523, 565
Euclia 232, 250–1
Eugenius 342
Euphemia 423
Euphenissa 530
Euphranor 530
Euphrates 630, 640
Euphrosinus 529
Euthine, *see* Judith
Eutychus 380
Eve 203, 670, 718
Exuos 275
Ezekiel 631, 642
Ezrael 606–8

Falconilla 369
feast at Cana 161
Festus of Galatia 386
Finees, *see* Phinees
Firmilla 382
flute girl 449, 453
Fortunatus 331–5
Frontina 382

Gabriel 114, 117, 564, 663, 701, 711, 714, 717
Gad 440, 455–8
Gamaliel 160, 170, 185, 190, 197

Gaul 385
Gemellus 423
Gennesaret 318
Gestas 176, 218, 220
Gion 630, 639
Graphathas 665
Gratinus of Sinope 273–4
Gundaphorus 440, 448, 454–8

Habakkuk 195, 614
Hades 187, 192–5, 200, 613, 656
Hanan (son of), *see* Annas (the scribe), son of
Hellespont 274
Hermias 372
Hermippus 374, 375
Hermocrates 374
Hermogenes 364, 366, 527
Hermopolis 96
Herod Agrippa I 527
Herod Antipas 154, 161, 170, 209, 212
Herod the Great 65–6, 82
Herodias 224
Hierapolis 513
Hierocrates 670
Hieronymus 377–9
Honorius 647
Hyrcania 490
Hyrtacus 530

Iconium 364, 368
India 447, 454–511, 703
Iphidama 232, 245, 248–9, 251–6, 259, 283
Iphidamia, *see* Iphidama
Iphitus 400
Ireus 513
Isaac (patriarch) 573, 614, 631, 640, 708
Isaac (rabbi) 172, 184
Isaiah 186, 188, 191, 193, 201, 631, 642
Italicus 411

Jacob (a Jew) 172
Jacob (patriarch) 573, 614, 631, 640, 708
Jairus 170, 184
James (brother of Jesus) 66, 79, 91, 98, 103, 108, 114, 115, 137, 675, 716
James (son of Alphaeus) 98, 447
James (son of Zebedee) 98, 316–17, 413, 447, 558, 612, 697, 702, 715
Jehoshaphat, field of 696, 699
Jehoshaphat, valley of 698
  see also Josaphat, valley of
Jephonias 707, 718
  see also Yophana
Jeremiah 202, 614, 631, 642
Jericho 364
Jerusalem 80, 364, 401, 703

Jesus 33–4, 36, 39–40, 42, 149, 448, 600–12, 655–68, 697, 722–3
  appears: to Nicostratus 420; to Paul 384; to Peter 410, 424; to Theon 402
  in differing guises 317; as Andrew 259; as Elijah 182; as Gabriel 564; as John 278; as a naked boy 411; as an old man 415; as Peter 415; as a ship's captain 285–8; as a twelve-year-old boy 300; as a young boy 252, 291, 299, 331, 378, 415, 458, 532, 698
  physical appearance described 543
  resurrection appearance to Joseph of Arimathaea 221–2
  as twin of Judas Thomas 452, 461, 493
Joachim 57–60, 88, 98
Joanna 669, 695
Job 631, 642
John (son of Zebedee) 98, 162, 219, 222, 311–47, 413, 447, 515, 517, 558, 612, 644, 658, 687–8, 698–9, 701–3, 707, 709, 710, 715, 716, 719–20, 722
John the Baptist 37, 66, 141, 186, 191, 201–2, 224
John Mark 523
Johoiada 12
Jonah 614
Jordan 518
Josaphat, valley of 713, 715
  see also Jehoshaphat, valley of
Joseph (brother of Jesus) 98
Joseph (carpenter) 37, 60–5, 76, 78–9, 81–2, 88–9, 92–3, 97–8, 103, 109, 114, 170, 448
Joseph (high priest), see Caiaphas
Joseph (patriarch) 641
Joseph of Arimathaea 154, 160, 162–3, 178, 181, 185, 190, 197, 199, 215, 218, 221, 668, 691, 714
Joseph of Capernaum 98
Joseph's Garden 156
Joshua 614
Josias 528
Judah (brother of Jesus) 98
  see also Jude; Judas
Judas (apostle) 447
  see also Jude (disciple)
Judas (brother of Jesus) 114, 115
  see also Jude; Judah
Judas (a Jew) 172
Judas (scribe) 170
Judas Iscariot 163, 219, 301, 669
  death 301–2
Judas Thomas, see Thomas
Judas Zelotes 558
Jude (brother of Jesus) 528, 529
  see also Judas; Judah

Jude (disciple) 715
  see also Judas (apostle)
Judith 57
Justus (brother of Jesus) 114, 115

Karinus 191, 196, 198
Kerkoutha 663
Kushan 488

Labdanes 703
Lacedaemon 282
Laodicea 327
Lazarus 161–2, 187, 192–3, 201, 573
Lazarus (beggar) 340
Lazarus (a Jew) 172
Leah 669
Lectra 364
Lentulus 542
Leontius 281
Lesbius 279
Lesbonax 224
Leucius 92, 191, 196, 198, 708
Levi (chief priest) 33–4
Levi (scribe) 170, 183, 184
Levi (son of Alphaeus) 158
Levi (teacher) 90
Levites 179, 181–2, 198
Licianus 210
Longinus 223, 382,
Longus 387–8
Losania 217
Lot 631, 642
Lucilius 549, 550
Luke 385, 387–8, 702, 715, 717
Lycaonia 517, 518
Lycomedes 311, 313–14, 328
Lydia 114, 115
Lysias 527
Lysimachus 275, 401
Lystra 364

Macedonia 401
Magi 65
Mambre 660
Mamilch 179, 183–4
Marcellus 404–5, 413, 415, 417, 421, 423
  vision of Peter after his crucifixion 426
  vision of Peter and Simon 415
  wife 311
Marcia 493–4, 496, 502–3, 504–6
Mariamne 515–16
Mark 644, 702, 717
Mars 531
Martha 515, 561–2, 669
  daughter 561
Mary (virgin) 37, 59–66, 82, 88–9, 92–3, 98, 103–4, 114–16, 149, 163, 183, 640, 658, 661, 695–723

Index of Subjects and Proper Names

Mary (daughter of Anna & Cleophas) 98
Mary (daughter of Cleophas) 98
Mary (daughter of Salome & Anna) 98
Mary (mother of James) 669
Mary (sister of Martha) 561-2, 669
Mary Magdalene 121, 147, 157, 163, 225, 561, 669, 698, 700
Matarea 105
Matthew 91, 108, 137, 273, 447, 521-3, 528, 558, 703-4, 715, 717
Matthias 20, 283-4, 291-2, 299, 672
Matthias Justus 715
Mauch 663
Maximianus 715
Maximilla 232, 245-6, 248-51, 253-7, 259, 266, 282-3
Medias of Philippi 276
Megara 282
Melioth 665
Melito 708
Melkir 669
Mermeoth 664-5
Mermidona, *see* Mermidonia
Mermidonia 273, 283-99
Meson 490
Mesopotamia 510
Micah 195, 631
Michael 117, 189, 195, 300, 302, 517, 563, 624, 631, 638, 661-3, 711, 714 721-2
Miletus 311, 322
miracles at Jesus' death 212
Misdaeus 473-82, 485-7, 495, 497, 499-501, 503-4, 506-7, 510-11
Mnesara 502-5
Moses 610-12, 614, 641, 699
Mount Mauria 660
Mount of Olives 660
Mygdonia 479-84, 486-7, 491-7, 502-4, 510
Myra 371, 374-5
Myrmidonia, *see* Mermidonia
Myrna 520
Myrta 383

Naddaver 530
Naoutha 663
Narcissus 401, 404, 410, 413
Nathan (son of Naum) 214
Nathanael 43, 558, 663
Nazaraeans 3
Nazareth 81, 83
Nephonos 665
Nephthalim 170
Nerkela 513
Nero 386, 388, 426
Neshra 717
Nicaea 274

Nicanora 513, 516
Nicaria 423
Nicatera 513
Nicocleides 513
Nicodemus 160, 162, 170, 174, 185, 190, 197, 199, 215, 219, 715
Nicolaus 276, 281
Nicomedia 274
Nicostratus 419-20, 422
Noah 643
Nympha 374-5

Oertha 663, 665
Onesiphorus:
    Acts of Andrew 300-1
    Acts of Paul 364-5
Onomatath 665
Ophiani, land of the 515
Ophioryme 516
Orba 523

Pamphylia 376
Panchares 364
Parmenius 91
Parthenius 387
Patras 245-61, 264, 279, 282
Patroclus 385-6, 388
Paul 364-88, 399-401, 546, 547, 549-53, 576, 620-44, 702-3, 707, 710, 715, 721
    description of 364
Perga 376
Perinthus 274
Persia 528
Peter 45, 137, 147, 158, 292, 299, 316-17, 385, 397-426, 433-8, 447, 518, 558, 562, 600-12, 644, 658, 661, 670, 672, 675-6, 679, 695, 697-8, 698-9, 700, 702-3, 707, 713, 715, 721, 722
    address to the cross 424
    vision of Jesus 424
Petronilla (Peter's daughter) 397-9
Petronius 156
Pheretas 387
Philetus 527
Philip (apostle) 162, 385, 447, 515-18, 530, 531, 558, 702, 715, 717
Philip (son of Alphaeus) 98
Philip (tetrarch) 161, 209, 212, 225
Philippi 274, 275, 379-82
Philogenes 669
Philomedes 276
Philopator 280
Philostrate 401
Phinees 172, 179, 183, 184, 198
Phulbana 522
Phulbanos 522

Pilate 154, 157, 160, 162, 163, 170, 197, 206, 207, 209, 215, 218, 224, 225
Pisidia 376
Pison 630, 639
Plato (bishop) 522–3
Polymius 519
Polyxena 524
Pompey 412
priests 156, 179, 181–2, 198
Prisca 379
Procla 210, 223
Ptolemy 397–8
purification of a house 413
Puteoli 403

Quartus 399
Quo Vadis? 384, 424

Raab 225
Rachaab, see Raab
raising of Lazarus 161–2
Ramiel 614
Raphael 564, 663
Rebecca 89
resurrection account 157
resurrection appearance of the good thief 222
Reuben 57, 88, 715
Rhodeon 373
Rome 385, 399, 401, 402, 404, 703
  and Peter 396
Ruben, see Reuben
Rufina 399–400
Rufus 299, 695
rulers of the synagogue 180, 182

Sabinus 717, 719–20
Salem 103, 106
Sallust 549
Salome 16, 18, 64, 93, 114, 143, 149, 669, 695
Salome (third husband of Anna) 98
Samiel 614
Samuel (high priest) 61
Samuel (a Jew) 172
Sarah 561–2
Sarra (daughter of Caiaphas) 219
Satan 186, 192, 195, 200
  in guise of a young man 104
Satanael 663
scribes 156
Scythia 531
sealing 248–9, 369, 374, 387, 458, 468–9
Seleucia 372
Semes 170
Semmath 268
Seneca 547, 549–53
Sennes 529
Sephora, see Sepphora

Sepphora 89, 714
Seth 186, 191–2, 201
shepherds at Jesus' birth 94
Sidon 375–6, 437
signs of the end of the world 646–51
Simeon (brother of Jesus) 98, 114, 115
Simeon (priest) 183–5, 190
  see also Symeon
Simeon (son of Philogenes) 669
Simmias 364
Simon (brother of Jesus) 528, 530
Simon (the Canaanite or Cananaean, or Zelotes) 103, 447, 702, 715, 717
Simon (son of Clopas) 516
Simon Magus 380, 401–23, 433, 555, 558, 560
Simon Peter, see Peter
Siophanes 671
Siphor 473–6, 479, 482, 486–7, 497–9, 501, 504–5, 510
Smyrna 324, 327, 379
Solomon 721
Sophia 532
Sosias 282
Sostratus 273, 280–1
Sotinen 96
Spain 399, 403, 524
Stachys 513, 516, 518
Stacteus 342
star at Jesus' birth 94
Stephanus 380
story of criminals crucified with Jesus 220–1
Stratocles 245–9, 251–2, 258–9, 261–2, 266
Stratonicus 422
Stratonike 380
Suanir 529
Susanna 89
symbolism of Peter's crucifixion 425
Symeon (priest) 66, 89
  see also Simeon
Synesis 523
Syrice, see Stacteus

Tabitha 717
Tarsus 620
Tartarouchus 626
Tartarus 203, 615, 627, 661
Tatirokos 608
Temlakos 605
Tertia 497–9, 502–5
Tertullus 328
Thaddaeus 538, 668, 670, 702
Thamyris 365–6, 372
Thebes 704
Thecla 365–74
Theoclia 365, 372
Theocritus 527

Index of Subjects and Proper Names 739

Theodosius 647
Theodosius (consul) 616
Theon 402–4
Theophanes, *see* Siophanes
Theophilus 162, 380, 550
Thessalonica 275, 277
Thomas (apostle) 135, 137, 163, 442, 447–511, 538, 558, 562, 646, 649, 651, 671, 702, 703, 707, 715–16
  appears to Misdaeus 510
Thomas (the Israelite) 75, 80
Thrace 274
Thrasymachus 376
Threptus 380
Tiberia 703
Tiberias 14
Tiberius 161, 170, 207, 214, 225
Tigris 630, 640
Timothy 401, 644
Titus (apostle) 364, 385, 387–8
Titus (emperor) 214
Titus (thief) 103, 105
Tripolis 438
Trophima 279–80
Tryphaena 369
Tyre 376, 436

Uriel 564, 603, 614, 663
Urion the Cappadocian 386

Varardach 528
Varianus 267
  see also Virinus
Varinus 91
Varus 280
Vatienus 551
Vazan 499–505, 507–8, 510
Velosian 215, 216
Veronica 215, 216
  and the likeness of Jesus 215
  see also Berenice
Verus 314, 336, 346
Vespasian 214
via sacra 422

Vienne 217
virgin birth 93
Virinus 277
  see also Varianus
visions:
  of Jesus to Andrew 294, 297
  of Jesus to Matthias 284
  of Jesus reported 503
  voice from heaven to Paul 399
Volusian, *see* Velosian
Vualdath 519

Xanthanael 663
Xanthippe 423, 524
Xenophon 328
Xenophon (deacon) 474–5
Xerxes 528, 530

Yophana 720
  see also Jephonias
Ysachar 88

Zacchaeus 433
Zacchaeus (tax-gatherer) 20
Zacchaeus (teacher) 76–7, 81–2, 90, 104
Zacharias 60, 61, 66, 84, 109, 644
Zacheus, *see* Zacchaeus
Zael, *see* Zahel
Zahel 89, 714
Zaroes 528–9, 530
Zathael 663
Zebedee (husband of Mary, daughter of Salome & Anna) 98
Zebeus 529
Zechariah 631
Zecharias, *see* Zacharias
Zelomi 93
Zeno (child) 78, 82, 90, 103
Zeno (presbyter) 380
Zeno (son of Onesiphorus) 364
Zeras 172
Zeuxis 345
Ziphagia 523

3. Index of Biblical and Other Citations

For a table of synoptic parallels to the Gospel of Thomas see pp. 133–5.

(a) OLD TESTAMENT

GENESIS
1: 11   564, 566, 568
1: 14   559
1: 26–7   559, 564, 566, 568
3: 22   435
5: 24   184
6: 1–4   292
6: 6   435
8: 21   435
9: 11   292
18: 21   435
21: 1–3   58
22: 1   435

EXODUS
23: 20–1   184
25: 10   198

DEUTERONOMY
19: 15   184
21: 22–4   154
21: 23   184
32: 35   178
34: 5–6   184

I SAMUEL
1: 6   57
1: 28   58
2: 11   58

2 KINGS
2: 1–18   180

JOB
38: 10–11   559

PSALMS
1: 3   58
1: 4   667
3: 1–8   569
13: 3   578
24: 6   612
24: 7   188, 193, 200
24: 7–8   202
24: 7–9   612
24: 8   188, 193
24: 9–10   202
33: 6   344
39: 6   341
45: 14   697
49: 18   579
49: 19b   579
49: 20   579
49: 21b   579
54: 7   608
59: 10   608
62: 12   603
78: 10   579
81: 6   584
98: 1–2   195
107: 15–16   202
107: 16–17   193
118: 22   417
118: 26   171, 189
121: 1   659
132: 8   697
148: 7   94

ECCLESIASTES
3: 8   474

ISAIAH
1: 3   94
5: 23   587
7: 13–14   417
9: 1–2   186, 191
9: 2   201
19: 1   96
25: 8   193
26: 19   188, 193
28: 16   417
29: 13   40
30: 1   620
53: 2   416
53: 4   414
53: 8   416
54: 1   577
65: 25   95

JEREMIAH
1: 18   576
10: 11   184
15: 20   576
31: 35   621

EZEKIEL
33: 11   343
37: 4–14   602

DANIEL
2: 34   417
3: 54   559
7: 13   417

AMOS
8: 9   155

MICAH
7: 18–20   195

HABAKKUK
3: 2   94
3: 13   195

(b) OLD TESTAMENT
APOCRYPHA AND
PSEUDEPIGRAPHA

TOBIT
4: 15   567

WISDOM
3: 2   579

ECCLESIASTICUS
15: 16–20   581

ASCENSION OF ISAIAH
10: 7–16   563
11   49
11: 13   417

APOCALYPSE OF ELIAS
43: 10   565
87: 32   566

ODES OF SOLOMON
19   49
21: 3   570
42: 16   570

(c) NEW TESTAMENT

MATTHEW
1: 20–1   62
1: 21   49
2: 1–12   65
2: 1   63
2: 13   37
2: 15   12
2: 16   66
2: 23   12
3: 10   574

Index of Biblical and Other Citations

3:12   588
3:13-14   13
3:14-15   15
3:16-17   156, 186
3:17   202
4:5   13
4:24   560
5:4   365
5:5-8   483
5:5   628
5:6   629
5:7   365
5:8   365
5:9   365
5:10   611
5:11   488, 580, 588, 673
5:12   582, 583
5:22   13
5:44   36, 567
5:48   575
6:9   502
6:10   448
6:11   12
6:25   462
6:26   459
6:30   571
6:34   458
7:5   13
7:7   312, 469, 581
7:14   571
7:15   478, 585
7:21   567
8:2-4   40
8:2-3   560
8:11-12   220
8:11   438
8:16   560
8:20   258
8:22   426
8:23-7   287
8:26   571
9:1-8   175
9:2-8   559
9:15   42
9:20-2   560
9:32-3   560
9:34   291
9:37   582
10:1-4   15
10:7-10   285
10:12   434
10:15   572
10:16   13, 291, 585
10:22   588
10:28   42
10:41-2   583
11:4-5   560

11:5   287
11:8   462
11:12   14
11:15   480
11:22   572
11:24   572
11:25   14
11:28-9   9
11:28   480
11:29-30   459
12:9-14   12
12:10-14   559
12:24   291
12:27   291
12:35   45
12:40   14
13:16-17   575
13:30   588
13:38   575
13:55   288
14:13-21   287
14:17-21   560
14:23-7   560
14:31   571
15:5   14
15:7-8   40
15:14   584, 587
15:30   560
16:2-3   14
16:8   571
16:17-19   416
16:17   14
16:27   459, 600, 603
17:4   611
17:5   611
17:20   407
17:24-7   560
18:6   404
18:15-16   587
18:21-2   13
18:22   14
19:16-24   11
19:23-4   586
19:23   462
19:24   300
19:26   220
19:28   570, 575
20:12   472
20:28   29
21:21   407
22:8   582
22:14   438
22:15-18   40
22:24   559
23:8-9   582
23:24   584
23:35   12, 51

24:1-51   578
24:3   600
24:4   600
24:5-8   588
24:5   600
24:22   574
24:24   574, 601
24:26   600
24:27   600
24:30   600
24:31   574
24:32-3   600
24:35   296
25:1-13   584
25:6   270
25:10   584
25:14-30   11
25:46   572, 574
26:24   601
26:27-8   565
26:29   575
26:31   44
26:34   562
26:38   42, 187, 192, 201
26:41   42
26:45   42
26:52-3   481
26:61   173
26:64   559, 603
26:69-75   562
26:74   14
27   505
27:15   176
27:19   172
27:24-5   173, 176
27:24   154, 157
27:25   178
27:33   561
27:34   155
27:38   561
27:46   292
27:48   155
27:51   155
27:54   155
27:62-6   156
27:65   14
27:66   156
28:1-2   156
28:1   157
28:2-4   178
28:5-7   179
28:7   561
28:10   561, 562
28:11-15   157
28:12-14   179
28:17   562
28:18-20   567

742   Index of Biblical and Other Citations

28:18   570
28:19   575

MARK
1:4   15
1:5-6   15
1:9-11   10
1:34   560
1:40-5   560
1:40-4   40
2:1-12   175
2:3-5   559
2:16-17   36
2:20   156
3:3-5   559
3:22   291
3:31-5   15
4:26-9   673
4:35-41   287, 560
5:1-20   560
5:7   466
5:25-34   560
5:25-9   175
5:34   588
5:35-43   559
6:8-9   285
6:11   434
6:32-44   287
6:38-44   560
6:47-52   560
7:6-7   40
7:32-5   560
8:17   585
8:18   480
8:22-6   560
9:1   501
9:40   36
9:44   637
9:46   637
9:48   637
10:17-22   338
10:25   300
10:28-30   673
10:32-4   149
10:46a   149
10:46-7   175
12:10   417
12:13-15   40
13:1-37   578
13:9   565
13:20   574
13:21   296
13:26   417
13:35   565
14:12-16   16
14:12   154
14:23   565

14:27   44
14:30   44
14:61   155
14:65   155
15:5   155
15:15   154
15:16-20   155
15:22   561
15:24-7   155
15:27   561
15:33   155
15:34   155, 296
15:38   155
15:40   49
15:43   154
15:46   156
16:1-8   157
16:1   561
16:3-4   157
16:4   561
16:6   561
16 [shorter ending]   575
16:10   156, 561
16:11-13   562
16:14   28-9, 562
16:15-18   179
16:15   575
16:19   559

LUKE
1:1   16
1:13   58
1:20-2   61
1:26-8   564
1:28   61
1:31   61
1:35   61
1:35   49
1:36   37
1:41-4   61
1:42   61
1:48   61
1:64   61
2:1   63
2:7   66, 559
2:25-6   67
2:28-35   183
2:30-2   191
2:34   184
3:17   574, 588
5:12-16   560
5:12-14   40
5:17-26   175
6:4   28
6:7   45
6:22-7   580
6:23   583

6:24   586
6:27   567
6:35   567
6:39   587
6:45   45
7:14-15   559
7:14   418
7:22   287, 650
7:29   45
8:22-5   287
8:26-39   560
8:43-8   560
8:49-56   559
9:2   567
9:3   285
9:10-17   287
9:50   36
9:58   258
10:3   291
10:4   285
10:5   434
11:3   12
11:9-10   581
11:15   291
11:19   291
12:15-16   586
13:24   571
13:29   438, 575
14:8-10   29
14:24   582
15:7   343
15:31-2   9
16:8   581
16:19-31   340
16:23   573
17:1   574
17:14   40
17:20   600
17:23   600
18:14   65
18:24   586
18:25   300
20:20-3   40
20:21   571
21:1-36   578
21:10-11   579
21:12   565
21:18   296
21:33   296
21:34   462
22:19   565
22:30   575
22:42   448
23:33   561
23:34   176
23:35-7   177
23:39-43   155, 177

Index of Biblical and Other Citations

23:43   190, 196, 220
23:44–8   177
23:47–8   156
23:48   156
23:50–3   177
23:54   154
24:1   561
24:2   561
24:3   561
24:11–41   562
24:25   578
24:37   562
24:39   562, 563
24:44–5   568

JOHN
1:1   566
1:4   581
1:13   559
1:14   472, 494, 559, 564, 582
1:29   186, 191
1:49   42
2:1–12   287
2:1–11   559
2:12   559
3:2   40
4:34   57
5:1–7   175
5:21   569
5:24   570, 574
5:25   575
5:28   575
5:39   39
5:45   39
5:46   40
6:9–13   560
6:15   162
6:37–9   11
7:18   588
7:30   40, 45
8:44   502
9:1–5   560
9:29   39
9:35   575
10:1–2   585
10:12   585
10:28   574
10:36   581
10:38   414, 566, 577, 581
10:39   40
11:10   155
11:39–44   559
11:50   157
12:26   582
12:32   563
12:35–6   673

12:36   581
12:37   575
12:38   577
12:44   574
13:15   583
13:31–2   569, 579
13:34   567
14:2   673
14:4   673
14:6   673
14:10   566, 572, 581
14:11–20   566
14:11   581
14:12   564
14:13   579
14:15   571, 579, 581
14:20   568, 577, 581
14:21   571
14:23   579
14:27   576
14:28   564
15:4–5   568
15:10   571, 579
15:18   580
15:20   42
15:21   565
16:10   575
16:17   575
16:23b   673
16:25   575
16:26   673
16:29   673
16:32   575
17:2   574
17:20   578
17:21   566, 581
17:22   566, 581
17:23   566, 581
18:30   173
18:31   173, 174
18:33–8   173
18:38   173
19:12   176
19:13   155
19:17   561
19:18   561
19:19–20   177
19:26–7   709
19:28   155
19:30   155
19:31–7   155
19:31   154
19:41   156
20:11   561
20:14–15   561
20:15   561
20:17   561

20:19   157, 402, 457, 562
20:20   563
20:21   457, 576
20:22   576
20:25   155
20:26   457, 562
20:27   155, 558, 562, 563
20:28   451, 508
20:29   575, 673
21:1–8   158

ACTS
1:8   576
1:9   588
2:17–18   576
2:22   576
2:33   559
2:39   576
3:19   312
5:38–9   174
9:2   577
9:4   576, 577
9:5   576
9:6   576
9:8–9   576
9:8   576
9:15   576
9:18   576
10:42   459, 566
12:3–5   565
13:9   576
13:10   578
13:47   577
15:7   558
15:20   567
15:29   567
16:36   588
20:29   585
20:35   28
21:39   577
22:3   576, 577
22:5   577
22:6–7   577
22:7   576
22:11   576
23:1   580
23:34   577
24:15   580
26:6   577
26:7   575
26:12   577
26:14–15   576
26:14   576, 577
26:17   576
26:18   577
27:7–8   576
27:34   296

Index of Biblical and Other Citations

28:28 577

ROMANS
2:6 575
2:11 571
8:17 365, 567
8:29 467, 472
10:5 581
12:19–20 178
13:12 581
16:17 588
16:18 588
16:20 467

I CORINTHIANS
2:6 573
2:8 573
2:9 26, 426, 463
4:15 583
7:3 232
7:10 28
7:29 365
9:14 28
11:19 574
11:24–5 565
11:25 565
11:26 565
15:9 576
15:25–6 42
15:55 42, 188, 193
16:13 403
16:23 452

2 CORINTHIANS
5:10 572
12:1–10 616
12:1–5 620
12:4 628
12:12 576
13:14 190

GALATIANS
1:13 576, 577
1:16 576
1:23 577
2:2 573
2:8–9 576
3:12 581
4:26 577
4:27 577

EPHESIANS
1:10 564
1:21 559
3:6 577
4:28 471
5:8 581
5:11 581
6:9 571
6:14 509

PHILIPPIANS
1:27 580
2:9 458
2:16 573
3:5 576
3:19 580, 587

COLOSSIANS
1:25 564
3:9–10 467
3:9 471
3:25 571
4:16 543

I THESSALONIANS
1:4 572
4:15–18 28
4:17 580
5:5 581
5:23 570

2 THESSALONIANS
2:9 576

I TIMOTHY
2:7 580
6:15 559

2 TIMOTHY
4:1 566

TITUS
1:16 581

HEBREWS
1:1 559, 569
1:3 559
1:14 623
2:4 576
8:1 559, 588
10:11–12 588
12:2 559
12:22 557

JAMES
1:1 575
1:3 579
1:10–11 586
2:1–2 586
2:1 571
2:16 588
5:16 582
5:19–20 586

I PETER
1:7 579
1:10–11 569
1:12 567
2:9 570
3:9 471
3:19 157, 165, 573
4:5 566

2 PETER
1:10 572
2:9 572
3:7 572

I JOHN
1:1 558, 563, 577
1:5 581
2:4 573, 579
2:19 574
3:13 580
4:17 572

2 JOHN
verse 4 580

3 JOHN
verse 4 580

JUDE
verse 6 572

REVELATION
2:3 565
3:12 577
6:9 565
6:13 578
8:3–4 564
8:5 578
8:7 578
8:10 578
9:1 578
11:13 578
11:19 578
14:10–11 585
16:7 604, 609
16:18 578
16:19 578
16:21 578
17:14 559, 582
19:2 604, 609
19:16 559
20:2 628
20:4 565
20:13 601
21:2–10 577
21:12 575

(d) New Testament Apocrypha

ACTS OF PAUL
37 570

ACTS OF PETER AND PAUL
40–2 205

ACTS OF PHILIP
140 425

ACTS OF JOHN
93 563
100 566, 581

Index of Biblical and Other Citations

APOCALYPSE OF PETER
1   566

EPISTLE OF THE APOSTLES
40   613
47   140

GOSPEL OF PETER
10(39)   566
13(55)   561

GOSPEL OF THOMAS
2   498
13   463, 464, 509
16   30
17   26, 426
22   425, 482, 509
28   673
52   510
69   673
82   30

INFANCY GOSPEL OF THOMAS
2   659
6-8   478

6   559
14   478, 559
15   478

PASSION OF PETER AND PAUL
(Pseudo-Marcellus)
19   205

PSEUDO-MATTHEW
38   559

(e) APOSTOLIC FATHERS

EPISTLE OF BARNABAS
11: 1   573, 583
15: 8   567

1 CLEMENT
5: 7   576
20: 2-3   559
20: 6-7   559
36: 1   588

2 CLEMENT
4: 5a   13
5: 5   563, 573, 574

6: 7   563, 573, 574
9: 1   570
9: 5   569, 570
12: 2, 4, 5   18-19

DIDACHE
1: 2   567
16: 7   565

HERMAS
Similitudes 9: 20   586
Visions 1: 1.8   586
            3: 9.6   586

IGNATIUS
ad Eph. 7.2   570
ad Smyrn. 3.1.2   10
            3.2   563
            7.2   560
ad Trall. 7.1   560
            11.1   560

JUSTIN
Dial. Trypho 47   30

4. Index of Ancient Authorities

Abdias of Babylon 525
Abercius of Hierapolis 392
Adamantius 9
Ambrose 5, 19
Augustine 25, 231, 303, 320, 391, 439, 538, 547, 617

Catalogue of the Sixty Books, *see* List of the Sixty Books
Celsus 49
Cerinthus 14
Clement of Alexandria 3, 5, 9, 16, 18, 19, 20, 21–3, 30, 49, 129, 148, 306, 350, 390, 567, 593, 595, 598–9
Clement of Rome 431
Clementine Homilies 30
Codex Claromontanus 593
Commodian (Commodianus) 351, 563
Cynewulf 240
Cyril of Jerusalem 70, 124

Decretum Gelasianum, *see* Gelasian Decree
Didascalia Apostolorum 390
Didymus the Blind 3, 5, 30
Doctrina Addai 538

Epiphanius 3, 5, 14–16, 17, 25, 120, 165, 231, 236, 303, 439, 617, 685
Epiphanius the Monk 232, 233
Eusebius 3, 10, 11, 19, 150, 164, 205, 231, 303, 350, 390, 528, 538, 593
Evodius, Archbishop of Rome 695
Evodius of Uzala 232, 305

Filaster, *see* Philaster

Gelasian Decree xxiii (contents), 19, 25, 86, 108, 124, 231, 350, 390, 538, 617, 645, 652, 683, 691
Gregory the Great 544
Gregory of Nazianzus 21, 24
Gregory of Tours 232, 233, 234, 236, 240

Hegesippus 528
Hippolytus 16, 18, 70, 124, 350, 355, 685
Hrosvit of Gandersheim 86

Ignatius 49
Innocent I 231, 303

Irenaeus 29, 77, 697
Isho 'dad of Merv 100

Jacob of Voragine 304
Jerome 3, 5, 9, 11, 19, 25, 85, 91–2, 350, 538, 544, 547, 652
John Cassian 304
John of Damascus 21, 23–4
John of Salisbury 351
Josephus 697
Justin Martyr 30, 49, 150, 164, 567

Latin Homily on the Ten Virgins 600
Leonides 231
Letter of Pelagia 35
Leucius 229, 232, 235
Leucius Karinus (Charinus) 165, 229, 306
List of the Sixty Books xxiv (contents), 19, 350, 617, 682, 683

Macarius Magnes 593, 599
Manichaean Psalter 231, 234, 303
Marcion 544
Melito 150
Merinthus 14
Methodius 593, 599
Muratorian Fragment 544, 553, 593

Nicephorus 355
Nicetas the Paphlagonian 233
Nicetas of Thessalonica 441

Origen 3, 5, 9, 10, 19, 21, 24, 30, 49, 70, 124, 150, 236, 350, 390, 617, 685

Pamphilus the Martyr 11
Papias 29–30
Philaster (Philastrius) of Brescia 231–3
Pilgrimage of Etheria 538
Plato 20
Prudentius 617
Pseudo-Abdias 235, 236, 303, 304
Pseudo-Chrysostom 353
Pseudo-Cyprian 350
Pseudo-Linus 547
Pseudo-Melito 304–5

Rufinus 431, 528, 538

Sozomen 593, 617
Stichometry of Nicephorus xxiv (contents), 70, 124, 234, 303, 350, 352, 391, 439, 593, 682, 683
Syriac Didascalia 150

Tertullian 25, 205, 350, 357, 544

Theodore 543
Theodoret 543
Theophilus of Antioch 593, 599
Turribius of Astorga 303, 439

Xenocharides 231